# Law and Administration

# Law in Context

Editors: William Twining (University College, London) and
Christopher McCrudden (Lincoln College, Oxford)

# Law and Administration

Carol Harlow
*Professor of Public Law at the London School of Economics and Political Science*

Richard Rawlings
*Reader in Law at the London School of Economics and Political Science*

Butterworths
London, Edinburgh, Dublin
1997

| United Kingdom | Butterworths a Division of Reed Elsevier (UK) Ltd, Halsbury House, 35 Chancery Lane, LONDON WC2A 1EL and 4 Hill Street, EDINBURGH EH2 3JZ |
| --- | --- |
| Australia | Butterworths, SYDNEY, ADELAIDE, BRISBANE, CANBERRA, MELBOURNE and PERTH, |
| Canada | Butterworths Canada Ltd, TORONTO and VANCOUVER |
| Ireland | Butterworth (Ireland) Ltd, DUBLIN |
| Malaysia | Malayan Law Journal Sdn Bhd, KUALA LUMPUR |
| New Zealand | Butterworths of New Zealand Ltd, WELLINGTON and AUCKLAND |
| Singapore | Reed Elsevier (Singapore) Pte Ltd, SINGAPORE |
| South Africa | Butterworths Publishers (Pty) Ltd, DURBAN |
| USA | Michie, CHARLOTTESVILLE, Virginia |

A CIP Catalogue record for this book is available from the British Library.

ISBN 0 406 04589 5

Typeset by Doyle & Co, Colchester
Printed and bound in Great Britain

M. Barthélemy, the Dean of the Faculty of Law in the University of Paris, relates that thirty years ago he was spending a week-end with the late Professor Dicey. In the course of conversation M. Barthélemy asked a question about administrative law in this country. 'In England', replied Dicey, 'we know nothing of administrative law; and we wish to know nothing.'

W. A. Robson, 'The Report of the Committee on Ministers' Powers'
(1932) 3 Political Quarterly, p. 346.

# Preface

When, in the late 1970s, this book was first contemplated, our intention was a book about law, or 'law in context' study of administrative law, rather than a 'lawbook'. In this new edition, we have pinned our colours more firmly to the mast, describing ourselves as 'functionalists'. By this we mean that our main interest lies, as it has always lain, in observing the contribution made by law and lawyers to the practice of government and administration. Our book sets out, in other words, to make lawyers, and more especially law students, aware of the environment in which administrative law has to operate. From the opposite side of a divide which, we believe, ought not to exist, we aim to teach political scientists and students of public administration something about the role of law and legislation in administration.

That is not to say, however, that our attitude to law is purely mechanistic. We believe that administrative law raises fundamental questions about our constitutional and political arrangements to which standard texts customarily pay insufficient attention. This may be necessary in a text aimed primarily at practitioners, whose need to know the rules, often in considerable detail, takes precedence. In the case of student texts, the argument is made that students must learn the law before they criticise it. This is to put the cart before the horse. The danger is that background theory, by which is meant the underlying values of a legal or constitutional system, will be absorbed uncritically along with the rules. The constitution, as Sir Stephen Sedley has said, is reduced to a jumble of unrelated facts. We believe that the broad constitutional questions of legitimacy and accountability which underlie our subject must be faced squarely and honestly. Like democracy, the values of administrative law have to be understood if they are to withstand challenge.

We are, in this respect, unashamed believers in diversity. Like Professor Loughlin, we see public law partly as 'a sophisticated form of political discourse'. Discussion, debate and disagreement are the very nature of politics. In the first edition, our concern was very much with showing the breadth of opinion in English public law, at that time too often ignored or pushed to one side. Today, this point of view has become more generally accepted. In this edition, therefore, we feel able to make our own views more explicit.

This book does not set out, however, to propound a single, consistent theory of the state or constitution – a civic republican, post-modern, or legal positivist perspective on administrative law. In Chapters 2 to 4, therefore, a variety of views about administrative law are presented and subjected to critical scrutiny. These chapters also attempt to integrate law and legal theory with related disciplines, notably those of political science and public administration.

Unlike many other texts, our book contains no map of the state in the sense of a description of the way in which central and local government, agencies and other bodies are organised. It is not, however, our intention to convey a monolithic vision of a faceless Weberian bureaucracy. We have preferred to concentrate on the evolution of state forms and the way in which administrative law reflects and responds to them. Historically, the British contribution to public administration has been to view it as an art rather than a science. Traditionally, British government is 'club' or 'group' government, comfortable with discretion, less reliant than the objective Weberian model on standardisation and rules. It does no harm to remember that the influence of individual ministers, regulators, ombudsmen and judges is considerable; personal style and opinion infuses their decision making.

A key theme of this book is the clash between these two styles of public administration as this has been reflected in administrative law. Thus Chapter 4 traces the struggle to eliminate discretion and the movement for rational decision-making, while Chapters 6 and 7 trace the growing power of rules. We find a rapid 'juridification' of public administration through a myriad of complex rules and complicated procedures. Challengeable in a confusing network of complaints procedures, these rules inevitably stimulate a secondary process of juridification through litigation and the interpretative jurisdiction of courts. In Chapters 12 to 14, we look at the tradition of alternative dispute resolution and its contribution to administrative law. In Chapters 15 to 17, we turn to judicial review. Our first edition went to press shortly after *O'Reilly v Mackman* introduced into procedural law a sharp distinction between 'public' and 'private'. This underpinned the development of an exclusive supervisory jurisdiction vested in an administrative division of the High Court. In this edition, we see how the changing face of public administration has put in issue the public/private dichotomy on which this jurisdiction is founded. We also track the rise of judicial review, both quantitatively and doctrinally. We focus on the role of judicial discretion, illustrated in a case study of procedural fairness. The expansion of judicial review highlights questions of legitimacy and judicial accountability. These issues are ventilated in Chapter 17.

Our first edition came out on the cusp of a political era, just as a paradigm change was taking place. The welfare state had reached its zenith and under the influence of New Right political theory, the Government of Margaret Thatcher was embarking on 'rolling back the boundaries of the state'. At that point, in the preface to the first edition, we summarised the themes of our book 'in three currently fashionable terms: "process", 'legitimacy" and "competency"'. In retrospect, 'participation' and 'accountability' were strongly emergent themes which should have been separately listed. By 'process' was meant the vision of administration as an entity, or dynamic interaction of output and input functions, rather than, as lawyers tend to see it, as a set of disparate decisions. This vision found expression in three long modular studies of planning, welfare and immigration administration.

Today our list of currently fashionable themes would need further extension to include the distinctive ideology of New Public Management, with its emphasis on economy, efficiency and effectiveness. The subject matter of this edition has changed in other ways. Since we first wrote, both contract and regulation have moved to the centre of the subject area, a change reflected in Chapters 8 to 11. Structurally, we have replaced the modular studies by shorter case studies more closely integrated into the argument of the book, such as the studies of social security adjudication, of telecommunications regulation and of criminal injuries compensation.

When we first wrote, the European dimension of the state and the European contribution to national administrative law were barely perceptible. In this new edition, their influence is everywhere apparent not only in the jurisprudence of the European Court of Human Rights at Strasbourg and European Court of Justice at Luxembourg but, more important, through the Community's legislative and regulatory capacity. The growing influence of the ECHR is reflected not only in the case study of parole procedure but, more generally, in the emergence of a distinctive rights based theory of judicial review. The authority of the ECJ is nowhere better illustrated than in its expansive doctrine of state liability, discussed in Chapter 18. In respect of legislation, we could single out the EC law of public procurement, or regulation of government contracting, described in Chapter 9.

Just as our first edition appeared on the cusp of a political era, as the pendulum swung sharply from left to right, so the second appears as the pendulum swings back from the right to the centre. Some changes are already apparent, such as the termination of compulsory competitive tendering or enhanced regulation of financial markets. We can also expect some radical constitutional changes. We have not attempted to anticipate the problems of devolution or prophesy the style, or the effects, of incorporating the European Convention on Human Rights. We hope that the promised freedom of information legislation will be forthcoming but again, we have not attempted to anticipate it. Once more there will be developments whose importance, as last time with regulation, we underestimate, and others which we fail entirely to foresee. Already, juridification is emerging as a problem with which society has not learned to grapple. We are confident that there will be plenty of room for a third edition.

Carol Harlow
Richard Rawlings

August 1997

# Acknowledgments

As usual, the authors have accumulated many debts. First, we must thank our families for their patience and encouragement during a long period of gestation. Secondly, we thank Susan Hunt, who typed innumerable drafts accurately and rapidly, and Elizabeth Durant for their help. We would also like to thank our publishers for support and patience.

In the course of preparation, we have had many research assistants. Special thanks go to Elizabeth Start and Jesse Elvin, who undertook the thankless task of verifying references and finalising the manuscript. Elizabeth also helped prepare case studies, as did Liora Lazarus, Lee Jackson, Tobias Krohn and Katie Wood, all of whom we take this opportunity of thanking. Finally, we thank those colleagues who read drafts and commented, and the many friends and contacts in government and the law who generously supplied information and advice.

The authors and publishers would like to thank the following for permission to reproduce copyright material: T. Allan (*Modern Law Review*, 'Rugby, Recreation Grounds and Race Relations: Punishment for Silence'); T. Allan (Oxford University Press, Clarendon, *Liberty and Justice: The Legal Foundations of British Constitutionalism*); M. Aronson (Hart Publishing, 'A Public Lawyer's Responses to Privatization and Outsourcing' (in M. Taggart (ed.), *The Province of Administrative Law*)); R. Austin (*Current Legal Problems*, Oxford University Press, 'Judicial Review of Subjective Discretion – At the Rubicon; Whither Now?'); I. Ayres and J. Braithwaite (Oxford University Press, *Responsive Regulation: Transcending the Deregulation Debate*); J. Baldwin, N. Wikeley and R. Young (Oxford University Press, Clarendon, *Judging Social Security: The Adjudication of Claims*); R. Baldwin and C. McCrudden (Weidenfeld & Nicolson, *Regulation and Public Law*); R. Baldwin (Weidenfeld & Nicolson, 'Civil Aviation Regulation: From Tribunal to Regulatory Agency' (in R. Baldwin and C. McCrudden (eds.), *Regulation and Public Law*)); R. Baldwin (Oxford University Press, *Rules and Government*); R. Baldwin and K. Hawkins (*Public Law*, Sweet & Maxwell, 'Discretionary Justice: Davis Reconsidered'); R. Baldwin (*Public Law*, Sweet and Maxwell, 'A British Independent Regulatory Agency and the "Skytrain" Decision'); R. Barker (Methuen, *Political Ideas in Modern Britain*); J. Black (*Modern Law Review* 'Constitutionalising Self-Regulation'); L. Blom-Cooper (*Current Legal Problems*, Oxford University Press, 'Public Inquiries'); G. Borrie (Fabian Society, *Justice and the Administration*); J. Bowdery (Centre for the Study of Regulated Industries, *Quality Regulation and the Regulated*

*Industries*); J. Bradshaw (Heinemann Educational, 'From Discretion to Rules: The Experience of the Family Fund' (in M. Adler and S. Asquith (eds.), *Discretion and Welfare*)); S. Breyer (Harvard University Press, *Regulation and its Reform*); L. Bridges, C. Game, O. Lomas, J. McBride and S. Ranson (Avebury, *Legality and Local Politics*); R. Brownsword and I. Harden (*Legal Studies*, Butterworths, 'Rights and the Red Book'); F. Bulmer (Conservative Political Centre, *CCT: The Continuing Challenge*); P. Cane and P. Atiyah (Weidenfeld & Nicolson, *Accidents, Compensation and the Law*); P. Cane (*Public Law*, Sweet & Maxwell, 'Standing, Legality and the Limits of Public Law'); B. Carsberg (Institute of Economic Affairs, 'Injecting Competition Into Telecommunications' (in C. Veljanovski (ed.), *Privatization and Competition: A Market Prospectus*)); M. Cave and P. Williamson (Oxford University Press, 'The Reregulation of British Broadcasting' (in M. Bishop, J. Kay and C. Mayer, *The Regulatory Challenge*)); R. Cotterell, (Oxford University Press, Clarendon, 'Judicial Review and Legal Theory' (in G. Richardson and H. Genn (eds.), *Administrative Law and Government Action*)); P. Craig, (*European Review of Public Law*, 'Procedures and Administrative Decision Making: A Common Law Perspective')); R. Cranston, (Oxford University Press, Clarendon, 'Reviewing Judicial Review' (in G. Richardson and H. Genn (eds.), *Administrative Law and Government Action*)); R. Crossman (Fabian Society, *Socialism and the New Despotism*); T. Daintith (*Current Legal Problems*, Oxford University Press, 'Regulation by Contract: The New Prerogative'); K. C. Davis (Louisiana State University Press, *Discretionary Justice*); S. de Smith, H. Woolf and J. Jowell (Sweet & Maxwell, *Judicial Review of Administrative Action*); A. V. Dicey (Macmillan, *Introduction to the Study of the Law of the Constitution*); M. Dimock (Praeger, *Law and Dynamic Administration*); S. Domberger (Oxford University Press, Clarendon, 'Economic Regulation Through Franchise Contracts' (in J. Mayer and D. Thompson (eds.), *Privatization and Regulation: The UK Experience*)); L. Duguit (Allen and Unwin, *Law in the Modern State*); P. Dunleavy and B. O'Leary (Macmillan, *Theories of the State: The Politics of Liberal Democracy*); A. Dunsire (*Public Administration*, Blackwell, 'Challenges to Public Administration in the 1980s'); R. Dworkin (Oxford University Press, Clarendon, *A Matter of Principle*); M. Elliot (*Modern Law Review*, 'Chasing the Receding Bus: The Broadcasting Act 1980'); M. Fagence (*Citizen Participation in Planning*); Financial Law Panel (*Transactions with Local Authorities*); S. Fredman and G. Morris (*Public Law*, Sweet and Maxwell, 'The Costs of Exclusivity: Public and Private Re-examined'); M. Freedland (*Public Law*, Sweet and Maxwell, 'Government by Contract and Public Law'); W. Friedmann (Penguin, *Law in a Changing Society*); J. Fulbrook (*Industrial Law Journal*, Oxford University Press, 'The Job Seekers' Act 1995: Consolidation with a Sting of Contractual Compliance'); D. Galligan (Oxford University Press, Clarendon, *Due Process and Fair Procedures: A Study of Administrative Procedures*); D. Galligan (*Public Law*, Sweet & Maxwell, 'The Nature and Function of Policies within Discretionary Power'); D. Galligan (Croom Helm, 'Rights, Discretion and Procedures' (in D. Galligan and C. Sampford (eds.), *Law, Rights and the Welfare State*)); G. Ganz (*Public Law*, Sweet & Maxwell, 'Allocation of Decision-Making Functions'); J. Garner (*Public Law*, Sweet & Maxwell, 'The Council on Tribunals'); H. Genn (Legal

Action Group, *A Strategy for Justice*); C. Graham and T. Prosser (Oxford University Press, *Privatising Public Enterprises*); C. Graham (*Utilities Law Review*, John Wiley & Sons Ltd., 'Consumers and Privatized Industries'); R. Gregory and G. Drewry (*Public Law*, Sweet & Maxwell, 'Barlow Clowes and the Ombudsman'); R. Gregory, P. Giddings, V. Moore, J. Pearson (Edwin Mellen Press, *Practice and Prospects of the Ombudsmen in the United Kingdom*); J. Griffith (Blackwell, *Judicial Politics Since 1920*); J. Griffith (Barry Rose, 'Constitutional and Administrative Law' (in P. Archer and A. Martin (eds.), *More Law Reform Now!*)); S. Grosz (Wiley Chancery Publishing, 'Access to Environmental Justice in Public Law' (in D. Robinson and J. Dunkley (eds.), *Public Interest Perspectives in Environmental Law*)); S. Grosz (*New Law Journal*, Butterworths, 'Pergau Be Dammed'); L. Hancher and M. Moran (*European Journal of Political Research*, Kluwer Academic Publishers, 'Introduction: Regulation and Deregulation'); Hansard Society (*Report of the Hansard Society Commission on the Legislative Process*); Hansard Society and European Policy Forum (*Report of the Commission on the Regulation of Privatised Utilities*); I. Harden (Open University Press, *The Contracting State*); C. Harlow (*Modern Law Review*, 'Ombudsmen in Search of a Role'); C. Harlow (*Modern Law Review*, 'Accidental Death of an Asylum Seeker'); F. Hayek (Routledge, *The Road to Serfdom*); Lord Hewart (Benn Ltd., A. & C. Black, *The New Despotism*); M. Hill (Harper Collins, *The State, Administration and the Individual*); P. Hogg (Carswell, *Liability of the Crown*); P. Hogg (*National Journal of Constitutional Law*, 'Compensation for Damage Caused by Government'); C. Hood (*Public Administration*, Blackwell, 'A Public Management For All Seasons'); Lord Howe (*Public Law*, Sweet and Maxwell, 'Procedure at the Scott Inquiry'); A. Hutchinson (*University of Toronto Law Journal*, 'Mice Under a Chair: Democracy, Courts and the Administrative State'); A. Hutchinson and M. Jones (*Journal of Law and Society*, Blackwell, 'Wheeler-Dealing: An Essay on Law, Politics and Speech'); Lord Irvine (*Public Law*, Sweet & Maxwell, 'Judges and Decision-makers: The Theory and Practice of *Wednesbury* Review'); D. Jabbari (*Oxford Journal of Legal Studies*, Oxford University Press, 'Critical Theory in Administrative Law'); S. James (*Public Administration*, Blackwell, 'The Political and Administrative Consequences of Judicial Review'); W. Jennings (*Public Administration*, Blackwell, 'In Praise of Dicey'); W. Jennings (London University Press, Hodder & Stoughton Educational Ltd., *The Law and the Constitution*); T. Jones (*Journal of Law and Society*, Blackwell, 'Administrative Law, Regulation and Legitimacy'); J. Jowell (*Public Law*, Sweet and Maxwell, 'The Legal Control of Administrative Discretion'); JUSTICE/All Souls (*Review of Administrative Law*); JUSTICE/Public Law Project (*A Matter of Public Interest. Reforming the Law and Practice on Interventions in Public Interest Cases*); Sir Peter Kemp (*Parliamentary Brief*, 'The Mandarins Emerge Unscathed'); H. Laski (Oxford University Press, 'M. Duguit's Conception of the State' (in A. Goodhart et al., *Modern Theories of Law*)); H. Laski (Allen and Unwin, *Government and Politics*); H. Laski (Allen and Unwin, *A Grammar of Politics*); Sir John Laws (*Public Law*, Sweet and Maxwell, 'Law and Democracy'); N. Lewis (*Public Law*, Sweet and Maxwell, 'Supplementary Benefit Appeal Tribunals'); N. Lewis (*Public Law*, Sweet and Maxwell, 'IBA Programme Contract Awards');

S. Livingstone (Gill and MacMillan, 'The Impact of Judicial Review on Prisons' (in B. Hadfield (ed.), *Judicial Review: A Thematic Approach*)); O. Lomas, (*Modern Law Review*, 'The Twenty-Fifth Annual Report of the Council on Tribunals – An Opportunity Sadly Missed'); M. Loughlin (*Public Law*, Sweet & Maxwell, 'Innovative Financing in Local Government: The Limits of Legal Instrumentalism – Part II'); M. Loughlin (Oxford University Press, Clarendon, *Public Law and Political Theory*); M. Loughlin (University of Toronto Law Journal, 'Procedural Fairness: A Study of the Crisis in Administrative Law Theory'); N. MacCormick, (Stanford University Press, *H. L. A. Hart*); R. MacDonald (*McGill Law Journal*, 'Judicial Review and Procedural Fairness in Administrative Law'); G. Majone (*West European Politics*, Frank Cass & Co., 'The Rise of the Regulatory State in Europe'); Sir Anthony Mason (Oxford University Press, 'Courts, Constitutions and Fundamental Rights' (in R. Rawlings (ed.), *Law, Society and Economy*)); R. Megarry (*Law Quarterly Review*, Sweet & Maxwell, 'Administrative Quasi-Legislation'); J. D. B. Mitchell (Harper Collins, *The Contracts of Public Authorities*); D. Mullan (*University of Toronto Law Journal*, 'Fairness: the New Natural Justice'); W. Muller and V. Wright (*Western European Politics*, Frank Cass & Co., 'Reshaping the State in Western Europe: The Limits to Retreat' (in W. Muller and V. Wright (eds.), *The State in Western Europe. Retreat or Redefinition*)); D. Nelken (*Current Legal Problems*, Oxford University Press, 'The Use of "Contracts" as a Social Work Technique'); P. Nonet and D. Selznick, (Harper Collins, *Law and Society in Transition: Toward Responsive Law*); A. Ogus (Oxford University Press, Clarendon, *Regulation. Legal Form and Economic Theory*); D. Oliver (*Public Law*, Sweet & Maxwell, 'Is Ultra Vires the Basis of Judicial Review?'); D. Pannick (*Political Quarterly*, Blackwell, 'The Law Lords and the Needs of Contemporary Society'); M. Partington (Legal Action Group, 'Lessons from Tribunals' ( in R. Smith (ed.), *Shaping the Future: New Directions for Legal Services*)); M. Pirie (Adam Smith Institute, *The Citizen's Charter*); M. Power (Demos, *The Audit Explosion*); R. Posner (Little Brown, *The Economic Analysis of Law*); T. Prosser (*Juridical Review*, W. Green & Son, Sweet & Maxwell, 'Privatization, Regulation and Public Services'); T. Prosser (*Journal of Law and Society*, Blackwell, 'Poverty, Ideology and Legality: Supplementary Benefit Appeal Tribunals and their Predecessors'); Sir Idwal Pugh (*Public Law*, Sweet & Maxwell, 'The Ombudsman – Jurisdiction, Powers and Practice'); M. Radford (*Modern Law Review*, 'Auditing for Change: Local Government and the Audit Commission'); R. Rees and J. Vickers (Oxford University Press, 'RPI – X Price-Cap Regulation' (in M. Bishop, J. Kay and C. Mayer, *The Regulatory Challenge*)); C. Reich (Random House, *The Greening of America*); A. Reiss (*Michigan Law Review*, 'Book Review of K. C. Davis, Discretionary Justice'); R. Rhodes (*Political Quarterly*, Blackwell, 'The Hollowing Out of the State: The Changing Nature of the Public Service in Britain'); G. Richardson (Oxford University Press, Clarendon, 'The Legal Regulation of Process' (in G. Richardson and H. Genn (eds.), *Administrative Law and Government Action*)); J. Richardson (Croom Helm, 'Doing Less by Doing More: British Government 1979-1993' (in R. Rhodes and V. Wright (eds.), *The State in Western Europe*)); W. Robson (*Political Quarterly*, Blackwell, 'The Report of the Committee on Ministers' Powers'); W. Robson (*Public Law*, Sweet and Maxwell, 'Administrative Justice and Injustice: a Commentary on the Franks Report'); W. Robson (Stevens, Sweet & Maxwell, *Justice and Administrative Law*); L. Rovizzi and D. Thompson (Oxford University Press, 'The Regulation of Product Quality in the Public Utilities' (in M. Bishop, J. Kay and C. Mayer, *The Regulatory Challenge*)); R. Sainsbury (Oxford University Press, Clarendon, 'Internal Reviews and the Weakening of Social Security Claimants' Rights of Appeal' (in G. Richardson and H. Genn (eds.), *Administrative Law and Government Action*)); B. Schwartz and H. W. R. Wade (Oxford University Press, Clarendon, *Legal Control of Government*); J. Shklar (Harvard University Press, *Legalism*); A. Shonfield (Royal Institute of International Affairs, *Modern Capitalism: The Changing Balance of Public and Private Power*); A. Sparke (Butterworths, *The Compulsory Competitive Tendering Guide*); J. Steltzer (Institute of Economic Affairs, 'Regulatory Methods: A Case for Hands Across the Atlantic?' (in C. Veljanovski (ed.), *Regulators and the Market*)); R. Stewart (*University of Chicago Law Review*, 'Madison's Nightmare'); F. Sutcliffe (*Anglo-American Law Review*, Barry Rose, 'Contracting Out Public Services: UK Policy v. EC Law'); G. Teubner (Walter de Gruyter, 'Juridification – Concepts, Aspects, Limits, Solutions' (in G. Teubner (ed.), *Juridification of Social Spheres*)); R. Titmuss, (*Political Quarterly*, Blackwell, 'Welfare "Rights", Law and Discretion'); C. Turpin (Longman, *Government Procurement and Contracts*); C. Veljanovski (Institute of Economic Affairs, 'The Regulation Game' (in C. Veljanovski (ed.), *Regulators and the Market*)); C. Veljanovski (European Policy Forum, *The Future of Industry Regulation in the UK*); M. Vile (Oxford University Press, Clarendon, *Constitutionalism and Separation of Powers*); P. Vincent-Jones (*Legal Studies*, Butterworths, 'The Limits of Contractual Order in Public Sector Transacting'); J. Vickers and G. Yarrow (MIT Press, *Privatization: An Economic Analysis*); H. W. R. Wade (Stevens, Sweet & Maxwell, *Constitutional Fundamentals*); H. W. R. Wade and C. Forsyth (Oxford University Press, Clarendon, *Administrative Law*); M. Weber, C. Wright and H. Gerth (Oxford University Press, *Essays in Sociology*); Lord Woolf (*Public Law*, Sweet & Maxwell, 'Droit Public – English Style'); P. Xavier (*Telecommunications Policy*, Elsevier Science Ltd., 'Price Cap Regulation for Telecommunications').

# Contents

# Table of statutes

Page references printed in **bold** type indicate where the Act is set out in part or in full.

# Table of cases

xxiii

Decisions of the European Court of Justice are listed below numerically. These decisions are also included in the preceding alphabetical list.

# Chapter 1

# State, government and law

## 1. Law and politics

Behind every theory of administrative law there lies a theory of the state. Laski once said that constitutional law was unintelligible except as the expression of an economic system of which it was designed to serve as a rampart.[1] By this he meant that the machinery of government is necessarily an expression of the society in which it operates and that it is impossible to understand the one except in the context of the other. In 1941, Sir Cecil Carr made a similar point in a series of lectures at Harvard University on the subject of administrative law, in the course of which he said:[2]

> We nod approvingly today when someone tells us that, whereas the State used to be merely policeman, judge and protector, it has now become schoolmaster, doctor, housebuilder, road-maker, town-planner, public utility supplier and all the rest of it. The contrast is no recent discovery. De Tocqueville observed in 1866 that the State 'everywhere interferes more than it did; it regulates more undertakings, and undertakings of a lesser kind; and it gains a firmer footing every day, about, around and above all private persons, to assist, to advise, and to coerce them' (Oeuvres, III, 501). Nassau William Senior, a Benthamite ten years older than Chadwick, a colleague of his on the original Poor Law Commission, had justified this tendency. A government, he thinks, must do whatever conduces to the welfare of the governed (the utilitarian theory); it will make mistakes, but non-interference may be an error too; one can be passively wrong as well as actively wrong. One might go back much earlier still to Aristotle, who said that the city-state or partnership-community comes into existence to protect life and remains in existence to protect a proper way of living. What is the proper standard? That is an age-long issue which is still a burning question of political controversy. The problems of administrative law are approached in the light of that fire. Those who dislike the statutory delegation of legislative power or the statutory creation of a non-judicial tribunal will often be those who dislike the policy behind the statute and seek to fight it at every stage. On the one side are those who want to step on the accelerator, on the other those who want to apply the brake.

In this lecture, Carr plainly accepts not only that the problems which administrative law is asked to resolve are also political questions, but also that they are customarily judged by subjective rather than objective standards, everything

---

1   H. Laski, *A Grammar of Politics* (London: Allen and Unwin) 1925, p. 578.
2   *Concerning English Administrative Law* (Oxford: OUP) 1941, pp. 10-11.

1

being dependent on the viewpoint of the observer. To his American audience, this would probably have seemed unexceptional.[3] English lawyers, on the other hand, would certainly have found it unpalatable. Yet, as Loughlin indicates in the following passage, nineteenth-century writers were alive to the relationship between constitutional law and political theory and were themselves well grounded in the latter.[4] Writing much later, Loughlin himself is able to take the close nexus between public law and political theory for granted:[5]

> [P]ublic law is simply a sophisticated form of political discourse [and] controversies within the subject are simply extended political disputes. Since many argue that public law is rooted in its social, political, economic, and historical context this approach should ensure that our inquiry is embedded in the realities of the times. The adoption of this method of inquiry, in addition, will force us to try to articulate what, if anything, is special about law's claims. Furthermore, though to many people this method of inquiry may seem both novel and radical, this is not in fact the case. There is a long history of seeking to express and articulate the issues of public law in the context of the development of society.

Standard public law texts do not usually admit the relationship between law and political science, however. Indeed, it is fair to say that a majority do their utmost to separate law from its political context.[6] The dominant view has been that law is not a branch of political science, a view accepted by lawyers and political scientists alike:[7]

> Judicial theory has not constituted a major part of the body of political ideas in Britain. The law has been considered to be a world neutrally detached from the contests of political ideas and argument. Particular laws and particular legal judgments may have had recognized political consequences which have been applauded or resisted, but the general character of the judicial system and the general assumptions of law have been little considered in debates about the political character and goals of the nation. Dicey had of course given an account of the basis of rights and of the rule of law which was allied to his preferences for limited and central government, and the discussions of administrative law and of delegated legislation continued to be carried on with reference to such preferences. The phrase 'the rule of law' was later in the century employed by Hayek to express and legitimize his own political ideas and beliefs. But in general, legal ideas were invisible in the elaboration of political argument.

This vision of the world of law as apolitical, neutral and independent of the world of government, politics and administration, has its roots deep in Western

---

3   See N. Duxbury, 'The Theory and History of American Law and Politics' (1993) 13 OJLS 249, reviewing the famous studies by M. Horwitz, *The Transformation of American Law, 1780-1860* (New York: OUP) 1992; *The Transformation of American Law, 1870-1960: the Crisis of Legal Orthodoxy* (New York: OUP) 1992.

4   See e.g. F. Maitland, 'A Historical Sketch of Liberty and Equality' in *Collected Papers* (1911) vol. 1, p. 1; Sir Frederick Pollock, *Essays in the Law* (1922) Nos. 2 and 3, pp. 31-110.

5   *Public Law and Political Theory* (Oxford: Clarendon) 1992, p. 4 (hereafter M. Loughlin, *Public Law*).

6   See, for criticism of this approach, J. Griffith, 'The Teaching of Law and Politics' (1982) 16 The Law Teacher 1. M. Loughlin, *Public Law*, pp. 32-36 tries to explain the divide.

7   R. Barker, *Political Ideas in Modern Britain* (London: Methuen) 1978, p. 95.

constitutional and legal theory. To take the first point first, implicit in the Rule of Law ideal is the concept of law as somehow neutral and impartial, 'above' both ruler and party politics:

> A cardinal feature of the rule-of-law model, and a bulwark of institutional autonomy, is the disjunction of political will and legal judgment. Law is elevated 'above' politics; that is, the positive law is held to embody standards that public consent, authenticated by tradition or by constitutional process, has removed from political controversy. The authority to interpret this legal heritage must therefore be kept insulated from the struggle for power and uncontaminated by political influence. In interpreting and applying the law, jurists are to be objective spokesmen for historically established principles, passive dispensers of a received, impersonal justice. They have a claim to the last word because their judgments are thought to obey an external will and not their own.[8]

In this way the Rule of Law ideal locks into the classic liberal ideal of a state whose limited function is to act essentially as a neutral arbiter between all citizens. Oakeshott[9] establishes this point when he summarises freedom in terms of limited power ('no leader, faction, party or "class", no majority, no government is in our society allowed unlimited power'). Equally, the Rule of Law ideal locks closely into the constitutional theory of Separation of Powers;[10] indeed, it is often difficult to distinguish the two. From Separation of Powers theory we derive both the idea that judges do not 'make' law but simply 'declare' it and also the perception of the judiciary as 'independent' or somehow detached from 'government'.[11] This eighteenth-century perspective on the control of power underlies all modern constitutions, has survived two centuries of political centralisation,[12] and is fundamental to an understanding of the development of administrative law.

By including in *A Grammar of Politics*[13] a chapter about the judicial process, Laski was therefore affirming his belief that the legal system *forms part of* the wider political scene, a point made by Carr in a different fashion. Yet so strongly entrenched are the ideas of independence and neutrality in British constitutional theory that to question them – as Laski, in describing the judiciary as a branch of government seemed to do and as Griffith, in *The Politics of the Judiciary*,[14] famously did – may seem heretical. But one does not have to be a Marxist to believe that the idea of apolitical law is itself political. The idea merely reflects ideas about the functions of the ideal state. Both sets of ideas developed in conjunction with nineteenth-century laissez-faire, or market, economic theories,

---

8  P. Nonet and D. Selznick, *Law and Society in Transition: Toward Responsive Law* (New York: Harper and Row) 1978, p. 57.
9  M. Oakeshott, *Rationalism in Politics and Other Essays* (Oxford: Blackwell) 1962, p. 41; M. Loughlin, *Public Law*, pp. 63-104 explains and comments on Oakeshott's theory of the State.
10  Montesquieu's formulation of this doctrine justifies his title as 'the father of constitutions': see J. Shklar, *Montesquieu* (Oxford: OUP) 1987.
11  On which see, R. Miliband, *The State in a Capitalist Society* (London: Quartet) 1969, pp. 124-130.
12  See, M. Vile, *Constitutionalism and Separation of Powers* (Oxford: Clarendon) 1967.
13  H. Laski, *A Grammar of Politics*, note 1, Ch. 10.
14  J. Griffith, *The Politics of the Judiciary* (London: Fontana) 4th edn., 1991; J. Griffith, *Judicial Politics since 1920: A Chronicle* (Oxford: Blackwell) 1993.

in which economic activity was not regulated but left to individual enterprise.[15] They are not immutable.

## 2. State, Crown and government

In 1981, two years after Margaret Thatcher became Prime Minister, an 'unofficial Royal Commission' was set up under the auspices of *Justice* and All Souls College, Oxford to consider the current state of English administrative law. This is how the Committee saw the state in which they found themselves:[16]

> In 1900 government interfered hardly at all in the way people ran their daily lives; and it provided virtually no personal social services. Today quite the reverse is true. The state has assumed an ever increasing range of responsibilities. Through nationalisation it controls most of the basic industries and the goods and services they supply. It runs a comprehensive system of social services providing benefits from just before the cradle (by way of pre-natal services and a maternity grant) to the grave (with a death grant) and in between it provides education, a health service, sickness benefits, unemployment benefits and old age pensions . . . The state also seeks to control much of the environment in which we live . . . This enormous growth in the nature and ambit of state power can be illustrated in a number of ways. First, there has been a vast increase in public expenditure. In 1870 it was £100 million, 9% of the gross national product and £3 per head of the population. A hundred years later it was £20,000 million, 43% of the gross national product and £400 per head of the population. Today it is over £52,000 million, 42% of the gross domestic product and about £1,000 per head of the population . . . Secondly, there has also been a massive increase in the number of those employed to administer our affairs. In 1900 there were 50,000 civil servants employed by central government; in 1980 there were 548,600 non-industrial civil servants. If to that is added about 600,000 officials in local government and about 100,000 who administer the health service, there are some 1.25 million officials without including administrators in such bodies as the water and sewerage authorities and the nationalised industries.

Descriptive though this passage is, one can glimpse behind the description a concern with what the state is – and perhaps also what it ought to be – doing. Why, for example, does the Committee emphasise that, before 1900, the state hardly interfered with the way people ran their lives? After all, the state has always proscribed certain behaviour as criminal, described other behaviour as immoral and often prescribed people's religious or political beliefs. If you read the passage carefully, however, you can see that the Committee's concern is with the state as engaged in industrial enterprises (the producer state) and as a provider of services and benefits (the welfare state). In this context, the Committee's main concern was to ascertain whether the rights and liberties of the individual were adequately protected against what they saw as a vast increase that had taken place this century in the power of the state and in the range of its activities.

15  Discussed by E. Kamenka and E. Tay, 'Beyond Bourgeois Individualism: the Contemporary Crisis in Law and Legal Ideology', in E. Kamenka and R. Neale (eds.), *Feudalism, Capitalism and Beyond* (London: Edward Arnold) 1975.
16  *Justice*/All Souls Review of Administrative Law, Interim Report 1981, paras. 18-22.

To find out more about the functions and character of the state we shall need to look outside legal textbooks and turn instead to the work of political scientists and historians. According to a standard textbook of political science,[17] the modern state has five characteristics:

1. The state is a recognisably separate institution or set of institutions, so differentiated from the rest of society as to create identifiable public and private spheres.
2. The state is sovereign, or the supreme power, within its territory, and by definition the ultimate authority for all law, i.e. binding rules supported by coercive sanctions. Public law is made by state officials and backed by a formal monopoly of force.
3. The state's sovereignty extends to all the individuals within a given territory, and applies equally, even to those in formal positions of government or rule-making. Thus sovereignty is distinct from the personnel who at any given time occupy a particular role within the state.
4. The modern state's personnel are mostly recruited and trained for management in a bureaucratic manner.
5. The state has the management to extract monetary revenues (taxation) to finance its activities from its subject population.

In this definition many ideas which we have already met are recognisable and the reader will be able to fit legal labels to other elements, such as sovereignty. Think about the authors' definition of law in terms of 'binding rules supported by coercive sanctions', however. Is it somewhat limited and perhaps outdated? Later chapters will suggest that this is only one among many conceptions of law.

It is a common criticism of public law that it has failed adequately to conceptualise the state,[18] and certainly the term has little legal resonance. If we turn to de Smith's popular textbook on *Constitutional and Administrative Law*[19] we find that the word 'state' does not even figure in the index. Predictably, we get instead a description of the Queen as 'the symbol of national identity', followed by a discussion of the prerogative powers of the Crown, defined innocuously as 'those inherent legal attributes which are unique to the Crown'. Here we find the assertion that for 'the Crown' we can substitute 'the Queen'. This sidesteps many questions. If Crown equals Queen, where do government departments fit? How, if the Crown comprises only central government departments, do local government and autonomous agencies fit into the framework of the state? We shall find later that whether or not an agency is part of the state may determine whether its

17   P. Dunleavy and B. O'Leary, *Theories of the State: The Politics of Liberal Democracy* (London: Macmillan) 1987, p. 2. This is an 'institutional' definition of the State. The authors (pp. 3-4) point out that 'functional' definitions, based on what the State actually does, are also possible.
18   Associated with the classic study by K. Dyson, *The State Tradition in Western Europe* (Oxford: Martin Robertson) 1980, the criticism goes back to H. Laski, *Grammar of Politics*, note 1, and 'The Responsibility of the State in England' (1919) 32 Harv. LR 447. See now, J. Allison, *A Continental Distinction in the Common Law: A Historical and Comparative Perspective on English Public Law* (Oxford: Clarendon) 1996, Ch. 2.
19   Though retained by the present editor, the approach is that of the original author: see S. de Smith, *Constitutional and Administrative Law* (Harmondsworth: Penguin) 3rd edn., 1973, pp. 103, 114, 140. The present editor's views are expressed in R. Brazier, *Constitutional Reform: Re-shaping the British Political System* (Oxford: Clarendon) 1991.

activities are subject to judicial control.[20] Again, what is the legal status of 'Ministers of the Crown'? If a minister is merely an 'emanation' of the Crown[1] he may be able to rely on prerogative powers and immunities whose extent is unclear. A host of other fundamental questions about our governmental system remain unanswered. De Smith is clearly unhappy both about the extent of prerogative powers which cannot be clearly identified and also that the conditions under which they are exercisable are obscure. He has to content himself, however, with the laconic observation that 'The accidents of litigation will doubtless resolve some of these problems, and throw up new ones, before the century is out.'[2]

Criticism of this position is really two-pronged. On the one hand, public lawyers are blamed for sidestepping theoretical and political issues. They are content to map the institutional contours of the state: central government departments, local government, agencies, boards, etc.[3] Sedley sees this as a significant defect which has the effect of demoting all constitutional issues to questions of fact. 'British constitutional questions are answered not from a prior consensus of principle, written or unwritten, but by a body of descriptive law which functions by collapsing what ought to be into what is.'[4] Prosser makes a similar point when he protests that:[5]

> Britain has an extended and powerful state apparatus; nevertheless the *concept* of state as the means for ... 'the rationalist pursuit of order in a society subject to ceaseless change' is absent, and certainly there is no systematically developed legal concept of the state as a sort of moral unifier standing above the struggles of civil society. If anything, the state is seen as a vaguely threatening monolith taken from the pages of George Orwell.

The second object of attack is the legal concept of 'The Crown'. With his striking metaphor of the 'republican crown', Jacob[6] points to the danger of allowing a sprawling state apparatus to grow up behind the screen of the personalised image of the monarch like an extension of the royal household. The monarchical imagery is absurd, and the legal fiction that power is *not* vested in the Prime Minister, Cabinet and other organisms of the modern state but in a royal dignitary

20  Originally decided by the House of Lords in *Mersey Docks and Harbour Board Trustees v Gibbs* (1866) LR 1 HL 93. And see J. Black, 'Constitutionalising self-regulation' (1996) 59 MLR 24.
1   *Merricks v Heathcoat-Amory* [1955] Ch 567. But see now, *M v Home Office* [1993] 3 WLR 433, below, p. 61.
2   S. de Smith, *Constitutional and Administrative Law* (Harmondsworth: Penguin) 2nd edn., 1973, p 140.
3   For an excellent map, consult D. Foulkes, *Administrative Law* (London: Butterworths) 8th edn., 1995.
4   S. Sedley, 'The Sound of Silence: Constitutional Law Without a Constitution' (1994) 110 LQR 270, 273.
5   T. Prosser, 'The State, Constitutions and Implementing Economic Policy: Privatization and Regulation in the UK, France and the USA' (1995) 4 Social & Legal Studies 507, 510. Prosser is quoting the influential work by K. Dyson, above.
6   J. Jacob, *The Republican Crown. Lawyers and the Making of the State in Twentieth Century Britain* (Aldershot: Dartmouth) 1996. See also V. Bogdanor, *The Monarchy and the Constitution* (Oxford: Clarendon) 1995; P. Hennessy, *The Hidden Wiring, Unearthing the British Constitution* (London: Gollancz) 1995.

incapable, in Blackstone's famous aphorism, not only of *doing* but even of *thinking* wrong, is dangerous. It allows government to benefit from our modern perception of the titular head of state as without political power and confined to dignitary functions.[7] Attached to the symbol of the Crown – as later chapters will reveal – are very real political powers in the shape of ancient privileges and immunities deriving from an earlier and more authoritarian monarchy. But the term is 'a convenient cover for ignorance'[8] which disguises the real location of power, blinds us to its true nature and renders its control in consequence more difficult:[9]

> Had the State emerged as a separate entity, then government could have been detached from the trappings of medieval monarchy, and the way would have been open for a reassessment of the equation 'Sovereignty = privilege' which is central to English thought . . . The State is a corporate body established to maintain public services, and is in theory, therefore, responsible rather than irresponsible.

## 3. Public and private law

A variant of this argument introduces a distinction between 'public' and 'private' law. In the next chapter, we shall explain how English law has developed as a 'private law' model of public law. By this is meant that there is no special administrative court; cases involving the state and its officials are decided by the 'ordinary courts of the land' – a fundamental premiss of Dicey's conception of the Rule of Law state (below, p. 40). In a celebrated article, however, Mitchell,[10] a great admirer of the French system of administrative law, argued that the absence of systematised public law meant that the common law had failed to develop principles appropriate for the control of a modern state. Mitchell linked two phenomena: the institutional lack of a special administrative jurisdiction and the substantive inadequacy of the rules applicable to the state.

By way of illustration, we can turn to the mundane case of *Town Investments v Department of the Environment*.[11] The question was whether a government department was entitled to reduced rent in terms of the Counter-Inflation (Business Rents) Orders 1972. The landlords argued (with some justice, since the property was sub-let) that the Department of the Environment (DoE) was not carrying on a business there; the DoE responded that the lessee was the Crown, which was carrying on the 'business of government'. This argument was upheld by the House of Lords, which ruled that, although 'the vocabulary used by lawyers in the field of public law has not kept pace' with the evolving constitution, the term 'government' was apt 'to embrace both collectively and individually all of the ministers of the Crown and parliamentary secretaries under whose direction the

---

7  See W. Bagehot, *The English Constitution* (London: Fontana) 1963, ed. R. Crossman.
8  The phrase is borrowed from F. Maitland, 'The Crown as Corporation' (1901) 18 LQR 131.
9  C. Harlow, 'The Crown: Wrong Once Again?' (1977) 40 MLR 728, 729-30.
10  J. Mitchell, 'The causes and effects of the absence of a system of public law in the United Kingdom' [1965] PL 95.
11  *Town Investments v Department of the Environment* [1976] 1 WLR 1126 (Foster J and CA); [1978] AC 359, HL. The citations are from Lord Diplock.

work of government is carried on by civil servants'. Arguably here the House did indeed struggle to evolve a theory of government consonant with the reality. But this did not help it to a just outcome. The DoE had argued that, because of the operation of the royal prerogative, the Crown was entitled to the benefits of the legislation even when the Orders expressly excluded the Crown from their operation; in other words, the Crown would be able to lease property at commercial rates while holding its landlords to the counter-inflation measures. The House agreed.

Now Mitchell's argument becomes relevant. A separate public law system would undoubtedly provide a different answer, distinguishing the 'governmental' functions of the state, where special privileges are permissible, from its 'commercial' activities, where they are not.[12] More interested in outcome than logic, the Court of Appeal had achieved this result by holding government to be divisible; the Minister, who could not then claim Crown immunity, was the lessor. To summarise, one approach to the problems of the Crown and the royal prerogative is through a doctrine of state which would allow rules of public law appropriate to our century to be developed. Thus, Samuel attributes weak control of state power to the fact that the common law treats state officials as 'citizens in uniform' and draws a highly misleading analogy between state power and individual rights.[13] But the problem can be approached from the opposite angle. After all, the prerogative powers *are* special rules of public law even if, contrary to the wishes of most of the modern commentators, they operate to shelter government from responsibility. It can then be argued that the judges have made skilful use of the idea of personal liability (explained in Chapter 2) both to cut down on governmental privilege and to confine the bodies which can claim them. The real strength of the 'private law' model is being discounted through dislike of the tools employed.

Recently, the judiciary has started to draw boundaries between public and private law though, as we shall see in Chapter 16, the division is mainly concerned with procedure and remedies. A rule of 'exclusivity' has been created, which routes all applications for judicial review of administrative action into a specialised division of the High Court. This development has been trenchantly criticised for erecting procedural obstacles in the way of the citizen.[14] Lord Woolf has backed the exclusivity rule as providing a stout support for an extended system of judicial review.[15] Cane too sees[16] the distinction as a helpful tool for analysis, provided that it is not too rigidly adhered to. The authors, on the other hand, accept the

12  C. Harlow, [1997] 40 MLR 728, above.
13  G. Samuel, 'Public and Private Law: A Private Lawyer's Response' (1983) 46 MLR 558. And see below, p. 44.
14  C. Harlow, '"Public" and "Private" Law: Definition Without Distinction' (1980) 43 MLR 241; J. Alder, 'Hunting the Chimera – the End of O'Reilly v Mackman' (1993) 13 LS 183. See also H. Wade and C. Forsyth, *Administrative Law*, 7th edn., (Oxford: OUP) 1994 (hereafter Wade and Forsyth), pp. 680-695.
15  Lord Woolf, 'Public Law – private law: Why the divide? A personal view' [1986] PL 220; *Protection of the Public – A New Challenge* (London: Stevens) 1990; 'Droit public – English style' [1995] PL 57.
16  P. Cane, 'Public Law and Private Law: A Study of the Analysis and Use of a Legal Concept', in J. Bell and J. Eekelaar (eds.), *Oxford Essays in Jurisprudence* 3rd series (Oxford: Clarendon) 1987.

efficacy of the common law and its structures and concepts to provide appropriate answers to problems involving the state. Perhaps more important, in the post-modernist world described at the end of this chapter, the authors feel that both argument and distinction are fast becoming outmoded. Since the consequences of the 'absence of a system of public law' are plainly visible throughout this book – in Chapter 8, for example, we shall find that there is no special law of administrative contracts; in Chapter 18 that state liability is governed by civil law principles – the reader can be the judge.

## 4. Towards the corporate state

Theories of the state are, on the other hand, central to the science of politics. Political science has charted the rise of the sovereign nation-state and noted its changing functions; from the residual or 'nightwatchman' state to the 'cradle-to-grave' welfare state depicted by the *Justice*/All Souls Committee.[17] Contrary to what was implied by the Committee, the skeleton of the 'interventionist state' was in place before the end of the nineteenth century; both Dicey and Maitland realised this[18] and it is confirmed by modern historians:[19]

> Britain, in the nineteenth century, saw a remarkable series of extensions of State intervention in society. Not only were many Acts of Parliament passed which were intended to have a major impact upon the behaviour of individual citizens, but means were devised to enforce these Acts much more effectively than had ever been the case before. The basis of the modern civil service was laid, local government was reformed and a variety of effective ad hoc bodies were created . . . Many of the key reforms of this period involved compromises with the older system of decentralized government. To enforce new laws without radically altering the administrative machinery, agencies were set up to inspect and supervise the activities of local organizations. The Poor Law Act of 1834, for example, set up a Poor Law Commission to supervise the activities of the local Guardians of the Poor and to organise them into Unions of parishes. Then, gradually through the century, the extent of central intervention increased. The Commission was transformed into the Poor Law Board and then, in 1871, into the Local

17  See P. Dunleavy and B. O'Leary, *Theories of the State: The Politics of Liberal Democracy* (London: Macmillan) 1987. And see D. Held, 'Central perspectives on the modern state' in G. McLennan, D. Held and S. Hall (eds.), *The Idea of the Modern State* (Milton Keynes: Open University Press) 1983; D. Fraser, *The Evolution of the British Welfare State* (London: Macmillan) 1973. For a historical account, see Q. Skinner, *The Foundations of Modern Political Thought* (Cambridge: Cambridge University Press) 1978 (2 vols.).

18  F. Maitland, *The Constitutional History of England* (Cambridge: Cambridge University Press) 1908, p. 501 called us 'a much governed nation', while in A. V. Dicey, *Law and Public Opinion in England* (London: Macmillan) 1905, 2nd edn., 1963, pp. 64-65, Dicey divided the nineteenth century into periods, choosing 1870 for the beginning of what he termed the 'collectivist' influence on legislation.

19  For an introduction see O. McDonagh, 'The Nineteenth-Century Revolution in Government: A Reappraisal' (1958) 1 Historical Journal 52; H. Parris, 'The Nineteenth Century Revolution in Government: A Reappraisal Reappraised' (1960) 3 Historical Journal 17; H. Parris, *Constitutional Bureaucracy: the Development of British Central Administration Since the Eighteenth Century* (London: Allen and Unwin) 1969; O. McDonagh, *Early Victorian Government* (London: Weidenfeld and Nicolson) 1977 and 'Pre-transformations: Victorian Britain' in E. Kamenka and E. Tay (eds.), *Law and Social Control*, (Melbourne: Edward Arnold) 1980. See generally W. Cornish and G. Clark, *Law and Society in England, 1750 -1950*, (London: Sweet and Maxwell) 1989.

Government Board, with a Cabinet Minister as Chairman. The relationship between citizen and administration, as far as the recipients of poor relief were concerned, remained a local one. But even at this level it was increasingly the case that the administrators were full-time officials, while the lay Guardians faded into the background. The lash of State control was felt by the more prosperous, who were forced to contribute to increasing levels of 'poor rates' as the Guardians were forced by the Government to raise standards . . . A similarly indirect pattern of relationships between the State and citizens developed in the public health field. Here the initial legislation was largely permissive. Then, as this was seen to be ineffective, local agencies were required to take prescribed steps to curb dangers to public health . . . In this area too, a corps of professionals began to be built up, operating at both local and national level to deal with, and draw attention to, public health problems: the medical officers . . . Public health legislation was one of the most significant nineteenth-century contributions to the extension of the coercive power of the State; its key characteristic was the prevention of actions that might harm others. Factory legislation had similar characteristics. To be effective, such legislation had to bring in its wake a most significant extension of State bureaucracy. A new kind of policing role had to be played by officials appointed to ensure that legislation of this kind was carried out. An important Victorian addition to the apparatus of the State was, therefore, the government inspector. Capitalists were to be free to pursue profits. They were to be involved in decentralized government through the local authorities and the various ad hoc bodies, but were to operate in both these spheres within a framework of rules and restrictions laid down by central government and enforced by a cadre of inspectors.[20]

We can begin to see just how radical a change of outlook was required by the growth of government in the nineteenth century. Until the Industrial Revolution, the functions of the state had been assumed to be limited and largely negative in character. Its role was to act as a 'policeman', providing the framework in which citizens could go about their business. According to Locke (1632-1704),[1] the state's functions are limited to the preservation of the rights of its members against infringement by others. Each individual has a right to security of his person and property and to liberty of action in so far as he does not use this liberty to infringe the rights of others. The task of the state is to repress any violation of these rights by the use of force, to deter any man from injuring another in respect of his person, property or freedom and, where it is not successful in deterring, to punish. It is this and nothing more; a state exceeds its legitimate function if it endeavours to go beyond these limits. This idea has never been abandoned. It finds support in a body of modern writing, notably that of Hayek.[2] and Nozick.[3] There are glimpses of nostalgia for this simple picture behind *Justice*/All Souls. But modern societies cannot easily conform to Locke's model; invariably, they are more like those portrayed by Hill and have to find solutions to the problems this creates.

Writing in 1978, when the centralised state had reached its zenith, Barker argued that by the end of the nineteenth century, all the major political parties had,

20  M. Hill, *The State, Administration and the Individual* (London: Fontana) 1976, pp. 23-24.
 1  See *Two Treatises of Government* 1689. For a helpful introduction, see, J. Dunn, *Locke* (Oxford: OUP) 1984.
 2  F. A. Hayek, *The Road to Serfdom* (London: Routledge) 1944 and *Law, Legislation and Liberty* (London: Routledge) 1982.
 3  R. Nozick, *Anarchy, State and Utopia* (Oxford: Blackwell) 1974.

for practical purposes, abandoned the ideal of limited, and accepted the necessity for interventionist, government:[4]

> Whereas the old conception of government had been static the new was, if not dynamic, then at least ambulatory. The old conception had viewed government as administering laws, keeping the peace and defending the frontiers. But it was not a part of government's function to act upon society, nor was it expected that legislation would do much more than sustain clear and established customs. In contrast the new conception was of government as the instigator of movement. This conception of movement was not restricted to the parties of progress or reform; the Conservative and Unionist Party at the beginning of the twentieth century was increasingly characterized, despite opposition, by a commitment to tariff reform, a programme of discriminatory trade duties designed to . . . provide funds for new military and social expenditure at home. Government was not merely to regulate society, it was to improve it.

How did this change of ideology come about? Hill suggests that the apparatus of the state may have insinuated itself, like a 'Trojan horse', into an unsuspecting society:[5,6]

> The first stage was the discovery of some 'intolerable' evil, such as the exploitation of child labour. Legislation was passed to prevent this. In the second stage, however, it was discovered that the legislation was ineffective. New legislation was passed with stronger provisions and inspectors were employed to ensure enforcement. Third, many of the new groups of professionals recruited to enforce legislation themselves became lobbyists for increases in the powers of their agencies. Fourth, this growing corps of professional experts made legislators aware 'that the problems could not be swept away by some magnificent all embracing gesture but would require continuous slow regulation and re-regulation'. Finally, therefore, a quite elaborate framework of law was developed with a complex bureaucratic machine to enforce it. The professionals helped to transform the administrative system into a major organization with extensive powers, almost without Parliament realizing it.

A variant of Hill's Trojan-horse theory is often used to explain the unsystematic development of English administrative law. In Chapter 14, for example, there will be found a description by Professor Robson of the development of administrative tribunals which exactly parallels what Hill says about the growth of the modern administrative state. A similar explanation – that Parliament simply did not notice what was happening – could be given of the practice of delegating rule-making powers to government departments. It was realisation of this development which caused sufficient alarm in the inter-war period to justify the establishment of the Donoughmore Committee (below, Chapter 2). But this Committee's incrementalist approach to reform allowed attrition of legislative power through overload to continue. Today, as we shall see in Chapter 6, it has become one of the most serious, yet unsolvable, problems of modern government. Hill himself is not

---

4   R. Barker, *Political Ideas in Modern Britain* (London: Methuen) 1978, p 11. See now, for a helpful account, 2nd edn., 1997, Ch. 2.
5   See also A. Briggs, 'Towards the Welfare State', in Paul Barker (ed.), *Founders of the Welfare State* (London: Heinemann) 1984.
6   M. Hill, *The State, Administration and the Individual* (London: Fontana) 1976, p. 27.

entirely convinced, however, that the process of insinuation was fortuitous. He suspects a deliberate process of social engineering.

In the following passage, Friedmann spells out the implications of the growth in state functions for the administrative process as he saw it in 1964:[7]

> The growth of the administrative process has been a universal phenomenon of contemporary society, although both speed and manner of its development have varied greatly from country to country. A minimum of administration is, of course, inherent in the very notion of government. The most ardent advocates of laissez faire policy concede to government the minimum functions of defence, administration of justice and police. But, regardless of political philosophy, the needs of an increasingly complex society have forced upon one country after another a multiplicity of additional functions: to the protection of elementary standards of health and safety, both for the public in general and employees – which accounted for the first major growth of public services in nineteenth-century England – were rapidly added a vast number of additional social services, from elementary measures of public assistance to the highly diversified social-security systems of the mid-twentieth century; the supervision of public utilities, labour relations, and many other economic and social processes intimately affecting the public interest . . . The mixed economies which today characterize the political and economic systems of many States . . . have a combination of managerial and regulatory administrative functions. Certain industries and public utilities are operated by the State itself – either through government departments or with increasing frequency through semi-autonomous public corporations, responsible to government but equipped with more or less far-reaching managerial autonomy . . . At the same time, the bulk of industry and business, which remains in private ownership, is subject to varying degrees of public supervision and regulation, while another set of public authorities administers the various social services.

To meet increased obligations, the state needed more administrators; 'bureaucracy' developed, with its own ideology. Study of bureaucracies and the way in which they operate derives essentially from the work of Weber (1864-1920). In his seminal work *Economy and Society*,[8] Weber describes the goals of the bureaucrat. (Weber is careful to associate bureaucracy with industry as well as with public administration. Later writers and politicians have been less scrupulous in this regard.)

> Bureaucratization offers above all the optimum possibility for carrying through the principle of specializing administrative functions according to purely objective considerations. Individual performances are allocated to functionaries who have specialized training and who by constant practice learn more and more. The 'objective' discharge of business primarily means a discharge of business according to calculable rules and 'without regard for persons' . . . The second element mentioned, 'calculable rules', also is of paramount importance for modern bureaucracy. The peculiarity of modern culture, and specifically of its technical and economic basis, demands this very

7    W. Friedmann, *Law in a Changing Society* (Harmondsworth: Penguin) 2nd edn., 1964, pp. 273-274.
8    M. Weber, *Economy and Society*, Parts 1 and 2 (Berkeley: University of California) 1968. For presentation and discussion of Weber's ideas, see E. Kamenka and M. Krygier (eds.), *Bureaucracy* (Melbourne: Edward Arnold) 1979. And see D. Beetham, *Bureaucracy* (Buckingham: Open University Press) 2nd edn., 1996.

'calculability' of results . . . [The] specific nature [of bureaucracy], which is welcomed by capitalism, develops the more perfectly the more the bureaucracy is 'dehumanized', the more completely it succeeds in eliminating from official business love, hatred, and all purely personal, irrational, and emotional elements which escape calculation. This is the specific nature of bureaucracy and it is appraised as its special virtue.[9]

Weber's description of bureaucracy can be read in two ways: on the one hand, it serves as an 'ideal-type' or pattern of the way in which administration would develop in modern society. His second lesson concerns the nature of bureaucracy as a self-serving institution impervious to outside opinion. Weber was, however, optimistic that bureaucracy could be controlled through the development of democratic institutions. He saw, or believed that he saw, this process embodied in the British constitutional doctrine of ministerial responsibility. Arguably, in the period between the nineteenth-century reforms of the civil service inaugurated by the Northcote-Trevelyan Report and the twentieth-century Fulton Report,[10] the underlying pattern of central government was political control of, and accountability for, a civil service which was Weberian to the extent that it saw itself as neutral and impartial: a servant to any master.[11]

Inaugurated with the Factories Acts and daring reforms of Edwin Chadwick, a planned society was under way, later to be associated with the Fabian reformers and their vision of public administration as a *science*. World War II was partly instrumental in creating a highly regulated state[12] which, after the war, evolved ever more complex systems of land-use planning, state housing and welfare services. At its zenith in the 1970s, by which time the concept of planning had expanded to cover everything from land use to the national economy, a planner could be grandly described as 'a helmsman steering the city'.[13]

By the 1970s, political scientists were using the term 'corporatism' to describe a mode of government in which a centralised state combines with the giant enterprises of modern capitalism to channel power into the hands of a powerful elite.[14] Notice how Reich in the following passage poses individuals against giant corporations, an interesting variant on the concern of traditional administrative law for individuals:[15]

---

9   M. Weber, C. Wright Mills and H. Gerth, *From Max Weber: Essays in Sociology* (London: Routledge) 1946, p. 215.
10  The Northcote Trevelyan *Report on the Organisation of the Permanent Civil Service* (C 1713, 1853) reprinted 1984 and as Appendix B of the Fulton *Report on the Civil Service* (Cmnd. 3638, 1968).
11  See K. Dowding, *The Civil Service* (London: Routledge) 1995, pp. 7-21. See also J. Jacob, *The Republican Crown* (above, pl 6, note 6), Chs. 3, 4, and 5.
12  On which see C. Allen, *Law and Orders* (London: Stevens) 3rd edn., 1965.
13  Cited P. McAuslan, 'Planning Law's Contribution to the Problems of an Urban Society' (1974) 37 MLR 134, 140. See also P. Hall, *Urban and Regional Planning* (London: Allen and Unwin) 2nd edn., 1982 and *Great Planning Disasters* (London: Weidenfeld and Nicolson) 1981.
14  A fuller discussion can be found in K. Middlemas, *Politics in Industrial Society* (London: Deutsch) 1979, Ch. 13, 'Corporate Bias'; P. Birnbaum, 'The State Versus Corporatism' (1982) 11 Politics and Society 477 discusses different models, as do P. Dunleavy and B. O'Leary, *Theories of the State: The Politics of Liberal Democracy* (London: Macmillan) 1987.
15  C. Reich, *The Greening of America* (New York: Random House) 1970, p. 89.

The American Corporate State today can be thought of as a single vast corporation, with every person as an involuntary member and employee. It consists primarily of large industrial organizations, plus non-profit institutions such as foundations and the educational system, all related to the whole as divisions to a business corporation. Government is only a part of the state, but government coordinates it and provides a variety of needed services. The Corporate State is a complete reversal of the original American ideal and plan. The State, and not the market or the people or any abstract economic laws, determines what shall be produced, what shall be consumed, and how it shall be allocated. It determines, for example, that railroads shall decay while highways flourish; that coal miners shall be poor and advertising executives rich. Jobs and occupations in the society are rigidly defined and controlled, and arranged in a hierarchy of rewards, status, and authority. An individual can move from one position to another, but he gains little freedom thereby, for in each position he is subject to conditions imposed upon it; individuals have no protected area of liberty, privacy or individual sovereignty beyond the reach of the State. The State is subject neither to democratic controls, constitutional limits, or legal regulation.

Traditional democratic controls came to seem inadequate to tame this new Leviathan of planning, difficult to reconcile, Shonfield argued,[16] with:

> . . . the existing structure of Western democratic institutions. Who controls the planners? It is not just a matter of getting parliamentary approval for the broad outline of a scheme for raising the standard of living of a nation by a certain amount over a stated period of years. A plan is a living body of economic policy, adapting itself constantly to changing circumstances, sometimes undergoing drastic alteration in its component parts in order to secure particular objectives which come in time to acquire a new order of priority. The traditional Western parliament, a non-expert body, by instinct non-interventionist unless there is some manifest abuse or need for legislation, is hardly equipped for the job of supervising the systematic intervention which planning implies. That is perhaps the justification for the tacit consensus among the planners that it is, on the whole, best to bypass the parliamentary process.

In Hill's view, however, the growth and centralisation of the state owe more to a deliberate process of 'social engineering' than to belief in planning as scientific. state intervention can be, and was, used consciously to remodel society. Society does not stop short, for example, at prohibiting child labour but goes on to make positive provision for education, welfare, health and nutrition of children. Ultimately, if parents do not carry out their responsibilities, children may be removed into the care of the state. Cynics may prefer to substitute the term 'social control' for the more positive 'social engineering',[17] as more appropriately

---

16  A. Shonfield, *Modern Capitalism: the Changing Balance of Public and Private Power* (Oxford: OUP) 1965, p. 230.
17  See E. Kamenka and E. Tay, 'Social Traditions, Legal Traditions' in *Law and Social Control* (New York: St. Martins Press) 1980, or 'Beyond Bourgeois Individualism: the Contemporary Crisis in Law and Legal Ideology' in E. Kamenka and R. Neale (eds.), *Feudalism, Capitalism and Beyond* (London: Edward Arnold) 1975. K. Ziegert, 'A sociologist's view', in *Law and Social Control*, pp. 60, 63, attempts a definition. See further J. Higgins, 'Social Control Theories of Social Policy' (1980) Journal of Social Policy 1.

conveying a sense of authoritarianism. Thus Piven and Cloward[18] see the primary objective of poor relief in all capitalist societies as social control. A body of welfare law then 'regulates the poor' by:

> defining and enforcing the terms on which different classes of men are made to do different kinds of work; relief arrangements, in other words, have a great deal to do with maintaining social and economic inequities. The indignities and cruelties of the dole are no deterrent to indolence among the rich; but for the poor man, the spectre of ending up on the welfare or in the poor-house makes any job at any wage a preferable alternative.

Planning is often seen as integral to collectivism and linked to socialism (as in Hayek's influential tract *The Road to Serfdom*). Neither social engineering nor social control are confined to one end of the political spectrum, however; in practice governments of all political persuasions are inclined to indulge. The history of social assistance is a history of social control, from the Elizabethan Poor Law, through Chadwick's nineteenth-century reform based on the parsimonious notions of 'stigma', 'less eligibility' and 'the deserving poor',[19] to the modern Child Support Agency, a state collection agency set up by a Conservative government with the aim of re-establishing parental responsibility for child maintenance. In short, social engineering has become a regular and accepted technique, perhaps even a function, of modern government resisted only by libertarians like Nozick. Shonfield's picture of the reluctant legislator is today wholly unrealistic.

It is fear of these authoritarian techniques of modern government which infuses the *Justice*/All Souls report.[1] The same fears motor the international movement for the protection of human rights and the drive to develop a modern and principled administrative law.

## 5. Rolling back the frontiers

Until recently, the growth of public bureaucracy and public enterprise was seen as the one certain thing about our future . . . No one predicted the age of privatisation or foresaw that the UK would return to regulated private ownership for virtually all of its major public utilities barely a generation after the nationalisation boom of the 1940s.[2] Looking back on the period of Margaret Thatcher's government, Rhodes identifies a steady process of erosion:[3]

> The phrase 'the hollowing out of the state' suggests the British state is being eroded or eaten away. I freely admit the term is controversial and it may even be inaccurate.

---

18  F. Piven and R. Cloward, *Regulating the Poor: The Functions of Public Welfare* (London: Tavistock Publications) 1971, p. xvii.
19  A. Brundage, *The Making of the New Poor Law 1832-39* (London: Hutchinson) 1978.
 1  Above p. 4.
 2  C. Hood, 'Emerging Issues in Public Administration' (1995) 73 Public Administration 165.
 3  R. Rhodes, 'The Hollowing Out of the State: The Changing Nature of the Public Service in Britain' (1994) 65 Pol. Q. 138.

Please note, however, I refer to processes which contribute to a hollowing out of the state and I do not suggest the era of the hollow state has arrived. I will try to show it is a revealing expression which teaches us something about what is happening to British public administration. I use the phrase to cover four interrelated trends.

(1) Privatisation and limiting the scope and forms of public intervention.

(2) The loss of functions by central and local government departments to alternative service delivery systems (such as agencies).

(3) The loss of functions by British government to European Union institutions.

(4) Limiting the discretion of public servants through the new public management, with its emphasis on managerial accountability, and clearer political control through a sharper distinction between politics and administration.

Although we have talked loosely about the growth of the state and discussed the association of state with Crown and central government, we have not so far attempted a map. Many would want to include local authorities in their definition of state and we could go on to provide a further catalogue to include the police – neither wholly centralised nor part of local government – the National Health Service, etc. We have already met references to inspectorates and the idea that the state has 'regulatory' functions which may be exercised through agencies which are at least partly autonomous. Friedmann's description of the engagement of the state in industry (steel or coal) and the management of public utilities (water and gas) reminds us that the boundaries of the state may change. When Friedmann wrote, much industry was state-owned and run, independent in respect of managerial functions but working closely with ministers over policy and funding; today so many have been 'privatised' or transferred from the public to the private sector[4] that one might be forgiven for overlooking this aspect of state activity entirely.

In the post-war period, the three growth areas of modern government, in descending order, were local government, the National Health Service (NHS) and administrative agencies. Only the NHS was technically a national service, funded and operated on a national basis, primarily the responsibility of a central government department accountable to Parliament through ministers since its conception by the post-war Labour government of Clement Attlee, though much of the organisation was always downloaded to area and district health authorities. Today, we would need to add to this relatively simple picture a number of smaller units, such as hospital trusts and general practice fundholders. The NHS remains a public service but the picture has become more complex while the legal relationships between the various entities have changed[5] and are likely to change again.

Local government in the post-war period gradually assumed great importance as a service provider, given responsibility amongst other important functions for

4    C. Graham and T. Prosser, 'Privatising Nationalised Industries: Constitutional Issues and New Legal Techniques' (1987) 50 MLR 16; T. Prosser, *Nationalised Industries and Public Control* (Oxford: Blackwell) 1986; C. Veljanovski, *Selling the State* (London: Weidenfeld and Nicolson) 1987.

5    D. Longley, *Public Law and Health Service Accountability* (Buckingham: Open University Press) 1992.

public housing, education and social services. But as the government share of local government expenditure steadily augmented, so central government control of local authorities increased exponentially[6] and local authorities became in large part agents for the implementation of central government policy. Since 1979, however, the role of local government has been eroded even more rapidly than it grew, sometimes to the profit of central government, more often to small 'community' entities such as housing trusts. Schools, for example, have been allowed to 'opt out' of local government control, gaining limited autonomy, accountable to and funded directly by, the Department of Education. The School Curriculum and Assessment Authority has responsibility for a centralised syllabus which sets standards supervised by an inspectorate. Devolution, in short, has brought a paradoxical increase in central government power. Elsewhere local authorities have lost functions to the private sector through the contracting out of services (see Chapter 9).

If a heady combination of practical economics – reduction of expenditure, public sector borrowing and taxation – with ideology inspires the attrition of local government functions and 'downsizing',[7] party political advantage cannot be wholly discounted, more particularly in the abolition of the metropolitan authorities and Greater London Council.[8] Monk and Kleinman[9] argue that, during the first two terms of Margaret Thatcher's government, housing policy strove for the limited economic goal of reducing expenditure on public housing. From 1987, however, 'a more thorough-going ideological approach' was evident, in which a switch from public provision to the private sector was deemed more economical and efficient and an 'ideology of home ownership' developed. The following passage[10] from Michael Heseltine, then Secretary of State for the Environment, incidentally illustrates the readiness of politicians to indulge in social engineering:

> There is in this country a deeply ingrained desire for home ownership. The Government believe that this spirit should be fostered. It reflects the wishes of the people, ensures the wide spread of wealth through society, encourages a personal desire to improve and modernise one's home, enables people to accrue wealth for their children and stimulates the attitudes of independence and self reliance that are the bedrock of a free society.

One ideological basis for disempowering local government lies in that strand of 'New Right' thought which tends to view all institutions interposed between the citizen and state as interlopers in a free market between individuals and capitalist

---

6 M. Loughlin, *Local Government in the Modern State* (Sweet and Maxwell) 1986; *Legality and Locality: the role of law in central government relations* (Oxford: Clarendon) 1996.

7 C. Foster and F. Plowden, *The State Under Stress* (Milton Keynes: Open University Press) 1996, Ch. 1.

8 By the Local Government Act 1985. They had been created after the Redcliffe Maud Commission (*Reform of Local Government in England* Cmnd. 4276, 1970) by the Local Government Act 1972 with the exception of London, to which the London Government Act 1963 applied. An assembly and mayor for London is now likely.

9 S. Monk and M. Kleinman, 'Housing' in P. Brown and R. Sparks (eds.), *Beyond Thatcherism: Social Policy, Politics and Society* (Milton Keynes: Open University Press) 1989, pp. 121-122.

10 HC Deb., vol. 976, Pt. 1, col. 1445.

producers.[11] Again, because the New Right is less concerned with democratic control and more with control through markets, there is a preference for agencies entrusted with a specific task and answerable to its consumers for performance:[12] in other words, a housing trust rather than a local authority whose housing functions are mixed with others, radically different in character, and where consumers cannot easily indicate their preferences. At this point we are moving away from democratic accountability through elected councillors towards a combination of direct input by consumers with managerial accountability of agencies. These ideas are developed in Chapter 5.

Agencies or 'quangos' (an acronym for quasi- or semi-autonomous non-government organisations) are hardly new. If we return to Hill (above, p. 9), we will see that independent boards, committees and commissions were already in being in the nineteenth century.[13] At first their existence can best be explained by the 'Trojan horse' principle. Agencies may be justified by the need to avoid party political or ministerial control; because they exercise adjudicatory functions, for example, it is thought proper for tribunals to be independent of government. Yet the Civil Aviation Authority, which like many other agencies possesses licensing powers described as 'quasi-judicial', combines these with policy-making and is subject to ministerial direction and guidance on policy, a combination of functions which has sometimes in practice proved difficult to handle (below, pp. 83–90). Some agencies, such as the Health and Safety Executive, whose job is to promote industrial safety, have policy-making functions and statutory powers of supervision and control, including the power to issue 'stop' orders comparable to the injunctive powers of courts.[14] Others merely tender advice to the Minister, like the Social Security Advisory Committee and Council on Tribunals, which have to be consulted before new regulations in the area are promulgated. Others possess rule-making powers which may be combined with executive and/or adjudicatory functions. The Advisory, Conciliation and Arbitration Service (ACAS), which deals with trade unions and industry, is empowered to negotiate agreements and codes of practice and to act as an arbitrator.[15] The Commission for Racial Equality and Equal Opportunities Commission possess rule-making powers but are also empowered to conduct investigations which have been described by courts as prosecutorial in character.[16]

11  C. Harris, 'The State and the Market' in P. Brown and R. Sparks (eds.), note 9 above. See also R. Scruton, *The Meaning of Conservatism* (Harmondsworth: Penguin) 1980, pp. 162-4. A different explanation is advanced by C. Foster and F. Plowden *The State Under Stress*, above, note 7, pp. 137-140.

12  P. Dunleavy and B. O'Leary, *Theories of the State: The Politics of Liberal Democracy* (London: Macmillan) 1987, pp. 120-122, 305-307.

13  See also, H. Street, 'Quasi-Government Bodies since 1918' in G. Campion (ed.), *British Government Since 1918* (London: Allen and Unwin) 1957.

14  See R. Baldwin, 'Health and Safety at Work: Consensus and Self-Regulation' in R. Baldwin and C. McCrudden (eds.), *Regulation and Public Law* (London: Weidenfeld and Nicolson) 1987.

15  L. Dickens, 'The Advisory, Conciliation and Arbitration Service: Regulation and Voluntarism in Industrial Relations' in R. Baldwin and C. McCrudden (eds.), *Regulation and Public Law* (London: Weidenfeld and Nicolson) 1987.

16  See Ch. 12 below.

Administrative tribunals, it is said, 'just grew like Topsy', and the allocation of functions to agencies is no more coherent nor logical. It is hard to discern a typical agency and no apparent rhyme or reason lies behind the choices.[17] Broadcasting provides an excellent example. The British Broadcasting Corporation (BBC) was established as the monopoly purveyor of broadcasting inside the country by Royal Charter, a device adopted specifically to denote independence from interference by government and day-to-day scrutiny by Parliament. Later, this state monopoly was broken in two main stages. In 1954, the provision of new TV channels by independent contractors was for the first time permitted and the Independent Television Authority set up to regulate this 'private' broadcasting. Subject to minor changes, the system endured until 1990, when it was broken down again to make space for cable and satellite television, more local and regional broadcasting, and commercial radio stations. Each time, the need for independence of political control by government and the House of Commons was flagged by the appointment of a Royal Commission or committee of inquiry established to ensure a measure of consensus about proposed reforms. Each time, new agencies were introduced until today we possess a confusing network of agencies with a miscellany of functions. The BBC is still extant and still possesses executive functions as a service provider. The ITA, on the other hand, became first the Independent Broadcasting Authority, to which was added a Cable Authority, and later the Independent Television Commission (ITC), whose chief function is to grant and monitor franchises for commercial TV; a Radio Authority exercises the same function for commercial radio. The ITC is under an obligation to protect good taste and decency but a Broadcasting Standards Council has been added to draw up a code of standards of taste and decency and consider complaints, while a Broadcasting Complaints Council considers questions of privacy and fairness (these may soon be merged). In consequence, private broadcasters are subject to both regulators, while the BBC operates under BSC standards and its own internal guidelines.[18] Even this much-simplified outline contains a reference to five separate quangos as well as to commissions and committees of inquiry, of which there have been at least five.[19] And this account of our complex domestic arrangements leaves entirely out of account the regulation of the media at European level,[20] the shape of things to come.

As early as 1968, the Fulton Committee had 'enthusiastically endorsed the pattern of government growth by bureaucratic stasis at the centre and growth at the fringes of Whitehall by its doctrine of "hiving off" units from civil service

---

17  N. Lewis, 'Regulating Non-Government Bodies: Privatization, Accountability, and the Public-Private Divide' in J. Jowell and D. Oliver (eds.), *The Changing Constitution*, (Oxford: Clarendon) 2nd edn., 1986, pp. 230-237.

18  Sections 6(1)(a), 151-161 of the Broadcasting Act 1990. See also E. Barendt, *Broadcasting Law* (Oxford: Clarendon) 1993, pp. 112-113.

19  The most recent are the Annan Committee report, *The Future of Broadcasting* (Cmnd. 6753, 1977); the Peacock Committee, *Report on Financing the BBC* (Cmnd. 9824, 1986). *Broadcasting in the Nineties: Competition, Choice and Quality* (Cmd. 517, 1988) and *The Future of the BBC: Serving the Nation, Competing Worldwide* (Cmd. 2621, 1994) are White Papers.

20  W. Sauter, 'The Telecommunications Law of the European Union' (1995) 1 Eur. Law J. 92.

departments to non-departmental bodies'.[1] By the time Margaret Thatcher came
to power she had a mandate for 'quangocide'. A contemporary pamphlet[2] spoke
of misuse of public funds through duplication of departmental functions and
deplored the fact that, 'In spite of the progress already made, there remain a
further 2,400 official bodies whose administration costs *alone* exceed a well-
researched estimate of £1,500 million annually'. The Pliatzky Committee was set
up to look into quangos;[3] a few bit the dust.

Yet, as we shall see later, quangos have taken on a new life as 'regulatory
agencies', established in the wake of the government's privatisation programme
to monitor and represent the public interest while suggesting a new autonomy
from central government. By 1994, agencies were said to be responsible for the
expenditure of more than £47 billion, of which 50% had been transferred since
1979 from local authorities. In 1996, a report[4] showed that their number had
fallen to 1,194 but expenditure had risen sixfold since 1979, a discrepancy
explained by the fact that low-cost advisory bodies (the Physical Activity Task
Force or National Breastfeeding Campaign) had been axed while the expenditure
of executive (the London Docklands Development Corporation or Next Steps
agencies) and regulatory agencies (Ofgas or Oftel) has risen steadily.

Because of its inevitable association with 'welfarism' and with the previous
statist economic regime, now seen as markedly unsuccessful or inefficient,[5]
Margaret Thatcher also had the civil service in her targets. The civil service was
subjected to attacks on its unions, pay cuts and a series of efficiency scrutinies.[6]
The implementation of the Ibbs Report,[7] which in 1988 recommended 'a quite
different way of conducting the business of government', led to the 'hiving off'
of government business to a novel type of administrative (or Next Steps) agency:

> The central Civil Service should consist of a relatively small core engaged in the
> function of servicing Ministers and managing departments, who will be the 'sponsors'
> of particular government policies and services. Responding to these departments will
> be a range of agencies employing their own staff, who may or may not have the status
> of Crown servants, and concentrating on the delivery of their particular service, with
> clearly defined responsibilities between the Secretary of State and the Permanent
> Secretary on the one hand, and the Chairmen or Chief Executives of the agencies on
> the other. Both departments and their agencies should have a more open and simplified
> structure.

1   Report of the Fulton Committee, *The Civil Service* (Cmnd. 3638, 1968). And see C. Hood, 'The
    Politics of Quangocide' (1980) 8 Policy and Politics 247.
2   P. Holland, *The Governance of Quangos* (London: Adam Smith Institute) 1981, p. 7.
3   Report on Non-Departmental Public Bodies (Cmnd. 7797, 1980).
4   *Public Bodies 1996* (London: HMSO) 1996. Quangos are reviewed every four years.
5   G. Fry, *Policy and Management in the British Civil Service* (London: Prentice Hall) 1995, pp. 37-
    38. See also G. Drewry and T. Butcher, *The Civil Service Today* (Oxford: Blackwell) 2nd edn., 1991.
6   See e.g. the 'GCHQ case', *Council of Civil Service Unions v Minister for the Civil Service* [1985]
    AC 374.
7   Efficiency Unit, *Improving Management in Government: The Next Steps. Report to the Prime
    Minister* (London: HMSO) 1988, para. 44. For comment, see R. Baldwin, 'The Next Steps:
    Ministerial Responsibility and Government by Agency' (1988) MLR 622 ; and G. Drewry, 'Forward
    from FMI: The Next Steps' (1988) PL 505 and 'Next Steps: The Pace Falters' (1990) PL 322.

The central civil service shrank to 565,000 by 1993 and a year later to 524,000 as departmental functions were privatised or hived off to agencies. The retention of a 'Senior Civil Service' was intended to safeguard core values and provide for policy development and implementation. For this 'respected and valued' few, short-term, performance-related contracts of employment, similar to those used for the recruitment of agency chief executives, were introduced. Departments and agencies were to draw up 'annual efficiency plans', indicating how they proposed to stay within their budgets for the coming three years.[8] The White Paper, as a top mandarin noted, gave formal recognition to changing structures but also highlighted the diversity of services operated by or on behalf of government:[9]

> What the White Paper finally recognises is that there are two (or perhaps many more) Civil Services. Essentially, on the one hand, there are top people we all think we know about, now about 3,500, to be entitled the Senior Civil Service, plus their supporters; on the other hand, about 500,000 invisible people, who do the work. The White Paper at last addresses the existence of an enormously diversified set of services, delivering what needs to be done in the best way it can be done, whether publicly or privately. It finally buries the idea of the old monolithic Civil Service, which has hampered thinking for so long, leaving those described as civil servants simply bound together by familiar concepts of independence, impartiality etc., and by accountability through Ministers to Parliament and the iron hand of the public expenditure system.

Could these 'familiar concepts' survive the assault on the unity and integrity of the public service? Already in 1982 an observer was describing the 'disintegration of the model of representative and ministerial government which took shape in Britain in the course of the last century'.[10] 'Semi-autonomy' undermines the doctrine of ministerial responsibility by blurring the division of responsibilities between Ministers and the chief executives of agencies. Worse still, the informal, discretionary 'old-boy-network' system of appointments allows the government powers of patronage wholly incompatible either with true autonomy or with the Weberian model of objective bureaucracy. In 1979, when Labour was in power, more than 200 quango seats were held by TUC Council members; in 1994, 25% of members of the 40 largest quangos were known members of the Conservative party, and the media was drawing attention to the fact that many leading industrialists known to contribute to Conservative party funds held multiple and well-remunerated quango apointments.[11] In 1994, a Committee was established under the chairmanship of Lord Nolan, a Law Lord, to investigate and make recommendations to deal with alleged breaches of conventional practices governing

---

8  *The Civil Service: Continuity and Change* (Cm. 2627, 1993/4) and *The Civil Service: Taking Forward Continuity and Change* (Cm. 2748, 1994/5).

9  Sir Peter Kemp, 'The mandarins emerge unscathed' (1994) 2 Parliamentary Brief 49.

10  N. Johnson, 'Accountability, Control and Complexity: Moving Beyond Ministerial Responsibility' in A. Barker (ed.), *Quangos in Britain: Governments and Networks of Public Policy-Making* (London: Macmillan) 1982, p. 206.

11  See S. Jenkins, *Accountable to None: The Tory Nationalization of Britain* (London: Hamish Hamilton) 1995.

the conduct of MPs.[12] The Nolan Committee is now a standing body with a mandate more generally to observe and report on standards in public life.

Despite the rush to privatise and hive off central government functions, however, there is some sense that government has steadily become more centralised. This perception may partly result from increased willingness to indulge in social control and engineering; service delivery may have been downloaded but central government is seen as more intrusive:[13]

> One of the many problems in discussing the retreat of the state is that we have no means of *measuring* the role of the state in modern societies. Big state budgets and big state bureaucracies are by no means the only way to affect the way in which society behaves. For example *regulation* has become a central and cheap policy of the modern state. This presents enormous problems to researchers in deciding whether there has been a rolling back of the state or, put more colloquially, whether government is getting off people's backs. Not only is the task difficult in terms of quantative measures, it is difficult conceptually – for example do we have less or more government when the government *imposes* new rules of competition, or *imposes* the contracting out of services, or confers new statutory *rights* on the consumers of utilities? This may sometimes be presented by central policy-makers as 'less' government, yet from the bottom up it may seem like tighter state regulation of activities which were hitherto unregulated or were at most self-regulated. 'Less government' may be seen as 'more government', depending upon where one sits!

The triangular partnership of government, industry and labour may be dead, but many would argue that hiving off or downloading central government functions has merely disguised the extent of state regulatory activity, which gains new potency from the interconnection between centralisation and decentralisation, private and public.[14] If the essence of corporatism (above) is centralisation and a state in which public and private are inextricably tangled, then this is neo-corporatism. The march of the modern state towards centralism and corporatism, no longer accepted as desirable, has merely been camouflaged by the intermediate device of the administrative agency.

Advocates of pluralist alternatives to statist centralisation would certainly see the new arrangements as broadly corporatist. Pluralism – defined briefly as a 'defence of multiplicity' or recognition of the need for diversity within society and its political institutions[15] – provides an alternative set of justifications for

12  See A. Doig, 'From Lynskey to Nolan: The Corruption of British Politics and Public Service?' (1996) 23 J. of Law and Soc. 35; A. Doig and J. Wilson, 'Untangling the Threads of Sleaze: The Slide into Nolan' in F. Ridley and A. Doig (eds.) *Sleaze: Politicians, Private Interests and Public Reactions* (Oxford: OUP in association with the Hansard Society for Parliamentary Questions) 1995. And see Eighth Report of the Public Accounts Committee, 'The Proper Conduct of Public Business', HC 154 (1993/4); Audit Commission, *Protecting the Public Purse; Probity in the Public Sector: Combating Fraud and Corruption in Local Government* (London: HMSO) 1993.

13  J. Richardson, 'Doing Less by Doing More: British Government 1979-1993' (1994) 17 West European Politics 178, 181–182.

14  N. Lewis and P. Wiles, 'The Post-Corporatist State?' (1984) 11 J. of Law and Soc. 65.

15  P. Dunleavy and B. O'Leary, *Theories of the State: The Politics of Liberal Democracy* (London: Macmillan) 1987, p. 65. See also C. Reich, *The Greening of America* (New York: Random House) 1970.

breaking 'the state' down into smaller and more accessible units or for hiving off state functions and downloading them to 'grass roots' level.[16] In later chapters we will find strong traces of pluralist influence pervading recent developments in administrative law.

## 6. A European dimension

In parallel with 'downsizing', power has been leaching away from the national government through a transnational process of centralisation and neo-corporatism. As Horsman and Marshall put it:[17]

> neither the nation nor the state is about to disappear . . . there are no substitute structures that can perform all the functions traditionally associated with the nation-state . . . What we are seeing . . . are the outlines of a global system that has been in the making since the French Revolution; in the process, the principal defining element of it – the autonomous nation-state – is losing its privileged position [and] this involves political and social change on a very grand scale.

The process of internationalisation has been reinforced by international organisations such as the United Nations, and treaties and international conventions, such as the GATT or the European Convention on Human Rights (ECHR) to which this country belongs or is a signatory. In Chapter 4 for example, we shall see how the influence of the ECHR, reflecting the strength and universality of the international human rights movement, has contributed to a resurgence in judicial review.

The impact of the European Union[18] is more direct. Cooper has classified it as:[19]

> . . . more a transnational than an supra-national system. Although there are some who dream of a European state (which would be supra-national), they are a minority today – if one takes account of ordinary people, a very small minority. The dream is one left over from a previous age. It rests on the assumption that nation states are fundamentally dangerous and that the only way to tame the anarchy of nations is to impose hegemony on them.

In describing the advocates of European integration as a minority, Cooper may be guilty of under-stating the opposition to his more pluralist and decentralised outlook. The dominant ideology is avowedly integrationist; Judge Mancini has

---

16 See P. Dunleavy and B. O'Leary, above, pp. 13-71, 320-349. See also R. Dahl's classic, *Dilemmas of Pluralist Democracy: Autonomy versus Control* (New Haven: Yale University Press) 1982.

17 M. Horsman and A. Marshall, *After the Nation-State: Citizens, Tribalism and the New World Disorder* (London: Harper Collins) 1994, p. 264.

18 Correctly, the European Union refers to the 'three pillar' arrangements put in place by the Treaty of European Union, while the legal system is that of the European Community. Hereafter the abbreviation EC will be used for simplicity.

19 R. Cooper, *The Post-Modern State and the World Order* (London: Demos) 1996, pp. 25, 30.

famously talked of integrationism as a 'genetic code transmitted to the court by the founding fathers'.[20] The values of economic liberalism are entrenched at constitutional level in the Treaty,[1] setting parameters within which Member States must operate. Theoretically these parameters are friendly to privatisation and 'downsizing' and could be seen as reinforcing the private side, management ethos of the New Public Management described more fully in Chapter 5. They could make a return to the 'producer state' or state as service provider difficult, as we shall see more clearly when we come to consider the impact of EC public procurement law.

The major EC policies – the single market, monetary union, abolition of frontier controls and common European citizenship – all have centralising tendencies. As Muller and Wright explain,[2] in this respect:

> . . . the impact of the Community has been paradoxical: increased market leads to diminished national regulatory activity (with less national differentiation) but Community protection of markets leads to increased regulation . . . We may expect the regulatory role of Brussels to increase, albeit at a slower rate, despite vague promises to respect the principle of subsidiarity, because such a role conforms fully to the logic of the open market. It is not, of course, merely in the financial and industrial sectors that the impact of Europe is being felt. Sensitive areas such as health, education, social welfare, environmental issues have been slowly dragged into the regulatory net of Brussels. The Schengen Agreement, signed first by five, now by eight countries on the European continent, provides for the abolition of internal frontier controls on goods and people, combined with measures for cooperation amongst police, immigration, customs and intelligence services and for common policies on rights of entry and residence. To an extent which is not fully appreciated, the EU is slowly redefining existing political arrangements, altering traditional policy networks, triggering institutional change, reshaping the opportunity structures of members states and their major interests. These interests are now increasingly entangled in relationships at four territorial levels: the international, the European, the national and the local, and for some of these interests it is by no means clear that the national level is the most important.

The concept of 'subsidiarity' inserted by the Preamble to the (Maastricht) Treaty of European Union (TEU), which provides for decisions to be 'taken as closely as possible to the citizen in accordance with the principle of subsidiarity', is meant as a counterweight to this centralising tendency. For all its ambiguity, the phraseology of the Preamble and TEU Art. A hints at delegation to units smaller than the nation-state. Here we have a pointer towards a decentralised and truly federal Europe. EEC Art. 3(b), on the other hand, is more limited in its scope, requiring the Community to take action 'only if and in so far as the objectives of

---

20  F. Mancini and D. Keeling, 'Democracy and the European Court of Justice' (1994) 57 MLR 175, 186. See also D. Wincott, 'The role of law or the rule of the Court of Justice? An institutional account of judicial politics in the EC' (1995) 2 J. of Eur. Pub. Policy 583, 584.

1  E. von Mestmacker, 'On the Legitimacy of European Law' (1994) 58 RabelsZ 617.

2  W. Muller and V. Wright, 'Reshaping the State in Western Europe: The Limits to Retreat' in W. Muller and V. Wright (eds.), *The State in Western Europe Retreat or Redefinition*, Special Issue, 17 W. European Politics No. 3 (1994) p. 6.

the action cannot be sufficiently achieved by the Member States'. How these provisions will be interpreted and developed is at present far from clear.[3]

The impact of EC membership is felt throughout government and we will see traces of it throughout this book. During the 1980s, policy-making expanded in every area of EC competence and the areas of competence themselves expanded. As we shall see in Chapter 7, this enormous change had a direct impact on national law-making and rule-making processes. We shall also see that the integration of EC case law (jurisprudence) into national structures, together with the power of individuals to challenge the validity of national law in national courts,[4] subject to a final ruling on validity by the ECJ on a reference under EEC Art. 177, has bitten deeply into national legal autonomy. The significance for administrative law has been a gradual progression towards a common set of legal remedies in national law, engineered by the Art. 177 rulings of the ECJ; we shall see this illustrated in the celebrated *Factortame* case (below, p. 171).

In contrast, the effect of the EC on national administrations is largely *indirect*; as Muller and Wright indicate,[5] regulation is the primary output of the EC. Except in certain limited fields, such as competition policy, where the Commission may take 'decisions', a form of EC law directed at individuals, and implement them, Brussels functionaries do not themselves execute decisions as national administrators do. Even when the EC is the primary policy-maker or issues regulations directly enforceable within the Member States, enforcement is still the task of national agencies and administrations.[6] For example, it is estimated that the Common Agricultural Policy has had the effect of transferring to Brussels up to 80% of the policy-making and regulatory powers, yet the subsidies for which it is responsible and has to account to the European Parliament are distributed on its behalf by national agencies. To borrow a celebrated metaphor, the Community steers, it does not row.

## 7. What should public lawyers do?

The time has come to reconsider our opening sentence. What is the connection between administrative law and theories of the state? The classical view, expounded in the next chapter, sees little relation. Theories of the state are at best 'background theory', a term used to denote the political setting and values in the context of which public law is studied.[7] Whatever the context, the function of public law is the control of abuse of state power, primarily through the judiciary whose values, although shaped by background theory, will seldom be openly articulated. This focus establishes the judicial process as the principal object of academic scrutiny

---

3    I. Ward, *A Critical Introduction to European Law* (London: Butterworths) 1996, p. 41. See also J. Peterson, 'Subsidiarity: A Definition to Suit Any Vision?' (1994) 47 Parl. Affairs 116.

4    This is the doctrine of 'direct effect'; see, T. Hartley, *The Foundations of European Community Law* (Oxford: Clarendon) 3rd. edn., 1994, pp. 195-233.

5    See above, note 2.

6    T. Daintith, 'European Community Law and the Redistribution of Regulatory Power in the United Kingdom' (1995) 1 Eur. Law J. 134, 136-137.

7    C. Harlow, 'Changing the Mindset: The Place of Theory in English Administrative Law' (1994) 14 OJLS 419.

and the task of the academic as the development of an orderly body of legal principles and legal concepts ('shallow theory'). Given his definition of law (above, p. 5), it is not surprising that this should be O'Leary's position.[8]

For Sedley,[9] whose views on the demotion of all constitutional issues to questions of fact have already been cited, it is insufficient to allow the common law preoccupation with facts to dictate outcomes. Where O'Leary sees theory as the prerogative of the political scientist or philosopher, Sedley believes that theorising plays an essential role in public law, that we should think carefully about where we are going and where we want to go:

> What public law can achieve on a constitutional plane in the next generation will be in large part a function of its particular character and history, and we risk losing control of our own enterprise and our own future if we do not adequately understand the dynamic of the system which we operate.

With Craig[10] and Allan[11] Sedley believes that public law should consciously incorporate a set of democratic values, an idea which returns behind Bentham to re-insert the 'ought' into law under the guise of 'principles'. This understanding, which prompts the question what these values should be, permeates many of the ideas propounded in Chapter 4.

A more radical explanation is that of the American scholar Frug, who has argued[12] that the real purpose of administrative law doctrine, however much it may talk in terms of control, is to justify bureaucracy and administration; the relationship between the two is essentially symbiotic in character. Frug identifies four models of administrative law, related to differing visions of bureaucracy. The first, formalist model views bureaucracy as a mechanism for carrying out the wishes of its creators, who keep it firmly under the control. This vision broadly corresponds to that of classic English administrative law, premised on and responsive to, a liberal-democratic conception of the constitution and of the civil service as 'neutral and impartial: a servant to any master'. As we saw, this classic view was inaugurated by the Northcote-Trevelyan Report and installed by nineteenth-century writers, especially Dicey.

Frug associates his second 'model of expertise' with Franklin Roosevelt's New Deal policies. This model recognises both the extent of administrative discretion and the ineffectiveness of external control but welcomes bureaucracy as an essential tool for effective policy-making. It is sometimes described as 'instrumentalist' because law is seen as an 'instrument' for the implementation

---

8  B. O'Leary, 'What Should Public Lawyers Do?' (1992) 12 OJLS 404.
9  S. Sedley, 'The Sound of Silence: Constitutional Law Without a Constitution' (1994) 110 LQR 270, 277.
10  P. Craig, *Public Law and Democracy in the United Kingdom and the United States of America* (Oxford: Clarendon) 1990.
11  T. Allan, *Law, Liberty, and Justice, The Legal Foundations of British Constitutionalism* (Oxford: Clarendon) 1993.
12  G. Frug, 'The Ideology of Bureaucracy in American Law' (1984) 97 Harv. LR 1277. And see C. Edley, *Administrative Law: Rethinking Judicial Control and Bureaucracy* (New Haven: Yale University Press) 1990.

of policy.[13] We shall consider the American influence and follow this viewpoint in Chapter 3.

Frug moves next to a 'judical review' model, terminology which may confuse the English reader by conflating this model with the classical, positivist school of English administrative law. But Frug's judicial review model differs in seeking to limit the courts' power of intrusion, leaving control primarily with the administrative hierarchy. The seminal work of American author K. C. Davis, which exemplifies this attitude, is placed in Chapter 4. Frug sees the credibility of the judicial review model as challenged, from the left by pluralists and by critical legal theory, and from the right, by an aggressive market model – his fourth model.

This is, however, to telescope two wholly discrepant views of state and administration which have in common only their hostility to judicial review and its values. To reformulate the argument, pluralists (as we have seen in this chapter) fear monopolist, multi-national corporations against which the political left – not necessarily pluralist – tried to mobilise the power of the state and organised labour, acting on behalf of and controlled by the people. In common with pluralists, the New Right fears the corporatist network of bureaucratic departments and nationalised industry, quangos and trade unions. It also aims to dismantle and privatise the proliferating organisms of the state. On the other hand, the New Right fears the power of organised labour. In this book, therefore, these very different attitudes are treated separately. It is fair to characterise the ideas discussed in Chapter 3 as broadly left-leaning; the 'New Right' market model of public administration is presented in Chapter 5.

Public administration is both a valid object of study by administrative lawyers and something to which they need to remain responsive. It is important that administrative law should not be out of synchronisation with its administrative context. Hood has suggested[14] that the changed landscape of public administration poses important questions for public law today. Should discretion in public administration, for example, be checked by legal counter-measures designed to protect entitlements, such as the principles of legitimate expectation or acquired rights? Are traditional mechanisms of accountability, notably ministerial responsibility, adequate to respond to the new forms of downloaded government? Do some of the novel forms of accountability themselves form part of our system of public law?

As lawyers, the authors are naturally concerned that legal techniques shall be used to the best advantage in the administrative process, whether to control or forward the goals of administration. We have tried to apply the functionalist method in questioning 'the effectiveness of various possible legal rules and arrangements'.[15] Like Craig, we are concerned with the search for values, accepting law's educative and symbolic roles.[16] Our response to the question

---

13  See M. Loughlin, 'The Pathways of Public Law Scholarship' in G. Wilson (ed.), *Frontiers of Legal Scholarship* (Chichester: John Wiley) 1995.

14  C. Hood, 'Emerging Issues in Public Administration' (1995) 73 Pub. Admin. 165, 167.

15  F. Cohen, 'The problems of a functional jurisprudence' (1937) 1 MLR 5, 22.

16  See P. Atiyah, *Pragmatism and Theory in English Law* (London: Stevens) 1987.

'What should public lawyers do?' would be that they have a responsibility critically to evaluate the institutions, processes and systems of administration, exposing to public gaze the values on which both are premised. They must also articulate their own values. These are the fundamental assumptions of the chapters which follow.

# Chapter 2

# Red light theories

## 1. Public law and scientific method

Administrative law started to emerge as an independent subject during the nineteenth century. Contemporaneously, the views of thinkers like Jeremy Bentham (1748-1832)[1] and John Austin (1790-1859) were becoming influential. Both men saw themselves as rationalists, concerned to excise mysticism and the doctrines of natural law from the philosophy of law. They believed that law was capable of reduction to rational, scientific principles. This method was introduced to the field of public law by Professor A. V. Dicey (1835-1922), the first professor of law at Oxford University.[2] Dicey has been described as:[3]

> . . . the first to apply the juridical method to English public law. Blackstone's incursions into this field were jejeune. Austin was essentially a civilian. Pollock and Salmond have made a science out of English private law. Maitland's scattered contributions were of the greatest possible value, but his main work was done in the historical field . . . [Dicey's] style, too, though somewhat verbose and repetitive, was eminently readable. His influence upon the development of public law in England has been immense. His authority to-day is greater than that of any other public lawyer; it is probably true to say that in no country have the views of a public lawyer of a past generation the same weight as Dicey's possess in England.

Over a period when linguistic philosophy dominated in British thought, it was natural to find a jurisprudence much concerned with linguistic analysis.[4] Thanks largely to Dicey, this method extended to public law.

It is none the less important to remember that, in the history of ideas, simplification is dangerous. Legal theorists tend to wander across the boundaries inside which we try to pen them. How is 'positivism' to be defined or 'formalism' pinned down, and are the two terms synonomous? Who were the American

---

1   For Bentham's influence on positivism, see Loughlin, *Public Law*, pp. 17-20. And see P. Schofield, '"Professing Liberal Opinions": The Common Law, Adjudication and Security in Recent Bentham Scholarship' (1995) 16 Legal History 350.
2   See his inaugural lecture, 'Can English Law be Taught at Universities?' (1883). And see R. Blackburn, 'Dicey and the Teaching of Public Law' [1985] PL 679.
3   W. I. Jennings, 'In Praise of Dicey (1885-1935)' (1935) 13 Pub. Admin. 123, 133.
4   The masterpiece of the school is H. Hart, *The Concept of Law* (Oxford: Clarendon) 2nd revised edn., 1994.

'realists'?[5] Who or what is a 'functionalist' and is functionalism different from instrumentalism?[6] Much ink has been lavished on such questions. Bentham, to whom modern Anglo-American legal theory owes a particular debt, called himself a rationalist, yet it has been said that 'in some ways, his principle of utility was a canon of value not susceptible of proof but only justifiable if at all by a metaphysical argument, and therefore idealist in character'.[7] For our purposes here it is enough broadly to differentiate two legal traditions.[8] We shall loosely group *positivism* and *formalism* as comprising theories which focus on law as a logically coherent system of principles and rules and a logical and discrete system of legal reasoning. In contrast, whatever their differences, *realists* and *functionalists* have in common that they are primarily interested in what Felix Cohen once called 'the human meaning of law' – in other words, law in action or the way in which law functions in society.[9]

American observers like Davis, who visited England in 1961, were struck by the endurance of the positivist tradition amongst English lawyers and more particularly the judiciary. Davis described English judicial review as restricted by an old-fashioned, positivist corset, 'astonishing to one with a background in the American legal system'. English judges strove to avoid consideration of the policy aspects of the issues they decided, an attitude which he saw as running deep in the legal profession. The typical lawyer, he said:[10]

> responds with consternation to an inquiry into the soundness of the policies embodied in a judicial decision, and, if he persists, the inquirer is gently reminded that judges do not consider policy questions and that only Parliament can change the law; the task of the judge is wholly analytical – to discover the previously existing law, and to apply it logically to the case before the court.

It is fair to see the classical tradition of English administrative law as predominantly positivist, while the American tradition was much less clearly so (a point to be borne in mind when reading the American literature).[11] Jaffé,[12] in a study of English and American judges, attributed the difference to constitutional factors, remarking that it had always been anticipated that the federal American judge

---

5  See N. Duxbury, *Patterns of American Jurisprudence* (Oxford: Clarendon) 1995.
6  See M. Loughlin, 'The Pathways of Public Law Scholarship' in G. Wilson (ed.), *Frontiers of Legal Scholarship* (Chichester: John Wiley) 1995.
7  D. Lloyd, *The Idea of Law* (Harmondsworth: Penguin) 2nd edn., 1972, p. 76.
8  See, for a fuller exposition, M. Loughlin, *Public Law*. Loughlin prefers the terminology of 'normativism' and 'functionalism'. W. Rumble, 'The Legal Positivism of John Austin and the Realist Movement in American Jurisprudence', (1981) 66 Cornell LR 986, relates the two movements.
9  F. Cohen, 'Transcendental Nonsense and the Functional Approach' (1935) 35 Col. LR 809, 843.
10  K. C. Davis, 'The Future of Judge-Made Public Law in England: A Problem of Practical Jurisprudence' (1961) 61 Col. Law Rev. 201, 202.
11  See, P Atiyah and R. Summers, *Form and Substance in Anglo-American Law: A Comparative Study of Legal Reasoning, Legal Theory and Legal Institutions* (Oxford: Clarendon) 1987. We are not, of course, implying that there is no American formalist public law: see especially the works of Dickinson. See K. Werhan, 'The Neoclassical Revival in Administrative Law' (1992) 44 Admin. LR 567.
12  L. Jaffé, *English and American Judges as Lawmakers* (Oxford: Clarendon) 1969, p. 83.

would 'assume a role in the polity far greater than that played by his confrerè in Britain'. The positivist ideal of law as 'autonomous', a discrete discipline founded on semantic analysis, relates closely both to classical liberalism, with its view of the state as autonomous and objective, and the constitutional principle of the Rule of Law, in many ways a different formulation of the same ideal.

The analytic, formalist or positivist style of legal reasoning dominated English law in the inter-war and early post-war periods – formative periods in the law of judicial review – and it is by no means defunct. Much of the time of law students is still spent on close semantic analysis of judicial decisions, criticism of the reasoning and predictions of where the decision may lead. Many administrative lawyers still see this process of classification as a core element in their discipline, though today it is probably a majority which sees the lines as hard to maintain. Although it will already be plain that formalistic analysis is not the primary end of this book, this does not mean that we can simply brush it aside.

## 2. Hair-splitting distinctions and terminological contortions?

### (a) judicial/administrative

Central to the development of administrative law in England is the distinction between administrative and judicial functions, formerly used as the criterion for deciding when the rules of natural justice applied to decision-making. The attempts made by the Donoughmore Committee to distinguish the two provide an excellent example of formalistic reasoning. The committee had been set up by the government in the wake of a panic sparked off by Lord Hewart, then Lord Chief Justice, who had launched a scathing attack on what he called the 'new despotism'. Bemoaning the destruction of the balanced constitution, his analogy was with Stuart autocracy:[13]

> Writers on the Constitution have for a long time taught that its two leading features are the Sovereignty of Parliament and the Rule of Law. To tamper with either of them was, it might be thought, a sufficiently serious undertaking. But how far more attractive to the ingenious and adventurous mind to employ the one to defeat the other, and to establish a despotism on the ruins of both! It is manifestly easy to point to a superficial contrast between what was done or attempted in the days of our least wise kings, and what is being done or attempted today. In those days the method was to defy Parliament – and it failed. In these days the method is to cajole, to coerce, and to use Parliament – and it is strangely successful. The old despotism, which was defeated, offered Parliament a challenge. The new despotism, which is not yet defeated, gives Parliament an anaesthetic. The strategy is different, but the goal is the same. It is to subordinate Parliament, to evade the Courts, and to render the will, or the caprice of the Executive unfettered and supreme.

Lord Hewart reserved his most savage ridicule for the concept of 'administrative justice', in his mind a 'grotesque misnomer', renamed by him 'administrative

---

13   *The New Despotism* (London: Benn) 1929, pp. 17, 44.  See, to similar effect, F. Mount, *The British Constitution Now* (London: Heinemann) 1992.

lawlessness'. 'The exercise of arbitrary power is neither law nor justice, administrative or at all.' In this context, the committee's terms of reference, phrased directly in terms of separation of powers, were:[14]

> to consider the powers exercised by or under the direction of (or by persons or bodies appointed specially by) Ministers of the Crown by way of (a) delegated legislation and (b) judicial or quasi-judicial decision, and to report what safeguards are desirable or necessary to secure the constitutional principles of the sovereignty of Parliament and the supremacy of the law.

In its own words, the questions that the committee was trying to answer were:[15]

> (a) To what extent should judicial functions be entrusted (i) to Ministers and (ii) to Ministerial [administrative] Tribunals: (b) What are the right methods for the exercise of such functions? What are the proper safeguards?

How was the committee to set about such an amorphous task? They could, of course, have tried to accumulate empirical evidence on the way these bodies operated to see whether Hewart's strictures were justified.[16] Instead, they tried to devise definitions which would enable governmental decision-making to be split into three separate categories of 'judicial', 'quasi-judicial' and 'administrative'. The committee's reasoning mirrors, and probably borrowed, judicial reasoning of the period:[17]

> A *true judicial* decision presupposes an existing dispute between two or more parties and then involves four requisites: (1) the presentation (not necessarily orally) of their case by the parties to the dispute; (2) if the dispute between them is a question of fact, the ascertainment of the fact by means of evidence adduced by the parties to the dispute and often with the assistance of argument by or on behalf of the parties on the evidence; (3) if the dispute between them is a question of law, the submission of legal argument by the parties; and (4) a decision which disposes of the whole matter by a finding upon the facts in dispute and an application of the law of the land to the facts so found, including where required a ruling upon any disputed question of law.

If you think carefully about the committee's definition, you can see that it is procedural in character. In other words, a decision is not classified as 'judicial' because of its innate or substantive characteristics but because it has been taken by a judicial or 'trial-type' process. (Later, in Chapter 15, we will be able to compare this approach with Fuller's attempt at defining adjudication.) The answer to the question set by the committee has thus been foreclosed. The definition is circular. We could paraphrase the reasoning as follows: *When a decision which should be taken by a judicial procedure is entrusted to a*

14  *Report of the Committee on Ministers' Powers* (Cmnd: 4050, 1932) p. 1.
15  *Report*, p. 82.
16  As the Franks Committee on Tribunals and Inquiries (below, Chapter 14) did, and as the Donoughmore Committee did for delegated legislation.
17  *Report*, pp. 73-74.

*Minister or tribunal it must be taken by a judicial procedure.* The committee continued:[18]

> *A quasi-judicial decision* equally presupposes an existing dispute between two or more parties and involves (1) and (2), but does not necessarily involve (3), and never involves (4). The place of (4) is in fact taken by administrative action, the character of which is determined by the Minister's free choice.
>
> *Decisions which are purely administrative* stand on a wholly different footing from . . . judicial decisions and must be distinguished accordingly. Indeed the very word 'decision' has a different meaning in the one sphere of activity and the other. When a person resolves to act in a particular way, the mental step may be described as a 'decision'. Again, when a judge determines an issue of fact upon conflicting evidence, or a question of law upon forensic argument, he gives a 'decision'. But the two mental acts differ. In the case of the administrative decision, there is no legal obligation upon the person charged with the duty of reaching the decision to consider and weigh submissions and arguments, or to collate any evidence, or to solve any issue. The grounds upon which he acts, and the means which he takes to inform himself before acting, are left entirely to his discretion.

It is hard to discover exactly what the committee is saying here. Their main point seems to be that a judge is under a 'legal obligation' to adopt the four-stage pattern of decision-making described earlier, although custom and practice rather than obligation dictates this. A politician or administrator, on the other hand, merely 'resolves to act'. Not only is this a travesty of the way in which administrators approach policy and decision-making – a point discussed at length in Chapter 4 – but the committee is once more guilty of circular reasoning. It has defined an administrative decision as one in which there is no *duty* to use judical procedures – the very question which it was set up to decide.

Much of the modern law of judicial review has been devoted to prising administrative law from the 'dead hand' of the Donoughmore Committee and imposing procedural requirements on administrative decision-making. This does not undercut the criticisms of de Smith,[19] the leading post-war commentator, of judicial efforts at classification:

> It is sometimes impossible to discern why a court has characterised a given function as judicial or administrative. Often, it is true, the method of characterisation can be seen as a contrivance to support a conclusion reached on non-conceptual grounds. But in many cases the terms seem to have been used loosely and without deliberation; and in some cases definitions propounded in earlier reported cases appear to have dominated the juristic analysis of the case in hand and indeed the conclusion reached by the court . . . recent English caselaw has tended to blur rather than clarify the distinctions between the two most important classes of function, the judicial and the administrative.

18  *Report*, p. 74.
19  S. de Smith, *Judicial Review of Administrative Action* (London: Stevens) 4th edn., J. M. Evans, 1980, pp. 58-59.

## (b) Public/private

In the latest edition of de Smith's great classic, *Judicial Review of Administrative Action*, the editors have pushed this passage into an appendix and feel able to say, 'Servitude to these classifications has now largely been abandoned. In regard to natural justice, the notion that a fair hearing is reserved to a 'judicial' or 'quasi-judicial' situation has been firmly 'scotched' as a heresy'.[20] (Whether this is so can be judged after reading Chapter 15.) This is not true, however, of the analytic method of reasoning. In modern administrative law a similar distinction has evolved between 'public' and 'private' law. Designed to provide an answer to the preliminary question in which court the litigant should sue, the test ought to be simple and easy to apply. We find instead a modern example of the 'hair-splitting distinctions' and 'terminological contortions' which earlier exasperated de Smith. The case law has generated a whole new chapter of nearly 50 pages in the latest edition of de Smith, whose editors somewhat defensively admit:[1]

> . . . what the commentators do agree on is the difficulty in identifying the path which the divide follows and its extensive influence on many aspects of administrative law. The distinction between public and private law now plays a crucial role in determining:
> (1) when it is necessary to bring proceedings by way of judicial review, under R.S.C. Order 53, with its distinctive procedural requirements;
> (2) by whom and against whom proceedings which raise public law issues can be brought;
> (3) the principles which the court will apply and the role it will play in order to determine those issues; and
> (4) the remedies which may be granted.
> Because of the importance of the distinction it is obviously regrettable that there has been so much uncertainty. This chapter tries to improve this unsatisfactory situation. It cannot do so by identifying an exhaustive set of criteria which will identify the difference between public and private law. Instead the chapter seeks to highlight the principles which have and are in the process of emerging as the courts struggle, in a variety of contexts, to determine that boundary.

This is almost an admission that pure analytic reasoning is doomed to failure.

In deciding whether a decision is public or private in nature, courts sometimes rely on *institutional* definitions, according to which any activity undertaken by a public body is 'public'. This was essentially the tactic used in the *Town Investment* case (above, p. 7). When a government department or local authority is in issue, the answer may be fairly clear, but in less obvious cases this often involves the court in classifying a given body as 'public' because another court has in the past said that it was (the automatic operation of the doctrine of precedent earlier criticised by de Smith). To escape this difficulty, a *functional* test may be substituted whereby public law applies to decisions which seem to be inherently 'governmental' in character. This route (which we argued for in *Town Investments*)

---

20   S. de Smith, Lord Woolf and J. Jowell, *Judicial Review of Administrative Action* (London: Sweet and Maxwell) 5th edn., 1995, para. 1-001. (Hereafter de Smith, Jowell, Woolf.)

 1   de Smith, Jowell, Woolf, paras 3-002, 3-003. One of the editors has defended the distinction: see Sir Harry Woolf, 'Public Law – Private Law: Why the Divide? A Personal View' [1986] PL 220.

allows the courts more room for manoeuvre, since there is no limit on what functions the state must or should exercise. Since neither test is precise and it is difficult to predict which will be applied, the suspicion must be that, here again, de Smith's belief that conclusions are often reached 'on non-conceptual grounds' is correct.

de Smith hints that formalistic reasoning may be used to cover reasons for a decision which a functionalist or realist would answer overtly, realistically and with due regard to policy – essentially Jaffé's point. But for a formalist the admission is unthinkable. It undercuts the idea of law as autonomous and as a discrete system of reasoning. None the less formalism does sometimes provide a useful shield against accusations of playing politics.[2] It is, in other words, a technique which a judiciary committed both to the Rule of Law ideal and the doctrine of Sovereignty of Parliament can employ to avoid encounters with the government of the day over policy and politics. We will find this technique used to great effect in the celebrated case of *M v Home Office*.[3]

Analytic reasoning at its best does possess a rational strength,[4] and in Chapter 4 we shall find a growing insistence that this rigorous quality must not only be maintained but, crucially, strengthened. But Shklar, herself a political theorist, describes the wider consequences of the 'scientific' method for legal reasoning:[5]

> The urge to draw a clear line between law and non-law has led to the constructing of ever more refined and rigid systems of formal definitions. This procedure has served to isolate law completely from the social context within which it exists. Law is endowed with its own discrete, integral history, its own 'science', and its own values, which are all treated as a single block sealed off from general social history, from politics, and from morality. The habits of mind appropriate, within narrow limits, to the procedures of law courts in the most stable legal systems have been expanded to provide legal theory and ideology with an entire system of thought and values. This procedure has served its own ends very well: it aims at preserving law from irrelevant considerations, but it has ended by fencing legal thinking off from all contact with the rest of historical thought and experience.

Are there perhaps common elements in Shklar's description of lawyerly habits of thought and Weber's description of bureaucracy (above, p. 12)? The modern bureaucratic method is based closely on rules, often caustically dismissed by the public as 'red tape', to which the actors are obliged to conform. Is this really a variant of Shklar's 'legalism'? Perhaps both bureaucracy and legalism were the hidden threat concealed within the Trojan horse of the modern state.

2   C. Harlow, 'Accidental Death of an Asylum Seeker' (1994) 57 MLR 620.
3   [1993] 3 WLR 433 (below, p. 61).
4   See N. MacCormick, *Legal Reasoning and Legal Theory* (Oxford: Clarendon) 1978.
5   J. Shklar, *Legalism* (Cambridge, Mass.: Harvard University Press) 1964, pp. 2-3. See also T. Daintith, 'Legal Analysis of Economic Policy' (1982) 9 J. of Law and Soc. 191, 191-193.

Griffith,[6] in an essay written when positivism and legal formalism were at their height,[7] agrees that a 'conventional' legal training based on the positivist method induces an inflexible cast of mind. The effect is to cut lawyers off from other social scientists:

A lawyer is *bound* by certain types and habits of belief . . . A man who has had a legal training . . . is never able to look at institutions or administrative practices or even social or political policies, free from his legal habits of belief. It is not easy for a lawyer to become a political scientist. It is very difficult for him to become a sociologist or a historian . . . he will fight to the death to defend legal rights against persuasive arguments based on expediency or the public interest or the social good . . . he believes, as part of his mental habits, that they are dangerous and too easily used as cloaks for arbitrary action.

Bouchard, a Canadian, sees lawyers as 'part of the problem' of modern administrative law, accusing them of looking at administration 'through the wrong end of the telescope' and giving undue importance to 'lawyers' values':[8]

They are trained mainly in the resolution of private disputes and in the representation of private individuals having difficulties with other individuals or having been accused of violating the law. Such training can only lead to an over-emphasis on formal responses to deviant conduct, to over-judicialisation and to over-reliance on adversarial processes, all of which are undesirable in the context of administrative law.

Later, we shall find that the development of public administration during the 1990s has led to the re-assertion of contract in public law, often under the influence of the private, commercial firms of lawyers to whom, increasingly, government legal work is entrusted. We use the terms 'juridified' and 'juridification' to cover the consequential formalisation of relationships defined by law and couched in legal terminology. Again, there is a clear relationship with Shklar's legalism.

To summarise the argument in modern terms, we might say that lawyers, grounded in philosophies of legal positivism and trained in analytic jurisprudence, have contributed to 'thin' or rights-based theories of state and constitution, which over-rate the virtue of autonomy and individualism and leach out community values. In this way, they have resiled from their own ideal of autonomy both by failing to facilitate or preside neutrally over a discourse of other, related disciplines[9] and, signally, to admit new participants to the discourse.

6    Griffith's contribution to administrative law is discussed in Ch. 3. For the view that Griffith is at least partially a believer in formalism, see Loughlin, *Public Law*, p. 198.
7    J. Griffith, 'The Law of Property (Land)' in M. Ginsberg (ed.), *Law and Opinion in England in the 20th Century* (London: Stevens) 1959, pp. 117-119.
8    M. Bouchard, 'Administrative Law in the Real World: A View from Canada' in M. Taggart (ed.), *Judicial Review of Administrative Action in the 1980s, Problems and Prospects* (Auckland: OUP) 1986, pp. 194-195. See also J. Willis, 'The McRuer Report: Lawyers' Values and Civil Servants' Values' (1968) UTLJ 351.
9    G. Teubner, 'Altera pars Audiatur: Law in the Collision of Discourses' in R. Rawlings (ed.) *Law, Society and Economy* (Oxford: Clarendon) 1997.

## 3. The Diceyan inheritance

Behind the formalist tradition, we can often discern a preference for a minimalist state. It is not surprising, therefore, to find many authors believing that the primary function of administrative law should be to control any excess of state power and subject it to legal, and more especially judicial, control. It is this conception of administrative law that we have called 'red light theory'.[10] A definition of administrative law borrowed from the influential text of Sir William Wade, the pre-eminent contemporary disciple of Dicey, embodies these themes:[11]

> A first approximation to a definition of administrative law is to say that it is the law relating to the control of governmental power. This, at any rate, is the heart of the subject. The governmental power in question is not that of Parliament: Parliament as the legislature is sovereign and, subject to one exception, is beyond legal control. The powers of all other public authorities are subordinated to the law, just as much in the case of the Crown and ministers as in the case of local authorities and other public bodies. All such subordinate powers have two inherent characteristics. First, they are all subject to legal limitations; there is no such thing as absolute or unfettered administrative power. Secondly, and consequentially, it is always possible for any power to be abused. Even where Parliament enacts that a minister may make such order as he thinks fit for a certain purpose, the court may still invalidate the order if it infringes one of the many judge-made rules. And the court will invalidate it, *a fortiori*, if it infringes the limits which Parliament itself has ordained.
>
> The primary purpose of administrative law is, therefore, to keep the powers of government within their legal bounds, so as to protect the citizen against their abuse. The powerful engines of authority must be prevented from running amok. 'Abuse', it should be made clear, carries no necessary innuendo of malice or bad faith. Government departments may misunderstand their legal position as easily as may other people, and the law which they have to administer is frequently complex and uncertain. Abuse is therefore inevitable, and it is all the more necessary that the law should provide means to check it . . .
>
> As well as power there is duty. It is also the concern of administrative law to see that public authorities can be compelled to perform their duties if they make default . . . The law provides compulsory remedies for such situations, thus dealing with the negative as well as the positive side of maladministration.
>
> *Function distinguished from structure*
> As a second approximation to a definition, administrative law may be said to be the body of general principles which govern the exercise of powers and duties by public authorities. This is only one part of the mass of law to which public authorities are subject. All the detailed law about their composition and structure, though clearly related to administrative law, lies beyond the proper scope of the subject . . .
>
> What has to be isolated is the law about the *manner* in which public authorities must exercise their functions, distinguishing function from structure and looking always for general principles . . .
>
> *Administrative justice*
> What gives unity to the subjects mentioned above . . . is the quest for administrative justice. Diverse as some of them are, this is the connecting theme. At every point the question is, how can the profession of law contribute to the improvement of the technique of government? It is because all the various topics offer scope for this

missionary spirit that they form a harmonious whole. Subject as it is to the vast empires of executive power that have been created, the public must be able to rely on the law to ensure that all this power may be used in a way conformable to its ideas of fair dealing and good administration. As liberty is subtracted, justice must be added.

In the light of overt suspicion of the 'vast empires of executive power' coupled with the expectation that government will 'run amok'; of the emphasis on 'control'; the concern for vanishing liberty; the references both to the rule of law and to parliamentary sovereignty, Wade's definition of administrative law as 'the law relating to the control of governmental power' comes as no surprise. In his definition – though not in practice in the later editions of his textbook – Wade narrows his focus to include 'only the *general principles* of the law relating to the *control* of governmental power'. In every respect his definition exemplifies the classic tradition of English administrative law, deriving directly from the writings of its greatest exponent, Dicey. Wade would welcome the association. He has said, 'I yield to no one in admiration of Dicey's brilliant summing up of the Constitution in the nineteenth century', and described the spirit of Dicey's work as 'enduring'.[12]

Dicey's *Introduction to the Law of the Constitution*, published in 1885, might almost be described as a substitute for a written constitution. His influence on the development of administrative law has been equally pervasive.[13] Dicey's ideas lock up together to form the ideal of a 'balanced' constitution, in which the executive, envisaged as capable of arbitrary encroachment on the rights of individual citizens, will be subject, on the one side, to political control by Parliament, on the other, to legal control through the common law by the courts.

## (a) Dicey and the Rule-of-Law state

The ancient philosophical ideal of the Rule of Law can be traced back to Aristotle's government of 'laws not men', and has been promoted and explored by generations of political philosophers. The ideal, with its emphasis on the importance of formal, predictable rules is likely to prove attractive to lawyers. They too have adopted this paradigm as the basis for theories of constitutionalism.[14] The concept of 'legality', in other words that the administration must observe the law and act 'legally', is fundamental to modern administrative law.[15] The Rule of Law provides a convenient theoretical justification for the judicial power to

---

10  In *Public Law*, pp. 184-190, Loughlin calls this the 'conservative normativist' tradition.
11  H. W. R. Wade and C. Forsyth, *Administrative Law* (Oxford: Clarendon) 7th edn., 1994, pp. 5-7. (Hereafter Wade and Forsyth.)
12  H.W. R. Wade, 'Law, Opinion and Administration' (1962) 78 LQR 188, 189. This was Wade's inaugural lecture in Oxford University, where Dicey had held the Vinerian Chair.
13  More detailed analyses are to be found in Loughlin, *Public Law*, pp. 140-162; P. Craig, *Public Law and Democracy in the United Kingdom and the United States of America* (Oxford: Clarendon) 1990, Ch. 2. See also 'Dicey and the Constitution', All Souls Symposium [1985] PL 583-723.
14  See particularly, J. Raz, 'The Rule of Law and its Virtue' (1977) 93 LQR 195; T. Allan, *Law, Liberty, and Justice: Legal Foundations of British Constitutionalism* (Oxford: Clarendon) 1993.
15  See G. Zellick, 'Government Beyond Law' [1985] PL 283.

'review' governmental and administrative acts and to declare them lawful (in legal terminology, intra vires) or unlawful and in excess of power (ultra vires). We will find the House of Lords making an expansive appeal to the Rule of Law ideal in *M v Home Office* (below, p. 61). The attempt to capture the high ground in this way reflects the fact that the judges concerned knew that they were treading on dangerous political ground. separation of powers theory provides us with the concept of an 'independent' judiciary detached from government. 'Impartiality', however, blends into Montesquieu's famous description of the judicial power as 'neutral' in the sense of 'apolitical'.[16] We also derive from separation of powers theory the belief that judges do not 'make' law but simply 'declare' it. To make 'new law' or 'political decisions' brings criticisms of judicial activism which formalism can do much to allay.

In the work of Hayek, economist and political theorist,[17] there is a close link between the Rule of Law in the sense of law's objectivity and Hayek's strong belief in the 'nightwatchman' or limited state. In a passage which looks forward to modern faith in 'the market' yet back to the Donoughmore Committee's conception of administrative decision-making, Hayek, in his early classic, *The Road to Serfdom*[18] draws a 'general distinction between the Rule of Law and arbitrary government':

> Under the first, government confines itself to fixing rules determining the conditions under which the available resources may be used, leaving to the individuals the decision for what ends they are to be used. Under the second, the government directs the use of the means of production to particular ends. The first type of rules can be made in advance, in the shape of *formal rules* which do not aim at the wants and needs of particular people . . . Economic planning of the collectivist kind necessarily involves the very opposite of this. The planning authority cannot confine itself to providing opportunities for unknown people to make whatever use of them they like. It cannot tie itself down in advance to general and formal rules which prevent arbitrariness. It must provide for the actual needs of people as they arise and then choose deliberately between them.

Oakeshott, historian, political philosopher, and author of a distinguished essay on the Rule of Law[19] argues that law is culturally related, deriving essentially from custom, tradition and human experience.[20] Dicey's late nineteenth-century version of the Rule of Law doctrine is perhaps the most celebrated English version but it is one of many interpretations, neither the latest nor the definitive theory.

Dicey's statement of the Rule of Law contains three elements: (a) that the state possesses no 'exceptional' powers and (b) that individual public servants are

16  M. Vile, *Constitutionalism and Separation of Powers* (Oxford: Clarendon) 1967, pp. 85-90.
17  *Law, Legislation and Liberty* (London: Routledge and Kegan Paul) 3 vols, 1973-79. See also *The Constitution of Liberty* (London: Routledge and Kegan Paul) 1960. And see Loughlin, *Public Law*, pp. 84-93.
18  Above, n. 2, p. 10.
19  'The Rule of Law' in M. Oakeshott, *On History and Other Essays* (Oxford: Blackwell) 1983. And see Loughlin, *Public Law*, pp. 63-83.
20  See especially M. Oakeshott, *On Human Experience* (Oxford: OUP) 1975; *On History: and Other Essays* (Oxford: Blackwell) 1983.

responsible to (c) the ordinary courts of the land for their use of statutory powers. Let us look at this a little more closely:[1]

> When we say that the supremacy of the rule of law is a characteristic of the English constitution we generally include under one expression at least three distinct though kindred conceptions.
>
> [First] that no man is punishable or can be lawfully made to suffer in body or goods except for a distinct breach of law established in the ordinary legal manner before the ordinary courts of the land. In this sense the rule of law is contrasted with every system of government based on the exercise by persons in authority of wide, arbitrary or discretionary powers of constraint . . .
>
> [Secondly], not only that with us no man is above the law, but (what is a different thing) that here every man, whatever be his rank or condition, is subject to the ordinary law of the realm and amenable to the jurisdiction of the ordinary tribunals.
>
> In England the idea of legal equality, or of the universal subjection of all classes to one law administered by the ordinary courts, has been pushed to its utmost limit. With us every official, from the Prime Minister down to a constable, is under the same responsibility for every act done without legal justification as any other citizen . . .
>
> [Thirdly] that the general principles of the constitution (as for example the right to personal liberty, or the right of public meeting) are with us the result of judicial decisions determining the rights of private persons in particular cases brought before the courts; whereas under many foreign constitutions the security (such as it is) given to the rights of individuals results, or appears to result, from the general principles of the constitution.

By 1885, when Dicey published his lectures, the expansion of state power was well under way; Maitland, writing contemporaneously,[2] acknowledged this fact and, in his later works, Dicey too had regretfully to concede the point.[3] Yet Dicey did not consider that his theory needed modification to meet this situation. In 1908, in the seventh edition of his work, he wrote:[4]

> The innovations, such as they are, have been suggested merely by considerations of practical convenience, and do not betray the least intention on the part of English Statesmen to modify the essential principles of English law. There exists in England no true *droit administratif*.

### (b) 'The English have no administrative law'

Founded partly on misunderstandings, there is no doubt that Dicey's legendary hostility to 'administrative law' and his faith in the superiority of common law systems has been highly influential in the development of English administrative law:[5]

---

1   A. Dicey, *Introduction to the Study of the Law of the Constitution* (London: Macmillan) 10th edn. by E. Wade, 1959, pp. 187-196.
2   F. Maitand, *A Constitutional History of England* (Cambridge: CUP) 1885, pp. 385-501.
3   A. Dicey, *Lectures on the Relation Between Law and Public Opinion in England During the Nineteenth Century* (London: Macmillan) 2nd edn. by E. Wade, 1963, Lecture VIII, 'Period of Collectivism'.
4   *Law of the Constitution*, p. 391.
5   A. Dicey, *Law of the Constitution* (above, note 1), pp. 328, 388.

In many continental countries, and notably in France, there exists a scheme of administrative law – known to Frenchmen as *droit administratif* – which rests on ideas foreign to the fundamental assumptions of our English common law, and especially to what we have termed the rule of law. This opposition is specially apparent in the protection given in foreign countries to servants of the State, or, as we say in England, of the Crown, who, whilst acting in pursuance of official orders, or in the *bona fide* attempt to discharge official duties, are guilty of acts which in themselves are wrongful or unlawful ... [This] forms only one portion of the whole system of *droit administratif*, but it is the part of French law to which I wish to direct particularly the attention of students. I must, however, impress upon them that the whole body of *droit administratif* is well worth their study. It has been imitated in most of the countries of continental Europe. It illustrates by way of contrast, the full meaning of that absolute supremacy of the ordinary law of the land – a foreign critic might say of that intense legalism – which we have found to be a salient feature of English institutions ...

For the term *droit administratif* English legal phraseology supplies no proper equivalent. The words 'administrative law', which are its most natural rendering, are unknown to English judges and counsel, and are in themselves hardly intelligible without further explanation.

This absence from our language of any satisfactory equivalent for the expression *droit administratif* is significant; the want of a name arises at bottom from our non-recognition of the thing itself. In England, and in countries which, like the United States, derive their civilisation from English sources, the system of administrative law and the very principles on which it rests are in truth unknown ...

Anyone who considers with care the nature of the *droit administratif* of France, or the topics to which it applies, will soon discover that it rests, and always has rested, at bottom on two leading ideas alien to the conceptions of modern Englishmen.

The first of these ideas is that the government, and every servant of the government, possesses as representative of the nation, a whole body of special rights, privileges, or prerogatives as against private citizens, and that the extent of these rights, privileges, or prerogatives is to be determined on principles different from the considerations which fix the legal rights and duties of one citizen towards another. An individual in his dealings with the State does not, according to French ideas, stand on anything like the same footing as that on which he stands in dealings with his neighbour.

The second of these general ideas is the necessity of maintaining the so-called 'separation of powers' (*séparation des pouvoirs*), or, in other words, of preventing the government, the legislature, and the courts from encroaching upon one another's province. The expression, however, separation of powers, as applied by Frenchmen to the relations of the executive and the courts, with which alone we are here concerned, may easily mislead. It means, in the mouth of a French statesman or lawyer, something different from what we mean in England by the 'independence of the judges', or the like expressions. As interpreted by French history, by French legislation, and by the decisions of French tribunals, it means neither more nor less than the maintenance of the principle that while the ordinary judges ought to be irremovable and thus independent of the executive, the government and its officials ought (whilst acting officially) to be independent of and to a great extent free from the jurisdiction of the ordinary courts.

Dicey explicitly gave to the term *droit administratif* a very limited meaning. He meant by it that, in England, (1) public servants possess no professional privileges which (2) protect them from the jurisdiction of the ordinary courts of the land and (3) that the state does not possess special powers in its own name. Dicey, in short, favoured the view that the relationships between citizens and public officials are not radically different from the relations of citizens with each other. It was only towards the end of his long career that Dicey admitted the capacity of the separate French system of administrative courts to control abuse of power; later still he conceded 'a considerable step towards the introduction among us of something like the *droit administratif* of France', though maintaining that the jurisdiction of 'ordinary law courts' in cases of breach of the law by public officials 'is fatal to the existence to true *droit administratif*'.[6]

But the very existence of prerogative powers, available to validate government actions not specifically authorised by Parliament, tends to undercut what Dicey said, while his polemic skates lightly over the extent of statutory power. When Dicey's *Law and Opinion* was written, the web of statute and regulation which today confines and structures government was still fragmentary. For example, Dicey was able to conceptualise police powers as common law powers; in other words, largely judge-made and incorporated in precedent. Today, these powers are mainly statutory, embodied for the most part in the Police and Criminal Evidence Act 1984 but the subject of regular amendment and extension in a series of criminal justice measures: judicial rulings, though still occasionally significant, have declined in importance. Even in the context of his times, Jennings saw deficiencies in Dicey's ideology of equality:[7]

> What Dicey suggests by equality is that an official is subject to the same rules as an ordinary citizen. But even this is not true. An official known as a collector of taxes has rights which an ordinary person does not possess . . . All public officials, and especially public authorities, have powers and therefore rights which are not possessed by other persons. Similarly, they may have special duties . . . Dicey was not referring to that part of the law which gives powers to and imposes duties upon public authorities. What he was considering . . . was that, if a public officer commits a tort, he will be liable for it in the ordinary civil courts.

In pitting individuals against individuals, the Diceyan paradigm is sometimes described as a 'private law' model of 'public law'. As in a private law action in contract or tort, *individual* citizens assert their rights and protect their interests against named *individuals* who represent the public service: the 'state' does not feature in the equation. It must be remembered that the potency of the model was proven. In a famous set of eighteenth-century cases, the courts had held both that the common law acknowledges no general executive 'police powers' and that ministers could be personally liable for torts committed in the exercise of official functions.[8] Dicey showed no interest in the consequential problem that the Crown might thus be able to shuffle off financial responsibility for the wrongdoing of its

---

6   A. V. Dicey, '*Droit administratif* in Modern French Law' (1901) 18 LQR 302; 'The Development of Administrative Law in England' (1915) 31 LQR 148. Dicey was better versed in the subject of French administrative law than were many of those who came after him. See F. Lawson, 'Dicey Revisited' (1959) 7 Pol. Studies 109 and 207.

7   W. I. Jennings, *The Law and the Constitution* (London: University of London Press) 5th edn., 1959, p. 312.

8   *Entick v Carrington* (1765) 2 Wils 275; *Leach v Money* (1765) 19 State Tr 1001; *Wilkes v Wood* (1763) 98 ER 489; *Wilkes v Lord Halifax* (1769) 19 State Tr 1406. Dicey cites further cases.

servants. Take the case of Inspector Y, who arrests and prosecutes X without good reason. X sues Y, who is held personally liable. Suppose Y cannot pay. In Dicey's day, this would have been the end of the matter. The Crown did not become vicariously liable for torts committed by public servants until the Crown Proceedings Act 1947, while, before the Police Act 1964, the police authority could not be made vicariously liable for the torts of individual police officers. Once more we see how a gap exists which could be filled if the state were seen as a corporate entity with rights and duties vested in it. X might then sue 'the state' arguing that the organisation of the public service was faulty.[9] At common law, as we saw in Chapter 1, 'the state' does not exist; it must be divided for purposes of legal liability into the Crown and the local police authority.

*Malone v Metropolitan Police Comr*[10] illustrates another side to the problem. The plaintiff, who was accused of a criminal offence, was asking the court for a declaration that it was unlawful for the Commissioner, in the absence of statutory authority, to authorise the tapping of his telephone. After a careful examination of the authorities, the judge, Megarry V-C, refused to grant the declaration. In the course of his judgment he remarked that, at common law, every act is presumed lawful unless it is specifically prohibited. Treating the Commissioner of Police as an *individual* allowed him to benefit from a presumption designed for the protection of private persons. A further result of discounting the 'special' position of state officials was that the parliamentary authorisation which, in the case of governmental powers of this type is necessary for legitimation, was not required, even though the judge went to some lengths in expressing his view that Parliament *ought* to have legislated.

There are two possible ways round this paradoxical result. The first is to make sure that the common law *does* provide remedies for an obvious 'abuse' of power; as Wade put it, 'the public must be able to rely on the law to ensure that all this power may be used in a way conformable to its ideas of fair dealing and good administration'. Arguably, this case was wrongly decided.[11] The true position is that 'all governmental powers, save those of the representative legislature, shall be distributed and determined by reasonably precise laws'[12] and also that administrative bodies must act within their powers (intra vires). The second solution would be to take into account the inherent inequality of the state, openly admitting the difference between the Metropolitan Police Commissioner and a private citizen.[13] This is the 'public law' approach of continental administrative law systems.

---

9 This has been the position in French administrative law since 1870: see N. Brown and J. Bell, *French Administrative Law* (Oxford: Clarendon) 4th edn., 1993, pp. 73-83.

10 [1979] Ch 344.

11 See C. Harlow, 'Comment: *Malone v Metropolitan Police Comr*' [1980] PL 1. Subsequently, Malone won a case under the European Convention on Human Rights in the Court of Human Rights (*Malone v United Kingdom* (1985) 7 EHHR 14). The government did in fact legislate to regulate telephone tapping in the Interception of Communications Act 1985.

12 Significantly, Jennings, *The Law and the Constitution* (above, note 7), p. 48, calls this a fundamental tenet of the Rule of Law principle.

13 See G. Samuel, 'Public and Private Law: A Private Lawyer's Response' (1983) 46 MLR 558.

Later generations feel that Dicey left English administrative law with a great mistrust of executive or administrative action but without any theoretical basis for its control. By refusing to accept the reality of state power and acknowledge 'the state' as a legal entity possessing inherent powers of government, his theory disguised a vital and inevitable inequality between the state and its citizens. This inequality is of such fundamental importance that the rules of private law are unable to cope, yet Dicey stultified the growth of a 'special' public law apt to deal with it:[14]

> The fallacy of Dicey's assumptions lies in his contention that the rule of law demands full equality in every respect between government and subjects or citizens. But it is inherent in the very notion of government that it cannot in all respects be equal to the governed, because it has to govern. In a multitude of ways, government must be left to interfere, without legal sanctions, in the lives and interests of citizens, where private persons could not be allowed to do so . . . The refusal of the courts to make planning or policy decisions of government the subject of legal action, also shows that the inequality of government and governed in certain respects is an indispensable fact of organized political life. Where the borderline between governmental freedom and legal responsibility has to be drawn, is, indeed, a very difficult problem. It may be described as the key problem of administrative law. But we can only begin to understand it after having accepted, unlike Dicey, that inequalities between government and citizens are inherent in the very nature of political society.

This did not bother Dicey because his model was largely an ideal-type. Dicey argued for its superiority on the moral ground that individuals ought not to be able to shuffle off responsibility for their own misdeeds. His theory of administrative and constitutional law sprang from his belief in individualism and dislike of the collectivism which, by the end of the nineteenth century, was beginning to flourish around him:[15]

> [Dicey's] propositions condemn wide administrative powers. Wide administrative powers mean the exercise by administrative authorities of some at least of the major functions of the state. In the individualist constitution, the police state, the state 'holds the ring'. It creates crimes, and it gives remedies for wrongs. The administrative powers of punishing crimes and granting remedies are exercised by and under the control of the Courts. Collectivism places the Courts in a relatively inferior position. The hegemony of the lawyer is broken. Moreover, the legal profession in England is, subject to its own 'trade union' regulations, highly competitive or individualistic. For these reasons the 'Rule of Law' is intensely popular among most lawyers. This popularity is increased by the current contempt for foreign constitutions which runs, half submerged, throughout the book. English law, it is assumed, better protects the individual because it does not give him worthless paper guarantees which can be torn up like any other scrap of paper, but provides him with substantive remedies enforced by the Courts. Moreover, these Courts are free, independent and unbiased. There are no 'administrative courts', whose function it is, if we are to believe Dicey, to decide

---

14  W. Friedmann, *Law in a Changing Society* (Harmondsworth: Penguin) 2nd edn., 1964, pp. 276-277. See also J. Mitchell, 'The causes and effects of the absence of a system of public law in the United Kingdom' [1965] PL 95; Samuel (above, note 13) and Allan (p. 66  below).
15  W. I. Jennings, 'In Praise of Dicey (1885 – 1935)' (1935) 13 Pub. Admin. 123, 132.

cases in which the administration is concerned in favour of the administration and against the citizen. Thus Dicey's views were in accord with the strongly nationalistic sentiments which pervaded English society until 1919. Patriotism insisted that the British Constitution not only worked better than other constitutions, but was intrinsically better. Dicey showed where the superiority was to be found.

Thus, Dicey adopted a narrow view of the constitution as 'an instrument for protecting the fundamental rights of the citizen, and not an instrument for enabling the community to provide services for the benefit of its citizens'. Consequentially, he came to confuse 'discretionary' with 'arbitrary' powers, which were 'unconstitutional'. For Dicey, 'the constitution excludes wide discretionary authority; therefore it forbids large administrative powers; and 'therefore . . . the collectivism of the twentieth century parties, and collectivism generally, are unconstitutional'. Wide administrative powers, which Dicey feared because of their collectivist connotations were, in Dicey's model, restricted in two ways. On one side stood Parliament which, because it was still dominated by Whig ideas, would not tolerate administrative interference with individual rights; on the other stood the courts dominated by a similar ideology. This brings us back to the model of the 'balanced constitution', which lies behind 'red light' theories of administrative law.

### (c) Dicey and separation of powers

Although Dicey spoke disparagingly of the French theory of *séparation des pouvoirs*, Vile reminds us that the ideal of the balanced constitution, in which executive power is constantly subject to checks and balances from both Parliament and the law courts, is itself a variant on the theme of separation of powers. Noting its peculiar attraction for lawyers, Vile calls it[16] 'the theory of law'. Vile – not an ardent Diceyan – argues that Dicey's theory becomes untenable once it is admitted that the executive and legislature are one and the same:

> If the subordination of the executive to the law was the keynote of [Dicey's] work, it would be to reduce this principle to nonsense to assume that legislators and executive were identical, that the powers of government were 'fused'.

With the 'theory of law' Vile contrasts 'the theory of government', in which executive and legislative powers are fused, both being at the disposal of the government. This he associates particularly with Bagehot's description of *The English Constitution* (1867),[17] arguing that the theories were, until the end of the last century, capable of reconciliation:[18]

> The theory of parliamentary government, with its balance between government and parliament, the fusion of the legislative and executive powers, and the subordination

16  M. Vile, *Constitutionalism and Separation of Powers* (Oxford: Clarendon) 1967, p. 230.
17  W. Bagehot, *The English Constitution* (R. Crossman ed.) (Ithaca, NY: Cornell University Press) 1966.
18  *Constitutionalism and Separation of Powers*, p. 231.

of the executive to the law were all quite cheerfully accepted as principles of British government. They were in fact all capable of being reconciled to a considerable extent. The reconciliation between the theory of law and the theory of government was achieved through the principle of ministerial responsibility. This idea enabled the two theories to be knitted together, and the differing functional concepts they embodied to be brought into a working relationship. The 'executive' must act according to the law, the 'government' must exercise leadership in the development of policy; but if the government was subject to the control of parliament, and the executive to the control of the courts, then a harmony could be established between the two roles of the ministers of the Crown. Ministerial responsibility, legal and political, was thus the crux of the English system of government. Whilst it remained a reality the whole edifice of constitutionalism could be maintained; should it cease to be a workable concept the process of disintegration between the legal basis and the operation of the government would begin.

As Vile hints, the growth of the state gave predominance to the 'theory of government' as administrators gained powers to make regulations and to adjudicate upon matters affecting the state's subjects. Lawyers and administrators were pulling in opposite directions. Lawyers, trained in the Diceyan mode of thought, regarded these developments as threatening, respectively, Parliament and the courts. They were also conditioned to suspect administrative discretion. The 'balanced constitution' was an ideal-type which may never really have existed. In the present century, the growth of popular democracy has in any event tipped it hopelessly out of kilter.

Moreover, as we saw in Chapter 1, the state in which we live today has changed radically from that Dicey knew. The role of the state has changed, bringing a ceaseless growth in the extent and powers of the executive; state and government have steadily acquired new obligations and functions, and even when administration of state services has been hived-off to agencies or the private sector, the result has been to weaken accountability without diminishing executive power. Breakdown – or perceived breakdown – of the doctrine of ministerial responsibility which formed the political arm of Dicey's balance has brought fear of 'elective dictatorship'.[19] Each failure to secure accountability weakens Parliament, further weakened by scandals which led to the setting-up of the Nolan Committee on Standards in Public Life.[20] If Parliament, the historical protector against tyranny, has dwindled into an 'elective dictatorship' then what, in an unwritten constitution, remains?

Wade's approach is unequivocal.[1] The threat to the 'balanced constitution' justifies the courts in taking extraordinary preventive measures. His appeal to 'constitutional principle' reflects concern that the absence of limitation on parliamentary action may render government unaccountable. The Rule of Law

---

19  Lord Hailsham, in *The Dilemma of Democracy – Diagnosis and Prescription* (London: Collins) 1978, especially Ch. XVI. See also R. Brazier, *Constitutional Reform, Re-shaping the British Political System* (Oxford: Clarendon) 1991.

20  The Nolan Report, *First Report of the Committee on Standards in Public Life*, Cm. 2850 (1995) noted D. Oliver, 'Standards of Conduct in Public Life – What Standards?' [1995] PL 497; H. Berrington, 'Political Ethics: The Nolan Report' (1995) Government and Opposition 431.

1  H. Wade, *Constitutional Fundamentals* (London: Stevens) 1980.

ideal, which legitimates judicial intervention, becomes a vital weapon against an over-powerful state. In a millennial echo of Lord Hewart, Michael Beloff QC speaks of the political process disparagingly,[2] noting:

> the diminution in the power and effectiveness of political control over the Executive; the subservience of backbenchers disciplined by whips and ambition alike; the limitations on the powers of the opposition, hampered by lack of information – except at the discretion of disobedient civil servants; inadequate powers and resources for the Select Committees compared, say, with their American counterparts; the decline, it may be, of the number of MPs with stamina to inquire and the wit to criticise. It is for political scientists to debate the relative significance of these factors. But that there has been a vacuum cannot be doubted; and the judges have filled it.

## 4. Titanic battles: courts versus executive and Parliament

The cases which follow come from the tiny minority of judicial review cases which possess lasting constitutional resonance. Indeed, Wade has called one of them 'the most important case in constitutional law for the last two hundred years or more'.[3] In producing a 'developed system of administrative law', the judges have indulged in a certain amount of judicial interventionism, not acceptable to everyone.[4] The *Burmah Oil* case raises fundamental constitutional questions about the relationship of courts and government and about the Rule of Law principle. Some hints of this appear in Lord Radcliffe's judgment, where he questions the right of courts to 'import into the common law a legal right that has not hitherto been recognised to exist'. The point is also raised in the parliamentary debate below.

### (a) Poisoning of the fount of justice?

The Burmah Oil Company owned valuable oil installations in Burma. During the Second World War these were destroyed before the advancing Japanese on the orders of the British military authorities. After the war, ex-gratia compensation amounting to £11 million was paid by the British Government in respect of property loss caused to British individuals and companies in wartime Burma. Burmah Oil received nearly £5 million for 'reconstruction'. The word was carefully chosen; with the encouragement of the British government, Burmah Oil was pursuing an action against the government of Burma in the High Court of Burma, and the British government did not wish to prejudice the company's chances. But later it was explained that the sum was part of the total referred to above, and that, although it was hoped that the money would be used in reconstruction, it was an out-and-out payment to Burmah, to be dealt with as the company wished. Burmah got no compensation from the Burmese government.

---

2    M. Beloff, 'Judicial Review – 2001; A Prophetic Odessey' (1995) 58 MLR 143, 145.
3    H. Wade, 'The Crown – Old Platitudes and New Heresies' (1992) NLJ 42, p. 1275.
4    See A. Hutchinson, 'The Rise and Ruse of Administrative Law and Scholarship' (1985) 48 MLR 293; 'Mice under a chair: Democracy, courts and the administrative state' (1990) 40 UTLJ 374.

It then re-opened negotiations with successive British governments, who declined to find additional sums. Nearly 12 years later, when the English limitation period had expired, Burmah filed an action in Scotland claiming £31 million. The case went without trial to the House of Lords on a preliminary point.

The case centred on the use of the prerogative powers. In *A-G v De Keyser's Royal Hotel Ltd*[5] it had been decided that, where Parliament has legislated in a given subject area, the prerogative falls into abeyance for the duration of the statute. Now the question arose whether, in the absence of statute, the Crown had to pay compensation for the lawful exercise of its prerogative powers to requisition private property for the defence of the realm. A complicating factor was that Scots law was not necessarily identical with English common law because, as a civil law system, it recognises the civilian principle of 'eminent domain'. For this reason the writings of Scots jurists were considered. Basing themselves on a passage from Vattel, who distinguishes damage caused in the face of the enemy (battle damage), where no compensation is payable, from damage caused in preparation for hostilities, where compensation must be made, a majority of the House held that Burmah possessed a claim to compensation. Lord Upjohn's is a majority judgment, Note the long discussion of policy in the dissenting judgment of Viscount Radcliffe.

### Burmah Oil Co Ltd v Lord Advocate[6]

*Lord Upjohn*: . . . the practice of the Crown, so far as it can be ascertained, and the course of statutory enactment at any rate from Napoleonic times entitling the Crown to seize, use and destroy the subject's property supports the view that this could only be done upon payment. Furthermore, it is clearly settled that where the executive is authorised by a statute to take the property of a subject for public purposes the subject is entitled to be paid unless the statute has made the contrary intention quite clear . . .

Believing as I do in the great justice of the principle that if the Crown takes the property of the subject for the public good whether for use or destruction the Crown should pay for it, justice . . . demands that [the exception] should be a limited one. No doubt in the actual battle the property of the subject may be seriously damaged. It may be damaged by both sides and it may be quite impossible to find out, indeed, how the damage did in fact arise. But where even the day before the battle some property is razed to the ground to provide some better field of fire, or something of that sort, is it unreasonable to compel the Crown to compensate the subject for that loss providing he can prove how it took place? . . . I would think that it was quite clear that the destruction of the installations in this case fell within Vattel's first classification; it was done by way of precaution in the general prosecution of the overall strategy. It was not done in the heat of battle.

*Viscount Radcliffe (dissenting)*: It is just in that distinction between what is expected by public sentiment and what is actually obtainable by legal right that our present difficulty lies. We know that by long tradition private property appropriated for public use is treated as the subject of compensation and we look to the Government to secure this, either by moving Parliament to provide it or by some ex gratia payment which will afterwards receive Parliamentary sanction. The recent war, for instance, gave us both the Compensation

5    [1920] AC 508.
6    [1965] AC 75.

(Defence) Act, 1939, which, speaking generally, was intended to provide compensation to persons affected by defined acts in exercise of emergency powers (including prerogative powers of the Crown) and the War Damage Act, 1943, the purpose of which was to introduce a scheme of insurance as cover against war damage due to enemy action. The present case is strictly an anomaly because, relating to acts done in Burma outside the scope of the United Kingdom statutes and not . . . within the scope of any other statutes, it requires us to consider the acts of destruction as 'pure' prerogative acts without the control of legislative provisions that would obviously be available if the case were not wholly exceptional.

I cannot see that that circumstance entitles us to import into the common law a legal right that has not hitherto been recognised to exist. By what title do we do it? There is no principle of justice or equity made visible to us that has not by now been apparent for centuries: and if hitherto the justice of the matter has been administered through other channels, I do not think that there is any adequate reason to open the law courts to such claims. Indeed . . . the balance of public advantage and, perhaps, constitutional propriety argue against it . . .

Where war damage is concerned, the long-standing absence of any recognition that there is jurisdiction in the courts to award compensation is based on sound considerations of public policy. Such damage is a matter, being unpredictable in extent and range, that must be controlled by that department of the sovereign power that is responsible for the raising and expenditure of public money. There is not a legal line between those divisions of that damage that carry a legal right to compensation and those that do not. Damage inflicted by the enemy may be terrible individual loss, and it is certainly suffered in the common cause. Moreover, it is likely to fall with disproportionate weight on some citizens who suffer in that cause, a fact familiar in the last war to those whose homes or places of business were close to an object of strategic importance and so peculiarly exposed to air or missile attack. Damage inflicted by one's own side, accidentally or to prevent its capture and the enrichment of the enemy, does not seem to me different in kind unless the element of deliberation marks off the latter . . . And no one can find an equation between the personal loss that war inflicts and its inroads upon property . . .

None of this is an argument against the propriety or, indeed, urgent desirability of the state providing compensation schemes to take care, so far as possible, of all war damage, of person or property. But it is for those who fill and empty the public purse to decide when, by whom, on what conditions and within what limitations such compensation is to be made available. After all, states lose wars as well as win them: and at the conclusion of a war that has seen massive destruction, whether self-inflicted through the medium of a 'scorched earth' policy or inflicted by the enemy, there may well be urgent claims for reconstruction priorities that make it impossible in advance to mortgage the public treasury to legal claims for full individual compensation for such destruction as we have now to consider. Indeed, what in legal terms does 'compensation' mean in this case? The act of destruction was lawful, that is conceded . . . so we are not to think of damages and the legal rules for their assessment. Has the law any principle for measuring compensation as a legal right when an act has been done in circumstances so special that the ordinary conceptions of property do not apply to it? Can the state be asked to pay a requisition price for something for which there was at the time no conceivable purchaser? I do not think so.

Immediately afterwards, with the acquiescence of the Opposition front bench, the Government introduced the War Damage Bill, which provided only:

1(1) No person shall be entitled at common law to receive from the Crown compensation in respect of damage to, or destruction of, property caused (whether before or after the passing of this Act, within or outside the United Kingdom) by acts lawfully done by, or on the authority of, the Crown during, or in contemplation of the outbreak of, a war in which the Sovereign was, or is, engaged.

(2) Where any proceedings to recover at common law compensation in respect of such damage or destruction have been instituted before the passing of this Act, the court shall, on the application of any party, forthwith set aside or dismiss the proceedings, subject only to the determination of any question arising as to costs or expenses.

The retrospective element was a further cause for concern in the *Burmah Oil* case, because it was seen to imperil the Rule of Law. An important aspect of the Rule of Law doctrine is that the law must be certain in order that the subject can calculate the consequences of his actions. Opening the debate on the second reading, Mr MacDermot (Financial Secretary to the Treasury) argued[7] that it was the House of Lords which had changed the law. Like Lord Radcliffe, he argued that the issue was really a question of policy for the executive:

> The object of the Bill is to restore the common law of England and the law of Scotland to the position which was generally thought to exist before the decision and to provide that about 12 cases now pending . . . before the court are disposed of on the basis of the law as it has always been thought to be . . .
>
> The whole question of compensation for damage and destruction inflicted during war presents serious problems for a country whose Government are anxious to secure equitable treatment for their people. The incidence of losses is arbitrary, but it has seemed right to the Government of this country that the burden should as far as possible be shared. Damage and destruction may arise partly from identifiable enemy action or from defensive action of our own forces, or it may arise in the course of actual fighting in which the side responsible for the particular damage may not be identifiable . . . Moreover, the scale of losses in total wars in this century has been so formidable as to make the idea of their reparation in full impossible . . . This carries two implications: first, there must be some equitable scheme for distributing such compensation as may be afforded in relation to the losses suffered by individuals; and, secondly, opportunity must not be left open to any special groups amongst those who have suffered loss to claim redress on a preferential scale. Any entitlement to compensation on an indemnity basis of common law would, in effect, give preferential treatment to those enjoying it.

Here we find two arguments for retrospective legislation, which Mr MacDermot admitted to be 'generally undesirable'. The first is that the sums involved were too large to be paid (Burmah was claiming £30 million and other claims might have totalled £200 million in South-East Asia). The second concerns equality of treatment. Claims throughout the Far East had been dealt with in similar fashion. For example, in Malaya, the British government had contributed £20 million to claims of £160 million and in Borneo £2.25 million to claims of £ 12.5 million. It was inequitable to allow people to accept compensation and then pay in full those who stood out for their legal rights. This raises the difficult philosophical question of how to balance three diverse aspects of the Rule of Law principle: the

7    HC Deb., vol. 705, cols. 1091-4.

principle of equality of treatment, the principle of obedience to the law or the binding nature of judicial decisions and the 'principle of legality' or the rule against retroactivity.

Here, from the Conservative MP, Mr Jenkin,[8] is the constitutional argument against retroactive legislation:

> It has been said over and over again that ignorance of the law is no excuse if one commits a breach of the criminal code. In exactly the same way, ignorance of the law should never be used as a means of depriving a subject of his right to benefit under the law. Still more should we hesitate to legislate to make a retrospective interference with the rights of the subject when these rights have been judicially determined by the courts. We have strict rules about anyone's attempting interference with the judicial process, and very severe penalties for anyone who does. Indeed, one judge referred to it some years ago as 'poisoning the fount of justice at its source', and so it is.
>
> In exactly the same way, any retrospective interference with the judicial process is just as much a poisoning of the fount of justice, and none the less to be deplored, when it happens to be done by due legislative process. The French jurist Montesquieu based his celebrated doctrine of the separation of powers on the British constitution and as all constitutional lawyers know well, sadly misunderstood our constitution, but in one matter he was absolutely right, and that is, the separation of the powers of the Executive and of the Judiciary.
>
> A Bill such as this, with the express intent to overrule retrospectively a decision of the House of Lords, is dangerous because it blurs that very necessary separation and legal safeguard. Parliament, I say, should be extremely chary of the way in which it exercises its powers in this regard.

At the time, Goodhart observed[9] that 'Parliament, by enacting the War Damage Act 1965 did the claimants a service, because although it deprived them of a claim which might have proved almost valueless when the time came to assess the damages, it saved them from unnecessary legal costs'. Wade, however, approaches the question rather differently:[10]

> The House of Lords' decision . . . was immediately nullified by the War Damage Act 1965, which . . . provided in sweeping terms that no compensation should be payable at common law for damage or destruction of property caused by acts lawfully done by or on the authority of the Crown during or in contemplation of war, whether before or after the Act. By this unusual measure of retaliation Parliament demonstrated that it can, when it wishes, expropriate in a manner not permitted in some other countries which enjoy the protection of written constitutions and bills of rights.

Of the two arguments for retroactivity, it is the equality argument rather than the floodgates argument which dominated the debate over *Burmah Oil*. Only a handful of other parties could have been in an identical position to Burmah Oil and legal action would probably have been barred both by the fact that compensation had been accepted and by the expiry of the six-year limitation period. Yet we have

8  HC Deb., vol. 705, cols. 1183-4.
9  A. Goodhart, 'The Burmah Oil Case and the War Damage Act 1965' (1966) 82 LQR 97, 114.
10  Wade and Forsyth, pp. 808-809.

seen that if Burmah Oil had won full compensation a feeling of unfairness would have been created. In other words, the case possessed some of the characteristics of 'polycentricity' whereby a decision taken in one case has 'knock on' or 'ripple' effects on other decisions. This is an important problem for modern administrative law to which we shall return.

### (b)  Ouster clauses: the foreign compensation case

Parliament has traditionally been able to deploy a variety of devices designed to restrict or exclude judicial review of administrative action. In some ways a preferable alternative to retrospective legislation, they are equally damaging to the Rule of Law principle, though they strike at a different aspect. Retrospective legislation affects certainty; ouster impinges on the right of access to the courts. For this reason, modern statutes which seek to restrict judicial review usually do so *indirectly* by casting the relevant decision-making power in subjective terms, e.g. through the formula 'if the Minister is satisfied'. There are also more limited forms of ouster, such as the 'time-limit clause' which limits recourse to the courts to actions commenced within a specified time from the date of the impugned decision. The commonest example is the six weeks clause frequently used in planning and compulsory purchase statutes.

The notorious case of *Smith v East Elloe RDC*[11] concerned a compulsory purchase order made under the Acquisition of Land (Authorisation Procedure) Act 1946. Paragraph 15 of the First Schedule to this Act laid down that a compulsory purchase order could be challenged on specified grounds within six weeks. Paragraph 16 provided: 'Subject to the provisions of the last foregoing paragraph, a compulsory purchase order . . . shall not . . . be questioned in any legal proceedings whatsoever.' Nearly six years after the order was made, the applicant discovered facts sufficient, she argued, to invalidate it on the ground of fraud and bad faith. On appeal to the House of Lords, a majority ruled that the courts had no jurisdiction. Here Viscount Simonds defends a literal reading of the provision:

> My Lords, I think that anyone bred in the tradition of the law is likely to regard with little sympathy legislative provisions for ousting the jurisdiction of the court, whether in order that the subject may be deprived altogether of remedy or in order that his grievance may be remitted to some other tribunal. But it is our plain duty to give the words of an Act their proper meaning and . . . words are used which are wide enough to cover any kind of challenge which any aggrieved person may think fit to make. I cannot think of any wider words. Any addition would be mere tautology.

11  [1956] AC 736. See J. Alder, 'Time Limit Clauses and Judicial Review – *Smith v East Elloe Revisited*' (1975) 38 MLR 274 and 'Time Limit Clauses and Conceptualism – A Reply' (1980) 43 MLR 670; N. Gravells, 'Time Limit Clauses and Judicial Review: The Relevance of Context'(1978) 41 MLR 383 and 'Time Limit Clauses and Judicial Review – Some Second Thoughts' (1980) 43 MLR 173. See also *R v Secretary of State for the Environment, ex p Ostler* [1977] QB 122; *Pearlman v Keepers and Governors of Harrow School* [1979] QB 56. For a recent case, see *R v Cornwall County Council, ex p Huntington* [1994] 1 All ER 694.

The total 'ouster' or 'preclusive' clause attempts to render administrative decisions unchallengeable in the courts. As Viscount Simonds remarked, judges have traditionally been antagonistic to such clauses, developing a common law presumption that access to the courts is not to be denied save by clear statutory words.[12] This hostility is hardly surprising, because ousters raise directly the question of the allocation of decision-making functions within the constitution. In what circumstances should the executive, acting through Parliament, be able to exempt governmental activities from judicial intervention? Should non-judicial bodies be able to decide questions of law free from control by the ordinary courts or, turning the issues around, should the ordinary courts enjoy a monopoly of determining issues of law? While ousters may be favoured for reasons ranging from distrust of a conservative judiciary to the administrator's desire for finality and expertise, supporters of the balanced constitution would necessarily urge that the courts must retain overall control. In recent years, this view has gradually become dominant. Not only have the courts emphasised their opposition to ousters but government has largely conceded the issue. A start was made with s. 11 of the Tribunals and Inquiries Act 1958:[13]

> 11. (1) : . . . any provision in an Act passed before the commencement of this Act that any order or determination shall not be called into question in any court, or any provision in such an Act which by similar words excludes any of the powers of the High Court, shall not have effect so as to prevent the removal of the proceedings into the High Court by order of certiorari or to prejudice the powers of the High Court to make orders of mandamus . . .

Before reading *Anisminic*,[14] one needs to remember the points made earlier about formalistic reasoning and also to understand how limited at that period were the grounds for judicial review. Review differs from appeal, which broadly allows the decision appealed from to be re-opened. As de Smith[15] explains, 'Judicial review of administrative action was founded upon the premise that an inferior tribunal is entitled to decide wrongly, but is not entitled to exceed the jurisdiction it was given by statute'. This created a need to distinguish between errors of fact (generally final) and errors of law, some of which could be reviewed: error of law on the face of the record was an old ground for review, and errors affecting the jurisdiction of the tribunal to decide a case were generally reviewable; non-jurisdictional error of law was not. The result was a case law built upon technical distinctions of great complexity. de Smith commented, 'the concept of jurisdictional error has become one of the most elusive in administrative law,

---

12  See Viscount Simonds in *Pyx Granite Co Ltd v Minister of Housing and Local Government* [1960] AC 260. And see Denning LJ in *R v Medical Appeal Tribunal, ex p Gilmore* [1957] 1 QB 574. For thorough discussion of the modern law, see Wade and Forsyth, pp. 600-609; de Smith, Jowell, Woolf, paras 5.033–5.043.

13  Passed after the influential Franks Committee Report and today re-enacted as the Tribunals and Inquiries Act 1992: See below, Ch.14. Certiorari and mandamus are orders available during judicial review proceedings (below, Ch. 16).

14  *Anisminic Ltd v Foreign Compensation Commission* [1969] 2 WLR 163 (below, p. 54).

15  de Smith, Jowell, Woolf, paras 5-001, 5-002. See also Wade and Forsyth, Ch. 9.

largely because it calls for analytical distinctions which have, as judicial review developed, become difficult if not impossible to sustain'.

The effect of judicial invalidation of a decision is another elusive question. You will find Lord Reid describing a decision struck down for jurisdictional error as 'a nullity' and 'void'. In other cases decisions have been held 'voidable', meaning broadly, valid until set aside by a court. The distinction may have important consequences. A void decision may invalidate further decisions dependent upon it. It may create rights to compensation or affect the rights of third parties, which will be frozen out if the decision is merely voidable. In short, 'Behind the simple dichotomy of void and voidable acts (invalid and valid until declared to be invalid) lurk terminological and conceptual problems of excruciating difficulty'.[16]

### *Anismic Ltd v Foreign Compensation Commission*[17]

Egypt had agreed with the United Kingdom that it would provide limited compensation in respect of British property nationalised after the Suez crisis in 1956. The British government handed over responsibility for administering the share-out to the Foreign Compensation Commission (FCC), a statutory body established by the Foreign Compensation Act 1950. The FCC was required to act according to an Order in Council which included provisions concerning the nationality of claimants for compensation. These were intended to ensure that only British nationals, be they the original owners of the relevant property or their 'successors in title', obtained compensation. The property of Anismic, a British company, had been nationalised but was then sold by the Egyptian government to an Egyptian concern. The FCC interpreted the Order as excluding the company from the compensation scheme because of the Egyptian nationality of its successor in title. This determination was protected by a preclusive clause: 'The determination by the commission of any application made to them under this Act shall not be called in question in any court of law.' This clause was not caught by the Tribunals and Inquiries Act[18] as s. 11(3) specifically preserved it.

The House of Lords held by a majority (Lord Pearson dissenting) that the FCC had misconstrued the Order. It then had to decide: (1) had the FCC, in making its determination, fallen into an error 'which went to jurisdiction'? – if not, the preclusive clause would deny Anismic relief; (2) if there had been jurisdictional error, what effect did this have on the preclusive clause? To put this differently, was the effect of a preclusive clause to oust jurisdiction to rule on jurisdictional errors? By a majority (Lord Morris dissenting), the House decided that the FCC had committed a jurisdictional error against which, it was held unanimously, the preclusive clause offered no protection. Note the ingenious use of formalistic reasoning to distinguish *Smith v East Elloe RDC*.[19]

---

16   Para. 5-044. See further H. Wade, 'Unlawful Administrative Action: Void or Voidable?' (1967) 83 LQR 499 and (1968) 84 LQR 95.
17   [1969] 2 WLR 163.
18   Above, p. 53.
19   Above, p. 52.

*Lord Reid*: The respondent [the FCC] maintains that [the words of the preclusive clause] are plain words only capable of having one meaning. Here is a determination which is apparently valid; there is nothing on the face of the document to cast any doubt on its validity. If it is a nullity, that could only be established by raising some kind of proceedings in court. But that would be calling the determination in question, and that is expressly prohibited by the statute. The appellants maintain that this is not the meaning of the words of this provision. They say that 'determination' means a real determination and does not include an apparent or purported determination which in the eyes of the law has no existence because it is a nullity. Or, putting it in another way, if you seek to show that a determination is a nullity you are not questioning the purported determination – you are maintaining that it does not exist as a determination. It is one thing to question a determination which does exist: it is quite another thing to say that there is nothing to be questioned. It is a well established principle that a provision ousting the ordinary jurisdiction of the court must be construed strictly – meaning, I think, that, if such a provision is reasonably capable of having two meanings, that meaning shall be taken which preserves the ordinary jurisdiction of the court . . .

If the draftsman or Parliament had intended to . . . prevent any inquiry even as to whether the document relied on was a forgery, I would have expected to find something much more specific than the bald statement that a determination shall not be called in question in any court of law. Undoubtedly such a provision protects every determination which is not a nullity. But I do not think that it is necessary or even reasonable to construe the word 'determination' as including everything which purports to be a determination but which is in fact no determination at all. And there are no degrees of nullity. There are a number of reasons why the law will hold a purported decision to be a nullity. I do not see how it could be said that such a provision protects some kinds of nullity but not others; if that were intended it would be easy to say so . . .

The case which gives most difficulty is [*East Elloe*] where the form of ouster clause was similar to that in the present case. But I cannot regard it as a very satisfactory case . . . As [it] never reached the stage of a statement of claim[20] we do not know whether her case was that the clerk of the council had fraudulently misled the council and the Ministry, or whether it was that the council and the Ministry were parties to the fraud. The result would be quite different, in my view, for it is only if the authority which made the order had itself acted in [bad faith] that the order would be a nullity. I think that [her] case . . . must have been that the fraud was only the fraud of the clerk because almost the whole of the argument was on the question whether a time-limit in the Act applied where fraud was alleged; there was no citation of the authorities on the question whether a clause ousting the jurisdiction of the court applied when nullity was in question, and there was little about this matter in the speeches. I do not therefore regard this case as a binding authority on this question. I have come without hesitation to the conclusion that in this case we are not prevented from inquiring whether the order of the commission was a nullity . . .

There are many cases where, although the tribunal had jurisdiction to enter on the inquiry, it has done or failed to do something in the course of the inquiry which is of such a nature that its decision is a nullity. It may have given its decision in bad faith. It may have made a decision which it had no power to make. It may have failed in the

20  In the earlier case of *Smith v East Elloe RDC and John Campion* [1952] CLY 529, an action for trespass against the Council succeeded. But in *Smith v Pywell* (1959) 173 Estates Gazette 1009 an action for conspiracy against the town clerk and a ministry official failed. See G. Ganz, 'Malicious Exercise of Discretion' [1964] PL 372. Lord Reid is saying that this is relevant in deciding whether or not the error goes to jurisdiction.

course of the inquiry to comply with the requirements of natural justice. It may in perfect good faith have misconstrued the provisions giving it power to act so that it failed to deal with the question remitted to it. It may have refused to take into account something which it was required to take into account. Or it may have based its decision on some matter which, under the provisions setting it up, it had no right to take into account. I do not intend this list to be exhaustive. But . . . if it is entitled to enter on the inquiry and does not do any of those things which I have mentioned in the course of the proceedings, then its decision is equally valid whether it is right or wrong subject only to the power of the court in certain circumstances to correct an error of law . . .

It appears from the commission's reasons that they construed [the] provision as requiring them to inquire, when the applicant is himself the original owner, whether he had a successor in title. So they made that inquiry in this case and held that [the Egyptian concern] was the applicant's successor in title. As [that concern] was not a British national they rejected the appellants' claim. But if, on a true construction of the Order, a claimant who is an original owner does not have to prove anything about successors in title, then the commission made an inquiry which the Order did not empower them to make, and they based their decision on a matter which they had no right to take into account . . . It was argued that the whole matter of construing the Order was something remitted to the commission for their decision. I cannot accept that argument. I find nothing in the Order to support it. The Order requires the commission to consider whether they are satisfied with regard to the prescribed matters. That is all they have to do. It cannot be for the commission to determine the limits of its powers. Of course if one party submits to a tribunal that its powers are wider than in fact they are, then the tribunal must deal with that submission. But if they reach a wrong conclusion as to the width of their powers, the court must be able to correct that – not because the tribunal has made an error of law, but because as a result of making an error of law they have dealt with and based their decision on a matter with which, on a true construction of their powers, they had no right to deal. If they base their decision on some matter which is not prescribed for their adjudication, they are doing something which they have no right to do and their decision is a nullity.

*Anisminic* is a case which helped to set the tone of modern judicial review and whose significance is not reduced by its special facts. It has provoked sharp differences of opinion. Griffith, whose work as a green light theorist properly forms part of the next chapter, explains how the House of Lords expanded the notion of jurisdictional error:[1]

If an Act of Parliament says that A [a public authority] shall be the person to settle certain specified questions and that there shall be neither appeal to nor review by . . . the courts, then A's decisions are unchallengeable so long as (a) it is A, not another, who decides, (b) A decides those specified questions and not others and (c) A does not act in bad faith or with similar impropriety. The *Anisminic* decision goes much further than this and says in effect that A's decision can be set aside by the courts if they disagree with his interpretation of the rules which he is required to apply.

Griffith believes that this is improper:[2]

---

1   *Politics*, pp. 118-119. See also the speech of Lord Morris in *Anisminic* and *Re Racal Communications Ltd* [1981] AC 374.
2   *Politics*, p. 56.

Where Parliament enacts positively that certain questions should be decided finally
by a public authority, whether a Minister or a specialised tribunal or commission (as
in *Anisminic*), the courts should respect this decision and should not assume that
judges, however eminent, are the better deciders of complex issues.

Wade,[3] on the other hand, is inclined to pass this point over, persuaded by the
court's motivation:

The net result was that [the Law Lords] had disobeyed the Act, although nominally
they were merely construing it in a peculiar but traditional way . . . The judges
appreciate, much more than does Parliament, that to exempt any public authority from
judicial control is to give it dictatorial power, and that this is so fundamentally
objectionable that Parliament cannot really intend it . . . There can be abuse of
legislative power, not indeed in the legal sense, but in a distinct constitutional sense,
for example if Parliament were to legislate to establish one-party government, or a
dictatorship, or in some other way were to attack the fundamentals of democracy. To
exempt a public authority from the jurisdiction of the courts of law is, to that extent,
to grant dictatorial power. It is no exaggeration, therefore, to describe this as an abuse
of the power of Parliament, speaking constitutionally. This is the justification . . . for
the strong, it might even be said rebellious, stand which the courts have made against
allowing Acts of Parliament to create pockets of uncontrollable power in violation of
the rule of law. Parliament is unduly addicted to this practice giving too much weight
to temporary convenience and too little to constitutional principle. The law's delay,
together with its uncertainty and expense, tempts governments to take short cuts by
elimination of the courts. But if the courts are prevented from enforcing the law, the
remedy becomes worse than the disease.

Whatever Parliament had intended, the government reacted swiftly to *Anisminic*.
It tacked on to a Foreign Compensation Bill, coincidentally before the House of
Commons, an amendment designed to nullify the decision, this time *prospectively*,
by enabling an Order in Council to be made establishing the finality of a purported
determination by the FCC. The Minister argued[4] that the nature of the FCC's task
rendered judicial review inappropriate. Here we meet 'polycentricity' again, in
the shape of a fixed pot of resources to be conclusively divided by an expert
'arbitrator':

[The] Commission cannot avoid interpreting the Orders under which it carries out
the distributions entrusted to it. [The *Anisminic*] judgment would therefore make it
possible . . . for the Commission's determinations, made in perfectly good faith and
after the most careful deliberation, to be challenged in a wide range of cases. The
consequences of this . . . would be most unfortunate. The task of the Commission,
which is of a special character, is to determine claims and to arrange for distribution
on a rateable basis to successful claimants, of what are nearly always finite 'lump
sums' either received in the form of cash from foreign Governments, or . . . raised by
the disposal of foreign assets in this country . . . Until all obligations, or at any rate all

3   *Constitutional Fundamentals*, pp. 65-66.
4   HL Deb., vol. 299, col. 17 (Lord Chalfont, Minister of State at the Foreign and Commonwealth
    Office). Compare the *Caswell* case, below, Chapter 16.

those of any substance or magnitude, have been disposed of, it is impossible for the Commission to judge with any degree of certainty what will be the share attributable to each successful application and so to pay anything like a final dividend at all to them. If there is to be a risk that their determinations may be challenged in the courts . . . the claimants, who have usually already been waiting for a very long time . . . may well have to wait a further substantial period before they can touch their awards or at any rate the greater part of them.

Faced by angry letters to *The Times* from eminent lawyers and by a hostile amendment, supported by the Law Lords and carried in the Upper House,[5] the government backtracked. Section 3 of the Foreign Compensation Act 1969 provides for direct appeal to the Court of Appeal on a question of law concerning the construction of an Order in Council. No further appeal lies to the House of Lords. Otherwise, save in cases of natural justice, a determination (including a purported determination) is not to be called in question in any court of law.

### (c) Ouster ousted? A European dimension

After *Burmah Oil*, Wade queried the compatibility of the War Damage Act with the European Convention on Human Rights, to which the United Kingdom was at the time already a signatory. Article 1 of the First Protocol (1952) permits expropriation of private property only 'in the public interest'. Notice that Wade is here querying the propriety of *a statute*, a question which simply could not arise before a court in domestic law. The supra-national Convention can, however, bite on legislation. Article 6 of the Convention makes some ouster clauses suspect by providing that:

> In the determination of his civil rights and obligations . . . everyone is entitled to a fair and public hearing within a reasonable time by an independent and impartial tribunal established by law.

The Foreign Compensation Commission would certainly have passed this test. On other occasions this Article, together with Art. 13, which provides that:

> Everyone whose rights and freedoms as set forth in this Convention are violated shall have an effective remedy before a national authority notwithstanding that the violation has been committed by persons acting in an official capacity.

have been used with some success in the United Kingdom to extend and improve appeal procedures in administrative law. An alternative way to challenge a statutory ouster clause in some cases may, however, be through EC law.

---

5   From Wade, the Chairman of the Bar Council and the President of the Law Society: *The Times*, 1 and 4 February 1969. See also, HL Deb., vol. 299, cols. 640-54.

## Johnston v Chief Constable of the Royal Ulster Constabulary[6]

The Royal Ulster Constabulary (RUC), in reliance on Art. 53(2) of the Sex Discrimination (Northern Ireland) Order 1976, maintained a policy of excluding the use of firearms by female members of the force. The plaintiff sued in an industrial tribunal, arguing that the policy was incompatible with the equality provisions of the EC Treaty.[7] The defendants claimed a 'public interest' defence under EC law, and relied on a ministerial certificate certifying that the EC conditions for derogation from the principle of equal treatment had been met. If accepted, the certificate would have ousted the tribunal's jurisdiction and with it, the supervisory jurisdiction of the Court of Justice (ECJ) exercisable under the EC Treaty, Art. 177.[8] Before ruling on the equal treatment point, the ECJ ruled:

### The right to an effective judicial remedy

14. In Mrs. Johnston's view, a provision such as article 53(2) . . . is contrary to article 6 of the directive inasmuch as it prevents the competent national court or tribunal from exercising any judicial control.

15. The United Kingdom observes that article 6 of the directive does not require the member states to submit to judicial review every question which may arise in the application of the directive, even where national security and public safety are involved. Rules of evidence such as the rule laid down in article 53(2) . . . are quite common in national procedural law. Their justification is that matters of national security and public safety can be satisfactorily assessed only by the competent political authority, namely the minister who issues the certificate in question.

16. The Commission takes the view that to treat the certificate of a minister as having an effect such as that provided for in article 53(2) . . . is tantamount to refusing all judicial control or review and is therefore contrary to a fundamental principle of Community law and to article 6 of the directive.

17. . . . Article 6 of the directive requires member states to introduce into their internal legal systems such measures as are needed to enable all persons who consider themselves wronged by discrimination "to pursue their claims by judicial process". It follows from that provision that the member states must take measures which are sufficiently effective to achieve the aim of the directive and that they must ensure that the rights thus conferred may be effectively relied upon before the national courts by the persons concerned . . .

18. The requirement of judicial control stipulated by that article reflects a general principle of law which underlies the constitutional traditions common to the member states. That principle is also laid down in articles 6 and 13 . . . As the European Parliament, Council and Commission recognised in their joint declaration of 5 April 1977 (Official Journal 1977 No. C.103, p.1) and as the court has recognised in its decisions, the principles on which that Convention is based must be taken into consideration in Community law.

19. By virtue of article 6 of [the] Directive . . . interpreted in the light of the general principle stated above, all persons have the right to obtain an effective remedy in a

6   Case 222/84 [1986] 3 WLR 1038.
7   EC Treaty, Art. 119 and Directive EEC 76/207, generally known as the Equal Treatment Directive.
8   Under EC Treaty, Art. 177, a point of EC law which arises in the course of a hearing in a national court can be referred to the ECJ for an opinion. The highest appellate court must refer such a point.

competent court against measures which they consider to be contrary to the principle of equal treatment for men and women laid down in the directive. It is for the member states to ensure effective judicial control as regards compliance with the applicable provisions of Community law and of national legislation intended to give effect to the rights for which the directive provides.

20. A provision which, like article 53(2) . . . requires a certificate such as the one in question in the present case to be treated as conclusive evidence that the conditions for derogating from the principle of equal treatment are fulfilled allows the competent authority to deprive an individual of the possibility of asserting by judicial process the rights conferred by the directive. Such a provision is therefore contrary to the principle of effective judicial control laid down in article 6 of the directive.

21. The answer to this part of question 6 put by the industrial tribunal must therefore be that the principle of effective judicial control laid down in article 6 of [the] directive . . . does not allow a certificate issued by a national authority stating that the conditions for derogating from the principle of equal treatment for men and women for the purpose of protecting public safety are satisfied to be treated as conclusive evidence so as to exclude the exercise of any power of review by the courts.

The court went on to hold, first, that Directive 76/207 was directly effective and, second, that the impugned policy was too wide:

45. It does not appear that the risks and dangers to which women are exposed when performing their duties in the police force in a situation such as exists in Northern Ireland are different from those to which any man is also exposed when performing the same duties. A total exclusion of women from such an occupational activity which, owing to a general risk not specific to women, is imposed for reasons of public safety is not one of the differences in treatment that article 2(3) of the directive allows out of a concern to protect women.

Here then, EC law was able to render the ouster clause ineffective. Although this remedy is correctly available only when an EC right is in issue, EC law can have what Craig[9] calls a 'spillover effect for the resolution of analogous problems of a purely domestic character'. Such was the situation in *M v Home Office*,[10] where the House of Lords had to construe s. 21 of the Crown Proceedings Act 1947 which precludes a court from granting an injunction against the Crown in civil proceedings. Shortly before, in *Factortame (No. 1)*,[11] the House of Lords had ruled that interim injunctions were not available. In *Factortame (No. 2)*,[12] when a preliminary reference under Art. 177 was made to the ECJ, that court replied that injunctive relief must be made available for the protection of EC rights if it would otherwise be available in proceedings between citizens, even if this required the disapplication of an Act of Parliament. It is generally considered that this case had

9  *Administrative Law* (London: Sweet and Maxwell) 1994, pp. 209-210.
10  [1993] 3 WLR 433 (below).
11  *R v Secretary of State for Transport, ex p Factortame* [1990] 2 AC 85.
12  C–213/89 *R v Secretary of State for Transport, ex p Factortame (No. 2)* [1990] ECR I-2433, [1990] 3 WLR 818. For comment see, N. Gravells, 'Disapplying an Act of Parliament Pending a Preliminary Ruling: Constitutional Enormity or Community Law Right?' [1989] PL 568 and 'Effective Protection of Community Law Rights: Temporary Disapplication of an Act of Parliament' [1991] PL 568. These famous cases are further dealt with below, pp. 170–171.

a 'spillover effect' in *M v Home Office*. In reading the following extract, note how the court moved decisively on to the constitutional high ground, invoking the full force of Dicey's statement of the rule of law principle, combining this with a clever use of formalistic reasoning to conceal the innovative nature of the judgment.

## *M v Home Office*[13]

M was a citizen of Zaire who applied for asylum in the United Kingdom as a refugee within the Geneva Convention on the Status of Refugees. In November 1990, the Home Secretary (Mr. Kenneth Baker) notified him that the application had been turned down. Following an unsuccessful appeal, M applied for judicial review. The application failed but was renewed before the Court of Appeal on the basis of new evidence from a medical foundation. This appeal also failed, to be renewed before a judge in chambers by different counsel. Counsel for the Home Office guaranteed that removal would be postponed but, due to a confusion, M was put on a plane to Zaire. The judge issued an order for his immediate return but attempts to retrieve the error, first in Paris, later in Zaire, failed. M's lawyers instituted proceedings for contempt of court. Simon Brown J ruled that the court had no power to make a finding of contempt against a Minister of the Crown but was reversed in the Court of Appeal (Lord Donaldson MR, McCowan and Nolan LJJ) on the ground that the Home Secretary was acting in his personal capacity and was guilty of an interference with the administration of justice. On appeal to the House of Lords, the decision was upheld on a different ground. Mr. Kentridge QC appeared for M; Mr. Richards for the Home Office.

> *Lord Woolf*: Mr. Kentridge placed at the forefront of his argument the issue as to whether the courts have jurisdiction to make coercive orders against the Crown or ministers of the Crown. It was appropriate for him to do so for at least two reasons. First, and more importantly, because whether the courts have or do not have such a coercive jurisdiction would be a strong indicator as to whether the courts had the jurisdiction to make a finding of contempt. If there were no power to make coercive orders, then the need to rely on the law of contempt for the purpose of enforcing the orders would rarely arise. The second reason is that, on the facts of the case, the issue is highly significant in determining the status of the order which Garland J. made and which it is alleged Mr Baker breached. If that order was made without jurisdiction, then Mr Richards would rely on this in support of his contention that Mr Baker should not have been found guilty of contempt. As Mr Richards admitted, the issue is of constitutional importance since it goes to the heart of the relationship between the executive and the courts. Is the relationship based, as he submits, on trust and cooperation or ultimately on coercion?
>
> Mr. Richards submits that the answer to this question is provided by the decision [in] *ex p. Factortame (No.1)* and in particular by the reasoning of Lord Bridge. This speech was highly influential in causing Simon Brown J. and McCowan L.J. to take a different view from the majority of the Court of Appeal as to the outcome of the present proceedings. That case was not, however, primarily concerned with the question as to whether injunctive relief was available against the Crown or its officers.

13   [1993] 3 WLR 433.

. . . It is clear that what for the Crown was a question of greatest importance was for the applicants a side-show. The Crown was anxious to have reconsidered the dicta in two cases which indicated that in judicial review proceedings injunctive relief could be granted against officers of the Crown. The first case was *Reg. v. Secretary of State for the Home Department, ex p. Herbage* [1987] Q.B. 872. The second *Reg. v. Licensing Authority Established under Medicines Act ex p. Smith Kline & French Laboratories Ltd. (No.2)* [1990] 1 Q.B. 574, where the majority of the Court of Appeal approved the judgment of Hodgson J. in *Herbage*. In both those cases the Crown had been unable to appeal as it had been successful and so the *Factortame* case proved an ideal opportunity in which to vindicate its view that the dicta were wrong. Since the decision in *Factortame* there has also been the important development that the European Court has determined the second reference against the Crown so that the unhappy situation now exists that while a citizen is entitled to obtain injunctive relief (including interim relief) against the Crown or an officer of the Crown to protect his interests under Community law he cannot do so in respect of his other interests which may be just as important . . .

I was a party to the judgment of the majority in the *Smith Kline* case . . . I indicated that injunctive relief was available in judicial review proceedings not only against an officer of the Crown but also against the Crown. Although in reality the distinction between the Crown and an officer of the Crown is of no practical significance in judicial review proceedings, in the theory which clouds this subject the distinction is of the greatest importance. My judgment in the earlier case may have caused some confusion in *Factortame* by obscuring the important fact that, as was the position prior to the introduction of judicial review, while prerogative orders are made regularly against ministers in their official capacity, they are never made against the Crown . . .

Mr. Richards and Mr. Kentridge relied on principles which had been repeatedly reiterated down the centuries since medieval times. The principles on which Mr Richards founded his argument are that the King can do no wrong and that the King cannot be sued in his own courts. Mr. Kentridge on the other hand relied on the equally historic principle which is intimately linked with the name of Professor Dicey that 'When we speak of the "rule of law" as a characteristic of our country, [we mean] not only that with us no man is above the law, but (what is a different thing) that here every man, whatever be his rank or condition, is subject to the ordinary law of the realm and amenable to the jurisdiction of the ordinary tribunals. In England the idea of legal equality, or of the universal subjection of all classes to one law administered by the ordinary courts, has been pushed to its utmost limit. With us every official, from Prime Minister down to a constable or a collector of taxes, is under the same responsibility for every act done without legal justification as any other citizen. The reports abound with cases in which officials have been brought before the courts, and made, in their personal capacity, liable to punishment, or to the payment of damages, for acts done in their official character but in excess of their lawful authority. A colonial governor, a secretary of state, a military officer, and all subordinates, though carrying out the commands of their official superiors, are as responsible for any act which the law does not authorise as is any private and unofficial person.' (*Dicey on the Law of the Constitution*, 10th ed. (1959), pp.193-194.)

In the present proceedings what is in dispute is not the validity of the principles but the manner in which in practice they were reconciled by the courts. The fact that the Sovereign could do no wrong did not mean that a servant of the Crown could do no wrong. Prior to the Crown Proceedings Act 1947 it was long established that what would now be described as private law rights could be established against the Crown either by bringing a petition of right or, in the case of an action in tort, when a petition of right was not available, by bringing an action for damages against the servant of the Crown responsible for the tort in his own name . . .

In most situations today statutory duties are conferred on ministers in their own name and not upon the Crown in general . . . Furthermore, by the time of the introduction of the remedy of judicial review the position had developed so that the prerogative orders, including prohibition and mandamus, were being granted regularly against ministers without any investigation of whether a statutory duty, which had not been complied with, was placed upon the minister or some one else in the department for which the minister was responsible. Thus the Immigration Act 1971 places some duties on immigration officers and others on the Home Secretary, but even where it is the immigration officer who has not complied with the statutory duty it is the practice to make an order of mandamus against the minister. As a result of even more recent developments, illustrated by the decision in the [*GCHQ* case, below, p. 113] a distinction probably no longer has to be drawn between duties which have a statutory and those which have a prerogative source.

After the introduction of judicial review in 1977 it was therefore not necessary to draw any distinction between an officer of the Crown 'acting as such' and an officer acting in some other capacity in public law proceedings . . . The changes made in procedure introduced in 1977 by R.S.C., Ord. 53 for judicial review were first given statutory authority by primary legislation in section 31 of the Supreme Court Act 1981.

In section 31 the jurisdiction to grant declarations and injunctions is directly linked to that which already existed in relation to the prerogative orders. The jurisdiction to award damages by contrast is restricted to those situations where damages are recoverable in an action begun by writ. It has never been suggested that a declaration is not available in proceedings against a minister in his official capacity and if Order 53 and section 31 apply to a minister in the case of declarations then, applying ordinary rules of construction, one would expect the position to be precisely the same in the case of injunctions . . .

After discussing Lord Bridge's reasoning in *Factortame*, Lord Woolf continued:

The language of section 31 being unqualified in its terms, there is no warrant for restricting its application so that in respect of ministers and other officers of the Crown alone the remedy of an injunction, including an interim injunction, is not available. In my view the history of prerogative proceedings against officers of the Crown supports such a conclusion. So far as interim relief is concerned, which is the practical change which has been made, there is no justification for adopting a different approach to officers of the Crown from that adopted in relation to other respondents in the absence of clear language such as that contained in section 21(2) of the Act of 1947. The fact that in any event a stay could be granted against the Crown under Ord. 53, r.3(10) emphasises the limits of the change in the situation which is involved. It would be most regrettable if an approach which is inconsistent with that which exists in Community law should be allowed to persist if this is not strictly necessary. The restriction provided for in section 21(2) of the Act of 1947 does, however, remain in relation to civil proceedings.

The fact that, in my view, the court should be regarded as having jurisdiction to grant interim and final injunctions against officers of the Crown does not mean that that jurisdiction should be exercised except in the most limited circumstances. In the majority of situations so far as final relief is concerned, a declaration will continue to be the appropriate remedy on an application for judicial review involving officers of the Crown. As has been the position in the past, the Crown can be relied upon to cooperate fully with such declarations . . .

The Court of Appeal were of the opinion that a finding of contempt could not be made against the Crown, a government department or a minister of the Crown in his official capacity. Although it is to be expected that it will be rare indeed that the circumstances will exist in which such a finding would be justified, I do not believe there is any impediment to a court making such a finding, when it is appropriate to do so, not against the Crown directly, but against a government department or a minister of the Crown in his official capacity. Lord Donaldson considered that a problem was created in making a finding of contempt because the Crown lacked a legal personality. However, at least for some purposes, the Crown has a legal personality. It can be appropriately described as a corporation sole or a corporation aggregate: . . . In any event it is not in relation to the Crown that I differ from the Master of the Rolls, but as to a government department or a minister.

Nolan L.J. considered that the fact that proceedings for contempt are 'essentially personal and punitive' meant that it was not open to a court, as a matter of law, to make a finding of contempt against the Home Office or the Home Secretary. While contempt proceedings usually have these characteristics and contempt proceedings against a government department or a minister in an official capacity would not be either personal or punitive (it would clearly not be appropriate to fine or sequest the assets of the Crown or a government department or an officer of the Crown acting in his official capacity), this does not mean that a finding of contempt against a government department or minister would be pointless. The very fact of making such a finding would vindicate the requirements of justice. In addition an order for costs could be made to underline the significance of a contempt. A purpose of the courts' powers to make findings of contempt is to ensure that the orders of the court are obeyed. This jurisdiction is required to be coextensive with the courts' jurisdiction to make the orders which need the protection which the jurisdiction to make findings of contempt provides. In civil proceedings the court can now make orders (other than injunctions or for specific performance) against authorised government departments or the Attorney-General. On applications for judicial review orders can be made against ministers. In consequence of the developments identified already such orders must be taken not to offend the theory that the Crown can supposedly do no wrong. Equally, if such orders are made and not obeyed, the body against whom the orders were made can be found guilty of contempt without offending that theory, which would be the only justifiable impediment against making a finding of contempt.

In cases not involving a government department or a minister the ability to *punish* for contempt may be necessary. However, as is reflected in the restrictions on execution against the Crown, the Crown's relationship with the courts does not depend on coercion and in the exceptional situation when a government department's conduct justifies this, a finding of contempt should suffice. In that exceptional situation, the ability of the court to make a finding of contempt is of great importance. It would demonstrate that a government department has interfered with the administration of justice. It will then be for Parliament to determine what should be the consequences of that finding. In accord with tradition the finding should not be made against the 'Crown' by name but in the name of the authorised department (or the Attorney-General) or the minister so as to accord with the body against whom the order was made. If the order was made in civil proceedings against an authorised department, the department will be held to be in contempt. On judicial review the order will be against the minister and so normally should be any finding of contempt in respect of the order.

Commenting on this decision,[14] one of the authors wrote:

> To summarise, *M v Home Office* confirms that injunctions, whether final or interim, do lie against officials and Ministers of the Crown in public law or 'Crown side' proceedings. Such exceptions as remain are likely to prove extremely limited . . . A powerful back-up to mandatory orders exists in the form of contempt proceedings,[15] now held to lie against officials and ministers in their official as well as their personal capacities. Thus the decision does move our system of judicial review a long way towards the mandatory model for which Lord Woolf argued.
>
> A long way but not all the way because, at the end of his lengthy judgement, Lord Woolf . . . deduces that contempt proceedings are ultimately unenforceable. At the theoretical level, this admission that 'the Crown's relationship with the courts does not depend on coercion and in the exceptional situation, when a government department's conduct justifies this, a finding of contempt should suffice', surely undercuts the fundamental premise of Lord Woolf's judgment. A mandatory model of judicial review which cannot be enforced must be a contradiction in terms.

Many administrative law cases could be described as symbolic victories. The courts assert their power but no real remedy is forthcoming. At the end of the day, most of the cases in this section fall into that category. The Rule of Law principle has ultimately to concede to the paramount constitutional norm of parliamentary sovereignty and, even if this were not the case, ministers do not automatically resign and their committal to prison could not be a regular occurrence. But this is hardly the point. Like Dicey's model of personal liability, Lord Woolf's mandatory model of public law is an ideal-type. Both are designed to the same end; to remind public officials of their duties, responsibilities and obligations. In this sense they are symbolic. Defending at one and the same time the ideal-type and the apolitical paradigm of public law, Allan offers this spirited defence of Dicey's Rule of Law ideal:[16]

> Contrary to orthodox opinion, A.V. Dicey was wise to seek an interpretation of the rule of law which reflected the traditions and peculiarities of English common law. Whatever its faults, Dicey's work recognised the importance of expounding a constitutional philosophy, which could serve as a basis for the systematic exposition and consistent development of legal principle. More recent efforts to give analytical precision to the concept of the rule of law have not always been wholly successful – at least in Britain – and constitutional law has perhaps been weakened in consequence, because its foundations have come to seem uncertain and insecure . . . At the heart of the problem lies the difficulty of articulating a coherent doctrine which resists a

14  C. Harlow, 'Accidental Death of an Asylum Seeker' (1994) 57 MLR 620, 623.
15  Criminal proceedings for contempt of court are usually enforced by fines, though ultimately by imprisonment. The reasons why Lord Woolf called them unenforceable against a Minister involve s. 25(4) of the Crown Proceedings Act 1947, and are omitted from this extract.
16  T. Allan, *Law, Liberty and Justice, The Legal Foundations of British Constitutionalism* (Oxford: Clarendon) 1993, pp. 20-21.

purely formal conception of legality – according to which even brutal decrees of a dictator, if formally 'valid', meet the requirements of the rule of law – without instead propounding a complete political and social philosophy. The formal conception, which serves only to distinguish the commands of the government in power (whatever their content) from those of anyone else, offers little of value to the constitutionalist theorist. And the richer seams of political theory – ideal versions of justice in the liberal, constitutional state – are inevitably too ambitious (because too controversial) to provide a secure basis for practical analysis . . . It seems very doubtful whether it is possible to formulate a theory of the rule of law of universal validity . . . But it does not follow that we cannot seek to elaborate the meaning and content of the rule of law within the context of the British polity – exploring the legal foundations of constitutionalism in the setting of contingent political institutions. That was, of course, Dicey's purpose in *The Law of the Constitution*.

Dicey's account of the English constitution was never, as he himself seems to have believed, simply a description. It was an *interpretation*, inspired by his own values as well as those of the society in which he lived and worked. The ideology which formed the 'background theory' of his great works included an ardent belief in individualism, in laissez-faire economic policy and in the value of the common law. Dicey showed no interest in the idea that administrative law might regulate the relationships between public authorities – as today it is increasingly asked to do. He realised and feared the trend to collectivism but saw no need for structures which could counter it. In this respect he must bear some responsibility for the individualistic, citizen-versus-state approach of English administrative law.

# Chapter 3

# Green light theories

## 1. Foreign connections

In Chapter 2 we concentrated on one view of English administrative law as an instrument for the control of power and for the protection of individual liberty, the emphasis being on courts rather than on government. We found too that 'the state' was often regarded as intrusive. In this chapter, we look more closely at an alternative tradition, which we have called 'green light' theory. In using this metaphor, we do not wish to suggest that green light theorists favour unrestricted or arbitrary action by the state. What one person sees as control of arbitrary power may, however, be experienced by another as a brake on progress. While red light theory looks to the model of the balanced constitution, green light theory finds the 'model of government' more congenial. Where red light theorists favour judicial control of executive power, green light theorists are inclined to pin their hopes on the political process.

While red light theory relates to positivism and formalism, we shall find that many green light theorists favour 'realist' and 'functionalist' jurisprudence. Realism, as it developed in late nineteenth-century America,[1] stressed that law could be studied only in its social context, and realists included in their definition of law elements, especially of policy, which positivists would seek to exclude. The effectiveness of the legal system became an object of study not only for lawyers but also for political scientists and sociologists of law. A method known as functionalism was born:[2]

> The functional method poses such questions as: How do rules of law work? Are certain rules of law, so-called, merely ritual observances which have no verifiable relation to the decisions of judges who recite them? To what extent are laws actually obeyed? What are the limits of effective law enforcement? What are the social mechanisms and institutions that make certain rules of law effective and leave others dead letters? When rules of law are obeyed or disobeyed, what consequences actually follow from such conduct? More generally, these questions may be compressed in the formula 'What is the human meaning of the law?

---

1   See N. Duxbury, 'The Theory and History of American Law and Politics' (1993) 13 OJLS 249.
2   F. Cohen, 'The Problems of a Functional Jurisprudence' (1937) 1 MLR 5, 6. See also M. Loughlin, *Public Law and Political Theory* (Oxford: Clarendon) 1992, p. 60; P. Craig (1993) 'Book Review' 13 Legal Studies 275.

In making this point, we do not wish to attempt precise definitions or to sever one school of legal theory artificially from the other;[3] the essential point for our purposes is that both functionalists and realists interest themselves in the way in which rules come into being and actually operate. Nor do we intend to imply that all American administrative law is 'realist' in character. We have already noted the existence of a school of administrative law which is positivist in character and devoted to supporting the separation of powers framework of the US constitution. But the functionalist method did appear particularly appropriate to draw out the relationship between law and administration, more complex than the picture of the balanced constitution might suggest. A new definition to describe the relationship between law and administration was necessary; administrative law became the law relating to the administration (below).

But not all functionalists were content merely to describe. Reformers by temperament, they looked back to the example of Jeremy Bentham. Believing the end of government to be the 'greatest happiness of those for whom the powers of government are exercised', Bentham had long ago envisaged a more active role for government and legislature.[4] He believed it to be the duty of the sovereign to engage actively in legislation to ensure that the principle of utility prevailed through the legal system. Moreover, both Bentham and Austin discounted law courts as efficient vehicles for law reform, even of their own archaic procedure. Green light theorists were active in the design of new administrative procedures suited to the modern administrative process. These procedures were to be assessed in their particular administrative context rather than forced into a separation of powers framework or measured against general principles such as the rules of natural justice.

Writing at the London School of Economics in the inter-war period, and conscious of the close relationship between law, politics and social policy,[5] Laski, Robson and Jennings were able to draw inspiration from the work of lawyers in other countries.[6] In the United States, where realist and sociological jurisprudence was influential, the gaps between law, politics and administration were narrower. Many years after the event, Nonet, himself the author of an important functionalist study of the work of an American administrative organisation, described a new relationship between sociological and realist jurisprudence and the state interventionism which was the hallmark of President Roosevelt's inter-war government:[7]

---

3   We do not imply, either, that all 'realists' are anti-positivist: see J. Singer, 'Legal Realism Now' (1988) 76 Univ. of Calif. LR 465.

4   See P. Craig, 'Bentham, Public Law and Democracy' [1989] PL 407, 409.

5   J. Griffith, 'A Pilgrim's Progress' (1995) 2 J. of Law and Soc. 410. On the LSE tradition of legal scholarship generally, see R. Rawlings, 'Distinction and Diversity: Law and the LSE' in R. Rawlings (ed.), *Law, Society and Economy* (Oxford: Clarendon) 1997.

6   J. Griffith, 'The Teaching of Law and Politics', (1982) 16 The Law Teacher 1, and M. Dimock, *Law and Dynamic Administration* (New York: Praeger) 1980, p. 69, both make this point.

7   P. Nonet, *Administrative Justice: Advocacy and Change in a Government Agency* (New York: Rusell Sage Foundation) 1969, p. 83. And see G. Frug, 'The Ideology of Bureaucracy in American Law' (1984) 84 Harv. LR 1276, 1282; G. Lawson, 'The Rise and Rise of the Administrative State' (1994) 107 Harv. LR 1231.

With the advent of the New Deal, the legal order suddenly turned from an obstacle and an enemy into a friend and a positive support . . . The active state was emerging and a new idea of law, already embodied in the flowering legal realism, was now presenting it as an active instrument of political and social change.

The new ideas were less insular and less hostile to left-wing ideas than those of Dicey. Here Robson contrasts the so-called models of law and government:[8]

An opposition has for long existed in Britain between the idea of 'law' and the idea of 'government'. This is a heritage from the conflict in the seventeenth century between, on the one side, a sovereign claiming to rule by divine right and to exercise an undisputed prerogative in all matters of government, and, on the other side, a nation claiming a supreme law to which even the sovereign should be subject. That struggle between king and commons has become transformed in our own day into a conflict between the executive, on the one hand, and the judiciary and legal profession on the other. The lawyers still regard themselves as champions of the popular cause; but there can be little doubt that the great departments of state . . . are not only essential to the well being of the great mass of the people, but also the most significant expressions of democracy in our time. Considerations of this kind, however, could scarcely be expected to weigh with the predominantly upper middle class conservative legal mind.

A further influence in providing a new model for a collectivist state inside which green light theories of administrative law could flourish was the work of the French jurist, Léon Duguit (1859-1928). Duguit developed his theory of public law under the influence of the great French sociologist Emile Durkheim (1858-1917). Durkheim's work on the *Division of Labour* (1893) started life as a dissertation on 'the relationship of individualism and socialism'; Duguit's theory was premised on a socialistic state in which strong government was a necessity.[9] Duguit accepted the need for a state whose activities stretch far beyond the traditional areas of law, order, justice and defence. He believed in a collective state whose function was to secure the provision of public services. These he defined as including:

any activity that has to be governmentally regulated and controlled because it is indispensable to the realisation and development of social solidarity . . . so long as it is of such a nature that it cannot be assured save by governmental intervention.

Duguit's theory laid the basis, therefore, for a welfare state but also for a corporatist state in which planning and the control of private economic activity in the interests of the collectivity are legitimate state activities. For example, Duguit foresaw that transport, mining and electricity would ultimately become

---

8    W. Robson, *Justice and Administrative Law* (London: Stevens). This quotation is from the 3rd edn., 1951, p. 421.

9    Duguit's main works in this field were *Traité du droit constitutionnel* (5 vols., 1911) and *Les transformations du droit public* (1913). The Laskis translated the latter under the title of *Law in the Modern State* (London: Allen and Unwin) 1921 and our extracts are drawn from their translation at pp. 48-49. See also L. Duguit (trans. Laski), 'The Law and the State' (1917-18) 31 Harv. LR 1; M. Loughlin, *Public Law and Political Theory* (Oxford: Clarendon) 1992, pp. 109–113.

public services. Yet Duguit rejected the idea of the state as a corporate entity with a legal life and legal powers of its own. The state was merely a collection of individuals 'interdependent upon one another even for their daily and elementary needs'. Sovereignty itself was a misconception;[10] the state had 'duties' rather than 'rights' or 'powers'. This view transformed the character of 'public law':

> Public law is no longer a mass of rules which, applied by a sovereign person with the right to command, determine its relations between the individuals and groups on a given territory as a sovereign dealing with its subjects. The modern theory of the state envisages a mass of rules which govern the organization of public utilities and assure their regular and uninterrupted function . . . The one governmental rule is the governmental obligation to organize and control public services in such a fashion as to avoid all dislocation. The basis of public law is therefore no longer command but organization . . . government has . . . a social function to fulfil.

Yet Duguit's theory actually had much in common with that of Dicey, his great contemporary. In the former's theory:

> two things are clear: the state is reduced to the level of a private citizen since the activities of each are brought within the scope of an objective law; and, further, there is no distinction between the nature of public and of private law, since each is subject to the criterion of social solidarity.[11]

Duguit did not believe in absolute power, whether or not it was subject to control. Power was subject to inherent limitations, and the rulers, defined as those who possessed the power of implementing decisions, had only a limited mandate to act in the public interest or in the interests of social solidarity:[12]

> Government and its officials are no longer the masters of men imposing the sovereign will on their subjects. They are no longer the organs of a corporate person issuing its commands. They are simply the managers of the nation's business. It should thus be clear, contrary to the usual notion, that the growth and extension of state activity does not necessarily increase the government's power. Their business increases, their duties expand; but their right of control is extinct because no one any longer believes in it . . . In whatever manner the business of the state is managed, its fundamental idea is thus clear: government must perform certain definite functions. As a consequence a public service is an institution of a rigorously objective order controlled by principles equally imposed on the government and its subjects.

Like Dicey's, Duguit's theory was individualistic, though the individualism differed in its character. Laski, an admirer of Duguit who translated his works, describes them as:[13]

---

10   See also H. Laski, *A Grammar of Politics* (London: Allen and Unwin) 1925, pp. 44-88.
11   H. Laski, 'M. Duguit's Conception of the State' in A. Goodhart et al., *Modern Theories of Law* (London: Oxford University Press) 1933, p. 56.
12   L. Duguit, *Law in the Modern State*, translated by F. and H. Laski, pp. 51-54.
13   H. Laski, 'M. Duguit's Conception of the State', in A. Goodhart et al., *Modern Theories of Law*, above, note 11, pp. 56-57.

. . . a doctrine which makes against authoritarianism. The only justification for any public act is that its result in public good should be commensurate with the force that is involved in its exercise. But that, after all, is ultimately a matter for the private judgement of each one of us; and a real impetus is thus given to the initiative of the private citizen. Room is left for that reservoir of individualism upon which, in the last resort, so much of the welfare of society depends.

In Duguit's state the function of public law was first and foremost to provide the framework inside which the efficient operation of the public services could at all times be assured. Administrative law limited state action in two distinct ways: (a) through the notion that the state can act only in the public interest and for the public good; and (b) through the principle that the state must observe the law. Regulation and rules, which set out the principles of operation, at once become more important than the adjudication of disputes. Duguit's theory does, of course, find a place for adjudication. In case of doubt, administrative courts pronounce on the legality of administrative action. They have a third function. Duguit believed that the state was fully responsible for its acts and that every citizen was entitled to equality of treatment. Where a citizen suffered abnormal loss in the interest of the collectivity, compensation was due; loss caused by a state enterprise must be repaired by the state. Disputes between citizen and state were to be referred to administrative courts. These two ideas formed a complete new theory of administrative liability.

## 2. A new deal?

New accounts of administrative law showing the influence of these various ideas appeared in England.[14] These were *administration centred* – the role of administrative law was not to act as a counterweight to the interventionist state but to facilitate legitimate government action – and *collectivist* in character,[15] advancing the claim to promote the public interest or common good. As Jennings put it:[16]

> The task of the lawyer as such is not to declare that modern interventionism is pernicious, but, seeing that all modern states have adopted the policy, to advise as to the technical devices which are necessary to make the policy efficient and to provide justice for individuals . . . The problem to be discussed is the division of powers between administrators and judges and, given that judges must exercise some functions,

14 And also in American texts. See e.g. J. Hart, *An Introduction to Administrative Law with Selected Cases* (New York: F. S. Crofts) 1st edn., 1940, where the author defines administrative law as 'all the law that controls the administration as well as that made by the administration' and states that 'the subject matter that administrative law takes as its focal point is public administration'. M. Dimock, *Law and Dynamic Administration* (New York: Praeger) 1980 contains a useful survey of the development of American administrative law with a bibliography.

15 They were therefore inherently socialistic. See B. Barry, *Does Society Exist? The Case for Socialism*, Fabian Tract No. 536 (London: Fabian Society) 1989, p. 17, where Barry remarks, 'What has united socialists historically – and this is a statement which would include Marx, the Webbs, and everybody in between – is a belief in collectivism'.

16 W. I. Jennings, 'Courts and Administrative Law' (1936) 49 Harv. LR 426, 430.

the kind of courts and the judicial procedure necessary to make the exercise of the functions most efficient.

For Jennings, in 1933, administrative law consisted of all that Wade was to exclude:[17]

> Administrative law is the law relating to the Administration. It determines the organisation, powers and duties of administrative authorities. Where the political organisation of the country is highly developed, as it is in England, administrative law is a large and important branch of the law. It includes the law relating to public utility companies, and the legal powers which these authorities exercise. Or, looking at the subject from the functional instead of the institutional point of view, we may say that it includes the law relating to public health, the law of highways, the law of social insurance, the law of education, and the law relating to the provision of gas, water, and electricity. These are examples only, for a list of the powers of the administrative authorities would occupy a long catalogue.

One senses here the functionalist concern with how things actually work, leading Jennings towards a new, *descriptive* role for academic administrative law, with a growing emphasis on statutory and regulatory regimes rather than the general principles of case law. Jennings himself published studies of housing law.[18] Later authors added extended studies of new and developing areas of administrative activity: vertical rather than horizontal studies were made. Typically, such studies were inter-disciplinary in nature, drawing on the ideas of non-lawyers to explain and provide context for legal rules and to interpret concepts like 'discretion', which Dicey had feared but had never investigated. These studies were to promote a 'hiving-off' of administrative law into its component parts: welfare, planning, housing, immigration, etc.

Descriptive as Jennings's definition is, it should not be read to mean that administrative law possesses no checking function. Citing the definition with approval in the first textbook devoted to administrative law (1952), Griffith and Street explained that their book would focus primarily on three questions:[19] 'First, what sort of powers does the Administration exercise? Secondly, what are the limits of those powers? Thirdly, what are the ways in which the Administration is kept within those limits?' This certainly does not suggest a permissive attitude to power – an unlikely stance from Griffith who has described society as 'by nature authoritarian'.[20] As a realist, Griffith sought to uncover the relationship between public law and power and track the locus of power. For him, the key questions were what power should be used *for* and *how* it should be controlled.

For red light theorists, the answer lay in courts, the Rule of Law and Separation of Powers theory. Green light theorists, however, took a very different attitude to judges and lawyers. Openly advocating reform of the antiquated legal system, they viewed the legal profession as too old-fashioned to reform itself. Since

17   W. I. Jennings, *The Law and the Constitution* (London: University Press) 5th edn., 1967, p. 194.
18   W. I. Jennings, 'Courts and Administrative Law' (1936) 49 Harv. LR 426.
19   J. Griffith and H. Street, *Principles of Administrative Law* (London: Pitman) 5th edn., 1973, p. 4.
20   J. Griffith, 'The Political Constitution' (1979) 42 MLR 1, 6.

Robson's classic study of administrative adjudication, *Justice and Administrative Law* (1928), an early example of the functional approach,[1] green light theory has focused on alternatives to courts.[2] Robson described[3] the Donoughmore Committee as paralysed by 'the dead hand of Dicey', and damned its Report for rejecting the opportunity of a 'boldly-conceived system of administrative courts' headed by an administrative appeals tribunal, in favour of accepting 'the patchwork quilt of ill-constructed tribunals which at present exists, and endeavour[ing] to remedy some of their more obvious defects'. His polemic attacks legal reasoning and the profession generally. Here Robson is not complaining that lawyers are *wrong* in seeking to protect individual rights – though green light theorists undoubtedly queried their limited definition and narrow focus on the right of property.[4] Robson's complaint is that the tools which they use are inadequate for the task. And he goes further, alleging that a profession which is incapable of reforming the legal system, ought not to be let loose on the administrative process:

> The disappointing feature of the Report is its failure to make any significant contribution to the structure of the system. Instead of endeavouring to increase the sense of responsibility and independence of the administrative tribunals, the Report relies on a hostile judiciary to provide 'checks and balances'. It recommends, accordingly, that the supervisory jurisdiction of the High Court to compel ministers and administrative tribunals to keep within their powers and to hear and determine according to law be maintained; and further, that anyone aggrieved by a decision should have an absolute right of appeal to the High Court on any question of law.
>
> This is the means by which the rule of law is to be perpetuated and the liberty of the subject protected for all eternity. It sounds admirable. But when one looks a little deeper doubts begin to arise. In the first place, it is often extraordinarily difficult to discover any essential difference between a question of law and a question of fact. A question of fact in one generation sometimes becomes a question of law in the next; and a vast body of precedents is almost certain to arise on hair-splitting distinctions between questions of law and questions of fact in the field of public administration. When the courts want to interfere they will seek to find that a question of law is involved; and *vice versa*. Second, the procedure for getting a decision reviewed on a question of law by the courts is, to quote the Report, 'too expensive and in certain respects archaic, cumbrous and too inelastic'; and the Committee recommends a cheaper and more simple procedure. One must consider the implications of this criticism. Here are the judges and the lawyers complaining that they are not empowered in all cases to interfere with judicial decisions by administrative tribunals, and clamouring for more power. Yet in the large sphere where the right of judicial control over the executive *does* exist, the courts have done absolutely nothing to modernise, to cheapen or to bring into accord with modern needs a fantastic procedure which has

---

1   See J. Willis, *The Parliamentary Powers of English Government Departments* (Cambridge: Harvard University Press) 1933 for a parallel study of delegated legislation.

2   See C. Glasser and C. Harlow, 'Legal Services and the Alternatives: The LSE Tradition' in R. Rawlings (ed.) *Law, Society and Economy*, above, note 5. And see below, Ch. 12.

3   W. Robson, 'The Report of the Committee on Ministers' Powers' (1932) 3 Pol. Q. 346, 359 and 360-361.

4   E.g. Jennings (1936) 49 Harv. LR 429; J. Griffith, 'The Law of Property (Land)' in Ginsberg (ed.), *Law and Opinion in England in the 20th Century* (London: Stevens) 1959, and *The Politics of the Judiciary* (London: Fontana) 4th edn., 1991.

been obsolete for at least a century . . . It is difficult to believe that the legal profession retains any considerable capacity for reforming either the law or the practice of the courts.

When Robson talks of the well being 'of the great mass of the people' as being achieved through political action he was not arguing for a robotic administrative law and public administration devoid of values; very much the reverse. Like Street, he was working for justice in the welfare state,[5] but a real, ground floor justice accessible by the many.

Because they see their own function as the resolution of disputes and because they see the administrative function from outside, lawyers traditionally emphasise external control through adjudication. To the lawyer, law is the policeman; it operates as an external control, often retrospectively. But a main concern of many green light writers was to *minimise* the influence of courts. Courts, with their legalistic values, were seen as obstacles to progress, and the control which they exercise as unrepresentative and undemocratic. To emphasise this crucial point, in green light theory, decision-making by an elite judiciary imbued with a legalistic, rights-based ideology and eccentric vision of the 'public interest' – Griffith's phrase[6] – was never a plausible counter to authoritarianism. Here Hutchinson, writing many years later and in Canada, seeks to re-politicise the notion of 'control':[7]

> [Courts] take an overly historical approach to deciding disputes; they rely on an adversarial process; they limit the amount of relevant information on which decisions can be made; they are ignorant of bureaucratic concerns and workings; they allow access to only a limited number of individuals; they fail to monitor the impact of their decisions; they ignore the claims of collective interest; they adopt a negative cast of mind; and they are imbued with an individualistic philosophy. In short, the work of the courts is qualitatively incoherent and quantitatively ineffective. They engage in an inescapably political enterprise and function in a way that is incompatible with their self-imposed democratic responsibilities . . . [I]t will be necessary to give up on the courts entirely in the campaign to develop a better organisational ethic and democratic practice.
>
> In seeking to repoliticise the vast administrative regions of contemporary society and to oblige the ship of state to sail under democratic colours, it is necessary to throw liberalism overboard and cast off the moorings of the public/private distinction. On a democratic voyage of discovery there is no chart to follow and no grand manual of statecraft to consult. On the oceans of possibility, empowered citizens must be allowed to dream their own destinations and steer their own courses.

Green light theorists have generally shown interest in alternative, democratic forms of accountability. Laski advocated[8] citizen participation in the form of

---

5   H. Street, *Justice in the Welfare State* (London: Stevens) 2nd edn., 1975. On the link between socialism and law see D. Feldman, 'The Left, Judicial Review and Theories of the Constitution' in W. Watts Miller (ed.) *Socialism and the Law* (Stuttgart: Franz Steiner) 1992.
6   See *The Politics of the Judiciary* (London: Fontana) 4th edn., 1991, pp. 274-300.
7   A. Hutchinson, 'Mice Under a Chair: Democracy, Courts and the Administrative State' (1990) 40 UTLJ 374, 375-376, 403.
8   See further, W. Gwyn, 'The Labour Party and the Threat of Bureaucracy' (1971) 19 Political Studies 383, 389.

parliamentary advisory committees – a precursor of the modern, departmental Select Committees – to oversee the work of government departments. He also advised attaching to each department a 'users' committee of citizens affected by its operations plus a small, 'clearly impartial' investigatory committee to deal with serious charges against departments. A parallel could be drawn with Bentham's celebrated Public Opinion Tribunal[9] and with the case for an administrative court advanced both by Jennings and Robson.[10] In the early years of the century, committees were seen as a useful, procedural device to ensure public participation:

> If bureaucracy is to be controlled, the future lies with increasing the opportunities of the public to temper the rule of the official. The system of administration by committee, the basis of modern local government, is one of the healthiest features of to-day. For it affords a means of imposing a more or less personal responsibility to its members on the officials of the particular service administered by the committee . . . In short, any device to secure more directly government by the consent of the governed rather than by rule of the expert is to be commended to those who share Dicey's ideal of democracy and distrust and dislike of the expert.[11]

Griffith set out his personal creed in 'The Political Constitution'.[12] Dismissing the recently fashionable constitutional device of a Bill of Rights, justiciable and enforceable in the courts to enshrine and protect individual 'rights', Griffith argued for the collectivist view of 'rights' as group interests or 'claims' to be evaluated through the political process. Griffith emphasised the need for access to information, open government, a free and powerful press, and ultimately expressed faith in decentralisation through local government and a strengthened Parliament.[13] On the other hand, he prescribed a reduced role for the judiciary and a diminution in the amount of discretionary power at its disposal. Policy-making and accountability, in short, are political functions.

## 3. Green light theory and control

If the model of law is to be abandoned, then many feel that something other than the traditional model of government must take its place. Few administrative lawyers – or, indeed, citizens – would wish to set sail in a barque as frail as that of ministerial responsibility. Because it revealed the inadequacies of ministerial responsibility, Crichel Down is often described as the beginning of modern administrative law. Very briefly, Crichel Down had been acquired before World

---

9  See P. Kelly, *Utilitarianism and Distributive Justice* (Oxford: Clarendon) 1990, p. 69.
10  W. Robson, *Justice and Administrative Law* (London: Stevens) 3rd edn., 1951, pp. 426-429; W. I. Jennings, 'The Report on Ministers' Powers' (1932) 10 Pub. Admin. 348.
11  E. Wade, Appendix to 9th edn. of Dicey's *Law of the Constitution*, 1939, pp. 494-945. See also K. Wheare, *Government by Committee* (Oxford: OUP) 1955.
12  (1979) 42 MLR 1. See also J. Griffith, 'Judicial Decision-Making in Public Law' [1985] PL 564.
13  Both Jennings and Griffith made extended studies of Parliament, see: W. I. Jennings, *Parliament* (Cambridge: CUP) 1939; J. Griffith and M. Ryle, *Parliament: Functions, Practice and Procedures* (London: Sweet and Maxwell) 1989.

War II by the Air Ministry as a bombing range. Subsequently, when no longer required for these purposes, it was transferred to the Ministry of Agriculture. Later, a dispute arose when the Ministry, wishing to dispose of the land, tried to let it as a single unit to a new tenant instead of allowing its original owners to buy it back. Fierce objections from the latter forced a public inquiry, which established the responsibility of civil servants both for the policy and also for its execution.[14] Controversially, the Minister, Sir Thomas Dugdale, resigned, a paradox which Wade described[15] as an illustration of 'the rock-like solidity of the civil service and, in contrast, of the irrational vicissitudes of politics'.

Crichel Down exposed a world of administrative policy and decision-making apparently immune from political and parliamentary controls. In Griffith's phrase,[16] 'the fundamental defect revealed was not a failure in the constitutional relations of those involved nor the policy decisions nor even the length of the struggle [the complainant] had to wage. It was in the method and therefore in the mental processes of the officials'. But content to rely on 'that personal integrity which is so much more than an absence of corruption', Griffith concluded that the civil service must be left to put its own house in order. Here we find the characteristic reliance of green light theorists on political and administrative institutions. For those who were less trusting, yet did not wish to tip the balance too far in the direction of judicial control, the challenge was to provide alternatives. In the aftermath of Crichel Down, this was to become a major preoccupation for administrative lawyers (see below).

Discussing 'control' theories of administrative law, we did not stop to consider what was meant by the word. Control can be symbolic or real; it can mean to check, restrain or govern. Griffith and Street[17] clearly sense latent ambiguities. They say: 'A great deal turns on the meaning which is attached to the word "controls". Banks control a river; a driver controls his car. The influence of a parent over a child may be greater than the power of a prison guard over a convict.' If we try applying these metaphors to the administrative process, we will see that the 'controls' are direct and internal rather than indirect and external. To extend our metaphors, a river bank may be inspected by an officer of the catchment board (today more probably the official of a privatised water authority) to see that it is in good repair; a policeman may stop the driver and caution him for speeding; a health visitor may advise the child's parents to exert a different kind of influence; and the prison guard may be questioned by the board of visitors. These are all controls, but they are external.

Dicey's controls were *external*, as the concept of 'checks and balances' implies. Obviously, however, the first control of administrative activity is

---

14  See, Report of the Clark Inquiry into Crichel Down, Cmnd. 9176 (1954) and HC Deb., vol. 530, cols. 1182-302. See also Lord Boyle, 'Ministers and the Administrative Process' (1980) 58 Pub. Admin. 1.

15  Wade & Forsyth, p. 69. A full account of the Crichel Down case based on contemporary documentation is now available: see, I. Nicolson, *The Mystery of Crichel Down* (Oxford: OUP) 1986. Note that in 'Crichel Down, The Most Famous Farm in British Constitutional History' (1987) 1 Contemporary Record 35, Griffith changes his view from that in the 1955 article quoted below.

16  J. Griffith, 'The Crichel Down Affair' (1955) 18 MLR 557, 569.

17  *Principles of Administrative Law* (London: Pitman) 5th edn., 1973, p. 24.

*internal*: hierarchical and supervisory. Consider the doctrine of individual ministerial responsibility central to the argument over Crichel Down.[18] One function of the doctrine is to provide internal control because the minister must, as head of his department, supervise the activities of his subordinates by establishing policies and checking the way in which they are implemented. The doctrine also provides for external control through responsibility to Parliament, but this is envisaged as a last resort. And Griffith hints at the superiority of internal control when he prescribes as a remedy for Crichel Down 'more "red tape" not less'.

A second distinction is between *prospective* and *retrospective* control. Judicial review of administrative action is primarily retrospective, although it can possess a prospective element if the administration accepts that judicial precedent establishes the limits of its future conduct.[19] Legislation is primarily prospective. Like the banks of the river, legislation controls administrative activity by prescribing its limits. When an administrator asks 'May I do X?', the lawyer replies 'if the law permits'. He knows where to find the law: statute, regulations, precedent etc., and he knows how to rank it when it has been found. Lawyers like to assume that administrators approach law in the same way:

> To the public administrator, law is something very positive and concrete. It is his authority. The term he customarily uses to describe it is 'my mandate'. It is 'his' law, something he feels a proprietary interest in. It does three things: tells him what the legislature expects him to accomplish, fixes limits to his authority, and sets forth the substantive and procedural rights of the individual and group. Having a positive view of his mandate, the administrator considers himself both an interpreter and a builder. He is a builder because every time he applies *old* law to new situations he builds the law. Therefore law, like administration, is government in action. It is operational, functional, sociological.
>
> Like the judge, the administrator 'finds' the law . . . [He proceeds by asking] What is our statutory authority? What is the ruling case law as found in court cases that serve as precedents? What are our own sublegislative or policy interpretations of statutory authority by means of which we give effect to steps in the administrative unfolding of the law not specifically provided in the words of the statute?[1]

This passage contains clues to the fact that the author had a legal training. Generally speaking, neither administrators nor politicians seek their mandate in law but in policy; they are, in other words, policy-orientated. Administrators see law positively as a set of pegs on which to hang policies; viewed negatively, the law may be a series of hurdles to be jumped before policy can be implemented, in which sense it acts as a control. If law conflicts with policy, the administrator tries to change the law and, if this proves impossible, he may (improperly) sometimes set it aside or ignore it. Again, consider Dimock's neat pyramid of

---

18  See further C. Turpin, 'Ministerial Responsibility' in J. Jowell and D. Oliver, (eds.), *The Changing Constitution* (Oxford: Clarendon) 3rd edn., 1994 and *British Government and the Constitution* (London: Butterworths) 3rd edn., 1995, pp. 366-378; P. Hennessey, *Whitehall* (London: Fontana) revised edn., 1990, pp. 502-506.

19  See generally P. Atiyah, *Pragmatism and Theory in English Law* (London: Stevens) 1987.

1  M. Dimock, *Law and Dynamic Administration*, above, p. 68, note 6, p. 31.

legal norms; statute, case law, formal rules. There is much evidence that administrators do not always understand this hierarchy. They follow policy directives in preference to regulations, do not always know of the existence of case law or realise its significance. This partly represents divergent attitudes of the two callings, lawyer and administrator, which it is well to bear in mind. As we develop the argument in later chapters, however, an infinitely more complex pattern will emerge.

As prevention is proverbially better than cure, so fire-watching can be seen as more 'efficient' than fire-fighting. This is significant, since efficiency is an imperative both for functionalism and, as we shall see in Chapter 5, for modern public administrators. We shall see how, under the influence of Davis, the notion of legislative control has widened. Rule-making has developed into a primary technique for control of bureaucracies. And we shall find that the trend of post-war public administration generally has been to put in place controls which are internal and prospective.

Alongside the new internal controls we find new fire-watchers added. The Council on Tribunals (below, Chapter 14) was installed in the 1960s essentially to carry out fire-watching functions; the ombudsmen (below, Chapter 13) were primarily used for fire-fighting. There is an irony here, in that the introduction of this new, external machinery for control had been heavily promoted by lawyers. Yet the agencies, although external, were often only semi-autonomous. In consequence, the developments were frequently misunderstood by lawyers who, using the courts as their paradigm, doubted the independence and integrity of the new institutions. Again, because they lacked some of the compulsive attributes of law, relying on negotiation rather than command/control, they were often described as 'toothless watch-dogs'. Later re-organisation and privatisation of state services, outlined in Chapter 1 brought about a situation in which state control of public services is necessarily external. The reorganised audit machinery is both external and retrospective. The regulatory agency, a newcomer with a phenomenal growth rate, was introduced specifically as a firewatcher (below, Chapter 10).

## 4. Allocation of functions again

Discussing the allocation of functions in the English governmental and administrative system, Ganz criticised the way in which theories of the balanced constitution seek to distinguish 'legislative', judicial' and 'administrative' functions. Ganz described decision-taking as a spectrum, ranging from 'fixed rules at one end of the spectrum to a purely discretionary act at the other. No clear lines can be drawn where the one activity stops and the other begins as they shade off into one another imperceptibly'. In other words, legislative or rule-making powers and administrative (discretionary or policy-making) powers inevitably blend; the legislative process, too, normally starts in government departments[2] and may end there for implementation after the Royal Assent has been given. For Ganz, each stage of the process involved value-judgments:[3]

2　See M. Zander, *The Law-Making Process* (London: Weidenfeld and Nicolson) 4th edn., 1994.
3　G. Ganz, 'Allocation of Decision-Making Functions' [1972] PL 215 and 279 at 216.

Rules are themselves value-judgements whereas discretion is the power to make a value-judgement. In practice the difference may not be very great . . . where the rule contains words such as 'reasonable' which amount to a delegation of discretion to make value-judgements.

Everything, therefore, turned on the choice of the decision-maker:

When the problem arises of who should make decisions in a particular field the controversy should centre not on whether these involve the application of rules or discretion but on who should make the necessary value-judgements. Looking at this from the point of view of the legislature there is a wide area of choice.

Parliament may make the value-judgements itself and embody them in reasonably precise rules in statutes. This narrows the area of discretion to be exercised by whoever is charged with the application of the rules but does not eliminate it. The choice has to be made between the courts, administrative tribunals and sometimes even ministers or independent statutory bodies as interpreters of the rules laid down.

In many areas it is not, however, possible or even desirable to formulate value-judgements in the shape of detailed rules. Especially in a new field it may be necessary to make value-judgements on a case-to-case basis. This can be done by laying down rules embodying very broad standards or conferring wide discretionary powers. These powers may also be given to courts, administrative tribunals, Ministers or a specially created statutory body.

Here Ganz makes an important point concerning the paramountcy of the legislature. Like Griffith, Ganz believes strongly that courts should not interfere with the allocation of functions as established by statute; by so doing, they substitute the court for the rightful decision-maker chosen by Parliament. Again, like Griffith, Ganz forcefully links the procedural question of allocation of functions with the question of *values*. Where courts cross jurisdictional boundaries to impose 'judicial' procedures on the administration, they are in fact substituting their own values for those of the administration. This is a two-pronged argument. Administrative procedures would be more accessible and 'user-friendly' than courts; equally important, the new institutions would be less imbued with old ideas and ideologies.

Although Ganz's position is typical of green light theorists, it is also an archetypal evocation of the relationship between legislature and judiciary in the English constitution, acknowledged by Dicey. A classic restatement is to be found in a passage from the judgment of Lord Greene, Master of the Rolls during the post-war Labour government in the *Wednesbury* case, which follows.

### *Associated Provincial Picture Houses Ltd v Wednesbury Corpn*[4]

The Sunday Entertainments Act 1932 empowered local authorities to license cinemas for Sunday performances, subject to such conditions 'as the authority think fit to impose'. The defendants banned entry to children under 15. The plaintiffs sought a declaration that the condition was ultra vires.

4   [1948] 1 KB 223.

*Lord Greene MR*: When an executive discretion is entrusted by Parliament to a body such as the local authority in this case, what appears to be an exercise of that discretion can only be challenged in the courts in a strictly limited class of case . . . it must always be remembered that the court is not a court of appeal. When discretion of this kind is granted the law recognizes certain principles upon which that discretion must be exercised, but within the four corners of those principles the discretion, in my opinion, is an absolute one and cannot be questioned in any court of law. What then are those principles? They are well understood . . . The exercise of such a discretion must be a real exercise of the discretion. If, in the statute conferring the discretion, there are to be found expressly or by implication matters which the authority exercising the discretion ought to have regard to, then in exercising the discretion it must have regard to those matters. Conversely, if the nature of the subject-matter and the general interpretation of the Act make it clear that certain matters would not be germane to the matter in question, the authority must disregard those irrelevant collateral matters . . .

I am not sure myself whether the permissible grounds of attack cannot be defined under a single head. It has been perhaps a little bit confusing to find a series of grounds set out. Bad faith, dishonesty – those of course, stand by themselves – unreasonableness, attention given to extraneous circumstances, disregard of public policy and things like that have all been referred to, according to the facts of individual cases, as being matters which are relevant to the question. If they cannot all be confined under one head, they at any rate, I think, overlap to a very great extent. For instance, we have heard in this case a great deal about the meaning of the word 'unreasonable' . . . [a word which] has frequently been used and is frequently used as a general description of the things that must not be done. For instance, a person entrusted with a discretion must, so to speak, direct himself properly in law. He must call his own attention to the matters which he is bound to consider. He must exclude from his consideration matters which are irrelevant to what he has to consider. If he does not obey those rules, he may truly be said, and often is said, to be acting 'unreasonably'. Similarly, there may be something so absurd that no sensible person could ever dream that it lay within the powers of the authority. Warrington LJ in *Short v. Poole Corporation* [1926] Ch 66 gave the example of the red-haired teacher, dismissed because she had red hair. That is unreasonable in one sense. In another sense it is taking into consideration extraneous matters. It is so unreasonable that it might almost be described as being done in bad faith; and, in fact, all these things run into one another . . .

It is true to say that, if a decision on a competent matter is so unreasonable that no reasonable authority could ever have come to it, then the courts can interfere. That, I think, is quite right; but to prove a case of that kind would require something overwhelming, and, in this case, the facts do not come anywhere near anything of that kind. [The] proposition that the decision of the local authority can be upset if it is proved to be unreasonable, really [means] that it must be proved to be unreasonable in the sense that the court considers it to be a decision that no reasonable body could have come to. It is not what the court considers unreasonable, a different thing altogether. If it is what the court considers unreasonable, the court may very well have different views to that of a local authority on matters of high public policy of this kind. Some courts might think that no children ought to be admitted on Sundays at all, some courts might think the reverse, and all over the country I have no doubt on a thing of that sort honest and sincere people hold different views. The effect of the legislation is not to set up the court as an arbiter of the correctness of one view over another. It is the local authority that are set in that position and, provided they act, as they have acted, within the four corners of their jurisdiction, this court, in my opinion, cannot interfere.

Controversy surrounds the meaning of this famous passage. Are there two tests contained within it, namely (i) that the authority must act only after consideration of relevant factors (the ultra vires test) and (ii) that the authority must not act 'unreasonably', or did Lord Greene intend a single test? If the first interpretation is correct, then, after all procedural factors have been exhausted, the court is left with an overriding discretion to intervene not only in cases of bad faith or dishonesty but also where it sees extreme unreasonableness; 'if a decision on a competent matter is so unreasonable that no reasonable authority could ever have come to it, then the courts can interfere'. If the second interpretation is correct, the court can oversee the range of factors which the decision-maker must take into consideration or must not consider – e.g., he should not take into account wholly irrelevant questions, such as a school-teacher's red hair – but must stop short either of dictating the weight to be given to the various factors or of evaluating the final decision. The difference between these two approaches is well illustrated by the judgment of Lord Diplock in *Bromley London Borough Council v Greater London Council.*[5]

We might compare the operation of the *Wednesbury* test to a circle whose boundaries it is the court's duty to patrol. Provided the decision-maker does not put a toe outside the circle, he is protected from judicial review. In modern terminology, influenced by the vocabulary of the European Court of Human Rights, this magic circle has come to be called 'the decision-maker's margin of appreciation'. The judge, who cannot review the merits of a decision, retains less discretion than if he possessed an independent power of evaluation. Yet this distinction is not really so clear as it seems. As the court sets the boundaries, it can in practice adjust them virtually at will by adding or subtracting factors which the decision-maker should have considered or not considered. A striking example of the way in which this can be done is the *Burmah Oil* case,[6] where the House of Lords used its power to delimit the circle effectively to dictate the way in which prerogative powers could be used.

Lord Greene was in his time regarded as a 'highly conservative judge who took a most restricted view of the judicial function'. He was a 'literalist' or 'formalist' who maintained the inherently apolitical or neutral character of judicial decision-making.[7] That his inclinations were conservative is indicated by a famous lecture on 'The Judicial Office' delivered in 1938[8] in the course of which he said:

> Although there may be said to be certain broad considerations as to which there can be no real dispute amongst reasonable men, the conception of public interest may very well be bound up with questions of policy; and whether or not a particular policy is or is not in the public interest is a highly controversial one. It is a question which the Legislature can readily decide by reference to a vote in Parliament, for the course which the majority desire must, for the time being at any rate, be regarded as being in the public interest. But in a country where Parliamentary Government prevails the

5  [1983] 1 AC 768; below, p. 47.
6  Above, p 48.
7  J. Griffith, *Judicial Politics since 1920* (Oxford: Blackwell) 1992, pp. 51-57.
8  *The Judicial Office* (Birmingham: Holdsworth Society) 1938.

party in opposition one day may be the party in power the next; and how can a Court in these circumstances decide with any feeling of certainty what is in the national interest?

It may be said in answer to this criticism that the existence of rules relating to public policy which the Courts have elaborated in the past and still follow shows that the matter of national interest may be suitable for judicial consideration. But this analogy really proves the point. The consideration of 'public policy' is in truth an excrescence on the law. Its existence has been deplored; its extension has been prohibited; and few people would nowadays be found to deny the proposition that it is appropriate for the Legislature and not the judiciary to determine whether or not a particular course ought to be taken as being in the national interest or a particular act prohibited as being against public policy.

Griffith, however, sees Greene's position as a subtle one, deriving from his highly individual perspective on the allocation of functions in democratic societies:[9]

> Greene's special vision is to see the three constitutional institutions as being the elements of one machine serving a single purpose. The separateness of the judiciary is functional, not part of some system of checks and balances. He does not see the judiciary as having the duty to impose its own standards of behaviour on the executive. Greene's corporatism depends not on conscious collusion between the three elements but on their mutual recognition of the single purpose they serve. If we seek to define this purpose we shall get no nearer than saying it is the continuation of the government of the country along the lines already laid down, though extended over the years. The purpose is conservative and evolutionary, maintaining the basic structure of society and the relationship between classes within the economy. Ministers of the Crown, Parliamentarians and judges have distinct functions within the one machine but all work together towards a common end. Like all forms of corporatism the image is somewhat alarming.

Alarming or not, the position strangely echoes Griffith's own. Griffith has argued that draftsmen should be instructed to include in new legislation express provisions as to justiciability, bearing in mind that matters within the area of policy and politics are 'appropriate for politicians and not judges'. With a view to confining the ambit of judicial review, Griffith has demanded 'more positive, black-letter provision by statute which will define where the balance of public interest lies both in those situations where conflict is obvious . . . and where it is much less obvious but no less real'. While agreeing that public authorities must abide by rules of procedure laid down 'by or under statute in accordance with natural justice', he also believes that review should be confined to cases where public authorities 'act *ultra vires* in the narrow sense [of exercising] powers not given them by statute' and hopes to confine review in other cases to extreme instances of corruption or bad faith. Griffith has urged, too, 'a form of words which will positively state the grounds on which judicial control may properly be exercised', a plea for the establishment of paramountcy once and for all by codification.[10] Finally, Loughlin categorises Griffith too as a legal positivist.[11]

Nearly 50 years after *Wednesbury*, Lord Irvine of Lairg, at the time Labour's shadow Lord Chancellor, found it expedient to re-affirm the true sense of the *Wednesbury* test.[12] He called it 'shorthand for that constitutional school of thought which advocates self-restraint in public law matters. Moreover, it is shorthand which the vast majority of lawyers would still acknowledge to be the guiding principle of our system of judicial review'. Basing himself on the traditional axiom that 'the court does not act as an appellate authority, but as a judicial authority concerned only with the issue of whether the public authority has contravened the law by acting in excess of the powers which Parliament has confided in it', Lord Greene had:

> outlined substantive principles of judicial review which truly reflect the constitutional basis which he ascribed to them. First that a decision-maker has a broad discretion as to the factors which are to be taken into account before a decision is made, a discretion which is only restricted if the governing statute clearly requires that a particular factor *must* be considered, or *must not* be considered. Second, the celebrated principle of *Wednesbury* unreasonableness, that once the decision-maker has properly determined the range of relevant considerations, the weight to be given to each consideration is a matter within its discretion and a decision will only be struck down as unreasonable where it is so unreasonable that no reasonable decision-maker could have made it.

To summarise the argument, the tripartite 'model of law' or 'balanced constitution' on which classic administrative law is founded, is too simplistic a tool for analysis of the modern administrative state. We have already seen that the state does not consist of a single 'executive' power vested in central government. The map of the state is much more complex. Nor – as the Donoughmore Committee was already forced to admit in 1932 – can its functions be neatly categorised as legislative, judicial and administrative in character.

## 5. The Skytrain affair

One celebrated decision, *Laker Airways Ltd v Department of Trade*[13] epitomises the problems which can arise out of the loose structure of modern government, in which corporatist and centralist tendencies tussle with the arrival on the administrative law map of the regulatory agency, typically endowed with a blend of rule-making, adjudicative and sometimes executive functions. The *Laker* case involved the state, but the state represented by successive governments of different political persuasions, and the Civil Aviation Authority (CAA), a semi-

---

10  See J Griffith, 'Constitutional and Administrative Law' in P. Archer and A. Martin (eds.), *More Law Reform Now: a Collection of Essays on Law Reform* (Chichester: Barry Rose) 1983, pp. 58-59.

11  M. Loughlin, *Public Law*, p. 198.

12  Lord Irvine of Lairg QC, 'Judges and Decision-makers: The Theory and Practice of *Wednesbury* Review' [1996] PL 59, 63.

13  [1977] QB 643.

autonomous agency with ill-defined functions. According to Baldwin, the Court of Appeal conceived of the CAA:[14]

> as a traditional body with 'quasi-judicial' functions. They saw it as a court giving licences with rights to be protected by legal due process and as a judicial body deserving protection from executive interference. They failed to see the significance of the CAA as a new form of multi-faceted agency of government, attempting to combine judicial and executive methods in a delicately balanced legal framework whilst acting in a politically contentious area.

On the other side, the 'individual' is represented by Laker Airways. On the side-lines stand other international corporations, a state-owned enterprise (British Airways) and the United States Government – precisely the corporatist configuration which Reich (above, p. 13) deplored.

The case concerned the grant, followed by the withdrawal, of a licence to run a trans-Atlantic passenger service (Skytrain) in competition with other designated airlines. Ironically, this valuable licence represents an example of the 'new property' which Reich in the 1960s urged courts to protect, while at the same time providing a sign-post to an emergent contract-orientated public law. In 1979, Daintith noted[15] growing reliance by government on common law powers of contract, which he described as a 'new prerogative'. The 'arbitrary' character of these powers derived from the fact that 'the common law does not impose, either in general or on the Crown in particular, any constraint in the choice of contractual partners, and is prepared to offer its aid in the enforcement of almost any contractual terms'. Daintith went on to distinguish[16] two techniques available to government for the achievement of policy goals: on the one hand, 'the command of law, backed in the last resort by force'; on the other, 'the possession of wealth, carrying with it the promise of benefit for those who do'. Daintith chose the term *imperium* for the former attributes of sovereignty, *dominium* for the latter. Law-making and regulation fall into the first category; contract heads the second; franchising, as we shall see in Chapter 11, may blend the two modalities. The *Laker* case shows how government can skilfully blend imperium and dominium, using them to play the games of modern corporatism.

The case also raised important questions concerning the allocation of functions. We have seen Ganz argue that courts should follow the intention of Parliament in this matter; the truth is, however, that Parliament frequently fails to make its intentions clear. This particular case was very complex. The background to the disputed legislation, the Civil Aviation Act 1971, was one of continuous disagreement.[17] Before 1971, licensing was carried out by the Air Transport

---

14   G. Baldwin, 'A British Independent Regulatory Agency and the "Skytrain" Decision' [1978] PL 57, 79-80.

15   T. Daintith, 'Regulation by Contract: The New Prerogative' [1979] Current Legal Problems 41, 42.

16   T. Daintith, 'The Executive Power Today' in J. Jowell and D. Oliver (eds.), *The Changing Constitution* (Oxford: Clarendon) 2nd edn., 1987, p. 197.

17   See for details R. Baldwin, *Regulating the Airlines: Administrative Justice and Agency Discretion* (Oxford: Clarendon) 1985.

Licensing Board (ATLB) with right of appeal to the Minister. The question of possible reform was originally referred to a Select Committee (the Edwards Committee) which recommended delegation of licensing to an *independent* body.[18] This would have pleased the independent airlines, which felt that they did not get a fair deal from a government department. But the Board of Trade was convinced that the Minister must retain a firm grip on policy if international obligations were to be carried out and the national interest protected. His overall control must extend to licensing. So the 1971 Act was, like its predecessor of 1960, an uneasy compromise.

The 1971 Act established the CAA, which was responsible (inter alia) for licensing. Section 3(1) set out statutory policy objectives for the CAA. Section 3(2) allowed the Minister to issue 'guidance' to the CAA in the performance of its functions, while s. 4 allowed him to give express 'directions' in certain cases, specified by the section. Why did the draftsman distinguish 'guidance' from 'directions'? Does the ministerial power to give guidance in s. 3(2) prevail over the statutory criteria in s. 3(1) or vice versa? The sections are silent on these crucial questions.

> 3.(1) It shall be the duty of the Authority to perform the functions conferred on it . . . in the manner which it considers is best calculated—(a) to secure that British airlines provide air transport services which satisfy all substantial categories of public demand (so far as British airlines may reasonably be expected to provide such services) at the lowest charges consistent with a high standard of safety in operating the services and an economic return to efficient operators on the sums invested in providing the services and with securing the sound development of the civil air transport industry of the United Kingdom; (b) to secure that at least one major British airline which is not controlled by the British Airways Board has opportunities to participate in providing, on charter and other terms, the air transport services mentioned in the preceding paragraph . . .
>
> (2) Subject to the following subsection, the Secretary of State may from time to time, after consultation with the Authority give guidance to the Authority in writing with respect to the performance of the functions conferred on it . . . ; and it shall be the duty of the Authority to perform those functions in such a manner as it considers is in accordance with the guidance . . .
>
> (3) No guidance shall be given to the Authority in pursuance of the preceding subsection unless a draft of the document containing it has been approved by a resolution of each House of Parliament.
>
> 4. . . . (3) The Secretary of State may, after consultation with the Authority, give to the Authority directions to do a particular thing which it has power to do or refrain from doing a particular thing if the Secretary of State considers it appropriate to give such directions—(a) in the interests of national security; or (b) in connection with any matter appearing to the Secretary of State to affect the relations of the United Kingdom with a country or territory outside the United Kingdom; or (c) in order to discharge or facilitate the discharge of an obligation binding on the United Kingdom by virtue of its being a member of an international organisation or a party to an international agreement; . . . and in so far as any directions given in pursuance of this subsection conflict with the requirements of any provision of this Act except subsections (1) and (2) of this section those requirements shall be disregarded.

18   Cmnd. 4018 (1969).

Early in 1972 the Minister issued his first guidance under the 1971 Act. Later in the year Laker applied for a licence to run a Skytrain service to the United States, in competition with British Airways and British Caledonian. After a hearing at which all three parties were represented, a licence was granted and upheld on appeal by the Minister. Laker now needed 'designation' as a carrier on the Atlantic route. The British Government 'designated' Laker and requested ratification by the US Government. A hearing was held by an administrative judge after which the US Civil Aeronautics Board (CAB) recommended the issue of a 'foreign air carrier permit'. This recommendation was never ratified by the President. In January 1975, the CAA refused an application by British Airways to revoke the licence. But in Britain, the Government had changed. A Labour Minister told the House of Commons that the Skytrain service could not be allowed to start. The British Government now refused to 'designate' Laker as a permitted carrier. Consequently, the CAB withdrew its unratified US permit. In the litigation which followed, the Government claimed that the power to 'designate' was a prerogative power.

The Minister issued new guidance, duly approved in terms of s. 3(3). The relevant paragraphs read:

> Para. 7: In the case of long-haul scheduled services . . . the Authority should not . . . license more than one British airline to serve the same route . . . The Authority should review existing licences and exemptions in the light of this paragraph and take appropriate action . . .
>
> Para. 8: Nothing in paragraph 7 should, however, prevent the licensing of: . . . (b) . . . another British airline to provide a scheduled service within British Airways' sphere of interest . . . provided British Airways has given its consent . . .

When the case was referred to the Court of Appeal, the court granted declarations that the guidance was ultra vires:[19]

> *Lord Denning MR*: In carrying out its functions (including granting of licences) the Authority has to do its best to satisfy [the] objectives in s.3.(1) . . . Those objectives are expressed in very general terms. In putting them into practice, Parliament thought that some guidance would be desirable for the Authority. So it provided for it in section 3(2) and (3) . . . One of the matters much discussed before us is the scope of the 'guidance' authorised by those provisions. In my opinion the Secretary of State can give guidance by way of explanation or amplification of, or supplement to, the general objectives: but not so as to reverse or contradict them . . .
>
> Section 4 of the statute confers exceptional powers on the Secretary of State. It enables him to override the statutory requirements as to licences and also to by-pass the general objectives. But only in carefully defined circumstances . . . Section 4(3) confers large powers in respect of international relations. For instance, if the Secretary of State thought that one of our airlines was acting in such a way as to affect our relations with another country, he could direct the Authority to revoke its licence. Or if diplomatic pressure was brought for the purpose, he could direct the revocation of the licence. And he could do this without any inquiry or hearing at all. The Secretary of State would have to consult the Authority before issuing a direction, but that is all.

19  [1977] 2 WLR 234 at 242-251.

Once he gave a direction, it could not be challenged in the courts. The only way would be by a question in the House . . .

The word 'direction' in section 4 is in stark contrast with the word 'guidance' in section 3 . . . It denotes an order or command which must be obeyed, even though it may be contrary to the general objectives and provisions of the statute. But the word 'guidance' in section 3 does not denote an order or command. It cannot be used so as to reverse or contradict the general objectives or provisions of the Statute. It can only be used so as to explain, amplify or supplement them. So long as the 'guidance' given by the Secretary of State keeps within the due bounds of guidance, the Authority is under a duty to follow his guidance. Even so, the Authority is allowed some degree of flexibility. It is to perform its function 'in such a manner as it considers is in accordance with the guidance'. So, while it is obliged to follow the guidance, the manner of doing so is for the Authority itself. But if the Secretary of State goes beyond the bounds of 'guidance' he exceeds his powers: and the Authority is under no obligation to obey him . . .

*Ultra vires . . .*
The new policy guidance of 1976 cuts right across [the] statutory objectives. It lays down a new policy altogether. Whereas the statutory objectives made it clear that the British Airways Board was not to have a monopoly, but that at least one other British airline should have an opportunity to participate, the new policy guidance says that the British Airways Board is to have a monopoly. No competition is to be allowed. And no other British airline is to be licensed unless British Airways had given its consent. This guidance was not a mere temporary measure. It was to last for a considerable period of years.

Those provisions disclose so complete a reversal of policy that to my mind the White Paper cannot be regarded as giving 'guidance' at all. In marching terms it does not say 'right incline' or 'left incline'. It says 'right about turn'. That is not guidance, but the reverse of it.

There is no doubt that the Secretary of State acted with the best of motives in formulating this new policy – and it may well have been the right policy – but I am afraid that he went about it in the wrong way. Seeing that the old policy had been laid down in an Act of Parliament, then, in order to reverse it, he should have introduced an amending bill and got Parliament to sanction it. He was advised, apparently, that it was not necessary, and that it could be done by 'guidance'. That, I think was a mistake . . . It was in this respect ultra vires . . .

*Prerogative*
The Attorney-General contended that the power of the Secretary of State 'to withdraw' the designation was a prerogative power which could not be examined in the courts. It was a power arising under a treaty which, he said, was outside the cognizance of the courts. The Attorney-General recognised that by withdrawing the designation, the Secretary of State would put a stop to Skytrain, but he said that he could do it all the same. No matter that Laker Airways had expended £6 million to £7 million on the faith of the designation, the Secretary of State could withdraw it without paying a penny compensation . . .

The prerogative is a discretionary power exercisable by the executive government for the public good, in certain spheres of governmental activity for which the law has made no provision, such as the war prerogative (of requisitioning property for the defence of the realm), or the treaty prerogative (of making treaties with foreign powers). The law does not interfere with the proper exercise of the discretion by the executive in those situations: but it can set limits by defining the bounds of the activity:

and it can intervene if the discretion is exercised improperly or mistakenly. That is a fundamental principle of our constitution . . .

[Holding that the court could review the exercise of the prerogative powers, Lord Denning continued:]

It is necessary to see just how far Skytrain had got . . . The one thing that remained was for the President to sign the United States of America permit: but this was little more than a formality, seeing that the President was under a treaty obligation to sign it 'without undue delay' . . . The question is: Was it proper for the Secretary of State at that stage to stop it himself? Could he do it by withdrawing the designation . . . ?

In answering this question, it is important to notice that if there was a proper case for stopping Skytrain, there were available some perfectly good means of doing it. They were already provided by the Statute. One particular means was provided by section 4 of the Act. Under that section the Secretary of State could himself get the licence revoked. He could direct the Civil Aviation Authority to revoke it and they would have to obey . . . But in this case the Secretary of State did not give any direction under section 4. So, presumably, the circumstances did not exist to permit him to do so. Another means of stopping Skytrain would be for the British Airways Board to apply again to the Civil Aviation Authority asking for the licence to be revoked – for instance, on the ground that traffic would be diverted from them. But in that case there would have to be a fresh inquiry. There would have to be a hearing at which Laker Airways could state their case. An independent and expert body would make the decision.

Seeing then that those statutory means were available for stopping Skytrain if there was a proper case for it, the question is whether the Secretary of State can stop it by . . . withdrawing the designation? Can he do indirectly that which he cannot do directly? Can he displace the statute by invoking a prerogative? If he could do this, it would mean that, by a side wind, Laker Airways Ltd. would be deprived of the protection which the statute affords them. There would be no inquiry, no hearing, no safeguard against injustice. The Secretary of State could do it off his own head – by withdrawing the designation without a word to anyone. To my mind such a procedure was never contemplated by the statute. The Secretary of State was mistaken in thinking that he could do it . . . He misdirected himself as to his powers. And it is well established law that, if a discretionary power is exercised under the influence of a misdirection, it is not properly exercised, and the court can say so.

Arguably, the government made a tactical error in choosing to rely on prerogative powers. On the authority of an earlier case, *A-G v De Keyser's Royal Hotel*,[20] Lawton and Ormrod LJJ thought that the prerogative was superseded by statute. Lord Denning MR preferred the view that the court can review the exercise of prerogative powers, opening the way for such review[1] We have already suggested that it may be undesirable for the Government to possess residual powers of this type, uncontrolled by courts, whose extent is unknown.[2] Here Baldwin argues that the power is essential:[3]

20  Above, p. 48.
1  See *Gouriet v Union of Postal Workers* [1978] AC 435; *Council of Civil Service Unions v Minister for the Civil Service* [1985] AC 374 (the 'GCHQ case'; below, p. 113).
2  Wade, *Constitutional Fundamentals* (London: Sweet and Maxwell) 1980, pp. 43-47, argued that the power to designate was not a prerogative power but 'merely a piece of administrative action on the international plane'. The cancellation was therefore, in his view, ultra vires.
3  [1978] PL 57 at 80.

The argument that the prerogative could not be used to withdraw designation because of the existence of the licensing system and the description of the use of the prerogative as a 'side wind' seems wrongly to have assumed that the CAA was set up to control a licensing system which included all matters relating to designation and traffic rights. Civil aviation licensing has always operated in parallel to designation but always separately. The Government has always controlled designation and the possession of a licence has never been seen as a guarantee of designation. The idea that Laker had a valuable commodity in their licence wrongly assumed both that licensing gave a right and that it was conclusive of that right. It failed to recognise that the gaining and allocation of traffic rights is a complex system of regulation in itself. The prerogative to designate allowed the Government to engage in international bargaining concerning traffic rights, it was not merely a device used to interfere with CAA's licensing decisions. The Government may well have had excellent reasons for thinking that designation of Laker would adversely affect the British position in any renegotiation of the Bermuda Agreement.

The 'system of balance' was changed by the Civil Aviation Act 1980, which abolished guidance. The primary objective of the CAA is now that set out in s. 3(1)(a) of the 1971 Act, and a new section, s. 23(1)(a), provided that the Authority shall have regard 'to any advice received from the Secretary of State with respect to the likely outcome of negotiations with the government of any other country or territory for the purpose of securing any right required for the operation by a British airline of' any transport services outside the United Kingdom. Now Baldwin argued:[4]

> The CAA like other agencies is subject to government control . . . its expensive operation and its powers of judgement only have value within the governmental system in so far as the government in power respects the CAA's spheres of decision and policy-making. The contribution of the policy guidance system lay in insulating the CAA to some extent from the more disruptive forms of government interference – by appeals, traffic rights negotiations or other more clandestine methods of control. The abolition of guidance has, as a result, left the CAA exposed. The CAA's worth as a regulatory agency now depends upon little more than the restraint of Ministers. Past experience is not reassuring.

This case study nicely exposes Ganz's points over allocation of functions. Baldwin argued that the Minister was intended to control the licensing function directly or indirectly; Lord Denning believed that 'an independent and expert body' should make the decision. What evidence is available to courts in deciding this difficult point? Since the decision in *Pepper v Hart*,[5] they are able to turn to Hansard for help in cases of ambiguity; in 1971, however, this would not have been possible. Ganz also argued (above) that the value-judgments made in given situations depend on the choice of decision-maker. This emerges clearly from

---

4    R. Baldwin, 'Civil Aviation Regulation: From Tribunal to Regulatory Agency' in R. Baldwin and C. McCrudden (eds.), *Regulation and Public Law* (London: Weidenfeld and Nicolson) 1987, p. 176.

5    [1993] AC 593; noted in D. Oliver, '*Pepper v Hart*: a Suitable Case for Reference to *Hansard*?' [1993] PL 5.

*Laker*, where the procedural values of lawyers conflicted with the policy judgments of Ministers.

In this chapter we have seen the procedural emphasis of the Diceyan Rule of Law model described as old-fashioned, legalistic and inappropriate to modern administration. Here, Vile reminds us that procedures, too, reflect value-patterns:[6]

> Procedure, the rules governing behaviour, reflect certain value-patterns. The way in which things are done makes a very great difference. Men could be condemned to death, and in some countries are, by an administrative procedure. Roads could be built by a collegium determining by vote, after discussion, where every stroke of the pick should be made. The judicial method involving open discussion and an adversary procedure before a jury could be used to determine important questions of foreign policy and diplomacy. The results of allocating these tasks of government to be decided in this way would undoubtedly be disastrous. The present-day procedures in Britain and the United States, and the matters decided by them, have not been evolved by chance; they represent the collective judgment of centuries concerning the way in which certain things should be decided. This is not an argument against all innovation, but it should lead us to enquire into, and to examine the values which these procedures embody, and to look very closely at new procedures, and at the allocation of tasks to them, in order to be sure what we are doing.

If the arrangement of the last two chapters has suggested polarity, this is an over-simplification. The history of political ideas in Britain is peculiarly rich, the tradition of public law less so. It is none the less a plural tradition, even if this truth has sometimes been ignored, and it is this plurality of views which we have set out to explore. Even if we accept the description of post-war politics as a period of consensus, the clash of values which marked the Skytrain affair demonstrates how limited the consensus often was. Yet a measure of consensus did emerge, and that is the subject of the next chapter.

6   M. Vile, *Constitutionalism and Separation of Powers* (Oxford: Clarendon) 1967, p. 347.

# Chapter 4

# Forever amber?

## 1. Signposts

In 1946, Gower, a professed socialist, held out the prospect of a new age in which:

> the emphasis will change from private law to public law – from private contract to public regulation . . . the growth of Administrative Law in the Continental sense seems inevitable and the English lawyer will have to reconcile himself to something like that Droit Administratif which Dicey taught him to fear without understanding.[1]

In 1949, Keeton, a conservative professor, gloomily predicted the imminent demise of the common law[2] remarking of the Donoughmore Committee that in no important respect did it 'influence, much less delay, the onrush of administrative power, and the supercession of the ordinary forms of law which is today taking place'. He feared the imminence of people's courts, 'so far have we travelled in the past twenty years'. Yet Keeton himself warned the lawyers that their case was not infallible: 'It may well be that the administrator has as strong a case against [the lawyer] as he has against the administrator.' Schwarz and Wade[3] described administrative law in this period as being 'at its lowest ebb for perhaps a century. The leading cases made a dreary catalogue of abdication and error'. Blaming the 'lingering effect of the wartime spirit of abnegation and sacrifice',[4] they also diagnosed a failure of legal education.

Twenty-five years on, people's courts had emphatically not arrived; indeed, in the aftermath of the Franks Committee on Tribunals and Inquiries (below, Chapter 14), the balance of power had tilted sharply back in favour of the 'ordinary' courts. There was now widespread concern for the quality of administrative adjudication – in Street's phrase,[5] 'justice in the welfare state'. A humane administration, dedicated to a general welfare objective of social justice combining efficiency with fairness, became the goal for administrators and administrative lawyers alike. In 1974, Lord Scarman, reflecting on the still

---

1   L. Gower, 'The Future of the English Legal Profession' (1946) 9 MLR 211, 212-213.
2   G. Keeton, 'The Twilight of the Common Law' (1949) 45 Nineteenth Century and After 230. See, to the same effect, P. Devlin, 'The Common Law, Public Policy and the Executive' (1956) Current Legal Problems 1.
3   B. Schwarz and H. Wade, *Legal Control of Government, Administrative Law in Britain and the United States* (Oxford: Clarendon) 1972, p. 320. (Hereafter Schwarz and Wade.)
4   Ibid, p. 320.
5   H. Street, *Justice in the Welfare State* (London: Stevens) 1968.

imminent demise of the common law,[6] felt able to advise lawyers that the remedy lay entirely in their own hands; if they were more imaginative in their approach to developing areas like welfare law, the power of the common law could be renewed. And Schwarz and Wade were able to talk of a 'turn-round . . . brought about by discovering that Britain had in the past developed much more administrative law than the legal profession understood'.[7] When Yardley, like Wade, set control by courts in the centre of administrative law, he none the less defined its functions as 'the control of power, and the maintenance of a fair balance between the competing interests of the administration (central government, local government or specialised agencies) and the citizen'.[8] In short, as Bradley in 1981[9] was deploring the polarisation of public law and exhorting public lawyers to occupy the middle ground, the middle ground was in fact already densely populated.

This notion of consensus in administrative law does not imply, in Fukuyama's[10] well-known phrase, 'the end of history'. Quite the reverse. What constitutes the middle ground is liable to vary in the light of changing fashions. First, the rubric itself provides ample scope for dispute over key values and value-judgments. As we shall see, distinctive approaches to our discipline would continue to emerge and to jostle for recognition. Second, we have here to bear in mind the major breakdown in political consensus in the years following the 1979 General Election. To anticipate the argument of the following chapter, one consequence of the re-ordering of the role of the state by the Conservatives, notably by a resort to and enhancement of market-style disciplines, has been to broaden and deepen the debate on an appropriate style of public law.

In 1958, Robson was able to observe broad political agreement on a need to protect the individual:[11]

> Politicians have at last become aware of the need to safeguard more effectively the individual citizen in his dealings with the state. Conservative opinion, which in the past had shown blind and unfailing confidence in the ability of the courts to establish and maintain a genuine system of administration according to law, has recently shown signs of distinct uneasiness at the difficulties which for various reasons often make it impossible to secure judicial review of executive action in the ordinary courts . . .
>
> The posture of the Labour Party has also changed. The party's commitment to central economic planning and regulation, the nationalisation of industry, a vast development of the social services, and the general policies of the Welfare State and Socialism, have predisposed Labour supporters to regard a strong executive armed with extensive discretionary powers as necessary for the realisation of their objectives. Neither the leaders nor the rank and file of the party had appreciated that the greater the powers which are given to public authorities, the more essential does it become to safeguard the citizen against their harsh or improper exercise.

6  Sir Leslie Scarman, *English Law – the New Dimension* (London: Stevens) 1974.
7  Schwarz and Wade, p. 321.
8  D. Yardley, *Principles of Administrative Law* (London: Butterworths) 1981, p. viii.
9  A. Bradley, (Book Review) (1981) 1 Legal Studies 329.
10  F. Fukuyama, *The End of History and the Last Man* (London: Hamish Hamilton) 1992.
11  W. Robson, 'Administrative Justice and Injustice: A Commentary on the Franks Report' [1958] PL 12, 130.

Here we find some important signposts to the strong development of administrative law which would gain impetus in the 1960s. From a contemporary perspective also, there are here some useful benchmarks to show how far we have since travelled.

First, consider from the left of the political spectrum Richard Crossman's famous Fabian pamphlet *Socialism and the New Despotism*, published in 1956. In Robson's[12] words, this represented 'the first glimmering sign of uneasiness' at the assumption prevalent among Labour politicians that political controls sufficed to protect the citizen (in our terminology, green light theory). Whereas one year earlier the socialist *New Statesman* magazine had contended that 'judicial review is the last doctrine that the Labour Party should champion', much of what Crossman wrote would have been acceptable to the late Lord Hewart.[13] According to Crossman:[14]

> The growth of a vast, centralised State bureaucracy constitutes a grave potential threat to social democracy. The idea that we are being disloyal to our Socialist principles if we attack its excesses or defend the individual against its incipient despotism is a fallacy . . . For the Socialist, as much as for the Liberal, the State Leviathan is a necessary evil; and the fact that part of the Civil Service now administers a Welfare State does not remove the threat to freedom which the twentieth-century concentration of power has produced . . .
>
> In Britain we are faced with the following dilemma. Since the abuses of oligopoly cannot be checked by free competition, the only way to enlarge freedom and achieve a full democracy is to subject the economy to public control. Yet the State bureaucracy itself is one of those concentrations of power which threaten our freedom. If we increase its authority still further, shall we not be endangering the liberties we are trying to defend? . . .
>
> Some of you may imagine that Ministers are already responsible to Parliament. In fact that responsibility is rapidly becoming a constitutional fiction . . . To restore Parliamentary control of the Executive, however, is not sufficient for our Socialist purpose of liberating the community from the abuse of arbitrary power. The next step will be to reform the Judiciary, so that it can regain its traditional function of defending individual rights against encroachment. That function has been steadily narrowed for the last hundred years, as small-scale capitalism has been transformed into oligopoly and the flimsy structure of the Victorian state has developed into the Leviathan which now dominates our lives . . .
>
> What is required is nothing less than a new statement of what we mean by personal freedom and how we should safeguard it under socialism . . .

Such ideas gained practical sustenance the following year in a Labour Party Policy Statement and a Fabian Research Study tellingly entitled respectively, *Personal Freedom* and *Justice and the Administration*. Particular emphasis was placed on a need to 'clean up' the formal system of administrative adjudication (a project on which, contemporaneously, the famous Franks Committee on Tribunals and Inquiries was engaged):

12  W. Robson [1958] PL at 13.
13  *New Statesman*, 1 January 1955; W. Robson [1958] PL at 13.
14  R. Crossman, *Socialism and the New Despotism* (Fabian Tract No. 298) 1956, pp. 6, 12, 18-20.

The Labour Movement has always recognised that the freedom of individuals is unreal and stunted unless the community accepts the responsibility of providing a system of social security and improved conditions of housing. Labour's attack on inequality and its efforts to plan the economy and the use of land in the public interest have likewise been aimed at the enlargement of personal freedom . . . But these very measures have at the same time brought with them elements of restraint and restriction on freedom, new concentrations of power, and the exercise of judicial power by bodies outside the ordinary courts of law – in other words, the danger of a 'new despotism'. The Labour Party's Policy Statement *Personal Freedom* has recognised that one of the great problems of the age is how to reconcile the rights of individuals with the social needs and claims of a community . . .

Much of the criticism levelled against [administrative tribunals] is justified. Many of them are appointed by government departments, some refuse parties the right to legal representation, reasons for their decisions are not always given, and provisions for appeal are unsatisfactory . . . Substantial reform . . . is necessary if these tribunals are all to be recognised as both performing a vital function in society and also providing adequate safeguards for individuals . . .[15]

From the other side of the line came a critical pamphlet from a group of Conservative practitioners and academics. *The Rule of Law*,[16] published in 1955, was a prospectus for major law reform, centred on the idea of an Administrative Division of the High Court. Briefly, there would be a right of appeal against administrative decisions to this court, which, inter alia: (1) would be able to decide all questions of law, ouster clauses (above, p. 52) notwithstanding; (2) would be empowered to call for a statement of the facts and reasons upon which the administrative decision was based; (3) would determine whether there was any evidence on which the decision could reasonably have been based, notwithstanding the subjective statutory formula 'if the minister is satisfied' (see below); and (4) would extend the principles of natural justice to all administrative decisions. If the growth of administrative adjudication could not be stopped or the jurisdiction absorbed by the ordinary courts, then *The Rule of Law* well illustrates the increasing acceptance by conservative opinion that it should be made the object of judicial supervision, so as to guarantee development in harmony with common law principles.[17] In later chapters we shall see, first, that in the short term this prospectus was instrumental in the setting up of the Franks Committee; and, second, that in the longer term its essential elements have come to be incorporated in our system of judicial review.

Although de Smith could question whether the balance was being struck too far against the administration,[18] there could be no doubting the pamphlet's 'amber' tinge. The authors described their object as being 'to reconcile freedom and

---

15  G. Borrie, *Justice and the Administration* (Fabian Research Pamphlet No. 185) 1957, pp. 1, 9.

16  *The Rule of Law* (Inns of Court Conservative and Unionist Society), pp. 48-57. The 'cleaning-up' of administrative tribunals was also stressed.

17  The various solutions proposed by conservatives to the challenge of tribunals are represented in C. Allen, *Law and Orders* (London: Stevens) 1945; C. Hamson, *Executive Discretion: an Aspect of the French Conseil d'Etat* (London: Stevens) 1954; and E. Iwi, *Laws and Flaws* (London: Odhams Press) 1956.

18  S. de Smith, 'A Conservative Approach to Administrative Law Reform' (1955) 2 British J. Admin. Law 5.

justice for the private citizen with the necessities of a modern government charged with the promotion of far-ranging social or economic policy. We firmly believe that such a reconciliation can be brought about'.[19]

The traditional emphasis of English administrative law on redress of grievance, more especially for individuals, was reinforced in 1961 by an influential report, *The Citizen and the Administration*, drawn up by JUSTICE, a pressure group of lawyers dedicated, according to its constitution, to the 'preservation of the fundamental liberties of the individual'. In the preface, Lord Shawcross (a former Labour Attorney-General) pursued the by now familiar theme that the extension of administrative discretion necessitated greater protection for the citizen. Stressing that, with the growth of the state, 'large areas of discretion are created in regard to all sorts of matters affecting the lives and rights of ordinary people', he coined the famous phrase: 'The little farmer, with four acres and a cow, would never have attempted to force the battlements of Crichel Down'.[20]

The Report pursued two lines of reform. First, the principle of impartial adjudication should be extended to cover those many discretionary decisions subject at most to informal (internal) techniques of review. In addition to new specialist tribunals, there should be a general tribunal to deal with miscellaneous appeals from discretionary decisions. This, we will find, is an idea which has often been proposed but which government has steadfastly refused to countenance. Second, JUSTICE demanded that the institution of the Ombudsman should (with modification) be imported from Sweden to plug the gap in citizen protection left by the traditional controls and deal with complaints of maladministration.

In the same period that judicial review was at its 'lowest ebb', a few extra-judicial writings were beginning to suggest – as Lord Scarman would later assert – that the common lawyers could and should do better. The flavour of *Protection From Power*,[1] a series of lectures delivered by Lord MacDermott, may be gleaned from the title. The author was concerned with those concentrations or regions of power which, by 'their weight or their nature, conduce to the oppression of the individual'.[2] A famous passage from Sir Alfred Denning's *Freedom Under The Law*[3] pinpoints a need for the thorough overhaul or modernisation of the machinery of judicial review:[4]

> Our procedure for preventing the abuse of power is not [efficient]. Just as the pick and shovel is no longer suitable for the winning of coal, so also the procedure of mandamus, certiorari, and actions on the case are not suitable for the winning of freedom in the new age. They must be replaced by new and up to date machinery . . . Of all the great tasks that lie ahead, this is the greatest. Properly exercised the new powers of the executive lead to the welfare state: but abused they lead to the totalitarian state. None such must ever be allowed in this country . . . Let us prove ourselves equal to the challenge.

19 *The Rule of Law*, pp. 11-12.
20 JUSTICE, *The Citizen and the Administration* (1961), p. xiii.
 1 Lord MacDermott, *Protection from Power Under English Law* (London: Stevens) 1957.
 2 Ibid, p. 4.
 3 Sir Alfred Denning, *Freedom Under The Law* (London: Stevens) 1949.
 4 Ibid, p. 126. For an example of what Denning had in mind, see *Pyx Granite Co Ltd v Minister of Housing and Local Government* [1958] 1 QB 554, CA.

Modernisation of judicial review procedure was an enterprise only begun in earnest some 20 years later. Reform through the case law foreshadowed a more complete study by the Law Commission, resulting in important reforms to judicial review procedure implemented in 1978. These developments are fully dealt with in Chapter 16.

It is, however, common currency that in the 1960s judicial review entered on a period of expansion and innovation. A series of cases – *Ridge v Baldwin*,[5] *Padfield*,[6] *Conway v Rimmer*[7] and *Anisminic*[8] – is seen to have laid the foundations for a development of judicial review which not only continues but has in recent years appeared to gather pace. The reasons for the change in mood are naturally contestable. Some see the Tribunals and Inquiries Act 1958 which followed the significant Franks Report (below) as helping to smooth the path of judicial activism; others emphasise key changes in judicial personnel, focusing particularly on the appointment of Lord Reid in the House of Lords and Denning LJ to the Court of Appeal; the return of a Labour government in 1964; social, cultural and educational changes associated with 'the swinging sixties'; and, more profoundly, on the continued development and increased complexity of state forms and administrative powers outlined in Chapter 1 and mentioned by Crossman.[9] Whatever the reason, the mood changed decisively.

## 2. The battle against discretion

There is a latent ambiguity in the word 'arbitrary' which implies a hint of the capricious or despotic, even though it may mean merely a decision which is not bound by rules. In other words, discretion and arbitrariness may easily be conflated, a confusion traceable to the writings of Dicey. To put this differently again, discretion (the power of choice) may be confused with unreasonable or capricious choices (arbitrariness). It is in fact the overlap between the two meanings in the celebrated *Wednesbury* test[10] which gives rise to the question whether it comprises one or two rules. You will see the same shift of emphasis in Wade's definition,[11] where he admits that not all abuses of power 'carry an innuendo of malice or bad faith; they are simply a characteristic of a state governed by rules'. This slippage suggests that abuse and misuse of power are one and the same thing, inadmissible to those unable to accept that an abuse of power is an exercise of discretion at all.[12]

K. C. Davis opened his celebrated book, *Discretionary Justice*, first published in 1969,[13] by dissociating himself from 'the extravagant version of the Rule of

---

5  [1964] AC 40; below, p. 500.
6  [1968] 2 WLR 921; below, p. 98.
7  [1968] AC 910; below, p. 108.
8  [1969] 2 WLR 163; above, p. 54.
9  Above, p. 93.
10  Above, p. 79.
11  Above, p. 37.
12  D. Feldman, 'Discretions, choices and values' [1994] PL 279, 291.
13  *Discretionary Justice* (Westport, Connecticut: Greenwood Press) 1969.

Law'.[14] His concern was not particularly with the legitimacy of judicial decision-making. Rather he saw the Diceyan paradigm as too court-orientated and the control which it purported to exercise as both indiscriminate and too limited. It operated on the surface, 'pushing bricks on the nice part of the house'. Like Griffith after the Franks Report,[15] Davis was troubled that administrative lawyers were studying only areas of administrative activity which were already relatively open and controlled. Davis was concerned with opening windows on to arbitrariness which, he believed, thrived in darkness:[16]

> If we stay within the comfortable areas where jurisprudence scholars work and concern ourselves mostly with statutory and judge-made law, we can at best accomplish no more than to refine what is already tolerably good. To do more than that we have to open our eyes to the reality that justice to individual parties is administered more outside courts than in them, and we have to penetrate the unpleasant areas of discretionary determinations by police and prosecutors and other administrators, where huge concentrations of injustice invite drastic reforms.

As Davis's work became better known in the United Kingdom, this aspect of his critique of traditional administrative law struck a chord. Davis's new theories provided a valuable stimulus for work on what had been peripheral areas of administrative law:[17] council housing, welfare law and prisons. The influence of this aspect of Davis's work has been immeasurable. In the first edition of this book, we included a study of parole procedure as introduced in Oregon, USA under the direct influence of Davis,[18] contrasting the secret and discretionary English parole process. Chapter 7 shows how far the system has today changed towards a model of accessible rules. Morgan, writing more generally about the prisons system, has remarked on the change from a secretive service operating through virtually untrammelled discretion to a system in which the prisons administration can begin to be held accountable through a framework of accessible rules and guidelines.[19] Welfare law also began to escape its Cinderella status during the 1970s. In bringing this previously neglected area inside the perimeters of administrative law, reformers again focused on rule-making as a technique for controlling the arbitrary operation of widely-dispersed administrative discretion in the hands of junior officials.

Of course, these developments are not solely attributable to the influence of Davis. One year before his book was published, the House of Lords moved to control ministerial discretionary power.

14  Ibid, pp. 27-28.
15  J. Griffith, 'Tribunals and Inquiries' (1959) 22 MLR 125.
16  *Discretionary Justice*, p. 215.
17  See the review by A. Bradley, 'Research and Reform in Administrative Law', (1979) 13 JSPTL (NS) 35; K. Hawkins, 'Using Legal Discretion' in K. Hawkins (ed.), *The Uses of Discretion* (Oxford: Clarendon) 1992, p. 17.
18  C. Harlow and R. Rawlings, *Law and Administration* (London: Weidenfeld and Nicolson) 1984, Ch. 5. And see I. Blalock, 'Justice and Parole: The Oregon Experience' in D. Fogel and J. Hudson (eds.), *Justice as Fairness: Perspectives on the Justice Model* (Cincinnati: Anderson Publishing) 1981.
19  R. Morgan, 'Prisons Accountability Revisited' [1994] PL 314. To measure the change, compare G. Zellick, 'The Prison Rules and the Courts' [1981] Crim. LR 602.

## Padfield v Minister of Agriculture, Fisheries and Food[20]

The Agricultural Marketing Act 1958 established the milk marketing scheme. Producers had to sell their product to the Milk Marketing Board, which periodically fixed prices on a regional basis. In case of dispute, s. 19 provided a formal procedure. The Minister had to establish a committee of investigation consisting of a chairman and four or five members. If he received a complaint either from the public or from the representative consumers' committee, it could, 'if the Minister in any case so directs', be referred to the committee of investigation. On receipt of the committee's report, the Minister could, 'if he thinks fit so to do after considering the report', revoke or amend the scheme. A dispute arose over the basis of prices in the South Eastern region, producers in that area complaining that an additional element in the price fixed for their milk was too low, since it did not adequately reflect increased costs in transporting milk from other regions. Since an increase paid to the complainants would be at the expense of other areas, the Board had declined to fix new prices. The Minister refused to refer the matter to the committee of investigation. His reasons were contained in a letter which stated that, if the complaint were upheld, the Minister would be expected to give effect to the committee's recommendations by laying a statutory order before Parliament. The appellant (a South Eastern region producer) sought mandamus to compel a reference. By a majority, the House of Lords issued the order:

> *Lord Reid*: The Minister is, I think, correct in saying that the board is an instrument for the self-government of the industry. So long as it does not act contrary to the public interest the Minister cannot interfere. But if it does act contrary to what both the committee of investigation and the Minister hold to be the public interest the Minister has a duty to act. And if a complaint relevantly alleges that the board has so acted, as this complaint does, then it appears to me that the Act does impose a duty on the Minister to have it investigated. If he does not do that he is rendering nugatory a safeguard provided by the Act and depriving complainers of a remedy which I am satisfied that Parliament intended them to have . . .
>
> If [the Minister's letter] means that he is entitled to refuse to refer a complaint because, if he did so, he might later find himself in an embarrassing situation, that would plainly be a bad reason. I can see an argument to the effect that if, on receipt of a complaint, the Minister can satisfy himself from information in his possession as to the merits of the complaint, and he then chooses to say that, whatever the committee might recommend, he would hold it to be contrary to the public interest to take any action, it would be a waste of time and money to refer the complaint to the committee. I do not intend to express any opinion about that because that is not this case. In the first place it appears that the Minister has come to no decision as to the merits of the appellants' case and, secondly, the Minister has carefully avoided saying what he would do if the committee were to uphold the complaint.
>
> It was argued that the Minister is not bound to give any reasons for refusing to refer a complaint to the committee, that if he gives no reasons his decision cannot be questioned, and that it would be very unfortunate if giving reasons were to put him in a worse position. But I do not agree that a decision cannot be questioned if no reasons are given. If it is the Minister's duty not to act so as to frustrate the policy and objects of the Act, and if it were to appear from all the circumstances of the case that that has

been the effect of the Minister's refusal, then it appears to me that the court must be entitled to act.

*Lord Morris (dissenting)*: The language here is, in my view, purely permissive. The Minister is endowed with discretionary powers. If he did decide to refer a complaint he is endowed with further discretionary powers after receiving a report . . .

I cannot, therefore, accept the contention of the appellants that they had a right to have their complaint referred to the committee and that the Minister had a positive duty to refer it. The Minister, in my view, had a discretion. It was urged on behalf of the respondent that his discretion was in one sense an unfettered one, though it was not said that he could disregard the complaint. The case proceeded on an acceptance by the respondent that he was bound to consider the complaint and then, in the exercise of his judgment, to decide whether or not to refer it to the committee.

If the respondent proceeded properly to exercise his judgment then, in my view, it is no part of the duty of any court to act as a Court of Appeal from his decision or to express any opinion as to whether it was wise or unwise . . . A court could make an order if it were shown (a) that the Minister failed or refused to apply his mind to or to consider the question whether to refer a complaint or (b) that he misinterpreted the law or proceeded on an erroneous view of the law or (c) that he based his decision on some wholly extraneous consideration or (d) that he failed to have regard to matters which he should have taken into account . . .

Lord Morris then examined the evidence and decided that these criteria were not met. He therefore favoured dismissing the appeal.

The final remarks of Lord Reid can be construed as imposing what American administrative law calls the 'no-evidence' rule, which allows the court to examine the decision and, in the absence of any evidence to support the Minister's conclusions, to make its own deductions: in shorthand, no evidence is deemed to equal bad evidence.[1] In time this would be taken further, permitting the court to make its own evaluation of the weight of evidence before the decision-maker,[2] a development ostensibly precluded by the *Wednesbury* rule.[3] In Chapter 15, we will see this control gradually expanded, as the courts inch towards a requirement of reasons for all administrative decisions while never yet going so far as to impose a general duty.[4] On the other hand, Lord Reid was careful in *Padfield* to reserve policy-making for the Minister; in other words, his judgment does not move far outside a traditional, separation of functions analysis:[5]

If the Minister directs that a complaint . . . shall be referred to the committee of investigation, that committee will make a report which must be published. If they report that any provision of this scheme or any act or omission of the board is contrary to the interests of the complainers *and* if not in the public interest, then the Minister is

---

1  For the present state of the law see, de Smith, Jowell, Woolf, para. 13-019. See also *Lonrho v Secretary of State for Trade and Industry* [1989] 1 WLR 525; *R v Secretary of State for the Home Department, ex p Fayed* [1997] 1 All ER 228; below, p. 527.
2  See particularly Lord Diplock's judgment in *Bromley London Borough Council v Greater London Council* [1982] 2 WLR 62.
3  Above, p. 79.
4  de Smith, Jowell, Woolf, paras. 9-039-9-060.
5  [1968] AC 997 at 1031.

empowered to take action, but not otherwise. He may disagree with the view of the committee as to public interest, and, if he thinks that there are other public interests which outweigh the public interest that justice should be done to the complainers, he would be not only entitled but bound to refuse to take action. Whether he takes action or not, he may be criticised and held accountable in Parliament but the court cannot interfere . . .

The decision also demonstrates the limitations of procedural review. After the decision, the Minister did refer the dispute to the committee of investigation, which duly recommended change. Immediately, the Minister explained to the House of Commons through a written answer that he would not be accepting the report.[6] There is another lesson contained here concerning the superiority of 'fire-watching' over 'fire-fighting' techniques. It is much harder to undo decisions retrospectively than to move to a structured decision through appropriate administrative procedures. We shall return to this point.

### 3. Rational decision-making

Administrative law was embarking on a quest for rational decision-making. Remember Lord Hewart's attack on 'administrative lawlessness' or discretionary administrative decision-making unstructured by procedure (above, p. 31). This contrasted with a picture of law as structured and rational. This dichotomy is too simple. Rules do not apply themselves; they are applied by human beings who inevitably feed in their own preferences and prejudices. On the other hand, if they are not to act arbitrarily and capriciously, administrators need to narrow down their choices when they take decisions by finding a way of 'avoiding distraction (or at least too much distraction) and focusing on the things that need attention at a given time'.[7] Simon based his model of 'bounded rationality', in which information-gathering is a prerequisite of rational decision-making on a maxim of 'No conclusions without premises'.

If we think back to the wording of the *Wednesbury* test,[8] we can see how it can fit within the terminology of rational decision-making. In other words, as even the Donoughmore Committee had to admit, the techniques used in judicial and administrative decision-making are not poles apart. There are, however, significant differences. While lawyers concentrate on procedures, policy analysts look for the causes and consequences of government action to see how it may be improved. Again, policy is dynamic. Rather than a single decision, policy-makers envisage decision-making as a flow-chart to which different actors and different answers have contributed along the line.[9] Lawyers, on the other hand, typically break the process of decision-making into a number of decisions, only one of

6    HC Deb., vol. 781, cols. 46-47 (WA, Mr. Cledwyn Hughes).
7    H. Simon, *Reason in Human Affairs* (Oxford: Blackwell) 1983, p. 21.
8    Above, p. 79.
9    See C. Ham and M. Hill, *The Policy Process in the Modern Capitalist State* (London: Wheatsheaf Books) 1984, p. 10; K. Hawkins, 'The Uses of Legal Discretion: Perspectives from Law and Social Science' in K. Hawkins (ed.), *The Uses of Discretion* (Oxford: Clarendon) 1992, pp. 41-43.

which may figure in a given adjudication. As Baldwin[10] argued after the *Skytrain* case,[11] by insisting on the intrusion of adjudicative procedures, courts break the flow of policy-making. Where social scientists would refer to policy or decision-making, lawyers are also likely to talk of discretion.

At this stage, we might query the ideal of rational decision-making as unrealistic. Hayek[12] once spoke, for example, of 'the fiction that all the relevant facts are known to some one mind, and that it is possible to construct from this knowledge of the particulars a desirable social order'. Moreover, the word 'desirable' here suggests a *value-judgment*, while 'reason' is seen by Simon[13] as a pathway to a goal; 'all reason can do is help us reach agreed-on goals more efficiently'. Rational choice is a *process* of 'selecting alternatives which are conducive to the achievement of previously selected goals' or 'the selection of the alternative which will maximise the decision-maker's values, the selection being made following a comprehensive analysis of alternatives and their consequences'. This is one reason why the case for rationality in administrative law typically manifests itself in a search for *processes and procedures* designed to furnish the premises on which decisions can be based. It is also a reason why 'process jurisprudence', as Americans call it,[14] tends to mimic positivism by denying substantive values.

## Discretion and rules

Davis's primary object was to harness the legal technique of rule-making inside administration to restructure administrative processes. Surprised by the inconsistency of decision-taking in the immigration services, Davis believed this could be easily rectified by the use of standardised forms. The forms would embody immigration department policies in the shape of rudimentary rules and would be used to check decision-making by junior officials who would tick boxes to indicate their reasons. Davis hoped that the rule-making process would bring policies into the open and allow citizens to participate in 'a miniature democratic process'. To summarise his aims, they were to open up the administrative process and to procure fairer, more consistent decisions.

Davis himself adopted a simple and pragmatic definition of discretion.[15] 'A public officer has discretion whenever the effective limits of his power leave him free to make a choice among possible courses of action and inaction.' In a famous metaphor, Dworkin added depth to this simple definition by pointing out that

---

10 R. Baldwin, 'Civil Aviation Regulation: From Tribunal to Regulatory Agency' in R. Baldwin and C. McCrudden (eds.), *Regulation and Public Law* (London: Weidenfeld and Nicolson) 1987, pp. 159-176.
11 Above, p. 86.
12 F. Hayek, *Law, Legislation and Liberty* (London: Routledge) vol. 1, 1973, p. 14. See also D. Galligan, *Discretionary Powers, A Legal Study of Official Discretion* (Oxford: Clarendon) 1990, p. 5.
13 *Reason in Human Affairs*, above, note 7, pp. 5, 77, 106.
14 See, N. Duxbury, 'Faith in Reason: The Process Tradition in American Jurisprudence' (1993) 15 Cardozo LR 601, 602: 'Process jurisprudence exemplifies the emergence of reason as the dominant ideological and theoretical motif in American legal thought.'
15 *Discretionary Justice*, p. 4.

discretion is not necessarily 'uncontrolled' or, in administrative law terminology, 'unfettered'. Discretion does imply choice, but the choice is seldom unlimited and must be evaluated in the context in which it arises:

> Discretion, like the hole in the doughnut, does not exist except as an area left open by a surrounding belt of restriction. It is therefore a relative concept. It always makes sense to ask, 'Discretion under which standards?' or 'Discretion as to which authority?'.[16]

Theorists trying to pin the butterfly to the specimen board were to waste much time trying for ever more nuanced meanings without ever reaching agreement over the core meaning of the word or improving on Dworkin.

## Discretion to rules: a spectrum

Davis never argued that discretion could or should be eliminated; it was simply one part of a decision-making process:[17]

> Even when rules can be written, discretion is often better. Rules without discretion cannot fully take into account the need for tailoring results to unique facts and circumstances of particular cases. The justification for discretion is often the need for individualized justice. This is so in the judicial process as well as in the administrative process.
>
> Every governmental and legal system in world history has involved both rules and discretion. No government has ever been a government of laws and not of men in the sense of eliminating all discretionary power.

When Davis spoke of rules, he was not thinking primarily of rules as legislation or regulation. He was more interested in internal control through the hierarchical structures of the bureaucracy itself, believing that the administration should be encouraged to 'structure' its discretion by formulating its policies as rules. These could then be used for the guidance of the 'line bureaucracy'. Rules may still need to be divided into the legislative (which have binding force) and the non-legislative (which do not), but we shall reserve this point for Chapter 6. Here we are more interested in knowing that 'rules' are precise and specific while 'principles' and 'standards' are less specific and more flexible. Jowell[18] describes discretion as a scale on which the decision-maker may have wide powers of choice (strong discretion) or limited powers (weak discretion):

> Discretion is rarely absolute, and rarely absent. It is a matter of degree, and ranges along a continuum between high and low. Where he has a high degree of discretion, the decision-maker will normally be guided by reference to such vague standards as

---

16  R. Dworkin, *Taking Rights Seriously*, (London: Duckworth) 2nd impression (corrected) 1978, p. 31. See further, M. Adler and S. Asquith (eds.), *Discretion and Welfare* (London: Heinemann Educational) 1981.

17  *Discretionary Justice*, p. 17. For a contrary interpretation of Davis, see R. Baldwin and K. Hawkins, 'Discretionary Justice: Davis Reconsidered' [1984] PL 570.

18  J. Jowell, 'The Legal Control of Administrative Discretion' [1973] PL 178, 179-180.

'public interest' and 'fair and reasonable'. Where his discretion is low, the decision-maker will be limited by rules that do not allow much scope for interpretation. For example, a police officer's discretion is high when he has the power to regulate traffic at crossroads 'as he thinks fit.' If he were required to allow traffic to pass from East to West for three minutes and then from North to South for two minutes, subject to exceptional circumstances, then his discretion would be greatly reduced. A traffic light possesses no discretion at all.

So far we have not defined the terms 'principle' and 'standard'. In the next extract Jowell indicates that they are loosely-woven rules:[19]

### Rules

Roscoe Pound defined a rule . . . as a 'legal precept attaching a definite detailed legal consequence to a definite detailed state of fact.' . . . The process of legalisation involves the transformation of policies into rules. Policies are broad statements of general objectives, such as 'To provide decent, safe and sanitary housing,' 'To prevent unsafe driving.' The policy is legalised as the various elements of housing and driving are specified, providing, for example, for hot and cold running water, indoor toilets, maximum speed limits and one-way streets. A rule thus is the most precise form of general direction, since it requires for its application nothing more or less than the happening or non-happening of a physical event. For the application of the maximum speed rule, all we need do is determine factually whether or not the driver was exceeding thirty miles per hour . . .

### Principles

Principles arise mainly in the context of judicial decision-making. They involve normative moral standards by which rules might be evaluated. They are frequently expressed in maxims, such as 'No man shall profit by his own wrong,' 'He who comes to court shall come with clean hands.' They have developed in the judicial context over time, and are less suited to administrative decision making because they do not address themselves to economic, social or political criteria, but to justice and fairness largely in the judicial situation. A principle that may arise in the administrative context would be the maxim: 'Like cases shall receive like treatment.'

### Standards

The feature of standards that distinguishes them from rules is their flexibility and susceptibility to change over time. In 1955, for example, 'average' and 'prudent' university administrators probably had little difficulty in determining a standard requiring 'neat' dress in university lecture halls. Obviously skirts for women, and collar and ties for men, were essential criteria of 'neatness'. Some years later, however, the standard could alter, allowing trousers for ladies, open collars for men, or indeed anything if not nothing at all . . .

In addition to Pound, Jowell is here basing himself on the jurisprudence of Dworkin. Dworkin[20] once described rules as 'applicable in all-or-nothing fashion' in contra-distinction to 'principles' which guide adjudicators when rules run out. Today, it is more common to admit that rules vary in style and character. Not

19   J. Jowell [1973] PL 178, 201, 204. We have changed the order slightly.
20   'The Model of Rules I', in R. Dworkin, *Taking Rights Seriously* (London: Duckworth) 1978, p. 24.

every rule is so clearly formulated as to exclude discretion; in other words, the distinction between all-or-nothing rules and non-conclusive (discretionary) principles is simply 'a matter of degree'.[1]

To summarise the argument so far, we could describe the simple rules/discretion dichotomy with which we started as elongated into a two-dimensional scale on which some of the points are represented by rule-typology:

discretion —> standards —> principles —> rules.

Now we can see that discretion is present at every point on this scale. Not only do the different rule-typologies allow for differing amounts of discretion but differing types of rule are matched by differing types of discretion. On the one hand, the power to interpret rules (usually known as 'judgment discretion') differs in kind, though it may be very considerable, from the power to devise and impose standards;[2] on the other hand, it is possible to describe judgment discretion as an inherent quality of rules which can never be wholly eliminated. This is another way of saying that the application of rules to facts can never be purely mechanical. 'Lawyers know that rules must be interpreted and that rules can lead to wrong results in particular cases. Thus lawyers know with special acuteness that discretion is necessary.'[3] This understanding collapses the rules/discretion dichotomy but also challenges the concept of rule-types as points on a linear scale.

Seeing rules and discretion as points on a spectrum, Davis believed that the aim should be to achieve a good balance between them:[4]

> The problem is not merely to choose between rule and discretion but is to find the optimum point on the rule-to-discretion scale. A standard, principle, or rule can be so vague as to be meaningless, it can have a slight meaning or considerable meaning, it can have some degree of controlling effect, or it can be so clear and compelling as to leave little or no room for discretion. The degree of discretion depends not only on grants of authority to administrators but also on what they do to enlarge their power. In general, [the] thesis is that the degree of administrative discretion should often be more restricted; some of the restricting can be done by legislators but most of this task must be performed by administrators.

What factors would or should influence administrators in selecting? A common approach has been to look to the quantity of discretion required; strong discretion suggests standards, weak discretion rules:

---

1   This is part of the battle over positivism mentioned in Ch. 2. See H. Hart, *The Concept of Law* (Oxford: Clarendon) 2nd edn., 1994, J. Raz and P. Bulloch (eds.) p. 262.
2   W. Twining and D. Miers, *How To Do Things With Rules* (London: Weidenfeld and Nicolson) 3rd edn., 1991.
3   C. Schneider, 'Discretion and Rules: A Lawyer's View' in Hawkins, *The Uses of Discretion*, above, p. 97, note 17, pp. 48-49.
4   *Discretionary Justice*, p. 215.

Most agencies making decisions do so in a manner which can be located on a continuum somewhere between discretion at one end and rules at the other. Competing values push the character of the decision between these two ends of the continuum. Thus accountability, efficiency, rationality and entitlement push the agency towards rules, and generosity, relevance, individuality, sensitivity and choice push it towards discretion.[5]

Bradshaw's case depends, however, on identifying criteria by which a rational choice can be made. Writing two decades later, Schneider concludes that the tension between rules and discretion can never be resolved; no magic formula can be devised for choosing the 'optimum point on the scale':[6]

[I do not offer] any formula to follow in choosing between discretion and rules. On the contrary. My general position is that the choice will be complex and uncertain and that it will depend on factors that will be difficult to assess and that will vary from circumstance to circumstance (so that it is not unreasonable for lawyers to look to particular contexts in evaluating discretion and rules). I will argue that, in the world in which we live, there typically is not a choice between discretion and rules, but rather a choice between different mixes of discretion and rules. The first reason for this is that discretion and rules rarely appear in unadulterated form in any large area of legal significance. Typically, I will suggest, there is no such thing as an important legal decision from which all elements of discretion have been removed. Yet I will also suggest that, typically, there is no such thing as an important legal decision in which judicial discretion is free to roam wholly unchecked.

The second reason we rarely face a decision between discretion and rules is that there are compelling advantages and compelling disadvantages to both discretion and rules. We will commonly want to secure the advantages of *both* discretion and rules while avoiding their disadvantages. Worse, it will usually be unclear just how to secure those advantages and to avoid the disadvantages in any particular situation. This will generally mean that we must grope toward some satisfactory mix of discretion and rules.

Since Davis wrote, there have been many attempts to fit rule-type to function. Economic models have been constructed based on the concept of rational economic behaviour, which construe 'optimality' in terms of cost.[7] Writing in 1995, Black[8] devised a four-dimensional model, defining rules according to substance, character (permissive or mandatory), status and structure. Yet structure had to be again broken down, to cover additional factors such as precision/ vagueness, complexity/ simplicity and so on. The complexity of these models throws doubt on Davis.

5   J. Bradshaw, 'From Discretion to Rules: the Experience of the Family Fund' in M. Adler and S. Asquith (eds.), *Discretion and Welfare* (London: Heinemann Educational) 1981, p. 139.
6   C. Schneider, in K. Hawkins, *The Uses of Discretion* (above, p. 97, note 17), p. 49.
7   C. Diver, 'The Optimal Precision of Administrative Rules' (1983) 93 Yale LJ 65.
8   J. Black, '"Which Arrow"?: Rule Type and Regulatory Policy' [1995] PL 94, 96.

*Retreat from Davis*

Reviewing *Discretionary Justice*, Reiss, a sociologist, thought Davis unduly optimistic about the power of rules to counter misuse of discretion. Davis had closed his eyes to how people really behave:[9]

> Davis relies on rule making as the principal means for confining discretion, on openness of discretionary processes as the major means for structuring discretion, and on supervision and review as the major means for checking discretion. These are, of course, the classic means and processes operating in modern bureaucracies. What is absent from his treatment, however – a deficiency that may puzzle behavioral scientists – is both a consideration of the relative importance of these factors and a consideration of how bureaucracies can turn these means to ends of justice or can find ways to circumvent them so that decisions go against the interests of individual parties . . .
>
> Indeed, examination of the structure and nature of bureaucracies seems crucial for determining the quality of administrative justice. While it is a cardinal principle in the Weberian theory of bureaucracy that rules are a way of ensuring consistent treatment of all individual parties, it also is a principle that bureaucracies neutralize civic power. Paradoxically, then, protection exists only so long as bureaucratic officials behave properly. When they do not, the capacity for citizens to affect official actions is very limited. How can one ignore the fact that the power to litigate is the power to neutralize much administration, and that for every formal procedure there is an informal one of circumvention?
>
> Welfare lawyers are particularly frightened of discretion because of its potency as a weapon for social control. They feel that social workers and benefit officers use discretionary power to manipulate their clients. It is important to realize, however, that rules as well as discretion can be used to manipulate people and that administrators well understand how to play games with rules. 'Bad' clients find that officials stand on the letter of the law or lodge unnecessary appeals designed to postpone payment; 'good' clients may receive the benefit of loopholes and ambiguities. Both sides can play the game. Some seek to 'neutralize administration' by tying it in its own rules; e.g. by lodging unnecessary appeals which use up resources and time and may even be designed to overload the system to provoke concessions. Consultation procedures may be contested at every stage in the hope that a development plan or new regulations can be postponed indefinitely. On the other hand, resort to discretion in the form of 'selective enforcement' is necessary to mitigate the severity of rules or deal with the perennial problem of the 'over-inclusive rule', such as a parking regulation which catches a samaritan who has stopped his car to help a blind man across the road.

Fifteen years later, Goodin, examining[10] some of the common arguments against discretion – such as the danger of arbitrariness, uncertainty and of manipulation or exploitation by its possessor – rammed this point home. These problems could not be overcome (as Davis suggested) simply by replacing discretion with rules. Some discretions (such as judgment discretion) are *inevitable*, in the sense that 'they are logically necessary to the operation of a system of rules at all. Such

9   A. Reiss, 'Book review of K. C. Davis, *Discretionary Justice*', (1970) 68 Michigan LR 789, 794-795.
10  R. Goodin, 'Welfare, Rights and Discretion' (1986) 6 OJLS 232. See also R. Goodin, 'Vulnerabilities and Responsibilities: An Ethical Defense of the Welfare State' (1985) 79 American Political Science Rev. 775.

discretions are truly ineliminable: they cannot be eliminated except by eliminating the system of rules itself'. Thus, the choice to make rules can be shifted 'all around the system . . . from lower-level officials to higher ones, or onto judges, or onto Parliament, or whatever', but it cannot be eliminated. Again, all the objectionable features of discretionary powers – secrecy, inaccessibility, arbitrariness – are possible in a system of rules and the very consideration that dictated discretion, drives the administrator to use rules in an identical fashion. Goodin instances a discretion which is objectionable because reasons do not have to be given for its use; a rule demanding reasons is introduced; the rule may allow 'boiler plate reasons',[11] which merely restate the rule as reasons. Thus, Goodin contends that discretionary powers and the problems associated with them are to a large extent insurmountable without wholesale correction of a negative administrative ethos:[12]

> Of the many problems posed by officials possessing discretions . . . a regime of rules [is the proper solution] to only one. It is important to see what rules can do: they can prevent the manipulation and exploitation of those dependent on state services by officials responsible for the administration of those services. It is equally important to see what they cannot do. They cannot (necessarily, or without substantial costs in other respects) prevent intrusiveness, arbitrariness or insecurity. For much the same reasons that discretionary decisions *must* display those attributes, rule-based decisions *can*, and *probably will*.

## 4. Openness and citizen participation

Without digressing to discuss it, we noted Davis's desire to open up the administrative process, bringing policy-making into the open and allowing citizens to participate in 'a miniature democratic process'. Here, Davis was reflecting the experience of America, where rule-making procedures were formal and regulated either by specific statutes or by the Administrative Procedure Act 1946. This Act provides for notice of proposed rule-making together with a public hearing. Interested persons are afforded an opportunity to participate, and a concise statement of all views presented forms part of the record. The less onerous procedure of 'notice and comment' is applicable to informal rule-making. The rise of demands for similar provision in Britain is dealt with in Chapters 6 and 7. The United States has since gone further by passing a federal Freedom of Information Act, opening access to public documents, in 1966 and the Government-in-the-Sunshine Act, providing for access to meetings, in 1976. Taken together, these provisions have gone a long way in the United States to create a culture of openness and participation in public affairs.

Arguably, modern participation theory sits more comfortably in the American federal system, where pluralism has always been strongly represented in political

11  E.g., 'you are not entitled to welfare benefit/to a taxi licence/to a tax rebate because you do not come within the terms of para. 1(b) of Reg. No. 000'. The applicant still does not know why.
12  (1986) 6 OJLS at 237.

thought.[13] In Britain, it cuts across our dominant political traditions, constructed around a theory of *representative* government, according to which we all participate in government through our elected representative(s).[14] This fits comfortably with a constitution dominated by the doctrine of parliamentary supremacy, creating a built-in bias to centralisation[15] A British obsession with 'strong government' reflects a preoccupation with political stability epitomised in the nation-state. The roots of participation theory reach, in contrast, into a form of pluralism which, as we said in Chapter 1, is concerned to break the state down into smaller and more accessible units.

Neither the administrative nor political culture of the United Kingdom favours 'Government in the Sunshine'.[16] The prevailing doctrine of representative government joins force with the doctrine of ministerial responsibility, which enjoins the total anonymity of civil servants to preserve their neutrality, to reinforce an ingrained culture of secrecy. We have never recovered from a blanket ban on disclosure imposed by the draconian Official Secrets Act 1911, which made virtually all disclosure of information received in the course of government employment a criminal offence. It was 1968 when, in *Conway v Rimmer*,[17] the judiciary for the first time seriously questioned the right of government to withhold documents requested for the purposes of litigation on the ground of 'public interest immunity'.[18] In 1972, an official committee set up under the chairmanship of Sir Oliver Franks to consider reform of the archaic Official Secrets legislation[19] warned that a government 'which pursues secret aims, or which operates in greater secrecy than the effective conduct of its proper functions requires . . . will lose the trust of the people'. Reform has not yet been conceded. Disclosure is still today governed by an Official Secrets Act, remodelled and updated in 1989, and the main inroads on the culture of secrecy have come through informal government guidelines whose provisions are dealt with in Chapter 13. The Franks prediction came near to fulfilment, however, with an unprecedented inquiry, set up to investigate the use of public interest immunity in the course of criminal proceedings to stifle information about

13  See, R. Dahl, *Dilemmas of Pluralist Democracy: Autonomy versus Control* (New Haven: Yale University Press) 1982.
14  C. Harlow, 'Power from the People? Representation and Constitutional Theory' in P. McAuslan and J. McEldowney (eds.), *Law Legitimacy and the Constitution* (London: Sweet and Maxwell) 1985.
15  This line of reasoning underlies *Wheeler v Leicester City Council* [1985] AC 1054 (below, p. 117). See also pp 583–588 below, where a fuller consideration of the representative function of local authorities is contained.
16  I. Harden and N. Lewis, *The Noble Lie. The British Constitution and the Rule of Law* (London: Hutchinson) 1986; J. Michael, *The Politics of Secrecy: the Case for a Freedom of Information Law* (London: National Council for Civil Liberties) 1979.
17  [1968] AC 910. For the modern law on public interest immunity see *R v Chief Constable of the West Midlands Police, ex p Wiley* [1995] 1 AC 274. Public interest immunity is further discussed in the context of police complaints in Ch. 12 below.
18  Compare the *Johnston* case, above p. 59.
19  Report of the Committee on Reform of s. 2 of the Official Secrets Act 1911, Cmnd 5104 (1972). The citation is from para. 12. See, W. Birtles, 'Big Brother Knows Best' [1973] PL 100.

covert ministerial policies concerning arms exports. When finally published, the five-volume Report of the Scott Inquiry severely criticised ministerial conduct and contained important recommendations about the relationships between Ministers, civil servants, legal advisers and Parliament.[20] The fact that 'the beleagured Major government . . . in the end, and in the face of apparently overwhelming odds, managed to survive almost unscathed one of the biggest political crises in Britain in recent years' brought renewed pressure to open up government and strengthen the ailing doctrine of ministerial accountability. We return to this point.

By 1970, when Davis was writing, citizen-participation was beginning to creep seriously on to the political agenda in Britain. Pateman[1] dates this to the last years of the 1960s, when 'the word "participation" became part of the popular vocabulary, gaining ground in education (France), welfare (America) and planning (Britain and America)'. Barker[2] records a parallel shift away from 'managerial conceptions of public ownership' coupled with renewed interest in earlier theories – such as 'guild socialism' and the ideas of William Morris – which made the citizen something 'more than a claimant on resources and an occasional elector'. Fagence[3] links the citizen- participation movement with the dislike and fear of corporatism in the modern state which we noted in the work of Reich (above, pp. 13–14). Modern technological societies, in which decisions are taken out of the hands of the people and reserved for an elected elite and its expert advisers are faced with an inescapable dilemma: big is efficient but small is beautiful:

> As society has developed, and has become culturally and technologically sophisticated, there has grown an insistence that decision-making should be infused with a more democratic expression. Thus, within the last decade or two modern society has tended to advocate the simultaneous growth of participatory democracy and expertise in decision-making. Clearly it is not possible to maximise both of these value preferences; it is not that they are exclusive and incompatible one with the other, but that they are capable of neutralising each other with the result that the decisions made are less than satisfactory to the demands of the participants and the technical requirements of the problem to be solved. Despite these antagonisms, the tensions in society dictate that meaningful attempts should be made to reshape the traditional decision-making processes to accommodate strategies of citizen participation; the movement of such advocacy has gained a momentum which is now irresistible, and it has attracted a high emotional content so that any denial of opportunities for citizen involvement is challenged as a betrayal of democratic tradition.

---

20  *Inquiry into the Export of Defence Equipment and Dual-Use Goods to Iraq and Related Prosecutions*, HC 115 (1995/6). The citation is from G. Drewry, 'Judicial inquiries and public reassurance' [1996] PL 368, 372. See also A. Tomkins, 'Government Information and Parliament: Misleading by Design or by Default?' [1996] PL 472; N. Lewis and D. Longley, 'Ministerial Responsibility: The Next Steps' [1996] PL 490.

1  C. Pateman, *Participation and Democratic Theory* (Cambridge: CUP) 1970, p. 1.

2  *Political Ideas in Modern Britain* 1978, p. 208.

3  M. Fagence, *Citizen Participation in Planning* (Oxford: Pergamon) 1977, p. 3.

Sewell and Coppock identified[4] 'growing concern that the public – or at least significant segments of it – has developed an increasing feeling of alienation towards governmental decision-making'. Representation through elected representatives and traditional techniques, such as the committees favoured by green light theorists, increasingly came to seem inadequate and even elitist. Pressure and interest groups burgeoned.[5] During the 1970s there was growing demand for new channels of communication, in addition to the traditional devices of ballot box, public meetings and letters to editors or public officials. Public opinion polls and surveys; referenda; public hearings; workshops, seminars and task forces; telephone phone-ins, debates and phone-in polls were all tried. Planning inquiries, developed as a forum for the exchange of views, came under fire as too legalistic and orientated towards the protection of private interests (below, Chapter 12). The Skeffington Report of 1969[6] marks a high point of experimentation with citizen-participation and its techniques of consultation.

In *The Ideologies of Planning Law* (1981), McAuslan developed the idea of clashing values of different interest groups, detecting three competing 'ideologies'. McAuslan describes participation theory as 'radical and populist' but he demonstrates clearly how the new ideology cuts across the priorities and preoccupations of both red and green light theory:[7]

> Firstly . . . the law exists and should be used to protect private property and its institutions; this may be called the traditional common law approach to the role of law. Secondly, the law exists and should be used to advance the public interest, if necessary against the interest of private property; this may be called the orthodox public administration and planning approach to the role of law. Thirdly, the law exists and should be used to advance the cause of public participation against both the orthodox public administration approach to the public interest and the common law approach of the overriding importance of private property; this may be called the radical or populist approach to the role of law.

Linked to pluralist theories of democracy, participation theory is collective in character. Its demand for openness in government is designed to allow people to engage in informed public debate and participate in decision-making.[8] In this sense, as McAuslan indicates, it is at variance with the individualistic model of our legal process, designed to protect private rights. In Stewart's influential interest-representation model of administrative law,[9] however, judicial review plays a significant part in guaranteeing that 'all affected groups have the right to participate in agency decision-making procedures and obtain judicial review to

4   W. Sewell and J. Coppock (eds.) *Public Participation in Planning* (London: Wiley) 1977, p. 1.
5   See J. Richardson and G. Jordan, *Governing Under Pressure* (London: Martin Robertson) 1979; G. Alderman, *Pressure Groups and Government in Great Britain* (London: Longman) 1984.
6   Report of the Skeffington Committee, *People and Planning* (London: HMSO) 1969.
7   P. McAuslan, *The Ideologies of Planning Law* (Oxford: Pergamon) 1981, p. 2. See also P. McAuslan, 'Administrative Law, Collective Consumption and Judicial Policy' (1983) 46 MLR 1.
8   T. Prosser, 'Towards a Critical Public Law' (1982) 9 J. of Law and Soc. 1.
9   Famously articulated in R. Stewart, 'The Reformation of American Administrative Law' (1975) 88 Harv. LR 1667. See also '*Vermont Yankee* and the Evolution of Administrative Procedures' (1978) 91 Harv. LR 1821 and 'Madison's Nightmare' (1990) 57 Univ. of Chicago LR 335.

ensure that the agency has adequately considered their interests'. New models of adjudication which saw courts as providing a forum for the articulation of political views began to appear.[10] Cotterell explains:[11]

> An alternative claim is that democracy requires popular participation in and access to public decision-making and courts help to provide this. Potentially, they can do this in at least two distinct ways. First, they can enforce procedures in governmental decision-making that allow popular input into decision-makers' deliberations. Secondly, they can supplement administrative processes with judicial hearings, which provide different kinds of opportunity for influence on administrative matters by citizens as litigants. Courts are relatively open to public view, accountable (through appeal systems), and in some senses participatory. They not only allow, but normally require, opposing voices to be heard. Hence some writers have suggested that they actually embody democratic values or have the potential to do so.

As participation theory gained ground, public interest litigation became a growth industry,[12] putting pressure on the legal process to become less individualistic and accommodate collective action. We shall follow this aspect of the movement in Chapter 16.

## 5. Discretionary justice

Davis's concern was with rationalisation of those areas of policy and decision-making which rarely reach tribunals or courts. The primary concern of jurists, however, has always been with the rationality of the judicial process. Hart's classic, *The Concept of Law*,[13] possibly the century's most influential jurisprudential work, epitomises this concern with the internal coherence of law as an artificial system of legal reasoning. Thus the judicial process could hardly escape the movement for rational decision-making.

In a critique of the *Padfield* case,[14] Austin had accused the courts of ignoring a basic distinction between 'objective' and 'subjective' discretion:[15]

> The decision-maker's discretion is 'objective' where the source of his power imposes defined or ascertainable predetermined criteria by which, and solely by which, he must make his choice. The decision-maker's discretion is 'subjective', however, when the source of his power confers upon him the freedom to determine his own criteria for choosing between the alternative courses of action open to him. Subjective

---

10 P. Weiler, 'Two Models of Judicial Decision-Making' (1968) 46 Can. Bar. Rev. 406. See further below, Ch. 16.

11 R. Cotterell, 'Judicial Review and Legal Theory', in G. Richardson and H. Genn (eds.), *Administrative Law and Government Action: the Courts and Alternative Mechanisms of Review* (Oxford: Clarendon) 1994, p.18.

12 See C. Harlow and R. Rawlings, *Pressure Through Law* (London: Routledge) 1992.

13 H. Hart, *The Concept of Law* (Oxford: Clarendon) 1961.

14 [1968] 2 WLR 924. Above, p. 98.

15 R. Austin, 'Judicial Review of Subjective Discretion – At the Rubicon; Whither Now?' (1975) 28 Current Legal Problems 150, 152-154.

discretions are usually conferred by such phrases as 'if in his opinion', 'if he thinks fit', 'if he deems', 'if he considers' and numerous other similar expressions . . .

That this distinction is a relevant one to make becomes apparent when it is realised that the application by the courts of the doctrine of substantive *ultra vires* [16] in reviewing discretionary powers, depends upon the existence in the empowering legislation of criteria against which the decision-maker's choice can be measured. In the absence of such criteria, the doctrine of substantive *ultra vires* is impotent . . . However, some recent cases . . . have hinted at a disturbing possibility, namely that if the source of the power does not impose any objective criteria, the courts will imply such criteria; the disturbing element in this development is that the courts may simply be replacing their own subjective views for those of a person such as a Minister who is better qualified and equipped to exercise the power. In short, they may supply their own criteria rather than implying them from the terms of the empowering legislation.

Lord Hailsham once described law as dependent 'upon the strict application of a clearly formulated rule of law, and not dependent on the subjective opinion of the individual judge'.[17] If Austin is right, then the reasoning of *Padfield* does not meet this criterion. But Austin is faced with an emerging pattern of judicial review which was ultimately to undermine the doctrine of ultra vires.[18] In *Padfield* the Minister was (1) required to follow prescribed procedures by referring cases to the established committee and (2) effectively needed (no positive duty was imposed) to give reasons for his decision if he was to avoid review. Judicial review has operated to confine and structure the exercise of discretionary power through a process of reasoned decision-making.

As judicial review began to impinge more on discretionary decision-making, the contrast between the decision-making patterns required of administration and those of courts, which remained inherently discretionary in character, stood out. It did not seem unreasonable to insist that judicial review as well as administrative decision-making 'makes sense only if the judge is in a position to enunciate or explain the rule on which his decision is based'.[19] The test of *Wednesbury* unreasonableness began to seem deficient. Turning back to Jowell's account of the spectrum of rules, we find this sentence: 'Where he has a high degree of discretion, the decision-maker will normally be guided by reference to *such vague standards as "public interest" and "fair and reasonable"*' (our emphasis). Fifteen years later, the same author was attacking the loose texture of *Wednesbury* unreasonableness and arguing that 'intellectual honesty requires a further and better explanation as to why the act is unreasonable'.[20] Characterised as casuistic and, in the technical sense, unprincipled, the principles of judicial review came under attack.

16  According to the ultra vires doctrine, power must be used in a manner and for purposes which are reasonably incidental to or consequent on statutory authorisation; substantive ultra vires is the term for 'doing the wrong thing'.
17  Lord Hailsham, *The Dilemma of Democracy – Diagnosis and Prescription* (London: Collins) 1978, p. 106.
18  See D. Oliver, 'Is Ultra Vires the Basis of Judicial Review?' [1987] PL 543.
19  J. Kahn (trans. Harlow), 'Discretionary Power and the Administrative Judge' (1980) 29 ICLQ 521, 525.
20  J. Jowell and A. Lester, 'Beyond *Wednesbury*: Substantive Principles of Administrative Law' [1987] PL 368, 371.

In public law cases, the court's discretion lies not only in its powers of statutory interpretation but also in the malleable nature of the principles of judicial review,[1] once graphically described as possessing 'no more substance at the core than a seedless grape'.[2] Strict application of the doctrine of parliamentary supremacy means that a rule in statutory form must be applied unquestioningly.[3] In this sense, rules trump principles. A common criticism of *Padfield* is that the court breached this fundamental principle, re-writing the statute to substitute the words 'the minister *must*' for the legislative formula 'the minister may'. If, however, the rule to be applied is not contained in statute, there is greater latitude for discretion. We saw this illustrated in *Burmah Oil*,[4] where the courts treated as overriding the principle that property should not be sequestrated without due compensation, effectively writing the requirement into the prerogative power.

Further opportunities for judicial discretion arise where a statute is silent on the point in issue or in fitting statutory provisions to unusual fact-situations. This type of gap affords a court strong discretion.[5] Judicial discretion enables forays deep into political territory. Griffith in particular has argued that the 'hole in the doughnut' is filled with policy choices drawn from an inchoate judicial philosophy of political conservatism which he would like to see curtailed. It is indicative that Griffith saw *Padfield* as 'perverse' and as 'biting into the red meat of statutory powers'.[6]

By encouraging a more logical and coherent approach, some proponents of judicial review felt that these arguments could be met. A change in terminology from 'reasonableness' to 'rationality' in the celebrated *GCHQ* case seemed to augur the desired new direction. Significantly, the change occurred in a highly charged political case, in which the judges were asserting the justiciability of prerogative powers. It was therefore important for judicial review to appear scientific, objective and apolitical. Lord Diplock's judgment in this case is usually cited as the basis of the modern doctrine of judicial review.

Although his three principles largely conform with tradition, note that he leaves room for the development of further principles.

## *Council of Civil Service Unions v Minister for the Civil Service*[7]

The Civil Service Unions had members working in the General Communications headquarters when the Foreign Secretary suddenly announced to the House of Commons that employees working in GCHQ would no longer be allowed to join a

1   See Lord Wilberforce in *Bromley London Borough Council v Greater London Council* [1983] 1 AC 768.
2   E. Gellhorn and G. Robinson, 'Perspectives on Administrative Law', (1975) 75 Columbia LR 771, 780. The theme is pursued in Ch. 15 with a study of procedural fairness.
3   A. Lester, 'English Judges as Lawmakers' [1993] PL 269, 272-5 invites the judges to strike off the fetters of the 'Victorian' literal rule. And see D. Pannick, 'The Law Lords and the Needs of Contemporary Society' (1982) 53 Pol. Q. 318.
4   Above, p. 47.
5   See R. Dworkin, *Law's Empire* (London: Fontana) 1986, Ch. 1 for discussion and illustration.
6   J. Griffith, *Judicial Politics*, p. 106. See also J. Griffith, *Politics of the Judiciary*, p. 63 and Ch. 4.
7   [1985] AC 374.

union.  A legal challenge was mounted on the grounds that the decision was unreasonable and disproportionate, and that the unions had not been consulted.  For the Minister it was argued that the matter fell under the Royal Prerogative and was not justiciable.  The House of Lords rules (1) that the prerogative powers were in principle justiciable; and (2) that the Council had a legitimate expectation that the would be consulted.  In the instant case, however, they found for the Government on the ground that security and the defence of the realm were involved.

*Lord Diplock*: I see no reason why simply because a decision-making power is derived from a common law and not a statutory source, it should *for that reason only* be immune from judicial review.  Judicial review has I think developed to a stage today when . . . one can conveniently classify under three heads the grounds upon which administrative action is subject to control by judicial review.  The first ground I would call 'illegality', the second 'irrationality' and the third 'procedural impropriety'.  That is not to say that further development on a case by case basis may not in course of time add further grounds.  I have in mind particularly the possible adoption in the future of the principle of 'proportionality' which is recognised in the administrative law of several of our fellow members of the European Economic Community . . .

By 'illegality' as a ground for judicial review I mean that the decision maker must understand correctly the law that regulates his decision-making power and must give effect to it.  Whether he has or not is *par excellence* a justiciable question to be decided, in the event of dispute, by those persons, the judges, by whom the judicial power of the state is exercisable.

By 'irrationality' I mean what can by now be succinctly referred to as '*Wednesbury* unreasonableness'.  It applies to a decision which is so outrageous in its defiance of logic or of accepted moral standards that no sensible person who had applied his mind to the question to be decided could have arrived at it.  Whether a decision falls within this category is a question that judges by their training and experience should be well equipped to answer, or else there would be something badly wrong with our judicial system . . .

I have described the third head as 'procedural impropriety' rather than failure to observe basic rules of natural justice or failure to act with procedural fairness towards the person who will be affected by the decision.  This is because susceptibility to judicial review under this head covers also failure by an administrative tribunal to observe procedural rules that are expressly laid down in the legislative instrument by which its jurisdiction is conferred, even where such failure does not involve any denial of natural justice . . .

While I see no a priori reason to rule out 'irrationality' as a ground for judicial review of a ministerial decision taken in the exercise of 'prerogative' powers, I find it difficult to envisage in any of the various fields in which the prerogative remains the only source of the relevant decision-making power a decision of a kind that would be open to attack through the judicial process upon this ground.  Such decisions will generally involve the application of government policy.  The reasons for the decision-maker taking one course rather than another do not normally involve questions to which, if disputed, the judicial process is adapted to provide the right answer, by which I mean that the kind of evidence that is admissible under judicial procedures and the way in which it has to be adduced tend to exclude from the attention of the court competing policy considerations which, if the executive discretion is to be wisely exercised, need to be weighed against one another: a balancing exercise which judges by their upbringing and experience are ill-qualified to perform.  So I leave this as an open question to be dealt with on a case to case basis  . . .

In his standard text, Craig, who is sympathetic to the concept of a principled and orderly legal universe infused by liberal values,[8] charts the progress of a new judicial review based on the concept of *irrationality*. Craig feels that this development could 'subject administrative discretion to a set of more specific substantive principles. This would have the benefit of forcing the courts to articulate more openly the premises on which they are reasoning'. Loose general standards ought to give way to principles because the latter are more precise and would leave less room for unstructured judicial discretion. Below MacCormick exposes the fallacy that principles are both inevitable and non-controversial:[9]

> Even if it be the case . . . that moral values and principles have some objective truth and universal validity, it remains also the case that people inveterately disagree about them . . . Political principles are . . . also subjects of inveterate disagreement. Legal systems result from a patchwork of historical assertions of contentious and changing political principles, political compromises and mere political muddles. That from which laws emerge is controversial, even if some or all of the controversies concern moral issues on which there may in principle be a single right answer. So the idea that judges have only a 'weak' discretion since their task is to 'find' *the* right priority ranking of legal principles and deduce from it *the* right answer is utterly unsustainable . . .
>
> In all cases, judicial discretion exists only within the framework of some predetermined standards. Where these standards are legal rules, the discretion extends only within rather a restricted field, though rarely eliminated completely. Where the rules give no guidance or give ambiguous guidance, recourse may be had to other standards of judgment. But since these standards are all less precise than rules, the discretion involved in interpreting and extrapolating from them is greater.

At this stage, we need to feed in to our discussion the idea that rules should be 'principled' in the sense in which Jowell used the term (above, p. 103). To put this differently, many people expect rules to have a moral content. Cotterell indeed argues persuasively[10] that a serious problem for contemporary legal systems lies in the fact that much modern regulation patently does not live up to these ideals. No longer linked to simple, explicable standards of right and wrong, it has become instead a vehicle for intricate economic policy or a means of expressing complicated scientific standards. Classic separation of powers theory, however, reserves the policy-making process for the executive branch. As Austin and Griffith argue, if judges in interpreting a statute supply their own view of its 'purposes', they may easily cross the sacred line between policy and interpretation. Dworkin seeks to meet this problem by severing the legal universe of rules and principles from the political world of policy. 'Policy' relates to the general or

---

8   P. Craig, *Administrative Law* (London: Sweet & Maxwell) 3rd edn., 1994, p. 441 (hereafter Craig *Administrative Law*). See also P. Craig, *Public Law and Democracy in the United Kingdom and the United States of America* (Oxford: Clarendon) 1990.

9   N. MacCormick, *H.L.A. Hart* (Stanford: University Press) 1981, p. 130.

10  R. Cotterell, 'Law's Community: Legal Theory and the Image of Legality' (1992) 19 J. of Law and Soc. 405.

public interest, is characteristically concerned with economic or social priorities, and is not required to be consistent. 'Principles' are concerned with justice and fairness, and are governed by the principles of integrity and consistency. The expectation that law should be principled in the moral sense is described by Dworkin as the principle of 'political integrity'.[11] Significantly, he sees law-makers as well as adjudicators as bound 'to make the total set of laws morally coherent'.

For Allan, the principle of integrity forms an inherent element of the rule of law.[12] He expresses no doubts over judicial legitimacy in this vision of a principled administrative law:

> I shall argue that Ronald Dworkin's account of the distinction between principle and policy makes a helpful contribution to the task of defining the nature and limits of public law. Questions of principle are those which concern the scope and content of individual rights, as opposed to the general welfare or the public interest. Matters of public interest or public policy should be determined by the political branches of the government – executive or legislature. Questions of right, by contrast, are peculiarly the province of the courts. As counter-majoritarian entitlements or 'trumps' over general utility or the public interest, the relative insulation of the judges from the ordinary political process ought to be specially conducive to their protection and enforcement. I shall suggest that administrative law may be helpfully interpreted as a system of public law rights and the legitimate boundaries of judicial review may be found in the process of defining and enforcing those rights.

Galligan[13] seeks to impose similar standards on administrators who, 'in rationally pursuing the objects of their power, must be responsive to moral principles. These may be seen as part of the axioms of rational action, or as providing subsidiary goals to be achieved, or simply as constraints on the pursuit of goals'. Galligan prioritises a general precept to 'treat the rights and interests of individuals with understanding and respect', an all-encompassing principle which generates others, such as substantive and procedural fairness and non-discrimination. His moral principles typify the process values of liberal lawyers.[14] But, as the next case indicates, the case for principled judicial review was developing from a procedural to a substantive argument. Basing their argument on the *GCHQ* case,[15] Jowell and

---

11  R. Dworkin, *Law's Empire* (London: Fontana) 1986, Ch. 6.
12  'The Rule of Law' in T. Allan, *Law, Liberty and Justice: The Legal Foundations of British Constitutionalism* (Oxford: Clarendon) 1993, p. 7.
13  D. Galligan, *Discretionary Powers, A Legal Study of Official Discretion* (Oxford: Clarendon) 1990, p. 5. J. Mashaw, 'Mirrored Ambivalence' (1983) 33 J. of Leg. Ed. 23, 29 lists as general principles of administrative law: (1) agency processes and structures must respect individual rights to fair and rational treatment; (2) individual substantive and procedural rights are limited by the need to effect those public purposes that administrative agencies have in their charge.
14  On Dworkin's liberal values, see P. Kelly, 'Ronald Dworkin: *Taking Rights Seriously*' in M. Forsyth and M. Keens-Soper (eds.), *Political Classics: Green to Dworkin* (Oxford: Clarendon) 1996. On liberalism and process values, see G. Richardson, 'The Legal Regulation of Process' in G. Richardson and H. Genn, *Administrative Law and Government Action* (Oxford: Clarendon) 1994; C. Harlow, 'A Special Relationship? The American Influence on English Public Law' in I. Loveland (ed.), *Lessons from America* (Oxford: Clarendon) 1995. And see C. Sunstein, *The Partial Constitution* (Cambridge: Harvard University Press) 1993.
15  Above, note 7.

Lester were prepared to argue[16] that 'official decisions are in practice appropriately reviewed for substance as well as process'. They saw the new categories of illegality and irrationality as 'clear[ing] the way for the courts to develop general principles of substantive administrative law based upon what Lord Diplock called "accepted moral standards"'.

## Wheeler v Leicester City Council[17]

The applicant was a member of Leicester (Rugby) Football Club who applied for judicial review of the council's decision to suspend the club from operating on council property for a one-year period. The ban was imposed to punish the club for refusing to condemn a tour to South Africa joined by three of its players. The tour breached the 'Gleneagles Agreement', designed to discourage sporting links with South Africa but was not unlawful. The council invoked s. 71(b) of the Race Relations Act 1976, which required it 'to promote . . . good relations between persons of different racial groups'. Forbes J and the Court of Appeal (Browne Wilkinson LJ dissenting) applied the *Wednesbury* test, ruling that the sanction was not so unreasonable that no reasonable local authority would have applied it. The House of Lords reversed the decision of the Court of Appeal.

*Wheeler* undoubtedly fell into Dworkin's category of a hard case. Of the nine judges who heard it, three found for the council and six for the club. The reasons given were diverse.

> *Lord Roskill*: I greatly hesitate to differ from four learned judges on the *Wednesbury* issue but for myself I have been disposed respectfully to do this and to say that the actions of the council were unreasonable in the *Wednesbury* sense. But even if I am wrong in this view, I am clearly of the opinion that the manner in which the council took that decision was in all the circumstances unfair within the third of the principles stated in *Council of Civil Service Unions v Minister for the Civil Service* [1985] AC 374. The council formulated those four questions [18] in the manner of which I have spoken and indicated that only such affirmative answers would be acceptable. They received reasoned and reasonable answers which went a long way in support of the policy which the council had accepted and desired to see accepted. The views expressed in these reasoned and reasonable answers were lawful views and the views which, as the evidence shows, many people sincerely hold and believe to be correct. If the club had adopted a different and hostile attitude, different considerations might have arisen. But the club did not adopt such an attitude . . .

> *Lord Templeman*:[19] My Lords, the laws of this country are not like the laws of Nazi Germany. A private individual or private organisation cannot be obliged to display zeal

16  J. Jowell and A. Lester, 'Beyond *Wednesbury*: Substantive Principles of Administrative Law' [1987] PL 368, 369-370.
17  [1985] AC 1054.
18  The questions were: 1. Does the Leicester Football Club support the government opposition to the tour? 2. Does the Leicester Football Club agree that the tour is an insult to the large proportion of the Leicester population? 3. Will the Leicester Football Club press the Rugby Football Union to call off the tour? 4. Will the Leicester Football Club press the players to pull out of the tour?
19  [1985] AC 1081.

in the pursuit of an object sought by a public authority and cannot be obliged to publish views dictated by a public authority.

The club having committed no wrong, the council could not use their statutory powers in the management of their property or any other statutory powers in order to punish the club. There is no doubt that the council intended to punish and have punished the club. When the club committee made their dignified and responsible response to these questions, a response which the council find unsatisfactory, to the council, the council commissioned a report on possible sanctions that might be taken against the club . . .

In my opinion, this use by the council of its statutory powers was a misuse of power. The council could not properly seek to use its statutory powers of management or any other statutory powers for the purposes of punishing the club when the club had done no wrong.

Consider the following comment: 'Such conclusory statements do not pass argumentative muster; they fail to satisfy even minimal standards for reasoned argument and decision-making.'[20]

After *Wheeler*, Jowell and Lester argued[1] for the assimilation by English law of the 'proportionality' principle from the jurisprudence of the ECJ and Court of Human Rights, where its use is familiar. Their argument ran: the test of *Wednesbury* unreasonableness forces a decision-maker to weigh or balance the case for and against the course of action he is proposing but it is procedural because it leaves the final decision to the administrator. Broadly, the proportionality test requires an administrator to 'balance' means against objectives, rejecting any course of action where the action is disproportionate to the ends to be achieved.[2] The proportionality principle goes further than the *Wednesbury* rule in two ways: first, it may end with blocking a course of action entirely on the ground that it is a disproportionate method of attaining the legislator's objectives; secondly, it openly transfers to the court the power to conduct the balancing exercise. It is thus a move to substantive review. The use of this test in *Wheeler* would have allowed the court to balance the usefulness of the ban for improving race relations against the infringement of the members' rights. This leads to an argument, here expressed by Allan, that administrative policies can only be operated within a framework of protected rights and interests which create legitimate expectations:[3]

The error of the majority judgments in [the Court of Appeal], it is suggested, lies in their failure to address the question of parliamentary intention within the general constitutional context. Whether or not the draftsman, or government, or relevant parliamentary majority had envisaged the narrower or wider construction of [the Race

20  A. Hutchinson and M. Jones, '*Wheeler*-Dealing: An Essay on Law, Politics and Speech' (1988) 15 J. of Law and Soc. 263, 267–269.

1  [1987] PL 368. See also J. Jowell and A. Lester, 'Proportionality: Neither Novel nor Dangerous' in J. Jowell and D. Oliver (eds.), *New Directions in Judicial Review* (London: Stevens) 1988.

2  The classic example in English law is the tariff system of sentencing, but see also *R v Barnsley Metropolitan Borough Council, ex p Hook* [1976] 3 All ER 452 (market stall-holder deprived of licence for urinating in market).

3  T. Allan, 'Rugby, Recreation grounds and Race-Relations: Punishment for Silence' (1985) 48 MLR 448, 450-451. See also T. Allan, 'Racial Harmony, Public Policy and Freedom of Speech' (1986) 49 MLR 121.

Relations Act] . . . was really beside the point. The rule of law requires that statutory provisions be generally interpreted and applied in accordance with the fundamental freedoms enshrined in the common law . . .

It follows that . . . limits may properly be placed on the scope of a local authority to pursue its responsibilities for securing racial harmony. It may often be legitimate, in exercise of its general functions, to take account of the requirement of its racial policy. It does not follow that these functions can be exercised in a manner which endangers freedom of speech and conscience generally considered to be fundamental. Nor does the existence of explicit electoral support justify such an exercise; the effect would be to annihilate individual rights and freedoms. The authority which a policy derives from its endorsement by the majority of voters is constrained by the legitimate interests of the minority in the same way that, in construing legislation, the doctrine of parliamentary sovereignty is applied in conformity with the constitutional demands of the rule of law.

In this passage, Allan refers to three types of right: the 'legitimate interests' of citizens; 'fundamental freedoms enshrined in the common law'; and 'individual rights and freedoms'. Allan applauded the judgment of Browne-Wilkinson LJ in *Wheeler*, founded on freedom of speech. Here Browne-Wilkinson LJ[4] analyses the dispute as a conflict between 'the right of a democratically elected body to conduct their affairs in accordance with their own views and . . . the right to freedom of speech and conscience enjoyed by each individual in a democratic society':[5]

The right to freedom of speech depends on the fact that no one has the right to stop the individual expressing his own views, save to the extent that those views are libellous or seditious. These fundamental freedoms therefore are not positive rights but an immunity from interference by others. Accordingly, I do not think that general words in an Act of Parliament can be taken as authorising interference with these basic immunities which are the foundation of our freedom.

## 6. Rights as trumps?

Because they are awarded constitutional status, Allan saw this cluster of rights as binding local authorities when making policy. Remember too that Allan sees issues of rights as falling particularly within the province of the judiciary. But pointing to the complexity of the issues at stake, Hutchinson and Jones see rights as an area of political dispute:[6]

'Free speech' is an evocative and potent term. As an ideal, like due process and natural justice, it exercises a tenacious grip on the political imagination and consciousness. Yet its ideological attraction and resilience are largely attributable to its historical adaptability and political plasticity. Free speech only takes on meaning in particular contexts . . . The two major justifications – liberal and democratic – for freedom of speech can be distinguished by the different limitations they suggest on the authority and power of the state to intervene in speech matters. Liberals want individuals left alone to cultivate their personalities through diverse acts of self-expression . . .

4   [1985] AC 1054 at 1061.
5   [1985] AC 1054 at 1065.
6   (1988) 15 J. of Law and Soc. 263, 267-269.

democrats protect political speech so that people can engage in informed public debate and effect a substantial degree of self-governance. Government must facilitate the expression and hearing of a full spectrum of values and ideas at large in society . . . The problem of the liberal is to explain why speech is special . . . the parallel problem for the democrat is to explain how majoritiarian principles ought to be set aside in the interest of the minority . . . In *Wheeler and Others v Leicester City Council* it was not that the rugby players were required to speak but that the council's threat was intended to force the players to express a political opinion that they did not hold or else be punished . . . the decision was not intended to have a chilling effect on ideas or speech. It was, instead, intended to allow the council to make a statement through a body which was seen as an ambassador for the community. In such a case it is extremely uncertain that the free speech principle must or should be extended to protect the rugby players' desire to remain silent . . . In essence, *Wheeler and Others v Leicester City Council* brought into sharp focus a deep and enduring disagreement between two competing conceptions of social justice. It pitted the council's espousal of an egalitarian justification against the courts' adherence to a libertarian ethic.

It is also difficult to square Allan's thesis with the structure of our constitution, in which protected status cannot be granted to any institution other than Parliament or to any category of right.[7] Moreover, how are the judges to determine which rights are in this sense 'fundamental' and which are not? As the United Kingdom is a founder-member of the Council of Europe and signatory of its Convention on Human Rights (ECHR), the answer might seem to lie in the ECHR. But successive governments have left the judiciary with an awkward dilemma. On the one hand they have indicated willingness to be bound by the ECHR, ratifying the original text with some protocols and periodically renewing the right of individual petition; on the other, they have consistently refused to incorporate the ECHR into the domestic laws of the United Kingdom. In *Brind* the House of Lords, applying the classic *Wednesbury* test, decided against indirect incorporation by the judiciary.

## *R v Secretary of State for the Home Department, ex p Brind* [8]

The Home Secretary, acting under statutory powers contained in the Broadcasting Act 1981, made an order prohibiting the broadcasting of the voice of any member of banned organisations. Sinn Fein, a legitimate political party, was also listed. The order was challenged on public interest grounds by journalists. Three main arguments were advanced in support of the journalists' case: (1) that in making the ban, the Home Secretary had acted 'unreasonably' and in breach of a recognised principle of English administrative law; (2) that his action amounted to an excessive intrusion on free speech and was thus in breach of Art. 10 of the ECHR; and (3) that the ban was unnecessary and 'disproportionate' to the ends which he hoped to achieve and therefore contravened a recognised principle of European public law established in the jurisprudence both of the European Court of Human Rights and the ECJ. The House of Lords ruled that the ECHR did not form part of United Kingdom law and was not directly enforceable in a British court.

7   See further below, Chapter 17.
8   [1991] 1 AC 696.

Lord Bridge: The obligations of the United Kingdom, as a party to the [European] Convention, are to secure to every one within its jurisdiction the rights which the Convention defines including both the right to freedom of expression under article 10 and the right under article 13 to "an effective remedy before a national authority" for any violation of the other rights secured by the Convention. It is accepted, of course, by the applicants that, like any other treaty obligations which have not been embodied in the law of statute, the Convention is not part of the domestic law, that the courts accordingly have no power to enforce Convention rights directly and that, if domestic legislation conflicts with the Convention, the courts must nevertheless enforce it. But it is already well settled that, in construing any provision in domestic legislation which is ambiguous in the sense that it is capable of a meaning which either conforms to or conflicts with the Convention, the courts will presume that Parliament intended to legislate in conformity with the Convention, not in conflict with it. Hence, it is submitted, when a statute confers upon an administrative authority a discretion capable of being exercised in a way which infringes any basic human right protected by the Convention, it may similarly be presumed that the legislative intention was that the discretion should be exercised within the limitations which the Convention imposes. I confess that I found considerable persuasive force in this submission. But in the end I have been convinced that the logic of it is flawed. When confronted with a simple choice between two possible interpretations of some specific statutory provision, the presumption whereby the courts prefer that which avoids conflict between our domestic legislation and our international treaty obligations is a mere canon of construction which involves no importation of international law into the domestic field. But where Parliament has conferred on the executive an administrative discretion without indicating the precise limits within which it must be exercised, to presume that it must be exercised within Convention limits would be to go far beyond the resolution of an ambiguity. It would be to impute to Parliament an intention not only that the executive should exercise the discretion in conformity with the Convention, but also that the domestic courts should enforce that conformity by the importation into domestic administrative law of the text of the Convention and the jurisprudence of the European Court of Human Rights in the interpretation and application of it. If such a presumption is to apply to the statutory discretion exercised by the Secretary of State under section 29(3) of the Act of 1981 in the instant case, it must also apply to any other statutory discretion exercised by the executive which is capable of involving an infringement of Convention rights. When Parliament has been content for so long to leave those who complain that their Convention rights have been infringed to seek their remedy in Strasbourg, it would be surprising suddenly to find that the judiciary had, without Parliament's aid, the means to incorporate the convention into such an important area of domestic law and I cannot escape the conclusion that this would be a judicial usurpation of the legislative function.

But I do not accept that this conclusion means that the courts are powerless to prevent the exercise by the executive of administrative discretion, even when conferred, as in the instant case, in terms which are on their face unlimited, in a way which infringes fundamental human rights. Most of the rights spelled out in terms in the Convention, including the right to freedom of expression, are less than absolute and must in some cases yield to the claims of competing public interests. Thus, article 10(2) of the Convention spells out and categorises the competing public interests by reference to which the right to freedom of expression may have to be curtailed. In exercising the power of judicial review we have neither the advantages nor the disadvantages of any comparable code to which we may refer or by which we are bound. But again, this surely does not mean that in deciding whether the Secretary of State, in the exercise of his discretion, could reasonably impose the restriction he has imposed on the broadcasting organisations, we are not perfectly entitled to start from the premise that any restriction of the right to freedom of expression requires to be justified and that nothing less than an important competing public interest will be sufficient to justify it. The primary judgment as to whether the particular competing public interest justifies the particular restriction imposed falls to be made by the Secretary of State to whom Parliament has entrusted the discretion. But we are entitled to exercise a secondary judgment by asking whether a reasonable Secretary of State, on the material before him, could reasonably make that primary judgment.

Applying these principles to the circumstances of the case . . . I find it impossible to say that the Secretary of State exceeded the limits of his discretion. In any civilised and law-abiding society the defeat of the terrorist is a public interest of the first importance. That some restriction on the freedom of the terrorist and his supporters to propagate his cause may well be justified in support of that public interest is a proposition which I apprehend the applicants hardly dispute. Their real case is that they, in the exercise of their editorial judgment, may and must be trusted to ensure that the broadcasting media are not used in such a way as will afford any encouragement or support to terrorism and that any interference with that editorial judgment is necessarily an unjustifiable restriction on the right to freedom of expression. Accepting, as I do, their complete good faith, I nevertheless cannot accept this proposition. The Secretary of State, for the reasons he made so clear in Parliament, decided that it was necessary to deny to the terrorist and his supporters the opportunity to speak directly to the public through the most influential of all the media of communication and that this justified some interference with editorial freedom. I do not see how this judgment can be categorised as unreasonable. What is perhaps surprising is that the restriction imposed is of such limited scope. There is no restriction at all on the matter which may be broadcast, only on the manner of its presentation. The viewer may see the terrorist's face and hear his words provided only that they are not spoken in his own voice. I well understand the broadcast journalist's complaint that to put him to the trouble of dubbing the voice of the speaker he has interviewed before the television camera is an irritant which the difference in effect between the speaker's voice and the actor's voice hardly justifies. I well understand the political complaint that the restriction may be counter-productive in the sense that the adverse criticism it provokes outweighs any benefit it achieves. But these complaints fall very far short of demonstrating that a reasonable Secretary of State could not reasonably conclude that the restriction was justified by the important public interest of combatting terrorism. I should add that I do not see how reliance on the doctrine of 'proportionality' can here advance the applicants' case . . .

Even if *Brind* closed the door to judicial incorporation, it could not close the door on the ECHR, increasingly invoked to fill gaps in the common law and persuasive in dictating particular interpretations of statute law.[9] Rights-talk has become universal, bringing our courts under pressure from rights-conscious litigants and determined pressure groups well-versed in the techniques of the international human rights movement.[10] Since applicants to the European Commission and Court of Human Rights must show that they have exhausted their domestic remedies before filing their application,[11] cases on their way to Strasbourg necessarily start in domestic courts. Incorporation of the ECHR into national law

---

9 A. Lester, 'English Judges as Lawmakers' [1993] PL 269.
10 C. Harlow and R. Rawlings, *Pressure Through Law* (London: Routledge) 1992, esp. Ch. 6.
11 Art. 26 ECHR. And see D. Harris, M. O'Boyle and C. Warbrick, *Law of the European Convention on Human Rights* (London: Butterworths) 1995, pp. 608-621.

is likely during 1997–98. Until legislation is in force, however, the judges, who might have preferred incorporation earlier,[12] have been faced with a problem how to treat the increasing number of human rights cases reaching them.

Cases involving EC law are also litigated in national courts. The EC Treaty and secondary legislation originally protected gender equality in EEC Art. 119 and the sacred 'four freedoms': free movement of workers and goods; freedom to supply services; and freedom of establishment within the community. The 1997 Treaty of Amsterdam extends the list, notably to racial discrimination. EC law increasingly impinges on public law cases. The ECJ makes considerable use of the proportionality principle,[13] and where EC law is in issue British courts must also employ it.[14] Again, although the European Union is not a signatory to the ECHR,[15] Art. F(2) of the (Maastricht) TEU provides that the Union 'shall respect fundamental rights, as guaranteed by the [ECHR] and as they result from the constitutional traditions common to the member States, as general principles of Community law'. This too was endorsed and amplified at Amsterdam.

Let us illustrate this problem through a practical example. Assume that a policy operated by the Ministry of Defence prohibits all persons of homosexual persuasion from serving in the armed forces for reasons of efficiency and morale. This policy has recently been examined and approved by a parliamentary select committee. X is dismissed summarily on suspicion of homosexual orientation. S/he applies for judicial review on the grounds of unreasonableness and of breach of ECHR Arts. 8 (respect for private and family life) and 14 (discrimination in the exercise of a protected right). Reviewing this policy, the court has a range of options. It could say:

(i)  that the issue falls within the area of prerogative defence powers and is non-justiciable (see the *GCHQ* case[16]);

(ii)  that no one should be dismissed without a fair hearing as to their sexual proclivity (natural justice, below, Chapter 15);

(iii)  that the policy is valid if it is not so unreasonable that no reasonable Defence Minister would adopt such a policy (*Wednesbury*);

(iv)  that dismissal is too grave a penalty for homosexual orientation and that the Minister must show either forbidden sexual activity or likelihood of harm before dismissal (proportionality);

(v)  that the policy is disproportionate in that it bars those of homosexual tendency who never put their feelings into practice, and must be adjusted accordingly (proportionality);

12  See particularly, Sir Thomas Bingham, 'The European Convention on Human Rights – Time to Incorporate' (1993) 109 LQR 390.
13  See G. de Burca, 'The Principle of Proportionality and its Applications in EC Law' (1993) 13 Yearbook of European Law 105.
14  *Torfaen Borough Council v B & Q plc*: C-145/88 [1990] 2 QB 19, ECJ. See also *Milk Marketing Board v Cricket St Thomas Estate* [1991] 3 CMLR 123.
15  The ECJ has ruled that the Community is not competent to ratify the ECHR: see *Accession by the Community to the European Convention for the Protection of Human Rights and Fundamental Freedoms*, Opinion 2/94 of 28 March 1996. See also House of Lords Select Committee on the European Communities, *Human Rights Re-examined* HL 10 (1992/3).
16  *Council of Civil Service Unions v Minister for the Civil Service* [1985] AC 374.

(vi)  that the policy is either unreasonable or sufficiently unreasonable to require endorsement by Parliament (*Wednesbury*);[17]

(vii) that the policy cannot be adopted because it is contrary to EC law, in this case, EEC Directive 76/207 (the Equal Treatment Directive);[18]

(viii)that the policy contravenes the ECHR and/or the case law of the Court of Human Rights (but see *Brind*[19]).

First, note how each choice on this scale is a step on the road to substitution of a judicial view of policy for that of the executive. Secondly, note what strong discretion is left to the executive by the traditional *Wednesbury* test (iii)(vi). Can the proportionality principle be manipulated in the same way to achieve a similar result?

Those who do not wish to abandon the traditional terminology of unreasonableness but who also accept some judicial role in the protection of human rights,[20] may favour the introduction of a 'hard look' rule in cases where a breach is alleged. This entails extending the *Wednesbury* test to a scale on which variant standards mark different government functions. In cases involving fundamental human rights, 'the threshold of unreasonableness' would be lowered; in areas of high government policy, involving prerogative powers or former judicial 'no go areas',[1] the threshold would be raised to what has ineptly been termed a 'super-*Wednesbury*' test. We can add two new positions to our scale, the first of which involves re-writing (i) above:

(ix)  that the issue falls within the area of prerogative defence powers and is justiciable only if it defies logic or accepted moral standards (*Smith*,[2] below);

(x)   that the policy involves such a grave intrusion on human rights that it merits an intensive review process.[3]

Now let us see how the courts have actually treated this issue, which came before them in the following case.

### R v Ministry of Defence, ex p Smith[4]

The appellants were a lesbian and four homosexual males, who were administratively discharged from the armed forces in accordance with an MOD policy document dated March 1994 when their homosexual tendencies became

17  This was the solution of the Court of Appeal in *R v Secretary of State for Social Security, ex p Joint Council for the Welfare of Immigrants* [1996] 4 All ER 385.
18  The ECJ has ruled discrimination against transsexuals illegal (*Perkins*, unreported). See also Art 6A EEC, inserted at Amsterdam.
19  [1991] 1 AC 696. Above, p. 120.
20  Sir John Laws, 'Is the High Court the Guardian of Fundamental Constitutional Rights?' [1993] PL 59.
 1  See C. Harlow, 'Public Interest Litigation in England: the State of the Art' in J. Cooper and R. Dhavan (eds.), *Public Interest Law* (Oxford: Blackwell) 1986.
 2  *R v Ministry of Defence, ex p Smith.* Below, note 4.
 3  See, *Bugdacay v Secretary of State for the Home Department* [1987] AC 514.
 4  [1996] 1 All ER 257.

known. All had exemplary service records. They sought judicial review on the basis: (1) of a breach of the ECHR; (2) of a breach of EEC Directive 76/207; and (3) that on any test of reasonableness the policy was irrational. Affirming the Divisional Court, the Court of Appeal dismissed the appeal.

> *Sir Thomas Bingham MR*: . . . The court may not interfere with the exercise of an administrative discretion on substantive grounds save where the court is satisfied that the decision is unreasonable in the sense that it is beyond the range of responses open to a reasonable decision-maker. But in judging whether the decision-maker has exceeded this margin of appreciation the human rights context is important. The more substantial the interference with human rights, the more the court will require by way of justification before it is satisfied that the decision is reasonable in the sense outlined above . . .
>
> It was argued for the ministry . . . that a test more exacting than *Wednesbury* was appropriate in this case[5] . . . The Divisional Court rejected this argument and so do I. The greater the policy content of a decision, and the more remote the subject matter of a decision from ordinary judicial experience, the more hesitant the court must necessarily be in holding a decision to be irrational. That is good law and, like most good law, common sense. Where decisions of a policy-laden, esoteric or security-based nature are in issue, even greater caution than normal must be shown in applying the test, but the test itself is sufficiently flexible to cover all situations.
>
> The present cases do not cover the lives or liberty of those involved . . . [but] the appellants' rights as human beings are very much in issue. It is now accepted that this issue is justiciable. This does not of course mean that the court is thrust into the position of primary decision-maker. It is not the constitutional role of the court to regulate the conditions of service in the armed forces of the Crown, nor has it the expertise to do so. But it has the constitutional role and duty of ensuring that the rights of citizens are not abused by the unlawful exercise of executive power. While the court must properly defer to the expertise of responsible decision-makers, it must not shrink from its fundamental duty 'to do right to all manner of people'.

Return to our scale. How many of the criteria were considered and which were applied?

Shortly after *Brind*, in which he acted as counsel for the unsuccessful applicant, Lord Lester QC returned to an earlier theme. In a lecture[6] accusing the common law of 'ethical aimlessness', Lester invited the judiciary to supply ethical and social values where these were lacking. In a country whose unwritten constitution is founded in the concept of parliamentary sovereignty, how can this be done? Dworkin's conception of 'rights as trumps' originated, after all, in the United States, a constitution with a Bill of Rights, where the tradition of judicial review differs significantly from our own.[7] Writing extra-judicially, the judges began to supply their own answers.

5 See *Nottinghamshire County Council v Secretary of State for the Environment* [1986] AC 240; *R v Secretary of State for the Environment, ex p Hammersmith and Fulham London Borough Council* [1991] 1 AC 521.
6 'English Judges as Lawmakers' [1993] PL 269. For Lester's consistent position on incorporation, see 'European Human Rights and the British Constitution' in J. Jowell and D. Oliver (eds.), *The Changing Constitution* (Oxford: Clarendon) 3rd edn., 1994. For the contrary case, see J. Allan, 'Bills of Rights and Judicial Power – A Liberal's Quandary' (1996) 16 OJLS 337.
7 For an attempt to overcome this difficulty, see P. Craig, *Public Law and Democracy in the United Kingdom and the United States of America*, (Oxford: Clarendon), 1990.

For Sir John Laws,[8] the rights guaranteed by the ECHR are to be seen '*as a series of propositions*, [which] largely represent legal norms or values which are either already inherent in our law, or, so far as they are not, may be integrated into it by the judges'. Fundamental rights, Laws asserts, have the status of 'higher-order' law:[9]

> The democratic credentials of an elected government cannot justify its enjoyment of a right to abolish fundamental freedoms. If its power in the state is in the last resort absolute, such fundamental rights as free expression are only privileges; no less so if the absolute power rests in an elected body. The byword of every tyrant is 'My word is law'; a democratic assembly having sovereign power beyond the reach of curtailment or review may make just such an assertion, and its elective base cannot immunise it from playing the tyrant's role . . .
>
> A people's aspiration to democracy and the imperative of individual freedoms go hand in hand. Without democracy the government is by definition autocratic; though it may set just laws in place, and even elaborate a constitution providing for fundamental rights, there is no sanction for their preservation save revolution . . . the need for higher-order law is dictated by the logic of the very notion of government under law.

This position is described by Griffith as 'unbalanced'.[10] Griffith prefers Sedley's emphasis[11] on *outcomes*; the 'outcome – or result we want – is symbiotic with principle, because it is only for their concrete effect that we consider principles worth having and fighting over'. For Sedley, courts offer space for the struggle and for the articulation of human rights; as judges cannot be barred from the debate on values and principles, it is better that they should participate and express their views openly.

Advocates of reasoned adjudication at first seemed to be encouraging the 'structuring' of strong judicial discretion by the development of logical and principled judicial reasoning. Their influence can be seen in the Law Reports when we read modern judgments, coherent, well-structured and accessible. We have also seen the argument for reasoned adjudication fuse with a wider argument about judicial legitimacy. As judicial review 'bit more strongly into the red meat' of policy-making and statutory interpretation, theorists began to advocate the primacy of 'principles' over 'policy'. To put this differently, they were seen as replacing the emotive words 'politics' and 'reasonableness' by a hierarchy of seemingly rational rules and principles. An extreme position emerged that undemocratic or 'unconstitutional' legislation which did not conform to the 'higher legal order'[12] might in the last resort be disregarded. Spirited opposition

---

8  'Is the High Court the Guardian of Fundamental Constitutional Rights?' [1993] PL 59, 61. And see *R v Secretary of State for the Home Department, ex p McQuillan* [1995] 4 All ER 400, Sedley J.

9  Sir John Laws, 'Law and Democracy' [1995] PL 72, 89-90. And see R. Dworkin, *Life's Dominion* (London: Harper Collins) 1993, p. 123.

10  J. Griffith 'Judges and the Constitution' in R. Rawlings (ed.), *Law, Society and Economy* (Oxford: Clarendon) 1997. Sir John seems to resile from his position in 'The Constitution: Morals and Rights' [1996] PL 622.

11  Sir Stephen Sedley, 'Human Rights: a Twenty-First Century Agenda' [1995] PL 386 and 'The Sound of Silence: Constitutional Law without a Constitution' (1994) 110 LQR 270.

12  Laws, above, note 9; Lord Woolf of Barnes, 'Droit Public – English Style' [1995] PL 57, 67-69.

from Griffith,[13] unpersuaded by appeals to reasoned or principled theories of adjudication, demonstrates that the polarities of red and green light theory are still in place.

## 7. Forever amber?

In this chapter, we have depicted 'amber light theory' as borrowing from both red and green light theory and moving forward to strengthen the 'fire-watching' and 'fire-fighting' functions of administrative law, finding solutions outside as well as inside courts. These themes will be developed in every subsequent chapter. In a new text on Australian judicial review, however, Aronson and Dyer assert[14] that:

> the last fifteen years or so have belonged to the red light brigade in the political, economic and administrative arenas. The legal profession is looking increasingly like one of the last bastions of liberalism, if not an institution for lost causes. This is especially marked in the administrative lawyers' reactions to increasing managerialism within the public sector, and to its downsizing, corporatisation, outsourcing and privatisation.

Before we can assess this view, we need to be clearer what developments are being referred to. Outlined in the next chapter, they too will make an appearance in every subsequent chapter. At this stage it suffices to mark a propensity for conflict between lawyerly values forged in an era of political consensus and the values of a government committed to radical, conservative change. Is this conflict, as Hood suggests,[15] endemic? Can administrative law respond? Must its values change? Or is administrative law doomed, as reviewers of the first edition suggested, to 'remain forever amber'?[16]

13  'Judges and the Constitution', above, note 10. See also Lord Irvine, above, p. 83, note 12.
14  M. Aronson and B. Dyer, *Judicial Review of Administrative Action* (Sydney: LBC Information Services) 1996, p. 5.
15  C. Hood, 'A Public Management for All Seasons' (1991) 69 Pub. Admin. 3.
16  L. Hancher and M. Ruete, 'Forever Amber?' (1985) 48 MLR 236, 243.

Chapter 5

# A blue rinse

## 1.    Themes and values

Behind every theory of administrative law there lies a theory of the state, or so we
asserted in Chapter 1. For this reason Chapter 1 included a sketch of the way in
which the modern state has been organised, together with some discussion of
attitudes to the state since the turn of the century. But if the proposition contains
even a grain of truth, then the remarkable transformation in the structure and
organisation of the British state since 1979 must be of the utmost significance for
our system of administrative law. The purpose of this chapter is to connect
prevailing theories of government to the doctrinal and institutional development
of administrative law. Here we are content to explore new ideas and identify some
of the fresh challenges and opportunities, leaving them to be pursued later.

An article by Dunsire describing changing themes in public administration
provides a convenient starting point:[1]

> From a writing-desk in Britain today, certainly, and also perhaps in the United
> States, one historical circumstance dominates thought about public administration:
> fiscal crisis, cuts, retrenchment. With that clue, using hindsight, the period from the
> early fifties to the late sixties can be seen to have been a period of steady government
> growth, the problems those of organizing and managing expansion; multiplication of
> agencies and programmes, coordination, planning. The latter sixties to mid-seventies
> were a period of relative standstill; and hence, perhaps, of reorganizations, mergers,
> consolidation, review, improvement. Since the later seventies, an undoubted contraction
> – not only an 'end to growth', but a drastic reduction in real resources available to
> public administration has been taking place ... Cause, effect, or simple accompaniment
> of this historical trend, there are perhaps three important movements of thought in the
> late 1970s to be noted. The first is the spreading critical appraisal of the role of the state,
> which on the Left speaks of a crisis of legitimation, and on the Right of 'getting
> government off the backs of the people'. Both join in the attack on 'bureaucracy'.
> The second movement of thought impugns the 'rationality' of earlier orthodoxy in
> Public Administration writing, rejects its pseudo-technical claims, and politicizes
> appreciation of public administration generally. The third group of ideas dissolves
> the clarity of the separation of 'public' and 'private' in earlier thinking, questions the
> usefulness of the state/non-state distinction, and takes a more holistic view of society
> and its processes.

1    A. Dunsire, 'Challenges to Public Administration in the 1980s' (1982) 39 Pub. Admin. Bulletin
     8, 9-10.

Notice that Dunsire locates the emergence of opposition to centralisation and statism in the 1970s. Yet the election of Mrs Thatcher's government in 1979 is the date usually chosen as marking the triumph of 'New Right' ideology[2] and the end of 'post-war consensus'.[3] Over the last 15 years, commentators tell us, British government has been re-invented and transformed. When Prime Minister John Major presented the Citizens' Charter as 'one of the central themes of public life in the 1990s', he inaugurated a 'ten year programme of radical reform' aimed at a steady raising of standards of public service. The White Paper[4] mentioned a medley of interlocking 'themes, principles mechanisms and implementation vehicles'. It focused on:[5]

> . . . four main themes: quality, choice, standards and value . . . **Quality** referred to a sustained new program for improving the quality of public services. **Choice** meant that wherever possible competing providers would be the best spur to improved quality. Choice also meant that, even where competition was not possible, the users of services would be consulted about the level and nature of those services. **Standards** evoked the notion that citizens must be told what the service standards are and be able to act where service is unacceptable. And last but not least, **value** referred to taxpayers' rights to receive public services on a value-for-money basis within a tax bill the nation can afford.

The revolution in public governance which has taken place since 1979 could fairly be portrayed in terms of choice, which figures high on this list of themes and principles. Lewis[6] sees choice as 'the ruling political sentiment'. The collective welfare state has been remodelled as a market in democratic goods, ideas encapsulated in Hirschman's use[7] of the three primary choices open to consumers – Exit, Voice and Loyalty – as the basis of a theory of political participation by citizens. McAuslan has argued[8] that the programme of administrative reform undertaken by the Thatcher government was premised, though not always explicitly, on public choice theory, which operated as the underlying binding for an apparently disparate set of changes. Dunleavy and O'Leary[9] explain the link between New Right politics and public choice:

2   See I. Crewe and D. Searing, 'Ideological Change in the British Conservative Party' (1988) 82 American Political Science Rev. 361; A. Gamble, 'The Thatcher Decade in Perspective' in P. Dunleavy, A. Gamble and G. Peele, *Developments in British Politics* (London: Macmillan) 3rd edn., 1990; P. Whiteley, P. Seyd, J. Richardson and P. Bissell, 'Thatcherism and the Conservative Party' (1994) 42 Political Studies 185.

3   See A. Seldon, 'Britain, Europe and the World, 1945-80' in Bill Jones et al, *Politics UK* (London: Harvester Wheatsheaf) 2nd edn., 1994, p. 42.

4   *The Citizen's Charter. Raising the Standard* Cm. 1599 (1991) p. 2.

5   *Implementing the UK Citizen's Charter* (Ottawa: Canadian Centre for Management Development) 1992, p. 3.

6   N. Lewis, *Choice and the Legal Order, Rising above Politics* (London: Butterworths) 1996, p. xi.

7   A. Hirschman, *Exit, Voice and Loyalty, Responses to Decline in Firms, Organizations and States*, (Cambridge: Harvard UP) 1970.

8   P. McAuslan, 'Public Law and Public Choice' (1988) 51 MLR 681.

9   P. Dunleavy and B. O'Leary, *Theories of the State. The Politics of Liberal Democracy* (London: Macmillan) 1987, pp. 75-77.

Public choice theory is the most frequent name given to a distinctive methodology in political science, also known as collective choice, rational choice theory, social choice theory, or mathematical political theory. In principle you do not have to adopt new-right values in order to use public choice patterns of argument . . . However, a majority of public choice writers in fact espouse political values and policies normally associated with conservatism (in America) or market liberalism (in Europe).... Probably the large majority of public choice writers do not dissent much from the *laissez faire* prescriptions espoused by Milton Friedman in *Capitalism and Freedom* (1962). So there has to date been a strong correlation between using a public choice methodology and espousing new-right values, even if there is no necessary or intrinsic connection between the two. Public choice has four distinct intellectual antecedents: neo-classical economics, mathematical political models, social contract theory and the ideas of Jeffersonian administration.

*Neo-classical economics* has dominated post-war economics in all Western countries, a period in which the discipline has rapidly emerged as the most prestigious and apparently rigorous of the social sciences. Its extension into public choice theory reflects a wider movement for economic modes of analysis to 'invade' the areas covered by other disciplines such as human geography, law and political thought. In economic theory public choice is best understood in terms of its antonym: private choice . . . A paradigm case of private choice is that of the individual making choices in a market. The individual seeks to maximise his/her personal utility, whether as a consumer or a producer. He/she makes his/her decisions about consumption and investment, work and leisure so as to maximise benefits and minimise costs. Conventional micro-economics and welfare economics . . . elaborate at length on this logic of the private choices of maximising individuals. In contrast, public choice theory studies collective, social or non-market decision-making. The subject-matter of public choice thus includes many aspects of political science: the study of the state, constitutions, collective action . . . bureaucratic behaviour . . . Applying the methods and techniques of neo-classical economics to the study of these subjects is what makes public choice so distinctive . . . Three sets of problems precipitated the development of public choice as a distinctive approach: the search for a social welfare function, a concern with 'market failures', and problems in the economics of public finance . . . While conventional economics explored the subject of market failures in commercial contexts, public choice theory developed to demonstrate that political markets might have their failures too. For example, individuals reveal their preferences for public policies by voting at elections, but they may do so imperfectly because the structure of the political marketplace produces unintended harmful consequences. They later extended their analysis to explore what goes wrong inside the governmental machine itself, arguing that in welfare terms 'state failures' can be as much of a problem as market failures.

The most powerful influence from micro-economics on the public life of the last two decades has probably been the conceptualisation of state activities in terms of market. Market-mimicking is a constant theme within publicly-funded enterprises where true competition is difficult of achievement; in the National Health Service, for example, hospital services are now contracted for by group practices or area health authorities. By exploring the dangers of 'free riding',[10] public choice theorists have been able to undercut faith in collective action,

---

10   M. Olson, *The Logic of Collective Action* (Cambridge: Harvard University Press) 1965.

collective consumption and public subsidy. Olson's conviction that citizens were rational, selfish actors and that interest groups were largely organised to secure to themselves a share of collective benefits or public goods, led on to a re-evaluation of the nature of state institutions. Far from the ideal of the public interest supported by collectivists and crucial to amber light theory, Olson perceived public officials as largely dedicated to their own interests or the interest of their agencies to the point that government and legislators came to be seen as a motley crew of self-serving 'rent seekers'.[11] For public choice theorists, the benchmark for politics and public administration was the rational choices of private citizens.

Public choice theory demands both a change in the role of the state and a narrowing of its functions to maximise the area open to private interests. Today, in Osborne and Gaebler's celebrated metaphor,[12] 'The state steers, it does not row'. The term 'New Public Management' (NPM) has been coined to describe this decisive change in administrative style. In 1991, Hood explained the rise of NPM in terms of:[13]

> . . . four other administrative 'megatrends', namely:
> (i) attempts to *slow down or reverse government growth* in terms of overt public spending and staffing.
> (ii) the shift towards *privatization and quasi-privatization* and away from core government institutions, with renewed emphasis on 'subsidiarity' in service provision.
> (iii) the development of *automation*, particularly in information technology, in the production and distribution of public services; and
> (iv) the development of a more *international* agenda, increasingly focused on general issues of public management, policy design, decision styles and inter-governmental cooperation, on top of the older tradition of individual country specialisms in public administration.

This chapter focuses on two aspects of NPM. The first is a shift in dominant *values* associated with a more limited conception of government. Hood has expressed this diagrammatically as a conflict between three clusters or families of administrative values:[14] *sigma* values of economy and parsimony ('keep it lean and purposeful'), *theta* values of integrity and equity ('keep it honest and fair') and *lambda* values of security and reliability ('keep it robust and resilient'). When we find that Hood's category of classic theta values includes:

(i)   recall systems for removing public officials from office by popular vote;
(ii)  'notice and comment' and 'hard look' requirements in administrative law;
(iii) independent anti-corruption investigatory bodies . . .

11  See also J. Buchanan and G. Tullock, *The Calculus of Consent: Logical Foundations of Constitutional Democracy* (Ann Arbor: University of Michigan Press) 1962.
12  D. Osborne and T. Gaebler, *Reinventing Government* (New York: Addison Wesley) 1992.
13  C. Hood, 'A Public Management for All Seasons' (1991) 69 Pub. Admin. 3.
14  Ibid, 10-12.

we can deduce that a clash is on the agenda between the theta values which can be associated with amber light theories developed by administrative law during and since the 1970s (see Chapter 4) and the 'lean and mean' sigma values associated 'with the matching of resources to narrowly defined tasks and circumstances in a competent and sparing fashion' and prioritised by NPM.

We focus secondly on novel or refashioned *techniques of control and accountability*, functioning in part to vindicate relevant values.[15] As functionalists, the authors share the view that some at least of the techniques of NPM fall within the boundaries of administrative law and contribute to the evolution of a New Public Law,[16] a belief reflected in this chapter. Thus, we briefly examine the changing role of audit, once a book-keeping exercise designed to check fraud and waste, now refurbished to promote 'value for money'. Again, the Citizen's Charter, a central plank in Conservative ideology, has penetrated the traditional administrative law concept of dispute-resolution and has been in its own way as influential as the values of 'openness, fairness and impartiality' propounded by the Franks Committee. Contract law, too, is changing to reflect public law principles (see further Chapter 8).

Finally, and directly associated with the revolution in public management, we find *regulation and regulatory agencies* and the move already mentioned towards an *agency-orientated* system of administrative law more characteristic of the United States (with all the growing pains which the development implies).

## 2. Functional values: economy, efficiency and effectiveness

Foremost amongst Hood's sigma values we find the 'cold, calculating and relentlessly functional' values of economy, efficiency and effectiveness, otherwise known as 'the three Es'. All three are malleable concepts, their definition clearly arguable and, like the common law concept of reasonableness, they are frequently used with imprecision. Efficiency can refer to productive efficiency, simply, the relation between input and output; production is efficient when an article is manufactured at the cheapest cost. Allocative efficiency, on the other hand, refers to the relationship between producer and consumer; in this sense production of an article made cheaply is inefficient if consumers are unwilling to buy it. Economy too is frequently equated with cheapness;[17] arguably, however, production is not economic if it does not fulfil the purpose for which goods were made. Economy and efficiency together cover the idea of productive efficiency while effectiveness can be equated with allocative efficiency. Taken together, the three concepts add up to value for money.[18]

---

15  P. Hoggett, 'New Modes of Control in the Public Service' (1996) 74 Pub. Admin. 9.
16  On which see W. Eskridge Jr. and G. Peller, 'The New Public Law Movement: Moderation as a Postmodern Cultural Form' (1991) 89 Michigan LR 707 (a special issue devoted to the New Public Law); C. Scott, 'The "New Public Law"' in C. Willett (ed.), *Public Sector Reform and the Citizen's Charter* (London: Blackstone) 1996.
17  See *Bromley London Borough Council v Greater London Council* [1983] 1 AC 768.
18  M. Mulreany, 'Economy, Efficiency and Effectiveness in the Public Sector: Key Issues' in T. Hardiman and M. Mulreany, *Efficiency and Effectiveness in the Public Domain* (Dublin: Irish Institute of Public Administration) 1991.

Introduction of these economic criteria into public administration enables public expenditure to be monitored and evaluated by reference to the overriding criterion of value for money, a process which has latterly assumed great importance in British public administration. It has also allowed outputs to be measured by reference to performance indicators. The 'Three Es' also form the basis of the 'Next Steps' initiative.[19] Increased reliance on the Three Es as the governing principles of public administration has proved controversial, however. Sometimes comparators are simply not comparable. For example, how can one place a pecuniary value on a twelfth-century church and 'weigh' it against projected increases in productivity to be derived from a new airport, as was once done by the Roskill Inquiry into a Third London Airport?[20] Quantification clearly has its limitations as a tool for evaluation. Crude performance indicators may bring unexpected results, as when a target to meet all police calls within 15 minutes brings an increase in traffic accidents. Short-term economies may bring long-term inefficiencies, as when patients are discharged to free up hospital beds into an inadequate care situation which results in further and more serious illness. Or should we argue that death would be more cost-efficient? Critics have argued that the criteria undercut the very concept of public service. 'Efficiency is not an exclusive criterion to be applied in policy formation: considerations of income distribution are also important. Policies which improve efficiency may increase inequalities in income distribution . . . There is often a trade-off between efficiency and considerations of equity and equality.'[1] Just as fairness and independence are associated with administrative law, so equity and equality are often seen as key public service values, emerging, for example, as the basis of ombudsman reports (below, Chapter 13).

## (a) An audit society . . .

One of the techniques seized on by Conservative government as a transmission-belt for its key values has been *audit*; indeed, the transformation of public audit into a proactive system entrusted with the duty of 'auditing for change' was widely seen as the first phase in the 'Thatcher revolution'. Public audit has deep roots, represented for most of this century by the Comptroller and Auditor-General, an independent officer of the House of Commons, responsible to the powerful Public Accounts Committee for the audit of central government;[2] at

---

19  P. Kemp, 'The 'Next Steps' Project: Efficiency and Effectiveness in the UK Civil Service' in T. Hardiman and M. Mulreany, *Efficiency and Effectiveness in the Public Domain* (Dublin: Irish Institute of Public Administration) 1991. See also D. Goldsworthy, *Setting Up Next Steps* (London: HMSO) 1991.

20  P. Self, '"Nonsense on Stilts": Cost-Benefit Analysis and the Roskill Commission' (1970) 41 Pol. Q. 249.

1  Mulreany, 'Economy, Efficiency and Effectiveness in the Public Sector', above, note 18, pp. 30-31.

2  See J. McEldowney, 'The Control of Public Expenditure' in J. Jowell and D. Oliver (eds.), *The Changing Constitution* (Oxford: Clarendon) 3rd edn., 1994; *The Role of the Comptroller and Auditor General*, Cmnd. 8323 (1981) and J. McEldowney, 'The National Audit Office and Privatisation' (1991) 54 MLR 933. And see, 'The Public Accounts Committee' in G. Drewry (ed.), *The New Select Committees: A Study of the 1979 Reforms* (Oxford: Clarendon) 2nd edn., 1989.

local level, the district auditor was an important official, with powers to question expenditure and surcharge councillors.[3] A new institutional focus was provided when the National Audit Act 1983 established a National Audit Office to work with the Comptroller. At the same time, the Local Government Finance Act 1982 replaced the district audit service with the Audit Commission.[4] Under the Local Government Act 1992, the Commission has responsibility for appointment and supervision of locally appointed auditors and for standard-setting,[5] though it does not itself carry out audits nor are its members necessarily accountants.[6] It has also acquired the role of overseeing the development of performance indicators for local government, to serve as the basis for league tables of performance. Greeted with suspicion as a tool to increase the central government grip on local government, the Audit Commission has emerged as strikingly independent, despite its link with central government through the Secretary of State for the Environment, who participates in appointments and may give it directions, and to whom it reports.[7]

While the ambit of government audit was being extended and its institutions re-modelled, the function of audit was also being expanded. The simplest form of audit is 'certification audit', a function carried out by the Comptroller and Auditor-General, who certifies for central government departments that the account properly presents the income and expenditure account, that expenditure is lawful in the sense of intra vires, and that it is procedurally correct. The new technique of 'Value-for-Money' (VFM) audit is more far-reaching.[8] To quote the Chairman of the Audit Commission:[9]

A public audit should be much more than just a check on probity and regularity. As well as being handled in accordance with the law, funds should be spent wisely. This means obtaining the best possible value for the money spent, and the success with which this is done should be assessed during the audit. [Our value for money] methodology identifies good practice through national studies, using comparisons of performance . . . These are then reported nationally, and audits carried out at a local level to help elected authorities, governing boards and managers understand what they do well, and what they could do better. Auditors identify practical ways of improving services which help local managers target their efforts . . . The Commission believes that this methodology . . . is of great benefit to the public services to which it is applied. It gives managers a wealth of information . . . It gives the Government an objective view of local performance . . . It gives the public confidence that money spent on local services will not be wasted.

3   The system, which dates back to the Poor Law Amendment Act 1834, was structured by the Local Government Act 1972, since when auditors must refer recommendations of surcharge to a court.
4   See M. Radford, 'Auditing for Change: Local Government and the Audit Commission' (1991) 54 MLR 912.
5   *Code of Audit Practice for Local Authorities and the National Health Service* (London: Audit Commission) 1995. And see Radford (1991) 54 MLR at 914.
6   About 70% of district audits are now carried out by District Audit, a 'Next Steps' Agency of the Audit Commission.
7   See s. 11 of and Sch. 3 to the Local Government Finance Act 1982.
8   For a fuller account, see E. Normanton, 'Reform in the Field of Public Accountability and Audit: a progress report' (1980) 51 Pol. Q. 175.
9   D. Cooksey, Audit Commission *Annual Report 1993*, pp. 1-2.

Unlike financial audit, which is merely a protection against corruption, obvious waste and illegality, VFM 'is intended both to evaluate and to shape the performance of the auditee in three dimensions: economy, efficiency and effectiveness'. The effect is to substitute *quantifiable* criteria for earlier notions of performance, effectiveness and accountability. Power argues[10] that the primacy of 'The Three Es' has led to the growth of 'an audit society' and that the key to audit's success in expansion has been VFM. He illustrates his point with the 'league tables' published to allow parents to exercise their power of choice in education.[11] These have the effect of substituting easily calculable examination results for community knowledge and first-hand experience of a school's environment. Significantly, dispute has broken out about the factors to be included: e.g., can data as to pupils' background be included to represent 'value added', etc.?

Educational reform epitomises the values of NPM associated with Margaret Thatcher's governments. The Education Reform Act 1988 has been described as introducing the most wide-ranging and profound changes since 1944, with a fundamental shift towards central control. It also 'subjects the provision of education to competitive market forces in the search for improved standards, efficiency and accountability'.[12] Thus, we find on the one hand enhanced parental governance in individual schools, 'league tables' encouraging competition and an illusion at least of parental choice and official encouragement of subsidiarity in the form of 'opt-outs' from local authority control. On the other hand, a new National Curriculum has been installed whose delivery entails a framework of rules to confine and structure professional discretion. A new regulatory agency, the Office for Standards in Education (OFSTED) has replaced the familiar figure of the government inspector, who had played a central role in developing standards and providing accountability in this and many other fields of public activity during the nineteenth century. Setting of standards and oversight ('steering') is one of OFSTED's chief functions. To a cynic, the Act and its successors could be seen as screening behind more attractive values of 'public choice'[13] a steady process of centralisation and authoritarianism. Standard-setting and regular testing are key elements in establishment of control.

This type of standard-setting is a form of performance indicator (PI), another device central to the transformation of government and closely linked to VFM audit. The technique of performance indicators is facilitated by the development of information technology. PIs can be used either as 'tin-openers' or, more assertively, as 'dials'. A 'tin-opener' provides an invitation to investigate any unit shown to depart from a statistical norm. 'Dials' provide both a reading of 'performance' and norms against which performance can be assessed directly; in more familiar language, they allow discretion, albeit in limited areas, to be

10  M. Power, 'The Audit Society' in A. Hopwood and P. Miller (eds.), *Accounting as a Social and Institutional Practice* (Cambridge: CUP) 1994.
11  See the Education (Schools) Act 1992.
12  P. Meredith, 'Educational Reform' (1989) 52 MLR 215.
13  See P. McAuslan, 'Public Law and Public Choice' (1988) 51 MLR 681; P. Brown, 'Education' in P. Brown and R. Sparks, *Beyond Thatcherism* (Milton Keynes: Open University Press) 1989.

structured and confined. Equally, 'dials' can be used prescriptively to establish performance targets and 'ratchet up' performance (one of the avowed objectives of the Citizens' Charter programme explained below). The Charter programme is replete with examples of PIs, ranging from 'accuracy targets' in the payment of welfare benefits to 'waiting time targets' for the police to answer calls. In a contractual setting, PIs can be formulated as specific obligations, so that we shall find them used in contracting-out, franchising and regulation, where a regulator might use PIs to set standards for the regulated industry to maintain. Carter summarises their manifold uses in the specific context of Next Steps agencies:[14]

> Sustaining the entire [next steps] agency exercise is the use of performance measures as instruments of hands-off managerial control and democratic accountability: central departments, particularly the Treasury, need PIs to exercise control without breathing down the necks of the new chief executive. Parliament and the public need PIs to ensure that agencies are delivering the desired services efficiently and effectively. Specifically, each agency is required to publish performance targets in its Framework Agreement, which will be the subject of a quarterly review by the sponsoring department and the scrutiny of parliamentary committees and individual politicians.

Audit shapes the activities which it controls in significant ways. As Power puts it:[15]

> Far from being passive, audit actively constructs the contexts in which it operates. The most influential dimension of the audit explosion is the process by which environments are made auditable, structured to conform to the need to be monitored ex-post . . . The standards of performance themselves are shaped by the need to be auditable . . . At the same time, organisations may be encumbered with structures of auditability embodying performance measures which increasingly do not correspond to the first order reality of practitioners' work . . . The general point is that the system of auditing knowledge is increasingly self-referential. It models organisations for its own purposes and impacts to varying degrees upon their first-order operations . . . Concepts of performance and quality are in danger of being defined largely in terms of conformity to auditable process.

As Power notes, this can be controversial if the goals and values of management as expressed in PIs and enforced through audit do not tally with those of the professionals engaged in service-delivery:[16]

> Performance in the sense of effectiveness is difficult to assess where practitioners are unaccustomed to thinking in such terms. For example, nurses, policemen and women, prison officers, research workers and others have traditionally used highly localised standards of quality control. In all these cases, too, concepts of success and failure are problematic: rising levels of ill-health, crime and prison disorder have many causes and cannot simply be regarded as 'failures' of the service in question. For all

---

14　N. Carter, 'Learning to Measure Performance: The Use of Indicators in Organisations' (1991) 69 Pub. Admin. 85, 87.
15　M. Power, *The Audit Explosion* (London: Demos) 1994, pp. 8, 37, 39, 48.
16　Ibid, p. 13.

its proclaimed sensitivity towards context, VFM demands that effectiveness be quantifiable. It does this by standardising measures of effectiveness (on the one hand) and/or by reducing effectiveness to standardisable measures of economy and efficiency.

Thus, one effect of audit is to impoverish the discipline of public administration, as a single form of accountability for *performance*, the golden thread of the revolution in government, is all that is sought. On the other hand, and this time within the parameters of audit, audit prioritises the quantifiable criteria of efficiency and economy over the less easily quantifiable value of effectiveness. Auditors hesitate to enter the governmental field of policy-making. McEldowney, for example, blames the NAO for timidity in advancing audit-based models for departmental decision-making and describes it as 'risk averse from entering the area of government policy':[17]

> VFM examinations have concentrated too heavily on 'economy and efficiency' rather than that of 'effectiveness'. The questions raised about effectiveness are linked to the ability of auditors to perceive and quantify the link between intentions and outcomes of decisions within government. Given the complexity of decision-making, it is thought that it is often difficult to quantify and assess the intention behind the decisions and their outcome.

Arguably, however, this lies outside the remit of VFM audit. The Audit Commission, for example, has been widely praised for the success of its impact on the management culture of local government, supposedly producing recurrent savings of many thousand million pounds.[18] Yet its decision to examine the role of chief executive, councillors and council met (well- justified) criticism as lying outside its remit;[19] to put this differently, VFM audit had trespassed on territory reserved for democratic audit.

We are beginning to see how, from its small beginning as a book-keeping exercise, financial audit has emerged as a hydra-headed technique. The rapid spread in audit practices initiated in large measure by concern with economic stability and control of public expenditure also reflects a changed conception of administration and government. Today, it manifests itself in management audits, teaching audits, environmental audits, stress audits and many others. It has become instrumental to the propagation of a private sector ethos:[20]

> The reinvention of government is informed by two opposite tendencies. On the one hand, there are centrifugal pressures for the decentralisation and devolution of services and for turning parts of government into enterprises, whether through full privatisation or partial 'enterprisation' . . . On the other hand, there are equally powerful pressures

---

17  J. McEldowney, 'Audit Cultures and Public Authority Risk Aversion' in R. Baldwin and P. Cane (eds.) *Law and Uncertainty: Risks and Legal Processes* (London: Kluwer Law International) 1996, p. 196. See also S. Roberts and C. Pollitt, 'National Audit VFM Study' (1994) 72 Pub. Admin. 527.

18  B. McSweeney, 'Accounting for the Audit Commission' (1988) 59 Pol. Q. 28; M. Radford, (1991) 54 MLR 912 is more critical.

19  McEldowney, 'Audit Cultures', above, note 17, p. 198.

20  Power, *The Audit Explosion*, above, note 15, pp. 15-17.

to retain control over functions that have been made autonomous ... These competing pressures ... constitute a distinctive idea of government. Consistent with the liberal mission, the UK state is increasingly committed not to interfere or engage in service provision directly; it seeks to fulfil its role by more indirect supervisory means. In many cases the state has become regulator of last resort, operating indirectly through new forms of control (such as the independent regulator) which have the appearance of being apolitical. The great attraction of audit and accounting practices is that they appear to reconcile these centrifugal and centripetal forces better than the available alternatives . . . The word [audit] symbolises a cluster of values: independent validation, efficiency, rationality, visibility almost irrespective of the mechanics of the practice and, in the final analysis, the promise of control. All these apparent virtues have come together to make audit a central part of the 'reinvention of government'.

Here, Power stresses the artful way in which audit insinuates itself under the guise of neutrality, a process closely resembling the legal tactic of formalistic reasoning. A further parallel is identified by Perks:[1]

Professional accountants need uncertainty, lack of clarity, professional judgment and general mystification to maintain their distinction from ordinary people. But if it were generally realised that accounting principles have more to do with ritual and magic than with clarity and consistency, there would be a general loss of confidence in the accountancy profession and the financial statements that it produces.

Very similar arguments have been advanced against legal realism. Not only does this insight help to explain how law and accountancy have successfully established their claim as a technique of control, but also how the one discipline may borrow the techniques of the other, which may in time come to be superseded by it.[2]

### (b) Contract culture

A further link can be made between NPM and contract. Contract can provide an additional means of enforcing standards in services which have been downloaded:[3]

Accountability is linked to performance assessment. If managers are to be in greater control over the resources required to achieve targets, then they will be held accountable for their performance. Schools will be held accountable for the achievement of the national curriculum. Contractors will be held accountable for fulfilling their contracts. There is a necessary emphasis on performance assessment and performance indicators.

Audit helps to construct definitions of quality and performance as well as monitor them; contract and franchising also involve specification of standards and

1   R. Perks, *Accounting and Society* (London: Chapman and Hall) 1993, p. 158.
2   See further J. Freedman and M. Power, 'Law and Accounting: Transition and Transformation' (1991) 54 MLR 769; T. Murphy, 'The Oldest Social Science? The Epistemic Properties of the Common Law Tradition' (1991) 54 MLR 182, 191.
3   J. Stewart and K. Walsh, 'Change in the Management of Public Service' (1992) 70 Pub. Admin. 498, 505.

exercise of control through the monitoring of performance. In both cases, the judgment of quality and performance is a potentially difficult and contested exercise. Public expectations rise and citizens differ in their view of what is an acceptable level of service. Even in contracts for simple services, such as refuse collection, the quest for 'quality assurance' can prove an exacting task demanding lengthy documentation (below, Chapter 9). In complex professional services replete with value choices, such as medicine or social services, the more sophisticated approaches demanded are not necessarily forthcoming.[4]

Contract shares with audit the capacity to superimpose its own specific conception of accountability and undermine competing forms of accountability.[5] For Deakin and Walsh,[6] 'Contracts and markets have been crucial to the process of reinventing the public service in Britain which began a decade ago and is still in full flow. In this process, the concept of contract is as much a metaphor and the basis for a new legal rhetoric as formal legal mechanism'. The setting of contracts, the devolution of management responsibility and the use of Next Steps agencies all depend on the shift from local, internal, qualitative methods of control and accountability to the external, retrospective, quantified forms of controls which in large measure audit represents. In short, the introduction of NPM has had the effect of replacing hierarchical control with the diffused, sporadic and horizontal controls of the market. There is an inevitable clash with traditional public law methods of ensuring accountability.

The rise of contract is also a mark of the influence of NPM on administrative law. As Freedland notes,[7] Next Steps agencies, competitive tendering, contracting out, internal markets and market testing all represent in different ways a shift towards a 'contractual mode of governing'. Appropriated as an essential legal tool for structural and managerial re-ordering, contractual and semi-contractual relations have taken on a central role in public management, to the point where the term 'contract culture' has been applied to the new relationships.[8] This usage expresses the idea of service providers controlled through a network of contracts and contrasts sharply with the hierarchical relationship symptomatic of an (earlier) bureaucratic mode of government. The contract culture is not necessarily restricted to contract in the full legal sense of an agreement enforceable in the courts. It includes agreements 'intended to be binding' but falling – like many types of administrative rule – below the Plimsoll Line for formal, legal recognition:[9]

> The most interesting examples of a shift to a contract-based way of viewing new institutional relationships occur in the new executive or next steps agencies. When an executive agency is created by separation from its parent department, the relationship between the two is governed by a so-called Framework Document, which defines the functions and goals of the agency and the procedures whereby the department will set

4   K. Walsh, 'Quality and Public Services' (1991) 69 Pub. Admin. 503.
5   P. Birkinshaw, I. Harden and N. Lewis *Government by Moonlight* (London: Unwin) 1990.
6   N. Deakin and K. Walsh, 'The Enabling State: The Role of Markets and Contracts' (1996) 74 Pub. Admin. 33.
7   M. Freedland, 'Government by Contract and Public Law' [1994] PL 86, 88.
8   N. Flynn, *Public Sector Management* (London: Harvester Wheatsheaf) 2nd edn., 1993.
9   Freedland [1994] PL 86, 90.

and monitor the performance targets of the agency. Although it is asserted that the Framework Documents are not strictly speaking contracts, it is increasingly accepted that they are contracts in every sense but the technical one, so much is the nature of these arrangements like that of the contracts whereby activities are contracted out to the private sectors . . . the law seems to remain one step behind, even out of step, with this new set of realities.

Contract is essential to the functioning of a market or market-mimicking system, the discipline of which is seen as so much stronger than political controls. Just as contract ideology expresses a concern with individual rights and freedom of choice[10] central to NPM, so the contract culture expresses the idea of a cultural shift – powerfully formulated in the Citizen's Charter – towards a model of administration more akin to private sector management. Contract operates to structure and confine discretion by the making of rules, but through the simulation of markets rather than the hierarchical and participative rule-making favoured by amber light theories of administrative law. As Harden observes:[11]

> Responsibility for deciding what services there shall be should be distinguished from responsibility for delivering the services. This separation of the roles of 'purchaser' and 'provider' offers the opportunity not only to pursue economy, efficiency and effectiveness, but also to enhance individual rights and the accountability to government for policy decisions . . . this decision takes the form of an agreed definition of rights and duties, which is intended to be binding, if not necessarily legally enforceable . . .
>
> The approach works by creating a structural bias in favour of two constitutionally valuable developments: the reduction of unnecessary administrative discretion and the delegation of decision-making authority to accountable and effective units. However, if the contractual approach is to produce the latter result, the separation of functions must correspond to a genuine organisational independence. In turn, this can exist only if there is an appropriate legal and constitutional framework . . .
>
> Although contract is not a panacea for the problems of discretion, it does offer an opportunity to make real progress towards greater accountability by clearly identifying who is responsible for policy, what it is, whether it is being carried out in practice and if not, why not.

A problem arises because the common law has shown muted interest in government contracting, a point made earlier and amply documented in Chapter 8. In addition to what was said earlier, it is sufficient to note that, consistent with the classification of contract as private law, judicial review of the exercise of contractual functions is largely undeveloped. Yet significant issues of control and capacity clearly arise in this context. The exercise of monopoly public power by a private organisation, for example, renders suspect the contract paradigm of a voluntary, consensual obligation. The doctrine of privity constrains contracts to a bi-polar relationship, a limitation creating problems for the new decentralised model of government typified by triangular relationships between a public body as purchaser which contracts with a private firm as provider of services to the citizen/consumer.

---

10   See R. Epstein, *Simple Rules for a Complex World* (Cambridge: Harvard University Press) 1995.
11   I. Harden, *The Contracting State* (Milton Keynes: Open University Press) 1992, pp. xi, 14, 29, 71.

Ironically, whereas in a previous era, concern was expressed over the capacity of the common law to meet the great advance in state activity, the talk today is of its appropriate response to the rolling back of the state and assignment of public activities to the 'private' sphere. Calls are increasingly heard for a special public law contract to reach across the conceptual divide:[12]

> The rapid extension of the 'contract State' raises urgently the question as to whether the private law of contract is sufficient to ensure that public functions are properly supervised, or whether their exercise should be subject to judicial review. Put another way, should the State be able effectively to 'contract out' of its public law duties and responsibilities by reconstituting its functions in terms which have been regarded historically as exclusively the province of private law? . . . In reality, the public and private domains are now so intermeshed that it is no longer feasible to operate a [judicial review] procedure which is based upon their separation . . . The use of contract . . . has created a serious, growing and logically indefensible gap in accountability . . . . Supervision of the contracting power should not be available only at the suit of those who have failed to secure, or retain, a contract; the users of a service also have an interest in ensuring that there is no misuse of a contracting power and that services provided pursuant to a contract are delivered . . . Judicial means of supervision are particularly crucial given the lacuna in other forms of accountability.

The poverty of contract law and the rise of the contract state creates a crisis of legitimacy for courts concerned with contemporary canons of government and resolution of thorny contractual and quasi-contractual problems has become a priority for modern administrative lawyers. We shall follow these developments in greater detail in Chapter 8.

## 3. The regulatory state

Regulation, a sustained control exercised by a public agency over an activity that is socially valued,[13] goes back centuries. In the course of the last decade, however, commentators like Majone have begun to talk about the emergence in Western Europe of 'the regulatory state'.[14]

> Administrative regulation – economic and social regulation by means of agencies operating outside the line of hierarchical control or oversight by the central administration – is rapidly becoming the new frontier of public policy and public administration throughout the industrialised world. The absence of an efficient regulatory framework is increasingly seen as a major obstacle to modernisation . . .
> The growth of administrative regulation in Europe owes much to . . . newly articulated perceptions of a mismatch between existing institutional capacities and the

12  S. Fredman and G. Morris, 'The Costs of Exclusivity: Public and Private Re-examined' [1994] PL 69, 70, 79.
13  P. Selznick, 'Focusing Organisational Research on Regulation' in R. Noll (ed.), *Regulatory Policy and the Social Sciences* (Berkeley: University of California Press) 1985. For alternative meanings, see below, p. 295.
14  G. Majone, 'The Rise of the Regulatory State in Europe' (1994) 17 West European Politics 77, 83, 85. See also M. Loughlin and C. Scott, 'The Regulatory State' in P. Dunleavy et al., *Developments in British Politics 5* (London: Macmillan) 1997.

growing complexity of policy problems: policing financial markets in an increasingly interdependent world economy; controlling the risks of new products and new technologies; protecting the health and economic interests of consumers without impeding the free flow of goods, services and people across national boundaries; reducing environmental pollution. It is sufficient to mention problems such as these to realise how significant is the supranational dimension of the new economic and social regulation.

One element has been greater formalisation and external involvement in schemes of self-regulation. An example would be the regulation of financial services under the Financial Services Act 1986, which represented a shift from an informal 'club' style of regulation, premised on a high degree of mutual trust, to an elaborate combination of statutory and self-regulation. So as with media regulation (above, p. 19) and for similar reasons, we find a plethora of autonomous agencies, presided over by the Securities and Investments Board (Chapter 10).

Then there is privatisation. Clearly, the transfer of ownership to the private sector need not imply the full transfer of control and accountability functions from the public sector, nor has it in cases where the market after privatisation is seen as fragile or lacking in competition, as with utilities which deliver key services within the economy. Today, the landscape is littered with regulatory offices: the Office of Telecommunications (OFTEL) (1984); the Office of Gas Supply (OFGAS) (1986); the Office of Water Services (OFWAT) (1989); the Office of Electricity Regulation (OFFER) (1989); and the Office of the Rail Regulator (OFRAIL) (1993). In the context of privatisation, regulation may be described as the quid pro quo for the grant of monopoly or semi-monopoly status and special powers. It is also a central feature of the model of 'reinvented' government. The state which steers but does not row spawns a multiplicity of regulatory bodies with a general remit to monitor decision-making by the private sector and to represent the public interest. The process whereby 'rolling back the state' has ushered in a new breed of what are now fashionably termed 'non-departmental public bodies' – the so-called independent regulators – is commonly seen as a paradox. This should not disguise the difficult questions involved in maintaining control of what has been devolved. Regulatory agencies share with audit and with legal control their notionally apolitical and autonomous character, exemplifying the point made elsewhere that professions or bodies which seek to legitimate themselves through expertise generally also seek to distance themselves from policy-making and politics, where lack of representative credentials might render them suspect. On the other hand, their remit is in part to represent the public interest, traditionally a government prerogative.

It is sufficient here to identify some major themes to be developed in subsequent chapters. The first concerns agency discretion and the exercise of regulatory power. As we shall see later, the legislative mandate of an agency may incorporate various types of competitive and economic goals, as well as social objectives. This necessarily involves choices of emphasis and means of pursuit. It has been suggested that the K. C. Davis model of 'discretionary justice' is poorly suited to this kind of setting:[15]

---

15  R. Baldwin and K. Hawkins, 'Discretionary Justice: Davis Reconsidered' [1984] PL 570, 574, 580, 594, 598.

[Davis's] concern with individualistic justice slants his account and restricts its wider applicability. He concentrates on decisions that are made by individuals rather than by organisations or groups, and decisions that affect private citizens and not, say, sectors of the population. His conception of decision is also individualistic in the sense that he is concerned with the exercise of discretion in the handling or disposal of *cases* and does not address the ways in which choices are made about *policy*. Policy, after all, may be regarded as speaking to the handling of classes of case or as decisions about how to decide. Thus, there emerges a concept of administrative justice that diminishes policy considerations and makes it easy both to focus attention on those demands typically made of administrators by lawyers (fairness, openness, predictability etc.) and to minimise the importance of public decision-making of such factors as efficiency, adaptability, the accessibility of remedies and the furtherance of public rather than private interests.

A concept of administrative justice which does not pay full regard to policy matters is too limited because it overlooks the substantial recourse to administrative discretion exercised by organisational actors and by legislatures in, for example, wide and diverse areas of social and economic regulation . . . A proper appraisal of discretionary justice must recognise the part played in decision making by moral, political, organisational and economic values, in addition to legal ones . . . Instead, therefore, of extolling the virtues of controlling discretion in the interests of 'justice', the questions before administrative lawyers should be redrafted on a wider basis. The first issues in looking at any discretionary power should be political ones, what values should be advanced? What sort of accountability should be sought here? . . . To look to the rules and not to accountability is unjustifiably to give priority to one particular type of control mechanism.

Regulation in practice is widely understood as operating in 'the shadow of the law':[16]

It is a mistake to regard the formal legal framework as regulation. The legal framework provides only the scaffolding of regulation in practice. No legal system, apart from the most totalitarian, operates a penal strategy with automatic recourse to the formal law. Rather, the law operates as the sanction of last resort against which compliance is sought through negotiation, bargaining and threats.'

The familiar concern of administrative law with procedural safeguards and accountability follows naturally as the second theme. The advantages of regulatory bargaining chime with green light theorists, such as Ganz, who see the development of new and flexible administrative procedures as a prime task of administrative law. We have also noted a strong argument for transparency or openness and a participative form of regulatory decision-making.[17] The case presented for informality, weak channels of accountability, limited judicial review and an absence of procedural safeguards might, on the one hand, be described as a return

---

16  C. Veljanovski, 'The Regulation Game' in C. Veljanovski (ed.), *Regulators and the Market* (London: Institute of Economic Affairs) 1991, p. 13.
17  C. Graham and T. Prosser, *Privatizing Public Enterprise: Constitutions, the State and Regulation in a Comparative Perspective* (Oxford: OUP) 1991.

to corporatism (above, p. 22) or, on the other, in terms of governmental resort to powers of *imperium*.[18]

A third theme concerns the potential for dynamic patterns of control and accountability displayed in this area of administrative law. This is a familiar idea in the literature of regulation, as for example in the popular theory of 'agency capture', whereby agencies go through a life-cycle of youth, maturity and old-age, exhibiting appropriate levels of assertiveness.[19] Over the last decade, utilities regulation in Britain has provided a fine illustration of agency evolution, moving beyond benign and straightforward regulation focused on price control and towards an assertive model, probing and scrutinising more of each utility's activities. In the 1990s, we find growing stress on 'regulating for quality'.[20] In the context of privatised utilities, Citizen's Charter philosophy underlines the continuing role of government in their structuring and organisation.

## 4. The Citizen's Charter

The Citizen's Charter programme follows on and brings together the radical changes in government and ideology we have been discussing, the entirely foreseeable focus being taxpayers' rights to receive public services on a value-for-money basis within a tax bill the nation can afford. Often derided as Prime Minister John Major's 'big idea', the Charter was launched by means of a government White Paper in July 1991.[1] It consists of an array of political and administrative initiatives intended to raise the standards of delivery of public services and to empower the citizen to take action when the service delivered is substandard. Inside a policy of fiscal restraint, the Charter requires no substantial increase in public expenditure; rather, it is about 'finding better ways of converting the money that can be afforded into even better public services'.[2] The distinctive feature of the programme, however, is the requirement that all relevant agencies develop statements (charters) which indicate the standards of service that the citizen can expect to have delivered by the agency. This is in itself a considerable enterprise, since the programme extends not only to central government departments and agencies but also across local government, police and courts, the National Health Service and the (now mainly privatised) utilities. Both theoretically and in practice, the Charter has had the effect of re-writing the relationship between state and citizen in contractual terms, a theory of liberal individualism in which the state supplies services as a quid pro quo

---

18  T. Daintith, 'The Techniques of Government' in J. Jowell and D. Oliver, (eds.), *The Changing Constitution* (Oxford: Clarendon) 3rd edn., 1994.

19  See, for discussion, G. Wilson, 'Social Regulation and Explanations of Regulatory Failure' (1984) 32 Pol. Studies 203.

20  L. Rovizzi and D. Thompson, 'The Regulation of Product Quality in the Public Utilities' in M. Bishop, J. Kay and C. Meyer (eds.), *The Regulatory Challenge* (Oxford: OUP) 1995.

1  *The Citizen's Charter, Raising the Standard*, Cm. 1599 (1991). See C. Willett (ed.), *Public Sector Reform and the Citizen's Charter* (London: Blackstone) 1996.

2  See Francis Maud, HC Deb., vol. 203, col. 181 (WA) (5 February 1992).

for taxes paid by the citizen.[3] Later chapters will reveal just how great the transformation of administrative law has been.

*The Citizen's Charter*

| *Themes* | *Principles* | *Mechanisms* |
|---|---|---|
| Value | Standards | Privatisation |
| Quality | Openness | Wider competition |
| Choice | Information | Contracting out |
| Standards | Choice | Next Steps Agencies |
| | Non-discrimination | Performance-related pay |
| | Accessibility | Public information on standards |
| | Redress | Published performance levels |
| | | Improved complaints procedures |
| | | Reformed inspectorates |
| | | Audit |
| | | Enhanced regulation |

The Charter reinforces the idea that 'choice, wherever possible between service providers, is the best spur to quality improvement'. Choice also means in this context that, even where competition is not possible, the users of services are to be consulted about the level and nature of those services. This reflects a determination behind the programme to drive the philosophy of the 1980s reforms into the hard core of public services, where competitive pressures may remain limited. Choice appears as one of the seven 'principles of public service . . . which every citizen is entitled to expect'. The goal is once more to substitute 'marketised' decision making structures for a public bureaucracy associated with the industrialised welfare state and, further, to move towards individual choice in place of universal or standardised service provision. But the Charter goes further. It blurs the boundary between public and private sector by giving citizens some of the rights which private customers enjoy, the intention being to encourage the public sector to adopt the mechanisms which have been the private sector's response to those rights. In the next extract, the language of consumption and choice, contracts and competition, the metaphor of 'new democracy', of service

---

3   A. Barron and C. Scott, 'The Citizen's Charter Programme' (1992) 55 MLR 526; R. Bellamy and J. Greenaway, 'The New Right Conception of Citizenship and the Citizen's Charter' (1995) 30 Government and Opposition 469.

choice to replace an 'old corruption' of producer interests, all provide clues to Pirie's identity as an advocate of public choice theory:[4]

> The talk within the public sector is of serving the public, but in the absence of effective consumer pressures, the reality is one of producer domination . . . The imbalance is further heightened by the fact that public services often operate under monopoly or near-monopoly conditions. This means there is not the constant incentive to outdo rivals, or to pick up valuable innovations and practices from competitors . . . It is against this background that the notion of a Citizen's Charter makes its appearance. The central idea behind it is that citizens, or consumers of state services, shall be equipped with rights which seek to provide substitutes for the rights which they would have in a private market . . . Its assumptions are threefold. They are that the citizen is entitled to receive some level of service in return for the taxpayer funds used to finance it; that the citizen is entitled to know what level of service that is; and that he or she is entitled to some form of redress if that level is not attained . . . [The Charter's] instrument is the individual transaction which each citizen makes with the public service. The citizen has had little power to affect that service hitherto, but the Charter will supply those powers . . . The point of the Charter is that it is consumer pressure which improves supply. Transactions by individuals achieve a positive affect on the service in general . . .

The Charter programme has in fact been characterised[5] as 'a blending of New Right concerns with restricting the power of bureaucracy and extending individual choice, with more widespread concerns to make government bureaucracies more responsive to the needs of users'. Its managerial origins are also evident in this account from the responsible minister:[6]

> In the post-War period, two things have changed. The users of public services have come to expect higher standards as their own standard of living and education has risen. At the same time, the cost of public services has risen swiftly . . . In 1991, for example, government spent some £77 million a day on education, and £90 million a day on the National Health Service. Contrast this with 1963, when the comparable costs were £37 million and £30 million respectively . . . Yet despite their importance, and indeed their costs, our public services have been the subject of a peculiarly sterile political debate, the electorate has been presented with a false choice, between higher taxes or poorer services. Meanwhile, the private sector, by contrast, has continued to demonstrate that the control of costs and the pursuit of quality go hand in hand . . .
>
> We have had to restore the principle that the Government's job is to *govern* not to administer; to *steer* not to row. We have been reforming government; in fact we have been reinventing it . . . There has been a genuine, though somewhat unnoticed *revolution* in Whitehall. We have introduced the entrepreneurial spirit into the corridors of power . . . We understand now, with a decade of experience under our belts, that it is not simply *ownership* that matters. As fundamental as the division between 'public' and 'private' is the distinction between 'competition' and 'monopoly'. Since many important services will continue to have to be provided by the state with public funds, the key to improving them and controlling costs is having to *operate*

---

4   M. Pirie, *The Citizen's Charter* (London: Adam Smith Institute) 1991, pp. 5, 7-8, 23.
5   A. Barron and C. Scott, 55 MLR 526.
6   William Waldegrave, Speech to the Institute of Directors, 20 July 1992.

*competitively*. This pressure must operate in the private and public sector alike . . . Where, for whatever reason, the service must remain a publicly-owned monopoly, we shall look for other ways of exerting equivalent discipline to that of competition. Indeed, we must, since where there is no choice, the supplier has a higher, not a lower, responsibility to do well. *Management* improvements are the key. We are getting decent financial management systems in public services; we have established in most public services proper purchaser/provider relationships as the basis for their operation; we have freed managers . . . Where – as they sometimes should – services stay in government hands or are operated by government, we shall make sure, through the Citizen's Charter, that they deliver the best possible value, and the highest practicable quality . . .

[The Charter] means that instead of looking at services through the eyes of the provider, we must see them through the eyes of the user. It means determining services from the bottom up, not from the top down . . . What has stood in the way of the public services finding a capacity for constant improvement and renewal is the failure to empower either those responsible for delivering services or those who rely upon them. [The Charter builds in] a pull downwards and outwards – to the local provider, the user, and the local community . . . It puts pressures on the providers of services to treat customers well and to be called to account if they do not. And it empowers the providers with the managerial responsibility which, for too long, has been denied them.

Amongst the management techniques developed in the private sector with the aim simultaneously of reducing costs and enhancing quality is Total Quality Management (TQM) – an ideology of production which, as the name implies, is dedicated to an all-embracing design of processes and orientation of employees towards improving product quality; and, less radical, quality assurance or the introduction of systems to ensure that products or services comply with specifications (a simple example being the quality mark of the British Standards Institute). Quality assurance in the public sector entails identifying those features of a service which are considered as significant to users (e.g., speed of delivery); assessing any related problems or deficiencies; implementing improvements and monitoring the situation and, last but not least, publishing the standards to 'customers'.[7]

The seven principles are generally designed to increase consumer awareness and invite responsiveness, lubricating the model of market-type discipline. Thus, the programme demands *transparency*: full, accurate information should be readily available, including targets and results achieved presented whenever possible in comparable form. It contains a commitment to run services for customer convenience (an attack on theories of bureaucratic self-interest and unionism). Finally – and we shall amplify this point in Chapter 12 – well-publicised and readily available complaints procedures are requested. In New Right philosophy, complaints become a key performance indicator and assist management with quality assurance.

Remember Hirschmann's concepts of 'Exit, Voice and Loyalty' (above, p. 129). In the context of the Charter, 'citizenship' takes on a peculiar and limited form. In the post-war period of welfarism, citizenship had come to be given the

---

7    C. Pollitt, *Managerialism and the Public Services* (Oxford: Blackwell) 2nd edn., 1993.

extended definition of T. H. Marshall,[8] which added to the earlier concept of civil and political rights and obligations attached to membership of a community, the new social rights associated with the welfare state. In stark contrast, the Charter citizen is essentially an economic actor – a taxpayer and, consistent with an atomistic view of society, an individually autonomous *consumer*. To its opponents, 'Citizen's Charter' is a misnomer, a legitimating device to help cloak the radical transformation of state forms; 'public customers' charter' has been suggested as less appealing but more appropriate.[9]

The broad scope of the Charter programme is faithfully reflected in the range of mechanisms for implementation. We find promises of further privatisations, contracting-out and market-testing, additional Next Steps agencies and performance-related pay linked to Charter standards of service. Some of these promises we have already seen implemented, others, especially in the realm of contract, will be dealt with in later chapters. There is renewed emphasis on certain techniques of control and regulation, directed to the provision of information, the use of information in the setting of standards, and the public assessment of performance. Thus, the White Paper[10] heralds tougher audit powers, more independent inspectorates, new powers for the utilities regulators and, in limited areas such as the rail service, compensation schemes to tempt citizens into remedial action. Here again we find themes which will impact directly on administrative law. Still more ambitious, the programme has come to be defined as encompassing those changes in attitudes and culture in the public service and the structural and managerial reforms – privatisation, market testing, the establishment of agencies – which we have so far characterised as techniques of NPM.[11]

## 5. Reinventing administrative law?

In the first edition of this book,[12] we were able to remark on the dramatic changes in the political climate which were then bringing to the fore new political theories[13] and alterations in administrative practice. Yet few – including the authors – could have anticipated the depth of change in public institutions – the prime subject of study for administrative lawyers. A decade on, what was then unthinkable has, as reforms of the civil service demonstrate, often become the mainstream of policy debate. The Conservative revolution in state forms easily bears comparison with any structural or managerial transformation in the past, such as the great Northcote-Trevelyan civil service reforms of the nineteenth century or the programme of welfarism and public ownership associated with the 1945 Labour government of Clement Attlee.

---

8  T. Marshall, *Citizenship and Social Class and Other Essays* (Cambridge: CUP) 1950.
9  R. Hambleton and P. Hoggett, 'Rethinking Consumerism in the Public Service' (1993) 3 Consumer Policy Review 103, 111.
10  Citizen's Charter 1991, pp. 282-249.
11  The Citizen's Charter, Second Report, Cm. 2540, 1994, p. 89. See N. Lewis, 'The Citizen's Charter and Next Steps: A New Way of Governing?' (1993) 64 Pol. Q. 316.
12  C. Harlow and R. Rawlings, *Law and Administration* (London: Weidenfeld and Nicolson) 1984, p. xxiv.

By the late 1990s, the main outlines of the new state forms were all in place. The privatisation agenda reached what is likely to prove its zenith when British Rail joined 47 major privatised activities plus many smaller ones. But even if privatisation is terminated or slowed, it is unlikely that it can be undone. Over 60% of all civil servants now work in agencies or organisations operating on agency lines. Nothing suggests that this will change. Performance-related pay and performance indicators have spread from agencies to local government and to the core civil service (above, Chapter 1). Contracting out and franchising are characteristic of both local and central tiers of government, though the compulsory element may be on the way out since the election of a Labour government. Agencies, so the Charter Task Force informed us, were by 1994 'in the forefront of delivering the Citizen's Charter'; there were 38 charters in place covering the main public services, setting out standards of service and what people could do if those standards were not met.[14] These were the tip of an iceberg reaching into every public sector institution or body operating on behalf of the public service. Again, there is nothing to suggest that this is likely to change under Labour, equally committed to standards, though less enamoured, perhaps, of choice.

New Public Management, in short, is no longer new; it has become a permanent feature of the landscape. The structural and managerial revolution clearly establishes a strong framework for the future role and development of government. Its all-pervasive ethos and vocabulary has been adopted at home by both major political parties.[15] Its discourse has spread throughout Europe, reinforced by the market ideology entrenched at constitutional level by the EC Treaty.[16] Of course, the fashionable nostrums of the 1980s may eventually prove as ephemeral as faith in big government. At present, however, this seems unlikely. Even critics concede that, for the foreseeable future, a general ethos has been established likely to prevail whichever political party is in office.

A caveat is, however, necessary. Although, as we have tried to show, blueprints exist for much governmental machinery, one should not lightly assume that the equipment can be put only to one use. The Next Steps programme, for example, has been dubbed a piece of 'transferable technology' of equal value to a Labour government.[17] Again, although the Charter as constituted expresses a particular brand of market philosophy and economic citizenship, Charterism in the sense of setting standards of public service – an avowed Labour priority – could certainly be used to promote ideals of welfarism or participatory democracy.[18] To pin this to our own functionalist objectives, while machinery should be evaluated to see whether it does the job it was intended for, we should not exclude the possibility

---

13  E.g., D. King, *The New Right, Politics, Markets and Citizenship* (London: Macmillan) 1987.
14  Second Report on the Citizen's Charter, 1994.
15  C. Foster and F. Plowden, *The State Under Stress* (Buckingham: Open University Press) 1996.
16  W. Muller and V. Wright (eds.), 'Reshaping the State in Western Europe: The Limits to Retreat' (1994) 17 West European Politics.
17  P. Hennessy, *The Hidden Wiring, Unearthing the British Constitution* (London: Gollancz) 1995, p. 131.
18  R. Plant and N. Barry, *Citizenship and Rights in Thatcher's Britain: Two Views* (London: Institute of Economic Affairs Health and Welfare Unit) 1990.

that it cannot do, should not do, or indeed, is not already doing, something else rather better.

What of the implications for administrative law? To spell these out in detail is unnecessary, as they can be traced throughout the rest of the book. Privatisation and regulation need to be read together. In Chapter 1, we saw how privatisation has moved nationalised industries into the private sector. Their place has to a large extent been filled by regulatory agencies. This development, sketched in above, is the subject of detailed analysis in Chapters 10 and 11. Privatisation of public functions and the recasting of public bodies in the image of private companies has worked to undermine the public/private dichotomy.[19] Downsizing of the state through the 'Next Steps' programme gives agencies – which may or may not form part of the public sector – responsibility for the execution of government policy. Downsizing and the techniques of NPM have increased the reliance of administration on rulemaking.[20] The desirability of this trend, introduced in a wholly different context in Chapter 4, is considered in Chapters 6 and 7. Contract law is no longer, as in the past it tended to be, peripheral to administrative law and a new law of administrative contract is surely on the point of development (below, Chapters 8 and 9).

Administrative law theory has struggled to keep pace with changes in public administration,[1] unsure whether to treat them merely as the context for a relatively self-contained system of administrative law founded on principles laid out in Chapter 4, or categorise them as innovations to the structure and values of administrative law. In classic 'red light theory', where judicial review takes the central place, it is relatively easy to ignore the revolution in public administration. The shift from judicial review to contract law described below might be regretted as bringing a diminution in control,[2] but the challenge remains essentially simple: it is to widen the frontiers of judicial review so as to bring all bodies which exercise public or quasi-public functions within its boundaries.[3] We follow this exercise in Chapter 16. Arguably, however, Conservative reforms, running counter to the thrust of modern administrative law, impinge far more directly. Not only have the central ideals of justice and fairness been dethroned by the economic triad of 'economy, efficiency and effectiveness', but the dominance of law and legality as mechanisms for control has bowed before audit and its battery of performance indicators. It is not clear that this can be reversed.

For those administrative lawyers who prefer to define their subject in terms of participation and accountability,[4] the new techniques of public management,

---

19   See esp. *R v Panel on Take-overs and Mergers, ex p Datafin plc* [1987] QB 815; *Roy v Kensington and Chelsea and Westminster Family Practitioner Committee* [1992] 1 AC 624; *Mercury Communications Ltd v Director General of Telecommunications* [1996] 1 WLR 48. And see below, Ch. 16.

20   See C. Hood and C. Scott, 'Bureaucratic Regulation and New Public Management in the United Kingdom: Mirror-Image Developments?' (1996) 23 J. of Law and Soc. 321.

1   See P. McAuslan, 'Public Law and Public Choice' (1988) 51 MLR 681; C. Harlow, 'Changing the Mindset: The Place of Theory in English Administrative Law' (1994) 14 OJLS 419.

2   M. Freedland, 'Government by Contract and Public Law' [1994] PL 86.

3   M. Beloff, 'Judicial Review – 2001: A Prophetic Odyssey' (1995) 58 MLR 143.

4   E.g., T. Prosser, 'Towards a Critical Public Law' (1982) 9 J. of Law and Soc. 1; D. Galligan, *Discretionary Powers, A Legal Study of Official Discretion* (Oxford: Clarendon) 1990.

such as audit or the rights of access to information granted by the Citizen's Charter programme, become an inherent part of administrative law. But we find criticism of the efficacy and appropriateness of market discipline as a form of accountability, particularly where, as remains true of many public services, the extent of choice which citizens exercise is limited. Policy-making involves choices, but is not normally an area which management sees as appropriate for citizen input. Administrative rules and contracts which specify operators' obligations can set limits to accountability or squeeze out other forms of accountability (as has partially occurred with political accountability in the case of Next Steps agencies). From this perspective, the very process of handing administrative choices to the private sector may be suspect and may justify extending legal controls. History suggests that the idea of setting up courts to combat a private market ethos is implausible, but perhaps history will once again prove an unreliable prophet.

Chapter 6

# Getting things taped

## 1. A surfeit of rules

Over a generation there has been an explosion in rule-making. The inevitability of this development is generally accepted; rule-making is seen as an essential feature of a modern, bureaucratic society. The output structures of government have been defined in terms of rules: as rule-making, rule-application, rule-determination (adjudication) and discretion.[1] At the same time, lawyers, administrators and politicians express concern over the growing volume of rule-making, which actually makes it difficult to know what the law is. Figures produced for the Hansard Society in 1988 showed that around 2,222 pages of statute law with 6,342 pages of statutory instruments were produced annually,[2] and these figures relate only to the most formal types of rule-making. They leave altogether out of account 'bureaucratic law' – the departmental circulars, memoranda and codes of practice which clutter filing cabinets and computer files.

Galanter describes[3] the rule-making explosion as part of a general enlargement of the legal world, comprising, on the one hand, more lawyers and more litigation and, on the other, a growing amount of complex legal regulation and various legal material, with information technology rapidly multiplying the amount of information about law and the speed of circulation. Why? Galanter suggests: education bringing higher expectations of institutional performance and 'a pronounced decline of confidence in government, business and other major institutions'. To paraphrase, there has been a shift from trust in government (in fashionable terminology, group government) to the objective, accountable, governance (grid government) described in Chapter 5. The inevitable concomitant is regulation in all its forms.[4]

---

1   This classification is borrowed from D. Easton, 'An Approach to the Analysis of Political Systems' (1957) 9 World Politics 383. See also G. Almond and G. Bingham Powell Jr., *Comparative Politics: System, Process and Policy* (Boston: Little Brown) 2nd edn., 1978, pp. 9-12.

2   *Making the Law, The Report of the Hansard Society Commission on The Legislative Process* (London: Hansard Society) 1993, p. 11.

3   M. Galanter, 'Law Abounding: Legalisation around the North Atlantic' (1996) 55 MLR 1, 2. Teubner calls this process the 'juridification of the social spheres': see below, p. 300, note 20.

4   See C. Hood and C. Scott, 'Bureaucratic Regulation and New Public Management in the United Kingdom: Mirror-Image Developments?' (1996) 23 J. of Law and Soc. 321.

Cotterell deplores[5] the modern move from principled law, its image resonant through simplicity, towards a body of legislation and regulations which reads 'more like the contents of a manual of bureaucratic practice than a body of legal rules or principles'. He blames a tendency to be too specific: 'The striking, though hardly exceptional, Nightwear (Safety) Order 1978 made under consumer safety legislation then in force, is almost entirely made up of definitions of items of children's nightwear in terms of chest, sleeve, and inside-leg measurements.' This trend relates to the spectrum which we constructed in Chapter 4: at one end, unstructured discretion or 'no-rules' imply trust and flexible standards of reasonable conduct, at the other end, we find rules, specific and binding in character. Cotterell also blames the 'fusion of legal forms and scientific standard-setting'.[6] Scientific standards are quite unlike the flexible standards of neat dress selected by Jowell to characterise standards (above, p. 103). They are extremely precise, and may, like the performance indicators which we met in Chapter 5, be expressed as mathematical formulae; algebra does in fact figure in some financial legislation. Cotterell cites the Cosmetic Products (Safety) (Amendment) Regulations 1987, which demand that 'The ratio of aluminium atoms to that of zirconium atoms must be between two and ten' in a particular cosmetic ingredient. (Note that even the specificity of this rule permits a measure of discretion.) A variant on the theme comes from Scheuerman who, in a study of welfare law, presents[7] a Hayekian 'worst case scenario'. 'Not only does contemporary law rarely look like the ideal of cogent formal law as it was developed by the giants of modern political thought, but contemporary law seems to be undergoing a gradual *deformalisation* as well.' The reference here is to the use of the 'open-ended' standards associated with 'outline legislation' (below).

Traditionally, the focus of lawyers was on 'law' rather than 'rules'. To put this differently, lawyers were interested in form. They focused on the formal processes of law-making and delegated legislation, and tended to use these as a demarcation line between 'law' and 'non-law'. What lawyers needed to know was whether rules were 'binding'. As Robert Megarry, a young barrister later to be a judge, sadly remarked shortly after World War II:[8]

> Not long ago, practitioners could live with reasonable comfort and safety in a world bounded by Acts of Parliament, Statutory Rules and Orders and judicial decisions. One of the tendencies of recent years is for this world to become an expanding universe.

He noted the growth of what he called 'administrative quasi-legislation' or 'announcements by administrative and official bodies'. Today, we would probably substitute the American 'bureaucratic law' or the European 'soft law' for 'quasi-

5    R. Cotterell, *Law's Community. Legal Theory in Sociological Perspecive* (Oxford: Clarendon) 1995, p. 280. The same point was made many years earlier by C. Allen, *Law and Orders* (London: Stevens) 1945. Further examples of complex rules are to be found in W. Twining and D. Miers, *How To Do Things With Rules* (London: Weidefield and Nicolson) 3rd edn., 1991, p. 30.

6    See also R. Livock, 'Science, Law and Safety Standards: A Case Study of Industrial Disease' (1979) 6 J. of Law and Soc. 172.

7    B. Scheuerman, 'The Rule of Law and the Welfare State: Towards a New Synthesis' (1994) 22 Politics and Society 195, 199, 207.

8    R. Megarry, 'Administrative Quasi-Legislation' (1944) 60 LQR 125, 126-129.

legislation'.[9] Soft law includes the relatively formal – directives, circulars, guidance, guidelines and codes of practice – but the term may equally extend to departmental notices and memoranda. Megarry cites the example of concessions made by the Inland Revenue to the taxpayer, but seems unaware that these concessions ran to several volumes, some of which were openly published, others contained in departmental memoranda or even letters to individuals. Megarry puzzled:[10]

> It is true that arrangements such as these, operating in favour of the individuals concerned at the expense of taxpayers as a whole, are technically not law, but although no Court would enforce them, no official body would fail to honour them, and as they are not merely concessions in individual cases but are intended to apply generally to all who fall within their scope, the description of 'quasi-legislation' is perhaps not inept. Announcements operating against the individuals concerned, on the other hand, will normally be open to challenge in the Courts and so can be said to have the practical effect of legislation only to the extent that the expense, delays and uncertainties of litigation in general, and of opposing the unlimited resources of the Administration in particular, make those affected prefer to be submissive rather than stiff-necked.

The conservative young barrister had hit on a practice which was to escalate into one of the problem areas of modern administrative law, but his attitude remained that of the 'model of law' discussed in Chapter 2, which equated 'rules' with 'law' and judicial procedures, relegating discretion to the 'lawless' side of the line. What concerned Megarry was the legal status of this body of 'quasi-law'; notably, he did not question the propriety of this blatant example of 'selective enforcement', apparently merely because it operated for, not against, the subject. As we shall see, this is a dangerous assumption.[11]

Since the nineteenth century, a first objective for lawyers has been to arrange legal norms logically and in a hierarchical fashion.[12] This is no more than the practical expression of Dicey's doctrine of parliamentary sovereignty. At the apex of the hierarchy stand Acts of Parliament. Immediately below we find delegated legislation. Griffith and Street once described[13] this as a confusing 'ragbag of rules, regulations, orders, schemes, byelaws, licences, directives, warrants, instruments of approval or minutes', all 'children' and 'grandchildren' of statute. Lawyers will immediately add the judge-made rules of the common law, though where these stand in a vertical hierarchy is not immediately obvious; while the common law can never directly override statute, the cases met in Chapter 4 show that judicial interpretation may qualify statute law very

9  Though see G. Ganz, *Quasi-legislation: Recent Developments in Secondary Legislation* (London: Sweet and Maxwell) 1987. See also K. Wellens and G. Borchardt, 'Soft Law in European Community Law' (1989) 14 ELR 267; J. Mashaw, *Bureaucratic Justice* (New Haven: Yale University Press) 1985, Ch. 3.
10  Above, note 8.
11  See *IRC v National Federation of Self Employed and Small Businesses Ltd* [1982] AC 617.
12  See H. Hart, *The Concept of Law* J. Raz and P. Bullock (eds.)(Oxford: Clarendon) 2nd edn., 1994.
13  J. Griffith and H. Street, *Principles of Administrative Law* (London: Pitman) 3rd edn., 1973, p. 32.

considerably, while delegated legislation may actually be invalidated by an application for judicial review. *Laker's* case[14] illustrates how the prerogative powers fit into the hierarchy. They are clearly subordinate to statute but remain in abeyance to be revived if the statute law is repealed. Like the common law, the prerogative can also be used to fill gaps in statute or regulations. All these rules possess a place in the lawyer's hierarchy and (except perhaps with the prerogative) their legal status is relatively clear.

Less clear is the position of two recent additions. In Chapter 4, we looked at the status of the ECHR, finding that failure to incorporate had created a problem for the judges in deciding what weight to attach to the ECHR.[15] Incorporation will not solve all the problems, especially if, as is likely, the 'weak' or interpretative model is chosen, allowing explicit words in statute to over-ride the ECHR. Further problems have come with the accession of the United Kingdom to the European Community. The extent to which the various types of EC law were to be binding inside the Member States has been a controversial issue for EC law to settle,[16] while the exact position of EC law in the United Kingdom legal herarchy is a matter for debate amongst constitutional lawyers (see below).

But rules are not simply binding (law) or non-binding (quasi-legislation). We have already agreed that they form part of a spectrum. The great contribution of Davis to administrative law was to articulate the administrative uses of rule-making and draw upon it as a way to structure and control administrative discretion. By so doing, he changed attitudes, extending the horizon of administrative lawyers from 'law' to 'rules'.

Let us follow the distinction a little further. Lawyers commonly differentiate 'rules' from 'decisions'. According to this distinction, rules are not only legislative in character but they apply *generally* or across the board. Decisions on the other hand are *individuated*[17] and are often made as part of an adjudicative process. Craig[18] warns of the duality of meaning: a 'legislative' instrument is identifiable by the procedure by which it came into being, but the adjective also 'signifies that the rule has a generality of application which distinguishes it from a mere executive order'. This may be a source of confusion. Later we shall find that 'rules' are frequently contained in contracts, licences and franchises; indeed, these forms are such a common feature of the New Public Management discussed in Chapter 5 that they could well be classified as governmental output functions. But because they are not 'general' in character, lawyers would not normally include them in a definition of legislative instruments. There is then an implication that contracts, because they are conceptualised in the common law as agreements between two parties, do not come within the definition of 'rules'. Given the predominance of standard form contracts, this is inherently misleading. In the 'contract culture' described in Chapter 5, contracts may contain rules of wide application and some government contracts may combine the functions of

---

14  Above, p. 86.
15  *R v Secretary of State for the Home Department, ex p Brind* [1991] 1 AC 696. Above, p. 120.
16  See D. Curtin, 'The Province of Government: Delimiting the Direct Effect of Directives in the Common Law Context' (1990) 15 ELR 195.
17  D. Galligan, 'The Nature and Function of Policies within Discretionary Power' [1976] PL 332.
18  P. Craig, *Administrative Law*, p. 270.

contract and regulation. Licences too are often specific to individuals, yet because they are authorised by statute, we find them included in Griffith and Street's ragbag of delegated legislation. In Chapter 9 we shall describe franchises and licences issued by regulators as instruments of rule-making. Similarly, the codes of practice typical of self-regulation – e.g., statements of practice issued by the Press Council which purport to establish standards of good behaviour for the press, or the Advertising Standards Agency's Code of Practice – though limited in application, are rules.

Drawing lines between law x&d rules can create problems. For example, the rules of natural justice apply to individuated decision-making but less strongly, if at all, to decisions of a regulatory character.[19] When space has to be made for participation and consultation in informal rule-making procedure, this raises the question whether the rule is of limited application, in which case participation rights are apt to be reserved for those likely to be affected (as, e.g., the *GCHQ* case,[20] where the appropriate union had to be consulted) or extends more widely to the public at large. Again, in EC law the distinction between rules and decisions is very marked. EEC Art. 189 speaks of three types of Community legislation: regulations, directives and decisions, the first two general, the last individual in character. But a decision applicable to individuals may in fact embody administrative policies indirectly affecting groups or even members of the wider public who do not have standing to challenge the decision's validity.[1]

The traditional concern of administrative law with executive rule-making as an exercise of legislative power helps to foster a vision of Parliament, the legislator, as 'making' the law. Of course, the parliamentary contribution to law-making is important; it marks 'the giving of assent on behalf of citizens to measures that are to have binding applicability'[2]. In all other respects, however, parliamentary input into legislation is rather modest. It represents a small part of a continuum of policy-making and implementation in which the action passes from one body to another.[3] Cabinet, civil servants, politicians and lawyers, as well as interest groups, all participate in the legislative process. Many other bodies, such as local government, which possesses powers to make byelaws, regulatory agencies which often possess independent rule-making powers, and the Law Commission, with advisory and drafting responsibilities, also participate in law-making. Courts make law. As Dimock, expressing the American Realist viewpoint, once said:[4]

> One of the main shortcomings of jurists who try to reduce management to a hierarchy of rules is that they overlook the stimulus/response nature of law. Like

19  *Bates v Lord Hailsham of St Marylebone* [1972] 1 WLR 1373.
20  Above, p. 113.
1  T. Hartley, *Foundations of European Community Law: an Introduction to the Constitutional and Administrative Law of the European Community* (Oxford: Clarendon Press) 3rd edn., 1994, pp. 367-377. And see Case 16/62. *Confédération Nationale de Fruits et Légumes v Council* [1962] ECR 471.
2  See P. Norton (ed.), *Legislatures* (Oxford: OUP) 1990; P. Norton, 'Adapting to European Parliament and Policy in Britain: the House of Commons as a Policy Influencer' (1984) 13 Teaching Politics 201.
3  M. Zander, *The Law-Making Process* (London: Butterworths) 4th edn., 1994; D. Miers and A. Page, *Legislation* (London: Sweet and Maxwell) 2nd edn., 1990.
4  M. Dimock, *Law and Dynamic Administration* (New York: Praeger) 1980, p. 98.

everything in nature, law grows. It is spelled out when courts speak, and it is equally spelled out when the legislature or the administrative agency speaks. Law is not the monopoly of a profession or even of one branch of the government. It is something that grows and responds to society itself and all three branches take part in that response.

Modern administration usually incorporates several types of rule-making, blending formal law and soft law. Central to our system of police procedure, for example, is the Police and Criminal Procedure Act 1984 (PACE). PACE is actually a modern codification of the common law rules founded on the report of a Royal Commission,[5] traditionally considered to be a consensual method of law-making. Long though PACE is (it runs to 122 sections and contains 7 Schedules), it is not sufficiently detailed to cover every aspect of pre-trial procedure. Like virtually all modern statutes, PACE therefore authorises 'secondary' legislation in the form of ministerial regulations. When PACE was enacted, however, some procedures, such as the tape-recording of confessions, were not ready for operation. Sections 60 and 66 of PACE therefore empowered the Home Secretary to issue Codes of Practice governing the tape-recording of interviews, search of premises and vehicles, detention at police stations, and seizure of property.

Since these are very sensitive subjects at the heart of civil liberties, Parliament was not willing to delegate too generously. Section 67 therefore lays out formal procedures for the introduction of the Codes. By s. 67(1), the Home Secretary has (i) to publish a draft of any Code issued under ss. 60 and 66 and (ii) to consider any representations made; he may then modify the draft. Codes of Practice under PACE must be laid in draft before Parliament and approved by resolution (below). Revisions require the same procedure. PACE also dictates the legal effect of the Codes. Failure to comply with a Code may lead to disciplinary proceedings, though not automatically to criminal or civil proceedings (s. 67(8)). The Codes are admissible in evidence and 'shall be taken into account' in determining any question where the court thinks them relevant (s. 67(11)).

The purpose of this statutory authorisation is to avoid the type of problem which arose in the pre-Act case of *Collins v Wilcock*.[6] Here the court had to consider the terms of a circular which authorised an administrative practice of 'cautioning' women suspected of prostitution offences as an alternative to arrest and prosecution. Oblique reference was made to this practice in the Street Offences Act 1959 but it was not explicitly authorised. The defendant was charged with assault on a police officer in the execution of his duty when she responded with force to the officer's attempt physically to detain her for cautioning. The court held that the officer was acting illegally. It would take more than a mere circular to legitimate the cautioning practice. 'If it had been intended to confer any such power on police officers that power could and should have in our judgment have been expressly conferred by statute.'

Formal rules are by no means the only rule-making which takes place in the context of PACE. The Codes also contain 'Notes for Guidance', which amplify the Codes. Both are public in the sense that they have to be made available at

5    Report of the Royal Commission on Criminal Procedure (the Philips Commission) Cmnd. 8092, 1981.
6    [1984] 3 All ER 374. The circular in dispute was HO Circ. No. 109/1959.

police stations. The difference is that the legal status of the Guidance is less clear.[7] Again, PACE established common procedures and is designed to be operated on a national basis, yet the policies, objectives and working practices of the various regional police authorities may differ. A series of Home Office Circulars plays a central role in ensuring uniformity. The best known of these used to be the so-called 'Judges' Rules', informal guidance to police officers of the formula thought appropriate by the judiciary for cautioning a suspect before charge about his right to remain silent. This had no legal force, although clearly the police were unwise blatantly to disregard the Judges' Rules, until replaced by para. 11.2 of the Codes of Practice under PACE, which possessed limited statutory force. When the Criminal Justice and Public Order Act 1994 made changes to the accused's 'right of silence', the old caution became inappropriate and was replaced in a new Code.

A major advantage of informal rule-making lies in flexibility. Legislation and regulations are binding but also in principle general.[8] Codes of practice can be negotiated or worked out locally and extended nationally if successful. To take our example further, the Metropolitan Police are currently experimenting with new guidance to police officers governing charge and caution. Despite the warning of *Collins v Willcock*, they are starting informally. With the help of the Crown Prosecution Service, points have been allocated to each offence according to gravity and published internally as a Case Disposal Manual. Faced with an offender, the officer is supposed to run mentally through a list of aggravating and mitigating factors before making his decision to charge, caution or issue a formal warning.

The strengths and weaknesses of Davis's rule-making theory emerge rather strongly from this example. On the one hand, the new arrangements encourage consistency and help eliminate prejudice; on the other, they seem unsuited for rapid decision-making by a constable on the beat. Doubts must also arise about the legitimacy of 'tertiary' rules made in this fashion, which gloss the law of police procedure. This introduces an important question raised by Baldwin in his study of rules in government[9] whether given types of rule are more, or less, appropriate to particular situations.

In this and the following chapter we treat legislation and rule-making as part of a single, dynamic process. We consider the advantages and disadvantages of various rule-making processes and also, though to a more limited extent, their fitness for purpose. Chapter 7 contains a case study of parole which not only underlines the interplay of various rule types but traces the evolution of a system based almost wholly on discretion to a system bounded and structured by rules.

## 2. Formal rule-making

As we saw, formal rules made by the executive possess a recognised place in the hierarchy and their legal status is clear. There is either formal parliamentary

7    M. Zander, *The Police and Criminal Evidence Act 1984* (London: Butterworths) 3rd edn., 1995, p. 173.
8    The distinction is reflected in the terminology of 'Public General Acts'. Private Acts of Parliament are an exception to the point made in the text.
9    R. Baldwin, *Rules and Government* (Oxford: Clarendon) 1995.

authorisation for their making in statute or, less commonly in the case of Orders in Council, they are made under the prerogative powers of the Crown.[10] At least in theory there is control of what has been made. Statutory instruments are governed by the terms of the Statutory Instruments Act 1946 and have to be laid before Parliament for approval and scrutiny. They must be published and fall within the public domain. They may (or may not) be invalidated by failure to follow the proper procedures, such as laying before Parliament or consultation (below). Delegated legislation forms part of the traditional subject matter of administrative law simply by virtue of the fact that it is made by the executive, in practice usually in the name of a Minister.

By the end of the nineteenth century, the need for delegated legislation was accepted. The preferred model, by no means always observed, was a division of functions in which Parliament controlled policy and the administration was left to finalise matters of detail. Lord Thring, a leading parliamentary draftsman of the time, argued[11] that the province of Parliament should be:

> to decide material questions affecting the public interest, and the more procedure and subordinate matters can be withdrawn from their cognisance, the greater will be the time afforded for the consideration of the more serious questions involved in legislation.

By 1932, when the Donoughmore Committee was asked to make recommendations concerning the practice of delegated legislation, it believed that delegated legislation was here to stay:[12]

> ... with the haphazard habit characteristic of English political life the constitutional practice had grown up gradually, as and when the need arose in Parliament, without any logical system. The power has been delegated by Parliament for various reasons, because, for instance, the topic involved much detail, or because it was technical, or because the pressure of other demands upon Parliamentary time did not allow the necessary time to be devoted by the House of Commons to the particular Bill. The limits of delegated power, the methods of ministerial procedure, and the safeguards for the protection of the public or the preservation of Parliamentary control thus appear often to have been dictated by opportunist considerations, peculiar to the occasion.

Today, there is mounting dissatisfaction with the quality of both legislation and delegated legislation. The volume, making it difficult for even the professional lawyer to find and interpret the law, is clearly an important factor. Over a 60-year period, legislation has grown from 34 Acts with 440 sections using 375 pages in 1931 to 69 Acts with 1,985 sections using 2,222 pages in 1991.[13] The length and complexity of modern statutes is also worrying. The Courts and Legal Services

---

10  See *Council of Civil Service Unions v Minister for the Civil Service* [1985] AC 374, above p. 113, where the Minister, acting in the name of the Crown, possessed powers originating in the prerogative to make rules governing the organisation of the civil service.

11  Cited by C. Allen, *Law and Orders* (London: Stevens) 3rd edn. 1965, p. 35.

12  Cmnd. 4060 (1932), p. 16.

13  *Making the Law*, above, p. 152, note 2, p. 11. Figures are not strictly comparable because of a recent change of format to larger A4 pages.

Act 1990, for example, contains 125 sections and 20 Schedules in 201 pages and repeals approximately 100 existing statutes without consolidating them – a bad practice which makes it hard to know what law is in force.

### (a) The case for legislation

The argument for legislation turns partly on Lord Thring's constitutional argument about statute but partly also on the indeterminate legal status of informal rules (people should know where they stand). Take, for example, the long-standing practice of collective labour agreements. 'British industrial relations have always been regulated by "codes" in the sense of voluntarily agreed rules which may have a legal effect: the collective agreement, the union rule book, the TUC's inter-union "Bridlington" procedure, and the more recent TUC "Guides".'[14] Now s. 3 of the Employment Act 1980 empowered the Employment Secretary to issue 'codes of practice containing such practical guidance as he thinks fit for the purpose of promoting the improvement of industrial relations'. Under s. 3(8) the codes are admissible as evidence and can be used to assist in the determination of questions in the course of legal proceedings, although breach of the codes does not in itself give rise to legal liability. Section 3 provides for the codes to be laid in draft and approved by each House of Parliament before being brought into operation by statutory instrument. The first two codes received additional parliamentary scrutiny because they were the subject of a report by the Select Committee on Employment. Yet this relatively formal rule-making did not please everyone. During the passage of the Bill, John Gorst MP called the codes 'unconstitutional', expressing concern about their status as 'law'. The codes:[15]

> . . . constitute the first step down a slippery slope. If we have semi-judicial edicts that are quasi-binding on the courts and that have been produced by Ministers who haven't had the courage to enshrine them in the law, worse developments will follow. The codes will bring the spirit of the law into industrial relations but not the certainty and precision of the letter of the law.

This concern for certainty and precision was echoed by Baroness Sear in the House of Lords:[16]

> What is happening is that when we have a really controversial piece of legislation we tend to say . . . 'We will not have this in the Act. We will put it into a code of practice.' When you put it into a code of practice you do not have to be so clear about what 'it' really is, because it does not have the force of law . . . this is a thoroughly muddle-headed way of dealing with new developments . . . an escape route from difficult matters which we don't wish to thrash out in legislation.

---

14  R. Lewis, 'Codes of Practice on Picketing and Closed Shop Agreements and Arrangements' (1981) 44 MLR 198.
15  HC Deb., vol. 992, cols. 675-6.
16  HL Deb., vol. 44, col. 1522.

Courts have often taken the view that ministers are answerable to Parliament for policy, and that Parliament's approbation must be assumed where regulations have been submitted to parliamentary oversight.[17] Occasionally, however, they do insist that a policy has such grave consequences that it must be explicitly authorised by Parliament. Such a situation arose in *R v Secretary of State for Social Security, ex p Joint Council for the Welfare of Immigrants*.[18] Regulation 70 of the Income Support (General) Regulations 1987 allowed emergency payments to 'persons from abroad', a term which included asylum seekers for whom no specific provision was made. Subsequently, the Asylum and Immigration Appeals Act 1993 changed the rules on asylum. The rules on benefit were then amended by the Social Security (Persons from Abroad) Miscellaneous Regulations 1996, which removed the rights of certain categories of asylum seeker to claim. These regulations had to be submitted to the Social Security Advisory Committee which, under s. 174(2) of the Social Security Administration Act 1992, has to be consulted about changes in the regulations. The SSAC was told that 'a growing number of unfounded applications from those who are actually economic migrants' was creating a bottleneck to the prejudice of genuine refugees; economic migrants needed to be discouraged. Despite a negative opinion from the SSAC, the regulations were duly laid before Parliament and came into force.

However, judicial review proceedings were brought by the Joint Council for the Welfare of Immigrants, whose main argument was that Parliament could not have not intended the very broad statutory enabling powers to be used in such a way that 'persons might be deprived of their common law or statutory rights, or in such a way as to interfere with fundamental human rights'. By a majority, the Court of Appeal accepted this argument, rejecting the counter-argument that the Minister was acting within a 'carefully defined system of parliamentary control' and was thus accountable only to Parliament.

*R v Secretary of State for Social Security, ex p Joint Council for the Welfare of Immigrants*[19]

> *Simon Brown LJ*: I do not pretend to have found this an easy case. Powerful arguments are advanced on both sides . . . As stated, I for my part have no difficulty in accepting the Secretary of State's right to discourage economic migrants by restricting their benefits. That of itself indicates that the Regulations are not invalid merely because of their 'chilling' effect . . .
>
> It is, moreover, as I recognise, one thing, as *in Ex parte Leech*, to condemn direct interference with the unquestioned basic rights there identified; another to assert that the Secretary of State here is bound to maintain some benefit provision to asylum seekers so as to ensure that those with genuine claims will not be driven by penury to forfeit them, whether by leaving the country before their determination or through an inability to prosecute them effectively. The present challenge, I therefore acknowledge, involves carrying the *Ex parte Leech* principle a step further and this, moreover, in a

17 *Nottinghamshire County Council v Secretary of State for the Environment* [1986] AC 240; *R v Secretary of State for the Environment, ex p Hammersmith and Fulham London Borough Council* [1991] 1 AC 521.
18 [1997] 1 WLR 275 (Simon Brown and Waite LJJ, Neill LJ dissenting).
19 [1997] 1 WLR 275 at 401.

field where Parliament has been closely involved in the making of the impugned Regulations.

I have nevertheless concluded that this is a step the court should take. Parliamentary sovereignty is not here in question: the regulations are subordinate legislation only . . . Parliament has for its part clearly demonstrated by the Act of 1993 a full commitment to the United Kingdom's Convention obligations. When the regulation-making power now contained in the Act of 1992 was first conferred, there was no question of asylum seekers being deprived of all benefit and thereby rendered unable to pursue their claims . . . [T]he fact that asylum seekers have hitherto enjoyed rights to benefit seems to me not entirely irrelevant. After all, the Act of 1993 confers on asylum seekers fuller rights than they had ever previously enjoyed, the right of appeal in particular. And yet these Regulations for some genuine asylum seekers at least must now be regarded as rendering these rights nugatory. Either that, or the Regulations necessarily contemplate for some a life so destitute that to my mind no civilised nation can contemplate it. So basic are the human rights here at issue that it cannot be necessary to resort to the European Convention on Human Rights . . .

Parliament cannot have intended a significant number of genuine asylum seekers to be impaled on the horns of so intolerable a dilemma: the need either to abandon their claims to refugee status or alternatively to maintain them as best they can but in a state of utter destitution. Primary legislation alone could in my judgement achieve that sorry state of affairs.

The Convention referred to in this passage is the UN Convention on the Status of Refugees to which the United Kingdom is a signatory. Unlike the ECHR, this Convention was explicitly recognised by s. 2 of the 1993 Act, which provides that nothing in the Immigration Rules shall lay down any practice which would be contrary to the Convention. *Leech's* case[1] concerned a prisoner's right of access to his solicitor. The Court of Appeal described this as a 'constitutional right' which could only be taken away by express words or necessary implication. Thus, these cases can be directly linked to the development of a 'rights based' jurisprudence described in Chapter 4 (above, p. 122), a link made still more clearly in *Witham*,[2] where there was a challenge to the validity of an Order made by the Lord Chancellor in terms of s. 130 of the Supreme Court Act 1981 uprating the court fees payable by litigants. The argument was that, as poor persons, some on income support, the applicants could not meet the relevant fees, and were thus deprived of their 'constitutional right' of access to a court. Equating this right with freedom of opinion (ECHR, Art. 10) Laws J said:

In the unwritten legal order of the British state, at a time when the common law continues to accord a legislative supremacy to Parliament, the notion of a constitutional right can in my judgment inhere only in this proposition, that the right in question cannot be abrogated by the State save by specific provision in an Act of Parliament, or by regulations whose *vires* in main legislation specifically confers the power to abrogate. General words will not suffice.

Adding that he found great difficulty 'in conceiving a form of words capable of making it plain beyond doubt to the statute's reader that the provision in question

1    *R v Secretary of State for the Home Department, ex p Leech* [1994] QB 198.
2    *R v Lord Chancellor, ex p Witham* [1997] 2 All ER 779 at 783-784.

prevents him from going to court . . . save in a case where that is expressly stated', Laws J ruled the Order ultra vires. The Lord Chancellor immediately announced that those on income support would continue to be excused court fees.

Parliamentary sovereignty ensures, however, that not every case will have such a happy outcome. After the *JCWI* case,[3] the government moved a new clause to the Asylum and Immigration Bill, conveniently before the House, to read:

> 11(1) Notwithstanding any enactment or rule of law, regulations may exclude any person who has made a claim for asylum from entitlement to any of the following benefits, namely-(a) income support . . ..

The effect was to reinstate the 1996 regulations from the date of Royal Assent. For good measure, s. 9 of the new Act removed the right to housing benefit and assistance in respect of homelessness. The effect was to leave most asylum-seekers destitute. The campaigners did not simply go away; a new test case was brought involving different legislation. In *R v Westminster City Council, ex p A*,[4] the Court of Appeal intervened again, ruling that destitute asylum seekers fell within the provisions of the National Assistance Act 1948 and could apply to local authorities under s. 21(1) for care and attention, including accommodation. These cases illustrate how pressure for specific, complex and formal law-making may come from the increase in lawyers and legal activity.[5]

## (b) Complex laws

A different argument relates legislative complexity directly to the increasing sophistication of our society:[6]

> We find ourselves in a computerised age where various interest groups compete very fiercely for limited resources . . . Given opposing interests, a Government wishing to legislate on a particular topic will be faced with opposing interests fighting to gain concessions.

There is an echo here of 'public choice' analysis of legislation as a series of bargains between government and interest groups.[7] Such groups are unlikely to be satisfied unless the bargain is recorded as legislation. Certainly, McCrudden, in a study of the Commission for Racial Equality,[8] had to conclude that the assets of codes of practice – more consensual, more participatory, more flexible and often easier to enforce – will in the long run be undermined by the absence of explicit parliamentary authority. Another dimension of this argument can be

3   Above, note 18.
4   (1997) Times, 17 February.
5   See further, C. Harlow and R. Rawlings, *Pressure Through Law* (London: Routledge) 1992.
6   A. Graham, 'Well On in the Act – A Government Lawyer's View of Legislation' (1988) 9 Stat. Law Rev. 4, 5.
7   E.g., B. Ackerman, 'Interpreting Statutes in the Regulatory State' (1989)103 Harv. LR 407. For public choice theory, see above, p.130.
8   C. McCrudden, 'Codes in a Cold Climate' (1988) 51 MLR 409.

traced in Chapter 9, where we find that government contracts and franchises are typically extremely complex, as central government and regulators wrestle for ultimate control through performance indicators and vainly try to provide for every eventuality.

Complexity and prolixity are in reality the enemies of transparency and participation. In legislation, controversial matters may be concealed inappropriately in Schedules or placed late in the statute, when they may never be debated or even read, undercutting democratic legitimacy. Government increasingly resorts to the guillotine[9] to ensure passage of the overloaded legislative programme. Haste leads to the tabling of amendments at a late stage, a procedure described in the House of Lords as 'legislate as you go'.[10] Between 1979 and 1983, an average of 1,106 government amendments were moved in the Lords each session which, in the next two years, escalated to 2,668. This means that as much as 50% of legislative text may result from amendments moved at a late stage. During the Committee stage of the controversial Deregulation and Contracting Out Bill (below) 200 amendments were moved; 100 government amendments passed in contrast to two moved by the Opposition. It has been sensibly suggested that proper timetabling of the stages of Bills could end such tactics.[11] Alternatively, the position may be ameliorated by the new practice of publishing draft bills for consultation.

Lord Renton, who chaired an important Commons Report on the quality of legislation, has blamed a tendency to push everything into primary legislation.[12] Discussing the Water Act 1989 (418 pages long with 194 sections and 27 schedules) he observed in it:

> . . . a good deal of law which consists of mere instruction to government departments . . . This is not a suitable device for legislation. Internal matters of this kind are best dealt with by the ordinary machinery of government . . . and departmental circulars can play an important part.

Lord Howe, who has chaired the Cabinet Legislation Committee and been Leader of the House of Commons, has also described the system as 'overloaded' and believes that, to improve quality, 'we must make fewer laws and make the laws fewer'.[13]

## 3. Outline legislation: the case for delegating primary power

The alternative is 'outline legislation', which gives Ministers power to make regulations virtually uninhibited by policy guidance from the legislature. There

---

9 See G. Ganz, 'Recent Developments in the Use of Guillotine Procedure' [1990] PL 496. A guillotine allocates a fixed amount of time for debate of given clauses.

10 See above, p. 163 for an example.

11 *Public Bill Procedure*, Second Report of Procedure Committee, HC 49-I (1984-5), paras 31ff. For comment, see D. Miers, 'Legislation and the Legislative Process: A Case for Reform' (1989) 10 Stat. Law Rev. 26, 31-32.

12 Lord Renton, 'Current Drafting Practices and Problems in the United Kingdom' (1990) 11 Stat. Law Rev. 11, 14. See also *Report of the Renton Committee on the Preparation of Legislation*, Cmnd. 6053 (1975).

13 G. Howe, *Conflict of Loyalty* (London: Macmillan) 1994, pp. 622-623.

has been a tendency recently to delegate policy-making powers.[14] For example, the Child Support Act 1991, with around 100 regulatory powers, did not contain on its face provision for the controversial Child Support Agency. Again, s. 40(1) of the Education Act 1986 permits the Secretary of State by regulation to:

> make provision requiring local education authorities, or such person as he may prescribe, to secure that the performance of teachers to whom these regulations apply . . . is regularly appraised in accordance with such requirements as may be described.

Here, Parliament has not troubled to satisfy itself about either the terms and conditions of appraisal or even the body to be entrusted with the appraisal function.

More draconian are ouster clauses excluding the jurisdiction of the courts, on which, as we have seen (above, p. 54) the courts have taken decisive action and so-called 'Henry VIII clauses', which allow the executive to amend or repeal primary legislation. Under the Counter-Inflation Act 1972 and the regulations made thereunder, the Minister was empowered to define the limits of his own jurisdiction, to amend earlier legislation, and to define conclusively the meaning of terms used in the statute. This type of clause, described as 'a threat to Parliamentary Sovereignty',[15] is allegedly becoming more common:[16]

> Ministers now take power to amend and even repeal primary legislation almost as a matter of common form. Such orders, which cannot be amended, are not subject to any effective parliamentary control, whether or not they are expressed to be subject to either negative or affirmative resolutions. Nor is any limit placed on the extent of the exercise of these extraordinary powers.

Lord Rippon cites s. 147 of the Local Government Finance Act 1988, which provides:

> (1) The Secretary of State may at any time by order, make such supplementary, incidental, consequential or transitional provisions as appear to him to be necessary or expedient for the general purposes or any particular purpose of this Act or in consequence of any of the provisions or for giving full effect to it.
> (2) An order under this section may in particular make provision for amending, repealing or revoking (with or without savings) any provision of an Act passed before or in the same session as this Act.

The House of Lords is fighting back with a new Delegated Powers Scrutiny Committee.[17] Its terms require departments to submit memoranda justifying the

---

14  J. Hayhurst and P. Wallington, 'The Parliamentary Scrutiny of Delegated Legislation' [1988] PL 547, 573.

15  V. Korah, 'Counter-Inflation Legislation: Whither Parliamentary Sovereignty?' (1976) 92 LQR 42.

16  Lord Rippon, 'Henry VIII Clauses' (1989) 10 Stat. Law Rev. 205, 206 and 'Constitutional Anarchy' (1990) 11 Stat. Law Rev. 184.

17  Established by Resolution on 10 November 1992 (HL Deb., vol. 540, col. 91), the committee originated in the Select Committee of the House of Lords on the Work of the House, HL 35-I (1991-2) (the Jellicoe Committee). See C. Himsworth, 'The Delegated Powers Scrutiny Committee' [1995] PL 34.

delegation and proposed sub-delegation of legislative power in primary legislation, including the use of 'Henry VIII' clauses. It reports inappropriate delegations of legislative power to the House.

The sweeping order-making powers of the controversial Deregulation and Contracting Out Act 1994, described during debate as 'a Henry VIII clause squared', provoked both Houses. Section 1 provides:

> 1.(1) If, with respect to any provision made by an enactment, a Minister of the Crown is of the opinion—(a) that the effect of the provision is such as to impose, or authorise or require the imposition of, a burden affecting any person in the carrying on of any trade, business or profession or otherwise; and (b) that, by amending or repealing the enactment concerned and, where appropriate, by making such other provision as is referred to in subsection (4)(a) below, it would be possible, without removing any necessary protection, to remove or reduce the burden or, as the case may be, the authorisation or requirement by virtue of which the burden may be imposed; he may, subject to the following provisions of this section and sections 2 to 4 below, by order amend or repeal that enactment . . .
>
> (4) An order under this section shall be made by statutory instrument and may do all or any of the following—(a) make provision (whether by amending any enactment or otherwise) creating a burden which relates to the subject matter of, but is less onerous than that imposed by, the existing provision; (b) make such modifications of enactments as, in the opinion of the Minister concerned, are consequential upon, or incidental to, the amendment or repeal of the relevant enactment; . . . but no order shall be made under this section unless a draft of the order has been laid before and approved by a resolution of each House of Parliament.

Expecting trouble, the government referred their Bill to the Select Committee on Procedure for consideration. The Committee was far from happy; indeed, Opposition Members ultimately boycotted the Committee on the ground that its deliberations were proceeding in parallel with debates on the Bill, assuming the outcome.[18]

Describing the Bill as creating a 'fast track procedure', the Committee set out 'to ensure that no Act of Parliament is repealed or amended under this new power without examination at least as thorough as if the change had been made by a Bill passing through the House'. A new Select Committee of 16 senior Members was proposed to scrutinise orders made under this Act; satisfy themselves that these fell within the powers delegated; and report to the House any unsatisfactory orders. Provision was included for a 90-minute debate. This did not satisfy the Opposition, which insisted that repeal always requires the same procedure as that used in the original measure.[19] Equally dissatisfied, the House of Lords secured a concession to extend the period of scrutiny to 60 days from the norm of 40 for delegated legislation, and allocated the task of monitoring deregulation orders to its new Delegated Powers Scrutiny Committee.[20]

The Deregulation Committee was set up with 18 members under Standing Order 124A in 1995, and promptly reported unfavourably on the first deregulation

---

18  *Delegated Legislation*, Fourth Report of Procedure Committee, HC 152 (1995-96), para. 16.
19  HC Deb., vol. 237, cols. 203-6 (8 February 1994).
20  Himsworth [1995] PL 34 at 43.

proposal[1] on the ground that 'it did not contain a full list of those consulted'. By the end of 1996, the Deregulation Unit of the Cabinet charged with monitoring legislation with a view to deregulation had introduced 44 measures, of which only three had attracted the notice of Parliament. Behind the scenes, we learn of a new, 'exciting and positive way of dealing with a specialised class of legislation' based on a procedure 'mutually agreeable to the Committee and Whitehall'.[2] A working relationship has evolved between the Unit, which provides advance notice of its future plans, and the Committee. A majority of Orders laid is amended, often after lengthy discussion. Perhaps most important, the new procedure provides access for the public:[3]

13. *Access*: A novel element in the deregulation procedure – and I think an exciting and constructive one – is the extent to which those with expert knowledge of the subject, and those who will be affected by the legislation, can have access to the process. We have taken full account of written submissions received, and have taken oral evidence when the case for doing so appeared only marginal. The input of the public and relevant organisations has been important, and in several cases has led us to suggest improvements to the legislation. I see the possibility of this dialogue between Parliament and people – largely absent from the consideration of much primary legislation – as the most valuable feature of the new procedure.

14. *A bipartisan approach*: The extent and manner of deregulation may raise contentious issues. It is very much to the credit of my colleagues on the Committee that proposals which could have been divisive, on party political or conscience grounds, have been tackled in a spirit of co-operation between Government and Opposition Members of the Committee, and on the basis of the evidence before us. We have not so far had a Division in the Committee, and I believe that this approach has made our work more effective and our unanimous recommendations more compelling.

In the next section we shall see why the Committee feels this procedure holds a general lesson.

## 4. Secondary legislation

Ideally, legislation and the delegated legislation needed to implement it should form part of a single scheme. This is, however, a counsel of perfection and one which tends to undercut the reasons for resort to delegated legislation in the first place. None the less, the Law Society has recently argued that the drafting function should be transferred to parliamentary draftsmen under the aegis of a

1  The Deregulation (Greyhound Racing) Order 1995.
2  *Consideration of Deregulation Proposals and Draft Orders* First Special Report of the Deregulation Committee, HC 311 (1994/5).
3  *Delegated Legislation*, Fourth Report of Procedure Committee, HC 152 (1995-96), App. 8, p. 73 (Mr. Barry Field).

Ministry of Justice, as it is in some Commonwealth countries,[4] where statute and regulations may be prepared in tandem. They feel that:[5]

> the style of drafting is on the whole worse than that for primary legislation and this can perhaps be explained by the fact that secondary legislation is not prepared by specialist Parliamentary draftsmen but by departmental lawyers who despite best efforts and training perhaps do not have the opportunity to build up the necessary skill and expertise.

Aside from parliamentary overload, the strongest justification for regulations is probably that of technicality. Many statutes, like the Health and Safety at Work etc Act 1974, the Consumer Protection Act 1987 or the Food Safety Act 1990 need to incorporate, codify or make reference to, complicated technical and scientific standards. As we suggested earlier, it is hard to make such regulations comprehensible, let alone accessible. The picture has now become more complex with the advent of transnational regulation through the EC.[6]

Over the years, parliamentary machinery for scrutiny has been improved, with the impetus for reform often coming from Parliament. The provisions governing publication and 'laying' (below) are today contained in the Statutory Instruments Act 1946. The first Commons Committee on Statutory Instruments was established in 1944 with a mandate not only to scrutinise the text of regulations but to ensure that they conformed to certain overriding principles. Delegated legislation cannot, for example, be used to impose taxes, and the Committee looks also for measures which seem to make 'an unusual or unexpected use' of statutory enabling powers. Theoretically, this is different from the remit of the courts, which is to annul measures which exceed the legal ambit of the powers delegated. The *JCWI* case[7] indicates, however, that these two concepts may not always tally.

A survey of the arrangements in 1971 led to a measure of rationalisation when the Special Orders Committee of the House of Lords merged with its Commons equivalent as a joint 'Scrutiny Committee', the Commons Members of which make up the Select Committee on Delegated Legislation to deal with those instruments which need to be laid only before the House of Commons. The Scrutiny Committees regularly express disquiet at the volume of delegated legislation; in 1995, it was estimated that around 1,500 instruments were annually subject to positive parliamentary procedure (a rise of about 50% in 15 years), with the numbers subject to negative procedure doubling in the same time, from 700 to over 1,300.[8]

---

4    See W. Iles, 'Legislative Drafting Practices in New Zealand' (1991) 12 Stat. Law Rev. 16, 'New Zealand Experience of Parliamentary Scrutiny of Legislation' (1991) 12 Stat. Law Rev. 165 and 'The Responsibilities of the New Zealand Legislation Advisory Committee' (1992) 13 Stat. Law Rev. 11. See also *Rule Making by Commonwealth Agencies*, Report No. 35 of the Administrative Review Council (Canberra: Australian Government Publishing Service) 1992, Ch. 4.

5    In *Making the Law*, above, p. 152, note 2, p. 285.

6    See e.g., C. Scott, 'Continuity and Change in British Food Law' (1990) 53 MLR 785; S. Weatherill, 'Compulsory Notification of Draft Technical Standards: the Contribution of Directive 83/189 to the Management of the Internal Market' (forthcoming).

7    Above, p. 161, note 18.

8    *Delegated Legislation*, Fourth Report from Procedure Committee, HC 152 (1995-96), para. 10. On the different procedures, see J. Griffith and M. Ryle, *Parliament* (London: Sweet and Maxwell) 1989, p. 444.

Yet experts feel that the reforms to date are still ineffective and that parliamentary 'control' remains illusory. The Procedure Committee has recently reported:[9]

> ... widespread concern at the growing volume and complexity of delegated legislation, and the obvious deficiencies in its consideration and scrutiny by Parliament. While instruments subject to affirmative procedure are at least guaranteed debate, many of those subject only to negative procedure go unregarded, undebated and often unnoticed by Members. The procedure for debating and deciding on instruments is palpably unsatisfactory, and offers the House scarcely any opportunity for constructive and purposeful discussion.

The last sentence here refers to the 'negative procedure', whereby a statutory instrument enters into force *unless* a motion to annul is successfully moved. Only about one in five of the 'prayers' is debated under this procedure. In 'affirmative procedure', regulations need confirmation by the House but this may occur *before* the Scrutiny Committee has reported on them and the vote may be purely formal after a debate in Standing Committee. No procedure for amendment exists; unless the Scrutiny Committee can negotiate amendments before the instrument reaches the House, it must either stand or fall.[10] The Committee called for an increase in the 40-day scrutiny period to tally with the 60 days allowed to the Deregulation Committee, and a new Standing Order to forbid a final decision in advance of the recommendations of the Scrutiny Committee. The experience of the European Legislation and Deregulation Committees had 'demonstrated that scrutiny by committees can work', but scrutiny demanded a higher profile.

It has been argued that no government can afford to concede to the House of Commons the power of control it is asking for, because to do so might mean losing control of the legislative process. (Perhaps this is an argument for more stringent judicial control.) In other words, to strengthen the Scrutiny Committee until it could function properly would mean creating a Select Committee of the type established to monitor the operation of departments.[11] These committees are known to develop a critical personality which frequently cuts across party lines; note in this context the comment from the Deregulation Committee concerning consensus. One MP, at least, discounts the argument that this might defeat the whole purpose of delegating legislative powers to the executive.[12]

> If these very necessary reforms were to make ministers a little more reluctant to use statutory instruments instead of putting detail in Bills, that is no cause for alarm. It is far more alarming that ministers should find it so convenient to write the law long after Parliament thinks it has done so itself, and that they should have so little difficulty in ensuring a smooth passage through Parliament for what is in effect legislation by the executive.

9  HC 152, para. 1. See also *Making the Law*, above, p. 152, note 2, p. 71.
10  A. Bennett, 'Uses and Abuses of Delegated Power' (1990) 11 Stat. Law Rev. 23, 26.
11  See generally, G. Drewry (ed.), *The New Select Committees* (Oxford: Clarendon) 2nd edn., 1989.
12  A. Beith, 'Prayers Unanswered: A Jaundiced View of the Parliamentary Scrutiny of Statutory Instruments' (1981) Parliamentary Affairs 165, 173.

## 5. Climbing the ladder: EC law

The precise legal effects of United Kingdom accession to the European Community in 1972 are even today a matter for debate. The European Communities Act 1972, passed when the United Kingdom joined the EEC in 1972, operates in three distinct ways. First, s. 2(1) provides for all 'rights, powers, liabilities, obligations and restrictions from time to time created or arising under the Treaties' to be directly applicable and enforceable inside the United Kingdom. Secondly, s. 2(2) and (4) read with Sch 2 of the Act, empower the government, in cases where EC law is not directly applicable or effective, to carry out its obligations under EC law by implementing it through delegated legislation. In practice, implementation of directives is 50% by regulations and Order in Council empowered by s. 2(2).[13] Third, by s. 3, the case law (jurisprudence) of the ECJ is incorporated directly into our judicial hierarchy.

The traditional view of these provisions is that they position EC law as delegated legislation, empowered by the 1972 Act. As Lord Chancellor Gardiner said in the debate on entry:[14]

> Adherence to the Treaties would involve a considerable body of implementing legislation . . . This UK legislation would be an exercise of Parliamentary sovereignty, and Community law, existing and future, would derive its force from it.

But as the European Community has grown in influence, expanded its competence and gained new law-making powers after the Single European Act in 1986, it has become difficult to maintain this position. The argument is complicated by the jurisprudence of the European Court of Justice (ECJ), which has described the 'new legal order' of the EC as the superior legal order; in other words, in any matter in which the EC has competence, EC law takes precedence over the laws of the Member States.[15] Of critical importance is the fact that the ECJ has the last word on this crucial matter, as s.3 of the 1972 Act makes it mandatory for a final appellate court to make a reference under EEC Art. 177 to the ECJ in a case involving a disputed point of EC law.

The dramatic nature of the change became evident for the United Kingdom with the *Factortame* cases,[16] where Spanish boat owners and fishermen challenged

---

13  See T. St. J. Bates, 'The Conversion of EEC Legislation into United Kingdom Legislation' (1991) 12 Stat. Law Rev. 109. But for the view that EC law may affect the domestic allocation of regulatory power, see T. Daintith, 'European Community Law and the Distribution of Regulatory Power in the United Kingdom' (1995) 1 Eur. Law J. 134.

14  HL Deb., 8 May 1967, col. 1197. And see *Membership of the European Community: Report on Renegotiation* (Cmnd. 6003, 1974). For comment, see O. Hood Phillips, *Constitutional and Administrative Law* (London: Sweet & Maxwell) 7th edn., 1987, p. 71; L. Collins, *European Community Law in the United Kingdom* (London: Butterworths), 4th edn., 1990, p. 26; A. Bradley, 'The Sovereignty of Parliament – in Perpetuity?' in J. Jowell and D. Oliver, (eds.) *The Changing Constitution* (Oxford: Clarendon) 3rd edn., 1994.

15  *Van Gend en Loos v Nederlandse Belastingadministratie* Case 26/62 [1963] ECR 1.

16  *R v Secretary of State for Transport, ex p Factortame* [1990] 2 AC 85; refd sub nom *R v Secretary of State for Transport, ex p Factortame (No 2)*: C-213/89 [1991] 1 AC 603. See, N. Gravells, 'Disapplying an Act of Parliament Pending a Preliminary Ruling: Constitutional Enormity or Community Law Right?' [1989] PL 568 and 'Effective Protection of Community Law Rights: Temporary Disapplication of an Act of Parliament' [1991] PL 180.

the validity under EC law of the Merchant Shipping Act 1988, passed to regulate fishing quotas and rights of EC nationals to fish in British fishing grounds. A licensing scheme made by the Secretary of State for Transport in terms of the Act discriminated against foreign boat owners. Anxious about the losses they were suffering, they also demanded an interim injunction to postpone the operation of the legislation for the duration of the legal challenge. The position on the interim injunction was regulated by s. 21 of the Crown Proceedings Act 1947, which stated that injunctions were not available against the Crown in civil proceedings. In *Factortame* the House of Lords interpreted this section strictly, to preclude the possibility of injunctive relief against the Crown. When the question was referred to the ECJ for a preliminary ruling under EEC Art. 177, however, the ECJ replied that protection for rights under EC law in national courts must be the same in a case involving the State as in any other case; if the only barrier between the applicants and adequate protection was an Act of Parliament, this must be disapplied. The House of Lords went on to award an interim injunction and the Merchant Shipping Act was disapplied. Reinforcement came four years later,[17] when the Equal Opportunities Commission tested the validity of provisions in the Employment Protection (Consolidation) Act 1978, which excluded part-time workers from protection against unfair dismissal and redundancy. It was argued that these discriminated indirectly against female workers, contrary to EEC Art. 119 and the Equality Directives. The House of Lords ruled that the legislation was indeed discriminatory and must be disapplied.

These decisions make it hard to view EC law merely as delegated legislation. Where EC law is in issue, statute law no longer occupies the apex of the hierarchy; it has been partially supplanted by EC law, which has had to be inserted at or somewhere near the top of the legal hierarchy. At the same time as it has decreased the law-making competence of Parliament, the 'new legal order' has increased the powers of the judiciary. Not only can legislation for the first time be attacked in United Kingdom courts, but the powers of the ECJ to interpret EC legislation impact indirectly on national legislation. Lord Bridge's judgment in *Factortame (No 2)* is hard to reconcile with Lord Gardiner's earlier view:[18]

> If the supremacy . . . of Community law over the national law of member states was not always inherent in the EEC Treaty it was certainly well established in the jurisprudence of the Court of Justice long before the United Kingdom joined the Community. Thus whatever limitation of its sovereignty Parliament accepted when it enacted the European Communities Act 1972 was entirely voluntary. There is nothing in any way novel in according supremacy to rules of Community law in those areas to which they apply . . .

EEC Art. 189 makes provision for two types of legislative act: *regulation*, 'binding in its entirety and directly applicable in all Member States', and *directives*, binding only 'as to the result to be achieved'. A directive leaves to the Member States 'the choice of form and method' to be employed in implementation.

---

17  In *R v Secretary of State for Employment, ex p Equal Opportunities Commission and Day* [1995] 1 AC 1.
18  [1991] 1 AC at 658-659.

However, the development of the doctrine of 'direct effect' by the ECJ blurs the distinction, and in practice makes the provisions of the EEC Treaty as well as directives, provided they are sufficiently clear, precise and unconditional, enforceable against Member States by individual litigants in national courts.[19] National legislation must be interpreted to conform with EC law,[20] and, as we saw, national law and regulation which is out of line with EC law must be disapplied.

Membership of the Community imposes further restrictions on national governments and legislatures. In areas of Community competence, the EC may have a monopoly of regulatory action, excluding the possibility of independent national action and pushing the Member States towards harmonisation and standardisation.[1]

The multi-tiered legislative process and its resultant network of rules is problematic. At European level, the Council of Ministers, a nominated executive body, is the primary law-maker, though increasingly it shares this power with the Parliament (EP). The complexity of the seven different law-making procedures and 20 or more different decision-making procedures in the EC is a source of concern.[2] The legislative process, though consultative and negotiatory in its early stages, is not notable for its transparency; in particular, the Council deliberates in secret. To the United Kingdom House of Commons,[3] 'European law accounts for a large and growing proportion of the law of each Member State, yet it increasingly seems to be made in a private club'.

In addition, the EC Commission possesses very considerable powers to make 'delegated' legislation, confusingly also termed 'regulations' and 'directives'. These powers are exercised under the supervision of an intricate and secretive web of committees collectively known as the 'Comitology',[4] whose favourable opinion may be a formal requirement for validity. Up to 400 committees exist, composed for the most part of Commisssion experts, national civil servants, and independent experts, reporting either to the Council or Parliament. Over 80% are involved in rule-making, and their output is considerable: in 1994, for example, the Commission adopted a total of 7,034 legal acts, of which 3,064 were regulations and 33 directives.[5]

---

19  *Van Duyn v Home Office* Case 41/74 [1974] ECR 1337 (Treaty); *Defrenne v Sabena* Case 43/75 [1976] ECR 455 (directives). See generally, T. Hartley, *The Foundations of European Community Law* (Oxford: Clarendon) 3rd edn., 1994, Ch.7.

20  *Marleasing v La Comercial Internacional de Alimentatión SA* Case C-106/89 [1990] ECR I-4135. See J. Steiner, 'From Direct Effects to *Francovich*: Shifting means of Enforcement of Community Law' (1993) 18 ELR 3; E. Szyszczak, 'Making Europe More Relevant to its Citizens' (1996) 21 ELR 351.

 1  See A. Dashwood, 'The Limits of European Community Powers' (1996) 21 ELR 113 and, generally, R. Pedler and G. Schaefer, *Shaping European Law and Policy* (Maastricht: European Institute of Public Administration) 1996.

 2  T. Hartley, *Foundations*, above, note 19, pp. 38-48, note 1. And see A. Dashwood, 'Community Legislative Procedures in the Era of the Treaty on European Union' (1994) 19 ELR 343.

 3  *The 1996 Inter-Governmental Conference; The Agenda, Democracy and Efficiency; The Role of National Parliaments*, 24th Report of Select Committee on European Legislation, HC 239-I (1994/5) para. 61.

 4  Established by the Comitology Decision of 13 July 1987, Decision 87/373, OJ L197 (18.7.87). And see *Commission v Council* Case 16/88 [1989] ECR 3457.

 5  28th General Report on the Activities of the European Union 1994 (Brussels: European Commission) p. 467.

It is not really surprising that the clarity and accessibility of EC legislation, published in nine languages and passing through so many stages of negotiated policy-making and drafting, are poor.[6] The EP has called the output 'opaque and confused', while English practitioners have commented that the EU has unhappily 'adopted the worst habits of the common law sytems according to which legislation, once enacted, is amended time after time without the issue of an updated text'.[7] At the Edinburgh summit in 1993, the European Council's Legal Service was told to monitor draft legislation regularly with a view to improving clarity and a Resolution was adopted on quality.[8] With an echo of Cotterell, however, an experienced observer has suggested that scope for improvement is limited because of the increasingly technical nature of many of the rules.[9]

From the national standpoint, the House of Commons has censured[10] several aspects of the legislative process, treating the 'considerable gap between aspiration and reality' with some cynicism. 'Too many of the documents we have considered in the past year have been stuffed with jargon, badly translated, or victims of the sort of muddled thinking that even the most limpid translation cannot cure.' Smugly, they added, 'It is a matter for special regret that the European Parliament is now a significant offender'.

Until recently, accommodation of EC regulation into the domestic legislative process was not taken particularly seriously; it was 'a kind of optional extra' to Parliament's usual business.[11] The House of Commons early established the 'parliamentary reserve' whereby:[12]

> No Minister of the Crown should give agreement in the Council of Ministers to any proposal for European Community legislation—(a) which is still subject to scrutiny . . . ; or (b) which is awaiting consideration by the House . . .

Detailed scrutiny of the texts was, however, another matter. The aim of the first Commons Select Committee on European Secondary Legislation[13] was merely to replicate scrutiny of delegated legislation. Judge has remarked on[14] the limited

---

6  R. Barendts, 'The Quality of Community Legislation' (1994) 1 Maastricht J. of Comparative Law 101. On interpretative problems, see T. Hartley, 'The European Court, Judicial Objectivity and the Constitution of the European Union' (1996) 112 LQR 95; R. Wainwright, 'Techniques of Drafting European Legislation: Problems of Interpretation' (1996) 17 Stat. Law Rev. 7.

7  M. Cornwell-Kelly and G. McFarlane, 'EC brief' (1995) 145 NLJ 144.

8  Council Resolution 8 June 1993 on the quality of drafting of EC legislation, incorporating the '10 Commandments' for the legislative draftsman. See T. Burns, 'Better Lawmaking? An Evaluation of Law Reform in the European Community' in P. Craig and C. Harlow (eds.) *The European Lawmaking Process* (Dublin: Sweet and Maxwell) 1997.

9  J.-C. Piris, 'After Maastricht, are the Community Institutions More Efficacious, More Democratic and More Transparent?' (1994) 19 ELR 447, 474.

10  *The Role of National Parliaments in the European Union*, 28th Report of the Select Committee on European Legislation, HC 51-xxviii, para. 112.

11  T. St. J. Bates, 'The Scrutiny of European Legislation at Westminister' (1975-6) 1 ELR 21.

12  Resolution of the House of 3 October 1980, HC Deb., vol. 991, col. 843, now Resolution of 24 October 1990, HC Deb., vol. 178, col. 399.

13  Set up on the recommendation of the Foster Committee: see Second Report from the Select Committee on European Community Secondary Legislation, HC 463 (1972/3).

14  D. Judge, 'The Failure of National Parliaments?' (1995) 18 West European Politics 79, 85.

ambition of this objective, 'when it is remembered that the processing of secondary legislation has traditionally raised profound issues of executive accountability, and has generally demonstrated the supremacy of the executive over the legislature'. The later Select Committee on European Legislation found problems not only with the bulk of the material it was expected to scrutinise but also with access and timing. Mainly in consequence of the Committee's experience, the Select Committee on Procedure in 1988 published an important report on scrutiny of EC legislation.[15] Criticism was directed particularly at the unavailability of official Council texts which greatly hampered scrutiny.[16] A revision of procedures followed this Report. The hope was that the debates would be better attended and Members generally would be better informed. Although the new procedures have not yet been fully digested, they are beginning to shake down and it is generally felt that they afford opportunities for stronger scrutiny of EC rules than was previously the case.[17]

Today, there are two new European Standing Committees liaising with the normal departmental Select Committees to deal with European affairs.[18] In addition, a 'scrutiny committee', the Select Committee on European Legislation, reports on every EC document 'of legal and political importance' and refers them either to the House or to one of the European Standing Committees for debate. The number of documents scrutinised is mounting; from 833 in 1992 to 980 in 1995 and 633 in the first six months of 1996, of which around 40% are referred.[19] The most effective vehicle for scrutiny is still the House of Lords Select Committee on the European Communities, established in 1972 with a wide remit to consider policy as well as draft legislation.[20] The reports of this Committee, which sits in six sub-committees, each competent over particular aspects of EC activity, have gained wide respect in Brussels as well as inside the country. The ambit of Sub-Committee E (Law and Institutions) is particularly wide; it is required to consider and report on any EC proposal which would lead to significant changes in United Kingdom law or have far-reaching implications for United Kingdom law, a remit which allows it to consider proposals at an early stage. In practice, everyday monitoring of Commission rule-making activities tends to be undertaken by interest groups likely to be affected, such as the Confederation of British Industry or Institute of Directors, who might have prior knowledge through representation on the EC 'comitology' or their Brussels lobbying activities.[1] Conveniently, these groups are often directly represented in the House of Lords.

15 *European Community Legislation*, Fourth Report of the Select Committee on Procedure, HC 622-I (1989/90). For the government response, see Cm. 1081 (1990).
16 See also *The Scrutiny of European Business'* HC 51-xxviii (1995/6), claiming the position has, if anything, worsened.
17 See for an overview, T. St J. N. Bates, 'European Community Legislation before the House of Commons' (1991) 12 Statute Law Rev 109, 119-121.
18 E. Denza, 'Parliamentary Scrutiny of Community Legislation' (1993) 14 Stat. Law Rev. 56.
19 *The Scrutiny of European Business*, 27th Report of the Select Committee on European Legislation, HC 51-xxvii (1995/6).
20 See Report of the Maybray-King Committee HL 194 (1972-3). For evaluation, see T. St. J. Bates, 'Select Committees in the House of Lords' in G. Drewry (ed.), *The New Select Committees* (Oxford :Clarendon) 2nd edn, 1989; Denza, above, note 18.
 1 See S. Mazey and J. Richardson (eds.), *The European Lobbying Process* (Oxford: OUP) 1993.

All the Committees have, however, suffered problems of access. Documentation reaches them late, incomplete, and badly translated, putting pressure on the parliamentary process. The House of Commons Select Committee has complained at:[2]

> . . . the way in which legislative proposals often came forward shortly before the Council decided on them, and long before an official text reached national Parliaments, let alone the citizens who would be directly affected. We criticised the way in which the Council was prepared to discuss legislation on the basis of unofficial texts that were not available to the public at all. We noted the unpredictability of Council agendas, obscure drafting, the lack of legislative consolidation, translation delays, and the submission of some Commission proposals long after the legal deadline.

For many reasons, which include the vagueness and lack of clarity of many directives and the clash of European and English drafting styles, the implementation of directives into domestic law is technically difficult and often leaves much to be desired.[3] For example, with the Equal Pay and Equal Treatment Directives (EEC 75/117 and 76/207), the government, for political reasons, refused to promulgate new domestic legislation, instead tinkering with the Equal Pay Act 1970 and Sex Discrimination Act 1975. This led to much litigation, including successful infringement proceedings brought by the Commission against the United Kingdom under EEC Art 169.[4] The Government used s. 2(2) to implement the judgment in these proceedings by Order in Council, allegedly to avoid parliamentary debate and deflect attention from the minimal nature of its response. The resultant regulations have been described by the EOC as 'incomprehensible legal gobbledegook', and foreseeably led to further litigation. Again, the Transfer of Undertakings Regulations 1981 were made hastily under Commission pressure to implement an overdue directive. Seven years later, in *Litster v Forth Dry Dock and Engineering Co Ltd,*[5] the House of Lords struggled to make sense of these regulations, and it was said that 'In construing the Regulations with which this appeal is concerned, one gets little help from the terms of the Directive to which they were intended to give effect'.

Warning of the problem of 'under-implementation', bringing the risk of invalidity and even state compensation to parties unfavourably affected,[6] the Hansard Society urged that the task of scrutiny be taken on by the House of Lords: 'It would be unrealistic for the House of Commons European Legislation Committee to vet bills or delegated legislation in such detail.' More important still was thorough training in EC law for all departmental lawyers; 'these are questions for lawyers rather than politicians'.[7]

---

2   HC 51-xxviii, para. 2.
3   For some of the problems, see P. Craig and C. Harlow (eds.) *The European Lawmaking Process* (Dublin: Sweet and Maxwell) 1997.
4   *EC Commission v United Kingdom* [1982] ECR 2601.
5   [1990] 1 AC 546, per Lord Oliver at 567.
6   See *Francovich and Bonafaci v Italy* Joined Cases C-6, 9/90 [1991] ECR I-5357 and *Brasserie du Pécheur SA v Germany, R v Secretary of State for Transport, ex p Factortame* Joined Cases C-46/93 and C-48/93 [1996] QB 404, discussed further in Ch. 18.
7   Hansard Society Report, p. 133 and Ch. 8 generally.

Chapter 7

# Below the waterline

## 1. Some reasons for rules

At the start of the last chapter we referred to the explosion in rule-making as 'inevitable' and as an essential feature of a modern, bureaucratic society. The lesson of the chapter was also that rules beget more rules. In this way, rule-making contributes both to 'bureaucracy' and public perception of that bureaucracy. In other words, it is part of the process of juridification and expansion of the legal world described by Galanter.[1]

The commonest explanation for rule-making in modern government is that most bureaucracies are hierarchical; that is to say, policy decisions are made at the top while routine decisions are delegated. Rules permit administrative organisations to communicate internally. In this respect, the advent of NPM has undoubtedly hastened the trend to administration by rules. Rules facilitate delegation. Managers formulate policies or record practice in the shape of guidelines and instructions which can then be circulated and applied by subordinates to individual cases.[2] This practice tends to clash with the traditional administrative law principle that discretion may not be delegated, although we should note that, in the public service, the 'non-delegation' rule was tempered by the understanding that officials act in the name of Ministers. Traditional understandings are thrown out of gear by the modern practice of downloading to agencies.[3]

Rules also facilitate openness, as the agency's policies can be published, communicated, or merely become known to the public. Today it is often argued that rules are 'transparent' whereas discretion fosters secrecy; the truth of this assertion will be questioned in Chapter 8. Again, rules are not transparent if they cannot be accessed by the public. High on Megarry's list of complaints over 'quasi-legislation', came the 'haphazard mode of promulgation'.[4] He requested 'some uniform official method of publication' for 'Administrative Notifications

---

1  Above, p. 152
2  See H. Molot, 'The Self-Created Rule of Policy and Other Ways of Exercising Administrative Discretion' (1972) 18 McGill LJ 310.
3  For the principle see *Carltona Ltd v Works Comr* [1943] 2 All ER 560. For comment on recent developments see M. Freedland, 'Privatising *Carltona*: Part II of the Deregulation and Contracting Out Act 1994' [1995] PL 21.
4  R. Megarry, 'Administrative Quasi-Legislation' (1944) 60 LQR 125, 126. See also G. Ganz, *Quasi-Legislation: Recent Developments in Secondary Legislation* (London: Sweet and Maxwell) 1987, pp. 36-41.

and Decisions'. There is still no Official Journal, such as exists in the European Community and perhaps it is doubtful whether such a mass of disparate materials could be uniformly published. Access to government information has, however, been greatly facilitated by a White Paper on Access to Information, itself a form of tertiary legislation.[5] We shall look at this in Chapter 13.

Equally important is a downward pressure created by dissatisfaction with the formal rule-making procedures described in the last chapter. There we saw an unavoidable pressure towards the top of the hierarchy. While the motives, such as the argument for democracy and the need for enhanced scrutiny, were in principle good, the result was to increase pressure on an already overloaded Parliament. In this chapter we track a converse, downward pressure, as overload, delay and expense, and the complex legal language used in formal rule-making combine to create a shift to 'bureaucratic law'. Statutory drafting was, we saw, hardly user-friendly, the usual excuse being that it must be precise. One senior civil servant[6] has, however, described the first drafts by parliamentary counsel of a new law as producing 'a mental effect somewhat analogous to the physical sensation of touching a block of dry ice . . . for a time, our own intellectual capacities were fully extended in trying to identify the pattern of his thinking and accommodate our own to it'. Yet the administrators had been working with their own draft, which actually formed part of the instructions to parliamentary counsel who 'with great good nature – and I fear considerably against his better judgment' consented to read it as a starting-point. Geoffrey Howe, himself a lawyer, has described how, as a Minister, he proudly drew up a 'plain English' draft of an Industrial Relations Bill and handed it to Parliamentary Counsel. But this draft was never considered; 'the idea of accepting some external input was too revolutionary to be tolerable'.[7] Expressed in terms of statute and regulation, the public servant may no longer understand his or her own policies. Memoranda and guidance become necessary guides to explain the law both to the public servants who initiated and have to administer it and to the public on whom it impacts.

In his comprehensive study of rules in government,[8] Baldwin distinguishes eight types of tertiary rule: procedural rules, such as the codes of practice made under PACE[9] or the model procedural code sponsored by the Council on Tribunals;[10] interpretative guidance published as explanation of official policy; instructions to officials inside a department or amongst a group operating the same service, such as the Home Office circulars to Chief Constables[11] or Prison Department circulars to Governors;[12] prescriptive rules aimed by regulators at the

---

5  White Paper on Open Government, Cm 2290 (1993) noted Birkinshaw, '"I Only Ask for Information" – the White Paper on Open Government' [1993] PL 557.

6  D. Johnstone, *A Tax Shall be Charged* (London: Civil Service Department) 1975, p. 53.

7  G. Howe, *Conflict of Loyalty* (London: MacMillan) 1994, p. 60.

8  R. Baldwin, *Rules and Government* (Oxford: Clarendon) 1995, pp. 81-85. See also, R. Baldwin and J. Houghton, 'Circular Arguments: The Status and Legitimacy of Administrative Rules' [1986] PL 239.

9  Above, p. 157.

10  Below, p. 471.

11  Above, p. 158.

12  Below, p. 185.

public or the regulated; evidential rules offering guidance to courts, such as the Highway Code, which has no binding force but may be taken into consideration in judging liability; commendatory rules, by which Baldwin means guidance notes recommending good practice but without legal backing, such as those issued by the Health and Safety Executive on how to achieve safety standards; voluntary codes of practice, such as the 'Bridlington agreements' between the trade unions briefly mentioned in the last chapter or, more topical, the codes of practice issued by the Advertising Standards Authority and Press Council[13] or the complaints procedures negotiated and put in place under the supervision of the ombudsmen (discussed further in Chapter 13); and, finally, rules of practice which explain how the law will in practice be operated. Exhaustive though this list is, it may not be entirely exhaustive (though it might be thought that the categories overlap).

In this chapter, we shall concentrate on three main issues raised by tertiary rules, illustrating them in a case study of the parole process. They are:

(i)   status – are the rules binding?
(ii)  consultation and access to the rulemaking process;
(iii) publication and access to the rules when made.

As we shall see, these are not discrete topics but themes which run through the whole discussion.

## 2. Are rules binding?

Megarry described[14] informal rule-making as:

> something of a curate's egg. On the one hand, announcements by official bodies on points of procedure and the way in which it is proposed to deal with doubtful points of interpretation have much in their favour, while on the other hand there are substantial objections to administrative quasi-legislation which overrides clear law.

When a less authoritative body, such as a local planning authority or area health authority, turns to a superior body, typically a government department for guidance, the junior partner will tend to regard guidance as authoritative. Interpretative rules may then in practice become mandatory. An additional problem arises if the interpretation is incorrect. Take, for example, land use planning, knit together by a series of circulars issued to planning authorities by the DoE.[15] In *Newbury District Council v Secretary of State for the Environment*[16] the council had attached a condition to planning permission which was challenged as not being 'reasonably related' to the planning permission, as the law requires.

13  See generally on self-regulation, Ch. 9.
14  R. Megarry, 'Administrative Quasi-Legislation' (1944) 60 LQR 125, 129.
15  These are published as Vol. 4 of *The Encyclopedia of Planning Law*, a looseleaf publication updated regularly and available to the general public through public libraries.
16  [1980] 2 WLR 379. The House of Lords upheld the Minister's decision on the ground that he had in fact arrived at a correct interpretation of the legal provisions.

The Minister, to whom appeal lies in planning cases, had relied heavily on a departmental circular in holding the condition unreasonable. Newbury argued that the circular glossed the law and was inaccurate. Lord Fraser called the circular 'erroneous in law' and the House agreed in thinking that the Minister's decision, if based on it, would have been unlawful.

When the accuracy of interpretative rules or the lawfulness of the policies embodied in them is disputed by third parties, a different problem arises. The rules may be seen merely as internal instructions possessing no independent legal force. In *Royal College of Nursing v DHSS,*[17] a departmental circular was issued to health authorities, advising on the legality of delegating to nurses certain functions thought to be reserved for doctors under the Abortion Act 1967. The College succeeded in challenging the legality of the circular, although the authority of the Department to issue it and the College's standing to challenge what was effectively an internal instruction to employees, were both questionable and were in fact questioned by some members of the House of Lords in the later case of *Gillick v West Norfolk and Wisbech Area Health Authority.*[18] Here a mother wished to challenge the validity of a DHSS circular to health authorities which stated that doctors were free to give contraceptive advice to girls under the age of 16 without their parents' consent or knowledge. The question arose whether she had standing to bring such an action as a private law case, a difficult point settled at first instance in the plaintiff's favour.[19] In Baldwin's terminology (above), the circular could be classified as interpretative guidance rather than as a prescriptive rule affecting members of the public directly and thus amenable to challenge. This analysis is supported by the opinion of Lord Templeman on appeal to the House of Lords that the case should never have been justiciable since the circular did not amount to a decision by which anyone was actually affected. As Lord Fraser put it, there was no 'present likelihood of any of the daughters seeking contraceptive advice or treatment without the consent of their mother'.[20] For the same reason, Lord Bridge viewed the *Royal College* case unfavourably, as effecting 'a significant extension of the court's power of judicial review' by creating a power to answer 'hypothetical questions'.[1] Writing extra-judicially, Sir John Laws has argued that the High Court has innate jurisdiction in such cases to hand down an advisory opinion, thus avoiding the problem of inaccurate interpretative rules circulating while immune from challenge, and this solution is also supported by the Law Commission.[2]

Like Megarry before him, Baldwin refers to the extra-statutory concessions made by the Inland Revenue. Today published in many volumes, these concessions are none the less of doubtful legal status and have troubled the courts on many occasions. Megarry thought extra-statutory concessions unenforceable; are they

---

17  [1981] AC 800.
18  [1986] AC 112.
19  But see C. Harlow, 'Gillick: a Comedy of Errors?' (1987) 50 MLR 768.
20  [1986] AC 112 at 163.
 1  Ibid, 193–194.
 2  Sir John Laws, 'Judicial Remedies and the Constitution' (1994) 57 MLR 213; Law Commission, *Administrative Law: Judicial Review and Statutory Appeals*, Law Com No. 226 (London: HMSO) 1994, paras 8.9–8.14.

then unlawful and, if so, who can challenge them? Some cases do show courts looking on these Revenue practices with disfavour. In *R v Customs and Excise Comrs, ex p Cook*[3] the Inland Revenue had agreed, as a concession, to accept excise duty in instalments rather than by a single, immediate payment. The Lord Chief Justice remarked: 'One approaches this case on the basis, and I confess for my part an alarming basis, that the word of the Minister is outweighing the law of the land.' Yet the court did not actually halt the 'illegal' practice because it thought that the applicants had no standing. In the celebrated *Federation* case[4] where third parties tried unsuccessfully to challenge a Revenue concession, we can see the House of Lords treating a similar, discretionary concession as reasonable and sensible. Parliament has on occasion condoned similar practices: for example, the Select Committee on the PCA has encouraged the Inland Revenue to make concessions without express statutory authority, while the Public Accounts Committee has accepted the need for extra-statutory concessions. The Inland Revenue itself, its many bound volumes of extra-statutory concessions testifying against its own argument, has on the other hand been heard to argue that, without government authority, interest on over-payments of tax cannot be paid.[5] So is 'selective enforcement' unlawful or is it not? As usual, there is no conclusive answer! Much depends on who challenges and in what context the point arises.

### 3. Rules, individuation and legitimate expectations

We are beginning to see that rule-making may bring administration into conflict with judicial rules about the exercise of discretionary power. The sharp distinction between discretion and law/rules in English administrative law has meant that discretion is traditionally seen as involving a power of free choice. As Galligan puts it:[6]

> There is an idea buried deep in the hearts of various constitutional theorists and judges that 'to discipline administrative discretion by rule and rote is somehow to denature it'. According to this idea, there is something about the nature of discretionary power which requires each decision to be made according to the circumstances of the particular situation, free from the constraints of preconceived policies as to the ends and goals to be achieved by such power. The circumstances of the situation will indicate the proper decision and policy choices must remain in the background.

Galligan describes discretionary powers as 'individuated'. By this he means that someone entrusted with discretionary power has an obligation to consider the merits of the *specific case* which confronts him; he cannot simply apply a rule.

---

3   [1970] 1 WLR 450.
4   *IRC v National Federation of Self Employed and Small Businesses Ltd* [1982] AC 617; below, p. 542.
5   See Report of the Public Accounts Committee, HC 300-I (1970/1), pp. 408-410.
6   D. Galligan, 'The Nature and Function of Policies within Discretionary Power' [1976] PL 332.

Paradoxically, this is what rules are all about. In modern societies, citizens are seen to have a right to equal treatment.[7] Bureaucracies need to evolve systems to deal with mass programmes, and rules promote uniformity. Recognised as a principle of good administration by many systems of administrative law,[8] equality of treatment becomes an important reason for rule-making. It must also be remembered that policies may have to be devised with the aim of rationing scarce funds. Exceptions may have devastating effects on departmental budgets and, if funds run out, may create unfairness. The best way to secure equality is to formulate guidelines. On the other hand, the generality of rules may make it difficult to cater for hard cases; the driver who parks on yellow lines while helping a blind man cross the road requires a more individual treatment.

Galligan suggests a compromise position between the lawyer's tendency to see discretion as a 'lawless' area of total freedom and the administrator's need for rules. Judges should acknowledge that:[9]

> discretion entails a power in the decision-maker to make policy choices, not just to deal with the individual case, but to develop a coherent and consistent set of guidelines which seek to achieve ends and goals within the scope of powers. In short, 'discretion' must include the discretion to make rules.

Modern case law has been working towards precisely this solution.

*British Oxygen Co Ltd v Ministry of Technology*[10]

The Industrial Development Act 1966 empowered the Board of Trade to award discretionary investment grants in respect of new 'plant'. The Board had a rule of practice not to approve grants on items valued individually at less than £25. British Oxygen Co asked for £4 million in respect of gas cylinders each valued at £20, but was refused. BOC sought declarations that the equipment was eligible for a grant.

> *Lord Reid*: I cannot find that these provisions give any right to any person to get a grant. It was argued that the object of the Act is to promote the modernisation of machinery and plant and that the board were bound to pay grants to all who are eligible unless, in their view, particular eligible expenditure would not promote that object. That might be good advice for an advisory committee to give but I find nothing in the Act to require the Board to act in that way. If the Minister who now administers the Act, acting on behalf of the Government, should decide not to give grants in respect of certain kinds of expenditure, I can find nothing to prevent him. There are two general grounds on which the exercise of an unqualified discretion can be attacked. It must not be exercised in bad faith, and it must not be so unreasonably exercised as to show that there cannot have been any real or genuine exercise of the discretion. But, apart from that, if the Minister thinks that policy or good administration requires the operation of some limiting rule, I find nothing to stop him.

---

7  See A. Wheale, *Equality and Social Policy* (London: Routledge and Kegan Paul) 1978.
8  This principle is strongly developed in EC, French and German administrative law: see J. Schwarze, *European Administrative Law* (London: Sweet and Maxwell) 1992, Ch. 4.
9  [1976] PL 332.
10  [1970] 3 WLR 488.

It was argued . . . that the Minister is not entitled to make a rule for himself as to how he will in future exercise his discretion . . . The general rule is that anyone who has to exercise a statutory discretion must not 'shut his ears to an application' . . . I do not think there is any great difference between a policy and a rule. There may be cases where an officer or authority ought to listen to a substantial argument reasonably presented arguing a change of policy. What the authority must not do is to refuse to listen at all. But a Ministry or large authority may have had to deal already with a multitude of similar applications and then they will almost certainly have evolved a policy so precise that it could well be called a rule. There can be no objection to that, provided the authority is always willing to listen to anyone with something new to say – of course I do not mean to say that there need be an oral hearing. In the present case the respondent's officers have carefully considered all the appellants have had to say and I have no doubt that they will continue to do so.

Perhaps this is not a very big step to take. But what is to happen in the reverse case, where the administration wishes to depart from policies on which a third party seeks to rely? We have met this idea earlier in the *GCHQ* case,[11] which involved a sudden change of policy in respect of union rights. The trade union was said to have a 'legitimate expectation' to be consulted before this drastic step was taken. As with the *BOC* case, you can see that this is 'a halfway house'; procedural rights and not substantive entitlements are implied.

In other cases the concept of legitimate expectation has taken applicants somewhat further. In *A-G of Hong Kong v Ng Yuen Shiu*,[12] the Hong Kong government had announced changes in its policy of repatriating illegal immigrants. The promise of a personal interview and individual consideration of each case was made, on the strength of which illegal immigrants were asked to give themselves up. When the applicant responded, he was given no opportunity to present a case. The Privy Council ruled that the promise had created procedural expectations which must be observed; no repatriation without interview. Notice that here the expectation was created by a general statement of policy. In *R v Secretary of State for the Home Department, ex p Asif Khan*,[13] the Khans had written to the Home Office making inquiries about current policy on entry for adoption. A reply set out four conditions which had to be satisfied. The Khans' application to adopt satisfied these conditions but was rejected on another ground. The Court of Appeal held that the policy could not be changed unless the applicant had been notified and given an opportunity to make representations as to the new condition, which must be seriously considered. This time the expectation arose out of an individual undertaking, paralleling the concept of estoppel, whereby a promise or representation not amounting to a contract may bind the promisor if the promisee acts on it to his detriment.[14]

11   Above, p. 113.
12   [1983] 2 AC 629.
13   [1985] 1 All ER 40.
14   See Craig, *Administrative Law* pp. 661-72. In addition to the *Liverpool Taxis* case (below, p. 201), see *Lever Finance Ltd v Westminster City Council* [1971] 1 QB 222; *Western Fish Products Ltd v Penrith District Council* [1981] 2 All ER 204.

### *R v Secretary of State for Health, ex p United States Tobacco International Inc*[15]

US Tobacco negotiated permission to market an oral snuff, subject to the condition that it would not be marketed to young persons. On the strength of this assurance they built a factory in Scotland. Later, the Minister, acting on the advice of an expert advisory committee, changed the rules by making regulations which banned oral snuff. US Tobacco argued that the regulations were ultra vires, in that the parent Consumer Protection Act 1987 was not apt to make regulations concerning public health. Not surprisingly, this argument failed. The firm fell back on an argument based on an individual expectation: namely, that they ought to be allowed to continue in business so long as they observed the original conditions. This argument also failed on the ground that, provided he acted fairly and reasonably, the minister could not fetter his statutory discretion. US Tobacco did at least succeed in re-opening the matter on the grounds that they had not been given access to the scientific advice underpinning the ministerial decision and had had no real opportunity to combat it.

> *Taylor LJ*: In view of the total change of policy the Regulations would bring about and its unique impact on the applicants, fairness demanded that they should be treated with candour. To conceal from them the scientific advice which directly led to the ban was, in my judgment, unfair and unlawful.
>
> It may well be that, in the end, the decision reached by the Secretary of State may prove to be wise and in the public interest, but such a draconian step should not be taken unless procedural propriety has been observed and those most concerned have been treated fairly. Although the Regulations were subject to annulment by negative resolution of the House of Commons but were not so annulled, Parliament would be concerned only with the objects of the Regulations and would be unaware of any procedural impropriety. It is therefore to the courts, by way of judicial review, that recourse must be had to seek a remedy.

Although the case law[16] provides no single answer, on balance it provides support for the 'halfway house' position that 'legitimate expectations' are procedural in character.[17] Baldwin and Horne suggest that difficulties in the case law stem from the contractual and individuated basis of the doctrine. This means that the courts look, on the one hand, for an interest worthy of protection and, on the other, for an undertaking or representation based on conduct. Like Galligan earlier, they argue for a more general 'principle of good administration' permitting the development of coherent guidelines in the interest of consistency:[18]

---

15  [1991] 3 WLR 529.
16  See also *Re Findlay* (below, p. 188), and *ex p Hargreaves* (below, p. 189); and *Re Preston* [1985] AC 835; *R v Secretary of State for the Home Department, ex p Ruddock* [1987] 2 All ER 518; *R v Ministry of Agriculture Fisheries and Food, ex p Hamble (Offshore) Fisheries Ltd* [1995] 2 All ER 714.
17  Some authors see a substantive element. See P. Craig, 'Legitimate Expectations: A Conceptual Analysis' (1992) 108 LQR 79; C. Forsyth, 'The Provenance and Protection of Legitimate Expectations' (1988) 47 CLJ 238 and '*Wednesbury* protection of substantive legitimate expectations' [1997] PL 375 discussing *R v IRC, ex p Unilever plc* [1996] STC 681.
18  R. Baldwin and J. Horne, 'Expectations in a Joyless Landscape' (1986) 49 MLR 685, 701-2.

. . . statutory powers are not given to public bodies to be exercised capriciously. Reasonable and fair action thus involves a modicum of consistency. Certain types of treatment will create legitimate expectations on this basis. This includes an express or implied undertaking to behave in a certain manner in exercising powers. . .; prior treatment which has a precedential quality. . .; and publication of rules or policies known to be relied on.

Like the doctrine of proportionality, this proposal tackles the problem from the other end, requiring the administration to take the applicants' legitimate expectations into consideration at the decision-making stage.[19] While this solution does not resolve the procedure/substance argument, it may often render it immaterial.

## 4. Parole: discretion, repression and due process

Shot through with discretionary power, criminal justice systems provide fertile ground for the application of the rule-making theories of K. C. Davis.[20] For centuries, prisons have remained 'dark and windowless' places filled with 'outlaws' who, having broken the law, forfeit its protections. For centuries, English courts showed no willingness either to acknowledge prisoners' rights or to become involved with what went on inside prisons, maintaining that it would be 'fatal to all discipline if governors and warders had to perform their duty with the fear of an action before their eyes if they in any way deviated from the rules'.[1] But just as changing attitudes led in the United States to the re-structuring of some American parole systems using Davis's theories as a blueprint,[2] so this case study shows similar forces at work in the United Kingdom. The case study can also be used to test points made in the last chapters about rule-making. While reading on, we suggest that the reader considers the following questions: has discretion really been eliminated? What sort of discretion remains and at what levels in the hierarchy? Has the 'optimum point' on the rules/discretion spectrum been achieved? Who makes the rules and how are they made? What has the respective contribution of formal and informal rules and of the standards and principles of case law been? What improvements should be made?

Illustrative of the general attitude, the first successful application for judicial review of the prison discipline system[3] came only after serious riots at Hull prison in 1976; until this case, the judicial/administrative distinction (above, Chapter 2) had been used to deny justiciability.[4] An unprecedented challenge to the Prison

---

19  de Smith, Jowell, Woolf, para 13-035.
20  See D. Galligan, 'Guidelines and Just Deserts: A Critique of Recent Trends in Sentencing Reform' [1981] Crim. LR 297; L. Wilkins, 'Sentencing Guidelines to Reduce Disparity', [1980] Crim. LR 201; N. Lacey, 'Discretion and Due Process at the Post-Conviction Stage' in I. Dennis (ed.), *Criminal Law and Justice* (London: Sweet and Maxwell) 1987.
1  *Arbon v Anderson* [1943] KB 252, 255 per Goddard LJ.
2  See particularly, I. Blalock, 'Justice and Parole: The Oregon Experience' in D. Fogel and J. Hudson (eds.), *Justice as Fairness, Perspectives on the Justice Model* (Cincinnati: Anderson Publishing Co) 1981.
3  *R v Board of Visitors of Hull Prison, ex p St Germain* [1979] QB 425.
4  See G. Richardson, *Law, Process and Custody: Prisoners and Patients* (London: Weidenfeld and Nicolson) 1993, pp. 18-19.

Rules followed in *Raymond v Honey*.[5] The argument was over rule 33(3), which empowered the governor at his discretion to stop any letter or communication which he thought objectionable (an example of strong, subjective discretion). The House of Lords held the rules ultra vires; there was nothing in the Prison Act 1952 authorising interference with 'so basic a right' as access to the court in the shape of free correspondence between prisoners and their solicitors. The cases were widely seen as a response to the case law of the European Court of Human Rights which, in a series of applications by British prisoners, had held the United Kingdom to be in breach of the ECHR, specifically in respect of prisoners' correspondence with their legal representatives,[6] regarded by the Commission and Court as an essential ingredient in access to justice (ECHR Art. 5).

In the United Kingdom, criminal justice stands high on the political agenda and public opinion is strongly divided over penal policy. Tension exists between reformers, often those who administer the prison system and settle its policies, for whom rehabilitation of the prisoner and safety of the public are the legitimate policy objectives; judges as sentencers, for whom equality of treatment, often expressed as a 'tariff', is important and who also have a concern for the Rule of Law; and politicians, who frequently seek votes by stressing punishment and deterrence as the primary goal of the penal system. From this viewpoint, the Home Secretary's extensive discretionary powers operate as a device for infusing a closed system, largely controlled by experts, with a healthy dose of public opinion, supposedly representative of the public interest.

Today much has changed in prison law. There is a growing dependence on rules, both formal (legislation and the Prison Rules) and informal (e.g., the Circular Instructions published by the Home Office). Informal 'white papers', widely circulated for comment inside and outside the service, are used in rule-making and reform. Statistical studies, including risk prediction tables, allow procedures to be monitored and their usefulness to be evaluated. Performance indicators are set. Morgan, an outside expert, argues the case for more rules, less discretion and, above all, less external political interference from Ministers, as the basis of 'a just, humane and orderly system'.[7] In other words, Morgan associates discretion with political interference:

> What the developing arrangements require is the firm guiding hand of a more prescriptive 'statutory' framework with the occasional light touch on the 'judicial' tiller which a new Prison Act might prompt. Such a constitutional framework would

5 [1982] 2 WLR 465. The Prison Rules had been laid before Parliament published as SI 1964/1988. The plaintiff lost the case on the facts.
6 Especially *Golder v United Kingdom* (1975) 1 EHRR 524, *Silver v United Kingdom* (1983) 5 EHRR 347. For the effect of the ECHR, see G. Douglas and S. Jones, 'Prisoners and the European Convention on Human Rights' in M. Furmston, R. Kerridge, and B. Sufrin (eds.), *The Effect on English Domestic Law of Membership of the European Communities and Ratification of the European Convention on Human Rights* (The Hague: Martinus Nijhoff) 1983.
7 R. Morgan, 'Prisons Accountability Revisited' [1993] PL 314. The reference in the extract Woolf is to the Woolf Report, *Prison Disturbances April 1990. Report of an Inquiry by the Rt. Hon Lord Justice Woolf (Parts I and II) and His Honour Judge Stephen Tumin (Part II)*, Cm. 1456 (1991).

dovetail well with the management accountability which Woolf proposed and the Prison Service is developing. We need not fear . . . the loss of flexibility which such a framework might seem to suggest. For the last 40 years the Prison Service has been fettered by an absence of law, rather than the reverse.

## (a) Parole: privilege, entitlement or . . .

Parole is the process whereby a prisoner may be released on trial within the period of sentence, subject to a recall power by the prison authorities if his behaviour is unsatisfactory. The original objective of parole was rehabilitation; it was based on the belief that a prisoner should only be allowed back into the community if the custodian deemed him suitable for release. The White Paper on which the English parole system was based in 1965 tells us that[8] 'prisoners who do not of necessity have to be detained for the protection of the public are in some cases more likely to be made into decent citizens if, before completing the whole of their sentence, they are released under supervision with a liability to recall if they do not behave.' Parole was therefore never a 'right' but a 'privilege' to be earned by good behaviour, and this justified the absence of procedural protections whether at the stage of release or recall. Nor was parole a favourite with the judges, who saw it as ironing out the differences between individuated sentences by shortening the time actually served.[9]

The starting point for a study of English parole procedures is ss. 59-62 the Criminal Justice Act 1967.[10] The Act established a tripartite division of responsibility for the parole system. At the apex of the system is the Home Secretary, in whom ultimate responsibility is vested and who, as Morgan complains, everywhere retains considerable discretionary power. The 1967 Act established a Parole Board to advise the Home Secretary, a statutory body consisting of a chairman and not less than four members appointed by the Home Secretary (in practice there are today nearer to 65 and the composition balances professionals (judges, psychiatrists, probation officers) with lay ('independent') members.[11]) The Board operated through small panels of three or four members who met to consider cases. After 1991, their jurisdiction was limited and their major responsibility was (i) release on licence in cases of mandatory and discretionary life sentences and (ii) recall from licence for all parolees. In 1995, the Parole Board became an executive agency, with corporate, management and financial plans.

The third link of the 1967 structure was formed by Local Review Committees (LRCs) whose duty it was to consider the case and make recommendations to the Home Secretary and Parole Board. LRCs were necessary because the parole

---

8   *The Adult Offender*, Cmnd. 2852, 1965.

9   N. Lacey, 'Government as Manager, Citizen as Consumer: The Case of the Criminal Justice Act 1991' (1994) 57 MLR 534, 539.

10   Previously, ss. 27 and 26(2) of the Prison Act 1952 allowed unfettered discretion to the Home Secretary to direct release on parole or otherwise. For a concise account, see S. Livingstone and T. Owen, *Prison Law: Text and Materials* (Oxford: Clarendon) 1993.

11   See Sch. 5 to the Criminal Justice Act 1991, as amended by Sch. 10 to the Criminal Justice and Public Order Act 1994.

system handled in the region of 25,000 cases annually and the system demanded an 'individuated' decision in every case. LRC procedures, governed by the Local Review Committee Rules 1967, were rough and ready, consisting of an interview at which the prisoner could make representations, followed by a written report. Today, the need for LRCs has gone and they have been wound up, though members were often 'recycled' as local Parole Board representatives (see below). A unanimous report from the LRC allowed the Home Secretary to parole the prisoner or dismiss his application without referring the case to the Parole Board,[12] and, in practice, the LRC's decision was invariably implemented. Although he rarely did so, the Home Secretary could reject the Parole Board's recommendation for parole, but he could not parole someone whom the Board had not recommended.[13]

The Act dealt separately with life sentences, providing in s. 61(1) that the release on licence of a life prisoner should not only depend on a recommendation from the Parole Board but should also involve consultation with the trial judge and Lord Chief Justice. In practice, a joint working group of the Home Office and Parole Board considered the cases after the first three years and the opinion of the judges was only sought when parole seemed a real possibility. A practice also grew up whereby a 'tariff' (or 'penal element) deemed necessary to meet the needs of punishment and deterrence, was set by the trial judge as the minimum period to be served. When this tariff was decided remained somewhat haphazard; in other words, the procedures were characteristically informal and discretionary. By 1995 the Parole Board had negotiated an agreement that the sentencing judge's comments together with material on which the sentence was based would form part of the prison file. The Home Secretary retained discretion as to a further period (the 'risk element').

## (b) . . . legitimate expectation?

This was the position when, in 1983, in a speech to the Conservative Party Conference, Mr. Leon Brittan, then Home Secretary, unexpectedly announced the introduction of a stiffer sentencing policy for serious crimes. Prioritising retribution and deterrence, Brittan changed the practice whereby the first review of life sentences came after three years; in future, he announced,[14] he would determine the date himself after consultation with the judiciary and review would be held back until three years before the expiry of the 'tariff' period, while certain murders would automatically carry minimum sentences of not less than 20 years. It was estimated that this change, which would bite retrospectively, apparently affected some 500 prisoners.

---

12  Section 35 of the Criminal Justice Act 1972.
13  For a fuller account of this period, see the Annual Reports of the Parole Board (London: HMSO) or E. Hall Williams, 'Parole in England and Wales: A Success Story' (1979) 10 Univ. of Toledo LR 465 (1979).
14  See HC Deb., Vol. 48, col. 281 (14 November 1983).

*Re Findlay*[15]

Prisoners affected by the Brittan statement were quick to apply for judicial review. They argued that there had been procedural impropriety in that the Parole Board had not been consulted about the changes; and because the policy operated to 'fetter' the Home Secretary's discretion, contrary to the 1967 Act which required an 'individuated' decision based on a recommendation by the Parole Board. The prisoners had acquired a 'legitimate expectation' that their cases would be considered at a certain time and this could not be retracted. A strong case one might think and, dissenting in the Court of Appeal, Browne-Wilkinson LJ thought so too, ruling the policy too rigid because it excluded consideration of all circumstances other than the nature of the offence 'unless there were genuinely exceptional circumstances or compelling reasons for making an exception'. The House of Lords, on the other hand, thought that the Home Secretary had not acted unlawfully.

> *Lord Scarman*: For myself, I have difficulty in understanding how a Secretary of State could properly manage the complexities of his statutory duty without a policy . . . The question, therefore is simply: did the new policy constitute a refusal to consider the cases within the specified classes? The answer is clearly 'no'. Consideration of a case is not excluded by a policy which provides that exceptional circumstances or compelling reasons must be shown because of the weight to be attached to the nature of the offence, the length of sentence and the factors of deterrence, retribution, public confidence, all of which it was the duty of the Secretary of State to consider . . .
>
> [Counsel] did not suggest that the statute gave rise to any greater expectation than that their cases would be considered on their becoming eligible for parole. Their cases have been considered and will continue to be considered under the new policy. Unless, therefore, the policy is unlawful (which I have held it is not) this argument avails them nothing . . .
>
> It is said that the refusal to except [the applicants] from the new policy was an unlawful act on the part of the Secretary of State in that his decision frustrated their expectation. But what was their *legitimate* expectation? Given the substance and purpose of the legislative provisions governing parole, the most that a convicted prisoner can legitimately expect is that his case will be examined individually in the light of whatever policy the Secretary of State sees fit to adopt provided always that the adopted policy is a lawful exercise of the discretion conferred upon him by the statute. Any other view would entail the conclusion that the unfettered discretion conferred by the statute upon the minister can in some cases be restricted so as to hamper, or even to prevent, changes of policy. Bearing in mind the complexity of the issues which the Secretary of State has to consider and the importance of the public interest in the administration of parole I cannot think that Parliament intended the discretion to be restricted in this way.[16]

This statement merits careful consideration. How does the retrospective impact of the new policy square with Allan's vision of the Rule of Law? In the light of the case law on legitimate expectation (above, p.182), does the assurance given

15  [1985] AC 318. Notice that this case antedates the *GCHQ* case, above p. 113.
16  [1985] AC 318 at 1168-1170.

in this case differ from that in *Ng Yuen Shiu*?[17] Should the case now be decided differently?

In *R v Secretary of State for the Home Department, ex p Hargreaves*[18] a similar argument was presented in a case concerning release of prisoners on home leave. Rule 6 of the Prison Rules 1964 had provided that 'A prisoner to whom this Rule applies may be temporarily released for any period and subject to any conditions'. Each prisoner received on admission a notice concerning home leave, which told them:

> You may be eligible to ask for Home Leave . . . You can apply for short home leave after serving one-third of the total term of sentenced imprisonment . . . You can apply for long home leave 2 months before your release date . . .
>
> REMEMBER: Home leave is a privilege for sentenced prisoners under Prison Rule 6. Its purpose is to help restore self-confidence by placing trust in you under conditions of freedom and to help you to re-adjust to life outside prison by giving you the opportunity to maintain links with family and friends . . .

At the same time, each prisoner signed a 'compact'[19] agreeing to observe the rules in exchange for a promise of 'thorough care . . . including consideration for home leave when you become eligible'.

In 1994, following the report of a working party set up to consider absconding and re-offending, the Home Secretary announced changes.[20] The broad discretion was replaced by the Prison (Amendment) Rules 1995, which provided 'a simple set of fair but firm criteria' covering release on temporary licence for 'precisely defined and specific purposes'. The new scheme included a mandatory and stringent risk assessment procedure. In consequence, the applicants' expectation of home leave was severely reduced. After ruling out the applicability of ECHR Art. 8 (Respect for Family Life), the Court of Appeal applied *Re Findlay*, holding that the 'compact' was insufficiently clear and unambiguous to ground any expectation of home leave.

The effect of these two cases on the policy-making process is to allow the Minister to change policy informally through guidelines. These 'rules' are published by means of a statement or written answer to the House of Commons but not validated through the more formal procedures of a statutory instrument. The more permissive attitude to *ministerial* discretion contrasts with the court's standard in 'process review'. In *Norney*[1] the Home Office had formed a practice of referring discretionary life cases to the Parole Board only on expiry of their 'tariff' period. Given the average time taken to process applications, this resulted in an additional six months' sentence. The Divisional Court criticised the practice as '*Wednesbury* unreasonable' and 'manifestly unjust'. An immediate change of practice resulted, though, on grounds of fairness to other prisoners, the court refused to order that the applicants' case be put to the head of the queue.

---

17  Above, p. 182.
18  [1997] 1 All ER 397. See also *R v Ministry of Agriculture, Fisheries and Food, ex p Hamble (Offshore) Fisheries Ltd* [1995] 2 All ER 714 (Sedley J), here disapproved.
19  As recommended by the Woolf Report, *Report of an Inquiry into Prison Disturbances April 1990* (Cm. 1456, 1991).
20  HC Deb., vol. 250, col. 244.
 1  *R v Secretary of State for the Home Department, ex p Norney* (1995) Independent, 4 October.

## (c) Rules and transparency

In his article on accountability (above, p. 185), Morgan depicts the Prison Service as relatively open 'after years of criticism of its obsessive secrecy'. The secrecy in which parole decisions were shrouded had long been a ground for complaint. In 1975, the then Home Secretary (Mr Roy Jenkins) took an important step in the direction of transparency when he insisted that the criteria on which the Board based its decisions should be published.[2] Since then, they have been annexed to each annual report of the Parole Board.[3] Here is the Home Office in 1981 defending its corner:[4]

> Inevitably the individual prisoner who is trying to weigh up his chances will find . . . [the] material insufficiently precise to enable him to foresee with any certainty what the outcome of his case will be. There can be no such precision or certainty in a system of discretionary release . . . A bureaucratic system would work differently, comparing one case with another and building up continuously on precedent. This system would have its own disadvantages which are common to bureaucratic methods, such as inflexibility, substantial resource needs and delay. The Parole Board . . . [believes] it to be better to consider each prisoner's case as separate and individual. This system is more responsive to varying circumstances and more humane in the sense that each prisoner is considered as a person rather than as a 'case'.

In support, the Home Office could rely on *Payne v Lord Harris of Greenwich,*[5] where a prisoner who had been turned down for parole and wanted to know how to prepare a second application, applied to the court for a declaration that he should know the reasons for the refusal. The Act required reasons for *revocation* of a parole licence, but not for refusal to grant parole, a difference defended by the Home Office on the ground that parole was, at the time of the Act, merely a 'privilege'. The Court of Appeal held that the legislation and rules constituted a complete code which should not be modified 'by grafting on a court-designed duty to act fairly'. Not an advocate of transparency, Lord Denning MR reasoned curiously:[6]

> I should think that in the interests of the man himself – as a human being facing indefinite detention – it would be better for him to be told the reasons. But, in the interests of society at large – including the due administration of the parole system – it would be best not to give them.

while Shaw LJ felt:[7]

> It is not easy, even if it were desirable, to give expression to or to define the subjective reasons in the minds of the members of the board; it is often virtually

2   See HC Deb., vol. 897, col. 25.
3   Today the Tables are published regularly as part of a series of research studies evaluating their performance: see C. Nuttall et al., *Parole in England and Wales*, Home Office Research Study No 38 (London: HMSO) 1977; D. Ward et al, *The Validity of the Reconviction Prediction Score*, Home Office Research Study No 94 (London: HMSO) 1987.
4   *Review of Parole in England and Wales* 1981.
5   [1981] 1 WLR 754.
6   [1981] 1 WLR 754 at 759.
7   [1981] 1 WLR 754 at 763.

impossible to communicate them in exact terms via a third party. Not only is there no statutory requirement to disclose to a prisoner the reasons for an adverse recommendation as to release on licence, but I doubt whether there is any statutory authority to make such a disclosure.

Later, the Home Office admitted that there might be 'much to be said from the point of view of humane administration for giving reasons',[8] yet both the Parole Board and Home Office continued to fight the giving of reasons. Reasons might invite applications for judicial review in which discovery of the file might be ordered. Ultimately, this 'would substitute for a system under which parole is a privilege to be earned a system under which it would be a right to be claimed'.

But even as it was published, the Home Office defence of secrecy in terms of individuation was at odds with the emergent parole system. The goals had changed. In 1980, the May Committee[9] had conceded that 'prison can never truly be rehabilitative'. The escalating prison population was also creating pressure. Just as the Brittan statement was decreasing the chances of parole for long-term prisoners, s. 33 of the Criminal Justice Act 1982 had reduced the minimum sentence to be served from 12 to six months, irritating the judiciary because of its effect on sentencing tariffs. Parole for short-term prisoners had effectively become an entitlement, though never a right. Thus, when the Carlisle Committee, set up to consider the parole system, reported in 1988,[10] it saw 'an unacceptable discrepancy' between parole for long-term, short-term and life prisoners, creating 'unreality in the criminal justice system and hand[ing] to the executive too much control over the length of sentence served'.

Between 1983 and 1986, the Parole Board's load had shot up from 265 to 10,603 cases until by 1991 parole was a mass system, with the Board and LRCs handling 33,000 cases annually. For the majority of the prison population, therefore, the Criminal Justice Act 1991 replaced parole with 'early release', unconditional after 50% of sentence for all those sentenced to four years or less (s. 33(1)); discretionary after 50% of sentence, mandatory after two-thirds of sentence, for long-term prisoners (s. 33 (2)). The main part of the Board's work was now life sentence cases, both on release and recall. In mandatory life sentences (murder), s. 35 provided for discretionary release after 50% of sentence on recommendation by the Parole Board after reference by the Home Secretary, plus consultation with the judges; for discretionary lifers, release was mandatory on recommendation of the Parole Board after the 'tariff' had been completed (s. 34(2)(b)). The effect on caseload was dramatic. By 1995/6, the backlog had been reduced until the Board had only 4,403 determinate sentence cases to consider and the two types of life sentences produced only 668 and 752 cases respectively. But the Home Secretary retained a significant area of 'strong' discretion, including the crucial decision whether or not to refer any case to the Board (s 34 (4)).

The Crime (Sentences) Act 1997 took this process further by introducing the concept of 'real sentences'. Short-term prisoners sentenced to three years or under will now earn by good behaviour only a small number of 'early release'

8  *Review*, paras. 72-81 and App. M.
9  Report of the Committee of Inquiry into the Prison Services (Cmnd. 7673, 1980).
10  *The Parole System in England and Wales*, Cm. 352, 1988. The citation below is from para. 194.

days (s. 11). Long-term prisoners (other than lifers) will have their cases referred to the Parole Board after serving five-sixths of sentence and must be released if the Parole Board so recommends (s. 12). These provisions are not yet in force. When they are, the Parole Board's existence will mainly be justified by its work in life sentence cases.

Life prisoners are now divided into two classes: those convicted of murder, who may be released on licence after a recommendation by the Parole Board *plus* consultation with the Lord Chief Justice and trial judge (s. 29(1)); and all other lifers, where the Parole Board may direct release (s. 28) after the 'tariff' has been served, in which case the Home Secretary 'must' order release. We shall return to this point.

Even before Carlisle, the Parole Board had expressed disquiet at the absence of clear criteria for release; the vague standard of 'risk to the general public' which governed the question was capable of being infinitely stretched. As *Re Findlay* and now *Hargeaves* show us, different Home Secretaries might view sentencing policy very differently[11] and could use their strong discretion to change the rules of the ball-game without reference to Parliament. In 1989 the Board had demanded statutory criteria, inviting Parliament to indicate clearly whether the presumption was *for* or *against* parole, a matter which had been cast in doubt by the interaction of the legislation with the 1983 Brittan statement. Section 32(6) of the 1991 Act empowered the Home Secretary 'to give directions', which had to be laid before Parliament, to the Parole Board, and set out the overriding criteria for parole as:[12]

> (a) the need to protect the public from serious harm from offenders; and
> (b) the desirability of preventing the commission by them of further offences and of securing their rehabilitation.

It may be thought that the objectives set out in the badly drafted (b) are internally incompatible and suggest opposite presumptions as to parole. In 1992, the Home Secretary's directions to the Parole Board prioritised the former:[13]

> 1.1 The decision whether or not to recommend parole should focus primarily on the risk of a further offence being committed at a time when the offender would otherwise be in prison. This should be balanced against the benefit, both to the public and the offender, of early release back into the community under a degree of supervision which might help rehabilitation and so lessen the risk of re-offending in the future.

But does this guidance flesh out the statutory rule or distort it? It should be remembered that the directions have their basis in s. 32(6) of the Act: how authoritative would they be as an interpretative aid? To reinforce the protection of the public as the primary concern in parole assessment, a new set of Directions was laid in 1996. Finally, for life prisoners (now an extended category under the Act)

---

11 See M. Wasik and K. Pease, 'The Parole Veto and Party Politics' [1986] CLR 379.
12 The statutory criteria are not expressed to apply to recall from parole but in *R v Parole Board, ex p Watson* [1996] 1 WLR 906 the Court of Appeal held that it was proper for them so to apply.
13 Secretary of State's directions for the release and recall of determinate sentenced prisoners, 1992: Appendix A, AR Parole Board 1992. HC 712 (1994) To reinforce the protection of the public as the primary concern in parole assessment, a new set of Directions was laid in 1996.

s. 28(6)(b) of the Crime (Sentences) Act 1997 clarifies the position by providing against release on licence unless 'the Board is satisfied that it is no longer necessary for the protection of the public that the prisoner should be confined.'

The 'Training Guidance' published annually in the Board's Report contains more detailed criteria for decision-making. It advises the Board, subject to (a) and (b) above, to consider each case on its individual merits. Amongst the criteria to be taken into account are the following:[14]

(a) the offender's background, including any previous convictions and their pattern, and responses to any previous periods of supervision;
(b) the nature and circumstances of the original offence; . . .
(d) any risk to the victim or possibility of retaliation by the victim, victim's family or local community; . . .
(f) any available statistical indicators as to the likelihood of re-offending; . . .
(i) remorse, insight into offending behaviour, attitude to the victim and steps taken, within available resources, to achieve any treatment or training objectives set out in a sentence plan;

### (d) Judgment discretion

Bearing in mind what we know about open-textured rules (Chapter 4), let us look more closely at these guidelines. Take the use of statistical evidence, governed by para (f). The Home Office regularly compiles Risk Prediction Tables.

Let us first let us look back at the statutory criteria in s. 32(6)(b). Over what period is the risk of new offences to be predicted? The Carlisle Committee (above) had recommended the remaining period of sentence, and suggested weighting crimes according to their seriousness; the Prediction Tables used by the Parole Board, on the other hand, were set at two years and standardised according to crime.[15] More discretion!

Home Office Guidance provides that, as with home leave applications (above), an individuated prediction of the risk of re-offending, calculated according to a points system based on the tables, has to be contained in the file of every potential parolee. This is how the risk score is used in practice:[16]

The police report will also contain a list of the prisoner's previous convictions and usually a short account of his social history and employment record . . . This information provides a background to the last offence and will show whether that offence was part of a previous criminal pattern of behaviour . . . This is highly relevant to the question whether he is likely to reoffend after release and, if so, what sort of crime he is liable to commit.

Obviously many previous convictions indicate (in the absence of other factors) a high probability of reoffending . . .

14  AR 1992, pp. 23-24.
15  See J. Copas et al., *Predicting Reoffending for Discretionary Conditional Release*, Home Office Research Study No. 150 (London: HMSO) 1996; D. Wright and J. Copas, 'Prediction Scores for Risk Assessment' in R. Baldwin (ed.), *Law and Uncertainty: Risks and the Legal Process* (London: Kluwer) 1997.
16  AR 1992, HC 712 (1993) p. 26.

Now take Factor (b), which deals with nature and circumstances of the original offence. How much discretion is left to the Board here? Can the Board, as the Home Secretary can, take public opinion into account in a case like that of Myra Hindley, imprisoned for life for her part in a series of gruesome child murders, whose periodic applications for release on parole are invariably the subject of negative press campaigns?

We now know that the mention of remorse in Factor (i) is taken very literally as the subsequent history of Mr Payne shows.[17] A model prisoner, Payne consistently protested his innocence. He was refused parole until 1990, when the Parole Board recommended him for the first time. When the Home Secretary turned down the recommendation, Payne absconded from an open prison. Inquiries produced from the Home Office the explanation that 'his continuing protestation of innocence makes it impossible to assess the risk to the public'. Criteria for mandatory lifers, not published at the time, now substitute the following text:[18]

> g. insight into attitudes and behavioural problems, attitude to the offence and degree of remorse and steps taken to achieve the treatment and training objectives set out in the life sentence plan.

Could both or either of these guidelines be challenged through judicial review? In *ex p Zulfikar,*[19] where parole was denied to someone who refused to admit his guilt on the ground that he had 'failed to address his offending behaviour', this phrase was described as 'a piece of jargon' and it was held that a blanket refusal to consider parole where guilt was denied is unacceptable. The Board substituted that: 'the lack of understanding of the causes and consequences of the offence and the lack of victim empathy indicated a risk of reoffending'. This time the court weighed the prisoner's conduct in prison against the prediction tables, ruling that the risk of reoffending had not been sufficiently reduced. This case indicates the limitations of reasoned decisions; challenged on one ground, the administrator can re-phrase his decision more acceptably.

### (e) Parole and due process

It is an important principle of administrative law that individuals should be permitted to participate in decisions concerning them; indeed, this is one of the rules of natural justice which form the basis of our system of judicial review. Yet no full hearing has ever been required in parole or early release cases. Under the 1967 scheme, the prisoner was limited to 'making representations' to the LRC (later a member of the Parole Board) which, in practice, amounted to an interview. The modern procedure is largely documentary and centres on a 'parole dossier'. Compilation of the dossier is the responsibility of the prison staff and detailed instructions, with a list of the numerous reports to be included and deadlines to be met, are contained in Home Office Circulars No.26/1992 and No.85/1992,

17  *Payne v Lord Harris of Greenwich*, above, p. 190, note 5.
18  AR 1995/6, HC 506 (1996), pp. 20-21.
19  *R v Secretary of State for the Home Department and the Parole Board, ex p Zulfikar* (1995) Times, 26 July.

distributed to all staff affected by the provisions and available on request from the Home Office. The instructions are detailed and specific; paras. 24-5 provide for the prisoner to have access to a copy of the dossier no less than two weeks before the date arranged for the interview and to copy the dossier at his own expense. The general rule is stated to be 'all information in the parole dossier should be disclosed to the prisoner' and para. 26 lists the four exceptions. Just how innovatory these new practices are can be seen from *Payne's* case.

The new procedures are based on the more generous standards of the Court of Human Rights.

## Weeks v United Kingdom[1]

The applicant had been sentenced to an indeterminate life sentence when, aged 17, he had stolen 35 pence from a shop, threatening the shopkeeper with a starting pistol loaded with blank cartridges. Although not a model prisoner, he finally obtained parole after ten years but his licence had to be revoked after two further offences. Weeks applied to the Commission and Court of Human Rights, under ECHR Art. 5(1) and (4):

> 5(1) Everyone has the right to liberty and security of the person. No one shall be deprived of his liberty save in the following cases and in accordance with a procedure prescribed by law: [including] (a) the lawful detention of a person after conviction by a competent court . . .
> 5(4) Everyone who is deprived of his liberty by arrest or detention shall be entitled to take proceedings by which the lawfulness of his detention shall be decided speedily by a court and his release ordered if the detention is not lawful.

The Court of Human Rights refused to accept the government's argument that the original life sentence handed down by the sentencing court remained operative, ruling that, to satisfy Art. 5(1), discretionary lifers were entitled to regular review throughout their imprisonment and any revocation must be the subject of a judicial ruling. The judgment repudiated existing procedures on the ground that the Parole Board, whose sole power was to make recommendations, was not a judicial body. It also cast doubt on the adequacy of judicial review – the only judicial process available – on the ground that this amounted largely to a review of procedure, giving no opportunity to consider the merits of the case. These deficiencies breached Art. 5(4) ECHR:

> The language of Article 5(4) speaks of the detained individual being entitled to initiate proceedings. Under the British system of parole of life prisoners, although only the Home Secretary may refer a case to the Board, referral is obligatory in recall cases except where a person recalled after a recommendation to that effect by the Board has chosen not to make written representations . . . In these circumstances, the recalled person can be considered as having sufficient access to the Parole Board for the purposes of Article 5(4) . . .

1  (1987) 10 EHRR 293. See also *Thynne, Wilson and Gunnell v United Kingdom* (1990) 13 EHHR 666, a broader ruling.

The Board deals with individual cases on consideration of the documents supplied to it by the Home Secretary and of any reports, information or interviews with the individual concerned it has itself called for . . . The prisoner is entitled to make representations with respect to his recall, not only in writing to the Board but also orally to a member of the Local Review Committee . . . The individual is free to take legal advice in preparing such representations . . . Furthermore, he must be sufficiently informed of the reasons for his recall in to enable him to make sensible representations.

Whilst these safeguards are not negligible, there remains a certain procedural weakness in the case of a recalled prisoner. Thus, The Court of Appeal established in the *Gunnell* case that the duty on the Board to act fairly, as required under English law by the principles of natural justice, does not entail an entitlement to full disclosure of the adverse material which the Board has in its possession. The procedure followed does not therefore allow proper participation of the individual adversely affected by the contested decision, this being one of the principal guarantees of the Convention, and cannot therefore be regarded as judicial in character . . .

*Judicial review*[2]

The Court has in previous cases recognised the need to take a comprehensive view of the system in issue before it, as apparent shortcomings in one procedure may be remedied by safeguards available in other procedures . . . In this connection, an application for judicial review undoubtedly represents a useful supplement to the procedure before the Parole Board: it enables the individual concerned to obtain a control by the ordinary courts of both the parole Board's decisions (See, eg, the judgment of the Queen's Bench Division in *Wilson*)[3] and the Home Secretary's decisions.

The applicant, adopting conclusions reached by the Commission in its report, argued that the remedy of judicial review did not meet the requirements of accessibility and effectiveness under Article 5(4) . . .

The grounds on which judicial review lies, as summarised by Lord Diplock in his speech in the *Council of Civil Service Unions* case, are 'illegality', 'irrationality' and 'procedural impropriety'. By 'illegality' is meant incorrect application of the law governing the decision-making power and, in particular, breach of the relevant statutory requirements; 'irrationality' covers a decision that is so outrageous in its defiance of logic or of accepted moral standards that no sensible person who had applied his mind to the question to be decided could have arrived at it; and 'procedural impropriety' is a failure to observe expressly laid down procedural rules, a denial of natural justice or a lack of procedural fairness.

As the Commission pointed out, the scope of the control afforded is thus not wide enough to bear on the conditions essential for the 'lawfulness', in the sense of Article 5(4) of the Convention, of Mr. Weeks' detention, that is to say, whether it was consistent with and therefore justified by the objectives of the indeterminate sentence imposed on him. In the Court's view, having regard to the nature of control it allows, the remedy of judicial review can neither itself provide the proceedings required by Article 5(4) nor serve to remedy the inadequacy, for the purposes of that provision, of the procedure before the Parole Board.

To meet the Court's requirements, the Criminal Justice Act 1991 introduced reforms. The Parole Board appoints a panel which must be chaired by a judge, and holds a private hearing at which the prisoner is represented. The Parole Board Rules 1992 require a written decision within seven days and a further hearing within two years

2    Above, note 2.
3    Below, note 7.

if parole is refused. The prisoner will also know his tariff, usually established by the judge at trial in accordance with a new Practice Direction.[4]

But note how the Government conceded only what was essential; the European case law concerned *discretionary* life sentences and the Act maintained the distinction between discretionary and mandatory life sentences. The Government defended the distinction to the House of Lords:[5]

> The element of risk is not the decisive factor in handing down a [mandatory] life sentence. According to the judicial process, the offender has committed a crime of such gravity that he forfeits his liberty to the state for the rest of his days . . . The presumption is therefore, that the offender should remain in custody until and unless the Home Secretary concludes that the public interest would be better served by the prisoner's release than by his continued detention. In exercising his continued discretion in that respect, the Home Secretary must take account not just of the question of risk, but of how society as a whole would view the prisoner's release at that juncture.

Is the italicised phrase an added factor? And ought it to mean that the prisoner is not entitled to proper, judicial procedures?[6] In *R v Secretary of State for the Home Department, ex p Doody*,[7] a group of mandatory lifers had tariffs duly set after consultation with the judges. The prisoners were simply informed. They asked for the orders to be quashed on the ground that they were entitled to have access to the information on which the Home Secretary's decision was based; to an opportunity to make written representations; and to a reasoned decision. In a decision seen as affirming important principles of administrative behaviour, the House of Lords ruled in their favour.

Two later cases go much further. In *Thompson and Venables*[8] the applicants were young persons detained indefinitely 'at Her Majesty's pleasure' in terms of s. 53(1) of the Children and Young Persons Act 1933. The trial judge had indicated a tariff or 'penal factor' of eight years in consideration of their extreme youth, duly raised by the Lord Chief Justice to ten. Equating the children's position with that of mandatory lifers, the Home Secretary, acting under s. 35 of the Criminal Justice Act 1991, set a new tariff of 15 years. This decision was quashed in the Divisional Court on the ground that the two situations could not be equated. This ruling was upheld by the Court of Appeal and House of Lords, which held further that the Home Secretary had failed to take into consideration the welfare of the children and had disregarded his statutory obligation to keep their situation under review. Tightening their grip, the House added that the Home Secretary's function in setting a tariff was 'comparable to that of a sentencing judge'. In consequence, material obtained through public

---

4    Practice Direction (Crime: Life Sentences) [1993] 1 WLR 223.
5    HC Deb., vol. 195, col. 311 (16 July 1991).
6    Somewhat surprisingly, the Court of Human Rights accepted the reasoning in *Wynne v United Kingdom* (1994) 19 EHRR 333.
7    [1993] 3 WLR 154. See also *R v Parole Board, ex p Wilson* [1992] 2 WLR 707, CA. And see the similar case of *R v Secretary of State for the Home Department, ex p Hickey (No 2)* [1995] 1 WLR 734 (reasons for Home Secretary's refusal to refer back to the Court of Appeal a potentially invalid conviction have to be given).
8    *R v Secretary of State for the Home Department, ex p Thompson and Venables* [1997] 3 WLR 23.

petitions and representations and press reports of hostile public opinion was clearly irrelevant and inadmissible. In Lord Steyn's words:[9]

> ... the material in fact taken into account by the Home Secretary was worthless and incapable of informing him in a meaningful way of the true state of informed public opinion in respect of the tariff to be set ... By 'informed public opinion' I mean public opinion formed in the knowledge of all the material facts of the case. Plainly, the 'evidence' to which the Home Secretary referred did not measure up to this standard. .. Plainly a sentencing judge must ignore a newspaper campaign designed to encourage him to increase a particular sentence. It would be an abdication of the rule of law for a judge to take into account such matters. The same reasoning must apply to the Home Secretary when he is exercising a sentencing function.

It is instructive at this point to think again about the case of Myra Hindley, to be reconsidered after a successful application for judicial review.

The last in this significant line of cases bites deeply into the tiny area of unstructured discretion which still remains. In *R v Secretary of State for the Home Department, ex p Pierson*[10] the applicant had been convicted in 1985 of murdering both his parents and given two mandatory life sentences. The then Home Secretary had declined the original judicial 'tariff' of 15 years, substituting 20, on the ground that the offences had been premeditated. Following *Doody*, the Home Secretary announced changes[11] whereby prisoners would be told the length of their 'tariff' at the start of sentence, together with reasons for departure from it. Where, 'exceptionally', an increase in the penal element was proposed, a right to make representations would be granted. After representations, Pierson's 20-year tariff was maintained, though the Home Secretary had to concede that the crimes had not been premeditated. Once more comparing the Home Secretary's powers to a judge's sentencing powers, the House of Lords quashed the decision, finding that once the minimum period of detention had been fixed and communicated to a prisoner, there was no general power to change it. Since the factor of premeditation used to bring the case under the head of 'exceptional' had never existed, the increase was unlawful by virtue of its retrospectivity. What is left of *Re Findlay* or even *Hargreaves*?

The steady imposition of procedural standards in case law is reflected in legislation. The Crime (Sentences) Act 1997 confirms prisoners' rights to require the Home Secretary to refer a case to the Parole Board (s. 28(7)). It also stipulates that, in cases of revocation of licence, a lifer may make written representations (s. 32(3)(a)) and shall be given reasons why he is to be recalled (s. 32(3)(b)); all such cases must be referred on to the Parole Board whose recommendation is final (s. 32(5)(b)). Discretional justice is giving way to the Rule of Law.

In this case study we have seen a 'privilege' turned into a 'right' and watched a discretionary administrative process structured through the imposition of rules. What are the gains? The prisoner might say that rules have: (a) clarified his position; (b) brought policy into the open where it can be challenged; and (c) reduced the possibility of discrimination. What are the administrative gains? The new guidelines ought to

---

 9  [1997] 3 WLR 23 at 74.
10  [1997] 3 WLR 492.
11  HC Deb., vol., cols 861–864 (27 July 1993).

have: (a) encouraged consistency; (b) reduced the time taken for routine decisions, allowing more time for hard cases; and (c) allowed general policy to develop. What the Home Secretary might say can be spelled out in the Crime (Sentences) Act 1997 which, in the language of the press, introduces 'real time sentencing', by which is meant that prisoners will serve the sentence passed by the court, subject to a small discount for good behaviour. Mandatory life sentences are extended to rape and other serious offences, to be joined by mandatory minimum sentences for persistent offenders. Parole, and with it the Parole Board, has been abolished.

## 5. Access to the rule-making process

Our discussion of rule-making has so far been process-orientated; in other words, we have concentrated on how the rules are made and, in the case study above, how they are applied. Few questions have been asked about who makes the rules and, more importantly, should make them. Traditional constitutional theory, we saw, vests the law-making function in Parliament; lying behind and legitimating the doctrine of parliamentary sovereignty is the classical English theory of representative democracy, whereby power is delegated from the electors to a representative but independent legislature.[12] In this model we saw that executive law-making was treated with caution as a potential usurpation of the legislative function, acceptable only when legitimated by a parliamentary delegation of power. Bureaucratic rule-making was treated with equal suspicion and classified either as policy-making, the acceptable executive function or, more recently, as a technique for management accountability. Judicial law-making is, within limits, acceptable though best not openly mentioned.

There is little room for citizen participation here. When, for example, the first parliamentary scrutiny committees were being set up in 1952, one MP remarked:[13] 'It has been perhaps rather noticeable that all through this afternoon we have been discussing this merely from the point of view of Parliament and MPs. We have not let the public creep into the discussion at all.' A proposal to allow members of the public to complain of, or ask for changes in, regulations was dismissed on constitutional grounds: 'aggrieved persons have their grievances brought to the attention of the House by Members.' Contrast the Deregulation Committee's account of its procedures (above, p.167), where a matter of particular pride was 'the extent to which those with expert knowledge of the subject, and those who will be affected by the legislation, can have access to the process'. The passage also hints that the new right of access could with benefit be generalised. The change is as great as the change in judicial attitudes between *Payne* (1981) and *Doody* (1993).

The window of opportunity for the Deregulation Committee was opened by legislation. Section 3(1) of the Deregulation and Contracting Out Act 1994 provides:

12 On which see C. Harlow, 'Power from the People? Representation and Constitutional Theory' in P. McAuslan and J. McEldowney (eds.), *Law, Legitimacy and the Constitution* (London: Sweet and Maxwell) 1985.

13 HC 310 (1952/3), p. 141.

3.(1) Before a Minister makes an order under section 1 above, he shall: (a) consult such organisations as appear to him to be representative of interests substantially affected by his proposals; and (b) consult such other persons as he considers appropriate.

How has this change of attitude come about? It is not altogether a new development. Griffith and Street summarise a lengthy empirical account of informal government consultation procedures[14] by emphasising their importance. Consultation had a threefold purpose: first, to put the administration 'in full possession of the facts and viewpoints which bear on the particular matter'; secondly, 'to enable those affected, from powerful groups to ordinary individuals, to state their case against the proposed action and to urge that it be modified or dropped'; and, third, for public explanation. Amongst the methods appropriate, the authors mention advisory committees, direct consultation and public inquiries, particularly important as a vehicle for consultation in the area of land use planning.[15]

In some ways, this passage marks a transition. The authors' emphasis is on rationality; better informed decision-makers produce better decisions. From the opposite standpoint, a well-informed public may see policies as 'less apparently irrational'. Equally, the authors stress the rights of 'persons affected'. In both respects the authors are adhering closely to the outlines of the common law. For Richardson:[16]

. . . the common law's involvement in the regulation of process is based on a mutually supportive structure comprised of three elements: an instrumental justification for involvement, an emphasis on the application and validation stages of policy evolution and the adoption of an adjudicatory model of procedure . . . Procedures are required in order to protect individuals', largely substantive, interests: the possession of such an interest triggers the procedural requirement . . . Secondly, the common law rules are applied predominately at the application and validation stages where these individual interests are most likely to be directly affected. Thirdly, and finally, the adjudicatory model which prevails is widely regarded as particularly well designed for the protection of individual interests from interference resulting from uninformed and inaccurate decisions.

Like Galligan,[17] the author argues that the common law distinction between 'individuated' and 'legislative' decisions, has resulted not only in a better protection of individual interests, but also in the use of the adjudicatory model as a prototype for consultation procedures. We can see this model exemplified in the Deregulation and Contracting Out Act. Originally inserted as an amendment to safeguard particular parties, the provision forms a more general safeguard by providing advance warning of legislation to a public which may be affected. As with a Green Paper, a pool of informed opinion and criticism is provided against which to test proposals. The Act is unusually stringent in providing also for 'second round' consultation. If the Minister varies his proposals, he 'shall

---

14  J. Griffith and H. Street, *Principles of Administrative Law* (London: Pitman) 5th edn, 1973, pp. 118-136. The citation is at p. 137.

15  Below, Ch. 12.

16  G. Richardson, 'The Legal Regulation of Process' in G. Richardson and H. Genn, *Administrative Law and Government Action* (Oxford: Clarendon) 1994, p. 121.

17  Above, p. 180. And see D. Galligan, *Due Process and Fair Procedures: A Study of Administrative Procedures* (Oxford: Clarendon) 1996.

undertake such further consultation with respect to the variations as appears to him to be appropriate'. Although the language is mandatory (shall) and the provision can be monitored by the Deregulation Committee, the rule-maker still possesses strong discretion. No specific procedures are provided, raising the question whether the provisions are legally enforceable.

So far the word 'participation' has not surfaced. In Chapter 4, however, we noted the growth of pluralist democratic theory and consequently, of interest in direct citizen participation in policy and law-making. Mention must here be made of the influence of Habermas. Describing society as 'a self-controlled learning process', Habermas floats the Utopian ideal of a fully democratic State, whose policies and institutions 'would meet with the unforced agreement of all those involved, if they could participate, as free and equal, in discursive will-formation'.[18] This is hardly the picture of rule-making procedure which we have been accumulating. However, while he admits the Utopian ideal of Habermas to be unattainable in practice, Prosser argues that public law should work towards it. However deficient participation may be in practice, it aspires to, and allows us to work towards, 'the development of institutions for the expression of the ideal of discussion free from domination, with equal power to affect decisions given to all those affected'.[19] In this passage, the word 'affected' clearly has a far wider meaning than it possesses in traditional administrative law, and collective rather than individual interests are envisaged.

Although we have seen that persons affected by administrative decisions may 'make representations', English administrative law acknowledges no general or collective right to participate in rule-making. Except where consultation is a statutory requirement, courts have not enthusiastically supplied the deficiency. They will not necessarily ensure compliance, even when statutory procedures are apparently mandatory.[1] Nor have they been exactly anxious to flesh out the requirements of consultation. As we shall see in Chapter 15, this provides a sharp contrast with their position on adjudicatory procedures.

The courts have made occasional forays into the area, as we saw in the *GCHQ* case,[2] where a trade union was held to have a legitimate expectation of being consulted. Here the group was a small one and the expectation probably reflected the individual right to make representations in a decision affecting oneself. In the *British Coal* case,[3] a decision to close 31 of 50 existing deep mine collieries was suddenly announced without any pretence at conformity with the review procedure agreed with the unions in terms of s. 46(1) of the Coal Industry Nationalisation Act 1946. Holding the decision to be a justiciable public law decision, the Court of Appeal not only suspended the decisions pending adequate consultation but at the same time precluded the Minister from making funds available for the

---

18  J. Habermas, *Communication and the Evolution of Society* (London: Heinemann) 1979, p. 186, cited in T. Prosser, 'Democratisation, Accountability and Institutional Design: Reflections on Public Law' in P. McAuslan and J. McEldowney (eds.), *Law, Legitimacy and the Constitution* (London: Sweet and Maxwell) 1985.
19  T. Prosser, 'Towards a Critical Public Law' (1982) 9 J. of Law and Soc. 1, 11.
 1  de Smith, Jowell, Woolf, para. 5.076. And see *Coney v Choyce* [1975] 1 WLR 422; *R v Secretary of State for Social Services, ex p Association of Metropolitan Authorities* [1986] 1 WLR 1, below p. 204.
 2  Above, pp. 193.
 3  *R v British Coal Corpn, ex p Vardy* [1993] ICR 720.

implementation of this policy before the review procedure had been followed. This decision is the stronger in that the Trade Union and Labour Relations (Consolidation) Act 1992, passed to implement EC Directive 75/129 on collective redundancies, provides an alternative consultation procedure enforceable in private law for employees made redundant through the closures. Perhaps surprisingly, the court rejected the argument that the statutory private right exhausted the duty to consult, enforcing the wider, public law obligation on the ground that it alone could allow a discussion of policy issues. Yet Freedland sees[4] this victory as strictly limited and marred by a different form of particularism, in which a specific decision is artificially severed from a policy-making process, effectively denying the parties any realistic chance of input into that process, as well as any effective review of policy. A limited victory for proceduralism rather than for Habermas.

We saw earlier that a legitimate expectation could be based on a voluntary undertaking; similarly, a voluntary undertaking can found a duty to consult.[5]

## *R v Liverpool Corpn, ex p Liverpool Taxi Fleet Operators' Association*[6]

Liverpool Corporation had for many years limited the number of cab licences to 300; owners wanted the limit retained, drivers wanted it increased. The council assured the owners that they would not proceed without listening to their representations. When it tried to regulate matters by introducing a private Bill into Parliament to limit private hire cars, coupled with a corporation resolution to increase the number of taxi cabs, the owners sought and obtained an order of prohibition to enforce the informal undertaking by prohibiting the corporation from acting on the resolutions without hearing representations. Lord Denning drew on the rather different approaches of natural justice and contract to reach his result:

> *Lord Denning MR*: . . . when the corporation consider applications for licences under the Town Police Clauses Act 1847, they are under a duty to act fairly. This means that they should be ready to hear not only the particular applicant but also any other persons or bodies whose interests are affected . . . To apply that principle here: suppose the corporation proposed to reduce the number of taxicabs from 300 to 200, it would be their duty to hear the taxicab owners' association: because their members would be greatly affected. They would certainly be persons aggrieved. Likewise suppose the corporation propose to increase the number of taxicabs from 300 to 350 or 400 or more: it is the duty of the corporation to hear those affected before coming to a decision adverse to their interests . . .
>
> The other thing I would say is that the corporation were not at liberty to disregard their undertaking. They were bound by it so long as it was not in conflict with their statutory duty.
>
> It is said that a corporation cannot contract itself out of its statutory duties.[7] But that principle does not mean that a corporation can give an undertaking and break it as they

---

4    M. Freedland, 'Government by Contract and Public Law' [1994] PL 86, 97–98.
5    See on the link, Craig, *Administrative Law*, p. 669.
6    [1972] 2 WLR 1262.
7    For the rule that a public authority cannot fetter its discretion by contract, or otherwise contract out of its statutory duties see *Birkdale District Electricity Supply Co Ltd v Southport Corpn* [1926] AC 355. And see pp. 227–230 below.

please. So long as the performance of the undertaking is compatible with their public duty, they must honour it. And I should have thought that this undertaking was so compatible. At any rate they ought not to depart from it except after the most serious consideration and hearing what the other party has to say: and then only if they are satisfied that the overriding public interest requires it. The public interest may be better served by honouring their undertaking than by breaking it . . . Applying these principles, it seems to me that the corporation acted wrongly . . . In the first place, they took decisions without giving the owners' association an opportunity of being heard. In the second place, they broke their undertaking without any sufficient cause or excuse.

We have now accumulated three possible bases for a duty of consultation in rule-making: (i) statutory provisions; (ii) an obligation of fairness developed by analogy to natural justice;[8] and (iii) a voluntary undertaking by the rule-maker. Are these exhaustive? To put this differently, are conditions (i) to (iii) the only cases giving rise to a 'legitimate expectation' of being consulted or is the expectation distinct and self-standing? Evans, displaying a pluralist approach, certainly believes that it should be.[9] He invites courts to develop a requirement that interested groups and individuals should be afforded (a) prior notice and (b) the right to present oral or written arguments before decisions of a legislative nature are made, believing that, 'Participation at this level would significantly increase the opportunities for the examination and debate of governmental measures beyond those available through the traditional political process'.

Here the reference is probably to the more formal types of rule-making – though Evans does not make this entirely clear – rather than the policy changes or informal rules which were at stake in parole. Moreover, Evans has chosen what Americans call 'notice-and-comment' procedure, probably wise in the light of what occurred after the *Liverpool Taxis* case. When the corporation finally issued an invitation to submit representations, widely publicised and in wide terms, so many people turned up at the committee meeting that the majority could not be accommodated. To keep proceedings orderly, the committee decided to exclude the public, except the press, so that the operators, who had decided not to make representations but to listen to those made by others, were unable to attend the meeting.[10] This incident stands as a warning that, as is increasingly the case with controversial planning inquiries, it may be hard to provide a forum for consultation which is both fair and orderly and provides an appropriate place in the consultations for individuals as well as interest groups, to whom government is inclined to turn.

This may be one reason why civil servants prefer to rely on informality, a habit approved by Wade, who thinks that:[11]

. . . practice counts for more than the law. Consultation with interests and organisations likely to be affected by rules and regulations is one of the firmest and most carefully

8   Natural justice and fairness in adjudication are dealt with in Chapter 15.
9   In de Smith 4th edn., 1980, p. 181. See also A. Jergesen, 'The Legal Requirements of Consultation' [1978] PL 290. But see *Bates v Lord Hailsham of St Marylebone* [1972] 1 WLR 1373, where Megarry V-C, discussing the rule-making functions of the Law Society, confined the *Liverpool* case to its facts.
10  See *R v Liverpool City Council, ex p Liverpool Taxi Fleet Operators' Association* [1975] 1 WLR 701. Perhaps surprisingly, the resolution passed was held valid.
11  Wade and Forsyth, p. 896.

observed conventions. It is not a matter of legal right, any more than it is with Parliament's own legislation. But it is so well settled a practice that it is most unusual to hear complaint. It may be that consultation which is not subject to statutory procedure is more effective than formal hearing which may produce legalism and artificiality. The duty to consult is recognised in every sense except the legal one.

But while Wade senses 'no pressure for reform', evidence given to the Hansard Society suggested 'deep dissatisfaction with the extent, nature, timing and conduct of consultation'. They also lamented a possible decline both in consultation and publication of preliminary Green and White Papers. The disparity of consultation procedures was also an issue.[12]

> . . . there can be much consultation, some or none; it can be general or detailed; it can be formal, with Green and White Papers, or it can be informal, consisting of no more than a few "soundings" on the telephone. It can. . . be a genuine request for help, or merely an attempt to legitimise proposals that a Government has already made up its mind to pass into law. . . this variation in practice is not simply due to the differing nature of different bills, but results from the absence of a coherent policy regarding the role consultation should play in the legal process; civil service guidelines do not appear to be followed; and there are inconsistencies of approach between, and even within, Government departments and agencies and other statutory bodies. This results in a mixture of good and bad consultation practice, and, more fundamentally, in a distortion of the whole consultation process.

As the Deregulation and Contracting Out Act 1994 shows, even statutory requirements for consultation leave much to the rule-maker. Who is to be consulted is left to discretion,[13] while the degree of consultation and how seriously recommendations are taken is a question of good faith. Experience shows that the letter, rather than the spirit, of the law may be observed. Only in extreme cases have courts insisted that consultation must permit 'a real and not an illusory opportunity to make representations'; four days is not an appropriate time for consultation on a new schools system, for example.[14] The representations are, of course, not binding and may be given only nominal consideration. In *R v Secretary of State for Social Services, ex p Association of Metropolitan Authorities,*[15] for example, Webster J said:

> . . . the essence of consultation is the communication of a genuine invitation to give advice and a genuine consideration of that advice. In my view it must go without saying that to achieve consultation sufficient information must be supplied by the consulting to the consulted party to enable it to tender helpful advice . . . Sufficient, in that context, does not mean ample, but at least enough to enable the relevant purpose to be fulfilled. By helpful advice, in this context, I mean sufficiently informed and considered information or advice about aspects of the form or substance of the proposals or their implications for the consulted party, being aspects material to the implementation of the proposal as to which the Secretary

12  *Making the Law: the Report of the Hansard Society Commission on the Legislative Process* (London: Hansard Society) 1993, pp. 17-18 and 226.
13  *R v Secretary of State for Social Services, ex p Association of Metropolitan Authorities* [1986] 1 WLR 1 (right of AMA to be consulted over new regulations made under the Housing Benefits Act 1982).
14  *Lee v Secretary of State for Education and Science* (1967) 66 LGR 211. See also *Bradbury v Enfield London Borough Council* [1967] 1 WLR 1311.
15  [1986] 1 WLR 1 at 4.

of State might not be fully informed or advised and as to which the party consulted might have relevant information or advice to offer.

At first sight this reflects a more generous spirit indicating a brighter future for participation. If you think more about it, however, you can see how limited the protection really is. What if the consulted party wishes to make general points? Why should its advice be helpful?

So is this another area for structuring discretion and replacing judge-made law with procedural rules? If so, how formal should the rules be? Some favour the model of the American Administrative Procedure Act 1946 which applies in the absence of alternative statutory provision to all federal administrative authorities and agencies. Its highly formal and judicialised procedures can involve a trial-type hearing with subpoenas, evidence taken on oath, cross-examination and a full record (s. 7). The Act also provides a less intensive 'notice-and-comment' procedure, which obliges administrative agencies to give notice of proposed rule-making (s. 4). They shall then afford 'interested persons the opportunity to participate in the rule-making through submission of written data, views or arguments with or without opportunity to present the same orally in any manner'. The Act also provides an informal right 'to petition for the issuance, amendment, or repeal of a rule'.

This procedure seems to place groups, corporations and individuals on an equal footing. In reality, this is unlikely to be the case. Powerful groups tend to dominate both legal and political processes, the first often by virtue of wealth which facilitates successful litigation,[16] the second because they are well-placed to influence those in power. Just as corporatism privileged trade unions and management, so the phenomenon of 'agency capture' may mean that a regulatory agency listens to its clients rather than to its supposed beneficiaries. Craig[17] believes that financial help may be necessary to redress the balance, though he urges that the problem be kept in perspective: 'The introduction of a more structured system of participatory rights does at least give the less advantaged groups a chance to air their view that would otherwise not have been possible.'

Opinions vary as to the success of the AAPA. One positive evaluation sees it as having produced workable solutions and institutionalised due process in the administrative setting.[18] Others disagree.[19] AAPA procedures provide an open invitation for judicial review which has been extensively used to block agency action. (We return to this point in Chapter 15). Administrators find them frustrating and a recipe for expense and delay:[20]

> The primary impact of these procedural requirements is often not . . . the testing of agency assumptions . . . Rather these procedures either cause the abandonment of the program . . . the development of techniques to reach the same regulatory goal but without a hearing . . . or the

16  For some of the reasons, see M. Galanter, 'Why the "Haves" Come Out Ahead: Speculations on the Limits of Legal Change' (1974) 9 Law and Soc. Rev. 225.
17  *Administrative Law*, pp. 260-261.
18  A. Morrison, 'The Administrative Procedures Act: A Living and Responsive Law' (1986) 72 Vir. LR 253, 268-9. See also K. C. Davis, *Discretionary Justice* (Westpoint: Greenwood Press) pp. 65-68.
19  E.g., M. Shapiro, 'APA: Past, Present, Future' (1986) 72 Vir. LR 447.
20  R. Hamilton, 'Procedures for the Adoption of Rules of General Applicability: the Need for Procedural Innovation in Administrative Rulemaking' (1972) 60 Cal. LR 1276, 1312-3. See also Strauss, 'Rules, Adjudications and other Sources of Law in an Executive Department: Reflections on the Interior Department's Administration of the Mining Law' (1974) 74 Col. LR 1231; M. Dimock, *Law and Dynamic Administration* (New York: Praeger) 1980, p. 3.

promulgation of non-controversial regulations by a process of negotiation and compromise . . .
In practice, therefore, the principal effect of imposing rulemaking on a record has often been
the dilution of the regulatory process rather than the protection of persons from arbitrary action.

The Hansard Society do not ask for formal rules. At one level they advise a more
leisurely and consultative legislative process, which should include Green Papers
and a prolonged, two-stage consultation process at 'rough draft' and 'final draft'
stage, giving an opportunity for experts and those likely to be affected to make their
views known. They do not recommend any rigid procedure but favour published
guidelines 'drawing on best practice' and influenced by the 'advice and experience
of those most directly involved'. These would apply to all government departments
when preparing legislation and, with appropriate modifications, to secondary
legislation.[1] This is close to the preferred Australian solution, where the
Administrative Review Council has proposed[2] that with every 'delegated instrument
which is legislative in character' there should be: (i) advertisement of intention to
make the instrument; (ii) publication in draft; (iii) a summary of objectives; and
(iv) a cost/benefit assessment with an obligation to consider all submissions and a
public hearing in sensitive or controversial cases. Notice once more that these
recommendations cover only formal rule-making.

What are the costs and benefits of these approaches? The discretionary approach is
more flexible and leaves less room for judicial review, especially when the outcome of
judicial review will probably continue to be unpredictable. Much – and many would
say too much – is also left to the goodwill of government and administrators. The
American experience shows judicialised procedures to be cumbersome, causing delay,
expense and bureaucracy. Administrators learn to stick to the letter of the law or to
frustrate the scheme by circumventing the procedural requirements. This creates a
move from 'hard' to 'soft' law. The most recent American experiment authorises
agencies to adopt rules mediated prior to publication by interested parties.[3] A similar
technique authorised by the Protocol to the Treaty of Maastricht permits the Social
Partners (management and labour) to negotiate agreements which can be adopted as
rules by the Commission or by the Member States.[4] In the same way, the cautious but
innovative experiment of the Deregulation Committee could point to a future in which
informal procedures under the supervision of Parliament provide for a limited amount of
citizen input in the case of primary and secondary legislation. Such an approach would,
however, leave a vast iceberg of tertiary rules internal to departments, agencies and
regulators, unregulated save by occasional judicial forays based on the doctrine of
legitimate expectation. This outcome is hardly the 'miniature democratic process' for
which K. C. Davis argued. Or perhaps it is, in which case our democracy is not very democratic.

1   *Making the Law,* Recommendation 150 at p. 39, and generally, pp. 17-29. For secondary
    legislation see Recommendation 162, p. 42.
2   *Rule Making by Commonwealth Agencies,* Administrative Review Council, Report No. 35
    (Canberra: Australian Government Publishing Service) 1992, Ch. 5, pp. 30-43 and p. 22.
    'Legislative instruments' are purposely left undefined but their characteristics are listed at
    pp. 20-21.
3   A. Aman Jr., 'Administrative Law for a New Century' in M. Taggart (ed), *The Province of
    Administrative Law* (London: Hart) 1997.
4   S. Fredman, in P. Craig and C. Harlow (eds), *The European Law Making Process* (Dublin: Sweet
    & Maxwell) 1997.

Chapter 8

# A revolution in the making

## 1. Uses and norms

Contract has been seen as a chief instrument of the Conservatives' revolution in government (Chapter 5). At one level, the policy of contracting out stretches across, and so blurs, the public/private sector 'divide'. At another, private sector notions of contract are infused into public administration: the discipline of markets or market-mimicking, the individualist ethos of freedom of choice. Contract as a legal topic becomes the cutting edge of administrative law, exhibiting a strong sense, on the one hand, of dynamic and experimentation, and, on the other, of tension and uncertainty.

There is a revolution in the making, in two senses. First, contractual arrangements emerge as a chief building-block of contemporary government, operating to define and reconstitute roles and relations with the private sector, and, further, between and within public institutions; to introduce another metaphor, this is contract as genetic engineering. Secondly, this process, which has gained a logic and a momentum of its own, has been fostering major changes in the procedures for making, as well as the uses of, public contracts. New forms of legal regulation emerge, adding strains to the pre-existing conceptual framework. And, as we shall see, this phenomenon is underscored and cut across by certain other developments, most obviously in European Community law and policy.

Let us begin with a taxonomy; various uses by government of contractual arrangements in carrying out policies and activities: in employment, the terms and conditions of staff; in supply or sale of services, such as the provision of council housing; in outsourcing or procurement, that is, the purchase of goods or services like IT from an outside body. Outsourcing, we see immediately, has gained greatly in importance in recent years, with the policy of contracting out. But more than this, it is now recognised as a key force shaping public and private enterprise into the next century. Thus, it has come to be seen by management specialists not as a mere cost-cutter, but as a way of improving overall performance by concentrating skills and resources on core activities.[1]

Contract may also be used by government as an instrument of policy, for example to favour national suppliers, and generally as a tool for regulating behaviour. Regulation is often of the essence of the contract. A fashionable

---

1   Economist Intelligence Unit, *Vision 2010: Designing Tomorrow's Organisation* (London) 1997.

example, considered in the next chapter, is public franchising, whereby, via the machinery of auction, market rules are laid out as contractual conditions, as in the 'franchise agreement' now made with private operators of passenger services on the railways.[2] In a second category of case, the economic or bargaining power of government in procurement is used to regulate matters which are collateral to the main object of the contract. It is in this sense that the term 'regulation by contract' has been used: the imposition of public policies on private business, as in social protection. Conversely, it is a feature of 'the blue rinse' that while contract has come into its own in the elaboration of market-style discipline, its use for other, collateral purposes of policy has been strictly discouraged, a stance now firmly buttressed by EC law and policy.

The term 'regulation by contract' is used more expansively today to denote the new usage of contractual arrangements as the instrument of intra-governmental co-ordination. The best-known example is the 'framework document' defining the goals and functions of a Next Steps agency (Chapter 5). And what is here identified as the building-block of contemporary government is also the essential agent of the fragmentation of the traditional government framework, a chief ingredient of the 'hollowing' of the state. Thus, it is through a contractual model that the bureaucratic hierarchies and organisational forms familiarly associated with 'public administration' have been challenged or subverted. We are reminded that contract, as an organisational tool, has destructive as well as constructive properties, most obviously that of squeezing out other, political forms of accountability.

A convenient angle of approach to the subject is provided by a second taxonomy, which concerns the hierarchy of norms. Starting at the bottom, stress must be laid on the role of 'internal' or 'bureaucratic law' (administrative directions, codes of practice, established procedures) occupying space commonly filled in other jurisdictions by formal law, notably in the realms of central government procurement and employment of civil servants. Second, and typically occupying a principal role, is the 'law of the contract': the terms and conditions, also referred to as the 'contract technology'. A central theme is highlighted: contract as *a source of rules* (above, p. 155). This, of course, is a basic idea in jurisprudential theory, as in Hart's reference to making a contract 'as the exercise of limited legislative powers by individuals'.[3] But the present context gives this idea some important implications. For 'individuals' read 'government', and the potential for 'regulation by contract' becomes apparent.

In England it has been a basic premise that government contracts should be subject to the ordinary private law. Thus, the general common law of contract, governing such matters as capacity and formation, implied terms and performance,

---

2   Another important variant is the planning agreement, whereby restriction on the statutory power to impose conditions is avoided by the local planning authority entering into a contractual arrangement with the developer for a similar purpose. Long the subject of controversy in administrative law (see J. Jowell, 'The Limits of Law in Urban Planning' (1977) 30 Current Legal Problems 63), the technique has recently been encouraged: see s. 106 of the Town and Country Planning Act 1990, as substituted by s. 12 of the Planning and Compensation Act 1991; *Tesco Stores Ltd v Secretary of State for the Environment* [1995] 2 All ER 636.

3   H. L. A. Hart, *The Concept of Law* (Oxford: Clarendon) 2nd edn., Bullock and Raz, 1994, p. 96.

termination and remedies, provides a basic architecture or legal framework within which contractual activities like outsourcing are carried on. There is, however, potential for conflict with the common law jurisdiction of judicial review, by reason of the public/private law dichotomy.

It is important to consider both the continuities and shifts in the role and relation of the norms. Only very recently, for example, has it been accepted that civil service employment is based on formal contract. In the guise of standard forms, the 'law of the contract' has traditionally suppressed the role of the general law in relation to contractual liability and the resolution of disputes. And consistent with strong roles for 'bureaucratic law' and the 'law of the contract', national legislation has in the past been of limited importance: there is no 'Government Contracts Act'. Statutory intervention has been focused on particular contexts like employment, or on specific matters such as exclusion clauses (the Unfair Contract Terms Act 1977) as part of general law reform. Recent years, however, have seen major changes, especially in the case of local government. First, there has been indirect intervention, by tightening the legal and financial framework within which local government operates, with significant knock-on effects in terms of the capacity to contract, and of a growth of litigation. Second, there has been direct ordering of contract-making, as exemplified in compulsory competitive tendering (CCT), a policy to broaden the potential range of procurement, which has involved detailing the procedures for letting or tendering a contract.

Ending at the top of the hierarchy, the ambit in procurement of EC law has increased greatly in recent years, an integral part of the drive to the Single Market. This has had a differential impact on central and local government procurement: the former was still largely the province of 'bureaucratic law'. Contemporary shifts in the role and relation of the norms demonstrate a proliferation of formal, legal rules in areas previously the territory of administrative practice and procedure. There is also more evidence of recourse to the ordinary courts, a break with a strong national tradition of alternative dispute resolution. The contractual process is being juridified.

In this book you will find emphasis on contract as a government activity or output function, and not merely as a source of legal liability. We emphasise contract technology, and the more elaborate procedures governing contract-making, as well as the challenge for the 'ordinary courts'. In relation to the issues of cost and complexity, there will be found in the materials on contract-making much which is highly technical: so much so, that on occasion it may seem surprising that anything much gets done. It is tempting to gloss over the complications, but that would be to ignore the problem of too much juridification.[4] We would also query the argument, associated with NPM, that the contractual separation of roles – purchaser and provider – aids transparency in government. The detail is apt to frustrate access save by the privileged few. Further, while there is obvious potential for enhancing accountability by reference to specification and performance standards, the contract process also has a capacity for concealment when appeal is made to privity of contract and commercial confidentiality. The

---

4    Above, p. 138.

sceptic will not want to take on trust developments which broadly entail replacing a sense of trust in government with a formal science of accountability.

## 2. Pseudo-contract

One feature of the contemporary scene demands special attention. We saw in Chapter 5 that the language of contract can be used in an extended way, encompassing and so modelling a variety of arrangements which are not true contract in the legal sense of an agreement enforceable in the courts. Elsewhere, the usage is variously 'near', 'private' or 'quasi-' contract. The authors prefer the label 'pseudo-contract'.

The expansive terminology of recent years reflects and reinforces a cultural shift in the idea of government. Pseudo-contract as a tool of administration has colonised major new territories. Its hallmark is lack of fit between emergent administrative forms and the traditional legal framework. On the one hand, appeal is made to the paradigm of contract, recasting relations in the terms of separation, specification and evaluation. On the other hand, what are formalised arrangements in comparison with the old techniques of public administration are denied formal legal recognition. This is fertile territory for advocates of a special public law of contract.

The expansive use of language links with the expansive use of 'regulation by contract' as the tool of organisation. The lack of fit is exemplified by the framework document of a Next Steps agency:[5]

> A contract must be between at least two parties, each of which possesses contractual capacity. In the case of organisations, contractual capacity is connected with the more general concept of 'legal personality' . . . Since an agency is not legally separate from the department . . . framework documents cannot be private law contracts because agencies do not have legal personality separate from that of the body their contract would be with . . . Legal identity precedes and cannot be derived from a contractual relationship.

In Freedland's words, there is 'a sort of double legal fiction, whereby a non-corporation is deemed to enter into non-contracts'.[6] In the next chapter we see a similar point arising in local government, as internal trading is promoted by compulsory competitive tendering.

A variation on the theme is the 'internal market' operated by the Conservatives in the National Health Service.[7] Three categories of arrangement between purchaser and provider may be distinguished: (i) the ordinary private law contract, between a private purchaser and NHS provider; (ii) the pseudo-contract, between a health authority and one of its management units for accounting purposes; and (iii) the hybrid or 'NHS contract' created by the National Health

5   I. Harden, *The Contracting State* (Buckingham: Open University Press) 1992, pp. 38, 44, 46. Legal personality would, however, be secured if statutory corporations were created.
6   M. Freedland, 'Government by Contract and Public Law' [1994] PL 86, 89.
7   D. Hughes, 'The Reorganisation of the National Health Service: The Rhetoric and Reality of the Internal Market' (1991) 54 MLR 88.

Service and Community Care Act 1990, between one Health Service body and another. According to s. 4 of the Act:

> Whether or not an arrangement which constitutes an NHS contract would, apart from this subsection, be a contract in law, it shall not be regarded for any purpose as giving rise to contractual rights or liabilities, but if any dispute arises with respect to such an arrangement, either party may refer the matter to the Secretary of State for determination.

The hybrid involves legal recognition or consequences, but with the common law incidents of contract expressly excluded. In other words, the private law model of contract is adapted to suit the particular purpose in public law. In the words of the Secretary of State:[8]

> It is not intended that those contracts, as we call them, should be subject to litigation in courts of law . . . I trust that no member . . . seriously contemplates different parts of the NHS commencing legal actions against other parts to enforce the terms of a contract. That would be a lawyer's charter and paradise, but of little benefit to patients. It is intended that the contracts be binding inside the Health Service and be adhered to by the parties.

Pseudo-contract has increasingly been used to model the relations of government and individual, a process all the more striking since this is traditionally regarded as the heartland of administrative law. We see immediately the link with the idea of citizen as consumer expressed in the Citizen's Charter: the portrayal of the relationship in contractual terms – services in return for taxes – and the care taken by the Major government to avoid a model of justiciable service delivery rights (Chapter 5).[9] But there is another, important, dimension: the individual as subject to regulation by (pseudo-) contract;[10] in other words, public services in return for civic duties or responsibilities; ultimately, contract as a tool of social control, contrary to its classic liberal meaning.

Pseudo-contract as a tool of social work became widespread in the 1980s.[11] Examples include agendas or check-lists of tasks for clients such as alcoholics or drug addicts; behaviour modification schemes incorporating rewards and sanctions tailored to 'progress'; and conditions or requirements for the use of care facilities. In practice, such contracts have varied from complex written forms to simple oral agreements. But a central theme, illuminating the symbolic value of contract, is

---

8 Kenneth Clark, HC Standing Committee E, Session 1989–1990, vol. 3, col. 349. See P. Allen, 'Contracts in the National Health Service Internal Market' (1995) 58 *MLR* 321.

9 There is also a long tradition in the common law of denying contractual status to the supply of utilities services to the public, so limiting the liability for economic losses: see *Willmore v South Eastern Electricity Board* [1957] 2 Lloyd's Rep 375. The conceptual explanation, that the compulsion of statutory requirements is inconsistent with the existence of a contract, endures post-privatisation: *Norweb plc v Dixon* [1995] 3 All ER 952.

10 One illustration has already been given: the 'prison compact' in issue in *ex p Hargreaves*. Above, p. 189.

11 J. Corden, 'Contracts in Social Work Practice' (1980) 10 British Journal of Social Work 143; B. Sheldon, 'The Use of Contracts in Social Work', Practice Note Series 1, BASW (1980).

the acceptance of responsibility by the client, as also the structuring and confining of professional discretion:[12]

> A Social Work contract was taken to have particular advantages for the *relationship* between the social worker and client. The first of these was that it treated clients with *respect* and helped them become more *responsible* for their choices . . . This emphasis on the responsibility of the clients in a welfare state was sometimes expressed . . . to include 'a duty not to become destitute if he can help it'.
>
> A further benefit was that contracts were thought to supply a definite spur to *motivation* and *achievement*. Because contracts provided a clear specification of the goals of social work intervention they made it possible (sometimes all too possible) to see what progress had been achieved. Clients would be motivated by their involvement in drawing up the contract, by their consent to what it contained, by the incentive of the reciprocal promises of the Social Work Department and, where applicable, by fear of sanctions if it broke down.
>
> A final set of functions related to control by the social worker and her *accountability*. Contracts were capable of helping both social workers and clients gain more control of their interaction so as to better achieve their aims. For the social worker they could be used to help keep the clients to their agreements . . . They prevented social workers from being at the beck and call of clients and placed limits on the extent to which social workers had to persevere with unpromising cases . . . On the other hand, contracts . . . provided a basis for complaint if social workers did not keep to their part of the agreement. They would be open to scrutiny by outsiders, including courts, and could help the emergence of 'discretionary rights'. They . . . might even begin to provide a measure of 'productivity' of social work.

But in a situation of unequal power how real is agreement? One of the more controversial Conservative reforms to the Welfare State was the Job Seeker's Allowance, which replaced unemployment benefit and income support for the unemployed. The scheme was designed to 'focus the efforts of job seekers on looking for work', and also to secure better value for money for the tax payer.[13] To this end, the 'Job Seeker's Agreement' was created as a condition precedent of receiving benefit, having effect 'only' for this purpose (Jobseekers' Act 1995, ss. 1, 9). The element of compulsion is immediately apparent; so too the hybrid nature of such agreements.

An agreement would be in writing and signed by the claimant and employment officer, the officer only 'contracting' if satisfied that compliance would secure the general statutory requirements of availability for work and actively seeking employment. Conditions would typically include targets of job applications, preparing a c.v., and seeking information about potential employers. Provision was made for determination by an adjudication officer in cases of dispute, including the issue of whether compliance might reasonably be expected, and for appeal to a social security appeal tribunal (Chapter 14). Thus the agreement would be inherently one-sided, and, while labelled as consensual, the subject of

---

12   D. Nelken, 'The Use of "Contracts" as a Social Work Technique' (1987) 40 Current Legal Problems 207, 215–217.
13   Michael Portillo, HC Dec., vol. 252, col. 47 (10 January 1995); Government White Paper, *Job Seeker's Allowance* (1994) Cm. 2687, para. 1.5.

adjudication, a spectacle which shows the tensions implicit in the notion of contract as a form of social control. Fullbrook pursues the argument:[14]

National insurance has of course always been about contractual contributions, but the Jobseekers' Act now supplements this with another set of contractual obligations of a very different order. The 'contract culture' is of course in vogue . . . But Government rhetoric on 'agreement' is difficult to square with legislative phraseology such as 'directions', 'such conditions as [an adjudication officer] considers appropriate', 'matters as may be prescribed', and the all-encompassing 'Any determination of an adjudication officer under this section shall be binding'. (Section 9(9)). There seems little leeway here for a 'meeting of the minds' but rather more the concept of 'take it or leave it'. And unlike the field of consumer law where a contractee may perhaps shop elsewhere or even abjure the goods on offer, the job seeking pseudo-contract is the sole means towards any prospect of income maintenance for a claimant and their family. And this after perhaps years of national insurance contributions. It is probably unrealistic to consider that contract terminology should be confined to agreements between autonomous individuals negotiating on level playing fields. But even the language of contract seems wholly inappropriate to the rigid framework of the Jobseekers' Act.

Recent developments in education law serve to highlight both the potential for, and limitations of, pseudo-contract as a form of regulation. The original notion of 'home-school agreements' as a means of parental involvement or participation[15] has given way to one of control. Thus, s. 13 of the Education Act 1997 empowers local education authorities to insist on the signing of agreements as a precondition of school admission. The scheme envisages the detailing of parental as well as school responsibilities, having regard to guidance issued by the Secretary of State. The approach has the political support of Labour as well as the Conservatives. Note, however, the ouster clause: an agreement 'shall not be capable of creating any obligation in respect of whose breach any liability arises in contract or in tort'. There are also the administrative implications to consider: the prospect of millions of bits of paper. The Advisory Centre for Education (ACE) expresses some basic concerns:[16]

Parental involvement is not promoted by binding contracts. Where parents are supportive of their child and his or her school, then the requirement to sign a contract is patronising. They are not likely to bring into line parents who are unable to support their child's school nor ensure children's good behaviour . . . It is very difficult to divorce the issue of home-school contracts from the wider debate on home-school relations, parents' rights and parental involvement in education. The debate about contracts is ultimately a debate about the distribution of power, responsibility and rights within education.

14 J. Fulbrook, 'The Job Seekers' Act 1995: Consolidation with a Sting of Contractual Compliance' (1995) 24 Industrial Law J. 395 at 400. See also G. Thomas, 'Job Seekers' Allowance' (1996) Legal Action (October) 18.
15 See *A New Partnership for our Schools*, Report by a Committee of Enquiry (T. Taylor, Chairman), Department of Education and Science, 1977.
16 ACE, 'Reading Between The Lines – Home-School Contracts Explained' (1996) ACE Bulletin (December) 6 at 7.

## 3. The ordinary law and vires

Government contract is important to administrative law, not only for the scale and diversity of activity, but also as a key battleground for competing theories and ruling intellectual passions. In terms of historical development, the legal architecture or analytical framework shows the dominant influence of Dicey, whose basic premise, that government liability should closely parallel private liability, represents a constitutional value: the principle of equality before the law. Hogg is a contemporary proponent:[17]

> The application of the ordinary law by the ordinary courts to the activities of government conforms to a widely-held political ideal and preserves us from many practical problems. Moreover, my review of the law leads me to the conclusion that, for the most part, the 'ordinary' law does work a satisfactory resolution of the conflicts between government and citizen. Indeed, the parts of the law that seem to me to be most unsatisfactory are those where the courts have refused to apply the ordinary law to the Crown. In short, I conclude that Dicey's idea of equality provides the basis for a rational, workable and acceptable theory of governmental liability.

Hogg takes a pessimistic view of a special public law of government liability, as a set of exceptions and privileges producing some highly executive-minded decisions.[18] Again, the reference to 'practical problems' highlights a need clearly to delineate separate systems. In a society typified by combinations of, or networks between, public and private actors, one in which government is fragmented and legal status may change very rapidly, there are good pragmatic reasons to hold the systems together.

In 1954,[19] Mitchell pleaded for a distinctive body of law which would be more sensitive to the distinctive characteristics of government. It was, on the one hand, necessary to recognise a principle of governmental effectiveness, such that 'no contract would be enforced in any case where some essential governmental activity would be thereby rendered impossible or seriously impeded'. On the other hand, a principle of compensation should be developed in situations where the administration reneged on its own contractual obligations. For Mitchell it was a question of 'the balance between the community and the citizen', with compensation as 'a check', the existence of which would 'prevent the frivolous exercise of the power and provide a safeguard for individual rights'. His argument epitomises the optimistic vision of a special regime of government liability, extrapolated from the special French system of administrative law, to include better protection for the citizen. Remember the criticism that Dicey, by refusing to accept the reality of state power and so disguising the inequality between the state and its citizens, had disabled effective legal control of the state machine (Chapter 2). Ultimately, Mitchell's plea for a special law of administrative

---

17  P. Hogg, *Liability of the Crown* (Toronto: Carswell) 2nd edn., 1989, pp. 2–3.
18  The argument is developed, and evidence provided in C. Harlow, '"Public: and "Private" Law: Definition Without Distinction' (1980) 43 MLR 241.
19  J. Mitchell, *The Contracts of Public Authorities* (London: L. Bell) 1954.

contracts translates into the demand for a distinctive, rational system of public law (complete with a distinct system of courts):[20]

> It seems important to urge recognition of the fact that the contracts of governmental agencies cannot always be governed by the same rules as those which regulate contracts between individuals . . . Hitherto in England problems of public law have largely been considered in relation to administrative adjudication and legislation. In truth the proper adjustment of the rights of the individual and the state is not confined within such limits and the proper protection of both state and citizen seems unlikely to be achieved solely by the application of private law rules to matters for which they were not designed . . .
>
> Equality of treatment by the law only operates to produce justice where there is in fact approximate equality between the parties involved. Just as inequalities have been recognised elsewhere, so the position of the state and its agencies should be recognised in its strength and weakness, both by the imposition of added burdens and of special privileges . . . The problem of the contracts of public authorities is therefore only a part of the larger problem of the relationship between men and the state. The acceptance of administrative contracts so far as it requires the acceptance of special treatment of the state and its organs, no matter what parallels may be drawn, does in fact involve a radical change. It involves the acceptance of the need for a general body of substantive public law . . . Since the law relating to the contracts of public authorities seems in this country to be assuming greater importance, and yet to be in an early state of growth, it may be in this connexion that the development of public law may be fostered.

The project failed of course, run aground, like Robson's parallel proposal for a separate system of tribunals, in the shoals of Diceyan 'background theory'. But unburdened of the idea of separate courts, we hear today strong echoes of the argument, most obviously by reason of the contractual 'revolution' in government, a phenomenon which Mitchell could never have anticipated.

At various points in this chapter we will see the interaction of, or conflict between, the analytical framework of ordinary private law and, on the one side, the needs of public policy and administration, and, on the other, demands for protection from the overarching economic power of government. Perhaps confusingly, we will see the courts moving in certain situations towards a public law model, and in others dismantling old exceptions or privileges in favour of ordinary private liability. We will need to keep in mind also the emergence of detailed legislative rules on contract-making, both domestic and European. Simply put, there are now special rules for many public contracts. As we shall see, however, they are not exhaustive of the topic.

Finally, any discussion of government liability in England is complicated by the legal fiction of 'the Crown' (above, pp. 5–7). While today the subject is commonly approached in the terms of 'public' and 'private' law, a more traditional arrangement would talk in terms of 'Crown Proceedings'. The Crown's distinctive legal position has been reduced, most obviously by the Crown Proceedings Act 1947, but certain peculiarities remain.

20  Ibid, pp. 7, 22–23, 242–244. See further, J. Mitchell, 'The Causes and Effects of the Absence of a System of Public Law in the United Kingdom' [1965] PL 95; 'The Constitutional Implications of Judicial Control of the Administration in the United Kingdom' (1967) CLJ 46.

## (a) From incapacity to restitution

It is elementary that a party must have the capacity to contract. The Crown is said to have all the powers of a natural person, including the power to enter into contracts, subject of course to the principle that Parliament may subsume or restrict the scope of the Crown's common law powers in statute. But, in addition, the Crown has enjoyed certain immunities in civil proceedings. Prior to the Crown Proceedings Act 1947, there was no legal right to sue the Crown. In contract, as distinct from tort, petition of right procedure could be used to mount a claim for damages (the *Amphitrite* case[1] discussed below is an example). Under the Act an action can now be pursued in the ordinary way, but it is expressly provided in s. 21 that no injunction or order for specific performance lies against the Crown in 'civil proceedings', although in lieu a declaration can be made.[2] Again, the payment of money by way of damages or otherwise cannot be enforced against the Crown by the normal processes of execution or attachment (s. 25). Conversely, no such restrictions inhibit orders in favour of the Crown.

All this highlights typical questions about the meaning of the Crown and the legal position of Ministers and agencies. As Crown agents, Ministers have general authority to make contracts on behalf of the Crown. But do they in addition have an independent capacity to make contracts in their own name? Arrowsmith correctly identifies three main options:[3]

(1)  there is no such capacity, the Crown being the only government entity which is a party to the contract;
(2)  the primary liability is with the Crown but the Minister may also be a party to the contract; and
(3)  as with other artificial legal entities there is such capacity.

Looking back to *Town Investments*,[4] briefly considered in Chapter 1, remember how the landlord argued that the Environment Minister signatory of the lease was himself the tenant, so that counter-inflation legislation did not apply. Essentially, this was an argument for option 3, the Crown and the Minister being treated as separate legal persons with separate capacity, and the relationship between them being determined by the general law of principal and agent. Led by Lord Diplock, a majority of the House of Lords disagreed, preferring option 1. Thus, the lease being executed under his official designation by the Minister, 'the tenant was the government acting through its appropriate member or, expressed in the term of art in public law, the tenant was the Crown'. The decision is open to serious criticism. A unitary theory of government of the type postulated enables any organ historically associated with the Crown to shelter behind Crown privileges, whatever its functions.

---

1   [1921] 3 KB 500. Below, p. 231.
2   In *M v Home Office* we saw Lord Woolf circumnavigate this provision in respect of judicial review. Above, p. 61.
3   S. Arrowsmith, *Civil Liability and Public Authorities* (South Humberside: Earlsgate Press) 1992, pp. 56–59.
4   Above, p. 7.

Unlike the Crown, statutory bodies such as local authorities have no general capacity to contract. The ultra vires principle applies to contract as to other activities and the scope of the power will be dependent upon the construction of the relevant legislation. Cases have been few and far between, a product of the traditional model of central-local government relations, which provided local authorities with a broad and flexible legal framework so limiting the impact of the ultra vires doctrine.[5] The courts have notably not required specific authorisation for a procurement contract, for example, provided that, in Lord Selbourne's words, it 'may fairly be regarded as incidental to, or consequential upon, those things which the Legislature has authorised'.[6] The approach is embodied today in s. 111 of the Local Government Act 1972:

> Without prejudice to any powers exercisable apart from this section but subject to the provisions of this Act . . . a local authority shall have power to do anything (whether or not involving expenditure, borrowing or lending of money or the acquisition or disposal of any property or rights) which is calculated to facilitate, or is conducive or incidental to, the discharge of any of their functions.

But a familiar theme of recent years is the undermining of traditional relationships by the assertion of a strong central will.[7] At one level, more structured and restrictive legislation has worked to bring the ultra vires principle to the fore. Specifically, the development of detailed statutory codes renders appeal to general provisions such as s. 111 more difficult. At another level, we find local authorities seeking to protect their expenditure programmes through 'creative accounting' and innovative financing techniques. This is the backdrop to a contemporary flood of litigation on the power to contract, involving some very special kinds of arrangements.

## (i) Interest swaps

The interest swap market was one of the fast-growing futures markets in the international world of finance in the 1980s. The basic idea is simple. Two parties agree to exchange a series of payments calculated by reference to differential rates of interest on a notional principal sum. The liability of one party is calculated by reference to a fixed rate of interest (the fixed rate payer) and the liability of the other (the floating rate payer) by reference to a varying market rate such as the London Inter-bank Rate (LIBOR). The financial outcome of the contract then depends upon future movements in interest rates. The market is a sophisticated one, far removed from the world of the contract law texts. Interest swaps can be used for various purposes, ranging from pure speculation to risk-spreading and debt-management. Take a party which has borrowed at fixed rates

---

5   See, for general discussion, J. Griffith, *Central Departments and Local Authorities* (London: Allen & Unwin) 1966; M. Loughlin, *Local Government in the Modern State* (London: Sweet and Maxwell) 1986.
6   *A-G v Great Eastern Rly* (1880) 5 App Cas 473 at 478.
7   See, for an overview, M. Loughlin, *Legality and Locality. The Role of Law in Central-Local Government Relations* (Oxford: Clarendon) 1996.

of interest and therefore bears the risk that current rates will fall: one way of hedging liabilities is to enter into a parallel swap transaction. It is important to think in terms not simply of single, discrete transactions, but of multiple, overlapping, interconnected deals by which risk is redistributed through the market (an idea closely resembling reinsurance). In back-to-back contracts, for example, one party enters into a pair of separate but balancing transactions.

Local authorities have long resorted to the money markets to manage their interest risk. As regards the swap market, it was generally assumed – on the basis of advice from the Chartered Institute of Public Finance and Accountancy – that local authorities could legitimately enter into contracts as ancillary to the exercise of their borrowing and lending powers. By 1989 it was estimated that these accounted for a third of all the sterling-based business in the market. Nearly 100 authorities had become involved, using swaps to turn fixed rate loans (from the government's Public Works Loans Board) into floating rate debt. But the question whether swap transactions were within the powers of the authorities became pressing in the late 1980s as market rates rose and councils' profits on swaps began to turn into losses. The Audit Commission took counsel's opinion and issued a warning that swaps agreements were ultra vires. In Hammersmith the local auditor sought a declaration that the council's transactions were unlawful. Hammersmith was the obvious target by reason of the sheer scale of its dealings: it had entered into nearly 600 swap transactions and was dealing in notional sums totalling more than 100 times its annual turnover and almost 20 times its total debt. At one point this single London borough had 0.5% of the global swaps market.[8]

## *Hazell v Hammersmith and Fulham London Borough Council*[9]

The main issue was whether, in the absence of express powers, the transactions could be brought within the rubric of s. 111 of the Local Government Act 1972. This in turn involved the question of the relationship of s. 111 with a very detailed set of provisions on borrowing set out in Sch. 13 to the same Act. Led by Lord Templeman, the House of Lords held that s. 111 was insufficient, and rejected an argument that those contracts entered into for the purpose of risk management could be saved.

> *Lord Templeman*: [It was contended that] swap transactions which are intended to 'replace' or 'reprofile' existing interest obligations are within the words of s. 111 . . . 'incidental to' the discharge by the local authority of its admitted function of borrowing or an alleged function of debt management.
>
> A power is not incidental merely because it is convenient or desirable or profitable. A swap transaction undertaken by a local authority involves speculation in future interest trends with the object of making a profit in order to increase the available

8   See M. Loughlin, 'Innovative Financing in Local Government: The Limits of Legal Instrumentalism' [1990] PL 372; [1991] PL 568; V. Veeder, J. Barrett and M. Reddington, *The Final Report of the Independent Inquiry into the Capital Market Activities of the London Borough of Hammersmith and Fulham*, 1991.

9   [1992] 2 AC 1.

resources of the local authorities . . . Individual trading corporations and others may speculate as much as they please or consider prudent. But a local authority is not a trading or currency or commercial operator with no limit on the method or extent of its borrowing or with powers to speculate. A local authority is a public authority dealing with public monies . . .

Schedule 13 establishes a comprehensive code which defines and limits the powers of a local authority with regard to its borrowing. This schedule is in my view inconsistent with any incidental powers to enter into swap transactions . . .

Debt management is not a function [for the purpose of s. 111]. Debt management is a phrase which has been coined in this case to describe the activities of a person who enters the swap market for the purpose of making profits which can be employed in the payment of interest on borrowings . . . A swap contract . . . is more akin to gambling than insurance.

*Lord Ackner*: Schedule 13 to the Act contains extremely detailed provisions dealing with the powers of the local authority to borrow money. The Schedule provides a high degree of limitation and control of those powers . . . Given this *express* limited power then I would expect to find that any additional such power would also need to be given in express terms in the statute. No such power is to be found.

But is this an example of the 'bad' case making 'bad' law? Whereas Hammersmith became so heavily involved in swaps for the *purpose* of speculative trading (income generation), the House of Lords held the *type* of contract ultra vires. Loughlin pursues the theme:[10]

The Lords were evidently affected by their perceptions both of the nature of the swaps market and the reasons for local involvement in it. In both respects, however, their grasp of the issues seems limited . . .

[Consider] the highly coloured views of Lord Templeman . . . Terms such as 'gambling' assume a symbolic quality and become a substitute for rational analysis of whether or not the use of swaps involves the assumption of inappropriate or unacceptable risk . . . There is much evidence that swaps are regarded as everyday tools of financial management by large organisations and as instruments for the mitigation of risk . . .

The pejorative characterisation of the market . . . is also skewed by the circumstances of one exceptional authority's relationship to that market . . . More generally, the court seems to have been influenced by the fact that, since Hammersmith's motives in entering the market seemed speculative, the market itself must be viewed as such . . .

The difficulty in presenting a convincing justification may well result from the restrictive procedures of judicial processes. That is, the problem lies at the cognitive-normative interface and may be the product of a failure to develop the techniques required to bring to bear on normative legal issues a more realistic portrayal of the world in which these [financial] instruments are put to work.

In a later chapter, we shall consider the argument that adversarial, adjudicative procedure is unsuited to resolving issues of this type (below, Ch. 17). The case name is misleading: ranged against Hammersmith and the auditor, Hazell, are the banks which contracted with Hammersmith and which are now joined as respondents; Hammersmith has a strong incentive to have its own contracts

10   M. Loughlin, [1991] PL 372 at 591–595.

declared ultra vires. There are many interested parties not before the court, including all those other authorities involved in the swap market: unlike Hammersmith, many have dealt conservatively and some are in profit. And what of the impact of the case on the financial markets? At one level, there is the cost of future credit to local government, and, at another, the damage to the international reputation of the City of London. The Bank of England was sufficiently concerned to press the case – unsuccessfully – for what the Governor was pleased to call 'retro-corrective' legislation in order to restore 'the principle of the sanctity of conduct'.[11]

### (ii) Enforcement: type and purpose of the contract

It is one thing to declare the contract of a public body ultra vires, another to sort out the consequences. It was accepted in the swap litigation that all the transactions would be void in the sense of being unenforceable against the local authority. In subsequent litigation, which therefore dealt only with the question of restitutionary claims (see below), the judges expressed the same view: in the words of Lord Woolf, 'Because there is no contract damages are not available'.[12] But is this a general rule of ultra vires contracts? Or should a distinction be drawn between cases of absence of power, as in *Hazell*, and of abuse of power, the transaction which is of a type capable of being lawful but which is unlawful by reason of the purpose for which it was made?

At common law an unlawful contract made by a private corporation was not enforceable against it, so as to protect shareholders and creditors against disbursements for unauthorised purposes. This rule was changed by the Companies Acts,[13] leaving the awkward question of the appropriate judicial response in the case of public bodies. We need to note also a provision in the Local Government Act 1972 that in contracts of loan with local authorities the lender 'shall not be bound to enquire whether the borrowing of the money is legal . . . and shall not be prejudiced by any illegality . . .' (Sch. 13, para. 20).

Lord Templeman argues that the object of the ultra vires doctrine is here the protection of the public. In the extreme case of Hammersmith, validating all its deals would have meant huge losses for the borough. But what of the prejudice to the counterparty, such as the loss of expected profits (an interest the law of contract generally protects)? Arrowsmith advocates shifting the balance in favour of the particular, private interest:[14]

> Contracts which are unlawful for a breach of public law should generally be enforceable [against the authority] at least where the contractor is not aware that the contract is unlawful: the *prima facie* right of the contractor should prevail over the public interest. This should apply even if, as in *Hazell*, the contract is one which on its

11  R. Leigh-Pemberton, Minutes of Evidence, Second Report of the Treasury and Civil Service Committee HC 289 (1990–1991) at paras. 129–130.

12  *Westdeutsche Landesbank Girozentrale v Islington London Borough Council* [1996] 2 All ER 961 at 1003.

13  *Ashbury Railway Carriage and Iron Co Ltd v Riche* (1875) LR 7 HL 653; Companies Act 1985, s. 35(1); Companies Act 1989, s. 108.

14  S. Arrowsmith, *Civil Liability and Public Authorities* (above, note 3), pp. 64–65.

face could not have been lawfully made: the onus should be on the authority itself to ensure compliance with its legislative mandate, and not on the contractor. Alternatively, however, courts might wish to hold that the contract is enforceable only where it is one where it might have been lawful if made for a proper purpose, and the other party does not know of the improper purpose.

In other words, who should bear the *risk* that contracts entered into by statutory authorities are ultra vires? An alternative argument might be that the interests of public authorities and private lenders do not, in fact, conflict, since both derive benefit from a healthy lending market free of significant 'vires risk' for the banks.[15] The theme is pursued by the Financial Law Panel, a City grouping which seeks to identify and have removed areas of uncertainty in the law affecting financial services:[16]

> The difficulties [for parties] in dealing with local authorities (or, indeed, almost all public bodies) . . . stem from the fact that the ability of public bodies to contract is closely delimited and these limits may need to be applied to a wide variety of factual scenarios. Some, and sometimes most, of the crucial facts are within the exclusive knowledge of the public body and third parties are faced with the practical difficulty, and in some cases the impossibility, of determining in advance whether the proposed transaction risks being struck down at a later date upon the ground that it was beyond the powers of the public body. The 'vires risk' limits the size of the financial market to which local authorities have access and, in so far as the market is open to them, increases the cost to them on account of that risk.

The Panel was moved to express a view in the context of the following litigation. The case is important both in terms of the substance of local authority powers and as providing the Court of Appeal with the opportunity to tackle directly the question of enforcing ultra vires contracts. In the event, the 'vires risk' to the financial institutions was maximised.

## *Crédit Suisse v Allerdale Borough Council*[17]

The council wanted to build a new swimming pool but was constrained by its borrowing limits set by central government. Expressly in order to avoid the controls, the council formed a wholly-owned limited company which then took out a loan facility with the Swiss bank guaranteed by the council. The pool was made part of a leisure development incorporating 'time shares' intended to pay for the pool. But the expected profits on these failed to materialise and the company collapsed, owing the bank over £5 million. When the bank called in the guarantee, it was argued for the council that the scheme was ultra vires.[18] Leading counsel had in fact advised favourably on the scheme at the outset, and it was only

---

15   See P. Cane, 'Do Banks Dare Lend to Local Authorities?' (1994) 110 LQR 514 at 517.
16   Financial Law Panel, *Transactions with Local Authorities* (London) 1996.
17   [1996] 4 All ER 129.
18   Because the company was the borrower, there was no protection for the bank under Sch. 13, para. 20 to the 1972 Act.

after the pool was complete that the issue of ultra vires was first raised by the District Auditor.

The case for the council was that (1) it had no statutory powers to establish the company and guarantee its debt; (2) even if it had, it had abused those powers by entering into a contract for an improper purpose or by acting *Wednesbury* unreasonably. The bank was most keen to resist (1) precisely because of an argument that absence of power cases could be distinguished. Further, it was argued that ultra vires contracts made by public bodies should not be treated as void automatically, but that enforceability should instead be subject to judicial discretion, so allowing the court to uphold a contract where the other party acts in good faith. Here an analogy was drawn with the discretionary character of remedies in judicial review procedure, it being argued that since the enforceability of the guarantee turned on issues of public law, the same principles should be applied in considering the consequences of a breach of public law in civil proceedings.

In the event, the bank lost on all the main issues. It had relied for statutory powers on an express power to provide recreational facilities coupled with the implied power of s. 111 of the 1972 Act. But, as in *Hazell*, the scheme ran into the buffers of the 'comprehensive code' on borrowing also contained in that Act.[19] Further, it was held that an authority is not providing a service where it relies upon a separate legal entity (the company) whose acts are not, in law, the acts of the council, to provide the service. This meant that the giving of the guarantee was not 'incidental' to the discharge of a statutory function: rather, it was incidental to the setting up of the company, i.e. to an activity that was itself incidental. In sum, we find the Court of Appeal concede little by way of flexibility in the interpretation and application of local authority powers:[20]

> *Neill LJ*: In my opinion the bank's argument on the statutory powers points fails at each stage. The establishment of the company and the giving of the guarantee were part of an ingenious scheme designed to circumvent the no-doubt irksome controls imposed by central government. The council, however, could only do what it was empowered to do by statute. Neither the establishment of a company nor the giving of a guarantee fell within the express or implied powers of the council.

The doctrine of ultra vires was applied to maximum effect: no public law discretion, no distinct categories:[1]

> *Neill LJ*: I know of no authority for the proposition that the ultra vires decisions of local authorities can be classified into categories of invalidity. I do not think that it is open to this court to introduce such a classification. Where a public authority acts outside its jurisdiction in any of the ways indicated by Lord Reid in *Anisminic*,[2] the decision is void. In the case of a decision to enter into a contract of guarantee, the consequences in private law are those which flow where one of the parties to a contract lacks capacity. I see no escape from this conclusion.

---

19  See further on this reasoning, the conjoined appeal *Crédit Suisse v Waltham Forest London Borough Council* [1996] 4 All ER 176.

20  [1996] 4 All ER 129 at 149.

1  Ibid at 159.

2  Above, p. 54.

This is hardly satisfactory. Note how the counterparty suffers the worst of the public/private law dichotomy, being deprived of its private law rights by public law and being unable in a private law court to take advantage of public law discretions. Conceptual arguments related to the definition of public law simply should not be allowed to produce this type of result.[3]

The case cuts against government policy, raising doubts over the guarantees and indemnities offered by statutory authorities in the kinds of partnership agreement, joint venture and private finance initiative concession favoured in recent years. Although local government lawyers have argued that this was to be over-sensitive – due diligence and search should do – those advising lenders saw the perception of a real risk in terms of lack of capacity – 'an impediment to legitimate and desirable commercial activity between public and private sectors'.[4]

Expressed slightly differently, the common law is here seen to be out of touch with contemporary approaches to public administration. The predictable outcome is a dose of legislative pragmatism to mitigate the rigour of the ultra vires doctrine. To this end, the Local Government (Contracts) Bill currently before Parliament is designed to provide contracting parties with a safe harbour while preserving the public protection of ultra vires.[5] Provision is made (a) for a certification procedure as a protection for contractors and lenders who subsequently discover that an authority entered into a invalid agreement; which (b) will prevent it being argued in private law proceedings that a certified contract is unenforceable because ultra vires; while (c) preserving the right of local taxpayers or external auditors to challenge such contracts by means of judicial review or audit-related proceedings. To this effect:

(2) The local authority must have issued a certificate (whether before or after the contract is entered into)—

(a)  including details of the period for which the contract operates or is to operate,

(b)  describing the purpose of the contract, . . .

(d)  stating that the local authority had or has power to enter into the contract and specifying the statutory provision, or each of the statutory provisions, conferring the power, . . .

(f)  dealing in a manner prescribed by regulations with any matters required by regulations to be dealt with in certificates under this section, . . .

(4) The local authority must have obtained consent to the issue of a certificate under the section from each of the persons with whom the local authority has entered, or is to enter, into the contract.

3   C. Harlow, '"Public" and "Private" Law: Definition Without Distinction' (1980) 43 MLR 241.
4   Financial Law Panel, *Transactions with Local Authorities*, p. 18.
5   In contrast to the suggestion that statutory bodies like local authorities be given a general power of competence. See J. Goudie, 'Judicial Review' in D. Bean (ed.), *Law Reform For All* (London: Blackstone Press, Society of Labour Lawyers) 1996; and see, for the problems, Sir Robert Carnwath, 'The Reasonable Limits of Local Authority Powers' [1996] PL 244.

*(iii) Restitution: interest swaps again*

A claim in restitution generally requires (1) that the plaintiff conferred a benefit on the defendant; (2) that the benefit was conferred at the plaintiff's expense; and (3) that it would be unjust for the defendant to retain it. In the case of ultra vires contracts, it may be considered unjust for a public body to retain a benefit which has been conferred in return for a consideration which has failed.

Restitution is recognised as a growth area of English law: to the extent perhaps of a danger of being seen as a panacea for all ills. Various difficulties are highlighted by the litigation on interest swaps, which provided the opportunity for substantial and controversial doctrinal development. 'It is no exaggeration to say', observes Burrows, 'that one could write a book on the restitutionary consequences of the decision in *Hazell v Hammersmith*'.[6]

One set of considerations involves the character of the general law: little authority before this litigation on the restitutionary implications of ultra vires contracts involving public bodies, and, more fundamental, continuing controversy over the juristic foundations of a legal subject bedevilled by large amounts of arcane learning. Another set of factors concerns the fluid and interactive character of the interest swap market. To blow the whistle and seek to restore the market players to their original position is likely to prove an arbitrary, even futile exercise, precisely because of the redistribution of risk through the market. There is the mixing in the market of public and private bodies: a local authority transaction is ultra vires, a separate balancing transaction between two banks is perfectly valid. Bear in mind especially polycentricity and the problem of fit between, on the one hand, multiple dealing, and, on the other, adjudication, which tends to isolate and focus on particular transactions.

The ruling in *Hazell* launched a great raft of litigation. More than 100 writs were issued, mostly in the Chancery Division, claiming to recover payments made by one party or the other under the ultra vires contracts. Although many cases were settled, litigation of this magnitude cried out for a high degree of judicial management: the kind of structuring and organising of cases designed to reduce expense, repetition and delay, which is now an increasingly familiar phenomenon as complex 'class' or 'group' litigation multiplies, most obviously in the realm of torts.[7] To this end, certain typical cases were selected as 'lead' actions in order to establish the law.

*Westdeutsche Landesbank Girozentrale v Islington London Borough Council;*
*Kleinwort Benson Ltd v Sandwell Borough Council*[8]

The Labour council in Islington was unwilling to make further expenditure cuts and, being 'rate-capped', could raise limited sums from its ratepayers. Like other

---

6    A. Burrows, 'Swaps and the Friction between Common Law and Equity' (1995) Restitution Law Rev. 15.
7    Thus, it is not, as M. Loughlin [1991] PL 595–598 implies, a distinctively 'public law' development. See, for discussion, C. Harlow and R. Rawlings, *Pressure Through Law* (London: Routledge) 1992, Ch. 3; also, P. Bowsher (Chairman), *Guide for use in Group Actions*, 1991, Supreme Court Procedure Committee.
8    [1994] 4 All ER 890; [1996] 2 All ER 961.

councils in a similar position, it was attracted by the idea of swap transactions with an upfront payment to the council uninhibited by central government's statutory controls. Islington generated some £19.4 million in this way by entering – as the floating ratepayer – into seven swap transactions, six with other local authorities and one, the subject of the litigation, with Westdeutsche Bank. The strategy achieved a form of borrowing, since, in consequence of the upfront payments, the rate of interest paid to the council was reduced. The contract with Westdeutsche involved an upfront payment of £2.5 million and half-yearly interest payments on a notional principal of £25 million for a period of ten years. Westdeutsche believed it could not lose. This was its first swap transaction with a local authority in this country, and it was only prepared to proceed on the basis of a satisfactory balancing contract which negated the financial risk and provided an assured return. Such a contract was agreed with Morgan Grenfell allowing Westdeutsche a 'turn' of 0.24%. The agreements commenced in June 1987. By June 1989 Islington had made four net interest payments to Westdeutsche, totalling some £1.355 million. After the Divisional Court's ruling in *Hazell v Hammersmith*[9] in November 1989 that such contracts were ultra vires, Islington made no further payments. Westdeutsche now claimed in restitution £1.145 million, the balance of the upfront payment, plus interest.

The *Sandwell* case involved repeat players in the market. At issue were four transactions; the first, a five-year agreement made in 1983, had been wholly executed before the *Hazell* ruling. It was also a transaction on which Sandwell had gained, and Kleinwort now incorporated this benefit in a general claim for restitution.

It was possible to present the actions in alternative ways: in standard fashion as a personal restitutionary claim at common law by means of an action for money had and received; and as a proprietary claim in equity, on the basis of a fiduciary relationship or resulting trust. At first instance and in the Court of Appeal the proprietary claim was allowed, a decision which had dramatic consequences for restitution in general, implying a duty to account strictly for profits from trust property and priority in insolvency over general creditors; also, it provided a rationale for awarding compound (not simple) interest against the recipient.[10] Ultimately, however, this basis for restitution was rejected by the House of Lords in an appeal from Islington on the issue of interest. Fortunately, then, it need not detain us further: note, however, the high degree of uncertainty associated with restitution as a rapidly evolving legal remedy.

Turning to the common law claim, although it may be considered unjust to retain money when consideration has failed, the understanding has been that recovery is only possible when the failure is total. Hobhouse J noted the implications:[11]

> As regards the Islington swap . . . there has been partial performance by both sides and both sides have received benefits under the 'contract'. As regards the first Sandwell swap, the contemplated contract was in fact fully performed and neither party

9 Above, p. 218.
10 P. Birks, 'No Consideration: Restitution After Void Contracts' (1993) 23 W. Aus. LR 195; W. J. Swadling, 'Restitution for no Consideration' (1994) Restitution LR 73.
11 [1994] 4 All ER 890 at 925.

can [on this view], say that there was any failure of consideration, let alone any total failure. [The] principle of total failure of consideration does not suffice to give any right to recover the sums paid under those contracts.

The judge proceeded to develop what in England is a novel ground for restitution:[12]

> In the case of ultra vires transactions such as those with which I am concerned where there is not and never has been any contract, I prefer to use the phrase 'absence of consideration' . . . In my judgment, the correct analysis is that any payments made under a contract which is void ab initio in the way that an ultra vires contract is void, are not contractual payments at all . . . The principle is [that] it is unconscionable that the recipient should retain the money. Neither mistake nor the contractual principle of total failure of consideration are the basis for the right of recovery.
>
> Where payments both ways have been made the correct view is to treat the later payment as, pro tanto, a repayment of the earlier sum paid by the other party . . . The remedy is only available to a party on the basis that he gives credit for any benefit which he has received . . . In so far as the recipient has made cross-payments to the payer, the recipient has ceased to be enriched . . .
>
> This decision is sufficient to establish the prima facie right of the plaintiffs to recover in both of the actions which are before me. It also follows from the fact that I consider that the correct analysis is absence of consideration . . . that it is irrelevant . . . under the first Sandwell swap that the supposed contract was in fact fully performed and there was no failure of consideration at all in the contractual sense.

As Birks observes, 'the losing party under the supposed contract therefore becomes the winner in the law of restitution'.[13]

For administrative lawyers, the ruling is one of a number[14] which signal a more prominent role for restitution. The expansive feel is evident too in the treatment of defences. Take the well-known principle that restitution may be denied if to allow recovery would undermine the policy of the ultra vires objection to contractual enforcement.[15] In *Westdeutsche*, there was said to be no question of swap transactions, as non-borrowing contracts, being indirectly enforced by the restitutionary claim. Again, in a related test case, *Kleinwort Benson Ltd v Birmingham City Council*,[16] Kleinwort had entered into separate balancing transactions: Birmingham therefore argued that payments which had enriched the council should not be recovered, since Kleinwort would receive a windfall gain. But although the benefit must be conferred at the plaintiff's expense, it was held this falls to be assessed inside the parameters of the individual contract. The practical difficulty of unravelling the consequences of interacting but differential public/private law regimes is demonstrated.

12  Ibid at 924, 929.
13  P. Birks (1993) 23 W. Aust. LR 195 at 199. The notion of restitution for no consideration is more resonant of civil law jurisdictions. The Court of Appeal agreed with the ruling, and on this point there was no appeal to the House of Lords.
14  *Woolwich Building Society v IRC* [1993] AC 70; *British Steel plc v Customs and Excise Comrs* [1997] 2 All ER 366. See below, Ch. 18.
15  The so-called incapacity defence of *Sinclair v Brougham* [1914] AC 398.
16  [1996] 4 All ER 733.

It is also appropriate to stress for administrative law, first, the measure of flexibility which restitution may usefully bring to topics such as contractual incapacity; and, second, the price to be paid in terms of legal doubt and costly litigation. In the *Islington* case the council did not have the sympathy of the court:[17]

> *Leggatt LJ*: Islington say that they should receive a windfall because the purpose of the doctrine of ultra vires is to protect council tax payers whereas restitution would disrupt Islington's finances. They also contend it would countenance 'unconsidered dealings with local authorities'. If that is the best that can be said for refusing restitution, the sooner it is enforced the better. Protection of council taxpayers from loss is to be distinguished from securing a windfall for them. The disruption of Islington's finances is the result of ill-considered financial dispositions by Islington and its officers. It is not the policy of the law to require others to deal at their peril with local authorities, nor to require others to undertake their own enquiries about whether a local authority has power to make particular contracts or types of contract. Any system of law, and indeed any system of fair dealing, must be expected to ensure that Islington do not profit by the fortuity that when it became known that the contract was ineffective the balance stood in their favour. In other words, in circumstances such as these they should not be unjustly enriched.

## (b) A clash of values: contractual fettering of discretionary power

It is a recognised common law principle that a public authority must retain the freedom to exercise its discretionary power from time to time in the public interest. One aspect, considered in Chapter 7 is that an authority may not fetter its discretion by adopting a rigid rule, although it may develop and pursue a general policy. There is also a doctrine limiting the extent to which an authority may by contract or grant limit its future choice of action. Here, however, the question of degree – how far the courts should push the principle, thus rendering the contract void and unenforceable – is especially difficult.

The clash is not simply between the authority and the private interest of the counterparty, as where the latter has incurred expense preparing for performance. We must also consider competing values of security of contract or party autonomy and of government effectiveness or responsiveness in changing conditions. In the event, the case law is decidedly messy and uncertain. As de Smith observes: 'Breaking [the principle] down into a series of neat propositions presents problems: formulations are not uniform, the decided cases have arisen in a variety of contexts and not all are reconcilable with one another.'[18] There is, however, a judicial swing towards narrowing the application of the doctrine, i.e. treating such agreements more like ordinary contracts.

Two competing lines of authority are found in the early cases. One implies a very strict test whereby the contract is void if it overlaps the subject matter of a statutory power. In *Ayr Harbour Trustees v Oswald*,[19] the trustees had statutory powers to compulsorily acquire land for the construction of harbour works as the

17  [1994] 4 All ER 890 at 967.
18  de Smith, Jowell and Woolf, p. 516.
19  (1883) 8 App Cas 623. See also *Mulliner v Midland Rly Co* (1879) 11 Ch D 611.

need arose. They acquired part of Oswald's land and agreed not to construct works on that land as would impede access from his remaining land to the harbour, so reducing the compensation payable. The House of Lords held that the covenant was ultra vires the trustees. In Lord Blackburn's words:

> Where the legislation confers powers on any body to take land compulsorily for a particular purpose, it is on the ground that the using of that land for that purpose will be for the public good . . . A contract purporting to bind [the trustees] and their successors not to use those powers is void.

The second line of authority, traceable to *R v Inhabitants of Leake*,[20] demonstrates a less strict test of incompatibility between the purpose of the statutory power and the purpose for which the contract is made. A case like *Ayr* may be 'explained' in this way on the basis that the trustees, in a famous phrase, were renouncing 'a part of their statutory birthright'.[1] This was the approach ultimately approved by the House of Lords in *British Transport Commission v Westmoreland County Council*.[2] Briefly, the Commission argued that a footpath over a railway bridge could not be dedicated to the public because statutory powers enabled them to discontinue the bridge. No incompatibility was found, however, the test being applied leniently.

The test of incompatibility has considerable merit. On the one hand, it allows for the use of contract as a tool of statutory purpose, as in procurement or outsourcing. On the other, it operates to defeat blatant attempts to rewrite statutory obligations. A classic example is *Stringer v Minister of Housing and Local Government*,[3] where the local authority made a formal agreement with Manchester University to discourage development in the vicinity of the Jodrell Bank telescope. The contract was held ultra vires since it bound the council to contravene the planning laws by a failure to consider all the matters which Parliament required to be considered in planning applications. There are, however, continuing difficulties in the operation of the test. Let us take two examples.

### *Dowty Boulton Paul Ltd v Wolverhampton Corporation*[4]

In 1936 Wolverhampton conveyed land to an aircraft company for the building of a factory together with the right to use a municipally owned airfield for 99 years. By 1970 the airfield was rarely used and the Corporation wanted to use the area for housing. When the company pleaded the lease, the Corporation argued that it was ultra vires as fettering their statutory powers to provide housing. Pennycuick V-C was not impressed:[5]

---

20  (1833) 5 B & Ad 469.
 1  *Birkdale District Electric Supply Co Ltd v Southport Corpn* [1926] AC 355, per Lord Sumner.
 2  [1958] AC 126.
 3  [1970] 1 WLR 1281.
 4  [1971] 1 WLR 204.
 5  Ibid at 210.

*Pennycuick V-C*: That seems to me . . . a principle wholly inapplicable to the present case. What has happened here is that the Corporation has made what is admittedly a valid disposition in respect of its land for a term of years. What is, in effect, contended by [the Corporation] is that such a disposition – and, indeed, any other possible disposition of property by a corporation for a term of years, for example, an ordinary lease – must be read as subject to an implied condition enabling the Corporation to determine it should it see fit to put the property to some other use in the exercise of any of its statutory powers. Nothing in the cases cited [such as *Ayr*] supports this startling proposition. The cases are concerned with attempts to fetter in advance the future exercise of statutory powers otherwise than by the valid exercise of a statutory power. The cases are not concerned with the position which arises after a statutory power has been validly exercised. Obviously, where a power is exercised in such a manner as to create a right extending over a term of years, the existence of that right *pro tanto* excludes the exercise of other statutory powers in respect of the same subject-matter, but there is no authority and I can see no principle upon which that sort of exercise could be held to be invalid as a fetter upon the future exercise of powers.

The case demonstrates the problem which arises when, typical of a multi-functional body like a local authority, two potentially conflicting statutory powers are involved. Read literally, the judgment suggests that when a contract or lease is created in furtherance of a statutory power it can never be incompatible with a second statutory power. The formulation is too broad; the matter must ultimately depend on statutory interpretation.

## *R v Hammersmith and Fulham London Borough Council, ex p Beddowes*[6]

The council owned a housing estate consisting of nine blocks of flats badly in need of modernisation. Acting under a statutory power to dispose of land held for housing purposes, the ruling Conservative group (which had a majority of one) resolved to sell one block to a property developer and to enter into covenants over the others effectively precluding the council from exercising a statutory power to provide housing accommodation by means of new council tenancies. The contract, bitterly opposed by the Labour opposition, was signed a few hours before Labour took control of the council after the local elections. A resident sought judicial review on the basis that the covenants were an unlawful fetter on the council's powers as a housing authority. By a majority, the Court of Appeal dismissed the challenge:

*Fox LJ*: The council formed the view that persons buying owner-occupier flats in [the first] block (and in the other blocks as the development proceeded) should have a guarantee as to the user of the rest of the estate for owner-occupation . . . In the absence of certainty as to the development of the whole estate, marketing might be difficult and the whole project might flop . . . That, it seems to me, is a coherent policy which is not manifestly unreasonable . . .

What we are concerned with in the present case are overlapping or conflicting powers. There is a power to create covenants restrictive of the use of retained land; and there are powers in relation to the user of the retained land for housing purposes. In these circumstances, it is necessary to ascertain for what purpose the retained land is held. All other powers are subordinate to the main power to carry out the primary purpose . . .

Now the purpose for which the . . . estate is held by the council must be the provision of housing accommodation in the district. The council's policy in relation to the estate, as I have set it out above, seems to me to be consistent with that purpose. The estate is in bad repair and the policy is aimed at providing accommodation in the borough of higher quality than at present by means of a scheme of maintenance and refurbishment . . .

It seems to me that if the purpose for which the power to create restrictive covenants is being exercised can reasonably be regarded as the furtherance of the statutory object, then the creation of the covenants is not an unlawful fetter. All the powers are exercisable for the achieving of the statutory objects in relation to the land, and the honest and reasonable exercise of a power for that purpose cannot properly be regarded as a fetter upon another power given for the same purpose.

Surely this formulation is too broad? The wide definition of the 'primary purpose' basically deprives the no-fettering principle of legal effect. Covenents which were not in furtherance of a statutory power would anyway be unlawful. The important issue is raised of upholding the values in a representative democracy of political responsiveness and electoral choice.[8] How far should the courts go in limiting contracts which (seek to) undermine the policy preferences of the political opposition? There is much to be said for the dissenting judgment, which does not sanitise political controversy:[7]

*Kerr LJ*: It seems to me that the court must consider with the greatest care whether the decisions of the . . . council – evidently taken by a majority of a single vote or so throughout – were actuated by policy reasons based upon the proper discharge of the authority's powers and functions as a housing authority, or by extraneous motives . . .

Policies are liable to be reviewed, as the result of events or political changes or both. They should remain open to review under our democratic institutions, save to the extent that an immediate policy decision renders it reasonably necessary to fetter future policy decisions . . .

I feel bound to conclude that the decision to contract . . . for the development of [the first block], subject to these covenants, was an unreasonable and impermissible exercise of the powers and functions of a housing authority in the *Wednesbury* sense. Its predominant motivation was to fetter the political aspects of the future housing policy for [the estate], and not the implementation of the then . . . housing policy for reasons which were reasonably necessary at the time . . . Accordingly, I would quash the . . . consequent contract.

## 4. The Crown: executive freedom of action?

The demand for freedom of action is liable to be pressed most strongly in cases involving the Crown. It has underpinned the denial of contract status to civil servants, which has long been a distinguishing feature of English administrative

---

7    Ibid at 273, 275 and 276.
8    Consider this case in the light of *Tameside*, below, p. 584.

law. A special defence of 'executive necessity' to an action for breach of contract against the Crown has been derived from *The Amphitrite*. Conversely, it is the Crown's distinctive legal position in these matters which has proved so troubling. In the event, traditional notions of 'Crown service' have been all but abandoned in recent years under the onslaught from contractualisation and NPM (see below). Although it has not been overruled, *The Amphitrite* is an antiquated authority of dubious validity. It has been described as unnecessarily draconian,[9] precisely because it goes beyond the general test of incompatibility for contract failure.

## *The Amphitrite*[10]

During World War I the government operated an emergency arrangement whereby neutral ships in British ports were allowed to leave only if their place was taken by other ships of the same tonnage. Mindful of this, the Swedish owners of the *Amphitrite* obtained an official assurance that if the ship carried approved goods to Britain she would be allowed to leave. The ship was not released and the owners claimed damages for breach of the undertaking. The judge accepted the Crown's argument that it did not amount to an enforceable contract:

> *Rowlatt J*: No doubt the Government can bind itself through its officers by a commercial contract, and if it does so it must perform it like anybody else or pay damages for the breach. But this was not a commercial contract; it was an arrangement whereby the Government purported to give an assurance as to what its executive action would be in the future in relation to a particular ship in the event of her coming to this country with a particular kind of cargo. And that is, to my mind, not a contract for the breach of which damages can be sued for in a Court of law. It was merely an expression of intention to act in a particular way in a certain event. My main reason for so thinking is that it is not competent for the Government to fetter its future executive action, which must necessarily be determined by the needs of the community when the question arises. It cannot by contract hamper its freedom of action in matters which concern the welfare of the state.

*The Amphitrite* highlights a lack of legal machinery for compensation in the face of the compelling needs of government. In contrast, the case for importing some flexible remedies, for Mitchell always borrowed from French administrative law,[11] accepts the idea that public authorities may be required in the public interest to vary or suspend contracts but admits a compensatory principle. Surely, however, the value here of a distinct system of public law is limited? The reason why the antiquated rule in *The Amphitrite* has survived[12] may be found in administrative practice. Government contracts typically contain variation clauses

---

9  P. Craig, *Administrative Law*, p. 707.
10  [1921] 3 KB 500.
11  See, for an introduction, N. Brown and J. Bell, *French Administrative Law* (Oxford: Clarendon) 4th edn., 1993, pp. 192–201.
12  There is limited case law. See in particular *The Steaua Romana* [1944] P 43; *Robertson v Minister of Pensions* [1948] 1 KB 227; and *Crown Lands Comrs v Page* [1960] 2 QB 274.

which make provision for compensation, as also so-called break clauses, permitting the government to terminate the contract at any time.[13] In other words, the 'law of the contract' allows for exactly the kind of public interest considerations and remedies associated with the French *contrat administratif*.

Consistent with the principle of equality before the law, the obvious solution to *The Amphitrite* is to draw the Crown further under the general law of contract. A contract could be treated as valid, so as to allow an action for damages, while refusing an action for specific performance or an injunction.[14] Hogg develops the policy considerations.[15]

> An argument that has been advanced in favour of a public law of contract is that the Crown ought to be able to escape from its contractual obligations when public policy calls for non-compliance ... The better view, in my opinion, is that the Crown should be bound by its contracts in the same way as a private firm. If one assumes that the Crown will occasionally have a sound reason of public policy for breaking a contract (a large assumption), the private law of contract now insists that the injured party be compensated. In that way, the cost of the change in government policy is borne by the government and not by the innocent private contractor. It is also probably true that the fact that the Crown's contractual undertakings are binding reduces the cost of government operations, because a private contractor need not demand a higher price from the government to cover the risk of a unilateral government decision not to fulfil the obligation ...
>
> A government, unlike a private contractor, controls the Legislature, and is able to commandeer unilaterally the goods and services that it requires, and stipulate the terms upon which property is to be sold or leased, employees are to be hired, and generally regulate other matters that could be dealt with by contract. To me, this argues for the position that, when the government chooses to play by the rules of contract, it should be bound by the same rules as other participants in the marketplace ...
>
> It is conceivable that a case might arise where the government cannot accept the decision of a court holding the Crown liable for breach of contract. For example, the court might award damages that were so high as to place an intolerable cost on a desired public policy. The solution to this case is legislation ... Through legislation ... the will of the community can be made to prevail over private contract rights. That is the ultimate safeguard of public policy.

Note the parallel with the 'Titanic battle' involving *Burmah Oil*.[16] We shall find in Chapter 18 that it is not necessarily simple to legislate retrospectively to deprive people of their property rights.

---

13 See C. Turpin, *Government Procurement and Contracts* (Harlow: Longman) 1989. And see below, pp. 236–240.
14 Another possible method of granting compensation would be through the doctrine of frustration. But this presupposes that the contract is at an end. See, for competing views, C. Harlow, '"Public" and "Private" Law: Definition Without Distinction' (1980) 43 MLR 241; P. Craig, *Administrative Law*, pp. 704–705.
15 P. Hogg, *Liability of the Crown* (Toronto: Carswell) 2nd edn., 1989, pp. 100–161, 172.
16 Above, p. 47.

## From Crown service to contracting employment

Recent developments in the terms and conditions of civil servants are of general interest in administrative law.[17] First, the shift to contract status exemplifies the process of juridification, at the expense of concepts of trust or professional norms. Second, the courts have struggled to delimit judicial review in the face of a piecemeal administrative framework, leading to confusion regarding 'public' and 'private' forms of action. Third, there has been a comfortable fit between judicial policy, concerned to keep 'staff cases' out of judicial review, and recent government policies designed to promote the ethos of, or narrowing of differences with, employment relationships in the private sector.[18] To underscore the point, the common law has proved a valuable resource for executive action.

To Wade, the law long regarded the civil service 'as if it consisted of a handful of secretaries working behind the scenes in a Royal Palace'.[19] The service was in a 'primitive state of legal evolution': in fact the structures of internal or bureaucratic 'law' were well developed, involving detailed codes of practice and discipline, while the lack of job security according to formal law contrasted with a high degree of job security in practice. The law of 'Crown service' is more evocative of Empire and military adventure. In the seminal case of *Dunn v R*,[20] a consular agent in Nigeria claimed damages on the basis that he had been prematurely dismissed. The Crown successfully argued that:

> Servants of the Crown hold office only during the pleasure of the Crown, except in cases where it is otherwise provided by statute . . . The action of a civil servant of the Crown might, if he could not be dismissed, in some cases bring about a war. A contract to employ a servant of the Crown for a fixed period would be against the public interest and unconstitutional. It is not competent for the Crown to tie its hands by such a contract.

The case exemplifies the executive demand for freedom of action. It is authority for the prerogative power to dismiss at will, standing foursquare with *The Amphitrite*. It also spawned the view that Crown servants did not have a contract of service as such, on the basis that the mutuality of obligation necessary for a contract was lacking.[1] A difficult body of case law developed, concerning such matters as remuneration and whether a Crown servant had the right to recover arrears of pay.[2] Ultimately, it was employment legislation in the 1960s and 1970s which gave significant legal protection, as in the right not to be unfairly dismissed, generally enforceable through industrial tribunals rather than through the ordinary courts.[3]

---

17  See, for an overview of employment law in the public sector, S. Fredman and G. Morris, *The State as Employer* (London: Mansell) 1989.
18  As in such matters as appraisal and performance-related pay, and local bargaining. See, for discussion, M. Freedland, 'Contracting the Employment of Civil Servants – a Transparent Exercise?' [1995] PL 224.
19  Wade and Forsyth, p. 69.
20  [1896] 1 QB 116. See also *Dunn v Macdonald* [1897] 1 QB 401.
 1  *Mulvenna v Admiralty* 1926 SC 842. But see *Reilly v R* [1934] AC 176 per Lord Atkin.
 2  *Lucas v Lucas* [1943] P 68; *Kodeeswaran v A-G of Ceylon* [1970] AC 1111.
 3  Civil servants were also given the benefit of the Equal Pay Act 1970 and the Sex Discrimination Act 1975. See now the Employment Rights Act 1996.

The issue of contract would resurface in the 1980s in paradoxical fashion. The *GCHQ* case[4] having established that the exercise of prerogative powers over civil servants was justiciable, the Crown looked vulnerable to challenges from its staff via judicial review. Further, this route of challenge suggested certain advantages: the remedy of certiorari to quash a decision in cases of dismissal; the requirements of natural justice, more readily implied in judicial review than in civil proceedings.[5] But as the existence of a contract operates to restrict the availability of judicial review,[6] the Crown lawyers now had the incentive to reverse their traditional stance and plead a contract; precisely this happened in *R v Civil Service Appeal Board, ex p Bruce*.[7] The court responded by saying that there was nothing unconstitutional about civil servants being employed by the Crown under a contract: the issue was whether there was intention to create legal relations. The extra mile was soon travelled.

## *R v Lord Chancellor's Department, ex p Nangle*[8]

A complaint was made of sexual harassment against a civil servant; following an investigation he was transferred to another department and denied a salary increment. Confronted by the argument that, because he had a contract, he could not challenge the fairness of the procedures by way of judicial review, he not unnaturally invoked para. 14 of the Civil Service Code: 'for the most part, the relationship between the civil servant and the Crown remains one regulated under the prerogative and based on personal appointment. As such, a civil servant does not have a contract of employment enforceable in the Courts . . .'

> *Stuart-Smith LJ*: Is the applicant employed by the Crown under a contract of service? If he is it is accepted . . . that he has no remedy in public law, the case being indistinguishable from *R v East Berkshire Area Health Authority ex p Walsh*[9] . . . The point at issue is whether there was . . . an intention to enter into legal relations. It is . . . common ground that the Crown can enter into a contract of employment with its servants: . . . *R v Civil Service Appeal Board, ex p Bruce*[10] . . .
>
> The Lord Chancellor's Department's Staff Handbook runs to some 162 paragraphs. After a brief introduction there are three main heads: 'Conduct and Discipline', 'Career' and 'Conditions of Service'. Many of these terms and conditions are of a similar nature to those that might be found in any contract of employment . . .
>
> The question whether there is an intention to create legal relations is to be ascertained objectively . . . It is possible for a party to believe mistakenly that he is contractually bound to another when in fact he is not, and conversely to believe that he is not when he is . . . In our judgment [para. 14] is merely descriptive of what was believed to be the position . . . the relationship of employer and employee, master and

4   Above, p. 113.
5   See, for discussion, S. Fredman and G. Morris, 'Public or Private? State Employees and Judicial Review' (1991) 107 LOR 298.
6   Below, p. 240. See in the employment context, *R v East Berkshire Health Authority, ex p Walsh* [1985] QB 152.
7   [1988] 3 All ER 686. The point was not taken on appeal: [1989] 2 All ER 907.
8   [1992] 1 All ER 897.
9   [1985] QB 152.
10  [1988] 3 All ER 686.

servant, which plainly exists here, must of its very nature be one that involves an intention to create legal relations, unless such intention is clearly excluded either expressly or by necessary implication . . . In our judgment, read in its proper context para. 14 does not have this effect.

Alternatively, the matter was held to be merely an exercise of internal discipline, such as might occur in the case of any large employer, with 'no element of public law'[11] which could give rise to any entitlement to judicial review remedies. The policy of judicial abstentionism in 'staff cases' is made evident.

So it was no longer a constitutional quantum leap when in 1996 a revamped 'senior civil service' was explicitly contracted on individual terms and conditions (Chapter 5). Yet is there, as Freedland suggests,[12] still a sense of equivocation as between the general law and practice of contracts of employment on the one hand, and, on the other, the old peculiarities of the Civil Service employment relationship? Although much criticised, there is a line of authority for the proposition that the power to dismiss at will cannot be excluded by contract.[13] Following protracted negotiations,[14] the government explained its position on the new contracts in the traditional format of a message to staff. Effectively, the decision was made both to stand on the line of authority and to underwrite administrative practice to the contrary effect. The government 'has gone as far as it can, given the legal position relating to its power under the Prerogative, to dismiss at will, to ensure that, in practice, civil servants are in no worse a position than employees in the private sector'. Have the Crown lawyers done the trick? Or are there circumstances in which judicial review would lie, based on legitimate expectation?

> The Crown cannot exclude or fetter its power under the Prerogative to dismiss at will by contract and cannot therefore enter into a contractual obligation, or otherwise bind itself, to give notice of termination. Generally, in practice, however, the Crown does not rely on its power to dismiss at will but gives notice of termination of employment, or where it does not give notice, pays an amount equivalent to pay in lieu of notice. The primary exception to this is where the grounds for dismissal will justify, under common law, summary dismissal (for example for gross misconduct). The Government has no intention of altering that practice in future.
>
> The statements of intention made above do not and cannot amount to a waiver or restriction of the Crown's power to dismiss at will or impose any obligation on it to give notice. However, to remove any doubt about, and to reinforce, its existing practice relating to the giving of notice of termination, the Government has agreed to do two things:
> (a) It has amended the Civil Service Management Code to make clear the notice periods that would in practice normally be given. These notice periods are set out

---

11  See further *R v East Berkshire Health Authority, ex p Walsh* [1985] QB 152; *R v Secretary of State for the HomeDepartment, ex p Benwell* [1985] QB 554; *McLaren v Home Office* [1990] ICR 824.

12  M. Freedland (1995) PL 224 at 227.

13  See in particular *Rodwell v Thomas* [1944] KB 596 and *Riordan v War Office* [1959] 1 WLR 1046.

14  Quoted in Association of First Division Civil Servants, *Advice to Members on the Government's Revised Pay and Contract Arrangements for the Senior Civil Service* (May 1996).

in . . . the [individual] contract which provides that notice of termination will in practice normally be given except when the contract is terminated by agreement, or on grounds which would justify summary dismissal at common law, or where summary dismissal follows disciplinary proceedings.

(b) It has included in the contract a legally enforceable obligation that, if it does not give the notice it states in the contract of employment would normally be given in practice, it will make a payment for sum equal to, or equivalent to, the remuneration that would have been paid if such notice had been given. A scheme to this effect has been made under the Superannuation Act 1972 . . .[15]

## 5. Procurement and outsourcing: central government

Central government procurement is a key element of the functioning economy. According to recent estimates, the annual expenditure is nearly £40 billion.[16] Spending has increased significantly in the last few years as a proportion of all government spending, with the popularity of outsourcing. Traditionally, the judicial exercise of control has been weak, there being a distinct preference for alternative dispute resolution, much less disruptive of the continuing relationships between the government and its contractors. EC law is only slowly making inroads.

### (a) Networks and policy

The Treasury has responsibility as lead department, with implementation entrusted to the Central Unit on Procurement (CUP) which was established in 1985 to help and advise departments to obtain value for money and to monitor their progress.[17] Procurement strategies are now common in individual departments and each will have a Head of Procurement (a number of them recruited from the private sector). In recent years, the administrative guidance issued by the CUP has become voluminous, coming on top of a substantial body of principles and procedures which had evolved over many years, distilled and promulgated by the Treasury.[18] High priority has been given by the Unit to facilitating information-sharing and collaboration between departments: the dissemination of experience and best practice.

Value for money has always been a principal objective in procurement. Predictably, however, it was given increased emphasis under the Conservatives. *Setting New Standards*, a White Paper issued in 1995, crystallised the policy. Best

---

15  Above, p. 182.
16  Excluding some £20bn spent annually within the NHS internal market. *Setting New Standards: A Strategy for Public Procurement* (1995) Cm. 2840, p. 2.
17  Following the Government Purchasing Initiative, *Government Purchasing: A Multidepartment Review of Government Contract and Procurement Procedures: Report to the Prime Minister* (London: HMSO) 1984.
18  See C. Turpin, *Government Procurement and Contracts* (Harlow: Longman) 1989, Ch. 3. The relevance for administrative law may be gleaned from some CUP titles: *Model Forms of Contract*, 1990; *Specification Writing*, 1991; *Quality Assurance*, 1994; and *Disputes Resolution*, 1995.

value for money was defined as 'the optimum combination of whole life cost and quality, to meet the customer's requirement', and not merely as the lowest price.[19] The Paper demonstrated the close links between procurement strategy and the concerns of NPM:[20]

> The government's strategy for procurement is to achieve continuing improvement in value for money . . . and to enhance the competitiveness of suppliers, through the development of world class professional procurement systems and practices. The strategy forms part of the government's continuing quest for efficiency and effectiveness set out in the White Paper 'The Civil Service: Continuity and Change'. Top management in departments will be responsible for its delivery.
>
> Key elements in the strategy are:
> * Best practice procurement will be a central element in departments' business at all management levels. Departments will seek to match the cost savings achieved by best practice private and public sector organisations and will collaborate to achieve best value for money . . .
> * Departments will be intelligent customers with well defined objectives and requirements.
> * The emphasis will be on integrated procurement processes, covering the whole cycle of acquisition and use from start to finish, to ensure quality and economy over time, not short term lowest price . . .
> * Training and skill development will be enhanced to produce world class professional procurement staff . . .
> * Relationships with suppliers will combine competition with cooperation. Contracts with suppliers will be designed wherever practicable to promote continuous improvement and benefit sharing.

Competitive tendering has long been the dominant method of procurement, and is now seen both at home and in the EC as part of a more commercial approach to purchasing. In true Citizen's Charter fashion, the White Paper incorporated a statement of good customer practice. Note the deliberate distancing from the courts of law:[1]

> Government departments . . . will do their best in all dealings with suppliers and potential suppliers:
> * To preserve the highest standards of honesty, integrity, impartiality and objectivity;
> * To be fair, efficient, firm and courteous; . . .
> * To manage the bidding process so as to avoid/minimise the burdens on suppliers, while preserving genuine competition and avoiding discrimination;
> * To make available the broad criteria intended for the evaluation of bids, to evaluate bids objectively, and to notify the outcome promptly;
> * Within the bounds of commercial confidentiality, to debrief winners and losers on request on the outcome of the bidding process and the reasons for not being selected to bid or losing, so as to facilitate better performance on future occasions;
> * To achieve the highest professional standards in the management of contracts;

---

19 *Setting New Standards: A Strategy for Government Procurement* (1995) Cm. 2840, p. 6. 'Whole life cost' takes into account all aspects of cost over time, including capital, maintenance, management and operating costs.
20 Ibid, p. 1.
 1 Ibid, p. 41.

- To respond promptly, courteously and efficiently, to suggestions, enquiries and complaints . . .

Individual departments may elaborate these principles in fuller statements of their relationships with suppliers . . . Procurement, both in the bidding and in respect of any contract which may be entered into, involves rights and obligations which are enforceable in law. The present statement is not intended to create further such rights and obligations: it is a statement of good practice.

The reference in the Paper to combining competition with co-operation discloses an enduring tension in procurement policy between, on the one hand, a distanced or arm's length relationship of government and contractor, and, on the other, a long-term, facilitative, and interdependent one. In a classic study, Turpin argued that:[2]

> The aims and principles of government procurement require a middle way between a detached, impersonal conduct of business and an almost symbiotic relationship. The Ministry of Defence has described the relationship between the Ministry and industry in terms of 'a general background of mutual interest and close co-operation – tempered by hard bargaining and an arms' length approach to the negotiation of individual contracts.' . . .
>
> It is important to remember the basic difference between procurement by government and procurement by the private sector. A private sector firm is generally selling its own products or services in competition with others. Its purchasing officers are impelled to seek value for money and in effect transmit to its suppliers the market pressures operating on the firm they work for. Government, by contrast, is almost always purchasing as a final buyer . . . In government, good procurement is essentially a product of skill and sound management in the purchasing organisation, not a response to market forces.

The development of professional training and skills was given special emphasis in the White Paper. It fits an attempt to move beyond bureaucratic procedures, hierarchical and rule-based, to private sector analogues, commonly associated with professional purchaser discretion. Further, the strategy has been read as:[3]

> [Indicating] clearly that the way forward for obtaining value for money in government procurement is not seen in further legal regulation. In fact, whilst legal regulation may be appropriate as a first step to reform for states with an undeveloped procurement system, and which lack trained and experienced personnel, it seems likely that to achieve value for money internally a move away from legal and bureaucratic controls is generally appropriate for a more advanced system.

It is important to keep this argument in mind when reading about the EC procurement rules, which limit flexibility at national level.

---

2   Turpin, *Government Procurement and* Contracts (above, note 18) pp. 70–71.
3   S. Arrowsmith, *The Law of Public and Utilities Procurement* (London: Sweet and Maxwell) 1996, pp. 4–5.

## (b) A procurement community

Features such as a continuous flow of information, shared understandings, and migration of personnel between purchasing departments and their major suppliers, led Turpin to introduce the concept of a 'procurement community'.[4] Developments under the Conservatives show, first, efforts being made through market liberalisation to break down barriers to entry to the community; and, second, in the rise of outsourcing, new links being forged and the community occupying new ground.

The concept is useful in explicating the national tradition of non-legal control of procurement. Enough has been said to identify a highly developed system of internal or bureaucratic 'law': a classic example of executive self-regulation. External control has largely been the province of Parliament – not always effective – and of audit (Chapter 5). Turpin drew attention to the community ethos in favour of alternative dispute resolution: negotiation, agreement, or if necessary arbitration. The non-development in England of a special legal regime of government contracts can be partially attributed to a dearth of litigation.

There is in the procurement community a strong sense of corporatism. For example, the Review Board for Government Contracts was set up in 1968 to deal with the problem of pricing non-competitive (highly specialised) contracts in defence procurement. The Board has operated as rule-maker, establishing acceptable rates of return on capital; as complaints handler, on behalf of the industry; and as adjudicator of disputes. It epitomises the consensual and informal character of arrangements, being established not by statute or regulations, but by agreement between the government and the CBI; further, the operation of the system has depended upon the inclusion of a condition to this effect in individual contracts.

## (c) Standard terms

The 'law of the contract' brings to mind the informal rule-making procedures met in the last chapter. Thus, the use of standard terms epitomises the idea of contract as a source of rules. It also fits the concept of a procurement community, providing for tried and tested solutions and shared understandings, and for flexibility through review and adaptation in consultation with contractors' organisations. Turpin explains:[5]

> The 'law' created by the agreement of the parties is 'subordinate' law, in that the conditions for its creation are regulated by the general law of the land; and it is 'particular' law, applicable only to the parties who have by their contract brought it into existence. It is in operation as law only during the continuance of the contract. In government contracting, however, there are many basic terms that are not freshly devised for each contract, but are supplied from sets of standard conditions adopted by government departments for regular use. In this case, the 'rules' applicable to each contract have a continuing existence in the government's standard conditions. It is only

4    *Government Procurement and Contracts* (above, note 18).
5    Ibid, pp. 105–106.

by their incorporation in each individual contract that they take effect as law for the parties, but the standard conditions have a quasi-obligatory character with respect to all relevant contracts in so far as government contracts staff are directed to incorporate them.

The main standard forms provide a framework for the detail of individual specification, comprising a set of model conditions selectively included in particular contracts. Reference has been made to variation and termination clauses incorporating public interest considerations and flexible remedies; other important provisions designed to combat excessive profits deal with equality of information and post-costing. To emphasise, it is 'contract technology' which has taken the place of special principles of law.[6]

## 6.  Competitive tendering: contract and judicial review

Let us expand the argument. Judicial review is weak in the very area – contract – where administrative development has been strong. The conceptual framework of the common law, that government contracts are subject to general private law doctrines, facilitates the use of informal administrative or negotiated rules. A public law system would supervise and monitor such arrangements; here the result has been judicial reluctance to apply to the contract function judicial review principles which apply to other government activities. The inhibition is connected with the consensual basis of contract and freedom of contract.[7]

The case for legal protection of the public interest is compelling. First, there is the ideal of fair access to the benefits of the government market, as expressed in principles of equal treatment and open competition. Second, the existence of corporatist arrangements or informal networks only fuels the argument for firm rules against bad faith and improper influence. A different argument for judicial review stems from the use of contract as a tool for regulating behaviour: why should this method but not others be exempt from jurisdiction?

This is not, however, a convincing case for judicial review simply because of the public status of a body: an institutional test. It is not immediately obvious either that, in ordinary commercial contracts like leases, corporate interests dealing with public bodies should have greater protection than any other contracting parties, or that, when operating in competition with private enterprise, public bodies should be subject to additional constraints. It is important to bear in mind also the practical problems of expense, delay and potential hardship to a successful bidder associated with legal action.[8] A suitable alternative would be the Ombudsman system; however, 'action taken in matters relating to contractual or other commercial transactions' is specifically excluded from investigation by the

---

6    Street argued many years ago for a Government Contracts Act, on the basis that standard terms should be 'legislative' in form as they are in effect: H. Street, *Government Liability* (Cambridge: Cambridge University Press) 1953, pp. 104–105.

7    See P. Cane, *An Introduction to Administrative Law* (Oxford: Clarendon) 3rd edn, 1996 (hereafter Cane, *Introduction*) pp. 257–260.

8    See, in the context of company takeovers, *R v Panel on Take-overs and Mergers, ex p Datafin*. Below, p. 344.

Parliamentary Commissioner[9] and a similar restriction applies in the case of the Local Government Ombudsman. The justification given is that Ombudsmen are concerned with the relations between government and governed, and should be excluded from activities like outsourcing in which public bodies are not acting in a distinctively governmental fashion.[10]

There has in the last few years been some movement away from the old assumption that decisions relating to procurement are not reviewable. It is most clearly marked in a system of local government increasingly restrained and limited by statute. In the *Lewisham* case,[11] a challenge to a decision not to deal with a company was successfully made on the basis of irrelevant considerations. In *R v London Borough of Enfield, ex p T F Unwin (Roydon) Ltd*[12] decisions to remove a firm from the council's list of contractors and to prevent it from tendering for renewal of an existing contract were held subject to the requirements of procedural fairness. In neither case did the court stop to consider whether there was an 'element of public law' to the contractual decisions, a functional test commonly associated with limitations on, or reluctance to exercise, the supervisory jurisdiction.[13]

However, the decision in *R v Lord Chancellor's Department, ex p Hibbit and Saunders* stands foursquare against treating contractual powers in the same way as other governmental powers for the purpose of judicial review. It is illustrative also of the conceptual difficulty which arises when a 'public law' oriented jurisdiction is faced by an administrative system increasingly premised on private law techniques. Thus *Hibbit* is one of many cases, some already highlighted, others to come, in which the court has been asked, and has attempted, to set the boundaries of judicial review, at a time and in a context where the boundary lines of public and private spheres of organisation are fast being overridden. The dispute involved the proper ambit of post-tender negotiations, a major issue in the design of procurement procedures pitting administrative pressures for flexibility and value for money against concerns of a level playing field and equal treatment.

## *R v Lord Chancellor's Department, ex p Hibbit and Saunders*[14]

Tenders for court reporting services were invited by the Lord Chancellor's Department (LCD), which then entered into discussions with the four lowest price bidders, inviting them to submit new, lower bids on the basis of which the

9 Parliamentary Commissioner Act 1967, Sch. 3, para. 9; Local Government Act 1974, Sch. 5, para. 3.
10 See *Observations by the Government on the Select Committee Review of Access and Jurisdiction*, Cmnd. 7449, 1979.
11 *R v Lewisham London Borough Council, ex p Shell UK Ltd* [1988] 1 All ER 938; below, p. 245.
12 [1989] COD 466. Previously, in *R v Hereford Corpn, ex p Harrower* [1970] 1 WLR 1424, the applicant was held entitled to force the council to adhere to its own Standing Orders regulating procurement. The Local Government Act 1972, s. 35, which requires that competitive procedures be provided for in this manner, is an early example of legislative intervention in procurement.
13 *R v East Berkshire Health Authority, ex p Walsh* [1985] 1 QB 152; *R v Lord Chancellor's Department, ex p Hibbit and Saunders* [1993] COD 326. Not that the 'public law' element found is always obvious: see e.g., *R v Barnsley Metropolitan Borough Council, ex p Hook* [1976] 1 WLR 1052; *R v Wear Valley District Council, ex p Binks* [1985] 2 All ER 699.
14 [1993] COD 326. See below.

contract was awarded. The incumbent firm, which was not one of those invited to tender again, cried foul. A statement in the contract documents that the Department reserved the right 'to enter into discussions with any tenderer to clarify the submitted bid' was said to create a legitimate expectation that discussions would only be conducted for the purpose of clarification, thus ruling out a second round of bidding. The firm had also complied with a specification relating to staff which, without telling it, the LCD had waived: the firm claimed that, in consequence, it had submitted a less competitive bid than would otherwise have been the case. The court accepted the substantive argument. 'Clarify' meant 'to make clear'; it did not mean 'increase or reduce'. The breach of legitimate expectation was 'unfair' and caused 'prejudice'. But the court dismissed the challenge for lack of jurisdiction:

> *Rose LJ*: The crucial question is whether [the unfair treatment] entitles them to judicial review. Three matters are common ground. First that the Lord Chancellor is susceptible to judicial review. Secondly, that that susceptibility exists only in relation to those of his decisions which are either in some way statutorily underpinned or involve some other sufficient public law element as to which there is no universal test . . . Thirdly, that the test to be applied is, in the words of Woolf LJ in *ex parte Noble*:[15]

>> 'To look at the subject-matter of the decision which it is suggested should be subject to judicial review and by looking at that subject-matter then come to a decision as to whether judicial review is appropriate.' . . .

> Mr. Pannick [for the applicants] submitted that . . . as the applicants are only one of many unsuccessful bidders, the decision challenged is of a general nature reflecting the policy or practice of the department in conducting a tendering exercise . . . It seems to me that . . . the absence of any alternative remedy, like the presence of an alternative remedy in private law, is immaterial to the question of whether a public law remedy exists . . . It is correct that the decision challenged affects many others, apart from the applicants, though the same can be said of any large tendering exercise by any government department or local authority. The fact that a commercial function is being performed does not take the case outside the ambit of public law . . . But in my judgment it is not appropriate to equate tendering conditions attendant on a common law right to contract with a statement of policy or practice or policy decisions in the spheres of Inland Revenue, immigration and the like, control of which is the especial province of the State and where, in consequence, a sufficient public law element is apparent . . . It follows that . . . it is impossible, in my opinion, to give them the relief they claim by way of judicial review. The decision challenged lacked a sufficient public law element to found such relief.

> *Waller J*: It is not sufficient in order to create a public law obligation simply to say that the Lord Chancellor's Department is a governmental body carrying out governmental functions and appointing persons to public office. If a governmental body carrying out its governmental functions enters into a contract with a third party . . . the obligations that it owes will be under that contract unless there also exists some other element that gives rise in addition to a public law obligation . . .

---

15   *R v Derbyshire County Council, ex p Noble* [1990] ICR 808.

There cannot be any justification . . . for distinguishing between pre-contractual negotiations and the contracts themselves. A governmental body is free to negotiate contracts, and it would need something additional to the simple fact that the governmental body was negotiating the contract to impose on that authority any public law obligation in addition to any private law obligations or duties there might be . . .

The fact that the decision sought to be reviewed is the placing of a contract with a particular firm seems to me to add force to the contention that there is unlikely to be any public law element in that decision. It would be extremely unsatisfactory to set aside the decision to make a contract, but leave the contract unaffected. The likelihood must be that, if that is to be the result, the decision itself does not have any public law element within it.

Private law may, however, be capable of finding a remedy through the medium of implied contract. This avenue was explored in *Blackpool and Fylde Aero Club Ltd v Blackpool Borough Council*,[16] which involved bids for a local authority concession. It was held to be a breach of an implied contract, whereby a party bidding before the deadline had a right to have that bid considered, when the plaintiff's bid was mistakenly treated as late and excluded from the competition. The fact that the purchaser was a public body was treated by the court as a relevant factor in finding the contract. This highlights a potential in administrative law for stretching private law doctrines; in effect, a blending of public and private law. We shall return to this point in the next chapter. There is, however, a practical limitation on securing an element of procedural fairness by way of implied contract. It is vulnerable to pre-emptive action by the use of exclusion clauses: judicial review is not.

Surely the pressures will increase for a reworking of the conceptual limitation on judicial review? The role of the common law principles is naturally bound up with the juridification of procurement stemming from domestic and EC policies expressed in detailed statutory codes. Heightened litigiousness, as well as the increased resort to contractual techniques in government, work to fuel the development whenever gaps in the codes appear. In the recent case of *R v Legal Aid Board, ex p Donn & Co*[17] it was held that the decision-making procedure of a Legal Aid Committee in awarding a contract to represent plaintiffs was amenable to judicial review. The 'public dimensions' of the matter took it outside the realm of a commercial function. The case indicates the probable incremental development of judicial review in this area.

## 7. Collateral purpose: contract compliance

Procurement and outsourcing point to the potential of the *dominium* power of government, the deployment of wealth in aid of policy objectives, in contrast to *imperium* or the command of law (Chapter 3). Use of the techniques of 'contract compliance' or 'regulation by contract' (above, p. 208) raises concerns about legal control and accountability. Conversely, its suppression under the

16  [1990] 3 All ER 25.
17  [1996] 3 All ER 1.

Conservatives is a fine example of imperium in the service of market ideology.[18] Later, we see a similar development at EC level.

'The new prerogative' was the term used by Daintith to describe the workings of incomes policy under the minority Labour government in the 1970s.[19] Private employers seeking to win government contracts had to undertake to comply with the policy, and, if successful, had to accept compliance as a legally enforceable term. Companies in breach of the policy found themselves on a government 'blacklist'. The tactic was not authorised by statute, in which case it must have been legal, but promulgated through a White Paper. The usage epitomises the rise in this period of 'the corporate state' discussed in Chapter 1. It also points forward to later concerns with contract as a source of rules. Thus, Daintith wrote:[1]

> In the traditional conception of contract, the legal obligations imposed are individualised by reference to [the] particular [joint] objectives. With the widespread adoption, in ordinary commerce, of the standard form contract, the distinction between the consensual, individualised contract and the imposed, general regulation is already blurred. Government contracting shares fully in this movement but also, [in this kind of example], goes far beyond it. For it incorporates, into standard terms and allocation procedures, clauses and requirements reflecting public interest which by their breadth and importance pass far beyond the mutual objectives of the contracting parties and which, therefore, might normally be promoted by statutory regulation. This is why [I refer] to prerogative: government has discovered means of using its increasing economic strength vis-à-vis private industry so as to promote certain policies in the style, and with results, which for a long time we have assumed must be the hallmark of parliamentary legislation: that is to say, officially promulgated rules backed by effective general compulsion. This means the power to rule without parliamentary consent, which is the hallmark of prerogative.

It had been commonly assumed that the Crown was free to take advantage of the general capacity to contract for this kind of purpose. In Ganz's words,[2] 'No question of legality can arise. The government is subject to no greater legal restraints in placing its contracts than the individual . . .' The position would probably be different today, despite the courts' reluctance to allow contract rules to be diluted by judicial review. First, this is the paradigm case for showing that the choice of contract as the tool for regulating behaviour ought not to exclude judicial review; if the tools of imperium were used, judicial review would be available. Second, a 'blacklisted' company would not have broken the law and by analogy with the *Wheeler* case[3] should have some protection for its rights.

---

18  There have in addition been significant changes in central government practice, most notably the abandonment in 1983 of the Fair Wages Resolution, first promulgated by the House of Commons in 1891 and affording to workers engaged on government contract work a modicum of protection. See O. Kahn-Freund's classic, 'Legislation Through Adjudication: The Legal Aspects of Fair Wages Clauses and Recognised Conditions' (1948) 11 MLR 274.

19  T. Daintith, 'Regulation by Contract: The New Prerogative' (1979) 32 Current Legal Problems 41.

1  Ibid, pp. 41–42.

2  G. Ganz, 'Comment' [1978] PL 333 at 338. See further, R. Ferguson and A. Page, 'Pay Restraint: The Legal Constraints' (1978) 128 NLJ 515.

3  Above, p. 117.

*Imperium versus dominium*

Contract compliance is a viable alternative to criminal sanctions or individual complaint and adjudication as a way of regulating behaviour. Its proactive, or fire-watching, qualities are valuable, as also the scope for flexibility or negotiated compliance. It is commonly associated with social concerns such as race or sex discrimination; it has emerged in the US as a distinctive technique of administrative action, and it has also been sanctioned by statute in the case of Northern Ireland.[4] Such strategies raise basic political and ideological questions: social engineering – however beneficial – versus the central value for money principle of NPM. And is it legitimate to target only one group in society: those who contract with government?

In the 1980s many councils, led by the Greater London Council, went down the route of contract compliance to enforce equal opportunities. Special compliance units developed to monitor and advise contractors, with the ultimate sanction of termination of contract or disbarment from tendering. Some councils refused to contract with firms which had business dealings in South Africa or connections with the nuclear industry.[5] The practice was eventually challenged by the United Kingdom subsidiary of a powerful multinational with other subsidiaries operating in South Africa.

*R v Lewisham London Borough Council, ex p Shell UK Ltd*[6]

Lewisham had a policy of not purchasing Shell products whenever equivalent ones were available on reasonable terms. It also set about persuading other councils to follow suit. Lewisham sought to justify the boycott on the basis of its duty under s. 71 of the Race Relations Act 1976 to promote good race relations within the borough. The court, however, focused on the pressure put on Shell to end trading links and held that there was an improper purpose. Note the close parallel with the *Wheeler* case:[7]

> *Neill LJ*: I [must] consider what principles of law should be applied if it can be shown that the statutory powers of the council were exercised for more than one reason or purpose. On this point the law seems to be clear . . . Where the two reasons or purposes cannot be disentangled and one of them is bad or where, even though the reasons or purposes can be disentangled, the bad reason or purpose demonstrably exerted a substantial influence on the relevant decision the court can interfere to quash the decision . . .

4   Fair Employment (Northern Ireland) Act 1989. See for general discussion, J. Carr, *New Roads to Equality: Contract Compliance for the United Kingdom* (London: Fabian Society) 1987, No. 517; P. Morris, 'Legal Regulation of Contract Compliance: An Anglo-American Comparison' (1990) 19 Anglo-American LR 87.
5   See, for details, Institute of Personnel Management, *Contract Compliance: The United Kingdom Experience* (London) 1987; also Inner London Education Authority Contract Compliance Equal Opportunities Unit, *Contract Compliance: A Brief History* (London) 1990.
6   [1988] 1 All ER 938.
7   Ibid, pp. 951–952.

The purpose of the decision . . . was not merely to satisfy public opinion in the borough or to promote good race relations in the borough, but was in order to put pressure on Shell UK . . . to procure a withdrawal of the Shell Group from South Africa. Furthermore, as I see it, the wish to achieve this purpose exerted a very substantial influence on the decision . . .

It is to be remembered that . . . Shell UK . . . was [not] acting in any way unlawfully . . . The council, and indeed a great many other people, may strongly disagree with the policy adopted by the Shell Group . . . but I find it impossible in the light of the authorities to escape from the conclusion that by seeking to bring pressure on Shell UK to change the Shell policy towards South Africa, the council was acting unfairly and in a manner which requires the court to intervene . . .

The wish to change the Shell policy towards South Africa was inextricably mixed up with any wish to improve race relations in the borough and this extraneous and impermissible purpose has the effect of vitiating the decision as a whole.

One reading of *Shell* would be that the use of procurement power is still permissible in support of policies which are a council's legal responsibility, as distinct from national policies like foreign affairs. In contrast, a strict reading renders *all* collateral or secondary considerations irrelevant, subject of course to statute such as the Race Relations Act. It is just this approach which the Thatcher government chose to assert by legislation. The relevant provisions of the Local Government Act 1988 were designed to cover all types of procurement contract, regardless of their financial value. Section 17 required local authorities to disregard 'matters which are non-commercial matters for the purposes of this section':

17(5) (a) The terms and conditions of employment by contractors of their workers or the composition of . . . their workforces . . . (c) any involvement of the business activities or interests of contractors with irrelevant fields of government policy . . . (d) The conduct of contractors or workers in industrial disputes . . . (e) The country or territory of origin of supplies to, or the location in any country or territory of the business activities or interests of, contractors . . . (f) Any political, industrial or sectarian affiliations or interests of contractors . . .

17(7) Where any matter referable to a contractor would . . . be a non-commercial matter in relation to him, the corresponding matter referable to — (a) a supplier or customer of the contractor; (b) a sub-contractor of the contractor or his supplier or customer; (c) an associated body of the contractor or his supplier or customers; . . . is also, in relation to the contractor, a non-commercial matter for the purposes of this section.

17(8) In this section — . . . 'government policy' falls within 'irrelevant fields' . . . if it concerns matters of defence or foreign or Commonwealth policy . . .

This is a good example of the authoritarian provisions which have been a feature of local government legislation in recent years. A council's discretion is so closely confined that commercial considerations must prevail. Discretion is transferred to the Minister who can add to the list of prohibitions by statutory instrument (s. 19(1)). Standard administrative law techniques are used to buttress the controls. Reasons for decisions have to be provided (s. 20), and judicial review is made available to any potential contractor and to 'any body representing contractors' (s. 19(7)) – so facilitating test cases. In practice, this exercise of imperium power has nipped in the bud the use of contract compliance by local authorities.[8] We wait to see whether the Blair administration will be more flexible. The potential for contract compliance is in any case now stunted by developments at EC level.

## 8. Contract making: Europeanisation

EC law has in the course of a decade moved from the periphery to establish a central place in public procurement and outsourcing. Once more, the philosophy is one of market liberalisation. With this as the goal, national administrative law has been explicitly recast as the instrument of EC requirements. The rules effectively comprise a special Administrative Procedure Act, relevant factors and model forms being established for various stages in tendering a contract. Interesting for innovations in the realm of remedies, the regime also raises general questions about the efficacy and scale of the juridification of contract-making.

Public procurement was an obvious target for Community action in the drive to the Single Market. Of enormous economic significance, it had been dominated by local provision, with very low rates of import penetration.[9] Predictably, the Commission identified discrimination as an important factor, and its elimination a main priority.[10] Although there had been early attempts to tackle the issue, the relevant directives have lacked an effective enforcement mechanism and in practice had largely been ignored.[11] The programme of legislative reform which the Commission initiated in 1985 was designed to widen control by bringing in the utilities and to deepen it by strengthening existing requirements and establishing a new regime of sanctions. Different activities – works, supplies, services – were each made the subject of a specific directive. This received general underpinning from the Remedies or Compliance Directive.[12] 'Contracting authorities' were

8   See, for the leading case, *R v Islington London Borough Council, ex p Building Employers' Confederation* [1989] IRLR 382. There has been a tightly drawn exception in the case of race relations (s. 18).
9   In 1996 public procurement was said to represent 11% of EU Gross Domestic Product: Commission, *Public Procurement in the European Union: Exploring the Way Forward*, 1996. An earlier study indicated that whilst aggregate EC import penetration was 22% in the economy as a whole, the value of public contracts placed with non-national firms was 2% (4% in the UK): W. S. Atkins Management Consultants, *The Cost of Non-Europe in Public Procurement*, 1988 vol. 5A.
10  Commission White Paper, *Completing the Internal Market*, COM(85) 310. The entry into force in 1996 of the Government Procurement Agreement (GPA) of the World Trade Organisation underscores the potential here for globalisation. See G. de Graaf and M. King, 'Towards a More Global Government Procurement Market: The Expansion of the GATT Government Procurement Agreement in the Context of the Uruguay Round' (1995) 29 International Lawyer 435.
11  See Directive 71/305 (Works), Directive 77/62 (Supplies); and generally F. Weiss, *Public Procurement in European Community Law*, (London: Athlone Press) 1992. Certain Treaty articles, notably Art. 30 on free movement of goods, provided limited assistance: see e.g. Case 21/88: *Du Pont de Nemours Italiana Spa v Unita Sanitaria Locale No 2 di Corrara* [1990] ECR 1–889.
12  See Directives 93/37 (Works), 93/96 (Supplies), 92/50 (Services); 89/665 (Compliance). One very important exception to the regime is defence procurement: see, for details, S. Arrowsmith, *The Law of Public and Utilities Procurement* (London: Sweet and Maxwell) 1996, Ch. 17.

broadly defined to include central government, local government and quangos: thresholds were used to exempt minor contracts. Finally, the utilities were given their own, rather more flexible regime.[13]

### On the straight and narrow

The Commission has portrayed the EC Code as 'a complete system of directives that ensures clarity and competition in public procurement . . . Their purpose is . . . to align the procedures to be followed . . . by laying down a few rules generally regarded as being based on common sense.'[14] The design involves stress on the transparency of decision-making and the use of objective criteria specified in advance. Public purchasers are prescribed a path with a series of steps to follow, so confining and structuring their discretion. The regime rests on the familiar assumption that whenever there is broad administrative discretion arbitrariness or discrimination follows automatically.

Let us take as an example a proposed contract for public works.[15] There are requirements to advertise in the EC Official Journal and on the use of European technical specifications. One of three award procedures must be chosen: open procedure, all interested firms being allowed to tender; restricted procedure, tenders being invited from a list of firms drawn up by the authority; and negotiated procedure, the contractual terms being negotiated with chosen contractors, the use of which is strictly confined precisely because of the informality. Exclusion of firms from tendering is limited to certain designated criteria related to their standing and competence. Both the philosophy and procedural design are exemplified in the last crucial stage of awarding the contract. First, a commercial outlook is dictated: note the negative impact on contract compliance.[16] Second, rules are deployed in order to minimise the scope for abuse, and so that decisions can be more easily monitored:

> Criteria for the award of a public works contract.
> 20-1. Subject to paragraphs (6) and (7) below, a contracting authority shall award a public works contract on the basis of the offer which — (a) offers the lowest price or (b) is the most economically advantageous to the contracting authority.
> 2. The criteria which a contracting authority may use to determine that an offer is the most economically advantageous include price, period for completion, running costs, profitability and technical merit.
> 3. Where a contracting authority intends to award a public works contract on the basis of the offer which is the most economically advantageous it shall state the criteria

---

13  Directives 93/38 (Utilities), 92/13 (Utilities Remedies). See, for discussion, S. Arrowsmith, ibid, Ch. 9 and 10.

14  Commission, *Public Procurement in Europe: The Directives*, 1994, p. 3.

15  As stipulated by the Public Works Contracts Regulations, SI 1991/2680, as amended, one of a series of statutory instruments implementing the directives. See generally, Association of Metropolitan Authorities/Local Government Management Board, *Going Public in Europe: A Guide to the EC Public Procurement Directives* (London) 1995.

16  See further, S. Arrowsmith, 'Public Procurement as an Instrument of Policy and the Impact of Market Liberalisation' (1995) 111 LQR 235.

on which it intends to base its decision, where possible in descending order of importance, in the contract notice or in the contract documents.

4. Where a contracting authority awards a public works contract on the basis of the offer which is the most economically advantageous, it may take account of offers which offer variations on the requirements specified in the contract documents if the offer meets the minimum requirements of the contracting authority and it has indicated in the contract notice that offers offering variations will be considered . . .

5. A contracting authority may not reject a tender on the ground that the technical specifications in the tender have been defined by reference to European specifications . . .

6. If an offer for a public works contract is abnormally low the contracting authority may reject that offer but only if it has requested in writing an explanation of the offer [and has] taken any such explanation into account . . .

7. If a contracting authority which rejects an abnormally low offer is awarding the contract on the basis of the offer which offers the lowest price, it shall send a report justifying the rejection to the Treasury for onward transmission to the Commission.

A pathway model like this needs fencing. The principle of transparency is buttressed by a duty to give reasons and by information and record-keeping requirements. This helps the Commission to act through Art. 169 procedure, a standard EC enforcement remedy.[17] There are also special provisions on remedies in the Compliance Directive, which operates alongside the ordinary remedies of English law. Just like the famous cases of *Factortame* and *Francovich*,[18] they operate to erode the procedural autonomy of national law in order to establish the means for the vindication of EC rights.[19] Thus, the court has powers to make an interim order halting progress; to set aside a decision or amend any document; and to award damages to firms for breach of duty: once a contract is made, however, damages is the only available remedy. This regime places great reliance on private legal action to police it.

## *Efficacy: the limits of rules*

In a major review in 1996, the Commission had to concede a 'relatively limited' economic impact: public procurement in the Community has in fact continued to operate overwhelmingly along national lines.[20] Of general interest to administrative law is a series of difficulties with formal legal ordering demonstrated by the scheme.

---

17 See e.g. *Commission v Spain* Case C-24/91 [1992] ECR I–1989; *Commission v Belgium* Case C-87/94R [1994] ECR I–1395. In practice Commission action is limited by scarce resources. See further, J. Fernandez Martin, *The EC Procurement Rules* (Oxford: OUP) 1995.

18 Above, p. 60.

19 See S. Weatherill, 'Enforcing the Public Procurement Rules in the United Kingdom' in S. Arrowsmith (ed.), *Remedies for Enforcing the Public Procurement Rules. Public Procurement in the European Community*, vol. 4 (Winteringham: Earlsgate) 1993.

20 The share of imports in 1995 was 3% for direct cross-frontier business, and 7% for purchases made through importers or local subsidiaries: Commission, *Public Procurement in the European Union*, 1996, p. 5. The Commission considers that a period of stability in the framework is desirable and does not propose any fundamental changes. See, for a detailed assessment of the problems, J. Fernandez Martin, *The EC Procurement Rules* (above, note 17).

There is first the problem of the over-rigidity of rules (Chapter 6). Considerable compliance costs are imposed, which are hard to justify. Rather than improving the efficiency of purchasing, such a framework may inhibit efficient practices, the rise of more formal and compartmentalised relationships operating to undermine important values of co-operation and co-ordination between purchasers and providers. A second issue concerns transparency, a value too easily associated with government by contract (above, p. 209). At one level, practitioners rightly express concern about the readability of the legal framework.[1] So much for the Commission's few rules based on common sense! At another level, the regime fails to secure transparency in decision-making, despite the stress on this in the procedural design. Take the various criteria for the award of contract based on economic advantage (above, p. 248): there is ample scope for 'games with rules' and for 'boiler plate' reasons. This has been seen as an inherent limitation of legal regulation of procurement: it is, according to Arrowsmith,[2] 'probably impossible to stop purchasers who are determined to discriminate.' But it is also illustrative of the limitations of rules and of the irrepressible character of discretion as discussed by Goodin.[3] Finally, difficulties arise with the enforcement model of private legal action.[4] It is unrealistic to expect many tenderers to engage in formal conflict with prospective major customers. The remedy of damages, in effect a contribution to company costs, is an inadequate incentive. The courts are not well-equipped to assess relevant matters, as for example the relative economic advantage of competing bids. To emphasise, these various problems are associated with the juridification of contract making as an activity, and are simply magnified at EC level.

## 9. Conclusion

It is hard to exaggerate the scale and significance of the contractual revolution in government. Developments range from contracting-out to contracting employment, and from the rise of pseudo-contract to the formal legal ordering of procurement. The market ideology finds powerful expression in European legal requirements as well as at national level.

The argument for an analytically distinct law of government contract is difficult to sustain. Typically, the project has run into the buffers of the Diceyan principle of equality before the law; it may further be criticised for paying insufficient attention to the creative potential of 'contract technology' or 'the law of the contract'. Today it may be likened to chasing a receding bus. Forms of collective provision which increasingly involve mixes of public and private

---

1    E.g., R. Boyle, 'Regulated Procurement – A Purchaser's Perspective' (1995) 4 Public Procurement LR 105. Looking to the future, the Commission sees the development of electronic tendering playing a key role in increasing transparency and access to public procurement: Commission, *Public Procurement in the European Union*, 1996, Ch. 4.
2    S. Arrowsmith, *The Law of Public and Utilities Procurement* (London: Sweet and Maxwell) 1996, p. 73.
3    Above, pp. 106–107.
4    M. Bowsher, 'Prospects for Establishing an Effective Tender Challenge Regime: Enforcing Rights Under EC Procurement Law in English Courts' (1994) Public Procurement LR 30.

power undercut judicial attempts at differentiation. If the basic concern is about judicial supervision in the public interest weakening as government operates through private legal forms, then good reasons exist not only to hold the systems together but also to encourage the cross-fertilisation of public and private law principles. A distinct body of law is less useful in controlling mixed administrations than mixtures of law. Thus far, the courts have failed adequately to respond to the novel challenges presented by contract. Increased litigation generates pressure to develop the ambit of judicial review and to explore unfamiliar territory like the law of restitution. But a clear and consistent line on these matters has not yet been achieved.

Speaking more generally, the limitations of a court-centred approach (Chapter 2) are exposed in this area of administrative law. Once contract is approached as an activity or output function of government, the focus shifts naturally to 'contract technology', and to the statutory and administrative frameworks. The incorporation in these arrangements of public law values like openness, fairness, rationality and accountability is a pressing task – a theme developed in the next chapter. Again, alternative dispute resolution as in negotiation or arbitration is a key ingredient of contractual behaviour: unfortunately, however, the potential of other techniques like the Ombudsman remains unrealised in this area. Juridification, in the guise of proliferating complex legal forms as well as litigation, is beginning to present difficulties. We can see this in the formal procedure for contracts and its resulting paper chase. Contract is not a way to simplify but another route to over-regulation and complexity.

Chapter 9

# Government, contract and competition: two paradigms

The aim of this chapter is to look more closely at contracting as an activity of government. We have selected two types of regime of great importance in the rise of contract under the Conservatives: compulsory competitive tendering (CCT) and public franchising. CCT epitomises the use of *imperium* power against recalcitrant authorities, and further illuminates the problems of detailed legal ordering of the procedures for making contracts. It has entailed organisational and cultural changes in local government of the kind associated with 'the contract culture'. Public franchising demonstrates both the functional use of contract as a source of rules and serious deficiencies in the procedure and accountability of agencies, as in a lack of transparency. To emphasise, the use by government of private legal forms strengthens rather than weakens the case for arrangements protective of the public interest. The two regimes also illustrate another key element in the juridification of the administrative process: the exercise of legal skills in the administration or management of contracts for public services.

## 1. CCT: essential attributes

CCT represents a legal requirement to open up activities funded by the public purse to competition: in addition, that is, to a set of public procurement rules governing the tender process. Work typically undertaken 'in-house' is thus exposed to bids from private contractors, which may or may not be successful, though the legal framework can be so designed as to press authorities towards private provision. Councils have ended up having to satisfy two sets of requirements, CCT and the EC procurement rules. Legal paper has proliferated.

*Competing for Quality*, a major consultation paper issued in 1991, summarised the policy objectives. Consistent with the Conservatives' general programme, we might add to the list a reduction in the size of the public sector and in the power of trade unions:[1]

---

[1] Department of the Environment, *Competing for Quality. Competition in the Provision of Local Services: A Consultation Paper*, 1991, para. 1.4.

The reasons which led the Government to introduce and extend compulsory competitive tendering were significant public criticism of the performance and efficiency of in-house work forces and a belief that subjecting in-house provision of services to competition would expose the true cost of carrying out the work and lead to greater efficiency in the use of resources and, hence, to better value for money for local authorities and for the tax-payers who contributed to local authorities' finances.

In sharp contrast to central government, where policies of market testing[2] and outsourcing could be implemented through administrative direction, formal law or *imperium* was needed here, the councils being independent legal entities. The policy had huge potential, local government (and government in general) being traditionally more reliant on in-house provision than the private sector. Not surprisingly then, CCT evoked great hostility in local government circles: the legal regime has been characterised by dispute and distrust. The new Labour Government has pledged to replace CCT with a less prescriptive duty on local authorities to demonstrate 'best value' in the delivery of services.[3] We wait to see the impact on competitive tendering and contractual forms of administration.

## (a) Central control: purchaser and provider

The CCT regime has been highly centralised, with the Department playing a multi-functional role. Thus, the familiar administrative law elements of rule-making, monitoring, adjudication and enforcement have all been concentrated in the hands of the Minister, described as 'the guardian of the purity of the competition process'.[4] To emphasise, this executive model is far removed from the model of the 'independent regulator' and different tiers of regulation (Chapter 10). Inside the Department, the work has been the responsibility of one Division.[5] Note the close interplay between techniques of casework and the progressive development of rules: 'fire-fighting' and 'fire-watching' (below).

The purchaser/provider 'split' is of the essence of government by contract (Chapter 5). For the purposes of CCT, there is the additional complication of competition between public and private providers. The in-house units have had to be reconstituted as trading units: Direct Labour Organisations (DLOs) and Direct Service Organisations (DSOs). A battery of administrative and audit checks has been applied to them: at the centre, reports and accounts for each activity could be monitored, and powers prescribing a commercial rate of return exercised by the Minister. Again, councils have had to operate both as 'client'

2   Office of Public Service and Science, *The Government's Guide to Market Testing* (London: HMSO) 1993; P. Greer, *Transforming Central Government: The Next Steps Initiative* (Buckingham: Open University Press) 1994.

3   Hilary Armstrong, Minister for Local Government, HC Deb, vol. 295, col. 49 (WA) (2 June 1997).

4   K. Shaw, J. Fenwick and A. Foreman, 'Compulsory Competition for Local Government Services in the UK: A Case of Market Rhetoric and Camouflaged Centralism' (1995) 10(1) Public Policy and Admin. 63, 72.

5   Local Government Competition Division (LG3) of the Local Government Directorate of the Department of the Environment. In 1995-96 LG3 had some 40 staff. In Scotland and Wales responsibility for CCT has lain with the national departments in the usual way.

and 'contractor'. Internal trading would typically involve, on the one side, a lead department 'purchasing' for itself and for other departments, and, on the other, a multi-purpose DSO administering most or all of the services subject to competition.[6] As an authority cannot contract with itself, clearly this is a further example of pseudo-contract. The market in local services is actually a mix of real and pseudo-contract:   if a private firm bids successfully, the contract will be legally enforceable; not so for a DLO or DSO.

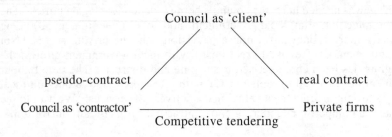

*(b) Turning the screw*

CCT has been introduced progressively. The first provisions contained in the Local Government, Planning and Land Act 1980 were intended to meet complaints from industry of unfair competition from in-house teams in construction and maintenance. Provisions in the Local Government Act 1988 were part of the government's more general drive towards market testing. A number of specified services – refuse collection, cleaning, catering, grounds maintenance and repair and maintenance of vehicles – were put out to competition. The Minister took power to add to the list by statutory instrument (s. 2):   white collar services such as finance, legal and personnel services, IT and housing management, were later included.[7] The Local Government Act 1992 strengthened ministerial control over practice and procedure (below). In 1995, the value of provision covered by the 1980 Act, the original activities under the 1988 Act, and the white-collar additions, was estimated at some £4 billion, £2.3 billion, and £6 billion respectively.[8]

Predictably, the technical problems increased as the net widened. According to the Audit Commission:[9]

---

6   K. Walsh and H. Davis, *Competition and Service: The Impact of the Local Government Act 1988* (London: HMSO) 1993, Ch. 2. There is a wide range of organisational arrangements: see DoE, *CCT and Local Authority Blue-Collar Services* (1997) chs. 12, 16–17.

7   Department of the Environment, *Competing for Quality in Housing:  Competition in the Provision of Local Authority Services* 1991.

8   Department of the Environment, *CCT and Local Government in England. Annual Report for 1995*, pp. 2-3.

9   Audit Commission, *Realising the Benefits of Competition* (London: HMSO) 1993, p. 3. See further, Audit Commission, *Preparing for Compulsory Competition*, Occasional Papers No. 7 (London: HMSO) 1989.

In some authorities, the 1980 legislation necessitated the setting up of contracting arrangements from scratch, but most were able to draw upon a long history of experience – defining the work to be carried out, finding appropriate contractors and making sure that work was carried out as required. This was the least difficult area to start contracting. The product is usually visible and readily defined. There are alternative suppliers in the private sector, with experience in working to such contracts . . .

The Local Government Act 1988 . . . broke new ground. For some of [the defined] activities, local authorities had little experience of working with contractors. Unlike the 1980 Act, the council had to specify services rather than visible products. There were few, if any, private companies with the experience or capacity to undertake some types of work . . . Even for activities such as building cleaning and catering, where a private sector market had existed for many years, the specialised requirements of local government were beyond the experience of many companies.

CCT for white-collar services magnified the issue. With activities like IT and legal and financial services, authorities have been permitted an 'excluded element' or percentage of the activity free from CCT, so allowing retention of, and proper training for, a core staff. But, typically, such exemptions could be cut back via statutory instrument. Precisely this happened in early 1997 following a consultation paper issued in the light of low levels of market penetration by private firms.[10] Ministers had concluded that the existing framework was 'not providing the challenging targets that were envisaged' and that changes were 'necessary to bring practice into line with the original policy intentions'. To emphasise, CCT was at the point of being applied with maximum effect when the Conservatives fell from power.

## 2. The character of instruction

Detailing the CCT regime is no easy task. First, the rules may be criticised on technical grounds: a 'Frankenstein's monster style jumble of legislative provisions which are clumsily composed and difficult to understand'.[11] Second, we find rules designed to anticipate non-compliance where 'the meticulous attention to detail shows the adoption by government of the approach more usually found in the operations manual prepared for use by persons directly employed by government departments'.[12] Again, the statutory amendments in 1992 were based on proposals in the consultation paper *Competing for Quality*,[13] which accuses (para. 1.6) many authorities of bending the rules to cushion their workforces against the full force of competition. The paper speaks of 'clarification' but it is possible to detect a rising spiral of command and disobedience as Government

10  SIs 1997/175 and 1997/176; Department of the Environment, *Compulsory Competitive Tendering: Consultation on Proposals for Changes to the Framework*, May 1996, p. 2. Below, p. 263.
11  See, for general accounts, S. Cirell and J. Bennett, *Compulsory Competitive Tendering: Law and Practice*, (London: Longman) 2nd edn., 1996, p. A11; A. Sparke, *The Compulsory Competitive Tendering Guide*, (London: Butterworths) 2nd edn., 1996; also S. Arrowsmith, *The Law of Public and Utilities Procurement* (London: Sweet and Maxwell) 1996, Chs. 12-14.
12  Current Law Statutes, Annotation on Local Government Act, 1988, 9/18.
13  Above, note 1.

became increasingly 'involved in policing the 'rules of the game' and plugging loopholes in its regulations . . .'[14]

The twin themes of central control and complexity are underscored in the hierarchy of rules (Chapter 6). Typically, the statutes are largely skeletal, conferring major rule-making powers. Initially the Minister operated by guidance: shorn of legal effect, it was open to disobedience and challenge in the courts.[15] The 1992 Act therefore gave power to make regulations providing that specified conduct represented anti-competitive behaviour: in effect, to make binding rules on virtually all aspects of the regime (see below).[16] The regulations exemplify the technical as well as prescriptive element which gives much contemporary law its quality of opacity:[17] to give a single example, the calculation of possible savings structured and confined by lengthy mathematical equation.[18] The Minister also took power in the 1992 Act to make regulations giving himself power to make 'statutory guidance' to be taken into account in deciding whether or not anti-competitive behaviour had taken place.[19] Thus, we identify a primary legislative power to formulate secondary rules empowering the creation of tertiary norms: these norms range over the statutory regime, in effect hem in the courts, and, not being statutory instruments, go free of formal parliamentary controls. This casts new light on the relationship between discretion and rules.

## (a) Competition and procedure

As with the EC procurement regime, a level playing field must exist. Once again, there is formal legal ordering of the different stages of tender and award of contract. But in practice the requirement is difficult to achieve and pressures are generated for more intrusive regulation. Let us take the example of packaging work: the size and mix of contracts put out to tender. Clearly the choice of package can influence the degree of competition: councils have been required to make work attractive to private firms. According to Circular 10/93 (paras. 7, 9-10), a piece of 'statutory guidance':

> Authorities should bear in mind that existing direct service organisation (DSO) or historic working practices may not be the most efficient or cost-effective way of packaging a contract. It follows from the duty of authorities to avoid anti-competitive conduct that work put out to contract should be packaged in such a way as to bring it

14  A. Cochrane, 'Local Government' in R. Maidment and G. Thompson (eds.), *Managing the United Kingdom* (Sage, London) 1993, p. 224.

15  See *R* v *Secretary of State for the Environment, ex p Knowsley Metropolitan Borough Council*, (1991) Independent, 25 September, CA.

16  Local Government Act 1992, s. 9(1); Local Government (Direct Service Organisations) (Competition) Regulations, SI 1993/848 (hereafter the 1993 Competition Regulations).

17  Above, p. 153.

18  See Competition Regulations 1993, reg. 8 and Schedule. The calculation which stretches over two pages cannot be included.

19  Local Government Act 1992, s. 9(3); 1993 Competition Regulations, Reg. 15. And see for statutory guidance, Department of the Environment Circular 10/93; now replaced by Department of the Environment Circular 5/96, *Guidance on the Conduct of Compulsory Competitive Tendering*.

within the scope of as wide a range of contractors as practicable. For example, packaging large amounts of work over a wide geographical area may deter competition from small locally based companies. This is particularly important when seeking tenders for activities such as grounds maintenance, building cleaning and jobbing maintenance, where many potential contractors are likely to be small companies.

An example of good practice was disseminated by the Audit Commission. Note the scale and diversity of contracting work:[20]

### Kent County Council
*Contract Packaging for Building Cleaning*
For first round education building cleaning contracts, the county was divided into six areas with an average of five group contracts in each area plus a number of single school contracts. The contracts, with a total value of nearly £6m, ranged in size up to a package of 36 schools, which encouraged interest from all sizes of contractor. Over all six areas, more than 80 potential contractors expressed an interest, of which 45 were included on the shortlist. In total, more than 250 bids were received for the work and the 30 group contracts were split between 11 contractors, including both external contractors and the DSO.

Detailed requirements of this kind have operated in tandem with a general prohibition on anti-competitive behaviour, providing strong underpinning for the value for money principle. Thus, the Local Government Act 1988 made it a condition of an award of work in-house that the authority 'did not act in a manner having the effect or intended or likely to have the effect of restricting, distorting or preventing competition' (ss. 6, 7). This then provided both the flexibility of the 'catch-all' provision and the basis for the progressive development of rules through regulations and statutory guidance. For example, Circular 10/93, para. 24 stated:

> Authorities should consider using, where available, standard contract documents - for example, a standard form of measured term contract which is widely approved and recognised by private and public sector employers, such as that published by the Joint Contracts Tribunal for building works contracts. Any departure from such standard contract documents, where they exist, may have the effect of restricting competition and authorities should consider carefully the justification for doing so.

Typically, the Audit Commission was early in the field, highlighting both the importance of judgment discretion (above, p.104) and the close combination of legal and audit techniques in the approach to government under the Conservatives (Chapter 5). Radford was critical of its proactive role:[1]

> One means by which the Commission can influence the way in which authorities conduct their affairs . . . is by issuing advice setting out its interpretation of the law

20 Audit Commission, *Realising the Benefits of Competition* (1993), p. 29.
1 M. Radford, 'Auditing for Change: Local Government and the Audit Commission' (1991) 54 MLR 912, 920-922, 924. Reference is being made to the Audit Commission, *Competition. Advice to Auditors* (London: HMSO) 1988.

... An area in which the Commission has been particularly active in expressing its view of authorities' legal duties [is] compulsory competitive tendering . . .

The Commission has published detailed guidance setting out the duties it considers to be incumbent on an authority to avoid contravening the anti-competitive prohibition. [Its] view of anti-competitive behaviour is far removed, and much more far reaching, than regarding it simply in terms of treating the in-house service and potential contractors fairly. The Commission's view appears to be that an authority must demonstrate that it is actively encouraging and facilitating the private sector to bid for contracts. . .

Practitioners in local government have objected to high profile legal opinions on the ground that it is not the business of the Commission to interpret the law and that it should be left to individual councils, which have considerable expertise in this area, to come to their own conclusions in the light of their particular circumstances . . . The Commission has emphasised that its advice is directed to auditors; it is made available to authorities for information, who are free to ignore it if they consider that they will remain within the law if they do so. But this is an over-simplification . . . Although in theory the Commission's legal opinions carry no more weight than those of any other lawyer, it is disingenuous to ignore their influence with both the government and courts . . .

It appears to many observers and practitioners that the Commission's advice is unduly negative and restrictive, and tends to reflect one view of several which might legitimately be possible. It is also presented as though there is no alternative view.

How far can a checklist approach sensibly go, the rules becoming ever longer and more intrusive? The Department had second thoughts, and finally opted for rule-substitution in a more open-textured approach of five key principles. Notably, this was presented as 'in line with the Government's deregulation initiative' (Chapter 10). But the principles would operate inside a detailed framework of regulation and were supplemented by examples of good practice from previous guidance and by new guidance on particular topics. It was explained that the new style 'does not diminish the ability of the Department to investigate anti-competitive behaviour or of the Secretary of State to take enforcement action'.[2] Deregulation, we learn, is an elusive concept.

Like the EC procurement rules, the principles involve great stress on transparency: the onus is put more clearly on authorities to demonstrate how their proposals for tendering avoid restricting, distorting or preventing competition. Note also the stress on specification in terms of outputs, at one with the general approach to 'reinventing government' expressed in the Citizen's Charter (above, p.144):[3]

(i)   Ensuring that the competition process is conducted, and is seen to be conducted, in a fair and transparent manner;

(ii)  Identifying the way in which the market operates for the service in question, and ensuring that tendering practices are consistent with securing a good competitive response;

2   Department of the Environment, *Competition News*, Issue 3, 1995; and see Circular 5/96, Appendix B.
3   Circular 5/96, paras. 8, 10.

(iii) Generally specifying the output to be achieved rather than the way in which the service is to be performed in detail, so that the evaluation of bids and the monitoring of performance can concentrate on the ability of contractors to achieve the full requirements of the specification, including real service quality;

(iv) Adopting clear procedures for evaluating tenders to ensure that the required quality can be achieved;

(v) Acting fairly between potential contractors to ensure that the conduct of tendering does not put any one of them at a disadvantage.

How competition is conducted within the broad framework of the statutory provisions and guidance is largely for individual authorities to decide. However, authorities should consider whether any aspect of their conduct might have the effect of restricting, distorting or preventing competition and to take action to avoid this. The Secretary of State will expect authorities to be able to provide a clear and soundly reasoned account of the way in which decisions have been taken and evidence that they have approached competition in a transparently fair and open manner.

## *(b) Administrative enforcement*

It has been for the Minister to determine whether an authority has broken the rules and to impose sanctions. Non-compliance might involve either the financial obligations on the DSO or the tendering procedures. Thus, casework would include trawling the reports and accounts on in-house activities and responding to complaints by private firms of anti-competitive behaviour. In practice most cases have been resolved informally in discussions between the Department and councils (see Table 9.1). Subsequent procedures were laid down in the Local Government Act 1988. Section 13 empowered the Minister to issue a formal notice requiring the authority to state a case. The Minister, if still not satisfied, was empowered by s. 14 to issue directions:

That . . . the authority—(a) shall cease to have power to carry out any work falling within the appropriate activity; (b) shall cease to have power to carry out such work falling within that activity as is identified in the Direction; (c) shall only have power to carry out work falling within that activity if such conditions as are specified in the Direction are fulfilled; or (d) shall, as regards such work falling within that activity as is identified in the Direction, only have power to carry it out if such conditions as are specified in the Direction are fulfilled.

The barring orders ((a) and (b)) are draconian remedies: in effect, the Minister could insist on private provision. More usually the conditions orders ((c) and (d)) have been used to reopen an award in-house by requiring re-tendering:[4] note that the problem of invalidating a contract could not arise, there being only a pseudo-contract. As the Table shows, the scale of casework has varied considerably, reflecting the dynamic character of the regime.[5]

4 See, for details, Department of the Environment, *CCT and Local Government in England, Annual Report for 1996*, pp. 10-14.
5 For example, the increase in 1996 is largely explained by the introduction of white-collar CCT; previously, developments on TUPE (see below) had reduced the number of complaints.

*Table 9.1:  CCT: department casework 1993-1996*

|  | 1993 | 1994 | 1995 | 1996 |
|---|---|---|---|---|
| *Anti-competitive behaviour* | | | | |
| Cases concluded | 157 | 100 | 66 | 89 |
| Notices (s. 13) | 20 | 20 | 12 | 19 |
| Directions (s. 14) | 12 | 9 | 7 | 10 |
| *Financial failure* | | | | |
| In house accounts analysed by DOE | 2,260 | 2,240 | 2,381 | 'about the same' |
| Financial objectives unmet | 335 | 350 | 324 | N/A |
| Notices (s. 13) | 79 | 102 | 125 | 68 |
| Directions (s. 14) | 11 | 39 | 49 | 54 |

*Source*: Department of Environment, *CCT and Local Government in England: Annual Reports.* (These figures relate to England and cover activities under both 1980 and 1988 Acts.)

This administrative method is very different from the EC procurement regime, with its enforcement model of private legal action (above, p. 249). There are clear advantages in terms of complainant access, cost and speed of process, and an integrated system of rule-making and application. Conversely, the issue is raised of the legitimacy of the ministerial, multi-functional model, more especially questions of impartiality and due process familiar in administrative law.

What then of the role of judicial review in constraining these extraordinary powers? Far from suggesting a 'hard look', the leading case actually cemented the Minister's position.

*R v Secretary of State for the Environment, ex p Haringey London Borough Council*[6]

An opposition councillor complained that Labour-dominated Haringey had awarded the refuse collection contract to the DSO despite lower tenders from two private firms. The DoE formed the view that Haringey had placed excessive weight on concerns about the financial status of the firms and insufficient weight on the potential savings. A s. 14(2)(a) barring order was made, on the basis of

6    (1994) 92 LGR 538.

anti-competitive behaviour. According to the Minister, the decision illustrated 'our determination to use the most severe sanction power available to us in cases of flagrant breach of the statutory requirements'. The court rejected an argument that the Minister was not entitled to police the quality of decisions in this way, in the light of 'the subjective nature of the Secretary of State's discretion, and the scope for differing views on [such] matters'. Haringey further contended that the Minister had failed to consider the less severe sanction of a conditions order, and had taken into account irrelevant considerations – the desire to make an example of Haringey. In effect, the issue was raised of proportionality (above, p.118):

> *Ralph Gibson LJ*: For the Secretary of State [it is said that] s. 14(2) confers . . . a wide discretion as to the form of direction that he may give once the conditions set out in s. 14(1) are satisfied: the exercise of that discretion is subject to control on *Wednesbury* . . . grounds, but is not subject to any specific statutory limitation, for example, to the effect that a s. 14(2)(a) direction may be given only if a s. 14(2)(c) direction is inappropriate . . . I am . . . driven [to agree]. When s. 14(1)(c) applies, the Secretary of State may issue directions as set out in s. 14(2)(a)(b)(c) or (d). There is no express limitation upon his discretion. . .
>
> One of the sanctions enacted by Parliament and put at the disposal of the Secretary of State . . . is to make a barring order. An intention to demonstrate to the country at large, and to those entrusted with the making of decisions on behalf of authorities in the tendering process . . . that an action by the local authority which is clearly in favour of the authority's direct services organisation and is in breach of the [anti-competitive] condition, *may* be met with the imposition of a barring order, seems to me to be an intention to promote the policy and the objects of the act. That policy and those objects are not merely that breaches of the [anti-competitive] condition, if reported, and well established in accordance with the Act, shall be visited only with such a sanction as may be held to be appropriate according to the degree of conscious wrongdoing on the part of the local authority (as to proof of which much difficulty would arise) but include the purpose of securing that all local authorities . . . shall, without the need for intervention by the Secretary of State, conduct their relevant activities in accordance with the . . . conditions laid down by Parliament.
>
> In so far as it is submitted that the Secretary of State was wrong in law in having any regard to the deterrent effect of the barring order in deciding that the appropriate direction in this case was in the form of a barring order, I do not accept it.

### (c) The biter bit

CCT developed then as a strong and dynamic legal regime, apparently strictly enforced: a model, we might say, of the use of law as an instrument of policy. There is, however, a missing piece in the jigsaw. EC law, in the shape of the Acquired Rights Directive, seeks 'to provide for the protection of employees in the event of a change of employer, in particular, to ensure that their rights are safeguarded'. In general, the new employer has to continue to employ the existing workforce, honour existing wages and other conditions of employment, and pay compensation for any redundancies or unfair dismissals as appropriate.[7]

---

7    Council Directive 77/187 [1977] OJ C61/26. See J. McMullen, *Business Transfers and Employee Rights*, (London: Butterworths) 3rd edn., 1997.

There is a clear clash of ideologies: worker protection on the one hand, and, encapsulated in competitive tendering, liberalising or free market policies on the other.   The threat posed to market testing in general, and CCT in particular, involves the reduced potential for savings on labour costs, and for efficiency gains tied to greater flexibility (see below). Tendering therefore becomes less attractive for private contractors: competitive pressures on in-house units are diminished.  No wonder that the Conservative government fought long and hard to hold the Directive at bay!  In the event, the affair epitomises the changed hierarchy of norms in administrative law inside the EC framework.

The chronology is important. The Directive pre-dates the drive to privatisation and contracting out, being agreed by the Labour Government in 1977.  The incoming Conservative Government was unenthusiastic but was locked into the Directive because of continuing support for it among Member States.[8] At first it proceeded on the basis that the Directive was irrelevant to CCT, to the extent of saying that it was anti-competitive behaviour by councils to take the Directive into account in the tendering process.   There was doubt over the ambit of the Directive, expressed to apply to 'the transfer of an undertaking, business or part of a business': when might this cover the transfer of an activity such as refuse collection?  Of more immediate significance were the Transfer of Undertakings (Protection of Employment) Regulations 1981 (TUPE) by which the Government implemented the Directive.  Exemption was given to undertakings 'not in the nature of a commercial venture', which was duly interpreted to exclude the application of TUPE to contracting out, although no such restriction was stated in the Directive.[9]  To emphasise, CCT could at this stage proceed unmolested.

A watershed came in 1992 with the Dutch case of *Stichting*,[10] where the Directive was held to apply in a paradigm non-commercial situation, a shift of public subsidy from one charitable organisation to another: a broad interpretation was given to the phrase 'transfer of an undertaking'. The Government's defence had been blown apart and the affair developed as the kind of collective, campaigning action which is a major feature of today's legal environment.   As Sutcliffe explains, the trade unions were suddenly:[11]

> . . . in the unfamiliar position of experiencing some law which is apparently to their advantage and that of their members, and are seeking to pursue it for all that it is worth. The TUC has set up a legal working group to explore the possibilities of TUPE and the Directive, and there has been extensive co-operation between the unions.  NUPE and the TGWU have supported appeals to the Employment Appeal Tribunal . . . and the unions are orchestrating a campaign to complain to industrial tribunals . . . NUPE and the TGWU have been actively lobbying in Europe to have the adequacy of the UK's implementation of the directive considered by the ECJ. The European Commission [has] initiated proceedings.

---

8  A proposal by the Commission ([1994] OJ C274) to amend the Directive met objections in the European Parliament. See, for the revised proposal, COM (97) 60.

9  SI 1981/1794, as amended; *Expro Services Ltd v Smith* [1991] ICR 577.

10  *Stichting v Bartol* Case C-29/91 [1992] ECR I-3189.

11  F. Sutcliffe, 'Contracting Out Public Services: UK Policy *v* EC Law' (1993) 22 Anglo- American LR 337, 361-363.  A key EAT case in the campaign was *Wren v Eastbourne Borough Council* [1993] ICR 955.  And see *Commission v United Kingdom* Case C-382/92 [1994] ECR 1-2435.

The infringement proceedings duly confirmed that the government was in breach of EC law.   In later cases the ECJ dismissed the policy argument concerning the undermining of contracting out and pursued an expansive interpretation.[12] At national level, the Court of Appeal followed suit, holding that a hospital service did not lose its identity on transfer, irrespective of new equipment or work methods, and was thus subject to the Directive.[13]   The relevance for CCT was hammered home, by the prospect of actions for damages under the EC *Francovich* principle.[14]

EC law was feeding into the national regulatory system, albeit the government moved slowly and reluctantly; a process which has been described as 'cumulative prevarication'.[15] The non-commercial exemption was removed by s. 33 of the Trade Union Reform and Employment Rights Act 1993. The guidance on what constituted anti-competitive behaviour by councils underwent a series of revisions: moving from a 'general rule' against TUPE considerations in 1992 to recognition in 1993 that it might be appropriate 'in neutral terms' to refer prospective contractors to the regulations; on, by 1996, to acceptance that councils may wish 'to indicate their preliminary view of the likelihood of the Regulations applying'.[16] While other rules on CCT were being tightened progressively against local authorities, here we find a softening.

To summarise, the government proceeded on traditional constitutional assumptions: effective control of the law-making process by the executive and sanctions against subsidiary bodies for non-compliance. The Directive introduced the trump card or a superior law which the government could not repeal; judicial review by the ECJ at the suit of individuals; possible sanctions against the government for non-compliance; and, eventually, changes in government practice. The biter bit.

## 3.  CCT: policy and performance

Despite the element of compulsion, CCT has not delivered a thriving market in local services. In-house teams have won the great majority of contracts, although the success rates and competition levels vary considerably between services (see Table 9.2).  There was by 1996 only slow growth in private firms' market share (1-2% a year) while DSOs were doing particularly well in tenders for professional services.[17]  To emphasise, this meant a preponderance of pseudo-contract.

12  *Rask and Christensen v Iss Kantinservice A/S*, Case C-209/91 [1992] ECR I-5755; *Schmidt v Spar-und Leihkasse* Case C-392/92 [1994] ECR I-1311.  But see now *Süzen v Zehnacker Gebäudereinigung GmbH Krankenhausservice* Case C-13/95 [1997] All ER (EC) 289.
13  *Dines v Initial Health Care Services* [1995] ICR 11. But see now *Betts v Brintel Helicopters Ltd* [1997] 2 All ER 840.
14  Below, p. 630.
15  M. Radford and A. Kerr, 'Acquiring Rights – Losing Power: A Case Study in Ministerial Resistance to the Impact of European Community Law' (1997) 60 MLR 23.
16  Department of the Environment, *Guidance*, 19 November 1992;   Circular 10/93, para. 43; Circular 5/96, para. 32.
17  See, for details, CCT Information Service, *Survey Report No. 14*, Appendix 1 (London) 1996.

*Table 9.2 CCT: tenders and awards*

| Activity | DSO Success % of contracts won | DSO Success % value of work won | Average number of contractors tendering |
|---|---|---|---|
| Building Cleaning | 41.5 | 71.8 | 4.9 |
| Refuse Collection | 62.2 | 64.8 | 3.6 |
| Other Cleaning | 64.4 | 71.2 | 3.5 |
| Vehicle Maintenance | 71.2 | 74.5 | 2.8 |
| Catering (Education and Welfare) | 69.6 | 78.1 | 2.2 |
| Catering (Other)• | 59.6 | 75.1 | 2.4 |
| Ground Maintenance | 53.3 | 71.1 | 4.3 |
| Sports and Leisure Management• | 79.4 | 88.0 | 1.8 |
| Average | 55.5 | 73.0 | 3.2 |

• Non-franchise contracts
(*Source*: CCT Information Service, *Survey Report No. 14*, 1996, pp. 10-12). The figures relate to England and Wales.

Predictably, dispute over the policy spills over into assessments of performance. Why the shortfall in private provision? Stress is laid by local authority organisations on the competitive merits of in-house provision, as also insufficient capacity in private firms.[18] From inside the Conservative Political Centre the same point materialises as complaints of 'tremendously slow progress ... because of a long war of attrition against government policy by significant sections of local government...'. Note how this is suggestive of more – not less – central control:[19]

[The] protracted nature [of the tendering process] is the first reason why private companies might be deterred ... There is [also] evidence ... that firms are selective

18  See Association of Direct Labour Authorities, *A Future for Local Public Service Provision* (London) 1997.
19  F. Bulmer, *CCT: The Continuing Challenge* (London: Conservative Political Centre) 1995, pp. 13-15. See also Department of the Environment, *CCT Non-Bidders* (London: HMSO) 1996.

about the contracts they tender for and that one of the key factors is the attitude of the local authority towards private firms. If contractors believe the council is hostile they do not bother tendering . . .

Many . . . hurdles have been imposed deliberately by authorities from the beginning of CCT – and are still widespread today. Amongst the most common are unduly complicated and lengthy contract documentation, excessive penalty clauses and high performance bonds . . . One other factor which deters contractors from bidding is the relatively short duration of the contracts awarded under CCT . . . Where the contract period is unreasonably short and the prospective reward from the contract is small in relation to the costs of tendering, many contractors will not bother to bid.

## (a) The paper chase

The expanded role of legal ordering in the provision of public services is exemplified by CCT. There is, in addition to the formal procedures for tendering, a premium on legal skills at the stage of managing the contract. Thus, on the ground, pseudo-contract moves closer to real contract:[20]

> Such exchanges cannot be contractual, because the providers lack separate legal personality, but in all other respects they formally (and increasingly) resemble contractual transactions with the private sector, with regard to pre-tender procedures, contract specification and documentation, monitoring of performance, adjustment and default procedures, and dispute-resolution . . .
>
> The most compelling evidence . . . lies in the increasing number of cases in which sanctions are applied in accordance with the 'contract', or in which internal disputes require dispute-resolution, with senior officers acting in an arbitration role . . . A further quasi-legal element concerns the manner in which arbitral decisions may be becoming 'precedents', regarded as binding in similar circumstances within the organisation..

To emphasise, such arrangements render the administrative process more formal and rule-bound. According to research by Walsh and Davis:[1]

> Greater formality was apparent in the growth of bureaucratic procedures, for example, for invoicing and for variation . . . There was increasing use of formal billing procedures. There was inevitable tension between the need for day-to-day flexibility and the need for systems that allowed close audit and control. Authorities were learning to balance the two, but systems were seen as increasingly bureaucratic . . .
>
> The direction of movement was towards greater formality of monitoring procedures as time went on, with informality of relationships built on a basis of clear structured processes . . . The process of inspection, though obviously not especially complex, does require care and generates a considerable amount of paper . . . The process was increasingly formal, especially in relation to payment for work done.

---

20 P. Vincent-Jones, 'The Limits of Contractual Order in Public Sector Transacting' (1994) 14 Legal Studies 364, 383-384, 386.

1 K. Walsh and H. Davis, *Competition and Service: The Impact of the Local Government Act 1988* (London: HMSO) 1993, pp. 11, 92, 100.

Size and complexity of documentation has increased. Contracts are typically extremely detailed, with large numbers of contract conditions.[2] Legal practice guides stress the need to anticipate difficulties. 'Pressures to plan fully and properly are increased by the direct responsibility of the client unit or department for the cost and quality of the goods or services obtained, and the knowledge that errors of judgment may have financial repercussions.'[3]   This then fuels routinisation, a growth in standard forms and uniform practices across local government. A cottage industry develops, further encouraged because departure from standard terms may be construed as anti-competitive behaviour (above, p. 257). Local authority associations produce standard core contract conditions; entrepreneurial councils, like Wandsworth and Westminster, sell copies of their draft contracts;  the Association of Chief Technical Officers produces basic documents for services such as refuse collection and grounds maintenance.

Let us look a little more closely at specification and quality of service. There is much use of systems of quality assurance of the type associated with the Citizen's Charter (above, p.147). Considerable effort has gone into tackling the problem of formulating standards of service: most councils report progress to 'clearer and more comprehensive service specifications'.[4] But, as a practitioner records:[5] 'It would be impossible in many contracts to entirely dispense with subjective judgments of quality to be made by council officers during the course of the contract.' The limitations are most obvious with professional services. What follows is part of an attempt to specify standards in a contract for legal services (in the event, all the work was awarded in-house). Note the central role of assessment and monitoring of performance:

> The Contractor is to exercise professional judgment and is required at all times to provide a full legal professional and advice service and undertake all steps necessary to satisfactorily complete a matter . . .
>
> In providing the service the Contractor shall be responsible for establishing and agreeing with the Contract supervisor clear and efficient procedures for taking instructions, progressing cases, informing the Client Officer of progress and maintaining case documentation and files in a professional manner. . .
>
> The Council will require all work to be done in accordance with the requirement of the law, best professional practice and in accordance with the Law Society's guide to the professional conduct of Solicitors . . . The Contractor shall establish and maintain an effective quality management system to the satisfaction of the Contract supervisor . . .
>
> The Council places great importance on high standards of customer care . . . The Contractor shall appoint sufficient case supervisors to ensure effective supervision of the Service . . . The Contractor shall ensure that case workers, or where appropriate a case supervisor, are directly accessible by telephone or in person to answer enquiries

2   See further R. Carnaghan and B. Bracewell-Milnes, *Testing the Market* (London:  Institute of Economic Affairs) 1993, pp. 94-97.
3   P. Vincent-Jones, 'The Limits of Contractual Order' (above, note 20), p. 378. See A. Sparke, *The Compulsory Competitive Tendering Guide* (London:  Butterworths) 2nd edn., 1996, Ch.4.
4   Department of the Environment, *CCT and Local Government in England, Annual Report for 1996* pp. 21-22.
5   A. Sparke, *Compulsory Competitive Tendering Guide* (above, note 3), p. 39.

from any person with a legitimate interest in a matter being dealt with by the Contractor
. . .

The Contractor will be required to keep Client Officers apprised of progress on each case as appropriate or when requested . . . The Contractor will be required to keep within the maximum time scale specified for each case type in the Appendices to this Specification.

Another useful illustration is dispute resolution and default procedure. As in the case of central government procurement, we would expect to find arbitration and variation clauses, as also clauses dealing with insurance and liability to third parties. Suppose that the Local Ombudsman finds against an authority by reason of the poor performance of a private contractor: under the Ombudsman scheme the authority is responsible for paying any compensation; in practice, the loss will probably be reallocated via an indemnity clause.[6] Authorities have to hand various contractual tools to deal with poor performance: performance bonds, default payments, termination clauses. Although the number of total contract failures has been small, part of the price of CCT has been paid in significant numbers of remedial actions and disputes.[7] There is considerable growth in the use of IT to generate monitoring programmes; to analyse complaints and defaults; and to operate totting up procedures, by which contract payments are reduced for poor performance.[8] To emphasise, more formal methods of enforcement have proliferated.

## (b) Costs and benefits: values

A policy like CCT invites very different criteria of assessment. Taking the Conservatives' own stress on 'the three Es', successive rounds[9] of tendering have demonstrated significant though variable cost-savings (see Table 9.3). These have resulted primarily from increased productivity, job cuts and changes in pay and conditions:[10] the drive to greater 'flexibility' in the labour market which in later years has been blunted by TUPE. Savings have been further reduced by transaction costs and the client-side costs of contract management.[11] The structuring and confining of discretion favoured by Harden[12] does not come cheap. Predictably, the impact of CCT on quality of service is hard to gauge,

---

6  Ibid, p. 35.
7  Defaults leading to financial penalties have been reported for 5.5% of DSO contracts and 7.5% of private sector contracts. See for details, CCT Information Service, *Survey Report No. 14* (London) 1996, Ch.2.
8  See K. Walsh and H. Davis, *Competition and Service* (above, note 1), Ch.10.
9  CCT procedures have been designed to be ongoing. Statutory periods of four to ten years have been set for contract periods, the work then being retendered. See SI 1995/2484.
10  The evidence is summarised in F. Sutcliffe, 'Contracting Out Public Services: UK Policy *v* EC Law' (1993) 22 Anglo American LR 337, 344-349. See further K. Shaw, J. Fenwick and A. Foreman, 'Compulsory Competitive Tendering for Local Government Services: The Experiences of Local Authorities in the North of England, 1988-1992', (1994) 72 Pub. Admin. 201.
11  Estimated by K. Walsh and H. Davis, *Competition and Service* (above, note 1), pp. 145-148, to be in the order of 1- 2% and 6-7% of total contract value respectively.
12  Above, p. 140.

though surveys suggest standards being kept up and improved over time.[13]  The policy must also be placed in context, interacting with other factors like budget constraint and IT.  The Audit Commission[14] accepts that CCT 'has played its part' in improving efficiency, 'but it is difficult to quantify it'.  Bennett and Cirell[15] amplify the theme in the case of professional services.  While 'in-house operations which have been subject to competition are now leaner and fitter than ever before ... one has to question whether or not the same ends could not have been obtained in a different, less conflict-orientated and less expensive manner'.  CCT is suspect even in the limited terms of cost-benefit analysis.

*Table 9.3: Blue-collar CCT: increase/decrease in annual costs by activity*

|  | *First round* | *Second round* |
|---|---|---|
| Refuse collection | - 11.3% | - 7.0% |
| Street cleaning | + 2.6% | - 10.4% |
| Building cleaning | - 12.7% | - 9.6% |
| Schools and welfare catering | + 2.8% | - 14.3% |
| Other catering | - 4.9% | - 4.0% |
| Vehicle maintenance | - 1.3% | + 2.4% |
| Grounds maintenance | - 10.9% | - 2.6% |
| Leisure management | - 5.0% | - 25% |
| Average | -6.5% | 9.1% |

(*Source*:  K. Walsh and H. Davis, *Competition and Service: The Impact of the Local Government Act 1988* (London, HMSO) 1993, pp. 142-143; Department of the Environment *CCT and Local Authority Blue-Collar Services* 1997).

To expand the theme, CCT points up the functional limits of contractual ordering in the provision of public services.  As Parker and Hartley observe:[16]

13  K. Walsh and H. Davis, *Competition and Service* (above, note 1), Ch. 12. Department of the Environment, *CCT and Local Authority Blue-Collar Services*, 1997, ch. 4.
14  Audit Commission, *Making Markets: A Review of the Audits of the Client Role for Contracted Services* (London: HMSO) 1995, p. 3.
15  J. Bennett and S. Cirell, 'Compulsory Competitive Tendering for White Collar Services' (1996) 5 Public Procurement LR 67, 76.
16  D. Parker and K. Hartley, 'Competitive Tendering:  Issues and Evidence' (1990) 10(3) Public Money and Management 9.

Contracting-out is one aspect of a more general problem of negotiating, writing, evaluating and monitoring a contract. Much of the debate about competitive tendering and contracting-out has neglected the difficulties and costs involved in the contractual process. Writing a complete contract to deal with all contingencies in an uncertain future is complex, costly, and, for some products and activities, it can be impossible. A compete contract requires the bidder to specify exactly the quantities to be supplied and their prices for every possible future contingency during the life of the contract. Where there is considerable uncertainty, contracts tend to be incomplete.

So too the compulsory nature of the scheme rests uneasily with the values of co-operation and compromise on which effective contracting depends. 'Who wants to work with an unwilling partner?'[17]

What then of process values, a key criterion of legitimacy for administrative lawyers? Contracting services has been advocated as an aid to transparency and to public involvement in determining provision (above, p. 209). CCT, however, demonstrates the way in which proliferating rules render the administrative process opaque and difficult to penetrate. It comes as no surprise to learn that in one survey[18] less than half of authorities had consulted consumers of services on requirements and standards. There is one exception, typical of the managerialist, individualist slant of the Citizen's Charter. According to Walsh and Davis,[19] complaints were widely seen as valuable in monitoring contracts.

The greater long-term impact of CCT arises from the requirement to operate on a trading basis and the resultant spread of an ethos of commercialism: in other words, a cultural shift in local government, from a public service base to a business organisation base.[20] Assessment of CCT solely in the terms of NPM glosses over the broad constitutional implications. The policy illustrates an important paradox of recent years: increased resort to law – imperium – in an effort at market liberalisation. We are back with theories of the state:[1]

> The ideological desire of the New Right – to restructure the local welfare state along business lines – has brought with it the increasing intervention of the central state in order to achieve its goal. Whatever the language of competition, markets and consumer sovereignty suggests, it can be argued that such rhetoric acts as 'a smokescreen behind which there is a progressive transfer of power to the centre' . . . From this point of view then, the long-term impact of CCT is to further erode local democracy in the UK.

## 4. Franchising and administrative law

Franchising as a tool of government, although not novel, has recently become much more important. It is operative today across a diverse range of activities,

---

17  Ibid, p. 13.
18  Audit Commission, *Making Markets* (above,note 14), p. 5.
19  K. Walsh and H. Davis, *Competition and Service* (above, note 1), pp. 103-104.
20  J. Greenwood and D. Wilson, 'Towards the Contract State: CCT in Local Goverment' (1994) 47 Parliamentary Affairs 405.
 1  K. Shaw, J. Fenwick and A. Foreman, 'Compulsory Competition for Local Government Services in the UK: A Case of Market Rhetoric and Camouflaged Centralism' (1995) 10 Public Policy and Admin. 63, 64.

from London buses to legal aid, and from cable television to that repository of contemporary social values, the National Lottery.[2] Harnessing private enterprise in the delivery of services, franchising epitomises NPM and the rise in administrative law of contract-type arrangements. It may be approached as either one technique of regulation, or a complement to, even a substitute for, regulation, in the sense of classical regulatory techniques like command and control (Chapter 10).

Franchising entails the allocation of temporary monopoly rights to carry on an activity, typically using the mechanism of an auction to control entry to the market.   The basic premise is that competition for the market effectively substitutes for competition within it: to enjoy monopoly rights, the private firm first has to engage in competition to secure those rights. As with contracting-out, with which it overlaps, franchising is appropriately considered as a *process*, involving both the design and operation of award procedures, and monitoring, negotiation, and sanction under the rubric of franchise management.   There is ample scope for agency discretion.

The rise of franchising is fuelled by loss of faith in the alternatives. Thus its use may be anticipated in conditions of market failure familiarly associated with nationalisation or the standard instruments of economic regulation (Chapter 10). Franchising allows competition for loss-making activities because negative tender prices can take the form of subsidy, as with the railways (below, p. 282).   The franchise as a source of rules can be used in defence of 'the public interest' as through specifications for quality and balance in commercial television (below, p. 272).   Then again, there is scope for explanation in terms of public choice, that is, franchising as the product of rent-seeking behaviour by private interest groups.[3]

An influential theory of public franchising derives from regulatory economics to the effect that market disciplines unleashed by a properly designed system of allocation undermine the case for conventional regulation: contract terms and conditions constitute the appropriate legal instrument of public control. Domberger argues that:[4]

> Franchising has attractive properties which suggest that if properly implemented it could go a considerable way towards meeting both objectives of productive and allocative efficiency . . . Franchising can be viewed essentially as a mechanism for increasing market contestability.   It does so by allowing firms to bid for the rights to supply *before* they have committed resources to the enterprise, i.e. by reducing the level of sunk costs associated with entry.   Of equal importance is the fact that

---

2   D. Miers, 'Regulation and the Public Interest: Commercial Gambling and the National Lottery' (1996) 59 MLR 489. Although government franchising is distinguished by its 'public' purpose, commercial franchising provides many instructive parallels.   See, generally, C. Joerges, *Franchising and the Law: Theoretical and Comparative Approaches in Europe and the United States* (Baden-Baden: Nomos, Verl.-Ges.) 1991; A. Dnes, *Franchising: A Case Study Approach* (Aldershot: Avebury) 1992.

3   K. Button, 'Economic Theories of Regulation and the Regulation of the United Kingdom's Bus Industry' (1989) 34 Antitrust Bulletin 489.

4   S. Domberger, 'Economic Regulation Through Franchise Contracts' in J. Mayer and D. Thompson (eds.), *Privatization and Regulation: The UK Experience* (Oxford: Clarendon) 1986.  See further H. Demsetz, 'Why Regulate Utilities?' (1968) 11 J. of Law and Economics 55; R. Posner, 'The Appropriate Scope of Regulation in the Cable Television Industry' (1972) 3  Bell Journal of Economics 98.

franchising is a mechanism for providing the regulator with information about the competitiveness of potential suppliers. Such information generation is entirely absent under traditional regulation and nationalisation and is a major advantage of the franchising method. Another advantage of franchising over traditional forms of regulation is that it provides a sanction on poor performance, namely the threat of franchise termination, which may in some circumstances be a more credible sanction than the threat of take-over faced by a regulated enterprise.

Conversely, the case for franchising weakens when the benefits of a competition for the market cannot be realised: 'Where, for example, potential franchisees cannot be found in numbers sufficient to produce competitive bidding; where the activity cannot be specified without excess uncertainties; where franchisors are unable to monitor or enforce franchise contracts; or where substitution of poor performers is not possible.'[5] To emphasise, franchising is no miracle cure for problems of public provision: in practice, it is typically deployed in conjunction with standard tools of regulation. Is there an 'optimum' balance of techniques?

Franchising has the potential to enhance accountability through specification. The record, however, on process values like fairness, consistency and transparency as a feature of the process can at best be described as mixed.[6] We choose to study two major systems: commercial terrestrial television and passenger services on the railway. The basic model illustrated involves: (i) wide discretion, encompassing procedure; (ii) exercise by executive agency; (iii) which has demonstrated hostility to public law concerns like transparency and voice; and (iv) is subject only to weak judicial review. To emphasise, this is poles apart from CCT and the reams of formal detail resulting from government distrust of local authorities. Speaking more generally, franchising highlights the challenge for administrative law presented by government by contract. First, there are the problems of reconciling the protection of the public interest, in terms both of value for money and process values, with precepts traditionally associated with private autonomy, such as commercial confidentiality. Second, the harnessing of private enterprise in the delivery of services may be said to strengthen, not weaken, the case for vindicating public law values. This suggests not merely stretching judicial review, but a remodelling of commercial precept: mixes of law for mixed administrations. Aronson argues that:[7]

> In the area of outsourcing, basic contractual details such as performance standards and price are frequently kept secret, for fear of prejudicing the contractor's competitive position. . . The natural assumption of anyone adhering to the public/private, public law/private law dichotomies [is] that any firm (government or private) conducting a commercial operation in a contestable market should be free of requirements to disclose information. There are several reasons for questioning this conclusion.

5   R. Baldwin and M. Cave, *Franchising as a Tool of Government* (London: Centre for the Study of Regulated Industries) 1996, p. 49.
6   A. Ogus, *Regulation. Legal Form and Economic Theory* (Oxford: Clarendon) 1994, p. 328.
7   M. Aronson, 'A Public Lawyer's Responses to Privatization and Outsourcing' in M. Taggart (ed.), *The Province of Administrative Law* (Oxford: Hart) 1997, pp. 58-62. His narrow definition of outsourcing as involving the provision of goods or services directly to the public covers franchising.

The effectiveness of outsourcing often requires greater transparency than currently stipulated. Agencies need information to enable them to bargain effectively. Information sharing between agencies . . . can . . . help them get better value for the tax payer. . . In an environment of truly competitive tendering, the losing bidders should be able to have a broad idea of how they must lift their game, if they are to be successful in any further or comparable tendering. The danger is otherwise that they might repeat the same mistakes, or eventually give up hope, thereby leaving the field that much less competitive . . .

One of the goals of privatization and outsourcing is to turn citizens into consumers, and to treat the consumer as sovereign . . . Devices for enhancing the consumer voice . . . include . . . systems for registering consumer views with a view to acting on them either under the contract, or when it comes up for renewal. In some contexts, it would also be appropriate to have a consumer input into the process of articulating some of the contract specifications . . . Information is not an end in itself, but it is a precondition to the effectiveness and legitimacy of virtually any other regulatory and participatory device . . .

[Such] arguments for greater access to information are all instrumental, being based upon enhancing competition . . . Other arguments are normative, and might be more readily recognisable in an administrative law context . . . Where there are government contracts, licences and privileges, there are opportunities for corruption, and where there are opportunities, corruption will occasionally happen. Its likely frequency must surely be significantly increased when one adds government secrecy to these risk factors . . .

If one accepts . . . the instrumental and normative arguments . . . for greater information needs in the case of government funded goods and services, then the private sector's concept of 'commercial, in confidence' needs at least as much adjustment as the public sector's concepts of accountability and legitimacy . . . This results in the paradox that there will be contexts in which the mechanisms for delivering governmental transparency should be expanded, rather than contracted, as government adopts privatization and outsourcing.

## 5. Continuity and change: commercial television

The broad range of possible allocation systems is demonstrated by the development of franchising in commercial television. On the one hand, there is 'public interest franchising': the system being geared to select the company which will best serve public interest goals. On the other, there is 'price bidding franchising': the highest bid in the auction being successful, or alternatively the bid which accepts to charge consumers the lowest price for the service.[8] Commonly there is a combination: given the monopoly, it is hard to ignore pricing, while price competition alone creates incentives to reduce quality. We see in commercial television, formerly, a heavy reliance on the public interest model; and, latterly, under the Broadcasting Act 1990, a marked shift in favour of price bidding.

Public interest franchising maximises agency discretion, a familiar theme in the literature of regulation (Chapter 10). Subjective judgment is involved: the choice and 'weighing' of different factors. Criteria may be prescribed in statute,

8 Respectively, monopoly price bidding and consumer price bidding. See A. Ogus, *Regulation* (above, note 6), Ch.15.

but this becomes progressively more difficult as the dimensions to the 'public interest' multiply. Franchising television is a classic example, more especially by reason of the problem of defining and measuring quality.[9] Under the original scheme of the Television Act 1954, a two-step procedure was adopted. The franchisor, successively the Independent Television Authority and the Independent Broadcasting Authority (IBA), was given virtually untrammelled discretion in the allocation of regional franchises. Standards of impartiality, decency, quality etc. had then to be stipulated in the contracts awarded to the successful bidders.[10]

Public interest systems are vulnerable to the charge of inattention to process values. Failure to meet standards of fairness, consistency and transparency is apt to prove the downside of agency discretion. These issues were raised by Lewis in a pathbreaking article about the IBA in 1975:[11] stress was put on the need for rational decision-making and structuring and confining of discretion (Chapter 4). With hindsight, a call for American-style procedure (notice and comment, open hearings, reasons) anticipates contemporary debates over 'regulation UK-style', the new style of utilities regulation (Chapter 10). At that time, Lewis could portray the IBA as an 'unusual creature in British public administration' by reason of the combination of private initiative with public control:[12]

> The award of programme contracts by the [IBA] is hedged around by few legal controls, unlike the position in the United States of America, Canada, Australia etc. . . . The paucity of external controls . . . raises fundamental public law issues which transcend the importance of the IBA. Our attitude to this vital regulatory body discloses much about the nature of our democratic ideals in general and the state of public law in particular . . .
>
> Controls over commercial broadcasting are not yet at their optimum level . . . One contribution to that improvement may be seen to be institutional restraints of the kind which exist already in Canada and the United States . . . [Consider] the selection procedure adopted [in] 1967 . . . None of the interviews was competitive, all were conducted in private and of course the deliberations of the Authority itself were strictly secret . . . Crude criteria for the selection process were laid down though they were not publicised until well after the event, yet in an atmosphere of prevailing mystery it was not possible to divine which were given priority and how seriously they were taken. The reasons for the choice of companies did not illuminate the dominating standards and would certainly not have satisfied a court of law were a requirement to state reasons imposed . . .
>
> It is very difficult to believe that the absence of competitive hearings with the opportunity for something approaching cross-examination, can ever provide a satisfactory setting for selection of contractors . . . Fairness to incumbent franchise-holders and to other applicants demands the twin virtues of open and clear standards and reasons for decisions unless an overwhelming case can be made out to the contrary.

---

9  See e.g. V. Goldberg, 'Competitive Bidding and the Production of Pre-Contract Information' (1976) 7 Bell Journal of Economics 250;  C. Veljanovski, 'Cable Television: Agency Franchising and Economics' in R. Baldwin and C. McCrudden (eds.), *Regulation and Public Law* (London: Weidenfeld) 1987.

10  See Television Act 1954, ss. 3, 6. The discretion of the agency was largely confirmed in the Independent Broadcasting Authority Act 1973, and the Broadcasting Acts, 1980 and 1981.

11  N. Lewis, 'IBA Programme Contract Awards' [1975] PL 317.

12  Ibid, at pp. 317-320, 322 and 324.

Fairness to the public . . . raises the question of open hearings and the need for secrecy in the general conduct of the Authority's affairs.

The theme was later developed by Elliott, with the franchising arrangements seen at one with the regulatory functions of the IBA and public service broadcasting by the BBC. But the ethos of public control was coming under increased challenge, given commercial pressures coupled with technological advance:[13]

> It is worth attempting to schematise the kind of regulation that is actually utilised in the field of broadcasting; it can be called the 'arm's-length top-down' model . . . Governments, and government appointees, do not make operational decisions in British broadcasting, but . . . delegate day-to-day management to executive staff. But the broad policies within which those executive staffs are asked to operate are imposed from above. They are determined by government and framed in legislation, and then entrusted to a government appointed body which acts as the custodian of the legislation and the representative of the public interest . . .
>
> As long as the structure of broadcasting is premised upon its public quality and thus regulatability, it is legitimate to press for accountability of the regulators . . . Top-down regulation . . . produces its own forms of accountability; a publicly appointed body, responsible ultimately to Parliament must be trusted. Yet it can hardly be claimed that the extent of that accountability has satisfied those who wish to influence broadcasting policy, or that the meaning assigned by the IBA to its perception of the public interest has been very clear . . . I see no difference in terms of public accountability, innovation, or responsiveness to public opinion between regulatory bodies *as presently constituted* and companies competing for consumer loyalty in the market. At the moment top-down regulation can be characterised, without any slur on the regulators, as the apotheosis of the great-and-the-good paternalistic mode of British public administration that needs far more justification than the anti-deregulation argument has yet given it.

It reflects the changing environment that the Independent Television Commission (ITC), established by the Broadcasting Act 1990, is not, unlike its predecessor, 'the broadcaster'. Franchisees are directly accountable for programme content and must make their own arrangements for transmission of services. The agency has developed a new role of post hoc regulator, with a range of sanctions at its disposal (see below).[14] Franchising is continued but the system has changed.[15]

First, let us consider the legal terminology. Previously, the system was one of 'contract awards': now it is 'licences'. The overlap of franchising with both contract and classical techniques of regulation is illustrated. Further, the White Paper[16]

---

13  M. Elliott, 'Chasing the Receding Bus: The Broadcasting Act 1980' (1981) 44 MLR 683, pp. 684, 688, 690, 692. See further A. Briggs and J. Spicer, *The Franchise Affair: Creating Fortunes and Failures in Independent Television* (London: Century) 1986.
14  See Independent Television Commission, *Annual Report* 1992, p. 5.
15  Reference is here made to 'Channel 3' and 'Channel 5' franchising. The Broadcasting Act 1996 establishes a different form of allocation system for digital terrestrial television: the ITC is directed by s. 8 towards strategic considerations, a choice of franchisees 'calculated to promote development' of this form of broadcasting.
16  *Broadcasting in the Nineties: Competition, Choice and Quality*, Cm. 517 (1988), para. 6.

explains the shift to a licence- based regime in terms of ITC policies being tested in the courts. Thus, there is underpinning for judicial review because the 'public law' nature of statutory licensing cannot be questioned, unlike contract (Chapter 8). It is envisaged that review will have a major impact: the agency will adopt 'a less heavy handed and discretionary approach than the IBA necessarily does at present'. As this chapter proceeds the practice can be tested against the sentiment.

Consistent with a policy of deregulation, s. 17 of the 1990 Act provides that 'the Commission shall, after considering all the cash bids submitted . . . award the licence to the applicant who submitted the highest bid'. But Parliament would not wear a pure price bidding system.[17] Franchises may be awarded otherwise if it appears to the Commission that there are 'exceptional circumstances', specifically cases where the quality of the service proposed by the preferred bidder is 'exceptionally high', or where it is 'substantially higher' than that proposed by the highest bidder (s. 17(3), (4)). Threshold requirements have first to be met. The ITC 'shall not proceed to consider whether to award him the licence' unless it appears to the Commission that the proposed service would comply with quality requirements (s. 16(1)(a)) and would be sustainable ('that he would be able to maintain that service throughout the period for which the licence would be in force') (s. 16(1)(b))). Section 16(2) provides:

> Where the service to be provided under the licence is a regional . . . service, the requirements referred to in subsection 1(a) are—(a) that a sufficient amount of time is given in the programmes included in the service to news programmes and current affairs programmes which (in each case) are of high quality . . .; (b) that a sufficient amount of time is given . . . to [other] programmes . . . which are of high quality; (c) that a sufficient amount of time is given . . . to a suitable range of regional programmes . . .; (e) that a sufficient amount of time is given . . . to religious programmes and programmes intended for children; (f) that (taken as a whole) the programmes so included are calculated to appeal to a wide variety of tastes and interests; . . .(h) that in each year not less than 25 per cent of the total amount of time . . . is allocated to the broadcasting of a range and diversity of independent productions.

There is much discretion in these criteria: the agency makes judgments about the appropriate design of the service. Thus, what amount of time is 'sufficient' or what is of 'high quality' is highly subjective. The assessment procedure and information requirements are set out in the *Invitation to Apply*, in effect a source of soft law or guidance (Chapter 6). Specification is far from cut and dried, despite pages of detail. Applicants have been warned that 'high quality . . . cannot be reduced to a single formula'. When bidding, the threshold cannot be known with certainty.[18]

---

17 See, on the legislative background, M. Cave and P. Williamson, 'The Reregulation of British Broadcasting' in M. Bishop, J. Kay and C. Mayer, *The Regulatory Challenge* (Oxford: OUP) 1995. Applicants had also to undertake to pay a proportion of their annual advertising revenue as a levy to the ITC.

18 Independent Television Commission, *Invitation to Apply for Regional Channel 3 Licences* (1991), para. 105. See, M. Cripps and N. Ireland, 'The Design of Auctions and Tenders with Quality Thresholds: the Symmetric Case' (1994) 104 Economic Journal 316.

The system was first used in 1991 for ten-year licences for Channel 3. The 'exceptional circumstance' criterion (s. 17) was not invoked, for fear, it is said, of judicial review.[19] So, after companies failing the threshold had been weeded out, the franchises went to the highest bidder. There was also greater acceptance of process values than previously, as the ITC was keen to emphasise:[20]

> There could have been no sterner test for the Members of the Commission and its staff than the awarding of the new Channel 3 licences by a statutory competitive tender process widely regarded at best as controversial and by many as deeply flawed ... It was always going to prove difficult to administer a system which combined the unmistakable fact of the size of an applicant's bid with the complex judgments involved in assessing the quality of the programme proposals and the applicant's ability to maintain the licensed service ...
>
> The ITC has pursued two general objectives in applying the requirements of the Act. Firstly, it has tried to operate a 'level playing-field' for all applicants for licences, to ensure not merely that it avoided bias in any particular direction, but that it was seen to do so. The most obvious form of such bias would have been in favour of the incumbent, which, apart from its unfairness, would have had the effect of diminishing the prospect of introducing 'new blood' to the system through the allocation of licences. Care was taken in setting requirements and deadlines and providing information to recognise the needs of the newcomer to the system as well as the already established player. Communication with potential and actual applicants was managed centrally in order to reinforce the policy that equal treatment should be accorded to all. Secondly, the Commission in every case encouraged and facilitated public comment on drafts of the key licensing documents before the decision was reached as to their final form ... It was ... considered important that those affected as viewers of television, as well as professionals or commercial interests, should not feel excluded from the process of setting the ground rules for licensing.
>
> A full statement of the terms and conditions for making an application were set out in [the] Invitation ... to Apply ... More than thirty separate ancillary documents, codes, guidance notes and rules required under the legislation were also provided, all of which were available on request ...
>
> In considering the applications, members were supported by teams of ITC staff. The assessment covered applicants' programme proposals, including networking, engineering proposals, business plans and ownership. The ITC had access to professional legal and financial advice. Each applicant's programme proposals were assessed without staff concerned being aware of the contents of business plans or the amount of cash bids. Individual Members were assigned a watching brief over specific licences as part of the assessment. However, the decisions on the awards were taken by the Members of the Commission collectively.
>
> Members also took into account public comment on the applications. Copies of the parts of each application concerned with proposals for the service and the composition and identity of the applicant were placed in 275 major public libraries ... The business plans of each applicant were provided on the basis that they were confidential to the Commission, and were, therefore, not available ... By the deadline ... comments had been received from 2,278 individuals, companies and organisations ... Where points

19   A. Dnes, 'Bidding for Commercial Broadcasting: An Analysis of UK Experience' (1993) 40 Scottish Journal of Political Economy 104, 105.
20   ITC, *Annual Report* 1991, pp. 4, 6, 9-11. And see, for the statutory underpinning, Broadcasting Act 1990, s.15.

about individual applications had been raised in the course of public comment which were material to the assessment, applicants were given the opportunity to respond.

To put it mildly, there were some surprises. Four incumbent firms lost franchises: TVS and TSW submitting the highest bid but failing at the threshold. Eight licences were not awarded to the highest bidder, a fact which underscores the continuing relevance of 'public interest' goals and suggests that rather more discretion may have been exercised than had been envisaged in Parliament.

*Table 9.4: Auction results for Channel 3 franchising*

| Winner | Winning bid (£m)* | Incumbent | Incumbent's bid (£m)* | Surplus bid** (£m) |
|---|---|---|---|---|
| Anglia | 17.804 | same | same | 3.726 |
| Border | 0.052 | same | same | 0.0 |
| Carlton | 43.170 | Thames | 32.694 | -2.144 |
| Central | 0.002 | same | same | 0.0 |
| Channel | 0.001 | same | same | -0.101 |
| Grampian | 0.720 | same | same | -1.989 |
| Granada | 9.000 | same | same | -26.303 |
| Harlech | 20.530 | same | same | 1.163 |
| LWT | 7.585 | same | same | -27.821 |
| Meridian | 36.523 | TVS | 59.758 | -23.235 |
| Scottish | 0.002 | same | same | 0.0 |
| Sunrise | 34.610 | TV-AM | 14.125 | 1.349 |
| Tyne Tees | 15.057 | same | same | 10.047 |
| Ulster | 1.027 | same | same | -2.073 |
| Westcountry | 7.815 | TSW | 16.117 | -8.302 |
| Yorkshire | 37.700 | same | same | 7.584 |

(*Source*:  Independent Television Commission, *Annual Report 1991*, p. 12.)
*Abbreviations*:  LWT = London Weekend Television;  TVS = Television South;
TSW = Television South West.
\*   Annual fee in 1993 prices.
\*\*  The difference between the winning and the next-best offer.

Companies' bidding strategies are seen by Cave and Williamson to reflect and reinforce uncertainties in the franchise process. Bidding was expensive, given the need to submit detailed programme plans and financial projections. It is estimated that many bids cost in excess of £1million to prepare:[1]

> Examination of the bids suggests that companies, especially incumbents, pursued a variety of strategies in trying to gain the licences. In the case of two substantial licence areas, Central Scotland, and [the] Midlands, there was only one application and the cash bid in each case was £2,000 [by Scottish and Central respectively]. Evidently the incumbent became aware that there was no competition for the licence and bid almost the smallest amount possible . . . Another group of incumbents appears to have submitted high bids . . . In two of these cases, however, . . . the Commission took the view that the cash bid was so high that it would be impossible for a company to sustain its programme service over the period of the licence. Two other major incumbents, Granada in North-West England and LWT in the case of the London Weekend licence, appear to have decided to submit relatively low bids . . . for potentially valuable regions . . . [They] were . . . probably hoping that their higher-bidding rivals would either fail the quality hurdle or be denied the licence by the exceptional circumstances clause. Their hunch was right . . .
>
> For the Government, [the auction] was a mixed success. The absence of a reserve price . . . enabled two successful companies to carry away valuable licences by making minimum bids . . . Another awkward aspect of the process was that what emerged was at best a quasi-competitive process. The regulatory body had the capacity to eliminate many applicants, and used that power copiously. The evidence of the bidding suggests that at least some companies anticipated that their rivals would be eliminated and made significant bids, but at a level much lower than would be suggested by observing other companies' behaviour in broadly equivalent regions.

We learn that the franchise auction is not the simple mechanism it first appears. Take the criterion of sustainability. A mathematical model of broadcasting finances has had to be constructed, and bids submitted to econometric models or 'sensitivity tests'. In order to ensure that financial support is securely in place, the ITC may have to seek further and better particulars. It is this kind of internal operating procedure which has been made the subject of legal challenge. Such litigation is obviously predictable, by reason not only of the character of the franchise process, but also the valuable monopoly, the resources of firms, and the potential for good publicity. It is worth bearing this in mind when considering the judicial response. Such litigation also opens a window on agency decision-making. And in this case it is a continuing lack of openness which is demonstrated.

*R v Independent Television Commission, ex p TSW Broadcasting Ltd*[2]

TSW's bid was more than twice the winning bid (Table 9.4), but was rejected as unsustainable. Not unnaturally, the company sought reasons. There was, however, no statutory duty to provide them: further, it emerged that, on the basis

---

1   M. Cave and P. Williamson, 'The Reregulation of British Broadcasting' (above, note 17), pp. 182-183, 186.
2   [1996] EMLR 291.

that the agency would not have to explain, no contemporary record of the reasons was made. After prompting in the Court of Appeal, a staff advisory paper was disclosed, along with affidavit evidence of the seriousness with which Commission members approached their task. TSW argued that the paper gave an unfair and inaccurate assessment of the bid, and that, since it helped to provide the basis of the franchise decision, there was procedural unfairness. Legitimate expectation was invoked, on the basis that the ITC had applied tougher criteria – in the guise of additional sensitivity tests – than had been indicated in the *Invitation to Apply*.

*Lord Templeman*: TSW were understandably outraged when their application was rejected. They had been the licence holder of the South-West region since 1981 and had made profits. They believed in their projection. They had reason to suspect that they were the highest bidders. The ITC were not expressly bound to give reasons for their decisions and did not do so. I do not blame them for their initial caution but having regard to the unique position of TSW I consider that TSW was entitled to be told the reasons for their rejection . . .

In view of the evidence, I do not consider that there is any scope for the courts to interfere with the decision reached by the ITC with regard to TSW. The members of the ITC carefully considered the application of TSW and in particular the crucial forecasts of revenue, costs, profitability and the amount of the bid. Having given the matter their best consideration, they found in the light of their general experience, and in the light of their particular experience of forty bids for Channel 3 licences, that it did not appear to them that TSW would be able to maintain their proposed service . . . They were therefore bound to reject the application . . .

The procedure adopted by the ITC for the consideration of applications was admirable. The papers and the evidence disclosed that the qualified staff and the experienced members of the ITC carried out their duties properly . . . TSW's criticisms of [the staff] paper . . . only amount to an ingenious invitation to the court to substitute its own views for those of the ITC . . . Judicial review does not issue merely because a decision maker has made a mistake and it is not permissible to probe the advice received by the decision maker or to require particulars or administer interrogatories or . . . to cross-examine, in order to discover the existence of a mistake by the decision maker or the advisers of the decision makers . . .

If this appeal were allowed, very serious and difficult questions would arise as to the powers of the ITC to take further action in the absence of further legislation. In any event there would be more delay. This does not mean that leave to apply for judicial review should be withheld where the applicant asserts a legitimate expectation in circumstances which, in private law, would have created an estoppel or misrepresentation . . . Of course, in judicial review proceedings, as in any other proceedings, everything depends on the facts. But judicial review should not be allowed to run riot. The practice of delving through documents and conversations and extracting a few sentences which enable a skilled advocate to produce doubt and confusion where none exists should not be repeated.

Lord Goff: [As regards procedural fairness] the principal flaw in the [challenge] is that it confuses the function of the Commission itself with that of the members of its staff who were employed to advise it. Obviously the assessment which has to be made pursuant to s. 16(1)(b) . . . must be made by the Commission, and by the Commission alone . . . When I read this evidence, I must confess that I was startled by the prominence which had been given [ to the staff] paper . . . This approach seemed to me to diminish, unwarrantably, the role played by the members of the Commission, including the Chairman and the Vice-Chairman . . . Advisory papers . . . may well place emphasis on points which are considered important and may well tend towards a certain conclusion. But those who draft advisory papers are not decision-makers, nor are they performing a judicial or quasi-judicial role. The duty to act fairly is laid not upon the staff but upon the decision-maker himself, here the Commission. This particular paper merely formed part of the data available to the Commission, to assist members of the Commission in reaching their decision . . . It follows that [the staff] paper . . . has nothing to do with procedural unfairness . . . The attack made on [the] paper . . . is not, on a true analysis, an attack upon the procedure of the Commission . . . The complaint is misconceived in that it fails to focus attention on the relevant decision, which is the decision of the Commission itself . . .

In my opinion, there is no substance in the point [of legitimate expectation]. [It] involves the proposition that by the form of its invitation, and in particular by the fact that it required applicants to carry out certain specified sensitivity tests, ITC precluded itself from adopting other sensitivity tests when it came to exercise the judgment which it was required to perform in the performance of its statutory duties under the Act. [The Commission Chairman] roundly rejected the proposition as preposterous, because the requested tests were 'premised on marginal variations from the applicant's own central case' and were 'manifestly not sufficent to test the assumptions inherent in the main case itself'. I entirely agree: moreover, any substance which the argument might have possessed was dissolved by the fact that TSW had made enquiries of ITC designed to identify the criteria which ITC would apply when considering applications, and ITC had (no doubt deliberately) failed to respond to those enquiries.

The case demonstrates 'light-touch' judicial review: respectful of the autonomy of the agency in complex matters, appreciative of the need for flexibility, and positively discouraging of future challenges.Or should the characterisation be 'soft-touch' review? The speech of Lord Goff might be said to encourage a lack of candour, as also to understate the role of expert staff. In the light of this, the views expressed in the original White Paper (above, p. 275) concerning judicial review seem a trifle naive.

In 1995 the ITC allocated the Channel 5 franchise. Process values were now further advanced: reasons were given and published. In the event, both the highest bidder (UK TV) and Virgin Television were disqualified at the threshold, leaving C5B, which had bid precisely the same amount as Virgin, the winner. Another bout of litigation duly followed.

### *R v Independent Television Commission, ex p Virgin Television Ltd*[3]

Virgin argued that it was C5B which should have been disqualified. Complaint was made of the proactive role of the ITC and, as in *ex p Hibbit*,[4] of the absence of a level playing field. After the bids were in, C5B had been allowed to increase its shareholders' funding commitment in response to agency inquiries about sustainability. The ITC is statutorily empowered to obtain further information, but Virgin cited the *Invitation to Tender*: 'No changes will be allowed in the cash bid or in the programme proposals, nor will the applicant be allowed to enhance

3   [1996] EMLR 318.
4   Above, p. 241.

his application once it has been submitted in any respect which the ITC considers unfair to other applicants.' It was suggested that, had the other bidders delayed funding, they could have mounted a more competitive bid. The disqualification of Virgin for failure to meet quality requirements was said to be *Wednesbury* unreasonable.

*Henry LJ*: Answering a request . . . for further information as to the extent and commitment of your funding is neither amending your application nor introducing new material to it. The application is unchanged, but the Commission in the performance of their statutory duty has required further information as to it. Any other construction of [the invitation to apply] would mean that no requests for further information could be made . . .

In this context, what does fairness mean? In our judgment we are here concerned with the Commission's duty to be even-handed, to treat all applications alike in the sense that the same rules are applied to them, and that each applicant receives or would receive the same treatment under those rules . . . Assuming that there was some advantage to C5B that does not mean that it was an unfair advantage. It simply means that the statutory scheme as amplified by the rules of tender worked out better for C5B than for the other bidders. There is nothing to suggest that C5B were allowed to have their shareholders' additional commitment taken into account because they were treated preferentially, but rather because the rules permitted it. There is nothing to suggest that the other applicants would not have been similarly treated had they acted as C5B did.

Turning to the treatment of Virgin, Henry LJ quoted from the speech of Lord Templeman in the *TSW* case[5] and continued:

That 'pick out a plum' school of advocacy is particularly dangerous (as well as being futile) in judicial review where, as here, there is neither full discovery nor cross-examination, nor the full rigour of pleadings . . . Matters of judgment were entrusted to an expert body by Parliament. That body was also made responsible for finding the facts on which such judgment would be based, in circumstances where the level of quality threshold was to be set by the Commission and no-one else. Of its nature such an exercise is . . . judgmental in character and, therefore, one upon which opinions may readily differ. Especially is this so within this area of decision-making where the exercise is not simply a quantitative exercise . . . but involves a qualitative analysis and judgment . . . It has to follow that a very heavy burden falls on the party seeking to upset a qualitative judgment of the nature described and arrived at by the qualified and experienced body which is the Commission . . .

It is quite plain that the Commission approached its task of evaluating the application and the evidence provided by Virgin to support it with model care. There must accordingly be a natural, as well as a judicial, reluctance to conclude that the decision was flawed. This is not a consequence of judicial conservatism or intellectual disinclination. It is a logical consequence of the perceived care and meticulous approach which the Commission brought to bear on its task of assessment and evaluation in accordance with what Parliament has entrusted to it. It is also a consequence of the limits which the court is required to observe in determining whether or not the decision-maker has arrived at a decision which has a sufficient factual basis . . .

5   Above, p. 278.

[Counsel for Virgin] employed the very technique which was roundly deprecated by Lord Templeman . . . This part of these proceedings consisted of an undisguised attempt to show that the Commission had 'got it wrong'. This is impermissible, in judicial review, unless it can be shown that the judgment which has been reached was based on a misapprehension of the facts which form the foundation of the Commission's judgment. Since the facts are for the Commission to find and there was, at the very least, evidence capable of supporting the Commission's view, [counsel's] task can be likened to that which according to legend confronted Sisyphus many years ago.

In what circumstances then might the ITC be successfully challenged?

## 6. 'Everything must go': the railways

The process of juridification associated with government by contract is nowhere better illustrated than in the case of the railways. Public ownership relies on an internal command structure for co-ordination and organisation; in contrast, 'the rail network has been privatised by lawyers, and it will be run on a regime dictated by legal documents'. The new service is governed 'by possibly the most complicated contractual matrix ever drawn up'.[6] To this effect, privatisation has involved a fundamental restructuring of the industry, characterised by a high degree of functional separation as well as interdependency.[7] In the new order inaugurated by the Railways Act 1993 the central player is Railtrack, now a private company which owns and manages most of the operational infrastructure, including the track and signalling equipment. Access is granted by Railtrack to the train operating companies, the winners of the franchises. Railtrack is responsible for the timetable and the franchisees for running the trains and for day-to-day station operations. Other important players include the Rolling Stock Companies (ROSCOs) which own and lease trains to the operators, and the Infrastructure Service Companies (ISCOs), responsible for maintenance. British Rail has been progressively diminished, operating in effect as a holding company until assets have been transferred into the private sector.

Public control and accountability functions are exercised by two new government departments: the Office of Passenger Rail Franchising (OPRAF), headed by the Franchising Director, and the Office of the Rail Regulator (ORR). The Regulator licences operators; approves and if necessary dictates access agreements; enforces competition law; and, generally, acts to protect the interests of rail users (Railways Act 1993, ss. 4, 8). The Franchising Director is responsible for the entire franchise process: tender, negotiation and award, monitoring and enforcement (ss. 5, 23-31, 57, 58). The offices are typical of the new breed of public agency: non-ministerial departments or small personalised units operating at arm's length from government (Chapter 5). Take OPRAF, which in 1996 had just over 100 staff under Director Roger Salmon. The agency

6   J. Edwards, 'Big Ticket' (1996) (June) Legal Business 22.
7   Government White Paper, *New Opportunities for the Railways*, Cm.2012, 1992.   See, D. Kennedy, *Competition in the British Railway Industry* (London: Centre for the Study of Regulated Industries) 1996.

has in practice been very reliant on outside, professional advice. Notably, a major item of cost has been fees to City Solicitors.[8]

The Government recognised that passenger rail services could not as a general rule cover their costs and would continue to require public subsidy. The sums involved are very large: the annual subsidy for the first three franchises awarded was over £100 million.[9] To emphasise, OPRAF has been responsible not only for allocating valuable concessions, but also for disbursing significant amounts of taxpayers' money. This is obviously relevant to the assessment of agency procedures which will be seen as scarcely adequate to protect the public interest.

## *Allocation: framework and policy*

Let us follow the franchise trail. This is the scheme as set out in the statute:

5(1). It shall be the duty of the Franchising Director to exercise any functions . . . under . . . this Act in the manner which he considers best calculated—(a) to fulfil, in accordance with such instructions and guidance as may be given to him . . . by the Secretary of State, any objectives given to him . . . by the Secretary of State . . . (b) to ensure that any payments [including any payments which the Franchising Director may be required to make pursuant to a franchise agreement] are such as he reasonably considers will achieve economically and efficiently any objectives given to him by the Secretary of State . . .

(3) Where the Secretary of State gives the Franchising Director any objectives under subsection (1)(a) above, the Secretary of State shall—(a) lay a copy of a statement of those objectives before each House of Parliament . . .

23(1) It shall be the duty of the Franchising Director from time to time to designate as eligible for provision under franchise agreements such services for the carriage of passengers by railway as he may determine . . .

'Franchise agreement' means an agreement with the Franchising Director under which another party undertakes either—(a) to provide, or (b) to secure that a wholly owned subsidiary of his provides, throughout the franchise term, those services for the carriage of passengers by railway to which the agreement relates . . .

25(4) The Franchising Director may, after consultation with the [British Railways] Board and the regulator, determine that . . . the Board . . . shall [not] be eligible for inclusion among the persons to whom the invitations are to be issued or who may be selected as the franchisee . . .

(5) The Franchising Director shall not make [such] a determination . . . unless he considers that it is desirable to do so—(a) for the purpose of promoting competition for franchises; . . . (c) for the purpose of encouraging new entry to the passenger railway industry . . .

26(1) Unless the Secretary of State otherwise directs, the person who is to be the franchisee under any franchise agreement shall be selected by the Franchising Director from among those who submit tenders in response to an invitation to tender . . .

(2) The Franchising Director shall prepare any such invitation to tender and shall issue that invitation to such persons as he may, after consultation with the regulator, think fit.

---

8    Some £13million to Linklaters and Paines between 1993 and 1996. See, for criticism, National Audit Office, *The Award of the First Three Passenger Rail Franchises*, HC 701, Session 1995-1996, Part 6.

9    Ibid, p. 5.

(3) The Franchising Director shall not issue an invitation to tender . . . to [or entertain such a tender from] any person unless he is of the opinion that the person has . . . an appropriate financial position and managerial competence, and is otherwise a suitable person, to be the franchisee.

28(1)   A franchise agreement may include provision with respect to the fares to be charged for travel by means of the franchise services . . .

(2) . . . If it appears to the Franchising Director that the interest of persons who use . . . franchised services so require, he shall ensure that the franchise agreement in question contains any such provision as he may consider necessary for the purpose of securing that any fares . . . which are to be charged are, in his opinion, reasonable in all the circumstances of the case . . .

29(1)   The Franchising Director may enter into a franchise agreement on conditions requiring—(a)  the rendering to the Franchisng Director by the franchisee . . . of payments of such amounts and at such intervals as may be specified in . . . the franchise agreement;  or (b)  the payment to the franchisee . . . of grants of such amounts and at such intervals as may be [so] specified . . .

(5) Subject to any requirements imposed by or under this Act, a franchise agreement may contain any such provisions as the Franchising Director may think fit.

(6) Any sums received by the Franchising Director in consequence of the conditions of the franchise agreement shall be paid into the Consolidated Fund.

(7)  Any sums required by the Franchising Director for . . . any . . . payment, in consequence of any  . . .  provision of a franchise agreement shall be paid by the Secretary of State out of money provided by Parliament.

The framework is typically skeletal, leaving open the basic model of allocation: neither a pure price-bidding system nor possible public interest goals are specified in the statute.  Discretion to make rules is reserved to the Minister, in contrast to the ITC which takes its mandate direct from Parliament.  Some agencies operate at greater arm's length from government than others.  This leaves ample scope for changes of approach in rail franchising under the new Labour Government.

We learn that rail franchising is contract-based, like the old IBA system, and that the Director has a wide choice of franchise terms including subsidy (ss. 23, 29).  The statute points towards a rolling procedure for the appraisal of bids (see below), specifying a threshold requirement in the form of pre-qualification (s. 26(3)).  Section 25 highlights the influence of policy on franchise design.  Assets and experience give the incumbent an obvious advantage, but the Conservative Government did not intend BR to win.  In the event, all 25 passenger franchises have been awarded to the private sector.[10]

The rule-making power has been used to express common themes in the Conservative 'revolution' in government: 'the three Es', value for money, competition. Take the 1996 version of the *Objectives, Instructions and Guidance* issued by the Minister:

10  Above, p. 275.

Dear Director:

Your principal objectives are:

- to secure that railway passenger services . . . are provided under franchise agreements as soon as reasonably practicable; and
- to secure an overall improvement in the quality of railway passenger and station services . . .

You should also:

- encourage efficiency and economy in the provision of railway services;
- promote the use and cost-effective development of the railway network; and
- promote the award of franchise agreements to companies in which [existing] railway employees . . . have a substantial interest.

The philosophy of public control under the Conservatives has been one of 'light-touch' franchising. This gears with the proclaimed virtues of the franchising technique as an alternative to 'heavy-handed' command and control regulation (Chapter 10). Thus, according to the general guidance as summarised by OPRAF:[11]

> In general the Franchising Director should ensure, within the resources available to him, that the franchise system provides good value for money, encourages competition in the railway industry and protects the interests of passengers . . . He should also leave maximum scope for the initiative of franchisees under franchise agreements imposing requirements no more burdensome than are required in his opinion to achieve his objectives, and he should act so far as possible to enable franchisees to plan the future of their businesses with a reasonable degree of assurance.

Rail franchising demonstrates the different kinds of rules in administrative law (Chapters 6 and 7). Both instructions (in italics) and guidance of a more specific character have also been issued:

> 18. *When setting minimum service levels for services being franchised for the first time, you should take as your starting point the service being provided by BR at the time when you draw up the specification . . .* Each service should be considered individually, taking account of all surrounding circumstances. For example, where you judge that services are essential but where they are unprofitable to run, you should set the minimum close to or at the current level of service. Conversely, where service levels have been set by BR on a commercial basis . . . you should leave maximum flexibility for franchisees while safeguarding what you believe to be a reasonable core service level . . .
>
> 20. *. . . Where bidders for a franchise offer additional contractual commitments to improve the level and/or quality of services provided beyond that which you have specified, you are to take account of those commitments when evaluating bids . . .*
>
> 21. *. . . You must require each franchisee to publish his own Passenger's Charter.* This should include the franchisee's own code of conduct for dealing with passengers, publishing performance information, handling complaints, and payment of compensation to passengers in the event of poor performance.

11  OPRAF, *Passenger Rail Industry Overview* (June 1996), p. 53.

## (b) Agency procedures

Procedure is typically a field of agency discretion. OPRAF has played a strong pro-active role, taking steps to generate competition and to advise, clarify and negotiate on bids. To this effect, a rolling procedure has been used. *Prequalification* sees prospective bidders invited to register an interest and tested in accordance with the legislation (s 26(3)). Detailed information on the franchise is made available to firms passing the threshold in the *Invitation to Tender*. *Indicative bidding* follows, a key time in OPRAF's words, 'for interacting with bidders', and leading to the choice of a short-list. *Evaluation* of formal bids leads to the selection of preferred bidders, subject to negotiations on detail. The decision was taken early on that the bid which required the lowest subsidy would generally be successful. The Franchising Director has, however, exercised discretion to extend franchise terms in return for additional investment; further, he was later instructed to take into account improvement in the quality of service (para. 20), a competing priority. Practical operations highlight the importance of procedural design. Take, for example, the award of the first franchise, South West Trains, to Stagecoach Holdings. According to the National Audit Office:[12]

> As bidders gained more knowledge about the industry so the range of subsidy levels proposed by bidders narrowed between indicative and final bid stage . . . In the case of South West Trains the range of bids in terms of subsidy payable over the life of the franchise varied from £341m at the indicative bid stage to £162m in the final bid. OPRAF believed this was a beneficial aspect of a multi-stage process and considered that an arrangement in which bidders submitted one final bid would not have worked as well: the immaturity of the market would have put the achievement of value for money in jeopardy since many bidders did not have a sufficient understanding at the outset of what they were bidding for.

A central feature of agency operations is the disdain for process values in the guise of publicly articulated criteria and reasoned decisions. The situation has been reminiscent of the old IBA contract awards. Thus, the precept of commercial confidentiality traditionally associated with private autonomy (above, p. 271) has been used to justify leaving opaque the how and why of individual awards. The pre-qualification document is emphatic:

> You are invited to lodge an application to pre-qualify in respect of any one or more of the Passenger Services summarised in . . . this document . . . The Franchising Director will treat as confidential any information so designated by an applicant . . . The Franchising Director reserves the right to refuse pre-qualification and shall not be obliged to give any reason for such refusal . . .
>
> If you pre-qualify, you will be asked to sign a confidentiality agreement as a pre-condition to receiving an [invitation to tender] . . . The Franchising Director will evaluate tenders in accordance with criteria to be set out in the [Invitation to Tender] and associated information . . .

12   National Audit Office, *The Award of the First Three Passenger Rail Franchises*, pp. 27-28. See further OPRAF, *Annual Report 1995-1996*, pp. 8-13.

The Franchising Director reserves the right not to accept a tender on the grounds of price or otherwise and without giving any reason for his decision.

A procedure in which not even the invitation to tender is published lacks legitimacy. The more transparent process commonly proclaimed as a virtue of 'government by contract' (above, p. 209) is conspicuous by its absence. Attention is here drawn to the speed and scale of rail franchising: the political imperative to complete the task ahead of the General Election. This is obviously a key factor in an explanation and assessment of OPRAF's methods: 'everything must go'.

### (c) The franchise and the courts

The franchise agreement defines the Director's requirements and governs his relations with the operator. A standard document has proved fit for purpose – routinisation – with variations reflecting the specific circumstances of individual franchises.[13] Common elements include incentive or penalty payments linked to the quality of service; prices, for certain designated classes of ticket (s. 28); and obligations on the franchisee to provide adequate capacity, participate in inter-operator arrangements, and provide the information necessary for monitoring. This personifies the functional use of public contract as a source of rules.

For example, the Passenger Service Requirement (PSR) forms a schedule to the agreement and breach of it can lead to the company defaulting on the franchise (see below). It comprises two components: a minimum level of services to be provided and a measure of flexibility above this level so as to allow the operator to develop services. Thus, rather than specify a detailed timetable, OPRAF has preferred to prescribe, route by route, certain service characteristics which are important to passengers: frequency of trains, stations to be served, maximum journey times, first and last trains.[14] The 'contract technology' reflects and reinforces the 'light-touch' philosophy of the franchising regime:[15]

> It is the Franchising Director's policy that operators should retain a substantial degree of freedom in managing their businesses, protecting the availability, quality and safety standards of rail services. A vital part of the franchising strategy is that operators have opportunities to introduce extra services for which there is public demand. It is also part of the policy that high quality operation is more likely to result if there are fair rewards for the operators . . .
>
> The franchise agreement sets out basic parameters within which operators must act. They include . . . the Passenger Service Requirement . . . and regulation of certain fares . . . operators have considerable freedom, to develop services outside these parameters. They may, for instance, run more trains than are set out in the PSR and they may adjust the structure of unregulated fares in accordance with the demands of the market . . . As in other industries, there are certain rules of the game . . . The important thing is that

---

13  See, for details, OPRAF, *Passenger Rail Industry Overview*, s. 3.
14  See, for details, *OPRAF Annual Report 1995-1996*, pp. 20-21.
15  OPRAF, *Bulletin*, No. 3, August 1995, pp. 1-2.

franchisees retain a significant degree of operational flexibility and considerable freedom to concentrate on those items in the profit and loss account over which they have control . . . The real thrust of the policy built into the franchising framework is to balance safeguards to ensure high quality of service with operational flexibility for franchisees.

In the event, a legal challenge was made to the minimum required service levels in the first seven franchises offered by the Director (see below). Affidavit evidence presented by OPRAF sheds further light on agency policy, in particular the relevance of subsidy:

> To set service requirements too close to current service levels could leave franchisees with inadequate flexibility to use initiative in developing new service patterns. It could also increase the overall call on the Franchising Director's budget: those bidding for franchises will take into account both the rights offered to them under the franchise and the obligation. The PSR is the principal such obligation . . .
>
> Instruction 18 [see below] led the Franchising Director to adopt the current timetables themselves as the starting point for drawing up PSRs. He concluded that minimum service levels should be set at, or below, the levels in those timetables. To set them below the levels in the timetable would be necessary in some instances in order to achieve flexibility and value for money . . . The Franchising Director considered that it was unnecessary to set higher PSR levels because he considered either that:- (a) The existing BR level of service would be likely to be maintained because it was commercially attractive, or (b) The service had a very low usage and, given the existence of reasonable alternatives, it was not appropriate that public money be used to guarantee it.

For administrative lawyers the issue is raised of the hierarchy of rules (Chapter 6). Reference must be made to the instructions and guidance under which the Director was supposed to be operating. They had been laid before Parliament, being incorporated in a single document with the objectives (s. 5(3)). Bear in mind that what is in italics is instructions:

> 18. *For the initial letting of franchises, your specification of minimum service levels . . . is to be based on that being provided by BR immediately prior to franchising . . .*
>
> 23. Although service specifications set for the initial franchises must be based on the timetable being operated by BR immediately prior to franchising, you should aim, over time, to tailor the provision of franchising services more closely to demand. In large part this tailoring should be driven by franchisees responding on a commercial basis to passenger demand . . . Any changes from the existing pattern of services should be made gradually.

### *R v Director of Passenger Rail Franchising, ex p Save Our Railways*[16]

Save Our Railways, a campaign group backed by the rail unions, sought to undermine the agency's approach on the basis of failure to comply with the Instructions and Guidance. The dispute centred on the effect of Instruction 18, and in particular the words 'based on. . .'. Individual PSRs were stated by OPRAF

16   (1995) Times, 18 December.

to be 'broadly based' on the current timetable. According to agency figures, expressed as a percentage of BR levels, the minimum requirements were: South West Trains – 89%-86%; Great Western – 86%; London-Tilbury-Southend Rail – 80%-69%; East Coast – 71%; Gatwick Express – 45%; Midland Main Line – 75%; Network South Central – 82%-77%. It was accepted that the Secretary of State had at all times known of and approved the agency's approach.

*Sir Thomas Bingham MR*: The . . . Instructions and Guidance need not be laid before Parliament, or published. To that extent they are treated as less significant than the prescribed objectives, perhaps because they may be more readily subject to change. There is, however, no reason to doubt that 'Instructions and Guidance' bear their ordinary meaning. An instruction is a direction with which the recipient must comply. Guidance is advice which the recipient should heed and respect; it should ordinarily be followed but need not if there are special reasons for not doing so. This response to the Instructions and Guidance of the Secretary of State forms part of the statutory duty of the Franchising Director. . .

The applicants' legal argument was that the Secretary of State's instruction in paragraph 18 . . . while not requiring minimum service levels specified on the initial letting of franchises to be in precise conformity with levels being provided by BR immediately prior to franchising, did require the level specified to correspond, at least approximately, to the levels provided by BR . . . In reading the Objectives, Instructions and Guidance the court is not construing a statute, nor even subordinate legislation. The document must be read in a practical down-to-earth way as a communication by a Secretary of State to a responsible public official. The language used is not to be invested with more precision than it would naturally bear . . . All this we take to be clear. But the statutory duty of the Franchising Director is, as we read s.5, to exercise his functions in the manner which he considers best calculated to fulfil the objectives given to him in accordance with the Secretary of State's instructions and guidance. Thus the Objectives, Instructions and Guidance define and circumscribe the Franchising Director's statutory duty. The court accordingly cannot, in case of dispute abdicate its responsibility to give the document its proper meaning. It means what it means, not what anyone – Franchising Director, Secretary of State or member of the public – would like it to mean.

'Based on' is not a term of art, and it is not an exact term. It permits some latitude. It is obvious that every train timetabled by BR need not continue to run. There may be changes, and within limits it is for the Franchising Director to rule on the extent of the changes. His is the primary judgment. But there is a limit to the changes which may be made without ceasing to comply with the instruction in paragraph 18 and the guidance in paragraph 23. The changes must in our view be marginal, not significant or substantial . . . We cannot read this document as a warrant for more than relatively minor change. Give or take relatively minor changes, the minimum service level specified was, as we understand the instruction, to correspond reasonably closely with the pre-franchising BR specification . . .

The Franchising Director's approach seems clear. He has been cautious in including loss-making services in his minimum service level specification because a subsidy would be payable to the operator required to run it. This is an intelligible and no way irrational approach. But it is not in our view an approach which gives effect to the instruction in paragraph 18 or the guidance in paragraph 23. No-one reading the Objectives, Instructions and Guidance could in our view have appreciated that this approach would be adopted or that the subsidy payment factor would be given so much weight.

In the event, the court concluded that, save in respect of South West Trains and Great Western, the Director 'did not correctly understand, or if he correctly understood did not comply with the Secretary of State's instruction'.   The Minister's approval could not alter the effect of the instruction: nor was his ability subsequently to amend the instruction an appropriate bar to relief.  The dispute is reminiscent of the famous *Laker* case[17] which also concerned franchising and the interplay, between Minister and agency, of objectives, instructions (directions) and guidance.  In both cases the procedural values of lawyers clash with the policy judgments of government.  Is *Save Our Railways* 'old-fashioned, legalistic and inappropriate to modern administration' – the kinds of criticism directed at *Laker*? Or is it entirely healthy – back to basics?  At one level the dispute is about, and the court demonstrates a restrictive attitude to, the scope of agency discretion; at another level, what is in issue is the preference for 'light-touch franchising', the attempt to increase agency discretion being in order to increase business discretion.

The confirmation that instructions etc. to agencies given under statutory powers are justiciable is important, given the fashion for 'hiving-off' under NPM. Paradoxically, the challenge in *Save Our Railways* represents the logic of the Government's own approach in terms of juridification:[18]

> PSRs have only become an issue as a consequence of the 1993 Act and the need to ensure that the obligation of the private sector franchisee as regards minimum services is formalised.  Prior to the enactment of the Act, BR retained the prerogative to cancel services with impunity.  It did not, and could not, guarantee services until more recently when the Passengers' Charter was created.  Thus, to the extent that a PSR is not significantly or substantially below the current BR timetable, it bears little difference from the position *ex ante* except that a PSR incorporated in a franchise agreement denotes an enforceable sanction.

The pressure group hoped that existing and future PSRs would be amended to meet the Instructions and Guidance.  The Minister,[19] however, preferred 'to clarify' the rules 'to ensure that they reflect beyond doubt the policy that we have always followed'.  OPRAF's approach, as explained in evidence, is precisely that stated in para. 18 of the amended version (above, p. 285).  This is a useful reminder of the limitations of judicial control of administration:  subsidiary norms are challengeable, but they are very easily changed.  As for Save Our Railways, it won the case but lost the campaign.

## 7.  Going on:  franchise management

Stress has been laid on franchising as a process or sequence of activities.  The prominence afforded the auction should not detract from important issues in the continuing franchise relationship.  The legitimacy of sales procedure is undermined if subsequently there is insufficient emphasis on compliance.  Take attempts by

17   Above, p. 83.
18   J. Goh, 'Privatisation of the Railways and Judicial Review' (1996) Utilities LR 42, pp. 42-43.
19   Hansard, HC Deb., vol. 268, col. 1238 (18 December 1995).

the franchisee to renegotiate terms. Although there must be scope for adaptation in the light of changed circumstances, the spectre is raised of opportunistic behaviour and over-bidders aiming to recoup monopoly profits.[20] An increasingly important issue in administrative law concerns the adequacy of arrangements for franchise management to protect the collective, public interest. Attention is drawn especially to the scale and form of agency discretion; the interplay of private and public legal forms; and the problems of exercising 'voice' as by consumers.

This stage of the process further highlights the interface of franchising and regulation. Such are the complexities of public services that the franchise as a source of rules is necessarily incomplete: the franchisor has a degree of flexibility in the enforcement function. By monitoring and negotiation, the agency is commonly involved in mandating aspects of the operation: precisely the kind of task familiarly associated with regulatory agencies (Chapter 10).[1]

## (a) Compliance: techniques and limitations

The wide range of possible techniques is shown by the ITC. Channel 3 licences require it to be supplied with such information 'as may reasonably be required', including financial and technical details. As regards the contentious issue of quality, the Commission looks to various sources to assess performance: staff monitoring, viewers' complaints, consultative councils, audience research. Particular stress is laid on formal performance reviews, which provide a focus for both appraisal and enforcement. Annual reports go into considerable detail about company performance, both individually and collectively. The agency has at its disposal a series of sanctions, including powers to give directions, issue notices of non-compliance and formal warnings, and extract financial penalties. As well as the threat of non-renewal of franchise, it may insist, in extremis, on reducing the franchise term or revoking the licence (Broadcasting Act 1990, ss. 33, 40-42). On occasion the watchdog has chosen to bite. The first fine imposed was £500,000, against Granada Television for breach of the ITC Programme Code. The ITC has intervened in the case of GMTV to negotiate changes in programming, as well as issuing a formal warning, for failure to meet franchise commitments.[2] In short, the agency has taken seriously its role of post-hoc regulator (above, p. 274).

None the less, it is sometimes argued that, by the nature of the arrangement, the franchisor is in a weak position to ensure compliance. The kind of quality standards familiar to the ITC present particular problems. Then there is the 'blank screens' argument, that sanction will be lax by reason of the danger of loss of

20 A common concern in the literature. See e.g., M. Zupan, 'The Efficacy of Franchise Bidding Schemes in the Case of Cable Television: Some Systematic Evidence' (1989) 32 J. of Law and Economics, 401.

1 See further M. Armstrong, S. Cowan and J. Vickers, *Regulatory Reform: Economic Analysis and British Experience* (MIT Press, 1994), Ch.4; R. Baldwin and M. Cave, *Franchising as a Tool of Government* (London: Centre for the Study of Regulated Industries) 1996, Ch. 2.

2 See, for details, ITC, *Annual Report 1994*, pp. 27-28. GMTV is the franchisee for national breakfast-time services.

continuity of service. 'Experience in the broadcasting field indicates that where substitutability is high this problem can be exaggerated.'[3] Williamson,[4] in classic work, highlights the issue of refranchising, observing that the advantages of incumbency are liable to undermine the competition. Note how this links back to the design of a system. It touches on the conduct of the auction, and the need to encourage 'new blood' as the ITC has done (above, p. 276). It also raises the question of the optimum length of the franchise term. On the one hand, a short term is good for discipline, minimising incumbent advantage and emphasising instead competition and agency leverage in enforcement; on the other hand, a long term is apt to encourage bidding and stimulate investment. The theme of franchising as a complex, judgmental process is underscored.

## (b) Discretion and legal form

The style of franchise management is naturally informed by the general philosophy of the franchise system. Take the railways, where the preference for light-touch franchising (above, p. 285) gears with the familiar regulatory model of negotiated compliance not strict enforcement. Thus:[5]

> The Franchising Director intends to develop a constructive and collaborative relationship with each franchise operator.. The Franchising Director intends to found this relationship on the following general principles: ... To manage the achievement of his objectives, not the activities of the franchise operator; ... to require the franchise operator to provide information only if this is required in relation to one of [his] objectives set out above; and ... to minimise the burden placed on the franchise operator.

Franchising not only connects private initiative with public control but also links the public and private legal forms of statutory and contractual remedies. Ogus[6] correctly draws attention to the weakness of a purely contractual approach, the conventional remedy of damages being 'inefficacious because the principal losses are incurred by consumers, not the franchisor'. The railway, however, illustrates contractual franchising which founds additional remedies. A franchise agreement will include such terms as customer compensation, a performance bond and termination for serious default. The Franchising Director is under a duty to act to prevent or rectify any breach of the agreement (Railways Act 1993, ss. 57, 58). The statutory procedure involves making either a provisional or a final order which specifies the action required to prevent or rectify the breach and which, in the case of a final order, may impose a financial penalty. An order is enforceable by civil injunction, while non-compliance is actionable by any person who suffers loss or damage. We see here a specially designed 'public contract'.

3   R. Baldwin and M. Cave, *Franchising as a Tool* (above, note 1), p. 34.
4   O. Williamson, 'Franchise Bidding for Natural Monopolies – In General And With Respect to CATV' (1976) 7 Bell Journal of Economics 73.
5   OPRAF, *Passenger Rail Industry Overview* (June 1996), p. 101.
6   A. Ogus, *Regulation. Legal Form and Economic Theory* (Oxford, Clarendon) 1994, p. 332.

The railway has been seen to exemplify the theme of juridification. A major issue here concerns interdependency: to encourage efficiency properly, enforcement must be sensitive to the fact that deficiencies in service may well flow from the actions of others in the industry. In practice this means an internal network of compensation provisions, another element in the huge contractual matrix (above, p. 282). To emphasise, legal skills are at a premium in franchise management.

Let us take two examples of action by the Franchising Director, both involving South West Trains.[7] In the first case, OPRAF established through its monitoring programme a series of minor breaches of franchise commitments on passenger information: in the event, in return for extended deadlines, SWT agreed additional commitments on refurbishment and passenger security. This illustrates the 'constructive and collaborative relationship' in operation: note the role of agency discretion and of bargaining in the shadow of formal enforcement powers. In the second case, OPRAF was dealing with a major breach of franchise: large numbers of cancellations resulting from a company cost-cutting exercise. The Franchising Director gave notice of a proposed statutory penalty of £1 million, but did not levy it because SWT then took 'appropriate steps' to remedy the breach. The company remained liable, however, for payments under a performance regime specified in the franchise. This illustrates the mix of statutory and contractual remedies. The affair also points up issues of 'voice'. Representations were invited from passengers about the draft order, and the parallel avenue of political redress opened up when questions were asked in Parliament.[8] To emphasise, the affair illustrates tensions between the bilateral model of the franchise relationship and collective or public expressions of concern. Looking to the future, we may anticipate that such issues of franchise management will gain increased prominence in administrative law.

## 8. Conclusion

Study of contract as a government activity demonstrates the importance to NPM and to the Conservatives' 'revolution' in government of the private legal form. Thus, in an era of mixed administrations, of heavy reliance on the creative interaction of public and private power, contract is at the heart of administrative law. To make the point slightly differently, the abolition of *compulsory* competitive tendering does not signal an end to outsourcing or contracting out. Again, franchising as a tool of government is here to stay. Illustrative of the functional use of contract as a source of rules, it is both a flexible technique and a useful alternative to classical techniques of regulation.

A policy like CCT is seen to operate at various levels: stimulus to efficiency and economy, instrument for cultural change, tool of central control. It has further involved experimentation with increasingly elaborate systems of tender and allocation, specification and enforcement. However, this extreme form of

7   OPRAF, *News Releases*, 14 March 1997.
8   HC Deb., vol. 292, cols. 5–9 (10 March 1997).

legal ordering has not only failed the test of market liberalisation but also shows the costs of complexity. Far from a solution, 'more law' in the shape of detailed rules and regulations is part of the problem.

Taggart[9] argues that in speaking up for process values administrative lawyers perform their most important role: requirements of transparency and voice and of fairness and rationality should be embodied in the design of institutions and regulatory schemes *from the outset* (Chapter 4). Nowhere is the point more convincingly illustrated than in the case of franchising, particularly when this involves the use of public funds. Stress has here been laid on franchising as a process or series of discretions, typically subject to weak judicial review. The view of Baldwin and Cave[10] that 'the extent to which procedural aims are achieved will depend upon the details of the arrangements chosen' would appear self-evident. Yet it glosses over the clash of values involved in the harnessing of private enterprise in the delivery of public services, as highlighted by claims to commercial confidentiality. In the brave new world of government by contract administrative lawyers must do more to make themselves heard.

9   M. Taggart, 'The Impact of Corporatisation and Privatisation on Administrative Law' (1992) 51 Aust. J. of Pub. Admin. 368.

10   R. Baldwin and M. Cave, *Franchising as a Tool* (above, p. 29, note 1), p. 50.

Chapter 10

# Regulation, agencies and self-regulation

Regulation is today one of the chief instruments of government for the achievement of policy objectives, epitomised in the rise of 'the regulatory state' (above, p. 141). For administrative law the development creates a special concern with the legal measures which express such arrangements, the infusion of process values, and the forms of control and accountability. English administrative law still has far to go in this context, as will be demonstrated.

## 1. Characterisation, classification, explanation

Regulation is a slippery concept: confusion arises because the term has acquired a variety of meanings. Sometimes it is used loosely to describe any form of behavioural control; effectively the main output function of government. Sometimes it is placed in opposition to markets, being used in economics to describe all activity of the state – including nationalisation, taxation and subsidy – which determines or alters the operation of markets. More manageably, to adopt Selznick's formulation, [1] regulation refers to sustained and focused control exercised by a public agency over activities that are socially valued.

It is in the last context that reference is made to 'the regulatory state'. First, regulation is differentiated from control of anti-social activities of the type commonly associated with the criminal justice system. In Majone's words, 'market activities can be "regulated" only in societies that consider such activities worthwhile in themselves and hence in need of protection as well as control'. [2] Second, there is more to regulation than simply passing a law. The stress on sustained and focused control points to the need for detailed knowledge of, and close and continuing involvement with, the regulated activity. 'Full-blown' regulation is usefully defined in this context as 'a combination of three basic elements: rule formulation; monitoring and inspection; enforcement and sanctions'. [3]

---

1   P. Selznick, 'Focusing Organisational Research on Regulation' in R. Noll (ed.), *Regulatory Policy and the Social Sciences* (Berkeley: University of California Press) 1985. See also, T. Daintith, 'A Regulatory Space Agency?' (1989) 9 OJLS 534; J. Kay and J. Vickers, 'Regulatory Reform: An Appraisal, in G. Majone (ed.), *Deregulation or Re-regulation? Regulatory Reform in Europe and the United States* (London: Pinter) 1990; G. Majone, 'The Rise of the Regulatory State in Europe' (1994) 17 West European Politics 77.
2   Majone, 17 West European Politics at 81.
3   C. Hood and C. Scott, 'Bureaucratic Regulation and New Public Management in the United Kingdom: Mirror-Image Developments?' (1996) 23 J. of Law and Soc. 321, 336.

What of the identity of the regulator and regulated? As the reference to government and markets illustrates, regulation is commonly associated with external control exercised over private business, so-called 'government' or 'public' regulation. In turn, an 'executive' model, in which public regulation is the direct responsibility of central or local government, may be contrasted with an 'agency' model, in which the control is exercised by means of bodies operating outside the conventional lines of political or democratic accountability. Then there is 'self-regulation' by the private sector. This may appear at first sight to fall outside the subject matter of administrative law. However, government may not only have an interest in policy and performance, it may in effect be delegating the regulatory function (below, p. 339). Putting this slightly differently, there are subtle blends or hybrids, for example self-regulation within a statutory framework, which command the attention of the public lawyer. Less familiar as a category is 'bureaucratic regulation', by which is meant the regulation of government bodies by other government bodies. Incorporating considerable parts of the machinery of administrative law – audit and inspection, ombudsman and regulatory agency – bureaucratic regulation finds a home in different chapters of this book. For present purposes, the classification usefully draws attention to the commonalities as well as differences between regulation in business and in government, and, further, to the place of public regulation and self-regulation in the broader process of 're-inventing government' (see below).

### (a) Competing theories

Economic regulation is broadly conceived as 'governmental efforts to control firms' decisions about price, output, product quality, or production process'.[4] It is justified according to classical, normative, public interest theories of regulation[5] in terms of 'market failure', circumstances in which the interaction of market forces fails to generate allocative efficiency. Typical justifications are the problem of externalities or spillovers, where the price of a product does not reflect major costs that its production and use impose on society (environmental protection); the need to compensate for inadequate information so that consumer preferences can be properly expressed (food and drinks labelling); so-called 'moral hazard', where someone other than a consumer pays for a service so that excessive consumption has to be avoided (medical costs); and excessive competition and predatory pricing. Again, market disciplines being at a premium, the case is a compelling one for regulation of monopolies, as also of anti-competitive practices.[6] According to standard economic theory, a monopolist may be expected to raise prices and reduce output (so reaping 'abnormal' profits);

4   S. Breyer and R. Stewart, *Administrative Law and Regulatory Policy* (Boston: Little Brown) 3rd edn., 1992, p. 1.
5   S. Breyer, *Regulation and its Reform* (Cambridge, Mass: Harvard University Press) 1982, Ch. 1; C. Sunstein, *After the Rights Revolution: Reconceiving the Regulatory State* (Cambridge, Mass: Harvard University Press) 1990, Ch. 2; A. Ogus, *Regulation. Legal Form and Economic Theory* (Oxford: Clarendon) 1994, Ch. 3.
6   Competition law, the general instrument for tackling these issues, falls outside the scope of this book. For an introduction, see R. Whish, *Competition Law* (London: Butterworths) 3rd edn., 1993.

while, if challenged by other firms, to engage in 'predatory' competition to retain dominance. In turn, the so-called 'natural monopoly' – classically a utility company – is seen in many texts as the regulatory paradigm:[7]

> The most traditional and persistent rationale for governmental regulation of a firm's prices and profits is the existence of a 'natural monopoly'. Some industries, it is claimed, cannot efficiently support more than one firm. Electricity producers or local telephone companies find it progressively cheaper (up to a point) to supply extra units of electricity or telephone service. These 'economies of scale' are sufficiently great so that unit costs of service would rise significantly if more than one firm supplied service in a particular area. Rather than have three connecting phone companies laying separate cables where one would do, it may be more efficient to grant one firm a monopoly subject to governmental regulation of its prices and profits.

Policies of redistribution, transferring wealth and resources from the advantaged, have not been in vogue. Yet distributional concerns remain on the regulatory agenda, illustrated by universal service obligations imposed on utilities (below, p. 317). Regulation is sometimes advocated as producing socially desirable results that, to the extent that there is cross-subsidisation, are inefficient. It is also important to bear in mind that much government regulation is designed to further social policy. An example is action against discrimination, and the work of the Equal Opportunities Commission and the Commission for Racial Equality.

As regulation has grown, so has concern about regulatory failure. The public interest theories are comfortable theories, indicating the design and operation of regulation in the pursuit of collective goals. They have, like many other assertions of public interest, been the subject of increased scepticism, concerning purpose as well as performance: all the more so, as economic and social regulation proliferated in the 1960s and 1970s in Western industrialised countries. Private interest or economic theories of regulation,[8] closely bound up with public choice analysis (above, p. 129), have abounded:[9]

> Politics has been defined as 'who gets what, when, and how' and in this sense all regulation is political. Because regulatory decisions produce groups of persons who will benefit and groups of persons who will lose, each side competes concerning the outcome of proposed policies ... This competition has been interpreted as a market process similar to private market decision-making. Interest groups demand more or less regulation according to the self-interest of their members and public officials supply more or less regulation according to what benefits their self-interest.

Producer interests, benefiting from homogeneity of interest and low organisational costs, may have such a powerful influence as to override more general preferences, as also the influence of groups representing consumers or diffuse interests like the environment.[10] As famously expressed by George

---

7 S. Breyer, *Regulation and its Reform* (above, note 5) p. 15.
8 See C. Sunstein, *After the Rights Revolution* (above, note 5) Ch. 3; A. Ogus, *Regulation* (above, note 5) Ch. 4.
9 R. Pearce, S. Shapiro and P. Verkeuil, *Administrative Law and Process* (Westbury NY: Foundation Press) 2nd edn., 1992, pp. 16–17.
10 The classic account is M. Olson, *The Logic of Collective Action* (Oxford: OUP) 1965.

Stigler, [11] 'regulation is acquired by the industry and is designed and operated primarily for its benefit', such theory underscores the problem of 'regulatory capture'.

Private interest theories have, in Majone's words, [12] 'greatly enriched our understanding of the regulatory process, but [have] not made the normative theory obsolete'. On the one hand, 'an important recent development' is the recognition that market failures 'provide only a *prima facie* case for intervention'. This expresses the notion of 'regulatory failure', circumstances in which the cure is worse than the disease, of which regulatory capture is one general cause. On the other hand, 'much of the recent growth of regulation can be explained in normative, public interest, terms'. Turning the argument round, private interest theories can be criticised as being overtly cynical and crude. According to Melville, [13] 'the "economic" view ... fails ... to recognise that [regulation] is a complex process of interaction, on the boundary of the public-private divide, with both regulator and regulated encompassing many different and often conflicting interests'.

Concerns about regulatory failure and the excessive burden of regulation filtered into Britain from the US. In 1982 Breyer surveyed the American scene: [14]

> The criticisms of regulation are typically of several sorts. First, some critics emphasise the enormous costs of regulation. Estimates of direct governmental expenditure range from \$3bn to \$6bn annually, but estimates of indirect costs, including the costs of compliance, vary from \$60bn to \$70bn annually to double or triple that amount ... Second, and more important, critics charge that too little is obtained in return for these large expenditures ... For example, there are numerous statistical studies that seek, but fail to find, any significant effect of workplace safety regulation on accident rates ... Third, critics have complained of unfair and unwieldy regulatory procedures. Some complain that the regulatory process is fraught with delay ... Fourth, the regulatory process has been criticised as fundamentally undemocratic and lacking legitimacy. Regulators are appointed – not elected – officials, yet they wield enormous power. How is their exercise of that power to be controlled? ... Finally, there are those who claim that the regulatory process is unpredictable, even random, in its effects. For example, the process can be used by one competitor to injure another ... Complexity of regulatory subject matter makes it impossible for regulators to consider all the relevant factors ... The more widespread, the more technical, the more costly the regulatory requirement, the more difficult it becomes to predict both the microeconomic and the macroeconomic effects of [a] change ...

---

11  G. Stigler, 'The Theory of Economic Regulation' (1971) 2 Bell Journal of Economics. See also R. Posner, 'Theories of Economic Regulation' (1974) 5 Bell Journal of Economics 335; and S. Peltzman, 'Towards a More General Theory of Regulation' (1976) 19 J. of Law and Economics 211.

12  G. Majone, 'The Rise of the Regulatory State in Europe' (1994) 17 West European Politics 77, 82–83.

13  A. Melville, 'Power, Strategy and Games: Economic Regulation of a Privatized Utility' (1994) 72 Pub. Admin. 384. See also M. Kelman, 'On Democracy-Bashing: A Skeptical Look at the Theoretical and "Empirical" Practice of the Public Choice Movement' (1988) 74 Virginia LR 199; D. Farber and P. Frickey, *Law and Public Choice: A Critical Introduction* (Chicago: University of Chicago Press) 1991.

14  S. Breyer, *Regulation and its Reform* (above, note 5) pp. 2–4.

These criticisms … do not apply to every regulatory program nor to every instance of regulation. They vary in their applicability from one time, place, and program to another. … Yet, criticism of regulation has grown apace … There is a perceived public demand for reform, and the reform issue now occupies a place of importance on the nation's political agenda.

The limits to centralised institutional capacity – in Hayek's words, [15] 'the fiction that all the relevant facts are known to some one mind, and that it is possible to construct from this knowledge of the particulars a desirable social order' – are identified as another general explanation of regulatory failure. The problem was compounded by the dominant form of government regulation in the US, rule-bound or 'legalistic' techniques of command and control, implemented by powerful regulatory agencies (below, p. 307). As explained by Stewart: [16]

> The legal commands adopted by central agencies are necessarily crude, dysfunctional in many applications, and rapidly obsolescent … Bureaucrats simply cannot gather and process the vast amount of information needed to tailor regulations to the nation's many variations in circumstances and the constant changes in relevant conditions. In order to reduce decision-making costs, national officials adopt uniform regulations that are inevitably procrustean in application … These dysfunctions not only overburden the regulated entities but also cause them to fail at their intended goal. Legal blueprints … inevitably fall short of postulated outcomes and produce unintended side-effects when officials attempt to apply them to unforeseen or changed conditions … Centralisation of information and decision-making … is generally far more costly for the government to administer than alternatives that place greater reliance on market incentives.

Over-legislation is commonly identified as a root cause of regulatory failure. But it is not, from the perspective of socio-legal theory, simply a problem of the abundance of law. For Teubner, [17] 'juridification … signifies a process in which the interventionist social state produces a new type of law, regulatory law, [which] "coercively specifies conduct in order to achieve particular substantive ends"'. It tends to be 'particularistic, purpose oriented and dependent on assistance from the social sciences'. (Compare green light theories of administrative law.) Teubner has drawn on autopoesis, [18] a theory of self-generating and self-referring systems, which are 'normatively closed, but cognitively open'. One of the implications is that while functional systems such as law, politics and economy 'can observe other systems and their environment, and be indirectly affected by them … no one system can declare its world view as the only view and … transcend the internal complexity and impenetrability of other highly developed systems'. [19] Basic conflicts are

15  F. A. Hayek, *Law, Legislation and Liberty* (London: Routledge) 1973, vol. 1, p. 13.
16  R. Stewart, 'Madison's Nightmare' (1990) 57 University of Chicago LR 335 at 343, 356. See further R Stewart, 'The Discontents of Legalism: Interest Group Relations in Administrative Regulation' (1985) Wisconsin LR 655.
17  G. Teubner, *Law as an Autopoetic System* (Oxford: Blackwell) 1993.
18  Ibid. And see N. Luhmann, *A Sociological Theory of Law* (London: Routledge) 1985; and, for an introduction, M. King, 'The Truth About Autopoeisis' (1993) 20 J. of Law and Soc. 218.
19  J. Black, 'Constitutionalising Self-Regulation' (1996) 59 MLR 24 at 45; see also in this context, M. Loughlin, *Public Law and Political Theory* (Oxford: Clarendon) 1992, Ch. 10.

suggested by Teubner's 'regulatory trilemma': regulatory law tends to be ignored, or to damage the life of the system being regulated, or to affect adversely the integrity of the legal system itself, premised on autonomy and generality. His brand of reflexive theory aims to mitigate these problems. It points to an effective use of intermediary institutions to mediate between different systems within society; to a change in regulatory strategy to regulate indirectly, to induce action rather than command: [20]

> One is forced to abandon ideas of effective outside regulation, the notion that law or politics could have a direct goal oriented controlling influence on sectors of society. The effect of regulatory law must be described in far more modest terms as the mere *triggering* of self-regulatory processes, the direction and effect of which can scarcely be predicted ... External influence on areas of social life is possible but – and this is crucial – only within the paths and the limits of the respective self-reproduction. These are described by the *regulatory trilemma*: [in respect of] *every regulatory intervention* which goes beyond these limits ...
>
> The matter is further complicated by the political instrumentalisation of law. In the activist state legal regulation involves not only the legal system and the respective social area of life but invariably also the political system. However, the legal system and the political system in turn are autonomous self-referential social systems ... If we adopt this perspective and regard juridification processes as complex relations between three self-regulating social systems, we begin to grasp why 'regulatory failures' must in fact be the rule rather than the exception and that this is not merely a problem of human inadequacy or social power structures but above all one of inadequate *structural coupling* of politics, law and the area of social life.

All of this has a very practical dimension. A growing perception of regulatory failure fuels demands for 'deregulation'. Private interest theories help us to understand the pressures for 'irrationality' in regulation, and so illuminate the path of regulatory technique and institutional design. The ideas articulated by Stewart reinforce the general movement towards indirect forms of administration, which is nowhere more strongly expressed than in regulation. Reflexive theory suggests constitutive approaches to self-regulation, designing processes and organisational structures to ensure that other, wider interests are taken into account in decisions.

### (b) Government regulation: design and technique

Some general classifications reveal the wide range of choice in government regulation. One set of regulatory alternatives involves industry-wide regulation, in ideal-typical form, standardised regulation throughout an industry, and 'partial-industry' regulation, in pure form allowing whole sections of an industry to go unregulated. A modified version, whereby the parts of an industry are regulated

20 G. Teubner, 'Juridification – Concepts, Aspects, Limits, Solutions' in G. Teubner (ed.), *Juridification of Social Spheres* (Berlin: Walter de Gruyter) 1987, pp. 16, 18–19, 21. See further G. Teubner, 'After Legal Instrumentalism? Strategic Models of Post-Regulatory Law' in G. Teubner (ed.), *Dilemmas of Law in the Welfare State* (Berlin: Walter de Gruyter) 1985.

to different extents, has been of special relevance in the case of utilities, owing to unreformed market structures and the importance of networks or transmission systems (below, p 320). Ayres and Braithwaite have expounded the advantages of partial-industry regulation, most obviously the prospect of careful targeting: [1]

> In some regulatory settings, regulating only an individual firm (or a subset of the firms) in an industry can promote efficiency by restraining monopoly power without giving rise to the evils of either captured or benighted regulation ... Partial-industry regulation may be seen as a form of regulatory delegation. The regulated firms in the industry bear the burden of ensuring that the unregulated firms comply. The compliance of unregulated firms is assured because competition forces them to match the offers of the regulated firm ... Dominant-firm regulation ... preserves the independence of fringe firms as a competitive check on the decisions of regulatory agencies. Although fringe firms will rarely have incentives to price above a dominant firm, fringe firms may have strong incentives to undercut dominant firm prices. By maintaining this potential for fringe price cutting, dominant-firm intervention may engender more competition and industry-wide intervention ... Partial-industry regulation uses public regulation as a check on private monopoly power and private competition as a balance against regulators being captured.

Secondly, regulators may be concerned with behaviour within a market – conduct regulation – or with the way in which the market is organised – structural regulation. The case for structural regulation often rests on asymmetry of information between the regulator and regulated. 'Since it is impossible to determine whether a professional, faced with a conflict of interest, is acting in the best interests of his client, a sensible solution ... may be to say that he cannot act in such a case.' [2] At the risk of stating the obvious, the categories are not mutually exclusive. Faced with a monopoly situation, a regulator may take action both to control prices and to open up the market. This, we will see, is precisely what has happened in privatised utilities such as the gas industry.

Thirdly, individual techniques may be classified according to the degree of state intervention. Ogus refers to a spectrum. [3] At the end associated with low intervention comes information regulation, as when suppliers are required to disclose details concerning the quality of their goods and services. (The 'market' in public services is lubricated in similar fashion in the Citizen's Charter (above, p. 144).) At the opposite end of the spectrum, individuals and firms may be prohibited from undertaking an activity without obtaining 'prior approval'. Thus, licensing has long been the stuff of administrative law. Between the extremes lies a very common form of conduct regulation, the 'standards' technique, whereby the activity is allowed to take place without prior control, but the operator who fails to meet the standard is open to criminal sanctions.

The model is a starting point only. As regards economic regulation, there are many other instruments in the armoury: competition rules and price control,

1   I. Ayres and J. Braithwaite, *Responsive Regulation: Transcending the Deregulation Debate* (Oxford: OUP) 1992, pp. 133–134, 137, 157.
2   J. Kay and J. Vickers, 'Regulatory Reform: An Appraisal' in G. Majone (ed.), *Deregulation or Re-regulation? Regulatory Reform in Europe and the United States* (London: Pinter) 1990, p. 225.
3   A. Ogus, *Regulation. Legal Form and Economic Theory* (Oxford, Clarendon) 1993, pp. 4–5, 150–152.

franchising (above, p. 269) and tradeable permits. And each category mentioned by Ogus can usefully be subdivided, again according to the degree of intervention. Mandatory disclosure requirements may be distinguished from the other main type of information regulation, the control of false or misleading information. A system of prior approval may ostensibly be designed to restrict competition (compare *Laker Airways*[4] ), to preserve minimum standards of quality (the solicitors' profession), or to do both (rail franchising). Regulatory standards come in various guises. A target standard prescribes no specific standard for a firm's processes or output, but imposes criminal liability should certain harmful consequences arise. A performance standard prescribes certain conditions for the output, but leaves a firm free to choose how to meet those conditions. A specification standard requires or proscribes certain conduct: a use or non-use by a firm of certain production methods or materials. And it is specification, as the most interventionist of the standards, which has been the classic target of criticism of fussy or 'legalistic' command and control regulation.

For Kay and Vickers,[5] regulatory directives or commands raise 'in acute form' the problem of information. When a broad goal is prescribed – 'run an efficient and economical service' – there is difficulty in establishing 'whether, within the limits of what is possible, the industry has complied with the directive'. When, in the alternative, a specification is issued – 'instal equipment of type X' – the problem arises of the regulator 'being in a poor position to judge whether type X is or is not the most efficient and economical means'. The regulator is at 'an informational disadvantage either in composing his instruction or in monitoring compliance with it, and there is no escape from at least one of these difficulties'. Compare Jowell's discussion of rules, principles and standards (above, p. 103).

Many regulatory programmes rest upon several different rationales; health and safety programmes, for example, can demonstrate concerns related to externalities and information defects, as well as unequal bargaining power and paternalism.[6] 'Regulation usually involves *blends* of responses to *mixes* of problems.'[7] This should not disguise the general search in recent years for less intrusive forms of regulation, epitomised by strategies of light-touch and incentive or market-orientated implementation.

### (c) Contemporary trends

There has over the last 20 years been a significant transformation in the style and institutions of regulation. Several features are represented in the development. One is obviously privatisation, the retreat on the one hand of 'the producer state' and, on the other, the emergence of a new breed of regulator in the utilities (below, p. 318). There is a distinct preference for an agency over an executive model of government regulation. The development, although not novel in Britain, represents a shift of emphasis in regulatory arrangements, and so highlights problems of 'fit'

---

4    Above, p. 83.
5    J. Kay and J. Vickers, 'Regulatory Reform' (above, note 2) p. 234.
6    R. Baldwin, *Rules and Government* (Oxford: Clarendon) 1995, Ch. 5.
7    R. Baldwin, *Regulation in Question* (London: LSE) 1995, p. 18.

with the traditional constitutional framework of controls (below, p. 330). Another feature is increased interest by government in the techniques of self-regulation (below, p. 339). A combination of sanctioned framework and local autonomy fits pervading theories of indirect forms of government: 'steering' not 'rowing'.

Allied to institutional change is change in, and challenge to, an old regulatory culture. Veljanovski refers to the paradox whereby privatisation has led to a more legalistic relationship between the state and the private sector. [8] Kay and Vickers [9] reflect on how 'older, informal structures [of regulation] have been breaking down under the pressure of powerful economic, technological, and ideological forces' – compare government contracting. On the one hand, there is as often as not a process of 're-regulation', whereby generally more explicit or formal regulatory structures are substituted, for example statutory for self-regulation (below, p. 340). On the other hand, since old habits die hard, some familiar British elements such as ministerial interference and a lack of transparency are seen persisting in the 'reinvented' regulatory structures.

### (d) The European connection

An important factor in the rise of 'the regulatory state' is the Europeanisation of law and administration. The scale of regulatory policy-making at Community level has grown to be enormous, ranging from environmental protection to competition law, and consumer product safety to the regulation of banking and financial services. As in public procurement (above, p. 247), the drive to the Single Market has been important, the profusion of national regulatory regimes long being recognised as a barrier to Member State trade. [10] Also, Community regulation is a relatively inexpensive instrument of government for the EC institutions, as well as enhancing their power and status. [11] In the event, the initial preference was for harmonisation or integrated regulation, the detailed setting of standards at Community level sector by sector: a process which, entirely predictably, proved slow and costly, and discouraging of innovation by producers. It has since the mid-1980s largely been overtaken by the so-called 'new approach', [12] whereby harmonisation is limited to minimum essential requirements and the task of either filling in the details or fixing standards above minimum requirements is reserved to the Member States or to expert committees (such as CENELEC, the European Standardisation Committee for Electrical Products). The development

---

8   C. Veljanovski, *Selling the State* (London: Weidenfeld & Nicolson) 1987, p. 165.

9   J. Kay and J. Vickers, 'Regulatory Reform' (above, note 2) p. 223. See further M. Moran and T. Prosser (eds.), *Privatization and Regulatory Change in Europe* (Buckingham: Open University Press) 1994.

10  Commission White Paper, *Completing the Internal Market*, COM(85) 310; and for discussion, J. Pelkmans, 'Regulation and the Single Market: An Economic Perspective' in H. Siebert (ed.), *The Completion of the Internal Market* (Tübingen: Paul Sieback) 1990.

11  G. Majone, 'The Rise of the Regulatory State in Europe' (1994) 17 West European Politics 77. And see, for a general introduction to Community regulatory law and policy, K. Gatsios and P. Seabright, 'Regulation in the European Community' (1989) Oxford Rev. of Economic Policy 5.

12  J. Pelkmans, 'The Approach to Technical Harmonisation and Standardisation' (1987) 24 J. of Common Market Studies 249; A. McGee and S. Weatherill, 'The Evolution of the Single Market – Harmonisation or Liberalisation' (1990) 52 MLR 578.

is premised on the principle of 'mutual recognition', established by the Court of Justice in the famous *Cassis de Dijon* case,[13] whereby a product lawfully manufactured in one Member State should be taken in principle to be of sufficient quality to be sold throughout the Community. Accordingly, from an economics perspective, there is now a potential for competition between national rules and between national regulators.[14]

All this naturally has a profound impact on regulation in the domestic system of administrative law (above, p. 25). Both the government and national regulators have a positive role to play, by virtue of the system of indirect administration of Community law. At the same time, the capacity of domestic regulators and legislators to dictate a regulatory strategy may be affected. Baldwin refers[15] to the scope for national regulatory jurisdictions being eroded progressively and in some sectors more than others, for example health and safety at work, where domestic regulators have publicly acknowledged their regimes to be 'driven by European rather than domestic laws'. But there are more subtle implications for national regulatory practice. The obligation on the government to demonstrate effective compliance with, and enforcement of, Community norms is another stimulus for greater formalisation of arrangements, as also centralisation or oversight of local regulatory power.[16] Meanwhile, limited harmonisation and mutual recognition are suggestive of less intrusive forms of regulation, intensified regulatory competition involving pressures on Member States to limit the costs imposed by local standards. The 'new approach' is seen contributing in this way to a general movement at national level for 'deregulation'. A recent emphasis on the principle of subsidiarity, whereby regulation within the Community should be pursued at the lowest level consistent with effectiveness, has given Member States some extra scope for setting national standards in accordance with their own perceptions of economic and social needs.[17]

### (e) Deregulation

Deregulation has been a fashionable nostrum in Britain under the Conservatives. Yet like regulation it is an elusive concept. For Hancher and Moran[18] its most striking feature is variety: in incidence, form and extent. Even its most obvious meaning, the relaxation or abolition of constraining rules, hides complexity:

---

13   *Rewe-Zentrale AG v Bundesmonopolverwaltung für Branntwein* Case 120/78 [1979] ECR 649.
14   J. Kay and J. Vickers, 'Regulatory Reform' (above, note 2); and see further W. Bratton, J. McCahery, S. Picciotto and C. Scott (eds.), *International Regulatory Competition and Coordination* (Oxford: OUP) 1996.
15   R. Baldwin, *Regulation in Question* (above, note 7), pp. 32–34.
16   T. Daintith, 'European Community Law and the Redistribution of Regulatory Power in the United Kingdom' (1995) 1 European LJ 134; F. McGowan and P. Seabright, 'Regulation in the European Community and its Impact on the UK' in M. Bishop, J. Kay and C. Mayer (eds.), *The Regulatory Challenge* (Oxford: OUP) 1995.
17   I. Maher, 'Legislative Review by the EC Commission: Revision Without Radicalism' in J. Shaw and G. More (eds.), *New Legal Dynamics of European Union* (Oxford: OUP) 1996. And see above, pp. 24–25.
18   L. Hancher and M. Moran, 'Introduction: Regulation and Deregulation' (1989) 17 European J. of Political Research 129, 129–131.

Three different kinds of rule change are in practice important: cancellation, substitution and systematization ... Cancellation or abolition is the kind of change most commonly associated with deregulation. It is, however, remarkably rare to find an instance where a rule is simply abolished and not replaced by an alternative. Rule substitution is a commoner process: an existing rule is replaced by one whose range of application is narrower. Alternatively, a specific regulatory regime for a particular sector of the economy may be abolished, leaving the industry involved subject to more generalised forms of regulations [as for example those] implementing competition policy ...

Systematization commonly involves the cancellation of rules, particularly through ... pruning sets of rules which have grown unnecessarily complex. But ... the pruning associated with systematization, far from involving a lightening of the regulatory regime, may actually be part of a more rigorous and well organised, if indirect, form of enforcement. In this process deregulation is a kind of regulatory reform, the goal being to make regulation more efficient ...

Much that passes for 'deregulation' is not so much a change in the content of rules, or a departure from regulatory objectives, as an adjustment to the means of enforcement. The state's retreat from a regulatory arena in such instances characteristically involves a shift from implementation by command to implementation via market mechanisms or through negotiation and bargaining.

Streamlining regulation or 'lifting the burden' on businesses was given high priority by the Conservative Government. In John Major's words, 'there should always be a presumption *against* regulation unless it is strictly necessary ... The temptation to over-regulate must be restricted'. [19] The Deregulation Unit, first established in 1985, and currently situated in the Cabinet Office, has had the task of co-ordinating initiatives across Whitehall. As regards rule-change, the work gained real impetus from the Deregulation and Contracting Out Act 1994, which we met earlier in the context of 'Henry VIII' clauses (above, p. 166). A programme followed of reviewing all primary and secondary legislation in the main fields of business regulation: by the end of 1996 over 1,000 regulations had been eliminated or simplified. [20] Again, the perception of over-regulation in the past has informed a major drive to have departments assess systematically the costs of new regulatory proposals. Compliance Cost Assessment (CCA) [1] was introduced, an appraisal technique designed to generate information on the total compliance costs for business sectors and individual firms, as also the effect on national competitiveness. The process of evaluation has latterly become more sophisticated and broadly-based. An administrative instruction in 1995 required a Regulatory Appraisal for all regulatory proposals affecting business. [2] In addition to CCA, information is included on the costs of other options and to

---

19 Deregulation Initiative, *Thinking About Regulating: A Guide to Good Regulation*, 1994, foreword. See further *Lifting the Burden*, Cmnd. 9571 (1985); Department of Trade and Industry, *Burdens on Business*, 1985.
20 The Deregulation Initiative, *Cutting Red Tape*, 1997, p. 1.
1 The Deregulation Initiative, *Checking the Cost of Regulation: A Guide to Compliance Cost Assessment*, 1996; J. Froud and A. Ogus, '"Rational" Social Regulation and Compliance Cost Assessment' (1996) 74 Pub. Admin. 221.
2 The Deregulation Initiative, *Regulation in the Balance: A Guide to Regulatory Appraisal Incorporating Risk Assessment*, 1996.

consumers and the government, and, further, on the potential benefits by means of a 'Risk Assessment' concerning the probability and magnitude of harm and the impact of different options on the risk. Notice, however, that such attempts at more 'rational' regulation, far from being a mechanical exercise, are shot through with discretionary judgment. Preparing a CCA will, in the words of the government manual, 'largely involve making *assumptions* about the consequences of regulation and producing *estimates* as to the extent of the impact on business'. Nor is it surprising to learn that in the control of hazardous activities 'public perceptions of risk and what is desirable to contain them are not always reconcilable with the objective, technical models used in risk assessment'.[3] Turning to enforcement, the keynote has been a business friendly model, 'ensuring compliance rather than over-zealous enforcement'. Citizen's Charter principles – information and advice 'in plain language', 'courteous and efficient service', accessible complaints procedures – have been invoked for the benefit of business. The Enforcement Code is actually entitled *Working With Business*.[4]

Of particular interest are statements of what constitutes 'good' regulation. Civil servants have been told that there are three themes.[5] The first, proportionality, gears with the evaluation process. From the viewpoint of administrative law, there is both a parallel with the legal doctrine and a lack of legal control – the evaluation process being an internal one designed primarily to assist government policy-making. 'Think Small First', the second theme, reflects concern that 'over-regulation harms small businesses most'. A special 'litmus test' for small business has been developed, to test impact. 'Go For Goal-Based Regulations' is the third theme. The basic idea will be familiar from government contract (above, p. 258): the regulation 'should specify the goal and allow businesses to decide how to achieve this goal'. In the event, significant numbers of detailed prescriptive rules have in areas such as health and safety and consumer protection been replaced by broader target standards.[6]

Suppose that a civil servant is asked to devise a new piece of regulation, say on the handling of meat products. How should he proceed? The following advice is provided by the government manual and there would also be a Deregulation Unit in the department on which to call:[7]

> Good regulation – ten points to think about.
> 1. Identify the issue ... Keep the regulation in proportion to the problem.
> 2. Keep it simple ... Go for goal-based regulation.
> 3. Provide flexibility for the future ... Set the objective rather than the detailed way of making sure the regulation is kept to.

3　The Deregulation Initiative, *Checking the Cost*, p. 8. A. Ogus, 'Risk Management and "Rational" Social Regulation' in R. Baldwin and P. Cane (eds.), *Law and Uncertainty: Risks and Legal Processes* (Boston, Mass: Kluwer) 1996, p. 139.
4　The Deregulation Initiative, *Thinking About Regulating*, pp. 10–12; Department of Trade and Industry and Citizen's Charter Unit, *Working With Business: A Code for Enforcement Agencies*, 1996.
5　The Deregulation Initiative, *Thinking About Regulating*, pp. 1–8.
6　The process is traceable to the Health and Safety at Work Act 1974: see for a comparative study R. Baldwin and T. Daintith (eds.), *Harmonisation and Hazard* (London: Graham & Trotman) 1992.
7　Deregulation Initiative, *Thinking About Regulating*, pp. 20–21.

4. Keep it short.
5. Try to anticipate the effects on competition or trade ... Try to find ways of regulating which cause the least market disruption ...
6. Minimise costs of compliance ... Think small first.
7. Integrate with previous regulations.
8. Make sure the regulation can be effectively managed and enforced ... If [it] cannot be enforced fairly at a reasonable cost, think again.
9. Make sure that the regulation will work and that you will know if it does not ... Consider how you will monitor the results, costs and any side-effects or changes in behaviour ...
10. Allow enough time ... for ... consulting people inside and outside government.

Turning the argument round, is there not a danger here of sub-optimal control? Allied to a presumption against regulation is a stress in evaluation on costs over benefits. Similarly, in the absence of American-style rule-making procedure (below, p. 333), consultation exercises have typically concentrated on the regulated industries, rather than groups representing consumers.[8] The discussion serves to highlight the political dimension in regulatory strategy and design. While other EU states have also pursued deregulatory policies in recent years, the United Kingdom under the Conservatives was 'notable for the ideological vigour of its commitment'.[9] It will be interesting to see how far this changes under the auspices of the new Labour government.

## 2. Regulatory agencies and legitimacy

The rise of the regulatory agency is one of the most striking features in the modern development of administrative law in Britain. Consider the position 25 years ago, when, in a comparative study,[10] Schwarz and Wade commented on the sharp distinction with administrative law in the US. The American system had long been agency-orientated, partly by reason of the New Deal (above, p. 69). Instruments of government regulation such as the Interstate Commerce Commission (1887) and the Federal Power Commission (1930) were a chief battleground for law as an instrument of administrative policy and in defence of private rights, and, latterly, for law as a resource for wider, collective interests (interest representation). In contrast, Schwartz and Wade observed, 'this kind of regulatory agency scarcely exists in Britain' and is 'difficult to compare with British institutions'. Perhaps this was an exaggeration, given the role of such bodies as the Monopolies Commission (1948) and the Independent Television Authority (1954), as well as a crop of agencies then on the horizon, including the Civil Aviation Authority (1972), the Office of Fair Trading (1973) and the Health and Safety Commission (1974). None the less, it conveyed an essential truth, that Britain has not had a strong tradition of using the agency model of government regulation.

8  Ibid, pp. 13–15, Annex F; A. Ogus, *Regulation. Legal Form and Economic Theory* (Oxford: Clarendon) 1994, Ch. 16.
9  T. Daintith, 'European Community Law and the Redistribution of Regulatory Power in the United Kingdom' (1995) 1 European LJ 134, 137.
10  B. Schwartz and H. Wade, *Legal Control of Government* (Oxford: Clarendon) 1972, pp. 9, 26, 41.

One explanation may be found in the dominant Westminster style of government. The use of boards and commissions had declined in the nineteenth century as government expanded and Parliament demanded more direct ministerial control of state activity. The centralist practices of parliamentarianism do not readily permit the development of independent regulatory agencies. In addition, agencies which combine powers treated as distinct in the 'balanced constitution' may be seen as constitutionally awkward or even monstrous. So Baldwin and McCrudden [11] refer to 'the tendency ... to treat regulatory issues as either administrative or executive (and so tasks for ministers), or as judicial (and so matters for determination by courts or court-like tribunals)'. We have seen this problem highlighted in the case of the Civil Aviation Authority, whose licensing powers fell between judicial and executive (above, p. 84). Another explanation is, of course, the post-war preference for public ownership as distinct from the private sector-plus-regulator model. Schwartz and Wade believed that 'it would never be thought right' in Britain to devolve the control of major industries such as rail or power 'where decisions of the utmost political and economic importance have to be taken and for which responsibility to Parliament is indispensable'. So far have we since travelled under the Conservatives!

Conversely, the explanations for the rise of the regulatory agency go beyond political fashions. Independence from, or an arm's length relationship with, government is said to facilitate the continuity of, and flexibility or responsiveness in, policy formulation and implementation, as also a disinterested expertise; in addition, that is, to helping to deflect criticism or political responsibility and reducing government overload. The specialist, multifunctional agency fits well the model of regulation as sustained and focused control.

We have already remarked that it is difficult to discern a typical agency. This is indicative not only of the British propensity to 'muddle through' in matters of institutional design, but also of the many and diverse operational choices. The broad canvas is usefully illustrated by the Equal Opportunities Commission (EOC), an issue-based regulator which operates in both public and private sectors. First, the Commission demonstrates the potentially wide-ranging powers of a regulatory agency. It issues codes of practice. It can play an investigative role, conducting 'formal investigations' with powers to compel the giving of evidence and the production of documents. It can issue non-discrimination notices against those who break its codes, backed up by the threat of an injunction. It conducts research, organises conferences, lobbies Parliament and gives grants to voluntary organisations. It provides legal advice and assistance to individuals, as well as taking its own cases. Secondly, EOC workings demonstrate the central role of agency discretion. It obviously has a limited budget: some £6 million in 1994/5. This means a 'Corporate Plan' [12] charting agency goals and performance targets, as well as particular fields of activity. Thirdly, the potential for change in agency perceptions and priorities, as influenced by changes in the external environment, is highlighted. For instance, the EOC has made only limited use of the formal investigation. The time and expense involved has been increased by a

11   R. Baldwin and C. McCrudden, *Regulation and Public Law* (London: Weidenfeld and Nicolson) 1987, p. 15.
12   Equal Opportunities Commission, *Annual Report 1994*, pp. 32, 34.

series of cases imposing severe procedural constraints. [13] On the other hand, the agency has in recent years put much effort into working constructively with small businesses, and into developing 'the business case for equality of opportunity'. [14] Another important aspect of its work is litigation, a more careful targeting of resources on test-cases, not least at the European level. 'This represents a policy decision by the Commissioners, who recognised the potential of EC law at an early stage'. [15] So, too, the agency has had to learn the art of creating networks, and of lobbying and standard-setting, at Community level, a further dimension of the spreading Europeanisation of law and administration.

## *Five models*

Let us draw together various threads in the argument. The independence of regulatory agencies from elected authority is commonly regarded as their chief virtue. But the broad delegation of rule-making and other powers exemplifies the dilemma in a system of indirect government of reconciling the values of independence and of control and accountability. All the more so in the case of Britain, precisely because, as Craig has put it, [16] 'We are now accustomed to the idea of ministerial responsibility as the "constitutional norm"'. The rise of regulatory agencies is a measure of change in, and challenge to, old canons of parliamentary government. Conversely, the agencies are still seen as 'constitutional anomalies which do not fit well into the framework of controls, checks and balances'. [17]

This raises the issue of the legitimacy of agency action. There are certain core values which regulators need to satisfy if, in Baldwin's words, [18] 'they are to merit and receive public approval'. Institutional legitimacy is typically seen as an indispensable condition for regulatory compliance and effectiveness, as in the view of the Constitutional Reform Centre [19] that 'many regulators operate without sufficient legitimacy to do their job with full confidence, weakening the regulatory environment and prompting agencies to operate defensively'. Legitimacy is also appropriately used as an evaluative concept, focusing attention on the sources

13 *Hillingdon London Borough Council v Commission for Racial Equality* [1982] AC 779; *Commission for Racial Equality v Amari Plastics Ltd* [1982] QB 1194; *Prestige Group plc* [1984] 1 WLR 335. See, for discussion, G. Appleby and E. Ellis, 'Formal Investigations: The Commission for Racial Equality and the Equal Opportunities Commission as Law Enforcement Agencies [1984] PL 236.
14 Equal Opportunities Commission, *Annual Report 1994*, p. 32.
15 C. Harlow and R. Rawlings, *Pressure Through Law* (London: Routledge) 1992, p. 285. Examples are *Johnston v Chief Constable of the Royal Ulster Constabulary* [1986] 3 WLR 1038 (above, p. 59); and *R v Secretary of State for Employment, ex p Equal Opportunities Commission and Day* [1995] 1 AC 1 (below, p. 545). See, for earlier criticisms, V. Sacks, 'The Equal Opportunities Commission – Ten Years On' (1986) 49 MLR 560.
16 P. Craig, *Administrative Law*, p. 89.
17 C. Veljanovski, 'The Regulation Game' in C. Veljanovski (ed.), *Regulators and the Market* (London: Institute of Economic Affairs) 1991, p. 16.
18 R. Baldwin, *Regulation in Question* (London: London School of Economics) 1995, p. 10.
19 Constitutional Reform Centre, 'Regulatory Agencies in the United Kingdom' (1991) 44 Parliamentary Affairs 504 at 507. See further J. Freedman, *Crisis and Legitimacy: The Administrative Process and American Government* (Cambridge: Cambridge University Press) 1978.

from which an agency may derive legitimacy. To this end, a number of competing models of regulatory legitimacy are commonly identified.[20] The criteria will be seen, however, to be of general application in administrative law, as illustrated by the similarities and overlaps with Frug's four models of bureaucratic legitimacy previously discussed (above, p. 26).[1]

According to the model of *legislative mandate*, agency action deserves support when authorised explicitly by the people's representatives in Parliament. And to step outside the statutory terms of reference is illegitimate or, in the language of judicial review, ultra vires. The problem, of course, is that the criterion affects simplicity, since rarely is an agency 'a mere transmission belt for implementing legislative directives in particular cases'.[2] A broad legislative mandate is typical, with objectives set out in general terms, pregnant perhaps with conflict. Nor would we expect anything else, precisely because 'these are bodies that are created to engage in complex tasks that are specialised and require the exercise of judgment'.[3] Yet the more agency discretion there is, the less a statutory mandate can be used to justify actions and policies.

Agency discretion sits well with a model of regulatory legitimacy based on *expertise*. In ideal-typical form, the model implies the rejection of formal law in a manner reminiscent of corporatist theories (above, p. 13). As described by Kagan:[4]

> regulatory decisions should not be prescribed in advance either by legislation or fixed legal rules. Regulatory officials must be free to formulate policies in response to the problems at hand, adapting decisions to varied and changing situations on the basis of their accumulating knowledge, making intuitive judgments as to what result will maximise the public interest.

The cult of the expert is not in fashion. Yet a proper level of expertise is a precondition of legitimacy, and it is the more technical and complex nature of decision-making today which fuels the agencies' rise (above, p. 141). Again, as judicial deference to regulatory expertise demonstrates, 'the kernel of the expert model is incorporated in administrative legal doctrine'.

The *efficiency and effectiveness* of agencies is typically seen as 'a crucial component of their claim to legitimacy, but very difficult to assess'.[5] As a source of legitimacy, 'the three Es' are epitomised in the paraphernalia of regulatory appraisal (above, p. 305). But Baldwin and McCrudden have emphasised the relationship between powers and performance:[6]

20  See T. Jones, 'Administrative Law, Regulation, and Legitimacy' (1989) 16 J. of Law and Soc. 410; R. Baldwin, *Rules and Government* (Oxford: Clarendon) 1995, Ch. 3.

1   As also with models of administrative justice devised by Mashaw. Below, p. 472.

2   R. Stewart, 'The Reformation of American Administrative Law' (1975) 88 Harv. LR 1667, 1675.

3   R. Baldwin and C. McCrudden, *Regulation and Public Law* (London: Weidenfeld & Nicolson) 1987, p. 34.

4   R. Kagan, *Regulatory Justice: Implementing a Price Freeze* (New York: Russell Sage) 1978, pp. 13, 15. See for the classic 'green light' defence of the expert agency, J. Landis, *The Administrative Process* (New Haven: Yale University Press) 1938.

5   Constitutional Reform Centre, (1991) 44 Parliamentary Affairs 504, 507.

6   R. Baldwin and C. McCrudden, *Regulation and Public Law* (above, note 3) p. 52.

A fundamental and recurring cause of inefficient regulation is the existence of a mismatch between regulatory institution or strategy and the task in hand ... It can hardly be argued that an agency is acting efficiently when it is either the wrong kind of body for the job, its strategies are misguided or its policies uncertain. Although the effectiveness of an agency is not guaranteed by a parliamentary grant of powers, it will clearly be crucially affected by it: adequate legislative empowerment of the agency in the initial statute is a necessary but not a sufficient condition of an effective agency.

Ambiguities in the legislative mandate make it difficult to determine how far an agency is successful in realising its objectives. There are other general problems in measuring performance. How is the performance of the regulator to be separated from that of the regulated? What would have happened in the absence of the regulator's efforts? The issue of efficient action or results as a value independent of distributional considerations is one which has been fiercely contested in economic regulation (below, p. 316).

A fourth model, that of *oversight*, expresses the idea that the exercise of broad agency discretion is rendered more acceptable by the presence of effective channels of accountability and external control. To this effect, the labelling of regulatory agencies as 'constitutional anomalies' underscores a concern that in Britain such safeguards are weak or insufficiently developed (above, p. 143). And there are other, general problems in reconciling the value of agency independence, as Jones explains: [7]

Any increase in accountability will result in less room for manoeuvre on the part of a regulatory agency and less flexibility in the application of its expertise to the problems confronting it. Too much emphasis on accountability might tend to defeat the purpose of creating an independent agency in the first place. The trite solution of this dilemma is to strike a balance between the competing values and not to choose to emphasise one at the expense of another. Achieving such a balance is no easy task, however, and there are a number of complicating factors. First, agencies ... habitually have a wide range of functions to perform and it may be that each function calls for a different degree of accountability. Secondly, there is a great diversity among regulatory institutions and there can be no guarantee that the best possible solution for [one agency] will be applicable to other agencies.

The equation suggested is too simple, yet the argument is a valuable pointer to a functionalist approach. A standard pattern would involve a combination of control instruments; in particular, one which included but did not place excessive reliance on judicial review, precisely because of limitations on the legitimacy and competency of court activity (below, p. 331). For a complex and specialised activity like government regulation, one of the main sources of legitimacy lies in the instruments of bureaucratic regulation.

Agencies can gain legitimacy by adopting fair administrative procedures, maximising consistency and equality of treatment, transparency and participation of outside interests. The model of *due process* is expressive of the search in amber light theories for a better quality of administrative justice (above, Ch. 4). In this

---

7    T. Jones, (1989) 16 J. of Law and Soc. 410, 417.

context, the contested nature of the relationship between the theta values of due process and the sigma values of efficiency and effectiveness (see Chapter 5) needs emphasis. Take formal participation requirements, which may be seen both as a recipe for delay and indecision and as a necessary instrument for institutional learning. Such perspectives have typically informed official approaches to, and criticism of, regulatory design in Britain.

At this point the discussion might be summarised in the following way. Each source of legitimacy from which regulatory agencies derive support, and against which they may be evaluated, is a necessary but insufficient criterion, and is in tension with others. In this case, according to Baldwin: [8]

> What matters is the collective justificatory power of the five forms of claim. A claim under one head may be weak but may be compensated for by a strong claim under another. Where strong claims can be made under all heads (a rare event) then a high level of legitimacy is assured; where only weak claims can be made under each heading then the power to justify will be low. Where a claim under one head can be improved by a reform that does not weaken claims under other heads then a convincing case for such a reform can be made ...
>
> Where it is necessary to consider a trade-off between two or more types of claim (e.g. a step that increases efficiency and diminishes accountability) ... the personal judgment has to be placed in the context of the anticipated reactions of others and a position of tempered idealism adopted. The implication is that the critic or designer of processes may be on unsure ground in seeking to argue for extreme trade-offs of legitimacy claims by making reference to a personal vision. Such a critic/designer should, accordingly, be wary of endorsing processes which score conspicuously badly on any of the five headings since those poor scores may tend to undermine the higher scores anticipated under other headings.

But this is too mechanical. Ultimately, there is no way of avoiding the contested nature of the trade-offs between such legitimacy claims. Different theories of the state are reflected in, and reinforced by, this selection of values (Chapters 2–5). With this in mind, let us consider practical illustrations of regulation and agency design under the Conservatives.

## 3. Regulation 'UK-style'

Many of the theoretical problems considered in the previous sections have been demonstrated in the process of utilities regulation which has also been seen to demonstrate the potential for dynamic patterns of control in agency regulation, and the attempts under the Conservatives to impose market and market-mimicking disciplines (Chapter 5). Again, the topic is a rewarding one precisely because of the dissonance between the new forms of ownership and control and the old maps of administrative law. An extract from Schwartz and Wade in 1972 points up the different contours of the subject under the regime of nationalised industries: [9]

---

8　Baldwin, *Rules and Government* (above, p. 302, note 6) pp. 48–49, 55–57.
9　B. Schwartz and H. Wade, *Legal Control of Government* (Oxford: Clarendon) 1972, pp. 39–41.

Nationalised industry is … a great economiser of legal friction. Complete nationalisation of the railways and of the coal, electricity, gas and steel industries, and partial nationalisation of road and air transport, have subtracted a vast area of economic activity from the field of judicial control. It is not that the government does not exercise power, but rather that the government's powers are so pervasive that the industry is in no position to contest them. Instead of issuing statutory directions and publishing them as the Acts require [the government] conveys its wishes privately and the boards are in no position to resist …

All this is beyond the reach of administrative law. It is a constitutional problem, since governments have been exercising much more power than they have accounted for in Parliament. At the same time, they disclaim responsibility when it suits them … Such cases [see for example *British Broadcasting Corporation v Johns*[10] and *Town Investments*[11]] as have arisen out of nationalisation and other similar measures have been confined to plotting the constitutional position of the industries … In general the litigation over the technique of regulating industry, which has contributed so greatly to the development of the subject in the United States, is eliminated by British methods of public administration.

Conversely, we see now the potential for *juridification*, the seeping of legal values and culture into regulatory relations. However, unlike the many Next Steps agencies involved in service delivery, the utility regulators have only limited contact with citizens in the sense that regulatory decisions are expressed through the medium of utility performance. There is the type of mix of public and private power which, as with the contractual 'revolution' in government, raises basic queries about the emphasis and conceptual framework of administrative law.

Utilities regulation is today a major area of political and commercial conflict. This is hardly surprising. As providers of basic services, the industries are vital to the infrastructure and competitiveness of the national economy, as well as a substantial part of it in their own right. Many diverse and potentially competing interests are involved: shareholders, business and domestic consumers, the environmental lobby. Turning the argument round, the utilities regulators now play a critical role in national economic management, exercise a power to make decisions worth literally billions of pounds to the stock market value of companies, and are second only to the Chancellor of the Exchequer in the influence they wield over the family budget. All this points up questions of process values and accountability of central relevance to administrative law.

## (a) Competition, regulation and discretion

The process of privatising the utilities served to highlight the two basic ways of tackling market dominance: through conduct regulation and through a structural remedy – reducing the danger of anti-competitive behaviour by the break-up of monopoly. In the case of utilities, the initial pattern was very much conduct regulation without restructuring. In turn, a mismatch is evident between the

10 [1965] Ch 32.
11 Above, p. 7.

imperatives of a successful privatisation programme – speedy implementation, attractive share price – and those of an efficient regulatory regime. [12] The leading example is British Gas, which was put into private ownership as a massive vertically integrated firm and with its monopoly of the domestic consumer market intact. [13] In the absence of competition the task of economic regulation is obviously made much more difficult. Then again, a regulator put in this position may be tempted to pursue an aggressive, adversarial approach. Exactly this happened in the case of Sir James MacKinnon, the first Director General of OFGAS, who conceived of himself as a form of 'surrogate competition' in an attempt to regulate effectively. [14]

Two important themes are highlighted. First, market structure is seen as both a potential regulatory problem and an explanation of the form of regulation. Later, in a case study of OFTEL, it is seen to be directly relevant to administrative law as a prime determinant of regulatory norms and procedures (Chapter 11). The second theme concerns the strong sense of dynamic in this area: neither market structures nor styles of regulation are set in stone. For example, British Gas has now been broken up, while there is from 1998 major competition in the domestic consumer markets for gas and electricity. And by the early 1990s, the character of the utilities regulation had generally become more assertive and extensive. [15]

K. C. Davis argued for 'balance' in the shape of an appropriate point on a scale between discretion and rules. [16] To Veljanovski, writing in 1991, this had not been achieved: [17]

> UK regulators are increasingly trading certainty for flexibility, and in the process risking 'stop-go' regulation ... Regulation UK style is evolving into a discretionary system where negotiations and personality are becoming its most important feature. It is turning into a 'game' between industry chiefs and regulators because regulation does *not* provide a clear and certain set of rules within which the industry can take economic decisions. Rather, investing in influencing regulators and changing the rules of the game are becoming an industry in themselves, consuming resources and increasing the burden of regulation.

Similarly, like rules, regulation suffers from problems of selective enforcement. In Britain the traditional preference is for informality and bargaining: a pragmatic

---

12   See, for general discussion, J. Vickers and G. Yarrow, *Privatization, An Economic Analysis* (Cambridge, Mass: MIT Press) 1988; C. Veljanovski, *The Future of Industry Regulation in the UK* (London: European Policy Forum) 1993, p. 5.

13   See C. Price, 'Gas Regulation and Competition: Substitutes or Complements?', in M. Bishop, J. Kay and C. Mayer (eds), *Privatization and Economic Performance* (Oxford: OUP) 1994.

14   To the extent of 'managed competition': the pressing of British Gas to give away business. See OFGAS, *Annual Report 1990*, Director General's statement.

15   See, for general surveys, Price Waterhouse, *Regulated Industries: the UK Framework* (London: Centre for the Study of Regulated Industries) 2nd edn., 1996; National Audit Office, *The Work of the Directors General of Telecommunications, Gas Supply, Water Services and Electricity Supply* HC 645, Session 1995–1996, 1996; Hansard Society and European Policy Forum, *Report of the Commission on the Regulation of Privatised Utilities* (London) 1996.

16   Above, p. 104.

17   C. Veljanovski, 'The Regulation Game' in C. Veljanovski (ed.), *Regulators and the Market* (London: Institute of Economic Affairs) 1991, pp. 23, 26.

style of regulation. [18] Compliance is achieved through negotiation rather than the imposition of prescribed sanctions. As Majone [19] indicates, the process of regulation 'is not simply one where the regulators command and the regulated obey. A "market" is created in which bureaucrats and those subject to regulation bargain over the precise obligations of the latter'.

## (b) Rationale and mandate

Utilities regulation was not designed to be complex: quite the reverse. The philosophy was spelt out in a seminal report commissioned from Professor Stephen Littlechild, an economist and currently the Director-General of Electricity Supply, concerning the arrangements for regulating the telecommunications industry. [20]

> Competition is indisputably the most effective means ... of protecting consumers against monopoly power. Regulation is essentially a means of preventing the worst excesses of monopoly; it is not a substitute for competition. It is a means of 'holding the fort' until competition arrives ...
>
> Once X [1] has been chosen the regulatory authority does not need to approve price changes nor vet the company's investment programme. There is less intervention in the company's business. Fewer regulatory staff are required. Regulation is cheaper. Decision-making is not held up or distorted by bureaucratic inertia or political pressure.

Regulation then was seen as not only inferior to competition but also as temporary, and so able to be more straightforward: 'light-touch' regulation. Great stress was here being laid on a non-discretionary approach, in order to minimise the burden of regulation and the likelihood of agency capture. Hayekian values of certainty and (market) autonomy as fundamental to the Rule of Law are implicit in the model (above, p. 39).

But as the case of gas illustrates, the antithesis drawn by Littlechild between (public) regulation and (private) competition proved to be false. Regulation to promote competition quickly became a central tenet of the agencies, as also the notion of competition as beneficial for regulation. In the words of Sir Bryan Carsberg, first Director-General of OFTEL: [2]

---

18  See e.g. G. Richardson, A. Ogus and P. Burrows, *Policing Pollution: A Study of Regulation and Enforcement* (Oxford: Clarendon 1982); J. Rowan-Robinson, P. Watchman and C. Barker, *Crime and Regulation. A Study of the Enforcement of Regulatory Codes* (Edinburgh: T. & T. Clark) 1990.

19  G. Majone, 'The Rise of the Regulatory State in Europe' (1994) 17 West European Politics 77, 89. See also P. Simpson, 'Regulatory Aspects of Utility Privatisations' (1992) Utilities LR 183.

20  S. Littlechild, *Regulation of British Telecommunications Profitability* (London: HMSO) 1983, para. 4.11; and 'Economic Regulation of the Privatized Water Authorities: Some Further Reflections' (1988) 4 Oxford Rev. of Economic Policy 40, 56.

1  A factor which is part of the regulatory price control formula, explained below.

2  B. Carsberg, 'Office of Telecommunications: Competition and the Duopoly Review' in C. Veljanovski (ed.), *Regulators and the Market* (London: Institute of Economic Affairs) 1991, pp. 100–101.

The first important message about competition ... is that it is a 'regulatory weapon'. A regulator does not need to wait, hoping that it will occur, but can take active steps to encourage it ... Competition encourages the development of innovative services, and it also encourages energetic realisation of the potential provided by technological developments ... Competition will find out what is possible and what is economic in these matters and do so more surely than regulatory assessment ... I could give many other examples of how a regulator's life can be made easier by competition.

The minimisation of regulatory discretion has proved to be unrealistic. Later, we focus on the price control, a cornerstone of the economic regulation, the operation of which has been anything but robotic. The regulation has proved to be more enduring, competition at best being slow to arrive. Nor does it follow that regulation will simply wither away as competition develops, as the study of OFTEL illustrates. From a public choice perspective there are significant dangers:[3]

With privatisation has come explicit economic regulation of the utility industries – which are state-enforced restrictions on the use and exercise of private property. It would be unrealistic to assume that the state will or can confine its role to a minimalist level of intervention designed solely to protect consumers and encourage competition. It will, because of the forces of politics and sectional interests, eventually graft on to the present regulatory scheme all sorts of inhibitions and restrictions that go well beyond those needed to ensure efficient production in the interests of the consumer.

## (c) Disputed objectives

Controversy over regulatory objectives is destined to continue. According to Sir Christopher Foster, economist and adviser on several privatisations, the regulators should limit themselves as far as possible to applying the criteria given by the maximisation of economic efficiency.[4] In contrast to the original Littlechild model, this assigns an important role to the regulator, since basic economics teaches that maximisation of profits by the dominant firm does not correspond with maximisation of efficiency. The approach is also designed to shore up regulatory *legitimacy*: to help structure and confine discretion and reduce the risk of arbitrariness, to ground decisions in technical expertise. To introduce social considerations 'inevitably leads to an incoherence where it becomes progressively harder for a regulator to defend what he is doing without contradiction ... He is ... likely ... to lose credibility if his motives are regarded not as economic, but as political or personal'.[5]

It is self-evident that the greater the diversity of aims, the more difficult it may be to develop a coherent, overall strategy. But should the economic criteria enjoy such a dominant position? Prosser,[6] a public lawyer by trade, does not think so.

3    C. Veljanovski, *Selling the State. Privatization in Britain* (London: Weidenfeld and Nicolson) 1987, p. 207.
4    C. Foster, *Privatization, Public Ownership and the Regulation of Natural Monopoly* (Oxford: Blackwell) 1992, esp. Chs. 6 and 9.
5    Ibid, pp. 7, 205.
6    T. Prosser, 'Privatization, Regulation and Public Services' (1994) 1 Juridical Review 3, 3, 12, 17.

Note the relevance to his argument of a jurisprudence of rights, increasingly common today in English administrative law (above, Ch. 4):

> The argument is ... that if the regulators depart from economic criteria they will be lost in a quagmire of subjective values ... This seems to me a curious view ... What we are concerned to do as public lawyers is in fact precisely to develop theories of non-arbitrary decision-making, which are not necessarily economic based but involve other conceptions of legitimacy and rights ...
>
> As regards substantive rights [there] is a much older legal tradition both in the English common law and in Scots law which is concerned with access to monopoly services and with avoiding discrimination in the terms on which such access is given. [7] [Although] largely forgotten in England ... there are a number of ways in which this right [of access and non-discrimination] could be developed through jurisprudential analysis; for example, through employment of Dworkin's concept of a right to equal respect and concern ... An alternative approach is to suggest that the very concept of a market implies the existence of prior rights without which market transactions would be impossible, something which Adam Smith understood very well ... The same values [of individual autonomy] used to justify market provision may also justify rights of access to the necessities of life through non-market mechanisms.

Let us consult the statutes. Typical of regulatory agencies we find a broad mandate and potentially conflicting objectives. Although the wordings differ, OFTEL, OFGAS, OFWAT and OFFER all have primary duties to ensure some form of universal service and that the regulated utility has sufficient financial resources to meet the obligations imposed on it. Secondary duties include promoting the interests of consumers; promoting, enabling or facilitating competition; promoting efficiency and economy; and other duties relating to health and safety, research and development (below, p. 353). In other words, the mandates, far from being confined to maximising economic efficiency, stress social considerations. Universal service basically involves meeting all reasonable demands, and that implies additional cost: emergency services, services to rural areas, provision for special needs. This may not support a coherent rights-based interpretation, especially given parallel powers to disconnect for non-payment, but it does underscore the relevance of distributional concerns and of access to essential services. Nor should the use of economic criteria be conflated with an absence of discretion, or with an absence of conflict. For example, a policy of consumer protection may produce a conflict with the promotion of competition: a price control designed to curb the profitability of the dominant firm may reduce the likelihood of market entry. Again: [8]

> Properly understood competition is a mechanism for the co-ordination and mutual accommodation of divergent and possibly conflicting interests ... It follows, therefore, that a regulator who acts as a substitute for competition must – explicitly or implicitly – take into account the interests of *all parties* with a stake in the industry – consumers,

7   A tradition typically associated with 'common callings' such as carriers, innkeepers and millers. See for discussion, P. Craig, 'Constitutions, Property and Regulation' [1991] PL 538.
8   A. McHarg, 'Whose Role Is It Anyway? Consumer Representation in the Electricity Supply Industry' (1994) 4(2) Consumer Policy Rev. 88.

shareholders, employees, suppliers and the community generally – and attempt to strike a reasonable balance between them.

The next link in the argument is a familiar one in administrative law. If discretion and conflict are endemic, then channels of accountability and process values are at a premium. We leave the point here to pick it up later on.

## (d) The structure of regulation

It is characteristic of our administrative law that machinery should evolve in piecemeal fashion and with no single set of clearly defined objectives. Utilities regulation has been peculiarly susceptible, given the scale and complexity of the privatisation process, as also a steep learning curve for government and agencies alike. Diversity in powers and performance is one trait which the regulation shares. None the less, it is possible to identify some standard components – what has become known as regulation 'UK-style'.[9]

- For each industry there is a *single, independent* regulatory agency, headed by a Director-General.
- While the privatisation statutes confer the legal authority to regulate and establish the general regulatory framework and duties of the Directors-General, practical operations have been predicated on a system of *licensing*.
- A cornerstone of the economic regulation has been the *price-cap formula*, 'Retail Price Index (RPI) minus X', intended to provide a strong incentive to greater efficiency.
- The Directors-General are themselves part of a regulatory framework or *network*, which includes the competition authorities.
- Latterly, there has been great emphasis on *quality* regulation as an integral part of economic regulation.

## (i) Independence and personalisation

There has from the very beginning been great stress on the need for regulatory independence and an apolitical appearance. Wigglesworth and Barnes argue that:[10]

> Failure to achieve the appropriate degree of independence from government runs the risk that some of the problems experienced under old-style public ownership may reappear under private ownership through detailed political interference – this time not through direct interference in the day-to-day operation of the [utility] company, but indirectly through political interference in the regulation process.

9  C. Veljanovski, 'The Regulation Game' in C. Veljanovski (ed.), *Regulators and the Market* (London: Institute of Economic Affairs) 1991. See further M. Armstrong, S. Cowan and J. Vickers, *Regulatory Reform: Regulation of Economic Activity* (Cambridge, MA: MIT Press) 1994.
10  B. Wigglesworth and F. Barnes, 'UK Policies and Regulations' (1992) Telecommunications Policy 721, 722.

The model chosen was the non-ministerial government department, headed by a Director-General (DG). As a compact agency, operating at arm's length from, but subject to the patronage of, the Secretary of State, it typifies fragmentation of the traditional government framework (Chapter 1). Once appointed by the Minister, the DG has a statutory period of tenure, subject only to dismissal for incapacity or misbehaviour. He exercises important powers not available to Ministers, most obvious the resetting of the price cap formula, and is responsible for the staffing and operation of the agency. Then again, it is important to grasp the constraints imposed by market structures and through tiers or networks of regulation (see below). Agency independence should not be conflated with institutional freedom.

In the event, most of the so-called 'Ofdogs' have been economists or accountants, and several have spent some years as academics. [11] The staff has contained a majority of generalists, together with significant numbers of economists, accountants, engineers and scientists. There is an increasing emphasis on lawyers: generally, in overseeing the regulation; in particular, in drafting licences and handling disputes as competition develops and regulation becomes more of a multilateral arrangement. Later on, regulatory style and legal input will be seen to go hand in hand.

There is a strong sense of personalisation in this kind of agency. At one level, the vesting of powers in the DG is seen to reflect the personalised traditions of constitutional government in the United Kingdom: powers vested not in 'the state', but in individual ministers. [12] At another level, media attention has naturally focused on the DG, underscoring what one critic unkindly calls a 'super-hero model of the independent guardian'. [13] There are here the classic concerns of administrative law: distinct personal powers of great importance, characterised on the one hand by wide discretion, and on the other by weak safeguards (see below). Thus, the highly personalised format threatens the legitimacy of regulation, as ultimately inimical to the Rule of Law. It also highlights the critical importance of non-legal factors: a point taken by a Labour Party spokesman, when in opposition: [14]

> Even the existing system could be deployed in favour of alternative policies where competition was not at the expense of social, economic or industrial objectives. New regulators should be appointed with a different ideological remit to change the direction of the utilities.

## (ii) The licensing technique

Post-privatisation, licence conditions provided the principal means for the regulatory authorities to order the market structure and establish market rules.

---

11  See, for details, National Audit Office, *The Work of the Directors General of Telecommunications, Gas Supply, Water Services and Electricity Supply*, HC 645, Session 1995–1996, Part 4.

12  T. Prosser, 'Regulation, Markets and Legitimacy', in J. Jowell and D. Oliver (eds.), *The Changing Constitution* (Oxford: OUP) 3rd edn., 1994; following K. Dyson, *The State Tradition in Western Europe* (Oxford: Martin Robertson) 1980.

13  P. Hain, 'Regulating for the Common Good' (1994) Utilities LR 90, 91.

14  Ibid, p. 93.

Here control has been exercised, first, on entry to the industries by the grant or withholding of the licence; and, second, on those firms allowed to enter by enforcement and modification of the terms and conditions contained in their licences. Licences emerge as a prime agent of juridification of the regulatory process. Here McEldowney points up the vital role played in the regulatory structure by lawyers and legal skills: [15]

> The regulation of the newly privatized industries and the respective legal framework which applies to each industry has provided lawyers unprecedented involvement in the technical drawing up of contracts, licences, and in the interpretation of the new regulators' authority ... Reliance on the use of licences and contracts has ... required skilled interpretation and careful drafting [to] provide in formal legal language the mechanisms of running the [industries].

Licences also emerge as a useful vehicle for the delegation by Parliament of substantial rule-making powers. As such, the system neatly demonstrates the major role of regulatory authorities in the elaboration of norms, formal or informal, which directly constrain the behaviour of firms and individuals.

Parallels may be drawn with public procurement and franchising. This is 'particular' law (above, p. 239), applicable in the formal legal sense only to the licensee and only for as long as the licence lasts. Yet the contrast with 'legislating', whereby rules have a generality of application, is not so easily drawn. It is the logic of the regulation that licence terms for a dominant firm affect various interests. Take 'interconnection', the terms on which a network or transmission system is made available to other market players: in an industry like telecommunications it is a sine qua non of competition. An important regulatory dynamic will be demonstrated in the study of OFTEL: a trend towards routinisation as competition expands. A greater emphasis on the general principles of competition law may also be expected: [16]

> The growth of competition and the number of licensees, allied with developments in technology, are tending to make regulation through detailed licences more cumbersome and inappropriate in some areas of the utilities. The conditions of licences should therefore be broadened and simplified. But, the counterpart of such a move should be legislation introducing general prohibitions against anti-competitive practices and abuse of a dominant position; ... Such legislation should be modelled on Articles 85 and 86 of the Treaty of Rome. Such a regime should be introduced for regulated utilities even if it is not adopted for the generality of industries ... Licence conditions and competition law [are] complementary in the utilities, and ... both licence enforcement and the enforcement of competition law in their respective industries should be the responsibility of the DGs ...
> The extent of the move to broader licences should vary both according to the sector and within sectors, depending especially on the extent to which effective competition had developed.

15  J. McEldowney, 'Law and Regulation: Current Issues and Future Directions' in M. Bishop, J. Kay and C. Mayer (eds.), *The Regulatory Challenge* (Oxford: OUP) 1995, pp. 408, 418–419.
16  Hansard Society and European Policy Forum, *Report of the Commission on the Regulation of Privatised Utilities* (London) 1996, pp. 9, 14. And see on the existing allocation of competition law powers in telecommunications, below, p. 377.

### (iii) A magic formula? RPI - X

Constraint on the profits and prices of the dominant firm has been seen as the paradigm case in the public interest mission of economic regulation. Further, the method commonly adopted in the utilities, the regulatory rule RPI - X, is appropriately described as 'the most distinctive feature of monopoly regulation in Britain'. [17] For the administrative lawyer several features command attention. First, the operation of the price control entails a major and ongoing exercise of agency discretion. This is seen both to reflect a demand for flexibility in the light of commercial factors, and to point up serious deficiencies in the formal structures of accountability and participation. Second, RPI - X regulation provides a leading illustration in administrative law of progressive rule-development: the gradual emergence of a hierarchy or sub-species of rules more closely to confine or structure discretion. Third, the subsequent development is seen to illustrate concerns about regulatory failure – detailed and intrusive norms, stifling of choice and innovation – and to generate countervailing pressures for deregulation, in the guise of rule-substitution.

In the choice of method, Littlechild was concerned to avoid the traditional American approach to price regulation based on assessment of a fair rate of return on capital employed by the regulated utility. For economists this model is seen to create an incentive for over-capitalisation of a firm – so as to achieve a greater absolute profit – and, conversely, to provide no inherent incentives for the firm to become more efficient. [18] The price in administrative law terms comes in the shape of heavy administrative costs, lengthy regulatory hearings and considerable litigation. [19] By rejecting rate of return regulation, Littlechild was rejecting the regulatory base on which many of the detailed procedural requirements under the American Administrative Procedure Act have evolved.

In its basic form, operative each year for a period of years, RPI - X requires the regulated firm to raise prices for a defined 'basket' of its wares by no more than the rate of retail price inflation minus X%, where the factor X represents a regulatory judgment of the cost-efficiency potential of the firm. It was chosen as the instrument both of straightforward regulation and of incentive regulation or the pursuit of greater efficiency. The original design was predicated on lengthy periods between resettings of the formula: in Littlechild's judgment a review every five years was appropriate. In Sir Bryan Carsberg's words: [20]

> The British price control approach ... is often contrasted with the rate of return approach as used in the United States because it is thought to have preferable incentive

17  R. Rees and J. Vickers, 'RPI - X Price-Cap Regulation' in M. Bishop, J. Kay and C. Mayer (eds.), *The Regulatory Challenge* (Oxford: OUP) 1995, p. 358. The method has been adopted, subject to variations, across a broad range of industries: telecommunications and airports, gas, water and electricity.
18  See, e.g., W. Viscusi, J. Vernon and J. Harrington, *Economics of Regulation and Antitrust* (Cambridge, Mass: MIT Press) 1995, Ch. 12.
19  S. Breyer, *Regulation and its Reform* (Cambridge, Mass: Harvard University Press) 1982, Ch. 2.
20  B. Carsberg, 'Injecting Competition into Telecommunications' in C. Veljanovski (ed.), *Privatization and Competition: A Market Prospectus* (London: Institute of Economic Affairs) 1989, p. 92.

properties. Because the price control rule is frozen for a period of five years, it gives [the firm] a strong incentive to become more efficient: if [the firm] can reduce its costs it will make more profit and will be allowed to keep it, and if it can reduce costs significantly below the level assumed in the setting of the price control rule, it can make profits above the normal level, whereas under US practice, little incentive exists to make cost savings because such savings have to be passed on to customers as soon as they are made.

How might the method be conceptualised by an administrative lawyer, bearing in mind that the price control will be incorporated in the licence, a legal instrument? One way forward is by reference to 'structuring' and 'confining' discretion as propounded by K. C. Davis, and the idea of discretion as a relative concept expressed in Dworkin's celebrated 'hole in the doughnut'.[1] Here the interplay is between an exercise of public power and managerial (or 'privatised') discretion, constrained by the formula. At first sight, RPI - X looks like a precise and specific 'rule': however, the design confines and so also conserves managerial discretion. Control on a 'basket' of services regulates the level of prices but not their structure: without more, the utility is free to change individual prices, affecting different classes of consumer, provided the average is met.

An alternative approach, popular among economists, envisages a long-term contract between the regulator and regulatee:[2]

> The shareholders in the utility are given the right to operate a monopoly through a licence. The price is fixed ... then, at a periodic review ... the prices are again reset. The customers are issued a price; the shareholders a cash-flow ... To the extent that the contract is well defined, it encourages efficiency.

This is a classic case of pseudo-contract, and it links with the general striving for clarification and precision in the contractual 'revolution' in government. Yet it also points up the conflicts of interest inherent in the regulation. On behalf of shareholders, stress had been laid on a 'regulatory bargain', investment on the basis of understandings as to the clear and certain nature of the regulation.[3] The regulators, however, have tended to emphasise their statutory duties to protect consumers and promote competition – so undermining the shareholders' 'expectations'. Speaking more generally, the contract analogy is apt to be misleading, precisely because of the dynamic character of the regulation:[4]

> At first sight the RPI - X method of price control looks simple, different from, and superior to rate-of-return regulation ... However, a number of parameters have to be set and from time to time reset: the coverage of the price cap; construction of the price index; ... the level of X; ... the frequency of price reviews; ... to name only the most obvious ...

1    Above, p. 102.
2    D. Helm, 'British Utility Regulation: Theory, Practice and Reform' (1994) 10 Oxford Rev. of Economic Policy 17, 22.
3    C. Veljanovski, *The Future of Industry Regulation in the UK* (London: European Policy Forum) 1993, pp. 59–60.
4    R. Rees and J. Vickers, 'RPI - X Price-Cap Regulation' (above, note 17), pp. 381–382.

RPI - X can be operated in various ways. 'Passive RPI - X' would involve the regulator simply checking that the formula was complied with year after year ... and resetting the parameters at review times ... 'Active RPI - X' involves continuing regulatory vigilance backed up by ... the imposition of tougher regulation. Price structure, quality, and perhaps even investment, are all under scrutiny ... The British pattern has been one of fairly active RPI - X.

It is in this context that we find increased complexity in the regulation. The development has included tougher X factors, additional factors as for investment, and burgeoning sub-rules on the structure of prices. [5] Most striking are repeated instances of 'regulatory chiselling', by which is meant changing the rules before the specified time-period is complete, in the light of substantial profits. This both puts in issue the incentive properties of the price control and underscores the scale of agency discretion. Later, 'active RPI - X' is illustrated in the case study of OFTEL, together with a counter-reaction in the context of a more competitive environment.

## (iv) Tiers of regulation

Although regulation 'UK-style' has been centred on the idea of the single, independent regulator, an industry-plus-agency model of arrangements is too simplistic. The concept of a regulatory framework is important, in the sense of the division and interconnectedness of regulatory functions between institutions. Ministers retain significant powers. One example concerns control on market entry in the case of telecommunications (below, p. 357); another involves rail, in the guise of Treasury control of the payment of subsidies. Then there is the parallel, sometimes overlapping, work of agencies. Leading illustrations are provided by the water industry, with responsibilities shared by OFWAT (economic regulation) and the Environment Agency; or the railways, with intersecting powers and duties assigned to the Rail Regulator and the Director of Passenger Rail Franchising (Chapter 9). It is particularly important that behind the DGs stand the competition authorities, in the shape of the Department of Trade and Industry, the Monopolies and Mergers Commission (MMC) and the Office of Fair Trading (OFT). [6] Hogwood [7] has in this context stressed:

> the 'interdependence' of the relationship between the wide variety of bodies and therefore the complex *networks* of organisations which are involved in the regulation of the privatised industries ... The full range of regulatory control often depends on the joint involvement of a number of regulatory bodies.

Let us take as an example the question of takeovers and mergers, with the powers of the Secretary of State to refer proposals to the MMC for consideration,

5   A useful survey is R. Baldwin, *Regulation in Question* (London: London School of Economics) 1995, Ch. 2.
6   General competition law applies to the utilities, in the shape both of national law and European Community law.
7   B. Hogwood, 'Developments in Regulatory Agencies in Britain' (1990) 56 International Rev. of Administrative Sciences 595, 604, 611.

and to determine what if any action should be taken. Here the emphasis is on a political model of decision-making. The Minister has wide discretion in deciding whether or not to follow the Commission's recommendations, there is no appeal against his decisions, and judicial review is characteristically 'light-touch' in this area. [8] A second example might be special statutory provisions concerning the powers of the DGs and the Director-General of Fair Trading (DGFT). In effect, these constitute a 'long-stop', covering anti-competitive practices which may elude licence restrictions. Thus, the industry regulators share concurrently with the DGFT his general powers (a) under the Fair Trading Act 1973, to refer a monopoly situation that may be contrary to the public interest to the MMC; and (b) under the Competition Act 1980, to prevent courses of conduct which have or are intended to have or are likely to have the effect of restricting, distorting or preventing competition. Thirdly, there is licence modification, which naturally assumes great importance in dynamic market conditions of developing competition. This, we learn, is the responsibility, but not the sole responsibility, of the DG. Change may take place either by agreement between the DG and the licensee, subject to reserve powers of the Minister, or following a reference by the DG to the MMC. The Commission in such a case must determine whether specified matters operate against the public interest and whether this could be remedied by licence modification; if so, the DG is required to impose a change, having regard to the proposals made by the Commission. [9]

The MMC provides the capacity for detailed investigation, via inquisitorial procedure. It has special strengths in technical expertise and analysis, by reason of a unique blend of specialist agency staff and part-time Commission members, drawn primarily from economics and business, accountancy and law. [10] In the event, it has been called upon in some of the sectors far more than in others. The utilities have seen a spate of takeovers and mergers in recent years, sometimes, as in electricity, involving vertical integration. Some bids, for example by the generators PowerGen and National Power for regional electricity companies, have been referred by the Secretary of State, others have not. [11] Over a longer period, the MMC was a catalyst in the break-up of British Gas, by means of a series of reports on monopoly references. [12] It is therefore appropriate to stress not only the problems of market structure associated with privatisation, but also, in McEldowney's words: [13] 'the flexibility inherent in the legal mechanisms used to regulate the industry. The legal basis for referral to the MMC and the resultant modification of the authorisation allowed gradual changes to be introduced.'

8  E.g. *R v Secretary of State for Trade and Industry, ex p Lonrho plc* [1989] 1 WLR 525.
9  See e.g. the Electricity Act 1989, s. 14.
10 See Monopolies and Mergers Commission, *The Role of the Commission*, 4th edn., 1992. See also P. Craig, 'The Monopolies and Mergers Commission: Competition and Administrative Rationality' in R. Baldwin and C. McCrudden (eds.), *Regulation and Public Law* (London: Weidenfeld and Nicolson) 1987.
11 See further, Hansard Society and European Policy Forum, *Report of the Commission on the Regulation of Privatised Utilities* (London) 1996, Ch. 6.
12 Monopolies and Mergers Commission, *Gas*, Cm. 500 (1988); *Gas and British Gas plc*, Cm. 2314, 2315, 2316 and 2317 (1993). And see the Gas Act 1995.
13 J. McEldowney, 'Law and Regulation: Current Issues and Future Directions' in M. Bishop, J. Kay and C. Mayer (eds.), *The Regulatory Challenge* (Oxford: OUP) 1995, p. 416.

The process of licence modification is especially noteworthy for administrative lawyers. A recent case, *R v Director General of Electricity Supply, ex p Scottish Power plc* [14] explores the relationship between the tiers. A licence modification concerning the calculation of supply price controls in Scotland was proposed by Professor Littlechild. One company (SP) reluctantly agreed, the other (HE) did not. The case of HE was referred to the MMC, which concluded that the calculation in its licence should be as both companies had contended. When Professor Littlechild refused to amend SP's licence accordingly, he was successfully challenged in the Court of Appeal. The case is a good example of a model of judicial review as an agent for rationality in the administrative process (Chapter 4):

> *Ralph Gibson LJ*: The decisive issue is whether ... a distinction drawn between HE and SP ... is founded upon an irrational basis ... The Director referred to his statutory duties to promote competition and to protect customers with reference to prices which required him to look 'at the whole picture not just one aspect' ... [Counsel for the Director] asserted that ... it is not possible to know what the MMC would have concluded for SP ... and that the MMC might have recommended a change adverse to SP as compared with the agreed modification of the SP licence. We can see no force whatever in this contention. The Director was as well, or better, placed than anyone in this country to decide whether, if SP's licence had been before the MMC, it was likely that the MMC would, having regard to their reasoning and decision with reference to HE, have proposed a distribution component more adverse to SP than that proposed by the Director himself and accepted by SP. More importantly, however, the Director was as well placed to make this decision for himself as he was to make the decision set out in his proposals to SP which SP accepted ... We can think of no reason why he could not ... make such proposal, if any, for amending SP's distribution price component as seen to him to be required or justified by the reasoning and decision of the MMC with reference to the distribution price controls in HE's licence. No such preventing reason has been put forward by the Director or on his behalf. If he had put forward such a proposal, SP would have been able to accept it or, if grounds for doing so appeared, to challenge it. In the alternative the Director could have referred the matter to the MMC. The simple refusal to propose the modification of the definition ... in the licence of SP, to which on the grounds of fairness SP was entitled, cannot be justified.

Seen in this light, the MMC functions as a check or machinery of appeal from the front line regulator, a line taken by its former Chairman, Sir Sidney Lipworth, who has stressed the impartiality of the Commission as 'an adjudicator between the regulator and the utility in the event of dispute'. [15] Yet the tiered structure serves also to highlight the importance of bargaining in regulatory process. Thus, licence modification and compliance may be negotiated by the DGs in the shadow of the MMC. Notice that both sides may have incentives to avoid a reference. First, there are the advantages familiarly associated with regulatory bargaining or regulation 'in the shadow of the law' (above, p. 143): flexibility and adaptability, speedy decision-making to eliminate commercial uncertainties. Secondly, there

14 (3 February 1997, unreported).
15 S. Lipworth, 'Utility Regulation and the Monopolies and Mergers Commission: Retrospect and Prospect' in G. Borrie and M. Beesley (eds.), *Major Issues in Regulation* (London: Institute of Economic Affairs) 1993, pp. 47–48.

are the disadvantages associated with a reference: not only onerous formal hearings, but also a loss of control for the regulator, and, for a dominant firm, the prospect of drastic consequences. These points are perfectly illustrated in the case of telecommunications, where the Commission is appropriately characterised as a brooding presence, rarely called upon, [16] and a powerful background influence. OFTEL was in these conditions able to edge licence terms and conditions progressively against the dominant firm. Then again, all the haggling can seem tedious. Very recently, OFTEL has been engaged in licence modification in order to avoid it in the future. In effect, it has with the consent of licensees metamorphosed into a full competition authority, which will itself decide what activities are contrary to the public interest. We leave the matter here, to pick it up in Chapter 11.

### (v) Regulating for quality

When the first two utilities, telecommunications and gas, were privatised no direct provision was made for the regulation of quality. 'It was felt, in line with the philosophy of the time, that it would be in BT's interests to maintain quality particularly with the prospect of competition ...' [17] Yet it is a familiar proposition in economic theory that an unregulated monopolist will be tempted to supply quality at other than allocatively efficient levels; further, 'the regulation of monopoly suffers from one inherent disability – tightening regulation of one activity leads to attempts by the firm to recoup the losses from unregulated activities'. [18] Seen in this light, RPI - X as the sole form of consumer protection is not only insufficient but may be damaging, the incentive under the formula to reduce costs providing a corresponding incentive to reduce quality. In the words of the National Consumer Council in 1989: [19] 'This is perhaps the most serious defect in this regulatory system. At best, [the formula] provides no positive encouragement to improve service quality. At worst, it actually pulls in the opposite direction ...' In the event, the problem was tackled in typically incremental fashion. Action to shore up standards had to be taken by individual regulators, in the case of OFTEL by negotiation and informal agreement with BT (below, p. 383). Later privatisation statutes, on electricity and water, gave the regulators specific powers to establish performance standards binding on the licence-holders. The Competition and Service (Utilities) Act 1992 brought up the quality regulation powers of the Ofdogs to the level of the strongest. Today, each of the offices puts great stress on this aspect of the work, there having developed a greater consumerist 'feel' to the regulation. Quality is in this context broadly defined to include standards of supply, for example reliability, and customer service issues, such as provision of information and complaints and billing procedures, as well as the quality of the product per se. In turn, the developments

16  But see Monopolies and Mergers Commission, *Telephone Number Portability*, December 1995.
17  C. Veljanovski, *The Future of Industry Regulation in the UK* (London: European Policy Forum) 1993, p. 36.
18  Ibid, p. 37.
19  National Consumer Council, *In the Absence of Competition* (London, HMSO) 1989, p. 46. See further L. Rovizzi and D. Thompson, 'The Regulation of Product Quality in the Public Utilities' in M. Bishop, J. Kay and C. Mayer, *The Regulatory Challenge* (Oxford: OUP) 1995.

led, in Bowdery's words, 'to a more formal and tightly specified regulatory process'.[20]

The 1992 Act is of general interest in administrative law, embodying the philosophy of the Citizen's Charter in the tools of standard-setting and compensation, information regulation and complaints procedure. An important distinction is drawn in the legislation between the overall standards of performance which a company must achieve and the standards to be achieved in individual cases. Individual or 'guaranteed standards' represent levels of service within certain quality dimensions which it is considered should be supplied on every occasion. Failure to do so incurs a liability to pay compensation, and, typical of Charter thinking, payment should where practicable be automatic, that is without the consumer having to make a claim. The vesting of powers to establish standards is a striking illustration of the agency discretion to make rules (above, p. 320). The regulators may prescribe individual standards in regulation, subject to ministerial consent, and may then adjudicate disputes. Overall standards may be incorporated in an agency order or determination, ultimately enforceable in civil proceedings in the same way as other licence conditions. Information regulation as an instrument for stimulating the quality of service is underwritten by duties on the Ofdogs to obtain and publish figures on company performance, and to ensure their dissemination to customers. Finally, the companies are placed under a legal duty to establish complaints procedures approved by the regulator. The DG is empowered to order periodic reviews of a procedure and to direct modifications, as well as to approve arrangements for publicity. Note here the pro-active role in design assigned to the regulator; significantly these are legal powers which a classical Ombudsman like the Parliamentary Commissioner for Administration does not possess (Chapter 13). Note also the imposition of Charter principles on (what is now) the private sector, and, further, the scope for a more formal regulatory style. This is not the usual Charter approach of non-legal standards. The bargaining power of the regulator is increased by the threat of the exercise of discretion to make binding rules. Bowdery aptly refers in this context to the hierarchy of regulatory instruments. As well as formal rules like licence conditions and contract obligations:[1]

> There appear to exist sets of informal rules which, although tightly specified, are not generally legally enforceable. An example of this is a regulated company agreeing to do something, possibly under threat of regulatory action if it does not, but in the absence of the regulator possessing any powers of enforcement. In addition a number of informal rules, which are not at all tightly specified, have operated, such as apparent assumptions that levels of quality should generally improve over time and certainly that there should be no sustained declines in any individual dimensions of quality of service.

The difficulties of regulating for quality deserve emphasis. 'It is likely that different consumers will make different decisions about the combination of

20 J. Bowdery, *Quality Regulation and the Regulated Industries* (London: Centre for Regulated Industries) 1994, p. 3.
1 Ibid, pp. 12–13.

prices and quality that suits them best, and that the balance favoured by the average consumer will change over time.'[2] The issue is highlighted of reconciling demands for product differentiation with the work of standard-setting agencies as proxies for market forces. Other, more specific, problems such as the monitoring of service quality are familiar from public procurement. Then there is the issue of the adequacy of the standard-setting model of the Charter. In the case of the utilities:[3]

> Problems of specification occur in standard setting as well as in information reporting in terms of both the danger of resources being allocated to those quality dimensions targeted at the expense of those not targeted, and the fact that the way in which a standard is measured is not always an accurate reflection of an underlying quality dimension. There appears also to be little evidence of any consideration of resource allocation issues between standards. Certainly little consideration appears to have been given to the relative marginal costs to companies of achieving specific standards.

Nor should the obvious attractions in this context of compensation schemes be allowed to obscure the limitations:[4]

> The first advantage of such a mechanism is that it ensures consumer-specific compensation: the individual customer who has suffered the loss in quality will be compensated. Second, the company is provided with more precise management information since it can spot the location of the quality failure. Third, with such a scheme the company is allowed to trade-off changes in quality against the incremental costs of achieving these. Thus the regulator does not fix a unique level of quality and the company can choose whether to improve service quality or pay out more compensation ...
> The main disadvantages of this approach are twofold. First of all the scheme can only work when the detriment is consumer-specific and quality failures can be easily verified. For instance it would not be practicable to compensate individual consumers for failures such as noisy telephone lines. Second, transaction costs – both to the company and to the consumer – will be higher than under other mechanisms [for quality regulation].

Consumer affairs are examined in more detail in the case of OFTEL (Chapter 11). But note that the individualist philosophy of the Charter also finds expression in the non-development in the 1992 Act of machinery for direct consumer representation. Let us focus now on the arrangements for oversight, transparency and voice.

## 4. Accountability and process

The delegation to regulatory agencies of broad decision-making powers is today in Britain an accomplished fact. We see too that while the public interest arguments for such delegation are strong, it gives rise to the classic public law

2    J. Kay and J. Vickers, 'Regulatory Reform: An Appraisal' in G. Majone (ed.), *Deregulation or Reregulation: Regulatory Reform in Europe and the United States* (London: Pinter) 1990, p. 236.
3    J. Bowdery, *Quality Regulation* (above, note 20), p. 34.
4    L. Rovizzi and D. Thompson, 'The Regulation of Product Quality' (above, note 19), pp. 351–352.

problems of accountability and process, themselves identified as touchstones of the legitimacy of agencies. Are the channels by which the regulators are answerable for their deeds adequate? Are the regulatory procedures fair and impartial? Do they, as Ogus prescribes,[5] constitute an adequate framework 'for making rules and decisions which serve the public interest and for resisting the undue influence of private interests'?

In this context we can look again at utilities regulation. Enough has been said to show, first, that a major part of the utility regulators' job is to balance conflicting interests; second, that this process entails very considerable agency discretion; and, third, that this discretion has underpinned dynamic regulatory regimes in which informal techniques of rule-making and negotiated compliance have loomed large. On the one hand, the 'closed' aspect of regulatory bargaining points up for the administrative lawyer important issues of transparency and 'voice'. On the other hand, according to an economic analysis of regulatory behaviour, the recourse by the agencies to informal techniques has been predictable. In addition to the incentives for negotiated compliance, 'The costs of informality are [low] because the regulator is subject to weak checks and balances ... This is because of three critical features of the legal, or lack of legal, constraints on the regulator – weak accountability, weak judicial review, and the absence of procedural safeguards'.[6] To push home the point, a lack of constraint is both a cause for complaint and a key explanatory factor. On one view, to the classical question 'quis custodiet ipsos custodes?' – Who regulates the regulator? – the truthful answer is 'no one'.[7]

## (a) Channels of accountability

Let us look more closely. The Conservative Government's view was summarised in 1992 by Lord Reay:[8]

> I accept entirely that the regulators should be accountable for their performance – and they are already accountable in a number of different ways. First, they must operate within the framework laid down by Parliament in the relevant legislation ... The regulators also have a continuing, direct accountability to Parliament: ... the legislation requires the Director General to make an annual report to the Secretary of State, which must be presented to Parliament. In addition, ... the directors can be called before the appropriate select committee ...
>
> Secondly, the directors' performance of their statutory duties is subject to judicial review and their decisions can be overturned by the courts if they fail to act reasonably ... Thirdly, the director cannot impose regulatory requirements without the consent of the utility or without independent backing ... The regulators are also constrained informally by public opinion: they consult widely before taking major decisions ... Fourthly, the directors are appointed by and are answerable in broad terms to the

5   A. Ogus, *Regulation. Legal Form and Economic Theory* (Oxford: Clarendon 1994, p. 111.
6   C. Veljanovski, 'The Regulation Game' in C. Veljanovski (ed.), *Regulators and the Market* (London: Institute of Economic Affairs) 1991, p. 16.
7   J. Garner, 'After Privatization: Quis Custodiet Ipsos Custodes?' [1990] PL 329, 337. See also the reply by C. Graham, 'The Regulation of Privatized Enterprises' [1991] PL 15.
8   HL Deb., vol. 536, cols. 1192–1193 (9 March 1992).

appropriate Secretary of State. If the director does not carry out his duties satisfactorily, he can be replaced.

Notice the traditional slant of the argument, a stress in terms of Dicey's 'balanced constitution' on control by Parliament and the courts. Yet it is precisely this model of the constitution which has been challenged by the combination of powers in regulatory agencies (above, p. 308). In truth, in the case of regulatory agencies in general, and the utilities regulators in particular, 'it would be difficult to claim that *post*-legislative agency accountability to Parliament, to the executive or to the public provides a secure foundation for legitimacy'.[9]

The independence afforded the Ofdogs as non-ministerial government departments represents a deliberate distancing from traditional parliamentary control in the form of ministerial responsibility. Detailed investigation of their efficiency and effectiveness by the National Audit Office[10] does not directly address the merits of policy objectives, while oversight by select committee does not provide consistent monitoring. Other 'external' controls are typically geared towards an agency's handling of individual disputes. As explained in Chapter 13, the Parliamentary Commissioner has jurisdiction over agencies like the Ofdogs yet is severely constrained in the exercise of powers. One or two cases each year hardly suggest a major impact. Again, such agencies come under the informal supervision of the Council on Tribunals,[11] but only in respect of the exercise of adjudicative powers in dealing with complaints as from consumers. Speaking more generally, a plethora of techniques, especially of bureaucratic regulation, may be seen as indicative of problems of fragmentation or piecemeal scrutiny: particular elements of agency operations being subject to oversight through diverse sources.

Judicial review of regulatory agencies is appropriately described in de Smith's famous phrase as 'sporadic and peripheral'.[12] We detect on different occasions a judicial willingness both to defer to the expertise and special role of regulators (the *ITC* cases[13]) and to engage in matters notwithstanding arguments from the regulator that judicial intervention is inappropriate (*Save Our Railways*[14]). But we see also that traditionally the review is circumscribed, being geared towards the procedures of regulators and not the substance or merits of decisions. The obvious contrast is with America and judicial examination under the so-called 'hard look' doctrine of the basis of regulatory decisions.[15] To Veljanovski, the

---

9  R. Baldwin and C. McCrudden, *Regulation and Public Law* (London: Weidenfeld and Nicholson) 1987, p. 39.

10  National Audit Office, *The Office of Telecommunications: Licence Compliance and Consumer Protection*, HC529, Session 1992–1993; *The Work of the Directors General of Telecommunications, Gas Supply, Water Services and Electricity Supply*, HC 645, Session 1995–1996.

11  See Council on Tribunals, *Annual Report*, HC 78, Session 1993/4 at para. 2.10.

12  S. de Smith *Judicial Review of Administrative Action* (London: Stevens) 4th edn., J. Evans, 1980, p. 3.

13  Above, pp. 278 and 280.

14  Above, p. 288.

15  S. Breyer, and R. Stewart, *Administrative Law and Regulatory Policy* (Boston: Little Brown) 3rd edn., 1992, pp. 363–394. And see *Vermont Yankee*, below p. 334, note 9. See also I. Harden and N. Lewis, *The Noble Lie* (London: Hutchinson) 1986, pp. 275–278.

impact of judicial review in England on the quality of decision-making by regulatory agencies 'is small and offers no protection'.[16]

The limited role of judicial review has been brilliantly illustrated in the case of the utilities regulation. The first decade of operations saw two cases against the agencies decided, one involving a disconnection of supply, the other about ending a 'chat-line' service.[17] On both occasions the court stressed the broad statutory discretion and declined to become involved in detailed questions of fact. To push home the point, controversial and important tasks such as price control have gone unchallenged.

The phenomenon is usefully linked by Ogus to the dominant theoretical framework in administrative law, as also the properties of adjudication (a theme developed in Chapter 17):[18]

> Judicial review has ... had a relatively small impact on regulation, a consequence no doubt of the Diceyan tradition of administrative law which concentrates on the protection of individual rights against illegitimate government interference, and thereby largely shuns a functionalist concern with public purposes ...
>
> [The] cautious approach to substantive review might not be inappropriate. If the gates are open too widely, the administrative costs of regulation may escalate and private interests will have an incentive to exploit the process for tactical purposes, thereby frustrating the implementation of public interest goals ... Regulatory rule-making often [involves] the 'polycentric problem': issues cannot be resolved independently and sequentially; they are, rather, interdependent and a choice from one set of alternatives has implications for preferences within other sets of alternatives. The decision-maker must take into account the whole network before she can reach a single decision. The adversarial setting of the judicial process does not lend itself to grappling with this problem, not the least because judicial intervention is generally sought after the rules have been promulgated.

Alternatively, the matter can be viewed in terms of the indirect 'ouster' of jurisdiction (above, p. 52). The legislation, couched in subjective and permissive language, is 'careful to protect the new regulators from judicial review',[19] reflecting a desire to avoid an American model of a central role for courts in the ordering of regulation. There is further the technical complexity of much of the subject matter, which naturally evokes tolerant or 'light-touch' review, and the use of informal techniques of regulatory bargaining, which renders judicial review less potent.

Here, as elsewhere, the 'impact' of judicial review principles remains elusive. In any assessment of the effects on agency decision-making the 'fire-watching' function ascribed to courts will be relevant (see further Chapter 16). We have learned too that recourse to informal techniques may signal a background

16 C. Veljanovski, *The Future of Industry Regulation in UK* (London: European Policy Forum) 1993, p. 69.

17 *R v Director-General of Gas Supply, ex p Smith* (31 July 1989, unreported); *R v Director-General of Telecommunications, ex p Let's Talk (UK) Ltd* (6 April 1992, unreported).

18 A. Ogus, *Regulation* (above, note 5), pp. 115, 117.

19 M. Beesley, 'Current Themes in Regulation' in C. Veljanovski, *Regulators and the Market* (London: Institute of Economic Affairs) 1991, p. 153.

influence in terms of 'defensive' administration, as when an agency is tempted to deny reasons for fear of judicial review (below, p. 369). Then again, stress has been laid on the dynamic character of these regulatory regimes. Set against strengthened principles of judicial review, a combination of increased competition and more assertive or innovative forms of regulation may portend a greater use of courts. Some recent cases involving OFTEL (below, p. 369 and p. 380), as also the *Scottish Power* case,[20] point in this direction.

## (b) Process values and agency discretion

An exercise of broad agency discretion fuels calls for transparency or openness, allowing all information to be brought forward and the basis of regulatory policy to be clear. It has been argued that, in utilities regulation, outside interests should be able to determine whether or not prices reflect costs and whether the commercial strategy of a privatised utility represents an abuse of monopoly power.[1] There is further a powerful demand for inclusive or participative procedures to ensure that all affected interests are allowed a 'voice', and to underwrite the legitimacy of regulatory decisions. Specifically, we see the outlines of a case for inclusive rule-making procedure policed by the courts, akin to an American-style 'interest representation' model of administrative law (above, p. 110).

There is an evident contrast between the situation of regulatory agencies in the US and the pragmatic style of regulation, typified by few procedural requirements, traditional in Britain. Whereas American regulation has been viewed, consistent with a process of judicialisation, as comparatively rigid, rule-bound, adversarial and participatory, regulatory process in Britain has long been recognised as informal, discretionary, co-operative and closed.[2] According to Steltzer:[3]

> America sees the regulatory process as one in which all interested parties should be permitted – nay, encouraged, even paid – to participate. Views are solicited from lawyers and experts representing the regulated firms, customers, competitors and potential competitors, local political bodies, consumer representatives (often self-appointed) and environmentalists and other special-interest groups. Nothing seems to please a regulatory body more than appending a massive list of intervenors to each decision ...
>
> The parties are all accorded due process: they file motions, they participate in hearings, they file briefs, and – in the end – some of them appeal the decision to and through the courts. To the quite proper charge that this process produces huge costs, inefficiencies and delays, its proponents respond: 'true. But these are worth bearing in a democratic society' ...
>
> The British see the regulatory process in an entirely different light ... To the British, regulation is a system by which the service provider negotiates with the regulator to decide upon the prices and service offerings that they – the company and the regulator

20　Above, p. 325.
 1　P. Simpson, 'Regulatory aspects of Utility Privatisations' (1992) Utilities LR 183, 185.
 2　K. Hawkins, *Environment and Enforcement* (Oxford: OUP) 1985; D. Vogel, *National Styles of Regulation* (Ithica, New York: Cornell University Press) 1986.
 3　J. Steltzer, 'Regulatory Methods: A Case for Hands Across the Atlantic?' in C. Veljanovski, *Regulators and the Market* (London: Institute of Economic Affairs) 1991, pp. 61–62.

– feel will be in the best interests of consumers, with a passing nod at other affected interests ...

True, in some cases a particular vigorous regulator ... successfully 'represents' all the parties absent from the regulatory bargaining process, perhaps by soliciting their views. In others, powerful, disgruntled customers ... can make themselves heard ... But, by and large, the British process is a closed one, devoid of hearings, intervenors and court appeals. It is, therefore, quicker, cheaper – and less likely to produce results that threaten incumbent firms, either with competitors or with effective demands from customers. [In sum] the two countries' approaches to regulation may converge, but will never meet.

To put this slightly differently, while at one level the two systems of administrative law have converged, the British system becoming agency-orientated, at another level they have remained disparate, the new British regulation incorporating elements of a traditional style.

We are reminded of an absence in Britain of generic legislation like the American Administrative Procedure Act (AAPA) to provide reasonably standardised requirements for rule-making and adjudication (above, p. 107). Grounded in a fundamental guarantee of due process, the AAPA not only provides the basis for a systematic attempt to establish a principled framework, but also underscores the importance of constitutional explanation for national differences in regulatory design. Graham and Prosser:[4]

find a startling difference between the constitutional approaches to [the] issues [of regulatory procedures] in the two countries. Although a considerable proportion of English public law concerns the procedures for the taking of decisions by public authorities, we find an absence of general principle to act as a guide for government in designing new regulatory bodies. Instead, procedural concerns have been largely ignored; when they have been taken on board, the approach to them has been ad hoc and inconsistent. In the United States, by contrast, there is a sound constitutional basis of principle for designing the procedure of regulatory institutions ...

The procedural problems in the regulation of public utilities, such as most importantly the tension between the need to ensure representation of all interested parties and the attraction of informal bargaining and negotiation, are similar in both countries. The perception of what, and indeed whether there is a problem is, however, radically different in the two countries, largely due to different constitutional expectations ... [The British] understanding of due process and procedures is highly impoverished.

The interest-representation model of administrative law reflects and reinforces values of pluralism central to American constitutional thought. In Richard Stewart's words, 'the hope was that decisions in furtherance of the public interest would emerge out of the judicially-supervised clash of actions'.[5] In similar vein, critics of British regulation such as Birkinshaw,[6] have advocated American-style

---

4   C. Graham and T. Prosser, *Privatising Public Enterprises* (Oxford: OUP) 1991, pp. 210, 239, 256.
5   R. Stewart, 'Madison's Nightmare' (1990) 57 University of Chicago LR 335, 345.
6   P. Birkinshaw, *Grievances, Remedies and the State* (London: Sweet and Maxwell) 2nd edn., 1994, Ch. 4.

requirements as contributing to administrative rationality through a process of intellectual challenge. But as Ogus[7] argues, this entails too easy an assumption:

> 'Open' rule-making procedures might inhibit attempts at cost-benefit analysis and reduce the importance of independent, expert judgments ... The extent to which 'open' procedures can be used to enhance or, conversely, to control, the influence of private interest groups is uncertain. On the one hand, formalisation might lead to less covert influence, and participation rights might serve to reduce inequalities in the power of pressure groups. On the other hand, the closer the rule-making procedures are to an adjudication model, the more likely it is that the decision-makers will strive for outcomes which constitute a compromise between competing special interests that are represented in the proceedings; and this may force them to lose sight of a broader conception of the public interest.

The interest-representation model has become much less fashionable in recent years in the land of its birth. The Supreme Court has stressed the broad discretion of agencies to determine the substantive content of administrative policies – the famous *Chevron* doctrine[8] – and to shape administrative procedures.[9] But nor was the model designed to appeal in Britain to a Conservative Government wedded to the functional values of 'the three Es': quite the reverse! In the case of utilities regulation, a formal due process model has been officially regarded as something actively to be avoided, liable to enmesh the regulators in legal complications, as well as generating substantial costs and delay.[10] Notice the linkage here with the original rejection of rate-of-return regulation (above, p. 321), as also the legislative drafting to thwart judicial review.

We learn that, in British regulation, procedural accountability is itself largely a function of agency discretion. The procedural framework is permissive, allowing a wide choice of informal rules and practices by which the process of formulating substantive rules may be structured. Typically, the privatisation statutes limited formal requirements to such matters as enforcement proceedings. Regulatory transparency lacks the legal underpinning familiar in the US. While the DGs are commonly *empowered* to publish information, their *duties* to do so are severely restricted. The individualist slant evident in the Competition and Service (Utilities) Act 1992 is relevant. Although the legislation provided for information and consultation in respect of utilities' performance, it passed over key polycentric tasks such as price control and interconnection.

The traditionally secretive and non-participative character of British government must be taken into account. The new model of independent regulation encourages

7  A. Ogus, *Regulation* (above, p. 329, note 5), pp. 114–115.
8  *Chevron USA Inc v NRDC* 476 US 837 (1984). See C. Sunstein, 'Law and Administration after *Chevron*' (1990) 90 Columbia LR 2072.
9  *Vermont Yankee Nuclear Power Corpn v NRDC* 435 US 519 (1978). And see for discussion in the British context, C. Harlow, 'A Special Relationship? American Influences on Judicial Review in England' in I. Loveland (ed.), *A Special Relationship? American Influences on Public Law in the UK* (Oxford: Clarendon) 1995. The model is discussed in the context of judicial procedures in Ch. 17.
10  See, on the policy background, C. Foster, *Privatization, Public Ownership and the Regulation of Natural Monopoly* (Oxford: Blackwell) 1992.

a greater degree of openness than was the case under public ownership. In the exercise of agency discretion some innovative approaches to procedure have been adopted (below, p. 360). But, turning the argument round, in such conditions a hotch-potch of practices is inevitable, some regulators more than others being convinced by different procedural virtues. Further, all the technical detail and complexity hardly makes for easy access by a wide variety of interests, the same difficulty as in government by contract.

The arrangements for consumer representation are also typically ad hoc, there being considerable variation between sectors, in part influenced by arrangements in the old nationalised industries, themselves criticised as ineffective. [11] Consider some competing models: [12]

> The first model is that of no specific institution designed to represent consumer interests, instead the job of representing the public interest is left to the regulator and, where appropriate, the development of competitive forces ... Here protecting the consumer is a matter of organising effective regulatory arrangements.
>
> The second possible model is to have an industry regulator but provide for consumer bodies whose main remit will be the handling of complaints, with a subsidiary role in advising the regulator on various policy issues ... The third model is to recognise the need for an independent consumer voice and provide some institutional means for ensuring that it is heard.

The first model fits well the straightforward regulation favoured by Littlechild. The consumer interest is equated with the public interest, the promotion of economic efficiency providing benefits for all consumers. The second model is typified by an agency such as OFTEL, which in effect represents the interests of consumers to itself, with assistance from a network of advisory committees (below, p. 382). The arrangement which most closely resembles the third model is the Gas Consumers Council, which is distinctive in being a statutory body separate from the DG. The argument for this model has been led by the National Consumer Council: [13]

> We believe that, in principle, there is a difference between the general 'public interest' which the regulator is established to guard, and the specific consumer interest which is part of that general public interest. Any mechanism for consumer policy representation needs, therefore, to be independent of the regulator ... If, as we have argued, regulation is about balancing competing interests, it will be important that the structure of the regulatory process helps maintain a real public interest balance. The regulated industry will have substantial resources, the regulator a lot less, and generalist consumer bodies very little. Locating the consumer representation function within the regulator exposes it to the danger of incorporation within the regulatory body. This would seriously reduce the consumer interest input into the regulatory balancing act ...
>
> There are some further advantages in separation. If either of the institutions is behaving ineffectively, then the other is likely to draw attention to it. And there is likely to be more public discussion of, and interest in, representations that pass from one body

11  T. Prosser, *Nationalised Industries and Public Control* (Oxford: Blackwell) 1986.
12  C. Graham, 'Consumers and Privatized Industries' (1992) Utilities LR 38.
13  National Consumer Council, *In the Absence of Competition* (London: HMSO) 1989, pp. 86–88.

to another than if the representation is simply an internal matter within the regulator's office ... [Again] unless [the regulator] has direct input from a body representing consumers in a partisan way, he will have to rely on information from the industry. As we have seen this is likely to be inadequate.

A recognition that so-called 'consumer advocacy' is necessarily a partisan activity is characteristic of American regulatory and rule-making activity. Implementation would no doubt raise tricky issues of the adequacy of representation, and of the uneven distribution of legal and organisational resources. It suffices to add that formally empowering the consumer voice in this fashion denotes a broader concept of due process than has generally obtained in Britain.

## (c) Proposals for reform

Let us consider some proposals for reform which, emanating from diverse sources and from across the political spectrum, help to underscore the importance of, and clash of values in, regulatory design. The chief argument for the defence is that agency discretion must not be fettered unreasonably. There is a premium on flexibility and responsiveness, such that the capacity to adapt to a dynamic environment is not constrained. Apart from the regulators themselves, this view has been articulated most forcefully by Sir Christopher Foster.[14] From this perspective, the problem of the regulatory procedures is one of fine-tuning. There is no special merit in striving for procedural uniformity, instead a checklist of good practice which a 'wise' regulator would adopt is appropriate. Foster includes the following suggestions:

* Being consistent in the procedures he adopts between apparently similar cases;
* Not reaching different conclusions in what may appear similar cases without explaining why ...
* [Issuing] some general guidance on the types of procedures [he expects] to adopt in different types of cases.
* [Taking care] to ensure that [his] consumer committees [are] representative of their consumers.

But if stress is laid on the values of consistency and predictability, the essential evil being seen as 'regulatory creep', a 'soft law' approach of this type will hardly do. Thus, more substantive concerns are evident in Veljanovski's call for 'a return to a stable rules-based system where the scope of the regulators' discretion is clearly defined'.[15] To this end he proposes a formal 'Regulatory Charter':

   The Government should provide a clear statement of the principles governing regulation. This would ensure that regulation is certain in application, clear in content

---

14  C. Foster, *Natural Justice and the Process of Natural Monopoly Regulation* (London: CIPFA) 1994, pp. 4, 20–21.
15  C. Veljanovski, *The Future of Industry Regulation in the UK* (London: European Policy Forum) 1993, pp. 82–84.

and open. It would re-affirm the Government's commitment to rules-based regulation in which the regulators' discretion is circumscribed. The Charter ... should clearly set out the principles of good regulation – protection against monopoly abuse, encouragement of efficiency and innovation, low burden of regulation in terms of costs and regulatory simplicity and predictability ...

Any significant modification to the utility's licence terms should only take place in formal regulatory proceedings by the MMC, at pre-determined intervals, which would be open to public scrutiny and third party representation ... The powers of regulators to negotiate licence modifications should be reduced, and the areas where they are permitted to exercise discretion on important regulatory matters circumscribed.

A reduction of the range of regulatory principles to a fixed set of rules is an unlikely prospect. Not only is a remarkable degree of foresight required, given the constraints on adaptability and flexibility, but there is also the potential for the kinds of games with rules discussed in Chapter 4. Nor, in a controversial area like the utilities, can we overlook a lack of political consensus. In this way, the following suggestion from the Labour Party of a 'super agency', while addressing the issues of personalisation and of regulatory overlap and division, discloses an awkward tension between the value of expertise and representation. [16]

There is a strong case for establishing a Utilities Commission to bring the existing regulators under one roof. A unitary system would promote policy consistency between the different regulators housed within it. Whilst being democratically answerable to government and parliament above, the Commission would act as a channel for organised consumer representation and individual grievances from below ... It could be governed by a board of representatives from all sectors, consumers, senior managers, trade unions, shareholders and academics – appointed by the Secretary of State to serve as expert advisers rather than representatives or delegates.

Perhaps, then, a more incremental approach is appropriate, and one which recognises that regulation of the privatised utilities involves learning. To engender greater consistency, but not standardisation by rules, we could envisage empowering the MMC to set common regulatory principles, replacement of individual regulators by small executive boards, and merging some of the regulatory bodies as industry boundaries weaken by reason of technological change and takeovers and mergers. [17] From administrative law there comes the idea of formalising existing best practice. Key themes in a major review of 'regulation UK-style' co-sponsored by the Hansard Society are transparency and 'voice'. The review follows K. C. Davis in a search for 'optimum balance'. [18] It also reflects the contemporary concern over commercial confidentiality, and the idea of remodelling commercial precepts in the image of public law (above, p. 271): [19]

---

16  P. Hain, 'Regulating for the Common Good' (1994) Utilities LR 90, 93.
17  See, for various shopping lists of reforms, D. Helm, 'British Utility Regulation: Theory, Practice and Reform' (1994) 10 Oxford Rev. of Economic Policy; 17; R. Baldwin *Regulation in Question* (London: London School of Economics) 1995; C. Graham, *Is There A Crisis In Regulatory Accountability?* (London) 1995, CRI Discussion Paper No. 13.
18  Above, p. 104.
19  Hansard Society and European Policy Forum, *Report of the Commission on the Regulation of Privatised Utilities* (London) 1996, pp. 56–62.

The DGs have themselves taken substantial steps with a view to improving their openness, consultation and clarity. Nevertheless, we were concerned at the lack of confidence indicted by the responses ... It is crucial for the legitimacy of the regulatory system that decision-making procedures be transparent, understood and seen to be fair and allow proper access by all interested parties to decision makers ...

There should be a statutory duty on DGs to produce and publish a Code of Practice governing their decision-making procedures ... It should be concerned with 'due process', and not be highly detailed and prescriptive. The DGs need sufficient discretion to be able to adopt procedures appropriate to specific circumstances ... It is essential that decision making should not become bogged down in legalistic procedural rules ... Effective and fair regulation requires both due process and also reasonable speed and cost ... Our proposals, set out below, concerning information, reasons, publication of information and consultation would form part of the Code ... The Code should be drawn up jointly by the industry DGs and should apply to all of them, to ensure clarity, consistency and the spread of best practice ...

Although the DGs do give published reasons for most of their decisions [there should be] a general statutory duty ... This might result in more decisions being challenged by judicial review. But, judicial review is far from easy to obtain and, in any case ... a few more judicial review challenges to decisions would be a price worth paying for greater openness ...

Sufficient, comprehensible and accurate information is essential for effective regulation. The provision of information is a *quid pro quo* of allowing privately-owned firms to supply utility services. Although at present the combination of statutory powers and licence conditions appears to offer considerable scope for the DGs to demand the information that they need, we favour a general statutory power for the DGs to be able to demand information from licensees ... At the same time, we propose a duty on the DGs to consider the costs of compliance with regulation, notably concerning the provision of information ... It is possible to exaggerate the problems of commercial confidentiality. We therefore propose a presumption that information given to the DGs by licence suppliers should be available publicly ... The actions of the DGs themselves must also be transparent. We would thus expect the DGs to expand their existing practices of publishing reports that they themselves have ordered in preparation for taking regulatory decisions – for instance, consultants' reports ... Similar criteria to those applied to information given by suppliers should be developed ...

Bodies representing the interests of consumers should be seen to be strong and independent. We therefore support giving such bodies a statutory existence, independent of the DGs, as industry consumer councils (as is the case of the Gas Consumers Council at present). The consumer councils should have their own financial and other resources ... [They] would have their own staff ... The bodies would be given a specific remit to represent small users and would also investigate customer complaints; they would be able to refer matters to the DGs.

Better to secure democratic legitimacy, we could envisage a system of general and periodic policy guidance from ministers, made subject to parliamentary approval: so, too, a House of Commons Select Committee on Regulated Industries, capable of specialisation and cross-sector comparison. There is, in other words, a good case for institutional and procedural reform consonant with, and making best use of, the strong parliamentary tradition.  Again, it is appropriate to underscore the concept of a regulatory framework. To this effect, the Government's draft Competition Bill, recently published, heralds extended power for the OFT to regulate competition and reform of the MMC as the 'Competition Commission'. Notably, consumers and companies would have the right to appeal 'Ofdog' decisions to the Commission. Finally, the dynamic patterns of control and accountability demonstrated in this area of administrative law should be kept in mind. A Government review of the power of the regulator is under way at the time of writing.

## 5. The challenge of self-regulation

Self-regulation is a phenomenon of great contemporary significance in law and administration. From a political science perspective, it may be seen as an example of modern *corporatism* (above, p. 13). State authority is delegated to self-regulatory organisations (SROs) which perform a vital intermediary function: that of developing and furthering public policy. Streeck and Schmitter [20] speak of 'private interest government', co-operative arrangements designed to make the self-interested, collective action of these bodies contribute to the achievement of public policy objectives. Typical of NPM, self-regulation is advocated as a way of overcoming the problems of overload and policy implementation associated with direct forms of state intervention, as also on ideological grounds because in comparison to government regulation it allows for a greater degree of freedom or autonomy. [1] It further raises basic questions about the scope and purposes of public law, not least in the traditional canon of judicial review.

Self-regulatory systems come in all shapes and sizes. The basic idea of self-regulation is as 'an institutional arrangement whereby an organisation regulates the standards of behaviour of its members'; [2] they are further usefully classified according to several main variables. One criterion is the degree of monopoly power, and the relevance of the regulation for third parties. For example, does the SRO regulate all the suppliers in a market, including non-members? A second variable is the degree of formality in systems. The body may or may not have been specially created for the purpose, it may or may not have statutory powers. And is there in effect a 'mini legal system': a well-established and generally recognised set of rules? Third, self-regulatory systems vary in terms of legal status. The rules may have binding force or they may be voluntary (backed with the government's threat to take powers if necessary). Alternatively, the SRO may be merely an unincorporated association, be constituted under a (private) Act of Parliament, or, as is more commonly the case, be a company limited by guarantee (so having a basic constitutional structure in the form of the company memorandum and articles). A fourth criterion is the degree of external involvement: participation in rule-making and enforcement, control in the sense of monitoring and supervision.

20  W. Steeck and P. Schmitter (eds.), *Private Interest Government: Beyond Market and State* (London: Sage) 1985.

 1  W. Streeck and P. Schmitter, 'Community, Market, State – And Associations? The Prospective Contribution of Interest Governance to Social Order'; and M. Hughes, 'Debureaucratisation and Private Interest Government: The British State and Economic Development Policy', both in W. Streeck and P. Schmitter (eds.) *Private Interest Government* (above, note 20).

 2  R. Baggott, 'Regulatory Reform in Britain: The Changing Face of Self-Regulation' (1989) 67 Pub. Admin. 436.

Relevant strategies include outside nominees on the SRO, an ombudsman to take complaints, and prior approval of the rules by government agency.

There comes a point, of course, at which the term 'self-regulation' is a misnomer, but the concept is sufficiently flexible to accommodate a considerable degree of external involvement: moreover, 'to treat it otherwise would be to ignore the interpenetration of the private and public sectors'.[3] To put this slightly differently, there is much scope for creative *blends* of self-regulation and government regulation, forms of so-called 'responsive regulation',[4] whereby different combinations of techniques are identified and applied depending on the social, historical, constitutional and legal context.

'Britain', it has been said, 'appears to be something of a haven for self-regulation'.[5] The phenomenon in part reflects the traditional regulatory culture: the attributes of co-operation, informality and discretion (above, p. 332), the high degree of trust associated with an elite or 'club' style of government. Self-regulation is today the principal instrument of control across a broad swathe of activities, including the press, advertising, and myriad professional occupations. In recent years, however, the phenomenon has been subject to increased scrutiny and the general trend has been towards a greater degree of formalisation and external involvement. In this respect, the regulatory culture has been changing: a 'striking feature' being 'the extent to which [self-regulation] has been redefined to encompass the public interest, the interests of users as well as practitioners'.[6]

## (a) Self-regulation and beyond: financial services

Take the hugely important area of financial services and investor protection. For a network of self-governing bodies expressing 'community' values – a local culture epitomised in 'the gentleman's agreement' – the Financial Services Act 1986 substituted a distinctive blend of statutory and self-regulation, in effect an elaborate system of rules and regulations.[7] The Securities and Investments Board (SIB) was established, to exercise statutory powers delegated by the minister. Individual appointments to the SIB were made by government, 'as to secure a proper balance between the interests of persons carrying on investment business and the interests of the public' (Sch. 7, para. 1). The SIB has promulgated basic rules relating to the conduct of investment business, further it has certified, monitored and supervised a number of SROs, often referred to as the 'practitioner level'. Latterly, there have been three SROs, organised on a functional basis and bearing the main burden of the regulation: the Investment Management Regulatory Organisation (IMRO), the Personal Investment Authority (PIA) and the Securities and Futures Authority (SFA). Oversight and disciplinary functions were built into the scheme at various levels. The Chancellor of the Exchequer has had to

3   A. Page, 'Self-Regulation: The Constitutional Dimension' (1986) 49 MLR 141, 144.
4   I. Ayers and J. Braithwaite, *Responsive Regulation: Transcending the Deregulation Debate* (Oxford: OUP) 1992.
5   R. Baggott, 'Regulatory Reform in Britain' (above, note 2), p. 438.
6   A. Page, 'Self-Regulation' (above, note 3), p. 164.
7   L.C.B. Gower, '"Big Bang" and City Regulation' (1988) 51 MLR 1; A. Page and R. Ferguson, *Investor Protection* (London: Weidenfeld and Nicolson) 1992; J. Black, *Rules and Regulations* (Oxford: OUP) 1997.

ensure that the SIB rules were not restricting or distorting competition to a significant extent, and to direct amendments if necessary. Certification has required acceptance by the SIB of the rules of an SRO and the way in which the rules were operating. An SRO has been afforded statutory powers to sanction and, ultimately, expel members (membership of an SRO conferring authorisation for the operation of an investment business).

Together with utilities regulation, the reform of financial services in 1986 was seen to epitomise a contemporary growth in 'intermediate territory' and organisations, encapsulated in the notion of 'the regulatory state' (above, p. 141). What, on the one hand, was a product of the retreat from 'the producer state', on the other was a perfect example of the advance of the state in some areas of control (above, p. 22). In Moran's words, [8] 'after almost two decades of "deregulation", the state is a more pervasive presence than ever in financial markets'. Furthermore, 'Mrs. Thatcher's administration ... ostentatiously rejected ... the corporatism of the 1970s. Yet in the ... self-regulatory organisations, the government has created powerful corporatist institutions'. This is not as contradictory as first appears: the old informal style being in decay amid recurring scandal and the growing internationalisation of the financial markets, and the subsequent regime being effectively a compromise short of full government regulation.

The political dimension in regulatory strategy and design is a recurring theme. Regulation of the City is one field of administrative law where the new Labour Government intends root and branch reform. The role of the SIB will be greatly enhanced,[9] with systems of self-regulation cut back and regulatory responsibilities for banking services reassigned from the Bank of England. The 'regulatory state' will have advanced further, in the name of investor protection.

### (b) Models of self-regulation

Black [10] usefully distinguishes for self-regulation four types of possible relationship with the state:

> [(i)] *Mandated* self-regulation, in which a collective group, an industry or profession ... is required or designated by the government to formulate and enforce norms within a framework defined by the government, usually in broad terms; [(ii)] *sanctioned* self-regulation, in which the collective group itself formulates the regulation, which is then subjected to government approval; [(iii)] *coerced* self-regulation, in which the industry itself formulates and imposes regulation but in response to threats by the government that if it does not the government will impose statutory regulation; and [(iv)] *voluntary* self-regulation, where there is no active state involvement, direct or indirect, in promoting or mandating self-regulation.

Financial services under the 1986 Act are an example of (i), while (ii) is illustrated by the development of trade association codes of practice approved by

8  M. Moran, 'Thatcherism and Financial Regulation' (1988) 59 PQ 20, 26; see further M. Moran, *The Politics of the Financial Services Revolution* (London: Macmillan) 1990.
9  Under the auspices of 'Newro'. HC Deb, vol. 294, cols. 508-511 (20 May 1997).
10  J. Black, 'Constitutionalising Self-Regulation' (1996) 59 MLR 24, 25.

the Office of Fair Trading.[11] Category (iii) is the most common – the Press Complaints Commission being a good example – although subsequently the SRO 'may become institutionalised, i.e. accepted, legitimated, or infused with value', in which case for the regulation to be effective a continued threat of state intervention may not be necessary. Category (iv), in which the industry desires self-regulation and takes the initiative, points up the limitations of a purely 'top-down' analysis. Even so, corporatist relations cannot be ruled out, since government may in fact rely on the body's regulatory function, as reflected in a decision not to take legal powers.

Judged by reference to 'the 3 Es', there are several reasons why an SRO may be preferable to regulation by a public, independent agency. A strong expertise and technical knowledge, coupled with a greater degree of mutual trust with the regulated, suggests lower information, monitoring and enforcement costs. Other typical justifications are provided by a former Chief Executive of the Lloyd's insurance market:[12]

- As the rules are made by those to whom they apply, they are likely to be more effective because they enable a regulation of the spirit rather than the letter of the law.
- The self-regulatory body can be quicker at rewriting rules than a government department and can therefore respond more flexibly to deal with problems and new developments.
- Self-regulation is cheap, because the regulated bear the burden of the costs of regulation.

The dangers are not hard to identify. From private interest theories of regulation come the charge of 'rent-seeking', epitomised in the ability of SROs to exploit their powers to establish anti-competitive conditions. 'With self-regulation, regulatory capture is there from the outset'.[13] Then there is the dilemma of accountability and control: the acquisition of power by bodies not answerable in the conventional way through the political process, the diffusion of the responsibility of government. In public law, corporatist theories have been taken up by critics such as Lewis,[14] the argument being that the delegation of state authority which self-regulation implies needs to be matched by appropriate techniques of accountability and control which, despite greater formalisation and external involvement, are still 'woefully inadequate'. The theme is one of 'regulated autonomy',[15] which breaks down into a shopping list of reforms –

11  See I. Ramsay, 'The Office of Fair Trading: Policing the Consumer Market-Place' in R. Baldwin and C. McCrudden (eds), *Regulation and Public Law* (London: Weidenfeld and Nicolson) 1987.
12  I. Hay Davison, *A View of the Room* (London: Weidenfeld and Nicolson) 1987.
13  J. Kay, 'The Forms of Regulation' in C. Goodhart and A. Seldon (eds.), *Financial Regulation – Or Over-Regulation* (London: Institute of Economic Affairs) 1988, p. 34.
14  N. Lewis, 'Regulating Non-Governmental Bodies' in J. Jowell and D. Oliver (eds.), *The Changing Constitution* (Oxford: Clarendon) 2nd edn, 1989; also C. Graham, 'Self-Regulation' in G. Richardson and H. Genn (eds.), *Administrative Law and Government Action* (Oxford: Clarendon) 1994.
15  P. Birkinshaw, N. Lewis and I. Harden, *Government By Moonlight: The Hybrid Parts of the State* (London: Routledge) 1990; and see, for a consumer perspective, National Consumer Council, *Self-Regulation* (London) 1986.

procedures for consultation and rule-making, complaint mechanisms and 'hard look' judicial review – familiar from work on government agencies. Self-regulation may be seen to pose in acute form the difficulty in a system of indirect administration of securing the public interest.

## (c) The Datafin project

The role of judicial review is of special interest precisely because of recent efforts to extend jurisdiction in the context of self-regulation. The difficulties confronting the courts are very considerable. Enough has been said to demonstrate a rather vague and elusive concept, and a mass of individual bodies more or less, or not at all, connected with the state. So not only are there the usual limitations of formal, legal process to contend with, but also the conceptual strain on a system of 'public law' of intervention in a 'private law' situation, raising issues over the legal and political autonomy of these bodies, which is after all a core value of self-regulation. Then again, simply to abstain may be to offend against the historical role of judicial review, protection of individuals from the abuse of power. And, speaking more generally, is there not a need to adjust the supervisory jurisdiction to meet the changing structure of government, by taking inside the fence bodies which exercise power on behalf of the government? From the authors' perspective, this is one more aspect of the general problem of 'reinventing' administrative law (above, p. 148).

One angle of approach is through the power which SROs can wield. Four broad positions may be identified concerning the application of judicial review. They serve to highlight a basic disagreement about the purpose of judicial review in contemporary society.[16]

(i)   Judicial review should operate to keep statutory and, arguably, prerogative bodies under supervision. This represents the traditional Diceyan paradigm, judicial review being geared towards, and confined to, the exercise of explicitly governmental and legal powers.

(ii)  Judicial review should apply to the exercise of regulatory power actually delegated by the state. This fits with a stress on indirect forms of administration, and encompasses some, but importantly not all forms of self-regulation.

(iii) Judicial review should extend to the exercise of monopoly power over an important sector of national life. This conveys a different sense of publicness to (ii), being premised not on a connection with the state but on the amount of power exercisable.

(iv)  The role of judicial review is to regulate all forms of power, public or private, exercised by the state or otherwise. This would cut across the established principles of private law, opening up, at least in theory, the decisions of companies to tests of unreasonableness and irrelevant considerations.

16  The different approaches can be tracked in H. Wade, 'Beyond the Law: A British Innovation in Judicial Review' (1991) 43 Admin. LR 559; P. Cane, 'Self-Regulation and Judicial Review' (1987) Civil Justice Quarterly 324; M. Beloff, 'Judicial Review – 2001: A Prophetic Odyssey' (1995) 58 MLR 143; G. Borrie, 'The Regulation of Public and Private Power' [1989] PL 552.

In recent years the judges have moved beyond (i) to (ii), holding that a non-government agency exercising non-statutory powers can be amenable to judicial review, and have flirted with (iii). Position (iv) is not seriously on the agenda. The assertion of jurisdiction in cases stated to involve 'public power' or, latterly, 'governmental interest', is dubbed by Aronson [17] 'the *Datafin* project' after the name of the seminal case.

## *R v Panel on Take-Overs and Mergers, ex p Datafin plc* [18]

The Panel was a non-statutory SRO which devised and operated the City Code on Take-overs and Mergers. The membership included nominees of the Bank of England and representatives from the major sectors of the City. The Panel had no direct statutory, prerogative or common law powers, nor was it in contractual relationship with the financial market or with individual dealers. Yet it was undeniably a major component of the regulation of the market; it was supported by statutory powers which presupposed its existence, and its decisions could result in the imposition of sanctions. The machinery was also an example of 'coerced' self-regulation; established originally in response to pressure from government, it now appeared to be 'institutionalised.'

The case arose from rival bids for a company, and a complaint from Datafin that the other side had, by acting in breach of the Code, secured an advantage. Datafin sought judicial review of the Panel's decision dismissing the complaint, on the grounds that the Panel had misconstrued the rules and that its fact-finding process had been irrational. But was the Panel susceptible to judicial review? And how should such a jurisdiction be exercised given the nature of the share market and of the Panel's activities?

Sir John Donaldson MR:

*The jurisdictional issue*
The Panel is a truly remarkable body, performing its function without visible means of legal support. But the operative word is 'visible', although perhaps I should have used the word 'direct'. Invisible or indirect support there is in abundance ... As an act of government it was decided that, in relation to take-overs, there should be a central self-regulatory body which would be supported and sustained by a periphery of statutory powers and penalties wherever non-statutory powers and penalties were insufficient or non-existent or where EEC requirements called for statutory provisions ...

In all the reports it is possible to find enumerations of factors giving rise to the jurisdiction, but it is a fatal error to regard the presence of all those factors as essential or as being exclusive of other factors. Possibly, the only essential elements are what can be described as a public element, which can take many different forms, and the exclusion from the jurisdiction of bodies whose sole source of power is a consensual submission to its jurisdiction ...

17  M. Aronson, 'A Public Lawyer's Responses to Privatization and Outsourcing' in M. Taggart (ed.), *The Province of Administrative Law* (Oxford: Hart) 1997.
18  [1987] QB 815.

The Panel ... is without doubt performing a public duty and an important one. This is clear from the expressed willingness of the Secretary of State for Trade and Industry to limit legislation in the field of take-overs and mergers and to use the panel as the centrepiece of his regulation of that market ... Its source of power is only partly based on moral persuasion and the assent of institutions and their members, the bottom line being the statutory powers exercised by the Department of Trade and Industry and the Bank of England. In this context I should be very disappointed if the courts could not recognise the realities of executive power ...

## The practical issue

... Consistently with its character as the controlling body for the self-regulation of take-overs and mergers, the Panel combines the functions of legislator, court interpreting the panel's legislation, consultant and court, investigating and imposing penalties in respect of alleged breaches of the code. As a legislator it sets out to lay down general principles, on the lines of EEC legislation, rather than specific prohibitions ... Against that background, there is little scope for complaint that the panel has promulgated rules which are *ultra vires* ... When it comes to interpreting its own rules, it must clearly be given considerable latitude both because, as legislator, it could properly alter them at any time and because of the form which the rules take, i.e. laying down principles to be applied in spirit as much as in letter in specific situations ... This leaves only the Panel's disciplinary function ... The only circumstances in which I would anticipate the use of the remedies of *certiorari* and *mandamus* would be in the event ... of the Panel acting in breach of the rules of natural justice ...

I wish to make it clear beyond a peradventure that in the light of the special nature of the Panel, its functions, the market in which it is operating, the timescales which are inherent in that market and the need to safeguard the position of third parties, who may be numbered in thousands, all of whom are entitled to continue trade on an assumption of the validity of the Panel's rules and decisions, unless and until they are quashed by the court, I should expect the relationship between the Panel and the court to be historic rather than contemporaneous. I should expect the court to allow contemporary decisions to take their course, considering the complaint and intervening, if at all, later and in retrospect by declaratory orders which would enable the panel not to repeat any error and would relieve individuals of the disciplinary consequences of any erroneous finding of breach of the rules. This would provide a workable and valuable partnership between the courts and the panel in the public interest ...

*Lloyd LJ*: I was unable to see why the mere fact that a body is self-regulating makes it less appropriate for judicial review. Of course there will be many self-regulating bodies which are wholly inappropriate for judicial review. The committee of an ordinary club affords an obvious example. But the reason why a club is not subject to judicial review is not just because it is self-regulating. The Panel wields enormous power. It has a giant's strength. The fact that it is self-regulating ... makes it not less but more appropriate that it should be subject to judicial review by the courts ... Nor is it any answer that a company coming to the market must take it as it finds it. The City is not a club which one can join or not at will ...

I do not agree that the source of the power is the sole test whether the body is subject to judicial review ... Of course the source of the power will often, perhaps usually, be decisive. If the source of power is a statute, or subordinate legislation under a statute, then clearly the body in question will be subject to judicial review. If, at the other end of the scale, the source of power is contractual, as in the case of private arbitration, then clearly the arbitrator is not subject to judicial review ... But in between these extremes there is an area in which it is helpful to look not just at the source of the power but at the nature of the power. If the body in question is exercising public law functions, or if the exercise of its functions has public law consequences, then that may ... be sufficient to bring the body within the reach of judicial review ... The essential distinction ... is between a domestic or private tribunal on the one hand and a body of persons who are under some public duty on the other.

*Datafin* was hailed by advocates of a broad approach to judicial review as a great leap forward. The judgment of Lord Donaldson in particular allowed for an expansive interpretation. In the words of one commentator, the reasoning 'was explosive because a public element can be found in most walks of life'.[19] Whereas previously, in establishing the limits of the supervisory jurisdiction, the courts had looked at the source of a body's power, the judges had now encompassed in the test the nature of the power being exercised. Equally, they had failed to provide appropriate guidance. The predictable outcome was a welter of litigation, and a complex and contradictory case law.

For David Pannick QC,[20] review was sanctioned whenever a body 'has such a *de facto* monopoly over an important area of public life that an individual has no effective choice but to comply with their rules, regulations and decisions in order to operate in that area' (position (iii)). But matters were not so simple. *Datafin* is appropriately described as 'both expansionary and restrictive'.[1] From the viewpoint of the regulator,[2] 'the decisive interest' of the case lay in 'the guidelines ... indicating that the jurisdiction would be sparingly exercised'. Two judicial strategies may here be identified. One is grounded in the discretionary nature or judicial control of the public law remedies (below, Chapter 16). The only remedy normally available will be a declaration: the exercise of jurisdiction will be 'historic' and not 'contemporaneous'. In the authors' terminology, judicial review is stripped of its fire-fighting function. The other strategy is the more familiar light-touch review, assigning to the agency a wide margin of appreciation in the twin tasks of rule-making and rule-application. Importantly, whereas the first strategy is keyed to the particular context of the share market, the second is of general application in the case of self-regulatory codes, and so displays great deference to the expertise and autonomy of self-regulatory bodies. The reasoning in *Datafin* can therefore be criticised as a poor solution: it both conjures the shadow, and denies the substance of, the supervisory jurisdiction. Alternatively, the viability of the project is put in question, since 'the further a regulatory regime travels from the legal paradigm' of fixed rules and due process, 'the less relevant is judicial review as an accountability device'.[3]

---

19  R. Cranston, 'Reviewing Judicial Review' in G. Richardson and H. Genn (eds.), *Administrative Law and Government Action* (Oxford: Clarendon) 1994, p. 48.

20  D. Pannick, 'Who is Subject to Judicial Review and in respect of what?' [1992] PL 1, 3; see also M. Beloff, 'The Boundaries of Judicial Review' in J. Jowell and D. Oliver (eds.), *New Directions in Judicial Review* (London: Stevens) 1988.

 1  P. Cane, 'Self Regulation and Judicial Review' (1987) 6 Civil Justice Quarterly 324, 346.

 2  Lord Alexander, 'Judicial Review and City Regulators' (1989) 52 MLR 640, 644.

 3  M. Aronson, 'A Public Lawyer's Response (above, note 17) p. 47. See further in this context, *R v Panel on Take-Overs and Mergers, ex p Guinness plc* [1990] 1 QB 146.

In the assertion of jurisdiction, two matters had been left unresolved. As regards the first, how to ascertain a 'public element', subsequent cases focused on the need to find 'not merely a public but potentially a governmental interest'[4] in the regulation (an approach akin to position (ii)). One test asked whether 'the Government would have assumed the powers being exercised "but for" self-regulation?' – a test it has been said which requires of the judges 'a greater perspicacity and insight into governmental intentions than most politicians and civil servants would claim'.[5] An alternative question might be whether the body has been 'integrated' in a system of regulation approved or defined by government, perhaps in a 'twin track system of control'?[6] This formulation, which demonstrates a concept of co-regulation or regulatory partnership as the key to judicial review, both fitted the facts of *Datafin* and marks a substantial limitation on the scope of the project. In the event, while such bodies as the Advertising Standards Authority and the financial services SROs have been found to demonstrate a 'governmental interest', a variety of other bodies have not, including the Chief Rabbi and the Football Association.[7]

Second, there was an unresolved tension in *Datafin* between the recognition of institutional power as a reason for subjecting a body to review and the exemption of bodies with a contractual source of power.[8] The idea of contract as a limitation on judicial review is familiar from the cases on government contracts, and was there shown to be increasingly problematic, precisely because of the proliferation of indirect forms of government (above, p. 241). As regards self-regulation, it had previously been held in *Law v National Greyhound Racing Club Ltd*[9] that the NGRC was not the kind of body which was susceptible to judicial review, the powers which it exercised over those engaged in the activity, in the instant case suspension of a licence, being derived from contract. In effect, the club had been treated as a 'domestic tribunal'. Post-*Datafin* the development continued. In one case, it was held that Lloyd's was not susceptible to judicial review in relation to its members' contracts; in another, that the Insurance Ombudsman was exempt, on the basis that membership of the Ombudsman scheme was voluntary.[10] But surely this is not the point. Ultimately, the issue is one of monopoly power, and therefore of the purpose of judicial review. The acid test is whether, in a case where the contract is both the source of regulatory power and a condition precedent to participation in the activity, the contract exception in *Datafin* should be disapplied.

---

4   Simon Brown J. in *R v Chief Rabbi of the United Hebrew Congregations, ex p Wachmann* [1992] 1 WLR 1036 at 1041.
5   R. Cranston, 'Reviewing Judicial Review' (above, note 19), at p. 49.
6   Simon Brown J in *Wachmann* (above, note 4) at 1041.
7   *R v Advertising Standards Authority Ltd, ex p Insurance Service plc* [1990] 2 Admin. LR 77; *R v Life Assurance Unit Trust Regulatory Organisation Ltd, ex p Ross* [1993] QB 17; *R v Chief Rabbi, ex p Wachmann* [1992] 1 WLR 1036; *R v Football Association Ltd, ex p Football League Ltd* [1993] 2 All ER 833.
8   See J. Beatson, 'The Courts and the Regulators' (1987) Professional Negligence 121; N. Bamforth, 'The Scope of Judicial Review: Still Uncertain' [1993] PL 239.
9   [1983] 1 WLR 1302.
10  *R v Lloyd's of London, ex p Briggs* [1993] 1 Lloyd's Rep 176; *R v Insurance Ombudsman, ex p Aegon Life Assurance* [1994] COD 426.

### R v Jockey Club Disciplinary Committee, ex p Aga Khan [11]

The Jockey Club exercised responsibility for the organisation and control of all aspects of horse racing. This was an example of 'voluntary' self-regulation, the club never having been drawn into a regulatory partnership with government. It was not a statutory body, nor did it exercise statutory powers. Its great power derived from a monopoly, the market not covered by the club being negligible, coupled with its rule-book (the Rules of Racing), which constituted a contract for those within the industry.

One of the applicant's horses failed a dope test after winning a major race and was disqualified. He sought judicial review, in effect preferring to test the decision for legality or fairness in public law to the chance of a contractual remedy. An attempt was therefore made to extend the frontiers of judicial review. The club, it was said, was exercising public functions: the contract was effectively a case of 'take it or leave it'. The application failed.

*Sir Thomas Bingham MR*: I have little hesitation in accepting ... that the Jockey Club effectively regulates a significant international activity, exercising powers which affect the public and are exercised in the interest of the public. I am willing to accept that if the Jockey Club did not regulate this activity, the government would probably be driven to create a public body to do so ...

But the Jockey Club is not in its origin, its history, its constitution or (least of all) its membership, a public body ... It has not been woven into any system of governmental control of horse racing, perhaps because it has itself controlled horse racing so successfully that there has been no need for any such governmental system and such does not therefore exist. This has the result that while the Jockey Club's powers may be described as, in many ways, public they are in no sense governmental ...

I would accept that those who agree to be bound by the Rules of Racing have no effective alternative to doing so if they want to take part in racing in this country ... But this does not ... alter the fact ... that the powers which the Jockey Club exercises over those who (like the applicant) agree to be bound by the rules of racing, derive from the agreement of the parties and give rise to private rights ... It would in my opinion be contrary to sound and long-standing principle to extend the remedy of judicial review to such a case ...

It is unnecessary for [the] purposes of this appeal to decide whether decisions of the Jockey Club may ever in any circumstances be challenged by judicial review and I do not do so. Cases where the applicant or plaintiff has no contract on which to rely may raise different considerations.

*Hoffmann LJ*: *Datafin* ... shows that the absence of a formal public source of power, such as statute or prerogative, is not conclusive. Governmental power may be exercised *de facto* as well as *de jure*. But the power needs to be identified as governmental in nature ... What one has [in *Datafin*] is a privatization of the business of government itself. [A] private [body is] established by the industry but [is] integrated into a system of statutory regulation. There is in my judgment nothing comparable in the position of the Jockey Club ...

In *Law* this court decided that the National Greyhound Racing Club Ltd. was not amenable to judicial review, notwithstanding that it controlled the greater part of the dog racing business ... The case was decided before ... *Datafin* ... and did not consider whether, notwithstanding the lack of any public source for its powers, the Club might *de facto* be a surrogate organ of government. I would accept that, if this were the case, there might be a conflict between the principle laid down in ... *Datafin* ... and the actual decision in *Law*'s case ... I would also accept that a body such as the Take-over Panel or IMRO, which exercises governmental powers, is not any the less amenable to public law because it has contractual relations with its members. In my view, however, neither the National Greyhound Racing Club Ltd. nor the Jockey Club is exercising governmental powers and therefore the decision in *Law*'s case remains binding in this case ...

The Jockey Club has power. But the mere fact of power, even over a substantial area of economic activity, is not enough. In a mixed economy, power may be private as well as public. Private power may affect the public interest and the livelihoods of many individuals. But that does not subject it to the rules of public law. If control is needed it must be found in the law of contract, the doctrine of restraint of trade, the Restrictive Trade Practices Act 1976, articles 85 and 86 of the EEC Treaty and all the other instruments available in law for curbing the excesses of private power ...

In the present case ... the remedies in private law available to the Aga Khan seem to me entirely adequate ... The Club has an implied obligation under the contract to conduct its disciplinary proceedings fairly. If it has not done so, the Aga Khan can obtain a declaration that the decision was ineffective ... and, if necessary, an injunction to restrain the Club from doing anything to implement it. No injustice is therefore likely to be caused in the present case by the denial of a public law remedy.

These judgments, although arriving at the same result, highlight the difficulties in the case law. On the one hand, the chief reason given by Sir Thomas Bingham for dismissing the application is the contractual source of power, the club's monopoly notwithstanding. On the other hand, Hoffmann LJ accepts that logically the test of 'governmental interest' renders the existence of a contractual source of power irrelevant. Then again, his strict application of that test marks a retreat from the idea that the purpose of judicial review is control of monopoly regulatory power, governmental or otherwise (position (iii)). Conversely, Lord Woolf,[12] writing extra-judicially, has argued that 'monopolistic powers' of 'public import' should be covered, at least where there is no alternative judicial remedy. In short, we find great confusion in this topic which only the House of Lords can resolve, and, underlying this, dispute or internal debate among the judges concerning the appropriate response in public law to the diffusion of power in contemporary society.

Is there room for a more radical approach? We could start by looking at the type of *function* being exercised (above, p. 34), and not a narrow public/private dichotomy, as the basis for determining the legal principles which should be applied. Thus Black draws on the fashionable jurisprudential theories of reflexive law and autopoiesis (above, p. 299) to argue for a principle of 'constitutionalised autonomy' for SROs which would explicitly recognise their intermediary role, not between the state and the individual within a hierarchical framework, but in a horizontal manner between the different spheres of society, for example, the state, the market and the community. 'Constitutionalised autonomy' would involve a recognition that 'the autonomy of the body is a social fact, but require

12  Lord Woolf, 'Droit Public – English Style' [1995] PL 57, 64.

the body to operate within a context of constitutional values implemented indirectly and strategically':[13]

> In order to develop such a principle, we need to develop a non-unitary notion of 'public' based on the understanding of the nature of SRAs as mediators ... As the role of SRAs is ... to mediate ... between systems within a heirarchical [framework] a notion of 'public' which is defined solely in terms of the SRA's relationship with the state is inadequate ... A body ... may also be public if the mediating role which it plays is a significant one within society. This is likely to be manifested as the exercise of power, although it need not be confined to that ...
>
> If we develop a more complex notion of public, then we can accept that there may be degrees of regulation, degrees of autonomy and that the appropriate degree of each may vary in different cases in relation to different functions or different decisions ... The essence of such a non-unitary concept of public is its flexibility. Only one of a body's functions may be regulatory; only some of its decisions may be public. This has implications not just for what is recognised as public, but what is looked for. The question that the courts should ask is not one big question of 'is this body public?', the answer leading to a once and for all categorisation from which all subsequent judicial treatment of the body flows ... The courts should focus on the nature of that decision or action and ask whether that act or decision is public, not whether the body is public. This would involve a recognition that one organisation can perform a range of functions: the Stock Exchange, for example, is at once a regulator, a market and a corporate actor. A quest for a single definition of public which can provide such a global and final categorisation is inapposite and leads only to confusion and contradiction ...
>
> In incorporating a more complex concept of 'public' [a principle of constitutionalised autonomy] emphasises the nature of SRAs as mini-systems of collective government. In requiring flexibility it demands a targeted and tailored approach, judicial responses being directed at the particular decision in question.

The argument fits with a general drift in judicial review towards contextualism or greater variability, evident in such key doctrines as *Wednesbury* unreasonableness[14] and, particularly, procedural fairness (Chapter 15). To this effect, the cognitive limitations of the judicial process, as also the concern about courts targeting fact situations at the expense of general principles of review, are given less weight (Chapter 17).

There is also scope for courts to mix-and-match 'public' and 'private' law doctrines, better to reflect the subtle mixes of 'public' and 'private' power. Cases such as *Mercury Communications*[15] already show a measure of hybridisation.[16] The message for judicial review is of a need both to broaden horizons and not to assume a monopoly of jurisdiction. Thus, Aronson has recently questioned 'whether only a public law response is appropriate for an issue involving public power', and 'whether only a private law response is

---

13  J. Black, 'Constitutionalising Self-Regulation' (1996) 59 MLR 24, 43.
14  Above, p. 84.
15  *Mercury Communications Ltd v Director General of Telecommunications* [1996] 1 WLR 48; below, p. 369.
16  See, for other examples, *Timeload Ltd v British Telecommunications plc* [1995] EMLR 459; *Stevenage Borough Football Club Ltd v Football League* (1996) Times, 1 August.

appropriate for an exercise of government power [through] contract'. He observes provocatively: [17]

> Judicial review was once regarded as one of administrative law's central devices for ensuring accountability. The *Datafin* project represented a hesitant and flawed attempt to apply judicial review to a situation of mixed power, shared by government and the private sector. It necessarily failed because it sought accountability to a model of legal regulation ... in a context of a regulatory reform movement which seeks increasingly to use other regulatory models. Its failure could also be attributed to an understandable lack of will on the part of the judiciary to involve itself too closely in economic or social regulation.
>
> More generally, administrative law's goals of accountability and participation are still important, but the way in which the state has restructured both itself and its delivery of goods and services, requires that the tools for achieving those goals might also have to be adapted. On occasions, it will even raise questions as to whether the best way of handling an issue might not be an adaptation of private law doctrines, such as tort or contract law.

## 6. Conclusion

As the tool and not the object of public law, regulation is the product of an exceptionally wide range of choices, both in terms of principle and technique. The activity has in Britain recently become much more prominent, which reflects in part the transformation in state forms, and in part changes in regulatory style and culture, more especially the processes of formalisation and juridification (which extend to self-regulation). Issues of regulatory design also underscore the political dimension in administrative law, which is traditionally downplayed.

The move to government by regulation provides public law with significant challenges. In tandem with government by contract, it serves to blur the public/private distinction, and thus strengthens the case for abandoning inflexible legal modes of classification. Deregulation, although welcome in many quarters, raises concerns about sub-optimal control, which require for resolution a more subtle approach to competition than was evident in the initial design of utilities regulation. Regulation is further an essential vehicle of the Europeanisation of national administrative law, giving rise to the challenges of reception or adaptation, and serving to emphasise the constraints on agency discretion.

At the procedural level, English administrative law is weak as regards regulation. Thus the design of 'regulation UK-style' exhibits serious deficiencies in the legal arrangements for accountability and participation. This puts in issue the legitimacy of agency action, where oversight and process values are identified as important criteria. A strengthening of judicial review in this field may be seen as a response, but ultimately only a partial response, to the gap in arrangements. Instead, the premium is placed on agency action to ground procedural accountability, a theme highlighted in the next chapter. Looking forward, we may anticipate under the new Labour

17  M. Aronson, 'A Public Lawyer's Responses; (above, p. 344, note 17), p. 70.

Government stronger or more intrusive forms of regulation in some key areas of economic and social policy. [18] Such further advance in 'the regulatory state' will need to be matched by an appropriate procedural development.

18  See, e.g., P. James, *Food Standards Agency: An interim proposal* (London: Cabinet Office) 1997.

Chapter 11

# Regulation, competition, juridification: a case study of OFTEL

It is time to look at regulation in action. We have chosen to study the Office of Telecommunications. As the first of the new breed of utility regulators, OFTEL is an important role-model in 'the regulatory state'. No regulatory regime better illustrates the theme of dynamic patterns of control and accountability in this field of administrative law (Chapter 5). So too the value of the functionalist method in administrative law is demonstrated: a traditional, legalistic emphasis on powers and duties, and on formal procedures and legal action, simply cannot do justice to the subject. The mandate must be treated as a starting point.

## 1. Mandate and anatomy

A broad legislative mandate has been seen as typical of the regulatory agency. OFTEL's is no exception, illustrating both the combination of primary and secondary duties, and the mixing of social policy and economic objectives criticised by Foster.[1] Section 3 of the Telecommunications Act 1984 places the DG and the Minister under a duty to act:

(1) . . . in the manner which he considers is best calculated—(a) to secure that there are provided throughout the United Kingdom, save in so far as the provision thereof is impracticable or not reasonably practicable, such telecommunications services as satisfy all reasonable demands for them including, in particular, emergency services, public call box services, directory information services, maritime services and services in rural areas; and (b) . . . to secure that any person by whom any such services fall to be provided is able to finance the provision of those services.

(2) Subject to subsection (1) above, the Secretary of State and the Director shall each have a duty to exercise [his] functions [under this Act] in the manner which he considers is best calculated—(a) to promote the interests of consumers, purchasers, and other users in the UK in respect of the provision and variety of, telecommunications services . . . and apparatus; (b) to maintain and promote effective competition . . .; (c) to promote efficiency and economy . . .; (d) to promote research . . . and . . . development . . .(g) to enable persons providing telecommunications services in the United Kingdom to compete effectively in the provision of such services outside the United Kingdom . . .

---

1   Above, p. 316.

The mandate remains essentially the same despite vast changes in the industry since 1984. The primary reason for this lies in the scope for agency discretion inherent in the widely drawn statutory formula. Secondly, as it turned out, the modalities by which the objectives were to be executed, more especially the licensing power, could be turned to advantage by the agency in broadening the ambit of its activities and introducing changes of policy. Thus, the increased competition which is now a feature of the industry is reflected in provisions concerning competition policy written in as terms of the licences (see below).

## (a) Mission statement

The statutory formula is also a poor guide to the character and emphasis of agency policy-making. The secondary duties, more especially promoting competition, lie at the heart of the regulatory development. The point is well illustrated by the agency's Management Plan.[2] It is stated with reference to s. 3:

> Two primary duties and eight other ones [are specified]. The section offers no guidance to the relative weight to be attached to each of the latter duties.
> In the light of these duties, OFTEL's primary focus is on customers. That focus translates into OFTEL's goal:
> 'To provide the best possible deal for the customer in terms of quality, choice and value for money.'
> OFTEL believes that a fully competitive market will deliver all elements of this goal – competition drives prices down, spurs innovation and automatically provides choice
> . . .
> OFTEL delivers this goal through five high level objectives aimed at promoting effective competition in the telecommunications industry and, in parallel, protecting consumers where effective competition has yet to develop.  These objectives are:
> • Promoting fair, efficient and sustainable network competition;
> • Promoting fair, efficient and sustainable services competition;
> • Securing licence enforcement and fair trading;
> • Securing a fair distribution of the benefits of competition between different groups of customers;
> • Protecting consumer interests, especially where effective competition is not yet fully developed.

OFTEL believes that 'its goal pursued through these five high level objectives delivers its statutory duties in the most effective way'. At this level of regulatory decision-making a successful challenge by means of judicial review is barely conceivable.

The Plan is in fact standard NPM fare, with much reference to 'fitness for purpose' and performance measurement. Agency discretion is exemplified by the choice of priority projects, a feature of the work programme which OFTEL considers critical to achieving its objectives. The flavour is given by a project on universal service.[3] Note the input from agency lawyers at various stages of design and implementation:

2   OFTEL, *Management Plan for 1996/1997 and Beyond*, 1996, Ch. 2, p. 1.
3   Ibid, Ch. 7, pp. 1-2. See further, OFTEL, *Universal Telecommunications Services*, 1995.

**Universal Service**

*Project objective*: to develop policy and implement effective arrangements to secure the funding and delivery of Universal Service in the UK in a fair and transparent way, in harmony with emerging European legislation.

*Fit with OFTEL's objectives*: Universal Service is central to OFTEL's objective of securing a fair share of the benefits of competition between different groups of customers. Universal Service will also protect customers with affordability problems, special needs, or those in remote rural areas.

Define service levels to ensure reasonably affordable access for all . . .

Keep under review Disability Act developments for telecommunications services . . .

Review Public Call Box policy and changes needed to secure reasonable access . . .

Revise cost estimates for proposed Universal Service Provision . . .

Publish consultation document with draft licence modifications . . .

Statutory consultation on licence modifications . . .

Establishment of Universal Service Funding Body . . .

Monitor and review . . .

## (b) Organisation and resources

A good regulatory regime needs suitable individuals and appropriate resources to ensure that it operates effectively. That OFTEL is an important role model among the new breed of independent regulators is due in part to the thoughtful and pro-active contributions of its DGs, Sir Bryan Carsberg (1984-1991) and Don Cruickshank. Mr. Cruickshank has notably stressed the need for regulatory transparency in conditions of market liberalisation (see below). As the pioneer, Sir Bryan was particularly concerned to establish the new regime's credentials; in promoting policies of competition and incentive regulation he made strenuous efforts to avoid the charge of regulatory capture. An official description serves to highlight the strong sense of personalisation in regulation 'UK-style':[4]

> During the eight years that he led OFTEL, Sir Bryan was the embodiment of the regulatory regime . . . The strong emphasis he placed on economic analysis as the basis for policy assessment brought a vital rigour to our decision making. This, together with Sir Bryan's commitment to ordered objective analysis, and his mastery of the accounting issues . . . gave a quality of cool rationality to our deliberations. This greatly enhanced OFTEL's effectiveness.

Operating in an increasingly complex and technical environment, a broad range of expertise is vital to OFTEL. It currently has five policy branches, or directorates, covering competition in networks, consumer policy and representation, licensing and fair trading, competition in services and international

4   OFTEL, *Annual Report 1992*, p. 1.

affairs.    These are backed by branches dealing in legal, economic and technical advice, as well as administration and publicity.  Multi-disciplinary teamworking is common practice.  Latterly, recruitment has become much more widely based, with many senior staff from consumer, business and industry backgrounds, as well as government service and the relevant professions.[5]

Several features command attention.  There is, first, the compact nature of the agency.  Staff numbers have gradually increased over the years, major factors being the licensing work associated with more operators and a growth in consumer complaints (see below).  A staff complement in 1996 of 168, of which 53 were senior staff, is, however, hardly generous.  OFTEL further expects staff numbers to decline as the market matures and competition becomes established: one product of a policy of deregulation.  Second, but related, OFTEL exemplifies the use by an agency of outside resources and networks, more especially private consultants, and, in the realm of consumer affairs, advisory committees (see below).  A third feature is the expanding input from lawyers.  The legal branch has grown significantly, both in terms of full-time staff (eight  in 1996) and through secondments from firms of solicitors.  Additionally, there is training for agency staff, which notably includes courses on administrative law, and on UK and EC competition law.[6] There is, finally, the funding of the agency: a budget of £9.5 million in 1996. This is provided by Parliament and is subject to the usual financial control, but OFTEL's costs are largely recouped from licence fees paid by the operators.  The division is indicative of a stress on the value of independence.

## 2. Market structure and regulatory style

Competition was slow to develop, but is now increasing rapidly.  This is both influenced by, and has affected, the style of regulation.[7]  There have been shifts in regulatory form, first from the benign to the more detailed and intrusive; and, latterly, via increasingly multilateral or multi-party proceedings, towards deregulation.  Juridification, in the broad sense of an injection of otherwise constricted legal values and culture, is a growing phenomenon.

### (a) Duopoly: regulatory bargaining

Stress has been laid on the distinction between privatisation and liberalisation. BT was transferred from public to private ownership with its dominant

---

5    See, for details, National Audit Office, *The Work of the Directors General of Telecommunications, Gas Supply, Water Services and Electricity Supply*, HC 645, Session 1995-1996, pp. 116-118 (hereafter *The Work of the Directors General*) OFTEL, *Annual Report 1996*, pp. 111-117.
6    See, for details, OFTEL, *Management Plan*, Chs. 9, 11.
7    It is also a key feature in recent controversy over the application to BT of the new Labour Government's 'windfall tax' on the privatised utilities.  See Finance (No. 2) Act 1997, ss. 1–5.

positions throughout the industry essentially intact.[8] Further, as regards the then core market of fixed link voice telephony, ministers opted for a highly asymmetric duopoly between BT and a fledgling subsidiary of Cable and Wireless, Mercury Communications. The rationale was a controversial one among economists: suppressing competition in order to protect, and so foster competition by, the infant company.[9] To this effect, other potential competitors were barred from the core market throughout the 1980s. The development highlights some basic characteristics of 'regulation UK-style': first, the continuing involvement of government in the structuring of industry post-privatisation; second, and related, the place of the DG inside a wider framework of controls (tiers of regulation); and, third, the central role of licensing or prior approval, the duopoly being constructed by the grant and withholding of permissions.

Attention is also drawn to the role of the regulator in the management of a transition to effective competition. Carsberg observed[10] in 1987: 'If the doors are thrown open wide, without adequate planning and preparation, the result is likely to be confusion, instability in prices and the provision of services, and perhaps a situation in which the original monopolist is able to re-establish its dominance.' But precisely because the market structure was so at odds with competitive forces, a heavy responsibility rested on the DG, whose attitude and energy was vital. An early statement of regulatory philosophy illustrates the creative approach to the legislative mandate:[11]

> The cornerstone of my conceptual framework is given to me by the Telecommunications Act 1984. It says that I have a duty to promote the interests for customers in the price, variety and quality of service ... The next step is, perhaps, a less obvious one, though it is extremely important and is also set down in the Act. It is that I should 'promote' the interests of customers, as far as possible, by 'promoting competition'. Whenever I become aware of a problem – some respect in which users are not getting as good treatment as is desirable – I ask first whether the problem can be alleviated by bringing about more competition or better competition. I believe that competition is frequently the best way of securing customers' interests. For example, a regulator can rarely establish with certainty how efficiently – including at how low

---

8   For contemporary analysis see J. Vickers and G. Yarrow, 'Telecommunications: Liberalisation and Privatization of British Telecom' in J. Kay, C. Mayer and D. Thompson (eds.), *Privatization and Regulation* (Oxford: Clarendon) 1986; M. Beesley, 'Regulation, Legislation and the 1984 Telecommunications Act' in M. Beesley (ed.), *Privatization, Regulation and Deregulation* (New York: Routledge) 1991.

9   See M. Beesley and B. Laidlaw, *The Future of Telecommunications* (London: Institute of Economic Affairs) 1989; also M. Armstrong and J. Vickers, 'Competition and Regulation in Telecommunications' in M. Bishop, J. Kay and C. Mayer (eds.), *The Regulatory Challenge* (Oxford: OUP) 1995.

10  B. Carsberg, *The Regulation of the Telecommunications Industry* (Edinburgh: David Hume Institute) 1987, p. 8.

11  B. Carsberg, 'Injecting Competition Into Telecommunications' in C. Veljanovski (ed.), *Privatization and Competition: A Market Prospectus* (London: Institute of Economic Affairs) 1989, p. 82. See also B. Carsberg, 'Office of Telecommunications: Competition and the Duopoly Review' in C. Veljanovski (ed.), *Regulators and the Market* (London: Institute of Economic Affairs) 1991.

a cost – a particular service can be provided. Competition will seek out the answer to that question far more effectively than the regulator can . . .

The second main leg of the conceptual framework is to use efficient kinds of regulation, regulation with the right incentive properties, for areas of activity where competition has not yet developed. . . I believe that effective regulation to prevent the abuse of monopoly power is regulation that mimics competition: for example, if a firm behaves in a way which would result in losses in a competitive environment, it should experience losses in a regulated environment also.

Regulatory bargaining is seen centre stage in this market structure. Characteristic of a bilateral relationship between regulator and regulated, the model is essentially one of compromise and co-operation. It is best illustrated by the focus on, and detailed development of, the BT price control: a series of negotiations taking place in the shadow of the Monopolies and Mergers Commission. In 1988 Vickers and Yarrow made an assessment:[12]

> Since BT and OFTEL would prefer not to go to the MMC (other things being equal) there exists a kind of bargaining game between them in which negotiating strengths depend partly upon the assessment of what would happen in the event of an MMC reference. The attitude of the Secretary of State can also play a part. Relative information conditions are of particular importance, because OFTEL's power rapidly diminishes the less it knows . . . The parameters of the negotiation are loosely defined by the 1984 Act, the licences and the conjectures regarding the attitudes of the MMC and the Secretary of State. Pro-competitive interests are especially fortunate that OFTEL has chosen – as it need not have done – to adopt a vigorous stance.

The argument can be put another way. The rise of the regulatory state was seen to imply a process of juridification: precisely because of the separation of regulation from operation of services (above, p. 313). Juridification is, however, a matter of degree, and may be seen as more limited here in the absence of market liberalisation. Thus, a preference is shown for an informal, 'closed' style of regulation at variance with process values espoused by lawyers (above, p. 332). As regards litigation, the duopoly policy not only limited the number of potential players, it also entailed close, fluid relationships with the regulator of the type which court action may disrupt.

## (b) Liberalisation: deregulation and transparency

The ending of the duopoly in 1991 is a watershed in government policy.[13] It paves the way for an unleashing of real competitive disciplines: a progressive eroding of BT's dominant positions. The industry, however, is also synonymous with

---

12  J. Vickers and G. Yarrow, *Privatization: An Economic Analysis*, (Cambridge, Mass: MIT Press) 1988, p. 236.

13  Department of Trade and Industry, *Competition and Choice: Telecommunications Policy for the 1990's*, Cm. 1461, 1991.

rapid technological change, which constantly expands the range of services available. An OFTEL survey in 1995 reveals:[14]

> The telecoms market in the UK is not a single market for a homogenous product but a large number of separate, overlapping markets for very different products. There are different sets of players in different market segments – a mosaic of competition. There are competitors to BT in almost all segments of the market, although to differing degrees and in many market segments BT is still dominant. BT is still the only nationally present operator competing as a vertically-integrated firm in all segments of the market.

Diversification feeds growth. An industry turnover of £20 billion in 1995 is projected to increase exponentially. We note, too, the swift emergence of a multi-operator regulatory environment: OFTEL now has over 200 licensees or 'clients', including over 50 major companies.[15] A distinctive feature is the substantial growth in network competition, as by cable operators in the residential market: OFTEL currently identifies this as its most important work.[16] Looking more broadly, the broadcasting, computer and telecommunications industries increasingly converge, as in the Internet and digitalisation. Cruickshank foresees an increasingly 'seamless communications environment'.[17]

A new policy by OFTEL of deregulation reflects and reinforces these developments. There was seen[18] to be 'a direct and rapidly growing conflict' between the policy goal of open and vigorous competition and the existing regulatory paradigm. Regulatory policies were 'still centred on managing a privatised utility. . . rather than letting competition determine the market's shape'. The case for reform was espoused by OFTEL in a major review of strategy published in 1995 after extensive consultation.[19] Regulation, it was said, could progressively move to a lower level as effective competition became established in various sectors of the market. OFTEL's role should change from one of policing adherence to detailed licence provisions to being more a competition authority regulating compliance with broadly-based competition provisions. We note the typical deregulatory form of rule-substitution (above, p. 305).

Let us develop the theme. First, in a liberalised market, licences will gain the general character that we associate with rules: in other words,[20] 'A more open form of competition – where the general conditions for entry are set and anyone can enter the market on those terms'. Second, potential exists across the regulatory regime for both pro-competition moves and less intrusive forms of regulation. Later, the application of the policy is tracked in such

---

14 National Audit Office, *The Work of the Directors General*, p. 66. In 1996 BT controlled about 80% of the total market. It had less than two-thirds of the market for international calls, but controlled 90% of local calls. See OFTEL, *Market Information*, 1997.
15 OFTEL, *Annual Report 1996*, p. 26.
16 OFTEL, *Management Plan*, Ch. 4.
17 OFTEL, *Annual Report 1996*, p. 11.
18 M. Sullivan and J. Prior, *Telecommunications Regulation in the UK* (London) 1994, pp. 10-11.
19 *Effective Competition: Framework for Action*,1995.
20 B. Wigglesworth and F. Barnes, 'UK Policies and Regulations' (1992) Telecommunications Policy 721, 723.

fields as price control and interconnection. Cruickshank vigorously expounds the philosophy:[1]

> The process of regulation aims to encourage competition wherever feasible. Regulatory rules are needed to get competition off the ground – to ensure that customers get a good deal and that new entrants are not unfairly prevented from competing. As competition gets under way, and the battle for customers becomes fiercer, the regulator has a vital role to play on behalf of customers and competitors in acting quickly to stamp out anti-competitive behaviour . . .
>
> But there are dangers associated with regulation and the regulator must not meddle more with the market than is justified in ensuring fair competition. The problem with detailed intrusive regulation where it is not necessary is that the market moves to reflect regulatory decisions rather than making its own. This can lead to nearly the same limitations in terms of lack of innovation and choice that characterise monopolised markets.
>
> Instead regulation must seek to replace monopolised markets by competitive markets from which regulation can withdraw. . . Above all our guiding principle must be that competition, wherever feasible, is the best regulator. Our aim is to establish a coherent framework which encourages entry, innovation, efficiency and sustainable competition, based on sound economic principles, so that the transfer from regulation to a competitive market can be efficient.

So, too, we see great store set upon transparency. This entails both regulatory and market transparency: regulatory transparency is broadly defined by OFTEL to focus on arrangements for consultation:[2]

> Consultation is central to OFTEL's approach to the regulation of the telecommunications industry . . . In principle, OFTEL will consult on all issues that have significant impact on consumers and operators. The only issues on which OFTEL would not consult are those which are of too little consequence to merit the expense to both OFTEL and the industry of mounting a consultation or of such a high level of commercial confidentiality that consultation would be damaging . . . The Director General's policy is to develop the maximum transparency in the consultation process – hence to include as full an exposition of his reasons for taking decisions as practicable.

Cruickshank signalled his intentions soon after taking office: he drew attention to a lack of openness in the regulatory procedures, as also of information for customers.[3] Recent procedural initiatives include, on major issues, public hearings; informal industry workshops; and panels of users. Other developments include the publication of the agency's Management Plan and a series of guidelines on regulatory action, as in enforcement of licences. The agency is today appropriately characterised as a market leader in process values.

The importance of agency discretion is further highlighted. Although some legal requirements are in operation, much of the procedural development is

---

1  OFTEL, *Annual Report 1996*, pp. 1-2.
2  National Audit Office, *The Work of the Directors General*, pp. 112, 123. See, further, OFTEL, *Consultation Procedures and Transparency*, 1995.
3  OFTEL, *Annual Report 1993*, para. 1.12.

voluntary.  Why the high priority on transparency?  Cruickshank[4] gives three main reasons: accountability of the regulator, quality of the policy-making process, and 'to give everyone a better understanding of how regulation works so the process is effective and efficient'.  We are reminded of the value of due process as a source of legitimacy of agency action (above, p. 311).  Again:[5]

> The transparency of the regulatory process – ensuring that . . . companies, their shareholders and consumers understand and contribute to the decisions the regulator makes – is important for all regulators.  But it is particularly important in telecoms where there is increasing competition in different segments of the market and where regulatory decisions can have different effects on different players.  OFTEL needs to have a clear picture of how possible changes in the regulatory regime will affect all the different players in the industry – both in the short and the long term.  It is vital, therefore, that proposals for change are fully aired and discussed with all the stakeholders in the industry.

The shift in regulatory forms is made clear.  No longer is policy change essentially a matter for regulatory bargaining with the dominant firm.  The multi-operator environment is underpinned by a regulatory model of broad consultation and agency decision.  Thus, as typically advocated by amber light theorists, there is a more American-style approach, albeit without the constitutional and legal underpinnings (above, p. 333).  It is, however, important to stress the limitations.  A level playing field cannot be assumed.  Licensees enjoy a privileged position in the broader discussion, if only because of a requirement to achieve change through the process of licence modification.  Then there is the problem of expectations and regulatory control.  Predictably, perhaps, survey evidence reveals a feeling among consultees that the process is 'not genuine', with OFTEL 'not taking due account of external views' in reaching its decisions.  The agency feels bound to assert that:[6]

> Decisions have in the end to be made by OFTEL in the light of its interpretation of its duties . . .  Discussion and the taking of views . . . is not . . . a way of reaching regulatory decision by majority vote.  In practice . . . there are adjustments to the working, and even to some elements of the direction, of OFTEL policy as a result of the points made . . . in the course of consultation.

The recourse to such open, inclusive procedures can be seen to illustrate the process of juridification in the context of liberalisation.  It is only natural that litigation should consequently grow, and recourse to lawyers increase, as interests in the industry diverge and the scope for consensus in the regulatory regime diminishes.  We will return to this general theme.

---

4   OFTEL, *Annual Report 1996*, p. 78.
5   National Audit Office, *The Work of the Directors General*, p. 64.
6   OFTEL, *Annual Report 1996*, p. 86; National Audit Office, *The Work of the Directors General* pp. 113-114.

## (c) Europe and globalisation

Telecommunications is an increasingly international, global business: national 'fences' will become increasingly irrelevant. OFTEL, as the national regulatory authority, will from 1998 be operating inside the framework of a European telecommunications market which is, with some exceptions, fully liberalised.[7] In particular, the regime will allow operators to provide services and networks throughout the Union under a harmonised regulatory structure. Typically, this entails implementation at the national level of a series of directives on key aspects of market operations – interconnection, universal service and licensing – as well as an evolving case law in the ECJ.[8]

Liberalisation is in progress on a global scale. A pact on telecommunications signed by 68 countries under the auspices of the World Trade Organisation (WTO) has been heralded as the most important international trade agreement for the 21st century.[9] Operative in 1998, it allows open competition in some 90% of the world market. This further illuminates recent structural changes in the industry, a wave of mergers, acquisitions and joint ventures, many with an international dimension for the purpose of meeting global demands. And nowhere is globalisation of the market better illustrated than in the case of the United Kingdom. As regards BT, there is a shift from a nationally focused operator to a global player in local markets across the world, as shown by attempts to merge with an American firm to establish the world's fourth largest carrier.[10] Conversely, we note the arrival in the domestic market of giant multinational companies and alliances: the likes of Deutsche Telekom and, from America, AT&T and Sprint, which are far less susceptible to pressures from the dominant firm. In 1996, a BT/Mercury duopoly in international facilities was ended: within six months over 40 international licences had been granted.[11] OFTEL's 'client-base' now looks very different.

Globalisation of an industry necessarily affects the scope, direction and style of national regulation. There will surely be further pressures here for deregulation. OFTEL has in the European context already had occasion to review national policy on matters such as interconnection in the light of new supra-national requirements.[12] Then again, the development will be more limited than in many other countries, precisely because of the early moves in Britain to liberalisation. General competition law will play a central role, more especially at the European level, where the institutional arrangements and jurisprudence are highly developed.

---

7  See W. Sauter 'The Telecommunications Law of the European Union' (1995) 1 Eur. Law J. 92; also, for an international comparison, C. Scott, 'Institutional Competition and Coordination in the Process of Telecommunications Liberalisation' in J. McCahery, W. Bratton, S. Picciotto and C. Scott (eds.), *International Regulatory Competition and Coordination* (Oxford: OUP) 1996.

8  See e.g. Case C-302/94 *R* v *Secretary of State for Trade and Industry, ex p British Telecommunications plc* (12 December, 1996). See, for discussion, A. Hunt, 'Regulation of Telecommunications: the Developing EU Regulatory Framework and its Impact on the United Kingdom' (1997) 3 European Public Law 93.

9  See M. Fredebeul-Krein and A. Freytag, 'Telecommunications and WTO discipline' (1997) 21 Telecommunications Policy 447.

10  Involving a joint company, Concert.

11  OFTEL, *Annual Report 1996*, p. 38.

12  See, for details, OFTEL, *Annual Report 1996*, pp. 102-107.

Later, we examine steps recently taken to revamp OFTEL as a competition authority applying broad-based EC norms. Globalisation will also reinforce the trend away from informal regulatory relationships characterised by a high degree of mutuality or trust. Reference need only be made to market entrants like AT&T, well-versed in the legal strategies typical of American regulation. Globalisation means juridification: in the shape of the corporate lawyer.

OFTEL itself is increasingly a player on the international stage. In the Union, the agency wants to ensure that nothing will jeopardise continued competitive development of the UK market. The DG also has a statutory duty to ensure that UK telecommunications companies are able to compete effectively abroad (above, p. 353); with moves to liberalisation around the world such work naturally assumes a high priority. In Cruickshank's words:[13]

> To support UK licensees effectively we must ... understand their global ambitions and make sure that our policies and decisions dovetail with the international regulatory scene. We cannot achieve this unless we develop a dialogue with licensees on their overseas plans and also with other regulators, such as the Federal Communications Commission in the USA, on their policies.

OFTEL now liaises closely with other leading national regulatory authorities. There is direct participation and assistance for the DTI in the development of a pro-competitive regulatory framework in Europe and at WTO level. The influencing of EU and international thinking are made 'priority projects':[14]

### Influencing EU Thinking

*Project Objective:* To ensure that OFTEL has a major influence and input in the development of telecommunications policy in Europe, in order to promote market opening in the EU and the interests of UK industry in Europe. To promote in particular the key UK themes of liberalisation, competition, effective enforcement and benefit to the customer.

It would be strange if things were otherwise. Telecommunications highlights the importance in a shrinking world of links between national authorities, and of lobbying and standard-setting at the international level. To this end, OFTEL illuminates the role of the regulatory agency in networking.

## 3. Aspects of the regulation

It is time to look more closely at some key elements of the regulatory regime. The importance of the discretion to make rules will be highlighted, as also the competing models of process and the expression of Citizen's Charter values in the response to consumers. The BT price control, which illustrates the changing style of the regulation, is an appropriate starting place.

---

13  OFTEL, *Annual Report 1993*, para. 1.53.
14  OFTEL, *Management Plan*, Ch. 3, pp. 2-3.

## (a) Price control: rule games

The regulatory rule RPI – X has been seen as a cornerstone of economic regulation 'UK-style'. Its application in telecommunications is especially noteworthy, the formula being originally propounded in the context of the industry. Fixing it is an archetypical polycentric decision, by reason of the major impact not just on the dominant firm but on the rest of the industry and its consumers. Let us consider the different periods in the life of the control.

The first period (1984-1989) is distinctive for the direct political input. The setting of the control, essential to the initial ordering of the market, is reserved to the minister via the power of prior approval. A choice for X of 3% for a five-year period is considered a benign decision by economists, and one which helps to promote a successful privatisation.[15] Characteristic of British government, this part of the regulatory process is 'closed'. Thus, the scale and scope of the control is made the subject of protracted negotiations with BT – corporatist bargaining – with little public consultation or explanation.

There is from the outset a move away from the straightforward model of regulation envisaged by Littlechild (above, p. 315). In the interests of consumer protection, the reach of the regulatory rule (expressed in the definition of the 'basket' of services) is extended beyond areas of natural monopoly to certain fields of duopoly competition.[16] But this also means potentially greater freedom to restructure prices inside the 'basket': notably at the expense of local users, favourably treated under the regime of public ownership. A secondary cap is introduced, RPI + 2 on residential line rentals, designed to allow a gradual 'rebalancing' of prices.[17] This is the beginning of the development of a system of rules: a fine example of the techniques of confining and structuring discretion in the regulatory environment.

Conditions are ripe for the regulatory 'bargaining game'. The independent regulator is both constrained within this framework and empowered to seek change through modification of licence. Carsberg stressed that he would seek the introduction of new licence rules if BT behaved unreasonably on any aspect of its pricing policy: specific threats to go to the MMC surfaced from time to time.[18] We catch sight of a set of informal pressures and 'voluntary' compliance tangential to the system of formal control. Expressed slightly differently, OFTEL exercises a wider influence than a purely legalistic interpretation would suggest: the very kind of agency discretion which RPI – X was meant to avoid.

In the next period (1989-1993), discretion has passed from the minister to the agency. The resetting of the control is achieved through licence modification:

---

15  D. Helm, 'RPI-X and the Newly Privatized Industries:  Deceptively Simple Regulatory Rule', Public Money (June 1987) 47.

16  See, for details, National Audit Office, *The Office of Telecommunications: Licence Compliance and Consumer Protection*, HC 529, Session 1992-1993, Part 4.

17  See, for discussion by economists, J. Vickers and G. Yarrow, *Privatization and Economic Analysis* (Cambridge, Mass: MIT Press) 1988, Ch.8.

18  B. Carsberg, 'Injecting Competition Into Telecommunications' in C. Veljanovski (ed.), *Privatization and Competition: A Market Prospectus* (London: Institute of Economic Affairs) 1989 at p. 92; C. Veljanovski, 'The Regulation Game' in C. Veljanovski (ed.), *Regulators and the Market* (London: Institute of Economic Affairs) 1991.

which means more regulatory bargaining. Several features command attention. First, there is increased complexity and stringency, managerial discretion being ever more divided. Thus X is set at 4.5 for a four-year period;[19] the 'basket' is extended; and more secondary rules are introduced to limit 'rebalancing'. Second, and related, the approach to the regulatory rule increasingly resembles rate of return regulation. The economic judgments and information comprised in the resetting are reminiscent of American practice. Third, the element of uncertainty is shown by a breakdown in the model of control soon afterwards. Fixed periods have been assessed as vital to RPI – X regulation, creating a strong incentive to efficiency (above, p. 321). However, BT operations outside the control prove far more profitable than the DG has anticipated. A further round of regulatory bargaining ensues, and so a classic example of 'regulatory chiselling': in order, in Carsberg's words, to bring the rate of return 'within acceptable levels'.[20] For 1991-93, the control is deepened to RPI – 6.25 and widened to include international services. In the light of this manoeuvre the rules themselves are seen to be unstable.

The third period (1993-1997) represents the high water mark of price control. The duopoly is ended, but competition still needs time to arrive: hence, in Carsberg's words, 'firm controls on BT . . . are needed to protect the customer'.[1] To this effect, X is raised to 7.5, while the basket now covers some two-thirds of BT's total revenue. The secondary rules are significantly strengthened: RIP – 0 on each individual basket price, save for RPI + 2 on line rentals. Writing in 1995, Xavier, a business analyst, lamented this process of rule-development in the name of consumer protection:[2]

> In the United Kingdom . . . attempts to fine tune the price cap scheme have resulted in a complicated, more intrusive, less transparent system than was originally intended. There is wide agreement that as competition increases there should be less rather than more regulation, and that regulation should be based increasingly on stable, clearly understood rules rather than on regulatory discretion. Observing its application in practice indicates that this has not happened in the case of price cap regulation . . .
>
> This outcome has to be considered against the repeatedly proclaimed desire . . . in the UK . . . to see regulation *decrease* rather than increase. . . It is doubtful, too, whether the cost of regulation has fallen substantially under price cap regulation . . . The benefits of price cap regulation will exceed costs only if the use of price cap regulation does not proliferate impediments which unduly delay the development of effective competition.

The procedures adopted at this time represent a hybrid or transitional stage between the models of regulatory bargaining and of consultation and decision.

---

19  Which more appropriately reflects the scope for cost-cutting especially by reason of technological advance. See for details, National Audit Office, *The Office of Telecommunications*, Part 4.
20  National Audit Office, *The Office of Telecommunications*, para. 4.25.
1  National Audit Office, *The Work of the Directors General*, p. 124.
2  P. Xavier, 'Price Cap Regulation for Telecommunications' (1995) 19 Telecommunications Policy 599, pp. 614-616. See further, I. Vogelsang, L. Jones and P. Tandon, 'British Telecom' in A. Fadil and A. Galal (eds.), *Welfare Consequences of Selling Public Enterprises* (New York: OUP), 1994.

On the one hand, detailed and timely consultation documents invite comment and advice on a wide range of economic calculations; on the other hand, information is lacking about the actual calculation of X.[3] To underline the point, there is both explicit recognition of the competing interests involved in the regulation, and a failure of explanation of how those interests are mediated. From the viewpoint of an amber light theorist: two steps forward, one step back.

### (b) Deregulation: consultation

The resetting for a further period (1997-2001) demonstrates the change in regulatory style under Cruickshank. Consider first the approach to the substance of control, which involves, in Cruickshank's words, 'a significant pulling back of detailed regulation to match the advance of competition.'[4] The agency must assess which markets are sufficiently developed to deliver the benefits of competitive prices: typically, the preferred option is 'the withdrawal of regulation where possible'. The reform is part of a package, which entails general competition powers for OFTEL as well as a new regime on interconnection (see below). We identify a basic shift in the role and functions of the agency.

So today the price control is greatly reduced in scope, and simplified: with the arrival of competition, it finally resembles the original design. Services for the larger business and high value domestic markets are deregulated, accounting for three-quarters of BT's total revenue.[5] Small business and most residential customers are protected by the cap RPI – 4.5, on the basis that competition in the local access market is insufficient. The major secondary rule, RPI + 2 on line rentals, is abolished.[6] And price control is now regarded as a temporary expedient: Cruickshank expresses the view that, after 2001, such will be the progress of market forces, none will be required.[7] The belief in competition as 'best regulator' is amply demonstrated.

Now consider the procedures. The old system of regulatory bargaining simply could not be sustained in the new multi-operator environment. OFTEL recognises the need for an open-plan method:[8]

> When the last review was done there was little competition in the UK telecoms market. The industry is now one characterised by many players who will all be affected by decisions on BT's price control. It is important therefore that the whole of the current review should be conducted with the maximum transparency . . . The aim is to ensure all interested parties have the opportunity to understand the issues arising from the review of the price control regime and to participate, through the consultation process, in the development of OFTEL's policy . . . Also fairness – constructing price

3   OFTEL, *The Regulation of BT's Prices*, 1992 and *BT's Cost of Capital*, 1992; and T. Gilland, 'Telecommunications: Regulation in a Dynamic Market' in T. Gilland and P. Vass (eds.), *Regulatory Review 1993* (London: Centre for the Study of Regulated Industries) 1993.
4   OFTEL, *Annual Report 1996*, pp. 3, 5.
5   OFTEL, *Pricing of Telecommunications Services from 1997*, 1996.
6   See, on this development, OFTEL, *Effective Competition: Framework for Action*, 1995.
7   OFTEL, *Pricing of Telecommunications Services from 1997*, Preface.
8   National Audit Office, *The Work of the Directors General*, p. 136.

controls inevitably involves a balancing of interests. Those affected – consumers, BT, operators – need to know the basis on which decisions are being made and how the balance is being struck.

The result is the kind of major procedure which takes several years to complete.[9] The design specifically allows for interaction between competing interests as well as for responses to OFTEL. Note too the stress on tackling the regulatory problem of asymmetry of information, vital to the proper assessment of market forces. Such a procedure requires careful planning:[10]

> OFTEL plans a first stage consultation . . . This document will be largely "green" although OFTEL will indicate what its present thinking is in order to give a focus to responses and subsequent discussion. It will address the definition of principles and objectives for a price control regime . . . OFTEL will follow its standard two-stage process in which commentators have time to review and respond to the responses of other commentators. This document will be followed by workshops and seminars with both consumer and industry groups, as well as by discussions with interested parties on specific topics.
>
> The results of this consultation will be combined with further work on the development of models of the impact of price controls in a second consultation document . . . This will give a clear OFTEL preference for a particular form of price control . . . It will also include OFTEL's first proposals for the value of X . . . the conclusions will be accompanied by draft modifications to BT's licence. This consultation will also be in OFTEL's standard two-phase process. It will also be followed by workshops and seminars with consumer and industry interests. OFTEL expects to hold detailed discussions with BT and the industry on the licence modifications . . . After digesting the responses to this consultation, OFTEL plans . . . to issue a statement and to start the statutory process of consultation on the finalised draft of BT licence modifications – this too will be a two-stage process . . .
>
> OFTEL is . . . concerned to set the BT price control review in the context of the interests and development of the total telecoms industry . . . It is therefore concerned that its analysis should as far as possible not be totally dependent on BT data. It aims to reinforce its BT data-based analysis by cross-checks through a number of parallel initiatives to gather information . . . Many of the telecoms operators in the UK market have worldwide experience and expertise in telecoms as major operators in other countries. They are well placed to make valuable input to OFTEL's data and modelling . . . This new review will go further than the last by including assessment of the impact of alternative price controls on the other operators.

### (c) Interconnection: judicial review and procedural discretion

The issue of interconnection has throughout been at the heart of OFTEL policy-making. Inevitably so, since the charges paid for the use of BT's network have accounted for a large proportion of other operators' costs. The topic perfectly illustrates the scope for, and problems of, the interaction of public regulatory and private contractual power. As such it has provided the setting for a leading case

---

9 See, for details, *OFTEL Annual Report 1996*, pp. 25-31.
10 National Audit Office, *The Work of the Directors General*, pp. 125, 127-129.

in judicial review. The topic further highlights the interplay of the substantive and procedural elements in agency discretion, and, latterly, the twin themes of regulatory transparency and deregulation.

Section 7 of the 1984 Act treated interconnection as another aspect of licensing. The scheme devised was for the regulator to impose a standard condition requiring the licensee to negotiate with a view to reaching agreement with any other operator requesting interconnection with its system. Ongoing regulatory control was secured in two ways: first, contracts between operators must comply with the rules set out in their licences, which can be modified in the usual way; and, second, through adjudication, a determination by OFTEL being incorporated in a contract if no agreement is reached. The model then was one of commercial bargaining structured by, and in the shadow of, agency regulation. But it was to prove burdensome, with many disputes and interventions.

For Sir Bryan Carsberg,[11] the important question was 'not really about whether you allow competition [but] about whether you assist competition, whether you do something to help new entrants into the market-place'. Assume that the setting of interconnection charges equal to the marginal cost of providing the use of the network broadly represents an allocatively efficient solution.[12] So-called 'entry assistance' would entail setting the charges below marginal cost in order to intensify the degree of competition. Regulatory intervention of this kind involves an agency directly in shaping the market, and Carsberg chose to do this. Consider the first major determination, which took place soon after privatisation in the conditions of duopoly. According to condition 13.5(A) of BT's licence, the DG was to determine terms 'reasonably necessary . . . to secure':

> That the Operator pays to the Licensee the cost of anything done pursuant to or in connection with the agreement including fully allocated costs attributable to the services to be provided and taking into account relevant overheads and a reasonable rate of return on attributable assets.

Adjudication involves a creative exercise of power which includes interpretation. All the more so, when the determination is an instrument of regulatory policy: for his part, Sir Bryan notably stressed the 'element of subjective judgment'. While the condition could be read differently, the DG opted for charges very favourable to Mercury, significantly below BT's marginal cost.[13] To the lawyer, the obvious question is: was this open to challenge? In fact, the affair demonstrates the scale of procedural discretion, and, further, a 'closed' and defensive approach redolent of an old regulatory culture. The only reason

---

11  B. Carsberg, 'Promoting Entry Into Regulated Industries' in G. Bourne and M. Beesley (eds.), *Major Issues in Regulation* (London: Institute of Economic Affairs) 1993, pp. 92-93.

12  The economic principles on which charges should be based have been hotly disputed. See e.g. M. Cave, 'Interconnection, Separate Accounting and the Development of Competition in UK Telecommunications' in M. Beesley (ed.), *Regulating Utilities: The Way Forward* (London: Institute of Economic Affairs) 1994.

13  M. Beesley and B. Laidlaw, 'The British Telecom/Mercury Interconnect Determination' in M. Beesley (ed.), *Privatization, Regulation and Deregulation*, (New York: Routledge) 1991; also M. Beesley and S. Littlechild, 'The Regulation of Privatised Monopolies in the United Kingdom' (1989) 20 Rand J of Economics 454.

given was a classic 'boiler plate' reason: the DG 'established the prices, based on BT's costs, which should be paid by . . . Mercury . . . for use of its network'. Although suspicion was raised, Carsberg only confessed much later that this was indeed the kind of avoidance of legal control which fuels the argument for a general common law duty to give reasons (see Chapter 15):[14]

> As with all things, my inclination was to explain exactly what I had done and why I had done it. The [licence conditions], however, did not make an explicit reference to entry assistance; they talked about this and that and covering costs. As an accountant, I knew that cost could mean almost anything, and so I asked counsel: 'Can I give discounts to Mercury?' He said, 'Yes, I think you can do it, but if I were you, I wouldn't explain it to anyone because if you do you will find yourself in court and you might prefer not to do that'. I took his advice, did not end up in court, and achieved the objective.

The lack of transparency became dysfunctional as the market liberalised following the duopoly review. Potential new entrants could not do their sums without the reasons. When a second BT/Mercury determination was issued in 1993, it was accompanied by an explanatory guide.[15]

## (i) A 'significant' case?

Yet, once again, the regulatory interpretation proved controversial. Whereas OFTEL and BT both considered that Condition 13 permitted charging based on average cost, Mercury read the terms 'fully allocated costs' and 'relevant overheads' as requiring a change to capacity charging based on marginal cost, so affording it greater flexibility and pricing. Further, the legal mix of private power and public control had been developed by the parties. The contract (in 1986), which was the product of the first determination, provided (in clause 29) for its own referral for a determination of a possible amendment if circumstances changed. The fresh determination was triggered in this way, following the duopoly review.

### *Mercury Communications Ltd v Director General of Telecommunications*[16]

Disappointed by the outcome, Mercury applied for a declaration by means of originating summons in the Commercial Court. The tactic serves to highlight important tensions between the norms of commercial law and of judicial review in this type of context. The legal question was whether the action should be struck out for abuse of process. One argument concentrated on the respective roles of the regulator and the judge. Adopting the perspective of contract law by reference to the principles of commercial arbitration, it was said that, effectively, there was

14 B. Carsberg, 'Telecommunications Competition in the United Kingdom: A Regulatory Perspective' (1992) 37 New York Law School L R 285, 291.
15 OFTEL, *BT/Mercury Interconnection Determination: Interconnect Charges and Explanatory Document*, 1993.
16 [1996] 1 WLR 48.

ouster of jurisdiction. This involved stress on the legal source of the determination as contractual, and was accepted by the Court of Appeal:

> *Saville LJ*: In principle . . . the Court should start on the basis that the parties to the agreement should be held to their bargain, namely that if they were unable to negotiate changes to their agreement between themselves, the question whether any and if so what changes should be made should be determined by the Director in accordance with the provisions of what is now the new clause 29. At the same time it seems to me that the Court has jurisdiction to entertain the matter . . .
>
> To my mind, therefore, the question is simply whether there are factors which in the present case should lead the court to conclude that, notwithstanding the bargain the parties made, it would be just to allow the proceedings to continue . . .
>
> I have concluded that [for the Court to intervene] would amount, in effect, to rewriting the contract between the parties on the basis that they could, with hindsight, have made a better agreement. That is not in my judgment a proper function of the Courts. The parties have agreed upon a method of resolving differences between them as to changes to their agreement. It seems to me that only in the most exceptional circumstances should the court change that method and substitute itself, in whole or in part, as the decision maker. I am not satisfied that such exceptional circumstances exist in the present case.

Things look different to the administrative lawyer. Irrespective of legal form, this is economic regulation, a situation of direct and indirect controls exercised in the public interest. The reasoning of the House of Lords to this effect is reminiscent of *Anisminic:*[17]

> *Lord Slynn*: What has to be done in the present case under condition 13, as incorporated in clause 29 of the Agreement, depends upon the proper interpretation of the words 'fully allocated costs' which . . . raises a question of construction and therefore of law, and 'relevant overheads' which may raise analogous questions. If the Director General misinterprets these phrases and makes a Determination on the basis of an incorrect interpretation, he does not do what he was asked to do. If he interprets the words correctly then the application of those words to the facts may in the absence of fraud be beyond challenge. In my view when the parties agreed in clause 29.5 that the Director General's determination should be limited to such matters as the Director General would have power to determine under condition 13 . . . and that the principles to be applied by him should be "those set out in those conditions" they intended him to deal with such matters and such principles as correctly interpreted. They did not intend him simply to apply such meaning as he himself thought they should bear. His interpretation could therefore be reviewed by the court. There is no provision expressly or impliedly that these matters were remitted exclusively to the Director General, even though in order to carry out this task he must be obliged to interpret them in the first place for himself. Nor is there any provision excluding altogether the intervention of the court.

A second argument concerned the exclusivity principle derived from the famous case of *O'Reilly v Mackman*,[18] it being said that, by reason of the DG's statutory

17  Above, p. 54.
18  Below, p. 554.

position, any justiciable issue was a public law matter and could be pursued only via an application for judicial review. Mercury was, however, allowed to proceed, and so avoid the special procedural constraints such as the three months' time limit and requirement to obtain leave from the court governing judicial review:

> *Lord Slynn*: The recognition by Lord Diplock [in *O'Reilly* v *Mackman*] that exceptions exist to the general rule may introduce some uncertainty but it is a small price to pay to avoid the over rigid demarcation between procedures reminiscent of earlier disputes as to the forms of action and of disputes as to the competence of jurisdictions apparently encountered in civil law countries where a distinction between public and private law has been recognised. It is of particular importance, as I see it, to retain some flexibility as the precise limits of what is called 'public law' and what is called 'private law' are by no means worked out . . . It has to be borne in mind that the overriding question is whether the proceedings constitute an abuse of the process of the court . . .
>
> The granting of a licence containing condition 13 was an act performed under section 7 of the statute. That does not mean that what the Director General does cannot lead to disputes which fall outside the realms of administrative law any more than that a government department cannot enter into a commercial contract or commit a tort actionable before the court under its ordinary procedures.
>
> In the present case, even though condition 13 is in the licence, the interpretation of its terms arises no less in a dispute between two telecommunications companies because of the provisions of the amended version of clause 29 which the parties agree they must adopt in their Agreement. The whole basis of the arrangements under clause 29 is that the parties shall discuss and negotiate in good faith changes in the Agreement, including modifications to charges. It is only if they cannot themselves agree the terms to be included that they contractually accept that the Director may decide, and that they as part of their contract will give effect to his decision. Thus what the Director decides becomes a part of the contract: the dispute in substance and in form is as to the effect of the terms of the contract even if it can also be expressed as a dispute as to the terms of the licence.
>
> Moreover . . . it seems to me that the procedure by way of originating summons in the Commercial Court is at least as well, and may be better, suited to the determination of these issues than the procedure by way of judicial review.

In sum, the House of Lords is seen developing a hybrid form of legal control; and, further, one in which the public and private law elements are so combined as to suggest a forceful control.

An assessment of the 'significance' of the case naturally depends on the criteria applied. Approached through the traditional legal way in terms of doctrine, it has ramifications for judicial review in general, helping to break down a strictness in procedure previously asserted (Chapter 16): all the more so, by reason of the mix of public and private power typical of the regulatory state and government by contract. Turning to the utilities, the case may be accounted a watershed in the process of juridification, signalling a judicial willingness to examine a substantive decision of the regulator. It is not entirely coincidental that around this time OFTEL doubled the size of its legal department. Consequently, concern has been expressed as to the possibilities of legal uncertainty and delay,[19]

---

19   A. McHarg, 'Regulation as a Private Law Function?' [1995] PL 539.

all the more troubling in a fast-changing regulatory environment. Note in this context the volume and difficulty of the accounting and economic evidence which in the view of the House of Lords rendered the Commercial Court an appropriate venue for the Mercury litigation.

Yet, in terms of the regulatory issue, interconnection, the case is of strictly limited significance. Prior to the ruling OFTEL had embarked on a three-stage strategy of reform. First, the determination had been made the basis for interim charges across the industry; the second stage, running into 1995, involved the accounting separation of 'BT-Network' from other parts of the company, and, further, a new set of charges; lastly, work continued on longer-term issues, including alternative approaches to interconnection (see below). The legal action, which was not pressed to trial, is therefore seen as a bargaining counter for Mercury, which threatened to unravel months of consultation. Conversely, the DG was able to threaten modification of licence, the dispute being seen to involve the timing of reform.[20] In short, the *Mercury* case highlights not only the potential for, but also the limitations of judicial intervention in the rolling administrative process which is agency regulation.

### (ii) Reform

The position on interconnection is now transformed.[1] The model of individuated agreements – negotiation and determination – can appear dysfunctional when set against the burgeoning contractual matrix of a competitive, multi-operator market. The immediate regulatory response to this was more direct control, the setting of most of BT's interconnection charges on an annual basis. As a 'necessary step' in the liberalisation of the market, the strategy was with accounting separation appropriately designed to provide 'the industry with greater transparency and confidence in the setting of . . . charges and . . . a firm basis for tracking cost allocations'.[2] But requiring OFTEL to be centrally involved in fixing charges is excessively burdensome for the agency and gives little scope for market forces to operate as competition develops at the network level. Recently, OFTEL has taken steps to reduce the need for detailed regulatory intervention in this area. Briefly, this involves a system of interconnection charge controls, within which BT has flexibility in relation to pricing, the degree of control depending on the competitiveness of the relevant service.[3] The regulatory philosophy of competition and deregulation is demonstrated, as also the interplay in the whole development of the familiar administrative law elements of rules, discretion and adjudication.

---

20  OFTEL, *Introduction to Interconnection and Accounting Separation Workshop*, March 1994, p. 8.

 1  See, for the policy development, OFTEL, *Interconnection and Accounting Separation*, 1993; *A Framework for Effective Competition*, 1994; *Effective Competition: Framework for Action* 1995; *Pricing of Telecommunications Services from 1997*, 1996.

 2  OFTEL, *UK Government Comments on Respondents' Comments to the FCC on the Merger of MCI Communications Corporation and British Telecommunications plc*, 1997, para. 45.

 3  In other words, network charge control, with interconnection charges based on incremental costs rather than fully allocated costs as previously. See OFTEL, *Network Charges from 1997*, 1996.

Finally, there is the pursuit of arrangements for the collective expression of voice. Many of the procedural innovations, such as industry or regional public meetings, were developed in relation to interconnection. The context of the early defensiveness on the issue makes the stress on transparent, multilateral processes all the more striking.

## (d) Licensing: compliance and enforcement

It is one thing to establish market rules, another to police them. The DG has a duty under the 1984 Act to ensure that licensees comply with their licence conditions. Such work, which typically involves issues of fair trading, naturally assumes a high priority as the number of operators multiplies. All the more so, when technological change facilitates more sophisticated and discriminating services, and the dominant firm becomes more innovative and market-sensitive in response to the heightened competition. Thus, inside the agency resources are redirected, pro-active steps taken to encourage compliance, and legal casework skills increasingly prized. Ultimately, the demand is pressed for a new set of competition rules. In short, nothing better illustrates the interaction of market change and agency style than the classic administrative law topic of regulatory enforcement.

## (i) Origins

Enforcement is one of the regulatory functions which typically requires a clear statutory framework. The design of the Telecommunications Act 1984 is unexceptional. Section 16 states that the DG 'shall' enforce if satisfied that an operator 'is contravening, or has contravened and is likely again to contravene, any of the conditions of his licence': an exception is made for trivial cases. The DG can make either a final enforcement order or a provisional one (which has temporary effect but can be confirmed). It must 'make such provision as is requisite' – for a provisional order 'as appears to him requisite' – 'for the purpose of securing compliance with that condition'. Section 17 establishes a rudimentary procedural code for the issuing of final orders or the modification or confirmation of provisional ones. The DG must give a period of formal notice and consider any representations. There are no sanctions for breaching a condition until an order takes effect: thereafter, the DG can secure compliance via civil proceedings. The statute contains an ouster clause (above, p. 52). Section 18 provides that if the operator wishes to challenge an order for lack of vires or substantial prejudice by reason of breach of the procedural code, he may apply within six weeks: otherwise 'the validity of a final or provisional order shall not be questioned by any legal proceedings whatever'. Note the exclusion of third parties.

BT's licence contained conditions on fair trading from the outset. It is appropriate to mention as accounting for the bulk of casework prohibitions on cross-subsidies; prohibitions of unfair preference between BT's businesses and those of competitors, and of unfair discrimination between customers (Condition 17); and rules on publication of charges and separate accounts. The provisions are notably strengthened and extended over the years in the effort to maintain effective control, more especially in the light of heightened competition. The early style may be gleaned from the statement: 'it has not been OFTEL's general practice to make the results of its actions publicly known. In most cases, therefore, the case and its outcome have been known only to OFTEL, the operator concerned and any other party involved (usually the complainant).'[4]   The approach under Cruickshank is typically different. 'To improve procedures for investigating complaints, being more transparent in the way OFTEL explains its enforcement activity, and being more proactive' is made a priority project.[5] We see in the new emphasis on enforcement work a regulatory form which is more juridified.

### (ii) Practice and procedure

Let us look more closely. Enforcement work is very variable as regards the amount of gathering of information, analysis and assessment which is required of the agency. Based on recent work-flow trends,[6] there are 35 to 45 live cases at any one time: four or five 'very big' cases, ten to 15 'complex' cases and 20 to 25 'more straightforward' cases. The agency draws attention to the growing difficulty as well as volume of casework as competition flourishes. Generic cases which give rise to a number of related complaints are more common.[7]

Consider a specimen case.[8] Evidence is submitted to OFTEL that some BT staff give out misleading information concerning the comparative costs of services, and generally make inaccurate statements about other companies. A possible breach of Condition 17 is investigated (above, p. 373), and the agency determines that BT has not taken adequate steps to discourage such practices, with the effect of placing competitors at a significant disadvantage. Thus, a provisional order is made, which requires BT to put in place measures necessary to prevent staff engaging in this kind of anti-competitive behaviour. Following the order, BT implements a compliance plan agreed with OFTEL; steps are taken by the agency to monitor the results and their effect on the market.

The case is instructive in several ways. We see first a clear advantage for regulatory action over action in the courts. Not only is there investigative procedure, but the agency is able to fashion a general remedy, and then test for compliance, as the courts are ill-equipped to do (see Chapter 16). Second, and related, a familiar trait in regulatory enforcement is demonstrated: the central role of bargaining. Effectively the formal legal order sets a framework for negotiation and agreement. Third, we learn of the potential for pressure group action or 'test-case' strategy in the field of regulatory enforcement. The evidence was collected by the Consumers' Association, which then made a complaint.

The reform of internal procedures involves some familiar techniques in complaints-handling (Chapter 12). Here, as elsewhere, there is scope for grafting

4   OFTEL, *Effective Competition*, pp. 28-29.
5   OFTEL, *Management Plan for 1996/1997 and Beyond*, 1996, p. 3.
6   OFTEL, *Management Plan*, Ch. 6, p. 5. The statistics include casework under the general competition legislation.
7   For example, product promotions. See OFTEL, *Annual Report 1996*, pp. 48-53.
8   See, for details of individual cases, OFTEL, *Annual Report 1996*, pp. 49-52.

onto the statutory requirements additional stages of review, better to target resources. Thus, OFTEL now operates by means of a preliminary inquiry phase, with a view to determining whether there is a case to answer. Appropriate for a regulatory agency, an advisory role is developed: operators can seek 'guidance' on whether a particular proposal is likely to create competition problems, and to refashion it in the light of OFTEL's 'informal view'.[9] Predictably, 'casework performance targets' and a 'management information system' feature prominently in the priority project; note, however, that the agency finds difficulty in establishing precise targets, precisely because of the great variation in casework.[10] Special attention is paid to speed of process and access to the agency. Initiatives include written guidance to licensees on the best formulation of complaints; a casework 'hotline'; and monthly 'competition surgeries', in which a senior member of the Licence Enforcement and Fair Trading Branch is available in person.

Greater transparency in enforcement is seen by OFTEL to have instrumental advantages. One is predictability: agency determinations clearly involve an exercise of adjudicative power. Particular stress is laid on the properties of 'firewatching' and of 'voice':[11]

- publication of casework will promote better understanding of OFTEL policies, of its interpretation of licence conditions and legislative provisions, and of what OFTEL considers (and what it does not consider) to be conduct or circumstances requiring enforcement or remedial action;
- publication should have a deterrent effect: licensed operators are more likely to adapt their behaviour if they are faced with the certainty of published adverse findings, even if adequate remedies are offered; and
- it will provide an opportunity for those affected by OFTEL's regulation to give their views to OFTEL.

To this end OFTEL now publishes a quarterly *Competition Bulletin*, which is like an interactive set of law reports. New and ongoing cases 'where input from the industry generally would be particularly useful in reaching a conclusion' are detailed. A section on concluded cases summarises outcomes, and gives general guidance on OFTEL's approach: in effect, a source of precedent. Operators are invited 'to discuss the principles underlying decisions in more detail' with the case officer listed.[12] The approach is further extended to the monitoring of compliance with previous orders. Consider the implications. There is, on the one hand, a stark contrast with the early closed style of case work; and, on the other, a major departure from the traditional legal model of enforcement or adjudication where participation is restricted (see further, Chapter 16). Encouraging input from the industry generally is, from the agency's viewpoint, another effective response to a multi-operator environment. Are there not dangers, however, in proceeding in this way in individual cases?

9 OFTEL, *Annual Report 1996*, p. 47.
10 OFTEL aims to resolve 75% of all competition complaints within six months of receiving the complaint, and none in more than a year. OFTEL, *Annual Report 1996*, p. 88.
11 OFTEL, *Effective Competition*, Ch. 6, p. 28.
12 OFTEL, *Competition Bulletin*, Issue No. 1, June 1996, p. 5.

The growth in pro-active work serves to illustrate the advantages of the multi-functional design of the regulatory agency. A structured programme is established 'for identifying and investigating parts of the telecommunications market or aspects of behaviour likely to have a significant adverse effect on competition'.[13] Then again, the agency may identify systemic issues arising from casework, which are carried on as policy issues: typically by means of more consultation papers.[14] Agency work on internal compliance or self-regulation is especially noteworthy:[15]

**Compliance Project**

*Project Objective:* To identify how far the internal compliance arrangements of BT and other [operators] possessing market power can be relied upon to meet OFTEL's fair trading objectives.

*Fit with OFTEL's Objectives*: This project will contribute towards promoting fair, efficient and sustainable competition in networks and services. It will also assist in the development of OFTEL as a fair trading and competition authority and may support its withdrawal from detailed and intrusive regulation.

Identify operators requiring assessment and key aspects of a compliance programme . . .

Review main elements of the relevant [operators'] existing compliance programmes against the chosen criteria . . .

Identify possible areas for development/improvement of existing compliance programmes and discuss with operators.   Ongoing . . .

*(iii) Structural problems*

The steps set out above strengthening enforcement procedures may be considered necessary but insufficient.[16] There are, from the perspective of general competition law, basic flaws in the system. The 1984 Act provides no retrospective sanctions such as fines for abuses of market power. Third parties affected by licence breaches are in a vulnerable position. Legal action may be taken only if an enforcement order is made and then breached, and liability in damages flows from the date of an order. 'As long as a regulated company mends its ways once it is caught, it can meanwhile ignore its licence . . . conditions with impunity.'[17] Again, enforcement is a monopoly system: subject to judicial review OFTEL has sole discretion to ground court action by the making of an order. Then there is the structure or general shape of the rules. A lack of 'fit' is shown between, on

13  OFTEL, *Management Plan*, Ch. 6, p. 2. Ten such pro-active investigations were initiated in 1996.
14  See, for details, OFTEL, *Effective Competition*, Ch. 6.
15  OFTEL, *Management Plan*, Ch. 6, p. 4.
16  See further Hansard Society and European Policy Forum, *Report of the Commission on the Regulation of Privatized Utilities* (London) 1966, Ch. 7.
17  National Consumer Council, *In the Absence of Competition* (London: HMSO) 1989, p. 78.

the one hand, an expanding series of *a priori* prohibitions, and, on the other, an industry which is increasingly dynamic, innovative and competitive. So it is that in *Effective Competition: Framework for Action*, OFTEL signals the need for major reform:[18]

> There are, and are increasingly likely to be, types of anti-competitive behaviour – such as predatory pricing, collusive activity, refusal to supply – which, however effective OFTEL's existing enforcement procedures, would not be caught effectively by the licence condition on undue discrimination and other 'fair trading' conditions.
> Due to the complex nature of the telecommunications market and the practices to be controlled in the market, it is very difficult to draft detailed "behaviour specific" licence conditions to deal with all possible manifestations of anti-competitive conduct. OFTEL's previous practice of plugging gaps through successive detailed licence modifications has resulted in BT's licence becoming increasingly long and complicated. This complexity leads to obscurity and uncertainty in the licensing regime. It also means that each licence deals only with problems that have already arisen and it has to be modified to deal with new problems that arise. Even short-term exploitation of a gap, which only a new form of anti-competitive practice by an operator brings to light, can cause considerable damage to competitors. Uncertainty and the threat of such damage can deter market entry. The considerable time it takes to plug such defects through licence modification can be extremely damaging.[19]
> OFTEL believes, therefore, that there is a clear need, particularly having regard to the special features of the telecommunications market in the UK, to have a general licence condition, giving the Director General the ability to deal with anti-competitive behaviour. OFTEL believes that such a condition is needed in order to provide a more effective deterrent and to enable OFTEL to act speedily and effectively.

### (e) Fair trading (by foul means?)

The scale of agency ambition, to be a competition authority, is laid bare. The upshot is a development which draws together many important strands in regulation and administrative law: on the one hand, the hierarchy of norms and the legitimacy of agency action, and, on the other, the processes of marketisation and Europeanisation, and of regulatory reform. It further grounds a controversial case in judicial review.

To recap, the pricing freedom now afforded BT is presented by OFTEL as part of a package of reforms. It 'can only be done if . . . OFTEL has effective powers to ensure that conditions for fair trading are not undermined by anti-competitive behaviour . . . BT cannot accept one without the other.'[20] Thus:

> 18A.1. The Licensee shall not do anything, whether by act or omission, which has or is intended to have or is likely to have the effect of preventing, restricting or distorting competition . . .

18 OFTEL, *Effective Competition*, Ch. 6, p. 30.
19 Alternatively, OFTEL could seek to use powers under the Fair Trading Act 1973 and the Competition Act 1980 to correct the offending behaviour (above, p. 324). But again these processes are not quick.
20 OFTEL, *Pricing of Telecommunications Services from 1997*, 1996, Ch. 2, pp. 2, 4.

For the purpose of this Condition, such an act or omission will take the form of: (a) Any abuse by the Licensee, either alone or with other undertakings, of a dominant position within the United Kingdom or a substantial part of it . . .(b) The making (including the implementation) of any agreement, the compliance with any decision of any association of undertakings or the carrying on of any concerted practice with any other undertaking which has the object or effect of preventing, restricting or distorting competition within the United Kingdom . . .

18A.2(a) An act or omission of a kind described in paragraph 18A.1 is not prohibited where: (i) it has or would have no appreciable effect on competition.

This catch-all provision involves, for BT, replacing many of the detailed licence conditions on fair trading. But it further illustrates the technique of making general rules by licence (or contract): the use of 'particular law' routinely applied. All new licences will contain the condition: all existing ones are modified accordingly. OFTEL's concerns are today 'not solely with potential anti-competitive behaviour by BT but with that of any operator with market power'. We see how the focus of enforcement action is likely to shift in a competitive industry.

Explicitly linked to the dynamic market structure, the new condition is clearly a solution to the problem of 'fit':[1]

[Because] the Fair Trading Condition ('FTC') . . . focuses on preventing behaviour which has an anti-competitive effect, and does not prohibit specified forms for behaviour outright, it gives licensees greater scope to compete legitimately in the market. In turn, this has the effect of providing greater incentives for investment and innovation, which is beneficial for consumers . . .

With the FTC . . . the scope of the condition is not 'frozen' in the licence, but capable of evolving . . . Consequently, the condition is unlikely to become increasingly inflexible – and possibly inappropriate – simply with the passage of time, as detailed, form based conditions have tended to do. In short, the FTC provides OFTEL with the tools which are essential for it to deal flexibly and speedily with potential anti-competitive behaviour, without having to impose intrusive . . . prohibitions.

'The regulatory state' has been seen as rich in paradox. OFTEL is keen to stress that the package of reforms constitutes 'a major step towards deregulation'.[2] Yet the FTC, in enhancing the enforcement power, is also a form of re-regulation. Again, note how the change to enforcement is agency-led, the government not being ready to take legislative action.[3] Regulatory action to deregulate itself demonstrates a high level of agency discretion.

The condition adopts the wording of the competition provisions (Arts. 85 and 86) of the Treaty of Rome. OFTEL explains that this is 'in order to give licensees as much certainty as possible in relation to its interpretation'. It is provided:

---

1   OFTEL, *UK Government Comments on Respondents' Comments to the FCC on the Merger of MCI Communications Corporation and British Telecoms plc*, 1997, paras. 49-52.
2   OFTEL, *Pricing of Telecommunications Services from 1997*, Ch. 2, p. 1.
3   The Government was at the time consulting on the general issue of domestic competition law. See Department of Trade and Industry, *Tackling Cartels and the Abuse of Market Power: Implementing the Government's Policy for Competition Law Reform*, 1996.

18A.3. Whether any act or omission is prohibited by this Condition shall be determined: (a) with a view to securing that there is no inconsistency with the general principles having application to similar questions of directly applicable competition law, in particular those laid down by the Court of Justice of the European Communities . . . and (b) having regard to—(i) any decision taken, or notice issued, by the European Commission in applying the competition rules contained in the EC Treaty and any relevant pronouncement of the Director General of Fair Trading or report of the Monopolies and Mergers Commission . . .

Non-binding guidelines which the DG issues on the application and interpretation of the power echo the theme.[4] Further, the condition applies to commercial activities in the United Kingdom irrespective of whether they have an impact on trade between Member States. Europeanisation here extends to the indirect impact or ripple effect of Community law on the national jurisdiction.

Let us examine the procedures.[5] The new scheme depends on formalising and supplementing agency practice in the enforcement of other licence conditions (above, p. 373). This involves the DG in the making of initial and final determinations ahead of, or in conjunction with, the provisional and final orders specified in the statute. There is provision for consultation with interested parties ahead of enforcement action: another illustration of a more multilateral process. Provision is also made for the DG to consult an advisory body before making a final determination. Briefly, its members are appointed by the DG, although they are intended to be independent experts, the first chairman being Jeremy Lever QC, a competition law specialist. The deliberations of the body are private and confidential, although the final reports are published. The DG need only 'take into account' any reports. The legal reasons are instructive. In promulgating the scheme, OFTEL is both changing the character of the regulation and constrained by the existing framework. Consider how the agency's chief lawyer at the time might advise Mr. Cruickshank, bearing in mind (i) that the 1984 Act provides no appeal from the DG in enforcement cases and (ii) the common law principle of no fettering of discretion (above, p. 181).[6] Is the advisory body the 'best' that OFTEL can offer by way of independent review?

Behind this lurks the issue of the legitimacy of agency action and the legislative mandate. Agency rule-making which concerns the day-to-day operation of controls is one thing; to use it to transform the character of an agency is something else. Consider the hierarchy of norms. There is, from a 'red light' perspective, good reason to cry 'foul', the institutional structure of the regulation having been laid down by Parliament in statute. Or should the courts be more receptive these days to rule-making by licence or contract, so underscoring the values of agency flexibility and responsiveness? In the event, BT agreed to the licence modification: after protracted bargaining, procedural concessions and the threat of an immediate reference to the MMC. The company, however, challenged the power of OFTEL to proceed in this fashion.

---

4   See OFTEL, *Guidelines on the Operation of the Fair Trading Condition*, 1997.
5   OFTEL, *Fair Trading Condition Enforcement Procedure*, 1997; *Procedural Notes of the Advisory Body on Fair Trading in Telecommunications*, 1997.
6   See further *H Lavender & Son Ltd v Minister of Housing and Local Government* [1970] 1 WLR 1231.

*R v Director General of Telecommunications, ex p British Telecommunications plc*[7]

BT deployed a battery of arguments. The scheme was described as a usurpation of power, which bypassed Parliament. It was said, too, that the condition ranged too widely, in effect reordering the statute. Thus, considerations relevant to Part III, which involves the competition powers shared with the DGFT (above, p. 324), are being extended to Part II, which governs the licensing function. Another argument focused on the need for legal certainty, and BT's concern that, in determining abuse of dominant position, a single regulator was gaining too much discretion. The attempt to Europeanise was also said to be defective and thus contrary to Community law, creating a risk of different interpretation with no mechanism for resolving such conflict. The High Court dismissed the challenge, with the result that the condition is now in general operation.

Phillips LJ:

*Demarcation*

Although the precise viewpoint and priorities of the DGT differ when he is exercising Part II anti-competitive powers and Part III anti-competitive powers, they are both aimed at promoting the same objective, freedom of competition. The duty imposed on the Secretary of State and the DGT by s.3(2)(b) of the 1984 Act . . . is not ring-fenced, nor do we see how it could have been, from the existing duties placed on the DGFT, and transferred to the DGT, under the 1973 and 1980 Acts. It was inevitable that the exercise of his Part II powers by the DGT in the field of telecommunications would do most of the job in that field which would otherwise have fallen to be done, as best it could, under the general powers of the 1973 and 1980 Acts . . . There is no obligation on the DGT, when performing his Part II duties, to attempt to avoid trespassing on what might otherwise be an area of activity under the 1973 and 1980 Acts.

*Specificity . . .*

We are less sanguine than is the DGT as to the adequacy of Community jurisprudence as a sure guide to what is and what is not permitted under Condition 18A. Compliance with Condition 18A calls for judgment of what is and what is not permissible, and to that extent it involves uncertainty. Any uncertainty that there may be is not, however, of such a character as to render the Condition *ultra vires* on the basis that it is void for uncertainty. Nor do we believe that it adds significantly to the uncertainty to which BT was already subject under the terms of the licence. It is fallacious to suppose that BT could proceed on the basis that they would be safe from interference if they complied with the existing conditions of the licence. They could expect that if they indulged in anti-competitive conduct that was not prohibited by existing licence conditions, not least if they were thereby infringing Community law, the result would be likely to be the adoption by the DGT of the modification process, with the delay and uncertainty attendant on it . . .

---

7    (20 December 1996, unreported).

*Arrogation of Power*

We now come to the aspect of this application that has caused us most concern . . . In particular we have asked ourselves why it is that the MMC should have a role in the scheme at the stage of the insertion of conditions by compulsory modification, but not in respect of the insertion of conditions at the outset. We have concluded that the answer lies in consent . . . Once . . . the licence has been granted, rights vest in the licensee . . . it is in [these] circumstances that the 1984 Act provides that, in the absence of consent, a modification can be forced on the licensee only where the MMC determines that the public interest so demands. Where there is consent there is nothing objectionable under the 1984 Act in allowing the DGT to decide what conditions are required in the public interest, having regard to those matters which his duties require and permit him to consider, subject always to the overriding power of veto of the Secretary of State.

In this case BT has consented to Condition 18A, provided that it is within the powers of the DGT to insert it, and the Condition has the support of the Secretary of State . . . We have concluded that the modification under which Condition 18A has been inserted in BT's licence was one which the DGT had power to make . . .

*Community law . . .*

It is a paradox of [the] argument that it is the very fact of the harmonisation of the language of Condition 18A with that of Articles 85 and 86 to which [counsel] objects. What concerns him is . . . that . . . when [conflict] does occur it will appear all the more reprehensible because the DGT will be seen to have reached an erroneous decision when attempting to apply the same, or similar principles, as those of Community law . . . It seems to us that such concern promotes a regard for the purity of Community law over appreciation of the beneficial practical consequences that the language of Condition 18A is designed, and is likely, to achieve . . . In fact there is built into Condition 18 . . . provisions aimed at ensuring that the DTG will adopt an approach to the language of the condition that mirrors the correct approach under Community law. So far as Community law is concerned, we think that the effect of Condition 18A is wholly beneficial.

No decision better illustrates the rise to prominence in administrative law of contractual ideas and regulation by agency. Conversely, the court showed no interest in playing a positive constitutional role in rule-making of the type seen in the *Fire Brigades Union* case.[8] It could prove a landmark decision in agency regulation. If one body can metamorphose, why not others?

## (f) Consumer affairs

'The interests of the consumer are at the heart of OFTEL's objectives.'[9] The agency has to this effect not confined itself to price control and liberalisation. It has evolved both a strategy for consumer representation and a range of regulatory

8   *R v Secretary of State for the Home Department, ex p Fire Brigades Union* [1995] 2 WLR 464, below, p. 596.
9   National Audit Office, *The Work of the Directors General*, p. 75.

mechanisms designed 'with reference to the widely acknowledged consumer policy principles of access, information, quality, equity, safety and redress'. Prominent is Citizen's Charter thinking; indeed OFTEL can claim to have pioneered such techniques as service standards and automatic compensation. There is scope for criticism of arrangements, especially in terms of such values as independence and representativeness.

OFTEL stresses the pluralistic nature of the system of consumer representation, 'which aims to maximise the number and type of communication channels between OFTEL and between different consumer interests'.[10] Its Consumer Affairs Directorate is afforded a broad remit, sharing in policy-formulation on issues affecting both business and residential consumers, particularly in respect of quality of service, price, and availability of choice. One of the responsibilities of the Directorate is liaison with six Advisory Committees on Telecommunications (ACTs), the only mechanism of representation which is a statutory requirement. Committees for England, Wales, Scotland and Northern Ireland are appointed by the minister, and committees for matters affecting the elderly and disabled people, and small businesses, by the DG. The 1984 Act also allows for Telecommunications Advisory Committees (TACs) at the local level, their primary role being to represent the interests of local users to BT, and views are fed in to the national committees. As well as market research and the large scale consultation exercises previously mentioned, OFTEL has set up special panels of users and has maintained links with various other 'players', notably bodies such as the National Consumer Council and business user organisations with a focus on telecommunications. In sum, this is a fine example of the growth of participatory arrangements far in excess of formal, legal requirements.

The ACTs are stated to be independent, but they are dependent on the agency for staff support and funding, and resources have been strictly limited. Then there is the problem of representativeness, all the more vexed in a broad-based, innovative market in which groups or segments of consumers have very different needs (and possibly conflicting interests). OFTEL's own descriptions indicate a mismatch:

> Different groups of consumers will differ in their ability to get what they want from the telecoms market – and so differ in the extent to which they need consumer representation to either help them exercise a choice or help protect them. Larger business customers, for example, may be seen as needing less 'representation' . . . than, say, low income, low spending residential customers.[11]
>
> The members of the ACTs make great efforts to be representative and fair. However, it has proved difficult to ensure a completely representative cross section of consumer interests on the committee. Committee members volunteer their time for free, and it is not always easy to encourage volunteers from all groups in the community . . .[12]

Here, as elsewhere, OFTEL sees the dynamic market structure as fundamental to reform. At one level, 'Consumer protection, while still a valid requirement, is

10  National Audit Office, *The Work of the Directors General*, p. 114.
11  OFTEL, *Meeting Consumer Needs in Telecoms: The Role of Consumer Representation*, 1996, para. 3.3.
12  National Audit Office, *The Work of the Directors General*, p. 115.

less important overall today than in 1984, whilst the need to make sure that consumers can take advantage of choice as it emerges and develops is growing in importance'. At another level, there is 'an important role for organisations that "represent" telecoms' consumer interests. The size and type of role they play will depend on the balance of emphasis between protection and choice, both currently and in the future'.[13] Nor is the committee structure an efficient and effective solution. Predictably, OFTEL has found difficulty in the co-ordination of effort and input, and in obtaining appropriately focused policy advice. Consider two alternative approaches. The first, suggested by OFTEL, involves reordering the formal representation in line with different consumer segments, while maintaining the close institutional links with the agency. Stress is typically laid on the values of flexibility and responsiveness; a structure of smaller 'core' ACTs is envisaged, 'able to expand and contract by co-opting appropriate experts onto sub-committees as issues arise'. The second approach is the model of the Gas Consumers Council (above, p. 335), whereby the consumer representative function is separated from the regulator. In OFTEL's view:[14]

In a rapidly developing competitive market, addressing problems needs flexible arrangements which allow a diversity of consumer opinions and views to be brought to bear. It has been argued that the presence of a large, exclusively telecoms-consumer focused organisation, could help to raise the profile of consumer views in telecoms matters. However, the profile of such an organisation is only one factor influencing the effectiveness of consumer representation – a louder voice, while welcome, may not always be a more effective voice . . .

The ability of a Consumer Council to influence policy would depend crucially on the point at which it is involved in the policy making process. The current arrangements allow the ACTs to be involved early in the policy development process. An independent Consumer Council would be more likely to adopt a reactive stance, and be less able to influence policy in a fast moving market like telecoms.

The argument is not entirely convincing. Is it perhaps suggestive of an agency interest?

### (i) 'Soft law' and information regulation

OFTEL has chosen to play an active role in the shaping of the relationship between the operators and their customers. Typically, the agency has made extensive use of soft law in the guise of codes of practice, despite there being no provision for this in the 1984 Act. The development originated soon after privatisation amid public concern that BT was allowing standards of quality to fall. Under pressure from OFTEL, BT produced a statement of the standard of service its customers could expect (the BT Commitment) and introduced a compensation scheme (the Customer Service Guarantee) for cases of breach. Note the regulatory rationale for redress, essentially one of incentive regulation

---

13 OFTEL, *Meeting Consumer Needs in Telecoms: The Role of Consumer Representation* 1997, paras. 2.6, 2.8.
14 Ibid, paras. 5.18, 5.19.

or market-mimicking: more 'management signal than . . . a realistic attempt to compensate customers for the disbenefits of service failures'.[15] None the less, in Carsberg's words,[16] 'Although the amounts were small, the effect was, not surprisingly, quite sharp, and the quality of services was dealt with quite well.' The scheme, covering such matters as installation, fault repair, deposits and billing, has over the years been extended and toughened.

This product of regulatory bargaining – in the shadow of licence amendment – prefigured the grant of formal powers by the Competition and Service (Utilities) Act 1992 (above, p. 326). Although the regulator's hand was strengthened, there was, according to Carsberg, 'no implication that things were unsatisfactory' – the legislation 'simply tied up a loose end'. Further, the statutory regime is, in the case of telecommunications, one of partial industry regulation; the provisions only apply in relation to firms exercising substantial monopoly power. The agency has in this context chosen to maintain existing practice, and, successfully, to encourage other firms to adopt similar codes.[17] Thus, agency action in the form of soft law has extended well beyond the scope of its statutory rule-making powers; all the more so recently, as the number of operators has escalated. Note here the regulatory potential for routinisation as well as flexibility. OFTEL has produced a Good Practice Guide to inform operators of what is expected.

There is, in line with Citizen's Charter principles, 'far more information for customers on service availability and quality than there was before privatisation'.[18] Information regulation is a typical weapon in the regulatory armoury but it has taken on a higher priority for OFTEL. While information serves to lubricate the market, increased competition buttresses the power of the technique. Greater use may be expected as the agency withdraws from detailed regulation. Thus:[19]

> Promoting better customer information on service quality and price . . . helps ensure consumers can make informed choices – it therefore supports the achievement of effective competition. It also provides objective information [for the regulator] on the extent to which customers are getting a good deal in terms of service quality . . .
> Data collected on a comparable basis across the telecoms industry is increasingly relevant to customers as the number of customers that have a choice of telecoms supply grows. . .

OFTEL has carried out surveys and published reports on a range of relevant topics. BT and Mercury have for a number of years published sets of performance indicators. As regards the industry as a whole, OFTEL sees itself operating 'as a catalyst' to ensure better information.[20] Reference may be made to comparable performance indicators of quality, and to pricing comparisons developed in

15  J. Bowdery, *Quality Regulation and the Regulated Industries* (London: CRI) 1994, p. 27.
16  B. Carsberg, 'Telecommunications Competition in the United Kingdom: A Regulatory Perspective' (1992) 37 *NY Law School LR* 285, 296.
17  OFTEL *Annual Report 1995*, pp. 67-68.
18  National Audit Office, *The Work of the Directors General*, p. 93.
19  OFTEL, *Management Plan for 1996/1997 and Beyond*, 1996, Ch. 8, pp. 2-3; National Audit Office, *The Work of the Directors General*, p. 94.
20  OFTEL, *Annual Report 1996*, p. 66.

conjunction with the Consumers' Association, introduced in 1996 and 1997 respectively.[1] Mr. Major would have approved.

### (ii) Complaints: performance indicator and tiers of review

Complaints as a field of agency action exemplifies the Citizen's Charter style and use of soft law and related techniques. We shall find, first, a hierarchical model of arrangements which combines internal and external review; and, second, a regulatory emphasis on 'firewatching', both in terms of the design of grievance procedures and feedback for substantive policies. Later, in Chapter 12, we shall see how such themes have increasingly infused broad swathes of public administration.

OFTEL has a statutory duty under the 1984 Act to consider any complaints or 'consumer representations' relating to United Kingdom telecommunications services or apparatus. It is a major function of the Consumer Affairs Directorate, with some limited assistance from the ACTs and, at a local level, the TACs. Analysis[2] of the statistics (see Tables 11.1 and 11.2) illustrates the changing nature of the industry. For instance, increased competition has seen the proportion of complaints against BT drop sharply (60% in 1996). Billing disputes have declined, as technological advance has permitted itemisation. Again, the larger complaint totals in recent years is officially explained as primarily a function of the growth in demand for, and diversity of services; as well as a higher public profile for OFTEL and new methods of recording complaints. Perhaps this is unduly optimistic: complaints relating to the quality of customer service, the largest category in 1996, have increased very considerably.

*Table 11.1:   consumer representations to OFTEL/ENACT*

| 1985 | 1986 | 1987 | 1988 | 1989 | 1990 | 1991 | 1992 | 1993 | 1994 | 1995 | 1996 |
|------|------|------|------|------|------|------|------|------|------|------|------|
| 8765 | 13660 | 24186 | 23782 | 31644 | 38530 | 41393 | 41026 | 23413 | 30831 | 38300 | 36050 |

(*Source*:  OFTEL Annual Reports)
*Note*: These figures cover all customer contacts—inquiries as well as complaints. Whereas contacts from people living in England are handled by OFTEL, those from people living in Scotland, Wales and Northern Ireland are dealt with by the relevant ACT.

---

1   See OFTEL, *Annual Report 1995*, p. 65 and Appendix 1; *Annual Report 1996*, p. 67.
2   See for details, National Audit Office, *The Work of the Directors General*, pp. 95-96; OFTEL *Annual Report 1996*, pp. 72-73.

*Table 11.2: Consumer representations to OFTEL/ENACT by category, 1995- 1996*

| Category | Complaints | | Enquiries | |
|---|---|---|---|---|
| | 1995 | 1996 | 1995 | 1996 |
| Disputed bills | 3,500 | 2,800 | 150 | 100 |
| Other problems with bills | 1,500 | 2,550 | 150 | 150 |
| Bill payment problems | 3,000 | 2,900 | 150 | 200 |
| Charges | 2,700 | 1,750 | 300 | 200 |
| Installations | 2,100 | 1,900 | 250 | 150 |
| Payphones | 300 | 250 | 0 | 50 |
| Phone books | 600 | 400 | 100 | 50 |
| Privacy | 1,500 | 1,550 | 250 | 250 |
| Quality of customer service | 3,300 | 4,600 | 150 | 150 |
| Quality of telecoms service | 2,100 | 2,400 | 100 | 200 |
| Repair service | 1,500 | 1,400 | 0 | 50 |
| Rental charges | 600 | 950 | 100 | 50 |
| Network and discount services | 900 | 950 | 100 | 100 |
| General requests for information | 900 | 950 | 3,900 | 2,800 |
| Miscellaneous | 5,400 | 4,400 | 2,700 | 1,800 |
| **Total** | 29,900 | 29,750 | 8,400 | 6,300 |

(*Source:* OFTEL, *Annual Report 1996*, p.73.)

What is the role of the regulator in individual disputes? OFTEL sees itself acting both 'as an advocate' on behalf of customers and as a 'route of appeal'.[3] It often secures the waiving of a charge, or a goodwill payment. Like many

---

3   National Audit Office, *The Work of the Directors General*, p. 75; OFTEL, *Management Plan*, para. 4.21.

Ombudsman systems, agency policy has been to encourage the service provider to consider the matter first and to resolve the dispute directly with the individual. There is no alternative. According to recent estimates, the companies receive each year some 800,000 complaints and queries.[4] The other side of the coin is the placing of this regulatory function under the jurisdiction of the Parliamentary Commissioner (Chapter 13). Note the tiers of complaints procedures: company procedures operating in the shadow of OFTEL; agency procedures operating in the shadow of the PCA (an example of bureaucratic regulation).

Then there is the role of the regulator in the design of company procedures, as prioritised by the Competition and Service (Utilities) Act 1992 (above, p. 327). It is made a licence requirement that operators include in a code of practice guidance on dealing with complaints. The BT Complaint Handling Scheme formally approved by OFTEL provides both a complaints review service within BT and opportunities for inexpensive arbitration. Note that the review service is expressed to be 'independent', which may seem a contradiction in terms. It denotes a typical form under the Citizen's Charter, internal review separate from the direct line management of the person complained against (below, p. 406). In OFTEL's experience the regulatory task has been made easier by increased competition. All operators 'now recognise that an effective and respected procedure for handling general complaints is a must in the market place. . . Commercial necessity demands it'.[5] There is here an important insight for administrative law: the potential for 'exit' concentrating minds on the arrangements for 'voice'. Typically, OFTEL also combines information regulation: comparable data on customer satisfaction with complaint handling designed to further market pressure and so improve performance.

The multi-functional design of the regulatory agency; the limited resources available to OFTEL; and the general problem in regulation of asymmetry of information should all be borne in mind. Private policing in the form of consumer complaints is a useful resource for OFTEL: agency practice exemplifies its use in regulatory policy development, as also self-assessment of performance. So there is much talk of complaints as 'market signals', and of 'tracking', and 'analysis'. Fire-watching, in the form of corrective action against the causes of complaints, goes on across a diverse range of topics:[6] typically by regulatory bargaining; ultimately through the exercise of formal powers. The priority afforded such work as the market diversifies is signalled by investment in a new computer system which allows for more comprehensive classification of complaints.

Not that OFTEL's complaints procedure has been free from criticism. A good example of the biter bit – bureaucratic regulation – is a National Audit Office report in 1993,[7] which drew attention to problems of delay, lack of explanation

---

4   OFTEL, *Management Plan*, para. 4.17.
5   Ibid, para. 4.19.
6   Recent examples include discounts on customers' bills, misleading product promotion, and deployment of BT's technical resources. See OFTEL, *Annual Report 1995*, pp. 71-73; *Annual Report 1996*, pp. 72-73.
7   National Audit Office, *The Office of Telecommunications: Licence Compliance and Consumer Protection*, HC 529, Session 1992-1993, Part 3 and Appendix 4.

and failure to resolve significant numbers of particularly challenging cases: proper training for staff was recommended. Subsequently, OFTEL has reorganised working practices and, in typical fashion, stiffened performance targets: it has also accepted what should be an obvious principle of access, namely that 'consumers . . . receive the same level of help and advice regardless of how they contact' OFTEL.[8] Other criticisms seem less convincing. The tiered format may be a source of confusion and delay, but from a functionalist perspective it allows for the targeting of agency effort on the 'tough nuts' and cases with wider implications. Later, in Chapter 13, this type of argument will be developed in the context of the Parliamentary Commissioner. A final question concerns the nature of the regulatory agency. It has been suggested by Lewis and Birkinshaw[9] that the complaint-handling role of regulators like OFTEL be reassigned to a new Utilities Ombudsman. To this effect we see the value of independence and separation of powers prioritised: 'a person who has bargained prices, objectives and standards may not be sufficiently disinterested to hold the ring as between the utility and its customers.' Per contra, what of the rationale of the specialist, multi-functional agency; and of the values of efficiency and effectiveness? There is a strong case for avoiding such fragmentation of the regulatory role.

### 4. Conclusion

A number of general trends in regulation are demonstrated by the OFTEL regime. A belief in deregulation finds powerful expression in a process of rule-substitution: from detailed norms aimed largely at the dominant firm to broad or overarching competition provisions of general application. A process of Europeanisation extends to regulatory networking and the adoption of a euro-style jurisdiction, as well as the reception in national law of cases and directives. We note too the attack on, and change in, an old regulatory culture: a model of agency regulation which implies a more legalistic relationship between the state and corporate sector, and, in particular, increased stress on process values.

This regulatory regime established the basic organisational pattern for 'regulation UK-style'. Operations display a high degree of agency discretion, as in the setting of the price control and the general field of licence modification. The importance to the regulatory model of non-legal factors, most obviously the personality of the regulator, is underscored. Then again, each regulatory agency is different. The tide of competition is further advanced in telecommunications than in the markets of the other privatised utilities.[10] And competition may be seen today as the hallmark of the OFTEL regime, in terms not only of the policy goal but also of the regulatory norms and procedures.

---

8    OFTEL, *Annual Report 1995*, p. 71.
9    N. Lewis and P. Birkinshaw, *When Citizens Complain: Reforming Justice and Administration* (Buckingham: Open University Press) 1993, p. 219.
10   See, for comparative market analysis, Price Waterhouse, *Regulated Industries: the UK Framework* (London: Centre for the Study of Regulated Industries) 2nd edn., 1996; also National Audit Office, *The Work of the Directors General*, above.

Alternatively, the regime may be considered in the light of the different criteria for the legitimacy of agency action (Chapter 10). Take the model of legislative mandate, which was seen to affect simplicity. OFTEL gives an excellent illustration, the statutory provisions being increasingly removed from the main trajectory of agency policy-making and implementation. Or take the model of efficiency and effectiveness, seen to present difficulties of measuring agency performance. OFTEL has presided over a remarkable transformation in the industry: not only is there now much more competition and many different services, but prices in real terms have fallen dramatically.[11]   Conversely, the extent to which this would have happened anyway by reason of technological advance and international developments is a natural subject of dispute.

The regime is especially noteworthy given the interest in fair procedure as a criterion of legitimacy in administrative law. Recurrent themes in this chapter are, first, the changing patterns of regulatory control and process, and, second, the close interaction of market structure and agency style. Thus, a shift in modalities is identified, as between a closed, bilateral approach expressive of flexibility and compromise, and open, multilateral procedures of consultation and decision. There is much to be admired in the development, which demonstrates a genuine commitment to a due process model of regulation, far beyond formal legal requirements.

Transparency should be a value, not an obsession. Some dangers and difficulties arise with the approach under Cruickshank. Major consultation exercises of the type pursued by OFTEL appear unwieldy. Structural imbalances in the organisation and resources of different interests are highlighted by problems concerning the independence and representativeness of consumer bodies. Potential conflicts arise when individual enforcement action is combined with a broad input or multilateral process. It may be good to talk, but it is important for the regulator to take prompt and decisive action where necessary.

Extending the argument, a process of juridification is a major feature in the regulatory development. The rise to prominence of enforcement work is a classic example, highlighting the need for legal casework skills and building up a system of precedent. A growth in recourse to courts is also under way; regulatory transparency feeds the potential for creative lawyering. There are the usual risks of cost and delay, and of disruption to relations within the industry; as also the problem of adversarial, bipolar process in matters of broad economic regulation. Attention is drawn to the continuing difficulties of the courts in reconciling public regulatory and private contractual power.

Finally, let us look forward. It seems inevitable that pressures for juridification will increase by reason of progressive Europeanisation and globalisation. The role and status of the national regulator will change as tiers of regulation multiply at the supra-national level, and as communications technologies converge. The study further demonstrates a propensity in dynamic market

---

11   By over 40% in the period to 1996. See OFTEL, *Pricing of Telecommunications Services from 1997*, Ch. 2.

conditions for the formal, legal and competitive frameworks of regulation to move out of kilter. The 1984 Act, designed to provide for the regulation of a fixed link duopoly, is no longer appropriate to the new horizons of the liberalised United Kingdom telecommunications market. Exactly how this problem is resolved will be a vital test of the capacities of national administrative law in a complex global and information age.

Chapter 12

# Complaining: is anybody there?

## 1. Alternative dispute resolution

Much of the energy of modern administrative law has been occupied with devising alternative machinery for dispute resolution. Alternative to what?[1] In the course of the next chapters, we shall see that this question can have more than one answer. We could be talking of inquisitorial alternatives to adversarial procedure, of inquiries as an alternative to tribunals, of ministerial appeals such as we find in the educational or planning systems, of administrative compensation schemes as an alternative to tort law or, in the case of contract, of arbitration instead of litigation. All these and many others have been tried. There is a natural tendency, however, for administrative lawyers to treat the question as relating to tribunals as alternatives to courts.[2]

At the turn of the century, concern was growing over what today would be called the 'access to justice' problem. A famous Victorian aphorism described justice, 'like the Ritz hotel', as open to both rich and poor. The simile was a telling one. Legal services for the poor were exceptional and virtually restricted in civil cases to charitable provision. Litigation, even in essential areas such as divorce and maintenance, landlord and tenant and industrial accident, was quite simply beyond the means of the majority of the population. Despite patchy efforts at reform, this situation did not change materially until after World War II, with the introduction of the Legal Aid and Advice Act 1949.[3]

Courts were not only inaccessible but were increasingly gaining a reputation for political conservatism. Judiciary and Bar Council were notable for their constant opposition to all measures of law reform. The courts' performance in carrying out 'regulatory' functions, (e.g. in deciding statutory appeals against railway and canal companies) was poor. Worse still was the experience of arbitration under the Workmen's Compensation Acts of 1897 and 1906, largely effected by county court judges. Intended as 'inexpensive' machinery for dispute resolution, the procedure led to a flood of conflicting decisions emanating from pro- and anti-employer judges, swamping the Court of Appeal. The experience

---

1   See W. Twining, 'Alternatives to What? Theories of Litigation Procedure and Dispute Settlement in Anglo-American Jurisprudence: Some Neglected Classics' (1993) 56 MLR 380.
2   H. Genn, 'Tribunals and Informal Justice' (1993) 56 MLR 393, 394. And see C. Glasser and C. Harlow, 'Legal Services and the Alternatives: The LSE Tradition' in R. Rawlings (ed.), *Law, Society and Economy* (Oxford: Clarendon) 1996.
3   See further B. Abel-Smith and R. Stevens, *Lawyers and the Courts* (London: Heinemann) 1967, Ch. VI or R. Egerton, *Legal Aid* (London: Kegan Paul) 1945.

391

induced government to experiment with alternatives. The Old Age Pensions Act 1908 set up local committees to arbitrate disputes, with appeal to the Local Government Board. Benefit disputes under the National Insurance Act 1911 were settled by local Courts of Referees with appeal to an Insurance Commissioner, bypassing the courts. These were not the *first* administrative tribunals,[4] but they do mark the start of modern welfare adjudication. 'The tribunals were providing a free service to their users and in front of them legal representation was unnecessary'.[5] The foundation of our modern system of administrative tribunals was being laid.

In the search for alternatives, green light theory came into its own. Many of the green light theorists whose work we studied in Chapter 3 were actively involved in working for reform of legal services. Laski campaigned for legal aid.[6] Robson, who criticised courts for doing 'absolutely nothing to modernize, to cheapen or to bring into accord with modern needs a fantastic procedure which has been obsolete for at least a century',[7] never ceased to argue for a systematised administrative justice 'in the main independent of the courts of law'. Robson believed that to submit tribunals to judicial control was to re-introduce 'the legalism and unfreedom of the formal judicature, the avoidance of which is one of the main objects sought to be obtained by the machinery of administrative justice'. His wide-ranging study of 'Trial by Whitehall'[8] compared and contrasted judicial and administrative decision-making, looking not only at areas, such as vehicle licensing and planning, where rights of appeal were vested directly in ministers, but also contributing studies of esoteric tribunals such as Railway Courts, Transport Tribunals, War Damage Tribunals and Tribunals for Children's Homes. His inquiries extended to domestic tribunals.

Amongst the objectives of Robson and those who followed him was to devise user-friendly machinery for the resolution of 'small claims'.[9] Street, an ardent protagonist of 'justice in the welfare state', identified the special needs of the typical clientele of administrative justice:[10]

> Here is a class of litigant often unfamiliar with the legal process and lacking the financial means to pay to be represented at hearings. Nervous, inarticulate, over-awed, mistrustful of bureaucracy, impatient of legal forms - he is indeed a special case ... He must be around the table with people, some of whom he sees as like himself, people to whom he can speak freely, who will be tolerant of his fumbling, discursive, often irrelevant, disorderly presentation of his case. Accessibility to justice in the land of

4   See further H. Arthurs 'Rethinking Administrative Law: A Slightly Dicey Business', 17 Osgoode Hall Law J. 1 and *Without the Law: Administrative Justice and Legal Pluralism in Nineteenth-Century England* (Toronto: Univ. of Toronto Press) 1985.

5   B. Abel-Smith and R. Stevens (above, note 3), p. 117.

6   Lord Chorley, for many years editor of the Modern Law Review, published many articles on law reform and legal services: see C. Glasser, 'Radicals and Refugees: the Foundation of the Modern Law Review and English Legal Scholarship' (1987) 50 MLR 688.

7   W. A. Robson, 'The Report of the Committee on Ministers' Powers' (1932) 3 Pol. Q. 346 (above, pp. 73–74).

8   W. A. Robson, *Justice and Administrative Law* (London: Stevens) 3rd edn., 1951.

9   See e.g. T. Ison, 'Small Claims' (1972) 35 MLR 18.

10  H. Street, 'Access to the Legal System and the Modern Welfare State: A European Report from the Standpoint of an Administrative Lawyer' in M. Cappelletti (ed.), *Access to Justice and the Welfare State*, (Florence: European Institute) 1981, p. 310.

welfare benefits is not merely helping the claimant; it is ensuring beforehand that there is a tribunal, an atmosphere, a procedure welcomely receptive and comforting to him.

Detailed studies of tribunals and their users of the kind called 'socio-legal', followed, fleshing out these needs. Such studies are often labelled 'bottom-up' studies. Mashaw's study of American welfare administration[11] is, for example, an archetypal 'bottom-up' study of administrative dispute-resolution. Mashaw does not focus on the handful of decisions taking by appellate courts but on the millions of decisions taken weekly by welfare administrators with a view to improving their quality. This style of work is represented in our case study of welfare adjudication in Chapter 14.

Even the keenest advocates of tribunals such as Robson were not at first prepared to move far from the legal paradigm; much of his classic study of administrative justice is devoted to identifying judicial qualities and the characteristics of adjudication. Many years later, Street was dismissive of conciliation as a technique for resolving welfare disputes, describing it[12] 'as an excuse for the adjudicator not discharging his hard appointed task of finding out what the facts in dispute are and applying the relevant law to them'. Classic red light theory, with its traditional bias, noted in Chapter 2, towards treating courts as a method of restraining administrative and executive excess, was more limited. From this 'top-down' perspective, the appellate courts assume undue importance and tribunals inevitably become court-substitutes. Tribunals exist, in Wade's phrase, to provide 'simpler, speedier, cheaper and more accessible justice than do the ordinary courts'.[13]

It was, as Griffith remarked at the time,[14] a perverse consequence of the Crichel Down affair that it prompted a review of procedure in tribunals and inquiries, already the most formalised area of administrative justice. The Franks Committee on Tribunals and Inquiries which followed Crichel Down in 1955 and which is discussed fully in Chapter 14, characterised tribunals as 'machinery for adjudication'. Not only did it extend the supervisory jurisdiction of the High Court and Lord Chancellor's Department but it also recommended the introduction of legal representation, legal advice and legal aid, a recipe for further formalisation. Although lawyers and legal aid never did become the norm in tribunals, the topic was to occupy the agenda of the Council on Tribunals for many years.[15] Over the next quarter-century, tribunals were pushed increasingly towards a court-substitute function until they came to be accepted as 'a third tier in the administration of civil justice'.[16] The judicialisation that Robson had feared was under way; the link with ADR had been broken.

11  J. Mashaw *Bureaucratic Justice; Managing Social Security Claims* (New Haven: Yale University Press) 1983.
12  'Access to the Legal System' (above, note 10), p. 310.
13  H. W. R. Wade and C. Forsyth, *Administrative Law*, p. 905.
14  J. Griffith, 'The Crichel Down Affair' (1955) 18 MLR 557.
15  See Annual Reports of Council on Tribunals for 1972/3 (HC 82, 1973/4) and 1974/5 (HC 679, 1975/6). See also Evidence of Council on Tribunals to Lord Chancellor's Advisory Committee in 1973/4 (HC 20, 1974/5).
16  B. Abel-Smith and R. Stevens (above, note 3), p. 264. See also, *Justice*/All Souls *Administrative Justice – Some Necessary Reforms* (Oxford: Clarendon) 1988 (hereafter *Justice*/All Souls).

## 2. Questions of procedure: inquiries

There is general agreement that tribunals and inquiries serve different purposes:[17]

> Tribunals had their origin in the need to adjudicate disputes ... more efficiently and cheaply than was possible in the courts. They are, or should be, essentially judicial and most of them, properly regarded, are courts of a special character adjudicating against a background of legal precedent ... Classically, inquiries were limited to investigation, making no final decision but providing the material upon which a decision could be made by a government minister. Inquiries had their origin ... in the need to provide an alternative to Private Bill procedure under which objectors to proposals for the acquisition of powers by Government or public authorities had to appear before parliamentary committees.

The argument over inquiry procedure goes back beyond Franks. Franks concentrated on planning and land inquiries, numerically the commonest, where the inquiry technique was more developed. Its reasoning shaped by the old-fashioned, Donoughmore analysis (above, p. 31), Franks saw its task as being to find 'a reasonable balance' between 'judicial' and 'administrative' functions':[18]

> Our general conclusion is that these procedures cannot be classified as purely administrative or purely judicial. They are not purely administrative because of the provision of a special procedure preliminary to the decision – a feature not to be found in the ordinary course of administration – and because this procedure ... involves the testing of an issue, often partly in public. They are not on the other hand purely judicial, because the final decision cannot be reached by the application of rules and must allow the exercise of a wide discretion in the balancing of public and private interest ... If the administrative view is dominant the public inquiry cannot play its full part in the total process, and there is a danger that the rights and interest of the individual citizens affected will not be sufficiently protected. In these cases it is idle to argue that Parliament can be relied upon to protect the citizen, save exceptionally ... if the judicial view is dominant there is the danger that people will regard the person before whom they state their case as a kind of judge provisionally deciding the matter, subject to an appeal to the Minister. This view overlooks the true nature of the proceeding, the form of which is necessitated by the fact that the Minister himself, who is responsible to Parliament for the ultimate decision, cannot conduct the inquiry in person.

While Franks stressed the hybrid function of inquiries and the policy element which was always present, the effect of bracketing tribunals and inquiries encouraged an assumption that 'what is right for a tribunal is also right for an inquiry'. At the time of Franks, the argument over inquiries centred on secrecy and the amount of information available to objectors; post-Franks it was to crystallise in terms of 'how much 'judicialization' the inquiry procedure can stand'.[19] Just such an argument may be found in *Bushell's* case,[20] when the courts drew a line under judicialisation in favour of the argument for policy.

17   *Justice*/All Souls, para. 10.2.
18   Cmnd. 218, paras. 272-274.
19   B. Schwarz and H. Wade, *Legal Control of Government, Administrative Law in Britain and the United States* (Oxford: OUP) 1972, p. 163.
20   *Bushell v Secretary of State for the Environment* [1980] 3 WLR 22; below, p. 518.

Franks had demanded a statutory code of procedure for planning inquiries. The result was inevitably to increase procedural formality. On the face of things, the inspector who conducts the inquiry has a wide discretion. In reality, this is structured by a detailed procedural code[1] suggestive of the stages in trial-type procedure; e.g. notice of an inquiry must be published, statements are to be served on applicants, documents must be discovered, the persons entitled to appear are listed and a right to counsel specified. The statutory code opened the inquiry process to increased court control. Case law stipulated that the Minister in deciding planning appeals should adopt a judicialised style of decision-making. The conceptual vocabulary of lawyers, distinguishing, for example, 'fact', 'law', 'policy', 'opinion', appeared in the cases. The judicial nature of the inquiry was emphasised; it was held, e.g., that the Minister's 'policy' decisions ought to be based on the inspector's findings of fact, that they must be supported by 'sufficient evidence' and that a decision to differ from the inspector's recommendations should be justified in an adequately reasoned letter of decision. These are developments towards 'rational decision-making' with which we are already familiar from Chapter 4. A similar trend towards formality was observed in local inquiries, where procedure was not statutory. The consequence was again a move towards trial-type, adversarial procedure: in short, judicialisation or juridification. We find a planning officer complaining,[2] 'We must behave as though every decision is going to be challenged even though only a handful of cases a year are'. Amongst the matters of which she complains is that an inspector must not 'base a fact or conclusion on something he has seen with his own eyes (which used to be thought the reason for his inspection of the site) which has not been discussed at the inquiry'.

Widespread confusion was also created about the purpose of planning inquiries (note that Grant is talking in this passage generically about planning appeals and inquiries):[3]

> The system serves three often contradictory purposes. First, it provides a means for challenging local planning authority decisions. It offers applicants for planning permission the opportunity to go over the head of the planning authority, and it gives them an important safeguard against arbitrary decision making at local level. Second, it provides a forum for public participation through the procedures of the local public inquiry, with an opportunity to question the assumptions of the main protagonists and to put forward alternative points of view. Third, it provides the Secretary of State with the means to supervise the development control functions of local planning authorities and to reassert national policy.

1  The Town and Country Planning (Inquiries Procedure) Rules 1974 (SI 1974/419) now replaced by Town and Country Planning (Inquiries Procedure) Rules 1988 (SI 1988/944) and Town and Country Planning (Determination by Inspectors) (Inquiries Procedure) Rules 1988 (SI 1988/945). See G. Graves, R. Max and T. Kitson 'Inquiry Procedure – Another Dose of Reform?' [1996] JPL 99.
2  P. Payne, 'Planning Appeals' (1971) 57 J. of the Town Planning Institute 114, 116-117.
3  M. Grant, *Urban Planning Law* (London: Sweet and Maxwell) 3rd edn., 1991, p. 553. This is the theme of P. McAuslan, *The Ideologies of Planning Law* (Oxford: Pergamon) 1980. See also P. McAuslan, *Land, Law and Planning* (London: Weidenfeld and Nicolson) 1975.

Not only are these objectives, as Grant points out, frequently incompatible but it may also be thought that the word 'inquiry' is a misnomer; it has indeed been held that an inspector has no duty to undertake an investigatory function. [4]

Judicialisation has produced a whiplash effect, provoking demands for streamlined procedures to cut the associated costs and delays. [5] The Conservative Government elected in 1979 promised a new planning era, committed to development and shorn of procedural complexity. The requirement of local inquiries was restricted by the Local Government, Planning and Land Act 1980. The General Development (Amendment) Order 1981 removed 'small householder development' from the planning system. Resolution of disputes through negotiation was encouraged, while planning appeals were delegated to inspectors and increasingly decided by means of written representations: the percentage has risen steadily over the years. [6] In short, alternative dispute resolution was back on the agenda; pre-appeal negotiations are in favour with refusal to settle penalised by costs, planning bargains and agreements encouraged and provision made to substitute 'informal hearings' where a formal inquiry has been requested. These procedures are popular because they are cheap and speedy and legal representation is unnecessary. On the other hand, they are less participatory and subject to abuse, offering none of the formal protections afforded by a planning inquiry. Third parties are virtually excluded and the wider public interest may also be prejudiced. [7]

Land use planning is not, however, the only case where inquiry procedure may be used. A special inquiry may be set up to investigate a disaster or other matter of public concern, as after the coal tip disaster at Aberfan or the football stadium disaster at Hillsborough or Lord Scarman's inquiry into policing after the Brixton riots (below). This may be done either by a Minister or under the Tribunals of Inquiry (Evidence) Act 1921. Smaller inquiries are used on a routine basis to examine railway accidents, and child abuse inquiries have become distressingly common. [8] Public authorities may also set up an internal inquiry into the operation of one of its departments, the report of which will not normally be published. In some ways and on some occasions, inquiries act very much as court-substitutes. Accident inquiries, for example, perform much the same function as coroners' courts, which incidentally use a variant of the same inquisitorial procedure. The subject matter of child abuse inquiries could re-surface before a criminal court or

4   *Federated Estates Ltd v Secretary of State for the Environment* [1983] JPL 812; *Bushell's* case, below, p. 518. See also Department of the Environment *Efficiency, Effectiveness of Local Plan Inquiries* (London: HMSO) 1994.
5   G. Dobry, *Review of the Development Control System* (the Dobry Report) (London: HMSO) 1974, 1975. See also *Planning Appeals, Call-in and Major Public Inquiries*, HC 181 (1985/6) which introduced a number of major reforms.
6   Delegation to inspectors was introduced in 1968 on the recommendation of Franks: Cmd. 218, paras. 392-394. Figures given by the Dobry Report for the years 1969-1978/79 show a decline in Ministers' cases and a rise in written representation procedure. See now, Housing and Planning Act 1986; Town and Country Planning (Appeals) (Written Representations Procedure) Regulations 1987 (SI 1987/701); DoE circ. 11/87.
7   See, e.g., *Tesco Stores Ltd v Secretary of State for the Environment* [1995] 1 WLR 759.
8   See *Child Abuse: A Study of Inquiry Reports 1980-89* (London: HMSO) 1991.

as the subject of an action in tort. Later, in considering the police complaints system (below, p. 414), we shall see that the subject matter of inquiries often overlaps with that of complaints systems as well as litigation.

If tribunals are, as the Franks Committee insisted, machinery for adjudication, then inquiries are more ambiguous. The primary function of an inquiry is to *investigate*: to search for and discover 'the truth'. As a barrister and experienced inquiry chairman, Louis Blom-Cooper sees this function as justifying 'inquisitorial' procedure, in which the chairman of the inquiry directs the proceedings and questions the witnesses. In a complex inquiry, such as the Scott Inquiry into the complicity of government in the illegal export of arms to Iraq,[9] counsel may be appointed to assist the inquiry. In a passage which certainly raises some questions about the objectives of the legal system, seen here as an adversarial contest, Blom-Cooper argues:[10]

> The adversarial procedure adopted in the legal system, admirable as it may be for the resolution of defined issues in dispute between identifiable parties, is wholly inappropriate [for an inquiry]. There are, in a public inquiry, no immediately discernible issues to be tried according to well-established rules of evidence ...
>
> Since the parties to litigation formulate their respective cases, call their own witnesses to support one party's case or refute the other party's case, and seek adjudication on the basis exclusively of such evidence, each party may seek to establish its own perceived version of the events. The result may be a satisfactory method for determining who should win or lose the forensic contest. It does not aim to establish an objective truth, still less to identify the relationship between that truth and a wider conception of the public interest. The public inquiry, on the other hand, is constructed – even instructed – precisely to elicit the truth. It will ask itself: what happened; how did it happen; and who, if anybody, was responsible, culpably or otherwise, for it having happened.

Here Blom-Cooper identifies a tension between trial-type, adversarial proceedings and inquisitorial procedure, less protective of witnesses. The point is brought home forcibly by Lord Howe, himself an angry witness at the Scott Inquiry:[11]

> Throughout the three working years of the inquiry, all the evidence was adduced in response to questions from Sir Richard Scott himself or from counsel to the Inquiry, Presiley Baxendale, Q.C. No distinction was drawn by either between examination-in-chief or cross-examination of witnesses. There was no cross-examination of any witness save by the Inquiry itself, no closing speeches, no face-to-face dialogue between the Inquiry and any representative of the outside world. When I first complained that this was to be an inquiry at which – as never before in modern times – 'defence lawyers may be seen but not heard', I had scarcely believed myself. But Sir Richard Scott had indeed explicitly discarded almost every one of the established principles.

9  *Inquiry into the Export of Defence Equipment and Dual-Use Goods to Iraq and Related Prosecutions*, HC 115 (1995/6) noted I. Leigh and L. Lustgarten, 'Five Volumes in Search of Accountability: The Scott Report' (1996) 59 MLR 695.
10  L. Blom-Cooper, 'Public Inquiries' (1993) 46 Current Legal Problems 204, 205-206.
11  Lord Howe,'Procedure at the Scott Inquiry' [1996] PL 445, 446-447; L. Blom-Cooper, 'Witnesses and the Scott Inquiry' [1994] PL 1. See also Annual Report of the Council on Tribunals 1995/6, HC 114 (1996/7) pp. 6–8.

The position of witnesses to inquiries had been considered by a Royal Commission chaired by Lord Salmon, a distinguished law lord, in 1966, which had recommended[12] that witnesses should receive notice of allegations against them, be given an opportunity to prepare a case assisted by legal advisers and that legal expenses be met out of public funds. Scott, however, challenges Howe's analysis both of the witness's position and the inquiry's function, saying, 'persons who are asked to assist an inquisitorial inquiry by giving evidence on matters being investigated do not have a "case" ... The conception that a witness needs to prepare "a case" introduces an element inherent in adversarial proceedings but alien to an inquisitorial inquiry at least at the investigation stage'.

In her study of administrative procedures,[13] Ganz asserts that judge-made principles of administrative procedure inevitably veer towards the tried and tested judicial procedures of any given society, hence the antipathy shown by British lawyers to inquisitorial procedure. The term 'inquisitorial' possesses an opprobrious undertone. This may show itself in hostility to the procedures of regulatory agencies. The judiciary has, for example, been accused of emasculating the investigatorial, 'formal investigation' procedure of the Commission for Racial Equality (and also the Equal Opportunities Commission), intended to allow 'own initiative' investigations into endemic discriminatory practices in industry,[14] which they have described as 'an engine of oppression' and likened to the Spanish inquisition. Similarly, Ganz refers to criticism of the Monopolies and Mergers Commission as centring on 'the inquisitorial nature of the proceedings', a term used to cover: private hearings; the absence of rights of cross-examination; the ill-defined nature of the 'charges'; and the dual role of the MMC as 'judge and prosecutor' – accusations similar to those made by Lord Howe.

To summarise the argument, one view of an inquiry is as machinery for *investigation*, a classification used to justify the substitution of inquisitorial procedure for traditional adversarial adjudication. In this analysis (Scott), what is happening is an unwarranted attempt to graft trial-type procedures on to machinery created for another purpose. An alternative view (Howe) would see the inquiry procedure as designed to undercut the procedural protections of adversarial proceedings. This is the dilemma which Blom-Cooper is unable to resolve.

## 3. Ombudsmen: the 'complaints man'

A secondary effect of Crichel Down was to stimulate demand for a new complaints machinery to handle disputes which, like Crichel Down, fell between courts and the political system.[15] In 1961, *Justice* published a seminal report[16] arguing the

12  Report of the Royal Commission on Tribunals of Inquiry, Cmnd. 3121 (1966). Technically, the Report referred only to tribunals established under the Tribunals of Inquiry (Evidence) Act 1921. Scott was an ad hoc, ministerial tribunal. The citation from Sir Richard Scott is from an unpublished lecture cited by Howe.

13  G. Ganz, *Administrative Procedures* (London: Sweet and Maxwell) 1974.

14  V. Sacks and J. Maxwell, 'Unnatural Justice for Discriminators' (1984) 47 MLR 334. See also, ss. 48-52 Race Relations Act 1976; *Hillingdon London Borough Council v Commission for Racial Equality* [1982] AC 779; *Commission for Racial Equality v Amari Plastics Ltd* [1982] QB 1194; *Mandla v Dowell-Lee* [1983] QB 1. Above, p. 308.

case for a Scandinavian-style 'complaints man' or Ombudsman with a general grievance-handling remit. The office of Ombudsman dates back to nineteenth-century Sweden (1809) but the idea gained wide appeal only after the establishment of the Danish Ombudsman in 1954, reaching fever pitch in the reformist 1970s.[17] Since then, Ombudsmen have been installed in public offices throughout the world,[18] one of the latest recruits being the European Ombudsman.[19]

The first Ombudsman to land on our shores was the Parliamentary Commissioner (PCA), seen today as 'part of the fabric of the United Kingdom's unwritten constitution',[20] a claim which we shall try to evaluate through a case study of the office in the next chapter. The Ombudsman technique has established itself as a central component of administrative justice; today we find in addition to the PCA (1967), a PCA and Commissioner for Complaints for Northern Ireland (1969), a Commission for Local Administration (CLA) (1974),[1] a Health Services Commissioner (HSC) (1974)[2] whose office doubles with the PCA, and a Prisons Ombudsman (1994). Required on occasion to co-operate formally (as when the PCA and CLA conduct joint investigations) Ombudsmen also meet regularly to exchange ideas. An International Ombudsman Institute has come into being which lists nearly 200 members in its *Directory of Ombudsmen* and promotes and publicises the office. Ombudsmen have proliferated in the private sector, achieving a wide acceptance and popularity within the country as an all-purpose method of handling complaints. Today we have several statutory Ombudsmen, including one for legal services established by the Courts and Legal Services Act 1990[3] and a Pensions Ombudsman installed by the Social Security Act 1990. In addition, we find Banking, Building Societies, and Insurance Ombudsmen,[4] a key difference being that these form part of schemes of self-regulation and are responsible to the industries which set them up and fund them.[5]

15  J. Mitchell, 'The ombudsman fallacy' [1962] PL 24.
16  *The Citizen and the Administration* (London: Stevens) 1961 (the Whyatt Report).
17  Classic accounts are W. Gellhorn, *Ombudsmen and Others; Citizens' Protectors in Nine Countries* (Cambridge, Mass: Harvard University Press) 1966; D. Rowat, *The Ombudsman. Citizen's Defender* (London: Allen and Unwin) 1968; F. Stacey, *Ombudsmen Compared* (Oxford: Clarendon) 1978.
18  G. Caiden (ed.), *International Handbook of the Ombudsman. Evolution and Present Function* (London: Greenwood Press) 1983.
19  Created by Art. 138c of the Treaty of European Union to investigate maladministration by Community institutions: see A. Marias Epaminondas (ed.), *The European Ombudsman* 1994.
20  First Report from the Select Committee on the PCA, HC 129 (1990/1) p. xii.
 1  Part III of the Local Government Act 1974 as amended by Part II of the Local Government and Housing Act 1989.
 2  National Health Service Reorganisation Act 1973 consolidated by Health Service Commissioner Act 1993. For an evaluation see, P. Giddings, 'Complaints, Remedies and the Health Service Commissioner' (1993) 71 Pub. Admin. 377.
 3  See R. James and M. Seneviratne, 'The Legal Services Ombudsman: Form versus Function?' (1995) 58 MLR 187.
 4  P. Rawlings and C. Willett, 'Ombudsman Schemes in the United Kingdom's Financial Sector: The Insurance Ombudsman, the Banking Ombudsman and the Building Societies Ombudsman' (1994) 17 J. of Consumer Policy 307; R. James and M. Seneviratne, 'The Building Societies Ombudsman Scheme' (1992) 11 CJQ 157; P. Morris and J. Hamilton, 'The Insurance Ombudsman and PIAS Ombudsman: A Critical Comparison (1996) 47 NILQ 119.
 5  See, generally, A. Mowbray, 'Ombudsmen – The Private Sector Dimension' in W. Finnie, M. Himsworth and N. Walker (eds.), *Edinburgh Essays in Public Law* (Edinburgh: EUP) 1991.

Since the original Swedish concept has been everywhere adapted to local conditions, Ombudsman institutions vary in constitutional position, operating methods and objectives; there is not one Ombudsman but many.[6] The variance is often reflected in the title. Thus the French title of 'Mediator' (1973)[7] points to the use of non-litigious or conciliatory techniques while the Spanish title, 'Defender of the People' (1978) indicates an important role in the protection of human rights.[8] Such a pronounced public advocacy role is uncommon. A common factor is that Ombudsman procedure is invariably inquisitorial. All the complainant has to do is complain; no expensive lawyers are necessary, no evidence has to be amassed and no case has to be proved. The Ombudsman takes over control of the investigation, typically possessing powers to trawl through government documents and offices and question officials informally in their offices. In this country, Ombudsmen also resemble inquiries, in that their recommendations (never judgments) are not usually enforceable. The PCA's function was once described – inaccurately as it turned out – very much in the language of ADR as 'a practical, very typically British-adapted arrangement designed to put wrong right in the quickest and most effective way'.[9]

A fuller account of this novel documentary and inquisitorial procedure is contained in Chapter 13. Here we need only note the familiar conflict between administrative/inquisitorial and adversarial/trial-type procedures, marked by the creeping spread of judicial review. Courts have from the outset shown willingness to scrutinise CLA decisions and to lay down the conditions for exercise of its discretionary powers to investigate.[10] Initial unwillingness to review the decisions of the PCA has given way to the judicial desire for omni-competence.[11] Jurisdiction has been established over the statutory Pensions Ombudsman.[12] Only the Insurance Ombudsman has so far avoided judicial scrutiny on the ground that he is a creature of contract, falling outside the supervisory public law jurisdiction.[13] What is noteworthy about the challenges is that many are premissed on adversarial procedure, typically asking for compliance with the rules of natural justice (Chapter 15). In *Seifert and Lynch*

---

6    See B. Serota, 'The evolution of the role of the ombudsman. Comparisons and perspectives' in G. Caiden (ed.), *International Handbook*, above, n. 180.

7    For an introduction see L. Brown and P. Lavirotte, 'The Mediator: A French Ombudsman' (1974) 90 LQR 212. See also W. Miller, 'Why a Mediator' in P. Morris (ed.), *Equality and Inequalities in France* (Wolverhampton: Wolverhampton Polytechnic) 1984.

8    On this function see, A. Bradley, 'The Role of the Ombudsman in Relation to the Protection of Citizens' Rights' (1980) 39(2) CLJ 304.

9    Lord Shackleton in debate on the Parliamentary Commissioner Bill, HL Deb., vol. 280., col. 1337 (7 March 1967).

10   See *R v Local Comr for Administration, ex p Bradford MCC* [1979] QB 287; *R v Local Comr for Administration, ex p Eastleigh Borough Council* [1988] QB 855; *R v Local Comr for Administration, ex p Croydon London Borough Council*[1989] 1 All ER 1033. And see M. Jones, 'The Local Ombudsmen and Judicial Review' [1988] PL 608.

11   *Re Fletcher's Application* [1970] 2 All ER 527n is superseded by *R v Parliamentary Comr for Administration, ex p Dyer* [1994] 1 WLR 621, which established jurisdiction though finding for the PCA. See further below, p. 448.

12   *Pensions Ombudsman v Haywood* [1996] 3 WLR 563; *Duffield v Pensions Ombudsman* [1996] PLR 285; *Hillsdown Holdings plc v Pensions Ombudsman* [1997] 1 All ER 862.

13   *R v Insurance Ombudsman Bureau, ex p Aegon Life Assurance Ltd* [1994] COD 426. And see above, p. 347.

*v Pensions Ombudsman*,[14] the PO's finding of maladministration was attacked
on the ground that he had not disclosed a relevant letter to the applicants or
allowed them an opportunity to comment on it. Lightman J held that the PO
must not only follow the statutory procedure but was also bound by the rules of
natural justice:

> A determination by the ombudsman can damage or destroy reputations, as well
> as impose financial penalties ... It is not open to the ombudsman to make a
> determination save in respect of the allegations in the complaint ... of which he has
> given notice to the appellants. It is highly desirable that the ombudsman, rather than
> simply transmitting copies of his correspondence with the complainant, (save in
> simple and obvious cases) expresses in his own words in plain and simple language
> what he perceives to be the substance of the allegation ... The respondents must know
> at least the gist of what he has learnt, so as to enable them to have a fair crack of the
> whip and a fair opportunity to provide any answer they may have. Whilst the
> procedure before the ombudsman is intended to be quick, inexpensive and informal,
> these are the minimum requirements for fairness and accordingly for a decision that
> can be allowed to stand.

## 4. Into the jungle: disputes, grievances and complaints

By the 1970s, administrative lawyers had become accustomed to three types
of alternative to trial-type procedure. Tribunals, accepted as 'machinery for
adjudication', generally dealt with small claims but had increasingly been
judicialised. Inquiries, accepted as an 'advanced and sophisticated',
specifically English contribution to administrative law and practice,[15] had
also suffered increasing judicialisation, though their hybrid character was
theoretically admitted. With the advent of the Ombudsmen, the net had
widened to trawl 'grievances' or 'complaints' as well as disputes. Describing
as 'its most surprising feature' the absence of legal staff in the PCA's office,
Schwartz and Wade conceded in 1972[16] that the PCA dealt with 'large
numbers of substantial cases with great thoroughness and fairness. The
complaint that he deals only with trivialities is unjustified'. Yet they were
unwilling to allocate the senior of the new arrivals more than a place on the
outskirts of administrative law:[17]

> The British public has habitually made much use of the traditional channel of
> complaint through members of Parliament ... But as the territory of administration
> expanded, and as Parliament's power weakened relatively to the government, the old
> methods became inadequate ...

14  [1997] 1 All ER 214.
15  *Justice*/All Souls Review 1988, para. 10.3.
16  B. Schwarz and H. Wade, *Legal Control of Government* (above, p. 394, note 19), pp. 64-66.
17  Ibid, p. 71.

Since he has no substantive legal powers, the Parliamentary Commissioner stands outside the field of administrative law. But he is closely connected with it, and his work will alter the aspect of many of its problems.

[Administrative lawyers] should also welcome him as an important ally in the campaign for administrative justice, who will work alongside an independent judiciary and legal profession and supplement the rule of law with the rule of administrative good sense and even of generosity.

The angle of approach was changing marginally as lawyers began to show some interest in statutory complaints procedures but the more visible parts of this machinery were relatively formal. Authors commonly 'descended' as far as tribunals, inquiries and Ombudsmen, expensive, often time-consuming machinery which was then christened 'informal'. To put this differently, if the core concept of the Access-to-Justice movement is the idea of 'unmet need', with a consequential emphasis on the extension of legal services to new clients and new types of dispute, then administrative tribunals as 'court substitutes', debates over tribunal representation[18] or legal aid, fit the Access-to-Justice model. The advent of the Ombudsman, with investigatorial powers and documentary procedures, was a step in the direction of ADR but acceptance of Ombudsmen, Rawlings has argued,[19] did not demand a great change in the traditional top-down, adjudicative perspective.

A 'topdown' analysis of the complaints problem might be that adjudicatory and complaints systems easily become overloaded. The legal process contains its own filters in the shape of cost and problems of access (though courts continue to suffer problems of delay and overload[20]). The response is to seek less expensive machinery, typically a tribunal but perhaps an administrative process. Thus, the Criminal Injuries Compensation Board whose operation is described in Chapter 18 provides an alternative to personal injury litigation. Seen as alternatives to the legal process, the sole rationale of such procedures is to process 'small claims' quickly, efficiently and cheaply.

Proponents of ADR, however, will read the landscape rather differently.[1] Not only do Ombudsmen offer an informal and cost- free alternative to courts but they possess other advantages, including a freedom to arbitrate, negotiate and redress the balance of power between individuals and large institutions.[2] These are not typical of adjudication.[3] Other standard administrative law techniques can be

18  H. Genn, 'Tribunals and Informal Justice' (1993) 56 MLR 393.
19  R. Rawlings, 'In the Jungle' (1987) 50 MLR 110.
20  See M. Sunkin, L. Bridges, G. Meszaros, *Judicial Review in Perspective, An Investigation of Trends in the Use and Operation of the Judicial Review Procedure in England and Wales* (London: Dartmouth) 2nd edn., 1995, discussed in Ch. 16 below. See also Lord Woolf *Access to Justice Report to the Lord Chancellor on the civil justice system* (London: LCD) 1996.
 1  See S. Roberts, 'Litigation and Settlement' in A. Zuckerman and R. Cranston (eds.) *Reform of Civil Procedure, Essays on 'Access to Justice'* (Oxford: Clarendon) 1995.
 2  R. Gregory, 'The Ombudsman in Perspective' in R. Gregory, P. Giddings, V. Moore, J. Pearson, *Practice and Prospects of the Ombudsmen in the United Kingdom* (Lewiston: Edwin Mellon Press) 1995, p. 11.
 3  But see the notion of judicial review as a 'bargaining game'. A more complex version of litigation as a negotiating technique is to be found in F. Snyder, 'The Effectiveness of EC Law: Institutions, Processes, Tools and Techniques' (1993) 56 MLR 19.

fitted into an ADR framework. Thus, public inquiries can be treated as primarily a stage in a decision-making process. [4] The 'MP filter' which restricts access to the PCA serves a crucial function of keeping MPs and the House of Commons in touch with their constituents. [5] A tribunal could not perform this additional function. Again, the provisions for conciliation – a classic form of ADR – in the police complaints system (below) are not conceived merely as a filter but operate simultaneously as a public relations exercise. The core commitment of ADR is to non-judicial fora for dispute-handling and the exploration of appropriate techniques.

Lawyers had been slow to notice that 'grievances' and 'complaints' do not necessarily demand the same treatment as fully-fledged 'disputes'. To rephrase this argument, it was easier for lawyers to accept the Ombudsman as an inquisitorial substitute in administrative justice than to view the MP, through whom all complaints to the PCA must still be referred, as machinery for redress of grievance. [6] Thus one way to look on the MP's 'complaints service' is simply as a filter, responsible for maintaining the workload of the PCA within manageable proportions. From a different angle, the MP is a more effective complaints system. The 'large numbers' of PCA complaints to which Schwartz and Wade made reference actually amounted in the year they wrote (1972) to 573, of which 318 fell outside the PCA's jurisdiction; [7] in contrast, MPs handle as many as 3 million constituency letters annually.

Commissioned to survey literature on 'administrative justice', [8] Rawlings set out to redress the balance. He noted that, 'even within the parameters of institutionalised complaining most people seek informal redress'. [9] Blaming the 'top-down' focus for ignorance of the 'unstructured, fluid and poorly publicised internal procedures which handle the great bulk of grievances ventilated by citizens against public bodies', he focused on 'bottom-up studies of how people usually behave when seeking redress'; on *non-judicial* means of dispute-resolution between citizens and administration; and on *informal* procedure for the redress of grievance.

Contributing a seminal study of the way in which government handles complaints, [10] Birkinshaw also moved to a 'bottom-up' approach, inverting the traditional approach which begins with courts and works down. Instead, Birkinshaw set out to:

> establish what [departments] did in relation to grievances from the public affected by their administration, and to study what connections there were between these

4   See R. Wraith and G. Lamb, *Public Inquiries as an Instrument of Government* (London: Allen and Unwin) 1971.
5   R. Rawlings, 'The MP's Complaints Service' (1990) 53 MLR 22.
6   Ibid, p. 149.
7   AR, 1972 HC 72 (1972/3) p. 3.
8   R. Rawlings, *Grievance Procedure and Administrative Justice, A Review of Socio-Legal Research* (London: Economic and Social Research Council) 1987.
9   Ibid, p. 3. See also F. Ridley, 'The Citizen Against Authority: British Approaches to the Redress of Grievances' (1984) 37 Parliamentary Affairs 1.
10  P. Birkinshaw, *Grievances, Remedies and the State* (London: Sweet and Maxwell) 2nd edn. 1995, p. xi, (Preface to the 1985 edition).

informal practices and the more formal procedures for complaint resolution or dispute settlement culiminating with Ombudsmen and Courts of Law.

Radical as this may sound to lawyers, for political sociologists it does not go far enough. Criticising the predominantly legalistic approach to the study of grievances, a new research study[11] saw even the new, 'bottom-up' research as flawed by legalism. In this narrow context, 'grievance is taken as a sub-component of dispute and dispute behaviour and is given a legalistic and institutional interpretation'. This accounts for 'the tendency to present the notion of grievance in an adversarial setting which may not be entirely helpful in developing a sociology of complaints and complaining'. In other words, the terminology of 'dispute', 'grievance' and even 'complaint' remains relatively legalistic and adversarial. This is precisely the attitude of Mulcahy and Tritter,[12] who describe complaint systems as low level grievance procedure, arguing that there is a need in a modern state to address the issue of how they are to be handled:

> Complaints systems are important and should be recognised as needing as much attention as other systems for dispute resolution. The systems represent the mass end of a disputes market; systems which users may choose to access rather than the courts. In addition, we have an overloaded court system. Access to the courts and tribunals is severely limited by financial and procedural factors as well as those based on knowledge. As the expanding state produces more opportunities for injustice low level procedures represent a cheap, accessible and often more appropriate way to resolve disputes.

This is an argument which needs to be considered very carefully. Dispute-resolution is the lawyer's trade; it is central to his function. It is natural for lawyers to see law through the spectacles of dispute-resolution and in terms of their clients' interests. Everything else is peripheral. If this were the whole story, much of what we have seen in earlier chapters – structuring through rulemaking, or regulation – is peripheral to administrative law because it is not concerned with dispute-resolution. As an explanation of lawyers' attitudes to ADR, however, the statement is helpful. Lawyers' concern is essentially with the pathological. A system may broadly function well; a lawyer's concern is typically not with the system but to protect his client if it malfunctions.[13] Adversarial procedure plus the right of access to a court are seen as the ultimate protections the law can bestow.[14] This is why lawyers are so often guilty of 'squaring the circle' by re-instating them.

---

11  P. McCarthy, B. Simpson, M. Hill, J. Walker, J. Corlyon, *Grievances, Complaints and Local Government, Towards the Responsive Local Authority* (Aldershot: Avebury) 1992, pp. 2-3 (hereafter, McCarthy et al.)

12  L. Mulcahy and J. Tritter, 'Rhetoric or Redress? The Place of the Citizen's Charter in the Civil Justice System' in C. Willett (ed.), *Public Sector Reform and the Citizen's Charter* (London: Blackstone) 1996, p. 109.

13  For one exception to this generalisation, see *R v Secretary of State for Social Services, ex p Child Poverty Action Group* [1990] 2 QB 540; below, p. 546.

14  See, *R v Lord Chancellor, ex p Witham* [1997] 2 All ER 779 above p. 162.

## 5. Jewels in the crown: a new look at complaints

In Chapter 5, we saw that complaining formed an essential component of the Citizen's Charter. We met the idea that the Charter was intended not only to raise the standards of delivery of public services but also to empower the citizen when the service delivered was sub-standard. This is done by complaining. In Hirschman's terminology of 'loyalty, voice and exit',[15] the Charter gives market citizens 'voice' but we should be careful not to confuse voice with participation. The Charter is a manager's and public customers' charter, closely linked to market ideology.[16] Rather than providing Voice, it sets out merely to correct market failures by providing remedies for individuals who have no power of Exit. This suggests a dual function for complaints: first and foremost, to inform managers (the 'jewel in the crown'); second, redress (the humble 'carrot' function).

Shortly after the Charter was unveiled, a Citizen's Charter Task Force was set up to advise on complaints procedure. Its own priorities were made clear in a series of discussion papers, culminating in a checklist for 'Putting Things Right':[17]

> Good complaints handling:
> * puts things rights for individuals who have received a poor service; and
> * allows organisations to learn from complaints and improve services.
>
> As public services embrace the principles of the Citizen's Charter, they are issuing statements of the standards the public can expect. An effective complaints system allows the public to tell organisations how they match up to those standards in practice. Only those who use a service know what that experience has been like, and if they express their dissatisfaction there is an opportunity to put the matter right.

The Unit recommended that all public services should 'define a complaint. This definition needs to be understood by all staff and users of the service'. They underscored the principle of easy access, insisting that all public services should 'have in place formal written guidance on how to recognise and handle all complaints, whether they concern operational or policy matters'. Staff should be familiar with these and be trained to 'fulfil their role and responsibilities within them'. Redress, including financial compensation, should be appropriate and consistently offered and the Unit 'should take the lead in producing guidance on redress in public services', a point to which we return in Chapter 18. The *Good Practice Guide* identified six basic principles of effective complaints systems:

* easily *accessible* and well-publicised
* *simple* to understand and use
* *speedy*, with established time limits for action, and keeping people informed of progress

---

15　A. Hirschman, *Exit, voice and loyalty, Responses to decline in firms, organizations and states* (Cambridge: Harvard UP) 1970 (above, p. 129).

16　C. Adamson, 'Complaints handling: benefits and best practice' (1991) 1 Consumer Policy Rev. 196.

17　*Effective Complaints Systems: Principles and Checklist*, Cabinet Office, 1993; *If Things Go Wrong...*, Discussion Papers 1-5, Cabinet Office, 1994; *Putting Things Right*, Cabinet Office, 1995; *Good Practice Guide* (London: HMSO) 1995.

- *fair*, with a full and impartial investigation
- *effective*, addressing all the points at issue, and providing appropriate redress
- *informative*, providing information to management so that services can be improved.

Fairness was seen as particularly important, both because of the absence of choice (exit) and because 'users of certain services – eg, the Inland Revenue or prison services – may have strong negative feelings about the service itself'. The Task Force urged that:

> All public services must be seen to be delivering their services on the basis of fair and equitable treatment of all their users. The same principle applies to the handling of complaints. All parties involved in a complaint – the users of services, those complained about, and others – must be assured that the complaint will be dealt with *even-handedly*. Users need to feel that they will be treated on an impartial view of the facts, and not on the basis of any irrelevant personal differences, discrimination or inherent resentment against them from having 'caused trouble'. Staff, and other parties involved, need to be assured that any complaint will be fairly investigated to establish whether there are grounds for complaint, and then responded to in an open and straightforward way. Demonstrably fair systems encourage people to complain and staff to respond positively, within the framework of policy.

This statement needs to be compared with judicial notions of fairness, discussed in Chapter 15.

In sharp contrast to lawyers and to the approach developed by international Ombudsman bodies,[18] which stress *independence*, the managerial approach emphasises high quality in-house complaints systems. But the Task Force did see a place for external review. While recommending conciliation and mediation at the review stage of complaints procedure, it warned against allowing mediation to close off the possibility of further review. Mediators too should be 'trained and independent'. External review, about which the Task Force was deliberately imprecise, seems to mean no more than access to someone outside the line management involved in the affair who must:[19]

- be clearly independent of the public service concerned...
- be free from interference by the organisation about how they carry out any investigation, once the remit and powers are set ...

### 6. Independence and externality: the Revenue Adjudicator and CLA

The Task Force's prototype was the Revenue Adjudicator (RA) for tax complaints, an office devised as an independent 'middle-tier' between internal procedure and the PCA.

---

18  See UK Ombudsman Association, *Criteria for the Use of the Term 'Ombudsman'* 1993, cited in R. Gregory, P. Giddings, V. Moore, J. Pearson, *Practice and Prospects of the Ombudsmen in the United Kingdom* (hereafter Gregory et al.) (Lewiston: Edwin Mellon Press) 1995, pp. 203-204.
19  *Good Practice Guide* (above, note 17), p. 29. There are seven more criteria, concerning resources, access, publicity and expertise.

## (a) The Revenue Adjudicator

The RA was introduced in 1993 by the Inland Revenue specifically to encourage adherence to Charter standards of service and complaints handling. No legislation was required since (like the Insurance Ombudsman) the office is contractual. In 1996 there were 41 support staff, mainly seconded from government departments. The budget is independent of the IR. The jurisdiction is, in theory, wide enough to cover all complaints about the IR (and now the Customs and Excise and Contributions Agency) but is in practice limited; the RA does not take complaints on tax law and liability, which go to the General and Special Commissioners; nor on property valuations (Valuation Tribunals); nor any complaint under investigation by the PCA, whose list is normally headed by tax complaints. The RA has no compulsory powers; to date, however, all of her recommendations have been complied with. This is a good record considering the high rate of adverse findings: of 1,615 and 2,581 complaints in the first two years (1993–95), 64% and 51% respectively were upheld.

The first three-year appointment brought criticism of a 'substantial and worrying independence deficit' sufficient to exclude the office from the Association of Ombudsmen despite the fact that the contract contains the protection that it may be terminated only for gross inefficiency or serious misconduct. Much has depended on the personality of the appointee. Elizabeth Filkin, the first RA, has a background in citizen's advice and 'is obviously strongly committed to securing the actual and perceived independence of the scheme'.[20]

The RA describes herself as a 'mediator ... striving to engineer and conciliate settlement'[1] and up to 50% of all complaints are in fact resolved by mediation. She has also devised an 'assistance' role to guide complainants through the internal complaints machinery where this has not been exhausted. Her methods are informal and designed to be 'user-friendly', reliant on telephone calls and personal interviews. Recommendations are based on:

• the concept of maladministration;[2]
• IR codes and guidance;
• Charter performance indicators.

Morris, an academic observer, notes additionally, 'a novel and subjective standard of "good professional practice" required of a public servant which involves ideas of integrity, fairness and good faith'.[3]

Evaluating this new office, Morris gives the RA high marks for openness, fairness and effectiveness and praises her impressive achievements. 'Taxpayers have been provided with a speeedy, high level and effective complaints service under the direction of an indivdual who is obviously strongly committed to

---

20  P. Morris, 'The Revenue Adjudicator – The First Two Years' [1996] PL 309, 312.
 1  E. Filkin, 'Mediation not Confrontation' Taxation Practitioner April 1994.
 2  As developed by the PCA, who has traditionally handled a large volume of IR complaints. See below, p. 425 for a definition of maladministration.
 3  [1996] PL at 315, citing a personal interview.

stimulating higher standards of administration throughout the Revenue'.[4] On the other hand, he sees the scheme as 'clearly flawed in terms of perceived independence and accountability', a comment which reflects on the Charter Unit's general preference for in-house schemes. Oliver has pointed out[5] that the RA is not the end of the road; accountability *is* secured because further complaint, including a complaint about the RA's performance, lies to the PCA and can ultimately be referred to the Select Committee. Whether reform could be achieved without a resultant loss in desirable informality is also very questionable.

### (b) The CLA

As we have already noted, the CLA is a public Ombudsman scheme established by the Local Government Act 1972 to handle complaints concerning local government. It is organised regionally and is funded directly from the Revenue Support Grant. Previously accountable to a representative body of local authorities, it now has only a duty to consult before publishing its Annual Report and accounts.[6]

The CLA has always been interested in promoting rule-making; only six years after its initiation, the CLA had sponsored a code of practice issued jointly with local authority associations for use in setting up complaints procedures. Like the Charter Unit later, this too recommended a relaxed and non-adversarial attitude to complaints:[7]

> Complaint should not be too narrowly defined. The definition should certainly cover the small minority of matters which are clearly complaints and may end as allegations of injustice caused by maladministration and be referred to a Local Commissioner. It should also, however, cover those other approaches to authorities, whether for advice, information, or to raise an issue which, if not handled properly, could lead to a complaint.

At first, local authorities were slow to introduce complaints procedures, but by 1992 the CLA was able to report[8] that an increasing number of authorities had done so for all their services as part of customer care and quality assurance programmes. Some authorities were going further and appointing an internal Ombudsman. A year later, the CLA published a guidance note on best practice and held seminars designed to stimulate the further development of effective

---

4    [1996] PL at 321.
5    D. Oliver, 'The Revenue Adjudicator – A New Breed of Ombudsperson?' [1993] PL 407.
6    Sections 24 and 25 of the Local Government and Housing Act 1989. In practice, consultation is with the Central Bodies Advisory Group of the local authority associations: the ACC, ADC and AMA.
7    *Complaints Procedures: A Code of Practice for Local Government and Water Authorities for dealing with queries and complaints* (London: Local Authorities Association) 1978.
8    Annual Report of the Commission for Local Administration 1990/91 (London: CLA), p. 5. See also, McCarthy et al., *Grievances, Complaints and Local Government*; J. Greenwood, 'Facing up to the Local Ombudsmen: Are Internal Complaints Procedures Adequate?' (1989) 15 Local Government Studies 1.

local complaints structures.[9] Communication skills were emphasised as a means of averting complaints:[10]

> Many complaints occur because of poor communications between the council, their staff and the public [or] because information about a council's services is not clearly and widely publicised. The clearer the customers' understanding of what they have the right to expect from a council, the more focused and appropriate their representations will be ... Complaints can be minimised if a council have appropriate and comprehensive policies; clear procedures for implementing those policies; properly trained staff; and good communications both internally and externally ... It is important to ensure that all communications are in simple and clear language which can be easily understood and that where relevant they are available in languages other than English; that any necessary forms are properly designed so that they are user friendly; that help is readily available for those who have difficulty in understanding procedures or filling in forms; and that staff are trained to respond positively and helpfully to those who need or seek their advice.

Sound advice, one may think, and in line with the thinking of the Charter Unit. Ironically, however, the CLA was soon to fall foul of a more managerial attitude. In a review[11] conducted for the DoE, which exercises a supervisory remit over local authorities, Sir David Chipperfield expressed a decided preference for *internal* complaints procedures. Chipperfield downplayed the CLA's contribution to 'fire-watching':

> The review of maladministration must always have a salutary effect on the quality of administration in local government, although how significant this is, compared with the effect of managerial changes and the greater appreciation of the importance of management which has affected all of English public life, is open to question ... The solution is not to involve the CLA but to get local complaint procedures working effectively; to do otherwise is to usurp the proper function of a local authority ... The CLA can be seen as usurping (although possibly with justification) a function which should properly belong to another.

The code of practice and guidance, said Chipperfield, had been overtaken by material issued by the Charter Unit and, if local government 'feels the need for advice on such management matters, it would be better to seek it from bodies which have a more all round approach to management' – the Audit Commission perhaps?

Measuring the CLA's effectiveness by a narrow quantitative test of the number of complaints which might otherwise have received a different outcome and criticising its 'legalistic procedures and the length of time it takes the CLA to resolve cases', Chipperfield suggested replacement of the external watchdog by statutory internal complaints procedures buttressed by the appointment of an

---

9 *Devising a complaints system – guidance on good practice*, note No. 1 (London: CLA) 1992. And see Annual Report of the Commission for Local Administration 1992/93 (London: CLA) p. 7.
10 *Devising a complaints system* (above, note 9), p. 3.
11 *Report of the Financial Management and Policy Review of the Commission for Local Administration in England. Stage One: Prior Options Review* (the Chipperfield Report) (London: Department of the Environment) 1995.

'adjudicator'. Responsible to and remunerated by the local council, this reviewer would be independent only in the sense of not being subject to 'the authority's management and direction'. Influenced by the Charter approach, the model of the Revenue Adjudicator was being suggested. This change, which would virtually eradicate the CLA's fire-watching function, flew in the face of the 1989 Act which had specifically authorised it, after consultation with local authority representatives, to provide 'such advice and guidance about good administrative practice as appears to the Commission to be appropriate'.

The generally hostile response to Chipperfield both from voluntary organisations representing users of local government services and, less predictably, from local government, led to a Second Stage Review which recommended against abolition. During the campaign, a conference of users' organisations made a strong case against internalising the handling of complaints. In a passage which casts doubt on the suitablity of the RA model outside a strong, centralised, government department, the advisers spoke of local complaints procedures as:[12]

> ... deeply flawed, with local authorities taking months to deal with cases in flagrant violation of the time limits set down. Complainants left to battle the system alone frequently become exhausted and disillusioned and may simply abandon their complaint. Others may be blocked because the local authority refuses to produce the necessary personal files, even when complainants are entitled to have access. A number of participants indicated that this situation is particularly difficult for the most vulnerable client groups such as children, the mentally ill, the disabled and others.

The combined fire-watching and fire-fighting functions of the Ombudsman emerge rather clearly from this passage. First, the Ombudsman is an *advocate* who stands up for individuals against unhelpful authority. Second, he is an *investigator*, with privileged access to vital documents. Third, he may act as *negotiator or conciliator*. Fourth, he is a *fire-watcher*, with an important role in maintaining the standard of internal complaints systems and encouraging good practice.

A typical set of CLA housing cases illustrates the point further. In the first group, all involving Brent's unsatisfactory housing department,[13] the CLA had received consistent complaints over the council's management of housing benefit. Despite Brent's assurances that the system would be reformed, complaints continued to pour in. In 1992/3 the CLA set down 69 complaints for investigation and issued a general report with the normal individual reports. There were 20 cases of maladministration, 18 of which caused injustice (as with the PCA, the statutory test). The CLA concluded that 'the culture of these services had encouraged the view that the needs and rights of the tenants were less important than those of the staff'. Not only did the CLA recommend compensation of £9,350 but (perhaps more important) it monitored Brent's procedures until it was able to report a 'radical transformation'.

---

12  *Review of the Local Government Ombudsman* (London: Public Law Project) 1996, p. 14.
13  Local Ombudsman Complaints 92/A/2978 and 19 others (Brent) 20 March 1995, (1995) 17 J. of Social Welfare and Family Law 477.

In a second housing case against Ealing,[14] 132 complaints were investigated over the two years 1992–94 and a lengthy general report was issued. Again, the report stipulated that recommendations for reform should be monitored after six months at a meeting between the CLA, the leader of the council and the chief executive. An experienced law centre adviser commented:[15]

> The detailed investigations and reports in relation to both councils demonstrate the strength and importance of the service provided by the local Ombudsman. When officers are covering up for their own failings, and being over-optimistic about their capacity to resolve problems, and members are largely in the dark, the Ombudsman provides a vital service in uncovering the truth and providing redress to individual complainants. Both reports recognise that the complaints were only the tip of the iceberg in terms of numbers of people affected.

Considering Chipperfield's proposals in this context and also the recommendations of the Charter Unit, would management go as far as the CLA went? What would the council's attitude be to an in-house adviser, if he were to recommend such far-reaching reforms? Not only may an organisation resist change but it may not realise that change is necessary. In defiance of rules and good practice, internal complaints machinery may not be in place.

To digress, health service complaints procedures, criticised by the Association of Community Health Councils as 'bureaucratic and biased in favour of the medical profession', prove this.[16] Patients are described as inhibited from complaining through fear of retribution, investigations can drag on 'for months or years and the outcome is often unsatisfactory, with explanations phrased in bureaucratic jargon'. To compound the problem, the machinery is complex and may overlap. Of course, such procedures fail to measure up to expectations generated by the Citizen's Charter, but how are they to be reformed? Vested interests – here, of the powerful medical profession – may oppose change; essential statutory intervention may be inhibited by low political salience. In such a situation, the overview provided by the Health Service Commissioner, who reports to a Select Committee with long experience of constituency complaints, is important. Powerful champions of patients' rights, often recommending and monitoring the implementation of reforms, the HSC and Select Committee are far more influential than a semi-autonomous, in-house adjudicator. Equally, they are far more effective than courts.

So should we move to a generalised two-tier system in which informal, internal complaints procedures are used to filter information in to management and filter 'grumbles' out of formal, external machinery for dispute-resolution? Birkinshaw and Lewis[17] advocate just such a 'systems-flexible' approach to public sector complaints-handling. They demand *statutory* complaints procedures within all government departments and agencies combined with 'proposals for the cooling

14 Local Ombudsman Complaints 92/A/3042 plus 14 others. (Ealing) 6 March 1995.
15 A. Griffith (1995) 17 J. of Social Welfare and Family Law 479.
16 P. Giddings, 'Complaints, Remedies and the Health Service Commissioner' (1993) 71 Pub. Admin. 377.
17 N. Lewis and P. Birkinshaw, *When Citizens Complain, Reforming Justice and Administration* (Buckingham: Open University Press) 1993, p. 214.

out of disputes within the administration without the necessity of calling in third parties', both to operate in conjunction with 'an enlarged ombudsman system'. Notice the move from the internal, informal, managerial approach of the Citizen's Charter to a system founded in statute.

## 7. Snakes and ladders

In the previous sections, we have met with a number of generalisations about complaints systems. In addition to the emphasis placed, for example, on independence, autonomy and externality, we have met the view that Ombudsman procedure is designed for the small claims of the administrative system. There has been an implication, too, that complaints systems should be pyramidal in design, filtering out the trivial and passing serious matters upwards. We can test these assumptions by looking at the structure of complaints machinery in the specially sensitive areas of prisons and police. Both border on the criminal process. Both are hotly political. Both involve closed societies. Both services are hierarchical and both are covered by strict disciplinary systems. Neither prisoners nor suspected criminals easily engage public sympathy and prisoners have only lately gained rights of due process.  All these factors necessarily impinge on the handling of complaints.

### (a) Prisons

Prisoners have a variety of ways to complain[18]. They may complain up the hierarchy to the governor. The Board of Visitors has jurisdiction in disciplinary cases. Habeas corpus is the classic remedy for wrongful detention, judicial review may also be available, an action for damages for negligence or false imprisonment may be tried.[19] Prisoners may write to their MP, who can, if appropriate, refer the complaint on to the PCA. They may petition the Queen. To this already complex pattern, a Prison Ombudsman (PO) has lately been added.

The PO originated in the Woolf Report[20] which, as befits a report drafted by a distinguished public lawyer, stressed the need for proper prison adjudicative structures:

> Within a prison in particular, it is an important requirement of justice that justice should not only actually be done but should be seen to be done. It will not be seen to be done if there is not proper procedure, if there are no established rules, if the prisoner is not made aware of those rules, and if there is not, at least at the final stage of the process, recourse to an independent element.

18  These are listed in S. Creighton and V. King, *Prisoners and the Law* (London: Butterworths) 1996, paras. 3.12-3.24, 6.43-6.54.
19  See M. Loughlin and P. Quinn, 'Prisons, Rules and Courts: A Study in Administrative Law' (1993) 56 MLR 497.
20  *Report of the Inquiry into Prison Disturbances*, Cm 1456, 1991, para. 14.297.

After some government resistance and a dispute over appointment, the PO finally took office in 1995. [1] In his first report, [2] Sir Peter Woodhead gave this account of his duties:

> The PO is charged with responsibility for investigating complaints made by prisoners about their treatment whilst in Prison Service custody. Complaints about other agencies such as the police, the courts, or the Immigration Service, therefore fall outside the PO's remit. Complaints about staff employed to work in prisons such as seconded probation officers or teachers, however, are eligible for investigation. Similarly, the actions of custody or escort officers employed by private companies fall within the remit.
>
> Nevertheless, there are some categories of complaint which are currently excluded from consideration. First, complaints relating to decisions by the Home Secretary or the Parole Board about the release of individual prisoners cannot be investigated by the Prisons Ombudsman [3]. However, complaints about the associated administrative actions of the Prison Service can be considered. So, for example, complaints about delays in reaching parole decisions or inaccuracies in parole reports fall within the remit.

There are four further criteria for investigation: (1) complaints must come from the prisoner and not a third party; (2) they should not be the subject of legal proceedings, other than incidentally; (3) they must already have been 'raised with the Prison Service at headquarters level', usually through the formal complaints system, though not the Board of Visitors; and finally the complaint must be 'relatively current', preferably within a month of an answer through the complaints system. Perhaps it is not surprising to find that only 253 (29%) of the 870 complaints received in the first six months was eligible for investigation. And exhausting internal prison procedures certainly disadvantages certain prisoners; just 17% of complaints about assault and 11% about segregation made to the PO were raised internally. Fear of making serious allegations against warders to the governor responsible for prison order may stifle a complaint to the PO of assault and ill-treatment. Better to bypass the oppressive requirement with a complaint through a friend or relative at the surgery of one's constituency MP.

The pyramid principle certainly does not apply to this situation. Instead, the picture is one of complexity, overlap and fragmentation, creating a confusing network of complaints systems which prisoners must find difficulty in understanding. Complaints also fall through the cracks, when no one investigator has jurisdiction. Of the few complaints to reach the PCA, for example, fewer still are investigated. In 1994/5, the PCA handled three prisons reports which covered: the handling of a parole review, delay in arranging a man's transfer to an open prison and a complaint over medical care. [4] Alternatives are available for each of

---

1 The PO is Sir Peter Woodhead KCB, a former naval officer. In 1996, there were three assistants, a civil servant, a lawyer and a pressure group worker. The office had six investigators seconded from the Home Office.
2 Six-month review, Prisons Ombudsman, 1995, paras. 3.2 - 3.9. At the time of this report, complaints about the clinical judgment of prison doctors fell outside the remit but were later included.
3 But see above, pp. 192–198.
4 Annual Report, HC 307 (1994-5).

these cases. A similar picture of fragmentation emerges from an earlier PCA report.[5] A prisoner complained that he had been unfairly held in segregation and had been unable to find out either what action was to be taken against him or what the effect on his future allocation would be. Segregation for more than three days requires authorisation of a member of the Board of Vistors – not within the PCA's jurisdiction. Nor can he question the decision of the Local Review Committee on a lifer's transfer to open prison. Worse, the *merits* of a discretionary decision taken by a department cannot be questioned in the absence of maladministration (a statutory restriction explained in the next chapter). The disempowered PCA was reduced to criticising the Prisons Service for *delay* in informing the prisoner of the reason for his segregation and of the decision on his future allocation.

The office of the PCA is both prestigious and expensive, yet an MP may receive and pass on to the PCA a trivial complaint. Many complaints are trivial. In 1991, for example, the PCA investigated a complaint about mishandling of a prisoner's earnings resulting in compensation of £15.77.[6] In 1993 he investigated a complaint of detention for two days longer than was lawful.[7] On the other hand, trivialities often hint at petty bullying on which no comment is forthcoming. Thus, a wide-ranging and lengthy investigation of allegations of interference with correspondence and destruction of legal papers with curtailment of exercise and other matters, resulted in 'the Home Office offering apologies for some shortcomings which I identified and taking steps to improve procedures'.[8] What really happened here?

The Chief Inspector of Constabulary in his Annual Reports to the Home Office regularly reports on serious maladministration: in 1995, for example, Sir David Ramsbotham staged a protest walk-out at Holloway Prison, refusing to complete his inquiries into conditions there until minimum standards had been complied with. No such complaint has ever reached the PCA. Despite the multiplicity of complaints procedures, serious breakdowns in prison discipline or complaints over conditions have almost invariably been dealt with by an inquiry. And is it not strange that no complaint commensurate in gravity with that handled by the Woolf Inquiry into Prison Disturbances has been handled by the PCA?

### (b) Police Complaints

Until 1976, the principal avenue for complaints about the police was the civil justice system. Criminal prosecutions were (and are still) theoretically possible[9] but in practice are rare and rarely successful. An important reason for this is the so-called '51% rule' operated by the DPP, with whom the decision to prosecute

---

5    5th Report of the PCA for 1993/4, HC 687 (1994) p. 40.
6    C 461/89, HC 347 (1991/2).
7    C 544/92, HC 826 (1992/3) p. 48.
8    HC 347 (1991/2) p. 22.
9    E.g. for (aggravated) assault, criminal damage, dangerous driving, conspiracy to pervert the course of justice, perjury etc. And see *R v Dytham* [1979] QB 722 (it is a misfeasance in public office for an officer to stand by and watch a grave assault). See further, J. Harrison and S. Cragg, *Police Misconduct: Legal Remedies* (London: Legal Action Group) 2nd edn., 1991.

lies, whereby a prosecution will only be brought if there is a better than even chance of conviction on the evidence and also that prosecution is in the public interest. Partly because of the high acquittal rate, this means that officers may not be prosecuted for acts which would incur prosecution if committed by members of the public, a position often criticised[10] and to which we shall return. Actions in tort (for assault, battery, wrongful arrest, false imprisonment, malicious prosecution and occasionally negligence) are commoner and their outcome more successful, though cost and problems of access to legal advice have always created real obstacles to their use; although legal aid is available, there are still only about 1,000 actions annually.[11] In short, the theoretically pleasing Diceyan model is difficult to use.

In addition, a police disciplinary system, a purely internal procedure, exists. Section 49 of the Police Act 1964 for the first time laid down a procedure for recording complaints from members of the public. Though this generated an increasing number of complaints (rising to over 19,000 in 1975) the outcome of prosecution or disciplinary proceedings was attained in only a handful of cases (in 1975 there were 128 prosecutions and 247 disciplinary charges). In the light of modern preoccupations, it is noteworthy that little was known about the nature of or reason for complaints, dismissed by the Police Federation as mainly wilful, malicious or trivial.[12] Trivial complaints did, however, create a serious problem. As all had to be investigated, a situation arose whereby 'many senior officers were ... deployed on time-consuming investigations into minor and trivial breaches of the police disciplinary codes producing detailed reports often of little moment ... [while] more junior colleagues ironically investigated serious breaches of the criminal law committed by members of the public'.[13]

Argument over a police complaints system rumbled on throughout the 1970s, nourished by growing public concern over police corruption and poor relations between the police and ethnic minorites, but largely conducted behind closed doors. There was no consultation exercise, as today there might be, to establish public priorities and wishes. The new system was finally introduced by the Police Act 1976. In the teeth of police opposition,[14] bought off with promise of increased protection in disciplinary proceedings and help to sue malicious complainants in defamation, the Act set up a Police Complaints Board (PCB) to handle complaints from members of the public alleging misconduct by individual officers. The PCB had nine full-time members appointed by the Prime Minister. The Chairman's office was strictly reserved for the 'great and good'; the first chairman was Lord

---

10  Glanville Williams, 'Letting off the guilty and prosecuting the innocent' [1985] Crim LR 115.
11  J. Harrison and S. Cragg (above, note 9). See also R. Clayton and H. Tomlinson, *Civil Actions Against the Police* (London: Sweet and Maxwell) 2nd edn., 1992.
12  See D. Humphry, 'The Complaints System' in P. Hain, D. Humphry and B. Rose-Smith (eds.), *Policing The Police* (London: John Calder) 1979, vol. 1, pp. 50-51. The Police Federation is the unofficial trade organisation of the police, disbarred from joining trade unions.
13  C. Corbett, 'Complaints Against the Police: The New Procedure of Informal Resolution' (1991) 2 Policing and Society 47.
14  Sir Robert Mark, *Policing a Perplexed Society* (London: Allen and Unwin) 1977; D. Humphry, above, note 12.

Plowden, an elderly and distinguished civil servant, who had chaired a Royal Commission; the second was Sir Cyril Philips, an academic who had chaired a Royal Commission into police procedure.

Complaints were to be made either orally or in writing at local police stations or directly to the PCB. They had to be investigated by a senior police officer from a different branch or another force under the supervision of the deputy chief officer and a final or progress report made to the PCB within four months. Delays had to be communicated to the complainant and the officer complained of. The latter had in addition to be given 'an early opportunity' of commenting on the complaint and to make a statement, admissible in disciplinary proceedings. On receipt of the final report, the supervising officer could: (a) send it to the DPP to consider criminal proceedings in accordance with s. 49(3) of the Police Act 1964 (compulsory unless he was satisfied that no criminal offence had been committed); (b) inaugurate proceedings before a disciplinary tribunal; (c) if he did neither, refer the case to the PCB, which in other cases was only informed of the outcome.

Controversy surrounded these procedures from the outset. Between 1978 and 1983, when the PCB was replaced, cases referred to the PCB averaged only a quarter of complaints received by the police. Why this was so was never properly explained. The NCCL (Liberty) alleged pressure on complainants; the police stood on their previous explanation of triviality; the PCB fruitlessly asked for 'research' and 'monitoring'. There was suspicion also over outcomes; fewer than 2% of cases led to disciplinary charges and about 10% to 'advice' on future conduct. As the PCB admitted,[15] this provided ideal material for those who had no confidence in the procedures and who were not notably assuaged by the explanation that 'chief officers rarely reach decisions with which we [the PCB] would disagree'. Serious problems arose also with the operation of the 'double jeopardy' rule, a common law principle designed to protect citizens from repetitive criminal proceedings in respect of the same offence. Section 11 of the Police Act 1976 protects police officers from disciplinary proceedings after acquittal by a criminal court. Trouble was caused when the rule was extended to cases *referred for consideration* by the DPP – a useful let out for some 'guilty' officers. This practice was finally ruled unlawful in *R v Police Complaints Board, ex p Madden and Rhone*.[16] The superiority of the external, independent legal process to contest the inbred system was demonstrated in *R v Lapite, R v O'Brien*.[17] In separate incidents, two men had died while in police custody. In each case an inquest returned a verdict of unlawful killing. Despite this compelling evidence of how a jury might react, the DPP declined to prosecute, using the '51% rule' as justification. Challenged in judicial review proceedings, she admitted to procedural improprieties and withdrew, offering to reconsider both cases. It was subsequently announced that all such cases would in future be scrutinised by the Attorney-General.

Finally, the perennial question of *independence* arose starkly. Despite regular assurances from the PCB that it was satisfied with the integrity of investigations;

15  *Final Review Report of the Police Complaints Board, 1977-85*, Cmnd 9584 (1985), paras. 3.9, 3.10.

16  [1983] 1 WLR 447. See also, 'Police Complaints Procedures', 4th Report from the Home Affairs Committee 1981-2, HC 98 (1982/3), paras 14,15.

17  Unreported, see G. Smith 'The DPP and prosecutions of police officers' (1997) 147 NLJ 1180.

and that 'in the vast majority of cases which came before them a thorough and fair investigation into the complaints allegations had been carried out', the charge that the police 'investigated themselves' never went away.

Discontent with the system was voiced by the Scarman Report on the Brixton Disorders,[18] the Royal Commission on Criminal Procedure[19] and the Home Affairs Committee,[20] and a Home Office working party chaired by Lord Plowden was set up to propose reform. Debate centred on two key issues: first, the need for a new, informal procedure, to filter out trivial complaints at local level by conciliation; and second, on the introduction into the investigatory stage of a truly independent element. Opinions varied as to how the latter might be achieved; a standing Commisssion, a lay assessor, a tribunal or an Ombudsman were all suggested. It must be said that the case for a Police Ombudsman, vigorously supported before the Home Affairs Committee by *Justice*, the NCCL and the CLA[1] has never really been refuted.

The present system,[2] introduced by Part IX of the Police and Criminal Evidence Act 1984 (PACE) is a dual one. Section 85 of PACE represents a systematic attempt to defuse trivial complaints. It allows a police complaint to be resolved informally provided (a) that the complainant consents and (b) that the conduct in question would not justify criminal proceedings or a disciplinary charge. Between 30% and 40% of all complaints are resolved informally and never cross the desk of the Police Complaints Authority. This classic example of ADR does not always provide satisfaction, however.[3] On the one hand it leads to allegations of pressure to withdraw and accept informal resolution; on the other to discontented officers required to apologise without any opportunity to clear their name. Moreover, the technique can be criticised for providing no adequate sanction for misconduct and no proper accountability.[4]

The second tier centres around PoCA[5] whose remit is (a) to supervise investigations into the most serious complaints including all cases of death or serious injury, which must by s. 87 of PACE be referred to it and (b) in all cases to consider whether disciplinary action should be taken (s. 89). It also possesses exceptional powers to take action of its own accord (s. 87(2)). PoCA reports annually and triennially to Parliament and its reports are reviewed by the Home Affairs Committee. The 14 members work full-time and all supervise investigations. The first Chairman was Sir Cecil Clothier, a barrister and previous Parliamentary Commissioner.

---

18 Cmnd. 8427 (1982).
19 *Report of the Royal Commission on Criminal Procedure*, Cmnd 809 (1981), para 4.119.
20 'Racial Disadvantage' 5th Report for 1980-81, HC 610 (1981) and 'Police Complaints Procedures', above, note 16.
1 HC 98, (1982-3) Memorandum 7.
2 See *Police Complaints Procedures*, Cmnd. 8681 (1982) and *Police Complaints and Discipline Procedures*, Cmnd. 9072 (1983). For a concise account of complaints procedure see J. Harrison and S. Cragg, *Police Misconduct* (above, p. 414, note 9), Chapter 3.
3 C. Corbett, above, note 13.
4 See L. Lustgarten, *The Governance of Police* (London: Sweet and Maxwell) 1986, pp. 155–158.
5 The correct abbreviation for the Police Complaints authority is PCA but here we use PoCA to distinguish the Parliamentary Commissioner.

PoCA, whose literature enthusiastically promotes its independent standing, believe that the new full-time status of its members has allowed them to:[6]

> ... evolve a common approach and uniform policies towards the handling of complaints and the implementation of the Act. We feel confident that in this way our influence on the handling of complaints by the police themselves, including the eventual disciplinary outcomes, has been more professional and more strongly felt than in times gone by.

The ten-year review[7] stresses PoCA's reform role, listing success in achieving reform in control of police use of firearms as well as less successful proposals for reform of the police disciplinary system (presently under review by the Home Office). PoCA is concerned by the hiving-off of police work to civilian authorities, over whom it has demanded jurisdiction.[8] On the debit side, PoCA expresses disappointment that, over a ten-year period, public sentiment has not substantially changed, the perception remaining that the system is 'not much different from what had gone before'. Despite costly public relations exercises, opinion polling shows that only 62% of a representative sample were aware of PoCA's existence, of whom fewer than 40% believed it to be 'independent or impartial'. A discouraging 32% felt that it always 'comes down in favour of the police'.[9] This has persuaded PoCA to monitor complaints statistics more precisely; to break them down by ethnic origin; and to make sustained efforts at publicity and community relations. An independent study concludes with the finding that a majority (69%) of complainants is unhappy with every aspect of the police complaints system; praise is almost always counterbalanced by negative comments.[10] But Table 12.1 provides little support for optimism, listing the growing number of complaints with the low percentage of outcomes resulting in disciplinary action. PoCA might, of course, argue that this is not the test; it is meeting performance indicators in about 60% of cases[11] and delays are regularly monitored.

*Table 12.1: Police complaints referred to PoCA 1986–1995*

CATEGORY A: SUPERVISED*

|                               | 1986 | 1989 | 1992 | 1995/96** |
|-------------------------------|------|------|------|-----------|
| Cases referred                | 3687 | 5008 | 4476 | 2761      |
| Cases accepted for supervision| 681  | 879  | 757  | 1142      |

* NB No outcomes are recorded in the Reports.

6   Memorandum submitted by Police Complaints Authority, 'Parliamentary Accountability of the Police Complaints Authority', 4th Report of Home Affairs Select Committee (1987/8), HC 583 (1988) p. 2, para. 6.
7   *PCA 10, Police Complaints Authority – The First Ten Years* (London: HMSO) 1995.
8   1995/6 AR, p. 44.
9   Annual Report of *The Independent* Police Complaints Authority (emphasis of PoCA) 1985, p.5; 1995/6 AR, p. 48. See also Triennial Review 1988-91 and *PCA10* (above, note 7).
10  M. Maguire and C. Corbett, *A Study of the Police Complaints System* (London: HMSO) 1991.
11  AR 1995/6, p. 20. An investigations target of 120 days with PoCA's response to be complete within 28 days.

CATEGORY D: DISCIPLINE CASES

|  | *1986* | *1989* | *1992* | *1995/96*** |
|---|---|---|---|---|
| Completed cases* | 6,646 | 5,283 | 9,200 | 9,816 |
| Complaints | 15,865 | 11,155 | 19,289 | 18,607 |
| Dispensations | 1,416 | 2,113 | 6,035 | 8,873 |
| Fully investigated complaints | 14,449 | 9,042 | 13,254 | 9,734 |
| Resulting disciplinary action (charges, advice, etc.) | 1,503 | 883 | 1,151 | 1,113 |
| Percentage of fully investigated complaints resulting in disciplinary action | 11.1 | 9.7 | 8.7 | 11.4 |

*Source*: *PCA 10, Police Complaints Authority – The First Ten Years* (London: HMSO) 1995, p. 9; Police Complaints Authority, *Annual Report 1995–1996*, pp. 15–17.

\* One case may include a number of separate complaints
\*\* 1 April 1995 – 31 March 1996.

Advisers blame the ineffective complaints procedure and the higher success rate of civil litigation for a recent upturn in civil actions against the police, regarded by some as 'the main forum in which the police can be brought to account for their misconduct', with a success rate of almost 50% in litigation against some 10% for complaints.[12] The fact that compensation cannot be awarded by PoCA is also a factor. If the Metropolitan Police is typical, litigation has recently escalated: from 52 actions in 1976 to more than 251 in 1991. The annual cost to the Metropolitan Police has also escalated: from £755,000 in 1992, when 136 cases were settled, 21 contested and 11 lost, to £1,560,000 in 1995 (212 cases settled, 50 contested, 22 lost). Not surprisingly, the Home Office is concerned because of the soaring costs.

A further reason for preferring a civil action to the police complaints system lies in the possibility of obtaining punitive and exemplary damages. By tradition, these are awarded in any case of 'oppressive, arbitrary or unconstitutional action by the servants of the government'.[13] So generous have the sums awarded by modern juries who try such cases been that appellate courts have had to step in to regulate awards. In *Thompson and Hsu v Metropolitan Police Comr*,[14] the Court of Appeal felt it necessary to remind juries that the purpose of an award of damages is to compensate the plaintiff rather than to punish the police. A scale was indicated, starting with £500 for the first hour of a wrongful arrest, which

12   R. Clayton and H. Tomlinson, *Civil Actions Against the Police* (above, p. 415, note 11), pp. 13, 15.
13   Lord Devlin in *Rookes v Barnard* [1964] AC 1129, 1226.
14   [1997] 3 WLR 403.

should never exceed twice the compensatory damages. Damages would also be appropriate for aggravating circumstances, such as 'humiliating, high-handed, insulting or malicious treatment'. These directions are likely to bring about a decrease both in awards and settlements; it is indicative that the result for Mr. Hsu was a reduction from the jury award of £220,000 to £35,000.[15]

The resurgence of the civil action locks into a problem over public interest immunity (PII). PII is the right to refuse to produce documents or evidence to a civil or criminal court if the public interest so requires.[16] Its application to police complaints files has had a chequered history. At first, the courts readily granted immunity in civil proceedings to documents created in the course of complaints investigations, perhaps without fully grasping the possible consequences. This line of cases culminated in the unfortunate 'no waiver' rule of *Makanjuola*,[17] where a complainant with a statutory right to a copy of her complaint was refused permission to produce it in a civil action against an officer who had procured sexual favours through a deception. This led to warnings by lawyers against using the complaints system.[18]

Unfavourable comments on the state of the case law[19] made during the Scott Inquiry (above, p. 397), after PII had been claimed for government documents in a prosecution on serious charges, led to a change of heart in the House of Lords. In *R v Chief Constable of the West Midlands Police, ex p Wiley*,[20] Lord Templeman warned that 'a rubber stamp approach' to public interest immunity was inappropriate. Reinstating the principle of *Conway v Rimmer*, the House ruled against 'class' claims to immunity, restricting them to specific documents, and approved waiver. Obviously, this facilitates civil proceedings.

It is doubtful whether improved complaints procedures would lead to a change of heart on the part of legal advisers. So long as the original causes of dissatisfaction – the absence of independent investigation, the '51% rule' and impact of the 'double jeopardy rule', the delays, the high standard of proof and lack of independence in disciplinary procedures – remain in being it is no wonder, critics argue,[1] that confidence in the procedures remains so low.

What are we to deduce from these studies? That duplication and fragmentation of complaints machinery leads to delay, as well-worn and bulging files are passed

---

15 This is part of a wider trend: see *AB v South West Water Services* [1993] 1 All ER 609; *John v MGN Ltd* [1996] 3 WLR 593.
16 *Conway v Rimmer* [1968] AC 910. See on police complaints, de Smith, Jowell, Woolf, paras. 1-143, 1-144. See also, Triennial Review 1985-88, HC 466, paras. 2.1-2.33.
17 *Makanjuola v Metropolitan Police Comr* [1992] 3 All ER 617. See also *Neilson v Laugharne* [1981] QB 736; *Hehir v Metropolitan Police Comr* [1982] 1 WLR 715. *Thorpe v Chief Constable of Greater Manchester* [1989] 2 All ER 827 concerns refusal of discovery of a disciplinary hearing adjudication.
18 J. Harrison and S. Cragg, *Police Misconduct* (above, p. 414, note 9), pp. 108-111 and 'Suing the police: should plaintiffs also make a complaint?' Legal Action, June 1991, p. 22.
19 Sir Richard Scott, 'The Acceptable and Unacceptable Use of Public Interest Immunity' [1996] PL 410. See also A. Zuckerman, 'Public Interest Immunity: A Matter of Prime Judicial Responsibility' (1994) 57 MLR 703; A. Tomkins, 'Public Interest Immunity after Matrix Churchill' [1993] PL 650.
20 *R v Chief Constable of the West Midlands Police, ex p Wiley* [1994] 3 WLR 433.
 1 See A. Hall, 'Time for a change?' Legal Action, August 1990, p. 7.

from one investigator to another without any satisfactory outcome. That a core of intractable cases exists for which none of the existing procedures provides, as in the notorious examples of Blair Peach, a young teacher allegedly killed by the police during a demonstration, [2] or of Joy Gardner, who died during a forcible deportation in 1993 [3] or of Stephen Lawrence, for whose murder no one has yet been convicted, a failure which is to be the subject of another special inquiry. In these cases, inquiries, inquests, criminal and civil proceedings are tried successively but fruitlessly, the interlocking web of remedies merely contributing to the unsatisfactory outcome.

Complexity leads to games of 'snakes and ladders' where complainants are referred from one office to another and end by fighting the complaints system rather than attacking the initial wrong. Ladders benefit both complainants and defendants. Unwelcome police investigation can be obstructed by a complaint against the investigating officer or by vexatious complaints in one forum after another; on the other side, the 'double jeopardy' rule can be used to block further action and disciplinary proceedings evaded by early retirement. Ladders also allow complainants to progress complaints, carefully weighing advantages and disadvantages: the PCA is free, litigation without legal aid is dangerous, especially if the police sue for defamation; litigation brings an outside element into prisons, Boards of Visitors are external but not necessarily wholly independent; court orders are mandatory, Ombudsmen recommend. Some complaints systems award compensation, others, like PoCA, do not. Are PCA recommendations more likely to be implemented than those of the Prisons Ombudsman (PO) or the Inspector of Prisons? And so on, endlessly.

## Conclusion: the complaints industry

What can we learn more generally from this discussion of complaints procedures? Are we now in a position to establish overall criteria for evaluation?

We have noted the view that tribunals exist for the provision of 'simple, informal, speedy, cheap and accessible' justice. As to values, lawyers are customarily content with the repetition of the three simple axioms of 'openness, fairness and impartiality' singled out by the Franks Committee as qualities of machinery for adjudication (below, p. 461). Though prioritising these, the *Justice*/All Souls Review grudgingly admitted that 'since Franks, other standards than openness, fairness and impartiality such as efficiency, expedition and economy' have become significant, [4] to which they added 'accessibility' in the limited sense of access to early advice and assistance. The Charter Unit agreed that complaints systems should be accessible and well-publicised; simple to understand and use; speedy and open; fair, with a full and impartial investigation, and effective in providing appropriate redress. Again, in a review-article based

---

2  *Southall 23 April 1979, The Report of the Unofficial Committee of Inquiry* (London: NCCL) 1980.
3  *PCA 10*, p. 14; AR 1995/6, p. 28.
4  *Justice*/All Souls Review (above, p 393, note 16), p. 214 and para. 9.25.

on long study of Ombudsmen, Giddings and others list essential criteria for successful complaints systems.[5] These include effectiveness, evidenced by public recognition and visibility; independence; accessibility, with clarity of jurisdiction. The investigator must also have adequate powers of investigation, including access to relevant information. A consensus begins to emerge.

The qualities required for a good complaints system include both 'sigma' values of economy, efficiency and effectiveness and 'theta' values of fairness and integrity (above, p. 131). High on everyone's list of priorities comes *independence*,though, as we have seen, this may be variously interpreted. Lawyers rate externality highly, a qualification which neither the Revenue Adjudicator nor private sector Ombudsmen really fulfil. The Charter Unit focuses on autonomy in the sense of freedom to make decisions without interference.

It is arrogant of lawyers to suppose that fairness is a value which 'trickles down' from courts into administration. True, due process is an important value for lawyers, but largely because values are also reflected in procedures. As our fondness for cricketing metaphors indicates, fairness is highly rated in British culture and a measure of consensus exists on its content. Equality before the law is a fundamental component of the Rule of Law ideal but administrators too recognise the value of equal treatment, recognised by the Charter Unit with its requirement of even-handedness.

Proliferating complaints and complaints procedures highlight basic questions about the design of effective systems of administrative law. Complaints are important because unresolved complaints cause much bitterness and easily escalate from grumbles into disputes. Functionalists in particular will expect the 'bottom layer' of complaints systems to be appropriate and efficient as well as just. This is the more important when we realise that a pyramidal structure for dispute-resolution is illusory. Not every case which reaches the Court of Appeal is significant; many are trivial. ADR, on the other hand, may inadvertently stifle a serious scandal by filtering out a grave complaint at an early stage – one reason why some Ombudsmen try to investigate all complaints within jurisdiction.

The culture of complaining is not necessarily admirable, nor from a public law perspective is it particularly constructive; market theorists dissemble when they equate complaining with participation. The 'bottom-up' approach to complaining inevitably stimulates the growth of a 'complaints industry'. In a complaints culture, complaints multiply, are sucked into, and overload complaints machinery as fast as it can be fashioned. And, however much the progenitors of the Charter tried to deny this, a culture of complaints is closely linked with a culture of rights enforceable through litigation. Perhaps, after all, complaints need to be firmly distinguished from 'grumbles' and other minor forms of dissatisfaction.

---

5    P. Giddings, R. Gregory, V. Moore and J. Pearson, 'Controlling administrative action in the United Kingdom: the role of ombudsman systems and the courts compared' (1993) 59 International Review of Administrative Sciences 291.

# Chapter 13

# Fire-fighter to fire-watcher? A case study of the PCA

## 1. In search of a role

At the end of Chapter 12, we concluded that a good complaints system must combine 'sigma' values of efficiency, effectiveness and, to a lesser degree, economy, with 'theta' values, especially fairness. We noted too the priority always accorded to independence, although we saw that this term might bear different interpretations. In this chapter, we try to evaluate the Parliamentary Commissioner for Administration (PCA), asking where this institution fits into the system of administrative justice. Is it a court substitute? Do its inquisitorial procedures provide a new model for administrative justice? Perhaps it is not really 'machinery for adjudication' and the real parallel is with audit? Before we embark on these and other questions, we need to know a little more about the office.

In the last chapter we saw that the word 'Ombudsman' literally means 'complaints man', indicating a general grievance-handling function. We also said that the office invariably took on local characteristics, so that there is not one Ombudsman but many.

In an attempt to draw the threads together, Gregory et al. identify the characteristics common to the office: [1]

  (i)  an expert, independent and non-partisan instrument of the legislature established by statute or in the constitution;

  (ii)  clearly visible and readily accessible to members of the public;

  (iii) responsible for both acting on its own volition and for receiving and dealing impartially with specific complaints from aggrieved citizens against alleged administrative injustice and maladministration on the part of governmental agencies, officials or employees; and

  (iv) furnished with practically unrestricted access to official papers, empowered to investigate, form judgements, criticise or vindicate, make recommendations as to remedies and corrective measures, and report on but not to reverse, administrative action.

---

1   R. Gregory, P. Giddings, V. Moore, J. Pearson, *Practice and Prospects of the Ombudsmen in the United Kingdom* (Lewiston: Edwin Mellon Press) p. 2 . And see G. Caiden, N. MacDermot and A. Sandler, 'The Institution of Ombudsman', in G. Caiden (ed.), *International Handbook of the Ombudsman. Evolution and Present Function* (London: Greenwood Press) 1983.

Now let us compare this list with the criteria evolved in Chapter 12 for a good complaints system – effectiveness; public recognition and visibility; independence; accessibility; and clarity of jurisdiction. Common elements appear, for example the stress on visibility and accessibility, qualities stressed by the Charter Unit. 'Impartiality' also seems to bear its Charter Unit meaning of freedom from interference by government agencies, combined here with a right of access to official papers, not an essential characteristic of adversarial justice. The authors hint at fire-watching functions when they speak of Ombudsmen 'acting on their own volition'; courts intervene only when invited to act by a litigant. Ombudsmen also take a more direct interest than courts in stimulating administrative improvement, pursuing their goals not only through their rulings but by rule-making, advice and monitoring. We have already seen the CLA carrying out fire-watching functions in the last chapter (above, p. 410). It should also be noted that Ombudsmen do not hand down judgments or issue orders; they 'make recommendations as to remedies and corrective measures', a further pointer to a fire-watching function. If we think back to what was said in Chapter 12 about inquiries, the phrase also suggests an investigatory rather than an adjudicative role.

Now let us move on to the PCA, established by the Parliamentary Commissioner Act 1967. Briefly, the Act provided for appointment by the Prime Minister. Today, after some wrangling, appointments are made after consultation with the Chairman of the Select Committee of the House of Commons, to which the PCA is responsible, and with the approval of the Leader of the Opposition. [2] Like High Court judges, the PCA holds office during good behaviour. Although we shall find that the individuals concerned have perceived their role rather differently, the PCA has invariably seen himself as *impartial*; in other words, he feels under an obligation to uphold public bodies whenever an investigation warrants it. A key administrative benefit of the scheme as it was set up, was that individual civil servants, falsely accused, should be able to clear their names. This view of the office as quasi-judicial has restrained the PCA from acting as 'citizen's advocate'. [3]

The PCA heads an office or department, staffed by approximately 90 people, a handful of lawyers and a majority of career civil servants seconded from central government departments, a practice which has proved highly effective. His investigators use documentary and investigatorial procedure, described in greater detail below, and this requires an understanding of civil service procedure.

The function of the office is to investigate complaints referred either by individuals or private corporate bodies who have suffered from maladministration. In other words, the office is at the disposal of the public and cannot be used to sort out disputes between public bodies or between public servants and the government as employer. The test also requires the complainant to be someone directly affected by maladministration; he cannot act as public advocate to notify the PCA of departmental incompetence. To succeed, a complaint must satisfy a two-pronged test of 'injustice' caused by 'maladministration'.

2   HC 33-I (1993/4) para. 31, p. xi.
3   See, A. Bradley, 'The Role of the Ombudsman in Relation to the Protection of Citizens' Rights' [1980] 39(2) CLJ 304; R. Rawlings, 'The Legacy of a Lawyer-Ombudsman', (1985) (June) Legal Action, p. 10.

Deliberately, the Act did not define maladministration, though the government spokesman, Mr Crossman, described it as including: [4]

> bias, neglect, inattention, delay, incompetence, ineptitude, perversity, turpitude, arbitrariness and so on.

Like the grounds for judicial review, maladministration has proved elastic. In some cases the term has been glossed by PCAs anxious to extend their competence, which they have done by referring to 'errors' or through phrases such as 'I was critical of' or 'left with a feeling of unease'. Not strictly maladministration, such findings have been used to insist on departmental action.

In his Annual Report for 1993, Mr. Reid, then PCA, proposed updating the 'Crossman Catalogue' to give a clearer indication, in the language of the 1990s, of what was expected of departments. To Crossman's list, Reid added these notably more bureaucratic examples: [5]

- rudeness (though that is a matter of degree);
- unwillingness to treat the complainant as a person with rights;
- refusal to answer reasonable questions;
- neglecting to inform a complainant on request of his or her rights or entitlement;
- knowingly giving advice which is misleading or inadequate;
- ignoring valid advice or overruling considerations which would produce an uncomfortable result for the overruler;
- offering no redress or manifestly disproportionate redress;
- showing bias whether because of colour, sex, or any other grounds;
- omission to notify those who thereby lose a right of appeal;
- refusal to inform adequately of the right of appeal;
- faulty procedures;
- failure by management to monitor compliance with adequate procedures;
- cavalier disregard of guidance which is intended to be followed in the interest of equitable treatment of those who use a service;
- partiality; and
- failure to mitigate the effects of rigid adherence to the letter of the law where that produces manifestly unequal treatment.

The flexibility of the definition was offset in the 1967 Act by complex limitations. First, the PCA's jurisdiction covered only central government departments and other public bodies specifically listed in the Act. Schedule 3 exempted from investigation some key governmental concerns, such as commercial transactions, civil service personnel matters and, originally, official action taken abroad. Second, s. 6(4) required that the complainant be resident in, or that the complaint relate to action taken while he was in, or relate to rights and obligations accruing in, the United Kingdom. Third, and most restrictive, s. 12(3) of the Act reads:

> It is hereby declared that nothing in this Act authorises or requires the Commissioner to question the merits of a decision taken without maladministration . . . in the exercise of a discretion vested in [a] department.

4   4 HC Deb., vol. 734, col. 51. See also G. Marshall, 'Maladministration' [1973] PL 32.
5   AR 1993, HC 290 (1993/4), para. 7.

We shall pick this crucial point up later. Other provisions, like the one-year time-limit for complaints and the provisions of s. 5(2) (below), could be waived by the PCA in certain circumstances.

The distinguishing characteristic of this particular Ombudsman is a quality not included in Gregory's catalogue. It is his unique position as an Officer of the House of Commons [6] and the close relationship between the PCA and Parliament which sharply differentiate the office from that of other Ombudsmen. [7] There is no direct access to the PCA; complaints lie only through an MP, who chooses whether or not to refer them. The PCA is responsible to a Select Committee of the Commons (SC) to which he makes regular reports. He lays his reports as parliamentary papers and dispatches individual findings to the referring MP. The SC reports to the House and its reports are occasionally debated on the floor of the House. [8] The SC follows investigations, summons witnesses and issues its own reports on matters arising. As one reads their reports, one can see that successive PCAs have set great store on their status as parliamentary officials. The relationship is at once an advantage and a disadvantage. On the credit side, it lends power to the PCA's elbow; the powerful SC looming over the PCA's shoulder is usually sufficient to frighten off disobedient civil servants.

On the debit side, the subservience entailed by the relationship has sometimes acted as a restraint. The PCA must be a particular type of person capable of walking a tight-rope between government and Parliament. The first PCA was Sir Edmund Compton, a former Comptroller and Auditor-General, and the office is modelled on his relationship with the powerful Public Accounts Comittee. Announcing his appointment to an office not yet in being, Mr. Crossman soothingly explained, 'It is a Parliamentary officer that we want, and Sir Edmund Compton is a most distinguished Parliamentary officer already'. [9] Sir Cecil Clothier later questioned whether he should investigate complaints which Parliament had debated on the ground that 'Parliament would not tolerate to be corrected by my subsequent investigation if I should arrive at a different conclusion'. [10] Other PCAs have fallen into a cosy relationship with their Select Committee (and vice versa). [11] Thus, the link in one sense threatens independence, perhaps the most crucial factor in legitimating complaints machinery. As the Minister (Mr. Crossman) told the Commons at Second Reading of the Bill, [12] the

6   See R. Gregory and A. Alexander, 'Our Parliamentary Ombudsman. Part II: Development and the Problem of Identity' (1973) Pub. Admin. 41.
7   R. Rawlings, 'Parliamentary Redress of Grievance' in C. Harlow (ed.), *Politics and Public Law* (London: Sweet and Maxwell) 1986. And see, R. Gregory and A. Alexander, 'Our Parliamentary Ombudsman. Part I: Integration and Metamorphosis' (1972) Pub. Admin. 313.
8   See, especially, HC Deb., vol. 251, cols. 1125-1164 (15 December 1994). And see R. Gregory, 'The Select Committee on the Parliamentary Commissioner for Administration 1967-1980' [1982] PL 49.
9   HC Deb., vol. 734, col. 54. Sir Edmund was followed by Sir Alan Marre and Sir Idwal Pugh, Permanent Secretaries; then came two lawyers, Sir Cecil Clothier and Sir Anthony Barrowclough; and two civil servants, Sir William Reid, from the Scottish Home and Health Department, and Mr. Michael Buckley, a civil servant who has chaired an NHS trust.
10   Sir Cecil Clothier, 'Legal Problems of an Ombudsman' (1984) 81 Law Soc. Gaz. 3108.
11   G. Drewry and C. Harlow, 'A 'Cutting Edge'? The Parliamentary Commissioner and MPs' (1990) 53 MLR 745.
12   HC Deb., vol. 734, col. 43.

PCA is 'in the strictest sense, a servant of the House'. As we saw in earlier chapters, the House is all too often the servant of the government.

The central theme of this chapter is that there has never been full agreement over the proper role and functions of the PCA. The classic Ombudsman model has been distorted by parliamentary jealousy for its privileges and traditions. At Second Reading of the Parliamentary Commissioner Bill in 1966, the main Opposition spokesman described the office as a threat to a system of parliamentary democracy in which MPs already provided 'an efficient and relatively sophisticated grievance machinery'.[13] The office contains a further built-in tension between its fire-fighting and fire-watching functions. We shall argue that this ambiguity has never been properly resolved, with the result that functions have become blurred and disagreement has emerged as to what the PCA ought to be doing. Two competing models have emerged, whose differing requirements are hard to balance. Some of the criticisms directed at the PCA's office result from this absence of a clear sense of priorities. Any evaluation of the PCA's performance requires us to look a little more closely at this disagreement.

## (a) Fire-fighting: the small claims court

The perception of Ombudsmen as fire-fighters infused the influential report *The Citizen and the Administration*,[14] which lay behind the legislation. As we saw in Chapter 4 (above, p. 94) this report formed part of the reaction fo *Crichel Down*. The report recommended an impartial officer to be called a parliamentary commissioner to investigate and report on complaints of maladministration. The lawyerly emphasis was not surprising; the report, whose director of research, Sir John Whyatt, was a former judge, was drawn up for *Justice*, a pressure group of lawyers dedicated, according to its constitution, to the 'preservation of the fundamental liberties of the individual'.

Whyatt, contended that traditional controls left a gap. Judicial review was too limited, leaving much maladministration (e.g., rudeness or delay) unredressed and too expensive save in the exceptional case. Equally, parliamentary procedures were ineffective; adjournment debates and parliamentary questions were uneven contests because only the executive possessed all the relevant information. Ad hoc inquiries, on the other hand, were a little-used Rolls-Royce machinery unsuited to everyday matters. Into the gap, an Ombudsman was to be inserted. This thinking exactly parallels that of the contemporary Franks Committee (below, p. 460). There are parallel ironies in what was to follow. The Whyatt Committee aimed squarely at the discretionary power with which the administration was increasingly endowed. Yet, as we shall see, discretionary decisions were to be excluded from the PCA's jurisdiction (s. 12(3), below). Again, Whyatt envisaged the Ombudsman as an alternative to courts. Yet the Labour government did not allow the PCA to supplant existing methods of obtaining redress, though we

13 HC Deb., vol. 734, col. 65.
14 (London: *Justice*) 1961.

do find Mr Crossman[15] voicing the traditional Labour Party view that the expense and popular awe of the courts might frighten people away, an argument extended by MPs, against the government's advice, to tribunals. Section 5(2) of the Act represents a modest attempt to avoid overlapping remedies. It provides that where a complaint relates to a matter giving rise to a right of appeal to a tribunal or to a court remedy, the PCA shall not investigate unless 'satisfied that in the particular circumstances it is not reasonable to expect [the complainant] to resort or have resorted to it'. In addition to this unstructured discretion, the PCA possesses an overarching power because s. 5(5) lays down that in determining whether to initiate, continue and discontinue an investigation, he shall 'act in accordance with his own discretion'. Thus the PCA possesses considerable freedom of manoeuvre or 'agency discretion'. This has at various times been exercised in very different ways. Sir Idwal Pugh, a former civil servant, exercised the discretion generously, inaugurating a practice of doubtful legal validity, of extracting from complainants a promise to refrain from legal action. The following passage from Sir Cecil Clothier illustrates a lawyer's response:[16]

> ... where there appears on the face of things to have been a substantial legal wrong for which, if proved, there is a substantial legal remedy, I expect the citizen to seek it in the courts and I tell him so. But where there is doubt about the availability of a legal remedy or where the process of law seems too cumbersome, slow and expensive for the objective to be gained, I exercise my discretion to investigate the complaint myself.

Another lawyer, Sir Anthony Barrowclough, took a rather different view in a case[17] where a dispute of fact had arisen whether a claim form had been received by the Ministry of Agriculture, Fisheries and Food (MAFF), as a farmer alleged and MAFF denied. Sir Anthony refused to investigate, advising the complainant that recourse to a civil action would be 'a relatively simple and inexpensive matter'.

Directed as it was towards the redress of grievance, the Whyatt report did not examine the fire-watching objectives of complaints machinery. The identification of administrative inefficiency with a view to its eradication passed the committee by. Neither *Justice* nor the House of Commons analysed the consequences for administration generally. They envisaged the new office as a sort of standing inquiry which could – as the Crichel Down Inquiry had done – penetrate the anonymity of ministerial responsibility. In advocating informal investigatory techniques designed to minimise administrative disruption, *Justice* recognised that departments expend resources meeting investigations. Perhaps it was not surprising, at a time before departmental Select Committees were operative, that the PCA was never envisaged as auditor-general or government inspector.

The office envisaged by the Whyatt report was effectively an administrative small claims court. The report conceived of the PCA as a court substitute, though decisively orientated to small claims. This perception is discernible in all of

15   HC Deb., vol. 734, col. 52.
16   HC 148 (1980/1) p. 1.
17   C45/88, AR 1988, HC 480 (1988/9), p. 17.

*Justice*'s later work on the office. In particular we shall find that, consistent with its initial position, the question of direct access to the PCA has been a constant source of concern to *Justice*, which has consistently lobbied[18] for open access, criticised the tendency to appoint career civil servants to the post and campaigned on grounds of independence for the appointment of a lawyer. It must be said, however, that with one possible exception (below, p. 446), the independence, objectivity and impartiality of the public service PCAs has never been seriously questioned. It was the first lawyer-Ombudsman, Sir Cecil Clothier, who remarked on retirement how greatly he had valued 'the privilege of having been treated as a Permanent Under-Secretary of State'.[19]

In its ten-year review[20] of the Ombudsman's progress, *Justice* concluded that the new institution had worked well, although within a very restricted frame of reference. By comparison with foreign Ombudsmen, who handled a proportionately greater number of investigations per head of population, the PCA was 'considerably under-utilised'. From Table 13.1 (below, p. 444) we can see that, although recently the workload has increased, the PCA has never yet received 2,000 complaints annually, a surprising comparison with, say, social security appeals (below, p. 457).

*Justice* concluded that direct access was an 'essential reform if the Commissioner is properly to fulfil the role of providing redress for citizens with complaints against central administration, and of acting as watchdog against administrative abuse'.[1] While elaborate investigations were appropriate for difficult cases, informal methods would produce immediate redress in routine cases. 'Maladministration' should be replaced with the wider formulation of 'unreasonable, unjust or oppressive action' and most of Sch. 3 abandoned, in particular, two statistically significant exclusions – personnel matters and commercial transactions:[2]

> The continuous growth of the administration . . . calls for a parallel development of effective checks and balances if the citizen is not to be submerged by bureaucracy. The [PCA] has the possibility . . . of becoming one of the most important of the safeguards for the citizen against the administration, and to that end should be developed to its full . . . The most important consideration is that as many as possible of bona fide grievances against government departments should be investigated ...

Neither government nor SC were to be persuaded down this road. Indeed, the SC re-asserted the original view that 'the primary responsibility for defending the citizen against the executive rests with the Member of Parliament' and advocated retention of the MP filter, although encouraging better publicity measures[3] and

18 In addition to *Our Fettered Ombudsman* (London: *Justice*) 1977, paras. 24-31, see *Justice*/All Souls Review *Administrative Justice – Some Necessary Reforms*, Report of the Committee of the *Justice*/All Souls Review of Administrative Law in the United Kingdom (Oxford: Clarendon) 1988, p. 90.
19 AR 1983, HC 617 (1983/4) p. 1.
20 *Our Fettered Ombudsman*, above, note 18.
1 Ibid, p. 1. And see pp. 16-19.
2 *Justice* 1977, pp. 6, 18.
3 *Review of Access and Jurisdiction*, HC 615 (1977/8) para 10.

approving an informal practice of sending direct complaints on to the constituency MP to decide whether to refer the complaint back formally. Fifteen years later, neither the SC nor MPs had changed their mind; 67.7% (159) of 235 MPs responding to a questionnaire supported the MP filter with only 23.8% (56) against.[4]

### (b) Fire-watching: inspection and audit

Ten years after the office had been established, Harlow was arguing that the PCA had yet to identify a distinctive role. The expensive machinery of the PCA and his office meant that it was wasted if treated merely as a small claims court; moreover, it had been calculated that each PCA investigation cost a government department about 80 hours of staff time. The Swedish Ombudsman can act without complaints, either by initiating his own investigations, for example after adverse press reports, or by inspecting institutions within his jurisdiction. Harlow argued that the PCA should be given similar powers:[5]

> The advocates of reform direct their attention to those barriers which seem to hinder the PCA from processing the maximum number of 'small claims' . ... These are fallacious arguments because PCA procedure is not really appropriate to handle a large number of [cases] . . . [His] investigatory procedure is thorough but costly: a PCA investigation may cost as much as £2000. It is [also] time-consuming . . . Obviously the PCA cannot abandon the investigation of individual complaints if only because, without complaints, grave administrative deficiencies would rarely come to light. But the arguments for removal of the 'MP filter' should be rigorously examined. The new compromise . . . allows the MP to settle the trivial administrative muddles, resubmitting only the hard nuts. Even then the PCA probably needs to develop a subsidiary procedure for very small cases to run alongside his 'Rolls Royce method'. . .
>
> When we turn to the second Ombudsman function . . . we find the PCA is uniquely well placed to undertake the task and that his procedures are entirely appropriate . . . Parliamentary questions are a blunt instrument. The classic doctrine of Ministerial Responsibility may actually shelter more administrative blunders than it exposes. The efficacy of court orders is limited by the absence of supervisory powers. The PCA, on the other hand, has available to him all the information on which the disputed decision was based. He has behind him the considerable authority of a Parliamentary Select Committee. [So] his *primary* role should be that of an independent and unattached investigator, with a mandate to identify maladministration, recommend improved procedures and negotiate their implementation. Changes in his jurisdiction and procedures should be made only if they facilitate the execution of this task.
>
> If this is right, the individual complaint is primarily a mechanism which draws attention to more general administrative deficiencies. [And] the essential question with regard to access is whether the PCA should be given power to intervene of his own initiative. It is submitted that he should.

In sharp contrast to *Justice*, Harlow was arguing for an elitist, strategic, role. The role of MPs in filtering simple and trivial complaints should be acknowledged.

4   G. Drewry and C. Harlow (1990) 53 MLR 745, 755.
5   C. Harlow, 'Ombudsmen in Search of a Role' (1978) 41 MLR 446, 450-453.

The PCA would concentrate on quality rather than quantity, developing his fire-watching characteristics. Time was to show that the flaw in this arrangement lay at the bottom of the pyramid, where both the response of MPs to their complaints function and their use of the PCA is unstructured, uncontrolled and sporadic. While some regard themselves as 'statutory pillar boxes', others exercise independent discretion and refuse to pass on complaints.[6] Nor is there any machinery whereby the PCA can rid his office of trivial complaints. Indeed, he would probably be loath to do this, as a trivial complaint has occasionally triggered a complex and demanding investigation (below).

Sir Cecil Clothier, a lawyer whose general attitude to complaints-handling was somewhat legalistic, believed that the PCA should concentrate his efforts to preserve the Rolls Royce quality of his investigations:[7]

> Since the complaints fully investigated by me are a small fraction of the total investigated by departments in direct communication with [MPs], it seems right that I should give them the most thorough and careful treatment of which my Office is capable. And the justification is to be found in the fact that in almost every second case investigated, there is a change in the department's previous stance. My concern is . . . to see that this careful process and my valuable resources are not wasted on trivial or unworthy causes.

In a ten-year review of the PCA's office,[8] the SC took faltering steps towards a firewatching function. It recommended that the PCA should be able, subject to the Committee's approval, to mount a systemic investigation where on the basis of previous complaints he believed that a particular department was working inefficiently, with a view to making recommendations for putting things right. Sir Idwal Pugh, then PCA, thought this the most important of the Committee's recommendations[9] but the government rejected the idea of an inspectorial power as 'unnecessary and undesirable':[10]

> It would place a heavy burden on the Commissioner if he were required in effect to 'audit' the administrative competence of government departments and would distract him and his staff from *their central purpose of investigating* complaints . . . Where the Commissioner investigates a series of complaints relating to a particular area of administration he is . . . able to form a clear view of the procedures in force there and to make recommendations . . . Any lessons to be drawn from investigations by the Commissioner are already studied by departments and acted upon . . . It should be for Ministers and their departments to decide what action is necessary to prevent further maladministration by a particular branch or establishment, and to be answerable to Parliament for the adequacy of the action . . . taken.

6   C. Harlow and G. Drewry (1990) 53 MLR 745, 749. See also R. Rawlings, 'The MP's Complaints Service' (1990) 53 MLR at 162-164.
7   HC 258 (1981/2), p. 2.
8   *Review of Access and Jurisdiction*, HC 615 (1977/8) para. 31. See also First Report of the Select Committee, HC 129 (1990/91) paras. 19-22.
9   HC 205 (1978/9), p. 5. R. Rawlings, 'Parliamentary Redress of Grievance' in C. Harlow (ed.), *Public Law and Politics* (London: Sweet and Maxwell) 1986, pp. 137-141, suggests a suitable structure.
10  *Observations by the Government on Review of Access and Jurisdiction* Cmnd 7449 (1997/78) pp. 5-6.

Arguably, a crucial opportunity was lost to put the Parliamentary Commissioner on a level with the Comptroller-General and Auditor, and his Select Committee on a level with the far more influential Public Accounts Committee. The government's position may, however, be revealing. As we now know, the Citizen's Charter was soon to arrive and Charter functions were to be internalised in the Cabinet Office. The managerial style of scrutiny may be less threatening to government than an external, *parliamentary* inspector. Indeed, the advent of the Charter initially posed a threat to the PCA, as the SC realised, quickly authorising a report in which his relationship to the novel programme was discussed.[11] It was agreed he should:[12]

> ... have regard to their [i.e., departmental charters] contents when investigating future complaints, or considering whether to investigate future complaints, about failure to attain the standard of service they describe. They will help to provide a standard by which to measure the maladministration alleged, but they leave the Parliamentary Commissioner... unfettered in his discretion to determine whether or not maladministration has taken place.

Although Charter standards might assist the PCA, the SC emphasised that the PCA might assist the Citizen's Charter Programme. This he would do by 'monitoring implementation of Charter principles by individual departments, and provid[ing] one form of the "independent validation of performance against standards" of which the Charter speaks'.[13] The PCA still possesses no power to investigate on his own account, however.

## 2. The investigation

In Britain, where adversarial procedure is the norm, the Ombudsman provides an alternative to the adversarial paradigm. Ombudsman procedure derives from a continental model. Legal representation is unnecessary and still exceptional (though increasing reference in reports to solicitors suggests a higher visibility for the office amongst lawyers). Perhaps the sharpest contrast is that the procedure is free for the complainant. Again, once the complaint is laid before the PCA, the investigation is wholly out of the complainant's hands; although he may be interviewed, this is not a statutory requirement.

The office of the PCA (OPCA) has evolved a three-stage, investigatory procedure, divided into (i) screening (ii) investigation (iii) report. Below, Sir Idwal Pugh describes the different stages[14] involved in handling a complaint:

> Before any investigation can begin, the complaint must be screened to determine whether it has been properly referred and whether it is within my jurisdiction . . . [If]

---

11  Second Report of Select Committee for 1991-2, *The Implications of the Citizen's Charter for the Work of the Parliamentary Commissioner for Administration*, HC 158 (1992/3).

12  Mr. Reid, Evidence, pp. 12-13.

13  HC 158, p. iv.

14  I. Pugh, 'The Ombudsman – Jurisdiction, Powers and Practice' (1978) 56 Pub. Admin. 127, 134-136. The statutory requirement referred to is in s. 7(1) of the 1967 Act.

accepted investigation begins. I am required by the Act to afford the principal officer of the department concerned . . . the opportunity to comment on the complaint. For this purpose I prepare a statement of complaint setting out the material facts of the case. I send this to the permanent secretary concerned together with a letter requesting his comments. If a complaint names a particular member of the department, a second copy of the statement of complaint will be sent so that he can have it...

When I receive the principal officer's reply, it is open to me to accept it and issue a report on the basis of that reply. In some cases I do so but usually only if the department fully accepts the validity of the complaint and makes full restitution. In other cases the principal officer's reply is only the starting point of the real investigation. This normally begins with a detailed enquiry into the statements or remissions which appear from an examination of the department's reply. It will consist of examining departmental papers, discussion with officers of the department concerned or further correspondence with the department. In about half the investigations members of my staff go on to take oral or further written evidence from the complainant. When all this has been done, a draft 'results report' on the case is prepared and is submitted to me and is often the subject of a case conference. This sets out all the facts of the case, the course of the investigation and the conclusion and findings on the complaint. If the complaint is upheld, it will also specify the remedy which is called for. I then send the draft report to the permanent secretary of the department concerned. I do this for the following reasons. First, so that he can check, as far as the department's records are concerned, that I have correctly reported facts. Secondly, so that he can confirm that the department will or will not agree to a remedy where one is included in the report. Thirdly, so that he may also decide whether or not in the very rare case to ask the minister in charge of the department to use the right which he has under the statute to prevent disclosure of information [when it] 'would be prejudicial to the safety of the State or otherwise contrary to the public interest'. I have never been called upon to comply with this part of the statute . . . This description of my investigations will reveal two things. Firstly, that they are extremely independent and secondly that they are extremely thorough.

A more up-to-date account is contained in a new booklet, *The Ombudsman in Your Files*[15] and is reinforced by guidance from the Office of Public Service. What emerges most clearly from a comparison is the continuity of practice, the more significant because the legislation stops at giving the department and 'anyone else concerned' a right to comment and procedure otherwise is largely a matter of agency discretion. In contrast to courts, however, PCA procedure is private and individuals are not named in his report.

The screening stage (first stage) is important, if only because such a high number of complaints is screened out at this stage. The office tries to be helpful to disappointed complainants, advising them where else to take their complaints. We shall see that a major factor here is the complexity of jurisdiction. A further factor, however, is the recent introduction by the PCA of a 'fast track' procedure, used where departments are considering or offer immediate redress or where informal inquiries lead to a satisfactory outcome. These settlements fall into the screening category for recording purposes.

15   *The Ombudsman in Your Files* (London: Cabinet Office) 1996, pp. 10-13; Cabinet Office Letter DEO(PM)(96)4.

The full investigation (second stage) is directed wholly by the PCA, whose office has access to the departmental files. There are no pleadings and seldom any hearings, though oral statements are frequent (above). There are no rules of proof or evidence and all information, including comments, may be quoted and relied on in the report. The responsibility to correct errors rests on the principal officer or chief executive of an agency. Section 8 requires anyone who can furnish information to do so and provides that no claim of PII, legal privilege or official secrecy shall prevail against the PCA except in the case of the proceedings of Cabinet and its committees.

The draft report (third stage) is sent to the principal officer (PO) and normally contains a recommendation as to remedy. In response, the PO should correct any errors, draw attention to omissions and discuss with the PCA proposed action in respect of the recommended remedy. Where compensation is involved, the department may also have to contact the Treasury (below, p. 609). The report is then ready to be sent to the referring MP and to the SC.

In accordance with Citizen's Charter standards, the latest guidance directs the department how to make best use of the investigation. It should record and analyse complaints for trends; set targets for reducing recurring failures; look for any repetition or pattern in failures to meet standards or in maladministration; and take action to change systems or procedures where necessary. The OPS must be notified of changes which may affect other departments. It must also consider why its own complaints systems failed to resolve satisfactorily any complaints which the Ombudsman considered justified. The OPS may then circulate a case summary together with a note on 'lessons to be learned'.

### 3. The 'big inquiry': Barlow Clowes

The *Barlow Clowes* affair[16] offers an opportunity to compare the investigatorial techniques of inquiries and Ombudsmen. Probably the most complex case a PCA has ever investigated, it involved two PCAs (Sir Anthony Barrowclough (a former QC) and Mr. William Reid (a former civil servant)). A statutory inquiry chaired by Sir Godfrey LeQuesne QC ran alongside.

Barlow Clowes (BC) dealt in 'bond washing', a trade which enables highly taxed income to be converted into tax-free or low tax capital gains. In 1988 BC had to be wound up after its funds had been fraudulently diverted to high risk ventures and the directors' private use. The issue was the extent to which the DTI in the exercise of statutory regulatory and licensing powers had known, or ought to have known, of this malpractice and taken steps to warn off potential investors.

The first complaint reached the PCA in 1988. In June 1989, when it seems that no decision whether to investigate had yet been taken, rumour and accusation had reached such a pitch that the minister, Lord Young, agreed to set up a statutory inquiry:

> to determine the facts of what actually happened within the Department, and to determine whether the Department is to blame in any way, and whether procedures could be improved in future.

16  *The Barlow Clowes Affair*, HC 76 (1989/90).

Why the PCA was by-passed is not known. His response was to hold himself in reserve, postponing his decision to investigate but warning investors that if they went to court, he could not proceed (see s. 5(2), above, p. 428).

In October 1988, the Le Quesne inquiry reported. PCA reports are normally published; ministerial inquiries can be private. Lord Young simply told Parliament[17] he had found 'the department's general handling of the licensing of Barlow Clowes ... was careful and considered and its actions reasonable'. The findings provided 'no justification for using taxpayers' money to fund compensation'. The government, however, agreed to co-operate if the PCA, who had a copy of the report, wished to investigate. Dissatisfied, a large number of MPs immediately turned to the PCA who responded positively.

With the PCA treading the same ground as the inquiry, duplication was a danger. However, his documentary procedures permitted him to use the inquiry's witness statements[18]. Unusually, we find intervention from lawyers on behalf of investors and detailed submissions from Barlow Clowes' solicitors. Again, the PCA and his officials took oral evidence from 'a large number' of witnesses, departmental and otherwise. Note the flexibility which allowed procedure, perhaps influenced by this PCA's legal background, to veer atypically towards the oral tradition of an inquiry. A lawyer was later to contrast[19] the style of Barrowclough, 'a QC and a man with a strong judicial instinct for analysis based upon practical experience', with that of Reid, 'a former career civil servant with no formal legal qualifications' who, two years later, completed a very similar investigation.[20] It was said that Mr. Reid, who found no maladministration, had too easily accepted departments' view of their own functions and placed the onus of policing the company effectively on investors. Note the inference both that lawyers are more independent than civil servants and also the leaning to adversarial procedures.

Citing s. 12(3) of the Act, the PCA noted that *discretionary* decisions to grant, refuse or revoke licences fell outside his jurisdiction. Only if he found maladministration could he proceed. But unlike Le Quesne, who had confined his remit narrowly to 'fact-finding', leaving evaluation to the minister, the PCA found maladministration on five counts. Construing causation in a way familiar to lawyers, he concluded that 'injustice' had been caused and that compensation was due. Drewry and Gregory provide a partial explanation for the discrepancy between the two distinguished lawyers: [1]

> Because the Office has time and resources, and the right of unrestricted access to persons and papers, the Commissioner was able to mount a fact-finding exercise far more formidable than M.P.s or the media could possibly have undertaken. Rarely, if ever, can any record of administration have been so closely scrutinised, and reconstructed in such detail, as in the Commissioner's report on the Barlow Clowes affair; some of the officials subjected to interrogation certainly felt not a little bruised by the

17  HL Deb., vol. 500, cols. 1255-1269 (20 October 1988).
18  HC 76, p. 1.
19  R. Bosworth-Davies, 'Credit where credit's due', (1994) 144 NLJ 871.
20  Case C438/89, HC 657 (1991/2) p. 39.
 1  R. Gregory and G. Drewry, 'Barlow Clowes and the Ombudsman' [1991] PL 192, 408 at 439.

experience. The Le Quesne investigation itself had been a good deal more searching than the normal investigation set in motion to brief ministers following representations from M.P.s. The Commissioner's 120,000 word report goes much further than Le Quesne, and sets out the results of a *de luxe* investigation in a class of its own.

What followed raises questions over the effectiveness of any grievance-handling machinery which comes up against the highest echelons of government. Mr. Ridley, now minister, rejected the PCA's findings,[2] criticising him both for ignoring the difficulty of the regulatory function and for measuring departmental action with the benefit of hindsight against 'a way of proceeding which, after the event, can be shown to be more satisfactory than what was actually done'. Taking legal liability as his own benchmark, the minister argued that the investigation should never have been undertaken since the complainants were not 'directly affected' (the legal test of standing to sue); the decision to recommend compensation departed from established principles of civil liability on the part of regulators[3] and causation had not been shown. None the less, 'in the exceptional circumstances of this case and out of respect for the Office of Parliamentary Commissioner', the government had agreed to substantial ex gratia compensation.

The minister also argued that the findings trespassed on both the discretionary and policy areas of decision-making, proscribed territory for the PCA because of s. 12(3), which forbids him to question the merits of a decision taken without maladministration (above, p. 425). Did the PCA exceed his jurisdiction? Drewry and Gregory conclude:[4]

> In relation to discretionary decisions, it has for the most part been the failure of officials to take into account all the relevant evidence which the Commissioner has had occasion to criticise. But to find fault with a department, as in this case, for giving 'greater weight' than it properly deserved to some consideration or other, or to join issue with it for giving 'undue weight' to a possible eventuality is, arguably, criticism of a rather different order, taking the Commissioner some distance along the road towards stating a preference for his own subjective judgement over that of the officials concerned. This is slippery ground. It is, after all, because they do not see eye to eye about the appropriate weight to be attributed to various elements in a situation that people disagree as to what should be done and therefore as to whether decisions are 'right' or 'wrong'. Yet it has always been maintained that it is not open to the Commissioner to find that a decision is simply 'wrong' in itself. In this instance, as regards what he was prepared to count as 'procedural maladministration' the Commissioner arguably pushed his competence close to its limits and certainly interpreted the term 'maladministration' with 'great flexibility'.

Sir Anthony certainly criticised the department for giving undue weight to the risk of a disorderly collapse, but such a balancing exercise can surely be accomodated within the *Wednesbury* principle.

---

2   HC Deb., vol. 164, cols. 201-212; *Observations on the Report of the PCA*, HC 99 (1989/90).
3   Then *Yuen Ken-yeu v A-G of Hong Kong* [1988] AC 175. See now, *Marc Rich & Co v Bishop Rock Marine Co Ltd* [1996] AC 211.
4   [1991] PL at 429.

At the time of Barlow Clowes, investor protection was a hot political issue and new regulation was just around the corner. Government sensed the danger of back-bench revolt. The intention of those MPs who referred complaints may partly have been to avoid political confrontation, borrowing the image of the 'independent' PCA to depoliticise the issue. This tactic, connived in by Lord Young, allowed the Government to save face later by offering compensation as an 'act of grace', while at all points denying liability.

After the Scott Inquiry (above, p. 397), Leigh and Lustgarten wrote: [5]

> To establish a judicial inquiry into a disaster or riot is one thing, but an inquiry into a failure of government inevitably raises difficulties about the division of constitutional labour. The inquiry must take care not to supplant the political process. One (somewhat artificial) place to draw the line would be to limit the task to investigation and reporting of factual matters. However, even factual findings are not guaranteed to be free from controversy where the political stakes are high. A desperate government may reject the findings of an inquiry it has set up, however perverse that may appear.

LeQuesne drew precisely the artificial line criticised by Leigh and Lustgarten. The PCA went further, drawing criticism of excess of jurisdiction. What then is the PCA's role: investigator or inquisitor?

## 4. The PCA's complaints service

It is now time to return to the criteria for a good complaints system – effectiveness; public recognition and visibility; accessibility and clarity of jurisdiction; independence; fairness – and measure this investigatory procedure against them.

### (a) Effectiveness

The first point to be made is that this is 'Rolls Royce' procedure. Its thoroughness brings it close to that used in a civil trial by the High Court. Later we will see that judicial review is largely dependent on the exchange of written questions and answers and you may think it far less penetrating. In the Divisional Court, for example, the discovery of documents has to be requested, which means that the applicant must know or suspect their existence. It is unlikely that either the existence or suspicious absence of documents will escape the informed investigators from the PCA's Office. On the other hand, the fact that the complainant will not himself have access, renders the independence of the PCA more important. In neither case will the respondent be cross-examined, though the PCA may interview and question.

There is a different contrast to be made with the informal, user-friendly methods used by other Ombudsman systems, many of which conduct their business on the telephone. The CLA has always emphasised informality. Their

5    I. Leigh and L. Lustgarten, 'Five Volumes in Search of Accountability: The Scott Report' (1996) 59 MLR 695, 697.

investigators make a practice of interviewing complainants in their own home and may be found queueing in local authority offices to test the quality of service. In contrast, the PCA concentrates on files. This has been justified on the ground that informal methods will have been tried by the complainant and the MP, who 'will think first of approaching the minister concerned through correspondence and then if necessary ... seeking a meeting to discuss a particular complaint'.[6] In 1994, however, the SC authorised the PCA to screen out at first stage complaints where telephone calls or faxed inquiries produce a satisfactory departmental reply.[7] The PCA's response was cautious;[8] in 1995, when he had settled 110 cases in this manner, he called informal procedures a useful tool but one suitable for limited circumstances, to be used with care, not indiscriminately. This again highlights his inspectorial approach.

Rolls Royce procedures, however, inevitably bring delay. In 1986, Sir Anthony Barrowclough admitted to delays averaging around one year; he thought that to go below nine or ten months would be 'unrealistic' and risk sacrificing accuracy and thoroughness';[9] perhaps this did not seem too long to a lawyer accustomed to the delays of litigation. In his last report, Sir Anthony mentioned 'increasing difficulty and complexity in the complaints', adding there were:[10]

> ... two crucial considerations which have to be borne in mind. One is that there is no appeal from the Parliamentary Commissioner's findings. The other is that the Parliamentary Commissioner has no power to impose his conclusions, or the remedies he believes appropriate, on an unwilling department or public body. It follows, to my mind, that the Commissioner's reports must aim to be impeccably researched and, as regards his findings and recommendations, lucidly and cogently argued. If these qualities are lacking, the complainant whose complaint is not upheld will go away dissatisfied. Equally, if the department or body concerned is able to pick holes in the Commissioner's account of the facts of the case, or to point to flaws in the Commissioner's reasoning, his chances of persuading the department or body to accept an adverse finding, and to provide an appropriate remedy, will be much diminished. Time spent on perfecting the investigation or the way in which the report is expressed will generally therefore, at least in my view, be time well spent.

The OPCA now regularly uses performance targets. For the years 1996-98, it aims to reduce screening time from 5.7 to 3 weeks, a target many would see as far too high for first stage and fast track procedure. The target for stages two and three is 39 weeks, a reduction from the previous average of 70-74 weeks.[11] Averaging these figures may, however, be misleading. Complex inquiries inevitably take longer.

In considering effectiveness, we also need to consider *redress*, given much emphasis by the Charter Unit. This has two facets: enforcement and remedy.

6  Sir Derek Andrew, Permanent Secretary, MAFF, 'A View from Whitehall' in R. Gregory et al., *Practice and Prospects* (above, p. 423, note 1), p. 101.
7  *Report on Powers, Work and Jurisdiction*, HC 33 (1993/4) para. 14.
8  AR 1995, HC 296 (1995/6) p. 7. Mr. Buckley shows more entusiasm: see HC 386 (1996/7), para. 4.
9  HC 312 (1986/7). In 1994 the Office set a target of nine months to deal with complaints but recorded an average of 17 months.
10  AR 1988, HC 301 (1988/9) p. 2.
11  Statistics from AR 1995, HC 296 (1995/6).

## (i) Enforcement

Unlike courts, the PCA makes recommendations, relying on the Select Committee for enforcement. If, after criticising a department, the PCA believes it will not provide adequate redress, he can issue a special, 'unremedied injustice' report to Parliament (1967 Act, s. 10(3)). Recalcitrant departments may encounter severe parliamentary pressure to give way, receiving written representations from MPs, facing parliamentary questions, and finding their highest officials cross-examined by the SC.

Perhaps surprisingly, not even *Justice* argues for change, concluding that mandatory remedies or enforcement through the courts would 'alter an essential aspect' of the office.[12]

> In practice we are satisfied that there is no problem to be tackled. Although there have been instances of non-compliance in the past ... the fact is that departments do now comply and do carry out his recommendations. In the background there is always the Select Committee and, if necessary, the authority of Parliament. The fact that the departments remain fully responsible for providing a remedy is an important strength of the present arrangements, since the PCA relies upon the co-operation of departments both in carrying out his investigations and at the stage of remedy.

There have been occasional battles involving ministers and matters of high policy but such cases are exceptional and even here the PCA can look to the media and public opinion. In the notorious 'Sachsenhausen affair', often unfairly cited as a failure, the Foreign Secretary defended the Foreign Office decision not to define Sachsenhausen as a concentration camp for compensation purposes, but conceded compensation.[13] In the 'Court Line affair'[14] the PCA strayed into high politics by criticising ministerial statements for implying that a troubled holiday firm would not collapse. The Labour government promptly rejected the finding and Eric Heffer MP called it 'a political judgment'[15] – a familiar reproach in the context of judicial review. Again, compensation was paid.

The battle of the Channel Tunnel was waged after delays in building the high-speed rail link through Kent had put the project in limbo and caused hard cases of planning blight. The Department of Transport (DoT) refused to consider extra-statutory compensation (See further, Chapter 18). The PCA saw this as maladministration, concluding that compensation should be awarded in cases of exceptional or extreme hardship. Unusually, the Permanent Secretary vigorously attacked the PCA for trespassing on the policy-making function, annexing a five-page memorandum to the Special Report[16] and refusing compensation. The PCA used s. 10(3) to lay his report before Parliament, stating his belief that injustice

12  *Justice*/All Souls Review (above, p. 429, note 18), paras 5.36-39.
13  HC Deb., vol. 758, cols. 112-116; Special Report of the PCA, HC 54 (1967/8).
14  HC 498 (1974/5). And see R. Gregory, 'Court Line, Mr Benn and the Ombudsman' (1977) 30 Parl. Affairs 3.
15  HC Deb., vol. 897, cols. 566-567.
16  *The Channel Tunnel Rail Link and Blight: Investigation of Complaints against the Department of Transport*, HC 193 (1994/5).

had not been and would not be remedied. Although the SC backed the PCA, asking for compensation in the most severe cases,[17] the Government supported the DoT, while agreeing to look again at a limited scheme 'for those affected to an extreme and exceptional degree'.[18]

The effectiveness of PCA remedies is heightened by his ability to advise on improvements and monitor the wider outcome of his reports. This is similar to the operation of the CLA, illustrated in the housing cases described in Chapter 12 (above, p. 410). A Special Report on the Driving and Vehicle Licensing Authority (DVLA), showed regulations drafted by the DVLA failed to implement an EEC Directive, wrongly depriving 234 heavy goods drivers of their livelihood. Note the emphasis on firefighting in the following passage from the SC Report:[19]

> The error in drafting was, to quote the Commissioner, 'a basic one' and was compounded by the failure of the accompanying instruction to interpret the regulations properly. The Committee was assured that steps had been taken to avoid such an error happening again. There was now a professional legal adviser within the DVLA to vet statutory instruments. Not only does the in house lawyer vet statutory instruments but also the desk instructions which interpret the efffect of those instruments for DVLA staff. DVLA's staff have also been trained in statutory instrument instruction writing... We are encouraged by the efforts made to ensure that such a failure does not recur. We note, however, that the original error was made not by the DVLA but by the Treasury Solicitor's Department. We are concerned that such an elementary mistake should occur in a Department whose task it is to draft such instruments and that the mistake passed unnoticed. We trust that the Treasury Solicitors have also undertaken thorough enquiries into how such a mistake could have occurred and will take whatever steps are necessary to ensure that there will be no repetition of this failure. We expect to be informed of the result of these enquiries.

If we compare these results to what could be achieved by a court order, we can see that a court could have invalidated the regulations and possibly awarded pecuniary damages. It could not have taken avoiding action nor taken action against a third party not involved in the proceedings.

*(ii) Remedy*

Initially, apology from a senior officer was seen as the primary remedy for maladministration. Apology remains important but is not always considered sufficient. As we shall see in Chapter 18, the SC and PCA have recently moved firmly to establish a general principle of redress by monetary compensation. This was effectively the point of disagreement in the Channel Tunnel affair.

The point arose still more forcibly in a dispute with the Child Support Agency (CSA), which exists to collect maintenance payments from absent parents. The CSA has been the target of a Special Report in which its management was strongly criticised.[1] It was also castigated for failing to provide appropriate remedies other than apologies. A separate complaint involved a case where the CSA had sent a

---

17  HC 270 (1994/5).
18  HC 819 (1994/5). The outcome is discussed in detail,below, p. 619.
19  Second Report of the Select Committee for 1992, HC 64 (1993/4) p. xi.
 1  *Investigation of complaints against the Child Support Agency*, HC 135 (1995/6).

maintenance inquiry form to the wrong individual. Censuring the CSA's 'slow and lackadaisical approach' to righting the wrong, the PCA described the effect on the complainant and his wife as 'traumatic'. On the question of redress, he said:

> The distress and anxiety which the Centre caused the complainant and his wife over a period of some eleven weeks and the effect on their relationship was such that in my view the Department's apologies did not provide adequate redress. I therefore invited the Permanent Secretary, in the exceptional circumstances of the case, to make the complainant an *ex gratia* payment as well. The Permanent Secretary added his apologies to those already given for CSA's error, but said that he did not agree that the circumstances were so exceptional as to warrant compensation for distress ...
>
> I was dissatisfied with the Permanent Secretary's response and ... wrote asking him to reconsider the matter. I pointed out that he has a clear duty to afford equitable relief against injustice which is shown to have arisen directly from maladministration by a government department [but] the Permanent Secretary replied that... it was the view of DSS that such mistakes should be considered as broadly comparable to legal challenges and similar principles applied in order that there should be consistency of outcome and ease of resolution. In the light of these considerations he accepted that, if the complainant were able to provide medical evidence to support his contention that he had suffered insomnia and depression as a direct consequence of CSA's actions, he would be prepared to reconsider the question of making some compensatory payment to him. After very careful consideration I decided to accept that proposition.

Note that the PCA (a non-lawyer) does not approach the matter by considering – as a lawyer would – whether a duty of care in negligence existed.[2] Even his concession met with the disapproval of the SC, which recommended compensation in all such cases.[3] We shall return to this point in Chapter 18.

The PCA also requires a general rectification of error. Sometimes large numbers of cases are involved. A series of cases involving incorrect calculation of pensions resulted in recalculation of more than 16,000 pensions.[4] We shall see later that this is a problem which courts find difficulty in negotiating (below, p. 598). Investigations may also produce a general change of policy. Early battles with the Inland Revenue over demands for tax arrears and interest on repayments ended in a change of Revenue practice.[5] A Special Report into Disability Living Allowance[6] revealed blunders committed by the Benefits Agency in implementing a change in benefits for disabled people. Not only did the PCA criticise the BA for failure to live up to standards set by the Citizen's Charter, but he disallowed compensation arrangements agreed with a previous PCA. A new solution changing and backdating compensation for all claimants affected by the serious delay in implementation was substituted. Then, in a later investigation of the CSA (above), the PCA expressed disappointment that it had 'not been able to avoid

---

2    Consider, e.g., *Alcock v Chief Constable of South Yorkshire Police* [1991] 3 WLR 1057. For more about actions in negligence and misfeasance in public office, see Ch. 18 below.
3    *The Child Support Agency*, HC 199 (1994/5) pp. xii-xiv.
4    See *A War Pensions Injustice Rectified* HC 587 (1970/1).
5    See HC 334 (1971/2), HC 454 (1974/5).
6    *Delays in Handling Disability Living Allowance Claims*, HC 652 (1992/3).

some of the systemic failures disclosed' in his earlier report into the failures of the BA, a sister agency.

An important statement by Mr. Reid captures priorities in redress of grievance: [7]

> Apologies, and acknowledgements of fault and the provision of financial recompense are undoubtedly important – but there is more to redress than that. Complainants need an assurance that, so far as is humanly possible, identified failings will not be repeated. Appropriate corrective action helps others to avoid sustaining comparable injustices and it improves the quality of service generally available. That is why I attach particular importance to getting rid of systemic defects, those which are liable to affect adversely hundreds or perhaps thousands of individual[s] ... That is why in their inquiries into a case my staff make a point of ensuring that any wider implications to an individual complaint have been identified and dealt with. That takes time, which I regret. There is still much truth in the old saying that 'Prevention is better than cure'.

*(b) Public recognition and visibility*

Lady Wilcox, late of the Citizen's Charter Unit, argues [8] that Ombudsmen should actively promote their services, seeking the help of the media to advertise their wares and appearing on 'phone-in' programmes and other high profile events. Ombudsmen should also accept telephone complaints, travel through the country, and establish local offices. In this way, their outreach can be extended to 'people who are not well informed about their rights and entitlements' and 'reach the more vulnerable groups in society, the socially disadvantaged and the underprivileged, whose need for help may be greater'. Bradley criticises [9] the PCA for failing 'to achieve any real place in the public's understanding'. Clearly, the parliamentary monopoly on access has an important bearing on both visibility and accessibility. A complaints system cannot be truthfully described as accessible if access is both indirect and dependent on the strong discretion of an intermediary (the MP).

If, on the other hand, we treat the PCA as the apex of a tiered complaints system – a point which we know to be both contestable and hotly debated – then in fact he possesses the inestimable advantage of a widely accessible and well-known outreach service: the MP and his surgery. [10] If we are to take the MP filter seriously, it is best to concentrate on educating the MP. Prodded by the SC, this is what the PCA now does, advertising his services through the Commons' *House Magazine*, leafleting new MPs and listing those who do not submit complaints. In 1994, the PCA (Mr. Reid) attributed an unexplained rise in complaints to the issue of a new, 'easier to understand' leaflet describing procedure in Official Information cases. [11]

---

7  HC 20 (1995/6) p. vii.
8  See Gregory et al., *Practice and Prospects* (above, p. 423, note 1), p. 213, pp. 61-6.
9  A. Bradley, 'Sachsenhausen, Barlow Clowes – and then?' [1992] PL 353.
10 R. Gregory and J. Pearson, 'The Parliamentary Ombudsman after twenty-five years' (1992) 70 Pub. Admin. 469, 496; R. Rawlings, 'The MP's Complaints Service', above, p. 431, note 6.
11 AR 1994, HC 307 (1994/5) p. 2. See also G. Drewry and C. Harlow (above, p. 426, note 11).

## (c) Clarity of jurisdiction

A good understanding of the Ombudsman's powers is only possible if the jurisdictional criteria are simple; unfortunately, however, the jurisdiction of the PCA has always been peculiarly complex. Section 5(1) of the 1967 Act empowers the PCA to investigate complaints of 'maladministration causing injustice' in the course of 'any action taken by or on behalf of a government department or other Authority to which this Act applies'. The inadvertent choice of a formula wide enough to embrace 'Next Steps' agencies was, in the event, fortunate!

One might suppose that the PCA had general jurisdiction over central government departments but even these cannot be investigated unless *specifically listed* by Sch. 2 of the 1967 Act as amended. Ironically, the Inland Revenue, always high on the list of most complained about departments, was a late addition. The Cabinet Office and the security services (MI5, MI6 and GCHQ) are significant exceptions, which bite especially on the PCA's new competence in cases of access to government information (below). The Act does not cover non-departmental agencies, though a random selection has in fact been added since 1967. The list, published in the PCA's promotional literature,[12] is long and full of anomalies. Evidence that not all MPs understand it comes from the high proportion of inadmissible complaints.[13] Describing the exceptions as 'bureaucratic and confusing', the PCA and SC hope to list only *exclusions* but perhaps because this creates a presumption of jurisdiction, the government has refused.[14]

Section 5(3) and Sch. 3 of the 1967 Act list further exclusions, of which *Justice* has singled out for attack the exclusion of personnel matters. The Schedule also excludes contractual and commercial transactions other than those arising from compulsory purchase, a more contestable exception criticised by the Salmon Commission on Standards of Conduct in Public Life.[15] We have seen in Chapters 8 and 9 how contracting out and franchising are increasing in importance; here again we find them falling outside traditional arrangements for accountability. Again, the SC's argument for inclusion[16] has met with no response.

Table 13.1 has some interesting features. First note that the case load has risen rapidly in the last few years, attributed by the PCA partly to the new right of direct approach in access to information cases (below). Note too that more complaints are rejected annually than actually investigated. The table records that *a majority* of complaints submitted still fall outside the PCA's jurisdiction. Perhaps it was understandable that at first jurisdictional criteria would prove puzzling but for a small claims court, this is a poor record. Annual Reports break down the reasons for rejection without shedding much light on the problem. A high proportion

---

12 *The Parliamentary Ombudsman – Can the Parliamentary Ombudsman Help You?* (London: HMSO) from 1991. A new leaflet advertising the PCA's Open Government function was issued by the Charter Unit: *Open Government, Access to Government Information Under the Code of Practice* (London: Cabinet Office) 1994.
13 G. Drewry and C. Harlow (above, p. 426, note 11), pp. 760, 766-767. And see Table 13.1.
14 See HC 33 (1993-4) paras. 49-50. For the government response, see HC 619 (1993/94).
15 Cmnd. 6524 (1976) para. 264.
16 HC 33 (1993-4).

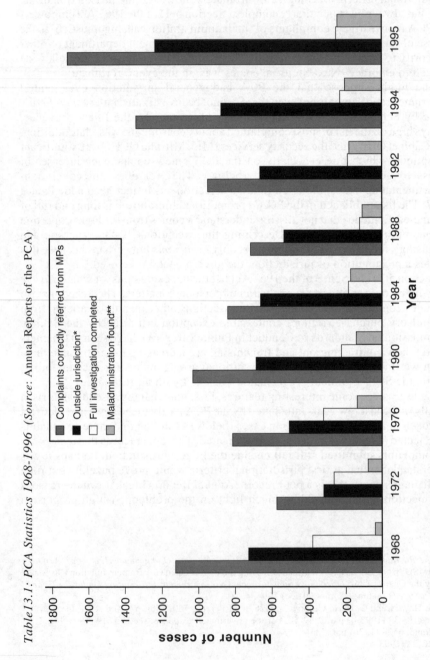

*Table 13.1: PCA Statistics 1968-1996 (Source: Annual Reports of the PCA)*

Legend:
■ Complaints correctly referred from MPs
■ Outside jurisdiction*
□ Full investigation completed
▨ Maladministration found**

*      Includes cases rejected through the exercise of the PCA's general discretion.
**    Includes cases where the complaint was not fully upheld but some element of maladministraiton was found.

always involves unlisted bodies, some, like the police, public bodies with their own low-visibility complaints system, others, like banks and financial institutions, private in character. A large group always comprises the judiciary and other legal bodies, where no formal complaints machinery is provided. Perhaps, however, we should be charitable; the figure may in later years include fast-track cases and other settlements which do not appear elsewhere in the statistics. Also, note that the number of investigations has actually *fallen* slightly over the years despite the rise in complaints. Finally, note the changing ratio of investigation to maladministration found. Is a strategy perhaps developing whereby easy cases are screened out at stage one, leaving for investigation cases which raise a prima facie case of maladministration? If so, this might justify the average time taken to screen of 5.7 weeks. We cannot say, but the figures are certainly suggestive.

Jurisdictional clarity is not helped by s. 12(3) (above, p. 425), which forbids the PCA from questioning *the merits* of discretionary decisions, reflected in the large group of cases screened out annually (43.25% of all rejections in 1995) because they 'did not concern administrative action'. Not only is this prohibition peculiarly hard for the public to understand but it also reduces the PCA's effectiveness. It means in practice that he may be unable to remedy an obvious injustice because it is not caused by 'maladministration'. If Parliament is really, in the Victorian phrase, the 'Grand Inquest of the Nation', why should a parliamentary officer and Select Committee be prohibited from questioning the judgment of ministers and bringing officials to account? The usual justification of ministerial responsibility is hardly convincing.

The first PCA, Sir Edmund Compton, initially took a narrow view of his powers. Citing s. 12(3), he would only investigate maladministration *in the process leading to* a discretionary decision and *not* the quality of the decision itself. But pushed by his SC,[17] he came to accept that where a decision was 'thoroughly bad in quality' he could infer that there *must have been* maladministration in its taking. Similarly, Sir Edmund found cases where the correct application of a rule produced 'manifest hardship' but believed he was debarred from questioning the merits of rules. At first, he characterised such decisions as 'injustice *without* maladministration', but later, to circumvent s. 12(3), he would check whether officials, aware of the hardship produced, had taken proper steps to review the rule. If not, he could make an adverse finding. This is an area in which there has recently been much movement and cases show the PCA and SC applying a broader brush in cases where strict application of rules causes unusual hardship. For example, in one case[18] where the Department of Transport (DoT) refused to buy property blighted by a road improvement scheme on the ground that it fell technically outside the rules, the PCA questioned the discretionary decision and recommended a discretionary payment. See also the last of Mr. Reid's categories of maladministration (above p. 425).

---

17  HC 350 (1967/8), p. 383.
18  C 521/91, HC 673 (1992/3) p. 58.

## (d) Independence

Two views on independence have already been recorded. On the one hand, that the PCA's standing as an Officer of Parliament does render him independent; on the other, *Justice*'s campaign for the appointment of a lawyer or someone external to the civil service. This point emerged starkly in Barlow Clowes. It emerged yet more starkly in an unusual set of complaints referred to Sir Alan Marre which also illustrates just how harshly the 'merits' restriction can operate. The cases involved discretionary payments to disabled people to help them bear the maintenance costs of a private car. In the first, a disabled person was in receipt of a discretionary payment of £100 annually. His car later became unroadworthy and the DHSS refused to provide a new one, despite representations made by his MP, his social worker and a charity. The PCA reported that there had been no maladministration and declined to review the rules which underlay the decision:[19]

> I am satisfied that all the various representations made on behalf of the complainant have been considered carefully; and that in deciding that a four-wheeled car cannot be provided to him the Department are acting in conformity with the rules they have laid down for the provision of such cars, which are strictly applied. Those who do not qualify are understandably deeply disappointed, and it would be open to me, as recommended by the Select Committee . . . to enquire whether the Department have taken any action to review their rules, but I know that the whole subject is already being reviewed . . .
>
> While I realise that my conclusion will bring no comfort to the complainant, I can only report that I do not find any maladministration by the Department . . . in handling his case.

In a similar but more controversial decision the complainant had been receiving a private car allowance on the ground that he needed a car to get 'to and from full-time paid employment'. He was made redundant and negotiated new employment in which he collected the work from the factory in his car, completed it at home and returned the finished work by car. His allowance was terminated on the ground that he no longer met the departmental criteria. Sir Alan Marre reported:[20]

> The distinction which the Department have drawn between these two sets of circumstances must seem to the complainant to be a fine one, as it does to me. But I know from other cases that it is the Department's policy to apply the conditions for payment of private car allowances quite strictly, and not to depart from those conditions, however sensible it may seem to do so in individual cases. That being so I do not consider I have sufficient grounds for criticising the Department's actions in this case.

Technically, Sir Alan was independent in the Charter Unit's sense of autonomy from departmental control. He had, however, been Permanent Secretary at the DHSS at the time when the policies were put in place. Was he impartial?

19   HC 49 (1974/5), p. 77.
20   HC 496 (1975/6), p. 132.

Assuming that he was, the test of natural justice in such cases is *objective*: 'justice must be seen to be done'.

These cases illustrate a different point about independence. Arguments for independence in the sense of externality often involve different codes of values. Here, for example, it is useful to think back to what was said in Chapter 7 about potential clashes between 'general' rules and 'individuated' decisions. Because of the nature of adjudication, lawyers' concern is more often with the latter. Here we are looking at an 'individuated' decision from the reverse side, seeing its potential impact on third parties. Policies are devised with the aim of rationing scarce resources and exceptions may have devastating effects on departmental budgets. The majority of PCAs have come from the civil service and rate the principle of equal treatment highly. Indeed, it has been held that the singling out of individual cases for special treatment means reconsidering every similar case. One early PCA investigation insisted that, after a High Court decision which changed the law affecting pension rights, a department must take out and reconsider every file which might be affected.[1] The decision itself would not have had this consequence, a point to which we shall return in Chapter 16.

### (e) Fairness

Discussing inquiries, we found criticisms that investigatorial procedure does not provide sufficient protection for those targeted by the investigation (above, p. 397). Does this criticism apply also to Ombudsman procedure, which is neither oral nor open? In line with Charter Unit thinking, modern guidance warns departments that any named individual must (i) be notified of the nature of the complaint and (ii) be given an opportunity to explain their position with the help of a trade union representative. Where the complainant is legally represented (which remains unusual), anyone complained about has a right to be legally represented.

Although the practice of showing the draft report to the department and any named official for comment has a statutory basis, it has been criticised as unfair. In the 'Preece affair',[3] the PCA (Sir Cecil Clothier) published a Special Report into the Home Office forensic science laboratory after a striking complaint of a miscarriage of justice. Preece's conviction depended largely on allegedly matching blood samples, processed by a forensic scientist later shown in an internal investigation to be guilty of 'gross professional' and 'grave technical' incompetence. Aware of this, the Home Office took no steps to re-open Preece's conviction, simply relying on press reports to bring forward anyone who might be unfavourably affected! This course of events was described by the SC as 'a disgrace to a civilised society'. Although the PCA also saw the failure as serious, the overall tone of his report is mild. He criticises the Controller but praises his

1   See *Judd v Ministry of Pensions* [1965] 3 All ER 642 and HC 72 (1973), p. 8.
2   See *R v Social Services Secretary, ex p CPAG and GLC* (1984) Times, 16 August. Below, p. 546.
3   *Investigation of a complaint about delay in reviewing a conviction for murder*, HC 191 (1983/4) and, for the SC, HC 423 (1993/4). For criticism, see R. Rawlings, 'The Legacy of a Lawyer-Ombudsman', Legal Action, June 1985, p. 10.

introduction of a quality control system. He criticises 'the passive and reactive role' of the Home Office but also describes it as 'in some respects prompt and efficient'. This was a case in which the supine performance of the Home Office had resulted in Preece serving four years in prison *following* the discovery of the forensic scientist's gross negligence. This may be a general defect with negotiatory and conciliatory procedure, designed to secure an effective and consensual outcome. As with police complaints, the legitimacy of the procedure in the eyes of the public may be undercut, a clash with the more punitive and deterrent outcomes associated with legal process.

In sharp contrast to adversarial procedures, the virtual absence of the complainant in these procedures should be noted. There is no statutory right to see the draft report, while the final report is made to the referring MP. This has been challenged by complainants who, as with police complaints procedure and disciplinary hearings, feel that PCA procedure pushes them to the sidelines. In *R v Parliamentary Comr for Administration, ex p Dyer*,[4] the Divisional Court rejected an application for judicial review based on the argument that natural justice had not been observed. The court justified the procedure on three main grounds: first, that the department but not the anonymous complainant is subject to public criticism; secondly, that the procedure is essential for the department to suggest and discuss redress with the PCA; and finally, to give notice under s. 11(3) if documents or information are to be withheld from further disclosure. This is one case where a court refrained from imposing its own, adversarial paradigm.

## 5. A new role: the PCA and Open Government

In Chapter 4, we recorded our view that the administrative and political culture of the United Kingdom has never recovered from the blanket ban on disclosure imposed by the draconian Offical Secrets Act 1911. There is still no general Freedom of Information legislation, though this is promised shortly,[5] and no across-the-board right of access by an individual to information held on file by public authorities which would permit correction of errors, though some statutory rights of access (e.g. to medical files) have been grudgingly created. The Official Secrets Act 1989 classifies information and centres round the idea of 'authorised' and 'unauthorised' disclosure. Unauthorised disclosure is the subject of a series of criminal offences of varying strictness. (It was once a disciplinary offence under 'Estacode', the unpublished civil service disciplinary code.) Civil servants sign an undertaking to comply with the Official Secrets Act and are in breach of their contracts of employment if they reveal information without authorisation. Similar restrictions, usually contractual in character, apply to other public employees and to government contractors, covered by the 1989 Act.

4    [1994] 1 WLR 621.
5    On the form it might take, see, *Labour Party, Because Britain deserves better* (London) 1997, p. 33.
6    See *Lion Laboratories v Evans* [1985] QB 526 and *A-G v Guardian Newspapers (No 2)* [1990] 1 AC 109 (the *Spycatcher* case).
7    See Y. Cripps, *The Legal Implications of Disclosure in the Public Interest* (London: Sweet & Maxwell) 2nd edn., 1994.

Controversial, and the subject of much debate in Parliament during the passage of the Bill, is the absence in this legislation of a 'public interest' defence[6] to protect publication of information which can be shown to be in the public interest and also 'whistleblowing' by public employees.[7] This is one reason why the PCA's statutory rights of access to documents and files have been so helpful in securing access, at least indirectly, to official information. Ombudsman investigations might reveal unsuspected policies formulated as informal rules. In general, policy documents, circulars, guidance and other internal material emerged only fortuitously or through an increasing number of 'leaks' from inside the service.

The main inroads on the culture of secrecy came through 'soft law' in the shape of informal government guidelines. The 'Croham Directive' of 1977 was an internal instruction which distinguished factual material from advice; publication of the former was now allowed.[8] Later, the Citizens' Charter Programme played a crucial part in dismantling the culture of secrecy. As we know from Chapter 5, the Charter required the publication of performance indicators and encouraged the giving of reasoned decisions. Partly as a manifestation of the new Charter culture and partly in response to a mounting campaign of pressure aimed at the unpopular 1989 legislation, a White Paper was published in 1993 proposing an informal Code of Practice on Government Information. Stating that 'Open Government is part of an effective democracy', the White Paper set out to handle information:[9]

> in a way which promotes informed policy-making and debate and efficient service delivery; providing timely and accessible information to the citizen to explain the Government's policies, actions and decisions; restricting access to information only where there are very good reasons for doing so ... [and] to establish a more disciplined framework for publishing factual and analytical information about new policies, and reasons for administrative decisions.

The Code is applicable to all departments, agencies and authorities falling within the jurisdiction of the PCA; once again, a list is published in the promotional literature. Although dismissed by some as 'a last-ditch attempt to forestall Freedom of Information legislation',[10] the Code could also be read as a sign that the climate of secrecy is slowly changing. In conjunction with the Citizen's Charter, the Code requires publication of the following information:[11]

- the facts and analysis which the government considers relevant and important in framing major policy proposals and decisions;
- explanatory material on departments' dealings with the public (including rules, procedures and internal guidance);
- the reasons for decisions;
- information relating to the running of the public services, including cost, targets, standards and complaints procedures;

---

8  R. Austin, 'Freedom of Information: The Constitutional Impact' in J. Jowell and D. Oliver, (eds.), *The Changing Constitution* (Oxford: Clarendon) 3rd, edn., 1994, p. 419.
9  *Open Government*, Cmnd. 2290 (1993), para. 1.7.
10  R. Austin (above, note 8) at p. 430.
11  *Open Government, Code of Practice on Access to Government Information* (London: Cabinet Office) 2nd edn., 1997.

- information relating to policies, actions and decisions in the department's area of responsibility.

This immediately brought into the public domain much 'soft law'; for example, in response to the requirement to publish internal departmental manuals, the Inland Revenue released *all* of its internal guidance manuals amounting to 11 volumes and the Benefits Agency published 56 internal codes.

But like all Official Secrets or Freedom of Information legislation, the Code contains a long list of exemptions. These fall under 13 headings:

(1)   Defence, security and international relations;
(2)   Internal (public service) discussion and advice;
(3)   Communications with the Royal Household;
(4)   Law enforcement and legal proceedings;
(5)   Immigration and nationality;
(6)   Effective management of the economy and collection of tax;
(7)   Effective management and operation of the public service;
(8)   Public employment, public appointments and honours;
(9)   Voluminous or vexatious requests;
(10) Publication which is 'premature', i.e., about to be published;
(11) Some research-related statistics and data;
(12) Privacy; and
(13) Commercial confidence.

According to the Office of Public Service, the most frequently cited reasons for exempting material are: (2) internal discussion and advice; (7) effective management and operation of the public service; (12) information given in confidence and (13) third party's commercial confidence. In cases of doubt, the Cabinet Office Guidance[12] authorises a 'proportionality' test, weighing 'harm or prejudice arising from disclosure' against 'the public interest in making information available'.

Wholly consonant with the informal nature of the scheme is the decision to use the PCA to adjudicate on complaints. Initially, commentators took the view that this was insufficient. Rights and entitlement coupled with judicial remedies were the preferred recipe. Hazell complained[13] at the failure to provide the PCA with any 'backstop' in the form of new statutory powers, a preference shared by the SC and ultimately by the new Labour government. Perhaps surprisingly, in the light of what has been said in this chapter, Hazell also thought the PCA 'ill equipped to carry out a judicial function', while for Birkinshaw, use of the PCA was part of a wider conspiracy to protect secrecy:[14]

> From the Government's perspective use of the Ombudsman was something of a master stroke ... To remove any taint of 'legalism' from their new scheme not only was

---

12   *Open Government Code of Practice on Access to Government Information; Guidance on Interpretation* (London: Cabinet Office) 1994.
13   R. Hazell, 'Freedom of Information: The Implications for the Ombudsman' (1995) 73 Public Administration 263, 264, 266.
14   P. Birkinshaw, *Freedom of Information* (London: Butterworths) 2nd edn., 1994, p. 203.

there to be a non-legal instrument operating under the discretion of officials but the scheme was to fall within the traditional operational conventions of British government. This meant that ultimately a minister was to be responsible or accountable to Parliament for the operation of the Code and the decisions of his officials. Where information was refused under the exemptions, a requester could ultimately bring a complaint to an MP who could refer the complaint to the Ombudsman, who would examine the complaint in a modified mannner.

But is this a fair assessment of PCA investigations? Birkinshaw admits[15] that the arrangements may have procedural advantages. PCA procedure is investigatorial, the PCA has assured access to documents and files, his investigators are familiar with civil service methods and attitudes. Again, enforcement of the Code lies in the hands of the SC, all familiar with techniques of wresting information from government through parliamentary questions. And modified in respect to what? Birkinshaw admits[16] that the PCA has 'set about this work in a spirited fashion'. He has stated to the SC[17] that 'injustice' will be deemed to have arisen from every refusal to provide information. 'It would be enough ... that the person or persons concerned had not been given information which, in accordance with the Code of Practice to which the Government is committed, they believed they were entitled to have.' The onus will lie squarely on the department to show why the document which it has withheld falls within one of the exceptions.

Originally, the Code provided a right of access to *information* as selected or 'filleted' by civil servants and not to *documents*. But the PCA was quick to criticise departments which took such action. In a case involving MAFF, a farmer bought an infected heifer. MAFF refused to release information on the breeder on the ground that a 'common law duty of confidentiality' was owed (exception (12) above). The decision was overridden by the PCA. When he discovered also that, although MAFF had decided in principle to accept ex gratia compensation claims from the owners of cattle slaughtered in these circumstances, they had never made that fact publicly known, he insisted that the guidelines for compensation be published.

In its first report on the experience of the Code,[18] the SC asked for amendment in this respect. The government refused, pleading exception (7); documents might be incomplete and supplementary information needed to interpret them. Moreover, the authors of documents could be 'identified and associated with a particular policy stance, thus compromising their impartiality and consequently their ability to establish a relationship of trust with current or future ministers'.[19]

How accessible is this new procedure proving? When it became operative in 1994, an explanatory leaflet in several languages was issued via Citizens' Advice Bureaux, lawyers, accountants, and MPs. A complaints form was attached, so that all MPs have to do is to endorse the form and hand it to the PCA's office. There has hardly been a flood of complaints for the extra staff to handle. 1994 brought 28 referrals and in each of 1995 and 1996 there were 44 complaints resulting in 16 and 12

15  P. Birkinshaw, ' "I only ask for information" '[1993] PL 557 at 563.
16  *Freedom of Information* (above, note 14), p. 211.
17  HC 33 (1993/4), p. xx. And see Vol II.
18  HC 84 (1995/6).
19  HC 75 (1996/7), p. vi. See also HC 556 (1995/6).

investigations. This may be because (according to OPS) most requests receive a favourable response: of 2,600 requests received by central government departments, only 89 were rejected in whole and 21 in part. The PCA has none the less expressed not only disappointment[20] at the public's mimimal use of the new facility but also surprise at the small use made by the press of the arrangements.

Yet the same Annual Report mentions a number of 'complex' test cases, differing from standard information requests, which typically concern personal files and affairs. One such request was for environmental impact assessments submitted to the European Commission in respect of a road-widening scheme and a second for the composition of working parties on air pollution. These show environmental campaigners taking advantage of the new arrangements. Another (unsuccessful) complaint[1] which was clearly political in character concerned a departmental review of broadcasting regulations covering interviews with members of restricted organisations in Northen Ireland after the ban had been lifted, reminiscent of the *Brind* case.[2]

In its response to the SC, the previous Government described the Code of Practice as:[3]

> a benchmark against which access to information in all areas of Government activity is being judged ... [Its] flexibility is one of the major strengths of a non-statutory code which would be lost if a statutory approach were adopted ... The Government believes there is clear evidence to show that the Code is working in the way that was intended. It is resulting in the disclosure of a good deal of official information, and a greater appreciation, throughout Central Government, of the need for openness in dealings with the public ... In particular, use of the Code has entirely avoided long and expensive disputes on appeal, in contrast to what might well be the case under a Freedom of Information Act, even one that was policed, in the first instance, by the Ombudsman himself.

If the case against soft law is lack of openness coupled with absence of judicial redress, we should remember that the case against hard law is juridification in both senses of the word. With the promise of legislation from the present government, we may be about to test the two models.

## 6. An Inspector-General?

We are now in a position to reconsider the two Ombudsman models set out earlier: small claims court or government inspector. And are the two models really alternatives? Over his 30 years of existence, the PCA has evolved a distinctive role, perhaps atypical of Ombudsmen. In its evolution, much seems to depend on the predilections of the current incumbent together with the interests of the SC. There are signs that the SC is becoming more active and that the PCA's relationship with his committee is evolving fast. The PCA's relationship with

---

20  AR 1995, HC 296 (1995/6) pp. 47-52.
 1  AR 1995, HC 606 (1995/6).
 2  Above, p. 120.
 3  Government response, HC 75 (1996/7) para. 7.

MPs and his parliamentary role are changing. Previously cynical, MPs may be recognising the value of his 'cutting edge'. [4]

Think about our evaluation of the PCA's performance against criteria for good complaints-handling – effectiveness, public recognition and visibility, accessibility and clarity of jurisdiction, independence and fairness, to which should be added adequate powers of investigation. What does the PCA do well and what are his deficiencies? As a complaints-handling system, Table 13.1 suggested that his record is dubious. His visibility remains low, a problem seemingly unaffected by strenuous efforts at publicity, and the indirect access rule renders accessibility difficult. Direct access advocated by *Justice* has consistently been blocked by the SC and is clearly not in the realms of practical politics. [5] The complex jurisdiction is rendered more complex by the inability or unwillingness of MPs to understand it; consistently, more complaints prove inadmissible than admissible. The PCA naturally continues to take complaints seriously and to seek tangible redress for a handful of fortunate individuals, but the consistent trawl expected of a good 'bottom-up' complaints system (see Chapter 12) is missing. Like Seneviratne, [6] we deduce that the PCA sees his role 'to be more one of providing an internal administrative audit than of acting as a ready channel for uncovering and investigating citizens' grievances'. Individual complaints operate as a useful spot check on departmental performance.

Where the PCA excels is in 'big inquiries'. Here his exhaustive investigatorial procedure, too costly, cumbersome and slow for trivial complaints, comes into its own. His relationship with the SC renders him highly effective. Even in hot political cases where governments have refused to accept his findings, his standing is such that only once (the 'Channel Tunnel affair') have recomendations for redress been overridden. The ripple effect of his investigations is now considerable. Recent co-operation with the Charter Unit has confirmed the PCA's insider status, allowing him unrivalled opportunity to see his recommendations implemented and monitor implementation. We can see this developing with Special Reports on the Child Support Agency (above) and on the Driving and Vehicle Licensing Authority (above). Thus the PCA is beginning to evolve a distinctive role as Special Investigator and Inspector-General and there are indications that his potential is beginning to be recognised. Both PCA and SC have demanded power for the PCA to institute investigations ex officio. They have also determined that he should publish occasional positive reports on good administration, [7] of which the important report on *Maladministration and its Redress*, dealt with in Chapter 18, was the first. The SC has successfully negotiated a division of labour with OPS and the Charter Unit; as we have seen, they promulgate codes and reports of investigations, while the PCA helps to monitor these, as he does with Citizen's Charter standards (above). The PCA has

4   R. Gregory and J. Pearson, 'The Parliamentary Ombudsman after twenty-five years' (1992) 70 Pub. Admin. 472.
5   E.g. *Review of Access and Jurisdiction*, HC 615 (1977/8); HC 158 (1991/2) p. xii. R. Gregory and J. Pearson (above, note 4), p. 488.
6   M. Seneviratne, *Ombudsmen in the Public Sector* (Buckingham: Open University Press) 1994, pp. 52 and 57-58.
7   HC 33-I (1993/4) p. xii.

not yet fully exploited his potential in standard-setting, [8] as Mr. Reid felt that a standard-setting role might imperil his impartiality as investigator in cases concerning the effect of rules and standards which he or his office had approved.

Sir Cecil Clothier once stated that complainants must 'advance some injustice which is personal to him and distinguishes him from the generality of the community'. [9] As in the 'War Pensions Affair' (above, p. 441), he handled group complaints only where each complainant could show 'injustice' and representative actions were often turned away as political. This is a test more restrictive than that used today in judicial review (below, Chapter 16). Mr. Reid, like Sir Idwal Pugh before him, treated multiple complaints as indicative of poor performance, using his discretion to make a selection of symptomatic cases. Before the Special Report on the CSA (above), the PCA received 95 complaints of which 70 were accepted. OPCA compiled a representative selection, using the wide discretion to filter others off to alternative complaints systems. Mr. Reid explained. [10]

> It was not the best use of my resources to investigate additional individual complaints unless they involved aspects of CSA work which had not previously been brought to my attention, or unless the complainant had been caused actual financial loss. I took the view that investigation of a number of representative cases should identify any administrative shortcomings needing to be remedied and that any resulting improvements to the system should bring general benefits in which others should share. Many complaints sent to me were about the policy underlying the legislation. That is outside my jurisdiction. Many complaints were about the financial assessment of support for children and single parents. The assessments are open to appeal to Child Support Appeal Tribunals. I have confirmed with the President of the Independent Tribunal Service that it stands ready to handle such appeals.

This attitude does not fit the image of the 'small claims court' assiduously fostered by *Justice*, in which each claim merits individual attention. Reid argued cogently, however, that only a number of representative cases was needed to identify any administrative shortcomings needing to be remedied. The PCA's inside position meant that *all* identifiable grievances would have to be redressed by the agency. This approach has been validated by the Divisional Court in *Dyer*[11] where it was held that the PCA was under no obligation to proceed with complaints which were trivial or inappropriate for investigation.

Aspects of the 1996 Report[12] also point to a need for selectivity. We saw in Table 13.1 that the number of complaints has recently increased, to just below the 2,000 mark in 1996. Many are multiple complaints, some bearing the stamp of the professional lobbyist: large numbers of identical complaints aimed at pressurising the recipient. Complaints are typically longer, with complex documentation taking more time to process. Complainants are less willing to

---

8  See *Justice*/All Souls Review, paras. 86, 88, where the Review team is seeking PCA support for its 'Principles of Good Administration'.
9  C. Clothier, 'Legal problems of an ombudsman' (1984) 81 Law Soc. Gaz. 3108.
10 *Investigation of complaints against the Child Support Agency*, HC 135 (1995/6), p. i.
11 See *R v Parliamentary Comr for Administration, ex p Dyer* [1994] 1 WLR 621.
12 Annual Report of the PCA for 1996, HC 386 (1996/7).

accept a negative outcome, following up with voluminous re-submissions, absorbing still more time and no doubt presaging further applications for judicial review. There are parallels here with courts and tribunals (below). Successful though the new screening process has proved in cutting the number of full investigations, still more stringent case management may be necessary if the office is not to be overloaded.

One way to deal with overload may be to follow the logic of devolution. Regional ombudsmen, respectively responsible to the Scottish Parliament and Welsh Assembly could combine the office of PCA and HSC at regional level. The effect might be, however, to reduce the standing of the several offices, reintroducing the small claims idea.

Alternatively, recall the 'systems-flexible' approach of Birkinshaw and Lewis[13] to public sector complaints-handling in which 'an enlarged ombudsman system' would operate in conjunction with internal complaints procedures, possibly instituted on a statutory basis. The PCA is in position to move to the apex of a genuinely pyramidal structure administered on a regional basis. An enlargement of access could allow him to investigate complaints referred by MPs, by the SC, by internal complaints adjudicators such as the Prisons Ombudsman or Revenue Adjudicator, even, perhaps, as Lord Woolf has suggested,[14] by the Divisional Court. In addition, government should concede the right to make ex officio investigations. Trivial complaints could be passed down to a tribunal or internal adjudicator; policy complaints might be referred, with the SC's approval, to a relevant Select Committee. In this way, complaints suitable for informal resolution would be filtered out more efficiently, while a welcome note of externality would be introduced into departmental complaints systems. If, as many believe, ministerial responsibility has had its day, it is time to replace it with real accountability to Parliament.

13 N. Lewis and P. Birkinshaw, *When Citizens Complain, Reforming Justice and Administration* (Buckingham: Open University) 1993, p. 214.

Chapter 14

# Tribunals: the rise and fall of judicialisation

In Chapter 12 we looked at the development of complaints procedures. Noting the connection between tribunals and the ADR movement, we none the less considered their role as court substitutes. In this chapter, we turn to look at more closely at the place of tribunals in the system of administrative justice. The period since the Report of the Franks Committee on Tribunals and Inquiries [1] was implemented by the Tribunals and Inquiries Act 1958, has been one of increasing judicialisation. Later in the chapter, we shall illustrate this process with a case study of social security adjudication and see how this later widened out into a presidential system capable of forming the nub of an independent tribunals service. But pendulums swing, especially when cost cutting is an issue. We shall also observe the growth of a negative reaction to judicialisation, bringing interest in ADR techniques, epitomised in social fund adjudication.

## 1. 'They just growed like Topsy'

Throughout this century specialist tribunals have proliferated, largely, though by no means exclusively, as an emanation of the welfare state. As we saw in Chapter 12, the roots of much of this development is to be found in the Liberal Party's great social reforms in the early years of the century. Later, particularly strong periods of growth are associated with Labour administrations, immediately post-war and again in the 1960s and 1970s. We shall see why this might be later in the chapter.

Some statistics will indicate the huge scale of current activity. In 1996, the Council on Tribunals was responsible for supervising almost 80 different categories of tribunal and over 2,000 tribunals altogether. [2] Annually, these tribunals hear over 300,000 cases (or over 1,250,000 if those cases are included which are withdrawn, settled or dealt with almost as a formality [3]). The total number of cases disposed of has long been many times the comparable total of civil cases in the High Court and county courts (already a multiple of six, when the Royal Commission on Legal Services reported in 1979 [4]).

---

1    Cmnd. 218 (1957).
2    Council on Tribunals, *Annual Report* 1995-6, HC 114 (1996/7), Appendix H.
3    See M. Sayers, 'The Importance and Variety of Tribunals' (1994) 1 Tribunals 2.
4    Cmnd. 7648 (1979) (the Benson Commission).

Overall figures conceal, however, variations in workload between tribunal systems. Whereas a few are rarely called upon, the statistics are dominated by just a few others (see Table 14.1). Again, individual systems are apt to demonstrate broad statistical fluctuations associated with change to, and development of, jurisdiction, or with change in social and economic circumstance. The tribunals on local taxation (successively rates, the community charge or poll tax and now council tax) provide a suitably dramatic illustration. [5]

*Table 14.1: Busy tribunal systems – 1994, 1995*

| Tribunal | Number of cases decided | | Tribunal | No. of cases decided | |
|---|---|---|---|---|---|
| | 1994 | 1995 | | 1994 | 1995 |
| * Data Protection Registrar | 39,589 | 32,672 | Medical Appeal Tribunals** | 18,379 | 17,217 |
| Disability Appeal Tribunals | 27,512 | 32,109 | Mental Health Review Tribunals | 6,750 | 7,089 |
| Education Appeal Committees | 30,413 | 35,601 | Rent Assessment Committees | 14,463 | 13,898 |
| *General Commissioners of Income Tax | 215,000 | 241,272 | Social Security Appeals Tribunals** | 86,056 | 81,633 |
| Immigration Adjudicators | 26,774 | 20,875 | *Traffic Commissioners | 576,435 | 220,532 |
| Industrial Tribunals | 21,003 | 21,828 | *Valuation Tribunals (local taxation) | 101,000 | 110,000 |

* A minority of cases in these tribunals require a hearing.
** Based on fiscal years (April to March).
Source: Council on Tribunals; Independent Tribunal Service. The figures are for England and Wales, except for MATs and SSATs, which are for Great Britain.

Table 14.1 does not reflect the diverse forms which have emerged in different areas of government activity and which it is the function of the Council on

5   1971 – 82,620; 1977 – 331,222; 1983 – 153,988; 1991 – 251,000; 1992 – 357,000; 1993 – 481,000; 1994 – 758,000; 1995–533,000. These figures include cases withdrawn or settled prior to a hearing. Source: Annual Reports of the Council on Tribunals.

Tribunals (below) so far as possible to rationalise. If we could follow this in detail, we should find that judicialisation itself was a matter of degree. Again, it presents only a small selection of tribunals, although the range of subject matter is obvious. Questions concerning individual welfare benefits arise before Social Security Appeal Tribunals (SSATs) and Disability and Medical Appeal Tribunals, while personal liberties are in issue in different ways before the Immigration Adjudicators and the Data Protection Registrar. The Traffic Commissioners, on the other hand, are concerned with commercial licensing, while the General and Special Commissioners of Income Tax are tax tribunals. The Table does not do justice to the enormous range and diversity of tribunals. Not all tribunals deal directly with disputes between the citizen and the administration; industrial tribunals and rent assessment committees resolve employer/employee and landlord/tenant disputes respectively, although the issues are of course resolved within the relevant statutory framework designed by government. These are genuinely 'court-substitutes'; machinery for the resolution of disputes beween subjects akin to county courts. Industrial tribunals point up the adaptability of tribunal machinery, expanding into new areas as new tasks arose. Created by the Industry Training Act 1964, they were chosen to hear claims arising under the Redundancy Payments Act 1965. In 1970 they were given jurisdiction to hear disputes concerning the Equal Pay Act and, by the Industrial Relations Act 1971, complaints of unfair dismissal. Subsequently, the Sex Discrimination Act 1975 and the Race Relations Act 1976 gave them power to deal with discrimination occurring in employment.

Tribunals occupy different positions in decision-making chains. Only some, like education appeal committees, directly check administrative determinations. Others, for example the Civil Aviation Authority, themselves take the initial decision, while others again hear appeals from inferior tribunals (e.g. the Immigration Appeal Tribunal from the Immigration Adjudicators). Even this classification is over simple. The CAA illustrates the point that a body may be a tribunal for some purposes but not for others; regulatory agencies, we observed, are sometimes seen as constitutional misfits precisely because they combine adjudicative with other powers traditionally treated as separate. Again, listing institutional structures tells us little about practical relationships. Official influence over tribunals may be secured by backdoor means, e.g. the manipulation of membership and training. As we saw in the 'Skytrain affair' (above, p.83), agencies like the CAA may, to a greater or lesser extent, be hemmed in by policy guidance issued by ministers. It is by no means the case, either, that uniformity has been produced – or indeed that Franks intended this. The 'system' is, and always has been, notably unsystematic!

A partial explanation for the lack of system lies in the absence of central co-ordination. Belying their function of court-substitute, not all tribunals come under the jurisdiction of the Lord Chancellor's Department. Rejecting Robson's boldly-conceived system of administrative courts, both Donoughmore and Franks failed to develop workable guidelines for allocation of functions: i.e. for determining (i) which issues require some form of adjudicative machinery and (ii) which form or agency is most appropriate for resolution of the particular issue. As we saw in Chapter 2, Donoughmore attempted the task by distinguishing 'judicial', 'quasi-judicial' and 'administrative' decisions, but the committee's circular reasoning provided no pointer for the future. Twenty-five years into the jungle, Franks accepted both that tribunals were here to stay and that the judicial/ administrative dichotomy did not yield a valid principle for allocation of decision-making functions. But the committee failed to develop prescriptive criteria of its own, commenting only that, in the absence of 'special considerations', courts, not tribunals, should adjudicate. It saw tribunals as generally preferable to ministerial adjudication, save where 'policy' could not be articulated easily in regulations amenable to administration by tribunals. But Franks concentrated on the existing system, suggesting that a new body, the Council on Tribunals, should tackle questions of allocation. Later on we will see how successive governments have prevented the Council from fulfilling this role.

What then is the rationale for tribunals? We have already met the traditional explanation, here set out more fully by Wade.[6]

> The social legislation of the twentieth century demanded tribunals for purely administrative reasons: they could offer speedier, cheaper and more accessible justice, essential for the administration of welfare schemes involving large numbers of small claims. The process of the courts of law is elaborate, slow and costly. Its defects are those of its merits, for the object is to provide the highest standard of justice; generally speaking, the public wants the best possible article, and is prepared to pay for it. But in administering social services the aim is different. The object is not the best article at any price but the best article that is consistent with efficient administration. Disputes must be disposed of quickly and cheaply, for the benefit of the public purse as well as for that of the claimant...
>
> An accompanying advantage is that of expertise ... Specialised tribunals can deal both more expertly and more rapidly with special classes of cases, whereas in the High Court counsel may take a day or more to explain to the judge how some statutory scheme is designed to operate ... Where there is a continuous flow of claims for a particular class, there is every advantage in a specialised jurisdiction.

Genn observes a tendency among the commentators to present technical justifications of this kind not only as reasons for, or objectives to be attained by, but as descriptive characteristics of, the tribunal system.[7] A growing body of empirical research[8] shows, however, that the account is increasingly open to question, a critical attitude supported by official sources, notably successive reports from the Council on Tribunals on difficulties such as inaccessibility and delay, which undercut the standard explanation.

---

6   Wade and Forsyth, *Administrative* Law, pp. 906-907.

7   H. Genn, 'Tribunal Review of Administrative Decision-Making' in G. Richardson and H. Genn (eds.), *Administrative Law and Government Action* (Oxford: Clarendon) 1994, p. 257.

8   This literature is too large to list an adequate selection here. Much is collected in R. Rawlings, *Grievance Procedure and Administrative Justice, A Review of Socio-Legal Research* (London: Economic and Social Research Council) 1987. From later studies not cited in the text, we would single out J. Peay, *Tribunals on Trial* (London: Economic Social Research Council) 1989; H. Genn and Y. Genn, *The Effectiveness of Representation at Tribunals* (London: HMSO) 1989.

Wade's account, confined to a choice between different forms of adjudication, is law-centred in the sense that tribunals are explained and evaluated by reference to the 'ordinary courts'. It also carries the implication, vigorously asserted by the Franks Committee, that tribunal decision-making should be viewed as an *external* control on administrators, not as a form of administration. The passage also contains a reference to 'proportionality', in the sense of matching disputes to resources. It is not simply that the 'ordinary courts' would find it difficult if not impossible to cope with the mass forms of adjudication engendered by the welfare state, but that the nature of such disputes does not justify the use of the courts. None the less, here as elsewhere the choice of procedure necessarily involves a value-judgment, and further, a value-judgment not always so clear-cut as Wade implies. Modern social security law shows that claims of low monetary value may be legally, as well as factually, complex. Does this then call for the 'highest standard of justice'? Again, in a mass adjudication system a single small claim may have considerable financial repercussions if replicated in other cases (the basis of 'test cases'). Once again, we are challenging the pyramidal concept of dispute-resolution.

## 2. Franks revisited

Forty years on, the obvious point of departure is still the Franks Report, correctly regarded as the 'watershed' for tribunal development in modern times. Here we shall stress the importance of certain proposals which the committee was unable or unwilling to accept, as well as the positive recommendations which it made.

The Committee's formation can be seen as a governmental response to a crisis of public confidence: Crichel Down. But that celebrated affair, seen as an outrageous case of civil service maladministration, was itself part of a general reaction to war-time and post-war controls manifested equally in *Ridge v Baldwin*;[9] reference has already been made in Chapter 4 to an emerging consensus on the need to protect the individual. Many years later, Lord Franks would observe: 'public opinion was ready to make changes and therefore our report was favourably received and acted on with speed'.[10]

Its terms of reference required the Franks Committee to examine statutory tribunals and administrative processes involving inquiry procedures (a brief which Franks interpreted strictly, determining that non-statutory inquiries of the type conducted in Crichel Down were excluded). Asked to consider only further decisions (i.e. decisions to confirm, cancel or vary original decisions), the Committee was unable to scrutinise far wider areas of departmental decision-taking. A modern critic has stressed the inability of Franks to tackle the overtly *collective* dimensions to public decision-making.[11] In this respect, the Committee is a prime example of the classical stress in English administrative law on *individual* redress of grievance. Arguably, however, the criticism says more about the recent trend towards regulation of process in collective decisions –

9    [1964] AC 40; below, p. 500.
10   Quoted in P. Hennessy, *Whitehall* (London: Fontana) revised edn. 1990, p. 572.
11   P. Birkinshaw, *Grievances, Remedies and the State*, (London: Sweet and Maxwell) 2nd edn., 1995, p. 56.

notably rule-making. Simply put, Franks reflected and reinforced the then prevailing concern with adjudication of individualism, while collective dimensions remained far over the horizon.

How then did the Committee approach its task? The foundations of reform were laid as follows:[12]

> 40. Tribunals are not ordinary courts, but neither are they appendages of Government Departments. Much of the official evidence ... appeared to reflect the view that tribunals should be properly regarded as part of the machinery of administration, for which the Government must retain a close and continuing responsibility ... We do not accept this view. We consider that tribunals should properly be regarded as machinery provided by Parliament for adjudication rather than as part of the machinery of administration. The essential point is that in all these cases Parliament has deliberately provided for a decision outside and independent of the Department concerned ... The intention of Parliament to provide for the independence of tribunals is clear and unmistakable ...
>
> 41 ... Parliament in deciding that certain decisions should be reached only after a special procedure must have intended that they should manifest three basic characteristics: openness, fairness and impartiality. The choice of a tribunal rather than a minister as the deciding authority is itself a considerable step towards the realisation of these objectives, particularly the third. But in some cases the statutory provisions and the regulations thereunder fall short of what is required to secure these objectives. Our main task ... will be to assess the extent to which the three objectives are capable of attainment in the field of tribunals and to suggest appropriate measures.
>
> 42. In the field of tribunals openness appears to us to require the publicity of proceedings and knowledge of the essential reasoning underlying the decision; fairness to require the adoption of a clear procedure which enables parties to know their rights, to present their case fully and to know the case which they have to meet; and impartiality to require the freedom of tribunals from the influence, real or apparent of departments concerned with the subject-matter of their decisions.

The Committee translated its view of tribunals as machinery for adjudication into two sets of recommendations. First, tribunals were to be remade in the image of the ordinary courts. Franks recommended that chairmen be legally qualified; that more 'orderly' procedures be followed; that hearings should be generally in public; that the right to legal representation be observed and the provision of legal aid extended; that full reasons be given; that systems of precedent be developed; and more. In short, by an application of the procedural values of openness, fairness and impartiality, the Committee aimed to push tribunals closer to an ideal-type of adjudication (below, p. 496). It should be noted at this point that a distinctive feature of the English tribunal system as it emerged is the importance attached to the role of lay participation in the appeals machinery. This feature is still much prized today as we shall see in the context of welfare adjudication.

Not every institution called a tribunal fits easily inside Franks' classification of machinery for adjudication. If some tribunals are court-substitutes, then others – such as the CAA, with both adjudicative and rule-making powers – are more clearly policy-orientated. To Farmer, the danger of the Franks classification lay

12   Cmnd. 218 (1957), para. 42.

in a stifling of innovation by a straight-jacket of legalistic procedure.[13] On this view tribunals were 'marginalised' as well as reformed by Franks, being 'confined to ensuring the correct application of rules whose content and objectives were decided elsewhere'.[14] To put this differently, adjudication brought a loss of power.

Although not all of the Committee's recommendations were implemented, a large measure of judicialisation resulted. Some changes, such as the duty to give reasons on request, were incorporated in the Tribunals and Inquiries Act 1958, while others, e.g. the opening-up of hearings to the public, came about either through delegated legislation or administrative action. The Council on Tribunals (see below) also provided an ongoing stimulus. When the Labour government introduced Rent Assessment Committees in 1965, for example, Richard Crossman, the responsible minister, agreed from the outset on the use of tribunals and little consideration was given to the use of the courts. The Labour Party had long regarded courts as intimidating and expensive institutions with an undue sensitivity to property rights. Crossman and his advisers wished to maximise the informality of the process, for fear of biasing it in favour of large landlords, but this preference ran counter to deeply entrenched administrative norms, reinforced by Franks. If Crossman did not accept some formalisation, his advisers foresaw conflict with the Lord Chancellor's Department and Council on Tribunals. The compromise procedures that resulted were not as formal as those of the courts but Crossman was not pleased with the degree of formality that had developed.[15]

Tribunals were also to be captured by the lawyers from without; they were to come under the supervision of the 'ordinary courts'. Franks recommended a statutory right of appeal on a point of law from most tribunals and a general appeal from all tribunal decisions; that 'ouster clauses' be cut back; and that (to use the modern terminology) judicial review should always be available. Also, by requiring tribunals to give reasoned decisions, the Committee believed it would be giving the courts a record on which effective judicial review could be based. Today, these measures are generally taken for granted. Judicial control of tribunals is routinely asserted; the tribunals themselves are seen as a lower tier in the administration of civil justice. In Wade's view, 'tribunals have found their place in the legal system, and ... they operate harmoniously with it instead of in opposition'.[16]

### 3. Policy or politics?

If we look back at the Franks recommendations, we will find an implication that tribunals are created to ensure that decisions are made *independently* of departments. Things are not so simple. Prosser, describing the introduction by the Unemployment Assistance Act 1934 of an appeals system for non-contributory

---

13  J. Farmer, *Tribunals and Government* (London: Weidenfeld & Nicolson) 1974, Ch. 8.

14  A. Boyle, 'Sovereignty, Accountability, and the Reform of Administrative Law' in G. Richardson and H. Genn (eds.), *Administrative Law and Government Action* (Oxford: Clarendon) 1994, p. 84.

15  K. Banting, *Poverty, Politics and Policy: Britain in the 1960s* (London: Macmillan) 1979, pp. 51-54.

relief (the forerunner of the social security tribunals described below), questions the belief in tribunals as a protection against arbitrary action. To the contrary, Prosser identifies the machinery as a legal buffer against political action:[17]

> It was decided to introduce [appeals machinery] for two main reasons: firstly to help avoid any possibility of ministerial responsibility for individual cases; secondly, and crucially, it was clear that the cuts in benefit were foreseen, as was mass opposition to them. ...The introduction of appeals machinery provided a means of defusing the opposition by directing it into channels where it could be controlled and have a minimal effect ...
>
>   This function of the tribunals implied a conflict between their symbolic role and their actual operation. They had to appear independent and prepared to protect recipients of assistance to ensure that they would be used in preference to other forms of protest. It was necessary also that they be carefully controlled to prevent them from undermining the [Unemployment Assistance] Board's policy. This was accomplished by appointing one member specifically to represent the Board and by ensuring that each of these members sat frequently enough to acquire expertise in handling appeals whilst the balancing workpeople's members were appointed from large panels so that each sat only occasionally. Secondly, the clerk to each tribunal (whose duties included advising the tribunal on its powers, the law, etc.) was invariably a senior officer of the Board, and it held conferences for the chairmen of the tribunals and issued to them the instructions given to its officers and unpublished memoranda ... Finally in the highly politically contentious area of the household means test the Board was prepared to press its policies onto the tribunals by direct means, either through the clerk or by sending its officers to talk to tribunal members before appeals were to be heard.

Prosser emphasises that the choice was 'never between appeal to tribunals and appeal to the court, but between appeal to tribunals and no appeal'. Nor was provision of a formal right of appeal a recognition of the 'rights' of those receiving assistance, or an attempt to provide an element of 'fairness' in the relationship between state and individual. It was a cynical, political manoeuvre to protect against political reaction. As we shall see, such manoeuvres can recur.

Set out below are the arguments of the Wilson Committee on Immigration Appeals (1967). Why, during a period when the State was imposing tougher immigration controls, should appeals be introduced to tribunals for intending immigrants refused entry to Britain? At the time, decisions were taken by immigration officers exercising a statutory discretion regulated by Home Office instructions; the committee's recommendations provided the framework for the statutory appeals system introduced in 1969 and still operative today. Again, various critics have contended that this was largely a matter of symbolic reassurance. To Bridges,[18] 'immigration appeals were a perfect legal buffer, enabling the State to maintain a liberal image while pursuing essentially illiberal policies'. However, in the report of the committee, we find a mix of instrumentalist and non-instrumentalist reasons for procedural protection:[19]

16  Wade and Forsyth, p. 920.
17  T. Prosser, 'Poverty, Ideology and Legality: Supplementary Benefit Appeal Tribunals and their Predecessors' (1977) 4 BJLS 59.
18  L. Bridges, 'Legality and Immigration Control' (1975) 2 BJLS 221, 224.
19  Wilson Committee on Immigration Appeals (Cmnd. 3387, 1967) at paras. 83-85.

The... main argument in favour of an appeal system rests on a basic principle. Its advocates contend that, however well administered the present control may be, it is fundamentally wrong and inconsistent with the rule of law that power to take decisions affecting a man's whole future should be vested in officers of the executive, from whose findings there is no appeal. In our opinion these critics have reached the heart of the matter. Even if, generally speaking, justice is being done under the present system, it is not apparent that this is the case. [The] immigrant, and his relatives and friends at the other side of the barrier ... are not aware of the safeguards provided by the immigration officer's responsibility through his superiors to the Home Secretary, and the Home Secretary's responsibility to Parliament: all that seems evident to them is that an immediate and summary power to refuse admission rests with one or two officials at the port. In this situation it is understandable that an immigrant and his relatives or friends should feel themselves from the outset to be under a disadvantage, and so should be less willing than they might otherwise be to accept the eventual decision ... Complaints quite often express the feeling that the person concerned never had a chance to confront his interrogators on equal terms. Allegations of this kind are hard to counter when the whole process has taken place in private. They reflect unfairly on the officials concerned, and cumulatively they give rise to a general disquiet in the public mind. The evidence we have received strongly suggests that among the communities of Commonwealth immigrants in this country, and among people specially concerned with their welfare, there is a widespread belief that the Immigration Service deals with the claims of Commonwealth citizens seeking admission in an arbitrary and prejudiced way. We doubt whether it will be possible to dispel this belief so long as there is no ready way of having decisions in such cases subjected to an impartial review.

Not only is there much truth in this passage but it reflects values today enshrined in ECHR Art. 6 that determinations affecting civil rights should be submitted to an independent court or tribunal.

## Education appeal committees

Our final example concerns the introduction by the Thatcher government of education appeal committees (EACs).[20] Previously, appeals against school allocation would have been handled internally with a very few cases going to the minister. Why, we might ask, was a form of adjudication like EACs chosen, given the intractable problems of individuation and rationing involved in these decisions? At one level, the tribunals can be seen as a necessary instrument of the government's policy of increased parental choice; at another, as a way to constrain policy-making by local authorities. As the Minister said at Second Reading: [1]

The principle that has guided us is clear. It is to give to parents the strongest possible right of choice about the schools at which their children shall be educated ... I accept, of course, that in this area there cannot be absolute freedom of choice ...

20 See further, M. Adler, A. Petch and J. Tweedie, *Parental Choice and Educational Policy* (Edinburgh: EUP) 1989; M. Halstead (ed.), *Parental Choice and Education* (London: Kogan Page) 1994; Advisory Centre for Education, *School Choice and Appeals* (London) 2nd edn., 1994.
1 HC Deb., vol. 573, cols. 33-34 (Mr. Mark Carlisle).

However, ... that .... does not mean that one should not attempt to provide for the strongest choice possible ... It will be a very large change in many areas. For the first time we are providing a statutory right to express a preference and a statutory duty on local authorities to comply with that preference.'

But is adjudicative machinery really appropriate for this type of decision? Predictably, the so-called 'best schools' tend to be oversubscribed, especially in an era of government league tables. Under Part VI of the Education Act 1996, the legal position is as follows. First, the local education authority (LEA) must publish an admissions policy (typically, the list of priorities for each school might include: (1) a siblings rule; (2) proximity to home; (3) exceptional circumstances (considered by a council sub-committee)). Second, the LEA must admit pupils up to a school's 'standard number' (calculated according to national criteria). Third, expressed parental preference must be met unless compliance would prejudice the provision of efficient education or the efficient use of resources. Fourth, disappointed parents have a right of appeal to an independent education appeal committee, the decision being binding on the authority. Fifth, case law establishes that this appeal process is two-staged. [2] In the first, factual stage, the committee must ascertain whether prejudice would actually result if the child is admitted. (In practice, the LEA may well argue that prejudice results after the 'standard number' has been reached.) In the second 'balancing' stage, as the national Code of Practice drawn up by the Local Authority Associations explains, the committee has 'to exercise its discretion, balancing between the degree of prejudice ... and the extent of applicability of the parental factors ...'. [3]

Today, this is a major tribunal system: in 1993, EACs decided some 28,000 cases; in 1995, around 35,000. [4] Although great stress is laid on establishing 'an atmosphere of informality where the parties can put their case quite simply', [5] the issues themselves can be quite complicated, particularly where, as increasingly, appeal committees are faced with appeals from a number of parents who wish their children to be admitted to a single popular school. As the National Code acknowledges, 'often it will not be possible for all the appeals to succeed and the committee will be expected to adjudicate between individual cases'. [6] This is a question of scarce resources; schools are not elastic and there may not be enough places to go round. To underline the point, at the so-called balancing stage, the committee will have to determine not only whether, but also *which of* the individual parental preferences outweigh the 'prejudice'. Here we encounter the notion of a 'polycentric decision', in which the success of one pupil impacts unfavourably on the chances of others. In later chapters we shall find the argument that polycentric decisions are inherently unsuitable for adjudication.

2   *R v South Glamorgan Appeals Committee, ex p Evans* (10 May 1984, unreported); *R v Comr for Local Administration, ex p Croydon London Borough Council* [1989] 1 All ER 1033.
3   Association of Metropolitan Authorities, *Code of Practice on Procedure for Admission, Exclusion and Reinstatement Appeals* (London) 1994, para. 22.
4   Annual Reports of Council on Tribunals, HC 22 (1994/5) p. 81; HC 114 (1996/7), p. 104.
5   AMA, *Code of Practice*, para. 14.
6   Ibid, para. 23.

The National Code in fact explains that multiple appeals of this kind depart significantly from the classical adversarial form of the *lis inter partes*:[7]

> It is desirable in these circumstances for an appeal committee comprising the same members to consider all the appeals for particular schools. It is also desirable that decisions should not be made on individual cases until all parents with outstanding appeals have had an opportunity of being heard in respect of an over-subscribed school or injustice could result ... Certainly it is difficult to see how a balancing process can be exercised otherwise. In these circumstances it may be necessary for the committee to adjourn its decisions in relation to that school until all appeals have been heard ...
> Appeal committees may wish to deal with multiple appeals in one of two ways ...
>
> *Grouped appeals*: where the ... authority's case in respect of a school is heard once. In this case the authority ... present their general case (the factual stage) in the presence of all parents and their representatives who may question that case. Thereafter, .... it will be appropriate to move to the second stage. Then the appeals of individual parents will be heard without the presence of the other parents, with the decisions deferred until the hearing of all appeals...
> *Individual appeals*: where the authority's ... case followed by individual parents' cases ... are heard in series. It will be necessary for the committee to hear the authority's case repeatedly ... This case would always be the same (first stage) and it will be the responsibility of the clerk to ensure that the authority ... does not introduce new evidence, nor elaborate on its case as the appeals proceed, as parents earlier in the process will not have had an opportunity to consider that evidence and to respond accordingly ... If material new evidence comes out in cross-examination of the authority's ... representative, the clerk must ensure that the appeal committee considers what bearing the evidence may have on all the appeals and decide how best to advise so that the committee deals with the matter fairly. This may entail adjourning the appeals to give parents the opportunity to consider and challenge the new evidence.
> With a number of individual appeals, it is of great importance, in exercising judgment, that the committee's recollection is accurate. It would be advisable to adopt arrangements which result in a note being taken of the main features in each case. The chair should, if possible, sum up the salient features after each appeal and, after the parties have withdrawn, the committee should briefly discuss the personal circumstances, perhaps forming a provisional list of priorities as the appeals progress.

The Council on Tribunals (discussed below) has stated that of the many tribunal systems under its supervision, none has caused it greater concern than school appeals and the practice of multiple appeals, as well as the nature of the two-staged appeal process, are identified as causing particular problems.[8] Every Annual Report of the CLA provides examples of complaints from parents about the appeals system. It is easy to see why. First, the appeal committee may well not have the luxury of comparing like with like: one appeal could be based on proximity, another on family circumstance (place of work of a single parent), another on medical and/or environmental factors (childhood asthma linked with pollution), and so on. The committee will have to 'balance' all these, one against the other, as also against the 'prejudice'. Secondly, whereas the degree of

---

7   AMA, *Code of Practice* (1994), para. 24.
8   Council on Tribunals, *Annual Report 1991-92*, HC 316 (1992/3), paras. 1.18-1.25.

'communication' between individual cases may be very strong, the scope for 'reasoned proofs and arguments' is confined at the vital 'balancing' stage within the parameters of each individual case. For perfectly understandable reasons, including personal confidentiality, parents, although vitally affected by other parents' cases, are not free to test those cases. Equally, the adjudicators' own list of priorities goes largely unchallenged by the participants. Other safeguards, not adversary presentation, must protect the adjudication from bias or prejudgment. If we look back to the simple Donoughmore classification (above, p. 32) we might ask: is this really a 'judicial' decision? And are Education Appeals Committees simply a substitute for a court?

Finally, the promulgation by Franks of what is today accepted as the orthodox view of tribunals, really rests upon a constitutional fiction. The intentions of Parliament and government are not – or not usually – separate. It is unrealistic to suggest that machinery inserted in a statutory scheme by civil servants who think of it as 'administrative' is transmuted during its passage through Parliament into 'machinery for adjudication'. (Although in Chapter 19 will be found such an example when the government wished to move to administrative determination in respect of criminal injuries compensation.) This perception explains both why Franks proposed an independent Council on Tribunals to allocate functions and also why the proposal fell on stony ground.

## 4. Tribunals watchdog: the Council on Tribunals

Some writers might argue that the short account of the council which follows is peripheral to the real subject of administrative law – the control of governmental power. Others have called it a 'toothless watchdog'. But the work of the council is significant, if only because of the number of bodies which fall under its supervision and the importance of their operations. It also draws together the themes of rule-making, adjudication and procedural fairness, all matters of concern to administrative lawyers. Its development reflects a movement in administrative law from fire-fighting to fire-watching. There is an interesting comparison here with the emerging role of the PCA. Finally, the way in which this administrative agency, imbued with the lawyerly values of openness, fairness and impartiality, has met with the colder climes of efficiency, economy and effectiveness, is emblematic of recent trends.

In evidence to Franks, Robson's functionalist concern with the 'irregular and unsystematic development of administrative adjudication' (above, Chapter 12) led him to propose not only an administrative appeals tribunal but also a permanent supervisory body to provide a 'focal point from which knowledgeable advice and guidance could be maintained'. This body should concentrate on structure and also the appointment, qualifications, tenure etc. of tribunal members. Wade meanwhile pressed the case that however informal a tribunal is intended to be, its proceedings must be orderly, and suggested that it was possible to identify generally acceptable procedural standards. He recommended the creation of a standing body which would be able to enforce procedural standards through a rule-making power. Franks proposed two Councils on Tribunals for which it envisaged a significant role.[9] While accepting that their recommendations would be advisory in character, Franks hoped the ambit of their advice would be considerable:[10]

> [The] main function ... should be to suggest how the general principles of constitution, organisation and procedure enunciated in the Report should be applied in detail to the various tribunals. In discharging this function they should first decide the application of these principles to all existing tribunals; thereafter they should keep tribunals under review and advise on the constitution, organisation and procedure of any proposed new type of tribunal. We recommend that any proposal to establish a new tribunal should be referred to the Councils for their advice before steps are taken to establish the tribunal. The Councils should have power to take evidence from witnesses both inside and outside the public service, and their reports should be published. All their functions should be statutory.

It was to be through the councils that tribunals, after the initial reforms anticipated by Franks, were to be moved towards the adjudicative ideal-type and future 'tribunals' were to be brought within the ethos. Their role was, however, seen as essentially reactive: to report on particular proposals, not to initiate their own suggestions. Franks also envisaged that the councils would have important executive powers; e.g. the appointment of tribunal members (as distinct from chairmen), the formulation of procedural rules and the review of remuneration for tribunal appointees. Yet they should be small, no more than ten members, the majority non-lawyers, with a part-time chairman, not necessarily a lawyer.[11]

In 1965, when there was only a single council with a Scottish committee, Garner found:[12]

> The staff of the Council is surprisingly small. The Secretary is a barrister and a civil servant of considerable experience; indeed, the fact that he has himself had a career in Whitehall and is well known to many civil servants in the various Ministries has clearly been of great assistance in getting the Council accepted in Government circles ... In addition to the Secretary the Council employs two lawyer assistants (both members of the Bar), an experienced executive officer, two secretarial assistants and a messenger. The vote in the current annual Estimate for salaries and national insurance, etc. is £19,000 and there is a supplementary sum of £1,000 to cover travelling and other expenses; accommodation and office expenses are not separately assessed on the Council. The most determined critic of Government expenditure can therefore scarcely accuse the Council of extravagance in either man-power or finance. Indeed, one might almost describe the office as being conducted on a 'shoestring' ... The Chairman [of the Council] is paid a salary (on a part-time basis) and the Chairman of the Scottish Committee also; the other members are entitled to claim fees and expenses ... The Council is not a professional or legal body; all the members were before their

---

9  Franks wanted separate councils, one for England and Wales and for Scotland, to keep the constitution and workings of tribunals under continuous review: Cmnd. 218 (1957), para.43. Instead, s. 1 of the Tribunals and Inquiries Act 1958 created a Council on Tribunals with a Scottish Committee.

10  Cmnd. 218, para. 133.

11  Cmnd., 218, para. 134.

12  J. Garner, 'The Council on Tribunals' [1965] PL 321, 321-325.

appointment well-known persons in other walks of life, and clearly they are chosen from as broad a section of the community as possible.

In 1980, during the course of an internal review into its own functions, the council said:[13]

> In making appointments the practice has been to strike a balance between legal and other skills and experience ... There is a preponderance of non-lawyers. One member is an academic with special experience of research in the field of social administration. Other members have a background of trade unionism, social work, consumer protection, public administration, business and agriculture ... Our secretariat is very small. In addition to the Secretary, the staff of the Council consists of one Principal, two Senior Legal Assistants, one Higher Executive Officer, three Executive Officers and clerical staff. For operational purposes our organisation is regarded as part of the Lord Chancellor's Department; we rely on that department to authorise our expenditure and we have no independent budget.

A little, but only a little, has changed since then. First, is it possible to choose 'from a broad section of the community' members who are well-known prior to their appointment? In fact, the membership of the council has been predominantly male (of the 19 members who sat during 1995, two were women), caucasian and middle-aged or elderly. The functions entrusted to the council were primarily legal in character and some, particularly statutory drafting, are also highly technical. Yet a minority of members has been legally qualified and not all of these have had practical experience. Here, however, the numbers have tended to increase (by 1995 roughly half were lawyers). With a few exceptions like Professors Wade, Bell and Foulkes, academics with a special interest in tribunals, the period of service has been comparatively short. The members are necessarily dependent on the small secretariat. This remains a 'shoestring' operation. In 1995 there was a staff of ten. The Chairman, Lord Archer, an ex-Solicitor-General is still part-time. Compare this with the scale of operations of the PCA. The secretaries to the council have been legally qualified, usually with previous public service experience, but they have had little professional support or legal assistance. A striking omission is any research capacity whatsoever, making the council dependent on the good nature of legal academics. There is no obvious career structure in the shape of a Tribunals Service from which staff could be seconded and inside which they could find promotion.[14] The Franks recommendations contained a vital defect: the council was never adequately staffed for the tasks which Franks wished to entrust to it.

This becomes clear when we consider the statutory power to 'keep under review the constitution and working' of Sch. 1 tribunals. This is done primarily through visits; each year the council visits approximately 100 hearings. Attention

---

13  Cmnd. 7805 (1980), paras. 3.4, 3.10.
14  See R. Wraith and P. Hutchesson, *Administrative Tribunals* (London: Allen and Unwin) 1973, pp. 300-306. They see the absence of a career structure as a serious weakness of the tribunal system and argue for a common tribunals service to provide staff (for example clerks, presenting officers) throughout tribunals. Such an arrangement could include the Council on Tribunals.

has already been drawn to the large numbers of tribunals falling under its supervision, and to the massive workload of some of these (above, Table 14.1). How could this inexpert, part-time body undertake such a case load? In practice, the style is endearing, amateurish and non-conflictual; the council never visits unannounced. Compare Street's comment, which still strikes a chord, with the work of the statutory Ombudsmen or Citizen's Charter Unit considered in Chapter 12 and Independent Tribunals Service (below):[15]

> I think it fair to say that the Council is playing no effective part in ensuring that the personnel are discharging their duties competently. Unannounced and frequent visits would be necessary. In order to assess the quality of the chairman's paperwork random examination of decision files would have to be made. In fact not only does the Council not do this, it has not even the power. I am not criticising the Council; I repeat that it has not the resources to do more than it is doing already. I am emphasing that its supervision of tribunals is so slight as to be ineffective.

Successive annual reports show the council performing four major functions: first, the supervisory role already referred to; second, a consultative role, laid down by statute, concerning proposed rules for procedure; third, an informal consultative role in relation to draft legislation; fourth, a promotional and propagandist role. It is not easy to tell how the council goes about these tasks. At one level, this reflects the bland nature of the 'promotional' annual reports, a feature which has only begun to diminish in recent years; at another, it is indicative of the nature of the agency's dealings with government departments. In a recent annual report the present chairman, Lord Archer, stated:[16]

> Of necessity, much of our work must be confidential. Some of it is a commentary on what, for legitimate reasons, has taken place in private. More importantly, we value the good relations which we enjoy with most government departments and which greatly facilitate our work. While on some matters there is a statutory obligation to consult us, on a much wider range of questions we are consulted voluntarily, and that process would not be encouraged if we failed to respect confidences.

What does emerge is that the council itself has not learned the managerial lessons of the Citizen's Charter. Its complaints-handling procedure is rudimentary. A promotional leaflet warns[17] the citizen that 'the Council has no power to change a tribunal decision or to provide any other redress', adding vaguely that the PCA (whose services are free) may be able to 'look into allegations of maladministration *by the administrative staff* of certain tribunals' (emphasis ours). This is hardly transparent and may help to explain why many inadmissible complaints concern courts and tribunals. In the climate of the 1990s, a more pro-active body might have fought for an adequate, and possibly centralised, tribunals complaints system.

Paper and procedural rules necessarily form the council's staple fare. From our embryonic description of tribunals it is evident that procedural standardisation has not gone very far; Franks had, in fact, rejected the idea of a standard code or

15   H. Street, *Justice in the Welfare State* (London: Stevens) 2nd edn., 1975, p. 63.
16   AR 1993-94, HC 22 (1994/5), p. viii.
17   Council on Tribunals leaflet, 'The Council and your Complaint'.

codes from which Parliament should choose when establishing a new tribunal because of the great variety of tribunals. In 1991, however, after ten years' work, the council published[18] an important compilation of model tribunal rules intended for the use of departmental draftsmen. The compilation is not intended as a code but as a 'store from which Departments and tribunals may select and adopt what they need'. The compilation is a major step towards a measure of harmonisation – but only if departments volunteer to use it.

The history of the council in terms of formal powers is a history of stasis; its position is essentially the same as 40 years ago, though at least it has not been abolished. It has expressed a desire to move on; in 1980, for example, it presented a case for bolstering powers in a special report[19] from which little resulted. Part of the council's work has been to compensate for the weakness of its formal position by developing practices of non-statutory or informal consultation and extensions of competence. Williams, a former member, feels[20] that it has 'built up a strong relationship with the departments, and it is common for there to be consultation on proposed primary as well as delegated legislation affecting tribunals or enquiry procedure'. External observers tend to be more sceptical: [1]

> The truth ... is that the Council attracts precious little interest or publicity and it is no secret that, as a result, at least some of its staff and members feel unloved, undervalued and unappreciated ... It is appropriate to consider why it is that the Council is so neglected and what might be done about it ...
>
> The Council has severely limited powers and functions, it operates on minimal resources and it is responsible for matters which do not readily fire the public's imagination. Undoubtedly these factors combined, go some considerable way towards accounting for the Council's lack of prominence. What remains to be considered is whether ... the performance of the Council within these limits may also be a contributing factor ...
>
> The Council's ability to produce annual and special reports is probably the most important resource it has at its disposal. It provides a valuable opportunity to exert pressure on decision makers and administrators through public exposure of its views, arguments and recommendations. Yet ... the Council do little more than recite facts and make the occasional grumble. Indeed, the Council gives no indication that it sees itself addressing a public audience and trying to inform, persuade and win support for its ideas ....
>
> It is stretching credulity ... to ask one to accept that the Council could not have gone further than it has in asserting itself ... If the Council wants more publicity it is going to have to create it itself, and it will not do so without ruffling the occasional feather ... After a quarter of a century of existence, the Council can be seen to face a choice. Either it will have to become more effective in seizing every opportunity to fight for what it believes, or it will have to accept that by continuing with its low key, 'softly softly' approach it will inevitably (and perhaps rightly), be confined to the margins of public life and left to carry out its limited functions in relative obscurity.

In short, the council is a 1950s relic lingering in the harsh world of NPM.

18 *Model Rules of Procedure for Tribunals* Cm. 1434 (1991).
19 *The Functions of the Council on Tribunals*, above, note 13.
20 D. Williams, 'The Council on Tribunals: The First Twenty-Five Years' [1984] PL 73, 88.
 1 O. Lomas, 'The Twenty-Fifth Annual Report of the Council on Tribunals – an opportunity sadly missed' (1985) 48 MLR 694, pp. 695, 697, 701, 703.

## 5. Justice for the claimant: a case study of welfare adjudication

In a famous American study,[2] Mashaw identified three different models of welfare adjudication. Like all ideal-types, Mashaw's models are not to be taken too literally, but they are none the less helpful. Mashaw calls his first model 'bureaucratic rationality' and describes it as hierarchical and primarily concerned with efficiency and effective delivery of services. This model incorporates the idea of administrators as executives who are not concerned with policy, a division which underlies the creation of 'New Steps' agencies for the delivery of services. We shall see this model exemplified in the machinery for Social Fund adjudication.

Mashaw's second model is the model of 'professional treatment', a term which points to its basis in the client/social worker relationship. Characterised by individuation and discretion, this is the model of welfare administration famously preferred by Richard Titmuss, who argued in an influential article that:[3]

> [A welfare system] needs an element of flexible, individualised justice for two fundamental reasons. First, because as far as we can see ahead and on the basis of all we know about human weaknesses and diversities, a society without some element of means-testing and discretion is an unattainable ideal. It is stupid and dangerous to pretend that such an element need not exist; that all will be resolved by the automatism of negative income tax, the money market, consumerism and the lawyer. Secondly, we need this element of individualised justice in order to allow a universal rights scheme, based on principles of equity, to be as precise and inflexible as possible. These characteristics of precision, inflexibility and universality depend for their sustenance and strength on the existence of some element of flexible, individualised justice.

Here, Titmuss is building on the familiar distinction between rules, which are general and, he argues, should combine precision with equality of treatment; and adjudication, which must incorporate broad discretion in order to do justice in individual cases. The essential problem is 'to find the right balance between general rules and individualised justice'. Titmuss admits that the British social security system is imperfect but warns of the dangers of moving too far in the direction of rules and legally enforceable rights; legalism may in the long run prove less humane. As we will see, his view by and large contrasts with that of welfare lawyers.

Mashaw's third model is more legalistic. He calls it the model of 'moral judgements', though we would describe it as a model, familiar to us, of 'due process'. In Chapter 4, 'due process' was identified as a key theme in the development of amber light theories and we noted the preference of lawyers for this procedural model. Mashaw's model of 'professional treatment' is, on the other hand, associated with the discipline of social work and is less acceptable to lawyers. There is a clash between the preference of lawyers and the Council on Tribunals for the model of due process fairness, comprising welfare 'rights' justiciable in tribunals, and the model of bureaucratic rationality introduced with the review procedures of the Social Fund. Are these more efficient than tribunals

2   J. Mashaw *Bureaucratic Justice; Managing Social Security Claims* (New Haven: Yale University Press) 1983.
3   R. Titmuss, 'Welfare "Rights", Law and Discretion' (1971) 42 Pol. Q. 113, 131.

and, if so, is there a trade-off in terms of fairness? Do they conform and ought they to conform to the adjudication model preferred by Franks, with its emphasis on openness, fairness and impartiality?

## (a) Claiming and internal review

Welfare administration is one of the most important output functions of the modern state. Elections are won and lost on welfare policy and it forms one of the most substantial items in the national budget: in 1993/4, the total expenditure on social security was £85,321 million.[4] In the same year, as 24% of the population was living on or below the income support line, over 5.6 million people claimed income support, an increase of 32,000 over the previous year. This figure has climbed from just under 3 million at the end of 1979 and 1 million in 1947. So welfare administration is big business and, like the welfare system which it shadows, welfare adjudication has a mass clientele. Notice how high Social Security Appeal Tribunals (SSATs) figure in the Table of busy tribunals (Table 14.1) (above, p. 457), determining more than 80,000 claims annually, a figure which has also risen exponentially but represents no more than a fraction of the number of decisions. As welfare administration has evolved into a mass service, so too has welfare adjudication.

When someone applies for income support, s/he makes a claim at the branch office of the Benefits Agency (BA) and fills in a form. The decision whether or not s/he is entitled is then made by an 'adjudication officer' (AO) of the BA. What happens if the claimant is dissatisfied with the decision and thinks that it is wrong? There are a number of ways to put the decision right. At the first stage, the system contains internal mechanisms for correcting wrong decisions. Any complaint or appeal sets in motion an internal administrative review designed to see whether the decision was correct or ought to be varied and this may take place either before or after an appeal.

This escape hatch is of some importance since internal monitoring shows that a very high proportion of decisions on welfare benefit are quite simply wrong. This is not – as the administrative lawyer's concentration on appeals tends to suggest – because the decision contains an error of law or reveals a misuse of discretionary power, but because a mathematical error or simple mistake of fact has occurred.

We know something about the high rate of error because the work of the AOs is regularly monitored by the Chief Adjudication Officer (CAO), who publishes an Annual Report commenting on standards. His function is to advise local adjudication oficers, monitor their decisions and to report annually to the Secretary of State. This process is not a 'review' but an 'audit', triggering reform of the system rather than correction of a single error. The CAO issues a 'comment sheet' on defective decisions, the aim being to maintain standards in local offices. The statistics are disquieting: between 30% and 50% of decisions merit a comment.[5]

---

4    *Social Security Statistics, 1995* (London: HMSO) 1995. See also C. Oppenheim and L. Harker, *Poverty, The Facts* (London: CPAG) 3rd edn., 1996.
5    Annual Reports of the CAO. See also Annual Report of the Council on Tribunals 1995/6, HC 114 (1995/6) paras. 2.172-5.

Wikeley and Young[6] argue that the fundamental reason for wrong decisions stems from the complexity of the rules and the frequency with which they change. But an important secondary reason for the low standards lies in the fact that welfare administration is not a very prestigious career. Officers are often poorly educated, badly trained and change jobs frequently. Error probably also derives from the way in which claims are processed. Although guidelines require officers to give prompt and courteous attention to claimants, to question them on their wants and give proper consideration to exceptional needs, this does not always occur. Not only are officers endemically overworked but a view of claimants as potential fraudsters and scroungers persists. In consequence, staff tend to discourage any claim unless specifically asked for by the claimant.[7] This has led the CAO to call for 'a climate in which good adjudication practices are actively pursued, measured and recognized by management at all levels'.[8] The publication of a Customer Charter in 1993, offering 'prompt, accurate advice and payment by an expert and committed staff', together with a Business Plan set an accuracy target of 92% for income support cases, is a management device for dealing with this problem.

The status of the 'adjudication officer' who makes the decision is rather uneasy. Although they are employees of the Benefits Agency, AOs are required to act 'independently' in coming to a decision on the merits of a claim. Their function has been described as 'quasi-judicial', because it is distinct from the administrative process of filling out and filing the application form and cannot simply be cancelled by a hierarchical superior.[9] An AO's decision is certainly not an 'adjudication' in the sense in which we have been using this term, however. The decision of a court is 'final and binding' but s. 26(1) of the Social Security Administration Act 1992[10] provides that the decision of an adjudication officer may be 'reviewed'. A review may take place if: (i) there has been a mistake about the facts; (ii) the claimant's circumstances have changed or are expected to change; or (iii) the adjudication officer made an error of law. Contrast the decisions of an SSAT or Social Security Commissioner, which can also be reviewed but only on grounds (i) and (ii); their determination of the law can only be set aside by appeal to a superior court or tribunal or by judicial review. The courts clearly see the distinction as important and have generally preferred to classify the AO's function as administrative.[11] A further reason to accept this view is that applicants are not entitled to a hearing before the AO, who normally proceeds entirely on the papers.

The fiction of adjudication is revealed by the study of the AO's work pattern to which reference has already been made. After lengthy interviews, the authors had to conclude:[12]

6   N. Wikeley and R. Young, 'The Administration of Benefits in Britain: Adjudication Officers and the Influence of Social Security Appeal Tribunals' [1992] PL 238, 246.
7   L. Howe, 'The "Deserving" and the "Undeserving": Practice in an Urban Local Social Security Office' (1985) 14 J. of Social Policy 49.
8   Annual Report of the Chief Adjudication Officer for 1988/9 (London: HMSO), para 1.14.
9   J. Baldwin, N. Wikeley and R. Young, *Judging social security: the adjudication of claims* (Oxford: Clarendon) 1992, p. 29 (hereafter, Baldwin et al.).
10  Replacing s. 14(2)(d) of the Supplementary Benefits Act 1976. See also para. 4 of the Supplementary Benefits (Determination of Questions) Regulations 1980.
11  *Jones v Department of Employment* [1989] QB 1.
12  Baldwin et al., Ch. 2, p. 69.

The truth of the matter is that most income support adjudication officers do very little adjudication: they simply authorize with their signature the decisions taken *de facto* by junior staff. The responsibility for taking decisions is in practice delegated to a level lower than is officially intended. The likelihood that mistakes will be made is great, especially since these low level clerical staff receive no special training in adjudication, in how to use the Adjudication Officer's Guide, or in how to interpret the complex regulations to be applied. It is not a case of adjudication officers seeking to shirk their responsibilities: they simply do not have time to carry out more than a superficial check, and then it involves only a minority of all the claims passing through their sections.

We shall return to this point. It is enough here to note that this makes scrutiny and review even more important.

Considering its importance and efficacy, administrative lawyers have generally shown little interest in review, regarding it as part of the administrative process.[13] Baldwin et al. were, however, impressed both by the integrity of the appeals officers and by the efficacy of the review system which, they found, had increased since the introduction of income support in 1988. In 1989, 31% of appeals were revised on review when only 12% were overturned after a hearing. The authors felt able directly to attribute this change to the move in modern legislation from strong discretion to a system closely structured by rules (below):[14]

> Under the old system, adjudication officers were able to resist the exhortations of appeals officers to revise decisions by saying it was all 'a matter of opinion'... The introduction of income support left adjudication officers more exposed by depriving them of the opportunity to dress up rushed decisions as legitimate exercises of discretion.

Internal review is an economical way to rectify errors. The procedure acts as a sieve for trivial complaints. Given the rate of error, it is possible to see an advantage to the claimant in a routine appeal! It is, after all, free and has the effect of placing the case automatically before a senior and more experienced official. This is another point to which we shall need to return. However, Sainsbury has argued that internal reviews have 'moved from being an element of routine administration to constituting the first tier of an appeals structure'; in other words, review provides a bottom tier in a pyramidal system. Concerned about the rise in the number of reviews, Sainsbury concluded that:[15]

> social security claimants' appeal rights have been weakened by the growth of internal reviews as the first tier of appeal. When reviews become a means of redress they cease to be part of the machinery of administration and become part of the machinery of adjudication. They should therefore be subject to similar criteria to the

---

13  But see, R. Coleman, *Supplementary Benefits and the Administrative Review of Administrative Action* (London: CPAG), many of whose conclusions remain relevant.
14  Baldwin et al., pp. 77-78.
15  R. Sainsbury, 'Internal Reviews and the Weakening of Social Security Claimants' Rights of Appeal' in G. Richardson and H. Genn, *Administrative Law and Government Action* (Oxford: Clarendon) 1994, pp. 288-289.

higher forms of adjudication such as tribunals and courts. When a comparison is made using such internal criteria, internal reviews emerge as inferior to tribunals.

Sainsbury sees three fundamental distinctions between the two processes: review is (i) internal and (ii) limited to the statutory grounds; while appeal is (i) external (ii) not restricted as to grounds and (iii) initiated by the claimant. He argues that recent extensions of the review process have allowed this distinction to become blurred. This view should be borne in mind as we move on to consider first, social security adjudication; secondly, the procedure for reviewing Social Fund decisions, a more obvious appeal substitute; and finally, some new government proposals.

### (b) Judicialising Social Security Tribunals

In Chapter 12, we noted the longstanding bias in English administrative law in favour of oral and adversarial procedures, strongly reinforced by the pervasive influence of Franks. In this case study, we shall find that the system of independent tribunals follows the classic pattern of trial-type procedures and is heavily reliant on lay participation. Social Fund review procedure is, by way of contrast, unashamedly documentary in character. But is it an 'inquisitorial', adjudicative procedure or a hierarchical, administrative review?

The SSATs which we have today merge two previous adjudication systems: Supplementary Benefit Appeal Tribunals (SBATs) and National Insurance Local Tribunals (NILTs). This is more than a nominal change. SSATs inherit the tradition of National Assistance Tribunals (NATs) established under the National Assistance Act of 1948, in turn based on the tribunals which existed under the Unemployment Assistance Act 1934.[16] The role of these tribunals could be compared to that of a teacher listening to a prefect's complaint about a pupil; she is concerned with the facts but she is not likely to question the school rules. Early welfare tribunals had no independent policy role.

The Franks Committee accepted the departmental view of NATs as 'an assessment or case committee, taking a further look at the facts and in some cases arriving at a fresh decision on the extent of need'.[17] They were thought to operate satisfactorily (perhaps this only meant that Franks received no grave complaints). The report described NATs as 'special' and exempted them from the general requirement of openness; 'if any or all of these appeals were to be held in public many applicants might be deterred from appealing or even from applying for assistance and the purpose of the legislation might thus be frustrated'.

There were other signs that Franks did not regard NATs as 'machinery for adjudication'. It did not create an appeal to the High Court on a point of law. It made no recommendations about legally qualified chairmen. The only real concession was the admission that 'legal representation should be permitted to the applicant who can satisfy the chairman of the Tribunal that he cannot

16   See T. Lynes, 'Unemployment Assistance Tribunals in the 1930s' and A. Bradley, 'National Assistance Appeal Tribunals and the Franks Report', both in M. Adler and A. Bradley, *Justice, Discretion and Poverty* (London: Professional Books) 1975, pp. 5-54. See also above, p. 462.
17   Cmnd. 218, paras. 180, 182-183.

satisfactorily present his case unless he is allowed to employ a lawyer'. It can be seen how these features might help to disguise dissatisfaction with tribunals. Claimants were not legally represented and were hardly likely to know of the prerogative order procedure which paralleled our modern application for judicial review. Neither lawyers nor journalists were present to articulate dissatisfaction. It may be that Franks was condoning amateurishness, perhaps because small sums were at stake.

Some years later, Herman, an American sociologist who surveyed the work of SBATs, still classified them as 'administrative', seeing their decisions as a natural extension of administration.[18] Mashaw's model of professional treatment was slow to change. In 1971, the Chairman of the Supplementary Benefits Commission wrote:[19]

> The Commission is grateful to all who act, in whatever capacity, as friendly counsellors to claimants and hope that this Handbook will make a major contribution, not only to removing misunderstanding where it exists, but also to intensifying and extending positive co-operation with anyone advising, representing or helping claimants . . . The concept of co-operation, in the Commission's view, goes to the heart of a successful operation of the scheme.

The Ministry of Social Security Act 1966 moved to flat rate entitlements for some, though not all, benefit payments. By 1976, Bradley was describing the functions of SBATs as being:[20]

> to decide *disputes* which the administration of social security has thrown up, disputes which break the surface because a citizen is sufficiently aggrieved by the official decision to appeal against it. It is an important function of tribunals to be able to settle such disputes in an impartial and fair manner. If their decisions are to be accepted, they must observe certain minimum standards both of procedural and of substantive justice.

Is Collison denying that 'disputes' can arise over benefit? Is Bradley saying that disputes *must* be resolved by a certain procedure if the solution is to give satisfaction? Or is he questioning 'the concept of co-operation'? As we suggested in Chapter 12, the difference is important if we are not to slip into unquestioning acceptance of a trial-type model of adjudication.

The Franks Committee had favoured informality, but had also warned[1] that informality without rules of procedure might produce 'an unordered character which makes it difficult, if not impossible, for the tribunal properly to sift the facts and weigh the evidence'. This was an apt description of SBATs, where ignorance of the simplest legal ideas, such as who ought to prove what or how things should be proved, was common. Members received no training at all, staff

---

18  M. Herman, *Administrative Justice and Supplementary Benefits* (London: LSE) 1972, pp. 13-14.
19  Lord Collision, Introduction to the 1st edn. of the Handbook for Claimants issued by the SBC. The SBC was a semi-autonomous agency set up by the Ministry of Social Security Act 1966. It combined administrative and advisory functions.
20  A. Bradley, 'Reform of Supplementary Benefit Tribunals – The Key Issues' (1976) 27 NILQ 96, 101.
 1  Cmnd. 218, para. 64.

received minimal training and legally qualified chairmen were exceptional. Unaware of the need for independence or procedural protections, tribunals were inclined to give free rein to prejudice.

In a significant study in 1973, Norman Lewis contrasted the performance of NILTs, which dealt with industrial injury claims, with that of SBATs. Lewis contended that Titmuss had greatly underestimated the advantages of legal input, praising the 'traditions of English lawyering which can, at its best, rise to lending order to administrative processes without ever meddling'. He concluded: [2]

> [The tribunals] appear to operate in marked contrast to the national insurance local appeal tribunals which are usually a model of balancing informal expertise with order and legality. This point is made to indicate that criticism of supplementary benefit tribunals is not based upon comparisons with courts of law but is made within a framework of acceptance of the valuable job performed by administrative tribunals at large. Nor is the objection to underdeveloped legal technique an attempt to promote the claims of the legal profession to intellectual leadership of the 'welfare rights movement'. It is simply that the system of appeals from the SBC is vastly important, that it is not operating upon the basis of anything resembling objective standards, that such a state of affairs works to the ultimate detriment of claimants and that some of the fault is a lack of legal expertise.

Let us follow Lewis's criticisms a little further. When a claimant enters a modern SSAT, she sees facing her across a table the chairman seated between two members. The chairman is a lawyer. The claimant and her representative sit opposite. The clerk sits on one side. The departmental presenting officer sits beside the claimant. This emphasises their equal status, removing any impression that he is an officer of the tribunal. Every member has the procedural guide, issued by the Independent Tribunal Service (below). There should be a copy of relevant statutes, regulations and guidance [3] in the room together with the collected summaries of relevant High Court precedents and Commissioners' decisions. [4]

This was emphatically not the procedure observed by researchers who attended tribunals in the early 1970s. They found tribunals which were heavily dependent on the clerk and departmental presenting officer, who in many tribunals sat opposite to the clerk, emphasising his official status. Observers were concerned by the way in which the power of choice was exercised. Benefit officers were in practice guided by departmental guidance but departmental policy was not supposed to bind the 'independent' tribunals. Some tribunals did not, however, understand the status of this 'soft law' or realise that SBC directives and codes of practice could not bind either the benefit officer or the tribunal. SBATs were meant to examine the discretionary decisions of benefit officers on their merits and could 'substitute for any decision appealed against any determination which a benefit officer could have made' (s. 15(1)(c) of the Supplemetary Benefits Act

---

2   N. Lewis, 'Supplementary Benefits Appeal Tribunals' [1973] PL 257, 258-259.
3   The main publications are: *The Law Relating to Social Security* (London: HMSO) 10 vols., loose-leaf; *Adjudication Officers' Guide* (London: HMSO) 10 vols., loose-leaf; *Income Support Manual* (London: HMSO) 1 vol., loose-leaf (all periodically updated).
4   D. Neligan, *Social Security Case Law – Digest of Commissioners' Decisions* (London: HMSO) 2 vols., loose-leaf.

1976, as amended). Yet the tribunal tended either to accept SBC policy unquestioningly or to give free rein to personal prejudices. To put this differently, its 'strong' discretion was not properly structured.

Here the composition of the tribunal was important. The SBAT was – as SSATs still are – supposed to represent the community. Chairmen were appointed by the minister from a panel approved by the Lord Chancellor. They did not need legal qualifications. Of the two members, one was selected by the minister from a panel nominated by trade unions and other representative organisations, the other was appointed by the minister from a list of people 'with knowledge or local experience of people living on low incomes'. In practice, such members were often drawn from social service organisations such as the Citizens Advice Bureaux (CABx), or local chambers of commerce. In an unofficial survey published by CPAG, Lister found [5] that, in the London area at least, members were unrepresentative of the population at large. Women and ethnic minorities were under-represented; 'there is, as in many such lay bodies, a clear bias towards men in the higher age and social class groups'. Equally, they were unrepresentative of claimants. There was a danger that tribunals would fail to recognise claimants' difficulties and might, as a group, possess prejudices which they did not recognise and could not restrain. The indeterminate nature of the 'rules' then came into play with lack of training reinforcing any latent bias. The fact that many members and chairmen were also magistrates may have reinforced their tendency to turn for advice to the clerk. Regular appearance in tribunals and access to departmental policy gave these DHSS officials a misleading appearance of expertise and might even suggest objectivity. But unlike the clerk in a magistrate's court, neither clerks nor presenting officers were legally trained. Their advice on the meaning of statute and regulations and their knowledge of High Court decisions was imperfect and the presenting officer, who had normally worked in a social security office deciding claims, was likely to feel a sense of loyalty to the DHSS and share its ethos.

A mounting tide of pressure from welfare lawyers, academics and action groups led the DHSS to commission a survey of SBATs conducted on its behalf by Professor Kathleen Bell. [6] Her survey pointed to some of the disadvantages of adversarial procedure in tribunals. She concluded that presenting officers did not understand their role; some could more aptly be described as prosecuting officers. Presenting officers needed to be of high calibre and properly trained if they were to balance their conflicting duties of 'adviser' and 'presenter'. Without legal qualifications clerks could not be relied on to redress the balance. Seconded to tribunals from regional DHSS offices for a period of service, they might later be absorbed again into the administrative work of the department. Clerks, unlike

---

5   R. Lister, *Justice for the Claimant: A Study of Supplementary Benefit Appeal Tribunals* (London: CPAG) 1974.

6   The main conclusions of this survey were published as *Research Study on Supplementary Benefit Appeal Tribunals: Review of Main Findings: Conclusions: Recommendations* (London: HMSO) 1975. For Bell's later views, see K. Bell, 'Social Security Tribunals – A General Perspective' (1982) 33 NILQ 132. See also M. Adler, E. Burns and R. Johnson, 'The Conduct of Tribunal Hearings' in M. Adler and A. Bradley, *Justice, Discretion and Poverty* (above, p. 476, note 16), p. 109.

presenting officers, remained with the tribunal while it was deliberating and after the appellant and his representative had left. Lister had found that clerks played a crucial role as a source of advice and information. Some clerks intervened of their own accord in proceedings where they felt the tribunal was going wrong. All this added up to independence without impartiality, a denial of the Franks criteria.

The Bell Report was an important stage in the move to orderliness and ultimately judicialisation of tribunals. It recommended a three-stage programme. Stage 1 was designed to strengthen existing tribunals, for example by appointing legal practitioners as 'Senior Chairmen' to supervise tribunals and institute training schemes. Stage 2 aimed to improve on existing tribunals by a planned programme of judicialisation: for example, Bell recommended legally qualified chairmen, better provision for representation and a higher calibre of member with strong commitment to the work. Stage 3 would bring the integration of SBATs with NILTs but, as a halfway measure, the appeals system would be restructured to allow a second appeal on a point of law to National Insurance Commissioners, who would be given jurisdiction in both sets of tribunals and rechristened 'Social Security Commissioners'. Bell complained: [7]

> At present no further right of appeal exists from decisions of SBATs to a second-tier appeal body. Furthermore, they are excluded from Section 13 of the Tribunals and Inquiries Act 1971 which provides for an appeal on a point of law to the High Court. [8] They are subject to review by certiorari but in fact this is a limited, complex and inaccessible remedy. The operation of these tribunals is kept under general review by the Council on Tribunals but although the Council has been much concerned with the problems discussed in this paper, it is an advisory body and has no power to alter any tribunal decision. Taking all the research findings into consideration I find no justification for leaving SBATs in a position in which they are virtually uncontrolled. A second-tier appeal body should, I submit, be treated as a matter of urgency and priority. The only reason this recommendation is placed in Stage III is that until the decision-making of SBATs and their recorded, reasoned decisions can be substantially improved it would be difficult, if not impossible, for a superior appellate body to do its work.

A majority of the Bell proposals could be implemented administratively; there were immediate moves to introduce training schemes and to appoint more legally trained chairmen. Five senior chairmen (legally qualified) were appointed on a regional basis to monitor tribunals and to supervise training who, by 1982, had assumed a 'watchdog' function. The new appeals structure was, however, provided by legislation: ss. 14 and 15 of the Social Security Act 1980 provided for appeal on a point of law with leave to the newly constituted Social Security Commissioners and thence with leave again to the Court of Appeal. The Commissioners' tribunal is well-used and accessible: between 1977 and 1980, there had been 150 appeals under s. 13 of the Tribunals and Inquiries Act; under the new procedure, there were 945 applications for leave to appeal to the Commissioners in the first year, 100 of which came from the DHSS; since then,

7   Bell Report 1975, pp. 24-25.
8   This was changed by SI 1977/1735, which added SBATs to the list of tribunals covered by s. 13 of the Tribunals and Inquiries Act 1971 (now s. 11 of the 1992 Act).

the figure has risen steadily: 2,639 appeals were decided in 1995. Both the DSS and welfare lawyers indulge in test case strategy, selecting their most favourable cases for appeal. [9] The Commissioners are specialists who understand the operation of the welfare system, so that a substantial volume of precedent is built up which can serve to regularise procedure, as well as to rule on the interpretation of the regulations.

Only a handful (under 50) of cases reaches the Court of Appeal with a further trickle of applications for judicial review, a remedy of last resort. A key decision of the House of Lords preserves the residual character of these external remedies. In *Chief Adjudication Officer v Foster*,[10] an appellant wished to argue before the Commissioner that ministerial regulations were ultra vires;. the Commissioner allowed the appeal on this ground. The Court of Appeal ruled, however, that the Commissioner, who possessed only an appellate jurisdiction, could not rule on the vires of regulations which formed a part of the statutory scheme; the point could only be raised by means of judicial review. Had this argument won the day, the standing of the Commissioners would have been seriously undercut and many important points of law would have been sucked into the Divisional Court. Fortunately, however, the House of Lords reversed the Court of Appeal, ruling that tribunals were competent to consider the validity of regulations.

To underpin the new judicialised structures, the appeals rules provided for the tribunal to record its reasons and findings of material questions of fact, together with any dissenting opinions.[11] A procedural guide was first issued in 1977; revised for the DHSS by the senior chairmen, it is re-issued regularly. This and the extension of training has done much to standardise procedures. For the first time, the guide laid great emphasis on the importance of reasoned decisions (by reading between the lines, a great deal can be learned about earlier practice).[12]

> 73. Having considered all the evidence, the tribunal should decide which facts it finds are established and, where there is a conflict in the evidence, indicate clearly the version it accepts ... It is not sufficient merely to record: 'The facts put forward by the Adjudication Officer (or the claimant) were agreed' or 'Facts as stated'.
>
> Commissioner's Decision R(SB) 8/84 paragraph 25 states -
>
> > 'It is useless to record the evidence in the chairman's note and then leave the claimant guessing as to whether or not his evidence was accepted'....
>
> The space labelled 'Tribunal's unanimous/majority decision' is not simply for a 'rubber stamp decision'. The Tribunal's decision should be fully, intelligibly and accurately set out in it. To use expressions such as 'Decision revised' or 'Appeal dismissed' or 'Case adjourned' is not sufficient. Similarly, in the case of a majority decision not only must it be clearly and unambiguously stated what that decision is, but

---

9   See T. Prosser, *Test Cases for the Poor* (London: CPAG) 1983; R. Smith, 'How Good are Test Cases' in J. Cooper and R. Dhavan (eds.), *Public Interest Law* (Oxford: Blackwell) 1986.
10  [1993] AC 754. See, for comment, D. Feldman, 'Review, Appeal and Jurisdictional Confusion' (1992) 108 LQR 45.
11  Supplementary Benefit and Family Income Supplements (Appeals) Rules, SI 1980/1605. The duty is reinforced by s. 10 of the Tribunals and Inquiries Act 1992, which provides statutory authority for a statement of reasons to form part of the record. See also J. Tinnion, 'Principles in Practice: The Statement of Reasons' (1995) 2 Tribunals 9.
12  *Social Security Appeal Tribunals, A Guide to Procedure* (London: HMSO) 1985, para. 73.

the dissenting member's reasons should also be recorded. The wording should be such that neither the claimant nor the AO is left in any doubt as to what the Tribunal has decided. A proper recording of decisions by the chairman is essential; it is his duty to see that this is done.

Early welfare adjudication then, had been characterised by the model of 'professional treatment' redolent of the unstructured discretion which characterised welfare administration. Against this background, the arrangements for appeals were informal and the main criteria for the adjudicator were knowledge of local conditions, fairness and common sense. By the 1970s, welfare had become a mass, national system and equal treatment an important administrative value, creating a system of officer discretion in practice heavily structured by rules. There had been a shift inside administration towards the model of 'bureaucratic rationality' not so far reflected in the appeals tribunals, of whom something more was clearly expected. Welfare lawyers now began vociferously to advocate a shift to the 'due process' model, change gradually taking place during the 1970s. A sharp switch in welfare administration away from unstructured officer discretion towards complex, legalistic rules took place in 1980.[13] Tribunal procedure remained relatively informal, although improvements were in hand. What more could be done? And what would claimants want?

### (c)  A presidential system

The Health and Social Services and Social Security Adjudications Act 1983 (HASSASSA) moved welfare adjudication sharply towards the court model. The debates on this measure, which was considerably amended during its passage, bring out familiar divisions about the purposes of tribunals. In committee, Mr. John (Labour) argued that tribunal members should be 'representative'. This extract should be compared with Bell's findings about the expectations of claimants (below):[14]

> [The Appellant] should be adequately represented and have a fair and sympathetic hearing. We shall therefore seek to write into the Bill . . . that there shall be representatives on the tribunal who can help and sympathise with the appellant and understand his point of view. The rule is still that people are unrepresented. They represent themselves and are often confused by procedures and by the doctrine of precedent that is increasingly being applied. It would help them if members of the tribunal were to have a knowledge of their conditions and their welfare.

By 'adequate representation', the Opposition members were not thinking in terms of lawyers and an extension of legal aid; indeed, they went on to argue for the retention of good chairmen who did not possess the legal qualifications specified by the government, insisting that it was knowledge of social security law and not

---

13  Social Security Act 1980 and Social Security (No 2) Act 1980. These statutes reflect a departmental review, *Social Assistance* (London: DHSS) 1978, into which the Supplementary Benefits Commission (above, p. 477, note 19) had considerable input. See further, C. Walker, *Challenging Social Policy* (London: Bedford Square Press) 1983.

14  HC SCB, 19 April 1983, col. 58.

legal qualifications which counted. But these arguments failed. HASSASSA provided for NILTs and SBATs to be amalgamated; for decisions as to benefit to be taken by an adjudication officer and for appeal to lie to a SSAT. Paragraph 8 of Sch. 4 empowered the Lord Chancellor to appoint a President and Regional and full-time chairmen for the tribunals and for these appointments to be held by barristers or solicitors of not less than ten, seven and five years' standing respectively. Appointments of tribunal members would also be made by the President. The greater independence of the tribunals was recognised by the fact that staffing, including the post of clerk, was to be the responsibility of the President (with consent of the minister and Treasury). Further appeal continued to lie to the Social Security Commissioners and Court of Appeal.[15] This was a context for rapid judicialisation.

No single person did more to fit SSATs for their new role than Judge Byrt, the first President of the ITS. Judge Byrt used to the full his powers to appoint and train chairmen, making tribunals conform more closely to the model of due process. Members are now more representative in regard to age and gender; by 1990, 36.4% tribunal members were women and nearly 50% under the age of 60.[16] Training has been steadily upgraded and increased. There is proper access to the regulations and precedent from the Social Security Commisssioners which go to make up social security law, as well as training in its use and interpretation.

Arguably, these changes were dictated both by the sharp move from discretion to rules in the 1980 legislation and the complex network of regulations which implement it, and also by the textual complexity of the rules. (It is instructive to look back to what Wade says about differing standards of justice in courts and tribunals (above, p. 459)). Baldwin et al. note the consequences of the transition:[17]

> The new regime has swept away many of the old (and potentially broad) discretionary powers and replaced them with a much firmer and narrower basis of legal entitlement. This means that a tribunal, whether or not it likes the look of a claimant, is obliged to apply the letter of the law without favour. Our own observations and interviews have convinced us that this is a fundamental change of substance: it is no mere tinkering with the old system. Consequently the typical tribunal appearance is nowadays a quite different experience from what it used to be. The pendulum has swung, and the key question is whether it has swung too far.

The new context of rules, in other words, was creating a need for a more expert tribunal, reflected in the statutory requirements of legally qualified chairmen. According to Bradley,[18] himself a chairman, tribunals could no longer 'range with

---

15   See N. Harris, 'The Reform of the Supplementary Benefits Appeals System' (1983) JSWL 212; C. Mesher, 'The Merging of Social Security Tribunals' (1983) 10 J. of Law and Soc. 135.

16   SSA 1975, s. 97, as amended by Health and Social Security Act 1984, s. 16(b), provides for panels 'composed of persons appearing to the President to have knowledge or experience of conditions in that area and to be representative of persons living or working there'.

17   At p. 155 See also C. Harlow, 'Discretion, Social Security and Computers' (1981) 44 MLR 546; C. Mesher, 'The 1980 Social Security Legislation: The Great Welfare State Chainsaw Massacre?' (1981) 8 J. of Law and Soc. 119.

18   A. Bradley, 'Recent Reform of Social Security Adjudication in Great Britain' (1985) 26 *Les Cahiers de Droit* 403.

freedom' in the area of policy and discretion; their task had been transformed. Tribunal work now called for greater technical ability in dealing with arguments based on entitlement under regulations. There was extra pressure to make an adequate record of the proceedings and the decision. The papers had become more legalistic, being drafted with heavy reliance on models issued by the CAO. Legally qualified chairmen were pushed into a dominant position, often forming a view on the papers submitted without too much further exploration of the facts.

This brings into question the tradition of lay members. Bell had recorded[19] the preference of appellants both for informality and for participation, noting the preference for social workers, who allowed them to participate in presenting their own case, as representatives. She also found that claimants 'felt more deeply about lay members than about any other single aspect of their experience'. Members, they thought, should play an active and *enabling* role towards claimants by showing sympathetic understanding of the problem, listening, asking relevant questions, drawing them out, and generally helping to sort out the case. This view of the function of the lay member survives in modern training. Paragraph 14 of the *Guide to Procedure* requires members to be 'interested, alert, knowledgeable, active, questioning and helpful'. It is questionable, however, whether tribunal members can really fulfil these expectations and it has even been suggested that they prefer not to play an active part in tribunal proceedings. Potter found[20] substantial improvement in the performance of chairmen, who now played Bell's 'enabling role' but saw a dimunition in the role of members. In the few instances where both members participated, 'their involvement had a marked effect on the appellant's perception of the tribunal and without exception ... all expressed their satisfaction with the hearing and rated the members' participation as good'. Vernon[1] associates an enabling role with inquisitorial procedure (or, we might add, ADR); 'Where the tribunal adopts an adversarial model of procedure the 'enabling role' is likely to be much reduced'.

The PO is not to be treated as a 'servant of the tribunal, and the tribunal is not bound to accept his interpretation of the law'. Equally, he is instructed to act as a 'friend of the court' rather than as departmental advocate:[2]

> An AO has a right to attend the sittings of the tribunal, to be heard, to call witnesses and to question any witness directly, but he does not act in the capacity of an advocate nor should he adopt a defensive role in respect of any decision the subject of an appeal, whether made by himself or by a colleague. It is his duty to ensure that all the relevant facts are before the tribunal and to refer to the tribunal all relevant decisions of Social Security Commissioners and to assist it in arriving at the correct decision in law on the facts of the case.

19  Bell Report 1975, p. 18; D. Bull, 'Social Workers as Advocate' (1982) 14 Social Work Today (December) 11.

20  J. Potter, 'Adjudication by Social Security Appeal Tribunals: A Research Study' (1992) Anglo-American LR 341, 342-343. See also N. Wikeley and R. Young, 'The marginalisation of Lay Members in Social Security Appeal Tribunals' (1992) J. of Social Welfare and Family Law 127.

1   S. Vernon, 'Principles in Practice: The role of lay members in the tribunal system' (1995) 2 Tribunals 5.

2   Social Security Appeal Tribunals, A Guide to Procedure HMSO, 1985, para. 35. The passage assumes the PO is an Adjuciation Officer.

This is a difficult balancing act for even a skilled and highly trained advocate, yet the PO remains a departmental official.

What then of the claimant? The Guide stresses the role of the Chairman as facilitator. 'When the claimant first enters the tribunal room, the chairman should do all that is possible to help him feel at ease'. In an article designed for tribunal staff.[3] Partington emphasises the chairman's 'considerable responsibility to ensure that... the parties to be heard have the appropriate chance to say what they have to say, to ask the questions that they wish to ask, and to make the submissions that relate to their case'. An important decision of the Social Security Commissioners[4] expands the Chairman's investigatorial function:

> A social security tribunal is exercising quasi-judicial functions and forms part of the statutory machinery for investigating claims in order to ascertain whether the claimant satisfies the statutory requirements which entitle him to be paid benefit. It is not restricted, as in ordinary litigation which are [sic] proceedings between parties, to accepting or rejecting the respective contentions of the claimant on the one hand and the adjudication . . . officer on the other . . . Its investigatory function has as its object the ascertainment of the facts and the determination of the truth.

Despite these counsels, the claimant may still be at a disadvantage both in explaining his case and also in knowing what to prove and how to prove it. In an adversarial system, if claimants are unrepresented, the chairman is bound to intervene in proceedings; if they are absent, their claim will go largely unheard. A high correlation between success rates, attendance and representation has been shown;[5] only about 7% of appellants who neither attend nor are represented succeed in their appeal. Genn states[6] categorically that 'in social security appeals tribunals, the presence of a skilled representative increased the likelihood of success from 30% to 48%'. In 1996, the success rate for appellants appearing in person was 46%; for those represented 53.6%; for those who did not attend 12.5%. It may be that the adversarial procedures in which we traditionally put our faith do not function particularly well in the absence of lawyers. Genn concludes:[7]

> A [difficult] situation faces appellants in tribunals who have no representation or who come with an unskilled representative. The relative simplicity with which proceedings can be initiated, the literature from tribunals stressing their informality, the physical appearance of hearings and the approach of the tribunal to the conduct of hearings can convey the impression that decision-making processes are carried out in a rather relaxed and informal manner. This impression is misleading. [Tribunal chairmen stress] the need for those appearing before them to 'make their case' by providing legally relevant factual information and evidence of those facts ...

3   M. Partington, 'Principles in Practice: Adjudication' (1994) 1 Tribunals 12, 13.
4   R(S)1/87, Commissioner Hallett.
5   H. Genn and Y. Genn, The Effectiveness of Representation at Tribunals (London: HMSO) 1989. See also A. Frost and C. Howard, Representation and Administrative Tribunals (London: Routledge) 1977.
6   H. Genn, 'Tribunals and Informal Justice' (1993) 56 MLR 393, 400. For the 1996 figures see, *DSS Quarterly Social Security Appeal Tribunal Statistics*, (1997).
7   *A Strategy for Justice*, (London: Legal Action Group) 1992, p. 9.

Thus, although unrepresented appellants are free to 'speak for themselves' before tribunals and many value this freedom, it has hidden dangers ...  Decision-making processes in tribunals require legally relevant and sufficient accounts. Applicants tell stories which may or may not be relevant. The result is often that they may feel satisfied with the process but ultimately lose their case.

Legal representation is, however, still exceptional in welfare tribunals and, in the absence of legal aid, is likely to remain so.

So is this an adversarial model, or does it inevitably veer to the inquistorial, as the growing dominance of the Chairman and the erosion of member's rights suggest?

New regulations introduced in 1996 [8] with the approval of the Chairman of the ITS (Judge Bassingthwaite) formalised practice and streamlined the system. To Lynes,[9] a 'simple and informal' procedure was deliberately bureaucratised. Oral hearings became the exception, unless specifically requested at an early stage and paper hearings were substituted. Significantly, members, and sometimes even Chairmen, no longer receive these papers in advance. Regulation 23(3)(c) authorises short cuts in the recording of decisions and reasons. The scene was being set for still more radical change. We shall return to this below.

### (d) Bureaucratic rationality: the model of Social Fund review

The principal objective of the 1985 review of social security [10] was to reduce the amount of expenditure on welfare. For the first time, welfare payments were not to be demand-led but disciplined by the introduction of fixed budgets for local areas. Again for the first time, many of the benefits took the form of loans. The Social Fund (SF) set up by the Social Security Act 1986 dispenses three types of payment:[11] (i) mandatory payments to meet specified situations, such as pregnancies or funerals, in respect of which appeal continues to lie to SSATs; (ii) grants to meet the expenses of release into the community from institutional care; and (iii) loans in other cases of exceptional need, including crisis loans. In respect of heads (ii) and (iii), there was a sharp reversion to discretion, reflecting the government perception that claimants 'knew too much about the rules' and were using their knowledge to divert funds into the pockets of people who were not 'in real need'. Crisis loans, for example, carry over into the SF some of the characteristics of early welfare administration in that the claimant must show that a loan is 'the only way that serious risk or damage to health and safety of the family can be avoided', a formula replete with officer-discretion. But the limited budget introduced a wholly new element into discretionary decision-making, reflecting the 'NPM' described in Chapter 5, and based on twin concepts of efficiency and management accountability.

Commenting on the Green Paper, the Social Services Advisory Committee, semi-official watchdog for the consumer, cautiously described the fund as possessing

8  Social Security Adjudication Regulations, SI 1801/1995.
9  T. Lynes, 'Social security tribunals: new procedures' Legal Action, June 1997, p. 24.
10  Green Paper, *The Reform of Social Security*, Cmnd. 9517-19, 1985; White Paper *Reform of Social Security: Programme for Action*, Cmnd. 9691, 1985. And see G. Beltram, *Testing the Safety Net, an enquiry into the supplementary benefit scheme* (London: Bedford Square Press) 1984.
11  For more detail, see, *A Guide to The Social Fund* (London: HMSO) from 1988.

'potential merit as a way of tackling an intractable problem' but expressed concern that the new fixed and limited local budgets would prove problematic. The problems would undoubtedly be compounded by the lack of appeal rights, a development which the SSAC saw as one of the most worrying aspects of the Green Paper proposals. [12]

> We quite agree that 'the first safeguard for claimants ... will be a professional approach in the administration of the Fund', and we also sympathise with the view that the present appeal system can be a cumbersome mechanism for handling very small financial issues. We appreciate, too, the practical and philosophical difficulties of constructing an appeal process over a fixed-budget discretionary system. However, the scale of present appeals, including in particular the extent to which decisions are reviewed in the claimant's favour before cases reach a tribunal, leaves us with little confidence that overnight a distinctively different approach can emerge, leaving the claimant fully satisfied that his case has been dealt with fairly. He is not likely to be satisfied, either, with an appeal to local management, who will inevitably be seen to be supportive of their own staff, whatever the facts of the matter ...
>
> Claimants have a right to an assurance that the facts of their case have been fully taken into account, and that discretion has been exercised fairly. We are not satisfied that internal reviews can be publicly seen to provide such an assurance. Besides the needs of claimants themselves, we suspect that Social Fund staff may also welcome some external validation of their judgements, since the system as proposed leaves them in a rather exposed position.

The White Paper replied:[13]

> Decisions which turn on whether it is reasonable to give or deny help in a particular case lend themselves far less readily to a separate, external assessment than do matters which turn on more specific criteria such as the amount of contributions paid or the income received. A necessary feature of any social fund review system is that it should operate quickly and effectively on the basis of knowledge and experience of local circumstances. The [present] adjudication system would not be able to provide these features.

The case for the SSATs was made with unusual force by the Council on Tribunals, arguing that the primary need was for the improvements to SSATs to have time to bed themselves in:[14]

> 5. The Council consider that the proposed arrangement for reviewing decisions lacks independence. The only separate review which a dissatisfied claimant could have would be by another official; apparently he would even be in the same local office as the person who made the original decision. This is not the way to gain the confidence of the public, still less of claimants, in these decisions and reviews ...

---

12  Fourth Report of SSAC for 1985 (London: HMSO) 1985, paras. 3.52, 3.75. The SSAC is officially described as 'an independent body' set up in 1980 to advise the Minister on social security issues and to consider and report on draft regulations. Appointed by the Minister, it issues annual and special reports.

13  Cmnd. 9691, para. 4.50.

14  *Social Security – Abolition of independent appeals under the proposed Social Fund*, Special Report by the Council on Tribunals, Cmnd. 9722, 1986.

6. However, the proposal goes further than depriving claimants of the right of an independent appeal. The accountability of social fund officers is also in question. There is no indication in the White Paper that there will be Ministerial accountability for particular decisions or for the actions of social fund officers, or that social fund officers will be independent of the DHSS. [This] ... would involve an important constitutional change in the field of social security, which is anyway difficult and sensitive ...

7. The need for an independent appeal system is also clear when one considers the figures. A quarter of appeals to SSATs about single payments [15] are successful, quite apart from the high proportion of decisions which are amended after an appeal is lodged but without it needing to reach a hearing. It is generally accepted that more than a quarter of all decisions on supplementary benefit are incorrect ... The number of single payment hearings is also very high, and has risen by 70% over recent years [from 21,453 in 1981 to 36,634 in 1984] ...

11. The discretionary nature of the Social Fund will not ... differ in principle from the discretionary systems in operation before 1980. The need for the application of local knowledge and experience is met under the present arrangements for hearings by local tribunals ... The only one of the Government's criteria which will certainly be met under the new arrangements is that of speed in reaching a final decision.

12. The people most affected by this proposal are amongst the most vulnerable in our society. Very good reasons are needed before the abolition of a right to an independent appeal in such circumstances, an appeal which has existed for over 50 years. It would probably be the most substantial abolition of a right of appeal to an independent tribunal since the Council on Tribunals were set up by Parliament in 1958, following the Franks Report. It is for these reasons we are so critical of the proposal. In our last Annual Report we described it as highly retrograde.

In addition to the flexible power of SFOs to review any decision at any time, s. 34 of the Social Security Act 1986 provided for two tiers of review at the request of the claimant: (i) the initial decision of an SFO may be reviewed by *the same or another* SFO; and (ii) a further review may be conducted by a Social Fund Inspector (SFI). Again, we must stress the importance of internal review: in 1995, there were 403,973 requests for first-stage review; 140,683 (or 45%) decisions were in fact revised. The SFIs are appointed by and accountable to the Social Fund Commissioner (SFC) and described as 'wholly independent' of the DSS and BA; in other words, this is the type of independence envisaged by the Citizen's Charter Unit (above, p. 406) falling midway between the Revenue Adjudicator and the ITS. There are around 100 SFIs, who receive three weeks' academic training, plus three weeks' supervised casework before they take up their job. Here the first SFC briefly explains her function.[16]

By statute I am required to monitor the quality of Inspectors' decisions and give such advice and assistance to improve the standard of their decisions and arrange such training as I consider fit ... I conduct a rigorous procedural examination of the cases I monitor, to reflect the approach which I believe the Bench would take. Consequently, my monitoring has revealed a higher proportion of Inspectors' decisions containing a defect which could leave the decision open to challenge. A procedural defect will not necessarily mean that the decision is wrong.

15 Single payments were discretionary lump sums paid in case of need under the Social Security Acts 1980, replaced by Social Fund loans.
16 *Annual Report of the Social Fund Commissioner for 1993/4 on the standards of review by Social Fund Inspectors* (London: HMSO) 1994, para. 1.1

I examine decisions at random, immediately after they have been issued. In addition, each of my six Team Leaders examines random decisions on my behalf. The information we obtain is used to inform my assessment of the quality of Inspectors' decisions and to indicate the areas in which further advice, assistance or training may be needed. In addition, I arrange for quality assessment exercises to be conducted to examine particular areas of the decision making process. The findings are fed back into the training programme for my Inspectors.

Of decisions checked that year, 85.3% (128) were acceptable, while 14.7% (22) fell intoothe class which 'contained a defect which may have rendered the decisions open to challenge' though not necessarily wrong. We can see from this that the purpose of the SFC is concerned with quality assurance and that this type of review is closer to audit than to appeal. Individual decisions can, of course, be corrected, if necessary by use of the powers under s. 34 (above).

Now let us turn to review by the SFI, initiated either by the claimant or by an AO, and starting with some statistics. In the first year of operation, only 2,954 applications were received. Since then, the number of applications for review has risen rapidly (below). A backlog developed, despite the appointment of new inspectors in 1993, though this has now been largely cleared. The clear up target is 24 hours for an express case and 15 days for a routine case, achieved in 1995/6 in 90% and 83% of cases. Only a minority of reviews is initiated by the applicant, and, in 1993/4, 27% of applications failed and had to be referred back merely because the applicant had failed to comply with the procedural requirements, possibly because of ignorance of the procedure, exacerbated by the refusal of the DSS to issue a leaflet explaining claimants' rights automatically to claimants.

The outcomes are summarised in Table 14.2.

*Table 14.2: Social Fund Review Applications*

|  | Total | Confirmed | Substituted | Referred back |
|---|---|---|---|---|
| 1993/4 | 26,433 | 37.9% | 47.9% | 14.2% |
| 1995/6 | 28,107* | 38% | 45% | 17% |

* Of 25,990 considered.
Source: *Annual Report by the Secretary of State for Social Security on the Social Fund 1995/6*, Cm. 3320 (1996).

Now let us look at the procedure. A first point to note is that review is largely documentary; only exceptionally is there an interview or a home visit. The Social Fund Manual (Direction 39) instructs the SFO to have regard to all the circumstances which existed at the time of the original decision, any new evidence, and any relevant change of circumstances. He must check that the law and any ministerial directions have been complied with, that relevant considerations were taken into account and that the decision was both fair and procedurally correct. Mullen notes the resemblance between this terminology and that used by the courts in judicial review:[17]

> Whether or not this is desirable, it is sometimes open to administrators conducting internal review of grievances to adopt a second guessing approach, asking themselves 'what decision would I have taken?'. The terms of section 34 appear to permit such an approach allowing review on matters of fact, law and discretion. The manual on the other hand seems to discourage second guessing and to imply a model of review more like that of the courts. The reasons for interfering with a decision are virtually the same as the grounds for judicial review – procedural irregularity, unfairness, relevant/ irrelevant considerations, *Wednesbury* unreasonableness, leaving the distinct impression that the Secretary of State has tried to restrict the scope of review.

The SFC's view of review procedure does not support Mullen. In 1990, she criticised the DSS decision letter informing applicants of the right of review:[18]

> The use of the term 'correct in law' is misleading. The role of the Social Fund Inspector is to satisfy himself that the decision was made correctly and was right in all the circumstances. The phrase 'correct in law' is narrow and restrictive and may well deter applicants from applying for review.

Elsewhere, she has described internal review as a 'two stage process' in which the first stage has the characteristics of a review while the second resembles appeal:[19]

> When the Inspector reviews, he addresses the same matters as does a court in Judicial Review. At the next stage the Inspector is asking himself whether the decision is the right one in all the circumstances of the case. There is no appeal against the Inspector's decision on the merits of the case. The only further recourse the citizen has, if he is not satisfied, is to apply for judicial review on procedural grounds. The aggrieved citizen has a right to expect that the Inspector will act in a fair and impartial manner, consistent with natural justice, and that the decision will be of a high standard. I place emphasis above all on the quality of the review and the standard of service provided by the IRS . . .
>
> By the time a case arrives at the IRS, all the facts of the case should have been established. The original application provides the basis for the first decision. As part of the review process, the applicant has the opportunity to attend an interview at which time further evidence may be provided. When the facts have not been established by the decision maker, or they are not recorded, or disputes of fact remain unresolved Inspectors will, if they are unable to resolve the issues, refer the case back to the BA.

From the start of her appointment, the first SFC laid great emphasis on reasons. These serve a dual purpose. For the claimant, reasons clarify the decision and may render appeals unnecessary; on the departmental side, they help both to render the review process workable and to legitimate it:[19]

17  T. Mullen, 'The Social Fund – Cash-Limiting Social Security' (1989) 52 MLR 64, 87-88.
18  AR 1989/90, para. 4.13.
19  AR 1993/4 (London: HMSO) 1994.

I remain firmly of the opinion that the proper way to conclude an open review process is for the applicant and the HEO(SF) to receive a detailed explanation of the decision reached by the SFI. It is vital that the explanation is readily understood by the applicant and/or his representative, and also by the DSS HEO(SF) who will often have to take some further action.

The Commissioner has made substantial efforts to communicate clearly with claimants. Impressed by complaints of a lack of intelligibility, the SFC consulted the plain English campaign, drafted new documentation and conducted training in the composition of decision letters. Five years later, the SFI returned to the subject,[20] complaining of the bad effects of a new computerised decision form, which tended to obscure the officer's reasoning. This seems to have been effective; a customer survey in 1995 showed a level of customer satisfaction of around 90%.[1]

A second priority for the SFC has been speed. In 1989/90, the clear-up time averaged 34 days for normal applications and 15 for crisis loans, which included 14 days for comment by the applicant; in the same year, social security appeals were averaging 19 weeks. In 1993/4, after the input of new inspectors, the Social Fund reviews had been reduced to about eight days.

In a major study, Dalley and Berthoud[2] conclude that the flow of substituted and returned decisions from the SFI has helped to maintain and improve the quality of local decison-making, even if officers sometimes denied this. In this respect they see the inspectorate as 'a centre of excellence' in decision-making, although they complain that its skills are not being sufficiently diffused. They argue for an extension of the inspection model, citing the precedent of the Schools Inspectorate operated until recently by the Department of Education. But this is to conceive the role of the SFI largely in administrative terms; the effect would probably be an expansion of the audit function at the expense of the SFI's adjudicative role. (We should remember here the argument over the role of the PCA in Chapter 13.)

*(e) Squaring the circle*

Until quite recently, the judicialised model propounded by Franks seemed to be in the ascendant in welfare adjudication.[3] The ITS was achieving a commendable measure of professionalism. Alongside, an internal review procedure, documentary and investigatorial was developing. Here Sainsbury contrasts the two:[4]

[As regards the] speed of decision-making ... reviews have inherent advantages over tribunals. In undertaking a review it is not necessary to prepare comprehensive documents for the parties, nor to organise a date for a hearing that suits tribunal

20  AR 1993/4 (London: HMSO) 1994, para. 4.13.
 1  AR 1995/6 (London: HMSO) 1996.
 2  G. Dalley and R. Berthoud, *Challenging Discretion: The Social Fund Review Procedure* (London: Policy Studies Institute) 1992.
 3  See, M. Sayers and A. Webb, 'Franks Revisited: A Model of the Ideal Tribunal' (1990) 9 CJQ 36.
 4  R. Sainsbury, 'Internal Reviews and the Weakening of Social Security Claimants' Rights of Appeal' (above, p.475, note 15, at pp. 298-9, 302.

members, appellants, and representatives. Similarly, there is no need to give appellants [statutory notice] nor is time taken up by documents being absorbed by the postal system ...

[A] tribunal system [may be] unable to respond quickly to... increases in demand and backlogs [build] up. Arguably it [is] easier for a system based on internal review by officials to respond since staff [can be] moved temporarily from other duties until the backlog [is] cleared ... There is little doubt that internal reviews are inherently quicker than tribunal hearings ...

The nature of reviews renders them inherently cheaper ... The costs of reviews include only the salaries of relatively junior staff and the usual administrative overheads. In contrast, tribunals not only require an administrative hierarchy but must pay tribunal members at least their expenses and often an attendance fee. In addition, appellants can usually claim travel and other expenses ... Though the relative costs of reviews and tribunals will be largely irrelevant to individual appellants, this will rightly be of interest and concern to government.

In the last decade, SSATs had come to seem a success story. Complacency vanished swiftly with a DSS Consultation Paper in 1996[5] which argued for simpler decision-making and streamlined appeals procedures. One aim was to simplify the existing decision-making structure within the ministry by abolishing the complex distinction between Adjudication and Benefit Officers, a move which might just be construed as undercutting independent adjudication. In respect of appeals, the recommendations were more hard-hitting. In particular, the scale of the attack on judicial independence caused concern:[4]

> With judicial appointments, there is an inevitable tension between independence and the need for proper accountability for the performance of the organisation. No judicial appointee may be responsible to, or subject to, the supervision or direction of any other, or of the Executive. Thus the President of the ITS, as a judicial appointee, cannot be called to account by Parliament for the efficiency of the organisation...
>
> Each individual tribunal is . . . independent. This prevents the judicial head of the ITS from exercising direct management responsibility. Whilst individual decisions cannot and should not be subject to interference, there needs to be a mechanism for systematic monitoring of quality and reporting on standards.

This passage led on to a proposal to bring the ITS 'in house', not surprisingly met by vigorous opposition. The ITS accepted the need for some streamlining, especially a filter system to weed out hopeless cases, but believed that reform was possible within the existing independent structure.[7] The Council on Tribunals added its own argument in favour of independence.[8] A silence, marking an election and change of government ensued.

The new government put change squarely back on the agenda with a draft Bill which provides for responsibility for all social security tribunals to be returned

---

5　*Improving Decision Making and Apppeals in Social Security*, Cm 3328 (1996).
6　Cm 3328, paras 6.5, 6.6.
7　ITS, *Submission of the President of the ITS to the consultation paper [Cm 3328] issued by the Secretary of State for Social Security entitled "improving decision making and appeals in social security"* (London) 1996.
8　*Tribunals, their organisation and independence* Cm 3744 (1997).

to their parent department, though a President, appointed by the Lord Chancellor, will remain in being, to supervise training and other matters. A new sifting process will be introduced to sort cases into categories, reserving only the most difficult for qualified legal chairmen and sending some to a single lay member, chosen from a panel to be maintained by the Lord Chancellor. Wide-ranging inquisitorial hearings will be discouraged; appeals tribunals are not required to consider any matter not raised in the appeal. Schedules to the legislation extend the number of matters which will be unappealable.

Some of these changes are acceptable. There might, for example, be general agreement that 'cases should only proceed to appeal if they cannot be otherwise resolved'. Similarly acceptable is the emphasis on speed and focused decision-making. That this might involve the virtual abolition of the tribunal's inquisitorial role is more surprising. Moreover, the changes do not fit the adversarial tribunal model. In bringing an adjudicative function under the control of the sponsoring department it is distinctly retrograde. Yet the investigatorial social fund model has not been substituted. Approximating to Mashaw's model of 'bureaucratic rationality', the re-structuring is primarily concerned with efficiency and effective delivery of services.

From the puny roots of the NATs with which our case study started, sprang a sophisticated, presidential tribunal system, the ITS, effectively a welfare court which took responsibility for SSATs, for child support appeal tribunals, disability appeal tribunals, medical appeal tribunals and vaccine damage tribunals. With a judicial president, and independence assured by the link with the Lord Chancellor, the ITS rapidly assumed training, supervisory and management functions.[9] It prepared the Procedural Guide and, with the Judicial Studies Board, developed a national training plan. It laid down and monitored standards of competency. It played a significant part also 'in the development of policy on adjudication when new legislation was in contemplation, such as child support or disability appeals'. The ITS could have provided the start of an integrated tribunals service for which Robson so strenuously argued.[10] Today this proposal merits reconsideration.

Court substitutes and alternative dispute resolution are presently high on the agenda - inevitably so when the cost of legal aid is £1,477 million and of civil courts around £325 million. The main inquisitorial alternative of the ombudsmen is also costly; the full overall costs of the PCA and HSC amount to £15 million plus £7 million for the CLA. The tribunal system does not come cheap either; SSATs alone cost £42.5 million. In an era of increasing pressure on public expenditure, these figures[11] take some justifying. The complaints culture has produced the further problem of an endless stream of trivial complaints and grumbles. Unless filtered out, these create congestion and delay.

---

9   See, M. Partington, 'Lessons from Tribunals', in R. Smith (ed.), *Shaping the Future: New Directions for Legal Services* (London: Legal Action Group) 1995, pp.251-2.

10  See also R. Wraith and P. Hutchesson, *Administrative Tribunals* (London: Allen and Unwin) 1973.

11  The figures formed the basis of the Middleton *Review of Civil Justice and Legal Aid* carried out for the Lord Chancellor during 1997.

Writing in 1993, Twining expressed[12] a wider concern that the legal system is incapable of living up to the ideal of 'justice for all'. This may be one reason why the Franks criteria, and more particularly the premium placed on independence in the sense of externality, are giving way before the values of NPM. Directly linked to the Rule of Law ideal, these criteria are important. Cheaper justice is desirable; justice on the cheap is not.

---

12  W. Twining, 'Alternatives to What? Theories of Litigation Procedure and Dispute Settlement in Anglo-American Jurisprudence: Some Neglected Classics' (1993) 56 MLR 380.

Chapter 15

# A flexible friend: procedural fairness

In Chapter 14 we looked at the way in which tribunals in the post-Franks era have been judicialised, a process started by the Franks Committee's decision that tribunals were 'machinery for adjudication'. The process of judicialisation, which culminated in the Independent Tribunals Service, was helped on its way by the Council on Tribunals; both were statutory creations. Franks had radiating effects and the Council on Tribunals used its consultative powers to push them. We saw that Franks made the administration more likely to think in terms of the tribunals for decision-making.

As 'control' theories of administrative law notably stress, however, the administrative process is shaped not only by government and Parliament but also by courts. In this chapter, we consider the contribution of courts to the judicialisation of administrative procedures through the influence of the doctrines of natural justice and, latterly, procedural fairness. We find again a general tendency to model the administrative process in the courts' own adjudicative image.

## 1. Rationale

In a classic account, the American jurist Lon Fuller identified the distinguishing characteristic of adjudication as being to confer 'on the affected person a peculiar kind of participation in the decision, that of presenting proofs and reasoned arguments for a decision in his favor'.[1] Fuller's general point was that the hallmark of this, and of the other forms of social ordering like contract, negotiation or legislation, was *procedural*. Each of the forms generates a set of procedural requirements, which requirements protect the integrity of the form. For example, shared understandings of the meaning of adjudication require the decision-maker to be impartial: the integrity of the process of adjudication becomes eroded if the reality strays too far from the ideal. Fuller's definition, in other words, implies that for a decision to be adjudicatory, certain procedural restraints must be placed on the decision-maker.

The model of procedure which facilitates the presentation of 'proofs and reasoned arguments', such as rights to notice, oral hearings and legal representation, is instantly recognisable: it closely resembles formal civil procedure in the

---

1   L. Fuller, 'The Forms and Limits of Adjudication' (1978) 92 Harv. LR 353. See further, J. Allison, 'Fuller's Analysis of Polycentric Disputes and the Limits of Adjudication' (1994) 53 CLJ 367.

Anglo-American tradition. But adjudication is not confined to the 'ideal-type'; it can encompass other proceedings, like those in administrative tribunals, which share some of the same features. We may conceive of a sliding scale of adjudication: the closer to the 'ideal-type', the more 'judicialised' the process will be. In practical terms, this is the significance of the invocation by the Franks Committee of the values of openness, fairness and impartiality. Again, because the twin strands of natural justice – 'no man judge in his own cause' and 'no man to be condemned unheard' – reflect procedure as it has developed in courts of law, whenever the two principles are imposed on the administration, the courts are asking for adjudication to be incorporated into the administrative process.

Fuller's ideas have been influential in English administrative law, not least in the quest by amber light theorists for rational decision-making. 'Judicialisation', like 'legalisation' or the resort to rules, was to help underpin the *integrity* of the administration – bringing official conduct under legal control. [2] Yet we find in the literature different justifications for the imposition by the legal system of procedural restraints on administrative decision-making. The first set of justifications is utilitarian and positivist in character, stressing the link between the grant of procedural protection and the quality of substantive *outcomes*. Participation is required in the service of accuracy and efficiency – a variant of instrumentalist arguments for law as a tool of effective administration. Thus, Posner and proponents of law-and-economics theory see the value of due process as quantifiable. The cost of withholding due process can be measured in terms of the probability of error if it is withheld. Alternatively, the cost of error can be calculated and weighed against the cost of procedural protection and participation: [3]

> While most lawyers consider that the question whether there is a right to a trial-type hearing in various administrative contexts ... turns on some irreducible concept of 'fairness', the economic approach enables the question to be broken down into objectively analysable, although not simple enquiries. We begin by asking, what is the cost of withholding a trial-type hearing in a particular type of case? This enquiry has two branches: first, how is the probability of an error likely to be affected by a trial-type hearing? If the legally dispositive issues are factual issues of the kind most reliably determined in trial-type hearings, the probability of error if such a hearing is denied may be high. Second, what is the cost of an error if one occurs? As a first approximation, if the stakes in the case are large, the cost of error ... will be large, so if in addition the probability of error is high, total error costs will be very high. Having established the costs of error, we then enquire into the cost of measures – a trial-type hearing or whatever – that would reduce the error costs. If those direct costs are low ... then adoption can be expected to reduce the sum of error and direct costs and thus increase efficiency.

This form of calculation demonstrates some obvious problems. What, for example, is the 'error cost' of wrongfully refusing entry to a would-be immigrant?

2   J. Jowell, 'The Legal Control of Administrative Discretion' [1973] PL 178.
3   R. Posner, *The Economic Analysis of Law* (Boston: Little Brown) 2nd edn., 1977 p. 430. See also *Matthews v Eldridge* 424 US 319 (1976).

Again – a question asked in other contexts – is there necessarily a 'correct' outcome? Enough has been said to show that many administrative decisions are not straightforward rule applications but rather involve questions of judgment or interpretation. Alternatively, can the comparative effectiveness of, say, an oral hearing in forestalling 'error' easily be determined? Considerable doubts exist concerning the competency as well as the legitimacy of courts in operating this type of model.

A second set of justifications for due process is rights-based. In other words, as Dworkin argues, [4] procedural protections are dependent on, or secondary to, substantive rights. This model is more likely than utilitarian theories to shift the balance in favour of the individual. It may be seen, however, as not going far enough. Thus, where an individual has only a bare 'interest' by reason of the existence of administrative discretion, the case for procedural protection is seen as considerably weakened. Galligan has developed the argument: [5]

> Where there is no right to a particular outcome ... procedures are ... a matter of policy, to be determined as the authority considers most expedient, taking into account a range of policy factors. Since there is no right to a particular outcome, there is no right to procedural protection. This means that with respect to many areas of administrative action, in particular those that are discretionary, there are no rights to specific levels of procedure ...
>
> [This] appears unduly restrictive ... in relation to interests which lack the status of rights. There seems to be something mistaken about an account which makes procedural protection a matter of policy choice, such that anyone denied a benefit or subjected to an imposition has no just basis for complaint, no matter how cursorily his situation has been considered ...
>
> [We need] to reassess the claim that procedural rights can be sustained only as complementary to primary rights ...

A third set of justifications sees process values as an end in themselves. This viewpoint is well-expressed by Tribe: [6]

> There is *intrinsic* value in the due process right to be heard, since it grants to the individuals or groups against whom government decisions operate the chance to participate in the processes by which those decisions are made, an opportunity that expresses their dignity as persons ... Both the right to be heard from, and the right to be told why, are analytically distinct from the right to secure a different outcomes; these rights to interchange express the elementary idea that to be a *person*, rather than a *thing*, is at least to be *consulted* about what is done with one ... At stake here is not just the much-acclaimed *appearance of justice* but, from a perspective that treats process as intrinsically significant, the very *essence* of justice.

---

4   See e.g. R. Dworkin, *A Matter of Principle* (Oxford: Clarendon) 1985, Ch. 4.
5   D. Galligan, 'Rights, Discretion and Procedures' in D. Galligan and C. Sampford (eds.), *Law, Rights and the Welfare State* (London: Croom Helm) 1986, pp. 140-141. See further, D. Galligan, *Due Process and Fair Procedures: A Study of Administrative Procedures* (Oxford: Clarendon) 1996.
6   L. Tribe, *American Constitutional Law* (New York: Foundation Press) 2nd edn., 1988, p. 666.

This 'dignitary' approach is common in the American literature.[7] Individuals are deprived of the conditions requisite for continued moral agency when they are denied the opportunity to participate in those decisions which affect them. Particularly influential has been the work of Mashaw,[8] who does not deny the instrumental value of procedural protection, but rather rejects this as its primary basis. Like Dworkin, he accepts the case for judicial 'balancing', on the basis that a weighing of competing factors recognises and confronts 'the fundamentally compromised nature of social life'.[9] Demands for absolute procedural rights, in the sense of a fixed or determinate content of procedural protection irrespective of the administrative context, should be resisted.

Bayles has constructed a theory of procedural justice that combines elements of the dignitary and instrumental approaches. The assumption is that process benefits exist which are independent of the impact on outcomes but which are not necessarily derived from the dignity and autonomy of the individual. Bayles identifies not only participation and equal treatment, but also timeliness, intelligibility and legitimacy or public confidence in the decision-making process as values which meet his criterion of what a 'fully rational person would accept'. On this model, procedures fall to be assessed in terms of the extent to which they promote process benefits as well as reduce direct costs and error costs. The provision of a hearing, for example, may help to underpin public confidence, even if it does not increase accuracy. In similar vein, we find Bayles placing great store on impartiality as a feature of procedural systems:[10]

> An impartial decision maker is a fundamental principle of procedural justice recognised in human rights codes, constitutions, common law, and legislation; it is one that rational persons would adopt ... Even the appearance of partiality should be avoided, because of the difficulty of determining whether it operates and its possible demoralisation effects - weakening confidence in impartiality and justice, making compliance appear pointless, and consequent non-compliance. The possibility of partiality should be accepted [only] when the risks of it are small, the costs to parties of an alternative decision maker are great and a failure to decide on the merits might also involve significant injustice.

Dignitary theories have in recent years gained increased prominence in Britain, largely through American borrowings. One source of dispute, of a familiar kind in comparative law, is how well this fits with our indigenous constitutional traditions. Is it correct to assume, as does Craig,[11] that theories of this type can in a British context be characterised as 'instinct'? Or are they more

---

7   A variety of philosophical underpinnings is used: e.g. while some writers ground the requirement of procedural protection in natural rights, others look to fundamental liberal values and yet others to social contract theory. See for discussion G. Richardson, 'The Legal Regulation of Process' in G. Richardson and H. Genn (eds.), *Administrative Law and Government Action* (Oxford: Clarendon) 1994.

8   See, in particular, J. Mashaw, 'Dignitary Process: A Political Psychology of Liberal Democratic Citizenship' (1987) 39 Univ. of Florida LR 433.

9   J. Mashaw, *Due Process in the Administrative State* (New Haven: Yale University Press) 1985, p. 155.

10  M. Bayles, *Procedural Justice* (Dordrecht: Kluwer) 1990, pp. 37, 130.

11  Craig, *Administrative Law*, p. 282.

appropriately portrayed as explicit advocacy of a value system? Such issues of procedural protection also serve to highlight the relevance of administrative law theory to practice. Case law stands to be shaped, in Tribe's words, both by 'alternative conceptions of the primary purpose of procedural due process and by competing visions of how that purpose may best be achieved'.[12] Thus competing versions of instrumentalism may themselves indicate different outcomes in the cases. Similarly, a stress on dignitary values might suggest a firm standard of protection, for example in those cases where the substantive merits of the individual's case are dubious. Administrative law theory may help us to explain and evaluate in this context the operation of the courts' own (adversarial) procedures; it may, on the other hand, be quite as difficult to implement as judicial principle.

## 2. From concepts to contexts

In Chapter 2 we drew attention to the attempt by judges to distinguish the 'judicial', 'quasi-judicial' and 'administrative' functions of government in order to determine whether natural justice applied.[13] This analytical theory is today commonly explained in terms of a restrictive, deferential response by the courts in a period, from World War I, of the consolidation of the administrative State.[14] It was not wholly devoid of merit, at least for green light theorists. By insulating 'administrative' functions from the common law doctrine, it implied a recognition that adjudicative (adversarial) procedures are of limited usefulness and thus left space for experimentation and innovation with alternative forms of social ordering.

Analytical theory came, however, to be criticised in three main ways. First, it was difficult, if not impossible, to separate different types of functions (illustrated in the 'terminological contortions' in the Donoughmore Committee Report (above, p. 31)). Secondly, with the growth of the state, increasing numbers of decisions were rendered devoid of procedural protections because they were classified as administrative. In *Nakkuda Ali v Jayaratne*,[15] for example, a Ceylonese textile trader, alleged to have acted fraudulently, was deprived of his trading licence by the Controller of Textiles. The Privy Council held that this exercise of statutory discretion did not require any kind of hearing; the Controller was acting neither 'judicially' nor 'quasi-judicially', but merely withdrawing a 'privilege'. Thirdly, analytical theory was presented as a break with tradition. Critics like Wade[16] harked back to a 'golden age' of natural justice in the nineteenth century in which, confronted by a nascent administrative state, the courts had demonstrated a robust approach to matters of procedural protection.[17]

---

12  Tribe, *American Constitutional Law* (above, note 6), p. 666.
13  See, e.g. *Franklin v Minister of Town and Country Planning* [1948] AC 87.
14  See S. Sedley, 'The Sound of Silence: Constitutional Law Without a Constitution' (1994) 110 LQR 270.
15  [1951] AC 66.
16  Wade and Forsyth, p. 508.
17  See the classic authority, *Cooper v Wandsworth Board of Works* (1863) 14 CBNS 180.

In the event, analytical theory was fatally undermined by *Ridge v Baldwin*, a landmark case described by C. K. Allen as 'The Magna Carta of natural justice'.[18] In a brilliant illustration of the common law method, Lord Reid by looking back now led the judges forward.

### *Ridge v Baldwin*[19]

The appellant had been dismissed as Chief Constable of Brighton by the Watch Committee acting under the Municipal Corporations Act 1882. Seeking financial compensation, not reinstatement, he applied for a declaration that the decision was void for breach of natural justice. In the Court of Appeal, it was held that the Watch Committee was exercising an administrative function and that the principles of natural justice were not applicable. The House of Lords reversed this decision.

> *Lord Reid*: The appellant's case is that ... before attempting to reach any decision [the Committee] were bound to inform him of the grounds on which they proposed to act and give him a fair opportunity of being heard in his own defence. The authorities on the applicability of the principles of natural justice are in some confusion ... It appears to me that one reason why [this is so] is that insufficient attention has been paid to the great difference between various kinds of cases in which it has been sought to apply the principle. What a minister ought to do in considering objections to a scheme may be very different from what a watch committee ought to do in considering whether to dismiss a chief constable ...
>
> The question [for] the watch committee ... was not [simply] whether or not the appellant should be dismissed. There were three possible courses open to the watch committee – reinstating the appellant as chief constable, dismissing him, or requiring him to resign. The difference between the latter two is that dismissal involved forfeiture of pension rights, whereas requiring him to resign did not ... The appellant's real interest in this appeal is to try to save his pension rights.
>
> [It was argued that] even if as a general rule a watch committee must hear a constable in his own defence before dismissing him, this case was so clear that nothing that the appellant could have said could have made any difference. It is at least very doubtful whether that could be accepted as an excuse. But, even if it could, the respondents would fail on the facts. It may well be that no reasonable body of men could have reinstated the appellant. But as between the other two courses open to the watch committee the case is not so clear ...
>
> If the present case had arisen thirty or forty years ago the courts would have had no difficulty in deciding this issue in favour of the appellant on the authorities which I have cited. So far as I am aware none of these authorities has ever been disapproved or even doubted. Yet the Court of Appeal have decided this issue against the appellant on more recent authorities which apparently justify that result. How has this come about?
>
> There have been many cases where it has been sought to apply the principles of natural justice to the wider duties imposed on ministers and other organs of government by modern legislation. For reasons which I shall attempt to state in a moment, it has been held that those principles have a limited application in such cases and those

18  C. K. Allen, *Law and Orders* (London: Stevens) 3rd edn., 1965, p. 242.
19  [1964] AC 40.

limitations have tended to be reflected in other decisions on matters to which in principle they do not appear to me to apply. Secondly ... those principles have been held to have a limited application in cases arising out of war-time legislation; and again such limitations have tended to be reflected in other cases.

In cases of the kind I have been dealing with the Board of Works or the Governor or the club committee was dealing with a single isolated case. It was not deciding, like a judge in a lawsuit, what were the rights of the person before it. But it was deciding how he should be treated – something analogous to a judge's duty in imposing a penalty. No doubt policy would play some part in the decision – but so it might when a judge is imposing a sentence. So it was easy to say that such a body is performing a quasi-judicial task in considering and deciding such a matter, and to require it to observe the essentials of all proceedings of a judicial character – the principles of natural justice.

Sometimes the functions of a minister or department may also be of that character, and then the rules of natural justice can apply in much the same way. But more often their functions are of a very different character. If a minister is considering whether to make a scheme for, say, an important new road, his primary concern will not be with the damage which its construction will do to the rights of individual owners of land. He will have to consider all manner of questions of public interest and, it may be, a number of alternative schemes. He cannot be prevented from attaching more importance to the fulfilment of his policy than to the fate of individual objectors, and it would be quite wrong for the courts to say that the minister should or could act in the same kind of way as a board of works deciding whether a house should be pulled down. And there is another important difference. A minister cannot do everything himself. His officers will have to gather and sift all the facts, including objections by individuals, and no individual can complain if the ordinary accepted methods of carrying on public business do not give him as good protection as would be given by the principles of natural justice in a different kind of case ...

... I would hold that the power of dismissal in the Act of 1882 could not then have been exercised and cannot now be exercised until the watch committee have informed the constable of the grounds on which they propose to proceed and have given him a proper opportunity to present his case in defence.

Although terminology associated with analytical theory was not abandoned, *Ridge v Baldwin* worked to liberate the courts from self-imposed conceptual restraints. Thus, the contemporary doctrine of procedural fairness, involving a *variable* 'duty to act fairly' not tied to the classification of governmental functions, began to emerge in subsequent cases.[20] In *Re H K (An Infant)*[1] an immigration officer had refused to admit a boy travelling from Pakistan on the ground that he appeared to be well over 16, under which age he would have possessed a statutory right to enter. Lord Parker CJ doubted whether the officer had acted in a 'judicial' or 'quasi-judicial' capacity, but thought that in any event:

... he must ... give the immigrant an opportunity of satisfying him [that he was under 16] and for that purpose let the immigrant know what his immediate impression is so that the immigrant can disabuse him. That is not ... a question of acting or being required to act judicially, but of being required to act fairly. Good administration and

20 Such as *Schmidt v Secretary of State for the Home Department* [1969] 2 WLR 337; *R v Gaming Board for Great Britain, ex p Benaim and Khaida* [1970] 2 All ER 528.
1 [1967] 2 QB 617. In the event, the application failed.

an honest or bona fide decision must ... require not merely impartiality, not merely bringing one's mind to bear on the problem, but acting fairly; and to the limited extent that the circumstances of any particular case allow, and within the legislative framework under which the administrator is working, only to that limited extent do the so-called rules of natural justice apply.

How far does this duty extend? As Wade observes,[2] 'acting fairly' is a phrase of 'such wide implications that it may ultimately extend beyond the sphere of procedure'. Immediately, the issue is raised of the constitutional role of the courts and the conventional restrictions on judges second-guessing official policy or the merits of decisions. The scope for different views is well-illustrated by *Chief Constable of the North Wales Police v Evans*.[3] A probationer constable was required to resign on the basis of an 'unfitting' lifestyle. In the Court of Appeal Lord Denning MR intimated that not only must there be a fair hearing but 'the decision itself must be fair and reasonable'. Lord Hailsham in the House of Lords was vexed:

> Since the range of authorities, and the circumstances of the use of their power, are almost infinitely various, it is of course unwise to lay down rules for the application of the [judicial review] remedy which appear to be of universal validity in every type of case. But it is important to remember in every case that the purpose of the [judicial review] remedies is to ensure that the individual is given fair treatment by the authority to which he has been subjected and that it is no part of that purpose to substitute the opinion of the judiciary or of individual judges for that of the authority constituted by law to decide the matters in question ... There are passages in the judgment of Lord Denning ... which might be read as giving the courts *carte blanche* to review the decision of the authority on the basis of what the courts themselves consider fair and reasonable on the merits ... I do not think this is a correct statement of principle. The purpose of judicial review is to ensure that the individual receives fair treatment, and not to ensure that the authority, after according fair treatment, reaches on a matter which it is authorised by law to decide for itself a conclusion which is correct in the eyes of the court.

### (a) Flexibility: competing models

The idea of variable protection – the 'flexible friend' – is antithetical to the general solutions implicit in the exposition of the two strands of natural justice – no bias and a fair hearing – as 'fundamental rules'. With procedural fairness the model of adjudication as 'presenting proofs and reasoned arguments' provides a familiar list of process rights, while the scope for variation may be visualised in terms of our sliding scale of adjudication – the closer the ideal type, the more 'judicialised' the process. Craig sees this in terms of a spectrum:[4]

> At one end of the spectrum the courts may decide that the applicant is entitled to the full panoply of procedural rights, including: notice of the charge or issue ...; an

2   Wade and Forsyth, p. 516.
3   [1982] 1 WLR 1155.
4   P. Craig, 'Procedures and Administrative Decision Making: A Common Law Perspective' (1993) European Review of Public Law (Special Issue) 55 at 62-63.

opportunity to appear in person; a right to introduce evidence himself; a right to discovery and cross examination; a reasoned decision from the administration; and a right of appeal, whether internally within the particular administrative hierarchy, or externally to a different institution. [Here] the process rights accorded to the individual render the procedure before the administration akin to a formal 'trial'. At the other end of the spectrum there may be cases where less is demanded of the administration: the individual may simply be held to be entitled to some notice of the case which is being developed by the administration, together with a right to make written representations in response to it. Other cases may fall at some intermediate point on the spectrum, where the individual is accorded less than in the case of the 'trial' type full panoply of process rights, but more than the minimum range of rights indicated in the second of the two examples.

Conceding that the duty is variable, by what criteria is the variation to be judged? Analytical theory highlighted issues of the applicability of judicial protection: although the content was never entirely fixed or determinate, [5] nevertheless the model implied highly judicialised procedure inside a restricted zone. In contrast, the broader ambit of the procedural fairness doctrine brings the quid pro quo of variant standards: the content question. Flexibility becomes the keyword as in this much quoted dictum of Lord Bridge in *Lloyd v McMahon*: [6]

> The so-called rules of natural justice are not engraved on tablets of stone. To use the phrase which better expresses the underlying concept, what the requirements of fairness demand when anybody, domestic, administrative or judicial, has to make a decision which will affect the rights of individuals depends on the character of the decision-making body, the kind of decision it has to make and the statutory or other framework in which it operates.

We find decisions explicitly premised on the idea of judicial 'balancing', raising the question of what exactly is to be weighed. Writing in the early 1980s, Hartley and Griffith suggested that many of the cases were explicable in terms of an 'interest theory': [7]

> The questions to be considered are: first, does the decision directly affect an individual person's interests; secondly, is the interest affected one which the courts are prepared to protect; and thirdly, how seriously is the interest affected? The interests of the individual, however, are not the only interests to be considered. There is also the public interest. This requires, for example, that the administrative process should not be unduly hampered by unreasonable procedural requirements. The interests of the individual concerned must be balanced against the public interest and the extent to which natural justice will apply (if it applies at all) will depend on the way the balance is struck.

---

5   See e.g. *Board of Education v Rice* [1911] AC 179; *Russell v Duke of Norfolk* [1949] 1 All ER 109.
6   [1987] AC 625.
7   T. Hartley and J. Griffith, *Government and Law* (London: Weidenfeld and Nicolson) 2nd edn., 1981, 334.

An alternative 'spectrum theory' of procedural content devised by Mullan[8] is of special interest because it represents in ideal-typical form the case for variation. Here is the model represented diagramatically with Mullan's explanation underneath.

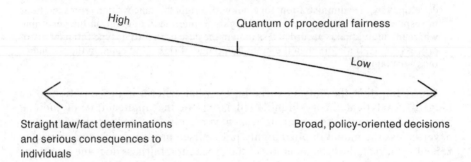

Why not deal with problems of fairness and natural justice simply on the basis that, the nearer one is to the type of function requiring straight law/fact determinations and resulting in serious consequences to individuals, the greater is the legitimacy of the demand for procedural protection but as one moves through the spectrum of decision-making functions to the broad, policy-oriented decisions exercised typically by a minister of the crown, the content of procedural fairness gradually disappears into nothingness, the emphasis being on a gradual disappearance not one punctuated by the unrealistic impression of clear cut divisions presented by the classification process?

Consider the character of these models: little reference is made to rights, let alone dignitary values. Both models demonstrate problems of definition and implementation. The interest theory, for example, implies an antithesis between 'private' and 'public' interests. But is there not (as Bayles would contend) a public interest in fair hearings? The problem with the spectrum theory is that 'broad, policy-oriented decisions' so often cause 'serious consequences to individuals'; the *Laker* case[9] is a good example.

Mullan's flexible approach avoids the pitfalls of classification: the difficulties entailed in drawing dividing lines; the arbitrary divisions between decision-making processes which may ensue; and the unrealistic results produced when two marginally different cases fall on opposite sides of a dividing line. Assume a general acceptance of the argument that some form of judicial 'balancing' is inevitable. The issue then becomes how far the courts should go in this direction. The 'spectrum theory' is an extreme version of functionalist argument which favours contextual, not conceptual, judicial review. From this perspective, judges

---

8   D. Mullan, 'Fairness: the New Natural Justice?' (1975) 25 Univ. of Toronto LJ 281.
9   Above, p. 83.

should be essentially pragmatic or result oriented, *tailoring* decisions to the particular subject matter in issue. The search for general principle, part of the nineteenth-century legacy of the common law, should be jettisoned in favour of diversity. The change resembles K. C. Davis's search for the 'optimum point' on a spectrum between discretion and rules (Chapter 4). In Mullan's words:[10]

> The development of the doctrine of procedural fairness is ... desirable primarily because it allows the courts to ask what kind of procedural protections are necessary for a particular decision-making process unburdened by the traditional classification process ... It recognizes that there is a very broad spectrum of decision-making functions for which varying procedural requirements are necessary and rejects the notion that such functions can be categorised satisfactorily into either one of two categories. The classification process was essentially accepted at a time when the administrative process was far less sophisticated. Its deceptive simplicity was perhaps adequate initially but it rapidly ceased to be realistic ... If individual decision-making functions have different characteristics then they deserve different procedural requirements.

There are, however, problems. We cannot assume the existence of a simple command theory of law: that judges dictate and administrators and politicians obey. Their relationship is far more complex (a theme developed in Chapter 16). A drift towards tailoring judicial review to particular contexts may cause the gap between court decisions and official behaviour to widen. And those who favour general principles of administrative law may contend that procedural fairness practises flexibility at the expense of other qualities associated with adjudication.

## (b) Principle and pragmatism

Such concerns are frequently expressed. Atiyah[11], for example, argues that the teaching or 'hortatory' function of law may be diminished if the judges over-emphasise their second role of dispute resolution which leads courts to strive for the most sensible solution in the particular case: *pragmatism*. In similar vein, Mashaw speaks of the 'symbolic' (value-creating) function of due process, as opposed to its 'regulative' (conflict-resolving) role.[12] We might describe the rise of procedural fairness as a manifestation of pragmatism in the administrative law field. There is then scope for an argument that courts, by prioritising the 'regulative' role, may fail to educate the administration in proper procedural restraints. In Clark's words:[13]

> Natural justice is more than a means to an end (a right decision in individual cases) ... The goal of administrative justice can never be attained by necessarily sporadic and *ex post facto* judicial review. The essential mission of the law in this field is to win

10 (1975) 25 Univ. of Toronto LJ 281 at 300-301.
11 P. S. Atiyah, *From Principles to Pragmatism* (Oxford: Clarendon), 1978.
12 J. Mashaw, *Due Process* (above, p. 498, note 9), p. 31. See also O. Fiss, 'Against Settlement' (1984) 93 Yale LJ 1073, prioritising the role of courts as the means through which basic norms in society are articulated, publicised and refurbished.
13 D. Clark, 'Natural Justice: Substance and Shadow' [1975] PL 27, 58 and 60.

acceptance by administrators of the principle that to hear a man before he is penalised is an integral part of the decision-making process.

The tensions can be illustrated by reference to a leading case on whether a breach of fair procedure can be 'cured' by a subsequent (fair) rehearing or appeal.

### Calvin v Carr[14]

Calvin was charged by the stewards with failing to run a horse on its merits, contrary to the Australian Jockey Club rules. The Committee of the Club subsequently upheld the stewards' decision to disqualify him from running horses for a year. Calvin claimed – and the Privy Council accepted for the purposes of argument – that the stewards had failed to give him a proper opportunity to be heard. It was, however, conceded that the hearing before the Committee was unimpeachable.

*Lord Wilberforce*: No clear and absolute rule can be laid down on the question whether defects in natural justice appearing at an original hearing, whether administrative or quasi-judicial, can be 'cured' through appeal proceedings. The situations in which this issue arises are too diverse, and the rules by which they are governed so various, that this must be so. There are, however, a number of typical situations as to which some general principle can be stated. First there are cases where the rules provide for a rehearing by the original body, or some fuller or enlarged form of it. This situation may be found in relation to social clubs. It is not difficult in such cases to reach the conclusion that the first hearing is superseded by the second ... At the other extreme are cases, where, after examination of the whole hearing structure in the context of the particular activity to which it relates (trade union membership, planning, employment, etc) the conclusion is reached that a complainant has the right to nothing less than a fair hearing both at the original and at the appeal stage ... These may very well include trade union cases where movement solidarity and dislike of the rebel, or renegade, may make it difficult for appeals to be conducted in an atmosphere of detached impartiality and so make a fair trial at the first - probably branch - level an essential condition of justice. But to seek to apply it generally overlooks ... both the existence of the first category, and the possibility that, intermediately, the conclusion to be reached, on the rules and on the contractual context, is that those who have joined in an organisation, or contract, should be taken to have agreed to accept what in the end is a fair decision, notwithstanding some initial defect.

In ... [intermediate cases] it is for the court, in the light of the agreements made, and in addition having regard to the course of proceedings, to decide whether, at the end of the day, there has been a fair result, reached by fair methods, such as the parties should fairly be taken to have accepted when they joined the association. Naturally there may be instances when the defect is so flagrant, the consequences so severe, that the most perfect of appeals or re-hearings will not be sufficient to produce a just result ... There may also be cases when the appeal process is itself less than perfect [ for example] there may be doubts whether the appeal body embarked on its task without predisposition ... In such cases it would no doubt be right to quash the original decision.

It is undesirable in many cases of domestic disputes, particularly in which an inquiry and appeal process has been established, to introduce too great a measure of formal

14  [1979] 2 WLR 755.

judicialisation. While flagrant cases of injustice, including corruption or bias, must always be firmly dealt with by the courts, the tendency ... in matters of domestic disputes should be to leave these to be settled by the agreed methods without requiring the formalities of judicial processes to be introduced.

It remains to apply the principles ... to the facts of the present case ... Races are run at intervals; bets must be disposed of according to the result. Stewards are there in order to take rapid decisions as to such matters as the running of horses, being entitled to use the evidence of their eyes and their experience. As well as acting inquisitorially at the stage of deciding the result of a race, they may have to consider disciplinary action: at this point rules of natural justice become relevant. These require, at the least, that persons should be formally charged, heard in their own defence, and know the evidence against them. These essentials must always be observed but it is inevitable, and must be taken to be accepted, that there may not be time for procedural refinements. It is in order to enable decisions reached in this way to be reviewed at leisure that the appeal procedure exists. Those concerned know that they are entitled to a full hearing with opportunities to bring evidence and have it heard. But they know also that this appeal hearing is governed by the Rules of Racing, and that it remains an essentially domestic proceeding, in which experience and opinions as to what is in the interest of racing as a whole play a large part, and in which the standards are those which have come to be accepted over the history of this sporting activity. All those who partake in it have accepted the Rules of Racing, and the standards which lie behind them: they must also have accepted to be bound by the decisions of the bodies set up under those rules so long as they can be said, by an objective observer, to have had fair treatment and consideration of their case on its merits.

In their Lordships' opinions precisely this can, indeed must, be said of the present case. The plaintiff's case has received, overall, full and fair consideration, and a decision, possibly a hard one, reached against him. There is no basis on which the court ought to interfere.

This speech naturally reveals a high degree of sophistication in the handling of procedural fairness, keying the extent of the protection to the particular context. Now consider the passage in the context of a teaching function. Imagine an administrator asked by an organisation falling within Lord Wilberforce's 'intermediate category' to devise procedural rules for a two-tiered system of appeal in disciplinary proceedings. How helpful would the speech be as a practical guide?

Leading practitioners confirm that in their experience 'it is often difficult to predict with confidence what fairness will be considered to require in any particular context'.[15] This can itself be seen as an encouragement to litigation. To put this differently, an assertion of Wade's that the courts have developed 'a kind of code' of fair administrative procedure is open to question.[16] According to official advice provided to civil servants:[17]

What the duty to act fairly amounts to is difficult to define in general terms. It will depend upon the facts and the circumstances of the case ... The circumstances in which

15  M. Beloff and P. Elias, 'Natural Justice – (The Audi Alteram Partem Rule) and Fairness' in M. Supperstone and J. Goudie (eds.), *Judicial Review* (London: Butterworths) 1992, p. 167.
16  Wade and Forsyth, p. 463.
17  Cabinet Office, *The Judge Over Your Shoulder* (London) 1st edn., 1987, paras. 14-16. And see below, p.573.

the courts will impose the duty to act fairly towards persons likely to be affected by a decision are now almost limitless. They extend not only to decisions affecting private persons but also to those affecting public bodies and authorities ... It is extremely dangerous to assume that further representations will have no effect and therefore refuse to hear them or consider them.

### (c) Techniques of tailoring

Another way to read *Calvin v Carr* is as 'transaction-typing', by which is meant a consistent approach to legal requirements in particular subject areas of administration. To paraphrase Lord Wilberforce, in different circumstances 'natural justice' means different things.[18] Here the relevant area might be defined as 'sporting disputes', a standard of 'light-touch' review being justified on the ground of agency expertise. Such definitions, however, may themselves prove controversial. Might it be suggested that transaction-typing is simply a more sophisticated species of conceptualism than the 'judicial', 'quasi-judicial', 'administrative' classification? Again, we must keep in mind that fashions change: the results of transaction-typing in one era may be different in another. This kind of argument was raised in the context of prison administration, an 'area' in which, in the post-*Ridge v Baldwin* world, it is possible to detect a sea change in judicial attitudes towards intervention. (See the case study on parole, above Chapter 7).

The potential of transaction-typing as a guide to procedural fairness is necessarily limited. Further tailoring is required at the 'micro' level, since precise procedural protections remain to be determined in individual cases within particular areas. The following prisons case highlights the sliding scale of adjudicative restraints.

### R v Secretary of State for the Home Department, ex p Tarrant and Anderson[19]

Five serving prisoners were charged with serious offences against prison discipline, including mutiny and assault. They complained that the Boards of Visitors responsible for determining the charges had refused requests for legal representation. The Divisional Court held that a prisoner was not entitled as of right to counsel in such proceedings. It was also held, however, that the Boards had discretion to allow legal representation, the exercise of which the courts would police.

> *Webster J*: As it seems to me, the following are considerations which every Board should take into account when exercising its discretion whether to allow legal representation or to allow the assistance of a friend or advisor. (The list is not, of course, intended to be comprehensive: particular cases may throw up other particular matters.)

18   For discussion, see M. Elliot, 'Appeals, Principles and Pragmatism in Natural Justice' (1980) 43 MLR 66.

19   [1985] QB 251.

1. The seriousness of the charge and of the potential penalty.
2. Whether any points of law are likely to arise ...
3. The capacity of a particular prisoner to present his own case ...
4. Procedural difficulties ... A prisoner awaiting [a Board of Visitors'] adjudication is normally kept apart from other prisoners ... pending the adjudication and ... this may inhibit the preparation of his defence ... In my view a Board ... should take into account any special difficulties of [this] kind ... and should particularly bear in mind the difficulty which some prisoners might have in cross-examining a witness, particularly a witness giving evidence of an expert nature, at short notice without previously having seen that witness's evidence.
5. The need for reasonable speed in making their adjudication, which is clearly an important consideration.
6. The need for fairness as between prisoners and as between prisoners and prison officers ...

It seems to me that in most, if not all, charges of mutiny ... questions are bound to arise as to whether collective action was intended to be collective ... In my judgment, where such questions arise or are likely to arise, no Board of Visitors, properly directing itself, could reasonably decide not to allow the prisoner legal representation ...

The decision in *Tarrant* was later approved by the House of Lords in *R v Board of Visitors of HM Prison, The Maze, ex p Hone*.[20] The speech of Lord Goff demonstrates acceptance of some of the administrative arguments liable to be raised against an imposition of tough procedural requirements:

Though the rules of natural justice may require legal representation before the board of visitors, I can see no basis for [the] submission that they should do so in every case as of right. Everything must depend on the circumstances of the particular case, as is amply demonstrated by the circumstances so carefully listed by Webster J. in ... *Tarrant* ... as matters which Boards of Visitors should take into account. But it is easy to envisage circumstances in which the rules of natural justice do not call for representation, even though the disciplinary charge relates to a matter which constitutes in law a crime, as may well happen in the case of a simple assault where no question of law arises, and where the prisoner charged is capable of presenting his own case. To hold otherwise would result in wholly unnecessary delays in many cases, to the detriment of all concerned including the prisoner charged, and to a wholly unnecessary waste of time and money, contrary to the public interest.

The variety of tailoring techniques is underlined by the following case. Less emphasis is placed on individuation, the attempt being made to specify different classes of personal interest for the purposes of evaluation.

### *McInnes v Onslow Fane*[1]

The plaintiff, who had been licensed as a boxing promoter, trainer and master of ceremonies, had been repeatedly refused a manager's licence by the British

---

20  [1988] AC 379.
 1  [1978] 3 All ER 211.

Boxing Board of Control. He applied once again, asking for an oral hearing and for prior information of anything which might be held against him. The Board, in refusing the plaintiff's application, also denied his other requests. The plaintiff failed in his claim that this was contrary to natural justice.

> *Megarry V-C*: I think it must be considered what type of decision is in question. I do not suggest that there is any clear or exhaustive classification; but I think that at least three categories may be discerned. First, there are what may be called the forfeiture cases. In these there is a decision which takes away some existing right or position, as where a member of an organisation is expelled or a licence is revoked. Second, at the other extreme there are what may be called the application cases. These are cases where the decision merely refuses to grant the applicant the right or position that he seeks, such as membership of the organisation, or a licence to do certain acts. Third, there is an intermediate category, which may be called the expectation cases, which differ from the application cases only in that the applicant has some legitimate expectation from what has already happened that his application will be granted. This head includes cases where an existing licence-holder applies for a renewal of his licence, or a person already elected or appointed to some position seeks confirmation from some confirming authority ...
>
> It seems plain that there is a substantial distinction between the forfeiture cases and the application cases. In the forfeiture cases, there is a threat to take something away for some reason: and in such cases, the right to an unbiased tribunal, the right to notice of the charges and the right to be heard in answer to the charges ... are plainly apt. In the application cases, on the other hand, nothing is being taken away, and in all normal circumstances there are no charges, and so no requirement of an opportunity of being heard in answer to the charges. Instead, there is the far wider and less defined question of the general suitability of the applicant for membership or a licence. The distinction is well-recognised, for in general it is clear that the courts will require natural justice to be observed for expulsion from a social club, but not on an application for admission to it. The intermediate category, that of the expectation cases, may at least in some respects be regarded as being more akin to the forfeiture cases than the application cases; for although in form there is no forfeiture but merely an attempt at acquisition that fails, the legitimate expectation of a renewal of the licence or confirmation of the membership is one which raises the question of what it is that has happened to make the applicant unsuitable for the membership or licence for which he was previously thought suitable.

What are the merits of this modified form of tailoring? On one view, provided that a measure of flexibility is retained – that is, it is not assumed that all renewal cases warrant greater protection than all application cases irrespective of the subject-matter in question – such ranking is in Craig's words 'both necessary and helpful'. [2] On the other hand, since a person's livelihood may be at stake in each class of case, the distinction between expulsion, expectation and application cases might be criticised for protecting vested interests, as also running contrary to the idea of the 'right to work'. [3] From this perspective, a more individuated approach would be preferable, tailoring procedural protection to *outcome*; in

2   Craig, *Administrative Law*, p. 297.
3   An argument pursued by Cane in *An Introduction to Administrative Law*, pp. 178-180.

other words, the effects on the applicant of denial of the application. Finally, examining *McInnes*, we find in the classification of personal interests a lack of attention paid to non-instrumentalist arguments for procedural protection such as Mashaw's dignitary values.

### (d) Judicial discretion and public interest

If, as we begin to see, the 'optimum' is not instantly recognisable, the judicary will have to make choices or exercise discretion. Procedural fairness, by releasing judges from the constraints of legal concepts, is seen to enlarge their freedom of manoeuvre. Since pragmatism implies discretion, it may alarm those who believe that the courts already choose to favour particular social groups. Griffith, a leading exponent of green light theory, compared the natural justice cases concerning disciplinary sanctions imposed on trade union members with those involving students: [4]

> The contrast ... is very great. In the [student cases] the courts seek assiduously to find some ground on which to disregard breach of the rules of natural justice. In the trade union cases they very rarely allow any such breach to be overlooked. Both groups of cases concern the right to work. Frequently both concern expulsions. The consequences of expulsion in both may be most serious to the livelihood of the individual ... It is right that the courts should protect the individual against a trade union which fails to proceed fairly against him. But why should the protection be denied to a student?

The argument shares with transaction-typing the idea that subject-orientated *clusters* of decisions are descriptively more accurate of the cases than is the image of firm general principles beloved of red light theorists. But transaction-typing is here seen as a vehicle not so much for achieving the 'optimum' in administrative justice as for the expression of a dominant judicial conception of the public interest.

Here we must consider cases touching on national security. In the *GCHQ* case [5] the demands of security were ultimately held to override a legitimate expectation of prior consultation. In *R v Secretary of State for the Home Department, ex p Hosenball*, [6] H was an American investigative journalist resident in Britain who was told that the minister, acting on information that H had sought out material prejudicial to national security, had decided to deport him. The Home Secretary, again pleading national security, also refused to disclose the particulars of the case against him. Following a hearing before an advisory panel at which H made representations and called witnesses, the deportation order was made. A plea of breach of natural justice was unsuccessful. Lord Denning said:

> There is a conflict here between the interests of national security on the one hand and the freedom of the individual on the other. The balance between these two is not

4  J. Griffith, *The Politics of the Judiciary* (London: Fontana) 3rd edn., 1985, p. 178.
5  Above, p. 113.
6  [1977] 1 WLR 766.

for a court of law. It is for the Home Secretary. He is the person entrusted by Parliament with the task. In some parts of the world national security has on occasions been used as an excuse for all sorts of infringements of individual liberty. But not in England. Both during the wars and after them, successive ministers have discharged their duties to the complete satisfaction of the people at large. They have set up advisory committees to help them, usually with a chairman who has done everything he can to ensure that justice is done. They have never interfered with the liberty or the freedom of movement of any individual except where it is absolutely necessary for the safety of the state.

*Hosenball* is widely criticised as a case where the court declined to fulfil its function of grafting on to a rudimentary adjudicative form additional procedural protections. A measure of the distance between the advisory panel and Fuller's ideal-type of adjudication may be found in the minister's original explanation of the machinery to Parliament: [7]

> The advisers will then take account of any representations made by the person concerned. They will allow him to appear before them, if he wishes. He will not be entitled to legal representation, but he may be assisted by a friend to such extent as the advisers sanction. As well as speaking for himself, he may arrange for a third party to testify on his behalf. Neither the sources of evidence nor evidence that might lead to disclosure of sources can be revealed to the person concerned but the advisers will ensure that the person is able to make his points effectively and the procedure will give him the best possible opportunity to make the points he wishes to bring to their notice ... Since the evidence against a person necessarily has to be received in his absence, the advisers in assessing the case will bear in mind that it has not been tested by cross-examination and that the person has not had the opportunity to rebut it ... On receiving [their] advice ... the Secretary of State will reconsider his original decision, but the advice given to him will not be revealed.

### *R v Secretary of State for the Home Department, ex p Cheblak* [8]

C was a Lebanese journalist resident in Britain. On the outbreak of hostilities in the Gulf War, he was one of a number of people detained with a view to deportation on the grounds of national security. The court refused to act on a complaint that the procedure involving the Home Secretary's advisory panel failed to secure to the individual adequate knowledge of the case to be answered:

> *Lord Donaldson MR:* The exercise of the jurisdiction of the courts in cases involving national security is necessarily restricted, not by any unwillingness to act in protection of the rights of individuals or any lack of independence of the executive, but by the nature of the subject matter. National security is the exclusive responsibility of the executive and, as Lord Diplock said in *Council of Civil Service Unions v Minister for the Civil Service*[ [9]] ... 'It is par excellence a non-justiciable question'...

---

7    Mr. Maudling, Home Secretary, HC Deb., vol. 819, cols. 376-377.
8    [1991] 1 WLR 890.
9    Above, p. 113.

Although they give rise to tensions at the interface, 'national security' and 'civil liberties' are on the same side. In accepting, as we must, that to some extent the needs of national security must displace civil liberties, albeit to the least possible extent, it is not irrelevant to remember that the maintenance of national security underpins and is the foundation of all our civil liberties ...

I have no doubt that the advisory panel is susceptible of judicial review if, for example, it could be shown to have acted unfairly within its terms of reference ... That legal representation is not permitted ... stems from the tribunal's terms of reference. If it is objectionable, as to which there may be more than one view, this is a matter for Parliament which approved the terms of reference and not the courts. That the respective detainee is not entitled to be given the fullest particulars of what is alleged against him would, in other circumstances, undoubtedly be objectionable as constituting a denial of natural justice. But natural justice has to take account of realities and something which would otherwise constitute a breach is not to be so considered if it is unavoidable ...

If there is a lesson to be drawn from these proceedings it is, I think, that detainees should try to have greater faith in the desire of the panel to safeguard their liberty to the maximum possible extent consistent with the risk to national security and should not rush off to the courts which are, at best, a second line of defence in special circumstances ...

This case is unsatisfactory by reference to all of the justifications for judicial imposition of procedural fairness. A utilitarian would note both the heightened chance of error and its high cost to the individual. To Dworkin, the substantive 'right' to liberty must demand high standards of procedural protection. Only a highly analytic interpretation of a 'right', in which Cheblak is seen as a non-British citizen with only a privilege to remain in the country, can avoid this conclusion. For Tribe and Mashaw, the dignitary value of procedural protection in this humiliating situation is evident. Finally, even a spectrum analysis would demand a greater degree of procedural fairness here given the close resemblance to individuated, adjudicative decision-making.

In this context reform has been spurred by the ECHR. The *Chahal* case[10] was part of a long-running dispute involving attempts by a Sikh activist to avoid deportation to India on grounds of national security. The advisory panel had proceeded in the usual fashion. An application for judicial review failed on the basis that the court could not review the evidence on national security and so was unable to decide whether the decision to deport was irrational.[11] The Strasbourg Court found violations of Art. 3 (risk of torture) and of the procedural guarantees in Arts. 5(4) and 13. In particular, the panel did not offer sufficient procedural safeguards for the purposes of 'an effective remedy'. The government in response has recently published the Special Immigration Appeals Commission Bill, which will establish a commission to deal with appeals involving considerations of national security. To emphasise, procedural protection is subject to improvement in this context, but not through the operation of the common law.

*(e) Competency and legitimacy*

10   *Chahal v United Kingdom* (1996) Times 28 November.
11   *R v Secretary of State for the Home Department, ex p Chahal* [1995] 1 All ER 658.

The rise of procedural fairness also invites consideration of the judicial function – as well as of the courts' own procedures. How far is it the courts' job to pursue the optimum form of procedure for different kinds of disputes? Are judges properly equipped to identify, assess and 'weigh' competing considerations? Are there not problems of legitimacy in the type of quasi-scientific undertaking which instrumentalist models of procedural fairness especially tend to imply? There is an argument that for 'tailoring' to be taken seriously, judges – to turn the aphorism around – would have to mould the judicial process in the image of administration.

Writing in the 1970s on the consequences for the legal system of adopting a spectrum theory, Loughlin foresaw that it might be necessary to admit, as American courts do, a wider range of evidence. But what then of the character of law?[12]

> Mullan argues that 'if individual decision-making functions have different characteristics then they deserve different procedural requirements.' However, bearing in mind the multifarious situations involving sensitive policy issues into which administration enters, such a role will result in a tremendous expansion of the number of factors which the court must consider in looking at administrative decision-making in the context of procedural fairness ... The result would be, in effect, to vest in the judiciary supreme authority to determine which decisions will be made by what process. As the court's role would be to deal almost solely with policy issues, a mode of argumentation similar to the Brandeis brief technique, (which would include socio-economic data to demonstrate potential or actual effects of alternative procedures for the goals of a particular administrative system), would become the dominant form of legal discourse ...
>
> Procedural fairness ... undermines the concept of the rule of law. The notion of generality of the legal order, achieved primarily by the use of general rules, is undermined by abandoning the formal rules of natural justice in favour of a flexible principle which cannot be individuated as its operation is governed by such notions as the most efficient way of attaining the presumed goals of a system. Also, autonomy of the legal order as an ideal is undermined as flexible standards like procedural fairness invite the court 'to make use of the technician's conception of efficiency or the layman's view of justice.' This destroys the distinctiveness of the methods and functions of administration and adjudication.

By way of contrast, the case for a pro-active judicial approach underpinned by radically improved information systems has been developed recently by Jabarri:[13]

> The balancing inherent in the more flexible 'duty to act fairly', in modern natural justice, potentially permits more of the detailed working of administrative systems to be considered by the court than was the case under the classification of function approach ... Law that has this openness to its environment can be described as intelligent, or in Teubner's term, 'reflexive' law. ... The problem ... is that [this]

---

12  M. Loughlin, 'Procedural Fairness: A Study of the Crisis in Administrative Law Theory' (1978) 28 *Univ. of Toronto LJ* 215, 236-237, 240.

13  D. Jabbari, 'Critical Theory in Administrative Law' (1994) 14 OJLS 189, 200-202. See, on reflexive law, G. Teubner, 'Substantive and Reflexive Elements in Modern Law' (1983) 17 Law and Society Rev. 239. And see above, p. 300.

requires the court to assess the consequences of its decisions upon administrative systems, if it is to avoid making decisions which appear to judges to produce unforeseen and damaging consequences for these systems ... The contention is that existing [judicial] information mechanisms do not endow judges with the expertise necessary effectively to respond to the complexity of administrative systems.

## 3. Non-adjudicative procedures

Properly to assess these arguments, we need to extend our horizons. So far in this chapter we have proceeded on the assumption that procedural fairness denotes the rendition of adjudicative-style restraint. Yet the concept is not in terms limited in this way and so, theoretically at least, could encompass the use of adjudication to devise and instal procedural requirements for *other* forms of deciding. Seen in this light, the rubric of 'fairness' would appear to import a qualitatively as well as a quantitatively different potential for the shaping of the administrative process by the courts.

Put another way, the change from analytical theory to procedural fairness could be read in different ways. The narrower interpretation is that the expansion of procedural protection does not mark a fundamental change in the nature of natural justice. In Craig's words, fairness is seen as 'simply fitting into an adjudicative framework'.[14] A more radical interpretation would be that abandonment of the 'judicial', 'quasi-judicial', 'administrative' classification ultimately frees the courts not only to discard discredited limitations on the area of review, but also to develop a new agenda of procedural choices no longer confined within a single framework of social ordering: adjudication. Compare this with classic green light theory, which also invites administrative lawyers to question the ideal-type of adjudication and to seek out alternative methods of administration. But, whereas such theory typically insists that courts play a limited role, 'fairness' broadly defined suggests they occupy a pivotal position: in effect, 'hands on', not 'hands off'. Thus, according to MacDonald:[15]

> The adoption of 'fairness' involves a fundamental reorientation in the law of judicial review ... It involves criteria far removed from the norms of classical adjudication ... Every exercise of delegated statutory power - investigating, prosecuting, contracting, mediating/conciliating, licensing, litigating, negotiating, land-owning, expropriating, taxing, benefit distributing, can fall within its ambit ...
>
> The concept of fairness is directed to what may broadly be identified as participation in decision-making ... Rather than ask what aspects of adjudicative procedures can be grafted onto this decisional process, reviewing tribunals must ask: what is the nature of the process here undertaken, what mode of participation by affected parties is envisaged by such a decisional process, and what specific procedural guidelines are necessary to ensure the efficacy of that participation and the integrity of the process under review?

Now consider a typology of judicial models of procedural protection:

14  Craig, *Administrative Law*, 291.
15  R. MacDonald, 'Judicial Review and Procedural Fairness in Administrative Law' (1980) 25 McGill LJ 520, 542-543, 549; (1981) 26 McGill LJ 1, 4, 19.

| Active Formalist<br>('Judicialised' Administration) | Inactive Formalist<br>(Analytical Theory) |
| --- | --- |
| Active Informalist<br>('Fairness' Redefined) | Inactive Informalist |

In this typology, judicial 'activism' denotes procedural supervision across broad swathes of the administration; 'inactivism', the reverse. 'Formalist' supervision consists of evaluating procedures against the 'formal' ideal-type of adjudication; 'informalist' supervision, evaluating procedures against a range of different techniques of social ordering. In turn, 'informalist' supervision is taken to imply that the standard of review (content) will vary dramatically.

Discounting activist formalism, which would mean 'judicialising' much of the administrative process, how might we describe the shift from analytical theory (that is, inactivist formalism par excellence)? Turning back to Mullan's spectrum theory, we see that it may encompass activist informalism, in the sense of a flexible supervisory role both inside and outside adjudicative contexts. In contrast, according to the narrower interpretation of the change, the development of procedural fairness is essentially contained within the same classification. Thus, there is a measure, but only a measure, first, of increased activism; and, second, of a sharing with informalism in the sense of greater variation of content.

This is, in Craig's words, how 'the system generally works at present'. The courts are apt not only to mould the administration in their own image, but also otherwise to *desist* from fashioning process. Take the case law on consultation (above, p. 199). Although we noted some important developments in recent years, the courts' demands remain comparatively muted when set against those made in individual, adjudicative contexts. We indicated that a strengthening of the duty to consult before rules are made was largely confined to situations where by statute Parliament has itself recognised the case for consultation.

Now we can pick up the arguments about competency and legitimacy. Loughlin[16] contended that the notion of procedural fairness which had developed in England was 'largely symbolic' in the sense that, confronted by the problems of competency and legitimacy associated with judicial 'balancing', the courts were compelled to caution. The argument was premised on the broader view of the potential of 'fairness', and thus serves to point up the multiple problems of tailoring which arise if that potential is sought to be realised. Jabbari's plea for improved information mechanisms is, however, specifically made on the basis of a want of fashioning of non-adjudicative procedures. In his words:[17]

---

16   M. Loughlin, above, note 12.
17   D. Jabbari, above, note 13, 211-213.

When requested to intervene in cases where non-adjudicative models of procedure are appropriate, the law has manifested a lack of readiness to devise non-adjudicative procedures, such as mediation or consultation, for that context ... To demand that fairness comprise non-adjudicative procedures is no more than a logical elaboration of the current evolution of the law ... Yet ... if a court is to be able to instal and monitor non-adjudicative procedures, it must be able to form an intelligent view of the precise characteristics of administrative decision-making which would render one procedure more appropriate than another in a given context. This brings us to ... the need for the reform of the information mechanisms of existing court procedure.

Process values can be seen as a way of emboldening the courts, the argument for a broad approach to fairness being explicitly grounded in the democratic values of participation and consent. According to Richardson:[18]

At the centre of the argument lies the notion of legitimate authority ... A government charged with co-ordinating social activities will be authoritative only if it acts in accordance with certain basic principles ... [Liberal pluralism] accepts that modern societies are complex and diverse ... Within such a society one of the principal liberal values must be 'the freedom of the citizen and of associations freely chosen by citizens' ... Such a value recognises personal freedom and the diversity that follows from it: it allows for differing concepts of the good. In addition, principles of equality, often expressed in terms of democracy, suggest that each person counts in the decisions of government. In order to satisfy these two principles of freedom and equal political significance, any exercise of government power must demonstrate that full regard has been paid to the diversity of values and interests represented within society ... The enforcement of common law principles reflective of full process in this sense would be supportive of democracy rather than hostile to it: they would be constitutional in the most fundamental sense ...

There is an alternative, more radical, approach which accords process an even more central role. According to [the] theory of strong democracy, the co-ordination required within a society is achieved by way of direct participation and self-regulation. The authority of 'state' action is achieved through the 'active consent of participatory citizens'. Even though the presence of prior values is denied by strong democrats, the commitment to strong democratic principles could itself ... be seen as such an independent value and some system of external review might be advisable to safeguard adherence to it ...

Admittedly the two approaches reflect very different attitudes towards the role of government, but both emphasise the fundamental role of process in the legitimization of government decisions, and thus provide an alternative view of the law's involvement in the regulation of process which could encourage the law to develop beyond the narrow parameters of interest protection set by the more traditional approaches ... A broader approach of this nature ... would carry the demands for fair process into the realm of policy formulation.

Enough was said elsewhere to indicate some formidable objections. For example, we observed in the context of rule-making the difficulty of devising procedures which take into account a broad range of views without impairing the efficiency of administration. Nor do the courts exist in a constitutional and

18  G. Richardson, 'The Legal Regulation of Process' in G. Richardson and H. Genn (eds.), *Administrative Law and Government Action* (Oxford: Clarendon) 1994, pp. 124-128.

historical vacuum. Concern about possible judicial 'interference' with the policy-making process is reflected in, and reinforced by, traditional patterns of judicial restraint; in a word, problems of competency and legitimacy are not simply to be wished away. Consider for example Jabbari's proposal. Is it correct to assume that more and different information would engender a 'solution'? Or might the development itself become a pressing problem for the courts?

### Functions and process. The planning inquiry

As we suggested in Chapter 12, inquiries represent a style of proceeding more flexible, broad and policy-orientated in character than the bipolar adversarial procedures of courts. Then again, the large-scale planning inquiry is an important context where conflicting objectives have long been evident. The highly controversial subject of building a motorway provides a good example. Residents, environmentalists, industrialists, the Department of Transport supposed to represent the public interest, may all have different arguments for and against possible alternatives. We find competing views of the function of the inquiry in this type of context. Is it to promote the taking of the best decision in the 'public interest' as officially determined? In this traditional, representative model, the inquiry may be seen essentially as a source of information to the minister responsible for taking the decision. Is it to protect the legal rights and interests of private property by serving as an institutionalised version of the dictates of natural justice? This view infused, and was promoted by, the Franks Report on Tribunals and Inquiries. Or is it to ensure an element of public participation in the decision-making chain? This view gels with a theory of process values such as that expounded by Richardson[19].

### Bushell v Secretary of State for the Environment[20]

At a motorway inquiry held under the Highways Act 1959, objectors wished to question witnesses for the department on the accuracy of traffic predictions contained in a departmental publication known as the 'Red Book' and used as the standard basis for predicting traffic growth. The inspector disallowed the questions. Before the minister issued his decision, but after the inquiry, a revised method was used. The minister refused to reopen the inquiry to allow challenge. The appellants applied for the minister's decision to be quashed on the grounds (a) that the refusal to allow cross-examination was a breach of natural justice and (b) that the minister had taken into account new evidence (i.e. the revised methods of traffic calculation and the question of 'need') which had not been disclosed to the objectors. The challenge was rejected by the House of Lords, Lord Edmund-Davies dissenting.

19  See further, P. McAuslan, *The Ideologies of Planning Law* (London: Pergamon) 1981.
20  [1980] 3 WLR 22.

*Lord Diplock*: The subject matter of the inquiry is the objections to the proposed scheme that have been received by the minister from local authorities and from private persons in the vicinity ... whose interests may be adversely affected. The purpose of the inquiry is to provide the minister with as much information about those objections as will ensure that in reaching his decision he will have weighed the harm to local interests and private persons who may be adversely affected by the scheme against the public benefit which the scheme is likely to achieve and will not have failed to take into consideration any matters which he ought to have taken into consideration ...

To 'over-judicialise' the inquiry by insisting on observance of the procedures of a court of justice which professional lawyers alone are competent to operate effectively in the interests of their clients would not be fair. It would, in my view, be quite fallacious to suppose that at an inquiry of this kind the only fair way of ascertaining matters of fact and expert opinion is by the oral testimony of witnesses who are subjected to cross-examination on behalf of parties who disagree with what they have said. Such procedure is peculiar to litigation conducted in courts that follow the common law system of procedure ... Refusal by an inspector to allow a party to cross-examine orally at a local inquiry a person who has made statements of facts or has expressed expert opinions is not unfair *per se*.

Whether fairness requires [this] must depend on all the circumstances ... Here the relevant circumstances ... include the nature of the topic upon which the opinion is expressed, the qualifications of the maker of the statement to deal with that topic, the forensic competence of the proposed cross-examiner, and, most important, the inspector's own views as to whether the likelihood that cross examination will enable him to make a report which will be more useful to the minister in reaching his decision than it otherwise would be is sufficient to justify any expense and inconvenience to other parties to the inquiry which would be caused by any resulting prolongation of it.

A decision to construct a nationwide network of motorways is clearly one of government policy in the widest sense of the term. Any proposal to alter it is appropriate to be the subject of debate in Parliament, not of separate investigations in each of scores of local inquiries before individual inspectors up and down the country upon whatever material happens to be presented to them at the particular inquiry over which they preside. So much the respondents readily concede.

At the other extreme the selection of the exact line to be followed through a particular locality by a motorway designed to carry traffic between the destinations that it is intended to serve would not be described as involving government policy in the ordinary sense of that term. It affects particular local interests only and normally does not affect the interests of any wider section of the public, unless a suggested variation of the line would involve exorbitant expenditure of money raised by taxation. It is an appropriate subject for full investigation at a local inquiry ...

Between the black and white of these two extremes, however, there is .. a 'grey area'. Because of the time that must elapse between the preparation of any scheme and the completion of the stretch of motorway that it authorises, the department, in deciding in what order new stretches of the national network ought to be constructed, has adopted a uniform practice throughout the country of making a major factor in its decision the likelihood that there will be a traffic need for that particular stretch of motorway in 15 years from the date when the scheme was prepared ... Priorities as between one stretch of motorway and another have got to be determined somehow. Semasiologists may argue whether the adoption by the department of a uniform practice for doing this is most appropriately described as government policy or as something else. But the propriety of adopting it is clearly a matter fit to be debated in a wider forum and with the assistance of a wider range of relevant material than any investigation at any individual local inquiry is likely to provide; and in that sense at least, which is the relevant sense for present purposes, its adoption forms part of government policy ...

I think that the inspector was right in saying that the use of the concept of traffic needs in the design year *assessed by a particular method* as the yardstick by which to determine the order in which particular stretches of the national network of motorways should be constructed was government policy in the relevant sense of being a topic unsuitable for investigation by individual inspectors upon whatever material happens to be presented to them at local inquiries held throughout the country.

*Lord Edmund-Davies* (dissenting): The inspector could - and should - disallow questions relating to the merits of government policy. But matters of policy are matters which involve the exercise of political judgment and matters of fact and expertise do not become 'policy' merely because a department of government relies on them. And, as the Franks Committee had put it in 1957: 'We see no reason why the factual basis for a departmental view should not be explained and its validity tested in cross-examination.' ... The general law may, I think, be summarised in this way: (a) In holding an administrative inquiry (such as that presently being considered), the inspector was performing quasi-judicial duties. (b) He must therefore discharge them in accordance with the rules of natural justice. (c) Natural justice requires that objectors (no less than departmental representatives) be allowed to cross-examine witnesses called for the other side on all relevant matters, be they matters of fact or matters of expert opinion. (d) ... the only restrictions on cross-examination are those general and well-defined exclusionary rules which govern the admissibility of relevant evidence ... beyond those restrictions there is no discretion on the civil side to exclude cross-examination on relevant matters. And there is a massive body of accepted decisions establishing that natural justice requires that a party be given an opportunity of challenging by cross-examination witnesses called by another party on relevant issues.

Then is there any reason why those general rules should have been departed from in the present case? ... The parameters of the inquiry, as agreed to by the department representatives, embraced *need* as a topic relevant to be canvassed and reported upon ... While I am alive to the inconvenience of different inspectors arriving at different conclusions regarding different sections of a proposed trunk road, the risk of that happening cannot, in my judgment, have any bearing upon the question whether justice was done at this particular inquiry.

Lord Diplock's approach to tailoring clearly reflects a reluctance to impose a strongly judicialised form of procedure. Cross-examination, which is high up on the scale of adjudicative procedures, is refused broad application and instead made to depend on the judicial view of all the circumstances. Particular importance is attached to the nature of the topic and whether it falls outside the proper scope of the inquiry. Yet the answer to this obviously depends on contested views of the inquiry function. Note here the way in which Lord Edmund-Davis classifies assessment methods in terms not of government policy but of fact and expertise.

*Bushell* illustrates how the dominant adjudicative framework of procedural protection can operate in a subtle way to close off other procedural choices. Cross-examination being deemed inappropriate, no procedural protection is imposed. A broader interpretation of 'fairness' would mean a duty of consultation to provide objectors with an opportunity of involvement without depriving the minister of the decision-making power.

Lord Diplock's speech indicates both a 'public interest' and instrumental view of the inquiry process – the aim being to facilitate the carrying out of public policies – and one which typically involves a cost-benefit analysis in the balancing of factors. How, then, does the speech stand with a model of due process premised on substantive rights? Dworkin has provided an answer: [1]

> It is uncontroversial (I suppose) that the decision whether to build a highway in a particular direction is ... a matter of policy. If it was in the public's overall interest to build the highway as the Department wished to do, giving full weight, in that determination, to the adverse impact on those particularly inconvenienced by the decision, then the decision to build the highway was the right decision to take. No individual or group has a right in the strong sense [that it would be wrong to build it even if it were wise policy to do so] against that decision ... If the question whether to build a highway in a particular direction is a question of policy, then is not the further question of what form and dimension of public hearings to hold in order to decide that question also a question of policy?
>
> Lord Diplock's ... language suggests that people particularly affected by a highway planning decision have no rights to any particular procedure in the conduct of any hearing at all, beyond what some statute might explicitly provide, so that the decision what procedures to provide is entirely a matter of cost-benefit policy considerations ... [My] argument ... suggests no flaw in Lord Diplock's argument ... Lord Diplock supposes that even if the public would lose overall by some highway decision, it may nevertheless gain by procedures that run a greater risk of allowing that mistake to be made than other, more expensive procedures would. Everything depends on whether the increased procedural costs of, for example, allowing local examination of every feature of the national programme are worth the gains in the actual design of the programme that would be *antecedentally* likely to result. If they are not, then the fact, available only by hindsight that the more expensive procedure would actually have produced a better programme, does not argue that the failure to follow that procedure deprived citizens of what utility would recommend ... Of course, the decision whether the more expensive procedures would be worth the cost is itself a policy decision ... Lord Diplock's point is precisely that [this] policy decision should be made by the government ... not by the courts.

The case for a more assertive judicial role is presented in this context by Brownsword and Harden: [2]

> The crucial part [of Dworkin's thesis] is that in which he invokes the division of labour to justify directing the litigant to refer the question to an institution which, unlike the Courts, does have jurisdiction to resort to arguments of policy. This [argument] is vulnerable in two ways. First, the policy-making institution may be disingenuous in its apparent pursuit of the common good. In reality the policy-makers may consistently advance policies which unfairly advantage or disadvantage some groups. If the judge realises that there is this risk of unfairness then he cannot be altogether happy about referring the policy question to this institution. Under the rights thesis this is a particularly poignant dilemma for the judge whose overall role is to secure fairness. The second weakness ... is this. The policy-making institution will necessarily approach the question within the framework of its own prior-formed

---

1   R. Dworkin, *A Matter of Principle* (Oxford: Clarendon) 1985, pp. 78-79.
2   R. Brownsword and I. Harden, 'Rights and the Red Book' (1981) 1 Legal Studies 94, pp. 97-99.

conception of the general welfare ... The institution may well be unable to transcend its own preconception of the common good and whatever defects there are in this preconception will be reflected in the instant decision ...

Conversely, the *Bushell* case may be seen as indicative of the courts' general approach to fairness. Thus, it fits well with the operational framework of the common law's involvement in the regulation of process identified by Richardson (above, p. 199). Galligan pursues the argument:[3]

> [Assuming] that there is in principle such a right [to make representations about the policy itself] the question is . . . just how far that right extends. It is helpful to break down policy to the facts on which it is based and the element of opinion and judgment which creates the policy . . . Policies are sound only to the extent that the facts on which they are based are accurate and reliable . . [In] *Bushell* . . . strict limits were imposed on the extent to which objectors . . . could challenge and try to rebut predictions about the future density of traffic. The predictions were vital to the Department's case for more roads and there were certainly grounds for suspecting they were erroneous . . .
>
> Yet there are reasons for limiting such challenges. Although the factual issue is sometimes clearly defined, often such hard facts give way to soft facts where matters of opinion, speculation and subjective judgment are integral elements . . . The principle of selective representation might . . . provide useful guidance here, for according to the principle the opportunity to be heard on the policy aspects is an individualised process and should depend on whether other opportunities have been available to that person . . . at other points in the policy process.

## 4. A duty to give reasons?

A long-standing bone of contention has been the absence of a general duty to provide reasons for administrative decisions. In 1971, *Justice* went so far as to say that no single factor had inhibited the development of English administrative law as seriously as this.[4] In 1988, the same organisation expressed a need for statutory reform, on the basis that it was 'not ... at all probable that the judges here will change their basic attitudes' and develop the obligation at common law.[5] Yet six years later, one commentator was able to identify 'a subtle but real shift in this area', while others spoke of 'a triumph of judicial expansionism'.[6] Further, the development has largely taken place under the rubric or, as Beloff and Elias prefer, the 'camouflage' of fairness.[7]

The case for requiring reasons is conveniently set out by *Justice* under four headings:[8]

---

3   D. Galligan, *Due Process and Fair Procedures* (above, p. 497, note 5), pp. 378–379.
4   *Justice, Administration Under Law* (London) 1971, p. 23.
5   *Justice*-All Souls, *Administrative Justice: Some Necessary Reforms* (Oxford: Clarendon) 1988, p. 72.
6   P. Craig, 'The Common Law, Reasons and Administrative Justice' (1994) 53 CLJ 282, 301; R. Gordon and C. Barlow, 'Reasons for Life: Solving the Sphinx's Riddle' (1993) 143 NLJ 1005, 1006.
7   M. Beloff and P Elias, 'Natural Justice – (The Audi Alteram Partem Rule) and Fairness' in M Supperstone and J. Goudie (eds.), *Judicial Review* (London: Butterworths) 1992, p. 203.
8   *Justice*-All Souls Review, pp. 69-70. See also G. Richardson, 'The Duty to Give Reasons: Potential and Practice' [1986] PL 437.

A.  *The functioning of the machinery of government*
1.  The need to give reasons imposes a healthy discipline on the decision-maker.
2.  Consequently, reasoned decisions are likely to be better thought out.
3.  Reasons are a check on arbitrary decision-making.

B.  *The viewpoint of parties affected by the decision*
4.  Reasons satisfy a basic need for fair play.
5.  Reasons enable the person affected to know whether it is possible to challenge the decision and, if so, upon what basis.
6.  Even if the decision is adverse, the person affected may be convinced by the reasons to accept it as a rational and unbiased exercise of discretionary power.

C.  *The viewpoint of the reviewing authority*
7.  The reviewing authority - whether appellate tribunal, court, or ombudsman – will be better placed to understand the decision ... if the decision is reasoned ...
8.  Proper reasons should expose excess of jurisdiction, error of law, unsubstantiated findings, and extraneous considerations.

D.  *The public at large*
9.  Public confidence in the decision-making process is enhanced by the knowledge that supportable reasons have to be given.

This list comprises a mix of instrumentalist and non-instrumentalist rationales. Thus, the first three justifications illustrate a concern with the quality of substantive outcomes, whereas the fourth suggests the idea of dignitary values. Again, the last justification can be seen to demonstrate the notion of process benefits identified by Bayles. The list is also expressive of the search in administrative law for rational forms of decision-taking (Chapter 4). Reasons are here seen to possess both a fire-watching function (improving the quality of initial decision-taking) and a fire-fighting function (facilitating the idea of administration under law). The imposition of a duty to give reasons may also represent an imposition of adjudicative-style restraint. A link with procedural fairness begins to appear!

The absence of a duty to give reasons reflects and reinforces the culture of official secrecy which has long characterised British government (Chapter 14). Arguments against imposing such a duty are typically expressed in terms of administrative costs or the downside of the utility calculus. Note too the potential for 'boilerplate' reasons:[9]

A. Efficient administration requires free and uninhibited discussion among decision-makers ...

B. A general requirement of reasons will impose an intolerable burden on the machinery of government.

C. Delays in the handling of business will inevitably follow and additional expense will be caused. The public at large will suffer ...

D. ... Many more decisions will be opened up to the possibility of legal challenge and a further step down the road of 'judicialization' of affairs will be taken.

9   *Justice*/All Souls Review, pp. 70-71.

> E. The imposition of a duty to give reasons will not necessarily mean that the true or complete reasons will be stated. Decision-makers will ... acquire the art of stating sufficient by way of reasons to preclude successful challenge but candour will not always be displayed.

What exactly is entailed in the obligation? As regards statutory requirements, the Franks Report on Tribunals and Inquiries once again proved an important milestone, a duty to give reasons being included as part of the package of judicialisation. The courts were assigned a major role, the relevant provision, currently s. 10 of the Tribunals and Inquiries Act 1992, specifying the applicability but not the content of the duty. In the event, it was soon established that the reasons given must be proper, intelligible and adequate, dealing with the substantive points which have been made.[10] We learned, however, that a standard such as adequacy is flexible and susceptible to change over time. Take planning appeals, where post-Franks the case law increasingly stipulated that the department adopt a judicialised form of decision-making. So it was held that the minister's decisions ought to be based on the inspector's findings of fact, that they must be supported by 'sufficient evidence' or that the justification for a decision to differ from the Inspector's recommendations should be clearly stated.[11]

The scope for judicial disagreement is highlighted by the leading case of *Save Britain's Heritage v Secretary of State for the Environment*.[12] A conservation group complained that the minister, in approving a major development in agreement with the inspector, had failed to indicate with due clarity and precision the extent to which he adopted the inspector's reasoning. In the Court of Appeal, Woolf LJ took a strong contextual approach, tailoring the statutory duty according to 'the nature of the decision ... the terms of the relevant legislation ... the importance of the issue' and the need for expedition. His conclusion that in the circumstances the reasons were insufficient was rejected by the House of Lords. Lord Bridge stressed the need to avoid a situation where the minister had 'to dot every i and cross every t', and called for 'a measure of benevolence' in the reading of decision letters.

The pessimism of *Justice* in 1988 reflected the limited contribution of the common law to the requiring of reasons. As well as no general duty, the common law exceptions, where in effect reasons were obligatory, were restrictively drawn.[13] In early cases such as *Padfield*,[14] the basis of the duty to give reasons was

---

10  *Re Poyser and Mills's Arbitration* [1963] 1 All ER 612.
11  Celebrated decisions in the series include *Lord Luke of Pavenham v Minister of Housing and Local Government* [1968] 1 QB 172; *Givaudan & Co Ltd v Minister of Housing and Local Government* [1966] 3 All ER 696; *Ashbridge Investments v Minister of Housing and Local Government* [1965] 1 WLR 1320; *Coleen Properties v Minister of Housing and Local Government* [1971] 1 WLR 433. See also P. McAuslan, *Land, Law and Planning* (London: Weidenfeld & Nicolson) 1975, pp. 558-579.
12  [1991] 2 All ER 10. See, to similar effect, *South Lakeland District Council v Secretary of State for the Environment* [1992] 2 AC 141.
13  See for details of a difficult case law, *Justice*/All Souls Review, Ch. 3; also, P. Craig, 'The Common Law, Reasons and Administrative Justice' above, note 6.
14  Above, p. 98.

treated as 'little more than a symptom of irrationality',[15] the court being more likely to infer irrationality in the absence of reasons. This was only to happen if the circumstances pointed 'overwhelmingly' towards one exercise of discretion and no explanation for taking the contrary course was given.[16]

Recent developments coincide with the greater insistence by government on the 'theta' value of transparency in the Citizen's Charter. (Note the broad commitment to reasons in the 1993 Code on Access to Official Information (above, p.449)). Although the courts still assert the absence of a general common law duty, broad exceptions have been established and then applied in an expanding range of cases. 'Fairness' is no longer seen as concerned only with procedure at the hearing.

One basis for the duty is to buttress a legal theory of 'control' – judicial review itself should not be frustrated by the absence of reasons. *R v Civil Service Appeal Board, ex p Cunningham*[17] concerned a prison officer who had been unfairly dismissed. The Board, a body established under the prerogative, made him an award of compensation less than half the going rate in the industrial tribunals and refused to give reasons. In the words of Lord Donaldson MR:

> The Board should have given outline reasons sufficient to show to what they were directing their mind and thereby indirectly showing not whether their decision was right or wrong, which is a matter solely for them, but whether their decision was lawful. Any other conclusion would reduce the Board to the status of a free-wheeling palm tree ... fairness requires a tribunal such as the Board to give sufficient reasons for its decision to enable the parties to know the issues to which it addressed its mind and that it acted lawfully.

In the leading case of *Doody* the House of Lords went further, recognising that the duty to give reasons may have an intrinsic value to the applicant. Expressed slightly differently, we see a development beyond instrumentalist or utilitarian concerns in the direction of dignitary theory. Emphasis is laid in grounding the duty on the nature and impact of the decision, in the instant case deprivation of liberty.

## *R v Secretary of State for the Home Department, ex p Doody*[18]

The applicants were mandatory life prisoners who challenged the 'tariff' system on grounds which included the failure to give reasons.

> Lord Mustill: What [the prisoner] does not know is why the particular term was selected, and he is now trying to find out: partly from an obvious human desire to be told the reason for a decision so gravely affecting his future, and partly because he hopes that once the information is obtained he may be able to point out errors of fact

15  D. Toube, 'Requiring Reasons at Common Law' (1997) 2 Judicial Review 68.
16  *R v Secretary of State for Trade and Industry, ex p Lonrho plc* [1989] 1 WLR 525.
17  [1991] 4 All ER 310.
18  [1993] 3 WLR 154.

or reasoning and thereby persuade the Secretary of State to change his mind, or if he fails in this to challenge the decision in the courts. Since the Secretary of State has declined to furnish the information, the respondents have set out to obtain it by applications for judicial review ...

What does fairness require in the present case? My Lords, I think it unnecessary to refer by name or to quote from, any of the often-cited authorities in which the courts have explained what is essentially an intuitive judgment ... From them, I derive that (1) where an Act of Parliament confers an administrative power there is a presumption that it will be exercised in a manner which is fair in all the circumstances. (2) The standards of fairness are not immutable. They may change with the passage of time, both in general and in their application to decisions of a particular type. (3) The principles of fairness are not to be applied by rote identically in every situation. What fairness demands is dependent on the context of the decision, and this is to be taken into account in all its aspects. (4) An essential feature of the context is the statute which creates the discretion ... (5) Fairness will very often require that a person who may be adversely affected by the decision will have an opportunity to make representations on his own behalf ... (6) Since the person affected usually cannot make worthwhile representations without knowing what factors may weigh against his interests, fairness will very often require that he is informed of the gist of the case which he has to answer ...

I find in the more recent cases on judicial review a perceptible trend towards an insistence on greater openness, or if one prefers the contemporary jargon 'transparency', in the making of administrative decisions ... I accept without hesitation ... that the law does not at present recognise a general duty to give reasons for an administrative decision. Nevertheless, it is equally beyond question that such a duty may in appropriate circumstances be implied ...

Turning to the present dispute I doubt the wisdom of discussing the problem in the contemporary vocabulary of 'prisoner's rights'... I prefer simply to assert that ... the Secretary of State ought to implement the scheme as fairly as he can. The giving of reasons may be inconvenient, but I can see no ground at all why it should be against the public interest: indeed, rather the reverse. This being so, I would ask simply: is refusal to give reasons fair? I would answer without hesitation that it is not ... As soon as the jury returns its verdict the offender knows that he will be locked up for a very long time. For just how long immediately becomes the most important thing in the prisoner's life ...

I can moreover arrive at the same conclusion by a different and more familiar route, of which *ex parte Cunningham* ... provides a recent example. It is not ... questioned that the decision of the Home Secretary ... is susceptible to judicial review. To mount an effective attack on the decision, given no more material than the facts of the offence and the length of the penal element, the prisoner has virtually no means of ascertaining whether this is an instance where the decision-making process has gone astray. I think it important that there should be an effective means of detecting the kind of error which would entitle the court to intervene, and in practice I regard it as necessary for this purpose that the reasoning of the Home Secretary should be disclosed.'

Looking to the future, we could anticipate a general duty to give reasons in cases affecting members of the public, subject to exceptions. One pointer is *R v Higher Education Funding Council, ex p Institute of Dental Surgery*,[19] in which a challenge to university research assessment grading on the ground of unfairness due to lack of reasons was rejected. The court stressed the element of academic

---

19   [1994] 1 All ER 651. See further, A. Lindsay, 'Reasons to be Cheerful' (1994) 57 MLR 954.

judgment entailed in the decision and its respect for the Council's expertise. The difficult case of *Fayed* deals with the interplay of common law and statute. The majority decision of the Court of Appeal is further evidence of the trend identified by Lord Mustill in *Doody* towards an insistence on greater transparency in administrative decision-taking.

## R v Secretary of State for the Home Department, ex p Fayed[20]

The Fayed brothers challenged the refusal of the minister to grant them citizenship. No reasons were given nor were the brothers given notice of the difficulties or reservations about their applications before the decision was made. The minister stood on s. 44(2) of the British Nationality Act 1981: 'the Secretary of State ... shall not be required to assign any reason for the grant or refusal of any application under this Act, the decision on which is at his discretion.' Not surprisingly, the Court of Appeal considered that in the absence of this provision there would have been a clear case of procedural unfairness, more especially because of the damage to reputation. Equally, however, an express statutory prohibition on the requirement of reasons could not be overlooked. The court divided on whether a duty to give notice was inconsistent with the ban. The majority thought that it could be differentiated:

> *Lord Woolf MR*: The suggestion that notice need not be given although this would be unfair involves attributing to Parliament an intention that it has not expressly stated that a minister should be able to act unfairly in deciding that a person lawfully in this country should be refused citizenship without the courts being able to do anything about it. This involves attributing to the protection which s 44(2) gives in relation to reasons far greater status than that to which it is entitled. English law has long attached the greatest importance to the need for fairness to be observed prior to the exercise of a statutory discretion. However, English law, at least until recently, has not been so sensitive to the need for reasons to be given for a decision after it has been reached. So to exclude the need for fairness before a decision is reached because it might give an indication of what the reasons for the decision could be is to reverse the actual position. It involves frustrating the achievement of the more important objective of fairness in reaching a decision in an attempt to protect a lesser objective of possibly disclosing what will be the reasons for the decision ...
>
> In many situations the giving of notice of areas of concern will do no more than identify possible rather than the actual reasons. Thus as long as the Minister seeks representations for more than one area of concern, the applicant in the absence of reasons will not know whether any particular area of concern played any part in the decision to refuse the application ... As the Minister has a discretion to give the applicant notice of an area of concern, that discretion must itself be exercised reasonably. If not to give notice would result in unfairness then the discretion can only reasonably be exercised by giving notice ... If the Secretary of State is correct in his contention, the effect of the restriction on the obligation to give reasons is far reaching indeed. In any readily identifiable situation it will totally exclude the court's power of review. It would apply for example if the Secretary of State was guilty of discrimination.

20  [1997] 1 All ER 228.

*Kennedy LJ* (dissenting): The plain intention of Parliament was to relieve the Secretary of State of the burden of giving reasons ... If [he] must nevertheless canvass with the applicant a matter or matters which in his view weigh against the grant of citizenship that, in every case where there is ultimately a refusal, means that the reason or reasons for refusal will have had to be disclosed. If, as may often be the case, the Secretary of State has only been troubled about one matter, then the unsuccessful applicant will be in no doubt as to the reason for refusal and the Secretary of State will in reality have been required to assign a reason for the refusal, which is precisely what s 44(2) says should not occur. Even if at the consultation stage the Secretary of State indicates that he is troubled by more than one matter the situation will be much the same ... [Counsel] rightly points out that the wording of s.44(2) relates to the decision-making stage of the process, and not to any earlier stage, but as [the judge] said: 'Although the principle of audi alteram partem and the provision of the reasons for the decision are distinct, they are closely related and derive from the concept of fairness' ... In my judgment the relationship is such that Parliament cannot have overlooked it. Undoubtedly the words of the statute do impinge upon what without them fairness would require, but not, as it seems to me, to a particularly surprising extent ... There will no doubt be many occasions on which the Secretary of State, for good reason, would prefer not to explain why he is minded to refuse or is in fact refusing citizenship.

## 5. Conclusion

Procedural fairness is an important element in the invigoration of judicial review, from *Ridge v Baldwin* on. Nowhere is the organic quality of the common law as reflected in shifts in the style and substance of judicial protection better illustrated. Nor is development slowing, as the sudden rise of the duty to give reasons demonstrates. At the same time we note the limitations, the modest contribution of the common law in non-adjudicative contexts.

A central theme is the scale and variety of judicial discretion. At one level this involves the choice of methodology: from categorising interests to interest balancing, and from transaction-typing to spectrum theory. At another level it involves, in Lord Mustill's words, 'essentially an intuitive judgment' in particular cases. At worst it may involve a failure to adhere to legal principle in hard cases, exemplified by falling below the standards of the ECHR in national security cases.

Expressed slightly differently, procedural fairness is in terms of legal principle soft-centred. As such it is fertile territory for complex and costly litigation. There is also a paradox, the change from analytical theory both extending the ambit of 'control' and, through the greater variation of content or standards which this entails, putting in issue the operation of 'control' through principle and precedent. Further, the case law often appears inchoate, one explanation being recourse to 'intuitive judgment' at the expense of theories of process. The approach has been broadly instrumentalist in character, with insufficient attention being paid to dignitary values. There are signs of change, as in the idea of an independent obligation to treat the citizen fairly suggested by *Doody*. More extensive development in this context is indicated by the fashionable 'theta' value of transparency.

Procedural fairness highlights concerns about the competency and legitimacy of judicial decision-making. As Fuller recognised, participation in adversarial process is necessarily restricted. Serious objection may be raised to the idea of judges as technicians implicit in the more radical arguments for judicial 'balancing' and broad interpretation of 'fairness'. In this way, a lighter judicial touch in non-adjudicative contexts is a realistic prospect.

Incrementalism and problems of 'control', judicial discretion, basic issues of constitutional function and institutional design: all these are recurrent themes across the broad field of judicial review. They will be pursued further in the next two chapters.

Chapter 16

# The judicial review process

Although this is not a book which sets judicial review at the centre of administrative law, we have learned a good deal about judicial review in its pages. This is, however, a book about the relationship between law and administration and the contribution law can make to administration. We have also described it as a functionalist book. In the two chapters on courts and their output which follow, we should not wish to deviate from these objectives. In this chapter, therefore, we treat judicial review as a process and try to evaluate its performance. We assume for these purposes that judicial review has two main functions: like courts in general it is machinery for redress of grievance and, at least in the eyes of red light theorists, it is a mechanism for the control of government and administration.

In his seminal study of the subject[1] de Smith famously described judicial review as 'sporadic and peripheral', even if the hundreds of cases scattered through the footnotes did not give precisely that impression. In the first edition of this book we remarked that 'research into *who* litigates, how *often*, and in respect of *which* governmental activities, has been singularly lacking'. And this despite the court-centred approach of many administrative lawyers and the special emphasis on 'control' of administration (Chapter 2). Today, much more is known about the use and operation of the machinery and this enables us to test de Smith's remark. Our conclusions are that, at least from a quantitative angle, de Smith's comment was justified. Litigant-driven, judicial review is indeed sporadic. A minority of cases concern central government and these are limited to a minority of departments. Its outreach, too, is limited by cost and chance. Like the PCA, judicial review is not a system for handling mundane complaints. Perhaps hopefully, Lord Woolf believes[2] that the High Court 'would have drowned under the clamour for judicial review but for the achievement of tribunals'. He has pressed the case for a tribunal to handle homelessness cases and immigration matters respectively, on the ground of the need to alleviate caseload pressures on the courts. This chapter therefore reveals a tension between the desire of some judges to open access to the judicial review process more widely – in some cases, as we shall see, by making judicial review procedure compulsory – and a managerial instinct to protect the integrity of that process by keeping litigants out. The judges tend to see themselves, too, as Franks portrayed them, at the apex of

1  S. de Smith, *Judicial Review of Administrative Action* (London: Stevens) 4th edn. (J. Evans), 1980, p. 3.
2  Sir Harry Woolf, *Protection of the Public: A New Challenge*, The Hamlyn Lectures (London: Stevens) 1990, pp. 68, 77.

a structured system of administrative justice, when the majority of the cases which they handle are peripheral in the sense of being unimportant to all save those directly concerned. Finally, these interests need to be balanced against a wider public interest in the effectiveness of the administrative process. In what follows, we have tried to show these tensions manifested at every stage of the judicial review process.

Introduced in 1978,[3] the Application for Judicial Review (AJR) was designed as an umbrella procedure. It was intended to tackle complexity in the matter of remedies, previously available in different courts and each with different rules. It allowed for the various common law remedies traditionally used to review the activities of administrative authorities and inferior tribunals with the exception of *habeas corpus* where the procedure is still by writ. Previously, the courts had at their disposal first, the prerogative orders: (a) *mandamus* (to order the execution of a public duty); (b) *certiorari* (to quash a decision); and (c) *prohibition* (to forbid the hearing of a case and, latterly, the taking of a decision): second, the ordinary remedies of *injunction* and *declaration* (especially valuable for establishing the law in 'test cases'). In addition, the court was empowered to award damages provided there was a recognised cause of action (Chapter 18). The regime is governed largely by delegated legislation in the form of the Supreme Court Rules (RSC Order 53) but in part by statute (Supreme Court Act 1981, s. 31).

The first point to note about these provisions is the space left for judicial discretion, which finds expression in open-textured rules about access to court and remedies. Critics[4] see a paradox: expressed judicial hostility to administrative arbitrariness and strong discretion while judicial review operates 'in a highly arbitrary and inconsistent manner'. The courts then become the target for the very same techniques of structuring, confining and checking which we saw operating in Chapter 4.

There is a second paradox. Access to court is a constitutional right according to judicial review cases like *ex p Witham*.[5] Yet, in contrast to ordinary civil proceedings, the leave of the court is necessary to make a substantive application, rendering access to judicial review a privilege rather than a right. Expressed slightly differently, the interest of applicants in redress of grievance, or in vindicating the rule of law, is one of a number of competing interests and is often overriden.

## 1.  Leave: discretion and managerialism

The leave stage demonstrates tensions between the traditional individuated model of adjudication and a form of judicial managerialism concerned with the exercise of control over the caseflow. One justification for leave concerns the prompt and efficient despatch of public business, the need to protect public

---

3   Following recommendations by the Law Commission, *Report on Remedies in Administrative Law* (Law Com. No. 73) Cmnd. 6407, 1976.

4   L. Bridges, G. Meszaros and M. Sunkin, *Judicial Review in Perspective* (London: Cavendish) 2nd edn., 1995, p. 198 (hereafter Bridge, Meszaros and Sunkin).

5   Above, p. 162.

administration from unmeritorious and/or costly litigation and from the uncertainty engendered by delay. A second justification concerns the efficient use of court time: in Lord Donaldson's words,[6] 'the public interest normally dictates that if the judicial review jurisdiction is to be exercised, it should be exercised very speedily and, given the constraints imposed by limited judicial resources, this necessarily involves limiting the number of cases in which leave to apply should be given'. The preliminary filter may deter unmeritorious applications and facilitate their disposal with the minimum use of resources.

For Lord Woolf,[7] the discretionary filter system is one of a number of 'safeguards' (including the strict time limit, the absence in the ordinary way of evidence or discovery, and the discretionary nature of remedies) in judicial review procedure which enable the courts 'to strike a balance between the interests of the administrators and the public'. More especially, the judges have been 'encouraged ... to develop their power to intervene to control abuse of power in a way which they would not have done otherwise'. This may appear a powerful argument – discretion as the *sine qua non* of expansion – but it is obviously not susceptible of proof. The related proposition, that the discretion 'is only to deal with the obvious case where, whatever the merits, the court should not intervene', is confounded by the evidence (below). And as Lord Woolf concedes, the basic premise, that public law and private law should be differentiated as serving fundamentally different purposes, is contestable. Take his litmus test for private law proceedings: 'it is the parties alone who are directly concerned with the outcome of the litigation.' Many judicial review cases fall into this category, notably in the field of immigration. Thus, while only some judicial review proceedings 'directly affect many members of the public', the 'safeguards' apply across the board.

Leave decisions will in the majority of cases be crucial, as Table 16.1 indicates. Either the challenge is not allowed to proceed or, where leave is granted, the case is withdrawn before a substantive hearing, probably through negotiation and settlement.

It is sufficient for our purposes that leave may be refused for various reasons which include:

- delay
- no sufficient interest (standing to sue)
- no arguable case
- no issue of 'public law'
- availability of alternative remedies
- challenge is premature.

The issue of delay highlights both judicial discretion and potential clash of values. An application must be made 'promptly' and in any event within three months of the date on which the decision or action being challenged was taken (RSC Order 53, rule 4; Supreme Court Act 1981, s. 31(7)). This contrasts with a

---

6    *R v Panel on Take-overs and Mergers, ex p Guinness plc* [1990] 1 QB 146.
7    Sir Harry Woolf, *Protection of the Public* (above, note 2), Ch 1.

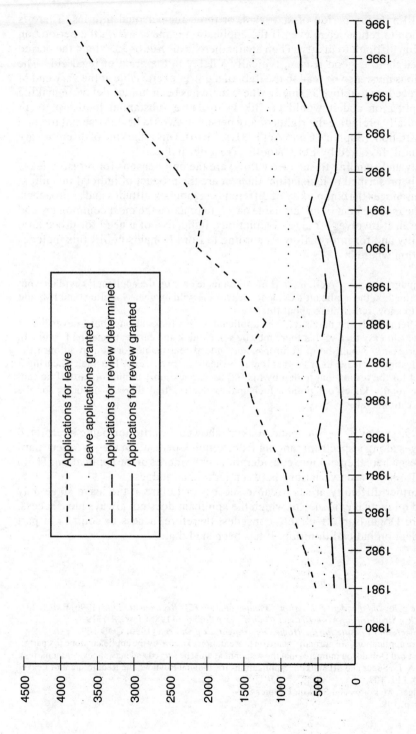

*Table 16.1: The Judicial Review Caseload 1981–1996*

*Source: Civil Judicial Statistics 1981–1985; Judicial Statistics 1986–1996.*

general limitation period of six years, or three for personal injuries. There is discretion to refuse leave even if the application is made *within* the period,[8] an exception difficult to justify. Then again, there is discretion to extend the period provided there is good reason, typically a delay in the grant of legal aid.[9] The provisions must also be read in the light of a power exercisable at the very end of AJR procedure to refuse a remedy where there has been 'undue delay' in making the application and it would be 'likely to cause substantial hardship to, or substantially prejudice the rights of any person, or would be detrimental to good administration' (Supreme Court Act 1981, s. 31(6)). This is the kind of discretionary 'safeguard' favoured by Lord Woolf. 'Trust our judges.'

Delay and standing to sue (see below) are the only reasons for refusing leave formally prescribed in legislation: the rest are the product of judicial invention. This introduces the complexity of difference in judicial attitudes and approaches. Take the requirement of an 'arguable case', in practice the most common ground of refusal. It involves a range of situations, indicative of a need for procedural flexibility and for information. According to Lord Donaldson MR this includes a situation where:[10]

> the judge may say, 'Well, there is no prima facie case on the applicant's evidence but nevertheless, the applicant's evidence leaves me with an uneasy feeling, and I should like to know rather more about this.'
>
> Alternatively, he may say, 'The applicant's case looks strong, but I nevertheless have an uneasy feeling that there may be some quick and easy explanation for this. In either case it would be quite proper and indeed reasonable for him to adjourn the application for leave in order that it may be heard *inter partes.*[[11]] At such a hearing it is not for the respondent to deploy his full case, but simply to put forward, if he can, some totally knock-out point which makes it clear that there is no basis for the application at all.

A 1992 survey by Le Sueur and Sunkin[12] showed the criterion being interpreted by judges along a spectrum ranging from a 'quick perusal' to the so-called 'hard look' test where there is more consideration of the merits of the application. There have also been wide variations between individual judges.[13]

A further difficulty arises because success or failure at the leave stage may depend on factual evidence to which the applicant does not always have access. As Lord Donaldson effectively concedes, therefore, access to court is in part dependent on judicial intuition. It has been said that:[14]

---

8  See e.g. *R v Independent Television Commission, ex p TSW Broadcasting Ltd* [1996] EMLR 291.
9  See *R v Stratford-on-Avon District Council, ex p Jackson* [1985] 1 WLR 1319.
10  *R v Secretary of State for the Home Department, ex p Doorga* [1990] COD 109.
11  Leave applications are normally heard on presentation of a case by the applicant alone (ex parte); here Lord Donaldson indicates that the respondent must be served and may appear (inter partes).
12  See A. Le Sueur and M. Sunkin, 'Applications for Judicial Review: The Requirement of Leave' [1992] PL 102.
13  Bridges, Meszaros and Sunkin, Chapter 8.
14  Ibid, p. 199.

good applications may be summarily refused access to the courts. Where this occurs, it causes injustice and it also has broader societal implications. It means, for example, that governmental illegality may go unchallenged, that standards of public administration may not be maintained, and that legal principle may not develop. For these reasons it is vital that the filter operates, and is seen to operate, fairly and consistently.

The number of leave applications has increased sevenfold over a 15-year period: those successful have roughly trebled (Table 16.1). One explanation for the discrepancy is judicial managerialism. Attitudes harden as pressure of work increases, resulting in what Gordon[15] has called 'ratcheting up'. This may be particularly the case where large numbers of similar applications are received. In *Puhlhofer v Hillingdon London Borough Council*[16] Lord Brightman ratcheted up the leave requirement to 'a very hard look', expressing his concern at 'the prolific use of judicial review for the purpose of challenging the performance by local authorities of their functions under the [Housing (Homeless Persons)] Act of 1977'. He expressed the hope that there would be 'a lessening in the number of challenges mounted against local authorities who are endeavouring in extremely difficult circumstances to perform their duty under the Homeless Persons Act, with due regard for all their other problems'. Was this powerful assertion of public interest really a piece of judicial gate-keeping? The homelessness case load fell from 66 applications for leave in 1985 to 32 in 1986, before rising again.

This form of rationing ties into the rule, also operated at the leave stage, against permitting judicial review where an alternative remedy is available. This rule is uncertain in its application. It has been targeted on statutory procedures, but may be disapplied if the court considers the alternative remedy inadequate.[17] No case better illustrates the competing demands of effective redress and regulation of the case flow than *R v Secretary of State for the Home Department, ex p Swati*.[18] A foreign visitor was refused admission at the port of entry. Under the statutory procedure, the so-called 'truncated appeal', he could appeal to a tribunal only from abroad (Immigration Act 1971, s. 13(3)). This hardly constituted effective redress of grievance. A practice developed in visitor cases of seeking judicial review: so much so that, by 1985, visitor cases accounted for over 20% of all leave applications in civil judicial review cases.[19] The Court of Appeal took action in *Swati* to halt this practice, even though the alternative procedure was unrealistic. Sir John Donaldson MR said:

> It is well established that in giving or refusing leave to apply for judicial review, account must be taken of alternative remedies available to the applicant ... the jurisdiction would not be exercised where there was an alternative remedy by way of appeal, save in exceptional circumstances. By definition, exceptional circumstances

---

15  R. Gordon, 'The Law Commission and Judicial Review: Managing the Tensions Between Case Management and Public Interest Challenges' [1995] PL 11.

16  [1986] AC 484.

17  *R v Chief Constable of the Merseyside Police, ex p Calveley* [1986] QB 424. See C. Lewis, 'The Exhaustion of Alternative Remedies in Administrative Law' (1992) 51 CLJ 138.

18  [1986] 1 WLR 477.

19  M. Sunkin, 'What Is Happening To Applications For Judicial Review?' (1987) 50 MLR 432 at 445–446.

defy definition, but where Parliament provides an appeal procedure, judicial review will have no place, unless the application can distinguish his case from the type of case for which the appeal procedure was provided.

The applicant may have no basis for complaint at being refused leave to enter. He may have cause to complain that the immigration officer erred in her assessment...we simply have no idea which is the case. All these matters will be open on a statutory appeal, but only the latter could form the basis of a judicial review...the applicant's case is wholly indistinguishable from the general run of cases where someone arrives in the United Kingdom and is dissatisfied because he is denied leave to enter. Accordingly, in my judgment, he should not be allowed to pursue it by way of judicial review.

Lord Woolf, pursuing the quest for a pyramidal framework for redress of grievance (Chapter 12), favours general expansion of the rule. According to *Access to Justice*, his report to the Lord Chancellor on the civil justice system, applicants for judicial review:[20]

> should be encouraged to resolve their complaints without resorting to litigation. There is an increasing number of grievance procedures and ombudsmen available for this purpose ... Before an application is made to initiate proceedings for judicial review, the proposed applicant should have taken advantage of any system of dispute resolution available, unless it would be unreasonable to do so.

Little is said of the problems stemming from the rigidity of such a framework. Remember the parallel development of tiers of complaint procedures. Is the convenience of those operating the machinery being prioritised at the expense of persons aggrieved? What happens when the alternative remedy proves to be inadequate? Judicial review time limits could be extended while the potential applicant investigates ADR. But persons driven to litigation are unlikely to see the system as providing speedy and effective redress of grievance.

It has been suggested[1] that the leave requirement be abolished. Many other jurisdictions, including Scotland, manage without it, so why not England and Wales? The judicial fear of opening a floodgate makes such a solution exceedingly unlikely. If, however, leave is to be used as part of a coherent strategy of case management, alongside rules on alternative remedies, then this ought to be openly stated, either in a revision of Order 53 or through a Practice Direction. In this, as in other areas of public administration, discretion should be structured by guidance or simple rules.

## 2. Litigants and litigation

Judicial review litigation is mostly about immigration, homelessness and crime (see Table 16.2) and this has been consistently the case throughout the 1980s and

20 Lord Woolf, *Access to Justice: The Final Report to the Lord Chancellor on the Civil Justice System in England and Wales* (London: HMSO) 1997, p. 251.
1 *Justice*/All Souls, *Administrative Justice. Some Necessary Reforms* (Oxford: Clarendon) 1988, pp. 153–154.

1990s.[2] To make the point differently, the major expansion of the judicial caseload in recent years is largely attributable to certain core areas of litigation. Take, for example, the 1995 statistics, which show an increase of 12% in leave applications over the previous year. This is largely accounted for by immigration. This fact is sufficient in itself to cast doubt on theories which see judicial review as a major control on maladministration. It also calls for explanation, which in part lies in the perceived inadequacies of the appeal procedures, especially in asylum cases.[3] Outside the core areas of housing, immigration and criminal cases, judicial review litigation is extremely diverse, lending credence once more to de Smith's description.

Of course statistics only tell part of the story. They cannot measure the 'ripple' effect of one decision on, perhaps, thousands of similar cases: a familiar premise of the test case. The mere existence of judicial review and the creation of precedent may influence future administrative behaviour: the fire-watching function. And it would be naive to argue, for example, that just because there are more tribunal cases, judicial review is of less significance. The courts, with their high prestige and backed by a powerful profession and significant media interest, possess an influence disproportionate to their caseload. Again, litigation has radiating effects, underpinning negotiation 'in the shadow of the law' in multiple venues outside the courts.[4]

Statistics may also mislead because they are incomplete. We need to bear in mind here that the High Court exercises jurisdiction also through appeals on a point of law[5] and actions in contract and tort. By any standards, however, judicial review procedure is, as grievance machinery, under-used and its potential undeveloped. Large swathes of public administration are untouched by the iron hand of the court. Each year only a few hundred cases result in court orders against the administration (Table 16.1); an infinitesimal number compared with the millions of decisions taken daily by public authorities and small beer compared with the caseload of other machinery for redress of grievance: tribunals (above, p. 457) or Ombudsmen, let alone the internal procedures brought to prominence under the Citizen's Charter (Chapter 12). Why, we are entitled to ask, does this not provoke the chorus of concern and criticism directed at under-use of the PCA (above, p. 429)?

A further point of interest emerges from the statistics: the majority of applications in the name of legally-aided individuals. Litigants in person also appear in significant numbers, though predictably with much less success.[6] On the other hand, both the arrangements for legal aid and requirements of standing have operated to conceal a broader range of applicants, tempting or forcing collective

---

2   See, for details, M Sunkin, 'What is Happening to Applications for Judicial Review?' (above, note 19) and 'The Judicial Review Case-load 1987–1989' [1991] PL 490; and Bridges, Meszaros and Sunkin, Chapter 2.

3   Justice, *Providing protection: towards fair and effective asylum procedures* (London) 1997.

4   See, M. Galanter, 'The Radiating Effects of Courts' in K. Boyum and L. Mather (eds.), *Empirical Theories of Courts* 1983; R. Rawlings, 'Courts and Interests' in I. Loveland (ed.), *A Special Relationship? American Influences on Public Law* (Oxford: Clarendon) 1995.

5   On which see Law Commission, *Administrative Law: Judicial Review and Statutory Appeals* (Report No. 226) 1994, Part XII (hereafer Law Commission No. 226).

6   See, for details, Bridges, Meszaros and Sunkin, Chapter 3.

*Table 16.2: Leave Applications by Subject-Area, 1994–1996*

| | 1994 | | | 1995 | | | 1996 | | |
|---|---|---|---|---|---|---|---|---|---|
| | *Received* | *Allowed* | *Refused/ Withdrawn** | *Received* | *Allowed* | *Refused/ Withdrawn** | *Received* | *Allowed* | *Refused/ Withdrawn** |
| Immigration | 935 | 162 | 723 | 1,220 | 258 | 722 | 1,748 | 301 | 1,012 |
| Homelessness | 447 | 265 | 231 | 417 | 193 | 174 | 340 | 144 | 199 |
| Criminal | 321 | 193 | 323 | 321 | 130 | 214 | 297 | 121 | 183 |
| Other | 1,505 | 640 | 852 | 1,646 | 812 | 896 | 1,516 | 691 | 822 |
| TOTAL | 3,208 | 1,260 | 2,129 | 3,604 | 1,393 | 2,006 | 3,901 | 1,257 | 2,206 |

Source: Lord Chancellor's Department, *Judicial Statistics*
* This figure includes applications refused but not renewed and applications withdrawn or otherwise not proceeded with at this stage.

interests to litigate in the name of individuals. There is further an increasing practice of judicial review cases brought expressly in the name of non-individual applicants.

The resolution of differences between public bodies has, for example, become an increasingly important function for the courts. The 1980s witnessed a whole series of legal battles between central and local government.[7] Again, judicial review is becoming a recognised avenue for pressure group action.[8] It would be strange if it were otherwise, given the close interest of many groups in the practical application of government policies; and, further, the opportunities for lobbying provided by courts as a surrogate political process. This development does something to balance the superior skill of government lawyers as 'repeat players'.[9] Then there are powerful business interests, as also trade unions, well able to afford the best legal advice. Their involvement in judicial review is not novel: see *Burmah Oil*[10] and *GCHQ*.[11] 'Commercial judicial review' has recently become a recognisable field,[12] reflecting and reinforcing the juridification of regulatory relations (Chapter 10). Cases like *Datafin*[13] and *Mercury Communications*[14] spring readily to mind. Litigation of this kind seems far removed from the model of imbalance or 'strong state' versus 'weak individual', and it will surely expand in an era of Europeanisation and globalisation as, indeed, we have already seen with the *Factortame* saga.[15]

### Accessibility and outreach

Bottom-up studies of complaints-handling are, as we saw in Chapter 12, preoccupied with questions of accessibility and outreach. Judicial review has not as yet received much attention in these terms. The little we do know, however, suggests that it scores poorly.[16] Access to legal advice; costs, which in this country fall on the loser, making them hard to predict at the start of the case; and difficulties with legal aid, especially for group claims, all pose serious problems. In addition, solicitors may be badly informed and many use the system just as infrequently as MPs use the PCA. Law centres and CABx also use judicial review infrequently; this must make access highly problematic for the most disadvantaged sectors of the community.

7  As, for example, on matters of finance and delegated legislation: *R v Secretary of State for the Environment, ex p Brent London Borough Council* [1982] QB 593; *Nottinghamshire County Council v Secretary of State for the Environment* [1986] AC 240. See, for an overview, M. Loughlin, *Legality and Locality: The Role of Law in Central-Local Government Relations* (Oxford: Clarendon) 1996.

8  C. Harlow and R. Rawlings, *Pressure Through Law* (London: Routledge) 1992, pp. 137–154.

9  See M. Galanter, 'Why the "Haves" Come out Ahead: Speculations on the Limits of Legal Change' (1974) 9 Law and Society Rev. 95.

10  Above, p. 47.

11  Above, p. 113.

12  As indicated by the start of the *Commercial Judicial Review Bulletin*, vol. 1, 1994.

13  Above, p. 344.

14  Above, p. 369.

15  Above, p. 170.

16  A theme developed in C. Harlow, 'Why Public Law is Private Law: An Invitation to Lord Woolf' in A. Zuckerman and R. Cranston (eds.), *Reform of Civil Procedure* (Oxford: Clarendon) 1995.

Judicial review is too centralised, being focused on the High Court in London.[17] Legal aid is hard to get and awards may be inconsistent; there are known to be wide disparities between areas.[18] All these factors operate to turn judicial review into something of a lottery, and not the 'cutting edge' envisaged by proponents of the control theory. According to solicitor Stephen Grosz, writing about environmental litigation, the position of groups, in the absence of specific rules covering 'public interest' cases, is particularly hard. Here he refers to a common practice among pressure groups of using a legally aided individual as a 'front man' for a test case:[19]

> Whilst it may be wrong to set up only applicants ... who are financially eligible for legal aid, it also seems wrong that, where there is a mixed group, those who are entitled to legal aid should not have it and should effectively be funded out of the pockets of those who are slightly better off.
>
> The present system...places a great burden of fund-raising on such groups. However, the courts take little notice of this. For example, in the *Oxleas Wood* case,[20] the Department of Transport applied to expedite the hearing of the appeal to the Court of Appeal. The appellants countered that they needed time to raise funds for the appeal, but this contention was rejected, on the basis that parties must come to court with the means to pursue the litigation ...
>
> In practice, our ... public law [system fails] to recognise or take account of the distorting effects of legal costs ... The cost of litigation and the risk of losing are the most serious barriers to fair and effective environmental litigation.

The problem has so far been only touched on, with a Law Commission recommendation that, where a 'public interest challenge' is allowed to proceed to a substantive hearing, costs should be awarded at judicial discretion from central funds.[1] Legal aid, meanwhile, is under the butcher's knife and, while the AJR is not directly affected, a gush of new funding is unlikely.

### 3. Opening the gates: the public interest model

With all these factors pointing to limited outreach, and sometimes to deliberate limitation, it is particularly striking to find the gradual emergence of a model of judicial review designed to fit so-called 'public interest challenges'. The first signs of the development are to be observed in a changed law of standing to sue.

---

17  Limited reforms are proposed by Lord Woolf, *Access to Justice: The Final Report to the Lord Chancellor on the Civil Justice System in England and Wales* (London: HMSO) 1996.

18  See L. Bridges, 'Costs and Obtaining Legal Aid' in Public Law Project, *An Applicant's Guide to Judicial Review* (London: Sweet and Maxwell) 1995; Bridges, Meszaros and Sunkin, Chapter 5.

19  S. Grosz, 'Access to Environmental Justice in Public Law' in D. Robinson and J. Dunkley (eds.), *Public Interest Perspectives in Environmental Law* (London: Wiley Chancery Publishing) 1995, pp. 205-206.

20  *Greenwich London Borough Council and Yates v Secretary of State for Transport* (19 February 1993, unreported)

1  Law Commission No. 226, Part X.

## (a) Standing to sue: theory and practice

Standing functions as a rationing device by requiring potential litigants to demonstrate some particular 'interest' in the matter in question, over and above that of the general public. It was traditionally seen as a separate issue or threshold requirement, raising directly the right to apply for a remedy; latterly, it has been linked more closely to the merits of the case and the grant of remedies (below). A contrast can be drawn with the action in damages where 'right' and 'remedy' are treated as part of the same issue and the right to bring an action is indirectly restricted (Chapter 18).

The notion of an 'interest' is obviously complex. A wide variety of individuals and organisations may subjectively feel themselves 'affected' by an administrative decision. Suppose that a local authority decides to increase its subsidy to the city's public transport system. As a result, fares fall but local taxes increase (the *Bromley* case[2]). Who might be said to have an interest in this decision? One answer might be, 'local taxpayers and users of public transport', but they are not necessarily the only groups. One person may be able to assert a variety of interests. An employer may be a taxpayer or a member of an environmental group; a taxpayer may oppose the decision because he lives in the inner city or because he is offended by urban deprivation.

Stewart[3] has distinguished 'material interests' which concern an individual's economic or physical well-being, from 'ideological interests' which include the affirmation of moral principles. If the classification is applied to our example, the open-ended nature of 'material interest' becomes apparent. A restrictive interpretation might confine decisions concerning an individual's 'well-being' to those which cause direct financial loss. If, however, the notion encompasses non-pecuniary detriment, where is the line to be drawn? The significance of standing to sue becomes apparent; it has been used by courts to select from the variety of possible interests those which they will protect. And, naturally, at different times different judges have been prepared to protect different interests.

The approach up until the 1970s was essentially two-pronged. First, applicants were required to show a private interest which had been directly adversely affected, reflecting and reinforcing the view that the primary function of judicial review is protection of the individual. For example, in *Gregory v Camden London Borough Council,*[4] the plaintiff sought to challenge a decision to build a school close by his property; the judge accepted that the decision was unlawful, but denied the plaintiff standing to obtain a declaration on the ground that his legal rights as land owner had not been infringed. Second, it was the Attorney-General who represented the 'public interest' before the courts and possessed public advocacy functions, having automatic standing to initiate or intervene in litigation. The 'relator action' allowed the Attorney to authorise a private party to litigate, acting in the name of the Attorney-General. The Attorney's powers then served as a reason why individuals could vindicate only personal, material interests; the public interest, it was said, had been entrusted by the electorate to the government

2   Below, p. 585.
3   R. Stewart, 'The Reformation of American Administrative Law' (1975) 88 Harv. LR 1667.
4   [1966] 1WLR 899. The dominant test for the prerogative orders was a 'person aggrieved'.

and was therefore appropriately represented in the courts by the chief Law Officer of the Crown who was directly accountable to Parliament.[5]

Following the reinvigoration of the grounds of review in cases like *Padfield*,[6] criticism of this procedural model became intense. Restrictive rules of standing contradict the idea, associated with amber light theory, of a general responsibility on the courts to control the abuse of legal power. It is seen as preferable, in Sir Konrad Schiemann's words,[7] that 'an illegality should continue than that the person excluded should have access to the courts'. The twin-pronged approach was decidedly non-pluralist in character, and thus contradicted the emergent idea in administrative law of interest representation (above, p. 107).

A liberalising trend developed, largely under the influence of Lord Denning.[8] Inspiration for change also came from the United States, where the Supreme Court had opened up the judicial system to a broad spectrum of interests and had gone some way to recognising direct standing for groups.[9] When AJR procedure was introduced in 1978, an American-style test of 'sufficient interest' was included on the advice of the Law Commission, concerned not to fetter judicial discretion; the formula was chosen because it 'allows for further development of the requirement of standing by the courts having regard to the remedy which is sought'.[10] This is reflected in the statutory provision which now contains the test (Supreme Court Act 1981, s. 31(3)). The test is mandatory: the court shall not grant leave unless it considers that 'the applicant has a sufficient interest in the matter to which the application relates'. But what is a 'sufficient interest'? Narrowly construed it could mean financial or legal interest; generously, it could comprise Stewart's intangible interest. The statutory formula contains no guidance concerning the relevant criteria and purpose of standing. In the event, in what is still the leading case, the House of Lords took the opportunity to re-write the law on standing.

### *IRC v National Federation of Self Employed and Small Businesses*[11]

The Federation wanted to challenge a tax amnesty negotiated between the Revenue and interested trade unions and granted to certain part-time workers in the newspaper industry. The group expressed the view that these people were being given preferential treatment over other taxpayers because the print unions could threaten industrial action. It was contended that the Federation lacked standing to launch the litigation. The House of Lords disagreed and recommended a relaxed approach to standing at the leave stage. In the event,

---

5   J. Edwards, *The Attorney-General, Politics and the Public Interest* (London: Sweet and Maxwell) 1984. And see *Gouriet v Union of Post Office Workers* [1978] AC 435.
6   Above, p. 98.
7   Sir K. Schiemann, 'Locus Standi' [1990] PL 342.
8   E.g. *R v Greater London Council, ex p Blackburn* [1976] 1 WLR 550; *A-G (ex rel McWhirter) v Independent Broadcasting Authority* [1973] QB 629.
9   See, especially, *Sierra Club v Morton* 405 US 727 (1972); *United States v Students Challenging Regulatory Agency Procedures* 412 US 669 (1973).
10   Law Commission, *Report on Remedies in Administrative Law*, Law Com. No. 73, Cmnd. 6407 (1976), para. 48.
11   [1982] AC 617.

the legality of the amnesty was upheld. The following speech has proved particularly influential:

> *Lord Diplock*: [The purpose of the leave stage] is to prevent the time of the court being wasted by busybodies with misguided or trivial complaints of administrative error, and to remove the uncertainty in which public officers and authorities might be left whether they could safely proceed with administrative action while proceedings for judicial review of it were actually pending even though misconceived ...
>
> At the threshold stage, for the federation to make out a prima facie case of reasonable suspicion that the Board in showing a discriminatory leniency to a substantial class of taxpayers had done so for ulterior reasons extraneous to good management, and thereby deprived the national exchequer of considerable sums of money, constituted what was in my view reason enough for the Divisional Court to consider that the federation, or for that matter, any taxpayer, had a sufficient interest to apply to have the question whether the Board were acting ultra vires reviewed by the court. The whole purpose of requiring that leave should first be obtained to make the application for judicial review would be defeated if the court were to go into the matter in any depth at that stage. If, on a quick perusal of the material then available, the court thinks that it discloses what might on further consideration turn out to be an arguable case in favour of granting to the applicant the relief claimed, it ought, in the exercise of a judicial discretion, to give him leave to apply for that relief ...
>
> If, in the instant case, what at the threshold stage was suspicion only had been proved at the hearing of the application for judicial review to have been true in fact (instead of being utterly destroyed), I would have held that this was a matter in which the federation had a sufficient interest in obtaining an appropriate order, whether by way of declaration or mandamus, to require performance by the Board of statutory duties which for reasons shown to be ultra vires they were failing to perform.
>
> It would, in my view, be a grave lacuna in our system of public law if a pressure group, like the federation, or even a single public spirited taxpayer, were prevented by outdated technical rules of locus standi from bringing the matter to the attention of the court to vindicate the rule of law and get the unlawful conduct stopped. The Attorney General, although he occasionally applies for prerogative orders against public authorities that do not form part of central government, in practice never does so against government departments. It is not, in my view, a sufficient answer to say that judicial review of the actions of officers or departments of central government is unnecessary because they are accountable to Parliament for the way in which they carry out their functions. They are accountable to Parliament for what they do so far as regards efficiency and policy, and of that Parliament is the only judge; they are responsible to a court of justice for the lawfulness of what they do, and of that the court is the only judge.

The *Federation* case is an important mile-stone in the development of a model of judicial review which can encompass the public interest in administrative legality. Or, as Sir Konrad Schiemann prefers,[12] a shift away from a 'closed' system, where only a person with private legal rights can take action, towards an 'open' system, where anyone can challenge anything claimed to be unlawful. The latter is the pure 'citizen action', the ideal-type of a pluralist system of law enforcement, as operated by 'private Attorneys-General'. The *Federation* case stands for a

---

12  Sir K. Schiemann, 'Locus Standi' (above, note 7) p. 346.

weakened version of this, representing a judicial willingness to consider some, but not all, instances of administrative illegality.

One consequence of the case is that relator actions in judicial review have withered on the vine. Ministerial discretion is no longer a key component of the process. Another consequence is increased judicial discretion, with less emphasis on 'rules' of standing as laid down in precedent. A central element here is a shift in the timing of the consideration of standing. To reiterate, it was classically treated as a preliminary issue: as the statute contemplates. Now, Lord Wilberforce explained, it would permeate and be permeated by questions of substance and remedy:

> There may be simple cases in which it can be seen at the earliest stage that the person applying for judicial review has no interest at all, or no sufficient interest to support the application; then it would be quite correct at the threshold to refuse him leave to apply...but in other cases this will not be so. In these, it will be necessary to consider the powers or the duties in law of those against whom the relief is asked, the position of the applicant in relation to those powers or duties, and the breach of those said to have been committed. In other words, the question of sufficient interest cannot, in such cases, be considered in the abstract, or as an isolated point: it must be taken together with the legal and factual context. The rule requires sufficient interest *in the matter to which the application relates*.

Issues of standing may therefore be raised both at the beginning and the end of AJR procedure (like those of delay (above, page 534)). At the second stage, Lord Donaldson has explained,[13] 'the strength of the applicant's interest is one of the factors to be weighed in the balance'. Cane said of the *Federation* case:[14]

> It has turned the question of standing very largely into a matter of fact and discretion. The question of legality is a question of fact which must be decided from case to case. It is very difficult to make reliable concrete statements about the content of the vague formulae in which most of the law of *ultra vires* is couched. The law of natural justice is all a matter of fairness in the light of all the facts of the case [and] the vague, fact-relative standard of 'unreasonableness' lies at the bottom of review of the exercise of discretionary powers and of decisions on questions of fact ...
>
> The retreat from rules to facts which the *National Federation* case illustrates...can be taken too far. Even if it achieves nothing else, the discipline of justifying decisions in terms of rules forces courts to measure the consistency inter se of their decisions against a pre-announced bench mark. Decisions on the facts cannot be cross-checked in this way; the result, at the least, is a considerable measure of uncertainty in the law, and at the worst, a feeling that apparently inconsistent decisions are explicable in terms of unexpressed and undesirable value judgments.

Later case law has generally maintained the liberal trend. In one case, a journalist was given standing as 'public-spirited citizen' and 'guardian of the public interest in ... open justice' to challenge a decision of local justices that they should have anonymity.[15] In another, a dissident peer was allowed 'because of his

13  In *R v Monopolies and Mergers Commission, ex p Argyll Group plc* (below, p.563).
14  P. Cane, 'Standing, Legality and the Limits of Public Law' [1981] PL 322, pp 335– 336.
15  *R v Felixstowe Justices, ex p Leigh* [1987] QB 582.

sincere concern for constitutional issues' to challenge the government's decision to ratify the Maastricht Treaty on European Union.[16] In a parallel development, public advocacy functions have been granted to many public bodies along the lines of those given to local authorities under s. 222 of the Local Government Act 1972 to take legal action including judicial review proceedings in the interests of their inhabitants. Among statutory agencies, the EOC has been given broad rein in judicial review cases. *R v Secretary of State for Employment, ex p EOC and Day*[17] was an important test case in which the House of Lords granted declarations that statutory limitations on employment rights were incompatible with EC anti-discrimination laws. In Lord Keith's words, it would be 'a very retrograde step now to hold that the EOC has no locus standi to agitate in judicial review proceedings questions related to sex discrimination which are of public importance and affect a large section of the population'. Here we have an example of a body which was not itself affected by the relevant legislation being able to challenge by way of judicial review, although the individual (Mrs Day) who was affected was held unable to proceed. Her claim was said by the House of Lords to be essentially a claim in private law which had to be brought in an industrial tribunal, an invocation of the rule about alternative remedies discussed above. Nothing better illustrates the contemporary shift in judicial review procedure from the objective of protecting the individual towards more elite 'public interest challenges'. Not only red light theorists will be dismayed by this prospect.

## (b) Representative proceedings

Much of the action has involved claims to standing by pressure groups in so-called 'representative proceedings'.[18] In the *Federation* case the group was an 'associational plaintiff', claiming to take action on behalf of its members. However, nothing turned on this. The Federation was accepted to be in no better position to obtain access to court by reason of being a collectivity; in the words of Lord Wilberforce, 'an aggregate of individuals each of whom has no interest cannot of itself have an interest'. In other cases, the group will be a 'surrogate plaintiff', claiming to represent the interests of other people. The issue is sharply posed of adequacy of representation. Does the applicant properly represent the interests of those who are adversely affected? What happens when the view of the 'public interest' presented is hotly contested? Let us look at some examples.

Founded in 1965, the Child Poverty Action Group (CPAG) campaigns to improve the lot of poor families. It is an initiator and promoter of litigation rather than merely an advocate for aggrieved individuals. As such, it has long experience of the problems of using 'frontmen' to manoeuvre inside individualistic procedures in the bringing of test cases. Disadvantaged people, faced by the long wait while the legal system produces a precedent, may be more easily bought-off by

---

16  *R v Secretary of State for Foreign and Commonwealth Affairs, ex p Rees-Mogg* [1994] 1 All ER 457.
17  [1994] 2 WLR 409.
18  See C. Harlow and R. Rawlings, *Pressure Through Law* (above, p. 539, note 8), pp. 148–151; also P. Cane, 'Standing up for the Public' [1995] PL 376.

settlement, so killing an action. In the 1980s, CPAG constructed two challenges which tested the judicial attitude to surrogate plaintiffs.

The first case[19] presented representative proceedings in a most favourable light. Large numbers of unidentified claimants were unaware of their rights; had any single individual made a claim, this would have been met; in effect, there would otherwise be immunity from suit. Yet audit had revealed serious error in the assessment of deductions, raising the prospect of back payments by the department. However, the department baulked at the idea of re-opening some 15 million files of claimants who had ceased to claim. These were reckoned to include 16,000 cases of wrongful deduction, totalling £440,000: a figure which would be dwarfed by the cost and disruption of a search operation. CPAG considered that advertising campaigns were not sufficient, and sought a declaration that the department was under a continuing duty to identify those claimants who had suffered a legal wrong. The case failed on the merits but standing was granted. Woolf J said that CPAG was:

> Very much a body designed to represent the interests of the unidentified claimants who stand to be deprived by the decision taken by the Secretary of State ... The Child Poverty Action Group, being the organisation designed to serve their interests in matters of this sort, has sufficient interest.

The challenge in the second case[20] was very wide-ranging, exception being taken to the delays experienced by many people in the handling of supplementary benefit claims. In effect, it was the organisation and staffing of the department which was being attacked, on the basis of a breach of duty in meeting claims within statutory time limits. At first instance, the department was allowed to waive the standing requirement: the Court of Appeal disapproved, correctly pointing out that it goes to the jurisdiction of the court. Woolf LJ further indicated a relaxed approach to representative proceedings, without giving a definitive ruling. The issues raised were 'not ones which individual claimants for supplementary benefit could be expected to raise'; CPAG was a 'prominent' champion of such claimants.

A single case, *R v Secretary of State for the Environment, ex p Rose Theatre Trust Co,*[1] demonstrates a different judicial attitude. The remains of the Elizabethan Rose Theatre were discovered in the course of construction work. Pressure was put on the Minister to schedule the site under the Ancient Monuments and Archaeological Areas Act 1979 but he declined to do so. Actors, archaeologists and residents came together in a litigation coalition and formed a company which sought judicial review. Standing was refused on the basis, consistent with the *Federation* case, that the collectivity had no greater interest than individual members. Schiemann J held that this was 'one of those governmental decisions in respect of which the ordinary citizen does not have a sufficient interest to entitle him to obtain leave to apply for judicial review'. Further, it was not the function of the courts 'to be there for every

---

19  *R v Secretary of State for Social Services, ex p Child Poverty Action Group and GLC* (1984) Times 16 August.
20  *R v Secretary of State for Social Services, ex p Child Poverty Action Group* [1990] 2 QB 540.
 1  [1990] 1 QB 504.

individual who is interested in having the legality of an administrative action litigated'. Note the gap that this implies in the model of control of abuse of legal power: decisions affecting everyone equally and no one in particular are effectively immune from challenge by judicial review, a point to which we return in Chapter 17. Note also the strong vested interest in representative proceedings. Pressure groups and their lawyers naturally prefer the discretion to litigate. Michael Beloff QC[2] refers to the 'Canute-like stand' of Schiemann J 'against the tide'; an impression strengthened by the following case.

## *R v Inspectorate of Pollution, ex p Greenpeace (No 2)*[3]

Greenpeace challenged the decision to allow British Nuclear Fuels (BNFL) to test its new thermal oxide reprocessing plant (THORP) at Sellafield in Cumbria. The group claimed to represent: (a) as an associational plaintiff, 2,500 local members who were concerned about the health risks associated with radioactive pollution; and (b) the wider public interest in preventing such pollution. The challenge failed on its merits but the judge confirmed that Greenpeace had standing to bring the proceedings:

> *Otton J*: I approach this matter primarily as one of discretion. I consider it appropriate to take into account the nature of Greenpeace and the extent of its interest in the issues raised, the remedy Greenpeace seeks to achieve and the nature of the relief sought ...
>
> Greenpeace is an entirely responsible and respected body with a genuine concern for the environment. That concern naturally leads to a bona fide interest in the activities carried on by BNFL at Sellafield and in particular the discharge and disposal of radioactive waste from its premises...The fact that there are 400,000 supporters in the United Kingdom carries less weight than the fact that 2,500 of them come from the Cumbria region. I would be ignoring the blindingly obvious if I were to disregard the fact that those persons are inevitably concerned about (and have a genuine perception that there is) a danger to their health and safety from any additional discharge of radioactive waste even from testing. I have no doubt that the issues raised by this application are serious and worthy of determination by this court.
>
> It seems to me that if I were to deny standing to Greenpeace, those it represents might not have an effective way to bring the issues before the court. There would have to be an application either by an individual employee of BNFL or a near neighbour. In this case it is unlikely that either would be able to command the expertise which is at the disposal of Greenpeace. Consequently, a less well-informed challenge might be mounted which would stretch unnecessarily the court's resources and which would not afford the court the assistance it requires in order to do justice between the parties. Further, if the unsuccessful applicant had the benefit of legal aid it might leave the respondents and BNFL without an effective remedy in costs ... Greenpeace ... with its particular experience in environmental matters, its access to experts in the relevant realms of science and technology (not to mention the law) is able to mount a carefully selected, focused, relevant and well-argued challenge ... I reject the argument that Greenpeace is a 'mere' or 'meddlesome busy body'. ... Its genuine interest in the issues raised is sufficient for it to be granted locus standi.

This is the kind of reasoning which sends a strong positive signal concerning collective forms of participation in the legal process.[4] Note the different kinds of factors identified as helpful to Greenpeace: seriousness of the issue, local or personal interest (said to differentiate the *Rose Theatre* case), character of the group. There is a strong functional element: the idea that interest representation is more efficient and effective for the court than individual proceedings. Values of pluralism are harnessed in the judicial service.

For what is the case authority? In the words of Otton J, 'it must not be assumed that Greenpeace (or any other interest group) will automatically be afforded standing in any subsequent application for judicial review in whatever field it (and its members) may have an interest. This will have to be a matter to be considered on a case by case basis at the leave stage and if the threshold is crossed again at the substantive hearing as a matter of discretion'. In this line of cases the courts are seen groping towards, but never clearly articulating, a theory of representative proceedings. Take the stress on Greenpeace as 'an entirely responsible and respected body'. It was not always thus: campaigning in the 1980s to raise the profile of environmental issues, Greenpeace had been castigated by the courts on several occasions for the tactics of disruption, notably against the plant at Sellafield.[5] And what will happen when a group which is not 'eminently respectable and responsible' seeks representative status? On one view,[6] there should be some kind of democratic audit by the judiciary, designed to ensure that the views put forward are a fair reflection of those the body claims to represent. This is an unhappy prospect and one which surely puts the court over the boundary between the legal and political process. The lesser test[7] that 'the legal claims being asserted are representative of those that arise from the challenged action' has considerable merit in judicial proceedings. To emphasise, while some circumstances may be thought compelling, on other occasions we could anticipate anxious scrutiny of a claim to representative status. This is an issue which will not go away. We shall leave it here, to pick it up in Chapter 17.

### (c) Standing: the field of choice

Standing has been treated in this book as one aspect of a broader question of access, its practical importance increasingly limited. So why not end this form of rationing? The answer, Cranston explains, lies in a mix of public and private interests:[8]

---

4   R. Rawlings, 'Courts and Interests' in I. Loveland (ed.), *A Special Relationship? American Influences on Public Law in the UK* (Oxford: Clarendon) 1995, p. 104. And see the case of the Pergau Dam, below p.591.

5   *British Nuclear Fuels Ltd v Greenpeace* (25 March 1986, unreported); *British Nuclear Fuels Ltd v Stichting Sirius* (30 October 1987, unreported).

6   P. Cane, 'Standing, Representation, and the Environment' in I. Loveland (ed.), *A Special Relationship? American Influences on Public Law in the UK* (Oxford: Clarendon) 1995.

7   M. Sunkin, 'The Problematical State of Access to Judicial Review' in B. Hadfield (ed.), *Judicial Review: A Thematic Approach* (Dublin: Gill & Macmillan) 1995, p. 19.

8   R. Cranston, 'Reviewing Judicial Review' in G. Richardson and H. Genn (eds.) *Administrative Law and Government Action* (Oxford: Clarendon) 1994, pp. 59–61.

While the traditional floodgates argument is sometimes disparaged, it would seem to have at least some support in the recent increase in the number of cases where judicial review has been sought … Multiplying the instances in which decisions may be challenged must add some uncertainty to administration … A caution in decision-making would be a not unnatural result if there were many more opportunities for administrative arrangements and political balances to be upset …

If declaring an act or decision unlawful will affect a particular individual or group of individuals, and if none of them decides to challenge it, there is a heavy onus to discharge in arguing that someone more remote from the actual decision ought to be able to do so. A more liberal [approach] in this situation would undermine individual autonomy and expectations … Why if government has decided to act in a certain way in relation to a particular individual should someone else be able to seek judicial review of the decision? Why, for example, should the person cautioned rather than prosecuted suddenly find that someone else is taking the matter to court? Why, for example, should a person suddenly find that his or her tax assessment is challenged as legally invalid because it is too low? These are matters of principle which cannot simply be brushed aside.

The Law Commission[9] proposes a new twin-track system, designed to reflect and reinforce the liberal trend in the case law. The first track, where standing would normally be granted as a matter of course, would cover those 'personally adversely affected' by a decision (a formulation sufficiently wide to cover some cases of associational plaintiffs). The second would cover so-called 'public interest challenges', concerning issues affecting the public generally or a section of it. The test would be whether the High Court 'considers that it is in the public interest for an applicant to make the application'.

Discretion would be piled on discretion. There is a need for guidelines, designed both to encourage consistency and to build on existing case law. A Practice Statement on representative proceedings might refer to the following considerations:[10]

- The case raises an important point as to the use of public power by a public body (the *Federation* case).
- The applicant has special expertise or knowledge in the issue in question (the *Greenpeace* case).
- The applicant represents a section of the public which is generally affected by the decision sought to be challenged (the *CPAG* cases).
- The applicant has a statutory role in relation to the subject matter of the proposed challenge (the *EOC* case).
- The case may not be pursued or concluded by a directly affected individual applicant (the *CPAG* cases).

It should be borne in mind that the Commission's further proposal (above p 540) that 'public interest challenges' would at the discretion of the judge have

---

9 Law Commission No. 226, pp. 41–44.
10 See *Justice*/Public Law Project, *A Matter of Public Interest. Reforming the Law and Practice on Interventions in Public Interest Cases* (London) 1996, p. 13. The Law Commission specifically rejected the case for guidelines.

costs protection: from the government viewpoint, an open-ended call on the legal aid budget. An alternative would be a continental-style list of preferred applicants, whereby certain expert groups are licensed to bring representative proceedings.[11] More dirigiste, it raises basic issues of selection and may be said to offend important values of pluralism and equal treatment.

### (d)  Interventions: a constitutional discursus

In a complex process like judicial review, procedural changes are apt to produce knock-on effects elsewhere in the system. This is brilliantly illustrated in the case of standing. 'Once it is conceded that the public interest may be served by allowing direct challenges by public interest groups, that same interest may be advanced by allowing them to intervene in litigation between an individual and the state where the litigation raises important issues.'[12] Put another way, standing and intervention are facets of the same problem of access and need to be considered in tandem. The common factor is, however, the apparent widening of access.

As the instrument of interest representation, the third party '*amicus* brief' can serve different purposes:[13] (i) to mitigate the problem of adequacy of representation by allowing for the protection of interests that might otherwise be unrepresented in the litigation; (ii) to lobby the court by demonstrating a wide spectrum of support for a particular proposition; (iii) the informational or educative function, the court being presented by specialist bodies with materials unlikely to be gleaned in the adversarial, bipolar process. An important variant of the amicus brief developed in America is the so-called 'Brandeis brief', which combines conventional legal argument with socio-economic data and analysis.

Intervention, like standing to sue, is not simply a technical matter, but bears on the role and functions of the judiciary. What is in issue if the lobbying function becomes too blatant is the 'separate identity' of courts, the idea fundamental to the Rule of Law that the court's 'duty is not to respond to pressure but to decide according to principle'.[14] At another level, the informational function may enhance the legitimacy of judicial decision-making, and, further, encourage, and be designed to encourage, judicial assertiveness and creativity. To this effect, a study by *Justice* and the Public Law Project warns against an 'excessive enthusiasm' for public interest interventions:[15]

---

11  R. Tur, 'Litigation and the Consumer Interest; the class action and beyond' (1982) 2 Legal Studies 135.

12  S. Grosz, 'A Matter of Public Interest: A *Justice*/PLP Report' (1996) 1 Judicial Review 147, 150.

13  The amicus brief is widely used in the United States and Canada: see S. Krislov, 'The *Amicus Curiae Brief: From Friendship to Advocacy*' (1963) 72 Yale LJ 694; G. Caldeira and J. Wright, 'Organised Interests and Agenda-Setting in the US Supreme Court' (1988) 82 American Political Science Rev. 1109; P. Bryden, 'Public Interest Intervention in the Courts' (1987) 66 Canadian Bar Rev. 490.

14  *Justice*/Public Law Project *A Matter of Public Interest* (above, note 10), p. 25. And see C. Harlow and R. Rawlings, *Pressure Through Law* (above, p. 539, note 8), pp. 155–158.

15  *Justice*/Public Law Project, *A Matter of Public Interest*, p. 23.

Once the Court admits an intervener with a specialist factual brief, perhaps including research materials which may be of a contentious nature, it could be said that it is starting to move a significant distance from its conventional role as adjudicator of a dispute conducted on adversarial grounds ... a development of this kind may encourage the court to adopt something akin to a legislative function.

For example, cases where a public interest intervener is likely to take part will almost inevitably concern issues of policy: perhaps government policy, or the policy of the law itself set out in past jurisprudence. On its face the question will be whether the government's policy satisfies the traditional public law tests or, where the policy is of the court's making, whether it ought to be changed. The admission of refined factual arguments put forward by an intervener may tempt the court to take a more interventionist position in relation to the former, and a more radical or contentious position in relation to the latter, than it has traditionally occupied.

The classical model of adversarial, bipolar procedure was by definition antithetical to such interventions. Participation was restricted to an official amicus curiae, typically a legal representative of the Crown appointed at the request of the court to assist it with legal argument. Order 53 makes provision for intervention only where a party is 'directly affected' (a formula narrowly defined[16]) or where the court considers that a person who desires to be heard in *opposition* to an application is a 'proper person to be heard' (r 5(3), r 9(1)). The prevailing judicial attitude was demonstrated in the *cause célèbre* of *Gillick v West Norfolk and Wisbech Area Health Authority*.[17] Whereas Mrs Gillick was allowed to challenge the legality of contraceptive advice to young girls, although her own family was not affected, the Children's Legal Centre, which operates as an advocate for young people, was refused permission by the House of Lords to intervene in the litigation. The problem of adequacy of representation is obvious.

Once the classical model had been successfully challenged at the stage of standing to sue, pressure to allow interventions was bound to intensify. In recent years, the mould has been broken. Typically, the first bodies to make headway had official or semi-official status: in the difficult area of discrimination law, the EOC and CRE;[18] and in asylum,[19] on the interpretation of the Geneva Convention on Refugees, the UN High Commissioner. Pressure groups were not far behind. In *R v Coventry City Council, ex p Phoenix Aviation*[20] the organisation Compassion in World Farming was allowed to file evidence relating to the treatment of live animals exported for slaughter, and to make legal submissions. Slowly but surely, a new area of legal practice is opening up.

Proposals for reform made by *Justice* and the Public Law Project[1] suggest a new rule of court to recognise public interest interveners as a distinct class of litigant. Close control would be exercised by the judges: leave to intervene would

16 *R v Rent Officer Service, ex p Muldoon* [1996] 1 WLR 1103.
17 [1986] AC 112. The application was brought in private law.
18 *Shields v E Coomes (Holdings) Ltd* [1978] 1 WLR 1408; *Science Research Council v Nassé, Leyland Cars v Vyas* [1980] AC 1028.
19 *R v Secretary of State for the Home Department, ex p Sivakumaran* [1988] AC 958.
20 [1995] 3 All ER 37. See also in the House of Lords, *R v Secretary of State for the Home Department, ex p Venables* [1997] 3 All ER 97 involving an intervention by *Justice*.
1 *Justice*/Public Law Project, *A Matter of Public Interest* (above, note 10) Ch. 2 and appendix.

be required, and the court would have to be satisfied that 'the proceedings raise a matter of public interest' and 'the intervention is likely to assist the court'. Costs, delay and prejudice to the parties would be relevant criteria in determining the leave application and in general an intervention would be in the form of 'a written submission that does not exceed twenty pages'. To the pressure group lawyer, these are modest proposals. Nevertheless, Schiemann LJ, author of the *Rose Theatre* decision, is not entirely convinced:[2]

> The authors do not articulate the dangers inherent in giving judges an ever wider discretion in determining who is to address them on what issues and indeed in determining on what matters they are prepared to spend time and energy. Nor does one see any warning of the results of having on the Bench judges of widely differing social judgments being called upon to make decisions where those social judgments are very much in play. Nor do the authors care to set out any awareness of the dangers of judges becoming more and more explicitly involved in making judgments of social policy. One of those dangers is that those involved in purely private pursuits will not regard the judge as an impartial arbitrator, but as someone who is applying his personal views to the dispute as opposed to applying the law. While one can of course point out that judges already make many decisions in which their value judgments are, often not explicitly and sometimes perhaps unknowingly, applied, that does not really meet the point.

Public interest challenges have increasingly gained a momentum of their own. Yet there seems no way back to a purely individualistic, private law model of AJR proceedings. We might hypothesise:[3]

> not only will judicial review proceedings tip further in the direction of collective legal action, but that increasingly they will be populated by a compendium of powerful repeat players – assocational groups, surrogate groups, corporations as well as government agencies – concerned to ensure that relevant precedents do not cut across collective interests, and, further, to use litigation strategically in the development of long-term policy strategies.

A new model of judicial review is evolving. We shall pick this up in Chapter 17.

## 4.  Channelling: a public/private divide

In Chapter 2, we noted that the first edition of de Smith's classic text on judicial review makes no mention of a jurisdictional distinction between public and private law but that the editors of the fifth edition have found it necessary to insert a substantial section on the topic (see above, p. 34). In this chapter we need to concentrate on the procedural consequences of this new divide. According to Dicey, the Rule of Law means that everyone, rulers and citizens alike, is subject to the jurisdiction of the 'ordinary' courts of the land. As we have emphasised throughout this book, in the common law system no separate system of

---

2   Sir K. Scheimann, 'Interventions in Public Interest Cases' [1996] PL 240, 243.
3   R. Rawlings, 'Courts and Interests' (above, p.548, note 4), p. 113.

administrative law courts for the resolution of public law disputes has been developed. As Allison argues,[4] the jurisdictional distinction is an alien concept in English law, which offends traditional conceptions of legality. Paradoxically, however, the common law did contain the seeds of a special system in the shape of the prerogative orders, largely used for what today we might call public law purposes (eg, the order of mandamus to compel the execution of a public duty). In modern times[5] these orders have been available from a Divisional Court, traditionally composed of three High Court judges and often presided over by the Lord Chief Justice to emphasise its importance. The Divisional Court, however, was not an administrative tribunal in the sense to which Dicey had objected; composed of 'ordinary' judges, it possessed no monopoly in cases involving the administration. Declarations and injunctions were available from the Chancery Division (look back to *Malone's* case[6] for an example) while actions for damages lay in the ordinary civil courts (below, Chapter 18).

The Law Commission in proposing AJR procedure in 1976[7] was looking for more, not less, procedural flexibility. The assumption was that applicants would have the option between AJR and ordinary action in cases where both were available on the facts of the case. Order 53, r. 1(2) and s. 31(2) of the Supreme Court Act 1981 both provide that declarations and injunctions 'may' (not 'shall') be awarded under Order 53. Reform of procedure paved the way for court reform. The impetus came from problems in the Divisional Court, which in the late 1970s was sinking under an increasing caseload.[8] Under the new AJR procedure it was envisaged that single judges would preside at full hearings. To this end, the practice was established of nominating a group of judges considered specialists in some aspect of administrative law to take Order 53 cases. Provision was further made for transferring into the 'Crown Office list' other High Court matters (e.g. Chancery Division cases or appeals on points of law from tribunals) considered to involve administrative law issues. A small cadre of 'nominated judges' was being established on which the system of judicial review today is predicated. The idea of judicial review as a significant and distinctive area of jurisdiction was being given a powerful boost. Wade[9] an arch-critic of the new system, describes judicial invention of 'procedural exclusivity' – the doctrine that in general AJR procedure is obligatory in 'public law' cases – in this context of reform as 'probably inevitable'. Too much had been invested in the new procedures.

4   J. Allison, *A Continental Distinction in the Common Law* (Oxford: Clarendon) 1996.
5   The historical position is outlined by de Smith, *Judicial Review of Administrative Action* (London: Sweet and Maxwell) 4th edn., J. Evans, 1980, appendix 1.
6   Above, p. 43.
7   Law Commission, *Report on Remedies in Administrative Law* (Law Com. No. 73), Cmnd. 6407 1976, para. 34. In contrast, the initial working paper, *Remedies in Administrative Law* (WP No. 40) 1971, had recommended an exclusive procedure.
8   See L. Blom-Cooper, 'The New Face of Judicial Review: Administrative Changes in Order 53' [1982] PL 250.
9   Wade and Forsyth, p. 681.

*O'Reilly v Mackman*[10]

Four prisoners challenged decisions by the Board of Visitors punishing them with loss of remission for involvement in a riot. Complaint was made of breach of natural justice. Either because they were out of time for judicial review, or because they wanted to be sure of an opportunity to cross-examine on disputed facts, the prisoners went by ordinary civil procedure (writ and originating summons) and not AJR procedure. The House of Lords held unanimously that the actions should be struck out for abuse of process:

> *Lord Diplock*: The public interest in good administration requires that public authorities and third parties should not be kept in suspense as to the legal validity of a decision ... for any longer period than is absolutely necessary in fairness to the person affected by the decision ...
>
> Nevertheless I accept that having regard to the disadvantages, particularly ... the absolute bar on compelling discovery of documents by the respondent public authority [in proceedings for] certiorari, and the almost invariable practice of refusing leave to allow cross-examination of deponents to affidavits lodged on its behalf, it could not be regarded as an abuse of ... process, before the amendments made to Ord. 53 in 1977, to proceed by an action for a declaration of nullity ... instead of applying for an order of certiorari; [although], by adopting this course, the plaintiff evaded the safeguards imposed in the public interest against groundless unmeritorious or tardy attacks on the validity of decisions made by public authorities in the field of public law.
>
> Those disadvantages, which formerly might have resulted in an applicant being unable to obtain justice ... under Ord. 53, have all been removed by the new rules introduced in 1977. There is express provision for interlocutory applications for discovery of documents, the administration of interrogatories and ... cross-examination. Discovery of documents ... is not automatic as in an action begun by writ, but ... discovery is obtainable on application whenever, and to the extent that, the justice of the case requires; similarly ... applications for interrogatories [and] for cross-examination... It may well be that it will be only on rare occasions that the interests of justice will require that leave be given for cross-examination... in applications for judicial review.[11] This is because of the nature of the issues that normally arise... The facts, except where the claim [is] that a ... public authority ... failed to comply with the procedure prescribed by the legislation ... or failed to observe ... natural justice or fairness, can seldom be a matter of relevant dispute on an application for judicial review since the ... authority's findings of fact ... are [generally] not open to review. Nevertheless the grant of leave to cross-examine deponents on applications for judicial review is [today] governed by the same principles as it is in actions begun by originating summons; it should be allowed whenever the justice of the particular case so requires ...
>
> Now that those disadvantages to applicants have been removed and all remedies for infringements of rights protected by public law can be obtained on an application for judicial review, as can also remedies for infringements of rights under private law if [these are] also ... involved, it would ... as a general rule be contrary to public policy, and as such an abuse of ... process ... to permit a person seeking to establish that ... a public authority infringed rights to which he was entitled to protection under public law to proceed by ... ordinary action and ... evade the provisions of Ord. 53 for the protection of such authorities.

10   [1983] 2 AC 237.
11   *George v Secretary of State for the Environment* (1979) 38 P & CR 609.

I have described this as a general rule for ... there may be exceptions, particularly where the invalidity of the decision arises as a collateral issue in a claim for infringement of a right ... arising under private law, or where none of the parties objects to [proceedings] by writ ... whether there should be other exceptions should ... at this stage in the development of procedural public law, be left to be decided on a case to case basis ... In the instant cases where the only relief sought is a declaration of nullity of the decisions of a statutory tribunal, the Board of Visitors ... as in any other case in which a similar declaration of nullity in public law is the only relief claimed, I have no hesitation ... in holding that to allow the actions to proceed would be an abuse of ... process ... They are blatant attempts to avoid the protections for the respondents ... which Ord. 53 provides.

This case epitomises the clash of interests to which we referred in the introduction to this chapter. It is obviously a case about rationing; time limits and the choice of a wrong procedure ended the case without reference to the merits (compare the *Federation* case, above). It is also a case about rationing in that it appears to restrict access to evidence, curtailing the important pre-trial procedure of discovery of documents and the opportunity of oral evidence and cross-examination at trial. In both respects, it is equally a case about judicial management; judicial review procedure is seen as more streamlined and efficient. What of the competing values of access to justice and vindication of the Rule of Law? Little is said. *Cocks v Thanet District Council,*[12] decided by the Law Lords immediately after *O'Reilly v Mackman*, effectively halted a practice of using claims for damages in county courts to enforce local authorities' duties to house the homeless. The key decision whether or not to provide accommodation was said to be a public law matter, challengeable solely through AJR procedure. Community lawyers advising the disadvantaged would now have to arrange for High Court proceedings in London.

It should be remembered that sufficient evidence must be brought forward at the leave stage to show an arguable case for judicial review. Lord Diplock justifies restrictions on the ground that judicial review is essentially concerned with disputes of law not fact. *M v Home Office*[13] is but one example which demonstrates that this is not always the case.[14] In this respect, judicial review proceedings may possess a highly contingent character, governed by the availability or otherwise of alternative sources of information. We shall see this point demonstrated in the *Pergau Dam* case.[15] In a country notable for the absence of freedom of information legislation, judicial review is not a helpful way forward.

But there is more to the channelling of cases into the Crown Office list in the wake of Order 53 than a rationing device. Many would see the new jurisdiction primarily as a status symbol and judicial power base[16] necessary for the evolution

---

12 [1983] 2 AC 286. And see further, Ch. 18.
13 Above, p. 61.
14 See further on interlocutory procedures, Law Commission No. 226, Part VII. The Commission, despite making criticisms of the restrictive approach to discovery, did not recommend amendment of the rules.
15 Below, p. 591.
16 M. Sunkin, 'What is Happening to Applications for Judicial Review?' (1987) 50 MLR 432; Lord Woolf, 'Droit Public, English Style' [1995] PL 57.

of a strong system of judicial review necessary, in the eyes of some members of the judiciary, to combat an increasingly powerful and centralised state (below, Chapter 17).

The most sustained defence of procedural exclusivity has been mounted by Lord Woolf. It could hardly have been otherwise. The doctrine is fundamental to his vision of a differentiated public law in which judicial discretion, in the form of the 'safeguards' (above, p.532), plays a vital role. There is here a paradox. The pragmatic style of judicial review favoured by Lord Woolf, whereby judicial discretion is assigned a positive role at various stages of the process, effectively depends on an analytic distinction or method of reasoning (above, p. 34). In Lord Woolf's words:[17]

> Cases which appear to involve a barren dispute as to procedure can involve a battle over a substantive issue of importance. This is because of the nature of the task which the courts are performing on an application for judicial review. That task is to ensure that bodies which perform public functions should do so in accordance with the requirements of the law. Many of those functions affect, to differing degrees, a great many people. This gives rise to a need to avoid the uncertainty that the existence of proceedings can cause, so as to protect not only the workings of government and other public bodies, but also all those members of the public whom the decision affects. In addition there is the need for there to be different, that is higher, standards to which public, not private, bodies should be required to conform by the courts when performing public functions. I do believe that these features provide a solid foundation for the procedural divide.

This passage does not stand close examination. The Rule of Law principle implies that everybody, and not only those concerned with public administration, must obey the law of the land. The activities of private corporations or individuals frequently affect 'a great many people'. As Cane observes,[18] Lord Woolf's justification of procedural protections for public bodies implies that what is at stake is less important than the sort of interests protected by private law. This is to reinstate the analytical distinction between 'rights' and 'privileges' in the new terminology of public law 'expectations' favoured by Lord Diplock.

Many of the problems stemming from the exclusivity rule could have been anticipated. Before *O'Reilly v Mackman* was decided, one of the authors warned of the analytical difficulties inherent in marking the dividing line.[19] This prophesy has been fulfilled in an era of mixed administrations, a recurrent theme of this book. The irony is that the possibility of maintaining a strict public/private dichotomy in the law was asserted by the courts precisely on the cusp of developments such as privatisation and contracting out. The wind of change was blowing but Lord Diplock set sail against the tide.

17  Ibid, p. 61. See also Sir H. Woolf, 'Public Law – Private Law: Why the Divide? A Personal View' [1986] PL 220.
18  P. Cane, *Introduction to Administrative Law* (Oxford: Clarendon) 3rd edn., 1996, p. 97.
19  C. Harlow, '"Public" and "Private" Law: Definition Without Distinction' (1980) 43 MLR 241.

The material costs of the exclusivity rule also have to be counted. It has produced a welter of litigation, much of which has ended in the House of Lords. This litigation is sterile in the sense that it is solely concerned with procedural form, whether one can sue and where one has to sue and not with the merits of the case. This is why Wade[20] has called *O'Reilly* 'a serious setback for administrative law', a 'step back' towards procedural technicality and the old forms of action abolished in the nineteenth century, which threatens to undermine the universal rule of the common law as expounded by Dicey.

From time to time, the judges, or perhaps some members of the judiciary, pioneer a retreat from exclusivity, as they did in *Winder*, a case which went to the House of Lords on the point of jurisdiction, though Winder lost on the merits. Cane[1] calls this a case of 'collateral review' in two senses. First, Winder was using the public law issue as 'a shield not a sword', raising it only as a defence. Secondly, private and public law were intermingled, the defence resting on Winder's contractual right. Bear in mind in this context the 'access to justice' problem of obtaining legal advice and representation.

## *Wandsworth London Borough Council v Winder*[2]

A council tenant fell into substantial arrears, having failed to meet a 50% increase in rents. His argument was that the increase was void for *Wednesbury* unreasonableness. He was, however, refused leave to apply for judicial review on the ground of delay. Westminster then applied to strike out the defence in possession proceedings, on the basis that the issue could be raised only via Order 53.

> *Lord Fraser*: Lord Diplock was careful [in *O'Reilly v Mackman*] to emphasize that the general rule which he had stated ... might well be subject to exception. The question for your Lordships is whether the instant appeal is an exception to the general rule ...
>
> The arguments for protecting public authorities against unmeritorious or dilatory challenges to their decisions have to be set against the arguments for preserving the ordinary rights of private citizens to defend themselves against unfounded claims...it would in my opinion be a very strange use of language to describe the respondent's behaviour in relation to this litigation as an abuse or misuse by him of the process of the courts. He did not select the procedure to be adopted. He was merely seeking to defend proceedings brought against him by the appellants. In so doing he is seeking only to exercise the ordinary right of any individual to defend an action against him on the ground that he is not liable for the whole sum claimed by the plaintiff. Moreover he puts forward his defence as a matter of right, whereas in an application for judicial review, success would require an exercise of the court's discretion in his favour ... I find it impossible to accept that the right to challenge the decision of a local authority

---

20 Wade and Forsyth, p. 682. See further, A. Tanney, 'Procedural Exclusivity in Administrative Law' [1994] PL 51; S. Fredman and G. Morris, 'The Costs of Exclusivity: Public and Private Re-Examined' [1994] PL 69.

1 *Introduction to Administrative Law* (above, note 18), p. 99. See further, C. Emery, 'Collateral Attack – Attacking *Ultra Vires* Action Indirectly in Courts and Tribunals' (1993) 56 MLR 643.

2 [1985] AC 461. See, for the substantive decision, *Wandsworth London Borough Council v Winder (No 2)* (1988) 20 HLR 400.

in course of defending an action for non-payment can have been swept away by Order 53, which was directed to introducing a procedural reform ...

If the public interest requires that persons should not be entitled to defend actions brought against them by public authorities, where the defence rests on a challenge to a decision by the public authority, then it is for Parliament to change the law.

Commenting, Lord Woolf declared himself 'appalled'[3] that a litigant blocked in AJR procedure by reason of 'safeguards', could still succeed on the same facts as a defence. Alternatively, one might deplore the opportunity for powerful respondents, often 'repeat players' in the judicial review game, to stand on technical points.

### *Roy v Kensington and Chelsea and Westminster Family Practitioner Committee*[4]

The local committee used its powers under regulations to reduce a doctor's practice allowance on the ground of insufficient time devoted to general practice. When the doctor sued for the amount deducted, *O'Reilly v Mackman* was invoked on the basis that, governed by regulations and discretionary decision, there was no private legal right to receive any particular remuneration. The Court of Appeal held that there was a contract for services and that therefore proceeding by ordinary action was appropriate. The House of Lords dispensed with the need for a contract:

> *Lord Lowry*: The actual or possible absence of a contract is not decisive against Dr Roy. He has in my opinion the bundle of rights which should be regarded as his individual private law rights against the committee, arising from the statute and regulations and including the very important private law right to be paid for the work that he has done ... if Dr Roy has any kind of *private law* right, even though not contractual, he can sue for its alleged breach.
>
> In this case it has been suggested that Dr Roy could have gone by judicial review, because there is no issue of fact, but that would not always hold good in a similar type of case and I do not forget that he might have been faced with the argument which succeeded in *ex parte Walsh* [i.e. that this was a private law matter[5]]. In any event, a successful application by judicial review could not lead directly, as it would in an action, to an order for payment of the full basic practice allowance. Other proceedings would be needed...
>
> Even if one accepts the full rigour of *O'Reilly v Mackman*, there is ample room to hold that this case comes within the exception allowed for by Lord Diplock. It is concerned with a private law right, it involves a question which *could* in some circumstances give rise to a dispute of fact and one object of the plaintiff is to obtain an order for the payment (not by way of damages) of an ascertained or ascertainable sum of money. If it is wrong to allow such a claim to be litigated by action, what is to be said of other disputed claims for remuneration? I think it is right to consider the whole spectrum of claims which a doctor might make against the committee. The existence of any dispute as to entitlement means that he will be alleging the breach of his private law rights through a failure by the committee to perform their public duty. If the committee's argument prevails, the doctor must in all these cases go by judicial review, even when the facts are not clear. I scarcely think that this can be the right answer ...

3   Lord Woolf, *Protection of the Public: A New Challenge* (The Hamlyn Lectures) (London: Stevens) 1990, p. 30.
4   [1992] 1 AC 624.
5   *R v East Berkshe Health Authority, ex p Walsh*[1985] QB 152; above, p. 234.

With regard to *O'Reilly v Mackman* [counsel for Dr Roy] argued in the alternative. The 'broad approach' was that the rule in *O'Reilly v Mackman* did not apply generally against bringing actions to vindicate private rights in all circumstances in which those actions involved a challenge to a public law act or decision, but that it merely required the aggrieved person to proceed by judicial review only when private law rights were not at stake. The 'narrow approach' assumed that the rule applied generally to *all* proceedings in which public law acts or decisions were challenged, subject to some exceptions when private law rights were involved. There was no need in *O'Reilly v Mackman* to choose between these approaches, but it seems clear that Lord Diplock considered himself to be stating a general rule with exceptions. For my part, I much prefer the broad approach ... Whichever approach one adopts, the arguments for excluding the present case from the ambit of the rule, or, in the alternative, making an exception of it are similar and to my mind convincing.

Each landmark case on exclusivity is hailed as a final solution but there is always another. The more open approach of *Roy* draws much of the sting of the exclusivity rule. Although it can clearly be accommodated as an 'exception', it underscores a more liberal trend, visible both in *Winder* and in the subsequent case of *Mercury Communications*[6] on utilites regulation. Unfortunately, however, this development is not enough to sort out all the problems. The law concerning exclusivity remains exceptionally complex. Judicial disagreements are common, as we can see in the *British Steel* case.[7] Moreover, the pendulum can always swing, as it has between *Winder* and the latest case of *Wicks*.

## *R v Wicks*[8]

The defendant was served with an enforcement notice under s. 87 of the Town and Country Planning Act 1971 in respect of some rebuilding work. He failed to comply with the notice, arguing that planning permission was unnecessary. In a criminal prosecution he argued that, in making the decision to serve the notice, the council had acted in bad faith and been motivated by irrelevant considerations. The judge ruled that the propriety of the decision to serve the notice could not be raised by way of defence in criminal proceedings. This ruling was upheld on appeal to the House of Lords. Lord Hoffmann said:

> While I am willing for the sake of argument to accept [the] submission [of the defendant's counsel] that there is a wide right for anyone prosecuted under a local byelaw to challenge its validity, the point at which we absolutely part company is when he submits that this right can be extrapolated to enable a defendant to challenge the vires of every act done under statutory authority if its validity forms part of the prosecution's case or its invalidity would constitute a defence. In my view no such generalisation is possible. The question must depend entirely upon the construction of the statute under which the prosecution is brought. The statute may require the prosecution to prove that the act in question is not open to challenge on any ground

---

6  Above, p. 369.
7  *British Steel plc v Customs and Excise Comrs*[1997] 2 All ER 366; below, p. 629.
8  [1997] 2 All ER 801.

available in public law, or it may be a defence to show that it is. In such a case, the justices will have to rule upon the validity of the act. On the other hand, the statute may upon its true construction merely require an act which appears formally valid and has not been quashed by judicial review. In such a case, nothing but the formal validity of the act will be relevant to an issue before the justices. It is in my view impossible to construct a general theory of the ultra vires defence which applies to every statutory power, whatever the terms and policy of the statute.

On the one hand, as Lord Hoffmann argues, a 'liberal' attitude to exclusivity would mean that prosecutions for breach of an enforcement order would be vulnerable to a defence of invalidity which might involve public law points of considerable complexity. On the other hand, a heavy burden has been placed on the citizen to raise potential illegality by means of AJR in the High Court. More flexible solutions need to be devised. In civil proceedings, as the Law Commission recommended,[9] a new procedure to convert proceedings started by writ into an AJR would be helpful. More radical and more useful would be a novel reference procedure, whereby any difficult public law point raised collaterally in the course of criminal or civil proceedings could be referred for a ruling to the Divisional Court.[10]

## 5. Remedies: reach and discretion

Judicial review was scornfully described by de Smith as a law of remedies.[11] The historical development epitomised the common law attitude that principles develop from procedures, or that substantive law grows out of adjectival law. Before the reform of Order 53, this was a major source of criticism, the many procedural technicalities being seen to distract attention from the grounds of review. In Dicey's formulation of the Rule of Law, however, the point wears a different emphasis. A cardinal feature of common law systems of administrative law is the possession of mandatory orders which lie to government and administration. Traditionally, these consisted of the orders of habeas corpus, which allows the court to assess the legality of a detention in custody, and mandamus (above). In recent times injunctions and interim injunctions, to prohibit administrative action for the period of court proceedings, have also become available generally against public authorities. Emphasis was laid in this context on the symbolism of *M v Home Office*,[12] expressed by Lord Woolf in terms of movement towards a model of judicial review premised on coercion, in contrast to one based on trust and co-operation.

One of the most important aspects of grievance machinery is that it should provide effective redress. Here the English system of judicial review has some notable strengths. Particularly striking are the strong 'stop orders', underwritten

9   Law Commission No. 226, paras. 3.20, 3.21.
10  See C. Emery, 'The Vires Defence – "Ultra Vires" as a Defence to Criminal or Civil Proceedings' (1992) 52 CLJ 308; C. Harlow, 'Why Public Law Is Private Law: An Invitation to Lord Woolf' in A. Zuckerman and R. Cranston (eds.), *Reform of Civil Procedure* (Oxford: Clarendon) 1995.
11  S. de Smith, *Judicial Review of Administrative Action* (London: Stevens) 3rd edn., 1973, p. 335.
12  Above, p. 61.

by *M* such that interim injunctions and other mandatory relief are now available against ministers of the Crown. There has been a European dimension to this development, in terms both of direct requirements of legal protection (*Factortame*, above, p. 170) and of indirect or 'knock-on' effects in domestic law (*M*). In Chapter 18 we see parallel developments in the realm of damages and restitution.

However, constraints associated with the classical procedural form of adversarial, bipolar adjudication, should be kept in mind. Evident in this context is judicial caution about devising collective remedies for collective injuries. In contrast to American courts in the celebrated education cases,[13] English courts have always declined to intervene in active administration. A further limitation of the judicial process is the absence of any procedure to monitor the implementation of decisions. The courts lack the ability of Ombudsmen to check the treatment of similar cases (above, p.440). Looking back to the 'errors' case brought by CPAG on behalf of an unidentified class of welfare claimants (above, p. 546), suppose the group had won and the court had held these claimants entitled to back payment. The most obvious legal remedy would be a declaration that the decision not to repay was unlawful. This, however, would have left the real outcome in ministerial hands. There are in practice two probable outcomes. Either the decision would be to implement, following the precedents established by the PCA to which we have already referred, or the position would be regularised by retrospective legislation depriving everyone of the fruits of the legal victory (below, p. 569).[14] The utility of a successful challenge is thus questionable.

English courts have not been enthusiastic to decide hypothetical issues, or to lay down rules merely because some individual or group thinks it appropriate. A departure from this classical dispute-orientated model of adjudication is signalled by proposals from the Law Commission for an advisory declaration.[15] The need for citizens and administrators to 'know where they stand' is here identified as part of the public interest in good administration. But further, the remedy is an obvious tool for 'public interest challenge'. It could be expected to underpin judicial creativity, allowing the courts to exercise 'abstract' judicial review free from the constraints of an ordinary law suit.[16] This then, like standing and intervention, is not a 'dry' or technical matter. It demonstrates how the role of judicial review is sculptured by the shape or reach of remedies.

---

13  Following *Brown v Board of Education of Topeka* 347 US 483 (1954). See further, C. Harlow and R. Rawlings, *Pressure Through Law* (London: Routledge) 1992, especially Ch. 2; A. Chayes, 'The Role of the Judge in Public Law Litigation' (1976) 89 Harv. LR 1281. And see below, p. 602 on the 'public interest model' of judicial review.
14  This solution is well documented in welfare cases. See C. Harlow, 'Administrative Reaction to Judicial Review' [1976] PL 16; T. Prosser, *Test Cases for the Poor* (London: Child Poverty Action Group) 1983. See now, s. 104 of the Social Security Act 1975 as amended 1990 and *Bate v Chief Adjudication Officer* [1996] 1 WLR 814.
15  Law Commission No. 226 paras. 8.9–8.14. And see for judicial developments in this direction, *Royal College of Nursing v Department of Health and Social Security* [1981] AC 800; *Gillick v West Norfolk and Wisbech Area Health Authority* [1986] AC 112. And see above, p. 179.
16  See further, Sir J. Laws, 'Judicial Remedies and the Constitution' (1994) 57 MLR 213.

*A precision instrument?*

Remedies in judicial review are held to be discretionary.[17] This in itself is a recognition of the distinctive character of the supervisory jurisdiction. Whereas private rights will typically be protected automatically by the courts,[18] in judicial review, even if the agency is held to have acted unlawfully, it is the court's prerogative to deny or fashion any relief. In an article entitled 'Should Public Law Remedies be Discretionary?'[19] Sir Thomas Bingham questions this prerogative. He answers: 'Well, yes, probably, in some cases, up to a point, provided the discretion is strictly limited and the rules for its exercise clearly understood.' Why? Because judicial review is more likely to gain legitimacy 'if it is seen as a precision instrument and not a juggernaut'.[20] How then, in practice, has the discretion been used?

In some cases the conduct of the applicant has been determinative. In one case,[1] the court refused to intervene when a fireman was disciplined for refusing to clean a superior officer's uniform: he should have complied with the order and, using internal procedure, complained later. In a student case, *ex p Roffey*,[2] failure in examinations led to disbarment from the course. The court refused to cure a breach of natural justice on the ground of delay in coming to the court. In another student case, *Glynn v Keele University*,[3] a naked sunbather was excluded from the university residence without a proper hearing: an injunction was refused on the basis that the end result was 'fair'. As Wade[4] points out, however, fair procedure must come first since 'it is only after hearing both sides that the merits can be properly considered'. Such cases point up the dangers of remedial discretion in terms of individual protection. The more stringent view, which favours a requirement only to grant redress for 'real and substantial injustice' involves a more limited role for judicial review. What, we may ask, of dignitary values?

Earlier in this chapter we saw a serious clash of values: access and the Rule of Law principle versus the efficiency of public administration and the legal process. Both the rationing principle and a protectionist mentality are clearly evident in the matter of remedy. A well known example is *R v Bristol Corpn, ex p Hendy*.[5] The Court of Appeal refused to compel the council to offer the applicant permanent council housing. Scarman LJ said:

> It would be improper for the court to make an order of mandamus compelling [a local authority] to do that which either it cannot do or which it can only do at the

---

17   Certiorari, mandamus, prohibition, declarations and injunctions all fall into this category. See on the distinctive position of habeas corpus, Law Commission No. 226 Part XI.
18   Injunctive relief is classically discretionary, however, and the point is disputed whether it can be withheld and damages substituted. See *Allen v Gulf Oil Refining Ltd* [1981] AC 1001.
19   [1991] PL 64.
20   Ibid, at p. 75.
 1   *Ex p Fry* [1954] 1 WLR 730.
 2   *R v Aston University Senate, ex p Roffey* [1969] 2 QB 538.
 3   [1971] 2 All ER 89.
 4   Wade & Forsyth, p. 528. See further, *R v Chief Constable of the Thames Valley Police Forces, ex p Cotton* [1990] IRLR 344.
 5   [1974] 1 All ER 1047.

expense of other persons not before the court who may have equal rights with the applicant and some of whom would certainly have equal moral claims.

The decision recognises the limitations of adjudication as a technique for dealing with the distribution of scarce resources. Later, we shall see this described as a 'polycentric' decision, whose knock-on effects cause particular problems for the bipolar adversarial process. Scarman LJ acknowledges the potential disadvantages to third parties not before the court, thus breaking through the mould of bipolarity. On the other hand, the court may be criticised for assuming as the framework for its decision the inevitability of a housing waiting list or indirectly legitimating, through failure to grant a remedy, delays in the administrative process. The effect is to countenance breach of the Rule of Law principle that legislative obligations have to be performed.

In Chapter 15 we discussed the concept of 'transaction typing', a consistent judicial approach in particular subject-areas of administration.[6] Now we find transaction typing introduced through the medium of remedial discretion. The student cases could, for example, be read in Sir Thomas Bingham's terms as a 'restricted area'[7] in which remedy will not easily be forthcoming. The same is true of decisions on the internal discipline of hierarchical forces such as the police and fire brigades. Take *Chief Constable of the North Wales Police v Evans*.[8] The House of Lords found a breach of natural justice. The probationer wished, however, to be reinstated. The House of Lords refused an order of mandamus on the ground that 'in practice it might border on usurpation of the powers of the Chief Constable'. Instead, a declaration was made that the probationer was entitled only to other remedies of unlawful dismissal. This has the indirect effect of channelling such cases out of the judicial review process, thus reinforcing the 'alternative remedy' rule.

As in recent times the boundaries of judicial review have been extended, so the power of remedial discretion has taken on a new prominence. This is the logic of Lord Woolf's argument about the judicial review 'safeguards' (above, p.532). Take the regulation of market activity in the City of London. In *Datafin*[9] we saw jurisdiction over the Take-Over Panel importantly asserted. On the other hand, the significance of justiciability was qualified, in part by a use of the novel form of 'prospective declaration'. A legal remedy was here being tailored in the light of the needs of effective regulation. A further factor was the position of third parties. Thus judicial review in *Datafin* was hardly a 'juggernaut'! Again, the *Argyll* case[10] concerned a take-over bid referred by the Minister to the Monopolies and Mergers Commission. The Commission Chairman, on the basis of certain assurances from the bidding company, determined, with the consent of the Minister, not to proceed with the inquiry. Under the statutory procedure, however, this was a matter for Commission members to decide. A rival bidder raised the illegality in an AJR but was refused certiorari. Lord Donaldson MR stressed that

6  Above, p. 508.
7  Sir T. Bingham, 'Should Public Law Remedies Be Discretionary?' [1991] PL 64, 74–75.
8  Above, p. 502.
9  Above, p. 344.
10  *R v Monopolies and Mergers Commission, ex p Argyll Group plc* [1986] 1 WLR 763.

'a public law court' had to approach its duties 'with a proper awareness of the needs of public administration'. Some of his reasons for refusing to quash may be thought more convincing than others:

> Good public administration is concerned with substance rather than form. Difficult although the decision on the fact of abandonment may or may not have been, I have little doubt that the Commission ... would have reached and would now reach the same conclusion as did their experienced chairman.
>
> Good public administration is concerned with the speed of decision, particularly in the financial field ... If relief is granted, it must be some days before a new decision is reached ... Good public administration requires a proper consideration of the public interest. In this context, the Secretary of State is the guardian of the public interest. He consented to the reference being laid aside, although he need not have done so ...
>
> Good public administration requires a proper consideration of the legitimate interests of individual citizens, however rich and powerful they may be and whether they are natural or juridical persons. But in judging the relevance of an interest, however legitimate, regard has to be had to the purpose of the administrative process concerned. Argyll [the rival bidder] has a strong and legitimate interest in putting Guinness in baulk, but this is not the purpose of the administrative process under the [legislation]. To that extent their interest is not therefore of any great, or possibly any, weight.
>
> Lastly, good public administration requires decisiveness and finality, unless there are compelling reasons to the contrary. The financial public has been entitled to rely on the finality of the announced decision to set aside the reference ... Account must be taken of the probability that deals have been done in reliance on the validity of the decisions now impugned.

Nowhere is the clash of values better illustrated than in *Caswell*, the leading authority on delay. There is on the one hand a strong case for individual protection in the form of financial interest; a claim buttressed in the circumstances by practical problems of access to justice. On the other hand, there are important practicalities of administration, the impugned decision being part of a system of rationing. To overturn administrative decisions retrospectively may have problematic effects on third parties not before the court. Once again, we have encountered the concept of a polycentric decision, which cannot be unpicked without consequences for other decisions in a chain reaction.

### *Caswell v Dairy Produce Quota Tribunal for England and Wales*[11]

Farmers, in accordance with Community legislation, are permitted to produce only the amount of milk allocated to them under a quota system. The applicants were dairy farmers in South Wales. The tribunal fixed their quota on the basis of current production levels, and indicated that when, as expected, the applicants increased their herd, they could reapply for additional quota. It was subsequently discovered that the quota could not be changed. Not until two years later did the

11  [1990] 2 AC 738.

applicants become aware of the remedy of judicial review through an article in the farming press. The tribunal was held by the judge to have erred in law in making an award without regard to the future. But what was the court to do? Sufficient provision had been made to deal with the applicants' claim for extra quota, but what then of other, similar claims? The judge fell back on the principle of 'undue delay' and the grounds of judicial discretion set out in s. 31(6) of the Supreme Court Act 1981. He refused both certiorari to quash the decision and mandamus to compel a new allocation. Only a declaration was available to mark the error. The frustrated applicants appealed unsuccessfully to the House of Lords. Evidently, it cannot be assumed that judicial review always provides effective redress of grievance. Sometimes compensation will have to be left to the ex gratia procedures which we shall describe in Chapter 18.

> *Lord Goff:* It is of importance to observe that s. 31(6) recognises that there is an interest in good administration independently of hardship, or prejudice to the rights of third parties, and that the harm suffered by the applicant by reason of the decision which has been impugned is a matter which can be taken into account by the court when deciding whether or not to exercise its discretion under s. 31(6) to refuse the relief sought by the applicant. In asking the question whether the grant of such relief would be detrimental to good administration the court is at that stage looking at the interest in good administration independently of matters such as these. In the present context that interest lies essentially in a regular flow of consistent decisions, made and published with reasonable despatch; in citizens knowing where they stand, and how they can order their affairs in the light of the relevant decision. Matters of particular importance, apart from the length of time itself, will be the extent of the effect of the relevant decision, and the impact which would be felt if it were to be reopened. In the present case the court was concerned with a decision to allocate part of a finite amount of quota, and with circumstances in which a reopening of the decision would lead to other applications to reopen similar decisions which, if successful, would lead to reopening the allocation of quota over a number of years. To me it is plain ... that to grant the appellants the relief they sought in the present case after such a lapse of time had occurred, would be detrimental to good administration.

## 6. Judicial review and administration. A tangled web

We cannot leave the machinery for judicial review without considering the impact of its operation on the administrative process. Unfortunately, however, assessment is difficult. We know very little in practice about the effects on respondent authorities of individual cases. We know even less about the more general or radiating effects of judicial activity on the workings of government.[12] The implication of traditional control theory, asserting the pivotal position of courts (Chapter 2), is that government dutifully follows the lead given by the judges. Matters could never be so simple. A more realistic hypothesis is that judicial review has only a sporadic, peripheral and temporary impact on government

---

12  See for a survey, G. Richardson and M. Sunkin, 'Judicial Review: Questions of Impact' [1996] PL 79.

policy.[13] One reason is the limited institutional capacity of courts (a theme developed in Chapter 17); another, the many competing pressures and priorities in administration. We should not be surprised if the effect on the quality of administrative decision-making is patchy, review eliciting negative as well as positive responses, or if practical reactions are adjusted as the perceived frequency and significance of this type of challenge increases.[14]

## (a)  Interplay: a matter of resources

Despite a lack of information, 'many judges remain undeterred ... from making assumptions about the effects of their intervention'.[15] A recurring theme of this chapter is the judicial propensity to temper review by reference to the perceived needs of the administration. *O'Reilly v Mackman* provided one example, the protections for public authorities being prioritised by Lord Diplock at the expense of considerations of access to justice. The restrictive approach of the courts to discovery and cross-examination only served to underscore the theme. In the realm of remedies, *Caswell* presented a particularly striking example. For Lord Woolf, all this highlights the need for judicial discretion:[16]

> If the safeguards did not exist the undesirable tendency ... of governments taking avoiding action to prevent judicial review could well increase, with the result that judicial review would afford less effective protection of the public. In seeking to draw attention to this possible counter-productive effect of judicial review I am of course not suggesting the court should ever be inhibited in interfering as forcefully as necessary with a governmental department if justice requires that intervention. All I wish to ensure is that judges appreciate the consequence of their intervention.

Not that judicial consideration of administrative impact is limited to matters of legal procedure. Quite the reverse. In Chapter 15, for example, we met the argument that the imposition of a duty to give reasons would improve the quality of administrative decision taking. We found, on the other hand, that courts were inclined to weigh the administrative costs. So, too, 'public interest' factors were identified as relevant considerations in the tailoring of 'fairness'. It could hardly be otherwise.

We have already met the situation in which a legal challenge is designed to secure additional resources, possibly for a large class of persons. The development of the representative 'public interest challenge' is likely to accentuate this trend. A recent case, the product of pressure group action, highlights the tension between the judicial function of protection of individuals and a practical

13  See to this effect, H. Rawlings, 'Judicial Review and the "Control of Government"' (1986) 64 Pub Adm. 125; R. Cranston, 'Reviewing Judicial Review' in G. Richardson and H. Genn (eds.), *Administrative Law and Government Action* (Oxford: Clarendon) 1994.

14  A. Barker, 'The Impact of Judicial Review: Perspectives from Whitehall and the Courts' [1996] PL 612, 613.

15  G. Richardson and M. Sunkin [1996] PL 79, 82.

16  Sir H. Woolf, *Protection of the Public: A New Challenge*, The Hamlyn Lectures (London: Stevens) 1990, p. 19.

understanding of the financial constraints on government. How far should the courts go in entertaining the 'sigma' values in administration of 'the three Es'? Alternatively, to what extent can courts grant remedies which impinge on the 'political' functions of government?

### *R v Gloucestershire County Council, ex p Barry*[17]

B, elderly and severely disabled, was assessed by the local authority as needing home care assistance including the provision of cleaning and laundry services. After central government reduced Gloucestershire's funding by £2.5 million, the council informed B, along with many others, that it was forced to prioritise and could no longer offer him the services. The case was taken up by the Public Law Project, with an eye on similar developments across local government. The key issue was whether the words 'necessary in order to meet the needs of that person' in s. 2 of the Chronically Sick and Disabled Persons Act 1970 imposed a duty on the council to provide an individual with the statutory services such that it was not entitled to take into consideration the resources available to it. Counsel for B sought only a declaration and not mandamus, a clear signal of the problems of implementation. The House of Lords by a majority refused even to grant a declaration:

> *Lord Nicholls*: A person's needs, it was submitted, depend upon the nature and extent of his disability ... This is an alluring argument but I am unable to accept it. It is flawed by a failure to recognise that needs for services cannot sensibly be assessed without having some regard to the cost of providing them. A person's need for a particular type or level of service cannot be decided in a vacuum from which all considerations of cost have been expelled ...
>
> Once it is accepted ... that cost is a relevant factor in assessing a person's needs for the services listed in s. 2(1), then, in deciding how much weight is to be attached to cost, some evaluation or assumption has to be made about the impact which the cost will have upon the authority. Cost is of more or less significance depending upon whether the authority currently has more or less money ...
>
> [It was argued that] if a local authority may properly take its resources into account in the way I have described, the s. 2(1) duty would in effect be limited to making arrangements to the extent only that the authority should decide to allocate money for this purpose. The duty, it was said, would collapse into a power. I do not agree. A local authority must carry out its functions under s. 2(1) in a responsible fashion. In the event of a local authority acting with *Wednesbury* unreasonableness ... a disabled person would have a remedy.

> *Lord Lloyd* (dissenting): In every case, simple or complex, the need of the individual will be assessed against the standards of civilised society as we know them in the United Kingdom ... Resources can, of course, operate to impose a cash limit on what is provided. But how can resources help to measure the need? This ... is the fallacy which lies at the heart of the council's argument ...
>
> Suppose there are two people with identical disabilities, living in identical circumstances, but in different parts of the country. Local authority A provides for his

17  [1997] 2 All ER 1. See also *R v Sefton Metropolitan Borough Council, ex p Help the Aged* [1997] NLJR 490; *R v East Sussex County Council, ex p T* [1997] ELR 311.

needs by arranging for meals on wheels four days a week. Local authority B might also be expected to provide meals on wheels four days a week, or its equivalent. It cannot, however, have been Parliament's intention that local authority B should be able to say 'because we do not have enough resources, we are going to reduce your needs.' His needs remain exactly the same. They cannot be affected by the local authority's inability to meet those needs...

By your Lordships' decision today the council has escaped from the impossible position in which they and other local authorities have been placed. Nevertheless, I cannot help wondering whether they will not be regretting today's decision as much as Mr Barry. The solution lies with the Government. The passing of the 1970 Act was a noble aspiration. Having willed the end, Parliament must be asked to provide the means.

Rights-based theories of judicial review would be unlikely to accept this outcome. We shall meet this clash of values again in *ex pB*.[18]

## (b)  Control: the forms of review

Stress was laid in Chapter 3 on the different forms of 'control': legal/political, internal/external, prospective/retrospective. Feldman has pursued the theme by reference to different techniques of judicial control or effects on government:[19]

(a) *Directing*. The traditional judicial function of compelling government to adhere to stated legal powers and duties.
(b) *Limiting*. Establishing the scope of, or setting the limits to the exercise of, discretion. For example, the common law rules against delegation and fettering of powers.
(c) *Structuring*. Making explicit values or goals which are to guide decision-making. This takes in common law principles of legality such as *Wednesbury* unreasonableness and the duty to act fairly.

Each of these techniques may have different implications in terms of the likely impact on the administrative process. With 'directing', the control applied is retrospective and specific. The agency is required to take steps to achieve legality, but there may be limited general impact or radiating effects. 'Limiting' is a broader activity with potentially a wider influence on the forms and structures of government.[20] 'Structuring', Feldman argues, affects administrators' day-to-day activities far more significantly than the other techniques, by reason of the greater exercise of prior control or provision of guidance. From this perspective, the fire-watching function of courts has assumed a new prominence in recent times through the development of grounds of review such as 'fairness'.

18  Below, p. 599.
19  D. Feldman, 'Judicial Review: A Way of Controlling Government?' (1988) 66 Pub Adm. 21.
20  See, for discussion in the context of delegation and the classic authority, *Carltona v Works Comr* [1943] 2 All ER 560; M. Freedland, 'The Rule Against Delegation and the *Carltona* Doctrine in an Agency Context' [1996] PL 19.

The typology points up some of the complexities in the model of judicial 'control'. The form of legal principle is, however, only one factor. As we have seen, in a 'public interest challenge', a test case may well be designed to achieve a marked 'ripple' effect, altering administrative practice in respect of large numbers of cases, although premised on a narrow point of statutory interpretation. We can describe the House of Lords in *Barry* as refusing a request to perform the 'directing' function. Thus, Lord Nicholls is content with only 'structuring' in the form of *Wednesbury* unreasonableness.

Another argument concerns the role of 'structuring'. As we saw in Chapter 15, the hortatory or educative function of law, ultimately the internalising by administrators of legal values, may itself be threatened by flexible application of such imprecise principles as 'fairness' and 'unreasonableness'. The 'intuitive judgment' of courts can be difficult to fathom, let alone predict. It is not surprising to learn that 'ministers and officials now complain that the principles of judicial review developed and applied by the courts are too uncertain'.[1] James, writing from an administrator's viewpoint, pursues the theme:[2]

> Difficulty is created by the sometimes inconsistent way in which judges apply the existing principles governing judicial review ... 'Judges exercise more freedom of manoeuvre [in judicial review] than in most of the other branches of English law' ...While judgments from the bench are apt to rhapsodise about the gradual development of judicial intervention, this creates great uncertainty for those public administrators not working in a narrowly defined executive field. This unpredictability leaves them with a choice between cautious paralysis – intolerable in an era of political activism – or a more hazardous approach of pressing forward where the hazy legal omens appear favourable.
>
> The present semi-molten arrangements ... leave a lot to chance. Since judges continue to develop the criteria for judicial review as they go along, administrators and litigants alike find themselves playing a complex game whose rules are liable to be adjusted by the umpire at the end of the match.

### (c) Formal and informal reactions

The sequels to particular cases illustrate the very different ways in which government may respond to judicial decisions. Negative reactions include secrecy – the use of 'boiler plate' reasons – and valedictory legislation or nullification. Many examples of the latter are scattered through this book. In *Burmah Oil*,[3] a strong form of retrospective legislation was used to rub out victory in the courts. A further example follows in the *Woolwich* case.[4] Another technique is to reaffirm or take the same decision twice as was done in *Padfield*.[5] This highlights

---

1    A. Le Sueur, 'The Judicial Review Debate: From Partnership to Friction' (1996) 31 Government and Opposition 8, 22.
2    S. James, 'The Political and Administrative Consequences of Judicial Review' (1996) 74 Pub Adm. 613, 623, 625, 634. The quotation is from R. Brazier, *Constitutional and Administrative Law* (London: Penguin) 7th edn., 1994.
3    Above, p. 47.
4    Below, p. 628.
5    Above, p. 98.

the limitations of procedural review which has the effect of returning the decision to the original decision-maker. To emphasise, each of these 'great' cases in the development of jurisdiction demonstrates the difficult relationship between judicial supervision and administrative behaviour.

Let us follow this process a little further. We know that by virtue of the doctrine of parliamentary sovereignty the legislative power 'trumps' judicial power. (In contrast, in the realm of European law, both the domestic legal and political processes are susceptible to 'trumping'[6]). But valedictory legislation does not deprive judicial review of all its 'impact'. One function of the judicial process may be to open up a particular policy to public debate, allowing interest representation in the policy-making process. Following the celebrated *Fire Brigades* case,[7] the government had to make substantial concessions in its valedictory legislation.[8] From the viewpoint of the administrator, 'changing the law is not as easy as it sounds. It all means extra work, disruption and delay'.[9] The emergence in cases like *Witham*[10] of a requirement to use primary and not delegated legislation when interfering with 'fundamental rights' (above, p.162) is thus significant. An example of judicial counter-reaction, the doctrine is ripe for development in the context of incorporation of the ECHR.

Legislative reversal is emblematic of the centrality of rule-making in the modern state (Chapter 7). Drafting technique is improving all the time and cunning games can be played with rules. Insulation by ouster clause of whole areas of administrative decision-making is effectively blocked by *Anisminic*.[11] However, it may be possible to draw the sting from test cases designed to benefit a large class of persons. In *R v Social Fund Inspector, ex p Stitt*[12] the Child Poverty Action Group successfully argued that the budgetary allocations under the Social Fund were unlawful. To satisfy the judgment, the Minister announced an additional expenditure of £10 million. Soon afterwards, provisions were inserted in the Social Security Act 1990 to the effect that legal rulings do not apply to other, similar, claims in the pipeline prior to the definitive decision.[13] An anti-test case rule contained in the Social Security Bill currently before Parliament would restrict the backdating of benefit in cases where an appeal is suspended pending the outcome of a legal challenge. Government is here seen resorting to the idea of individuation in order to limit possible financial impact. Only the person in the test case would obtain the full benefit.

Legislative reversal is a strong type of 'formal' reaction. By such reaction is meant a change to, or confirmation of, official agency policy.[14] Turning to

6   On judicial review procedure as a vehicle for Community law, see *R v Secretary of State for Employment, ex p Equal Opportunities Commission and Day* [1994] 2 WLR 409.
7   *R v Secretary of State for the Home Department, ex p Fire Brigades Union*[1995] 2 WLR 464; below, p. 596.
8   See G. Ganz, 'Criminal Injuries Compensation: The Constitutional Issue' (1996) 59 MLR 95.
9   S. James, (above, note 2) p. 620. A point epitomised by *R v Secretary of State for Social Services, ex p Cotton*, (1985) Times, 14 December; the subject of a case study in A. Le Sueur and M. Sunkin, *Public Law* (London: Longman) 1997.
10  Above, p. 162.
11  Above, p. 54.
12  [1990] COD 288.
13  See *Bate v Chief Adjudication Officer* [1996] 1 WLR 814.
14  G. Richardson and M. Sunkin, [1996] PL 79, 96.

'informal' or behavioural change, studies of judicial review in particular areas point up variations in the spread of impact. Let us take three examples, drawn from very different contexts. Prison administration is often seen as one of the success stories of judicial review. To this effect, attention may be drawn to changes in rules and practices as a result of litigation, and, further, to a greater emphasis in prison administration on legal values of formality and transparency. Livingstone, however, rightly stresses the limitations, as well as the interplay between law and administration. (The idea that judicial review works best closest to home is familiar from procedural fairness):[15]

> The formal legal impact of judicial review on prisons may be viewed as limited. Despite a decade of active litigation the Prison Rules 1964 remain in force in England, although they have been modified as to disciplinary adjudications and correspondence with lawyers, and the Prison Act has been left unchanged since 1952 ...
>
> What evidence there is does suggest a legalising of prison culture. There is the formalisation of release procedures for life sentence prisoners, the publishing of standing orders, the revising of the *Disciplinary Manual* ... All these developments fit in with an increasingly bureaucratic emphasis in prison management that no doubt reflects a decline in the belief that prison can actually do anything, positive or negative, to change prisoners' behaviour once they are released. They are also developments, however, that sit well with judicial review developments, stressing the need for clear criteria, formalisation and consistent decision-making in prison administration.
>
> It is arguably this emphasis on process that is judicial review's most enduring impact on prison administration. The courts have been happiest when ensuring prisoners access to the courts, reforming the quasi-criminal process of prison disciplinary proceedings and the quasi-sentencing function of life sentence release. In other words their impact has been greatest on the parts of prison administration that can be most closely analogised to the legal process. Judicial review has had less impact on either the framework of policy-making in relation to prisons or on the exercise of low level discretionary powers deemed essential to prison management ... Judicial review operates primarily to correct aberrations in bureaucratic decision-making but ultimately tends to find itself powerless before the arbitrariness which is often the normality of prison life. This is perhaps why it has had so little impact on prisoners' living and working conditions, a field that probably is best left to the more detailed investigative work of bodies like the ... Chief Inspector of Prisons.

Homelessness is identified as a 'core area' of judicial review and one in which the courts have tended to construe the legislation restrictively (*Puhlhofer*[16]). A study by Loveland confirmed that a chief determinant of local authority decision-making was the availability of empty properties for allocation to the homeless. A range of factors, such as agency relations and expediency, governed routine administration. In contrast, law in general, and judicial review in particular, had

---

15 S. Livingstone, 'The Impact of Judicial Review on Prisons' in B. Hadfield (ed.), *Judicial Review: A Thematic Approach* (Dublin: Gill & MacMillan) 1995, pp. 180–182. See further, G. Richardson, *Law, Process and Custody: Prisoners and Patients* (London: Butterworths) 1993; M. Loughlin and P. Quinn, 'Prisons, Rules and Courts: A Study of Administrative Law' (1993) 56 MLR 497. And see on parole, above, Chapter 7.

16 Above, p. 535.

not really penetrated at the ground floor, operational level: a common theme in the literature on impact.[17] Loveland paints a stark picture:[18]

> Legalistic perceptions of the 'law' will rarely be of more than minor significance. This is not to say that statute or case law has *no* hortatory role to play in structuring administrative behaviour ... It is clear that the threat of judicial review can have a marked short term effect on senior officers' perception of the way the administrative process should be controlled. But legalism is an intruder into the administrative arena. It does not prescribe administrative behaviour, but challenges it. It does not facilitate the decision-making process, rather it gets in the way. It is not respected, but ignored. And if it cannot be ignored it is grudgingly accepted as an unrealistic impediment to rational decision-making.

In the famous *Bromley* case[19] the House of Lords held that the Greater London Council had acted unlawfully and in breach of its fiduciary duty to ratepayers with regard to a reduction of fares on London Transport. What was the response among authorities? Some bowed to the spirit of the decision and changed direction; others resorted to creative lawyering to secure the policy.[20] Generally, the result of the case was a marked juridification of the administrative process, of the kind criticised elsewhere in this book. According to researchers:[1]

> The need to demonstrate the reasonableness of the policy process by routinely consulting political and legal interests has led to greater formality in the organisational arrangements of decision-making – in short, to greater bureaucracy. Accompanying the increasing rules and procedures [is] an extension in the amount of time spent in formal meetings and a growth in paperwork ...
>
> The taking of legal advice, of visiting counsel, has now become an established feature of the local authority's policy making process ... Some of the effects of judicialisation have in practice been detrimental to accountability either because the responsibilities for decision-taking have become confused or because the growth of paper work necessary to justify decisions can in practice prevent members digesting all the material upon which they need to take decisions ... The intrusion of the legal soothsayers erodes the authority of elected members in quite a fundamental way.

One measure of the increased seriousness with which central government regards judicial review is the steps taken to train staff to avoid taking attackable decisions. Already in 1982 the Treasury Solicitor was complaining publicly about the number of cases the Crown was losing. Perhaps predictably,

17  M. Sunkin and A. Le Sueur, 'Can Government Control Judicial Review?' (1991) 44 Current Legal Problems 161.
18  I. Loveland, 'Administrative Law, Administrative Processes, and the Housing of Homeless Persons: A View from the Sharp End' (1991) 10 Journal of Social Welfare and Family Law 4, 21–22. See further I. Loveland, *Housing Homeless Persons. Administrative Law and the Administrative Process* (Oxford: Clarendon) 1995, esp. Ch. 10.
19  *Bromley London Borough Council v Greater London Council* [1983] 1 AC 768, considered in Ch. 17.
20  See *R v Merseyside County Council, ex p Great Universal Stores Ltd* (1982) 80 LGR 639; *R v London Transport Executive, ex p Greater London Council* [1983] 1 QB 484.
1   L. Bridges, C. Game, O. Lomas, J. McBride and S. Ranson, *Legality and Local Politics* (Aldershot: Avebury) 1987, pp. 106, 110–111.

Sir Michael Kerry[2] identified as the root cause of government vulnerability the low level of legal awareness among officials. Challenge was here being made to traditional Civil Service views of law and lawyers as peripheral to the administrative process, encapsulated in the confining of departmental lawyers to legal as opposed to policy matters.[3] In the event, a new and systematic approach designed to anticipate legal challenge became a high priority for senior officials.[4] As well as in-house legal training, emphasis was laid on such steps as more pro-active use of lawyers at the planning stages of policy making; more thorough review of case work by managers; and greater use of counsel especially in the drafting of legislation. *The Judge Over Your Shoulder,*[5] a short guide to judicial review, was prepared by the Treasury Solicitor's Department in conjunction with the Cabinet Office. Designed for the benefit of non-lawyer civil servants, the pamphlet set out to 'highlight the danger areas' and 'enable warning bells to ring'.

How might this development be assessed? It reflects and reinforces the trend towards juridification of the administrative process. According to Cabinet Secretary Sir Robin Butler,[6] 'awareness of administrative law has greatly increased amongst civil servants'. A small pilot study suggests that if the 'new ethos [of judicial review] is having an effect it is to encourage officials to become more cautious in their work and more aware of the need to explain and justify action'.[7] This highlights the fact that judicial review may provoke both negative and positive responses. Bradley[8] criticises *The Judge Over Your Shoulder* for failure to extol the role of the law in promoting good administration. It can hardly be expected, however, that the response by government to judicial review will be anything other than ambivalent.

## 7. Conclusion

In the introduction to this chapter we introduced three dominant themes of rationing, public interest and judicial discretion. We also described judicial review as machinery for redress of grievance. It follows that criteria developed for complaints procedures (Chapter 12) may be used for its evaluation. The courts obviously score heavily in terms of independence, fairness (adjudication), public recognition and visibility. Judicial review also demonstrates important strengths as regards the criterion of effective redress, most obviously the mandatory orders. There are, however, major limitations. Despite their high visibility, courts are

2   M. Kerry, 'Administrative Law and the Administrator' (1983) 3 Management in Government 170; also 'Administrative Law and Judicial Review – The Practical Effects of Developments Over the Last Twenty-Five Years on Administration in Central Government' (1986) 64 Pub. Admin. 163.
3   B. Abel-Smith and R. Stevens, *Lawyers and the Courts* (London: Heinemann) 1967, p. 444.
4   See, for details, M. Sunkin and A. Le Sueur (above, note 17).
5   (London: Cabinet Office) 1987.
6   R. Butler, Foreword to *Judge Over Your Shoulder. Judicial Review: Balancing the Scales* (London: Cabinet Office) 1994.
7   M. Sunkin and A. Le Sueur (above, note 17) p. 175.
8   A. Bradley, 'The Judge Over Your Shoulder' [1987] PL 485. The tenor of the revised version, *Judge Over Your Shoulder. Judicial Review: Balancing the Scales*, is more positive towards judicial review.

difficult to access. There are problems of cost, technical jargon and remoteness. Legal advice is not always available. Courts are noted for their delays. Judicial review, in the light of *O'Reilly* and its progeny, is not noted for clarity of jurisdiction. The uncertain leave procedure is another barrier. Redress, though powerful when mandatory orders are forthcoming, is another area of uncertainty. Remedies may be adjusted, or denied altogether. Arguably, court remedies are quite as uncertain as the discretionary response to recommendations of the PCA. The PCA scores better in the area of fact-finding, where adversarial procedure combines with restrictive rules of discovery to limit the information necessary for intelligent decisions.

Situated on the interface of law, politics and administration, the judicial review process clearly requires a considerable degree of sophistication in its operation. The judges must pay due heed to the collective, public interest in good administration, and cannot pursue redress of grievance in isolation. Discretion, however, is a costly technique. The process sometimes resembles a lottery, especially at the vital leave stage. Techniques for rationing are various, and their purpose is not always clearly articulated. There is plenty of scope for judicial disagreement. Again, patterns of litigation demonstrate the illusory nature of a pyramidal structure for dispute resolution (above, p. 412). Considerable tensions are generated by moves towards a more elite system of 'public interest challenge' (Chapter 17).

Models of administrative law in which courts 'control' abuse of power require modification. It is not so easy to issue orders to government and administration and see them obeyed. Reactions may be positive but also negative. The radiating effects of litigation on administrative practice and procedure cannot be quantified. Realisation of the limitations of courts has led administrative law in several directions. It has fuelled a search for different techniques of 'control', in particular the fire-watching techniques of rule-making and regulation. It has fuelled a search also for alternative forms of dispute resolution, such as the Ombudsmen and the administrative review methods pioneered in welfare administration. There are, of course, contrary arguments in favour of advancing the institutional capacity of courts. These are underscored by the courts' own move to expand the judicial review process, procedurally through standing and intervention, and to extend justiciability, a trend illustrated by the *GCHQ* case.[9] This, however, highlights basic questions concerning the role and functions of courts and it is to this issue of legitimacy that we must now turn.

9   Above, p. 113.

# Chapter 17

# Justifying judicial review

## 1. Settling parameters

In Chapter 2, in the context of theories which prioritised the Rule of Law, we followed judicial review from the formalistic base to which a timid judiciary had retreated in the course of a century scarred by two devastating world wars. The temerity of the House of Lords in the 'trilogy of famous cases' (*Ridge v Baldwin,*[1] *Padfield,*[2] *Anisminic,*[3]) was to give judicial review a new lease of life.[4] We saw jurisdiction asserted over the prerogative powers in the *Burmah Oil* case,[5] a decision which goes to the heart of relationships between legislature and judiciary. This process reached a culmination in the *GCHQ* case,[6] where the House of Lords finally asserted the justiciability of the prerogative powers. The 'rule of law courts' was affirmed in *Anisminic,*[7] as it was a quarter-century later in *M v Home Office.*[8] In Chapter 4 we met a judicial review conducted in the terminology of rights, the dilemma for the judges being how far they ought to move in this direction prior to legislative authorisation through a Bill of Rights. Chapter 15 provided a study of judicial ideas of fairness. We saw that the principles of judicial review are fluid. Under the tutelage of the judges, natural justice dissolved into a more flexible principle of 'fairness' and developed offshoots, such as 'legitimate expectation'. Some important questions about legitimacy started to emerge. Why should administrative views of appropriate procedures be subordinated to judicial concepts of fairness, more especially when the latter are so inchoate? In Chapter 16, we concentrated on process. We saw the judges walking a tight-rope: much concerned with access, yet conscious of responsibilities towards the operation of the legal system; conscious of their responsibility to individuals, yet concerned to maintain an effective public administration. This again raised important questions about judicial values and the role of courts. It is now time to address these questions directly and to focus squarely on the function and proper ambit of judicial review.

1  Above, p. 500.
2  Above, p. 98.
3  Above, p. 540.
4  See J. Griffith, *Judicial Politics since 1920*, (Oxford: Blackwell) 1992, p. 63. For the crucial part played by Lord Reid in this transformation, see pp. 81-92. *Conway v Rimmer* (above, p. 420) is often added to the list.
5  Above, p. 47.
6  Above, p. 113.
7  Above, p. 54.
8  Above, p. 61.

Ours is essentially a majoritarian democracy in which the will of the people expressed through their elected representatives is supposedly paramount. This is a fundamental principle whose operation and observance can be traced throughout this book. It is recognised in the current Bill of Rights bill. Expansive doctrines of judicial review in a representative democracy are necessarily challengeable, as Sir Anthony Mason, former Chief Justice of Australia, observes: [9]

> The role of courts in the framework of government – the way in which they administer the rule of law – is in the process of evolutionary change, both in the United Kingdom and Australia. The forces driving that process of evolutionary change in both countries are broadly similar, though in the UK they are directly related to its membership of the European Community and its subjection to the legal regime which that membership entails.
> The courts in the UK and Australia have not advanced as far along this path of evolutionary change as have the courts in other modern democracies. The superficial explanation for that phenomenon is that neither country has adopted a Bill of Rights either entrenched in a Constitution or statute-based. Lying behind that explanation are a belief in majoritarian democracy and Professor AV Dicey's legal theory of Parliamentary sovereignty which may well have had a greater and longer-lasting impact in Australia and the United Kingdom than they have had elsewhere.

A common core of understanding probably exists, at least in western societies, about the judicial function. Around the periphery, however, perceptions differ very greatly. Modern cases, such as those already mentioned or the *Pergau Dam* case[10] and *Fire Brigades* case[11] discussed later in this chapter, push the judges very close to the heart of government. Inevitably they raise questions about the constitutional position of judicial review:[12]

> At the heart of much of administrative law – and certainly of the practice of judicial review of admininstrative action – stand fundamental and seemingly intractable theoretical questions about the role of courts in government. What, if anything, gives judges the general authority to review governmental action? What is sought from such review and what can it achieve? How if at all, is it compatible with ideas of democratic govenment, lawmaking, and policy implementation? In common law systems, courts have ultimate authority to interpret law, including administrative law. Equally, administrative law is assumed to provide an essential legal framework for most routine governmental activity. Thus, in this environment, the most basic and inescapable question becomes: what is the relationship between courts, polity and society? More specifically, how do courts that apply administrative law relate to the state, on the one hand, and the regulated population of individual citizens and varied social groups, on the other?

9   A. Mason, 'Courts, Constitutions and Fundamental Rights' in R. Rawlings (ed.), *Law, Society and Economy* (Oxford: OUP) 1997, p. 73.
10   Below, p. 591.
11   Below, p. 596.
12   R. Cotterell, 'Judicial Review and Legal Theory' in G. Richardson and H. Genn, *Administrative Law and Government Action* (Oxford: Clarendon) 1994, p.13. See also Sir Stephen Sedley, 'The Sound of Silence: Constitutional Law without a Constitution' (1994) 110 LQR 270.

We already know that sharply divergent views exist about the proper scope and function of administrative law in our society. Some of the positions are set out in earlier chapters where they were shown to range over a broad spectrum. It is not surprising to find the sensitive subject of judicial review at the centre of a similar debate over objectives and functions. The opposing positions are sometimes dismissed purely as political opinions. This attitude is, however, mistaken; as Stevens observes, modern expansive doctrines of judicial review and also the appeal to fundamental rights which we met in Chapter 4 provoke 'a clash with both the Labour and Conservative traditions',[13] a point we shall pick up later. We would say that the 'model of law' or 'balanced constitution' ideal, and the 'model of government' – in modern terminology perhaps conviction politics – dictate opposing answers to the fundamental questions we have raised.

In an attempt to situate judicial review within legal theory, Cotterell (above) identifies three basic positions. The first, which he christens the 'modest underworker', sees the judicial role as being simply to police the rule of law by interpretation. Later we shall see that this position can be broadly equated with Lord Wilberforce's description of 'narrow ultra vires' in the *Bromley* case[14]. The second position accords the judiciary much greater flexibility, allowing them to 'tap into values inherent in [a] fuller sense of democracy'.[15] This is broadly the position adopted by Sir Anthony Mason (above).

Cotterell's third proposition is grounded in the author's personal belief that law should foster a sense of community and shared values.[16] Cotterell sees courts as enabling popular participation in two distinct ways. The first way is through the enforcement of procedures in governmental decision-making that allow popular input into decision-makers' deliberations; in John Hart Ely's terminology, courts operate to buttress or shore up democracy.[17] This approximates to a 'process' theory of judicial review, such as we saw operating in our case study of the parole system.[18] In this book, however, we have seen that courts have operated the principle in a differential fashion. Today they are largely supportive of individual participation by reasoned proof in individuated decisions (natural justice and procedural fairness); as we saw in Chapter 7, they are so far less supportive of a right to collective input into decision-making of a general or collective character. Earlier, we found both Baldwin[19] and the

---

13  R. Stevens, 'Judges, Politics, Politicians and the Confusing Role of the Judiciary' in K. Hawkins (ed.), *The Human Face of Law, Essays in Honour of Donald Harris* (Oxford: Clarendon) 1997, p. 271.

14  Below, p.585.

15  R. Cotterell (above, note 12), p. 18. The citation is from D. Galligan, *Discretionary Powers, A Legal Study of Official Discretion* (Oxford: Clarendon) 1990, p. 236.

16  See further, R. Cotterell, 'Law's Community: Legal Theory and the Image of Legality' (1992) 19 J. of Law and Soc. 405; *Law's Community. Legal Theory in Sociological Perspective* (Oxford: Clarendon) 1995; and 'The Symbolism of Constitutions' in I. Loveland (ed.), *A Special Relationship? American Influences on Public Law in the UK* (Oxford: Clarendon) 1995.

17  J. Hart Ely, *Democracy and Distrust: A Theory of Judicial Review*, (Cambridge: Harvard) 1980.

18  See G. Richardson, 'The Legal Regulation of Process', in G. Richardson and H. Genn, *Administrative Law and Government Action* (Oxford: Clarendon) 1994. And see above, Chapter 7.

19  R. Baldwin, *Rules and Government* (Oxford: Clarendon) 1995.

Hansard Society[20] arguing for more widely recognised rights of participation in rulemaking (above, pp. 205-206).

The second way for judges to enable popular participation is to allow their own procedures to be used for this purpose, providing: [1]

> different kinds of opportunity for influence on administrative matters by citizens as litigants. Courts are relatively open to public view, accountable (through appeal systems), and in some senses participatory. They not only allow, but normally require opposing voices to be heard. Thus some writers have suggested that they actually embody democratic values or have the potential to do so.

In this passage, which reflects modern judicial views on access which we met in Chapter 15, we find the seeds of an emergent new model of judicial review. This we have labelled the 'public interest' model[2] and we return to it later in the chapter.

Cotterell's analysis is a helpful framework for our discussion, although, in what follows, it may be possible to discern other positions. This is not surprising. Unlike Dworkin,[3] the authors do not subscribe to the idea of a single, harmonious, correct answer to questions as fundamental as this one. Very different conceptions of judicial review can be held by sensible people.

## 2. Formalism and the 'drainpipe'

When, in the 1960s, the courts moved into the modern era, it was with a formalist model.[4] Visiting England at this period, the American jurist, K. C. Davis, was surprised[5] to find such a restrictive attitude to judicial review. 'Policy' was outlawed and a strict interpretation of the doctrine of precedent inhibited rapid changes of direction. This was the challenge taken up in the 'trilogy of famous cases' mentioned above.[6]

Elsewhere,[7] the authors have likened the classic model of judicial review to a drainpipe, narrow, inflexible lengths of tubing joined with rigid collars. The collars divided judicial review into three different stages, separating threshold requirements, such as leave, time-limits and standing, from the substantive issues

---

20   *Making the Law: Report of the Hansard Society Commission on the Legislative Process* (London: Hansard Society) 1992.

1    R. Cotterell, 'Judicial Review and Legal Theory' (above, note 12), p. 18.

2    C. Harlow, 'A Special Relationship? The American Influence on English Public Law' in I. Loveland (ed.), *Lessons from America* (Oxford: Clarendon) 1995.

3    R. Dworkin, *Taking Rights Seriously* (London: Duckworth) 1967 and *Law's Empire* (London: Fontana) 1986. For a relativist critique, see M. Weaver, 'Herbert, Hercules and the Plural Society: A "Knot" in the Social Bond' (1978) 41 MLR 660.

4    R. Stevens, *Law and Politics: The House of Lords as a Judicial Body 1800-1976* (London: Weidenfeld and Nicolson) 1983, Part 3.

5    K. C. Davis, 'The Future of Judge-Made Public Law in England; A Problem of Practical Jurisprudence' (1961) 61 Colombia LR 201, 202 and 216.

6    I.e., *Ridge v Baldwin*, *Padfield* and *Anisminic* to which some, including the authors, would add *Burmah Oil* and *Conway v Rimmer*.

7    C. Harlow and R. Rawlings, *Pressure Through Law* (London: Routledge) 1992, Ch. 7.

and finally from the separate question of remedies. Key elements in the formalist model were as follows:

1. There was no formal distinction between public and private law. As we saw in Chapter 16, this was inaugurated by the new Ord. 53. The unitary jurisdiction meant that 'public law' principles, such as the rules of natural justice, applied where appropriate to private and non-governmental bodies and, equally, might be applicable in private law actions.[8]
2. The primary objective of the model was the protection of litigants' legal interests. Administrative action was never reviewable merely because it was unlawful; to be reviewable, it must have caused injury to an individual interest.[9] In the drainpipe model, standing often depended on possession of a legal right (above, p. 541). The limitation also explains the emphasis on a distinction between 'rights' and 'privileges'.[10]
3. The grounds for review were restricted and grounded in the simple ultra vires doctrine[11] which meant no more than that a public body must not exceed or abuse its powers. This was construed wherever possible in favour of public authorities to validate 'whatever may fairly be regarded as incidental to, or consequent upon, those things which the Legislature has authorised'.[12] Decisions could also be quashed where there had been a breach of the rules of natural justice or an 'error of law on the face of the record', a ground rendered otiose by *Anisminic*.
4. The common law was remedy-orientated (Chapter 16). This meant that the ambit of judicial review was defined with reference to the scope of the existing remedies rather than to a grand design. Remedies also defined the scope of public law but in the limited sense that different remedies were obtained from different courts. Thus judicial review developed in a piecemeal fashion.

In the following passage, an epitome of classical judicial review is attempted by Allan:[13]

> Judicial review exists to safeguard legality. The rule of law requires that public authorities act only within the limits of their powers, properly understood. But a court may not interfere with action lawfully taken within the jurisdiction of a public authority. It is usually said that the court is concerned with the lawfulness of administrative decisions but not with their merits, which would be relevant only to an

---

8  See e.g. *Breen v Amalgamated Engineering Union* [1971] 2 QB 175; *Cooper v Wandsworth Board of Works* (1863) 14 CBNS 180, below p. 620.
9  There may have been an exception for invalid delegated legislation: see per Lord Reid in *Hoffmann-La Roche & Co AG v Secretary of State for Trade and Industry* [1975] AC 295.
10  de Smith, 4th edn. J. Evans, 1980, pp. 171, 188-189. See also *Nakkuda Ali v MF De S Jayaratne* [1951] AC 66; *Schmidt v Secretary of State for the Home Department* [1969] 2 WLR 337.
11  See D. Oliver, 'Is Ultra Vires the Basis of Judicial Review?' [1987] PL 543.
12  *A-G v Great Eastern Rly* (1880) 5 App Cas 473, 478. See also de Smith, 4th edn., J. Evans 1980 pp. 94-96.
13  T. Allan, *Law, Liberty and Justice, The Legal Foundations of British Constitutionalism* (Oxford: Clarendon) 1993, pp. 183-184.

appeal (granted expressly by statute). That distinction was emphasised by Lord Greene MR, in reviewing the exercise by a local authority of its discretion under the Sunday Entertainments Act 1932 [the *Wednesbury* case[14]]. The Court was not a court of appeal: 'When discretion of this kind is granted the law recognises certain principles upon which that discretion must be exercised, but within the four corners of these principles the discretion... is an absolute one and cannot be questioned in any court of law'. The court could intervene only where the authority had been influenced by irrelevant considerations, or had failed to take account of relevant matters; or where it had reached 'a conclusion so unreasonable that no reasonable authority could ever have come to it'.

Since, however, the exercise of discretionary power is properly subject to substantive, as well as purely procedural constraints, administrative and political choice may become closely intertwined with legal principle. In this field, therefore, the separation of powers is in practice neither straightforward nor self-evident; but it should not on that ground be rejected as futile. On the contrary it forms, as we have seen, an essential pillar of the rule of law. I shall argue that the court's jurisdiction is properly defined in terms of the rights of the applicant for review; the court's primary concern with his interest – as opposed to the wider objectives of the public authority – lies at the heart of the judicial function.

If this passage is read carefully, it will be seen that it contains an important ambiguity. The classical position, in which the judge exercises a balancing function, is that in the final sentence, where judicial review is 'defined in terms of the rights of the applicant'. This is close to a private law model of adjudication, where the court has to balance the plaintiff's legal interest against the defendant's legal obligations. To reiterate because it is important, the function of judicial review in the drainpipe model was primarily *to protect private interests*. Executive and administrative power was held within bounds by the principle that government must always be able to point to a source of authority for administrative action. (This is why we argued in Chapter 2 that *Malone v Metropolitan Police Comr* was wrongly decided.)

Allan's first sentence, however, describes judicial review as existing to 'safeguard legality' and ensure that 'public authorities act only within the limits of their powers', a standard 'control' theory of administrative law such as we met in the writings of Professor Wade in Chapter 2 (above, p. 37). We are not, of course, saying that the two positions are incompatible, but they do differ slightly. The distinction is important because the second approach leaves greater latitude for expansion than the first. Despite the restrictive reasoning of the following statement, the applicant's standing suggests that the wider position is being adopted.

## *R v Boundary Commission for England, ex p Foot*[15]

At the suit of the Leader of the Opposition, Mr. Michael Foot, the court was asked to review the findings of the Boundary Commission, an independent statutory

14   Above, p. 79.
15   [1983] QB 600.

commission set up by and answerable to the Home Secretary, which exists to review the boundaries of parliamentary electoral constituencies. Arguing that the Commission had failed to give proper weight to the principle of equal representation, the applicant asked for an order restraining the Commission from submitting its report. The court ruled first, that the question was justiciable but second, that the applicants had failed to show that the commission had reached conclusions which no reasonable commission could have reached.

> *Sir John Donaldson MR*: Since a very large number of people are interested in this appeal and since it is most unlikely that our decision, whether for or against the applicants, will meet with universal approval, it is important that it should at least be understood. In particular it is important that everyone should understand what is the function and duty of the courts. Parliament entrusted the duty of recommending changes in English constituency boundaries to the commission. It could, if it had wished, have further provided that anyone who was dissatisfied with those recommendations could appeal to the courts. Had it done so, the duty of the court would, to a considerable extent, have been to repeat the operations of the commission and see whether it arrived at the same answer. If it did, the appeal would have been dismissed. If it did not, it would have substituted its own recommendations. Parliament, for reasons which we can well understand, did no such thing. It made no mention of the courts and gave no right of appeal to the courts.
>
> There are some who will think that in that situation the courts have no part to play, but they would be wrong. There are many Acts of Parliament which give ministers and local authorities extensive powers to take action which affects the citizenry of this country, but give no right of appeal to the courts. In such cases, the courts are not concerned or involved as long as ministers and local authorities do not exceed the powers given to them by Parliament. Those powers may give them a wide range of choice on what action to take or to refrain from taking and so long as they confine themselves to making choices within that range, the courts will have no wish or power to intervene. But if ministers or local authorities exceed their powers – if they choose to do something or to refrain from doing something in circumstances in which this is not one of the options given to them by Parliament – the courts can and will intervene in defence of the ordinary citizen. It is of the essence of parliamentary democracy that those to whom powers are given by Parliament shall be free to exercise those powers, subject to constitutional protest and criticism and parliamentary or other democratic control. But any attempt by ministers or local authorities to usurp powers which they have not got or to exercise their powers in a way which is unauthorised by Parliament is quite a different matter. As Sir Winston Churchill was wont to say, 'that is something up with which we will not put.' If asked to do so, it is then the role of the courts to prevent this happening.

Before we move too far from the drainpipe model, it is important to stress that it is not unacceptable to green light theorists. (This is one reason why the *Wednesbury* judgment is set out in Chapter 3.) Griffith, for example, is generally protective of the political process, which he sees as more open, more accessible and more democratic than adjudication. He objects to the replacement of the discretionary decisions of politicians for which they are accountable to a democratically elected body, by judicial discretion for which no accountability exists. He has also argued stringently against the replacement of political debate by what he sees as the legalistic discourse of rights.[16] But Griffith is not advocating the abolition of judicial review,[17] believing only that review should be confined to cases where public authorities act outside their statutory powers in the classical sense of acting ultra vires (below). He also accepts that public authorities must abide by rules of procedure laid down 'by or under statute in accordance with natural justice'. His objective is to confine the ambit of judicial review, pinning the judges down and structuring their discretion by rules. Impractically, he asks for 'more positive, black-letter provision by statute which will define where the balance of public interest lies' and for express provisions as to justiciability in new legislation, bearing in mind that matters within the area of policy and politics are 'appropriate for politicians and not judges'. Remember *Anisminic*.

But Griffith is cynical of the view that judges possess only weak discretion, confined to the 'application of law to facts'. In reality, they are easily able to carry out forays into political territory:[18]

> In our system for two principal reasons, the judiciary have a wide scope for the making of political decisions. First, statute law does not seek with any precision to indicate where, between Ministers and judges, final decision making should lie. Secondly, judges themselves, in the common law tradition of judicial creativity, frequently invent or re-discover rules of law which enable them to intervene and to exercise political judgment in areas that hitherto had been understood to be outside their province. In the event, for these two reasons, legislators and Ministers and public authorities are continuously being surprised to discover that, in the view of the judges, they do not have the powers they thought they had.

## 3. Principles of judicial review: a 'seedless grape'?

Griffith is not the only one to see mutation inside the traditional model towards a wider and more penetrating judicial review; today the shift is generally conceded.[19] As we shall see, this is certainly the view inside the judiciary. From *Ridge v Baldwin*, where Lord Reid famously remarked, 'we do not have a developed system of administrative law – perhaps because until recently we did not need it'; to Lord Diplock in *O'Reilly v Mackman*, who thought the position had changed dramatically in the post-war era; to Lord Woolf, as we saw in Chapter 16, a principal advocate of the opening of standing, in 1996:[1]

> At one time it was thought that only those who are affected in some way which goes beyond the effect which the activity has on the public as a whole could bring proceedings, but now it is generally accepted that a much more generous approach to

---

16  J. Griffith, 'The Political Constitution' (1979) 42 MLR 1.
17  See his proposals in J. Griffith, 'Constitutional and Administrative Law', in P. Archer and A. Martin (eds.), *More Law Reform Now!* (Chichester: Barry Rose) 1983.
18  Ibid., p. 55.
19  A. Le Sueur, 'Justifying Judicial Caution: Jurisdiction, Justiciability and Policy' in B. Hadfield (ed.), *Judicial Review: A Thematic Approach* (Dublin: Gill & Macmillan) p. 199.
 1  Lord Woolf, 'Droit Public – English Style' [1995] PL 57, 62. See also H. Woolf, 'Judicial Review: A Possible Programme for Reform' [1992] PL 221.

an issue as to standing needs to be adopted. This is necessary to ensure that there is never a situation in which a public wrong can be committed without anyone having the right to seek redress.

How has this come about? For Wade, 'there has been little change in the law itself, but a very marked change of judicial spirit'.[2] More recently, for Le Sueur,[3] 'a myth of judicial intervention in high-level government policy has taken hold' which bears very little resemblance to what is actually taking place. Apart from European influences, allocating to judges new functions under the European Communities Act 1972 and causing some judicial heartsearching in the field of human rights, judges are merely carrying out their 'well-established supervisory functions'; judges are doing 'little that is new' and, 'as before, often hold contentious government policy to be entirely lawful'. It has to be said that these are big exceptions.

But can this view really stand? In Chapter 16, we watched the judges invent the exclusivity rule. We have seen them experiment with novel doctrines, notably the principle of legitimate expectation (above, p. 182). Lord Woolf, who is in a good position to know, describes[4] the changes as 'dramatic' and the courts' power 'to vary the extent of their intervention to reflect current needs, and by this means [helping] to maintain the delicate balance of a democratic society' as one of the strengths of the common law system.

## Courts and local democracy

We can see the extent of the change if we look at a series of controversial cases involving local authorities. Like *Wheeler v Leicester City Council*,[5] these pose serious questions about judicial attitudes to democracy. Our starting point is a classic 'drainpipe' case in which the validity of a council byelaw which prohibited singing within 50 yards of a dwelling-house was disputed.

## *Kruse v Johnson*[6]

*Lord Russell CJ*: [Byelaws] ought to be supported if possible. They ought to be, as has been said, 'benevolently' interpreted, and credit ought to be given to those who have to administer them that they will be reasonably administered...Surely it is not too much to say that in matters which directly and mainly concern the people of the country, who have the right to choose those whom they think best fitted to represent them in their local government bodies, such representatives may be trusted to understand their own requirements better than judges ... If, for instance, they were found to be partial or unequal in their operation as between different classes; if they were manifestly unjust; if they disclosed bad faith; if they involved such oppressive or gratuitous interference with the rights of those subject to them as could find no justification in the minds of

2   W. H. R. Wade, *Constitutional Fundamentals* (London: Stevens) 1980, p. 43.
3   A. Le Sueur, 'The Judicial Review Debate' (1996) 31 Government and Opposition 8, 18-20.
4   Lord Woolf, 'Droit Public – English Style' [1995] PL 57, 58.
5   Above, p. 117.
6   [1898] 2 QB 91.

reasonable men, the Court might well say, 'Parliament never intended to give authority to make such rules; they are unreasonable and ultra vires'. But a byelaw ... is not unreasonable merely because particular judges may think that it goes further than is prudent or necessary or convenient ...

This passage exactly parallels Lord Greene's liberal view of local authority discretion. It is instructive to turn back to *Wheeler v Leicester City Council* (above, p. 117). Are these decisions consistent?

In the recent case of *R v Somerset County Council, ex p Fewings*,[7] the council had acquired land under the Local Government Act 1972 for the purposes of 'benefit, improvement or development'. Following a local election in which Liberal Democrats were elected on an anti-hunting platform, it passed a resolution banning hunting on this land. Laws J quashed the decision on the ground that a public body has 'no rights of its own' and enjoys 'no such thing as an unfettered discretion' as this would put it 'above the law'; all its actions must be 'justified by a positive law'; it could act only 'to vindicate the better performance of the duties for whose fulfilment it exists'. A commentator calls this[8] an 'expansive use of public law'; certainly there is a contrast with the *Town Investments* case.[9] Why is the local authority not able to avail itself of powers of *dominium* when central government is? Cotterell's explanation is that judicial attitudes are hierarchical.[10] We might see them as accepting the democratic credentials of Parliament without question but not those of local government, seen as constrained entirely by statute, nor those of the elected government.[11] The case which follows is unusual in supporting local democracy against central government.

### *Secretary of State for Education and Science v Tameside Metropolitan Borough Council* [12]

A local education authority contested the powers of the (Labour) Minister under s. 68 of the Education Act 1944 to give directions in respect of selective entry to schools. Labour had introduced a scheme for comprehensive education shortly before the Conservatives had been elected with a mandate to restore selective entry. The Labour Minister, ignoring the mandate, took into account the short time available to introduce a selection scheme and the refusal of teachers' unions to co-operate with a selection procedure which they believed would be sketchy and unfair. Possibly influenced by the fact that, once abolished, selective entry could not easily be re-introduced, the House of Lords found for the council. Lord Diplock required the Minister to use a balancing test, arguing that he could use his statutory powers of direction *only* if the council had been unreasonable:

7   [1995] 1 WLR 1037, DC, Laws J. The Court of Appeal ((1995) 93 LGR 515) confirmed on the narrow ground that s. 12(1)(b) had not been considered.
8   G. Nardell, 'The Quantock Hounds and the Trojan Horse' [1995] PL 27, 29.
9   Above, p. 117.
10   R. Cotterell, 'Judicial Review' (above, p. 576, note 12), p. 29.
11   Sir Stephen Sedley, 'Human Rights: a Twenty-First Century Agenda' [1995] PL 386, 389.
12   [1976] 3 WLR 641.

*Lord Diplock*: Assuming, however, that [the Minister] had formed the view that cooperation by head teachers was likely to be only partial so that the selection process would be liable to greater possibility of error than where full cooperation could be obtained, the Secretary of State would have to consider whether the existence of such a degree of imperfection in the selection system as he thought would be involved was so great as to make it unreasonable conduct for the council to attempt to fulfil the mandate which they had so recently received from the electors. Again, there is no indication that the Secretary of State weighed these two considerations against one another ...

The mandate point arose again in *Bromley* but the case raises wider considerations.

### Bromley London Borough Council v Greater London Council[13]

The GLC, implementing a promise to electors in the manifesto of the governing Labour Party, reduced bus and tube fares by 25%. This was done by a grant to the London Transport Executive (LTE) which enabled the LTE to budget for a deficit.[14] The grant was financed by a precept to all London boroughs to levy a supplementary rate of 6.1p in the pound. This supplementary levy raised the rates to a level at which loss of central government grant would be incurred under the terms of the Local Government Planning and Land Act 1980. Bromley, a Conservative-controlled borough, applied for certiorari to quash the precept. Bromley failed in the Divisional Court (Dunn LJ and Phillips J), but succeeded unanimously in the Court of Appeal.[15] The House of Lords unanimously rejected the GLC's appeal:

*Lord Wilberforce*: The precept is attacked on two main grounds: (1) That it is beyond the powers of the GLC as defined by the Transport (London) Act 1969. (2) That even if the GLC has the necessary statutory powers, the issuance of the precept was an invalid exercise of its discretion under the Act. This ground itself may be divisible into two contentions (a) that the exercise of the GLC's discretion was unreasonable, or (b) that the GLC when deciding to issue the precept did not take relevant considerations into account, or did take into account irrelevant considerations or misdirected itself as to the law.

Both of these grounds depend upon the fact . . . that the GLC, though a powerful body . . . is the creation of statute and only has powers given to it by statute. The courts will give full recognition to the wide discretion conferred upon the council by Parliament and will not lightly interfere with its exercise. But its actions, unlike those of Parliament, are examinable by the courts, whether on grounds of vires, or on principles of administrative law (those two may overlap). It makes no difference on the question of legality (as opposed to reasonableness – see *Tameside*) whether the impugned action was or was not submitted to or approved by the relevant electorate: that cannot confer validity upon ultra vires action.

In this celebrated passage Lord Wilberforce distinguishes two judicial approaches: (i) judges can construe statute to determine the extent of administrative powers

---

13  [1983] AC 768.
14  See J. Dignan, 'Policy-making, Local Authorities and the Courts; the "GLC Fares" Case' (1983) 99 LQR 605.
15  [1982] 2 WLR 62.

('narrow' ultra vires); (ii) they may apply general principles of administrative law, such as the reasonableness doctrine ('wide' ultra vires). As indicated earlier, these approaches approximate to Cotterell's first two positions. Both may involve judicial creativity but the latter gives stronger and more open judicial discretion than the former, limited to interpretative or 'judgment discretion'. Lord Wilberforce, like Oliver LJ in the Court of Appeal, used the narrow approach, interpreting the word 'economic' to mean 'cost-effective' or 'making the most effective use of resources in the context of an integrated system'. Relying on a further statutory obligation under s. 7(3)(b) so far as possible to avoid deficit, Lord Wilberforce concluded:

> I find it impossible, in the light of the previous history and of the far from definite language used, to accept that Parliament could have intended that [there should be no limitation on the GLC's powers]. To say this is not to impose upon the London Transport Executive a rigid obligation to balance its accounts every year, nor... to maximise fares. There is flexibility in the words 'so far as practicable' and the obligatory establishment of a reserve gives room for manoeuvre . . . But, given this, it appears to me clear that neither the executive in making its proposals, nor the GLC in accepting them, could have power totally to disregard any responsibility for ensuring, so far as practicable, that outgoings are met by revenue, and that the London Transport Executive runs its business on economic lines.

> *Lord Diplock*: The GLC, like other local authorities, is an elected body . . . Broadly speaking, the electors comprise all adults resident in Greater London, of whom about 40 per cent are also rate-payers. Apart from income-earning assets, the GLC's principal sources of revenue are (1) rates for which it issues precepts to the London boroughs, who are under a statutory obligation to levy rates upon the ratepayers in the amount specified in the precept, and (2) grants from central government funds. Some 62 per cent of the total amount of the income of the GLC from rates is raised from ratepayers engaged in industry, business or commerce. They have no vote as electors. These structural characteristics of the GLC need to be borne in mind in applying, as I think one must, a purposive construction to the sometimes opaque and eliptical language adopted in the Transport (London) Act 1969 . . . .
>
> My Lords, the conflicting interests which the GLC had to balance in deciding whether or not to go ahead with the 25 per cent reduction in fares, notwithstanding the loss of grant from central government funds that this would entail, were those of passengers and the ratepayers. It is well established [16] that a local authority owes a fiduciary duty to the ratepayers from whom it obtains moneys needed to carry out its statutory functions, and that this includes a duty not to expend those moneys thriftlessly but to deploy the full financial resources available to it to the best advantage; the financial resources of the GLC that are relevant to the present appeals being the rate fund obtained by issuing precepts and the grants from central government respectively. The existence of this duty throws light upon the true construction of the much-debated phrase in section 1(1) 'integrated, efficient and economic transport facilities and services'. 'Economic' in this context must I think mean in the economic interests of passengers and the ratepayers looked at together, i.e. keeping to a minimum the total financial burden that the persons in these two categories have to share between them for

16  From the leading cases of *Roberts v Hopwood* [1925] AC 578 (local authority decision to remunerate women on a parity with men held unreasonable) and *Prescott v Birmingham Corpn* [1955] Ch 210 (local authority subsidy of fares for the elderly illegal).

the provision by the LTE in conjunction with the railways board and the bus company of an integrated and efficient public transport system for Greater London . . .

I think that the GLC had a discretion as to the proportions in which that total financial burden should be allocated between passengers and the ratepayers. What are the limits of that discretion ... does not, in my view, arise, because the GLC's decision was not simply about allocating a total financial burden between passengers and the ratepayers, it was also a decision to increase that total burden so as nearly to double it and to place the whole of the increase on the ratepayers. For, as the GLC well knew when it took the decision to reduce the fares, it would entail a loss of rate grant from central government funds amounting to some 50 million, which would have to be made good by the ratepayers as a result of the GLC's decision. So the total financial burden to be shared by passengers and the ratepayers for the provision of an integrated and efficient public passenger transport system was to be increased by an improvement in the efficiency of the system, and the whole of the extra 50 million was to be recovered from the ratepayers. That would, in my view, clearly be a thriftless use of moneys obtained by the GLC from ratepayers and a deliberate failure to deploy to the best advantage the full financial resources available to it by avoiding any action that would involve forfeiting grants from central government funds. It was thus a breach of the fiduciary duty owed by the GLC to the ratepayers. I accordingly agree with your Lordships that the precept issued pursuant to the decision was ultra vires and therefore void.

In this striking example of judicial creativity, Lord Diplock uses the 'wide' ultra vires principle in two distinct ways. First, as in *Tameside*, he re-formulates Lord Greene's doctrine of *Wednesbury* unreasonableness in a way which anticipates his speech in *GCHQ*,[17] using it to structure administrative discretion. Second, a common law concept of 'fiduciary duty' is introduced as a 'relevant consideration' in the light of which the statutory duty is to be interpreted. This is a principle of which de Smith, Jowell and Woolf say:[18]

> The breach of such a duty has rarely formed the *ratio* of a decision to strike down the expenditure concerned. The fiduciary duty could be interpreted in two ways: first, it could imply a duty to act on ordinary business principles and not to be 'thriftless' with ratepayers' money. Such a meaning comes close to permitting the courts themselves to decide the levels of expenditure which meet those standards. As the House of Lords has reminded us . . . courts are not, in judicial review, equipped to make such decisions. A second interpretaion views the fiduciary duty as a duty to take into account, in reaching a decision on expenditure, the interests of the ratepayers. Since the ratepayers' interests are likely to be adversely affected by a decision to increase expenditure, it is surely right that those interests should be considered by the local authority (although not necessarily slavishly followed). This second meaning of the fiduciary duty does not involve the courts in a function to which in judicial review, they are unsuited. It merely involves them in requiring that considerations which are relevant to the lcoal authority's powers, namely, the interests of the ratepayers, be taken into account. This is perfectly suited to judicial review.

Which of these two approaches did Lord Diplock adopt in *Bromley*? The end-result was surely precisely that prohibited by Lord Donaldson (above): as in an

17  Above, p. 113.
18  de Smith, Jowell, Woolf, para. 6-096.

appeal, the court has 'repeated the operations' of the council to see whether it arrives at the same answer. And is it really suggested that the GLC did not consider the interests of ratepayers? If so, where was the evidence?

This skilful rearrangement of principles forms part of what Allan Hutchinson has called 'the rise and ruse' of judicial review.[19] Lines can be drawn between terms such as 'politics', 'policy', 'principle' or 'purposive interpretation', but not very precise lines. Similarly, when judges use literal methods of interpretation and when they fall back on purposive methods is a matter for judicial discretion. The case for reasoned adjudication as a science, advocated in Chapter 4, begins to look somewhat thin. One might be tempted to share the suspicion of Gellhorn and Robinson[20] that 'the rules governing judicial review have no more substance at the core than a seedless grape'. Moreover, lingistic explanations such as that of de Smith, Jowell and Woolf, do not address our central question of the judiciary's credentials to develop or discover the norms. Lord Devlin, who supports openness in the matter of judicial lawmaking, also supports an 'activist' stance provided it stays within what he terms 'the consensus'. He justifies this on the ground that the judiciary is able to represent community values.[1] Precisely how, has never really been explained. Besides, the whole point about 'political' cases, such as *Bromley*, or *Wheeler*, or *GCHQ* is that they are the subject of differing, though strongly held, convictions. 'Consensus' on the merits is unlikely; if a limited consensus could be discovered, it would probably be procedural. This is really the strength of the 'process' school of judicial review (above).

Shortly after the controversial *Bromley* case, Oliver queried whether ultra vires was any longer the basis for judicial review. Without expressing a view on desirability, she answered her own question in the negative:[2]

> The central principle of administrative law has long been that the court's jurisdiction to review the acts and decisions of public authorites rests on the *ultra vires* rule. However, the trend in recent cases seems to be for the courts to pay little attention to questions of jurisdiction or the *ultra vires* rule (unless an ouster clause is involved): it was not relied on for example, in the judgements of Lords Diplock, Scarman or Roskill in the *G.C.H.Q.* case. It will be suggested in this article that judicial review has moved on from the *ultra vires* rule to a concern for the protection of individuals, and for the control of *power*, rather than *powers*, or *vires*.
>
> In considering whether *ultra vires* is the basis of judicial review, the phrase 'judicial review' is used in the sense of the substantive rules applied by the courts when using a supervisory jurisdiction ... These ... could be grouped together as, to use Galligan's words, 'principles of good administration'. They include the requirement of 'fairness' in its various guises, and they prohibit the fettering or delegation of discretion, abuse of power, arbitrariness, capriciousness, unreasonableness, bad faith, breach of accepted moral standards, and so on. They require, in other words, legality, rationality, procedural propriety and possibly proportionality.

19  A. Hutchinson, 'The Rise and Ruse of Administrative Law' (1985) 48 MLR 293.
20  E. Gellhorn and G. Robinson, 'Perspectives on Administrative Law' (1975) 75 Columbia LR 771.
 1  P. Devlin, 'Judges and Lawmakers' (1976) 39 MLR 1. For a fuller exposition, see, P. Devlin, *The Judge* (Oxford: OUP) 1979.
 2  D. Oliver, 'Is Ultra Vires the Basis of Judicial Review?' [1987] PL 543. See also C. Forsyth, 'Of Figleaves and Fairytales: The Ultra Vires Doctrine, The Sovereignty of Parliament and Judicial Review' (1996) 55 CLJ 122.

## 4. Structuring judicial discretion

Oliver is once again making the point that the rules of the game have changed. Can this be justified, or are judges indulging in too much judicial lawmaking and, if so, could their lawmaking capacity be fettered by Parliament, the legitimate lawmaker? No attempt at codification has ever been made in England; indeed, the question of grounds for review was notably absent from the programme of the Law Commission in 1991, which was confined to 'procedures and forms of relief', nor is there any mention of grounds in Lord Woolf's contemporary proposals for reform.[3] In Commonwealth jurisdictions it has been tried. Thus, s. 5 of the Australian Administrative Decisions (Judicial Review) Act 1977 reads:

### APPLICATIONS FOR REVIEW OF DECISIONS

5(1) A person who is aggrieved by a decision to which this Act applies that is made after the commencement of this Act may apply to the Court for an order of review in respect of the decision on any one or more of the following grounds:-

(a) that a breach of the rules of natural justice occurred in connexion with the making of the decision;

(b) that procedures that were required by law to be observed in connexion with the making of the decision were not observed;

(c) that the person who purported to make the decision did not have jurisdiction to make the decision;

(d) that the decision was not authorized by the enactment in pursuance of which it was purported to be made;

(e) that the making of the decision was an improper exercise of the power conferred by the enactment in pursuance of which it was purported to be made;

(f) that the decision involved an error of law, whether or not the error appears on the record of the decision;

(g) that the decision was induced or affected by fraud;

(h) that there was no evidence or other material to justify the making of the decision;

(j) that the decision was otherwise contrary to law.

5(2) The reference in paragraph (1)(e) to an improper exercise of a power shall be construed as including a reference to:-

(a) taking an irrelevant consideration into account in the exercise of a power;

(b) failing to take a relevant consideration into account in the exercise of power;

(c) an exercise of a power for a purpose other than a purpose for which the power is conferred;

(d) an exercise of a discretionary power in bad faith;

(e) an exercise of a personal discretionary power at the direction or behest of another person;

(f) an exercise of a discretionary power in accordance with a rule or policy without regard to the merits of the particular case;

(g) an exercise of a power that is so unreasonable that no reasonable person could have so exercised the power;

---

3   Law Com. No. 126 (1992), para. 1.1; H. Woolf, 'Judicial Review: A Possible Programme for Reform' [1992] PL 221.

(h) an exercise of a power in such a way that the result of the exercise of the power is uncertain; and

(i) an exercise of a power in such a way that constitutes abuse of the power.

5(3) The ground specified in paragraph (1)(h) shall not be taken to be made out unless—

(a) the person who made the decision was required by law to reach that decision only if a particular matter was established, and there was no evidence or other material (including facts of which he was entitled to take notice) from which he could reasonably be satisfied that the matter was established; or

(b) the person who made the decision based the decision on the existence of a particular fact, and that fact did not exist.

We know from our earlier consideration of rules that rule-interpretation may leave much discretion to the interpreter. This statute sets out to structure discretion but how far does it really achieve this? How precise are the provisions and how much discretion is left to the judiciary? The text follows the common law grounds for review quite closely yet its relationship with the common law is ambiguous. Whether the basis of judicial review lies in statute or common law is the subject of hot debate. [4] Section 4 provides that the Act shall have effect 'notwithstanding anything contained in any law' in force at commencement. Section 5(1)(a), on the other hand, is an example of legislation by reference; it merely incorporates the common law into the statute, leaving future development for the judges. What has in practice happened is that the statute has been strictly interpreted while the common law has evolved, in places overtaking and circumventing the Act; [5] that, indeed, is the purpose of s. 5(1)(j), the inclusion of which was apparently recommended by Wade. [6] We know too, if only from what Sir Anthony Mason (above) told us, that Australian courts have recently been experimenting with 'rights-based' review [7]; again, the legitimacy of what they are doing has come under similar scrutiny in Australia as in England. [8] Section 5(2)(g) incorporates the *Wednesbury* rule in its strictest version. Yet Australian courts, we are told, use the ground with some frequency and often 'where there is no shortage of similarly placed officials enthusiastically defending the reasonableness of the impugned decision'. [9] Could proportionality, at present a disputed ground (above, p. 118) be fitted into such a statutory scheme? We find the Australian debate proceeding alonf identical lines to that in England, with the judiciary characteristically split on the question. [10] We have to conclude that

---

4  M. Aronson and B. Dyer, *Judicial Review of Administrative Action* (Sydney: LBC Information Services) 1996, p. 103–115.

5  Ibid, p. 49.

6  Ibid, p. 208; *Prerogative Writ Procedures: Report of the Committee of Review*(th eEllicott Report) PP No. 56 (1973) paras. 41-43.

7  Ibid, p. 90.

8  See *Nationwide News Party Ltd v Wills* (1990) 108 ALR 681; *Australian Capital Television Property Ltd v Commonwealth of Australia* (1992) 66 AJLR 695. For comment see K. Ewing, 'Constitutional Constraints in Australia' [1993] PL 256 and H. Lee, 'The Australian High Court and Implied Fundamental Guarantees' [1993] PL 606.

9  M. Aronson and B. Dyer (above, note 4), p. 365.

10  Ibid, pp. 375-379.

little has been achieved in the way of greater certainty. The loose texture of this enactment leaves strong discretion to the judges; indeed, it is probably quite as flexible as the common law and certainly does nothing to extinguish concerns over the extent of judicial discretion.

## 5. Expertise and accountability

A different line of attack runs that, as de Smith, Jowell and Woolf put it, judges are simply not 'equipped to make such decisions'. Nor are their decisions based on the full consideration of appropriate evidential material that they require of administration. For Griffith[11] this is the worst of both worlds: an interventionist judiciary but one limited by procedures and practices designed to exclude the basic materials of effective political and administrative decision-making. In the absence of appropriate information, even the *Bromley* decision could only lead to approval of a modified deficit budget by a different court.[12] So either judicial procedure must change to become more inquisitorial (below); or the courts must back away from policy-making. As Cranston reminds us, courts are not the only machinery for accountability:[13]

> Public authorities are held to account as much, if not more so, through other mechanisms such as parliamentary select committees, investigations of the ombudsmen, or the activities of official audit bodies. These institutions may be as appropriate as the courts in reviewing the legality of a public authority's action and will have a greater expertise in deciding on other matters, for example, financial accountability. In some circumstances the political process itself will be a more effective and desirable avenue of accountablity or redress. The despised MP, for example, is often able to obtain satisfaction for an aggrieved constituent. And there is the important role of the media. Internal procedures within public authorities are also vital in ensuring that their activities are carried out within the limits of the law and that the position of individuals dealing with them is protected.

A general theme of this book, no modern case provides a better illustration of this line of reasoning than the *Pergau Dam* case.

### *R v Secretary of State for Foreign Affairs, ex p World Development Movement*[14]

The Foreign Secretary had (allegedly at the request of the Prime Minister) authorised aid in terms of s. 1(1) of the Overseas Development and Co-operation Act 1980 to the Malaysian government to help finance the construction of a dam.

11  J. Griffith, 'Judicial Decision-Making in Public Law' [1985] PL 564, 579.
12  *R v London Transport Executive, ex p Greater London Council* [1983] QB 484. And see above, p. 572.
13  R. Cranston, 'Reviewing Judicial Review' in G. Richardson and H. Genn, *Administrative Law and Government Action* (Oxford: Clarendon) 1994, p. 54.
14  [1995] 1 All ER 611.

The project was opposed by the environmental movement as destructive of natural resources, especially of rain forest. Section 1(1) provided:

> The Secretary of State shall have power, for the purpose of promoting the development or maintaining the economy of a country or territory outside the United Kingdom, or the welfare of its people, to furnish any person or body with assistance, whether financial, technical or of any other nature.

The Foreign Secretary's allocation of Overseas Development Administration (ODA)[15] funds to the project was opposed by the ODA and had been criticised in minutes from the Permanent Secretary (Sir Tim Lankester) in the light of British government appraisals which described the economic viability of the project as 'marginal' and 'a very bad buy'. Sir Tim had ultimately demanded written authorisation before making payments, facts which came to light through the reports of two Select Committees. The scheme had formed the subject matter of a 'value-for-money audit' by the National Audit Office, which reported unfavourably to the Public Accounts Committee (PAC).[16] The PAC learned that the payment was at all times seen as 'regular', the only issue being that of 'value for money'. A later report from the Foreign Affairs Committee of the House of Commons suggested an improper link between development aid and arms sales and was highly critical of the Ministry of Defence.[17]

In the light of this report, the World Development Movement (WDM), described by the court as 'a non-partisan pressure group' with official consultative status with UNESCO and in receipt of financial support from 'all the main UK development charities, the churches, the EC and a range of other trusts', asked for ministerial assurances that no further sums would be paid out. Not surprisingly, none was forthcoming. The WDM therefore applied for judicial review to quash these decisions. Both standing and legality were in issue:

> *Rose LJ*: The authorities referred to seem to me to indicate an increasingly liberal approach to standing on the part of the courts during the last 12 years. It is also clear from *ex parte National Federation of the Self-Employed*[18] that standing should not be treated as a preliminary issue, but must be taken in the legal and factual context of the whole case... Furthermore, the merits of the challenge are an important, if not dominant factor when considering standing.
>
> Leaving merits aside for a moment, there seem to me to be a number of factors of significance in the present case: the importance of vindicating the rule of law...; the importance of the issue raised, as in *ex parte Child Poverty Action Group and others*[19]; the likely absence of any other responsible challenger, as in *ex parte Child*

---

15  The ODA is a section of the Foreign Office with a separate budget whose funds were being used for the Pergau project. The Foreign Secretary at the time was Douglas Hurd.

16  See Seventeenth Report of the Public Accounts Committee 1993/4, *Pergau Hydro-electric Project*, HC 155 (1994/5). See also F. White, I. Harden and K. Donnelly, 'Audit, accounting officers and accountability: the Pergau Dam affair' [1994] PL 526.

17  Third Report from the Foreign Affairs Committee for 1993/4, *Public Expenditure: The Pergau Hydro-Electric Project, Malaysia, and the Aid and Trade Provision and Related Matters*, HC 271-I (1994/5).

18  Above, p. 542.

19  Above, p. 546.

*Poverty Action Group and others* and *ex parte Greenpeace Ltd*[20]; the nature of the breach of duty against which relief is sought ... and the prominent role of these Applicants in giving advice, guidance and assistance with regard to aid ... All, in my judgement, point in the present case to the conclusion that the applicants here do have a sufficient interest in the matter to which the application relates ... It seems pertinent to add this, that if the Divisional Court in *ex parte Rees-Mogg*[1]... was able to accept that the Applicant in that case had standing in the light of his 'sincere concern for constitutional issues', a fortiori, it seems to me that the present applicants, with their national and international expertise and interest in promoting and protecting aid to underdeveloped nations, should have standing in the present application.

Turning to the substantive question of whether the aid had been furnished for the purpose of 'promoting development', Rose LJ continued with an oblique reference to the *Wednesbury* principle:

> However, it is not disputed that the *weight* of competing factors (or whatever noun is applied to them) is a matter for the Secretary of State, once there is a purpose within s 1 of the 1980 Act.
>
> For my part, I am unable to accept [counsel's] submission that it is the Secretary of State's thinking which is determinative of whether the purpose was within the statute ... Whatever the Secretary of State's intention or purpose may have been, it is, as it seems to me, a matter for the courts and not for the Secretary of State to determine whether, on the evidence before the court, the particular conduct was, or was not, within the statutory purpose.
>
> As to the absence of the word 'sound' from s1(1), it seems to me that if Parliament had intended to confer a power to disburse money for unsound developmental purposes, it could have been expected to say so expressly.... Accordingly, where, as here, the contemplated development is, on the evidence, so economically unsound that there is no economic argument in favour of the case, it is not, in my judgment, possible to draw any material distinction between questions of propriety and regularity on the one hand and questions of economy and efficiency of public expenditure on the other. It may not be surprising that no suggestion of illegality was made by any official, or that the Secretary of State was not advised that there would, or might be, any illegality. No legal advice was ever sought.
>
> The Secretary of State is, of course, generally speaking, fully entitled when making decisions to take into account political and economic considerations such as the promotion of regional stability, good government, human rights and British commercial interests.... But for the reason given, I am of the view, on the evidence before this court, that there was, in July 1991, no such purpose within the section. It follows that the July 1991 decision is unlawful. This, of course, serves to reinforce the conclusion already indicated that the applicants have standing.

If we compare the position of Rose LJ with that of Otton J in the *Greenpeace* case,[2] we can see movement. The position of this applicant is not identical; this case relaxes the rules of standing further. What are standing rules for and what is left of them if, as Rose LJ suggests, it largely depends on the court's wish to intervene? Nobody suggests that members of the WDM were affected by the

20  Above, p. 547.
 1  Above, p. 545.
 2  Above, p. 547.

decision or that the WDM was 'representative' of persons affected. Like any group or individual in a democracy, it was merely voicing a complaint or opinion. [3]

As regards the second, substantive stage, this judgment is hardly tightly reasoned. Although he is interpreting a modern statute, it is not clear whether the judge is applying the 'narrow' ultra vires principle. Is the statute really ambiguous or has the word 'sound' been written in? We might also question whether this was the only, or even the principal head under which the Foreign Secretary could have justified his decision. Why was he not acting 'for the welfare of the Malaysian people'? And who is to be the judge and represent their welfare: the WDM and English Divisional Court or the elected Malaysian government, an equal partner in the negotiations?

It may be that the judge applied the *Wednesbury* test to this discretionary, ministerial decision, even if he does not explicitly say so. If so, was it Lord Diplock's 'strong' form or the modern paraphrase of Lord Greene's restrictive version approved by Sir John Laws? [4]

> First, the judges have to see that the power given by the statute is not transgressed by its donee; secondly, they have no business themselves to exercise powers conferred by it, precisely because they are not the donee. Hence the essence of the judicial review jurisdiction. It vindicates the rule of law not only by confining statutory power within the four corners of the Act, but also by ensuring that the statute is not usurped by anyone, including the courts themselves.

Lord Chancellor Irvine does not think that this is what the court did in *Pergau*: [5]

> Even on its own terms – that the decision whether the proposed development was in fact sound was for the court – the *Pergau Dam* decision dramatically illustrates the impact of treating a factor, such as the soundness of a proposed development project, not as a mandatory relevant consideration for the Secratary of State to weigh alongside other relevant considerations, but as the purpose of the statutory provision. The courts should take care to abstain, under the mantle of construction, from elevating what is, in truth, a mere relevant consideration into *a* or *the* purpose of a statutory provision, thus curbing a valuable and legitimate facet of administrative autonomy.

Now let us pick up the point about access to evidence both by the applicant and by the court which we first encountered in Chapter 16 (above, p 555). In this case, there was ample evidence. Why? Both the Foreign Affairs and Public Accounts Committees had completed full investigations. In stark contrast, as Stephen Grosz, solicitor to the WDM admits, the affidavit evidence available to the court in Ord. 53 proceedings was 'economical to the point of being parsimonious': [6]

---

3   See further, P. Cane, 'Standing up for the public' [1995] PL 276.
4   Sir John Laws, 'Law and Democracy' [1995] PL 72, 78.
5   Lord Irvine, 'Judges and Decision-makers: The Theory and Practice of *Wednesbury* Review' [1996] PL 59, 69.
6   S. Grosz, 'Pergau be dammed' (1994) 144 NLJ 1708, 1710.

The effectiveness of judicial review depends on the Government being candid in the evidence it gives to the court. A court can order disclosure of documents in judicial review proceedings only if it can be shown that the respondent's evidence is false or inaccurate. Since the judges considered that this could not be shown here, they refused to order disclosure. It was only because the matter had been investigated by two House of Commons committees that the WDM was able to mount the case at all.

It was only because the Government had provided the Foreign Affairs Committee with summaries of Sir Tim's minutes that the court was able to throw light on the advice Mr Hurd received, despite the inadequacy of the explanation given in the evidence filed in court. Few applicants will be so fortunate, yet the present procedure makes it difficult for them to go behind the evidence filed by the Government, be it ever so laconic.

Like Pannick in a similar critique of *Bromley*, Grosz argues for extensions to the court's powers. But could judicial review ever achieve the result these lawyers contend for? Pannick complains of: [7]

> ... paucity of reference to the social impact of the GLC's policy and the consequences of holding it unlawful; reduced passenger flow leading to even higher fares; an increase in road traffic causing more road accidents and greater pollution; a less frequent public transport service; and less jobs for London Transport staff. Nor is there any reference to the transport systems of other major cities in Europe, the subsidy of which was, no doubt, in the mind of Parliament in 1969. Whether or not the social and economic context and consequences of the decision argue against the substance of the Law Lords' judgment, it is objectionable that the judiciary should purport to construe admittedly ambiguous legislation without regard to the consequences of a decision for or against the GLC.

To go down this road would surely involve the court in 'repeating the operations' of the decision-maker. As in Scott, the Divisional Court would find itself in controversial or political cases embroiled in a full-scale inquiry. Many of the advantages of Ord. 53 procedure, more especially speed, would be lost. Moreover, the proposal raises fundamental constitutional questions over accountability. In classic constitutional theory, for policy matters such as this the Foreign Secretary was accountable to Parliament, while Sir Tim, his Principal Accounting Officer, was directly accountable to the Treasury. As judicial review expands into policy areas through expansion of the notion of 'legality', lines of accountability are becoming blurred.

Judicial review is a dynamic process and major changes, such as the move to exclusivity or the sudden widening of standing, can be accomodated within it. Although these may attract criticism, they seldom evoke reprisal. In the years since *Ridge v Baldwin*, the classic 'drainpipe' model has been transformed. It has transmuted into the 'hard edged' review deplored by Lord Irvine. Commentators identify a change in judicial purpose; 'the opinion of the court is determinative and the opinion of the decision-making body must conform to it if its decision is to survive challenge'. [8]

7    D. Pannick, 'The Law Lords and the Needs of Contemporary Society' (1982) 53 Pol. Q. 318, 322-323.
8    Lord Irvine, 'Judges and Decision-makers: The Theory and Practice of *Wednesbury* Review' [1996] PL 59, 63.

At one level, this development is what we might have expected; it is a facet of juridification, described throughout this book. We have seen a steady transition from discretion to rules; rarely has the trend been in the opposite direction. Modern rule-making practices, the rise of the contract culture and studies of the administrative process all exemplify this trend. Discretion, we learned, fell at one end of a spectrum. It was easily modified. Principles and standards were flexible, rules fixed. Thus, rules are often seen as providing certainty. As we saw in Chapter 4, however, this is an elementary error. Rules give rise to disputes over meaning in a way which discretion and 'soft law' cannot. The more formal the rules – and the present trend is to formalisation – the more likely it is that disputes over meaning will end in a court or tribunal. In the separation of powers theory which still dominates, judges declare the law. In other words, interpretation is the classic function of courts (and will always provide a good living for lawyers). In such a context, challenge for 'narrow ultra vires' is both acceptable and predictable.

It is at the level of principle that problems arise. Oliver correctly records a move from ultra vires to a long and expanding list of judge-made 'principles of good administration' (above). Principles are flexible and therein lies the problem. The principles have not been transmuted into rules and we have expressed doubt that they ever could. The principles of judicial review remain essentially soft-centred. Inevitably, this raises the question of their origin and of the authority of the judiciary to develop them (the principles/policy argument). Many of the principles are embedded in the common law. These fall into two classes. 'Rights' which are starting to be seen as constitutional in character have not as yet been sharply delineated. They raise further questions of legitimacy which we pick up later in the chapter. Other principles, like the rules of natural justice, are procedural in character. In recent years, we have seen such values acquire an added legitimation in the framework of the Citizen's Charter. Alongside the 'sigma' values of economy, efficiency and effectiveness, we have seen the promotion through the Charter of 'theta' values, notably transparency and participation. Proper procedures for handling complaints are encouraged. These developments in themselves justify a parallel development in the case law to establish process values in 'dark and windowless' areas of administrative law such as prisons and immigration. [9] To put this differently, far-reaching cases on procedural fairness and increasing firmness on the matter of reasons do little more than enforce recognised standards of public administration. Process review can easily be contained within existing understandings of the constitution. Rightly celebrated, the *Fire Brigades* case makes this point clearly.

## *R v Secretary of State for the Home Department, ex p Fire Brigades Union*[10]

Section 171(1) of the Criminal Justice Act 1988 placed the ex gratia criminal injuries scheme operated by the government under the prerogative, on a statutory basis. The Act was to come into force 'on such day as the Secretary of State may

9   G. Richardson, 'The Legal Regulation of Process', in G. Richardson and H. Genn, *Administrative Law and Government Action* (Oxford: Clarendon) 1994.
10   [1995] 2 WLR 1, CA; [1995] 2 WLR 464, HL.

appoint'. The Home Secretary introduced legislation to replace the 1988 scheme which failed to pass the House of Lords. Hoping to delay implementation indefinitely, he replaced the existing prerogative scheme with a new, less generous, 'tariff' scheme, effectively by-passing the 1988 Act. The lawfulness of this action was challenged by unions representing workers likely to be affected by the cuts in compensation. There was considerable disagreement both in the Court of Appeal and the House of Lords over the matter but both finally agreed by majorities that the procedure adopted had been improper.

*Lord Lloyd:* If one assumes that the postponement for five years was a valid exercise of the power conferred by Parliament, then of course the Home Secretary would be free to continue the existing non-statutory scheme in the meantime, as he has in the past, or substitute another scheme, whether more or less favourable to the victims of violent crime. But the assumption begs the question. It is the decision of the Home Secretary to renounce the statutory scheme, and to surrender his power to implement it, which constitutes the abuse of power in the present case ...

Ministers must be taken at their word. If they say they will not implement the statutory scheme, they are repudiating the power conferred on them by Parliament in the clearest possible terms. It is one thing to delay bringing the relevant provisions into force. It is quite another to abdicate or relinquish the power altogether. Nor is that all. The Government's intentions may be judged by their deeds as well as their words. The introduction of the tariff scheme, which is to be put on a statutory basis as soon as it has had time to settle down, is plainly inconsistent with a continuing power under section 171 to bring the statutory scheme into force ...

The duty of the court to review executive action does not depend on some power granted by Parliament in a particular case. It is part of the court's ordinary function in the day to day administration of justice. If a minister's action is challenged by an applicant with sufficient locus standi, then it is the court's duty to determine whether the minister has acted lawfully, that is to say, whether he has acted within the powers conferred on him by Parliament. If the minister has exceeded or abused his power, then it is the ordinary function of the Divisional Court to grant appropriate discretionary relief. In granting such relief, the court is not acting in opposition to the legislature, or treading on Parliamentary toes. On the contrary: it is ensuring that 'powers conferred by Parliament are exercised within the limits, and for the purposes, which Parliament intended'.

*Lord Mustill* (dissenting): It is a feature of the peculiarly British conception of the separation of powers that Parliament, the executive and the courts have each their distinct and largely exclusive domain. Parliament has a legally unchallengeable right to make whatever laws it thinks right. The executive carries on the administration of the country in accordance with the powers conferred on it by law. The courts interpret the laws, and see that they are obeyed. This requires the court on occasion to step into the territory which belongs to the executive, not only to verify that the powers asserted accord with the substantive law created by Parliament, but also, that the manner in which they are exercised conforms with the standards of fairness which Parliament must have intended. Concurrently with this judicial function Parliament has its own special means of ensuring that the executive, in the exercise of its delegated functions, performs in a way which Parliament finds appropriate. Ideally, it is these latter methods which should be used to check executive errors and excesses; for it is the task of Parliament and the executive in tandem, not of the courts, to govern the country. In recent years, however, the employment in practice of these specifically Parliamentary measures has fallen short, and sometimes well short, of what was needed to bring the executive into line with the law ...To avoid a vacuum in which the citizen would be left without protection against a misuse of executive powers the courts have had no option but to occupy the dead ground in a manner, and in areas of public life, which could not have been foreseen 30 years ago. For myself, I am quite satisfied that this unprecedented judicial role has been greatly to the public benefit. Nevertheless, it has its risks, of which the courts are well aware ... some of the arguments addressed [in the Court of Appeal] would have the court push to the very boundaries of the distinction between court and Parliament established in, and recognised ever since, the Bill of Rights 1688 ... 300 years have passed since then, and the political and social landscape has changed beyond recognition. But the boundaries remain; they are of crucial significance to our private and public life; and the courts should, I believe, make sure that they are not overstepped.

## 6. Adjudication and polycentricity

Drawing on the seminal work of Lon Fuller, Allison believes that there are good procedural reasons for a self-imposed judicial embargo on policy-making:[11]

> To avoid exceeding the limits of its own competence, a court confronted with a significantly polycentric dispute must refrain from two kinds of activism. First, the court must not change the law where an appreciation of repercussions is required for sensible legal development. Secondly, in so far as the court has a choice under existing law, it must avoid choosing a legal solution that necessitates an appreciation of complex repercussions.

Lon Fuller famously argued that certain problems, which he characterised as 'polycentric', are by their very nature unsuitable for resolution through adjudication. Such problems involve a complex network of *interacting* interests and considerations. As Fuller explained, each decision made communicates itself to other centres of decision, changing the conditions so that a new basis must be found for the next decision:[12]

> We may visualise this kind of situation by thinking of a spider's web. A pull on one strand will distribute tensions after a complicated pattern throughout the web as a whole. Doubling the original pull will, in all likelihood, not simply double each of the resulting tensions but will rather create a different complicated pattern of tensions. This would certainly occur, for example, if the doubled pull caused one or more of the weaker strands to snap. This is a 'polycentric' situation because it is 'many centered' – each crossing of strands is a distinct center for distributing tensions.

Fuller exemplified the task of establishing levels of wages and prices in a centrally-planned economy. A rise in the price of a single raw material may affect in varying degrees the demand for many different kinds of commodity, each of

---

11  J. Allison, 'The Procedural Reason for Judicial Restraint' [1994] PL 452, 455. See, for a slightly different angle, A. Le Sueur, 'Justifying Judicial Caution: Jurisdiction, Justiciability and Policy' in B. Hadfield (ed.) *Judicial Review: A Thematic Approach* (Dublin: Gill & Macmillan) 1995.
12  L. Fuller, 'The Forms and Limits of Adjudication' (1978) 92 Harv. LR 353.

these effects having further knock-on effects in the economy. Fuller's general point was that, as a technique of social ordering, adjudication cannot encompass and take into account the complex repercussions in this type of situation. 'It is simply impossible to afford each affected party a meaningful participation through proofs and reasoned arguments.' Each price rise would have a different set of knock-on effects and might require in each instance a redefinition of the 'parties affected'. As Cranston sees it:[13]

> Public authorities and the courts work on different assumptions. Public authorities are concerned with administrative efficiency, policy, and the 'public interest'. In recent times public authorities have also had to come to terms with new management techniques and market approaches. Estimation and probability are used by public authorities as a means of generalising. Judgements are made that particular policies can only be partly accomplished. The need to retain managerial flexibility to meet new circumstances is highly prized. Law is not seen as central to the enterprise. Viewed positively, it may be seen as a set of pegs on which to hang policies; viewed negatively it may be seen as a set of hurdles to be jumped.

## *R v Cambridge Health Authority, ex p B*[14]

B, a 10-year-old girl, was diagnosed as having leukaemia at the age of 5. Chemotherapy seemed to work but at age 8 she developed a rarer form of the disease. After further chemotherapy followed by a bone marrow transplant the disease went into remission but when in January 1995 she suffered a relapse the doctors treating her considered that she had six to eight weeks to live and that further remedial treatment would not be in her best interests. B's father sought other medical opinion and found a doctor prepared to act. The proposed treatment would be in two stages: (a) a further course of chemotherapy costing £15,000 with an estimated 10-20% chance of success; to be followed, if remission was achieved, by (b) a second bone marrow transplant costing £60,000 which also had a 10-20% chance of success. Because of the unavailability of beds in the only NHS hospital prepared to carry out the treatment, it could only be done privately. B's father sought judicial review of the health authority's refusal to allocate funds amounting to £75,000.

The annual budget of this health authority stood at £212 million, of which £145 million was committed on contracts with hospitals and care homes and on community health care. A further £55 million went to the family doctor service. A little less than £1 million was budgeted for 'emergencies' (the category stated to be relevant in *ex p B*). The whole budget represented an average bill of some £330 per head for the 450,000 people in the authority's area. In affidavit evidence, the senior officer responsible for contracting for the purchase of medical services outside the authority, himself a highly qualified physician, explained his decision:

> First and foremost I had to consider whether the proposed course of treatment was clinically appropriate for [B]. I also had to consider whether it would be an effective

13  R. Cranston, 'Reviewing Judicial Review' (above, p.591, note 13), p. 64.
14  [1995] 2 All ER 129.

use of the [authority's] limited resources, bearing in mind the present and future needs of other patients ... Having considered all the medical opinions put before me I decided to accept the clinical judgment [of B's doctors] that a further course of intensive chemotherapy with a view to a second transplant operation was not in the best interests of [B]. I have also been influenced in my decision by the consistent advice and directions of the Department of Health with regard to the funding of treatments which have not been proven to be of benefit. The ethical use of resources demands that new and expensive treatments are evaluated before they are transferred to the NHS for service funding. The doctors to whom I spoke were consistent in their advice that the proposed treatment was neither standard nor had been formally evaluated. I also considered that the substantial expenditure on treatment with such small prospect of success would not be an effective use of resources. The amount of funds available for health care are not limitless. The [authority] has a responsibility to ensure that sufficient funds are available from their limited resources for the provision of treatment for other patients which is likely to be effective.

In the High Court, the application for judicial review was partially successful when Laws J quashed the authority's decision, thereby requiring it to reconsider:

*Laws J*: It seemed to me that a fundamental right, the right to life, was engaged in the case. I invited counsel's attention to two authorities in Their Lordships' House: *Musisi*[15] and *Brind*[16]. In *Musisi*, the Court of Appeal ruled, 'the most fundamental of all human rights is the individual's right to life and when an administrative decision and a challenge is said to be one that may put the applicant's life at risk, the basis of the decision must surely call for the most anxious scrutiny'. In the light of these materials the first two questions I must decide ... are whether the respondents in the present case have (a) taken a decision that interferes with the applicant's right to life, and (b) if they have, whether they have offered a substantial public interest justification for doing so ... The fact is that without funding for [the new doctor's] treatment, the applicant will soon certainly die. If the funding is made available, she might not. As things stand at present, the respondents are the only apparent source of the necessary funds ...

If the necessary funds are made available for [the new doctor] to embark on B's treatment, she would enjoy what I will call a worthwhile chance of life. It may be very modest. It may be less than 10%. But to anyone confronting the prospect of extinction in a few weeks such a chance of longer, perhaps much longer, survival must be unimaginably precious ...

Merely to point to the fact that resources are finite tells one nothing about the wisdom or, what is relevant for my purposes, the legality of the decision to withhold funding in a particular case. But where the question is whether the life of a 10-year-old child might be saved, by however slim a chance, the responsible authority must in my judgment do more than toll the bell of tight resources. It must explain the priorities that have led it to decline to fund the treatment. It has not adequately done so here ... I accept that at present no sufficient justification has been shown to refuse this chance of life to B.

This case provides a perfect example of a complex polycentric decision. The interests of many parties are involved, not all of whom (such as doctors or even

15   [1987] AC 514 (alternatively known as *Bugdaycay*, below, note 17).
16   Above, p. 120.

the child, whose interests may differ from those of her parents) are before the court. A positive decision in the case will have a 'knock on' effect for other users and might ultimately affect the general tax fund. The judgment is challenging in two ways. First, it is emblematic of the rights-based approach to judicial review discussed in Chapter 4 (above, pp.119-127). Secondly, this is 'hard edged' review, the 'most anxious scrutiny' being reserved for the 'most precious' of rights.[17] As in *Bromley*, quashing the decision in effect put the onus of demonstrating a 'substantial' justification firmly on the authority. The judge stressed that it was no part of his function to make medical judgments, refusing a mandatory order because he conceded the possibility 'that the financial constraints, and other deserving cases, are more pressing than at present appear'. Yet this seems to be precisely the point which he had decided!

The line of reasoning failed to impress the Court of Appeal, where the application failed completely:

> *Sir Thomas Bingham MR*: This is a case involving the life of a young patient and that ... is a fact which must dominate all consideration of all aspects of the case. Our society is one in which a very high value is put on human life. No decision affecting human life is one that can be regarded with other than the greatest seriousness ...
>
> The courts are not, contrary to what is sometimes believed, arbiters as to the merits of cases of this kind. Were we to express opinions as to the likelihood of the effectiveness of medical treatment, or as to the merits of medical judgment, then we should be straying far from the sphere which under our constitution is accorded to us. We have one function only, which is to rule upon the lawfulness of decisions. That is a function to which we should strictly confine ourselves ...
>
> The learned judge held that ... evidence about money consisted only of grave and well-rounded generalities ... The learned judge said: 'They must explain the priorities that have led them to decline to fund the treatment', and he found that they had not adequately done so here.
>
> I have no doubt that in a perfect world any treatment which a patient ... sought would be provided if doctors were willing to give it, no matter how much it cost, particularly when a life was potentially at stake. It would, however ... be shutting one's eyes to the real world if the court were to proceed on the basis that we do live in such a world. It is common knowledge that health authorities of all kinds are constantly pressed to make ends meet. They cannot pay their nurses as much as they would like; they cannot provide all the treatments they would like; they cannot purchase all the extremely expensive medical equipment they would like ... Difficult and agonising judgments have to be made as to how a limited budget is best allocated to the maximum advantage of the maximum number of patients. That is not a judgment which the court can make. In my judgment, it is not something that a health authority such as this authority can be fairly criticised for not advancing before the courts ...
>
> I furthermore think, differing I regret from the judge, that it would be totally unrealistic to require the authority to come to the court with its accounts and seek to demonstrate that if this treatment were provided for B then there would be a patient, C, who would have to go without treatment. No major authority could run its financial affairs in a way which would permit such a demonstration.
>
> [One] criticism which the learned judge made was that the authority had wrongly treated the problem which they faced as one of spending £75,000 when, in the first

17   See M. Fordham, 'What is "Anxious Scrutiny"?' [1996] Judicial Review 81. The term originates in *Bugdaycay v Secretary of State for the Home Department* [1987] AC 514, a serious asylum claim.

instance, the treatment only involved the expenditure of £15,000 ... It is of course true that if the first stage were not successful then £15,000 ... would be the maximum that the authority would end up spending. It would not, however, be reasonable for the authority to embark on this expenditure on this basis since, quite plainly, they would have to continue if, having expended the £15,000, it proved successful ... Having weighed the matter up and taken advice, particularly bearing in mind the suffering which even embarking on the treatment would inflict, the authority thought that they should not fund the treatment at all. I regret that I find it impossible to fault that process on their part ... While I have every possible sympathy with B, I feel bound to regard this as an attempt, wholly understandable but nonetheless misguided, to involve the court in a field of activity where it is not fitted to make any decision favourable to the patient.

Here we have the 'orthodox' approach preferred by Lord Irvine (above). There is no reference to 'fundamental rights'; instead the focus is very much on 'lawfulness', 'excess of power' and '*Wednesbury* unreasonableness'. In a classic example of judicial restraint, the court sets out the parameters of the problem and seeks to avoid exceeding the limits of its own competence. In practical terms, this means choosing a legal solution which avoids an appraisal of 'complex repercussions', which in turn means refusing to open up the broader decision-making context (in the way that Laws J would have done) to external scrutiny through judicial review.

## 7. Reinventing judicial review

But this is not the direction in which the current is flowing. Elsewhere, the authors have likened contemporary English judicial review to a funnel,[18] generous with access, sucking in litigants and more recently intervenors. We watched these developments in Chapter 16. This is the 'public interest model', in which the courtroom is seen as a platform for public discussion and forum for debate of matters of public interest by litigants who are increasingly interest and pressure groups.[19] When we wrote this, grounds for review were less expansive, while remedies remained within the traditional drainpipe model. We argued that the model could not remain static; generous access would inevitably create pressure on later stages of the process.

Our prophecy is beginning to be fulfilled. Proponents of the 'New Judicial Review' have been successful in promoting steady expansion of the courts' jurisdiction. Previous 'no go' areas have been occupied, as we saw with the famous cases on prerogative powers. Le Sueur records a steady move from jurisdiction to the more flexible concept of justiciability to regulate the perimeters of judicial review.[20] In an earlier chapter, we saw the expansive approach applied to remedies in the landmark case of *M v Home Office*,[1] where an established

---

18  *Pressure Through Law* (above, p. 578, note 7), pp. 311-312.
19  See further, C. Harlow, 'A Special Relationship? The American Influence on English Public Law' in I. Loveland (ed.), *Lessons from America* (Oxford: Clarendon) 1995. The model originates in the United States Supreme Court: see R. Cortner, 'Strategies and Tactics of Litigants in Constitutional Cases' (1968) 17 J. of Pub. Law 287; R. Stewart, 'The Reformation of American Administrative Law' (1975) 88 Harv. LR 1667 (1975).
20  A. Le Sueur, 'Justifying Judicial Caution' (above, p. 582, note 20).
1  Above, p. 61.

statute was virtually re-written. In this chapter, we have seen the drainpipe split wide open in *Pergau Dam*. We note, too, pressure from practitioners for further procedural change in matters of proof and evidence. The growth of rights-based theories of judicial review has buttressed the public interest model. Consciously or unconsciously, courts under the leadership of a relatively interventionist judiciary, are beginning to function as a surrogate political process, responsive to the pressure created by generous access to the courtroom. Is this, as Lord Irvine argues, a dangerous break with constitutional tradition. Are courts assuming a larger constitutional role? Is this position justifiable in the light of forthcoming incorporation of the ECHR?

Sir John Laws claims[2] that courts are the guardians of democracy:

> The cornerstones of democracy and of inalienable rights ought not by law to be in the keeping of the government, because the only means by which these principles may be enshrined in the state is by their possessing a status which no government has the right to destroy.

Sir Anthony Mason agrees, rejecting as a 'shallow notion' the concept of untrammelled parliamentary sovereignty:[3]

> Our constitutional arrangements are more subtle and sophisticated than that. They envisage an effective system of democratic government in which powers are exercised in conformity with the rule of law in the interests of the people. And our conception of modern democratic government extends beyond simple majoritarianism to respect for the fundamental rights and the dignity of the individual.

Not every judge would echo these sentiments; indeed, what emerges from the case law is the diversity of judicial opinion. Laws J's judgment in the *Cambridge* case[4] marked the onward march of rights-based judicial review but was balanced by the withdrawal of the Court of Appeal behind the classic *Wednesbury* line. Paradoxically, in the *Fire Brigades* case,[5] Lord Mustill supported judicial willingness to fill a gap in political accountability but employed a 'hands off' approach; Lord Lloyd adopted a conservative interpretation of the judicial function, yet found it possible to review. This is perhaps the true 'politics of the judiciary'.

The public interest model of judicial review is fraught with dangers, of which its proponents seem largely unaware. It is not enough to rely, as Sedley does, on:[6]

> ... considerable public support for judicial control of an otherwise unaccountable executive, or of unresponsive public authorities. Administrations of all colours may have themselves to blame for a popular consciousness which, at least occasionally, casts them in the role of dragons and the judiciary in the role of St Georges.

2 Sir John Laws, 'Law and Democracy' [1995] PL 72, 92.
3 Sir Anthony Mason, 'Courts, Constitutions and Fundamental Rights' in R. Rawlings (ed.), *Law, Society and Economy* (Oxford: Clarendon) 1997, p. 73.
4 Above, p. 599.
5 Above, p. 596
6 S. Sedley, 'Governments, Constitutions and Judges' in G. Richardson and H. Genn, *Administrative Law and Government Action* (Oxford: Clarendon) 1994, p. 41.

Untested public support may be transient, leaving the judiciary too far out on a political limb. For Lord Mustill, when 'judicial creativity [is seen as] too wild and unpredictable, informed opinion creates a force in the opposite direction, tending to impel judicial methods back towards the norm. The result is a slow but repeated oscillation of judicial methods' [7] Lord Keith, dissenting in the *Fire Brigades* case, spoke in strong language of 'an unwarrantable intrusion by the court into the political field and a usurpation of the function of Parliament'.

Modern government 'derives its authority and legitimacy not by right of royal succession nor by divine right, but from the ballot box'. [8] The scope for political and administrative action is already severely limited, hedged about with economic and international restrictions. The danger is that courts will pin administration too tightly inside a judicial straitjacket, reformulating it as a quasi-judicial process. The legal process is, moreover, expensive, slow and uncertain, unsuitable for mass administration. Is Lord Woolf right in thinking that there should 'never be a situation in which a public wrong can be committed without anyone having the right to seek redress'? Judges are not omniscient, even where human rights are in issue; their credibility as decision-makers in dealing with complex polycentric cases is decidedly suspect. Courts may be wrong to suck litigants into the funnel without hope of an appropriate outcome. Surely some decisions must be final?

---

7   Lord Mustill, 'What Do Judges Do?' (1996) cited R. Stevens, 'Judges, Politics, Politicians' (above, p. 577, note 13), p. 274.
8   J. Griffith 'Judges and the Constitution' in R. Rawlings (ed.) *Law, Society and Economy* (Oxford: Clarendon) 1997, p. 308.

Chapter 18

# Golden handshakes: compensation and reparation

This chapter looks at circumstances in which government, usually in recognition of private property rights, though sometimes acknowledging a wider and more collectivist principle, concedes an obligation to compensate, using this word loosely and in its widest sense. Whether equitable or legal, such obligations necessarily impinge on the governmental prerogative of resource-allocation. Recognised as a central function of the 'nightwatchman' state, the raising of revenue is a power of *imperium* equal in importance to the legislative power discussed in Chapter 6. Central to the notion of sovereignty, it lies at the heart of the British constitution. Battles over the royal power to raise revenue led directly to the civil war, [1] and the Bill of Rights of 1688 left no doubt about its significance. This charter of parliamentary supremacy established control over the legislative power, prohibiting the 'pretended' prerogative powers of 'dispensing' and 'suspending' the laws. It went on to state firmly:

> That levying money for or to the use of the Crown by pretence of prerogative without grant of Parliament for longer time, or in other manner than the same is or shall be granted, is illegal.

A central tenet of our constitutional settlement had been established; the executive may raise revenue and allocate resources but only with the consent of Parliament (in modern times, the House of Commons [2]). Not only supply but also expenditure is strictly controlled and these are prerogatives of which the House of Commons is extremely jealous. There is potential here for a clash of interests with courts, who possess their own resource allocation function, incidental to the civil liability system whose operation is one of their most important functions. [3] We are by now familiar with Fuller's argument that polycentric decisions ought not to be resolved by means of adjudication and, in Chapter 17, the *Cambridge* case [4] demonstrated how individuated judicial decisions could impinge on resource allocation. It is not surprising to find Fuller expressing the view [5] that the award

---

1  See F. W. Maitland, *The Constitutional History of England* (Cambridge: Cambridge University Press) 1913, pp. 306–311.
2  W. I. Jennings, *Parliament* (Cambridge: Cambridge University Press), 2nd edn., 1970, Ch. 283.
3  See C. Harlow, *Understanding Tort Law* (London: Fontana) 1995; P. Cane, *An Anatomy of Tort Law* (Oxford: Hart) 1997.
4  Above, p. 599.
5  Cited by J. Allison, 'The Procedural Reason for Judicial Restraint' [1994] PL 452, 459.

of compensation to those affected by government action is not a matter for adjudication. We shall test this view later in the chapter.

The constitutional settlement of 1688 did not, however, solely establish the primacy of Parliament, setting in place institutional relationships with which we are still working. The great seventeenth-century cases in which the issues had been fought out [6] devolved from action taken by private citizens. The settlement was triangular in character, recognising all 'the true, ancient, and indubitable rights of the people of this kingdom'. It entrenched the 'modern, absolute, idea of individual property' [7] which had grown up during the century. Thus, Blackstone epitomised the rights of the people of England in 'three principal or primary articles: the right of personal security, the right of personal liberty, and the right of private property' whose preservation would encompass the maintenance of all other civil immunities. [8] Since courts see the protection of private interests as one of their main functions (above, p. 579), it is hardly surprising if the protection of private property emerged as a benchmark of the Rule of Law, or that courts see the protection of private property as a central objective.

The tension between private property and public interest, often mirrored in institutional conflict between government and courts, is a key theme of our account of state compensation. We set out also to illustrate the interplay between the institutions involved in compensation: the civil service and more especially the Treasury, courts, Parliament, the PCA and his Select Committee, from whom we shall find an increasing input. Are the principles they apply similar, or shall we once more find a clash of values?

We shall also find the public/private distinction central to the debate. The absence of a distinct system of public law in this country has meant that state and subject are bound equally by the common law rules of civil liability. To red light theorists, state liability is therefore a central plank in enforcement of the Rule of Law; indeed, the principle of personal liability lies at the heart of Dicey's exposition of the Rule of Law ideal. The compensation principle, on the other hand, is often based on a communitarian ideal. An example will be found in Duguit's theory of state liability (above, Chapter 3). Again, Cohen and Smith base [9] a theory of state liability solely on the concept of 'social entitlement' and collective insurance, grounded in a constitutional ideal of equality. There is a clear analogy here with the welfare function of the modern state. Later, indeed, we will find the argument that special compensation schemes, such as the criminal injuries compensation scheme outlined later in the chapter, are a basic ingredient of the welfare state in which we live today, and should be treated accordingly. This would, however, involve a drastic reshaping of our present system of civil liability. [10]

---

6  _R v Hampden, Ship Money Case_ (1637) 3 State Tr 826; _Bates's case_ (1610) 2 State Tr 371.
7  A. Macfarlane, _The Origins of English Individualism_ (Oxford: Blackwell) 1978, p. 57.
8  Blackstone's _Commentaries,_ 10th edn., 1787, p. 129.
9  See D. Cohen and J. Smith, 'Entitlement and the Body Politic: Rethinking Negligence in Public Law' (1986) 64 Can. Bar Rev. 1.
10  But see P. Cane (ed.) _Atiyah's Accidents, Compensation and the Law_ (London: Weidenfeld & Nicolson) 4th edn., 1987.

Individualism retained its dominance at the heart of the common law until, according to Dicey,[11] it came under attack from collectivist ideology during the nineteenth century, with the advent of new regulatory systems. It has been argued that the individualist bias of the common law has never been eliminated[12] but the collectivist tradition is not wholly absent;[13] indeed, we have already met it in the *Burmah Oil* case.[14] As Lord Moulton once remarked:[15]

> The feeling that it was equitable that burdens borne for the good of the nation should be distributed over the whole nation and should not be allowed to fall on particular individuals has grown to be a national sentiment. The effect of these changes is seen in the long series of statutes ... [which] indicated unmistakeably that it is the intention of the nation that ... the burden shall not fall on the individual but shall be borne by the community.

This principle may sometimes be freely acknowledged by the executive, as with the long tradition of ex gratia payment discussed below. It may, on the other hand, be imposed externally, either by the common law or by statute. Statutory compensation schemes vary greatly. At one end of the scale we find the occasional Foreign Compensation Acts which led to the *Anisminic* case and come into operation only occasionally;[16] at the other, the large scale industrial injuries scheme which is an important source of accident compensation. We use the example of compensation for property compulsorily purchased.

## 1. Grace and favour: administrative compensation

Government does not need specific statutory authority to settle claims for pecuniary compensation; the prerogative power can be used to make 'ex gratia payments'. It is in fact widely used to settle actions against the Crown and authorised by Treasury Guidance.[17] This raises the question whether ex gratia payments should parallel legal liability or be used more generously to provide redress where things have gone wrong. The Treasury is inclined to take legal liability as its benchmark, a point illustrated in *Barlow Clowes* and the dispute over compensation for worry and distress caused by the Child Support Agency.[18]

We know already that, as the Parliamentary Commissioner scheme got into its stride, ex gratia payments were often made in response to his reports. Generally, this was done on an individualised basis, the measure of compensation being the

---

11  A. V. Dicey, *Law and Opinion in England during the nineteenth century* (London: Macmillan) 2nd. edn., ECS Wade, 1963, Lecture VIII.

12  P. McAuslan, 'Administrative law, collective consumption and judicial policy' (1983) 46 MLR 1.

13  And see J. Ely Jr., 'That due satisfaction may be made: the Fifth Amendment and the Origins of the Compensation Principle' (1992) 36 Am. J. of Legal History 1.

14  Above, p. 47.

15  *A-G v De Keyser's Royal Hotel Ltd* [1920] AC 508.

16  Above, p. 54.

17  See *Government Accounting*, issued with a Treasury memorandum known familiarly as 'The Dear Accounting Officer' letter (DAO(GEN) 15/92).

18  Above, pp. 434 and 440 respectively.

amount of the complainant's actual loss. We also know that the PCA's insistence on equal treatment meant in practice that, where compensation had been granted to one person, every decision made on the same basis must be brought into line. The Treasury accordingly advises departments:[19]

> in the interests of equity, to consider whether they should offer compensation ... in discovered cases of official failure where there has been no complaint. Where, following a particular complaint or the discovery of a particular case, departments discover that other individuals or bodies have suffered in the same way, they should consider whether, in the interests of equity, they should offer compensation to others.

Generally, however, where a class of persons is affected by a court ruling or PCA finding, the government steps in with a legislative solution – as it did in the *Court Line Affair* described in Chapter 13. PCA investigations have nevertheless often revealed that no attempt has been made to identify other parties affected by a ruling; this was the case, for example, in the group investigation into Disability Living Allowance.[20] The *Slaughtered Poultry Affair*[1] was graver. After a scare over salmonella in eggs, some farmers had to slaughter their poultry. The PCA discovered that claims for statutory compensation had been deliberately, and with the knowledge of the Minister, handled so as to minimise the amount of compensation payable. The PCA upheld the complaint that compensation had been inadequate and censured MAFF for 'failure to devise and implement a scheme which fully complied with the requirements of the legislation and, in particular, for their unwillingness to reveal the basis on which their compensation package was proposed'. His intervention resulted in an extra £24,900 for the original complainant and re-calculation of sums due to other farmers in excess of £600,000. This raises the question whether the same result could have been achieved by litigation – a point dealt with later.

The Select Committee on the PCA has recently expressed dissatisfaction at:[2]

> ... the inadequacy of much of the redress offered by departments and agencies ... unwillingness to admit fault, refusal to identify and compensate all those affected by maladministration. The Ombudsman ... has done much to persuade departments to improve their procedures in the consideration of redress and their compensation to those adversely affected by maladministration. It is, however, apparent that many departments have yet to adopt practices which adequately reflect Charter principles ...
>
> Investigations into an individual complaint can often uncover maladministration which has affected the lives of hundreds, if not thousands, of people. Recent special reports by the ombudsman on delays in the granting of Disability Living Allowance, compensation to farmers for slaughtered poultry, and loss of employment caused by mistaken revocation of a licence to drive a heavy goods vehicle, all revealed the need to grant redress to many others adversely affected who had not complained. What was also apparent was the fact that at least in the case of the DVLA, no action was taken to locate the others affected until after the intervention of the Ombudsman.

19 'Dear Accounting Officer' (DAO(GEN) 15/92).
20 *Delays in Handling Disability Living Allowance Claims*, HC 652 (1992/3), above p. 441.
 1 *Compensation to Farmers for Slaughtered Poultry* HC 519 (1992/3), AR 1993, HC 290 (1994/5), p. 27.
 2 Third Report of Select Committee, HC 345 (1993/4).

Taking seriously the Citizen's Charter promise of 'better redress for the citizen when things go wrong', the SC set up a 'thematic inquiry' into compensation.[3] This revealed substantial departmental discrepancies in the practice of ex gratia payment. Some departments, like the Home Office, possessed unlimited authority; others, including the CSA, needed Treasury authority for all but the most trivial payments. Novel or contentious payments should always be referred to the Treasury for fear of setting precedents. The Treasury favoured 'strong', individuated, discretion – but only for the Treasury. It warned departments to:[4]

> ... avoid the codification of rules (or the definition of precedents) in forms which, over a period of time, might come to be regarded as applicable to cases removed from the original justification. An unduly liberal regime of compensation would impose an administrative burden on departments ... Departments needing to distribute codified internal guidance on ex gratia payments, in order to permit a measure of delegated authority to local staff, should design it to be exclusive to closely defined cases.

Treasury advice was found by the PCA to be often 'outdated, restrictive and doctrinaire', running counter 'not just to concepts of equity and fairness but also to the philosophy of the Government's Citizen's Charter' and the SC saw its Guidance as frequently 'inappropriate'. Despite Treasury caution, however, there were numerous administrative compensation schemes in operation. The schemes were diverse, revealing no common thread: e.g., a statutory Revenue scheme dealt with cases where undue delay caused loss to taxpayers while a similar DSS scheme handled back-payment of benefits; the Home Office compensated those who live in the region of open prisons for property loss; and so on. Some, like the MAFF scheme for slaughtered poultry and cattle were statutory in origin; others, like the IR scheme or payments for worry and distress made by the CSA, originated in PCA inquires. Many of the practices were unpublished and unknown to those for whom they were intended. This is 'soft law' at its worst!

Applying the Citizen's Charter approach to good administration, the SC set out to see these discretions structured by an input of principle, rules and transparency. In principle, it was said, a 'person who has suffered injury as a result of maladministration should be put back in the same position as he or she would have been had things gone right in the first place'.[5] (Note the close resemblance here to common law principles, based on the principle of 'making whole' or *restitutio in integrum*.) The SC wanted less meanness, recommending compensation in all cases of 'abnormal hardship' and that exceptional 'worry and distress' payments should be given 'automatic consideration'. 'Botheration' payments should be also be made where handling of a complaint had involved rudeness, malice, incompetence or other grave maladministration. Transfer of responsibility for redress to the Office of Public Service was recommended, with a 'Redress Team' to monitor and advise departments and agencies. In short, the PCA and SC were

---

3  *Maladministration and Redress*, HC 112 (1994/5).
4  'Dear Accounting Officer' (DAO(GEN) 15/92).
5  HC 112, p. vi. See also paras. 25, 45–47.

working towards a consistent approach to redress throughout the Civil Service with the decision-making on particular cases taking place as close as possible to the point at which the services were delivered'. To encourage transparency, departmental Charters should contain a section outlining compensation arrangements. There are signs that these policies are being put in place. The IR, Customs and DSS all now publish information about compensation in their material on complaining. The PCA also lists all cases in which he has obtained compensation.[6]

## 2. Betwixt and between: a case study of criminal injuries compensation

If, as we have indicated, compensation is a facet of resource allocation, then the lines of responsibility, though they start with government, undoubtedly end with Parliament, more specifically the House of Commons. The constitutional propriety of ex gratia payments made without parliamentary approval causes the Treasury to insist they be reserved for individual cases, or at least these affecting small classes. It may therefore be thought surprising that one comparatively large compensation scheme was set up and administered using solely prerogative powers.

### (a) Inception

The Criminal Injuries Compensation Scheme (CICS) was introduced in 1964 with all-party support by a Conservative government in response to pressure to 'do something for the victims of crime'. A working party was set up to consider what steps could be taken. The terms of the scheme which emerged were simply announced to the House of Commons and published in *Hansard* and elsewhere.[7] It came into operation on an ex gratia basis, perhaps justifiable so long as numbers remained small: in its first year of operation, only 554 applications were received and £33,430 paid out in compensation. Thereafter, the number of claims was to increase rapidly. In 1974, when extension of the scheme was under consideration by another Home Office working party, £5,224,580 was paid out and more than 10,000 claims were received. In 1988/9, a year when legislation was finally introduced to put the scheme on a statutory basis, awards had risen to £431,532,702 and claims totalled 43,385. In 1992/3, when the government moved to amend the scheme on the ground of cost, compensation totalled £909,446,123 and claims had risen to 65,977. These are large sums for which statutory authorisation is normally sought. So why was the scheme originally established and allowed to remain for so long on an ex gratia basis?

One answer seems to be that neither the working party, the government, nor speakers in the debates could devise an adequate principle to justify state liability. Advocates for the scheme made strenuous efforts to satisfy the critics. *Justice*

6   Annual Report of the PCA for 1996/7, HC 386 (1997/8) paras 23, 38, 48 and Appendix A.
7   See *Compensation for Victims of Crimes of Violence* (Cmnd. 1406 (1961)) and Cmnd. 2323 (1964). This White Paper formed the terms of the scheme. See also *Compensation for Crimes of Violence* (London: *Justice*) 1962.

made an analogy with (statutory) war and riot damage. The state forbids resort to violence, discourages the citizen from carrying arms or from taking the law into his own hands and may, for good measure, incarcerate the wrongdoer for a substantial period effectively shielding him from an action for damages, yet imposes a general duty to help in bringing criminals to justice. Thus, the state should provide the victim with an effective alternative. But as Lord Denning, then Master of the Rolls, pointed out in the House of Lords,[8] the payments did not reflect the pattern of legal liability, nor was there a clear moral obligation on the state to pay – at least, no obligation greater than that owed to other classes of victim, such as traffic accident victims, specifically excluded from the scheme for reasons of cost (CICS para. 11, below). The government also rejected any obligation, moral or legal, which might ultimately be used as an argument for extensive *legal* liability, probably because there would be no logical reason to exclude property damage. The working party timidly concluded:[9]

> We can find no constitutional or social principle on which State compensation could be justified, but we think that it could nevertheless be based on the more practical ground ... that although the Welfare State helps the victims of many kinds of misfortune, it does nothing for the victims of crimes of violence as such, notwithstanding that they are largely deprived of the means of self-protection and in most cases have no effective remedy at law. There is an argument for filling this gap, based mainly on considerations of sympathy for the innocent victim, but falling short of acceptance of any bounden duty to mitigate the victim's hardship; and we think this argument more likely to appeal to the public than any more abstruse principles that might be formulated.

We might pause to ask why 'sympathy' dictates compensation for physical injury but not for property damage. Again, we might question whether the welfare state does anything for anyone 'as such'? Criticising the 'appeal to the public instinct' as 'a complete abdication of the role of legislator [which] might as well have been used to justify feeding Christians to the lions in ancient Rome or the burning of witches in medieval England', Atiyah, the leading expert on accident compensation, insisted that:[10]

> The crucial issue was not whether victims of criminal violence ought to be compensated by the state, but whether there are any grounds for compensating such victims outside the normal processes of the welfare state. This question was only touched on in passing by pointing out that the welfare state did nothing for the victims of violence 'as such' – but why this should matter, provided it does *something* for them, it is impossible to see. Perhaps the Working Party were influenced by the belief that the benefits provided by the welfare system were inadequate. But if social security benefits are inadequate, the right solution is to increase them; and if less money were devoted to special categories of unfortunates, it might be possible without much, if any,

8  HL Deb., vol. 245, cols. 272–8.
9  Cmnd. 1406 (1961), paras. 17–18. For a theoretical view, see A. Ashworth, 'Punishment and Compensation: Victims, Offenders and the State' (1986) 6 OJLS 86.
10  P. Cane, *Atiyah's Accidents, Compensation and the Law* (London: Weidenfeld and Nicolson) 4th edn., 1987, pp. 293-294. See also D. Miers, *Compensation for Criminal Injuries* (London: Butterworths) 1990, pp. 1–11.

increased cost, to make benefits generally quite adequate. Abolition of special compensation schemes (including, of course, the tort system) would only be contemplated as part of a reform package; and one component of the reform package would be to redistribute in a more equitable manner many of the benefits that now go to victims in particular groups.

This is a strong assertion of the argument that compensation is merely a facet of welfare, the problem with Atiyah's fair, 'across-the-board' solution being that it would actually prove immeasurably more costly.[11] This is the true reason why governments buy votes by singling out special cases for action. But is it really impermissible for governments to justify their behaviour by reference to public sentiment? Are they not elected to do precisely this? Think back to the arguments which surround the parole system, creating problems that governments will be seen as 'soft on crime'. In this case too, successive governments were succumbing to a growing 'victims' lobby'.[12] These are arguments in favour of 'due parliamentary process'. Just as judicial review may provide protection for 'rights', so a statutory scheme should attract a greater measure of parliamentary scrutiny.

### (b) Discretion or rules?

Discussing the advantages of hard and soft law in earlier chapters, we saw flexibility as an important reason for the latter. The CICS was the first scheme of its kind in the world, and the government wished to see how it worked out and to make adjustments. Moreover, they were uncertain how much it was going to cost. This is the case for discretion. That the organisation and ambit of the scheme was governed by published rules, however, suggested something rather different. Atiyah[13] was quick to notice the contradiction, calling the denial of a 'right' to compensation 'quite meaningless, because the board administering the scheme has no discretion to refuse claims except within the terms of the scheme itself; and the payment of compensation – though not legally enforceable – follows automatically once the board has determined that it should be awarded'. Nor did the CICB believe that it had unfettered discretion:[14]

> The use of the words *ex gratia* means that an applicant has no right to sue either the Crown or the Board for non-payment of compensation. But, in practice, the position is exactly the same as it would be if the Scheme was embodied in a statute with the words *ex gratia* omitted. The Board's view of its legal obligation and duty under the Scheme is that, if an applicant's entitlement to compensation is established there is no power to withhold compensation.

11  These are reasons why the recommendations of the Pearson Commission on Civil Liability and Compensation for Personal Injuries, Cmnd. 7054 (1978) were not implemented and why 'no fault' medical compensation has not been introduced: see further, C. Harlow, *Understanding Tort Law* (London: Fontana) 1995, Chs 4 and 9.
12  P. Duff, 'Criminal Injuries Compensation' (1995) Juridical Review 102, 103; P. Rock, *Helping Victims of Crime: The Home Office and the Rise of Victim Support in England and Wales* (Oxford: Clarendon) 1991, Ch. 2.
13  *Accidents, Compensation and the Law* (above, note 11), p. 296.
14  Cmnd. 7752 (1979), para. 15.

Here the Board is suggesting that the rules of the scheme are sufficiently strict to render statute superfluous; entitlement and legal right are in practice synonymous. Yet the argument would not go away. In 1980, introducing a Private Member's Bill which he later withdrew, Lord Longford argued[15] that 'the establishment of a statutory system would command much more confidence among victims, and certainly could be used to promote much more effective publicity'. Lord Longford was making two important points. As we shall see later, informal rules can be (and were) amended from time to time without too much publicity. It was not until the Criminal Justice Act 1988, however, that the Scheme reached the statute book.[16]

A cursory look at the original text confirms the status of the scheme as 'soft law'. There were two parts, 'the Scheme' or rules of operation and a 'Guide' or 'Statement' designed 'for the benefit of applicants and their advisers as to how the Board are likely to determine applications'. Para. 12 explained that 'compensation will be assessed on the basis of common law damages and will normally take the form of a lump sum payment'. The 3 years' limitation period (para. 4) mirrored civil law, though the (moveable) threshold of £1,000 below which applications would not be entertained (para. 5), did not. The Guidelines balance clarity with flexibility. In comparison to statute or the complicated regulations on which SSATs have to adjudicate, the text is simple to construe and self-explanatory, a 'code of practice' or guidelines meant to inform the public and not to provide work for lawyers.

## (c) Administration

A further reason for an ex gratia scheme was to exclude appeal. There was a deliberate distancing from government; the Board was autonomous, its decisions not subject to ministerial review or appeal. (Here we can compare the scheme with parole, where ministerial discretion and input are substantial.) It was none the less accountable through annual reports submitted to the Home Secretary and laid before Parliament.

The government from the outset had favoured formal adjudicatory methods. The first stage in the application process was to submit a claim on an application form, processed initially by a single member of the Board on the papers. At first this was satisfactory; about 75% of applications were resolved at this stage. Gradually, the figure dropped until by 1995, under 2,000 cases were resolved at first stage, while hearings were referred or requested in over 11,000 and the Board had heard or resolved 10,000. Since 1993, an oral hearing before a panel has been requested in well over 10,000 cases each year. There has also been a steep rise in applications: from 2,452 in 1965/6, the first full year of operation, to 73,473 in 1993/4. Legal representation, at first exceptional, was fast becoming the rule.

Delay became endemic. In 1979/80, 74.8% of applications were resolved within the year; by 1994/5, only 4.5% of applications were complete in six months

---

15  HL Deb., vol. 401, cols. 233–5.
16  Sections 108–177, Schs. 6 and 7. See also P. Duff, 'Criminal Injuries Compensation: The Scope of the New Scheme' (1989) 52 MLR 518. The Act followed a Report from the Home Affairs Select Committee, *Compensation and Support for Victims of Crime* HC 43 (1984/5).

or less and far too many (41.5%) took more than one year; where a hearing was requested, this figure climbed to 51%. The three-member panel was reduced to a two-member panel, allowed to refuse a hearing on the papers. But despite documentary procedures designed to reduce delay and reduction in panel size, the Board was accumulating a serious backlog. The Annual Report for 1995 records the increasing pressure on the system:[17]

*Table 19.1: Time taken to determine hearings cases*

|                | 1979–80 | 1994–5 |
|                | %       | %      |
|----------------|---------|--------|
| Up to 3 months | 1.8     | 5      |
| 4–6 months     | 22.7    | 12     |
| 7–9 months     | 31.6    | 15     |
| 10–12 months   | 18.7    | 17     |
| Over 12 months | 25.2    | 51     |

The Board blamed:

the drop in the number of relatively straightforward decisions taken at the first decision stage. As a result of this a higher proportion than usual of cases at hearings were those which had been waiting some time, often by reason of the need to obtain further medical assessments and schedules of financial loss. Consequently, despite the throughput remaining at around 11,000 resolved cases, the number of cases dealt with in one year has reduced. Our hearings system, covering some 20 centres is operating at maximum capacity with Board Members and staff stretched to maintain the schedules.

Arguably, the CICB was getting the worst of all worlds. The input of lawyers into the adjudicatory process meant a steady progress towards formality, tempting applicants to turn to legal advisers. Ultimately, delays were created which paralleled those of other complaints systems, including the Divisional Court and PCA. We saw in Chapter 14 how pressure on SSATs may end the independent existence of the ITS. One reason why the Criminal Justice Act 1988 was never activated, was said to be the need to clear the accumulated backlog. The same justification was used for replacing the CICB by nominated adjudicators (below).

17   31st Report of the CICB, Cm. 3169 (1995/6).

## (d) Justiciability

Like Lord Denning, the government originally thought the absence of legal entitlement rendered ex gratia payments unsuitable for judicial determination. There was no appeal from the hearing panel and recourse to the prerogative was meant to exclude the courts. Paradoxically, it was this which led the courts to fill the gap with judicial review, opening it to unstructured judicial discretion. Tremors shook the legal world when, in *R v Criminal Injuries Compensation Board, ex p Lain*,[18] the Divisional Court held that the Board, as 'a servant of the Crown charged by the Crown, by executive instruction, with the duty of distributing the bounty of the Crown ... came fairly and squarely within the jurisdiction of this Court'. Inroads had been made both on the prerogative and on the scheme's discretionary nature.

Since the members of the Board (who by 1995 had risen to 40) were all distinguished lawyers experienced in personal injuries, it might be expected that few problems would arise. Yet the scheme has been submitted to the courts for a ruling on a point of law on many occasions. Decisions were treated with great respect by the Board and summarised in the annual reports. Unexpectedly, case law played an important part in structuring the scheme. But the sharp divergence of judicial opinion over resource allocation in the cases which follow should be noted.

## *R v Criminal Injuries Compensation Board, ex p Schofield*[19]

Paragraph 5 of the 1964 scheme provided:

> The Board will entertain applications for *ex gratia* payment of compensation in any case where the applicant ... sustained ... personal injury directly attributable to a crime of violence (including arson and poisoning) or to an arrest or attempted arrest of an offender or suspected offender.

A bystander was knocked down accidentally during a struggle to arrest a shoplifter. She argued that her injuries were 'directly attributable' to an arrest or criminal offence. The CICB refused compensation on the ground that:

> The purpose of the scheme is to compensate those who try to arrest an offender or who try to prevent the commission of a crime, or who assist a constable to do either of these things. It does not in our view cover bystanders who are accidentally injured by anyone who is engaged in the task of arresting an offender.

The application was allowed by a majority of the Court of Appeal. Here Bridge LJ (dissenting) argues that the 'soft' rules of the scheme are not adapted to review by a court:

---

18  [1967] 2 QB 864.
19  [1971] 1 WLR 926.

The scheme, as the document is entitled which enshrines the rules for the board's conduct, is not recognisable as any kind of legislative document with which the court is familiar. It is not expressed in the kind of language one expects from a parliamentary draftsman, whether of statutes or statutory instruments. It bears all the hallmarks of a document which lays down the broad guidelines of policy.

Because the scheme was purely administrative in character, Bridge LJ thought it would be wrong to intervene unless the Board's interpretation was 'wholly untenable'. He personally thought the explanation 'reasonably tenable', but his minority opinion permitted the Board to make errors of interpretation unless unreasonable and to withdraw from its published commitments. Does this square with modern principles of judicial review? A later case, discussed below, directly argues *Wednesbury* unreasonableness.

### R v Criminal Injuries Compensation Board, ex p P[20]

Paragraph 7 of the CIC Scheme excluded compensation for 'offences committed against a member of the offender's family living with him at the time'. After 1990, this rule was revised but not so as to allow claims where the offence occurred before 1979. The applicants claimed in respect of sexual abuse by their stepfather before 1979. When refused, they applied for review on the ground that the decision to maintain this inflexible rule was arbitrary, irrational and unfair. By a majority, the Court of Appeal held the claim justiciable, reasoning that even if 'a fixed amount of funds were available to implement the scheme, this did not justify an unfair (irrational) as opposed to a fair distribution under the scheme'. Like the Court of Appeal in the *Cambridge* case, Neill LJ would have preferred to have resource allocation to the authority:

> These decisions involve a balance of competing claims on the public purse and the allocation of economic resources which the court is ill-equipped to deal with. In the language of the late Professor Fuller ... decisions of this kind involve a polycentric task ... The Secretary of State had to make a judgment as to how to allocate the resources at his disposal ... I cannot see that the decision to continue the pre-1979 exclusion can be regarded as a 'justiciable' issue in the present case.

Once again, the CICB was getting the worst of both worlds. Notably, by 1978, a Home Office working party set up to review the scheme had favoured appeal on a point of law to the High Court. They also thought that the CICB should be brought under the supervision of the Council on Tribunals.[1] Judicialisation was under way.

---

20  [1995] 1 All ER 870.  The appeal was dismissed unanimously on the merits.

 1  *Review of the Criminal Injuries Compensation Scheme: Report of an Interdepartmental Working Party* (London: HMSO) 1978. The matter was reconsidered in 1986, when the supervision of the Council on Tribunals was conceded and a statutory right of appeal recommended: *Criminal Injuries Compensation Scheme: A statutory scheme. Report of an Interdepartmental Working Party* (London: HMSO) 1986.

## (e) Rationalisation?

In late 1993, a White Paper was published[2] proposing drastic change to the CICS. Delays and high operating costs of £14.25 million (9% of total expenditure) led the government to conclude that 'a scheme based on common law damages was inherently incapable of delivering the standard of service claimants should now reasonably expect'. Arguing that 'there is no objectively "right" sum of money which can compensate an individual for the pain and suffering which he or she has suffered as a result of an injury', the government proposed a simplified 'Banded Tariff' scheme, the bands to be calculated after averaging past awards. The present lawyer-dominated Board would be wound up and replaced by a simple administrative process coupled with a two-stage internal review: at the first stage, review by a more senior administrator, at the second an external appeals panel appointed by the Minister using documentary procedure. We have met this change in social security adjudication, with Social Fund review.

The tariff scheme came into force on 1 April 1994, to be immediately challenged by a group of unions whose members were likely to be affected. We saw the result in *R v Secretary of State for the Home Department, ex p Fire Brigades Union*.[3] By a bare majority, the House of Lords advised that the scheme was unlawful; the Home Secretary must seek the approval of Parliament. The opinion of the House was delivered on 5 April 1995; on 23 May 1995, a Criminal Injuries Compensation Bill was introduced into the Commons to validate the tariff scheme; by 8 November 1995 the scheme was in force and started up on 1 April 1996. A medium-term saving of approximately £200 million on the old arrangements was estimated to be likely. A year later, the average delay had fallen to six months with 75% of cases decided inside eight months.[4] The scheme had lost both its ex gratia and its legalistic character. The minister received wide discretionary power to 'make arrangements for the payment of compensation'. This included power for the making of a Scheme'. The Act[5] provides for standard amounts of compensation, to be specified in the scheme. It also allowed the minister to appoint an adjudicator. None of the details are contained in the Act; it is a paradigm 'outline' or 'framework' legislation.

## 3. Statute and just compensation: the case of property

Property, as we have seen, is a 'right' and one which some see as fundamental, provoking a characteristic clash between red and green light theorists. Requisition of property in wartime represents only a tiny corner of a huge area in which property may be 'taken' for public purposes. During the nineteenth century, roads and railways were constructed and, by the end of the century, land was needed for slum clearance schemes and new towns, while planning laws imposed for

2   *Compensating victims of violent crime: Changes to the criminal injuries compensation scheme*, Cm 2434 (1993).
3   Above, p. 596.
4   HC Deb., vol. 297, cols. 5–8 (30 June 1997) (WA).
5   Criminal Injuries Compensation Act 1995. For the history see the note in (1995) Current Law Statutes (London: Sweet & Maxwell) by D. Miers.

environmental reasons prohibited landowners from doing as they pleased with their own land. There was often a consequential fall in value. When Parliament gave authority for such undertakings it usually stepped in to provide compensation, at least for the 'taking' of property. Problems arose where compensation was insufficient or failed to cover ancillary losses, such as dimunition in value or loss of amenity.

In *Hammersmith and City Rly v Brand*,[6] the plaintiff, who owned a house close to a railway, claimed damages in nuisance for depreciation and loss of amenity through dust, smoke, vibration and noise. The construction of the railway was authorised by private Act of Parliament subject to conditions as to compensation contained in the Lands Clauses Consolidation Act 1845 and Railways Clauses Consolidation Act 1845. The judges split in a manner which was to become familiar. The majority supported Blackburn J, who felt that the nuisance action must be seen as superseded by the statutes. A minority stood behind the 'private interest' speech of Bramwell B, who thought express words necessary to remove the established common law right. Reasons of 'the public benefit' alone could be no excuse; since 'compensation comes from the public which gets the benefit', the public ought to pay.

The Franks Committee blamed[7] dissatisfaction with planning inquiries on compensation being below market value and Wade deplored the way in which the nineteenth-century House of Lords had 'paved the way for technological progress at the expense of individual rights'. They had drawn:[8]

an artificial contrast between those from whom part of their land was taken, and who were compensated for the injury to the remainder, and those from whom nothing was taken but who might suffer heavy uncompensated loss. This was an inducement to many people to resist projects for roads, airports and other public works by every possible means, thus causing many lengthy public inquiries into objections.

This traditional antithesis between private rights and public interest is too simple.[9] It suggests a one-dimensional equation in which government and administration represent one side, while the individual represents a private interest. But the public is not a single entity, nor can a single, identifiable public interest be identified. Governments have to weigh the diverse claims of different sections of the community, no one of which is paramount. The right of one citizen to purchase a council house may mean that another citizen cannot find a council house to rent. For a Conservative Minister, introducing the modern legislation in 1973,[10] the reality is a 'conflict of right with right'. A new power station brings jobs and increased comfort for some; to others it brings destruction of the environment and loss of amenity. A *legal right* to purchase a council house or of

6 (1869) LR 4 HL 171. The leading modern case is *Allen v Gulf Oil Refining Ltd* [1981] AC 1001.
7 Cmnd. 218, para. 278.
8 Wade and Forsyth, pp. 814–5. See also J. McLaren, 'Nuisance Law and the Industrial Revolution: Some Lessons from Social History' (1983) 3 OJLS 155; J. Brenner, 'Nuisance Law and the Industrial Revolution', 3 J. of Legal Studies 403 (1973).
9 See further P. McAuslan, *The Ideologies of Planning Law* (Oxford: Pergamon) 1980.
10 The Land Compensation Act 1973. See, HC Deb., vol. 847, cols. 35–7 (Mr. Geoffrey Rippon).

compensation for loss of environmental amenity automatically advances one claim at the expense of others. Land use planning is, in short, the paradigm polycentric issue.

Times change, and the modern position on indirect loss caused by planning decisions is much more generous, extending well past loss of amenity to depreciation in value and distress or upset caused by the need to move.[11] Yet compensation is still not liberal enough to settle every hard case. We saw (above, p. 440) that one of the fiercest of PCA battles was fought over compensation for planning blight caused through endemic delay in deciding a route for the Channel Tunnel Rail Link. This loss fell strictly outside the terms of the legislation but, applying the principle that a rule which causes hardship can be the subject of an investigation, the PCA (Mr. Reid) found maladministration in the failure to extend compensation to property blighted *through delay*:[12]

> By their very nature, all major transport infrastructure projects are likely to cause blight ... That is in my view unavoidable, and is not in itself evidence of maladministration. The [statutory] compensation schemes do not necessarily provide relief for every single person affected, to some degree, by a major new project. All such schemes must have limits; the compensation scheme which goes too far may increase blight and extend a problem to a wider population ... Where there is undue delay in settling a route which is to be constructed – no matter how good the reason for delay may be – DOT's duty must be to ensure that the effects of the continued uncertainty are kept to a minimum.

The PCA and SC felt that the DOT should have considered compensation in cases of 'exceptional or extreme hardship'. The government disagreed. The PCA returned to the matter in the Annual Report for 1995,[13] arguing that 'it should be possible to distinguish a small number of cases of exceptional hardship'. Finally, the government, complaining of difficulty in defining this vague term, came back with new 'Indicative Guidelines' for applicants who could show circumstances of exceptional hardship (e.g. divorce or retirement). When the PCA (Mr Buckley) conceded that these were '*capable of* meeting the requirement of good administration', they were agreed by the SC.

## 4. Courts, legality and liability

At the heart of Dicey's Rule of Law theory lies the principle of equal responsibility before the 'ordinary' courts of the land. Dicey insisted that public officials must take *personal* responsibility for their wrongs. When the 'gap' left in Dicey's theory by the doctrine of Crown immunity was closed by the Crown Proceedings

11  See the Town and Country Planning Act 1971, the Land Compensation Act 1973 and the Town and Country Planning Act 1990. The 1973 Act deals with depreciation due to factors such as vibration and s. 29 first introduced home loss payments.
12  *The Channel Tunnel Link and Blight: Investigation of complaints against the Department of Transport*, HC 193 (1995) para. 43. And see AR 1995, HC 296 (1995/6) p. 45.
13  *The Channel Tunnel Rail Link and Exceptional Hardship – Government Proposals for Redress*, HC 453 (1996/7).

Act 1947, it was not thought necessary to abandon the fundamental principle of personal liability. Improbably, s. 2(1) made the Crown vicariously liable[14] as if it 'were a private person of full age and capacity'. Modern extensions of the doctrine of vicarious liability partly undercut the deterrent element of Dicey's theory because the wrongdoer no longer pays personally for his wrong. However, Hogg, the leading authority on Crown proceedings, maintains that the principle retains its resonance:[15]

> Dicey captured, articulated and reinforced a fundamental attitude towards government which, at least in common law jurisdictions, is widespread both in the legal profession and in the community at large. A special regime of public liability, especially if it were administered by special courts, would lack an important symbolic and legitimating authority. In other words, at least for a common lawyer, I believe that some notion of equality with the citizen is embedded in our notion of a fair regime of public liability.

In other words, in common law countries the principle that the legal liability of government and private individuals is broadly similar, is a norm of constitutional value.

There is, then, no special system of state liability though there are some special rules. Misfeasance in public office in particular could be described as a special public law tort, in that it centres around the use of public office or public powers for improper purposes. Misfeasance is actionable when a malicious or deliberate exercise or non-exercise of statutory or common law powers by a public official causes loss to a plaintiff which has been foreseen. In the case of *Smith v East Elloe RDC*,[16] which we met in the context of ouster clauses, the allegation was that a planning decision had been motivated purely by personal animosity. This is one type of action covered by misfeasance in public office. Unfortunately, we do not know how far liability extends. Can the action be merely unlawful? or is gross illegality necessary? Modern cases establish liability where an official knowingly exceeds his powers.[17] We shall pick the point up later.

At common law, invalid administrative action could sometimes be actionable in trespass, subject to a defence of 'lawful authority'. In the leading nineteenth-century case of *Cooper v Wandsworth Board of Works*,[18] the plaintiff brought an action for trespass against the Board for ordering the demolition of his house, acting under powers granted by the Metropolis Management Act 1855. The Board argued that the plaintiff had not given the statutory notice of intention to build and

---

14  Vicarious liability is the liability of one person for the wrongful act of another, in practice restricted in the common law to the relationship of master and servant.

15  P. Hogg, 'Compensation for Damage Caused by Government' (1995) 6 National J. of Constitutional Law 7, 18. See also *The Liability of the Crown* (Toronto: Carswell) 2nd edn., 1989.

16  [1956] AC 736. For tort actions which followed the case, see G. Ganz, 'Malicious Exercise of Discretion' [1964] PL 372. See also *Rowling v Takaro Properties Ltd* [1988] AC 473, where a decision not to permit development by a foreign company was challenged as an improper use of a power by way of an action in damages.

17  Below, p. 630.  And see *Dunlop v Woollahra Metropolitan Council* [1982] AC 158; *Bennett v Metropolitan Police Comr* [1995] 1 WLR 488; *Three Rivers District Council v Bank of England (No 3)*[1996] 3 All ER 558.

18  (1863) 14 CBNS 180.

that it was lawful to demolish the house. The plaintiff replied that he was entitled to notice and to a hearing. The court found for the plaintiff on the basis of a breach of natural justice. Failure to observe the proper (public law) procedure rendered the Board's entry illegal (public law) and tortious (private law).

Order 53, r. 7(1) (now s. 31(4) of the Supreme Court Act 1981) makes provision for the award of compensation by the Divisional Court in an application for judicial review. This rule, however, was purely procedural and was not intended to create a novel and separate law of administrative compensation. It provides for compensation only where damages 'could also have been awarded in an action begun by writ' and is rarely used. In *R v Deputy Governor of Parkhurst, ex p Hague*,[19] a scarce example of a case in which a claim for damages was joined to a judicial review application, a prisoner had been segregated under r. 43(1) of the Prison Rules 1964, losing all his privileges. The Court of Appeal ruled the segregation unlawful as the proper procedures had not been followed and granted declarations accordingly. The court refused damages on two grounds: (i) the Prison Rules were not intended by Parliament to create a right to damages for breach of statutory duty; and (ii) the common law action for false imprisonment was inapplicable to the situation of segregation. In practice, the writ procedures of the High Court, with detailed pleadings and oral evidence, are considered better suited for damages actions which are therefore routinely transferred out of the Divisional Court *after* the court has determined the public law issues.[20]

The tort action none the less presents a temptation to attack indirectly, overriding the short limitation period for judicial review, as occurred in *O'Reilly v Mackman*.[1] It may be used to re-open questions which seem already to have been decided[2] or to circumvent more appropriate procedures. This is often called 'collateral review', a term applied when the legality of an act is attacked indirectly in criminal or civil proceedings. Since *Cocks v Thanet District Council*,[3] collateral review has been discouraged and sometimes labelled an 'abuse of process'. In *Jones v Department of Employment*,[4] the plaintiff brought an action for negligence in respect of a decision not to award him unemployment benefit which had subsequently been set aside by the social security tribunal. The Court of Appeal decided that the officer's duty 'lay in the field of public law' and he owed no common law duty of care. His decision could therefore be attacked only through the social security appeal system, with appeal to the Court of Appeal on a point of law. Slade LJ warned that the inevitable consequence of holding that a common law duty of care existed would be to circumvent this system. In the context of legislation under which there might be many thousands of appeals, it would make no sense to open the doors of the High Court to them.

Actions in tort against public authorities also leave the court to balance public and private law principles, weighing the general development of tort law in cases

---

19 [1991] 3 WLR 340.
20 de Smith, Jowell, Woolf, para. 19–012. Note that no power to transfer into the Crown list currently exists: Law Com. 226 (1992), para. 3.21.
1 Above, p. 554.
2 See e.g. *R v Chief Constable of Merseyside Police, ex p Calveley* [1986] QB 424; *Calveley v Chief Constable of Merseyside Police* [1989] AC 1228.
3 Above, p. 555.
4 [1988] 2 WLR 493.

involving private parties against principles of judicial review. There is overlap too between the concept of 'reasonableness' as used in the tort of negligence and 'reasonableness' in the *Wednesbury* sense. The deterrent effect of tort law on public officials who have to carry out statutory duties and exercise statutory powers is another issue. Finally, success in a tort action brings an award of damages, the impact of which on public finances (resource allocation) may have to be considered. In short, in cases of state liability, the courts are faced with polycentric questions.

In the celebrated *Dorset Yacht* case, the different senses of the term 'reasonableness' were considered. Collateral review received particular consideration from Lord Diplock (who was later to give the leading opinion in *O'Reilly v Mackman*). The House of Lords divided. Lord Reid, who famously described 'Her Majesty's civil servants' as made of 'stern stuff', could see no reason against liability. Lord Diplock thought tort law could have a deterrent or chilling effect and expressed concern for third party interests: Borstal trainees and other prisoners, as well as the general public interest in the reformation of young offenders and the prevention of crime. These groups might be unfavourably affected if, as a result of a liability finding, the Home Office, e.g., issued new instructions cutting down on external visits or early release. But this raises general questions about the 'bipolarity' of the legal process, already addressed in Chapter 17. Although Lord Diplock ultimately came down in favour of possible liability, his reasoning resembles his speech in the later *Bromley* case. [5] He addresses the relationship between the public law principle of legality and the common law principles of negligence, arguing that the latter must give way to the former.

## *Home Office v Dorset Yacht Co Ltd* [6]

Borstal trainees on an outside exercise on an island in Poole harbour absconded one night, boarded the respondents' yacht and caused damage. The respondents sued the Home Office as vicariously liable for the negligence of the officers in charge. Asked to rule on the preliminary point whether, in the absence of precedent, a duty of care was owed to the respondents by the officers, the House of Lords held by a majority that the Home Office could be liable.

> *Lord Reid*: In later years there has been a steady trend towards regarding the law of negligence as depending on principle so that, when a new point emerges, one should ask not whether it is covered by authority but whether recognised principles apply to it ...
>
>     If the carelessness of the Borstal officers was the cause of the plaintiffs' loss what justification is there for holding that they had no duty to take care? The first argument was that their right and power to control the trainees was purely statutory and that any duty to exercise that right and power was only a statutory duty owed to the Crown. I

5    Above, p. 585.
6    [1970] 2 WLR 1140.

would agree, but there is very good authority for the proposition that if a person performs a statutory duty carelessly so that he causes damage to a member of the public which would not have happened if he had performed his duty properly he may be liable ...

Parliament deems it to be in the public interest that things otherwise unjustifiable should be done, and that those who do such things with due care should be immune from liability to persons who may suffer thereby. But Parliament cannot reasonably be supposed to have licensed those who do such things to act negligently in disregard of the interests of others so as to cause them needless damage.

Where Parliament confers a discretion the position is not the same. Then there may, and almost certainly will, be errors of judgment in exercising such a discretion and Parliament cannot have intended that members of the public should be entitled to sue in respect of such errors. But there must come a stage when the discretion is exercised so carelessly or unreasonably that there has been no real exercise of the discretion which Parliament has conferred. The person purporting to exercise his discretion has acted in abuse or excess of his power. Parliament cannot be supposed to have granted immunity to persons who do that ...

It was suggested that a decision against the Home Office would have very far-reaching effects ... that it would make the Home Office liable for the loss occasioned by a burglary committed by a trainee on parole or a prisoner permitted to go out to attend a funeral. But there are two reasons why in the vast majority of cases that would not be so. In the first place it would have to be shown that the decision to allow any such release was so unreasonable that it could not be regarded as a real exercise of discretion by the responsible officer who authorised the release. And secondly it would have to be shown that the commission of the offence was the natural and probable, as distinct from merely a foreseeable, result of the release ... I think that the fears of the appellants are unfounded: I cannot believe that negligence or dereliction of duty is widespread among prison or Borstal officers.

Finally I must deal with public policy. It is argued that it would be contrary to public policy to hold the Home Office or its officers liable to a member of the public for this carelessness – or, indeed, any failure of duty on their part. The basic question is: who shall bear the loss caused by that carelessness – the innocent respondents or the Home Office, who are vicariously liable for the conduct of their careless officers? ... I can see no good ground in public policy for giving this immunity to a government department.

*Lord Diplock*: The analogy between 'negligence' at common law and the careless exercise of statutory powers breaks down where the act or omission complained of is not of a kind which would itself give rise to a cause of action at common law if it were not authorised by the statute. To relinquish intentionally or inadvertently the custody and control of a person responsible in law for his own acts is not an act or omission which, independently of any statute, would give rise to a cause of action at common law against the custodian on the part of another person who subsequently sustained tortious damage at the hands of the person released ... In the instant case, it is the interest of the Borstal trainee himself which is most directly affected by any decision to release him and by any system of relaxed control while he is still in custody that is intended to develop his sense of personal responsibility and so afford him an opportunity to escape. Directly affected also are the interests of other members of the community of trainees subject to the common system of control, and indirectly affected by the system of control while under detention and of release under supervision is the general public interest in the reformation of young offenders and the prevention of crime...

The conflicting interests of the various categories of persons likely to be affected by an act or omission of the custodian of a Borstal trainee which has as its consequence his release or his escape are thus of different kinds for which in law there is no common basis for comparison. If the reasonable man when directing his mind to the act or omission which has this consequence ought to have in contemplation persons in all the categories directly affected and also the general public interest in the reformation of young offenders, there is no criterion by which a court can assess where the balance lies between the weight to be given to one interest and that to be given to another. The material relevant to the assessment of the reformative effect upon trainees of release under supervision or of any relaxation of control while still under detention is not of a kind which can be satisfactorily elicited by the adversary procedure and rules of evidence adopted in English courts of law or of which judges (and juries) are suited by their training and experience to assess the probative value.

It is, I apprehend, for practical reasons of this kind that over the past century the public law concept of ultra vires has replaced the civil law concept of negligence as the test of legality, and consequently of the actionability, of acts or omissions of government departments or public authorities done in the exercise of a discretion conferred upon them by Parliament as to the means by which they are to achieve a particular public purpose ... It is not the function of the court, for which it would be ill-suited, to substitute its own view of the appropriate means for that of the department or authority by granting a remedy by way of civil action at law to a private citizen adversely affected by the way in which the discretion has been exercised. Its function is confined in the first instance to deciding whether or not the act or omission complained of fell within the statutory limits imposed upon the department's or authority's disretion. Only if it did not would the court have jurisdiction to determine whether or not the act or omission, not being justified by the statute, constituted an actionable infringement of the plaintiff's rights in civil law.

Here Lord Diplock argues that the tort action approaches the legality of administrative action indirectly, viewing it through the distorting glass of the civil liability system. He suggests that the 'public law' test of ultra vires, because it leaves more scope for administrative discretion, is better suited than the 'civil law' test of negligence for the determination of such issues. This terminology does not recommend itself to Lord Reid. He tells us that negligence can handle the problem. Errors of judgment are not lightly to be equated with negligence, but a stage comes 'when the discretion is exercised so carelessly or unreasonably that there has been no real exercise of the discretion'. But do these two approaches really differ substantially and does this formulation differ greatly from that of *Wednesbury* unreasonableness? Lord Diplock may be making 'a mountain out of a molehill'.

In *Anns v Merton London Borough Council*,[7] the plaintiffs, owners of a block of flats found to be structurally unsound, claimed damages for negligence in the exercise of the council's statutory powers of inspection under the building regulations. Two linked problems arose: on the one hand, the statute granted a power but abstained from imposing a duty to inspect foundations; on the other, what would the position be if the council decided not to inspect at all? Lord

7   [1977] 2 WLR 1024. Whether the council had inspected negligently or omitted to inspect was never ascertained as the case was decided on a preliminary point, with the House of Lords ruling against striking out. The case was remitted for trial but was settled before trial.

Wilberforce linked liability to the ultra vires principle, dividing statutory powers into 'an area of policy or discretion' in respect of which there could be no liability and an 'operational area' in which there could be liability where 'the act complained of lies outside the ambit of the power'. Like other conceptual dichotomies – administrative/judicial, rules/discretion, public/private – the distinction breaks down, as Lord Wilberforce had to admit, calling it 'a distinction of degree; many 'operational' powers or duties have in them some element of "discretion" '. The only safe conclusion was that 'the more "operational" a power or duty may be, the easier it is to superimpose upon it a common law duty of care'.

*Anns* also established the potential liability of public bodies for *omission* to exercise statutory powers. Like *Padfield*,[8] *Anns* blurs the boundary between statutory powers and duties.[9] A power is not a duty, it implies a choice and the distinction is presumably well understood by Parliament and parliamentary draftsmen.[10] Suppose a police authority decides not to police a demonstration or to close an airport for security reasons two days each week. We know that these decisions may, in certain circumstances, be reviewable.[11] Should the position be different in a negligence action?

In *Stovin v Wise*,[12] this question received the answer 'Yes'. The plaintiff had been injured in a motor collision with the defendant, who joined the highway authority as 30% responsible on the ground that it had failed to remove a bank which obscured visibility at a road junction. Acting under statutory powers, the authority had given notice to the landowner that it wished to carry out the work but the matter had then been allowed to lapse. For the majority, Lord Hoffmann thought that to derive a common law duty of care from the existence of a statutory power was 'to turn a statutory "may" into a common law "ought"'. Moreover, the difference between wrongful acts and omissions was justifiable. 'One must have regard to the purpose of the distinction as it is used in the law of negligence, which is to distinguish between regulating the way in which an activity may be conducted and imposing a duty to act upon a person who is not carrying on any relevant activity.'

Liability for breach of statutory duty is, however, not entirely straightforward. It accrues only where the court believes: (i) that this accords with the Parliament's intention; (ii) that the plaintiff can show that he falls within the class of persons the statute was meant to protect; (iii) that he has suffered consequential damage; and (iv) that there is no alternative appropriate remedy.[13] Not surprisingly, the

8  Above, p. 98.
9  Later, converging tests of liability were developed: see, *Governors of the Peabody Donation Fund v Sir Lindsay Parkinson* [1985] AC 210 where the test of liability in the exercise of statutory power was that the plaintiff had suffered a type of loss and came within a class of persons envisaged by the statute. This resembles the test of liability for breach of statutory duty (below).
10  See P. Craig, 'Negligence in the Exercise of a Statutory Power' (1978) 94 LQR 428.
11  See *R v Chief Constable of Devon and Cornwall, ex p Central Electricity Generating Board* [1981] 3 WLR 967; *R v Chief Constable of Sussex, ex p International Trader's Ferry Ltd* [1997] 3 WLR 132.
12  [1996] 3 WLR 388.
13  See generally K. Stanton, *Breach of Statutory Duty in Tort* (London: Sweet and Maxwell) 1986. Breach of EC law is deemed to be a breach of statutory duty: *Garden Cottage Foods v Milk Marketing Board* [1984] AC 130. And see B. Hepple, 'Tort Law in the Contract State' in P. Birks (ed.) *The Frontiers of Liability* (Oxford: OUP) 1994, pp. 74-76.

stringent conditions are rarely met. In public law cases, the court may rule that the duty is not owed specifically to the plaintiff but is a general, public law duty owed to the public at large.

## *X (Minors) v Bedfordshire County Council*[14]

The plaintiff was one of several children claiming damages from local authorities for breach of statutory duty and negligence. The cases fell into two groups: (i) cases involving assessment by schools of children with special educational needs in accordance with s. 8 of the Education Act 1944; and (ii) cases alleging failure properly to exercise powers to take care proceedings under the Children and Young Persons Act 1969 and subsequent legislation. The case reached the House of Lords as an appeal against striking out the writs. The House of Lords allowed the appeals, but only to the extent that the plaintiffs might be able to show a breach of a common law duty of care.

> *Lord Browne-Wilkinson*: Most statutes which impose a statutory duty on local authorities confer on the authority a discretion as to the extent to which, and the methods by which, such statutory duty is to be performed. It is clear both in principle and from the decided cases that the local authority cannot be liable in damages for doing that which Parliament has authorised. Therefore if the decisions complained of fall within the ambit of such statutory discretion they cannot be actionable in common law. However if the decision complained of is so unreasonable that it falls outside the ambit of the discretion conferred upon the local authority, there is no a priori reason for excluding all common law liability ...
>
> For myself, I do not believe that it is either helpful or necessary to introduce public law concepts as to the validity of a decision into the question of liability at common law for negligence. In public law a decision can be ultra vires for reasons other than *Wednesbury* unreasonableness ... which have no relevance to the question of negligence. Moreover it leads, in my judgement mistakenly, to the contention that claims for damages for negligence in the exercise of statutory powers should for procedural purposes be classified as public law claims and therefore, under *O'Reilly v Mackman* [1983] 2 AC 237 should be brought in judicial review proceedings: see *Lonrho plc v Tebbit* [1992] 4 All ER 280. However, although I consider that the public law doctrine of ultra vires has, as such, no role to play in the subject under discussion ... the exercise of a statutory discretion cannot be impugned unless it is so unreasonable that it falls altogether outside the ambit of the statutory discretion ... It follows that in seeking to establish that a local authority is liable at common law for negligence in the exercise of a discretion conferred by statute, the first requirement is to show that the decision was outside the ambit of the discretion altogether; if it was not, a local authority cannot itself be in breach of any duty of care owed to the plaintiff ... It is established that the courts cannot enter upon the assessment of ... policy matters. The difficulty is to identify in any particular case whether or not the decision is a 'policy' decision ...
>
> *Justiciability and the policy/operational dichotomy*
> In English law the first attempt to lay down the principles applicable in deciding whether or not a decision was one of policy was made by Lord Wilberforce in *Anns* ... I understand the applicable principles to be as follows. Where Parliament has conferred

14   [1995] 2 AC 633.

a statutory discretion on a public authority, it is for that authority, not for the courts, to exercise the discretion: nothing which the authority does within the ambit of the discretion can be actionable at common law. If the decision complained of falls outside the statutory discretion it *can* (but not necessarily will) give rise to common law liability. However, if the factors relevant to the exercise of the discretion include matters of policy, the court cannot adjudicate on such policy matters and therefore cannot reach the conclusion that the decision was outside the ambit of the statutory discretion. Therefore a common law duty of care in relation to the taking of decisions involving policy matters cannot exist.

*If justiciable, the ordinary principles of negligence apply*
   If the plaintiff's complaint alleges carelessness, not in the taking of a discretionary decision to do some act, but in the practical manner in which that act has been performed (e.g. the running of a school) the question whether or not there is a common law duty of care falls to be decided by applying the usual principles, i.e. those laid down in *Caparo Industries plc v Dickman* [1990] 2 AC 605, 617–618. Was the damage to the plaintiff reasonably foreseeable? Was the relationship between the plaintiff and the defendant sufficiently proximate? Is it just and reasonable to impose a duty of care?

Lord Browne-Wilkinson deduced that the social services cases were rightly struck out since 'the welfare sector involved is one of peculiar sensitivity, involving very difficult decisions how to strike the balance between protecting the child from immediate feared harm and disrupting the relationship between the child and its parents'. There could be no liability for breach of statutory duty without very clear indications from Parliament that this was intended and it was not 'just and reasonable' to impose a common law duty of care. In the education cases, a limited duty of care could exist based on the fact that 'the authority is offering a service (psychological advice) to the public ... once the decision is taken to offer such a service, a statutory body is in general in the same position as any private individual or organisation holding itself out as offering such a service'. This speech attempts to reconcile several difficult issues, including problems of deterrence, of the relationship between the public and private sectors and of resource allocation.
   By focusing on principles rather than on outcomes, it is easy to discount the resource allocation issue. We already know from the sums paid out in damages by the police that the resources required to meet claims in tort may be very considerable. The *Anns* case opened a floodgate. Ganz found[15] that the leading local authority insurer had 350 similar claims costing £1.4 million. Rising claims in negligence against local authorities were ultimately to bankrupt their main insurer. She believed this might be sufficient to inhibit local authorities from exercising important statutory powers. Perhaps this is partly why the House of Lords later resiled from *Anns*, restricting liability for economic loss and structural defects.[16] Civil actions in damages against government and administration often raise similar issues, particularly if a class claim is involved. The Ministry of Defence, for example, recently paid upwards of £16 million to female members of the armed forces dismissed because of pregnancy, after the Equal Treatment

15  G. Ganz, 'Public Law and the Duty of Care' [1977] PL 306.
16  *Murphy v Brentwood District Council* [1991] 1 AC 398.

Directive (EC 76/207[17]) made this illegal. And compensation claims have a habit of escalating. Take the settlement made to 1,200 haemophiliacs infected with the HIV virus through the use of unsterilised blood by the NHS of £72 million. This led to a further claim in 1997 from 3,000 haemophiliacs who had contracted hepatitis C during NHS treatment. Recently, Lord Reid's robust position in *Dorset Yacht* has been reconsidered. Describing public servants as 'applying their best endeavours' to the performance of their public duty, Lord Keith argued in *Yuen Kun-Yeu v A-G of Hong Kong*[18] that the threat of tortious liability could inculcate 'a detrimentally defensive frame of mind'. This is an argument for restricting state liability in favour of statutory or administrative compensation.

Of course, there is another side to this argument. First, we must not lose sight of the Diceyan system of accountability. In a famous article, a Canadian tort lawyer described tort law as an ombudsman[19] and we certainly hope it operates in a deterrent fashion in police cases. Secondly, polycentricity is not unique to public law. Group actions which possess the characteristics of polycentricity are becoming more common: for example, a case which establishes a manufacturer's liability for design faults may indirectly affect the rights of consumers throughout the world, help to introduce new safety systems and change insurance practice.[20] Yet it is not suggested that such cases are unsuitable for resolution by adjudication. [1] Thirdly, we must remember that government is not necessarily impartial in representing the public interest and does not always admit good claims. The intervention of a court may then be helpful. This is the controversy surrounding the *Burmah Oil* case and the rationale for 'the Battle of the Titans'.

## 5. Restitution and polycentricity

Decisions which change established principle also bring a problem of repercussions. In *Woolwich Equitable Building Society v IRC*[2] the House of Lords had to face this situation squarely. The House, in Lord Goff's discreet phrase, 'reformulated the law' to create a right to restitution (above, p. 226) where money has been paid to a public authority in the form of taxes or other levies and the demand subsequently turns out to be ultra vires. The change reflected dissatisfaction with the existing rule, at the time under review by the Law Commission,[3] according to which money paid under 'a mistake of law' was not

17  See Case 177/88 *Dekker v Stichting Vormingscentrum voor Jong Volwassenen* [1990] ECR I–3941. And see *R v Defence Secretary, ex p Leale and Lane and the EOC* (unreported) noted Fredman (1995) 111 LQR 220.
18  [1987] 2 All ER 705.
19  A. Linden, 'Tort Law as Ombudsman' (1973) 51 Can. Bar Rev. 155.
20  See D. Rosenberg, 'The Causal Connection in Mass Exposure Cases: a Public Law Vision of the Tort System' (1984) 97 Harv. LR 851.
 1  Though see Lord Pearson in *Morgans v Launchbury* [1973] AC 127; and see *McLoughlin v O'Brian* [1983] 1 AC 410, where the argument is advanced to deter courts from radical changes in the liability system.
 2  [1993] AC 70.
 3  Law Com. C.P. No. 120 (1991). See generally, P. Birks, 'Restitution from the Executive: A Tercentenary Footnote to the Bill of Rights' in P. Finn (ed.), *Essays in Restitution* (North Ryde, NSW: Law Book Co) 1990.

recoverable. Rightly described by a leading authority as 'a shabby rule',[4] it was, where public bodies were concerned, arguably contrary to Art. 4 of the Bill of Rights (above, p. 605).

Acceptable to all the leading commentators and to the Law Commission, this conspicuous piece of judicial law-making provoked a classic difference of judicial opinion on the respective roles of courts and government. Lord Goff expressed the view that courts are responsible for the development of common law principle, leaving 'policy' to the legislature. Strong dissents were voiced by Lord Keith and Lord Jauncey. Both showed concern over the possible disruption of public finances. Lord Jauncey thought that a wide restitution principle could cause 'very serious practical difficulties of administration and specifying appropriate limitations presents equal difficulties'.[5] For Lord Keith:

> formulation of the precise grounds upon which overpayments of tax ought to be recoverable and of any exceptions to the right of recovery, may involve nice considerations of policy which are properly the province of Parliament and are not suitable for consideration by the courts. In this connection the question of possible disruption of public finances must obviously be a very material one.

Parliament moved swiftly to tie up loose ends. Section 53 of the Finance Act 1991 retrospectively validates the disputed demands, exempting only a handful of cases. Law reform was left to the Law Commission.[6]

In Chapter 8, we saw that the decision in *Hazell v Hammersmith*[7] created many problems for the law of restitution, some of which had to be tackled in the *Islington and Sandwell* case.[8] The *Woolwich* principle, too, leaves many unanswered questions. Is it a special rule of public law, or does it apply more widely? If the former, to which bodies is it applicable? These questions are likely soon to be answered by statute. Again, is this a private law action, comparable to the tort action, or must a public law action be brought first? In *Woolwich*, the Court of Appeal had suggested[9] that a separate application for judicial review might be necessary but more recently the Court of Appeal has ruled to the contrary. In *British Steel plc v Customs and Excise Comrs*,[10] British Steel (BS) used hydrocarbon oil in its manufacturing processes. There was a long-standing dispute with the Inland Revenue (IR) as to whether this made BS liable to excise duty or not. BS finally challenged the IR's interpretation of the law in an action for restitution. Interpreting the case law rather strictly, Laws J ruled that BS must either follow the statutory procedure or challenge the decision in judicial review proceedings. The Court of Appeal ruled, however, that restitution was a common

---

4   P. Birks, '"When Money is Paid in Pursuance of a Void Authority…" – A Duty to Repay?' [1992] PL 580, 581.

5   See further J. Beatson, 'Restitution of Taxes, Levies and Other Imposts: Defining the Extent of the *Woolwich* Principle' (1993) 109 LQR 401.

6   Law Com. No. 227, *Restitution: Mistakes of Law and Ultra Vires Public Authority Receipts and Payments* Cm. 2731 (1994).

7   Above, p. 218.

8   Above, p. 224.

9   [1991] 3 WLR 790 (Glidewell and Ralph Gibson LJJ).

10   [1997] 2 All ER 366, CA, reversing Laws J ([1996] 1 All ER 1002).

law right which could be asserted in the normal way in civil proceedings. Similar differences of judicial opinion infused the see-saw 'exclusivity' case law in Chapter 16.

## 6. The Court of Justice and state liability

One principle emerges clearly from the case law we have looked at: public authorities cannot be liable in damages 'for doing that which Parliament has authorised'. There is no legal liability, in short, for losses flowing from or authorised by legislation, though such losses may – as we saw in the case of land compensation – be the subject of statutory compensation. The primary reason for the rule is constitutional; a contributory factor, however, is that liability in English law normally depends on proof of fault.[11]

Similarly, we have seen that there is no clear link between illegality and liability; it is not axiomatic that all illegal administrative acts give rise to liability. This was the point which arose in *Bourgoin v MAFF*.[12] Bourgoin was a French turkey producer who suffered financial loss when MAFF prohibited the import of turkeys, relying on powers to prevent the spread of infectious animal diseases, although the alleged motivation was economic. Had this been proved in an application for judicial review, the decision could have been ultra vires on the ground that a power had been used for an improper purpose. In the event, however, it was the ECJ which had annulled the decision as contrary to EC law.[13] The appellant's subsequent claim for damages in England was met by an application to strike out. The Court of Appeal divided. The majority accepted a 'collateral review' argument, ruling that the issue was one of public law challengeable only by means of an application for judicial review (for which the appellant would have been out of time.) This part of the judgment is disputable, since EC law requires that, in the case of directly effective rights, the national legal system must offer an effective remedy.[14] The Court of Appeal also ruled on the requirements for liability, ruling that, in the absence of negligence, malice or bad faith (misfeasance in public office) there could be no liability.

But can this judgment against no-fault liability stand with the subsequent jurisprudence of the ECJ? *Francovich*[15] was the aftermath of a failure by Italy to incorporate EEC Directive 80/97, designed to secure for workers a protected position in the event of their employer's insolvency. This omission had already been the subject of Art. 169 proceedings by the Commission in which Italy had been condemned[16] but, at the date of the action, was still unimplemented. The applicants, left with arrears of unpaid salary on the insolvency of their respective

11  P. Cane, *The Anatomy of Tort Law* (above p. 605, note 3) Ch. 2.
12  *Bourgoin v Ministry of Agriculture, Fisheries and Food* [1986] QB 716. The Ministry won the appeal but settled so that the case never reached the House of Lords.
13  Case 40/82 *Commission v United Kingdom* [1982] ECR 2793.
14  Case 45/76 *Comet v Produktschap voor Siergewassen* [1976] ECR 2043. Since then the ECJ has ruled that time limits imposed by national law which stand in the way of effective remedy must be set aside: Case C–32/93 *Webb v EMO Air Cargo (UK) Ltd* [1994] 3 WLR 941.
15  Joined Cases 6, 9/90 *Francovich and Bonafaci v Italy* [1991] ECR I–5357.
16  C–22/87 *Commission v Italy* [1989] ECR 143.

employers, turned to the Italian state for damages and a preliminary reference under EEC Art. 177 was made to the ECJ. The answer was returned that, even though this directive had no direct effect, the state could be liable in damages.

The conditions for liability in *Francovich* are wholly unlike the common law principles of liability set out in *Bourgoin*. The proposition advanced by the ECJ, based on the principles of liability developed in respect of Community institutions,[17] was that liability could accrue where:

(i) a directive was intended to confer rights on individuals;
(ii) the content of the rights was clearly spelt out in the directive;
(iii) a causal link between the failure to implement the directive and the loss suffered could be shown.

The majority of commentators believed this to be no-fault liability.[18] Describing the ruling as 'a minefield (or goldmine, depending on one's interest in the process)', one commentator saw the judgment as opening up 'a host of possible breaches by Member States of Treaty obligations which might lead to claims for damages by individuals'.[19]

Th ECJ has clarified the ambit of *Francovich* in a set of later cases.[20] *Brasserie du Pecheur and Factortame (No. 4)*[1] involved claims for loss of profit suffered by commercial companies resulting (i) from a German law on the purity of beer and (ii) from the British licensing scheme for fishing vessels both involving legislation which had previously been annulled by the ECJ.[2] In both cases the loss flowed from erroneous implementation of a directive. The ECJ now focused on the area of appreciation (discretion) left to the Member State, setting out three conditions for reparation:

(i) the rule of law infringed must be intended to confer rights on individuals;
(ii) the breach must be sufficiently serious;
(iii) a direct causal link must be shown between the breach of the obligation resting on the state and the damages sustained by the injured parties.

Notice the new requirement of a 'sufficiently serious breach' of obligation, for some a requirement of fault. How this operates in practice can be seen from *British Telecom*.[3] The applicant challenged the correctness of the transposition into United Kingdom law by the Utilities Supply and Works Contacts Regulations

---

17 See T. C. Hartley, *The Foundations of European Community Law* (Oxford: Clarendon) 3rd edn., 1994, pp. 482–98.
18 T. C. Hartley, *Foundations* (above, note 17), p. 468 classifies it as 'no fault' liability; D. Curtin, 'Directives: The Effectiveness of Judicial Protection of Individual Rights' (1990) 27 CMLR 709, describes it as 'risk' liability (see text below).
19 M. Ross, 'Beyond *Francovich*' (1993) 56 MLR 55, 64, 57.
20 See T. de la Mare, 'Making Sense of the EC Damages Cases' (1996) 1 Judicial Review 225.
1 Joined Cases C–46/93 and C–48/93 *Brasserie du Pecheur SA v Germany, R v Secretary of State for Transport Secretary, ex p Factortame* [1996] 2 WLR 506. The citations are from paras 46 and 51 of the judgment.
2 178/84 *Commission v Germany* [1987] ECR 1227; C–246/89 *Commission v United Kingdom* [1989] ECR 3125; C–246/89 *Commission v United Kingdom* [1991] ECR I–4585.
3 C–392/93 *R v HM Treasury, ex p British Telecommunications plc* [1996] 3 WLR 203.

1992 of Council Directive 90/531 on the co-ordination of national public procurement procedures. These are notably loosely worded and difficult to transpose. [4] In judicial review proceedings, BT claimed damages for consequential loss. In an Art. 177 reference, the ECJ acknowledged the need 'to ensure that the exercise of legislative functions is not hindered by the prospect of actions for damages whenever the general interest requires the institutions or member states to adopt measures which may adversely affect individual interests'. It ruled that the United Kingdom, which had acted in good faith though making an error in transposition, had not committed a 'manifestly serious' breach of EC law sufficient for liability. In *Factortame (No. 5)*, [5] on the other hand, the High Court ruled that the failure in transposition was sufficiently serious to merit compensation.

Like *Bourgoin*, *Hedley Lomas* [6] involved an excess of discretionary power and not, as in the earlier cases, a legislative error or omission. MAFF had systematically refused export licences for movement of live beasts to Spanish abattoirs contrary to EEC Art. 34, giving as its reason that conditions in Spanish abattoirs fell short of the standards required by EEC Directive 74/577. Spain had transposed the directive, though without providing any sanctions for breach. The questions put to the ECJ in a reference were (i) whether a public policy defence under EEC Art. 36 could justify the limitation of live cattle exports, and, if not, (ii) whether compensation would be payable. Ruling that the defence was not available and confirming the *Factortame* formula, the ECJ ruled on the crucial requirement of a sufficiently serious breach:

> where, at the time when it committed the infringement, the member state in question was not called on to make any legislative choices and had only considerably reduced, or even no, discretion, the mere infringement of Community law may be sufficient to establish the existence of a sufficiently serious breach.
>
> In that respect, in this particular case, the United Kingdom was not even in a position to produce any proof of non-compliance with the Directive by the slaughterhouse to which the animals for which the export licence was sought were destined.

All that was left, therefore, was for the national court to determine whether a direct causal link could be established between act and damage.

This jurisprudence negates the principle that public authorities cannot be liable in damages 'for doing that which Parliament has authorised'; where Parliament has neglected to comply with a directive or has, advertently or inadvertently, authorised a 'sufficiently serious' breach of EC law, liability is possible. Whether the jurisprudence has introduced into the common law the concepts of 'no fault' or 'risk' liability against which the English judiciary has always set its face, is less clear. The requirement of a sufficiently or manifestly serious breach suggests that

---

4   See S. Arrowsmith, 'An Assessment of the Legal Techniques for Implementing the Procurement Directives' in P. Craig and C. Harlow (eds.), *Lawmaking in the European Union* (Dublin: Sweet & Maxwell) 1997.

5   *R v Secretary of State for Transport, ex p Factortame (No 5)* [1997] 22 LS Gaz R 31.

6   C–5/94 *R v Ministry of Agriculture Fisheries and Food (MAFF), ex p Hedley Lomas (Ireland) Ltd* [1996] 3 WLR 787. *Francovich, Brasserie du Pecheur and Factortame* and *Hedley Lomas* are noted by Emiliou, 'State Liability Under Community Law: Shedding More Light on the *Francovich* Principle?' (1996) ELR 399.

it has not. The formulation of the criteria for liability in *Bourgoin* (broadly requiring proof of negligence or malice) is probably too narrow but similar results can be obtained with the ECJ formulation.

Where do we stand? Public authorities are, in the English system, subject to the ordinary principles of civil liability, largely based on negligence and other forms of fault. The common law does not recognise a general principle of administrative compensation,[7] but the administration does. We have traditionally been content to leave compensation to Parliament and the administration. Under the influence of Europe, however, things might be about to change. EC law is limited in its ambit but, as happened in the cases of *M v Home Office*[8] and of restitution,[9] the courts may be inclined to 'level up'.

## 7. Epilogue

It is fitting that this book should end with a chapter on compensation, since this topic epitomises so many of our themes. The action for damages was central to Dicey's theory of the Rule of Law, originating in an era before the application for judicial review had been invented. Contract and tort actions are also central to the private law paradigm of public law. We have not disguised our belief in the strength and resilience of this model and its capacity to deal with new problems. This resourcefulness emerges clearly in the radical decisions which revivify the law of restitution. We do not, of course, see the common law as perfect, any more than we approve of every change that is made. There is always room for improvement and criticism is a central part of the academic discipline. Unlike Mitchell,[10] however, we do not believe English public law to be stunted; like Griffith,[11] we do believe in the vitality of the 'political constitution'. Problems created in the political process have to be resolved there. Democracy is often dispiriting but who among us would wish to exchange it for government by judiciary?

There is a clash of values implicit in the previous paragraph which cannot be avoided in dealing with government liability.[12] A successful action in damages more often than not has resource implications which starkly raise the issue of allocation of powers. Courts cannot avoid ruling on polycentric issues but they need to be aware of the problems. If, over the centuries, the courts have erred on the side of parsimony, this may be no bad thing. If they have had to stay fairly close to the benchmark of private liability, this is a valuable discipline and, into the bargain, one which helps to balance the individualist judicial bias. This chapter has demonstrated the truth of Cranston's reminder that courts are not the

---

7  See A. Ogus, 'Do We Have a General Theory of Compensation?' (1984) Current Legal Problems 29.

8  Above, p. 61.

9  Case 199/82 *Amministrazione delle Finanze dello Stato v San Giorgio* [1983] ECR 3595, cited by Lord Goff in *Woolwich* [1993] AC 70 at 177.

10  J. Mitchell, 'The causes and effects of the absence of a system of public law in the United Kingdom' [1965] PL 95.

11  J. Griffith, 'The Political Constitution' (1979) 42 MLR 1.

12  C. Harlow, 'State Liability: Problem Without a Solution', (1996) 6 Nat. J. of Constitutional Law 67.

only machinery for accountability.[13] We have seen that compensation schemes often originate with Parliament or the administration. These often transfer decision-making to court-substitutes, usually a tribunal, although the PCA is also emerging as an important form of alternative dispute resolution in this area.

A major theme of this book has been 'juridification', in the sense of a move from discretion to rules. Both the re-structuring of the practice of ex gratia compensation and the study of criminal injuries compensation reveal this process in action. In both cases, departments and government started with 'strong', unfettered discretion. In the case of ex gratia payment, this is now structured by a 'soft law' code of rules and principles, policed internally by the OPS and Treasury and externally the PCA. In the case of criminal injuries, the discretion was from the outset structured by 'soft law' in the form of a published scheme. The trend from 'soft' to 'hard' law was demonstrated when the Home Secretary was forced, after judical intervention, to regulate the matter by legislation. This process of juridification is the natural result of the priority awarded by the NPM to the 'sigma' value of efficiency.

Juridification occurs also through a move from discretion to adjudication. We have seen many examples of this process in earlier chapters, notably with the judicialisation of administrative procedures through the rules of natural justice. Although the criminal injuries scheme was not intended to be justiciable, it was soon brought under the control of the courts. In the last section of the chapter, we have looked in some detail at a European influence on our administrative law. Advocates of the view that everything good originates in Europe would do well to ponder this example. Clearly, the attitude of the ECJ to state liability differs from that of the common law, creating scope for a clash of values which could have an unfavourable impact on our more restrained domestic system of liability.[14] The outcome of the *Factortame* litigation in an award of damages is sufficient to show that very large sums of money could be tied up in this way. There is also a considerable thrust towards juridification in the 'New Legal Order' of the European Community. On the one hand, the product of Brussels is a vast amount of regulation; on the other, the influence of both the ECJ and of ECHR Art. 6 is to promote a trend to formal adjudication premised on the procedures of the domestic legal system.

Administrative law is often regarded as bureaucratic in character, in contrast to the 'simple' rules of private law.[15] Every move to juridification tends therefore to create complaints of bureaucracy and red tape, provoking a whiplash effect. In this book, we have seen this effect most clearly in the move from public law to contract, not notably successful, we saw, in securing a de-juridification. Similarly, in Chapter 14, we noted the move to de-judicialise social security adjudication. In years to come, the rules/discretion dichotomy seems likely to be the subject of many battles. Whether an age of globalisation and of increased technology can

---

13  R. Cranston, 'Reviewing Judicial Review' in G. Richardson and H. Genn, *Administrative Law and Government Action* (Oxford: Clarendon) 1994. See above, p. 591.

14  C. Harlow, 'Francovich and the Problem of the Disobedient State' (1996) 2 European Law J. 199.

15  R. Epstein, *Simple Rules for a Complex World* (Cambridge, Mass: Harvard University Press) 1995.

launch a movement from rules to discretion is doubtful. Juridification is likely to be the enduring legacy of NPM.[16] The 'trust' society in which both Dicey and Titmuss[17] functioned has probably gone for ever. The next edition of our book may show that English administrative law has gone the same way.

16  C. Hood and C. Scott, 'Bureaucratic Regulation and New Public Management in the United Kingdom: Mirror-Image Developments?' (1996) 23 J. of Law and Soc. 321.
17  R. Titmuss, 'Welfare "Rights", Law and Discretion' (1971) 42 Pol. Q. 113.

# Index

636